Warman's
Flea Market
Price Guide

3rd Edition

ELLEN T. SCHROY

Published by

700 East State Street • Iola, WI 54990-0001
715-445-2214 • 888-457-2873
www.krause.com

Library of Congress Catalog Number: 99-63752
ISBN: 0-87349-629-9

Printed in the United States of America

Please call or write for our free catalog of publications.
Our toll-free number to place an order or obtain a free catalog is
(800) 258-0929

Editor: Karen O'Brien
Desiger: Jamie Griffin

Front Cover:
Nodder, football player, $10.
Pinback button, "Welcome Home Our Heroes," $5.
Republic Pictures 8mm film, Captain Marvel in Curse of the Scorpion, $20.
Toby mug, Royal Doulton, $35.
Book, The Hardy Boys, *The House on the Cliff*, $20.
Fiesta pitcher, $135.
Fisher-Price train, $35.

Back Cover:
This Shupp's Grove dealer grabbed your attention as you walked by with
this display of Redware on an old ladder. She merchndised is from all
angles with other types of collectibles.

Title Page:
An interesting display of watering cans.

Contents

A-Z Categories

Abbreviations

The following are standard abbreviations used throughout this book.

3D: three-dimensional

adv: advertising

approx: approximately

C: century

d: deep

dia: diameter

dj: dust jacket

doz: dozen

ed: edition, editor

emb: embossed

ext: exterior

ftd: footed

gal: gallon

ground: background

h: high

horiz: horizontal

hp: hand painted

illus: illustrated, illustration, illustrator

imp: impressed

int: interior

irid: iridescent

k: karat

l: long

lb: pound

litho: lithograph

MBP: mint in bubble pack

mfg: manufactured, manufacturing

MIB: mint in box

MIP: mint in package

mkd: marked

MOC: mint on card

n.d.: no date

No.: number

NOS: new old stock

NRFB: never removed from box

opal: opalescent

orig: original

oz: ounce

pat.: patent

pc: piece

pcs: pieces

pg: page

pgs: pages

pr: pair

pt: pint

qt: quart

rect: rectangular

Soc: Society

sgd: signed

sq: square

unp: unpaged

vol: volume

w: width

yg: yellow gold

#: number, numbered

For exciting collecting trends and newly expanded areas look for the following symbols:

❂ **Hot Topic**
✯ **New Warman's Listing**

Acknowledgments

Thanks to the many dealers and collectors who generously allowed me to photograph their items.

My husband and I spent almost every weekend this past spring, summer, and fall, visiting flea markets, antiques shows, and auctions. Everyone gladly obliged my pleas to photograph their items, most quipped "as long as I don't appear in the photo" or "am I dressed right?" My skills as a photographer are getting better, and perhaps Mother was right, practice might just be paying off. The clerk at K-Mart certainly got a good smile out of one roll I had developed "you selling on eBay?" as he handed me the developed roll. "No, writing a book" I answered back. "Guess it's about

collectibles and flea markets" — now that was success!

Spending time at so many fine flea markets also got us out in the fresh air, looking at what was being sold, what was not selling—trying to analyze why is the hard part.

Talented editor Karen O'Brien helped tremendously with that task when she suggested we put a questionnaire in *Antique Trader.* We both had a good time reading them. Keep paging on for the results! I hope you enjoy this book as much as I did researching and writing it.

Ellen L. T. Schroy

Ellen Tischbein Schroy

This reproduction pumpkin was clearly marked, but the telltale red rust also gives it away as a reproduction. This dealer offered it as a decorative accessory a few weeks before Halloween.

Quick covering saved the day when a shower popped up, notice the shoppers are still browsing.

INTRODUCTION

Remember the story about Camelot, and how it magically appears? Several of my favorite flea markets do just that—they seem to magically appear. Actually, the ladies of the Hempfield Woman's Club will disagree with the "magically appear" part for they know how hard it is to organize such an event, and how many volunteers it takes to get it all running smoothly. However, these ladies make it look so effortless, you can easily forget that some of them have been rumbling around that ballfield since 5 a.m. Their marvelous flea markets turn up Memorial Day and on Labor Day, and have been doing so since 1976. Hempfield Woman's Club president Judy Clough tells me they are fortunate that the East Hempfield Township has become a wonderful partner in this endeavor, adding help for traffic control, etc. The proceeds from these events are returned to the community through scholarships, donations to charities, etc. While their neighbors are out in the middle of the field selling wares, elbow to elbow with dealers and all types of vendors, several of the ladies have taken up residence under the pavilion, busily selling spaces for the next event, answering questions, and solving little problems.

And we've all driven by those flea markets filled lonely empty tables, just waiting for the dealers and shoppers to return, making the aisles come alive with merchandise. However, when we return on "flea market day" we know we will find all kinds of antiques, collectibles, new, and used goods. How a dealer decides what flea market to set up at, what to take, etc. is part of the magical mystery. Many times these dealers are traveling gypsies who wander from flea markets to antique shows to auctions. However, each time, they sell and buy, giving collectors a marvelous opportunity to browse through their wares at their own pace. Free enterprise can be found at each and every flea market. For those beginning their collections or lives as dealers, a flea market offers a lower cost experience, but also one that can be just as exciting or rewarding. Many of these experiences depend on the personality of the collector and the dealer and how well they connect. Watching this interaction can be fun too, nothing beats the smile of a collector as he clinches what he considers to be the best deal of the day. And the dealer is generally smiling back, glad his merchandise is going to have a new home, the proceeds helping to pay his table rent, allowing him to re-invest in even more

Tom Crawford, Allentown, PA, sets up a really sparkly booth filled with American and English stained and leaded glass.

collectibles to sell next time.

Grab your favorite tote bag, put in your hat, and let's take a walk through this magical world.

It's a family thing

One benefit of today's flea market is the emphasis placed on the family. While some dealers at higher-end markets twitch nervously at the sight of strollers and young children, most flea markets are promoted as events for everyone, young and old. Look around the next time you're at an outdoor flea market. Notice the number of parents pulling children in wagons. And, pay close attention to the smiles on those kids' faces.

Where else are kids encouraged to dig through a box of fast-food toys or spend a portion of their allowance on a 10-cent baseball card? An ice-cold drink or a soft pretzel is often all that's needed to give them a boost when they're wearing down.

No segment of the antiques and collectibles industry does a better job catering to the interests of children than do flea markets. These microcosms of the antiques trade offer youngsters appealing items at reasonable prices. For many adults, their love of collecting germinated in childhood and blossomed into adulthood. The legion of flea markets across the United States assures a bright future for the antiques and collectibles trade by creating tomorrow's collectors

Dealer Peter Byers was well prepared with a tent that provided shade or protection from impending showers in this booth filled with early American antiques and collectibles.

today.

And the fun isn't just for kids. If you haven't been to a flea market in a while, you're in for a treat. What are you waiting for?

Let the fun begin

The thrill of the hunt continues to drive the antiques and collectibles market. People delight in the search for treasured items. Nowhere is that hope more alive than at a flea market. Whether you're looking for a Beach Boys record you remember from your childhood or a goblet to fill the void in your collection of American pattern glass, flea markets offer the realistic hope that the search will be successful. Better yet, chances are good the item can be purchased for a reasonable price.

Don't assume this book is

another run-of-the-mill price guide. It's much more than that! *Warman's Flea Market Price Guide* contains valuable information about attending flea markets, and we've honed this edition specifically toward your needs as a flea market shopper or seller. We understand that flea markets are fun, family-oriented events. With that in mind, we've kept the tone lighthearted. A sufficient amount of information about each topic has been provided, complete with notes relating to periodicals, collectors' clubs, and reference books. However, the listings are the backbone of the work, since that's what flea market enthusiasts really want.

In compiling the listings for *Warman's Flea Market Price Guide*, we put our fingers on the pulse of the marketplace, carefully checking to see what's being sold at flea markets. There's not much sense in listing prices for potholders if no one is collecting them. Instead, we've focused on what's hot, like NASCAR collectibles, which has its own heading in this edition. Other new categories include Byers Choice, Corporate Collectibles, Hooked Rugs, Liberty Blue dinnerware, and Menus, to name a few.

Photographs are a key component of this work. *Warman's Flea Market Price Guide* contains more photographs, and this book illustrates more categories, than does any other flea market price guide. From the beginning of this project, photography has been a priority. While detailed listings are vital, clear photographs are invaluable for identifying an item. However, part of finding what you are looking for at a flea market can be part of the fun, searching through objects, scanning tables to find that perfect piece. This edition has more "on location" photographs, showing what it really like to browse at a flea market.

In preparation for this book we asked you, flea market buyers and sellers, to tell us what you think. That input allowed us to fine-tune the end product to fit your needs. This isn't just another general-line price guide with the upper-end merchandise stripped away and the words "Flea Market" added to the title. From start to finish, we've focused on creating the best flea market book possible. Included is inside information about what's happening on the flea market

scene, what's being offered for sale, and the value of that merchandise.

Our goal was to accurately reflect a typical flea market. We were literally thinking on our feet as we prepared this book. We walked hundreds of miles during a multitude of flea markets, talked to countless dealers, and listened to innumerable shoppers while observing the collectibles landscape.

You'll find an intriguing mix of merchandise represented here, from things that are readily available to scarce objects that, much to the delight of collectors, do occasionally surface at flea markets. Values in this price guide begin at 25 cents for trading cards and range upward from there, highlighting the diversity of items that can be found even within specific categories.

Methodology 101

How do you combine roughly 700 photographs, nearly 800 categories, and countless listings into one cohesive unit? We started with "A." It's a pretty basic concept, but one that works just fine. Categories are listed alphabetically, from ABC plates to Zeppelins. Within each section, you may find the following:

Category: In an effort to make this book as enjoyable to read as it was to write, we intentionally omitted dry discourses on a category's history. If you wanted to do research, you'd be at a library, not at a flea market. Levity aside, that doesn't mean we shied away from useful information. Instead, we utilize a mix of key facts and fun tips. If you're not smiling as you read this book, we haven't done our jobs. For anyone wanting additional insight into a topic, we include information on periodicals,

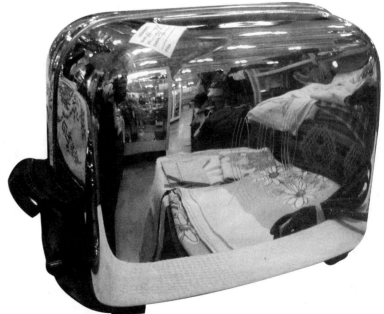

This toaster has a chrome body, rounded corners, and brown Bakelite handles, $90.

Cookie jars are popular finds at flea markets. This Puppy is a tan ceramic with black and white eyes, red tongue, and some wear, $15.

reference books, and collectors' clubs.

Periodicals: The advantage to periodicals is their ability to keep abreast of a changing marketplace. Newsletters are great sources of insider information. Weekly and monthly trade papers and magazines can also help you understand the market. We included those publications we consider helpful.

References: Due to the seemingly infinite number of books about the antiques and collectibles industry, we limited reference works to current titles

we believe provide the most useful historical information as well as accurate prices. Most of the titles listed are readily available from booksellers, and many are offered for sale at flea markets.

Collectors' Clubs: It's hard to keep a good thing to yourself. Collectors love to share their enthusiasm with others, and collectors' clubs offer the perfect avenue for that. We've included many clubs, but there may be others we are not aware of, and new groups may become active. Use our suggestions as a starting point, but don't hesitate to ask fellow collectors and dealers about other clubs they may know of.

Reproduction Alert: Reproductions remain a problem throughout the antiques and collectibles trade. When we were aware of reproductions within a specific category, we used this alert to call your attention to their existence.

Listings: Looking for the heart of this book? You just found it. The individual listings are short but sweet, giving detailed descriptions that aid in identification. You'll find the listings presented alphabetically, each with a current value.

What's a flea market?

Attempting to define a flea market is like trying to describe all restaurants with a single statement. Sure, McDonald's and the White House kitchen both serve food, but there's a world of difference between the two.

Flea markets suffer from the same identity problem. They come in innumerable varieties, from multi-thousand-dealer events at Brimfield, Massachusetts, to the local volunteer fire department's annual flea market and chili supper, featuring only a handful of merchants. The first may attract full-time dealers, while the latter may appeal to neighbors who have just cleaned out their garages. Yet, good sales and exciting buys can be made at both events.

Typically, flea markets are stereotyped as having low- to middle-market merchandise displayed in a haphazard manner. Imagine a herd of nude Barbies sprawled on the bare ground under a wobbly folding table holding a scattered array of chipped glassware and musty *TV Guides*. However, that's not always the case. In today's market, a shopper is just as likely to find a selection of 19th-century mechanical banks grouped in a professional setting, complete with risers and lights.

Additionally, a number of events considered flea markets are actually seasonal antique shows, such as the Sandwich Antiques Market in Sandwich, Illinois. Ask someone in the

Depression glass dealer Gerry Ruth, Depression Craze, Perkasie, PA, drives his mobile home to Renninger's Extravaganza and sets up a great looking booth, full of depression era glass and china.

Midwest to name his favorite flea market, and Sandwich is likely to be it. The Sandwich Antiques Market remains dedicated to providing both affordable and quality antiques and collectibles, while filtering out those dealers who carry bottom-of-the-line material. Is Sandwich a flea market? No, but it exhibits many of the qualities that attract flea market dealers and shoppers—a well-established event with indoor and outdoor spaces, good facilities, and the promise of finding a bargain.

The reputation of a particular market often dictates the quality of the merchandise presented. Better-known flea markets typically attract upper-end dealers who are just as comfortable at sophisticated antique shows, while lower-end markets tend to adopt a more laid-back approach. Booths may have a cluttered look, and there may be more merchants selling items from

outside the antiques and collectibles field, everything from Beanie babies to tie-dyed t-shirts.

Flea markets also run the gamut from daily markets held in strip malls to monthly shows at 4-H fairgrounds. Outdoor summer markets tend to be a favorite with shoppers. During good weather, the flea market becomes a haven for families wanting to do something together. Children who normally whine at the suggestion of going to an antique mall or auction will often put on a happy face when told the destination is a flea market.

Long live Flea Markets!

Flea markets are alive and well. That's good news in an industry that is undergoing none-too-subtle changes, due in large part to the Internet. In a day when many antique shows are losing dealers who have decided they

can more easily do business selling online, flea markets still appear to be strong. What's their secret? Actually, it's the Internet!

An increasing number of people have discovered fun and profit through selling antiques and collectibles on the World Wide Web. Although they might have started by cleaning out the attic, they're soon looking for additional sources of inventory. Flea markets have proven to be the perfect place to find inexpensive items for resale.

Nor have seasoned collectors abandoned flea markets. Shoppers still root through showcases and burrow under tables for prizes waiting to be found, sometimes at a fraction of their value. The thrill of the hunt continues to lure collectors and dealers to their favorite flea markets.

Those flea markets that serve

as tag-team partners with more traditional antique shows are also doing well. Consider the Springfield Antiques Show & Flea Market, held monthly in Springfield, Ohio. While shoppers find a variety of upper-end antiques there, from American art pottery to country furniture, the show also attracts a number of dealers selling more affordable wares. Looking for Beanie Babies? They're there. Need vintage hardware for a kitchen cabinet? No doubt, someone has it. Interested in Little Golden Books? Bring a large bag to carry them home.

Many promoters who combine traditional antique shows with flea markets are careful to limit the number of dealers selling new items, such as T-shirts and shrubbery. Because they are offered a range of items across a broad spectrum of prices, shoppers have the hope of finding exactly what they're looking for. Not even the Internet can dampen that enthusiasm.

The Flea Market Zone

If Rod Serling were still with us, he might sum things up this way: "There is a fifth dimension beyond that which is known to man. It is a dimension as vast as collectibles and as timeless as antiques. It is the middle ground between wanting and owning, between seeing and sacking, and it lies between the pit of person's coveting and the balance of his/her checkbook. This is the dimension of collecting. It is an

Local grower Dan Schantz visits the Perkiomenville flea market early on Monday mornings to sell some of his flowers.

area which we call The Flea Market Zone."

Is there a signpost up ahead? Collectors hope so, and they get excited when it reads "Flea Market" in large, bold letters. However, there are more efficient ways to find flea markets than by relying on chance. For starters, several guides have been published that cover American flea markets. These books are valuable for the detailed information they provide, listing flea markets, locations, dates, times, admission rates, dealer rates, and contact information. Check your favorite bookseller for titles and availability.

Trade publications are another excellent source of information. National and regional publications contain a fair number of advertisements for flea markets. In addition, don't overlook the free tabloids available at many flea markets, antique shows, and

antique malls. Ads for smaller flea markets and festival-related events can often be found in these publications.

Of course, nothing beats a good recommendation from other collectors and dealers. Ask around, especially when at a flea market you like. Talk to the dealers to find out which markets they prefer and which venues offer similar types of merchandise.

Do plan on checking with a local newspaper, chamber of commerce, or neighborhood know-it-all to double check that the super-duper tremendous flea market you heard about really will be held on the date you think. Some flea markets are better on certain days of the week. Don't be afraid to ask the locals when they go to shop for antiques and collectibles, not vegetables. The Columbus, NJ, flea market is great example—plan to go there

Booths at Shupp's Grove, Adamstown, PA, are large, big enough to park your van behind the booth. Some have tent enclosures, this particular one had a garage size awning and was filled with artfully displayed antiques and decorator items.

on a Thursday, not Saturday or Sunday if you're looking for really great antiques and collectibles. However, when you drive by, the sign says they are open on Saturday and Sunday too—yes in deed they are open, but usually the really good dealers are off at other antique flea markets.

Don't go quite yet

You've done your homework. You've found a great-sounding flea market. You managed to finagle a Saturday off from work. The rest of the family is dressed and ready to go. Have you forgotten anything?

How about a phone call?

Sure, the flea market guide states that Billy-Bob's Flea-Spectacular is open every

Saturday and Sunday. However, circumstances do arise that cause flea markets to change their hours, move to a different location, or even go out of business. There's nothing more frustrating than driving 100 miles in the wee morning light, enduring two hours of your kids drubbing each other in the back seat, and drinking three cups of lukewarm coffee, only to find a "CLOSED" sign hanging crookedly on the chain-link fence surrounding what used to be Billy-Bob's. Such experiences can generally be avoided by confirming the details of the market ahead of time.

When contacting the promoter, double-check the date, hours of operation, and admission fees. If you aren't familiar with the area, ask for directions. And remember, if the drive involves much distance, find out if you will

be changing time zones. Otherwise, a road trip from Illinois to Michigan could find you arriving 45 minutes after the gate opened instead of 15 minutes early, as you had planned. Time zones have crushed more than one collector's hopes of getting into a market with the opening surge of shoppers.

While you're at it, don't forget to check the weather forecast. It might be sunny when you leave your home in San Jose, but Pasadena could be in the midst of a thunderstorm. Rain and outdoor flea markets are natural enemies. A quick check of The Weather Channel would have shown you that a low-pressure system had stalled directly above the Rose Bowl Flea Market and Swap Meet. Sure, the event might be held "rain or shine," but that doesn't mean you feel like slogging through puddles on your day off.

Getting comfortable

Boy Scouts are pretty intelligent kids. They've got that neat hand sign, and they're good at expecting the unexpected. We should all be so smart.

Veteran flea market shoppers also know to be prepared. To begin with, they dress for success. Nothing will kill a day at a flea market faster than being uncomfortable, whether you're too cold, too hot, or suffering from achy feet. Dressing appropriately for the season and accounting for changes in the weather are essential components of an enjoyable hunt for flea market treasures. Two rules are key: dress in layers, and take a change of clothes.

Many flea market shoppers are early birds, wanting to jump into the action as soon as possible. When arriving at a Wisconsin flea market in the chill of the morning, a wool sweater and a cup of steaming coffee will keep you warm. But once the coffee cup is empty, Mr. Sun peeks from behind the clouds, and the temperature climbs, it's likely your wardrobe will become a hindrance. Suddenly you're concentrating on the hot, itchy sweater instead of the under-priced Art Deco candlesticks you just walked past.

At the very least, expect the temperature to fluctuate during the day. Layers of light clothing will prepare you for any variations in the weather. It's better to wear a light jacket that can be removed and carried in your cloth bag or backpack, serving as packing material if needed, than to be stuck in a heavy hooded sweatshirt all day because it's the only thing you tossed on that morning.

Never wear clothes that haven't been worn and washed several times. Everything should fit and be comfortable. A new pair of jeans might be a little tighter than you had imagined, or an unwashed T-shirt could cause an unexpected rash. And don't even think about breaking in a new pair of shoes at a flea market. You're

Depression glass offered by dealer Gerry Ruth, Depression Craze, Perkasie, PA, at Renninger's Extravaganza.

just asking for trouble (read: blisters) if you think your new Nikes are going to travel miles of hot pavement and acres of uneven terrain at an outdoor market without revolting against your toes or heels. Comfortable, well-worn walking shoes are your best bet.

Don't forget something to cover your noggin, also. On cold days, nothing keeps you warm like a stocking cap. In hot weather, a wide-brimmed hat will protect your head, face, and neck, lessening the possibility of sunburn and headaches. At the very least, a baseball-style cap affords shade for your face, and it can easily be stuffed in a back pocket when no longer needed.

In addition to those items you're wearing, pack a second set of clothes to keep in your vehicle. Give yourself the option of warmer or cooler clothes, depending on the weather. You may start the day wearing long pants, but by noon the shorts in

your car might feel more comfortable. A quick trip to change will be time well spent. Don't forget to pack an extra pair of shoes and socks as well. More than one rainy day at the flea market has been salvaged when the cloudburst stopped and the shopper changed out of soaked sneakers and into a dry pair of shoes and socks. Better yet, pack a pair of boots. You'll be glad you did when the other shoppers are slogging through a rain-soaked field with mud oozing between their toes.

The right stuff

The right clothes are important, but wise flea market shoppers know that it takes more than a comfortable pair of khakis to ensure a good day shopping. Here are some other items you'll find useful.

Cash: Money talks. Cash speaks a universal language that everyone understands. Do more

A simple sign tells the story here, canning jars for $2 in one basket, another holds those selling for 50 cents. The little wheelbarrow was for sale, but also made a great place to display flower pots. This well laid out booth belonged to Linda and Michael Bremer and was photographed at Renninger's June Extravaganza.

than just take along enough to get you through the day, keeping in mind that you'll probably eat and put gas in the car before returning home. Make sure you have a sufficient number of small bills, as well as some change in your pocket. Ones and fives come in handy when buying low-priced items, especially if a dealer has a handful of twenties or doesn't want to break your $100 bill for a postcard tagged $1.50. The quarters jingling in your pocket will speed the transaction at the concession stand when all you want is a glass of iced tea before heading down the next aisle.

Other funds: Although not all dealers accept checks, many do. Before leaving home, make sure you have a sufficient number of checks with you. Credit cards are honored by some dealers, primarily at the larger events; however, don't expect to use your VISA at many of the smaller flea markets. An ATM/debit card offers

the best of both worlds. When you unexpectedly find a Pairpoint cornucopia just as you are running low on cash, the dealer will likely hold it for you while you dart off to the nearest automated teller machine. Many large flea markets now have ATMs available on the property.

Meals and snacks: Flea market food ranges from fantastic to repulsive, and to make matters worse, what some markets charge for a hot dog and a cold drink might make you cry more than the onions. Depending on the market, a better solution might be to pack your lunch and keep it in a cooler in the car. A quick trip to the parking lot will take less time than waiting in line for a greasy cheeseburger.

Pack high-energy food that's easily digested and, if desired, can be eaten while you walk. As a snack, fruit is always a good option, as are many sports-

related energy bars. Don't forget to take along some drinks. A thermos of coffee, tea, or even soup is great for chilly mornings, while a cooler of iced soft drinks or juice will be worth its weight in gold by the end of the day. And don't forget the water. Not only will it quench you thirst, but it can also be used to clean and cool your face, neck, and hands on hot, sunny days.

After a long day of shopping, you may be too tired (or too poor) to stop at a restaurant. A cold drink and that box of crackers you stashed in your vehicle might be just what it takes to see you through the miles home. A small bag of hard candies might also give you the sugar rush needed to get home. That's a better option than trying to starve off light-headedness by scrounging for gummy bears stuck to the carpet in the back seat.

The car kit: If you've spent much time at flea markets, you know how important it is to pack some things in the car "just in case." Among the items to consider are sunblock, Chap Stick, a travel-size medical kit, pain reliever, antacid, a small package of facial tissue, a container of anti-bacterial wipes, hand cleaner, bug spray, and even a hairbrush for those windy days at outdoor markets.

A box of your most frequently used reference books can serve as your traveling library. And don't forget to toss in some empty boxes, newspapers, wrapping supplies such as bubble wrap and tissue paper, and tape to pack your purchases safely for the trip home. A clipboard or several sturdy pieces of cardboard will protect items that are easily bent.

Some shoppers also include a black light, Bakelite and gold test kits, plastic bags for holding small items, maps, a flashlight, a tow chain, gloves, hand warmers, an umbrella, and a small bag of tools with screwdrivers of various types and sizes.

Tools of the trade: Although your goal is to travel as lightly as possible, you will still want to carry a number of items with you. Begin with a cloth bag, fanny pack, or backpack for storing needed tools of the trade as well as your flea market finds. Some shoppers prefer to use collapsible carts.

A pen and a pocketsize notebook are useful for jotting down information on a dealer's location or for noting a specific item you want to quickly research using the reference books in your vehicle. A small tape measure can be used to determine whether the yellowware bowl you're considering is the size needed for your nesting set, or whether the Victorian marble-top table will fit next to your sofa. A collapsible jeweler's loupe will prove invaluable in reading small marks or enhancing details in vintage photographs. Some shoppers prefer a magnifying glass, with or without a battery-powered light.

A magnet can be used to determine if a painted frog

doorstop is cast iron or brass, and a set of batteries will come in handy for testing toys or other battery-operated collectibles.

Handing out a want list or cards printed with your name, telephone number and what you collect can help secure items after the event. Most business supply stores and copy centers can create inexpensive versions. You might also want to carry an inventory to refer to so you don't purchase duplicate items.

Durable paper towels can be tucked in your pocket, serving a multitude of functions. They can be used to wrap your newly acquired Davenport Cigars match safe so it doesn't get scratched, wipe a runny nose, clean up blood from a cut finger, or serve as a backup when the Port-A-John is out of toilet paper.

Communication: Cellular phones and walkie-talkies have become standard equipment for many flea market shoppers. The cell phone allows you to inform your spouse when you're running a little late, to ask a friend if he's interested in the Creature From the Black Lagoon model kit you just found, or to call to have someone check a reference book you forgot to pack. Walkie-talkies and other two-way radios allow teams of shoppers to stay in contact with each other,

checking to see if a Pepsi tray is a good buy or whether a team member still needs a specific Camp Snoopy drinking glass.

On your mark...

When it comes to flea markets, most veteran collectors attack the event with forethought. There's method to their madness. Here are some of the approaches used.

Run and gun: In the run and gun, the shopper hurries down the aisles, glancing in each booth for certain items, but not stopping unless he sees something he wants to buy. Sometimes he resorts to shouting, "Got any...?" as he's scurrying past. After going through the entire show, he'll begin a second loop, this time checking each booth more carefully.

Slow and steady: In this approach, the shopper figures he

An assortment of mugs can always be found at the flea market. Here is one with Santa holding bag of toys and teddy, small teddy on inside rim of cup, unmarked, $1.50.

The Bremers of Colts Neck, NJ, came up with an interesting way of displaying rolling pins by using wine racks.

has a better chance of finding something if he methodically looks at all of the merchandise in each booth. This method allows him to scrutinize the items in each booth, but by the time he gets to the last aisle, several hours may have passed. He feels what he might miss in those latter booths (because it's already sold by the time he gets there) will be offset by the treasures he discovers early on.

FDS (Favored Dealer Status): Knowing certain dealers carry the type of merchandise he's looking for, the collector will immediately head to those booths. This is generally a good approach, and the dealers are easy to find since most flea markets allow them to reserve the same booth space for each show.

Walking advertisement: In this method, the customer wears a shirt or sign noting what he collects. No one could miss a neon-orange shirt with large black letters that read, "Old Cameras Wanted." Dealers with cameras for sale will eagerly flag down the shopper. No doubt, the resulting sale will be a Kodak moment.

A little diplomacy

It's well understood that most flea market dealers are willing to lower their prices. Surely you've had this experience: You're shopping a flea market when, out of curiosity, you pick up an item. Immediately, you are hit with a rapid-fire, "Icandobe'eronthat!" Translated, it means, "I can do better on that." It doesn't matter if you're holding a $125 Blue Ridge teapot, a $10 PEZ dispenser, or the candy wrapper you just took off that refreshing mint you tossed in your mouth, the phrase speaks

volumes about the fact that flea markets are places where prices can be negotiated.

Some dealers will automatically volunteer to provide a discount, while others may have signs announcing, "Ask for a better price" or "No reasonable offer refused." Yet, often it's up to you to make the first move. Here are some rules for the game of dickering.

Rule No. 1: Politeness is everything. This is a good rule to follow in all your dealings at a flea market, from negotiating with a seller to ordering a hot dog at the concession stand. Put a smile on your face and enjoy the day. When seeking a better price from a dealer, a cheery countenance can work wonders. Talk to him with the same tone and manner you would use when asking a friend for a favor. You can never go wrong when treating people with kindness and respect.

Common courtesy will also put you in good stead when seeking additional information about an item that's for sale. You might want to know who previously owned a particular cedar chest or whether an oil painting has had touch-up work. Do as your mother told you, and mind your manners. A non-threatening approach will help put the dealer at ease and could put you both on the path to a sale.

Rule No. 2: Play with a poker face. Conceal your enthusiasm until after you've purchased the item. If you spot a Chef egg timer you recall from your grandmother's kitchen, don't squeal, "OH MY GOSH!" and immediately rush into the booth to gleefully snatch the piece off the table. To a dealer, that's tantamount to announcing, "I hereby waive all my rights to bargain on the price of this item." The dealer knows you want the egg timer, and he sees a sale coming at full price. Instead, wait until you get the little Chef character back to the car before jumping for joy.

Rule No. 3: Be willing to pay a fair price. Don't let your pride keep you from owning something you want, especially if it's already affordable. If you find a Hummel lamp worth $475 that's only priced $200, it's okay to ask if the dealer will negotiate the price. However, don't be offended if he tells you the price is firm. Pay the $200 and be happy with your bargain. Remember, collecting should be fun. Don't let the absence of a discount ruin your day.

Rule No. 4: Know how to bargain. There are a number of methods that work for buyers. The one we prefer is a straightforward, non-threatening approach. Politely call the item to the dealer's attention and ask, "Is this your best price?" The dealer then has the option of quoting a lower figure or telling you the price is firm. If a discount is offered, we recommend you either accept it or thank the dealer and walk away.

Some people delight in dickering back and forth until a

This flea market was held on the parking lot of a fire company. It was easy for dealers to set up tables and park their vehicles in the space.

price is agreed upon. If that's your style, and the dealer doesn't mind, the best of luck to you both. But keep in mind that some dealers will be insulted if you respond to their offer by undercutting it with a counteroffer.

Rule No. 5: Bargain seriously. Don't ask for a discount unless you are truly interested in buying the item. Otherwise, you're wasting both your time and that of the dealer. We've all seen it happen. Someone picks up a Hubley airplane tagged $165 and asks the dealer, "Can you do any better on the price?" The dealer says he really wants to move merchandise, so he'll take $85 for it. The customer then mumbles something unintelligible, sets down the plane and walks out of the booth. Obviously, the individual never intended to buy the toy.

And that's final!

They're just three little words, but they can have a big impact on your life. We're all familiar with the

phrase "All sales final." The general rule at most flea markets is that the deal is finalized when money changes hands. If you experience buyer's remorse or find an identical item for less just two booths later, don't expect the seller to refund your purchase price or give you a rebate.

Even if the item is later determined to be a reproduction, your avenues of recourse may be limited. While reputable dealers will refund the purchase price if an honest mistake has been made, others will point out that you should not have bought the piece if you weren't sure of its authenticity.

The best thing you can do is to carefully examine all merchandise before you buy.

Would you check on that?

You've found a McCoy cookie jar, the sticker price seems fair, and the dealer appears willing to negotiate. But before you strike a deal, there are some other steps

Decoration, pumpkin, orange, black, and white, green stem, mkd "Made in U.S.A.," $35

you'll want to take.

Examine the item: Carefully check over prospective purchases. If the price seems low, the piece may be damaged. Examine glassware and pottery for chips and cracks and old repairs. Check toys to see if all the parts are original and to determine whether the item has been repainted. Look for stains and holes in textiles and make sure you're dealing with an authentic item, not a reproduction.

Ask about it: Even if you are convinced the item is perfect, ask the dealer if he's aware of any damage. You might have missed a hairline crack or a carefully concealed repair. An honest dealer will tell you what he knows and most dealers are honest.

That Latin phrase

This is the part of the book in

which we get to use the Latin phrase every antiquer knows, *caveat emptor*—let the buyer beware. Although flea markets are enjoyable and hold the promise of turning up a prized collectible at a reasonable price, there are also some pitfalls that seem more troublesome than in any other segment of the market.

We want to stress that most flea market dealers are honest, reputable sellers who enjoy what they're doing and wouldn't think of jeopardizing their business by cheating a customer. However, it's important to discuss the proverbial "one bad apple" that can spoil the rest of the fruit in the barrel.

Reproductions:

Reproductions, fakes, and fantasy items are often found at flea markets. One must understand that sales of reproductions are not dependent on the items being represented as old merchandise.

Quite the contrary. At some flea markets, reproductions are stacked ten-deep on the table and are offered at wholesale prices. That repro tin windup penguin may be bought as new here, passed off as authentic there. *There* may be no farther than three aisles away, so *caveat emptor*.

Knowledge is your best defense. If the price seems too good to be true, even at a flea market, then maybe it is. When examining an item, use all your senses. Look at it. Are the details crisp, or does a cast-iron bottle opener have the worn molding of many recasts? Examine the hardware. Are the screws in a mechanical bank the right type for when the piece was made? Study the lithography. Is the printing of a die-cut sporting goods sign a little fuzzy, indicating a later printing method? Feel the piece. Does the wear on the base correspond to the age of the planter? Some old merchandise even has a slightly different texture than the reproductions. Using your nose can also provide some clues about the item. Does a small curly maple candle box have the smell of a 150-year-old piece, or is the scent that of freshly cut wood or new varnish?

Tall tales: Unscrupulous dealers always have a story to tell about their merchandise. Listen carefully, and *caveat emptor*. You might be told that a supposed hand-blown goblet traveled across the Atlantic Ocean with a family of Pilgrims aboard the Mayflower. But, if that goblet is pressed glass, you can rest assured it's not as old as the dealer suggests.

Some mistakes are made honestly, but they're mistakes nonetheless. How about the Lucy doll with a 1963 copyright date. The price tag read: "Lucy, 1963, all original, $45." But, Lucy's dress was fastened with Velcro tabs. Does anyone see a problem here? The Velcro shows the clothes to be of a more contemporary design.

Copyright dates are tricky things, and worth a brief mention. They indicate when a particular copyright was issued, not necessarily the date of manufacture for the object on which the copyright appears. G.I. Joes are good examples. Fuzzy haired Joes first appeared in 1970, but the copyright date on each figure says 1964, so do your homework.

Look for clues that indicate an item's true age. For instance, a Royal Staffordshire platter marked "Dishwasher Safe" is definitely from the second half of the 20th century, not from the 19th century, no matter how old the transferware pattern looks. Knowledgeable collectors are always on the lookout for price tags with incorrect information. Among the common mistakes are pressed glass said to be cut glass, molded pottery marked as hand-thrown, machine-molded glassware claimed to be mouth-blown, plastic tagged as Bakelite or celluloid . . . Need we go on?

Knowledge is your friend. The best purchases you will ever make are good reference books.

Some of your most productive time will be spent with dealers and collectors who allow a hands-on examination of authentic antiques and collectibles. Armed with knowledge, you can shop any market safely.

Absolutely positive

Don't let "The Bad and the Ugly" scare you away from flea markets. The nasties are far outweighed by "The Good" that can be found at these events. Topping the list of those positives is the family atmosphere at flea markets. Here's the perfect way to spend a day with loved ones. Because flea markets offer something for everyone, even children enjoy tagging along. The hunt for inexpensive collectibles will keep them interested for

A great flea market that springs up twice a year in Landisville, PA.

Due to the inexpensive nature of some of the merchandise, flea markets are good places for children to learn the value of money. Permitting them to spend their allowance on a collection of their own teaches them to make decisions regarding how that money is used.

The other side

What's more fun than shopping at a flea market? How about selling at one? Most flea markets are a mix of full-time dealers running a business and one-time sellers looking for a way to get rid of the stuff that has piled up in the garage. As such, these markets are perfect for anyone looking to make a little cash from the extra things around the house.

Here are some tips to help you succeed if you're new to the role of flea market dealer.

Finding fleas: The first thing you need to do is decide which flea market you want to try. Check flea market directories and trade publications to see which events are held in your area. Before making a commitment to take a booth, attend several flea markets. Ask the dealers what they like about the event and what they would change. Question them about what's selling well and what price ranges attract buyers. Decide whether your merchandise will fit in at a particular market. Inquire about other flea markets the dealers use, as well as the ones they like to shop. Don't

hours.

Although children seem to have a natural interest in the merchandise at flea markets, they don't always have the stamina to spend an entire day walking aisles and darting into booths. One popular solution is to take a wagon. Your youngsters will enjoy the ride, especially at outdoor markets. Toss in a coloring book or handheld video game, and you've made great strides toward boredom-proofing the day. Add a small cooler with juice and snacks, and you'll be a hero in their eyes.

Strollers can also be used,

and they're particularly good for infants. But whether you're pushing little Susie in a stroller or pulling Johnny Jr. in a wagon, don't be surprised if you get the evil eye from at least a few shoppers. Some adults think children should be banned from all markets. Don't let such cavalier attitudes ruin your day. Remember, you're spending time with your family, and there are few things in the world more important than that. Behaving courteously when maneuvering through the show and using common sense when parking your children to examine an item will certainly be appreciated though.

forget to find out how and where the flea market is advertised. The greater the number of people who hear about the market, the more customers you will likely have.

Next, study the environment. Are there plenty of shoppers? Are the facilities well kept? Are there affordable concessions and clean restrooms? All of these are important considerations for keeping shoppers happy. As a dealer, you'll quickly learn that an unhappy customer is less likely to make a purchase.

Calculating costs: It's important to know how much you'll have to spend to get started in the flea market business, whether you're interested in selling only once or want to set up every weekend. Talk to the promoter about rates and the availability of booth space. Do the dealers also rent tables for displaying their goodies, or will you need to bring some from home? Of course, don't overlook the incidental expenses, such as gas for travel, meals while away from home, and the cost of a motel if you're traveling any distance. All those things can quickly cut into your profit.

Factoring time: If you are retired, you might have unlimited time to devote to your new hobby. But if you're still holding down a 9-to-5 job, can you get away from your desk in time to get on the road and set up at your favorite flea market? Before committing to a particular market, ask the promoter about the event's set-up policy. Because dealers often arrange their booths before the show begins, you may need to spend Friday traveling to your destination and setting up, in preparation for the crowd that will spill through the gates early Saturday morning.

One other factor to consider is how early you plan to arrive at your booth during the show. When we asked flea market dealers for tips, they repeatedly told us, "Arrive early." After only one flea market experience, you'll appreciate the need to be ready before the show opens, in order to maximize sales to early shoppers as well as other dealers.

Some dealers also mentioned that it's important to be willing to stay late at a show. Leaving too soon might get you home in time to catch that made-for-TV movie you wanted to see, but it can also mean you miss out on sales to last-minute bargain hunters.

Deciding what to take: In addition to your merchandise, you'll need the following.

Tables—Unless tables are provided by the promoter, you'll need something to display your items on. Card tables and larger folding tables are ideal.

Chair—Don't forget something to sit on during lulls in the action.

Cash box and change—A small locking cash box and adequate change, both bills and coins, will be essential.

Accordion, Serenelli, The Ritz, 32, pearlized keys, black, silver, and white case, leather strap, fitted case with red lining, $150.

Spending money—In addition to the money for your cash box, you'll want to take along some extra funds for any purchases you might make or to buy lunch.

Wrapping material—Newspapers, tissue, and bubble wrap will protect your customers' purchases on the trip home.

Tape—This can be used to secure the wrapping material around an item or for posting signs in your booth.

Bags and boxes—You will need paper or plastic bags to hold sold merchandise if the customer doesn't have their own carry-all. Cardboard boxes are good for packaging larger pieces or multiple items.

Receipt books—You'll want to record your sales, and your customer will appreciate a copy of the transaction.

Price tags—Pack some extra price tags for any items you purchase for resale while traveling to the flea market or while at the event. You might also discover you've forgotten to mark some merchandise, and extra tags will come in handy.

Business cards—Don't be bashful about handing out business cards to anyone who is interested in your merchandise. It may result in a sale long after you've packed up and gone home. When a shopper has time to reconsider your *Wizard of Oz* book he walked away from at the show, knowing how to contact you

could put that one in the sold column.

Price guides—Pack a few of your favorite price guides, including one general-line guide that covers the market as a whole. (Of course, we strongly recommend this book!) They'll come in handy for determining whether an Annie lunchbox is a good buy or for showing a customer where to find information on a club for jelly glass collectors.

Showcase—Consider keeping any valuable small items in a showcase, which will discourage theft.

Sheets or tarps—You might also want to take some light, unfitted bed sheets to cover you merchandise when you're out of your booth, keeping ne'er-do-wells from being tempted by your miniature Blue Willow tea set. For outdoor shows, a light covering will also prevent dew from forming on your merchandise, while a water-resistant tarp will be more appropriate when the skies threaten rain.

Creating the display: There is no right or wrong way to display merchandise at a flea market. Some dealers achieve satisfactory results by simply placing their wares on a blanket on the ground. Others adopt a more professional approach, using tables with table covers, risers and lights. We believe the latter provides better exposure for your merchandise, and increased visibility can translate to increased sales.

One of the best things you can do to encourage sales is to price all of your merchandise. Some shoppers hesitate to ask for the price of an item that's untagged. Others may not ask out of principal, believing the dealer will quote a figure that's artificially inflated if the shopper is dressed nicely and appears to be financially fit. Don't run the risk of losing a sale because your merchandise isn't marked.

Providing customer service: The manner in which you treat your customers is the single most important factor in ensuring your success as a flea market dealer. Never underestimate the importance of greeting every individual who enters your booth. A genuine smile and polite conversation might be all it takes to win over a shopper who's debating whether to buy your hula girl nodder. Customers who are treated with courtesy will remember you, and a friend you make today might well be a customer you keep for life.

Another voice heard from: We all figure we're beating out collectors and dealers when we're buying at flea markets, but there is another character in the crowd that often will out-spend even a dedicated collector – and that's the decorator! Professional decorators, and budding amateurs too, frequent flea markets in search of accent pieces, and more and more are planning whole decors around their flea market find. We've got HGTV and some of the modern television shows, like *Trading Spaces*, to thank for this. It's great fun to watch them, trying to match color swatches, or whipping out their tape measure to see if that architectural fragment is big enough, or if that kitsch lamp is the right size. Add to that folks like me who sometimes take their flea market finds and transform them (or try to) into something more usable, giving a second lease on life to an outdated chandelier. Snapping up vintage linens to reuse as curtains turned out to be a rather inexpensive fix for my office. By adding small brass clip-on rings, I can simply take them off and fold up the linens to be used again in another way. At Christmas, I took some vintage cards found at a flea market for a few dollars, attached some to a wreath, added a bow and actually caught the mailman smiling back at a jolly Santa winking at him on the front door. More cards were placed on the bright red tablecloth on my dining room table, then covered with a light organza tablecloth, letting me enjoy the cards all during the season. I incorporated a few more cards into the centerpiece and felt I had a real theme going. It was quick, easy, and a cheerful reminder of a warm day's trip to a favorite flea market.

Here's wishing that you find bargains and exciting items awaiting you at the next flea market you visit.

Happiness is a bag of Fiesta in one hand and a bag of Harlequin in the other for Diane Davis of Bucks County, PA. Diane collects Fiesta and her daughter collects Harlequin - must make for two rather colorful kitchens. The photo was taken at Renninger's Spring Extravaganza, Kutztown, April, 2003.

Questions, Questions, Questions!

While I was busy collecting pricing information and visiting flea markets, Krause Publications editor Karen O'Brien helped design a questionnaire which ran in *Antique Trader.* Thanks to all who took the time to answer the questions for they have given us much to think about. Answers came from all the country, which is terrific. Karen read through them before sending them off to me where I have been sorting and reading them for weeks. As much as I'd like to travel to every flea market, it's just not possible. By reading and analyzing the surveys, I got to hear about what folks liked and disliked, what they are looking for, etc.

Of course those responding to the *Antique Trader* questionnaire were flea market enthusiasts and their answers reflected this. And if you believe as I do, that part of the great fun of visiting a flea market is finding a treasure, but it also offers us a way to participate in our right to have a free marketplace. Flea markets are often the entry level

Bowl, two handles, center dec of cavalier serenading two ladies, gold tracery border, mkd "Triumph, Made in U.S.A., Limoges, D'Or, It S284, Warranted 22K Gold," $20.

for antiques and collectibles, but some really fine pieces also find their way to flea markets. Whether a flea market is held informally or is a well organized events, held weekly or twice a year, it offer sellers a venue to lay out their merchandise. To buyers, being able to stroll up and down aisles filled with all types of merchandise is certainly easier than bouncing all over to yard and estate sales. I find it more rewarding to stop at a flea market full of dealers and look around than driving around trying to find yard sales which may only yield a few antiques or collectibles among their piles of used VCR tapes and out-grown baby clothing. However, when you happen upon a town hosting a flea market and the streets are filled with "yard sale" signs, I find myself thinking that Camelot

really does exist. Usually I head for the flea market first, and then to as many of the yard sales as I can reach from my first parking spot. Then it's onward to another parking spot and as many yard sales as I can hit til I'm ready to drop!

The first question we asked on our survey was to list the names and locations of flea markets – this list includes 280 flea markets spread from coast to coast. I've tried to add locations, based on the names the respondents gave, but would also advise you to check with a local newspaper or chamber of commerce to determine when a local flea market is open, if it's open rain or shine, etc. Numbers in parenthesis indicate that more than one person indicated this flea market as a favorite.

Flea Markets Around the Country

Alaska

Soldotna: Soldotna Flea Market, 538 Arena Drive

Alabama

Birmingham: Birmingham Fairground Flea Market, Alabama State Fairgrounds, Exit 120

Mobile: Flea Market Mobile, 401 Schillingers Rd.

Montgomery: Blue Ridge Treasure Hunt

Montgomery: Eastbrook Flea Market, 425 Coliseum Blvd.

Watumpike: Blue Ridge Treasure Hunt

Arkansas

Pine Bluff: 270 & 65 Flea Market, 8112 Sheridan Rd.

Redfield: Redfield County Fair Flea Market, S. Highway 365

Arizona

Glendale: Glendale 9 Swap Meet, 5650 N 55th Ave.

Phoenix: American Park N Swap, 3801 East Washington St.

Phoenix: Phoenix Fairgrounds Antique Market, Phoenix Fairgrounds

Canada

BC, Vancouver, Canada: Croatian Cultural Centre Flea Market, 21st Century Promotions

California

Alameda: Alameda Antique Flea Market, 1150 Ballena Blvd.

Concord: Solano Flea Market, Solano Way

Escondido: Escondido Swap Meet, West Mission Ave.

Fullerton: Troubleshooters Antiques & Collect Round-Up, Cal State University

Glendale: Glendale City College, Upper parking lot

Long Beach: Long Beach A& C Market, Long Beach Veterans Stadium

Napa: Napa Flea Market, 303 S.

Kelly Rd.

Oceanside: Oceanside Swap Meet, 3480 Mission Ave.

Pasadena: Rose Bowl Flea Market and Swap Meet, Pasadena Rose Bowl, Rosemont Ave. & Aroyo Blvd.

Petaluma: Petaluma Outdoor Antiques Faire, Sonoma-Marin Fairgrounds, 4th & KY St.

San Diego: Kobey's Swap Meet, San Diego Sports Arena, 3500 Sports Arena Blvd.

San Francisco: Cow Palace Cow Palace, Highway 101

San Mateo: San Mateo Flea Market, Several different flea markets held in this town

Santa Cruz: Skyview Flea Market, 2260 Soquel Dr.

Santa Monica: Santa Monica Outdoor Antiques Market, Parking lot, Airport Rd. & Bundy Ave.

Spring Valley: Spring Valley Flea Swap Meet, 6377 Quarry Rd.

Stockton: San Joaquin Delta College Flea Market, San Joaquin Delta College

Colorado

Redstone: Redstone Flea Market, 0373 Redstone Blvd.

Connecticut

Salisbury: Antiques in a Cow Pasture, Barn Star Productions

Deleware

Laurel Bargin Bill, Route 13 at Route 9 East

New Castle Farmer's Market, 110 N. DuPont Highway

Florida

Daytona: Daytona Flea Market, I-95 and US 92

Deland: Deland Flea Market Volusia County Farmer's Market, E New York Ave.

Fort Lauderdale: A-1 Flea Market, 1621 N. State Rd. 7

Fort Lauderdale: OaklandPark Blvd. Flea Market, 3161 West

Oakland Park Blvd.

Hollywood: Heritage Park

Hollywood: Ty Park

Jacksonville: Ramona Flea Market, 7059 Ramona Blvd.

Kissimmee: Highway 192 Flea Market, W. Irlo Bronson Highway

Kissimmee: Osceola Flea & Farmers Market, 2801 E. Irlo Bronsn Highway

Lecanto: Cowboy Junction

Melbourne: (2) Super Flea & Farmers Market, 4835 West Eau Gallie Blvd.

Mt Dora: (5) Florida Twin Markets, Renningers Highway 441, near intersection with Hwy 46

Okeechobee: The Market Place Flea Market, 3600 Highway 441 South

Orlando: Colonial Flea Market, 11500 E. Colonial Drive

Port Richey: USA Fleamarket, 11721 U.S. Highway 19

Sarasota: Flea Market & Collectibles Show, Sarasota Fairgrounds

St. Augustine: St. John County Beach Flea Market, I-95 and State Road 207, exit 94

Stuart: B & A Flea Market Soute, U.S. Highway 1, across from Martin Sq. Mall

Webster: Webster Westside Flea Market, 516 NW 3rd St., Highway 478 at NW 3rd St.

Webster: (2) Sumter County Farmer's Market, Inc., Highway 471

West Palm Beach: 45th Street Flea 45th Street

West Palm Beach: Beach Drive-In Theatre Swamp, 1301 Old Dixie Highway

West Palm Beach: Dr. Flea's Farmer's Market, 12 WS Congress Ave.

West Palm Beach: Headsley's

Georgia

Atlanta: Lakewood Antiques Market, 2000 Lakewood Way

Atlanta: Pride of Dixie, N. Atlanta Trade Center

Atlanta: Scott Antique Market, A &

C Show Atlanta Expo Center, 3650 Jonesboro Rd.

Savannah: Keller's Flea Market 5901 Ogeechee Rd.

South Augusta: South Augusta Flea Market, Doug Bernard Parkway

Summerville: Summerville Flea Market

Hawaii

Honolulu: Aloha Stadium Flea Market, Aloha Stadium

Iowa

Dubuque: Dubuque Flea Market, Dubuque County Fairgrounds

Fort Dodge: Hillbilly Sales

Marshalltown: market unspecified, location unspecified

Spirit Lake: Vick's Corner, Wa-Hoo Flea Market Highway 9 and 86

Walnut: Whole town

What Cheer: Collectors Paradise Flea Market, Keokuk County Fairgrounds

Idaho

ID, Filer Twin Fall County Fairgrounds Flea Market Twin Fall County Fairgounds

Illinois

Belleville: West Main Fea Market, 2615 West Main St.

Bloomington: Third Sunday Market, McClean County Fairgrounds, Interstate Center

Chicago: Buyers Flea Market, 4545 W. Division St.

DuQuoin: DuQuoin Co. Farigrounds, Hwy 51 South

Grafton: Water Street Flea Market, Water St.

Gray Lake: Lake County Antique & Collectibles Show & Sale, Lake County Fairgrounds

Grayslake: Zuako Antiques & Collectibles Mart

McLean: Old Route 66 Country Market, Route 66

Mendota: Fairgrounds

Pecatonia: The Pec Thing, Winnebago County Fairgrounds

Pontiac: Pontiac Thueseman's

Shows

Princeton: Princeton Flea Market, Fairgrounds

Rantoul: Gordyville Flea Market

Richmond: market unspecified

Rosemont: Wolff's Flea Market Rosemont Horizon, near intersection of I-90 and I-294.

Sandwich: Sandwich Antique Market Fairgrounds, State Rt. 34

St. Charles: Kane County Flea Market, Kane County Fairgrounds, St. Charles St.

Tinley Park: I-80 Flea Market, 19100 Oak Park Ave.

Wheaton: DuPage Flea Market

Indiana

Cedarlake: Big Bear Flea Market, I-70

Cedarlake: Uncle John's Flea Market, Rt. 41 South

Evansville: Cain's Flea Market, 322 W. Columbia St.

Evansville: Collectors Carnival, Vanderburgh County 4-H Fairgrounds

Fort Wayne: Memorial Coliseum Flea Market, Memorial Coliseum

Indianapolis: Indianapolis Flea Market, Indiana State Fairgrounds

Shipshewana: Shipshewana Auction & Flea Market, State Route 5

Veedersburg: Steam Corner Flea Market, 2164 S. U.S. Highway 41

Kansas

Hutchinson: Mid-America Flea Market, Kansas State Fairgrounds

Sparks: Sparks Flea Market, K-7 Highway and Mission Rd.

White Cloud: White Cloud Flea Market, 103 Main St.

Wichita: Mid-America Flea Market, Kansas Coliseum

Kentucky

Louisville: Kent Fairgrounds Flea Market, Kent Fairgronds & Expo Center

Richwood: Richwood Flea Market, 10915 U.S. 25

KY, TN, AL+: Longest Yard Sale U.S. 127 South

Louisiana

Lake Charles: Front Porch Antique & Flea Market, Ryan Street

Shreveport: Merchants Market, Pines Road

Massachusetts

Brimfield: Brimfield's Heart-O-The-Mart A & C Show, Several different flea markets held in this town

Hadley: Olde Haldey Flea Market, Route 47

Palmer: Tri-Town Flea Market, Route 20

Taunton: Taunton Flea Market, 93 Williams

Maryland

Baltimore: Best Yard Sale location unspecified

Baltimore: Patapsco Flea Market 1400 West Patapsco Ave

Mountain Road: market unspecified

Whitemarsh: market unspecified

Maine

Lincoln: Lincoln Flea Market, I-95 Access Road

Michigan

Allegan: market unspecified

Ann Arbor: Ann Arbor Antiques Market

Blissfield: Blissfield Markets, E. Jefferson

Centreville: Centreville Flea Market, St. Joseph County Fairgrounds

Lapeer: Lapeer Flea Market

Midland: market unspecified

Pontiac: Dixieland Telegraph & Dixie

Port Huron: Fort Gratiot Flea Market, 4189 Keewahdin Rd.

Utica: Red Barn Flea Market, 47326 Dequindre

Minnesota

Albany: Pioneer Days Flea Market

Barnum: market unspecified

Cromwell: market unspecified

Detroit: Lakes Shady Hollow Flea Market, Highway 59

Embarrass: market unspecified

Grand Rapids: market unspecified

Hibbing: market unspecified

Hill City: market unspecified

Kettle River: market unspecified

Mankato: National Guard Armory, 2nd & Plum St.

McGregor: market unspecified

Oronoco: Downtown Oronoco Gold Rush, Inc., Whole town

Remer: market unspecified

Rochester: Gold Rush

Tamarack: market unspecified

Wright: market unspecified

Missouri

Aurora: Houn' Dawg, 25 W Locust St.

Jolpin: Joplin Flea Market, 1200 block of VA Ave. in Old City Market

Kansas City: Jeff Williams Flea Market, Kemper Arena Compex, Governor's Building Kansas City: KCI Convention Center Flea Market, KCI Convention Center

Lake Ozark: Fiesta Flea Market, Highway 54

Lake Ozark: Osage Beach Flea Market

Lake Ozark: Village Flea Market

Neosho: Marco's

Rutledge: Rutledge Flea Market

Springfield: I-44 Swap Meet 2908 N. Neergard

Wentzville: Wentzville Flea Market

Mississippi

Waveland: market unspecified

Montana

Great Falls: Great Falls Farmer's Market, Civic Center

North Carolina

Charlotte: Metrolina Expo, 7100 Statesville Rd.

Greensboro: Super Flea Market, Greensboro Coliseum Complex

North Dakota

Fargo: market unspecified

Minot: Magic City Flea Market, State Fairgrounds

Nebraska

Brownville: Fall Flea Market, Main Street

Brownville: Spring Flea Market, Main Street

Omaha: 60th Street Flea

New Hampshire

Derby: Grand View Flea Market, Rt. 28 and Bypass 28 South

West Lebanon: Colonial Antiques & Flea Market

New Jersey

Berlin: Berlin Farmer's Market, 41 Clementon Rd.

Columbus: Columbus Farmer's Market, Rt. 206

Cowtown: market unspecified

Lambertville: Golden Nugget Antique Flea Market, Rt. 29

Lambertville: Lambertville Antique Flea Market, Inc., Rt 29

North Cape May: Victoria Commons Flea Market, Victoria Commons

Rutherford: Street Fair

Stanhope: Waterloo Antiques Fair, Waterloo Village

New Mexico

Albuquerque: North Valley Indoor Flea Market, Candelaria, NW

Carlsbad: Rose Peddle Flea Market, Standpipe Road

Moriaty: Moriaty Flea Market, Rt. 66

Nevada

Sparks: El Rancho Flea Market 555 El Rancho Dr.

New York

Alexandria Bay: market unspecified

Avon East: Avon Flea Market 1520 E Avon Rochester Rd.

Batavia: market unspecified

Bloomfield: market unspecified

Bouckville: Bouckville Antique Pavilion, Route 20

Clarence: Kelly Schultz Antique World & Marketplace, 10995 Main St.

Conklin: Jimay's Flea Market, 1766 Conklin Rd.

Deer Park: market unspecified

Delhi: market unspecified

Great Neck: market unspecified

Hammond: Market Barn location unspecified

Manorville: market unspecified

Millbrook: market unspecified

New York: The Annex Antiques Fair & Flea Market Ave of the

Americas, between 24th and
27th St., Manhattan

Ontario: market unspecified

Stanfordville: market unspecified

Stormville: Stormville Airport
Antique Show & FM, Airport, Rt.
216

Tupper Lake: market unspecified

Walcott: market unspecified

Warrensburg: market unspecified

Ohio

Allensville: Cross Creek Flea Market

Burton: market unspecified

Callipolis: Gallia County Flea
Market, Gallia Ct Fairgrounds

Cincinnati: Peddlers Flea Market,
4343 Kellogg Ave.

Hartville: Hartville Flea Market, 788
Edison St. NW

Hartville: Byler's Flea Market, 900
Edison St. NW

Middlefield: Middlefield Flea Market

N. Ridgeville: Jamie's Flea Market

Piketown: 23 South Flea Market US
23

Rogers: Rogers Comm Auction &
Open-Air Market, SR 154

Springfield: Springfield Antique
Show & Sale, Clark County
Fairgrounds

Oklahoma

Tulsa: Great American Flea Market
& Antique Mall, 9206-9244 East
Admiral Place

Oregon

Portland: America's Largest Antique
& Collectibles Sale, Multnomah
County Expo Center

Pennsylvania

Adamstown: Renninger's #1, Rt 272

Adamstown: Shupp's Grove

Adamstown: Stoudt's Black Angus
Antique Mall, Rt. 272

Barto: Jake's, 1380 Rt 100

Bedford: market unspecified

Hannahstown: market unspecified

Hazen: Warsaw Twp Volunteer Fire
Co. Flea Market, Rt. 28

Kutztown: Renninger's #2 Antique
Market, 740 Nobel St.

Lahaska: Rice's Market, 6326
Green Hill Rd.

Landisville: Hempfield Woman's
Club Flea Market, Amos Herr
Park, East Hempfield Township

Latrobe: Hi Way Drive-In Flea
Market, Route 30

Ligonier: Ligonier Fleatique, Route
30 & Route 259

Matamoras: Matamoras Drive-In

New Hope: New Hope Country
Market, Rt. 202

Perkiomenville: Perkiomenville Flea
Market, Rt. 29

Pittsburgh: Castle Shannon Flea
Market, Fire Hall

Pittsburgh: Eastland Mall, east of
Pittsburgh

Pittsburgh: Antiques Fair at the
Meadowlands, I-79S, Exit 41

Quakertown: Quakertown Farmer's
Market, 201 Station Road

Saylorsburg: Blue Ridge Flea
Market location unspecified

Somerset: market unspecified

Tarentum: market unspecified

Washington: The Meadows,
Racetrack Road

Rhode Island

Charlestown: General Stanton Inn,
4115A Old Post Rd

East Greenwich: Rocky Hill Flea
Market, 1408 Division Rd

Providence: Cedar Street Flea
Market, Cedar Street

South Carolina

Anderson: Anderson Jockey Lot &
Farmer's Market Highway 29
between Greenville and
Anderson

Beaufort: Laurel Bay Flea Market,
922 La Chere St.

Charleston: Lowcountry Flea Market
& Collectibles Show, Gaillard
Aud, 77 Calhoun St.

Pickens: Pickens County Flea
Market, 1427 Walhalla Highway

Madison: Memory Lane Flea
Market, Madison bypass curve

Tennessee

Crossville: Dixon's Flea Market,
Highway 70 North

Knoxville: Knoxville Expo Center,
Clinton Highway at Merchants
Road

Memphis: Memphis Flea Market,

Memphis Fairgrounds

Nashville: Expo Flea Market, 1-24
Expo Center (Smyra)

Sweetwate: Fleas Unlimited, Exit
60, I-75

Texas

Canton: First Monday Trade Days, 2
blocks north of downtown
square

Dallas: Buckarama, Fair Park

Ft. Worth: Henderson Flea Market,
1000 N. Henderston St.

Ft. Worth: Will Rogers Complex

Roundtop: Marburger Farm

Weatherford: First Monday

Utah

Salt Lake City: Redwood Swap
Meet, 3600 South Redwood
Road

Virginia

Chantilly: DC Big Flea, Chantilly
Convention Center

Front Royal: Double Tollgate Flea
Market, 490 N. Commerce Ave.

Hillsville: VFW Labor Day Gun
Show & Flea Market, VFW
Complex, U.S. Rt. 58-221 West

Lynchburg: Market Antiques Fair,
Old City Armory

Virginia Beach: Virginia Beach
Antique & Collectible Expo,
Virginia Beach Pavilion
Convention Center

Vermont

Chelsea: Chelsea Flea Market,
North and South Common of
Chelsea

Waterbury: Waterbury Flea Market,
Rt. 2

Washington

Everett: Puget Park Swap Meet,
13020 Meridian Ave. South

Seattle: Midway Swap Meet

Tacoma: America's Largest Antique
& Collectibles Sale, Tacoma
Dome

Washington DC

DC, Washington: Eastern Market,
7th St. & North Carolina, SE

DC, Washington: Georgetown Flea
Market, Wisconsin Ave. & S St.
NW

Wisconsin

Anjway: market unspecified

Antigo: market unspecified

Caldonia: 7-Mile Fair, 2720 West 7
Mile Road

Dells: market unspecified

Elkhorn: Walworth Flea Market,
Walworth City Fairgrounds

Lake Tomahawk: market unspecified

Milwaukee: Rummage O'Rama,
State Fair Park Grounds

Mukwonago: market unspecified

Princeton: market unspecified

Shawano: Shawano County
Fairgrounds, Flea Market
Highway 29

Warrens: market unspecified

West Virginia

Fayetteville: Bridge Day, New River
Gorge Bridge

Harpers Ferry: Harpers Ferry Flea
Market, Dual Highway 340

Wyoming

Casper: Casper Flea Market
Central, Wyoming Fairgrounds

Jackson Hole: Mangy Moose
Antique Show & Sale, Teton
Village

Question Two was "What are you shopping for at flea markets?" The list is long and varied. And oddly enough, it did not always match Question Three, which was "What do you collect?" Some of the respondents did agree with others that they loved looking for old books or jewelry.

As you can see by the following lists, the items are varied, but very interesting in their scope. I've tried to combine like items together, but thought you might enjoy looking at the variety of items, just as I did. What was really fun were the many ways folks told me that they were open to

finding interesting items, whether they listed them as "sleepers, unique items, etc." Those miscellaneous answers totaled the largest number. Does that mean many shoppers go to a flea market with an open mind, hoping to find something neat?

Survey Respondents Collect

A.C. Gilbert products
Advertising (8)
Animals, camels (2)
Animals, cats (2)
Animals, elephants
Animals, pug dog items
Antiquities, Greek, Roman, South American
Architectural
Art (2)
Art Deco
Automobilia (3)
Banks
Barber bottles
Beaded flowers
Bells (2)
Bicycles, balloon tires
Black Americana
Books (7)
Books, children's (2)
Bottles (4)
Breweriana (3)
Butter knives, twisted
Canes (2)
Chalkware
Children's dishes
Children's greeting cards
Children's paper
Child's mugs
China
China, 1950s dishes
China, Bluebird pattern
China, English pottery
China, Fiesta (2)
China, flow blue
China, Hall China
China, Hull Pottery
China, Lefton
China, Lenox
China, Nippon
China, Occupied Japan (2)
China, Rosemeade pottery
China, RS Prussia
China, slippers, shoes (2)
China, Van Briggle pottery
China, Wedgwood, green
Chinese, anything
Christmas
Clothing, dresses
Clothing, hats

Clothing, purses, vintage
Coins
Compacts
Corksrews
Cowboy stars, Roy Rogers, Hopalong Cassidy
Dolls (6)
Dolls, Black Americana
Dolls, Madame Alexander
Dolls, Muffies
Dolls, R. Tonner
Dolls, Vogue
Figurines
Fishing equipment
Flasks
Flower frogs
Folk Art (2)
Fruit jars (2)
Furniture, chairs
Furniture, painted
Garden
Garfield the Cat
Glass (6)
Glass from '20s, '30s, '40s
Glass, Carnival
Glass, cobalt blue (2)
Glass, depression (8)
Glass, depression glass, elegant
Glass, Fenton
Glass, Fire King
Glass, Fostoria
Glass, milk, old
Glass, opalescent
Glass, pattern, colored
Glass, Victorian
Gone with the Wind
Hallmark ornaments
Hand fans
Hat pins
Household
Inkstands
Inkwells
Iron
Ironstone
Jewelry (6)
Jewelry, charms, gold, old
Jewelry, costume (2)
Jewelry, dress clips
Kaliedescopes

Kitchen, mechanicals
Kitchenware (3)
Kliban cat items
Knife rests
Knives
Ladles
Lap desks
Letter openers
Llardo
M & M's
Magazine ads
Majolica
Match strikers
Medals
Metal
Misc (5): many things, curious items, misc smalls for resale, one of a kind,
Movie memorabilia
Mozart busts
Music
Orange/citrus theme
Paper
Parlor items
Perfume bottles
Peter Rabbit
Petroliana
Phonograph records, cylinders (2)
Pitchers (2)
Pixies
Political memorabilia (3)
Postcards (7)
Pottery (4)
Primitives
Prints, antique
Puzzles
Radios (2)
Raggedy Ann
Records, 78 rpm
Religious
Royal Doulton toby mugs
Royalty items (2)
Salt and pepper shakers (2)
Salt dips (3)
Sebastians (2)
Shot glasses
Signs
Silver (2)
Silver, candlesticks

Silver, sterling, spoons (2)
Smalls
Snoopy
Soda pop (2), signs, thermo
Souvenir spoons, sterling
Staffordshire historical china
Stamps (2)
Steiff bears
Stickpins
Swords
Teapots, figural
Teddy bears (2)
Telegraph sounders
Telephones (2)
Temple, Shirley (2)
Texana paintings on glass
Textiles, linens
Textiles, quilts, old
Textiles, vintage (2)
Tin dishes
Tins
Tip trays
Titantic movie memorabilia
Tobacco tins
Tokens
Tool miniatures
Tools (4)
Toothpick holders
Toys (2)
Toys, diecast
Toys, promos
Toys, sand
Toys, Tonka
Toys, Tootsietoys
Trade cards
Tumblers, old
Turtles
Valentines
Vases
Victorian hand vases
Wall Pockets
Watches
Water based decals
Wedding cake toppers
Wedding memorabilia
Whiskey, early, related glass
Whistles
World's Fair (2)
WWII military

A Custard Glass butter dish, with roses and decorative beading, $35.

Question Four lead to some wonderful stories. We asked for their most exciting flea market story. Here are some of the best:

Big finds department:

"Finding a Roycroft ashtray for $2." Jacqueline Fink, San Diego, CA

"Recently found both a Hall China teapot and a head vase for $1 each." Mary Sweeney

"Finding old steel Tonka toys for $1 each." Eileen Johnson, Duluth, MN

"Paid $1 for an old rabbit candy container." Audrey Belter

"I found a perfect "Button Band" cake basket on a take of assorted glassware for $10." Carolyn Martin, Florissant, MO

"Found a set of 4 cups, saucers, and cake dishes in Columbia, crystal, for $4." Rachelle V. Costa – quite a coup for this depression glass collector.

"In a dig deep bargain place in Texas, I found an old pull string talking Garfield for $1, in good condition." Linda Klodd, Granbury, TX, a dedicated Garfield collector.

"Found composition baby doll for $1. Repaired and dressed it, sold it at auction later for about $80." Margaret Artman.

"Finding a photo postcard that was my great grandfather holding my dad (as a baby).!" Betty Shappee, Escondido, CA

"I bought a pin and when I got home I noticed it was a Georg Jensen." Patricia Thom, Minoti, ND

"Found Y-1 Matchbox Yesteryear 1926 Allchin Traction Machine, paid asking price $1, value over $100." Ron O'Brien, Lansing, IL

"An orig edition book with Maxfield Parrish lithograph plates, found for 25 cents." Shannon Adamczyk, Getzville, NY

"In one booth full of a bunch of ugly old grubby "fresh dug" bottles, there was a beautiful satin glass reverse swirl salt shaker with orig lid for the humble sum of $2. Dealer obviously had no clue of it's real value, nor why I was so thrilled to get it. Turned out especially nice since I'd originally been reluctant to go." Betty L. Giddens.

Loves to shop:

Shopper Dot Marek loves the Longest Yard Sale, US Route 127. She says, "It took me 8 hours to go 30 miles in the Frankford, KY, area…lots of awesome finds in farmers fields, church parking lots, etc."

Jessie St. Pierre, Troy, MO, says "It's always exciting to go to a flea market and be able to leave with a truck full of great deals and wonderful treasures."

Laura Schmidt, Fairport, NY, writes "Everytime I go to flea markets, I get excited. I always find good buys and unusual things. I love the interesting people you meet at flea markets."

Seeing old friends: "Man selling disco records and singing with some. I went to high school with him in the 30's. Ha ha! Bought lots of records." Muriel E. Buchert, Indialantic, FL

Miscelleaneous:

"No one favorite. We get great buys consistently by being thorough and asking questions." Laura Schreuders, Mercerville, NJ

"A vendor got locked inside of an old outhouse." Diane Hones?, Birnamwood, WI

"Seeing my new sister-in-law buying a second smoking ashtray after I gifted her the first one, starting her collection!" Nancy Bell-Szwalle, Binghamton, NY

"I found a "3 Rivers Stadium" metal ornament for sale and bought it. This was after "3 Rivers Stadium" was imploded to build newer stadium, a part of Pittsburgh history." Pittsburgh resident, Patty Barnett.

I must admit to being somewhat surprised by the responses to Question Five: Do you generally haggle over prices? Less than 50% admitted to this. Some responded with a definite yes, with comments like "You Bet" and "Doesn't everyone" Janet Duncan, Grenada, MS, wrote "Always, always – except when I know it's a "real steal" – then I don't waste a second grabbing it up and running with it!" David Start, Gladstone, MO, wrote "Anything over $1. I think that's part of the fun of flea markets. My wife doesn't like to, but is getting better." I've to admit being in Mrs. Start's camp, but I also am the type of shopper who only puts so much cash into her pockets and frequently pesters my husband to fund the larger ticket item purchases. Besides, he's a better haggler. Other answers to this question were "Not to much, occasionally, sometimes, and if over priced." It also seemed to depend on how much the item was priced at. Some preferred to haggle only if it was over $1, while others thought $5 was the minimum, and another thought over $10 was a fair point to start haggling over. The question we didn't ask was if you tend to haggle more of the dealer greets you with a "I can do better" attitude. That certainly opens a door. And if you're a bargain hunter like I am, that marvelous phrase usually makes me linger a little longer in that booth. Some of the survey respondents quotes are as follows, bet you'll find yourself agreeing with some of these.

"Generally, except when the item is already priced as a steal or if the item is a really small item (price)." Carolyn Martin, Florissant, MO

"Gently, mostly ask if that's your best price." Charlotte Keane, Hollywood, FL.

"Always, always – except when I know it's a "real steal" - then I don't waste a second grabbing it up and running with it!" Janet Duncan, Grenada, MS

"Always, it would be incredibly stupid not to ask a vendor whether this is your best price." Geoff Seacrist, Brockville? PA

"Depends on the aura of the dealer's exhibit." Dorothy Johnson, Neptune Beach, FL.

"Depends on condition and sometimes knowing actually how much was spent." Don Martinson, Fargo, ND

"I will if I think the price is high for what it is. If I think it's a fair price, I usually pay it." Mary Sweeney, Glenfield, NY

"Not after my first offer, so much to see, so little time." Nancy Bell-Szwalle, Binghamton, NY

"Not always, depends on condition of item." Helen Schroeder, Morgan, MN

"Not in a nasty way. I'll usually try once to see how firm the price is." Shannon Adamczyk, Getzville, NY.

"No, if items are grossly over priced, I just move on." Patricia Thom, Minot, ND

"Not much, usually priced low at flea markets." E. M. Stoetzel, Sarasota, FL

"No, seller is selling to make money. If I want it, I pay their asking price." Pam Sigafoose, Port St. Lucie, FL

"No, unless its someone who doesn't know how to value things." Bruce Marsh, Wolcott, NY

"No! Never! Also hate buying items that are not priced." Darlene Goosman, Lynnwood, WA

"Not too often unless it is late in the day." Kyra Niegos, LaPorte, IN

"Only if the price is out of line. I sell myself, so I know when not to haggle." Jacqueline Flink, San Diego, CA

"The word is "discuss" Jeanette Norques, Hastings, MI

"Usually request a reduction. Generally expect one if I'm buying multiple items." Tina Wood, Montgomery, AL.

"Yes, of course, doesn't everyone?" D. K. Seitz, Londonderry, OH

"Yes, you can almost always get a better price." Jessie St. Pierre, Troy, MO.

"Yes, if I think they are too high. I admit to being a buyer and seller at flea markets, festivals, etc." Margaret Artman, Sidell, IL

Question Six asked "How often do you go to flea markets?" Again, the answers were varied. About a third told us they went to a flea market once a week, while another third went 2 to 3 times a month. About a tenth told us they go every chance they get. And a small percentage agreed they don't go as often as they would like to. Some folks like to stop at new flea markets when they are traveling and frequently make them destinations. Those living in warm climates tended to prefer outdoor flea markets during cooler months, leaving the really hot and steamy days to go places where they could enjoy air conditioning. Rachelle Costa, Deer Park, NY, wrote, "And if I see a sign somewhere in the street, I stop." Sounds like my kind of flea market adventurer. My

Box full of action figures, priced $2 or 3 for $5.

family laughs at me, but I'm sure my trusty Subaru can sniff out good flea markets and yard sales, and yes, I've followed my fair share of signs for events that turned out to be held a different day. I'm extremely fortunate to live in eastern PA where it is possible to get to a different flea market every day of the week.

Question Seven asked "Who accompanies you on your flea market shopping trips?" While a third answered they prefer to shop alone, over half said they preferred shopping with a spouse. Counting those who took along friends or family found identical numbers, about a quarter of those responding, and many of those who took their spouse, also included friends and family. Some take neighbors, brothers, or sisters. One responded "no one but my dog Tater, hopefully that way I am not distracted." Some of the other responses got me to thinking about my own experiences this past season. Because of this book and being a dedicated accumulator, I made a real effort to go to a flea market, auction, or antique show every weekend. I find these excursions to be terrific, because I'm out in the fresh air, meeting people, having a good time with my husband. One of us usually finds something we can't live without, sometimes we get "approval" before a purchase, but every now and then it's fun to spend a few dollars and happily carry a bag around with the other guessing what's in there.

One Monday morning, I decided to take my sister, Janet, who was visiting from Texas along to Perkiomenville. Believing that only the early bird does well there, I rousted her out of bed early and headed off. She was a good sport, but not nearly as much fun as having my husband along. He knows what I like and tends to point out things to me. Janet didn't possess this magic skill and I tried to watch her pick through things that might interest her. She went from being aghast over prices of toys she enjoyed as a kid to "didn't Mom have one of these" to the "oh, wish I could get this back to Texas" when

A clever way to display pins for sale. The tags are pinned to the back of the felt.

she found something she thought would look nice in her garden. I probably took more photos that morning, picked up a few Christmas presents, and watched shoppers a little more intently than usual. We also both fell under the spell of local grower, Dan Schantz and came home with the back of my car filled with flowers, rather than antiques. She politely declined my offer to go back to Perkiomenville during her next visit to PA, something about the snow flying and 20-degree outside temperature put her off.

Question Number 8 – Dealers do you have suggestions for shoppers – got a mixed reaction. Many of the responders were not dealers, so some didn't comment. Here are some of the answers we did receive. Most indicated they want to have some friendly verbal exchange with a dealer, which adds positively to their shopper experience.

Communication skills:

"Ask for what you collect or are looking for."

This is how the pinned jewelry looked from the back.

"Be as knowledgeable as you can be."

"Be engaging with vendors, kibitz, laugh, does wonders, admire good stuff."

"Be kind, your places change more often than you think. Have a sense of humor, no one needs this stuff – it's just for fun. Jackie Wright, Flagler Beach, FL

"Be pleasant." "Smile."

"Be polite. Don't bargain or at least make a reasonable offer (80% of the asking price.)" Carol Lauzon, Shohomish, WA

"Please don't make me listen to long

Thomas E. Nagy, Chelsea Hill Antiques, Hampton, CT, brought lovely antiques to Renninger's Extravaganza. His booth was visually appealing, yet secure from the threatening weather with a tent, plastic enclosures, and solid wood doors used to show off portraits and also act as a backdrop.

stores about what grandma had. Short is ok." Mary Duncan, E MO

"If there is something you are interested in, just ask. We can usually give a better price." Jessie St. Pierre, Troy, MO.

"If you don't understand why an object is so high, please ask rather than make negative comment!" S. Adamczyk, Betzville, NY

"I have sold a flea markets and I think people should stop and ask questions to learn. I have learned a lot that way." Patricia Thom, Minoti, ND

"I'm not a dealer, but have been, go for what you like if you're knowledgeable."

"Keep looking, keep learning about what you collect. Listen to others, even if it sounds unbelievable." David Norman, Perrin, TX

"Look items over very thoroughly before buying. Look closely for chips, repairs, reproductions, know your antiques."

Tell dealers what you're looking for. (3) "Just tell us what you are looking for – we may have it crammed under one of the tables!" Kyra Niegos, Court Lafourte, IN.

Bring cash:

Be there early, bring cash, try to be friendly. Bring cash, we don't like checks. Bring small bills. Don't ask if I take credit cards or will deliver furniture.

"Buy what you like and/or only if you think you can sell for more money than you paid for it. Stay in your own field of interest." M. Brown, Hollister, MO.

Bring small bills and change. Try for last day of 2-3 day shows, sellers often

reduce price rather than pack up to haul away large stock of non-sells.

Comments on how to handle merchandise:

"Don't block view of prospective buyers by conversing in front of tables."

"Careful how you handle my display – it can cost me time and money."

"Handle items carefully. Don't eat and pick-up glass or brass."

"Please handle our merchandise with some thoughtfulness. Some people can really mess up a display." Jacqueline Flink, San Diego, CA.

"Put things back where you find them. Ask questions on where to find things you don't see."

General etiquette:

"Don't hold your reunions in the middle of aisles; keep them open so the rest of us can get rid of our money."

"Get there early and go fast!"

"If early in the morning, have something smaller than a $100 bill. Be careful when handling glassware. Put items back in the place you found them."

"Remember I'm just as hot and tired as you."

Feelings on pets and children:

No dogs or cats. Please do not leave your children at your tables while they go off to shop. It is not a playground.

"Leave your children at home. Keep children controlled. Control your pets & your children – pay for what they break or in case of dog, raise a leg on." Dyanne Brox, Hamburg, NY.

Dealers views on pricing:

Make a reasonable offer (3). No sleepers anymore.

"Don't ask "best price" – it's tagged."

"Don't be rude. Talk. Don't look at price first. Don't say "I will give you," ask for better price, but don't expect 50-60% off. Stop saying "I'll be back" or "I just got here."

"Yes, I for one am always ready to deal. Many of my prices are marked to allow for some price lee way or marked "Firm" if not." Margaret Artman, IL

Question Number 9 – Shoppers, do you have suggestions for dealers? This one got answered big time, most of the responders filled in every inch of space for this one. And just like the comments from the dealers, they were meant in a kindly way. Some of the sentiments matched

from questionnaire to questionnaire. Would you believe almost 3/4ths of those answering the questionnaire had a common complaint? They want items priced!

Communication skills:

"Act interested and speak. Sometimes they can teach you about items you're not familiar with." Patty Barnett, Pittsburgh, PA.

Be approachable, smile, don't BS me – tell me what you do know, don't fabricate.

Be around when I shop to answer if you can when I ask questions.

Be friendly and accessible to shoppers. (4*)

Be polite (2), answer questions, pay attention to customers until finished, less use of word "rare"

Dealers Linda L. and Michael F. Bremer, set up a visually interesting booth, utilizing old shutters to display kitchen utensils.

"Be proud of your merchandise and take the time to explain it to un-knowing shoppers. Too many dealers sit quiet and bored or leave their booths to socialize." S. S. Adamcyzk, Betzville, NY.

"Be realistic about what you have – it's not the Mona Lisa." C. Meskauskas, Crockett, CA

Be set up early.

Most are friendly and helpful, plus willing to deal.

Pay attention to us. Just don't sit there and not talk or ignore us. At least say hi!

"Say hello, be friendly. Merchandise should be clean. Educate yourself with as much knowledge as you can." Patricia Thom, Minoti, ND.

"Smile! (2) I might not be buying today, but if you make me feel comfortable, I will definitely be back." Sharon Kelly, Stanfordville, NY "A smile is always nice." Susan Delby, Chicago, IL.

Display:

Arrange items neatly and visibly. Please don't make me "plunder." Mark prices clearly.

Display better (3) – some places look too "junky" "Please display your merchandise so that it appeals to everyone, and linens are a must." Don Martinson, Fargo, ND.

Display prices on items behind lock and key. E. Engelage, Ellis Grove, IL.

Don't overstuff booth. Hard to see individual items, buyer has fear of breaking items.

Make it easy for shoppers to get to merchandise. Keep things clean and clearly priced. " Make it easy for more than 2 or 3 people to enter your booth at a time." Jessie St. Pierre, Troy, MO.

Room to move around inside booth if allowed.

Show lots of stuff.

When things are displayed nice and enough walking room allowed that entices me to shop in their booth area.

Pricing:

As a shopper, I like a friendly dealer, willing to listen to my price offer, and always price every item.

As long as the prices are clearly marked and the dealer is friendly, I'm happy.

Be open and honest about your pricing.

Clean your merchandise for better prices. (3)

Clearly price each item. Don't put stickers on silver or brass. No rubber bands on silver.

Come down on prices.

"Don't put sticky price tags/labels on items. I've seen ephemera, toys in orig boxes, beer trays, etc., ruined by a little rectangle sticker!" Ed Natale, Wyckoff, NJ

"If dealer gives her best price, accept it and don't argue or "put down" the

merchandise." Maureen Morgan, West Springfield, MA.

"Make a couple of dollars and move your stuff. There is a lot out there." Mike Dryburg, Somerset, PA.

"Know your area, i.e. don't put New York prices on Memphis, TN, folks – they ain't interested. Overpriced items ain't gonna sell, no where! If you overpaid – you overpaid." Janet Duncan, Grenada, MS.

Hottest comment: Price items! "So many don't show a readable price, intending to "deal""

"I do not bother to ask prices on unmarked items."

'Mark prices clearly, don't guess." "Clearly mark your items – remark old faded out prices so senior eyes can read them."

"If you're busy with one shopper, you don't lose potential buyers who tire of waiting to ask your asking price for item."

"If no price tag, I don't even bother asking unless mot items are priced and this one item's tag is missing."

"I dislike having to ask, many times I'll pass an unpriced item by." "Mark price on all"

"Please just price all items as I REFUSE to ask."

"Please put prices on items. This is the only way to be fair to a buyer!" Mrs. Maxine Bianculli, St Cloud, FL

"Have items priced!"

"Always have everything priced. I walk away when items aren't priced."

"Make sure everything is priced. Buyers want to know price without having to ask for it." Pam Sigafoose, Port St. Lucie, FL.

"Price your items so I do not have to ask – actually I will not ask, just walk away – sale lost." Arlene Burger, Wilkliffe, OH

"Price items, if I go to a flea market and things are not priced, I'll walk away." Helen Schroeder, Morgan, MN

"Have all items priced, labeled, beforehand, if no price is on it if dealer is busy, I MOVE ON, if price is at least visibly labeled, you have another clue as to whether you are even interested. Betty L. Giddens, Ft Worth, TX.

"Please always display prices. Otherwise, I suspect the price varies with the shopper's appearance." Dorothy Johnson, Neptune Beach, FL.

"Rarely buy items not priced – if you know something about the item, put it on the price tag, not "nice" "old" or "great". LA Powers, Western Springs, IL.

"I hate booths with no prices and the dealer says "what do you offer"

"Give a good deal to a regular customer once in a while."

"Reduce your prices and it will sell."

Etiquette:

"Don't hold your reunions in the middle of the aisle. Keep them open so the rest of us can get rid of our money!" Gerald Willis, Duluth, GA.

"Don't be rude to potential buyers. People are just as smart as many dealers." M. Brown, Hollister, MO.

Do not mix craft items with antiques & collectibles. Do not shut down when a light rain begins. I won't sit around waiting for the rain to stop.

Don't stand and gossip with others and neglect customers.

Don't start packing up until market is closed.

"Handle things carefully – what is junk to you may not be to someone else. " Jackie Wright, Flagler Beach, FL

Have bags for people to put things in, wrapping newspaper too. (3)

Have plenty of change (2).

How about some entertainment?

"I have always dealt with nice people." J. Greenfield, Stoneboro, PA.

More food booths.

One way to display items is to spread them all out on a large blanket or tarp.

This Shupp's Grove dealer sets up a rainbow, grouping items by color, which resulted in a stunning booth, always full of shoppers.

"Please do not stand gossiping with others in the way of customers in aisles. Keep as much as you can off the floor, so we can see it, and handle it. Those boxes of old records on the floor are too heavy – they'll be there the next sale!" Gerald Willis, Duluth, GA.

"Stay with your booth. Have pieces well marked. Keep things clean." Dick Hentschel, Fennimore, WI

They get there at 5 a.m. to get a good spot and fold up at 12:30 – don't they realize most people sleep in on weekends and by the time they get up and get going, the dealers are folding up – that's crazy – they should wait at least to 4 pm. Carol Winold, Strongsville, OH.

They should be friendly and not so discourteous to wait on customers. Don't

mark a price on the back and then ask more without looking on the back.

Try not to act like it's a job you don't like when you're at the table.

On reproductions:

Look closely for chips, repairs, reproductions, know your antiques.

Some are not honest, will sell a repro for the real thing. Some things are overpriced!

"Don't cheat the customers. Don't well defective items. Tell the customers the truth. Don't scam!" David P. Norman, Perrin, TX

"Do not misrepresent items. " Ron O'Brien, Lansing, IL

"Don't mix new items with old trying to fool a person who is just beginning to collect." Jacqueline Fink, San Diego, CA.

David Stark of Gladstone, MO, included this list with his suggestions for dealers:

Be friendly.

Be helpful to those buyers who are novices and ask questions.

Expect to haggle unless you price marked firm.

Be friendly!

Mark the price on items.

Conclusion

Ann S. Kapp, San Antonio, TX wrote " I am not a dealer, just like the adventure of going to flea markets. Everything is mine from the moment I arrive. Some *items I buy with money, the rest I take home in my mind."* I think Ann has the right idea, don't you? Reviewing these questionnaires was a wonderful way to try to grasp how others feel about flea markets. It was soon apparent that who responded love flea markets as much as I do. Although many listed particular items they were searching for, I get the feeling many are happy to wander around and see what "speaks to them" while others are out there searching for the ultimate treasure to add to their growing collections. What we all do—is tap into the magic that surrounds each and every flea market, something that calls us time and time again

Shoppers browsing through tables of all kinds of collectibles at Landisville, PA.

❖ ABC Items

Generations of nannies and mothers have educated children by using colorful china with letters of the alphabet, numbers, etc. Most ABC plates were imported to the United States from England. They were highly popular between 1780 and 1860, when literacy rates were low. Originally available for only a few cents, they served a practical purpose on the table while also affording an inexpensive education. Often these charming children's wares incorporated nursery rhymes or sayings meant to inspire goodness in the user.

References: Irene and Ralph Lindsay, *ABC Plates & Mugs*, Collector Books, 1998; Margaret and Kenn Whitmyer, *Collector's Encyclopedia of Children's Dishes*, Collector Books, 1993.

Collectors' Clubs: ABC Plate & Mug Collectors, 67 Stevens Ave, Old Bridge, NJ 08857.

For additional listings, see *Warman's Antiques & Collectibles* and *Warman's Country*.

Cup, small, silver luster, floral sprig dec **135.00**

Mug
Bird perched on branch, alphabet on side, brown transfer with blue accents **245.00**
Elephant family with rowdy children, 2-1/2" h **150.00**
Franklin's Maxim, "Slough Like Rust Consumes Faster Than Labor

ABC Plates, Multicolored transfer of lion, emb letters around rim, 1870s, $285.

Wears," black transfer **165.00**
Tin, band of flowers, 1-7/8" h, 2-3/4" dia..**175.00**
Plate, pottery or porcelain
Braille, raised Braille dots on rim beside letter, dog design in center, dark green glaze, 6" dia **40.00**
Cat and mouse, Staffordshire, Elsmore and Son, 8" dia **225.00**
Child reading, Staffordshire, black transfer, short hairline, edge flakes, 5" dia...**35.00**
Duke Cambridge, 1867 opening of Town Hall, Preston, Lancashire **145.00**
Franklin Proverb, "Keep Thy Shop & Thy Shop Will Keep Thee," transfer dec center, 6" dia......................**50.00**
"Make Hay While The Sun Shines," 6" dia......................................**175.00**
"The Fall," polychrome center dec, Staffordshire, 8-1/4" dia, edge wear **195.00**
Two boys in cart pulled by dog, Staffordshire, 7" dia **125.00**
White, emb letters, beaded edge, 7" dia..**50.00**
Plate, tin
Children playing hoops, 3" d **210.00**
George Washington, c1890s, 6" dia **175.00**
Girl on swing, lithographed center, printed alphabet border **60.00**
Two kittens playing with basket of wood, 4-1/2" dia......................**180.00**
Who Killed Cock Robin? 8" dia ..**120.00**

❖ Abingdon Pottery

The Abingdon Sanitary Manufacturing Company of Abingdon, Ill., was founded in 1908. Although originally created to make plumbing fixtures, an art pottery line was introduced around 1933. In 1945 the company's name was changed to Abingdon Potteries, Inc., with production of the art pottery line continuing until 1950, when fire destroyed the art pottery kiln. The company then focused its attention on plumbing fixtures, eventually becoming Briggs Manufacturing Company.

References: Joe Paradis, *Abingdon Art*

Abingdon Pottery Low bowl, light blue glaze, blue stamp mark, $15.

Abingdon Pottery Vase, Art Deco stylized shell form, pink, #512, $24.

Pottery, Schiffer Publishing, 1996.

Collectors' Club: Abingdon Pottery Collector's Club, 210 Knox Hwy S, Abingdon, IL 61410, www.cookiejarclub.com/archives/abingdonclub.htm.

For additional listings, see *Warman's Americana & Collectibles*.

Ashtray, #456 ....**36.00**
Bookends, pr
Goose, #98................................**42.00**
Horse heads, black, #441, pr **75.00**
Bowl, 11-1/4" l, 8" w, Shell, #533, sea-green, c1940-48 ....**35.00**
Candlesticks, pr, 2 lite, rose glaze .**35.00**
Compote, #568, white, 5" h, base 2" sq **25.00**
Console bowl
#377, yellow, handle continues into bowl, 3-3/4" h, 14" w.................**55.00**
#532, green, leaf design, 10" l.....**30.00**
Cookie jar, cov
Daisy **45.00**
Little Miss Muffet, #622 ....**220.00**
Little Old Lady, Mammy, plaid apron, blue ink mark, 9" h.................**595.00**
Windmill, #678..........................**250.00**
Figure
Goose, #571, blue.......................**45.00**
Peacock, pink **40.00**
Flower pot, #151, white, hp floral dec, 5" h **25.00**
Planter
#484, fan with bow in center, white **40.00**
#616D, Mexican and cactus **70.00**
Salt and pepper shakers, Little Bo Peep, pr......................................**45.00**
String holder, mouse **90.00**
Tray, green, 10-3/4" x 8"..................**22.50**
Vase
#181, ivory, 2 handles **50.00**
#482, double cornucopia, white ...**35.00**
#512, pink glaze, 7" h...................**20.00**

#513, fan, salmon glaze, 9" h.......**30.00**

#520, Baden, light blue ground, white int., floral dec, gold trim, 2 handles, 8-3/4" h **30.00**

#560, Pink Cameo, Star Flower pattern, sgd "Special B, 4-16-42," 6-1/4" h **125.00**

Wall pocket

Book **50.00**

Calla Lilly..............................**60.00**

❖ Action Figures

Action figures are posable models with flexible joints. Generally made of plastic, the figures portray real or fictional characters, and their clothing, personal equipment, vehicles and other accessories are collected as well. The earliest action figures were the hard-plastic Hartland figures that depicted popular Western television heroes of the 1950s. During the late 1950s, Louis Marx also produced action figures for a number of their playsets, but it was G.I. Joe, introduced in 1964, that triggered the modern action figure craze. Mego established the link between action figures and the movies when the company issued series based on *Planet of the Apes* and *Star Trek: The Motion Picture*. Kenner jumped on the bandwagon with the production of *Star Wars* figures in 1977.

References: John Bonavita, *Mego Action Figure Toys*, Schiffer Publishing, 1996; Paris & Susan Manos, *Collectible Action Figures*, 2nd ed., Collector Books, 1996; John Marshall, *Action Figures of the 1980s*, Schiffer Publishing, 1998; Sharon Korbeck and Dan Stearns, *2003 Toys & Prices 10th ed.*, Krause Publications, 2003; Elizabeth A. Stephan, *Toy Shop's Action Figure Price Guide*, Krause Publications, 2000.

Collectors' Clubs: Captain Action Collectors' Club, P.O. Box 2095, Halesite, NY 11743; Captain Action Society of Pittsburgh, 516 Cubbage St, Carnegie, PA 15106.

Amy, Congo, Kenner, 1995, MIP.......**5.00**

Amanaman, Star Wars, Kenner, 1985 ....**110.00**

Aquaman, 1967, loose.................**160.00**

Box full of action figures, priced $2 or 3 for $5.

At-At Driver, Star Wars, Kenner, 1980, C-9 ....**750.00**

Banzai **10.00**

Ben Kanobi, 3" h, orig punched 12 back card, C-9.5 ....**695.00**

Betty Mustin, Mask, Kenner, MOC.**20.00**

Black Bolt, Fantastic Four, 1995, MIP **10.00**

Boba Fett, Star Wars, 2 circles, MIP **25.00**

Boss Hogg, Dukes of Hazzard, 3-3/4" h, MOC **15.00**

Bug-Eye Ghost, Ghostbusters, Kenner, 1986-91, MIP...............................**15.00**

B-Wing Pilot, Star Wars, Kenner, sealed in bag **15.00**

Captain Action, 12", parachute offer on box, MIP **700.00**

Dalek, Dr Who, 1976, loose **100.00**

Deadproof, #1, X-Men **25.00**

Death Star Commander, Star Wars, Kenner, loose **10.00**

Dorian, Mask, Kenner, MOC...........**20.00**

Dr Zarkow, Flash Gordon, Mego, 1976, loose...**55.00**

Feyd, Dune, LJN, 1984, MIP...........**40.00**

Hannibal, A-Team, Galoob, MOC ...**20.00**

Heads Up, Mask, Kenner, MOC......**20.00**

Hercules, swash buckling, loose.......**3.00**

House Ghost, Extreme Ghostbusters, 1997, MIP.......................................**4.00**

Human Torch, Fantastic Four **7.50**

Jill, Charlie's Angels, 8-1/2" h, Hasbro, 1977, MIP....................................**100.00**

Jon, Chips, 3-3/4" h, loose **10.00**

Joker, Legends of Batman..............**15.00**

Kato, Captain Action, MIP...............**20.00**

Kimo, Chuck Norris, 6", MIP **12.00**

Leia Organa, Star Wars, Kenner, 1978 ....**20.00**

Long Range, G.I. Joe Thunderclap driver, 1989, loose, 3-3/4" h **14.00**

Luke Skywalker, Star Wars, 1st issue, 12" h, MIP **38.00**

Luke Skywalker, X-Wing, 3"...........**12.00**

Mandrake, Defenders of the Earth, loose **8.00**

Mothra, Godzilla, boxed **10.00**

Mystique, Marvel, loose, 10" h **15.00**

Phantasm, Batman, animated, foreign card **24.00**

Picard, Star Trek, loose **10.00**

Power Droid, Star Wars, loose, 3" h.**8.00**

Quick Draw, Mask, Kenner, MOC...**20.00**

R2-D2, pop-up lightsaber, C-8.......**135.00**

R5-D4, 20/21 back, C-9 ....**260.00**

Rogue, Marvel, loose, 10" h...........**12.00**

Sabretooth #1, X-Men **10.00**

Spider-Man, super posable, 10" h ..**10.00**

Tornado, Mask, Kenner, MOC **20.00**

Tremor, Spawn, loose **12.00**

Vampire, Spawn, loose **17.50**

Walrusman, loose **10.00**

Werewolf, Spawn, loose **20.00**

Wicket, Star Wars, Kenner, 1983, C-9+ **120.00**

Wild Wolf, Mask, Kenner, MOC **18.00**

Willie Mays, Starting Lineup...........**20.00**

Wolf Bronski, Exosquad, Playmates, 1993-85, loose **8.00**

World War I Aviator Ace, GI-Joe mail-in **60.00**

❖ Adams

For collectors, the name Adams denotes quality English pottery. Since the company's inception in 1770, Adams potteries have been located in seven locations. Various marks have been used over the years, ranging from a simple "Adams" to more complex variations of the name. Some pieces were not marked.

ABC plate, 7-1/4" dia, horse head in center, alphabet letters around rim, chip on back **75.00**

Creamer, scene of three people in front of English buildings, dark blue transfer, wishbone handle, imp "Adams"..**165.00**

Cup and saucer, handleless, Adam's Rose pattern, imp "Adams" **225.00**

Dish, Cries of London-Ten Bunches A Penny Primrose, rect....................**50.00**

Mush mug, The Farmers Arms.......**90.00**

Pitcher, Adam's Rose pattern, scalloped rim **110.00**

Plate

Abbey pattern, mulberry..............**25.00**

Adam's Rose pattern, early.........**95.00**

Shakespeare Series, Sir John Falstaff, black transfer, blue and green accents, orange border.............**35.00**

Adams China Dinner plate, blue and white Oriental design, mkd "Pattern introduced by Wm. Adams in 1780," $15.

❖ Advertising

Advertisers of the 19th and early 20th centuries understood the necessity of catching the attention of potential customers. Colorful graphics were an important feature of mass-produced advertising items beginning in the late

1800s. Not only did bright, creative packaging attract attention, it also helped customers identify and locate particular brands during an era in which many people could not read. Those same colorful designs serve as head-turners for today's collectors, just as they did for buyers of a bygone era.

References: Ted Hake, *Hake's Guide to Advertising Collectibles*, Wallace-Homestead, 1992; Bob and Sharon Huxford, *Huxford's Collectible Advertising*, 4th ed., Collector Books, 1999; Don and Elizabeth Johnson, *Warman's Advertising*, Krause Publications, 2000.

Periodicals: *Creamers*, P.O. Box 11, Lake Villa, IL 60046; *Paper Collectors' Marketplace*, P.O. Box 128, Scandinavia, WI 54917; *Advertising Collectors Express*, P.O. Box 221, Mayview, MO 64071.

Collectors' Clubs: Advertising Cup & Mug Collectors of America, P.O. Box 680, Solon, IA 52333; Antique Advertising Assoc. of America, P.O. Box 1121, Morton Grove, IL 60053, www.pastime.org; Ephemera Society of America, P.O. Box 95, Cazenovia, NY 13035; Farm Machinery Advertising Collectors, 10108 Tamarack Dr, Vienna, VA 22182; Inner Seal Collectors Club, 4585 Saron Dr, Lexington, KY 40515; National Assoc. of Paper & Advertising Collectors, P.O. Box 500, Mount Joy, PA 17552; Porcelain Advertising Collectors Club, P.O. Box 381, Marshfield Hills, MA 02151-0381. Tin Container Collectors Assoc. P.O. Box 440101, Aurora, CO 80044.

For additional listings, see *Warman's Antiques & Collectibles*, *Warman's Americana & Collectibles* and *Warman's Advertising* as well as specific categories in this edition.

Advertising Doll, Chicken of the Sea Mermaid, Mattel, Shopping Pal, orig red and white box, $10.

Advertisement
Lee Overalls, fabric sample, 1920s **20.00**
Seeger Refrigerator Ice Box, 6-7/8" x 10" **5.00**
Sunbeam Automatic Cooker and Deep Fryer, 10-1/2" x 13-1/2"..............**7.00**

Banner, Holsum Bread, illus by Howard Brown, 58" w **125.00**

Billhook, Ceresota Flour..................**50.00**

Blotter
Fairbanks Portable Pumping Outfit, graphics of metal vehicle, road paving machinery, 7-1/4" x 9-1/2" **10.00**
Levi's, stiff cardboard, full color art, black and white imprint for local dealer, unused, 1960s, 2-3/4" x 6-1/4" **20.00**

Booklet, Dutch Boy Paint, 20 pgs, 5" x 6" **12.00**

Bookmark, Geneva National Mineral Water, celluloid, diecut water fountain, adv on back, c1905 ....**35.00**

Box, Mint Ju-ju-bees **5.00**

Box opener, Wrigleys, 1940s..........**70.00**

Bowl, Bird's Eye, General Foods **27.50**

Business card, Duluth Fire Appliance Co., Chas T Abbott, Manager, c1895, 3" x 5".....................................**18.00**

Candy pail, Riley's Rum & Butter Toffee, Halifax, England, 7-1/4" x 7", emb name, silhouettes of children playing with kite, slip lid **50.00**

Coat hanger, San Francisco Cleaning & Drying Works, wood **10.00**

Coffee cup, White Castle................**35.00**

Coffee measure, "Coffee Satisfaction is assured by A & P Coffee Service," aluminum, 3-3/4" l **8.00**

Coffee tin, Blanke's Portonilla Coffee, green and gold, bail handle, dome lid, c1900, 10" h, some losses..........**60.00**

Counter display, Sir Walter Raleigh Tin, 6 orig pocket tins **130.00**

Counter jar
Lance Crackers, clear, red tin lid..**20.00**
Planters Peanuts, 7" dia glass jar with lid, yellow and blue Mr. Peanut image, orig 8" x 8" x 9-1/2" corrugated cardboard shipping carton.......................................**90.00**

Emery board, Wead's Bread **20.00**

Fan, 9-1/2" x 10-1/2" w diecut cardboard, The Valley of Fair Play, black and white text on back for shoe tanneries and factories, Feb 1923 patent date ...**20.00**

Folder, Marcelle Face Powder, samples **18.00**

Jar, Horlick's Malted Milk, orig lids, set of 4 ....**125.00**

Liquor jug, Fleischmann's, dark blue pottery **90.00**

Advertising Box, Sovereign, Park Lane assortment, $12.

Mending kit, Real Silk Hosiery **5.00**

Pail, Picwick Peanut Butter, faded and dented, 12-oz, 3-1/2" h, 3-1/4" dia**25.00**

Paperweight, Whitewater Flour Mills, tinted sepia scene of Niagara Falls, brown rim lettered in white "Whitewaters, Kansas," 1920s......**35.00**

Pencil clip, Ardee Flour, red, yellow, blue logo, celluloid on brass wire clip, Hubbard Milling Co., Mankato, Minn, sponsor, early 1900s...................**25.00**

Pinback button, Metzer's Milk Infant Keeps Them Smiling, 1" d, c1930**12.00**

Plate, Quick Service Laundry, tin, c1900 ....**35.00**

Record, Get More from your Kenmore, 33-1/3 rpm...................................**10.00**

Ruler, Clark Bars, wood **8.00**

Salesman's brochure, Superior Matches, matchbook covers, "Glamour Girls Series" **45.00**

Salt and pepper shakers, pr, Tappan Kitchen Ranges, heavy glass with glossy yellow or pale blue finish, baker figure on one panel, black plastic threaded cap, 1940s **20.00**

Sign
Cat's Paw, emb black cat, scrolled ends, dirty **65.00**
Kellogg's Corn Flakes with Bananas, cardboard stand-up, easel back, 30" x 20", C.8+............................**275.00**
Snow Drift Fancy Patent Flour, Imperial Enamel Co., NY, heavy porcelain, two-sided, 1940s, 15" x 18"......**30.00**

Soap box, Rub-No-More, shows elephants....................................**40.00**

Spinner top, Hurd Shoes, black and white celluloid, wooden red spinner dowel, 1930s **20.00**

Stickpin, Grand Andes Range, diecut thin celluloid red, white, and blue U.S. flag, brass stickpin, 1905 patent date **10.00**

Tape measure, Sears, Roebuck & Co., white lettering, black ground, lightning bolt-style lettering for "WLS" (World's Largest Store,) red, white, blue, and green stylized floral design on back
..................................**15.00**

Tip tray, Clysmic Water, woman, deer and giant bottle of product **45.00**

Tray, Falstaff Brewing, merry group of cavaliers, c1920, 24" d **95.00**

Watch fob, Corby's Canadian Whiskey
..................................**175.00**

Whetstone, Lavacide, For Fumigation, celluloid, Innis, Speiden & Co., N.Y.,
..................................**35.00**

Whistle, Atwater Kent Radios **15.00**

Wrapper, Huskey Ice Cream Bar, snow dog **15.00**

Yardstick, Smith's Furniture Store ..**10.00**

❖ Advertising Characters

Just as advertisers used colorful labels to attract attention, the use of characters became quite important. When consumers didn't know what brand to buy, they often decided to trust the character or personality promoting a product. Today, many of these characters generate strong collector interest. From Mr. Peanut to the Campbell Kids, there is a plethora of items available to collectors.

References: Warren Dotz, *Advertising Character Collectibles*, Collector Books, 1993; ——, *What a Character*, Chronicle Books, 1996; Don and Elizabeth Johnson, *Warman's Advertising*, Krause Publications, 2000; Mary Jane Lamphier, *Zany Characters of the Ad World*, Collector Books, 1995; David and Micki Young, *Campbell's Soup Collectibles from A to Z*, Krause Publications, 1998.

For additional listings, see *Warman's Antiques & Collectibles*, *Warman's Americana & Collectibles* and *Warman's*

Advertising Characters Sta-Puft Marshmallow Man Man, figure, white, blue trim, $20, Big Boy dolls in background.

Oscar Mayer, toy wienermobile, plastic, Oscar pops up and down with movement, $125

Advertising, as well as specific categories in this edition.

┌─────────────────────────────┐
│   **Reproduction Alert**   │
└─────────────────────────────┘

Aunt Jemima, cookbook, *Aunt Jemima's Album of Secret Recipes*, 1935, 30 pgs, soft cover **35.00**

Buster Brown
Game, Buster Brown Game and Play Box, Andy Devine photo, unused
..................................**80.00**
Pinback button, Buster Brown Shoes, sepia letters, brown rim **24.00**

Charlie Tuna
Alarm Clock, wind-up, brass, Lux Time Co. **65.00**
Bracelet, 1-1/4" disk, c1970 ....**15.00**
Doll, vinyl, 7-1/2" h **30.00**
Watch, 1-1/8" goldtone case, blue leather double strap, 1971, mint with offer insert................................**55.00**

Dutch Boy Paint, marker, diecut thin cardboard, wooden base, Dutch Boy on front, black and white paint can on back, inscribed "Paint with Dutch Boy White Lead," c1930 ....**20.00**

Elsie the Cow, Borden's
Badge, white ground, blue lettering, 1-1/2" dia....................................**10.00**
Fountain glass, clear glass, frosted image of Elsie and name, tiny Borden Co. copyright, c1940, 6-1/4" h, pr **35.00**
Paper napkin, 6-1/2" x 6-3/4," white, multicolored graphic of Elsie in sunburst design, copyright Borden Co., 1960s **8.00**
Postcard, Elsie and Elmer, color, traveling scene..........................**25.00**
Salt and pepper shakers, Elsie and Elmer, china, c1940, pr..........**125.00**

Entenmann's, bank, 8-1/2" h, ceramic, piggy baker wearing hat and kerchief,

black eyes and shoes, glossy white body, orig box, early 1990s **30.00**

Exxon Tiger, mug, 3-1/2" h, white glass, full color tiger portrait, 1970s **8.00**

Florida Orange Bird, Tropicana, nodder
..................................**150.00**

Green Giant, telephone, Little Sprout, 14" h...**65.00**

Hamm's Bear, cup, Hamm's Beer, blue and red artwork of trademark bear relaxing in back yard, beret and glasses on one side, running with tray of beer on other, Dixie, c1970, 5" h, set of 4 ....**16.00**

Hawaiian Punch, Punchy figure, hard plastic, orange............................**12.00**

Johnny, Philip Morris Pinback button, 1930s **35.00**

Sign, emb tin, worn, 12" x 14" **95.00**

Keebler Elf
Doll, Ernie, plus, talking **25.00**
Mug, 3" h, hard plastic **20.00**
Watch, silvertone case, black leather strap, watch hands formed by Ernie's arms, 1980s, MIB **25.00**

Kellogg's, spoon, SP, emb "Kellogg's"
..................................**10.00**

Kool Cigarettes
Pinback button, Willie between donkey and elephant, 1930s.................**25.00**
Salt and pepper shakers, figural Willie and Millie, black and white plastic, yellow and red accents, c1950, 3-1/2" h **35.00**

Mr. Clean, figure, Procter and Gamble, painted vinyl, muscular, bald-headed figure with green earring in one ear, c1961, 8" h **135.00**

Nestle's Quik Rabbit, mug, 4" h, 3-dimensional hard plastic, c1970...**12.00**

Nipper, RCA Victor Coffee mug, plastic
..................................**8.00**

Snow dome................................**40.00**

Oscar Mayer, weinermobile, bank, plastic **30.00**

Pillsbury Doughboy, Pillsbury
Co.Cookie jar, 10-1/2" h, glossy white,
blue accents, c1970 ....**30.00**
Doll, vinyl, smiling, blue accent eyes,
button on cap, copyright 1971
Pillsbury Co., Minneapolis, 7-1/4" h
....**18.00**
Salt and pepper shakers, 4" h Poppin
Fresh, 3-1/4" h Poppie, names on
bases, copyright 1974 ....**28.00**

Reddy Kilowatt
Beanie Baby, 8" h.........................**20.00**
Magic Gripper, textured yellow rubber
disk, image of Reddy the Chef,
c1950, 4-3/4" dia, orig red and white
paper envelope 5-1/4" sq **20.00**
Pin, brass and red enamel figure,
c1950, 1" h, orig diecut card 2-1/4" x
2-3/4" **40.00**

Speedy Alka Seltzer, 5-1/2" h figure,
plastic, 1960s **24.00**

Tony the Tiger, pencil sharpener, soft
vinyl, orange head, threaded black
plastic base, c1960 ....**80.00**

❂ Advertising Logo Watches

What's more trendy than collecting
advertising watches? Collectors can search
for these at their favorite flea market as well
as save the required number of proofs of
purchase, coupons, etc., and obtain them
directly from the sponsor.

Burger King, 1970s, silvertone case,
blue suede strap, blue background on
face...**50.00**
Cambpell Kids, 1982, mechanical
windup, 1" goldtone case, black plastic
strap, face with boy in green shorts
carrying lunch box.......................**45.00**
Energizer Bunny, black plastic case,
black leather strap, pink bunny
drumming on face, 1992 ....**20.00**
Hawaiian Punch Punchy, Swiss digital,
rect goldtone case, wide red leather
strap with snaps, 1970s **110.00**
Little Hans, Nestle, silvertone case, Little
Hans in center of face, eyes move from
side to side, 1971.........................**50.00**
M & Ms, Mars Candy
Canadian, Minis, blue and yellow
sports style, black plastic strap,
1998, mint..................................**25.00**
50th Birthday, yellow case, red and
green strap, party hat on face,
Birthday Club package, 9" x 12"
printed envelope, mint **20.00**
Millenium, silvertone case, emb black
leather strap, "The Official Candy of
the Millenium" on crystal, red M&M
on face, 1998, mint...................**18.00**

Raid Bug Spray, Swiss wind-up,
goldtone case, can on face, bug on
revolving dial, 1970s **175.00**
Scrubbing Bubbles, Dow, Marcel,
goldtone case, wide blue plastic strap
with snaps, "Scrubbing Bubbles"
printed on face with character, 1970s
....**60.00**
Tony the Tiger, Kellogg's Frosted Flakes,
Swiss wind-up, silvertone case, black
vinyl strap with snaps, face with Tony,
1976, MIB..................................**215.00**
Toppie the Elephant, Tip Top Bread,
Ingraham, 7/8" chrome case, gray
leather strap, pink polka dotted
elephant wearing cape with "Toppie,"
1951 ....**110.00**

❖ Air Guns

"You'll shoot your eye out!" That admonition
is uttered by mothers everywhere, yet kids
continue their love affair with BB guns and
pellet guns. Air guns trace their roots to the
time of Napoleon, but most collectors set
their sights on examples manufactured
since the late 19th century. Air guns made
in the 1800s command premium prices,
while models from the 20th century are
kinder to the bank account. Collectors also
search for "go-withs" such as ammunition
containers.

Belt buckle, Crossman, brass, made by
Century, Canada **20.00**
Benjamin 30-30 carbine, rust-blistered
barrel **42.00**
Book
The American BB Gun by Arni
Dunathan **71.00**
The Complete Book of the Air Gun by
George C. Nonte, Stackpole Books,
1970.......................................**100.00**
History of the Daisy BB Gun by Cass
S. Hough, 1976.......................**58.00**
Daisy
Model 21 double barrel BB gun .**425.00**
Model 25 commemorative BB gun,
c1986, MIB **250.00**
Model 89 ....**90.00**
Model 1894 ....**65.00**
Instruction manual, Crossman Model
38T **4.00**
Postcard, depicts American Youth's Bill
of Rights poster, c1947, 5" x 7"....**31.00**
Red Ryder
1983, sundial, large compass, orig box
noting "A Christmas Story" **395.00**
1998, 60th anniversary BB gun, retail
production model, MIB **40.00**
Shot tube, shoots cork ball instead of
BBs, for Model 21/25/99..............**95.00**
Target, Daisy, metal, targets spin when
hit, 6" h, 8" w **62.00**
Token, brass, 2" dia **15.00**

Upton, Model 40, 1,000-shot, nickel-
plated, c1921.............................**350.00**

❖ Airline Collectibles (Commercial)

Come fly with me! The friendly skies
continue beckoning collectors today. As
airlines merge, change names, or even go
out of business, interest in related
memorabilia will increase.

Periodical: *Airliners*, P.O. Box 52-1238,
Miami, FL 33152.

Collectors' Clubs: Aeronautic & Air Label
Collectors Club, P.O. Box 1239, Elgin, IL,
60121; C.A.L./N-X-211 Collectors Society,
226 Tioga Ave, Bensenville, IL 60106; Gay
Airline Club, P.O. Box 69A04, West
Hollywood, CA 90069; World Airline
Historical Society, 3381 Apple Tree Ln,
Erlanger, KY 41018.

For additional listings, see *Warman's
Americana & Collectibles*.

Christmas card, Delta Airlines, Midnight
Clear, Delta DC-4, 1950s, used ...**14.00**
Coaster, 3-3/4" dia, American Airlines,
white china with silver dec, mkd
"American Airline Sterling China,
Wellsville, OH, USA," set of 8.....**250.00**
Coin purse, CAAC, "Fly CAAC," beaded
butterfly design, MIP **20.00**
Cup and saucer, Delta Airlines, for VIP
International flights, Mayer China.**25.00**
Dinner plate, Delta Airlines, for VIP
International flights, Mayer China.**20.00**
Cigar cutter, pocket, Pan Am, 1901**70.00**
Gumbo spoon, KLM Airline, silver
plated, zephyr mark, International
Silver Co., c1935, set of 6...........**25.00**
Magazine ad, 12" x 9", American
Airlines, small airport building with
plane, golf bags, adv winter golf
excursions **12.00**
Patch, Ozark Airline, 3" dia **10.00**
**Place setting, china, plate, bowl, cup
and saucer**
American Airlines, mkd "copyright Swid
Powell American Airline, Wessco,
Gwathmey Siegal" **40.00**
United Airlines **42.00**
Plate, 5-1/2" dia, Western Airlines...**15.00**
Playing cards, c1960-80, box 3/4" x 2-
1/4" x 3-1/2"American Airlines, U.S.
mail plane...................................**10.00**
Delta Airlines, white pyramid..........**8.00**
Eastern/Ryder, text with logo **8.00**
Ozark, snow-covered Rockies......**10.00**
TWA Collectors Series, Douglas DC-9,
1966......................................**12.00**
Postcard, unused
Air Canada, preparing for takeoff,

oversized **6.00**
Air Transat, Lockheed L1011, color,
    oversized **6.00**
Alitalia, Caravelle III S.E. 210, radio
    print on back **8.00**
KLM, Douglas DC-6B, airline issued,
    slight crease **7.00**
Lufthansa DC-10, airline issued.....**5.00**
Pan American, Super 6 Clipper, color
    ....**8.00**
Piedmont Airlines, Boeing 737-300
    series, color, oversized **6.00**
TWA Jetstream, French text.........**10.00**
Promotional brochure, show schedule
    of Las Vegas acts, Frontier Airlines,
    Elvis, Ella Fitzgerald, Don Ho, Patti
    Page, and other celebrities, 1970 **14.00**
Stewardess wings, United Airlines,
    silver accent wings, red, white and blue
    center logo, orig black and white card,
    c1960, unused, 2" w....................**20.00**
Toy car, TWA Airlines, airport service
    car, tin friction, 11" l....................**120.00**
Toy plane
    Corvair Inter-Continental Jet, friction,
    14" l, MIB **145.00**
    Pan Am Boeing 747, battery op,
    automatic stop and go action,
    flashing jet engines, realistic sound,
    13" l, MIB **225.00**
    Pan Am Boeing 747, friction, 7" l, MIB
    ....**225.00**
    Royal Dutch Airlines, KLM Corvair jet,
    friction, 14" l **95.00**
Travel bag, Pan Am World **10.00**

❖ Akro Agate

Akro Agate began producing marbles in
1911. The company moved from Ohio to
Clarksburg, W.Va., in 1914. By the 1930s,
competition in the marble industry was
fierce, and the company chose to diversify
its product line. Floral dinnerware and
children's play dishes were among their
most successful products.

Reference: Gene Florence, *Collectors
Encyclopedia of Akro Agate Glassware*, rev
ed, Collector Books, 1975 (1992 value

*Akro Agate Glass Ashtray, leaf shape, white with olive
green streaks, mkd on back, $2.*

update).

Collectors' Clubs: Akro Agate Art Assoc,
P.O. Box 758, Salem, NH 03079; Akro
Agate Collector's Club, 10 Bailey St,
Clarksburg, WV 26301.

For additional listings, see *Warman's
Americana & Collectibles.*

Reproduction Alert

Children's play dishes

Cereal bowl, large
    Concentric Ring, blue...................**30.00**
    Interior Panel, transparent blue....**40.00**
    Stacked Disk, transparent blue **40.00**
Creamer
    Chiquita, cobalt blue.....................**10.00**
    Interior Panel, transparent topaz..**20.00**
    Octagonal, sky blue, open handle**25.00**
    Stacked Disk, green **15.00**
    Stippled Band, large, green **30.00**
Cup and saucer
    Chiquita, opaque green..................**8.00**
    Interior Panel, green and white marble
    ....**42.00**
    Stippled Band, cobalt blue **35.00**
Pitcher
    Interior Panel, transparent blue....**35.00**
    Stacked Disk, opaque blue **15.00**
    Stippled Band, transparent green **18.00**
Plate
    Chiquita, opaque green..................**8.00**
    Concentric Rib, yellow....................**8.00**
    Interior Panel, opaque blue **15.00**
    Octagonal, large, green..................**8.00**
    Stacked Disk, blue **6.00**
    Stippled Band, large, topaz..........**10.00**
Set
    Concentric Ring, green plates and
    cups, white saucers and teapot lid,
    blue creamer, sugar, and teapot, orig
    box **215.00**
    Interior Panel, transparent topaz, cups,
    saucers, plates, creamer and sugar,
    teapot with lid, service for 4....**215.00**
Sugar, cov
    Chiquita, opaque green or transparent
    cobalt **8.00**
    Stacked Disk, green **10.00**
Teapot, cov
    Chiquita, transparent cobalt **30.00**
    Interior Panel, large, green, white lid
    ....**45.00**
    Octagonal, open handle, medium blue,
    green lid....................................**24.00**
    Stacked Disk, azure blue, white lid
    ....**10.00**
    Stippled Band, small, green.........**35.00**
Tumbler, octagonal **20.00**
Water set, Stacked Disk and Interior

Panel, transparent green, 7 pcs...**70.00**

Other

Ashtray, triangular, marbleized red and
    white..**35.00**
Bell, 5-1/2" h, blue.......................**115.00**
Cornucopia, #765, 3" h, green and white
    ....**12.00**
Flowerpot
    2-3/4" h, yellow.............................**35.00**
    4-1/4" h, blue marble....................**38.00**
Lamp, brown and blue marble, black
    octagonal top, Globe Spec. Co., top 4"
    dia, 12" h **75.00**
Marbles, Chinese checkers, orig box, set
    of 60 ....**130.00**
Mexicalli jar, covered, orange and white
    ....**40.00**
Planter, 5" x 3" x 2-1/4", Narcissus,
    green **12.00**
Powder jar, Colonial Lady, white **65.00**
Vase, 4-3/8" h, Daffodil, orange and
    white..**12.00**

❖ Aladdin Lamps

Many collectors use the term Aladdin to
refer to items produced by the Mantle Lamp
Company of America. Founded in Chicago
in 1908, the company was known for its
lamps. Vintage Aladdin lamps were made of
metal and glass, and Alacite was the name
given to their popular creamy, translucent
glass. Collectors insist that lamps possess
all the correct parts, including original
shades, which can be difficult to find.

References: J. W. Courter, *Aladdin
Collectors Manual & Price Guide #19*, self-
published (3935 Kelley Rd, Kevil, KY
42053), 1996; —, *Aladdin, The Magic Name
In Lamps*, rev ed, self-published, 1997.

Collectors' Club: Aladdin Knights of the
Mystic Light, 3935 Kelley Rd, Kevil, KY
42053.

Electric
    Alacite table lamp, ivory, embossed
    leaf design, cut-through scalloped
    base, wreath-shaped Alacite finial,
    22-1/4" h **92.00**
    Alacite wall lamp, white, U-shaped
    arm, 8-1/2" h..............................**93.50**
    G-217 table lamp, ivory Alacite, gold
    metal base, vase design with leaf
    spray in high relief, c1940.........**75.00**
    M-123, lady figural, metal, orig fleur-de-
    lis finial.....................................**405.00**
Kerosene
    B-26 Simplicity 'Decalmania" lamp, pink
    Alacite, c1948-53....................**325.00**
    Beehive, ruby, complete with B burner,
    wick, chimney, insect screen and
    shade, c1937 ....**795.00**
    Model 8, 401 shade **256.00**

Aladdin Lamps, Drape pattern, pink opaque, 14" h, $125.

Moonstone Quilt, green, B burner, wick, Chimney, c1937 ....**335.00**
Tall Lincoln Drape, ruby flashed, 1940s shade......................................**861.00**
Washington Drape, amber, plain stem, B burner, wick, chimney, shade, c1940......................................**195.00**

❖ Albums

Albums consist of a grouping of pages that are bound together and used for a similar purpose. Albums can range in size from small examples used for autographs to larger, more ornate types for storing photographs. They offer a unique glimpse into the life of their owner. An autograph album might show one's friends and their sentiments of a bygone era. Photograph albums filled with images of unidentified people are often found at flea markets. Usually the value of these individual "instant relatives" is minimal, but if the photographs happen to include a famous person, an interesting pose, or an unusual setting, the value the album is enhanced.

Autograph

Leather cover, used, wear to cover **65.00**
Velvet cover, "Autograph" emb on front, faded red, filled with autographs, some including caricatures.......**75.00**
Daguerreotype, gutta percha, scrolling motif, dark brown **50.00**

Photograph

Celluloid cover, swans, trees and couple in Victorian dress on bridge, fleur-de-lis border, front cover shades from celery to lime to orange, back cover ivory celluloid, spine is cut velvet, 26 5-1/2" x 3-3/4" openings and 16 2" x 3-1/2" openings, pages bordered in gold leaf, orig clasp, unused..........**165.00**
Celluloid cover, floral motif **85.00**
Leather cover, brass closure, family photos, worn **80.00**
Olympic logo, 1984, large format, MIB **10.00**
Velvet cover, maroon, "Our Friends" in nickel plate metal, c1890-1900, filled with old photos, 11" x 9".........**140.00**
Wood, "Our Honeymoon" in relief, Silver Springs, Fla., hp flamingo motif, unused, 9" x 6" **36.00**
Tintype, leather cover, holds 24 tintypes, 1-1/2" x 1-1/4" **225.00**
Tobacco Cards, Players Tobacco Album of Film Stars, 1935, complete **250.00**

❖ Aliens, Space-Related

From little green creatures to Martians, collectors are fascinated by science fiction and aliens. As you can see from this sampling, space-related items encompass a wide variety of collectibles, from scary and spooky to just plain fun. Any alien collection is sure to be out of this world!

References: Dana Cain, *UFO & Alien Collectibles Price Guide*, Krause Publications, 1998; Rex Miller, *The Investor's Guide to Vintage Character Collectibles*, Krause Publications, 1999; Frank M. Robinson, *Science Fiction of the Twentieth Century, An Illustrated History*, Collectors Press, 1999; Stuart W. Wells, III, *Science Fiction Collectibles*, Krause Publications, 1999.

Periodicals: *Starlog Magazine*, 275 Park Ave S, New York, NY 10016; *Strange New Worlds*, P.O. Box 223, Tallevast, FL 34270.

Collectors' Clubs: Galaxy Patrol, 22 Colton St, Worcester, MA 01610; Lost in Space Fan Club, 550 Trinity, Westfield, NJ 07090; Society for the Advancement of Space Activities, P.O. Box 192, Kent Hills, ME 04349.

For additional listings, see *Warman's Americana & Collectibles*.

Action figure

Alien, 18" h, Kenner, 1979, loose **150.00**
Clan Leader Predator, loose **5.00**
Hicks, Kenner, MIP **20.00**
Big Little Book, *The Invaders Alien Missile Threat,* by Paul S. Newman, Whitman #12, 1967 ....**8.00**
Cap, from movie *Alien*, 1992, black, neon green writing, adjustable strap, officially licensed by Universal Industries, Inc. **10.00**
Christmas ornament

Bird of Prey, Star Trek, Hallmark, 1994, MIB **30.00**
Kringles Bumper Cars, Santa, reindeer and space alien, Hallmark, 1991, MIB **50.00**
Comic book

Robotmen of the Lost Planet, Avon, #1, 1952......................................**125.00**
Moon Girl Fights Crime, EC Comic #7, 1949......................................**150.00**
Game, Alien, Kenner, 1979 ....**100.00**
Hood ornament, 5-1/2" h, space alien, plastic and pot metal, lights up **10.00**
Key chain, Toy Story, Pizza Planet vending machine, antennae light, orig Basic Fun blister pack....................**4.75**
Model, from movie *Alien*, Aurora, MIB **125.00**
Magazine, *Famous Monsters of Filmland* #143, Close Encounters, Alien, and Star Wars **8.00**
Puppet, Alf, red shirt and cap, Alien Productions, 1988, played with **10.00**
Stuffed Toy, 16" h, Alf, plush, 1986 **25.00**
Toy, Rocket Racer #8, Yonezwa, 11-1/2" l **775.00**

❖ Almanacs

While few of us today rely on almanacs for forecasting the weather, it wasn't too long ago that many folks did. They got much more than weather information from these charming little booklets. Beauty tips, household hints, and exercise regimens were also included.

Agricultural Almanac, 1932, John Baer's Sons, Inc., Lancaster, Pa. **15.00**
Bell Telephone System, 1941, 32 pages......................................**12.00**
Dr. Jayne's Medical Aliment and Guide to Health, 1870 ....**35.00**
Dr. Miles Almanac, 1934, red, white and blue cover, 32 pgs, cover loose, worn, 6" x 9-1/2" **7.50**
Goodrich Almanac for Farm and Home, 1937..**10.00**
Healthway Products Almanac, 1940, Illinois Herb Co. **12.00**

Herablist, 1938, 5-1/2" x 8-1/4" **16.00**
Hostetter's Illustrated United States Almanac, 1876, Pittsburgh, Pa., missing back cover, 7-3/4" x 5" **20.00**
Maine Farmer's Almanac, 1916, wear and stains **15.00**
MacDonald's Farmer's Almanac, 1922, Binghamton, N.Y. **5.00**
Old Farmer's Almanac, 1857, wear and stains **12.00**
Rawleigh's Almanac & Catalog, 1936, 6-1/2" x 9-1/2" **10.00**
The Herbalist Almanac, 1942, Meyer trademark, cover shows Indians bringing in herbs to dry, 5-5/8" x 8-3/8" **9.00**
The Ladies Birthday Almanac, 1937, Medlock's Drug Store, Roscoe, Texas **12.00**
Tribune Almanac and Political Register, 1863..**25.00**
Uncle Sam's Almanac, 1941, compiled by Frederic J. Haskin, 64 pgs, small tear on spine..............................**17.50**

❖ Aluminum, Hand-Wrought

The aluminum giftware market began in the 1920s, providing consumers with an interesting new medium to replace fancy silver and silver-plate items. In order to remain competitive, many silver manufacturers added aluminum articles to their product lines during the Depression. Many well-known metalsmiths contributed their skills to the production of hammered aluminum. With the advent of mass-production and the accompanying wider distribution of aluminum giftware, there was less demand for individually produced items. Only a few producers continue turning out quality work using the age-old and time-tested methods of metal crafting.

References: Everett Grist, *Collectible Aluminum*, Collector Books, 1994; Dannie A. Woodard, *Hammered Aluminum Hand-Wrought Collectibles*, Book 2, Aluminum Collectors' Books, 1993; Dannie Woodard and Billie Wood, *Hammered Aluminum*, self-published, 1983.

Periodical: *Aluminist*, P.O. Box 1346,

Aluminum, Hand Wrought Tray, flying geese dec, unmarked, 16-1/2" l, 9-1/4" w, $24.

Aluminum, Hand Wrought Basket, twisted handle, roses dec, reticulated fleur-de-lis motif, $15.

Weatherford, TX 76086.

Collectors' Clubs: Aluminum Collectors, P.O. Box 1346, Weatherford, TX 76086; Wendell August Collectors Guild, P.O. Box 107, Grove City, PA 16127.

For additional listings, see *Warman's Americana & Collectibles.*

Basket, pie-crust edges, dimpled handle, mkd on back "The Beauty Line, Designed Aluminum" with rose, 14" x 10-1/2"...**18.00**
Bowl
  Chrysanthemum pattern, Continental Silverlook, 11-3/4" dia..............**20.00**
  Pine Cone pattern, Wendell August Forge, 8" dia **45.00**
Bread tray, Chrysanthemum pattern, Continental Silverlook, 13-1/4" l...**25.00**
Candleholder, Buenilum, beaded edge base, aluminum stem with wood ball, 6" h **12.00**
Casserole carrier, holds Fire-King casserole, moving the handle lifts the metal lid......................................**35.00**
Coaster, Bamboo pattern, Everlast Forged Aluminum, set of eight, matching holder..........................**25.00**
Compote, ftd, fluted edges, emb fruit motif, 6" h, 6-1/2" dia...................**10.00**
Creamer and sugar, Chrysanthemum pattern, Continental Silverlook, matching tray...............................**35.00**
Desk set, Bali Bamboo pattern, Everlast Forge, 3-pc set **48.00**
Ice bucket, rosette finial, 8" dia **25.00**
Lazy Susan, Everlast, Art Deco leaping stag in relief, mkd on bottom........**30.00**
Nut bowl, footed, floral dec, 4" h, 9" l **20.00**
Pitcher, Regal, red, black handle....**15.00**
Plate, flying ducks and cattails, 5" d..**6.00**

Salad set, tulip dec, matching serving utensils, Buenilum Hand Wrought**24.00**
Serving dish, 3-part, Colonial, applied flower in center, 1 section with flower dec **14.00**
Tidbit tray, 3 tiers, Dogwood pattern, mkd "Wilson Specialties Co., Inc., Brooklyn, N.Y.," 10" h, 13" dia **30.00**
Tray
  Barley pattern, Wendell August Forge, #606, 14" x 9" **35.00**
  Paisley pattern, Keystone, emb floral dec, 20" dia including handles..**25.00**
  Rose design, scalloped and pierced open-work edge, 12-1/2" x 7"...**14.50**
Tray with 6 cordials, cordials with cutout floral dec and glass inserts, tray 12" x 3-1/2", cordials 3" h, set..............**75.00**
Water pitcher, handle knotted and riveted to pitcher, mkd with globe logo and "World, Hand Forged," wear, 8-1/2" h **35.00**

❖ American Bisque

The American Bisque Company was founded in Williamstown, W.Va., in 1919. Although the pottery originally produced china-head dolls, it quickly expanded its inventory to include serving dishes, cookie jars, ashtrays, and other decorative ceramic pieces. B.E. Allen, founder of the Sterling China Company, invested heavily in American Bisque and eventually purchased its remaining stock. In 1982 the plant was sold and operated briefly under the name American China Company. The business closed in 1983.

Trademarks used by American Bisque included Sequoia Ware and Berkeley, the former used on items sold in gift shops, and the latter found on products sold through chain stores. Their cookie jars are marked with "ABC" inside blocks.

For additional listings, see *Warman's Americana & Collectibles* and *Warman's American Pottery & Porcelain.*

Bank, 6" h, elephant........................**85.00**
Clothes sprinkler, figural, elephant, 6-1/4" h..**600.00**
Cookie jar
  Baby Elephant, bonnet...............**165.00**
  Bear with Cookie, mkd "USA" **80.00**
  Beehive, mkd "USA" 11-3/4" h ...**165.00**
  Candy Cane Babies **200.00**
  Churn Boy **225.00**
  Cookie Sack **95.00**
  Donald Duck, standing...............**385.00**
  Flintstone's Rubble House **650.00**
  Jack-in-the-Box..........................**195.00**
  Poodle **65.00**
  School Bus **250.00**
  Yogi Bear..................................**300.00**
  Wooden Soldier.........................**100.00**
Food mold, fish, white, red trim, incised

"ABC," ring for hanging, 10" l........**15.00**
Pitcher, chick, gold trim **48.00**
Planter
    Bear sitting on stump **18.00**
    Gold horn **35.00**
    Lamb **18.00**
    Tiger **28.00**
Teapot, Red Rose, gold trim, 6-1/2" h
    ....**55.00**
Vase
    6" h, white heart, blue bow **28.00**
    7-1/4" h, green, fern frond handles
    ....**20.00**

❖ Amusement Parks

Whhheeee!! What fun a trip to an amusement park can be. Doesn't everybody bring home some sort of souvenir? Today's collectors scout flea markets for these treasures, keeping the excitement of that vacation trip alive a little longer.

Ashtray, Disneyland, mkd "Walt Disney Productions Japan," some fading, 5"
    ....**8.00**
Bookmark, Coney Island, celluloid, diecut image of Ziz, young black girl entertainer, c1908, 3" h **150.00**
Charm bracelet, Disneyland, six charms, copyright Walt Disney Productions, MIB
    ....**40.00**
Desk calendar, mechanical, metal, Great Adventure Amusement Park, NJ, shows ferris wheel and other rides, paper label "Made in Japan," 3" h
    ....**24.00**
Pennant, felt, "Storyland, Asbury Park, N.J.," red ground, shows King Arthur's Court with knight on horseback, 26" l
    ....**22.00**
Pin, goldtone sailboat with Coney Island plaque, attached by chain to numerals 41 (1941)..**40.00**
Pin dish, Coney Island, metal, parachute jump in full relief, several rides and general views also emb, early 1940s
    ....**65.00**
Plate, Freedomland Amusement Park, pottery, 1960s, 5-1/4" dia **45.00**
Postcard

Amusement Parks, Pennant, Koziar's Christmas Village, Bernville, PA, yellow background, turquoise tabs, red end, red and white striped letters, multicolored park scene, $5.

Coney Island, postmarked
    Brooklyn/Coney Island 1939......**3.00**
Disneyland, 1969 ....**3.00**
Heinz Ocean Pier, Atlantic City, unused
    ....**10.00**
Palisade Amusement Park, postmarked
    June 12, 1911...........................**4.00**
Tumbler, Nathan's Famous Hot Dogs (Coney Island, Long Island and Yonkers), painted logo, 4-5/8"h **4.00**
Wallet, child's, Asbury Park, NJ, surfing and sailing scenes **20.00**

❖ Anchor Hocking

Founded in 1905, Hocking Glass Company was located in Lancaster, Ohio. In 1937 the company merged with Anchor Cap & Closure Company, forming the highly successful Anchor Hocking Corp. The company's primary output consisted of glass items for household use, including several Depression-era patterns. Much of their kitchenware and tableware is marked, enabling collectors to identify these pieces.

References: Gene Florence, *Anchor Hocking's Fire King & More*, 2nd ed, Collector Books, 2000; ——, *Collectible Glassware from the 40's, 50's, 60's*, 6th ed, Collector Books, 2002; ——, *Kitchen Glassware of the Depression Years*, 5th ed, Collector Books, 1995 (1997 value update); Joe Keller and David Ross, *Jadite: An Identification and Price Guide*, 2nd ed, Schiffer Publishing, 2000; Gary & Dale Kilgo and Jerry & Gail Wilkins, *Collectors Guide to Anchor Hocking's Fire-King Glassware*, K & W Collectibles, 1991; ——, *Collectors Guide to Anchor Hocking's Fire-King Glassware, Volume II*, K & W Collectibles, 1998.

Periodicals: *Fire-King Monthly*, P.O. Box 70594, Tuscaloosa, AL 35407; *Fire-King News*, K & W Collectibles, Inc., P.O. Box 374, Addison, AL 35540.

Collectors' Club: Fire-King Collectors Club, 1161 Woodrow St, #3, Redwood City, CA 94061.

For additional listings, see *Warman's Glass*, as well as *Fire-King* in this edition.

Batter bowl, set of nested bowls, transparent green, 7", 8", 9", and 10" dia. **95.00**
Berry bowl, Moonstone, opalescent hobnail..**18.00**
Bonbon, Moonstone, opalescent hobnail, heart shape **15.00**
Cereal bowl, Bubble, crystal.............**4.00**
Cigarette box, Royal Ruby **60.00**
Cocktail, Royal Ruby **10.00**
Condiment set, cruet and salt and pepper shakers, blue trim.............**25.00**
Cookie jar, cov, Sandwich, desert gold
    ....**37.50**
Creamer, Bubble, light blue.............**35.00**

Cup and saucer, Moonstone, amber
    ....**28.00**
Dinner plate, Sandwich, crystal......**20.00**
Egg cup, Jade-ite.............................**47.50**
Food chopper, red tin top, mkd "Anchor Hocking, Federal Tool Corp." **18.00**
Fruit bowl, Bubble, forest green **9.00**
Ice bucket, Royal Ruby...................**35.00**
Iced tea tumbler, Bubble, forest green
    ....**16.00**
Ivy ball, Royal Ruby **6.00**
Juice tumbler, Sandwich, forest green
    ....**4.00**
Mayonnaise dish with underplate, Jubilee.......................................**150.00**
Mixing bowl, Vitrock, 8-1/2" dia......**18.00**
Mug, Bo Peep.................................**12.00**
Punch set, Early American Prescut, bowl, stand, 12 cups, plastic hangers, plastic ladle **50.00**
Range salt and pepper shakers, opaque Delphite blue, some corrosion on salt lid, pr............................**25.00**
Salad set, hp salad bowl, two cruets, salt and pepper shakers, all marked "AH" on bottom, c1950 ....**25.00**
Sandwich plate, Sandwich pattern, desert gold, 12" dia **15.00**
Sherbet, Moonstone, green hobnail**10.00**
Sugar, Bubble, crystal **6.00**
Syrup pitcher, red top, mkd "Anchor Hocking, Federal Tool Corp.," 5-1/2" h
    ....**15.00**
Tom and Jerry set, large bowl with 5 matching cups, white ground, red décor **12.00**
Tumbler, crystal
    Bubble **5.00**
    Stars and Stripes, 5" h **45.00**
Vase
    Early American Prescut, 8-1/2" h..**8.00**
    Forest Green, 9" h.......................**12.00**
Water Pitcher, Forest Green **35.00**

❖ Angels

Many flea market shoppers are searching for angels to add to their collections. Perhaps they believe in guardian angels. In any event, they are finding them on all manner of objects, from figurines to artwork.

Collectors' Clubs: Angel Collector Club, 14 Parkview Ct, Crystal Lake, IL 60012-3540; Angels Collectors' Club of America, 12225 S Potomac, Phoenix, AZ 85044.

Advertising mirror "Angelus Marshmallows," angel holding box of marshmallows **80.00**
Candle climbers, gold, mkd "Made in Japan," gold foil label...................**25.00**
Candleholders, Clay Art, 4" x 3," pr
    ....**12.00**

Christmas decoration, porcelain head, chenille body, holding candle, 1950s, 4" h **22.00**

Christmas ornament
Bisque, mkd Edgerton Pottery, c1960, 3" h **24.00**
Wax over composition, human hair wig, spun glass wings, cloth dress, Germany **55.00**

Christmas stocking, cross-stitch cuff with angels, handmade, c1980 ....**18.00**

Christmas tree topper
Papier-mâché, blue dress, silver cardboard wings and crown, kneeling on silver sphere, silver tube **45.00**
Plastic, white, gold stars, 1940s, 4" h **28.00**
Plastic, white robe, gold lining, blue wings, electric cord in back, c1950, 8" h, some scratches **25.00**
Spun glass and cardboard, 6" h ..**24.00**

Chromolithograph, diecut 7" h, tinsel trim,
German **18.00**
8" h, tinsel and lametta trim **10.00**

Cookie cutter, aluminum, 5" h..........**5.00**

Figurine
Angel playing a harp, ceramic, gold label on bottom "Handmade in Japan" and "MY," 3-1/2" h **5.00**
Josef Originals, birthday angel 11, sewing, imp mark and paper label, 5" h **17.50**
Lefton, December, blue stone in center of pink flower, 1960-1983, 4-1/2" h **26.00**
Pair of hands with pink angel nestled in them, gold trim, applied roses, 5-1/4" h **35.00**
Young boy playing ball with angel ..**7.00**

Illuminated, GLO-rious Angel by Glolite, Chicago, Ill., hard plastic, silver, angel near mint cond, box fair cond.......**24.00**

Light switch cover, angel dec, Bernat **5.00**

Wooden angel, blue jacket, red and white plaid dress, copper wings, wooden stars and hearts, $2.

Matchsafe, celluloid **145.00**
Ornament, hard plastic, silver with gold hair and halo, white wings, 4-1/4 " h **12.00**
Perfume bottle, Avon, Angel Song with Lyre, Here's My Heart perfume, frosted glass, orig contents **8.00**
Pin, goldtone, small rhinestone accents **5.00**
Planter, Lefton China, angel on cloud **40.00**
Plate
Goebel, Heavenly Angel, 1st in a series, 1971, orig box **400.00**
Hummel, Herald Angel, 1977 Christmas plate, Schmid Bros., 7-3/4" dia..................................**32.00**
Postcard, group of angels hovering over stable manger scene, mkd "Series #444/1 Printed in Germany," divided back, unused **3.00**
Salt and pepper shakers, porcelain, 3-3/4" h, pr..................................**25.00**
Snow dome, Josef, porcelain base, 5-3/4" h, glass ball 4" dia **35.00**
Tie tac, angel head, brasstone, mkd "HNS" **12.00**
Wall pocket, Royal Copley, 6" h......**80.00**

❖ Animal Dishes, Covered

These clever covered dishes were first popular during the Victorian era, when they were used to hold foods and sweets on elaborate sideboards. China manufacturers produced some examples, but most were made of glass, representing many of the major glass companies. They can be found in colored and white milk glass, clear glass, and many colors of translucent glass.

Camel, white milk glass, Westmoreland **175.00**
Cat on drum, white milk glass, Portieux **195.00**
Cat on hamper, green milk glass, V mark **115.00**
Chick on sleigh, white milk glass.**115.00**
Cow, white milk glass, Kemple......**160.00**
Dewey, white milk glass, attributed to Flaccus, Spanish-American War, commemorative, chip on base ...**130.00**
Dolphin, white milk glass **145.00**
Duck, swimming, white milk glass, Vallerystahll **145.00**
Fish, flat, white milk glass, Atterbury **120.00**
Hen on nest
Marbleized, head turned to left, white and deep blue, Atterbury **185.00**
Mirage (pale orchid), Boyd, 5-1/2" l, 4-1/4" w, 5-3/4" h **20.00**
Transparent blue, Kemple Glass, mkd

Covered Dish Turkey, cobalt blue, reproduction. Notice how glossy the glass is, often a sign that this is a later copy of a period dish.

"K" **35.00**
Kitten, ribbed base, Westmoreland, white **130.00**
Lion, McKee, white milk glass, top only **25.00**
Lion, reclining, white milk glass, criss-cross base..................................**135.00**
Lovebirds, pink irid, "M" in shield for Mosser, 6-1/2" l, 5" w, 5-1/4" h **25.00**
Owl, green slag, Imperial Glass, mkd "IG" **60.00**
Rabbit, dark green, National Milk Glass Society mark, cracked..................**60.00**
Rabbit, light blue, National Milk Glass Society mark **145.00**
Robin on nest, medium blue milk glass, Vallerystahl..................................**165.00**
Robin on nest, white milk glass, air bubbles, Vallerystahl....................**95.00**
Setter dog, blue milk glass, Vallerystahl **265.00**
Swan, closed neck, white milk glass, Westmoreland **120.00**
Turkey, amethyst head, white body

Animal covered dish, Boar's head, white milk glass, glass eyes, on ribbed base. This rare dish sold for $1,200 at Green Valley Auctions.

....**220.00**
Turkey, white head, dark amethyst body
....**170.00**
Turtle, chocolate, with National Milk
Glass Society mark **130.00**

❖ Animation Art

A "cel" is an animation drawing on celluloid, a technique is attributed to Earl Hurd. Although the process was perfected under animation giants Walt Disney and Max Fleischer, individual artists such as Ub Iwerks, Walter Lantz, and Paul Terry—along with studios such as Columbia, MGM, Paramount/Famous Studios, and Warner Brothers—did pioneering work.

One second of film requires over 20 animation cels. The approximate number of cels used to make a cartoon can be determined by multiplying the length of the cartoon in minutes by 60 seconds by 24.

References: Jeff Lotman, *Animation Art: The Early Years*, Schiffer Publishing, 1995; ——, *Animation Art: The Later Years*, Schiffer Publishing, 1996; ——, *Animation Art at Auction: Since 1994*, Schiffer Publishing, 1998;

Periodicals: *Animation Film Art*, P.O. Box 25547, Los Angeles, CA 90025; *Animation Magazine*, 4676 Admiralty Way, Suite 210, Marina Del Ray, CA 90292; *Animato!*, P.O. Box 1240, Cambridge, MA 02238; *In Toon!*, P.O. Box 217, Gracie Station, New York, NY, 10028; *Storyboard/The Art of Laughter*, 80 Main St, Nashua, NH 03060.

Collectors' Club: Greater Washington Animation Collectors Club, 12423 Hedges Run Dr #184, Lake Ridge, VA 22192.

For additional listings, see *Warman's Americana & Collectibles*.

101 Dalmatians, The Colonel, 13" x 13-1/2" frame..............................**425.00**
Donald Duck, 9" x 6" frame..........**950.00**
Flintstones, Fred & Wilma with Barney and Betty Rubble, orig production cel, multi-cel setup, mounted on full celluloid, framed, glazed, 16" x 19"
....**425.00**
Jungle Book, Baloo, Walt Disney, 1967, gouache on celluloid, cel trimmed, unframed, 6-1/2" x 4" **925.00**
Scooby Doo, sgd "246/11 #60! SC36," 14-3/4" x 11-3/4" **150.00**
Smurf, #240 21 65 F-17, matted, 11" x 14"...**95.00**
Sylvester, orig production cel, gouache on full celluloid, accompanied by orig layout drawing, c1960, mounted, framed, glazed, 17" x 32"..........**450.00**
Teenage Mutant Ninja Turtles, certificate of authenticity, copyright dates 1985 to 1991, matted, 11" x 14"
....**85.00**

Winnie the Pooh with Rabbit and Piglet, 1960s orig film............................**350.00**

❖ Anri

This Italian ceramics manufacturer has had quite an impact on the market for limited-edition collectibles. Items by Anri can be found in various forms, with the work of several different artists featured.

Periodical: *Collectors Mart Magazine*, 700 E State St, Iola, WI 54990.

Collectors' Club: Club Anri, 55 Parcella Park Dr, Randolph MA 02368.

Egg, J. Ferrandiz, baby coming out of egg, dated, 1980s, firing check **18.00**
Figure
Bridesmaid **840.00**
Cowboy, 6-1/4" h **550.00**
It's My Baby, 6"..........................**590.00**
Looking to the Future **600.00**
Lumberjack, 8" h **560.00**
Mickey and Minnie Mouse, stamped "Walt Disney Company", 4" h, pr
....**690.00**
Santa, Joyful Giving **700.00**
Stolen Kiss, ink stamp, 3" h **400.00**
Talking to the Animals, 1969, 3" h
....**155.00**
The Bouquet, 5-3/4" h **300.00**
Tribute to Mother **550.00**
Umbrella and Raincoat, 6" h **580.00**
Windy Times, 6" h **560.00**
Limited edition plate, Disney Four Star Collection, Maestro Mickey, 1989, MIB
....**75.00**
Music box, Ave Marie De Lourdes by Ferrandiz **275.00**
Navitity figure
Dromedary **735.00**
Elephant **790.00**
Shepherd boys with goat **880.00**
Shepherd group **950.00**
Shepherd sitting with sheep.......**635.00**

❖ Anthropomorphic Collectibles

Even before the creation of Veggie Tales, tomatoes and cucumbers had a life of their own. Merchants discovered years ago they could attract a customer's attention by giving human characteristics to inanimate objects. Flea markets are a great place to find anthropomorphic collectibles. Don't hesitate if you see something you like, since this area of collecting is heating up.

Advertising trade card, Crème Oat Meal Toilet Soap, J. D. Larkin & Co., Buffalo, courting apes, chromolithograph, #5 of series, 1881, 3-1/8" w, 5-3/4" h **20.00**

Anthropomorphic, Salt and pepper shakers, oranges with faces, emb Florida, $15.

Condiment jar, banana boy, green bowtie and brown hat, slotted lid to insert spoon, worn, 5-1/2" h.........**55.00**
Condiment set
Tomato heads, mkd "Made in Japan," 3-1/2" w, 4" h **45.00**
Train, red ink stamp Japan mark, 9" l, 2-3/4" h, slight wear.................**35.00**
Embroidery pattern, 6 motifs of smiling vegetables, Alice Brooks #7059, unused, fading..............................**3.00**
Head vase, apple, illegible incised mark and 97608, orig chenille bee insert
....**30.00**
Rolling pin set, toothpick holder and salt and pepper shakers sit in rolling pin, 4-pc set..**23.00**
Salt and pepper shakers
Apples, full-figure, green-and-black dresses, applied black bead eyes, 1 with 2 holes, 1 with 3, cork stoppers, 2-1/2" h, pr.............................**24.00**
Cucumbers, green suits, 1 with 4 holes, 1 with 3, missing stoppers 4-1/4" h, pr..............................**45.00**
Goofy and Pluto, anthropomorphic car, orig label "Souvenir of Burlington, Iowa," red ink "Japan" mark, 4" l, 4-1/4" h **295.00**
Mushrooms, Napco, pr.................**36.00**
Pear and orange, 1-pc, Japan, 2-1/2" h, 3-1/4" w...................................**20.00**
Teapot with salt and pepper shakers, 1 boy and 1 girl shaker in teapot form, orig corks, unmkd, teapot 5" h, shakers 2-1/2" h, set..................................**76.00**
Toothpick holder, corn, based on animated character from Walt Disney World's "The Land," copyright 1981
....**39.00**
Transfer patterns, The Vitamin Ball, 24 characters include 10 couples, 12-pc orchestra, conductor and singer, Joseph Walker Co., orig packet with split along top.............................**32.00**

❖ Appliances

Appliances of all types fascinate collectors,

Anthropomorphic, Two plush peas in a pod, one with blue legs, other with pink, attached with Velcro to felt pea pod, $4.

with the most common question being, "Does it work?" Please exercise caution when attempting to see if an item functions. Damaged cords and frayed wiring can lead to unpleasant results. When considering a purchase, remember that original instructions, parts, and boxes add greatly to the value of vintage appliances.

References: Linda Campbell Franklin, *300 Years of Kitchen Collectibles*, 5th ed, Krause Publications, 2003; Helen Greguire, *Collector's Guide to Toasters & Accessories*, Collector Books, 1997; Gary Miller and K.M. Scotty Mitchell, *Price Guide to Collectible Kitchen Appliances*, Wallace-Homestead, 1991.

Collectors' Club: Electric Breakfast Club, P.O. Box 306, White Mills, PA 18473.

For additional listings, see *Warman's Americana & Collectibles.*

Advertisement, General Electric's New Line, shows can opener, toaster, coffee maker, iron, black and white, 9-1/2" x 12" **12.00**
Blender, Chronmaster Mixall, chrome and black motor, single shaft on hinged black base, orig silver-striped glass, 1930s **40.00**
Buyer's Guide, *Food is Fun,* Gas Appliance Manuf Assoc, 1963 .....**10.00**
Catalog, Trible's Appliance Parts Master Catalog, illus, 1959......................**25.00**
Chafing dish, American Beauty, American Electrical Heater Co., 3-part, nickel on cooper, black painted wood handles and knob, c1910.............**50.00**
Drink mixer, Weining Made Rite Co., lightweight metal, cream and green motor, single shaft, 1930s............**25.00**
Egg cooker, Hankscraft Co., yellow china base, instructions on metal plate on bottom, 1930s **35.00**
Flour sifter, Miracle Flour Sifter, electric, cream body, blue wood handle, 1934 ....**35.00**
Grill, Sunbeam, model FP, 12" x 12" x 4" **45.00**
Hair dryer
   Polar Club, AC Gilbert, orig box ...**15.00**
   Queen, Handy-Hannah Products Corp., Whitman, MA **15.00**

Hamilton Beach milk shake maker, green enameled base, orig container, $350.

Hot plate, El Stovo, Pacific Electric Heating Co., solid iron surface, clay-filled int., pierced legs, pad feet, c1910 ....**25.00**
Juicer, Vita-Juicer, 1930s, Kold King Distributing Corp., cream-painted cast metal **35.00**
Milk shake mixer, A.C. Gilbert Co., missing metal cup for mixing........**60.00**
Mixer, Montgomery Ward, electric beater with glass jar, green handle on beater **65.00**
Popcorn Popper, Rapaport, 5-1/2" sq black base, metal legs, round aluminum upper part, red knob, chrome handle, 1920s..................**25.00**
Toaster, 2 slice, chrome bodyGeneral Mills, wheat decor on side, black Bakelite base, early 1940s...........**35.00**
   Kenmore, black Bakelite handles, mechanical clock mechanism, early 1940s.......................................**30.00**
Waffle iron
   Coleman Waffle Iron, high Art Deco style, chrome, small black and white porcelain top impala insert, black Bakelite handles, early 1930s ..**85.00**
   Griswold, electric, 1920-1930, orig box **120.00**
   Universal, electric, porcelain top, replaced cord............................**65.00**

❖ Art Deco

The term Art Deco is derived from the French name for the Paris Exhibition of 1927, *L'Exposition International des Arts Décorative et Industriels Mondernes.* The style became quite popular, with its sleek, angular forms and simple lines reflected in everything from artwork to skyscrapers of the period.

Reference: Susan Warshaw Berman, *Affordable Art Deco Graphics,* Schiffer Publishing, 2002.

For additional listings, see *Warman's Antiques & Collectibles.*

Brush, pearlized pink, matching comb, Fuller, 1925 ....**65.00**
Chair, side, chromed metal rod frame, triangular back over triangular upholstered seat, 32" h, pr.........**100.00**
Clock, 16" l, mantle, circular geometric form, green variegated onyx, Whithal electric movement, c1925, some repair, minor loss...................................**100.00**
Coffee Set, silverplated, Wilcox, design attributed to Gene Theobald, faceted 10-1/2" h coffeepot, and sugar container with Bakelite finials, matching creamer, 20" l oblong tray, all mkd "Wilcox S.P. Co/E.P.N.S./International S.Co./W. M. Wounts/1981N." ...**1,150.00**
Demitasse cup and saucer, cream ground, multicolor floral dec, stamped on base, Honiton Pottery, Devon, England **90.00**
Figure
   Rearing horse in upright horseshoe, carved and polished black granite,

Art Deco Lamp base, 4" d, 8-1/2" h, carved and etched glass, red poppies and green leaves on striped yellow ground, hammered copper armature, shade missing, unmarked but attributed to LeGras, $600.

scratches, minor chips, 5-1/2" h
....**190.00**
Dancer, bronze, ivory dec, brass inlaid
malachite box base, French, c1920-
25, 11" h **275.00**
Fruit bowl, Lotus Fan dec, silver plate,
Rogers, c1923-25, 2-1/2" h, 11" dia
....**90.00**
Lamp, boudoir, Danse De Lumiere, 11"
h, molded glass figure of woman with
outstretched arms, bearing stylized
feather drapery, oval platform base with
internal light fixture, molded title and
patent mark, c1930, mold
imperfections **400.00**
Lamp, table, 19" h, 11" d concentric
ribbed pink satin shade with stylized
rosebud center, shade emb "Vleighe
France 1137," nickel-plated brass base
with emb geometric designs, minor
flakes on shade **520.00**
Magazine rack, bronze, upright circular
sides with openwork design of
greyhound in stride, scrolling leaf
border, c1930, 4-1/2" w, 11-7/8" l, 12" h
....**375.00**
Salad servers, fork and spoon, Swedish,
c1930-35, 11-3/4" l **50.00**
Tile, 8" sq, rust, tan, off-white and purple
design of lady, 4 short feet, mkd
"Longwy, France, Primavera" with
shield and crown **415.00**
Vase, 12-1/4" h, 5-1/2" d, Wiener
Werkstatte, bulbous, flaring neck,
painted white and black geometric
pattern, brown ground, stamped
"WWW/Made in Austria/HB".......**125.00**
Wall Sconce, 7" h, 3" d, nickeled brass
plate and curved arm, frosted glass
shade with raised geometric design,
rim chips to shade, minor dents to
sconce..**90.00**

❖ Art Nouveau

Sensuous female forms with flowing lines
are the signature motif of this style. The Art
Nouveau period started during the 1890s
and continued for the next 40 years, popular
in both Europe and America. Leading
designers of the time introduced the style's
sweeping lines into their works. Florals,
insects, and other forms from nature were
popular motifs.

References: Fiona Gallagher, *Christie's Art
Nouveau*, Watsun-Guptill Publications,
2000; Paul Greenhalgh, *Art Nouveau 1890-
1914*, Harry N. Abrams, 2000.

For additional listings, see *Warman's
Antiques & Collectibles*.

Ashtray, molded, clear glass, reverse
relief of Leda and Swan, c1925,
ground spot at base, nicks to bottom

*Art Nouveau Vase, spherical top emb with stylized
roses, four-sided base, artist's initials and "103",
Austrian, nicks and hairlines, 10" h, $75.*

edge, 3-3/8" w, 5-1/4" l, 7/8" h, ..**175.00**
Belt buckle, polychrome enamel, silver
mount, minor enamel loss..........**245.00**
Bird cage, beechwood, onion domed
body, wirework sides, scrolled feet, 33"
h **800.00**
Box, domed cov, paneled box of rust
brown shaded to colorless cased glass,
acid-etched dec with textured surface,
gilt highlights, bottom mkd "H 57,"
Continental, early 20th C, 4" h...**350.00**
Brush, silver-plate
Nude woman on back, 7-1/4" l.....**50.00**
Scrolls, initials, dated 1916, 7-1/4" l
....**50.00**
Woman's face, 5" l........................**75.00**
Bud vase, Vaseline, metal circle of nudes
supporting vase..........................**190.00**
Candlestick, 11-3/8" h, patinated metal,
figural, nymph standing on butterfly,
holding flower form candle sconce,
flower-form base, early 20th C...**115.00**
Cane, silver, 36" l, 7-1/2" across arc,
hunting dog head protruding from
swirls of marsh reeds, tarnished French
hallmarks, lignum vitae shaft, imp
below handle "Frizon 5 Av. Del Opera"
for Parisian seller, 3/4" white metal
ferrule, c1900 ....**800.00**
Clock, green bisque, gold and pink
highlights, gilt metal, imp Charenton
marks, France, c1900, hand missing,
nicks **825.00**
Desk set, onyx, two inkwells, blotter, note
pad, card holder and pen holder, inlaid
lapis lazuli band, imp hallmarks,
London, c1921, 6-pc set **300.00**

Dinner gong, mahogany, five graduated
bronze bells, exotic wood floral
marquetry on sides, bells restrung, 12"
w, 10-1/2" d, 10" h......................**450.00**
Figure, Fame, gilt-spelter, on marble
base, figure after E. Villianis, French,
17" h..**275.00**
Inkstand, brass, two-tiered letter holder,
hinged lid on inkwell, etched floral
decor, base imp "D.R.G.M. 237670
Ges Gesch," 3-7/8" h **120.00**
Lamp, polychromed, three lights with
frosted shades issuing from foliate
standard, classical maidens and child
below on sq base, hoof feet, 40" h
....**300.00**
Mirror, cast bronze, Rococo, kidney
shape, 19-1/2" h **250.00**
Picture frame, silver, English hallmarks,
4-3/4" h x 6-1/2" **90.00**
Umbrella stand, cast iron, emb floral
dec, old green repaint, 28-1/2" h,
....**150.00**
Vase
6" h, 6-1/2" d, silver plate, stylized relief
waterlily dec, English, c1900-15
....**175.00**
7-1/8" h, glass, quarter form, ruffled
rim, ribbed stem, bulbed base, green
glass cased to opaque pink int.,
slight irid sheen, rough pontil,
attributed to Union Glass Co.,
Somerville, MA **115.00**

❖ Art Pottery

The art pottery movement in America lasted
from about 1880 until the First World War.
During that time, more than 200 companies
produced decorative ceramics ranging from
borderline production ware to intricately
decorated, labor-intensive artware. The
latter would help establish America as a
decorative arts powerhouse. When buying
art pottery, remember that condition is
critical in determining price. Chips, cracks,
or damage of any kind can drastically

*Art Pottery Pewabic, squatty vessel, copper and purple
irid glaze, circular stamp mark, 4" dia, 3-1/2" h, $550*

Art Pottery, W. J. Walley, squatty flower frog vase, brown and green matte, stamped "WJW," 5" dia, $500.

reduce the price of an item.

References: Susan and Al Bagdade, *Warman's American Pottery and Porcelain*, 2nd ed, Krause Publications, 2000; Paul Evans, *Art Pottery of the United States*, 2nd ed, Feingold & Lewis Publishing, 1987; David Rago, *American Art Pottery*, Knickerbocker Press, 1997.

Periodicals: *Style 1900*, 333 N Main St, Lambertville, NJ 08530.

Collectors' Clubs: American Art Pottery Assoc, P.O. Box 1226, Westport, MA 02790; Pottery Lovers Reunion, 4969 Hudson Dr, Stow, OH 44224.

For additional listings, see *Warman's Antiques & Collectibles*, as well as specific categories in this edition.

Bowl
   Arequipa, light blue glossy glaze, molded flower and leaf dec, rolled rim, 9" dia **55.00**
   California Faience, medium blue, glossy glaze, 4-1/2" dia **125.00**
   Pewabic, hemispherical, gunmetal and turquoise dripping lustered glaze, circular stamp mark, 6-3/4" dia **1,800.00**
   Teco, 3 feet, green matte glaze, minor rust stains on interior, 3-3/4" h **330.00**
   Candlestick, Walley Pottery, bulbous top, flared base, striated brown-yellow high glaze, smooth green ground, looped handle, imp mark, 10" h **290.00**
Center bowl, Durant Kilns, turquoise crackled glaze, incised and dated 1917, very shallow bruise to side **450.00**
Flower Frog, California Faience, sailboat shape **75.00**
Inkwell, Owens Pottery, lime leaves, brown ground, sgd, 3-3/4" dia....**110.00**
Jardiniere, Pewabic, lustered cobalt blue glaze, stamped "Pewabic/Detroit," 9" dia, 8" h **2,200.00**
Mug, Walrath Pottery, reddish-brown

foliate dec, brown ground, imp mark, 4-1/2" h, pr.....................................**435.00**
Paperweight, Owens Majolica, stag head and "Edmiston Horney Company, Zanesville, Ohio," green glaze, 2-3/8" h, 3-7/8" w **82.50**
Pitcher, Merrimac Pottery, matte green glaze, restoration to rim chip, stamped mark, 6-3/4" h.............................**300.00**
Tile, Walley Pottery, relief turtle dec, thick crackle matte green glaze, imp mark, 7-1/2" dia **460.00**
Umbrella stand, Cincinnati Faience, 20" h, applied sea life, blue glaze, gold accents, sgd, c1890, 20" h.........**995.00**
Vase
   Arequipa, eight sided, tapering rim, emb leaves, matted red-brown glaze, imp mark, 8" x 5", small base bruise, minor glaze flakes inside rim ..**950.00**
   Avon Faience, flowers and stylized leaves, minor chips, 5-3/4" h ..**550.00**
   Bybee Seldon, vase, three handles, strong crystalline glaze over brown glaze, mkd with outline of Kentucky enclosing name, early 1930s, 5-7/8" h...**85.00**
   California Faience, bottle shape, flared rim, feathered blue matte finish, incised mark, 5" h **515.00**
Vessel, Denver Denaura, closed-in rim, emb with violets and leaves, matte green glaze, stamped mark "Denver Denaura/174," 5-3/4" dia, 2-3/4" h **1,900.00**

❖ Arts and Crafts

Decorative arts in America took on an entirely new look during the Arts and Crafts movement. This period, from 1895 to 1920, was greatly influenced by leading proponents Elbert Hubbard and his Roycrofters, the brothers Stickley, Frank Lloyd Wright, Charles and Henry Greene, George Niedecken, and Lucia and Arthur Mathews. Individualistic design and a re-emphasis on handcraftsmanship were important features of their work. Most Arts & Crafts furniture was made of oak. The market for good-quality furniture and accessories remains extremely strong.

References: Bruce Johnson, *Pegged Joint*, Knock on Wood Publications, 1995; Thomas K. Maher, *The Jarvie Shop: The Candlesticks and Metalwork of Robert R. Jarvie*, Turn of the Century Editions, 1997; David Rago, *American Art Pottery*, Knickerbocker Press, 1997; Paul Royka, *Mission Furniture from the American Arts & Crafts Movement*, Schiffer Publishing, 1997.

Periodicals: *American Bungalow*, P.O. Box 756, Sierra Madre, CA 91204; *Style 1900*, 333 N Main St, Lambertville, NJ 08530.

Collectors' Clubs: Foundation for the

Study of the Arts & Crafts Movement, Roycroft Campus, 31 S Grove St, East Aurora, NY 14052; Roycrofters-At-Large Assoc, P.O. Box 417, East Aurora, NY 14052; William Morris Society of Canada, 1942 Delaney Dr, Mississaugua, Ontario, L5J 3L1, Canada.

For additional listings, see *Warman's Antiques & Collectibles*.

Box, cov
   7-3/4" d, 3-3/4" h, round, pyrography dec, landscape of trees and mountains, browns and golds, orig green silk lining, small rim chip, unmarked, attributed to Arthur Grinnell **550.00**
   9-1/2" d, 6-1/2" h, round, hammered copper, floriform rim, ivory and silver pineapple shaped finial, medium orig patina, stamped "CAUMAN" ...**550.00**
Bowl, 5" d, 1-3/4" h, hammered silver, stamped "Sterling, Hand Beaten at the Kalo Shops, Park Ridge, Illinois," 4 troy oz **395.00**
Cabinet, 19" w, 15" d, 67" h, mirrored, single door painted with monk pouring wine, pewter strap hinges, paper "Shop-Of-The-Crafters" label on back, skinned finish **1,300.00**
Candlesticks, pr, 14-1/2" h, 7" d, brass, flat bobeches, flaring stems, wide circular base, orig inserts, attributed to Jessie Preston...........................**650.00**
Child's chair, Gustav Stickley, #342, 2-slat back, worn orig leather seat, orig finish, 23" h **460.00**
China Cabinet, 45-1/2" w, 17-1/4" d, 61-3/4" h, Rome Furniture Co, GA, two doors, orig glass in doors and in sides, three shelves, paneled back, paper label.......................................**1,200.00**

Arts & Crafts, Morris chair, oak, adjustable, lion's paw feet, recovered cushions, $450.

Cigarette Box, cov, 3-1/2" sq, 2" h, hammered pewter, enameled top with polychrome seascape with sailboat, cedar lined, sgd "Made in England/Tudric/Pewter/01021/Made by Liberty and Co." **775.00**

Coat Rack, 24" d, 67" h, brass, four-sided post, flaring base, four double hooks, old patina **200.00**

Desk Set, sterling on bronze, overlaid with pine bough motif, dark patina, pen tray, perpetual calendar/letter holder, blotter roller, inkwell, orig dark patina, stamp mark "Heintz," foil label **275.00**

Hall tree, L&JG Stickley, #89, single pole, copper hooks, corbelled base, 72" h **1,380.00**

High chair, Gustav Stickley, #388, ladderback, orig leather seat, 37" h **3,450.00**

Jardiniere, hammered coppery, corset shape, handles, orig patina, 12" h, 18" dia **430.00**

Magazine stand, mahogany, 4 shelves over arched toe board, orig finish, 38" h, 18" w **350.00**

Rocking chair, Gustav Stickley arm rocker, #311-1/2, mahogany, V-back, 5 vertical slats, orig worn leather cushion, 34" h **920.00**

Smoking Set, hammered copper, 12" d tray, match holder, cigarette holder, humidor with scrolled brass feet, stamped "Benedict Studios" marks, some cleaning to reddish patina, price for set **550.00**

Stool, Limbert cricket stool, #2001/2, canted legs, orig leather cover and tacks, orig finish, 7" h, 18" w, 10" d **632.50**

Umbrella stand, Gustav Stickley, #54, 4 tapered posts, orig copper drip pan, recent finish, unsigned, 34" h, 12" sq **575.00**

Vase

8" h, 3-1/2" d, sterling on bronze, corset shape, flowering branch, dark orig patina, stamp mark "Heintz" **450.00**

10" h, 3" d, sterling on bronze, cylindrical, overlaid with bird on branch, pewter finish, stamp mark "Heintz," small base dent **300.00**

Vice Cabinet, 20" w, 12-1/2" d, 32" h, backsplash, single drawer, carved door with green slag glass panel, new medium brown finish, replaced drawer bottom and glass **800.00**

Waste basket, mahogany orig finish, 16" h, 11" sq **490.00**

❖ Ashtrays

Now that smoking is unfashionable in certain circles, ashtray collectors are finding more to choices to pick from at their favorite flea markets. To narrow the field, many collectors specialize in a particular type of ashtray, whether advertising, souvenir, or figural.

Amber, glass, molded eagle in center, 9-1/4" **8.00**

Akro agate, burgundy and amber swirls, lip to hold book of matches **125.00**

Bellaire, Marc, 14" l, three island dancers, light purple and blue background, sgd and mkd "Calif Balinese B-47," c1950 ....**90.00**

Bum, holding no parking signs, cast iron, Wilton, 3-1/2" w at front, 4" w at back, 3-1/2" h..**75.00**

Capitol Metals Co., emb brass.......**10.00**

Carnation Ice Cream, glass **5.00**

Cigar wrapper, made with orig wrappers including King Edwards S&S, Dutch Masters and Robt. Burns de Luxe, wrappers under clear glass, 3 cigar slots, 4-1/4" dia **35.00**

Collie, chalkware, ashtray with 3 cigarette holders, 3-1/2" dia, dog 8-3/4" h, 7-1/2" w **22.00**

Coronation of Queen Elizabeth II, ceramic, 1953, gold trim, 3-1/2" sq **15.00**

Donkey, cast iron, 4-1/2" w, 4-1/2" h **130.00**

Esso, clear glass, blue and red dealer inscription, c1950, 4-1/4" x 4-1/4" x 1" h..**35.00**

Grand Canyon, silvertone metal, emb with attractions, 5-1/2" **12.00**

Harvard University, glass, 3-1/2" sq...**3.00**

Hawaii, Aloha, pot metal, emb, 1939 ....**20.00**

Hummel

Happy Pastime, #62, full bee mark, c1950-57 ....**245.00**

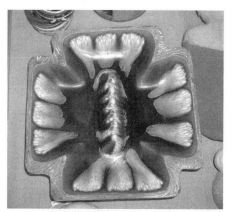

Ashtray, Ceramic, Maltese cross shape, green and white streaked glazed top, emb brown tree bark base, mkd "201 USA", $5.

Ashtray, Souvenir of NY, showing Empire State building in on left, Statue of Liberty in center, Rockfeller Center on right, blue and white porcelain, mkd "Fine Staffordshire Ware, Enco, Made in England," with history of landmarks, $25.

Joyful, #33, stylized bee mark, c1958-64...............................**220.00**

Singing Lesson, #34, full bee mark, c1950-57..............................**285.00**

Lion, chalkware, a few paint chips, ash mark in ashtray, 10-1/2" h, 9" w ...**30.00**

Penske Racing, 1984 Indy 500 Winner, helmet shape..............................**15.00**

Pool table shape, with Joe Camel shooting pool, 7-1/4" x 4-1/2"........**8.00**

Reddy Kilowatt, clear glass, red and white reverse-painted image on bottom, c1950, 4" dia **38.00**

Rooster, glass, multicolored swirls .**75.00**

Scottie, combination ashtray and cigarette holder, mkd "Made in Japan," 4" x 4" x 3" **80.00**

Tournament of Roses, ceramic **9.00**

White Horse Whiskey, glass..........**10.00**

❖ Aunt Jemima

The Pearl Milling Company first used the image of Aunt Jemima in 1889. The firm's owner, Charles G. Underwood, had been searching for a symbol his company could use for a new self-rising pancake mix. Reportedly, a team of blackface comedians performing a cakewalk to a song called "Aunt Jemima" served as his inspiration.

Collectors' Club: Black Memorabilia Collector's Assoc, 2482 Devoe Terrace, Bronx, NY 10468.

Bank, cast iron, hands on her hips, blue and white polka dot bandanna, red dress, white apron, 5-1/2" h.......**175.00**

Button, "Aunt Jemima Breakfast Club," tin litho, color image of smiling Jemima, red ground, black text "Eat a Better Breakfast," c1960, 4" dia **35.00**

Cookbook

Aunt Jemima Magical Recipes, 1954 ....**65.00**

Aunt Jemima, Six red and black plastic Aunt Jemima spice containers, made by F. & F. Mold & Die Works, Dayton, Ohio, $250.

Aunt Jemima's Pancake Recipes,
1950s **55.00**
Cookie jar, hard plastic, F&F Mold & Die
Works, Dayton, Ohio **450.00**
Creamer and sugar, plastic, Aunt
Jemima and Uncle Mose, F&F Mold &
Die Works, Dayton, Ohio............**150.00**
Doll, stuffed vinyl, 1940s, 12" h.....**165.00**
Hat, Aunt Jemima's Breakfast Club,
paper, fold-out style.......................**20.00**
Magazine tear sheet,
Aunt Jemima Pancakes, 1949, 13" x 5"
....**15.00**
Nelson family with Aunt Jemima
pancakes, 1956, full-page **25.00**
Pancake mold, round with 4 animal
shapes, aluminum, 1950s, 8-1/2" dia
....**125.00**
Paper plate, c1950, 9-1/4" dia **30.00**
Place mat, paper, Aunt Jemima's
Kitchen, full-color, unused............**20.00**
Pot holder, "There's Love in every Bite—
Aunt Jemima," 6" sq **24.00**
Salt and Pepper Shakers, Aunt Jemima
and Uncle Mose, plastic, mkd "F&F
Mold & Die Works, Dayton, Ohio, Made

Aunt Jemima, Cloth doll, Aunt Jemima on left, yellow polka dot dress, name printed on red and white striped apron, Uncle Moses on right, $65.

in USA," 5" h, pr............................**75.00**
Shaker, hard plastic, mail-away premium,
"Perfect Pancakes in 10 Shakes," emb
image of Aunt Jemima on lid, 8-3/4" h
....**90.00**
Sheet Music, *Aunt Jemima's Picnic Day,*
1914 ....**25.00**
String holder, chalkware, 1940s-1950s,
orig paint **395.00**
Syrup pitcher, Made in U.S.A., 5-1/2" h
....**65.00**
Thimble, porcelain, Aunt Jemima and
Uncle Mose, c1980, 1-1/8" h........**12.50**

❖ Autographs

Folks have been asking, "May I have your autograph?" for decades. Most celebrities will gladly oblige, but because many items have been signed with autopens and other mechanical devices, it's sometimes tough to know if a particular signature is authentic. Doing business with reputable dealers, asking questions, and conducting your own research will go a long way toward making your purchases good ones.

References: Mark Allen Baker, *All-Sport Autographs*, Krause Publications, 1995; ——, *Advanced Autograph Collecting*, Krause Publications, 2000; ——, *Collector's Guide to Celebrity Autographs*, 2nd ed, Krause Publications, 2000; *Standard Guide to Collecting Autographs*, Krause Publications, 1999; Kevin Keating and Michael Kolleth, *The Negro Leagues Autograph Guide*, Tuff Stuff Books, 1999; Kevin Martin, *Signatures of the Stars*, Antique Trader Books, 1998; Tom Mortenson, *Standard Catalog of Sports Autographs*, Krause Publications, 2000; George Sanders, Helen Sanders and Ralph Roberts, *Sanders Price Guide to Sports Autographs*, 2nd ed, Alexander Books, 1997; ——, *Sanders Price Guide to Autographs*, 5th ed, Alexander Books, 2000.

Periodicals: *Autograph Collector*, 510-A S Corona Mall, Corona, CA 91720-1420, *Autograph Review*, 305 Carlton Rd, Syracuse, NY 13207; *Autograph Times*, 1125 W Baseline Rd, #2-153-M, Mesa, AZ 85210-9501, *Autographs & Memorabilia*, P.O. Box 224, Coffeyville, KS 67337.

Collectors' Clubs: International Autograph Collectors Club & Dealers Alliance, 4575 Sheriden St, Suite 111, Hollywood, FL 33021-3575; Manuscript Society, 350 N Niagara St, Burbank, CA 95105-3648; Universal Autograph Collectors Club, P.O. Box 6181, Washington, DC 20044; Washington Historical Autograph & Certificate Organization, P.O. Box 2428, Springfield, VA 22152-2428.

For additional listings, see *Warman's Antiques & Collectibles* and *Warman's Americana & Collectibles*.

Autographs, Gordon Seltzer, #38, black signature on red, white, and yellow inflatable car with adv for Lipton Tea, $20.

Abbreviations
Dealers use the following abbreviations to describe autographed materials and their sizes.

Materials:
ADS -- Autograph Document Signed
ALS -- Autograph Letter Signed
AQS -- Autograph Quotation Signed
CS -- Card Signed
DS -- Document Signed
FDC -- First Day Cover
LS -- Letter Signed
PS -- Photograph Signed
TLS -- Typed Letter Signed

Aaron, Hank, baseball bat **135.00**
Barton, Clara, ALS, personal letter, 1 pg,
small 8vo, Glen Echo, MD, May 7,
1908 ....**450.00**
Belson, Louie, real photo postcard,
autographed 1948, several other
signatures...................................**65.00**
Berra, Ford and Rizzuto, sepia photo,
11" x 14".......................................**90.00**
Bush, Barbara, First Lady, Blair House
stationery, 3" x 2" **60.00**
Campbell, Earl, football **125.00**
Chagall, Marc, PS, mount below image
of artist and his wife viewing exhibit in
Israel, 7" x 9", David Harris
photographer's stamp on verso..**175.00**
Conick, Harry, Jr., black-and-white
glossy photo, 8" x 10" **35.00**
Crawford, Cindy, black-and-white glossy
photo, 8" x 10"..............................**60.00**
Dawson, Andre, baseball **25.00**
DeNiro, Robert, black-and-white glossy
photo, 8" x 10"..............................**60.00**
DiMaggio, Joe, black-and-white glossy
photo, 11" x 14".........................**175.00**
Elvis, record jacket, signed "Merry
Christmas, Elvis," Elvis Merry
Christmas Album, 1957.............**150.00**
Elkington, Steve, U.S. Open golf cap
....**35.00**

Fields, W.C., as Poppy playing cigar box cello, promotional photo, 10" x 13" **90.00**

Foreman, George, black-and-white glossy photo, 8" x 10" **40.00**

Gill, Vince, black-and-white glossy photo, 8" x 10"..**35.00**

Griebling, Otto, first day cover, hp watercolor cachet of clown, sgd on back..**45.00**

Harrison, Benjamin, DS, as Governor of VA, land grant, July 4, 1783, Richmond, 1 pg, folio, separations at folds repaired, framed **375.00**

Houston, Whitney, black-and-white glossy photo, 8" x 10" **60.00**

Jones, Spike, radio photo...............**75.00**

Kemp, Jack, black-and-white glossy photo, 16" x 20"..........................**60.00**

Morris, Robert, partially printed DS, promissory note for 100 pounds, signed by Bell on verso, 4-1/2" x 9-1/2", Feb 16, 1787, Philadelphia **460.00**

Parton, Dolly, black-and-white glossy photo, 8" x 10"..............................**35.00**

Rogers, Ginger, black-and-white photo, 8" x 10"..**70.00**

Roland, Ruth, silent film queen, wedding photo, inscription **45.00**

Ryan, Nolan, *Legends Magazine* cover **150.00**

Sousa, John Philip, card mounted to album page **125.00**

Stowe, Harriet Beecher, AQS, Biblical quote, 1 pg, 8vo, Andover Jan 24, 1864 ....**475.00**

Twain, Mark, (Samuel L. Clemens), ALS, 2 separate pgs, 4to, Hartford, April 11, 1883 ....**2,750.00**

Yeager, Chuck and Scott Crossfield, first day cover honoring Glenn Curtiss, canceled N.Y., 1980 ....**60.00**

Whitehouse, Eula, book, *Texas Flowers in Natural Colors*, 1st ed., 1936 ...**48.00**

Woods, Tiger, black-and-white photo, 8" x 10" **65.00**

❖ Automobilia

People have always had love affairs with their cars, and automobilia represents one of the biggest collecting areas in today's market. Flea markets are excellent sources for all types of materials relating to automobiles—parts, accessories, advertising, etc. Specialized flea markets held in conjunction with car shows offer the best opportunities for finding automobilia, but general flea markets can also hold some choice items for collectors.

Reference: Gordon Gardner and Alistair Morris, *Automobilia, 20th Century International Reference with Price Guide*, 3rd ed, Antique Collectors' Club, 1999.

Periodicals: *Automobile Quarterly*, 15040 Kutztown Rd, P.O. Box 348, Kutztown, PA 19530; *Cars & Parts*, P.O. Box 482, Sydney, OH 45365; *Classic Car Source*, www.classicar.com; *Hemmings Motor News*, P.O. Box 256, Bennington, VT 05201; *Old Cars Price Guide*, 700 E State St, Iola, WI 54990; *Old Cars Weekly, News & Markteplace*, 700 E State St, Iola, WI 54990.

Collectors' Clubs: Classic Gauge & Oiler Hounds, Rte 1, Box 9, Farview, SD 57027; Hubcap Collectors Club, P.O. Box 54, Buckley, MI 49620; International Petroliana Collectors Assoc, P.O. Box 937, Powell, OH 43065; Spark Plug Collectors of America, 14018 NE 85th St, Elk River, MN 55330.

For additional listings, see *Warman's Antiques & Collectibles*.

Ashtray

Chrysler, 1933.............................**45.00**

Tire, green glass insert, 1936 Texas exposition................................**125.00**

Badge, attendant's hatSinclair Grease, celluloid, 3" dia **350.00**

Texaco, 1930s era, with Scottie dogs **750.00**

Badge, driver's hat, Trailways Bus Lines, enamel **225.00**

Bank, shaggy dog, "Ford" on collar, marked "Florence Ceramics"........**65.00**

Blotter, Sunoco advertising, Disney's Goofy character, near mint...........**60.00**

Box, Mobil oil "Gargoyle" logo, designed to hold lubrication charts.............**45.00**

Calendar, 1966 Texaco station, "girlie" type, unsigned............................**15.00**

Can, motor oil, D-A Speed Sport, racing oil, yellow tin with black and white checkered flags, near mint full quart **50.00**

Clock

Atlas Tires and Batteries, wall clock, 1950s......................................**175.00**

Pontiac Service, glass front, dark blue painted rim............................**300.00**

Dealer brochure, Ford, 1954, shows all models, staple hole, unfolded 21" x 24" **30.00**

Display Cabinet

Auto Lite Spark Plug, 13" w, 18 1/2" h,

Automobilia, Camel Unitized Tire Patches, full, $45.

Automobilia, Buick emblem, blue and white, $5.

painted metal cabinet, glass front **125.00**

Gates fan belts, hangers inside for various sizes, painted tin front, 15" l, 30" w, 24" h **75.00**

Folder, advertisingBuick, 1950, 8 color pgs, shows models, 7-3/4" x 10-3/4" **25.00**

Oldsmobile, 1963, color, 6 models, 10-1/2" x 10-1/2" **5.00**

Opel Manta, 1974, specs on last pg, 7-1/2" sq.......................................**4.00**

Key Fob, Esso Tiger logo, 1960s, engraved serial number for lost key return..**10.00**

Lapel pin, Ford logo, cloisonne, 1-1/2" l **4.00**

Owner's manual, Ford Thunderbird, 1959 ....**40.00**

Pinback button

Hudson, 1939..............................**35.00**

Sherwood Auto Bob, multicolored, smiling youngster sledding in snow, Sherwood Brothers Mfg Co., Canastota, NY, orig back paper, 1-1/4" dia................................**250.00**

Promo Car, Mustang, 1964, hardtop **65.00**

Showroom catalogue, Chevrolet, 1952, 31 pgs, contains paint chips and upholstery samples, 9" x 12-1/4"**225.00**

Watch Fob, Good Roads, celluloid logo affixed to metal fob.......................**75.00**

❖ Autry, Gene

One of the famous singing cowboys most Baby Boomers remember, Gene Autry spawned a wide range of items for collectors to enjoy. Since he delighted us on the movie screen, radio, and television, an interesting variety of collectibles can be found at today's flea markets. A visit to the Gene Autry Western Heritage Museum in

Los Angeles is a must for all dedicated Gene Autry collectors.

Periodicals: *Cowboy Collector Newsletter*, P.O. Box 7496, Long Beach, CA 90807; *Gene Autry Star Telegram*, Gene Autry Museum, P.O. Box 67, Gene Autry, OK 73436; *Spur*, Gene Autry Western Heritage Museum, 4700 Western Heritage Way, Los Angeles, CA 90027-1462; *Westerner*, Box 5232-32, Vienna, WV 26105; *Westerns & Serials*, Route 1, Box 103, Vernon Center, MN 56090.

Collectors' Clubs: Gene Autry Fan Club, 4322 Heidelberg Ave, St Louis, MO 63123-6812; Gene Autry International Fan Club, 20 Cranleigh Gardens, Stoke Bishop, Bristol B59 1HD, UK.

Arcade card, black and white, 1940s, 3-1/2" x 5-1/2"Gene Autry and Champion **12.00**
   Head and shoulders pose............**10.00**
   Playing guitar **10.00**
Book
   Gene Autry and the Golden Stallion, Cole Fannin, 1954, 282 pages, hardcover, wear **7.50**
   Gene Autry and the Thief River Outlaws, Whitman, 1944, 249 pgs, hardcover, dj **35.00**
Cap pistol, silvered metal, simulated pearl handle, c1950, 8" l **35.00**
Comic Book, Gene Autry, Dell#115**22.00**
   #118 ....**22.00**
Cookie jar, McMee Productions, signature across back, copyright 1955 Autry Museum of Western Heritage, 15" h..**225.00**
Guitar, Emenee, orig box **75.00**
Handout, Sunbeam Bread, color photo of Gene and Champ, 1950s, 8" x 10" **5.00**
Home movie, Shoot Straight, Carmel-Hollywood, 16 mm, orig box.........**35.00**
Little Golden Book, *Gene Autry and Champion,* 1956...........................**25.00**
Magazine ad, BF Goodrich tires, June, 1950 ....**8.00**
Lobby card, Western Jamboree, Republic Picture, 14" x 11" **35.00**
Pennant, large..................................**55.00**
Pistol, heavy metal, orange plastic inserts on handle, name in raised letters on both sides, 6-1/2" l **55.00**
Record, *Merry Christmas with Gene Autry*, 45 rpm, 1950, orig box, 4-record set **40.00**
Sheet music, *Mister and Mississippi*, 1951 ....**22.50**
Songbook, *Gene Autry's Sensational Collection of Famous Orig Cowboy Songs and Mountain Ballads,* Cole, Chicago, 1932 ....**40.00**
Suspenders, clips with horses, straps with sliding metal guns, 18-1/2" l**195.00**
Toy pistol, metal, emb "Gene Autry" on

both sides, orange plastic inserts on sides of grips, trigger not functioning, rust **55.00**
Watch **110.00**
Writing pad, full-color cover, 9" x 5-1/2" **32.00**

❖ Autumn Leaf

A premium for the Jewel Tea Company, this dinnerware pattern was produced from 1933 until 1978. Autumn Leaf became so popular with American housewives that other companies began making accessories to complement the pattern.

Reference: Jim and Lynn Salko, *Hall's Autumn Leaf China and Jewel Tea Collectibles*, self-published, 1996.

Collectors' Clubs: Autumn Leaf Reissues Assoc, 19238 Dorchester Circle, Strongsville, OH 44136; National Autumn Leaf Collectors Club, 7346 Shamrock Drive, Indianapolis, IN 46217.

For additional listings, see *Warman's Americana & Collectibles.*

Bean pot, two handles **295.00**
Berry bowl, 5-1/2" dia........................**6.00**
Bread and butter plate, 6" dia **12.00**
Bud vase, 5-3/4" h **295.00**
Butter dish, covered, 1-lb..........**3000.00**
Cake plate, gold trim, 9-1/2" dia **30.00**
Canister, metal, plastic lid..............**25.00**
Coasters, set of 8 ....**48.00**
Creamer and sugar, cov, ruffled **35.00**
Cream soup bowl...........................**20.00**
Cup and saucer..............................**17.50**
Dinner plate, 9" d...........................**25.00**
Drippings jar...................................**40.00**
Flour sifter, metal, 1930s, light rust, worn **250.00**
Fruit bowl, stamped mark "Superior Hall Quality Dinnerware," 5-1/2" dia.....**12.00**
Jug, ball form, gold circle mark "Hall's Superior, Tested and Approved by

Autumn Leaf Gravy boat, underplate, $175.

Mary Dunbar, Jewel Homemaking Institute, Superior Ware," 7" h **70.00**
Mixing bowl, small rim chip, worn gold, 6-1/4" dia......................................**5.00**
Pie plate, dark spots from use, 9-1/2" dia **18.00**
Pitcher, gold trim worn, 7" h **40.00**
Range set **42.00**
Salad plate....................................**12.00**
Teapot, Aladdin, infuser, finial with 3 gold stripes, gold mark "Hall's Superior Quality Kitchenware" **120.00**
Tidbit server, 3 tiers **100.00**
Tumbler, 5-1/2" h **35.00**
Vegetable bowl..............................**40.00**

❖ Aviation Collectibles

Flying machines continue to fascinate us, and aviation collectibles are soaring at flea markets around the country. Collectors can find material related to hot air balloons, dirigibles and zeppelins, early flight, and modern planes. From paper items to toys, the sky's the limit in this category.

Periodical: *Airliners*, P.O. Box 52-1238, Miami, FL 33152.

Collectors' Club: World Airline Historical Society, 3381 Apple Tree Lane, Erlanger, KY 41048.

For additional listings, see *Warman's Americana & Collectibles.* Also see Airlines, Lindbergh, and other related categories in this edition.

Album, desk top, Pluna, Primeras Lineas Uruguayas de Navegacion Aerea, 7" x 4-1/4"..**55.00**
Ashtray, Aerolineas Argentinas, porcelain, 3-3/4" x 3-3/4"..............**14.50**
Bookends, pr, 5-1/2" h, cast iron, Charles Lindbergh, wearing helmet, emb, 1929 ....**115.00**
Cigarette lighter, desk type, chrome plated, lighter compartment in wing, c1937 ....**95.00**
Comic book, *Jim Ray's Aviation Sketchbook*, #2, 1946, ink stain on front, wear, yellowing, 64 pgs.......**18.00**
Dish, Lineas Aereas Paraguayas, inscribed "LAP," semi-porcelain, 6-1/4" x 4" **15.00**

Autumn Leaf Coffeepot, $125.

Game, Wings: The Air Mail Game, Parker Brothers, set of 99 cards, orig instruction sheet, copyright 1928, 4" x 5-1/2" **25.00**

Magazine tear sheet, Bendix Aviation Corp, 1947, *Saturday Evening Post* **2.00**

Gum cards, Aviation Pioneers, includes Hugo Junkers, Otto Lilienthal, and Orville Wright, biographies in German, set of 3 ....**15.00**

Model, diecast
  KLM 747, Matchbox, 1988, orig bubble pack, 3-3/4" wingspan, 4-3/8" l **35.00**
  Lufthansa 747, Matchbox, 1988, orig bubble pack, 3-3/4" wingspan, 4-3/8" l...**35.00**
  Pan Am 747, Matchbox, 1988, orig bubble pack, 3-3/4" wingspan, 4-3/8" l...**35.00**
  TWA 767-300, Herpa, German, scale 1:500, MIP **35.00**

Movie poster, Spirit of St Louis, starting James Stewart, Patricia Smith, Murry Hamilton, folded **90.00**

Palm puzzle, Vosin box aircraft in flight, silvered rim, plastic cover, full color paper playing surface, inscription "1908 80 Kahen/Frankreich," German, c1970 ....**35.00**

Pinback button, 1-1/4" dia, Captain Charles A Lindbergh **95.00**

Plate, Martin Aviation, Vernon Kilns, brown illus of 5 aircraft, c1940, 10-1/2" dia **55.00**

Postcard, Friendship Airport, Baltimore, Md., textured paper, tinted art, C.T. Art-Colortone, mid-1950s, 3-1/2" x 5-1/2", unused, set of 4 ....**18.00**

Teaspoon, Aviation Building, N.Y. World's Fair, 1939 ....**15.00**

Tobacco card album, 7-1/2" x 5", John Players & Son Imperial Tobacco, International Air Liners, 19 pgs, 50 cards **75.00**

Toy, monoplane, single motor, rubber tires, painted gray, restoration to wing, Steelcraft, 24" l......................**2,500.00**

Aviation Collectibles Toy, metal, blue body, red folding wings, red, white, and blue decals, yellow underbody, $15

❖ Avon

Ding, dong…Avon calling! After years of producing fine cosmetics in interesting containers, Avon has branched out, producing a wide variety of items that collectors look for. Expect to find items that are well-marked, and remember that original contents and packaging will increase values.

References: Bud Hastin, *Bud Hastin's Avon Products & California Perfume Co. Collector's Encyclopedia*, 16th ed., self-published, 2000, P.O. 9868, Kansas City, MO 64134.

Periodical: *Avon Times*, P.O. Box 9868, Kansas City, MO 64134.

Collectors' Clubs: National Assoc of Avon Collectors, P.O. Box 7006, Kansas City, MO 64113; Shawnee Avon Bottle Collectors Club, 1418 32nd NE, Canton, OH 44714; Sooner Avon Bottle Collectors Club, 6119 S Hudson, Tulsa, OK 74136; Western World Avon Collectors Club, P.O. Box 23785, Pleasant Hills, CA 94523.

For additional listings, see *Warman's Americana & Collectibles*. Also see Cape Cod in this edition for information on Avon's glassware line.

Reproduction Alert

After shave, figural bottle, orig contents, MIB
  Big Mack, truck, Windjammer after shave **80.00**
  Champion Spark Plug, Wild Country after shave **80.00**
  Chess piece, 6-1/2" h German Shepherd, Wild Country aftershave **25.00**
  First Volunteer, Tail Winds after shave **95.00**
  Haynes-Apperson, 1902. Tail Winds after shave **80.00**
  Thunderbird, 1955, Wild Country after shave **85.00**
  Touring T, Excalibur after shave ...**85.00**

Award, President's Club, 1993, Albee Award, MIB................................**125.00**

Barbie, Avon Spring Blossom Barbie, first in series................................**40.00**

Bell, frosted, orig box, 3-1/2" h..........**9.00**

Bottle, figuralBoot, empty..................**5.00**
  Liberty Bell, full..............................**10.00**
  Shoe, empty **5.00**
  Toby mug, empty............................**5.00**

Chamberstick, pewter, mkd "Avon American Heirlooms" **10.00**

Collector's plate, Freedom, 1974...**35.00**

Cologne bottle, Moodwind, dogwood flower design, paper label, 3" h....**15.00**

Compact, Gay Look, black faille cover,

Avon, After shave, Tai Winds, Volkswagon Bus, red body, silvered plastic motorcycle, c1975, $9.

  red lining, MIB **100.00**
Decanter, totem pole **7.00**
Goblet, Mount Vernon series, cobaltGeorge Washington..............**3.00**
  Martha Washington **5.00**
Jewelry
  Locket, faux pearls around edge, blue and lavender violets in center, space for 2 photos, 1-1/2" l **12.00**
  Pin, leaf shape, 50th anniversary.**40.00**
  Stick pin, key, goldtone, 2" l **15.00**
  Suite, bracelet, clip earrings and ring, imitation amethyst....................**15.00**
Magazine tear sheet, Avon for Men, 1967 ....**5.00**
Perfume bottle
  Elusive, clear, silver top, 3" h **9.00**
  Owl, frosted glass, 4-1/2" h............**9.00**
Plate
  For Avon Representatives Only, 1977 ....**5.00**
  Strawberry, 1978, 7-1/2" dia.........**12.00**
  Wildflowers of the Eastern States, Wedgwood, 8" dia....................**15.00**
  Wildflowers of the Southern States, Wedgwood, 8" dia....................**15.00**
Potpourri, figural pig, orig sticker......**5.00**
Soaky
  Mickey Mouse, 1969, orig bubble bath and box, 7" h **25.00**
  Pluto, empty, 6" h **20.00**
Soap
  Artistocat Kitten, 1970s, orig box.**65.00**
  Christmas Children, girl holds doll, boy holds toy rocking horse, 1983.....**9.00**
Statue, Mother's Love, 1982, 6" h...**15.00**
Stein
  Train, 1982, 8" h **25.00**
  Western, 1980, 8" h **25.00**
Thimble, porcelain, blue and red flowers, mkd "Avon" **6.00**

❖ Baby-Related Collectibles

Grandmas and politicians love them, and now more and more collectors are seeking items related to them. Perhaps it's nostalgia, perhaps it's the delightful colorful images. Whatever the reason, items related to babies and their care are quite popular.

Reference: Joan Stryker Grubaugh, *A Collectors Guide to the Gerber Baby*, self-published, 1998.

Baby bank, Kewpie, Lefton China, bisque, orig foil label, 1950s, 7-1/4" h **145.00**

Baby bottle, emb "Baby" and emb image of infant, bottom mkd Keystone, 6-3/4" h **30.00**

Baby ring, 12k yellow gold, 4mm garnet **75.00**

Baby scale, metal **65.00**

Baby spoon, sterling silver, monogrammed "F," marked GHF Sterling (G.H. French Co., Mass.), some wear, 3" l..........................**12.50**

Bib Clips, sterling silver, clothespin type **75.00**

Blanket, 38" x 45", light blue and white, jointed teddy bears in various poses, 1940s **100.00**

Bowl and spoon, sterling silver, Wm. B. Kerr & Co., early 20th C, acid-etched design of children riding different animals from seven countries, minor dents, Gorham monogrammed spoon, 5 troy oz **200.00**

Calendar, 1941, Mennen, baby products illus **15.00**

Crib quilt, Sunburst, pink, red, green, navy blue, and orange patches, reverse with paisley fabric, field outline and

Baby bath tub, enameled cast iron, cast iron stand, Hungarian, $195.

Toy, yellow dog, red ears, blue wheels, plastic, $3.50.

diagonal line quilting, PA, early 20th C, 41" x 40"....................................**865.00**

Feeding dish, sections, little girl feeding teddy bear, 8" dia **65.00**

Painting, Gerber Baby, sgd "D.H. S." for Dorothy H. Smith, titled "The Gerber Baby," orig mailing envelope, 10" x 11" **750.00**

Rattle, Palmer Cox Brownie head with bells, sterling and mother-of-pearl, late 19th C, 3-3/4" l **150.00**

Record book, pink and blue cover, 1950s, unused............................**15.00**

Sweater, hand-knitted, cream wool with satin ribbon trim, newborn to 3 months **35.00**

Talcum tin
Bauer & Black, oval, 4-1/2" x 3-1/2" **80.00**
California Perfume Co., toy soldier graphic, 2 small areas of paint loss, oval, 4" h.................................**75.00**

❖ Baccarat Glass

This French glassware manufacturer is still producing lovely wares, and their paperweights are well known to collectors. Vintage Baccarat glass commands high prices, but contemporary pieces can be found at flea markets for reasonable amounts.

Bonbon, 5-3/4" d, amberina, swirled mold, pedestal foot, emb "Baccarat" **150.00**

Box, cov, white airplane design on sides, etched mark, 2-1/4" h, 2-3/4" dia**125.00**

Cologne bottles, pr, colorless, frosted rosette ground, gold floral swags and bows, cut faceted stopper, 7" h..**365.00**

Figure
Baker, MIB....................................**95.00**
Bull **190.00**

Finger bowl, with underplate, ruby ground, gold medallions and floral décor **350.00**

Ice bucket, two reeded bands, swing handle, silvered metal mounts, ball finial on lid **200.00**

Paperweight, Pisces, sulphide, c1955 ....**150.00**

Toothpick holder, Rose Tiente.....**115.00**

Vase, colorless, swollen rectilinear vessel, dec with band of engraved water birds in stream, flowers on shore, pattern of raised curvilinear stripes, 6" h **290.00**

Wash bowl and pitcher, 12-1/2" h pitcher, 16-1/2" d bowl, colorless, swirled rib design, pitcher with applied handle and polished base, ground table ring on bowl, polished chip**250.00**

Wine decanter, Rose Tiente, Zipper pattern, matching stopper, 10" h**225.00**

❖ Badges

Name tags and identification badges have become quite popular with collectors, and each provides a brief glimpse into history. Examples found with photographs and other pertinent information about the original user are especially prized.

American Field Service, WWI volunteer organization, sterling....................**35.00**

Captain, Boy's State, American Legion logo **38.00**

Car, North Riding, metal frame, plastic front, shield dec...........................**15.00**

Chaffeur's
Illinois, 1951, 1-3/4" x 1-1/4" **25.00**
Oklahoma, 1938, pin-type back ...**35.00**

Dick Tracy Detective Club, brass, Dick Tracy in cener with star on each side **26.00**

Employee, National Cash Register Co., Dayton, Ohio, emb metal, 1-5/8" h, 2" l **90.00**

Fire Department, Inspector, U.S. Naval Air Station, fire truck in center of shield **50.00**

Hopalong Cassidy, six-pointed star, silvered metal, 2-1/4" dia..............**40.00**

Junior Police, Brattleboro, Vt., 1950s **35.00**

Nazi, wound type, silver..................**70.00**

Police, "Special Officer," brasstone, 1-3/4" x 2-1/2".............................**30.00**

Hunting, fishing, trapping license badge, New York, 1930, 1-3/4".................**55.00**

Service station attendant
Conoco, nickel over brass, cloisonné porcelain lettering, 1-5/8" h, 2-1/4" l **170.00**
Standard Oil, nickel over brass, cloisonné porcelain lettering, 1-5/8" h, 2-1/4" l **325.00**
Texaco, bronze finish, cloisonné porcelain logo, 1-3/4" h, 2" l ...**275.00**

Toy, "Special Police," 1950s, on orig card, 3-1/2" x 2-3/4" **15.00**

❖ Bakelite

Bakelite is an early form of plastic that was first produced in 1907. A registered trade name, Bakelite was derived from the name of its inventor, Leo H. Baekeland. Items made of Bakelite were formed in molds, subjected to heat and pressure, and then cooled.

Reference: Karima Parry, *Bakelite Bangles*, Krause Publications, 1999.

For additional listings, see *Warman's Americana & Collectibles* and *Warman's Jewelry*.

Ashtray, black and white, 8" dia **45.00**
Box, cov, amber and brown swirl **20.00**
Bracelet, bangle, red
  Carved floral, hinged, oval, c1930, 1-1/4" w...**450.00**
  Green dots dec, 3/4" w **425.00**
Bracelet, stretch, lemon slices, brown cylinder shapes **100.00**
Buckle, carved flower on each end, dark blue, rect..**20.00**
Button, translucent amber and brown swirl, orig card, set of 5................**15.00**
Cake server, green handle **12.00**
Corn cob holder, diamond shape, 2 prongs, red or green, pr **15.00**
Desk set, Art Deco, butterscotch, ink tray, two note pad holders **225.00**
Napkin ring, chick...........................**30.00**
Pie crimper, marbleized butterscotch handle **6.50**
Pin, horse head, marbled, brass bridle, 2-1/4" **500.00**

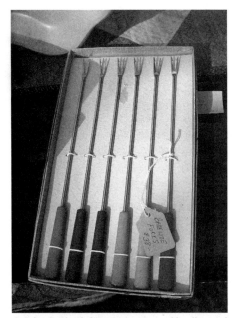

Bakelite Fondue forks, orange, green, gold, yellow, and red Bakelite handles, orig box, $38.

Salt and pepper shakers, gear shape, marbleized caramel, chrome lids, 2" h, pr **85.00**
Stationery box, Art Deco winged horse design, brown, American Stationery Co..**75.00**
Toothpick holder, figural dachshund, green **95.00**

❖ Ballerinas

Swirling images of dancing ladies grace many types of objects, all to the delight of ballerina collectors.

Barbie outfit, #989, leotard, paper tiara and skirt, 1965 ....**150.00**
Doll
  Effanbee, Nutcracker ballerina, 15" h
  ....**95.00**
  Lee Middleton, white tutu...........**185.00**
  Madame Alexander, Elise, 1970s, MIB
  ....**125.00**
  Madame Alexander, Karen, MIB
  ....**1290.00**
Figure, porcelain
  Dresden, hand painted, gold accents, layers of pink porcelain lace and porcelain roses, stamped "Large Crove D, Karl Klette"..............**175.00**
  Llardo, Julia, #1361 ....**230.00**
  Royal Doulton, NH 2116, 1952, 7-1/2" h..**400.00**
  Royal Dux, adjusting shoe, raised pink triangle mark, 7-1/4" h............**135.00**
Jewelry
  Charm bracelet, silvertone, 9 charms, mkd "Monet," 1950s, 8" l..........**55.00**
  Pin, figural, rhinestones, silver setting, 2-1/2" l **95.00**
Music box, bisque figure with glass eyes, cylinder base, French, 9" h **300.00**
Paper dolls, Little Ballerina, Whitman #1951, c1959, uncut **28.00**

Ballerina Figure, Lenox china, pink tutu, hand-painted with roses, green Lenox USA stamp, 6" h, $825.

❖ Banks, Still

The golden age of still banks was ushered in with the advent of the cast-iron bank. Usually in the form of animals or humans, they were often painted to increase their appeal, and many businesses and banks used them as a means of advertising. Tin-lithographed still banks were often used as premiums, being popular from 1930 to 1955.

Still banks, as listed below, are those with no moving parts. Mechanical banks, with some type of action, are thoroughly covered in *Warman's Antiques & Collectibles*.

References: Don Duer, *A Penny Saved: Still and Mechanical Banks*, Schiffer Publishing, 1993; ——, *Penny Banks Around the World*, Schiffer Publishing, 1997; Earnest Ida and Jane Pitman, *Dictionary of Still Banks*, Long's Americana, 1980; Beverly and Jim Mangus, *Collector's Guide to Banks*, Collector Books, 1998; Andy and Susan Moore, *The Penny Bank Book: Collecting Still Banks*, 3rd ed, Schiffer Publishing, 2000; Tom and Loretta Stoddard, *Ceramic Coin Banks*, Collector Books, 1997.

Banks, Still Train, papier-mâché, pink, yellow, and blue, "Saving for My Trip" written on front of cab, orig closure missing, c1970, 5" l, $4.

Periodicals: *Glass Bank Collector*, P.O. Box 155, Poland, NY 13431; *Heuser's Quarterly Collectible Bank Newsletter*, P.O. Box 300, West Winfield, NY 13491.

Collectors' Clubs: Mechanical Bank Collectors of America, P.O. Box 128, Allegan, MI 49010, www.mechanicalbanks.org; Still Bank Collectors Club of America, 4175 Millersville Rd, Indianapolis, IN 46205, www.stillbankclub.com.

For additional listings, see *Warman's Antiques & Collectibles* and *Warman's Americana & Collectibles*.

Reproduction Alert

Book, cover opens, made for Encyclopedia Americana, with key to open **65.00**

Banks, still Mickey Mouse, vinyl, red shirt, black pants, green base, $35.

Church, tin litho, U.S. Metal Co. **18.00**
Cookie Monster, sgd Jim Henson, orig
   Sesame Street box **24.00**
Cylinder, litho tin, black, white, red,
   yellow and blue designs of young
   children, white top with smiling sun as
   coin slot, late 1930s, 3" d, 3-1/2" h
   .... **35.00**
Elephant, diecast pot metal, painted
   ivory, 6" l, 5-1/2" h **235.00**
Glass, buffalo on one side, Indian on
   other, round, 7" h **22.50**
Globe, "As you save so you prosper" on
   pedestal, Ohio Art Co., 4-1/2" h .. **35.00**
Howard Johnson's restaurant, plastic,
   building shape, 1960s **28.00**
Hubert the Lion, Lefton **40.00**
Kewpie, Lefton China, bisque, orig foil
   label, 1950s, 7-1/4" h **145.00**
London tour bus, Warner Bros. **35.00**
Pabst Blue Ribbon Beer, miniature beer
   can, 1936-37 patent date, coin slot in
   top, 2-3/4" h **38.00**
Peter Rabbit, Wedgwood, 6 sides, 3-1/2"
   h **30.00**
Pinocchio on whale, musical, Schmid
   .... **35.00**
Safe, cast iron, orig paint, 3-3/4" w, 5-
   1/2" h **280.00**
Snoopy and Woodstock, lying on jack-
   o-lantern, Whitman Candies, 4-1/2" h
   .... **10.00**
Squirrel, Goebel **35.00**
The Jetsons, spaceship, licensed by
   Hanna Barbera **375.00**
Uncle Sam, register bank, 3-coin register

opens at $10, will hold up to $50, Ohio
Art Co. **35.00**

❖ Barber Bottles

At the turn of the century, barbershops used decorated bottles to hold oils and other liquids that were used on a daily basis. These colorful glass bottles included examples made of art glass, pattern glass, and milk glass, as well as a variety of commercially prepared and labeled bottles. Reproductions scared off many collectors in the early 1980s, but collectors have learned how to detect the fakes and are again seeking out interesting examples.

For additional listings, see *Warman's Antiques & Collectibles.*

> ### Reproduction Alert

Amber, Hobnail, 3-ring neck, curled lip,
   bulbous base, 1 nob broken, 6-3/4" h
   .... **200.00**
Amethyst, Hobnail, 7" h **250.00**
Aqua, Inverted Thumbprint, enameled
   deco of 18th C gentleman, 2 panels
   satin finish, 2 panels clear, metal top,
   9-1/2" h **280.00**
Clear
   Hazel Atlas, double plastic cap possibly
      Bakelite, 7" h, pr **45.00**
   Paper label, Empire Quinine Hair Tonic,

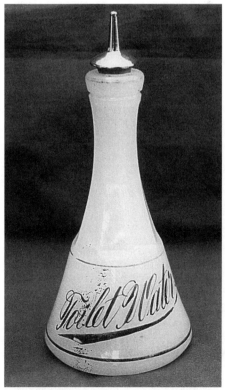

Barber Bottles, Toilet water, white opaque frosted glass, replaced metal top, raised diamond mark on bottom with "MAC", early 1900s, 8-1/4" h, $65.

Empire Barber and Beauty Supply
   Co., screw cap, contents, 1-gal, 12"
   h **25.00**
Coin Spot, cranberry opalescent, orig
   stopper, 8-1/2" h **395.00**
Cranberry glass, white enamel dec of
   young child, 8" h **175.00**
Green, all-over pattern of white
   enameled flowers with orange centers,
   white stopper, 9" h **250.00**
Lime green, ribbed mold, 7-1/2" h **365.00**
Milk glass
   Bay Rum, 7" h **260.00**
   Witch Hazel, painted letters and flower
      dec, 9" h **115.00**
Overshot, screw-on top, polished pontil,
   c1850 .... **150.00**
Purple, white enameled floral dec,
   missing stopper, 8-1/2" h **150.00**
Ruby stained, etched decoration, 6-1/2"
   h **250.00**
Vaseline, opalescent Daisy and Fern
   pattern, 7" h **360.00**
White, orange letters, "Bay Rum," 7" h
   .... **95.00**

❖ Barbershop and Beauty Shop Collectibles

Flea markets are great places to search for items related to barbershops and beauty shops. Following the decline of the barbershop as an important social institution and with the advent of uni-sex regional chains, early barbering and beauty products are becoming increasingly popular. Attractive advertising and interesting examples of barbering equipment add color and style to collections.

For additional listings, see *Warman's Americana & Collectibles* and Shaving Mugs in this edition.

Barber brush
   Half doll porcelain handle **20.00**
   Penguin handle, wood, paint chipped,
      1940s **35.00**
Barber pole, hand turned wood, some
   wear to paint **350.00**
Beer mug, Barber Shop Whistle Stop,
   "For Good Cheer, Whistle for Your
   Beer," applied googly eyes, barber pole
   handle with whistle, mkd "G.
   C....Japan," 5-1/4" h **50.00**
Counter map, Wardonia Razor Blades,
   rubber, 9" x 8" **18.00**
Display case, West Hair Nets, tiered
   display case, tin litho picture of flapper
   in touring car inside lid, 15" h, 6" w, 5"
   d **60.00**
Hair net, blond, orig envelope **3.00**
Magazine tear sheet, adv

Barber Shop Collectibles, Hair trap, Nioxin, white plastic, gold lettering, pierced center and sides, unused, 5" dia, $.50.

Eversharp Schick Safety Razor, 1958 ....**8.00**
Lady Schick, 1956.........................**6.00**
Norelco Speedshaver, 1957...........**6.00**
Remington 60 electric shaver, 1962 ....**6.00**
Remington Rollectric, 1958............**8.00**
Sunbeam Blade Electric Shavemaster Razor, 1957 ....**6.00**
Match book cover, Norman's Modern Barber Shop....................................**6.00**
Newspaper, *Barber's Journal*, 1881**12.00**

Comb disinfector, Barbicide, King Research Inc., glass, metal lid, 11-1/2" h, $30.

Poster, Packer's Tar Soap, scene of barber shaving customer, 1900, 9" x 12"..**40.00**
Razor tin, Yankee Blades, tin litho, eagles and center image of man shaving, red ground, 1-1/4" w, 2-1/4" l **200.00**
Safety razor, Burham, razor with 3 blades in orig envelope, tin litho safety razor tin, red ground, black lettering, unused.....................................**160.00**
Shaving brush, Ever Ready, black celluloid handle, dark bristles, orig box **15.00**
Shaving mirror, nickel silver, swing type, Geisha standing on ornate base, mkd "Golden Mfg Co., Chicago," c1890, 19" h **165.00**
Sign, Beauty Shoppe, two-sided flange sign, porcelain, Art Deco lady with finger wave hairdo, 12" h, 24" l ..**275.00**
Tin
Bouquet Talcum Powder..............**25.00**
Magic Shaving Powder................**25.00**
Towel steamer, nickel-plated copper, porcelain-over-steel base **325.00**

❖ Barbie

Mattel patented the Barbie fashion doll in 1958, with the first versions reaching store shelves in 1959. Her friends, including Ken and Skipper, joined the ranks in subsequent years. Accessories, clothes, room settings, and all types of related merchandise soon followed. A plethora of books cover Barbie, and her life is well documented. Her appeal is widespread, and she is the most collected doll ever created.

References: Sharon Korbeck, *Best of Barbie*, Krause Publications, 2001; Sharon Korbeck and Dan Stearns, *2003 Toys & Prices 10th ed.*, Krause Publications, 2003. J. Michael Augustyniak, *Collector's Encyclopedia of Barbie Doll Exclusives and More*, 2nd ed, Collector Books, 2000; Stefanie Deutsch, *Barbie, the First 30 Years*, Collector Books, 2001; Sibyl DeWein and Joan Ashabraner, *Collector's Encyclopedia of Barbie Dolls and Collectibles*, Collector Books, 2000; Connie Craig Kaplan, *Collector's Guide to Barbie Doll Vinyl Cases*, Collector Books, 1999; Patricia Long, *Barbie's Closet: Price Guide for Barbie & Friends Fashions and Accessories, 1959-1973*, Krause Publications, 1999; Marcie Melillo, *Ultimate Barbie Doll Book*, Krause Publications, 1996; Lorraine Mieszala, *Collector's Guide to Barbie Doll Paper Dolls*, Collector Books, 2000; Kitturah B. Westenhouser, *The Story of Barbie,* 2nd ed, Collector Books, 2000;

Periodicals: *Barbie Bazaar*, 5617 6th Ave, Kenosha, WI 53140; *Barbie Fashions*, 387 Park Ave S, New York, NY 10016; *Barbie Talks Some More*, 19 Jamestown Dr, Cincinnati, OH 45241.

Barbie Doll case, pink, silver stars, mkd "Barbie," played with condition, $10.

For additional listings, see *Warman's Americana & Collectibles.*

Accessories
Barbie Café Today, dated 1970, NRFB, age discoloration to box, fading, slightly scuffed **475.00**
Barbie Teen Dream Bedroom, dated 1970, MIB, discoloration to orig box **65.00**
Swimming pool, inflatable, no box**20.00**
Activity book, Skipper and Scott Beauty Sticker Fun, 1980 ....**5.00**
Car, Hot Rod, #1460, 1963 ....**195.00**
Carrying case, Barbie and Midge, pink, 1964 ....**30.00**
Clothing
#972 Wedding Day Set, VG **115.00**
#982 Solo in the Spotlight, VG.....**85.00**
#944 Masquerade, NRFB **265.00**
#1615 Saturday Matinee, NM/VG **310.00**
#1617, Midnight Blue, NM-VG ...**150.00**
Doll, Barbie
American Girl Barbie, brunette, bendable legs, #1658 Garden Wedding, box, VG..................**350.00**
Bubble cut, blond, straight legs, 1-pc red nylon swimsuit, red open toe shoes, orig box with gold wire stand, no box, VG **225.00**
Color Magic Barbie, lemon yellow hair, yellow metal barrette, undressed, no box, VG **365.00**
Happy Holidays, orig box, 1988, #1, NRFB.......................................**230.00**
Happy Holidays, 1989, NRFB **70.00**
Happy Holidays, 1994, NRFB, box slightly scuffed, sticker residue on plastic window **35.00**
Ponytail, #1, black and white striped 1-pc swimsuit, black #1 open toe

The World of Barbie Doll Case, blue, played with condition, $15.

shoes with holes, white rimmed glasses with blue lenses, pink cover booklet, reproduction #1 stand, box with replaced insert, VG **3,400.00**

Ponytail, #5, brunette, orig set, Pak outfit, no box, NM/VG **225.00**

Ponytail, #6, blond, red nylon 1-pc swimsuit, red open toe shoes, orig box with cardboard liner, black wire stand, light blue cover booklet, VG **215.00**

Doll, Barbie's family and friends

Francie, brunette, 2-pc yellow nylon swimsuit, orig clear plastic bag, cardboard hanger, NRFP, orig price sticker **250.00**

Julia, talking, gold and silver jumpsuit with belt, wrist tag, clear plastic stand, NRFB, nonworking, box age discolored, scuffed, and worn.**225.00**

Ken, brunette flocked hair, red swim trunks, worn wrist tag, booklet, yellow terrycloth towel, cork sandals in cellophane bag, black white stand, orig box, VG **155.00**

Skipper Pose'n Play, blond, blue and white outfit, wrist tag, orig clear plastic bag, cardboard hanger, NRFP **85.00**

Lunch box, The World of Barbie, vinyl, blue, multicolor images of Barbie, copyright 1971 Mattel, King-Seeley, used, 6-3/4" x 8-3/4" x 4" d **50.00**

Paper doll book, Whitman, uncut

Barbie and Ken Cut-Outs, #1986, dated 1970, NM **35.00**

Barbie's Boutique, #1954, dated 1973, NM **85.00**

Barbie Dolls and Clothes, #1976, dated 1969, NM **50.00**

Pencil case, Skipper and Skooter, Standard Plastic, 1966 ....**15.00**

Playset, Fashion Plaza, 1976 ....**80.00**

Record, 33-1/3 rpm, Sing-Along, unused, 12-1/2" x 12-1/2" **6.00**

❖ Bar Ware

Back in the days when recreation rooms were popular in homes, bars were often an important component of that scene. Of course, a well-equipped bar was a necessity. Novelty items and functional equipment from bars are now making their way to flea markets.

Reference: Stephen Visakay, *Vintage Bar Ware*, Collector Books, 1997.

For additional listings, see Cocktail Shakers in this edition.

Bar guide, *Esquire's Liquor Intelligencer*, 1938, wear, few pages loose, 5-1/2" x 7" **28.00**

Cocktail glasses, ruby, 2-1/2" h, set of 8 ....**125.00**

Cordial Set, six glass cordials with cut floral dec, 1-1/2" x 3", matching 12" x 3-1/2" aluminum tray **95.00**

Ice bucket, glass, hp horse and riding crops on both sides, hammered aluminum handle, gold band at top and bottom **10.00**

Jigger, frosted glass, Indian motif, Canada on back, 4-oz....................**4.00**

Mixer, clear glass, black lettering, recipes on side, 5-3/4" h **14.00**

Paper napkins, Ed Nofziger's Mad-Nagerie Sip 'n Snack, different animal illus, orig box, 6-1/2" x 6-1/2" **14.00**

Pitcher, sterling overlay of golfer on both sides **100.00**

Seltzer bottle, blue glass, "Babad's Miami Seltzer Co.," bottle made in Czechoslovakia **100.00**

Shot glass, Lucite, clear and black, glass magnifies female nude in bottom when held to light................................**50.00**

This flea market dealer had everything you need for your home bar, from measurers to cocktail shakers.

Sipper/stirrer, sterling, fashioned to resemble bamboo, orig box, 8-1/2" l, set of 4 ....**50.00**

Soda siphon, stainless steel, Sparklets Corp., N.Y., 1940s **80.00**

Tray and coasters, wood, tray shows man sleeping and "Silence, Genius at Work," coasters with humorous sayings, Canada, 1950s, tray 12" x 8", 6 coasters 3" dia **88.00**

❖ Baseball Cards

Baseball cards were first printed in the late 19th century. By 1900 the most common cards were those made by tobacco companies, including American Tobacco Company. Most of the tobacco-related cards (identified as T cards) were produced between 1909 and 1915. During the 1920s, American Caramel, National Caramel, and York Caramel candy companies issued cards identified in lists as E cards.

During the 1930s, Goudey Gum Company of Boston, and Gum, Inc., were the primary producers of baseball cards. Following World War II, Bowman Gum of Philadelphia, the successor to Gum, Inc., led the way. Topps, Inc., of Brooklyn, N.Y., bought Bowman in 1956, and Fleer of Philadelphia and Donruss of Memphis joined the competitive ranks in the early 1980s.

References: *All Sport Alphabetical Price Guide*, Krause Publications, 1995; *Baseball Card Price Guide*, 17th ed, Krause Publications, 2003; *Baseball's Top 500*, Krause Publications, 1999; *2003 Standard Catalog of Baseball Cards*, 12th ed, Krause Publications, 2003.

Periodicals: *Baseball Update*, 220 Sunrise Hwy, Suite 284, Rockville Centre, NY 11570; *Beckett Baseball Card Monthly*, 4887 Alpha Rd, Suite 200, Dallas, TX 75244; *Card Trade*, 700 E State St, Iola, WI 54990; *Diamond Angle*, P.O. Box 409, Kaunakakai, HI 96748; *Sports Cards Magazine & Price Guide*, 700 E State St, Iola, WI 54990; *Sports Collectors Digest*, 700 E State St, Iola, WI 54990; *Your Season Ticket*, 106 Liberty Rd, Woodsburg, MD 21790.

Collectors' Clubs: There are many local clubs for card collectors, but there is not a national organization at this time.

> **Reproduction Alert**

The following listings are merely a sampling of the thousands of baseball cards available. For detailed listings, see *2003 Standard Catalog of Baseball Cards*, 12th ed., by Bob Lemke, Krause Publications, 2003.

1961 Topps, Brook Rodgers, #10 ...**26.00**

1968 Topps, Casey Cox, #66 ....**65.00**

1969 Topps, Gene Oliver, #247, white

letter variation...............................**15.00**

1970 Topps, VG cond.
 Complete set, 720 cards............**350.00**
 Common player, 1-372.....................**.30**
 Common player, 272-546..................**.40**
 Common player, 547-633................**1.00**
 Common player, 634-720................**4.75**
 Pete Rose, #580............................**50.00**
 Don Sutton, #622............................**9.00**

1971 Topps
 Ernie Banks, #525........................**38.00**
 Lou Brock, #625 ....**22.00**
 Steve Carlton, #55 ....**16.00**
 Steve Garvey, #341......................**35.00**
 Jim Palmer, #570 ....**26.00**

1975 Topps
 Reggie Jackson, #300.................**15.00**
 Mike Schmidt, #70........................**38.00**
 Robin Yount, #223......................**112.00**

1984 Donruss
 Complete set, 660 cards............**180.00**
 Common player...............................**15**
 Roger Clements, #181 ....**12.00**

1995 Bowman
 Complete set, 439 cards............**240.00**
 Common player...............................**10**

1996 Topps, Ken Griffey, Jr., #M25 .**25.00**

1998 Fleer Update
 Complete set, 100 cards..............**50.00**
 Common player...............................**10**

❖ Baseball Memorabilia

"Play ball!" How those words excite fans and collectors alike. America's fascination with this popular national pastime guarantees a wide range of collectibles to choose from at flea markets.

References: Mark Allen Baker, *All Sport Autograph Guide*, Krause Publications, 1994; ⸺, *Sports Collectors Digest Baseball Autograph Handbook*, 2nd ed, Krause Publications, 1991; ⸺, *Team Baseballs*, Krause Publications, 1992; Mark Larson, *Complete Guide to Baseball Memorabilia*, 3rd ed, Krause Publications, 1996; Mark Larson, Rick Hines, and Dave Platta, *Mickey Mantle Memorabilia*, Krause Publications, 1993. Larry Canale, *Tuff Stuff's Baseball Memorabilia Price Guide, 2nd Edition*, Krause Publications, 2001.

Periodicals: *Baseball Hobby News*, 4540 Kearney Villa Rd, San Diego, CA 92123; *John L. Raybin's Baseball Autograph News*, 527 3rd Ave, #294-A, New York, NY 10016; *Sports Cards Magazine & Price Guide*, 700 E State St, Iola, WI 54990; *Sports Collectors Digest*, 700 E State St, Iola, WI 54990; *Tuff Stuff*, P.O. Box 1637, Glen Allen, VA 23060.

Collectors' Clubs: Glove Collector, 14057 Rolling Hills Ln, Dallas, TX 75210; Society for American Baseball Research, P.O. Box 93183, Cleveland, OH 44101

Reproduction Alert

A swing and a hit
Hillerich & Bradsby, Louisville Slugger Co. produces special black ebony bats to commemorate World Series games. The bats have gold facsimile signatures of the team members, and they are awarded to participating players and league dignitaries. Because they are produced in limited numbers, collector interest tends to drive the marketplace.
1965, Minnesota Twins   600.00
1992, Atlanta Braves   500.00
1993, Toronto Blue Jays   500.00

Autograph
 Mel Allen, on Yankee Stadium postcard **26.00**
 Don Clendenon, Tug McGraw and Ron Swoboda on 1969 New York Mets pennant...............................**60.00**

Baseball, autographed
 Bench, Johnny **50.00**
 Carew, Rod **50.00**
 Mays, Willie **100.00**
 Reese, PeeWee **125.00**

Baseball, team-signed
 All-Star Game, American league, 1967, faded.....................................**100.00**
 Minnesota Twins, 1991, 13 signatures **100.00**

Book
 Baseball Personalities, Jimmy Powers, 1949, 320 pgs, tattered dustjacket **15.00**
 Throwing Heat: The Autobiography of Nolan Ryan, Nolan Ryan and Harvey Frommer, 1988 ....**25.00**
 A Whole Different Game, Marvin Miller, Birch Lane Press, 1991 ....**10.00**

Brochure, season ticket plans, Washington Senators, 1963.........**15.00**

Cereal box ad, Post Sugar Crisp, three bears with baseball equipment, billboard with Ted Williams in background, 1955 ....**6.00**

Christmas ornament, Detroit Tigers, Sports Collectors Series, Topperscot, Inc., MIB.......................................**8.00**

Cocktail napkin, San Diego All-Star Game, July 14, 1992.....................**2.00**

Face mask, catcher or umpire, adjustable, 8-1/2" w, 8-3/4" h **40.00**

Game, Pitch Back Automatic Umpire, endorsed by Hank Aaron, 1960s, 10-1/2" w, 17-1/2" l **75.00**

Mug, figural, comic batter handle **70.00**

Patch, New York Giants, 1950s, flocking on vinyl, 3-1/2" dia........................**50.00**

Pennant
 Cincinnati Redlegs, red with pink and white detailing, one tassle missing, 29" l...**55.00**
 National Baseball Hall of Fame and Museum, Cooperstown, N.Y., 12" l **18.00**
 Schedule, Pittsburgh Pirates, 1936 ....**50.00**
 New York Mets, 1969, team-signed **60.00**

Place mat, paper, scalloped edge, photo showing aerial view of Yankee Stadium, "Yankee Stadium Baseball's Proud Heritage," early 1960s, 9-1/2" x 14-1/2" **7.50**

Postcard, Yankee Stadium, autographed by Mel Allen, Babe Ruth stamp with first-day cancellation **26.00**

Press guide, Minnesota Twins, 1963 ....**40.00**

Record, *Hank Aaron The Life Of A Legend*, 33-1/3 rpm, single record on Fleetwood label, interviews and career highlights, mid 1970s, unopened .**10.00**

Salt and pepper shakers, bisque, batter and umpire **95.00**

Schedule, Pittsburgh Pirates, 1936, back stamped "Kennedy Hardware Co., Sportsman's Headquarters" **50.00**

Toothbrush, bat shape, beige plastic, Cincinnati Reds, Oracare, early 1970s, 6" l **8.00**

Trade card, "Struck Out," comical baseball player, "W.M. Elder, Dealer in Drugs and Medicines", late 1800s, removed from scrapbook, 3-1/4" x 5-1/4" **35.00**

Whiffle ball, white vinyl ball 2-1/4" dia, black-and-white box 2-1/2" sq, photo of Tim McCarver on lid, c1960.........**10.00**

World Series pins
 1966, Dodgers............................**100.00**
 1974, Oakland A's......................**375.00**
 1982, St. Louis Cardinals **50.00**
 1984, San Diego Padres..............**75.00**
 1995, Atlanta Braves..................**100.00**

World Series program
 1948, Indians v Braves, no writing, some cover wear **85.00**
 1996, Yankees v Braves **10.00**

❖ Basketball Cards

This relatively new collecting area is growing quickly. As with baseball cards, it's important to know your subject in order to spot unusual and valuable cards.

 References: *Tuff Stuff Standard Catalog of Basketball Cards*, 6th ed., Krause Publications, 2003.

 Periodicals: *Sports Cards Magazine & Price Guide*, 700 E State St, Iola, WI

54990; *Sports Collectors Digest*, 700 E State St, Iola, WI 54990.

The following listings are merely a sampling of the thousands of basketball cards available.

Fleer
 1985 Series, 90 cards, with stickers **30.00**
 1998, #1 ....**15.00**
Johnson, Larry, stadium club **10.00**
Olympics Dream Team, 1992, orig collector's album, includes Larry Bird, Charles Barkley, Michael Jordan, Scottie Pippen, Karl Malone, coaches, set of 25 cards **15.00**
Skybox Series, 15 cards per pack, series of 36 factory sealed packs, 1990 ....**18.50**
Topps
 1995, complete #1 set..................**35.00**
 1997, factory set **25.00**
 1978, Julius Erving, #130.............**13.00**
 1995-96, Michael Jordan, #1 ....**2.00**
 1996-97, Grant Hill, #199...............**1.50**
 1997-98, Kobe Bryant, #171 ....**2.00**
 1997-98, Allen Iverson, $54 ....**3.00**
 2000-01, Vince Carter, #50 ....**3.00**
Upper Deck, 10 cards per pack, series of 30 packs, 1995.............................**15.00**

❖ Basketball Memorabilia

Since its introduction in 1891, players and spectators have enjoyed the game of basketball. So popular is the sport that phrases such as "Hoosier Hysteria" and "March Madness" have been added to the lexicon. The NBA is working hard to promote collecting among its fans, and the WNBA has created a whole new field of collectibles.

Periodical: Sports Collectors Digest, 700 E State St, Iola, WI 54990.

Action Figure, MOC
 Barkley, Charles, Headliners NBA**10.00**
 Drexler, Clyde, Rockets, Headliners NBA **5.00**
 Frazier, Will, Starting Line-Up, 1997 ....**15.00**
 Hill, Grant, Detroit Pistons, Headliners NBA **7.50**
Autograph, 8" x 10" photo
 Bird, Larry **34.00**
 Johnson, Magic **36.00**
 Mercer, Ron...................................**15.00**
 Van Horn, K...................................**25.00**
Autographed Jersey
 Bryant, Kobe **340.00**
 Jones, Eddie **185.00**
Bobbing head figure, New York Nicks, smiling player holding ball, Japan sticker, 1962, 5-3/4" h..................**225.00**

Christmas Ornament, Hallmark Treasury series
 Hill, Grant, 1998, includes Fleer Skybox trading card, 4-1/4" h ...**12.00**
 Johnson, Magic, 1997, includes Fleer Skybox trading card, 5-1/2" h ...**14.00**
 New York Nicks, 1997, ceramic, orig box **8.00**
 Seattle Sonics, 1997, ceramic, orig box **8.00**
Doll, Dennis Rodman, extra outfit, wig, vinyl, 12" h...................................**40.00**
Dribbler, Knicks, black, 1959, Japan **35.00**
Game, Cadaco, #165, 1973, unused, MIB..**30.00**
Photograph
 Grove City, OH, early 1930s, 5" x 7" **30.00**
 Petrovic Drazen, wire service photo of young Yugoslav player, 1989 ......**3.50**
Plaque, David Robinson, photo of him wearing Spurs jersey, copyrighted 1990 NBA, and cards, matted, display frame, 8" x 10"..**35.00**
Seals and Diecuts, Dennison, package of 4 pcs, unused, orig cellophane packaging **7.50**
Tie tack with chain, male basketball player **12.00**

❖ Baskets

Wonderful examples of all types of baskets can be found at flea markets. Check carefully for wear and damage, and make sure they are priced accordingly.

Baby basket, wicker, hood formed at one end, handles, some damage and splits **75.00**
Banana, large, two handles woven into sides, loosely woven, damage **45.00**
Cheese basket, woven splint, old patina,

Baskets, Figural chicken, yellow wooden beak, red wooden comb, eye, opens at middle, 3-1/2" h, $3.

some damage, string wrapped repair at rims, 21" dia **115.00**
Gathering, rye straw, oval, wear and damage, 15" x 21".......................**85.00**
Loom, woven splint, hanging type, natural, pink, and green, varnished, 9-1/2" w, 8-3/4" h............................**95.00**
Market, woven splint handle, 16" l ..**90.00**
Melon shape, woven splint, bentwood handle, 15" d **85.00**
Nantucket, oval, open, two carved handles, 10" l, 7-1/2" w, 3-3/4" h, handle repaired, late 19th/early 20th C **575.00**
Peach, wide slats, wooden base, 11-1/2" h **4.00**
Picnic, woven splint, two folding lids attached to sides with leather loops, c1950 ....**25.00**
Sewing, cov, round, ring-type handles, slight wear **45.00**
Shaker, woven splint, four handles, 19th C, 14-3/4" h, losses....................**695.00**

❖ Batman

"Holy cow, Batman! Why is everyone staring at us?" This famous super hero and his cast of cohorts can be found in abundance at local flea markets. Watch for examples related to contemporary movies as well as items with tie-ins to the television series and the comic characters.

References: Bill Bruegman, *Superhero Collectibles*, Toy Scouts, 1996; Joe Desris, *Golden Age of Batman*, Artabras, 1994.

Collectors' Club: Batman TV Series Fan Club, P.O. Box 107, Venice, CA 90291.

Action figure, Penguin, 1992, 9" h **100.00**
Batmobile, Corgi, #267, diecast, copyright 1983, MIB **190.00**

Batman comic book, DC Comics, The Brave & The Bold Presents Batman & the Green Lantern, No. 134, May, $5.

Batman, wood child's stool, red lettering, worn, $45.

Batmobile Gift Pack, batmobile and boat, Corgi, 1979, MOC **395.00**
Coloring book, 1963, used **20.00**
Comic book, Batman Comic, #22, April-May 1944, first appearance of Alfred the butler **125.00**
Cosmetics, Robin goes to a Weekend, Travel Time Cosmetics, Hasbro, 1960s, unused, MIB **65.00**
Costume, Switch & Go, orig box...**150.00**
Desk Set, calendar, stapler, and pencil sharpener, MIB...........................**150.00**
Figure
　Batman, Ertl, cast metal, 1990, sealed in orig blister pack with collector card, 2" h **15.00**
　Penguin, Batman Returns, Applause tag, plastic, 1992, 9" h.............**25.00**
Inflatable figure, plastic, 1989, 13" h **40.00**
Kite, Batman & Robin, plastic, 1982, sealed in orig package.................**20.00**
Notebook, spiral bound, Michael Keaton, unused...**1.50**
Pen set, Batman & Robin, DC Comics, 1978 ....**30.00**
Pez, Batman, #5, 1985, used **35.00**
Pin, plastic, 1989, pack of 12 assorted figures **12.00**
Puzzle, Batman & Robin, 1981, 130 pcs, unused, 10-3/4" x 8-1/2" **12.00**
Robot, tin wind-up, Biliken, Japan, MIB **175.00**
Scale model, Bat Car, Valtoys, 3-3/4" l, MOC **25.00**
Schoolbook cover, 1966, 20" x 13" **15.00**
Straw, figural, 18 assorted figures in box **9.00**
Toy
　Bat Cave, 1960s, orig box............**85.00**
　Pix-A-Go-Go, featuring the Penguin, National Periodical Publications, 1966, sealed in orig shrink wrap...........**75.00**

❖ Battery-Operated Toys

Battery-operated toys have amused children for decades. Originally inexpensive, these toys were made in large quantities, and many still exist today. Values increase quickly for examples in good working condition and for those playthings with interesting actions or with the original box.

Reference: Sharon Korbeck & Dan Stearns, *2003 Toys & Prices*, 10th ed, Krause Publications, 2003; Elizabeth A. Stephan, *O'Brien's Collecting Toys,* 10th ed, Krause Publications, 2001.

Big Top Champ Circus Clown, MIB **95.00**
BMW 3.5 CSL turbo car, tin, Dunlop and Bosch Electric advertising, MIB .**120.00**
Brave Eagle, beating drum, raising war hoop, MIB..................................**145.00**
Bubble Blowing Monkey, raises hand from pan on lap to mouth, MIB ..**195.00**
Button the Pup, MIB **375.00**
Captain Bushwell, vinyl head, Japan, 1970s, MIB **85.00**
Carnival Choo Choo, plastic, Hong Kong, 1970s, MIB........................**55.00**
Comical Clara, MIB **495.00**
Fighter Plane Bombardier, orig box **395.00**
Happy Miner, MIB....................**1,075.00**
Knock-Out Boxers, orig box........**295.00**
Lamborghini Countach car, red, MIB **120.00**
Love-Love Volkswagen Beetle, blinking light in back window, tin, orange, Mobil, Champion, Goodyear sayings, VW on hubcaps, MIB **145.00**
Luncheonette Bank, tin litho, plastic waitress, fabric clothing, serves coffee after coin is inserted, orig full color box, box professionally restored **500.00**

Snoopie, orig box, contains brown plush covered dog, red, white, tan, and black plaid jacket and hat, unplayed with condition, $35.

Battery Operated, Charlie Weaver Bartender, Rosko Toys, orig box, played with, $95.

Magic Snowman, white fabric, red facial accents and gloves, orig box with cellophane window, Modern Toys, Japan, c1960.............................**225.00**
McGregor, Scotsman smoking cigar, moves up and down from treasure chest, MIB **195.00**
My Fair Dancer, litho tin, dancer in naval outfit, seahorse graphics on base, MIB, 11" h...**225.00**
Picnic Bear, orig box **125.00**
Roller Coaster, plastic, Hong Kong, 1970s, MIB **55.00**
Rosko, bartender, shakes, pours and drinks, smoke rises from ears, MIB **75.00**
Santa Claus, orig box **225.00**
School Bus, tin litho, switch opens doors, headlights light **175.00**
Smoking Grandpa, smokes, but pipe doesn't light, Japan **85.00**
Sniffy Dog with Bee, Modern Toys, Japan, 1970s, MIB **55.00**
Space Explorer, turn-over action, Gakken, Japan, MIB.................**100.00**
Traffic Policeman, MIB.................**490.00**
Tumbles the Bear, Yanoman, 1970s, MIB..**85.00**
U.S. Army Helicopter, C-7 ....**90.00**
Walking Gorilla, MIB **1,275.00**
Waltzing Matilda, MIB **875.00**

❖ Bauer Pottery

Many people think of brightly colored California pottery when they hear the name Bauer, but the company actually produced utilitarian earthenware and stoneware for many years before expanding their product line. John Bauer founded the company in 1885 in Paducah, Ky., but the plant was moved to Los Angeles in 1909. Artware, dinnerware, and kitchenware became mainstays of the company until a strike in 1961 forced them out of business the following year.

References: Jeffrey B. Snyder, *Beautiful Bauer*, Schiffer Publishing, 2000.

Bowl, pumpkin orange granite glaze, 9" dia **60.00**

Bulb bowl, #200 Hi Fire Line, black, hand thrown by Fred or Jim Johnson, c1938, 5-3/4" dia **80.00**

Butter pat tray, black, scratches in center, 4-1/2" dia **35.00**

Coffee cup, green-gray, 4" d...........**14.00**

Coffee server, cov, pink granite......**85.00**

Dog Dish, large, cobalt **150.00**

Figure, duck, bill pointing down, 4-1/2" l **35.00**

Ice pitcher, Ringware, 2-qt, 2 small chips to handle **175.00**

Planter

Ball, yellow, 7-1/2" w, 5-1/2" h......**60.00**

Green, 7" l, 4-1/2" h **37.50**

Swan, ivory matte, imp mark, 12-1/4" l, 7-1/4" h **35.00**

Plate

Ringware, jade green, 9" dia........**40.00**

Plainware, black, imp mark, 1930s, 2 small nicks, 9-1/2" dia...............**20.00**

Relish, speckled white, 15-3/4" x 7-1/2" **30.00**

Rose bowl, Fred Johnson, hand-thrown, 8-1/2" dia **90.00**

Salad plate, Ringware, dusty burgundy, use wear, 7-3/4" dia, 1-1/2" h.......**35.00**

Teapot, Aladdin, pastel, 1930s......**215.00**

Vase

Avocado green, 1950s, 9" h.........**75.00**

Turquoise, by Fred Johnson, 7-1/2" h **95.00**

Vegetable bowl, Ringware, yellow, oval, 9" **95.00**

Water jug, Brusche, speckled pink .**65.00**

❖ Bavarian China

Flea markets are wonderful places to find examples of this colorful china. Several china manufacturers in the Bavarian porcelain center of southern Germany produced a wide variety of items that are collectively referred to as Bavarian china.

For additional listings, see *Warman's Antiques & Collectibles.*

Bowl, large orange poppies, green leaves **85.00**

Creamer and sugar, purple and white pansy dec, mkd "Meschendorf, Bavaria" **65.00**

Cup and saucer, roses and leaves, gold

Bavarian China, Dresser set, porcelain, "Favorite" pattern, blue band, floral dec, oval tray, lidded dresser jar, hair receiver, hat pin holder, and oval pin dish, $95.

handle **25.00**

Dinner plate, gold emb, stippled bands, "A" monogram, mkd "Hutshcenreuther selb Bavaria," price for set of 12.**320.00**

Hair receiver, apple blossom dec, mkd "T S. & Co." **60.00**

Portrait plate, elaborate portrait of lady, sgd "L. B. Chaffee, R. C. Bavaria," **100.00**

Ramekin and underplate, ruffled, small red roses and green leaves, gold trim **45.00**

Salt and pepper shakers, pink apple blossom sprays, white ground, reticulated gold tops, pr................**35.00**

Shaving mug, pink carnations, mkd "Royal Bavaria"...........................**65.00**

Sugar shaker, hp, pastel pansies...**60.00**

Teapot, yellow, colorful iris dec **60.00**

Vase, hp, red poppies, gold enamel dec, mkd "Classic Bavaria," 12" h **260.00**

❖ Beanie Babies

The original set of nine Beanie Babies was released in 1993. The resulting collector enthusiasm and speculation quickly priced many children out of the market. Intended as simple, inexpensive playthings, these bean-stuffed personalities took on a life of their own, with some examples commanding exorbitant prices. The current market has returned to a level more consistent with the fun factor of these toys.

References: Shawn Brecka, *The Beanie Family Album and Collectors Guide*, Antique Trader Books, 1998; Les and Sue Fox, *The Beanie Baby Handbook*, West Highland Publishing, 1997; Rosie Wells, *Rosie's Price Guide for Ty's Beanie Babies*, Rosie Wells Enterprises, 1997.

Ally the alligator **12.00**

Ants the anteater **3.00**

Aruba the fish **7.00**

Baldy the eagle **10.00**

Batty the bat **4.00**

Bessie the cow **60.00**

Bruno the terrier **6.00**

Cubbie the bear **20.00**

Daisy the cow **6.00**

Diddley the dog..................................**6.00**

Ears the bunny.................................**12.00**

Flip the cat **24.00**

Goldie the goldfish **55.00**

Gracie the swan **7.00**

Holiday bear, 1997 ....**20.00**

Hoot the owl.....................................**39.00**

Lizzy the lizard **19.00**

Peace bear **12.00**

Pinky the flamingo **10.00**

Quackers the duck..............................**8.00**

Rover the dog **16.00**

Seaweed the otter **10.00**

Snort the bull **7.500**

Tank the armadillo **70.00**

Weenie the dog.................................**18.00**

Wise the owl **7.50**

Ziggy the zebra **10.00**

Zip the cat **20.00**

❖ Beatles

The Fab Four created quite a sensation with their music during the 1960s. Beatlemania fueled the creation of a plethora of items paying tribute to the group and bearing the singers' likenesses. Record albums, concert ephemera, and even dolls can be found at local flea markets.

Reference: Jeff Augsburger, Marty Eck and Rick Rann, *Beatles Memorabilia Price Guide*, 3rd ed, Antique Trader Books, 1997.

Periodicals: *Beatlefan*, P.O. Box 33515, Decatur, GA 30033; *Instant Karma*, P.O. Box 256, Sault Ste. Marie, MI 39783.

Collectors Clubs: Beatles Connection, P.O. Box 1066, Pinealls Park, FL 34665; Beatles Fan Club, 397 Edgewood Ave, New Haven, CT 06511; Beatles Fan Club of Great Britain, Superstore Productions, 123 Marina, St. Leonards on Sea, East Sussex, England TN38 OBN; Working Class Hero Club, 3311 Niagara St, Pittsburgh, PA 15213.

For additional listings, see *Warman's Americana & Collectibles.*

Reproduction Alert

Arcade card, shows all 4 men, black-and-white, cream reverse with write-up on the group, 1965, major crease to 1 corner **5.00**

Bank, Yellow Submarine, plastic bust figures of each Beatle, 1960s, 7-1/2" h, price for set of 4, minor damage **1,400.00**

Banner, printed nylon, black images of four Beatles, blue printed "The Beatles," Memphis, 1966.........**1,150.00**

Beach towel, terry cloth, Beatles in bathing suits, c1960, 34" x 57" ..**115.00**

Cake decorating kit, figurals, playing instruments, set of 4, MIB **195.00**

Collector plate, The Beatles Live in Concert, 1st issue in the Beatles Collection, 1991, issued by Delphi (a division of The Bradley Exchange), #13108L, with paperwork, orig box **60.00**

Game, Flip Your Wig, Milton Bradley, 1964 ....**95.00**

Glass, pictures Beatles with instruments, insulating coating around middle, 1960s, 5-1/4" h **185.00**

Handkerchief, 8-1/2" sq **20.00**

Jigsaw puzzle, official Beatles fan club puzzle, black-and-white, shows band with instruments, 1964, 8-1/4" x 10-3/4" **40.00**

Lunchbox, Yellow Submarine **175.00**

Magazine

Accoustic Guitar, vol. 2 #1 (July/August 1991), Beatles cover, includes transcriptions for 3 Beatles songs **6.00**

Saturday Evening Post, August 27, 1966, Beatles cover, illus 6-page article on the group, loose cover, 11" x 14"...**20.00**

The Beatles Book Monthly #16, Nov. 1964, U.K. fan magazine, Paul and Ringo on cover, 6" x 8-1/2".......**18.00**

TV Guide, commemorative ed, 1995, includes story on Beatles **5.00**

Postcard, shows Beatles with printed autographs, 1964, unused, 2 pinholes **10.00**

Souvenir song album, features words and music to early recordings, biographical sketches and guitar chords, early 1960s, 32 pgs, small tears **25.00**

Sheet music, *Day Tripper*, 1964 .....**20.00**

Wallpaper Section, 20-1/2" x 21", unused, four images, facsimile signatures, c1964 ....**20.00**

❖ Beatrix Potter

Collectors are hot on the trail of this lovable English hare, and flea markets are a good place to spot him. Peter and the rest of the Beatrix Potter family are frequently sighted, since many of the items are in current production and, thus, readily available.

Baby cup, silver plate, "The World of Peter Rabbit by Beatrix Potter," F. Warne & Co. Ltd...........................**39.00**

Book

Ginger and Pickles, F. Warne & Co. Ltd., copyright renewed 1937, pictorial endpapers, paste-on picture on cover, owner's name inside cover **25.00**

Histoire de Jeannot Lapin, French, translated by Victorine Ballon and

Julienne Profichet, F. Warne & Co. Ltd., color illus and endpapers, hardcover, slight wear to edges **50.00**

The Tale of Squirrel Nutkin, F. Warne & Co. Ltd., copyright renewed 1931, 27 full-page color plates and endpapers, hardcover, 84 pgs, owner's name inside cover.............................**45.00**

The Tale of Two Bad Mice, F. Warne & Co. Ltd., copyright renewed 1932, hardcover, paste-on picture on cover **25.00**

Cookie tin, Peter Rabbit, 3" h, 7-1/2" dia **8.00**

Figure

Anna Maria, F. Warne & Co. Ltd., stamped "Beswick, England" and "Beatrix Potter's Anna Maria" on bottom, 3" h **350.00**

Benjamin Bunny, Beswick, 1st version gold mark BP-2.....................**480.00**

Flopsy, Mopsy and Cottontail, Beswick, 1st version gold mark BP-2 ....**330.00**

Lady Mouse, Beswick, gold mark, BP-2 ....**300.00**

Little Pig Robinson, Beswick, first version, blue stripes, gold mark **375.00**

Peter Rabbit, Beswick, 1st version gold mark BP-2.............................**240.00**

Timmy Willie, F. Warne & Co. Ltd., stamped "Beswick, England" on bottom, copyright 1949, 3" h **50.00**

Tommy Brock, Beswick, 1st gold mark, 3-3/8" h **450.00**

❖ Beer Cans

Prior to Prohibition, beer was stored and shipped in kegs. After the Prohibition Act was repealed in 1933, many breweries did not resume business. Those that did start up again wanted to expand their distribution areas, and brewers found themselves in need of an inexpensive alternative for holding their product. Cans fit the bill nicely. The first patent for a lined can was issued to the American Can Company in 1934. The rest, as they say, is history.

Reference: Thomas Toepfer, *Beer Cans*, L-W Book Sales, 1976 (1995 value update).

Collectors' Club: Beer Can Collectors of America, 747 Merus Ct, Fenton, MO 63026, www.bcca.com.

Ace Hi M.L., flat top, 7 oz **115.00**

Acme Beer, flat top, faded , 12-oz....**5.00**

Bantam, Goebel, flat top, 8 oz **27.50**

Budweiser, tab top, 10-oz................**5.50**

Colorado Gold Label, tab top, steel, 12-oz **6.00**

Coors, flat top, aluminum, full, 7-oz **11.00**

Fyfe & Drum, tab top, steel, 12-oz ...**4.00**

GB, Brace Bros., flat top, 1 side faded, 12-oz **25.00**

Hudepohl, 1975 Cincinnati Reds, tab top, steel, 12-oz.............................**4.00**

King Snedley's, tab top, 12-oz **10.00**

Lucky Lager, flat top, 7-oz.............**15.00**

North Star, pull top, 11 oz **4.00**

Piels Real Draft, "New Aluminum Can," air-sealed, 12-oz **4.00**

Rolling Rock, Labrobe, pull top, 7 oz **4.50**

Schmidt's Bicentennial, Cornwallis, tab top, 12-oz **1.50**

Topper, tab top, 12-oz......................**5.00**

Walter's Light, pull top, 12 oz..........**4.00**

West Virginia Pilsner, pull top, 12 oz **5.00**

Zodiac Malt Liquor, tab top, 12-oz...**2.00**

❖ Belleek

There's an old Irish saying that newlyweds who receive a wedding gift of Belleek will have their marriage blessed with lasting happiness. It's a great sentiment, and Belleek certainly does make a nice wedding gift. A thin, ivory-colored porcelain with an almost iridescent look, Belleek traces its roots to Fermanagh, Ireland, in 1857. The approximate age of a piece can be determined by looking at the mark. From 1863 to 1946 black marks were used; green marks were introduced in 1946.

Collectors' Club: The Belleek Collectors' Society, 9893 Georgetown Pk, Suite 525, Great Falls, VA 22066.

For additional listings, see *Warman's Antiques & Collectibles* and *Warman's English & Continental Pottery & Porcelain*.

Biscuit barrel, Basketweave pattern, cov, 6th green mark, 1965-80 ....**100.00**

Bread plate, Shamrock pattern, double handle, 3rd green mark, 10-1/2" l, 9-1/4" w **80.00**

Butter dish, cov, Limpet pattern, 1st black mark, 6-1/2" d top, 8-1/2" d base **475.00**

Cake plate, mask with grape leaves pattern, four looped handles, pale yellow edge, 3rd black mark, 10-1/2" dia **155.00**

Creamer

Cleary pattern, 3rd green mark....**60.00**

Pastel yellow ribbon and bow accents, green mark **60.00**

Creamer and sugar

Clover pattern, 6th green mark, 1965-80...**100.00**

Shamrock pattern, married pair, green marks, 1945-55.......................**120.00**

Cream jug, Lily of the Valley pattern, 2nd black mark, 1891-1926..............**195.00**

Cup and saucer, Shell pattern, 2nd black mark, 1891-1926..............**195.00**

Belleek Bowl, water lily dec, pink bud, applied gilded leaves and thistles, red Ott & Brewer crown mark, couple of minute flecks, some wear to gilding around rim, 10" dia, 4" h, $650.

Demitasse cup and saucer, green mark on cup, gold mark on saucer, c1956 ....**50.00**

Dish, Shamrock pattern, 3rd green mark **60.00**

Dresser vase, detailed rose and leaves, green mark, 3-3/4" h **185.00**

Figure
Harp, 3rd green mark, 6" h **70.00**
Pig, 2" h, 3" l **90.00**
Terrier, green mark, 3-1/2" h **45.00**

Honey pot, barrel type, clover leaves dec, 7th gold-brown mark, 1980-93 ....**80.00**

Mustache cup, Tridacna pattern, first black mark..................................**125.00**

Nut bowl set, Shell pattern, white ext, yellow int., black mark, 9 pcs **700.00**

Pitcher, Vine and Grape pattern, lavender and green, ivory ground, brown mark, 5-1/2" h....................**60.00**

Plate, Harp and Shamrock pattern, 5th mark, 9" dia **60.00**

Potpourri vase, Basketweave pattern, 6th green mark, 1965-80, 4-1/2" h **100.00**

Salt, open, star, 3rd black mark **60.00**

Sugar bowl, open, yellow ribbon and box accents, green mark.....................**45.00**

Tea set, Basketweave pattern, 6th green mark, 1965-80, repair to spout...**275.00**

❖ Bells

From the tinkle of a silver bell to the clanging of a ship's bell, the music of bells has enchanted collectors for decades. When considering a purchase, check for stress fractures and other signs of use, and also look to see if the clapper is original.

Collectors' Clubs: American Bell Assoc, Alter Rd, Box 386, Natrona Heights, PA 15065; American Bell Assoc International, Inc, 7210 Bellbrook Dr, San Antonio, TX 78227.

Bells, Disciples, Matthew, Mark, Luke, and John, brass, $45.

Ceramic
Aunt Jemima, Japan, 1940s, 3-1/2" h **75.00**
Hummel, 1978..............................**95.00**
Mermaid, 4-1/2" h........................**24.00**

Church, cast brass, wrought iron clapper, late 18th C, 20" h **990.00**

Cast iron, profiles of Franklin Roosevelt, Winston Churchill, and Joseph Stalin emb on sides, large "V" emb on handle, rim emb "cast with metal from German aircraft shot down over Britain 1939-45, R.A.F. Benevolent Fund," 6" h **125.00**

Desk, bronze, iron base, ornate mechanism, Victorian, 3" w, 5" h**135.00**

Door-mounted, brass, filigree mounting **45.00**

Glass
Czechoslovakian, green, gold dec, orig sticker "Handmade Bohemia Czechoslovakia," 7" h...............**85.00**
Daisy and Button, satin vaseline, 6-1/2" h...**75.00**
Fenton, Statue of Liberty, hand painted dec..**35.00**
Murano, gold wash, orig sticker, 4" h **65.00**
Princess House, cut design, 6-3/4" h **10.00**

Porcelain, Danbury Mint, Mother's Day, pink flowers **18.00**

Sleigh, leather strap, 7 graduated brass bells..**75.00**

❖ Belt Buckles

A collection of belt buckles consists of items that are small and easy to store, and which represent a variety of materials. What more could one want in a collection? Some of the more ornate examples are elaborately cast or set with precious and semi-precious stones.

Reproduction Alert

Belt Buckles, Civil war, Confederate, 2 pcs, $350.

Bakelite
O-shaped, red, silvertone knobs, 2-1/2" dia..**29.00**
Round, carved, black front, yellow back, 3" dia **55.00**

Boy Scouts, 1977 National Jamboree **15.00**

Hockey, brass **10.00**

Iron Maiden, "Number of the Beast," shows album cover, made in England, numbered, mint cond **41.00**

Lion Oil Co., silvertone, mountain lion and company name, owner's name and 1993 on back, 2-1/4" x 3-1/4" **35.00**

Marlboro, brass, oval, star and steer, copyright 1987, 2-1/2" x 3-1/2".....**20.00**

Masonic emblem, 2" x 2-7/8" **12.00**

National Finals Rodeo, Hesston, 1977, bull riding......................................**42.00**

Piedmont Airlines, goldtone, orig plastic wrap and box, 2-7/8" x 2-3/8".....**150.00**

Schlitz Light, brass and pewter, light blue enamel inlay, 1976...............**25.00**

Shriner emblem, silvertone **20.00**

Steam shovel, brass.......................**12.00**

Western, Wil-Aren Originals, 2-1/2" h, 3-3/4" w **20.00**

❖ Bennington Pottery

Although the company has been in existence for a century and a half, only their more contemporary items are included here.

Bowl, bowl, arched emb dec, brown glaze, hairline **30.00**

Bread plate, 6" d.............................**8.00**

Mug, brown Rockingham glaze **10.00**

Plate, abstract fish dec, 10" dia.......**70.00**

Wall plaque, owl, 8-3/4" x 7"..........**65.00**

Bennington Pottery, Cow creamer, brown mottled glaze, $65.

❖ Beswick

Beswick characters are well known to collectors and include figures from children's literature as well as animals and other subjects. James Wright Beswick and his son, John, organized the firm in the 1890s. By 1969, the company was sold to Royal Doulton Tableware, Ltd., which still produces many Beswick animals.

References: Diana Callow et al., *The Charlton Standard Catalogue of Beswick Animals*, 2nd ed, Charlton Press, 1996; Diana and John Callow, *The Charlton Standard Catalogue of Beswick Pottery*, Charlton Press, 1997; Harvey May, *The Beswick Price Guide*, 3rd ed, Francis Joseph Publications, 1995, distributed by Krause Publications.

Character jug
 Midshipman, 5-1/4" h **185.00**
 Old Mr. Brown, 1987-1992, 3" h.**200.00**
Child's feeding dish, Mickey and Donald on bicycle **140.00**
Decanter, monk, underplate and four mugs...**250.00**
Figure
 Amiable Guinea Pig, Beatrix Potter, 1995-1972 ....**250.00**
 Cecily Parsley, Beatrix Potter, gold mark.......................................**270.00**
 Grooming Kittens, two tabbies ...**135.00**
 Hereford Bull, 6" h......................**225.00**
 Jemima Puddleduck, Beatrix Potter, 1947..**95.00**
 Johnny Town Mouse, Beatrix Potter, 1954, 3-1/2" h **65.00**
 Mr. Jeremy Fisher, Beatrix Potter, gold mark.......................................**290.00**
 Mrs. Ribby, Beatrix Potter, 1951, 3-1/2" h...**75.00**
 Mrs. Tittlemouse, Beatrix Potter, 1st gold mark, 3-1/2" h **325.00**
 Palamino Horse, 7-1/2" h **200.00**
 Peter Rabbit, Beatrix Potter, 1st gold mark, 4-5/8" h **295.00**
 Scottie, white, ladybug on nose, HN804, 1940-69 ....**225.00**
 Squirrel Nutkin, Beatrix Potter....**220.00**
 Swish Tail Horse, #1182, orig Beswick

sticker, 8-1/2" h......................**225.00**
 Timmy Tiptoes, Beatrix Potter, gold mark.......................................**225.00**
 Tony Weller....................................**85.00**
 Trout, #1390, 4" h......................**150.00**
Mug
 Falstaff, inscribed "Pistol with Wit or Steel, Merry Wives of Windsor," #1127, 1948-73, 4" h...............**85.00**
 Hamlet, inscribed "To Be or Not To Be," #1147, 4-1/4" h **85.00**
Plate, Disney characters, 7" dia **95.00**
Shoe, old woman seated inside, Beatrix Potter, gold stamped mark, 3-3/4" w, 2-1/2" h...**175.00**
Tankard, A Christmas Carol, 1971..**50.00**
Teapot, Sairy Gump, 5-1/2" h **300.00**
Tulip vase, shape #843, semi-gloss white, 1940-43, 4" h **50.00**

❖ Bibles

Bibles are only occasionally found at flea markets, since most families either keep those that belonged to their loved ones, or donate them to a local church. From time to time, old large family Bibles do surface at flea markets and book sales. Prices can range from a few dollars to several hundred, depending on the illustrations, date, type of Bible, condition, etc. Potential buyers are often more interested in the genealogical information that might be contained therein. Before selling a family Bible, consider sharing its historical or genealogical information with family members. Additionally, historical societies and libraries are generally grateful for such information.

Bibles, Marble, spine and front engraved "Holy Bible," 5" w, 2" d, 6-1/4" h, $30.

Family Bible, dates start 1825, many engravings, 11" x 9-1/2" **250.00**
Family Worship Edition, King James Version, 1948, many color pictures, Nashville Bible House, Nashville, Tenn., ink spots on some pages ..**35.00**
Gilt engraved tooled leather, 1867, American Bible Society, N.Y., trace gilt to page edges, a few minor tears, 5-3/4" x 4-1/4"................................**60.00**
New Testament Bible ABC Book, full-color illus, The Book Concern, Columbus, Ohio, name on front cover, 16 pgs, 8-1/4" x 10-1/2" **8.00**
Presentation Bible, Masonic Edition, Masonic emblem on cover, copyright 1932, never inscribed.................**395.00**
Service testament and prayer book, U.S. Military issue, 1943, leather case imprinted with gold name of orig owner, tear to case at snap **80.00**
Soldier's pocket Bible, New Testament and Psalms, 1862, inscribed 1864/Lowell, Mass.....................**275.00**

❖ Bicentennial

Remember all that hoopla surrounding 1976? How many of you have stashed away some bit of Bicentennial memorabilia? These items are becoming more common at flea markets, and historically minded individuals are adding them to their collections. Perhaps these pieces of the past will turn into treasures.

Bowl, eagle dec, blue striped border, Mottahedeh, Chinese Export reproduction made for U.S. State Dept use **75.00**
Decanter, colorless, etched eagle, flag, 1776-96, 11" h...........................**25.00**
Dolls, Campbell Soup, hard plastic, Colonial clothes, 10-1/2" h, pr....**150.00**
Drinking glass, Elsie Family, Spirit of '76, red, white and blue patriotic dec, family in colonial garb, Elsie playing drum, Elmer playing fife, Beauregard playing small drum, 5-1/2" h, pr ...**28.00**
Guidebook, *Washington: The Official Bicentennial Guidebook*, ed by Nancy Love, 1976, softcover, 213 pgs **5.00**
Paperweight, rect, white lettering, rust ground **6.00**
Pitcher, Patriots, parian-type body, blue stripe at top, orig tag, Lenox **60.00**
Pendant, gold filled, diecut Liberty Bell in center, circled by enameled red, white, and blue stars, 24" l chain...........**45.00**
Pinback button, Spirit of '76, America's Bicentennial, 1776-1976, 3-1/2" dia **20.00**
Plate
 Avon, clear glass, bald eagle holding shield and arrows, "United States of

Bicentennial, Metal, oval, 1776 Bicentennial 1976, Washington Crossing the Delaware scene, legend of historic crossing on back, 15" l, $10.

America Bicentennial 1776-1976," 9-1/8" l, 6-3/4" w **5.00**

Bing & Grondahl, bald eagle in center, 13 colonies around edge, blue, gold trim, orig box.............................**50.00**

Fenton, powder blue, George Washington at Valley Forge, 3rd in a series of 4, 8-1/4" dia **35.00**

Frankoma, Patriots/Leaders, white sand glaze, 8-1/2" dia...............**30.00**

Gorham, silver, Paul Revere, George Washington, Minutemen, orig wood box **500.00**

International Pewter, We Are One, orig certificate and box **160.00**

Schmid, Mickey Mouse, orig box .**45.00**

Tray, anodized aluminum, mkd "The United States of America 1776-1976" and "Pepsi 1898-1976," 10-7/8" dia **25.00**

Tumbler, black and metallic gold deco, White House on one side, Capitol on other, "United States Bicentennial 1776-1976".....................................**5.00**

Bicentennial comic book, Dennis the Menace, Yankee Doodle Dennis, red, white, and blue cover, Dennis playing drum, $3.

U.S. mint set, silver, 1976, San Francisco, uncirculated................**30.00**

❖ Bicycles

"Look, Ma! No hands!" Gee, haven't we all shouted that once or twice? And how many of us wish we still had those really nifty old bikes, banana seats and all?

References: Fermo Galbiati and Nino Ciravegna, *Bicycle*, Chronicle Books, 1994; Jim Hurd, *Bicycle Blue Book*, Memory Lane Classics, 1997; Jay Pridmore and Jim Hurd, *The American Bicycle*, Motorbooks International, 1996; Neil S. Wood, *Evolution of the Bicycle*, vol. 1 (1991, 1994 value update), vol. 2 (1994), L-W Book Sales.

Periodicals: *Antique/Classic Bicycle News*, P.O. Box 1049, Ann Arbor, MI 48106; *Bicycle Trader*, P.O. Box 3324, Ashland, OR 97520; *Classic & Antique Bicycle Exchange*, 325 W Hornbeam Dr, Longwood, FL 32779; *Classic Bike News*, 5046 E Wilson Rd, Clio, MI, 48420; *National Antique & Classic Bicycle*, P.O. Box 5600, Pittsburgh, PA 15207.

Collectors' Clubs: Cascade Classic Cycle Club, 7935 SE Market St, Portland, OR 97215; Classic Bicycle and Whizzer Club, 35769 Simon, Clinton Twp, MI 48035; International Veteran Cycle Assoc, 248 Highland Dr, Findlay, OH 45840; The Wheelmen, 55 Bucknell Ave, Trenton, NJ 08619.

For additional listings, see *Warman's Americana & Collectibles.*

Bicycle

Ace Clyde and Motor Works, metal

label, as found cond **150.00**
Columbia, Fire Arrow **300.00**
Huffy, Radiobike **2,000.00**
Murry Jet X-64, girl's **195.00**
Roadmaster, Luxury Liner, restored **620.00**
Schwinn, Corvette **300.00**
Schwinn, Hornet.........................**425.00**
Schwinn, Mark II Jaguar **750.00**
Sears, Elgin, Skylark, very good orig cond **2,250.00**

Book, *Riding High*, A. Judson Palmer, autographed **65.00**

Catalog
Eclipse, Elmira, N.Y. **48.00**
Indian Bicycle **90.00**
Rollfast **70.00**

Dimestore soldier, Manoil, #50, bicycle dispatch rider...............................**50.00**

Display card, Sport Shoes, Xtrulock, 1930s, 11-5/8" x 15-1/2" **30.00**

Handle bar grips, wooden, for high wheeler, unused **65.00**

Ink blotter, Fisk Tires, 6-1/4" x 3-1/2" **15.00**

Magazine tear sheet
Columbia Bicycles, *Saturday Evening Post,* 1949................................**5.00**
Murray Bicycles, Strato-Flite, LeMans and Wildcat, *Boys' Life*, 1966 .....**3.00**
Raleigh, Chopper, *Boys' Life*, 1970**3.00**
Roadmaster, half sheet, *Saturday Evening Post*, 1951.....................**2.00**
Schwinn Bicycles, from back cover, reverse slightly scuffed **2.00**
Sears, The Screamer Bicycle.........**3.00**

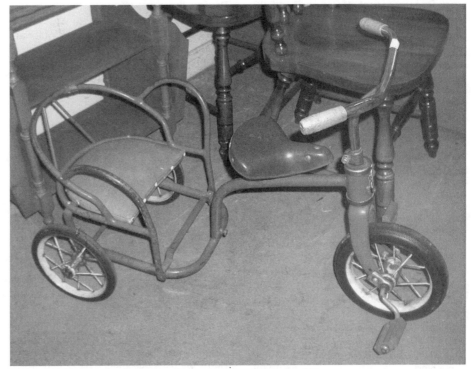

Red tricycle, black seat, back sulky seat with green cushion, slight rusting, $75.

Pin, bicycle shape
Goldtone, front wheel turns, faux pearls, 2-1/4" x 2-5/8" **8.50**
Silvertone, clear stones in center, 2" x 1-1/4" **15.00**
Pinback button, Schwinn, 7/8" dia.**28.00**
Program, Penn Wheelman Frolic, 1927, Minstrels, Orpheum Theater, 64 pgs
....**42.00**
Stickpin, United States Tire Co., brass stickpin of happy bug wearing hat and peddling bicycle, c1920, card with imprint of company 1-1/4" x 3".....**25.00**
Tie tac, Schwinn, gold plated, 1/2" h..**15.00**

❖ Big Little Books

The Whitman Publishing Company first trademarked these books in the 1930s, but the term is also used to describe similar books published by a number of other companies. Several advertisers contracted to use Big Little Books as premiums, including Cocomalt and Kool-Aid. Television characters were introduced to the format in the 1950s.

References: Bill Borden, *The Big Book of Big Little Books*, Chronicle Books, 1997; Larry Jacobs, *Big Little Books*, Collector Books, 1996; Lawrence Lowery, *Lowery's Collector's Guide to Big Little Books and Similar Books*, privately printed, 1981; *Price Guide to Big Little Books & Better Little, Jumbo, Tiny Tales, A Fast-Action Story, etc.*, L-W Book Sales, 1995.

Collectors' Club: Big Little Book Collector Club of America, P.O. Box 1242, Danville, CA 94526.

Buck Rogers, Moons of Saturn........**35.00**
Don Winslow of the Navy................**32.00**
G-Men Breaking the Gambling Ring, #1482, 1942 ....**60.00**
Lone Ranger and the Black Shirt Highwayman, 1939.......................**20.00**
Major Mat Mason, 1968..................**20.00**
Mickey Mouse and Bobo the Elephant, #1160, 1935 ....**85.00**
Mickey Mouse Runs His Own Newspaper, #1409, 1937.............**40.00**
Peggy Brown and the Secret Treasure, #1423 ....**30.00**
Radio Patrol, Outwitting the Gang Chief, 1939, spine torn **15.00**
Skeezix at the Military Academy, #1408, 1938 ....**35.00**
Snow White and the Seven Dwarfs, #1460, 1938 ....**60.00**
Tarzan the Mark of the Red Hyena, #2005, 1967 ....**35.00**
Terry and War in the Jungle, 1946, cover worn **25.00**
The Invaders, Allen Missle Threat, #2012, 1967 ....**30.00**
The Story of Jackie Cooper, 1933, spine missing **20.00**

❖ Billiards

Pool & Billiard magazine, Johnny Archer and Vivian Villameal, Players of the Year, 1993, $5.

"Rack 'em up, boys!" was the resounding cry heard in many pool halls. Today collectors enjoy poking around flea markets looking for vintage pool equipment as well as decorating accessories with a billliards theme.

Ashtray, Joe Camel shooting pool, 6-1/4" x 4-1/2" **20.00**
Balls, Catalin, complete set **60.00**
Bridge, brass mounted standard cue
....**70.00**
Cue case, wall-mounted, ornate Victorian type, painted and ebonized wooden frame **200.00**
Cue chalk, Electric Billiards, red and white box, mkd "Oliver L. Briggs & Son, Boston, Mass.," 7/8" sq **25.00**
Magazine tear sheet, The Irish Skirmishers Blind Pool, from *Puck*, Sept, 1882..................................**25.00**
Mirror, celluloid, advertising "The Wonders Pool Parlors,:" Scranton, Pa., multicolor graphics of topless women surrounded by cherubs, American Art Works, some light surface scratching, 1-3/4" x 2-3/4" **575.00**
Pool cue, Budweiser, Pabst **30.00**

❖ Bing and Grondahl

This Danish company has produced fine-quality Christmas plates for decades. However, many collectors have chosen to branch out and also include some of the company's other products, such as bells and figurines, in their collections.

Reference: Pat Owen, *Bing & Grondahl Christmas Plates*, Landfall Press, 1995.

Periodical: *Collectors Mart Magazine*, 700 E State St, Iola, WI 54990.

Bell
1976, Old North Church, Boston, Mass., 5" h...............................**25.00**
1978, Notre Dame Cathedral **55.00**
1991, Independence Hall, 4" h, MIB
....**30.00**
Cake plate, ftd, sea gull dec **100.00**
Cake plate, triangular, sea gull dec **90.00**
Coffeepot, cov, sea gull dec **200.00**
Compote, sea gull dec, 9-1/2" dia **100.00**
Cup and saucer, sea gull dec **85.00**
Dish, shell, sea gull dec, 6-3/4" **95.00**
Figurine
Boy with accordion, #1991, boy seated on barrel, 9" h **195.00**
English setter, #2015, 8-3/4" h...**350.00**
Fish woman, #2233, old woman sitting on bench, box of eels on one side, basket of flounder and other fish in front, old pail with scales, Axel Locher, 8" l, 7" w....................**500.00**
Girl with doll, #1721, 8" h..........**110.00**
Girl with flowers, #2298, 6" h **140.00**
Penguin, #1821, 3-1/8" h **150.00**
Skier, 8-1/2" h.............................**130.00**
Youthful Boldness, #2162, 7-1/2" h
....**175.00**
Gravy boat, attached underplate, seagull dec **130.00**

Bing and Grondahl Vase, blue, 1932, $20.

Bing and Grondahl Christmas plate, Christmas Peace, 1981, $50.

Limited edition collector plate,
Christmas
Christmas Peace, 1981 ....**35.00**
Country Christmas, 1973 ....**20.00**
Dancing on Christmas Eve, 1999
....**125.00**
Danish village church, 1960.........**85.00**
Limited edition collector plate,
Mother's Day, 6" d
Fox and Cubs, 1979....................**35.00**
Hare and Young, 1971..................**40.00**
Lion and Cubs, 1982.....................**55.00**
Raccoon and Young, 1983 ....**55.00**
Stork and Nestling, 1984..............**50.00**
Woodpecker and Young, 1980 .....**35.00**
Sugar bowl, cov, sea gull dec.........**90.00**
Teapot, cov, seagull dec................**190.00**
Thimble, soaring seagull, mkd "B & G
4831, Made in Denmark" **20.00**
Vase, Pomegranate, painted fruit, leafy
branches and butterfly in relief, shades
of blue, mustard, orange and green, gilt
highlights, B&G stamp in brown on
base, 4" h **275.00**

❖ Birdcages

Birds of a feather flock together, particularly
when kept behind bars. Birdcages have
long been used for the rather mundane and
practical purpose of keeping winged
creatures confined. Now, however,
designers are using them for their
decorative appeal.

Brass
Domed, round, ball finial, wooden
bottom, 1 glass water dish, 13"h, 12"
dia...**55.00**
Hendryx, pagoda style, doors slide up,
1 attached glass feeder, wood swing,
pull-out tray, sgd on bottom, 14"h,
12-1/2" sq **145.00**
Plastic, rectangular, pale green,
engraved floral dec on front and on top
around handle, metal bottom, 2 doors,
with feeders, ladder and perches, 10-
1/2" h, 11" w, 7-1/2" d **85.00**

Birdcages, brass, wooden dowel supports, center hanging loop, $85.

Wire
Black and gold, round, Japanned tin,
ship motifs on sides, orig swings,
perch and hanging pottery feeders, 3
scalloped legs, 18-1/2" h, 10" dia
....**150.00**
Domed, round, painted white, arched
cutout-work door with orig brass
screen and orig brass handle, 3 cast
iron owls clip to hold bottom to top,
orig perches and glass feeders, 14-
1/2" h, 12" dia **125.00**
Hendryx, round, domed top, attached
pedestal, 19" h, 11" dia **40.00**

❖ Birdhouses

Due to their folk art nature, many vintage
birdhouses can be found in collector's living
rooms, as opposed to their usual places in
pine trees and on fence posts. Vintage
birdhouses in good original condition are in
demand, but don't overlook some of the
high-quality contemporary examples on
today's market.

Metal
Contemporary, made from 5 Colorado
license plates, 9" h, 5" l, 5" w ...**18.00**
Vintage, made from 2-qt tin can, orig
gray paint, some rust................**22.50**
Pottery, cottage design in blues, greens
and reds, Louisville Stoneware, 10" h
....**55.00**
Wood
Martin house, 20-hole **60.00**
Vintage, traditional form, metal roof,
orig red paint, 7" h....................**65.00**
Wayne Sims, contemporary , church
design, rough cedar siding, 10" h

Home made birdhouse, wooden, green roof, white sides, yellow trim, $15.

....**20.00**

❖ Bisque

Bisque is a rather generic term used for
china wares that have been fired, but that
have not been glazed. Pieces usually have
a slightly rough texture, and they are highly
susceptible to chips.

Doll
Black, articulated arms and legs, hp
facial features, new dress, 4-1/2" h
....**20.00**
German, 1-pc body and head, sleep
eyes, closed mouth, glued wig, no
clothing, 2-1/2" h.......................**65.00**
Figure
Boy playing mandolin, mkd "Heubach"
....**75.00**
Colonial Boy, Occupied Japan, mkd
"Paulux," 1 finger missing, 6-1/4" h
....**18.00**
Elephant, 4" h...............................**9.00**
Fiddler, Occupied Japan, 3" h........**9.00**
Piano baby, lying on back, left foot in air,
white gown, blue trim, Heubach, 4" l
....**200.00**
Stopper, clown figure, removable hat,
mkd "Germany 6325," 3-3/4" h **25.00**

Two bisque piano babies reclining on stomachs, 9-1/2" long–damaged at leg and 10" l, $70.

Toothbrush holder, Mickey and Minnie Mouse, copyright Walt Disney, mkd "Made in Japan," worn paint, 4-1/2" h **245.00**

❖ Black Memorabilia

Black memorabilia is a term used to describe a very broad field of collectibles. It encompasses Black history and ethnic issues, as well as those items that have impacted our lives from a cultural standpoint. America's flea markets are great sources for Black memorabilia now that more dealers are recognizing the increased popularity of these items.

References: Douglas Congdon-Martin, *Images in Black: 150 Years of Black Collectibles*, 2nd ed, Schiffer, 1999; Kevin Keating and Michael Kolleth, *The Negro Leagues Autograph Guide*, Tuff Stuff Books, 1999; J.L. Mashburn, *Black Postcard Price Guide*, 2nd ed, Colonial House, 1999.

Periodicals: *Blackin*, 559 22nd Ave, Rock Island, IL 61201; *Lookin Back at Black*, 6087 Glen Harbor Dr, San Jose CA 95123.

Collectors' Clubs: Black Memorabilia Collector's Assoc, 2482 Devoe Terrace, Bronx, NY 10468; International Golliwogg Collectors Club, P.O. Box 612, Woodstock, NY 12498.

Reproduction Alert

For additional listings, see *Warman's Antiques & Collectibles* and *Warman's Americana & Collectibles.*

Advertising tin, Durham's Cocoanut **175.00**

Baby Rattle, 8" l, celluloid, figural, standing Black man, top hat and tails, holding bouquet of flowers, white, red, and black, mkd "Made in Japan"..**45.00**

Bank, Mammy, cast iron, 4-1/2" h ...**95.00**

Birthday Card, Black boy blowing out candles on cake, © Hall Brothers, 1940s, 4" x 5".................................**25.00**

Bottle Opener, 7" h, figural, minstrel, painted wood.................................**42.00**

Cigar box, Old Plantation Brand, emb, 11" l...**60.00**

Clock, luncheon type, black women dec, 1950s **45.00**

Comics page, Kemple Duke of Dahomey, 1911 ....**45.00**

Cookbook, *Dixie Southern Cookbook* **50.00**

Dart board, tin over cardboard, Sambo, name on straw hat, Wyandotte Toy Mfg., dents and scratch, 23" h, 14" w **80.00**

Dice, multicolor, spring activated, mkd

Black Memorabilia, Front: Bell, cloth doll type handle, $29; rear: Mammy cookie jar, McCoy Pottery, $165.

"Alco Britain HK" **90.00**

Doll, Cream of Wheat Chef, stuffed cloth, 1960s **80.00**

Game, The Game of Hitch Hiker, Whitman, 1937 ....**75.00**

Humidor, majolica, boy sitting on large melon, pipe in hand, small chip on foot and top, 10-1/2" h.......................**875.00**

Lunch box, Dixie Kid Cut Plug, litho tin **290.00**

Magazine, *Life*, Dec 8, 1972, featuring Diana Ross on cover...................**18.00**

Magic Lantern Slide, man playing banjo **24.00**

Needle Book, Luzianne Coffee adv**22.50**

Nodder, 4-1/4" h, painted metal, boy in yellow hat, smoking cigar, mkd "Occupied Japan".........................**55.00**

Notepad and pencil holder, painted hard plastic, Mammy, insert pencil as broomstick in one hand, orig paper label, 1950s...............................**150.00**

Photograph, unidentified subject
Little boy in front of train...............**75.00**
Man in formal dress, graduation, 1910 ....**45.00**

Piebird, black boy scout, yellow uniform, brown hat, mkd "England," 3-1/2" h, light stains **65.00**

Pinback button
I Raise You, black man in uniform holding cable with word "elevator" next to him, art by Goldberg.....**40.00**
Ten Days-Smoke Up, caricature of black man standing before judge, art by Tep, c1912, 7/8" d **35.00**

Pitcher, Mandy, Omnibus..............**160.00**

Poster
Paper, black man saying good-bye to wife and going off to war, colored

regiment marching by, 1918, framed, 19-1/2" h, 15-1/2" w.................**75.00**
Cardboard, "Ragtime Jubilee, Big Time Minstrel Review," 22" h, 14" w ..**25.00**

Pot hanger, chalkware, black boy and girl, wire hook, 7-1/2" x 5-1/2"....**125.00**

Ramp walker, multicolor, USA, c1920 ....**65.00**

Recipe holder, Mammy, wood........**45.00**

Reservation card, Coon Chicken Inn **100.00**

Salt and pepper shakers, pr
Jemima & Uncle Mose, F & F, damaged..................................**35.00**
Mammy & Chef, 5" h...................**55.00**
Mammy & Chef, ceramic, 8" h, Japan, 1940s......................................**115.00**
Native on Hippo........................**215.00**
Salty and Peppy, Pearl China.....**245.00**

Sheet music, Sam the Accordion Man **20.00**

Sign, diecut cardboard
Gold Dust Washing Powder, Gold Dust Twins shown on package, large letter 'L' on top, formerly part of larger hanging sign, 13-1/2" h, 9-1/2" w **60.00**
Hambone Sweets, color graphics on both sides, black caricature aviator smiling and puffing on cigar while seated in aircraft, titled "Going Over," orig string loop handle, late 1920s, 7" dia.....................................**38.00**

Tea towel, boy and girl eating watermelon, pr **25.00**

Toy
Dancing Dan, in front of lamp post on stage, microphone remote attached to stage, 13" h, MIB...............**375.00**
Trapeze Artist, squeeze type, painted wood **45.00**

Wall Pocket, Blackamoor, mkd "Royal Copley".......................................**70.00**

❖ Blenko

Blenko handcrafted glass was made in Milton, W.Va. Interesting crackle glass items and a reliance on strong colors have earned the company a place in the hearts of many. Original labels read "Blenko Handcraft" and are shaped like a hand.

Beaker, crackle, crystal body, applied blue rosettes, 9-1/2" h **135.00**

Bottle, amberina, style 64B, orig silver label, 10" h **40.00**

Decanter, amber, 8" h..................**115.00**

Paperweight, crab, orange, orig label, 4-1/8" dia **10.00**

Pitcher
Crackle, amberina, applied amber handle, 10" h **150.00**
Crackle, blue, long applied handle

....**110.00**
Crackle, red, yellow handle, 6" h..**55.00**
Williamsburg reproduction, aqua..**50.00**
Sculpture, owl, dark amber, orig label, 6-7/8" h..**75.00**
Vase
4" h, double neck, turquoise.........**50.00**
6-1/2" h, blue, 1960s **70.00**
8" h, ruby red, crimped, ftd, 1950s
....**150.00**
9" h, crackle, avocado green......**115.00**
9-1/4" h, emerald green, fluted, pontil
scar..**95.00**
9-1/2" h, crystal, four applied blue
rosettes, orig label **135.00**
10-1/2" h, crackle, reddish-orange
body, crimped top **135.00**
17" h, crackle, orange **135.00**

❖ Blue & White Pottery/Stoneware

Although termed blue-and-white, this category also includes blue-and-gray pottery and stoneware. Widely produced from the late 19th century through the 1930s, these items were originally marketed as inexpensive wares for everyday household use. Butter crocks, pitchers, and saltboxes are among the most commonly found pieces. Many examples feature a white or gray body with an embossed geometric, floral, or fruit pattern. The piece was then highlighted with bands and splashes of blue to accentuate the molded pattern.

Collectors' Club: Blue & White Pottery Club, 224 12th St NW, Cedar Rapids, IA 52405.

Reproduction Alert

Bowl
Apricot pattern, milk bowl, 4" h, 9-1/2"
dia...**80.00**
Flying Birds, berry bowl..............**125.00**

Butter crock
Colonial, with lid, 4-1/4" h **375.00**
Cows, minor base flakes, lid missing
large piece **225.00**
Daisy & Trellis, with lid, minor glaze
flake at bail **80.00**
Canister
"Cereal," basketweave, no lid **385.00**
"Coffee," basketweave, inner rim chips,
mended lid **75.00**
"Raisins," basketweave, with lid..**350.00**
Meat tenderizer, Wildflower, crazed,
replaced handle.........................**375.00**
Pitcher
Cherries and leaves, 8-1/2" h.....**195.00**
Daisy cluster, bulbous, 7" h........**495.00**
Dutch Boy & Girl, 6-1/2" h..........**125.00**
Swirl, relief scroll design, 11" h, short
hairline **90.00**
Salt box, hanging, 6" dia, 6" h
Good Luck pattern, orig lid present, but
broken, surface chipping **50.00**
Honecomb pattern with relief apricot,
replaced wood lid, surface chipping
....**65.00**
Relief butterfly design, matching lid,
base chips **100.00**

❖ Blue Ridge Pottery

Erwin, Tenn., was home to Southern Potteries, Inc., chartered in 1920. By 1938 the company was producing Blue Ridge dinnerware, marketing the items as "Hand Painted Under the Glaze." Most of their competitors used decals to create designs, and Southern Potteries was able to capitalize on this difference. The colorful, cheery floral patterns made Blue Ridge dinnerware a favorite with consumers. However, inexpensive imports and a move toward plastic dinnerware forced the company out of business in 1957.

References: Betty and Bill Newbound, *Best of Blue Ridge Dinnerware*, Collector Books, 2003; ——, *Collector's Encyclopedia of Blue Ridge Dinnerware*, Collector Books,

1994; ——, *Southern Potteries, Inc.*, 3rd ed, Collector Books, 1989 (1995 value update); Frances and John Ruffin, *Blue Ridge China Today*, Schiffer Publishing, 2000; ——, *Blue Ridge China Traditions*, Schiffer Publishing, 1999.

Periodicals: *Blue Ridge Beacon Magazine*, P.O. Box 629, Mountain City, GA 30562; Blue Ridge Quarterly, www.blueridgechina.com; *National Blue Ridge Newsletter*, 144 Highland Dr, Blountville, TN 37617.

Collectors' Club: Blue Ridge Collectors Club, 208 Harris St, Erwin, TN 37650.

For additional listings, see *Warman's Americana & Collectibles* and *Warman's American Pottery & Porcelain*.

Ashtray, Chintz **35.00**
Bon bon
Easter Parade, flat.....................**150.00**
Iris, center handle, 4-section......**150.00**
Cake plate
Nocturne, yellow, matching server
....**140.00**
Verna, maple leaf shape **125.00**
Celery, leaf, 11" l..........................**145.00**
Cigarette box
Ships **100.00**
Seaside **175.00**
Rooster..**195.00**
Cream and sugar, footed
Easter Parade, sugar only............**58.00**
Rose Marie..................................**140.00**
Rose of Sharon **140.00**
Dinnerware Set
Gloriosa, Skyline shape, 20 pcs **250.00**
Stanhouse Ivy, 45 pcs **425.00**
Winnie, Skyline shape, 31 pcs ...**325.00**
Pitcher
Alice, 8-1/2" w **330.00**
Sculptured Fruit, 6-1/2" h **135.00**
Plate, dinner
Christmas Tree, 10" dia **135.00**
Ham and Eggs, 9" dia **155.00**
Red Velvet, 10" dia **25.00**
Sweet Clover, 10" dia **22.00**
Plate, salad
Country Fair, green edge **30.00**

Blue and White Stoneware, bean pot, cov, molded figures of children at table, marked "Boston Baked Beans," wear, 6" h, $250.

Blue Ridge Pottery, creamer and sugar, Colonial pattern, yellow flower, $15.

Duff, set of 8	**225.00**
Flower Bowl	**30.00**
Honolulu	**30.00**
Relish tray, Iris, 4 sections	**150.00**
Salad bowl, Candlewick	**85.00**
Shaker, footed	
Dog Tooth Violet, pr	**115.00**
Floral Blossom, pr	**125.00**
Nova Leda, pr	**89.00**
Rose of Marie, pr	**95.00**
Rose of Sharon, pr	**35.00**
Snack set, Colonial, plate and cup	**.48.00**
Turkey platter, hp turkey in center, 17-1/4" l, 12-3/4" w	**330.00**

Blue Willow Plate, Johnson Brothers, dinner size, $12.

Boehm Plate, Young America, Symbol of the Republic, 1973, gold trimmed edge, orig box, $90.

❖ Blue Willow

This intricate pattern features a weeping willow along the banks of a river by a Japanese village. More than 200 manufacturers have produced items with variations of this pattern, generally blue on a white background. Josiah Spode first introduced the pattern in 1810, and it is still being used today.

References: Mary Frank Gaston, *Blue Willow*, 2nd ed, Collector Books, 1990 (2000 value update); Jennifer A. Lindbeck, *A Collector's Guide to Willow Ware*, Schiffer Publishing, 2000.

Periodicals: *American Willow Report*, P.O. Box 900, Oakridge, OR 97463; *The Willow Transfer Quarterly, Willow Word*, P.O. Box 13382, Arlington, TX 76094.

Collectors' Clubs: International Willow Collectors, P.O. Box 13382, Arlington, TX 76094-0382; Willow Society, 39 Medhurst Rd, Toronto Ontario M4B 1B2 Canada.

Blue Willow Teapot, tall sq body, base mkd "Ringtons Limited Tea Merchants Newcastle upon Tyne, Reg. No. 740055," $95.

Berry bowl, Homer Laughlin, small	**..6.50**
Bouillon and underplate, Ridgway	**85.00**
Cake plate, Newport Pottery Co., 1920	**250.00**
Cereal bowl, unmarked	**8.00**
Child's tea set, 14 pcs, orig box	**175.00**
Creamer and sugar, Allerton	**125.00**
Cup and saucer	
Buffalo Pottery	**25.00**
Shenango	**15.00**
Demitasse cup and saucer, mkd "Allerton"	**15.00**
Dessert plate, unmarked	**5.00**
Funnel	**85.00**
Gravy boat, mkd "Willow, Woods Ware, Woods & Sons, England," 8-1/4" l	**100.00**
Grill plate, mkd "Moriyama," 10-1/2" dia	**45.00**
Lamp, table, 1940s, 12" h	**250.00**
Mustard pot, cov, unmarked, rough edges, 3" h	**110.00**
Oil lamp, blue and white ceramic base, 1950s	**85.00**
Pie plate, 10" dia	**50.00**
Plate, dinner	
Booth's	**65.00**
Buffalo Pottery	**20.00**
Dudson, Wilcox & Till Ltd., Hanley, England, 10" dia, set of 10	**325.00**
Unmarked	**8.00**
Platter, unmarked, 11" x 13-1/2"	**165.00**
Soup bowl, unmarked	**10.00**
Teapot, cov, emb "Sadler, England"	**165.00**
Tray, metal, wear	**15.00**
Vegetable bowl, open, round, mkd "J. & G. Meakin"	**65.00**
Water set, 9" h pitcher, six 3-5/8" h tumblers, orig "Japan" paper labels	**245.00**

❖ Boehm Porcelain

From humble beginnings in a studio in Trenton, N.J., Edward Marshall Boehm has created exquisite porcelain sculptures. A second production site, Boehm Studios, was opened in Malvern, England, in the early 1970s and is still in business today.

Collectors' Club: Boehm Porcelain Society, P.O. Box 5051, Trenton, NJ 08638.

Limited-edition plate, Lenox China, 24 kt gold edge, orig box, certificate	
American Redstart, 1975	**70.00**
Baby Eagle	**90.00**
Mountain Bluebirds, 1972	**100.00**
Swan	**70.00**
Sculpture	
Baby cardinal, as is	**50.00**
Baby cedar wax wing	**80.00**
Black cap chickadee	**150.00**
Fledging gold finch	**90.00**
Fledging magpie	**90.00**
Fledging red poll	**80.00**
Fledging robin	**90.00**
Indigo Bunting	**170.00**
Great Dane, seated, paws extended	**275.00**
Grosbeck	**325.00**
Hummingbird, perched on flowering cactus	**200.00**
Open rose, pink edges, needs to be attached to base	**12.50**
Orchid oriole, pair of birds on flowering branch	**675.00**
Pink rose, small, individual flower	**..2.50**
Rabbit, sitting	**40.00**
Rabbit, sleeping	**35.00**
Rabbit, standing	**40.00**
Rabbit with young	**70.00**
Yellow throated warbler, hibiscus flower	**170.00**

❖ Bookends

These useful objects can be found in almost every medium and range from purely functional to extraordinarily whimsical.

Art Deco, bronze clad, Egyptian scribes, greenish-black, lighter green highlights, c1920 ....**350.00**

Bookends, Art Deco style, light green marble with white striations, rect blocks with round orb, $35.

Art Nouveau, nude winged dancing nymph, flowing scarf, copper colored cast iron, stamped "Designe Pat. 1154" **285.00**

Cherub holding butterfly and book, kneeling among ferns and cattails, bronze finish over white metal, orig felt base, 1924, 4" w, 2" d, 6-1/4v h.**330.00**

Cocker spaniels, chalkware, 5-1/2" h **30.00**

Elephant, Rookwood Pottery, ivory color, 1936, 5-1/2" h, 6" l **225.00**

Gardenia, Roseville Pottery, gray and white, pr......................................**200.00**

Horse, rearing, L.E. Smith, emerald green glass, 8" h **55.00**

Indian brave, chiseled face of native American, metal, green felt back, 6-1/2" h, 4-1/4" w, 2-1/8" d **75.00**

Indian chief bust, leather headdress **130.00**

Knights on charging horse, bronze, 1920s, 4" w, 8-1/4" h **285.00**

Native American motif, bronze, One Feather, sgd "F.W.E.T.," 4" w, 2" d, 6-3/8" h **350.00**

Nuart, boy in cap and knickers, girl with bonnet and dress, holding doll, book shaped back and base, bronze finish over pot metal, orig felt, 3-1/4" w, 3-3/4" d, 5" h **285.00**

Stagecoach, pulled by 2 teams of horses, "Old Coaching Days" on base, bronze-finish metal, 4-1/4" h, pr...**45.00**

Terriers, cast iron, orig paint and felt, 4-3/4" w, 2" d, 4-5/8" d **280.00**

❖ Bookmarks

Ranging from delicate filagreed clips to intricately embroidered fabric to simple cardboard shapes, bookmarks have assisted readers for decades. Interesting examples can be found at flea markets if one looks carefully.

Periodical: *Bookmark Collector*, 1002 W 25th St, Erie, PA 16502.

Collectors' Club: Antique Bookmark Collector's Assoc, 2224 Cherokee St, St. Louis, MO 63118.

Advertising

Cruver Co., diecut thin celluloid topped by red and yellow roses, green rose bud and leafy stems, lower half black and white text, 1912 Newark Industrial Exposition **35.00**

Erlanger Theatre, Chicago, showing Romeo & Juliet, with Norma Shearer and Leslie Howard, 1936, info on back regarding Chicago Public Library......................................**20.00**

Kirk Johnson & Co., pianos and organs, Lebanon, PA, little Victorian girl in pink dress, carrying bouquet of pink roses, 2" x 6".....................**15.00**

Poll Parrot shoes, die-cut cardboard, "They Speak for Themselves," 3-3/4" x 1-1/2" **12.00**

Cloth, Abraham Lincoln, oval silhouette, quote from Gettysburg Address, black on cream, with orig sales card, c1935, 5-1/2" h......................................**20.00**

Cross stitch on punched paper, "Love," beige, salmon and green dec, 6-1/4" l **9.00**

Embroidered, "Week of Birthdays," flowers in metallic red thread, poem, 8-1/2" x 2"......................................**75.00**

Photograph on paper, young woman **5.00**

Plastic

Donald Duck figural, "Book Mark, Disneyland," hand-painted **26.00**

Lord's Prayer, die-cut cross, page-holder type, 4-3/4" x 1-1/4".........**6.00**

Silver plated, Apollo Silver Co., scrolling letter "A", c1900...........................**35.00**

Bookmarks, Victorian, Thou God Seest Me, bird on floral branch, 1-11/16" w, 5" l, $2.

Sterling silver, Gorham, etched "C" with floral engraving.............................**25.00**

World's Fair, 1964-65 New York World's Fair, celluloid **35.00**

❖ Books

All types of books can be found flea markets. A book's value can be increased by a great binding, an early copyright, a first printing, interesting illustrations, an original dustjacket, or a famous author. At flea markets, prices for books can range from a dime to thousands of dollars.

Many book collectors are turning to their computers and using the Internet to find books. There are several sites devoted to antique books and also several ways to search for titles.

To remove a musty smell from a book, sprinkle baking soda onto several pages, close, and let it rest for a few days. When you remove the baking soda, the smell should disappear. Avoid books with mold, or you might be bringing home a big problem.

References: *American Book Prices Current*, Bancroft Parkman, published annually; Sharon and Bob Huxford, *Huxford's Old Book Value Guide*, 11th ed, Collector Books, 1999.

Periodicals: *AB Bookman's Weekly*, P.O. Box AB, Clifton, NJ 07015; *Biblio Magazine*, 845 Wilamette St, P.O. Box 10603, Eugene, OR 97401; *Book Source Monthly*, 2007 Syosett Dr, P.O. Box 567, Cazenovia, NY 13035; *Rare Book Bulletin*, P.O. Box 201, Peoria, IL 61650; *The Book Collector's Magazine*, P.O. Box 65166, Tucson, AZ 85728.

Collectors' Club: Antiquarian Booksellers Assoc of America, 20 West 44th St, 4th Floor, New York, NY 10036.

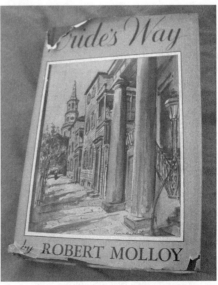

Books, Robert Molloy, Pride's Way, *MacMillan Co, 1945, tears to orig dj, $5.*

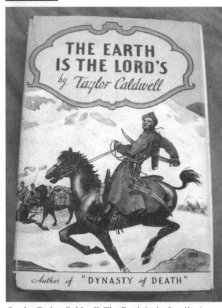

Books, Taylor Caldwell, The Earth is the Lord's, A Tale of the Rise of Genghis Khan, *Literary Guild of America, 1960, wear to orig dg, $8.*

TIAS Top 10
The following list ranks the most highly sought collectibles on the Internet during 2001. Books moved up on the list since their 2000 listing.
1. China
2. Cookie jars
3. Dolls
4. Furniture
5. Lamps
6. Carnival glass
7. Books
8. Plates
9. Depression Glass
10. Roseville
Source: www.tias.com
The following listings are a mere sampling of the many books that may be found at flea markets.

Agatha Christie, An Autobiography, Agatha Christie, Dodd, Mead, 1977, illus, 1st ed, dj **12.00**
A Lovely Find, Wm Allen Knight, Wilde Co., 1943, 41 pgs.........................**10.00**
America's Colorful Railroads, Don Bal Jr., Bonanza Books, 1980.................**15.00**
Ancient Evenings, Norman Mailer, Little Brown, 1st ed., sgd by author **20.00**
Billy, The Classic Hitter, Billy Williams, Rand McNally, 1974, 1st ed, dj **15.00**
Christmas in Germany, Peter Andrews, World Book, Inc., 1974, 64 pgs....**12.00**
East Wind West Wind, Pearl S. Buck, 1930, 3rd printing, dj **22.50**
Foil Travelers, Ballads, Tales, and Talk, Texas Folklore Society, No. 25, So Methodist Press, 1953 ....**8.00**

Footprints of the Pioneers in the Ohio Valley, a Centennial Sketch, 1788-1888, Venable, 1888, illus **125.00**
Jenny Lind's America, Frances Cavannah, Chilton Book Co., 1969**7.00**
John Jay Janney's Virginia, An American Farm Lad's Life in Early 19th C, Asa Moore Janney, EPM Publications, 1978, illus, map **4.50**
John Muir's Longest Walk: John Earl, A Photographer, Traces His Journey to Florida, John Earl, Doubleday, 1971, 1st ed **15.00**
Louisana Purchase, Robert Tallant, Random House, 1952 ....**7.00**
Moonspender, Jonathan Gash, St Martin's Press, 1987, 215 pgs, dj.**22.50**
Once A Wilderness, Arthur Poiund, Reynard & Hitchcock, 1934...........**6.00**
Petals Plucked from Sunny Climes, Silvia Sunshine, 1879, fold-out map of Florida **45.00**
Plowing on Sunday, Sterling North, MacMillan, 1934, 1st ed **10.00**
Ramona, Helen Jackson, Little Brown & Co., 1916, 457 pgs.................**7.00**
Romance of a Christmas Card, Kate Douglas Wiggins, Houghton Mifflin, 1916, 124 pgs **35.00**
Samson Occom and the Christian Indians of New England, Wm D. Love, Pilgrim Press, 1899, 1st ed.........**60.00**
Seven Pillars of Wisdom, T.E. Lawrence, Doubleday Doran, 1935, 1st ed, dj **25.00**
Temple Houston, Lawyer with a Gun: Biography of Sam Houston's Son, Shirley, Univ. of Oklahoma, 1981, 339 pgs **38.00**
The Correspondence of John Cleves Symmes, Founder of the Miami Purchase, Bonc, 1926, 312 pgs, ex-library **75.00**
The Flirt, Booth Tarkington, Scribners, 1916 ....**6.50**
The Glory of Giving, Grace Noll Crowell, Augsburg Pub Co., 1945, 45 pgs.**10.00**
The Illiterate Digest, Will Rogers, Albert & Chase, 1924, dwgs by Nate Collier **10.00**
The Shepherd, Frederick Forsyth, Viking Press, 1976 ....**12.00**
The Shoe, Willie Shoemaker's Illustrated Book of Racing, Willie Shoemaker, Rand McNally, 1976, 1st ed. **15.00**
Town Planning in Frontier America, Reps, Princeton Univ, 1969, 473 pgs, 135 plans, maps, photos **85.00**
Treasure of Christmas Crafts & Foods, Better Homes & Gardens, Meredith Corp, 1980, 384 pgs **12.00**
Twelve Brave Boys Who Became Famous Men, Esther E. Enock, Pickering &

Ingils, 1940s **8.00**
Wild Bill Hickock Tames The West, Stewart H. Holbrook, Landmark/Random House, 1952 ...**7.00**
Within the Iron Gates, F. Rafer, Times Mirror, 1988, illus..........................**6.50**

❖ Books, Children's

Flea markets are great places to look for children's books, and examples with interesting illustrations are particularly sought. Because condition is critical in determining price, check carefully for crayon illustrations by budding young artists. Likewise, make sure all the pages are there.

References: E. Lee Baumgarten, *Price Guide for Children's & Illustrated Books for the Years 1880–1960,* self-published, 1996; David & Virginia Brown, *Whitman Juvenile Books,* Collector Books, 1997; Diane McClure Jones and Rosemary Jones, *Collector's Guide to Children's Books, 1850 to 1950,* Collector Books, 1997; ---, *Collector's Guide to Children's Books, 1950-1975,* Collector Books, 2000; E. Christian Mattson and Thomas B. Davis, *A Collector's Guide to Hardcover Boys' Series Books,* self-published, 1996.

Periodicals: *Book Source Monthly,* 2007 Syossett Dr, P.O. Box 567, Cazenovia, NY 13035; *Martha's KidLit Newsletter,* P.O. Box 1488, Ames, IA 50010; *Mystery & Adventure Series Review,* P.O. Box 3488, Tucson, AZ 85722; *The Authorized Edition Newsletter,* RR1, Box 73, Machias, ME 04654; *Yellowback Library,* P.O. Box 36172, Des Moines, IA 50315.

Collectors' Clubs: Many specialized collector clubs exist.

A Child's Garden of Verses, R. L. Stevenson, Schribner, 1885, 1st ed. **145.00**
Alice's Adventures in Wonderland, Lewis Carroll, Harper, 1901, 1st ed., color plates, some lifting to cover **175.00**
Children's Praise & Worship for Sunday School, A. L. Byers, Anderson College, Ind., 1928 ....**6.50**
Elsie's Girlhood, Martha Finley, Dodd, Mead & Co., 1872, emb pansies on cover...**20.00**
Guess Who, Dick & Jane, Scott Foresman, 1951 ....**45.00**
How the Grinch Stole Christmas, Dr. Seuss, 1957, red and green cover **25.00**
Jo's Boys, Louisa May Alcott, 1918, 10 plates, top edges gold..................**10.00**
Joyful Poems for Children, James W. Riley, 1946, 1st ed......................**28.00**
Mattie's Home, S.W. Partridge & Co., London, red cover **25.00**

Mother Goose In Silhouettes, Katherine Buffum, 1907, 1st ed, few minor tears **37.50**
Pollyana Grows Up, E.H. Porter, H.W. Taylor illus, 1915, 1st ed **22.00**
Raggedy Ann in the Snow White Castle, Johnny Gruelle, Bobbs-Merrill, 1960, 95 pgs **21.50**
Rebecca of Sunnybook Farm, Kate Douglas Wiggins, Hough Mifflin, 1903 ....**25.00**
Stories from Hans Andersen, Edward Dulac, 15 color pictures **135.00**
The Birds' Christmas Carol and Polly Oliver's Problem, Kate Douglas Wiggin, Grosset & Dunlap, 1951, 220 pgs**25.00**
The Haunted Bridge, Nancy Drew, Grosset & Dunlap, 1937, 1st ed., illus by Russell Tandy **45.00**
The Little Mother Goose, Jessie Willcox Smith, Dodd Mead, 1918, color pic on front cover, 176 pgs.....................**80.00**
The Water Babies, Charles Kingsley, Dodd Mead, 1916, illus by Jessie W. Smith, color pic on front cov **70.00**
The Whispering Statue, Nancy Drew, Grosset & Dunlap, 1937, 1st ed., illus by Russell Tandy **45.00**
Tom Swift & Airline Express, Whitman #2166, orig wrap-around dj illus by T Kerrs...............................**45.00**
Treasure Island, Robert Louis Stevenson, illus by Paul Frame, Whitman, 1955 ....**5.00**
Uncle Arthur's Bedtime Stories, 1976, Arthur S. Maxwell, 5 vol set **25.00**

❖ Bootjacks

Designed to ease the removal of boots, bootjacks were primarily made of cast iron or wood. The heel of a boot is placed in the U-shaped opening at the front of the jack, the other foot is placed on the rear of the jack, and the boot is pried off the front foot. Examples range from crude, one-of-a-kind versions to examples with elaborate, artistic castings and carvings.

In 1852 the United States Patent Office awarded its first patent for a bootjack to Saris Thomson of Hartsville, Mass.

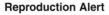

Reproduction Alert

Bootjacks, Wooden, plain, wrought iron nails, hole for hanging, $20.

Beetle, cast iron, mkd "Depose," French, 10-1/2" l......................................**50.00**
Double pistol, cast iron, mkd "From Younder E Bros.," **205.00**
Lee Riders, wooden, small pc of rubber missing, 12" l.............................**35.00**
Naughty Nellie
  Antique, cast iron, 9-1/2" l...........**80.00**
  Reproduction, cast iron, 9" l.........**10.00**
Scrolled design with horseshoe end, Victorian, cast iron, 11" l...........**195.00**
Scrolled design with V-shaped end, openwork design of intertwined stems, cast iron, 12" l **45.00**
Wooden, homemade
  Tiger maple, 10" l.........................**30.00**
  Pine, oval ends, sq nails, 25" l.....**30.00**
  Walnut, carved heart and openwork, 22" l...**45.00**

❖ Bottle Openers

Back in the "dark ages" before pull tops and twist off tops, folks actually used these wonderful bottle openers. Today collectors seek them out at flea markets. Some collectors prefer the figural types and try to find interesting examples with good paint. Other collectors concentrate on finding interesting advertising bottle openers.

Collectors' Clubs: Figural Bottle Opener Collectors Club, 3 Ave A, Latrobe, PA 15650; Just for Openers, 3712 Sunningdale Way, Durham, NC 22707.

For additional listings, see *Warman's Americana & Collectibles*.

Reproduction Alert

Bottle Openers, Advertising, Duquesne Brewing Co., Pittsburgh, PA, aluminum, hand shaped opener, 3-3/4" l, $5.

Atlanta 1996 Centennial Olympic Games, shows American flag, 4-1/2" l **12.00**
Bell Telephone hard hat, cast iron, MIB **50.00**
Benson & Hedges 100's, bottle opener and keychain, metal, 1-1/2" x 3-1/2" **10.00**
Biltmore Hotel, Los Angeles, mkd "Vaughn USA," slight rust **10.00**
Black boy and alligator, figural, cast iron, 2-3/4" h.............................**145.00**
Canada Dry, metal, 3-1/8" l **3.50**
Champagne bottle type, mkd "Rogar" **10.00**
Coca-Cola, wall-mount, Starr X type, cast iron, some rust.....................**22.00**
Coors, America's Fine Light Beer, Ekco, Chicago, U.S. Pat. Pending **6.00**
Drunk on a lamp post, cast iron, paint chips, 4-3/8" h **15.00**
Edelweiss Beer, A Case of Good Judgement, metal, 4-3/4" l **3.00**
Figural, wood, boy, blue hat, yellow yard hair, 3-1/2" l, slight wear to paint....**6.50**
Falstaff Beer, wall-mount, Starr X type, orig box **24.00**
Guitar-shaped bottle opener and nodder, opener sticks to magnet on front of nodder figure **25.00**
Heintz 57, bottle shape **14.00**
Leg shape, brass, 3" l....................**22.00**
Miller Brewing Co., metal, some rust **3.00**
Old Crow, wooden figure, bottle opener under head, corkscrew hidden in leg,

holding cane, 7-3/4" h, chip on hat brim
....**10.00**
Pabst, metal, some rust **2.00**
Parrot on stand, cast iron, mkd "JW"
(John Wright), 5-1/4" h **95.00**
Royal Crown Cola, Best Taste Calls for
RC **5.00**
SAS, Scandinavian airlines, hard plastic,
3-1/2" l..**9.25**
Singing cowboy, cast iron, 4-3/4" h
....**95.00**
Walt Disney World, 4-1/2" l **5.00**

❖ Bottles

Many types of bottles are found at flea markets. Prices vary according to rarity, condition, and color. Several excellent reference books are available to assist collectors.

References: Antique Trader Bottles: Identification and Price Guide, Michael Polak, Krause Publications, 2002.

Periodicals: Antique Bottle and Glass Collector, P.O. Box 187, East Greenville, PA 18041; Canadian Bottle and Stoneware Collector, 179D Woodridge Crescent, Nepean, Ontario K2B 7T2 Canada.

Collectors' Clubs: American Collectors of Infant Feeders, 5161 W 59th St, Indianapolis, IN 46254; Federation of Historical Bottle Collectors, Inc; 1485 Buck Hill Dr, Southampton, PA 18966; Midwest Antique Fruit Jar & Bottle Club, P.O. Box 38, Flat Rock, IN 47234; New England Antique Bottle Club, 120 Commonwealth Rd, Lynn, MA 01904.

For additional listings, see *Warman's Antiques & Collectibles Price Guide* and *Warman's Glass.*

The following listings are a mere sampling of the bottles that may be found at flea markets.

Acme Nursing Bottle, clear, lay-down
type, emb **70.00**
Bull Dog Brand Liquid Glue, aqua, ring

Bottles, Figural, violin shape, cobalt blue, white price tag, modern, $8.

collar..**6.50**
Calla Nurser, oval, clear, emb, ring on
neck..**8.50**
Cole & Southey, Washington, D.C., soda
water, aquamarine......................**110.00**
Dr. Ham's Aromatic Invigorating Spirit,
cylindrical, applied mouth, smooth
base, c1875-85, orange-amber, 8-1/2"
h **65.00**
Gogings Wild Cherry Tonic, sq, beveled
corners, tooled mouth, smooth base,
c1890-1900, medium amber, 8-3/4" h
....**90.00**
Kranks Cold Cream, milk glass **6.50**
Lysol, cylindrical, amber, emb "Not to be
Taken"...**12.00**
Missiquoi Springs, apricot-amber,
applied sloping collared mouth with
ring, smooth base, 1-qt **150.00**

Bottles, Hires Improved Root Beer, Makes Five Gallons of Delicious Drink, Manufactured by the Charles Hires Co., Phila, Pa, USA, emb lettering, light blue, 4-5/8" l, $20.

Bottles, Cologne bottle, MacGregor Cologne for Men, horsehead shaped clear bottle, goldtone cap, $2.

Mother's Comfort, clear, turtle type**25.00**
Neamand's Drug Store, clear **30.00**
Owl Drug Co., owl sitting on mortar,
cobalt blue...................................**70.00**
Pre Cream Rye, bartender's type ...**35.00**
Shaker Family Pills, Dose 2 to 4, A.J.
White, rect, paneled sides, sheared lip,
smooth base, c1890-1900, medium
amber, 2-1/4" h...........................**95.00**
Sloan's Liniment, castor oil...........**20.00**
Violet Dulce Vanishing Cream, eight
panels, 2-1/2" h **7.50**

❖ Boxes

Collectors love boxes of all kinds. Interior decorators also scout flea markets for useful boxes. The colorful labels of these vintage packages are delightful to display. Locked boxes offer the mystery of a treasure inside, but don't be lured into paying too much.

Adams Sappota Chewing Gum, 7-1/2"
x 8-1/2", two Victorian ladies, graphic
labels...**90.00**
Apple, pine, old red paint, conical feet, 9-
3/4" x 10" x 4" h **310.00**
Baker's Chocolate, wood, 12-lb size
....**25.00**
Book shape, green onyx, brass and
wood trim, wear and chips, 5" l..**165.00**
Candle, hanging, pine and hardwood, old
worn gray paint, 10-1/4" w **330.00**
Candy box, Whitman's Pleasure Island
Chocolates, cardboard, pirate scenes
on 5 sides, map on bottom, 1924 **28.00**
Collar box, gold paper ground, pink,
green and yellow flowers, clear
celluloid overlay, pretty woman in
center **175.00**
Dome top, cast brass, relief eagle and
crowns, English, 19th C, 4" l **175.00**

Boxes, Wooden box, Oriental dec of man driving cart over bridge, ivory and wood inlay, small ivory knob, $20.

Dresser, white ground, small pink flowers and green leaves, mkd "Nippon," rect **35.00**
Heart shape, silver-plated, small gold bow trim, velvet lining **35.00**
King Brand Rolled Oats **45.00**
Lacquer, red ground, Oriental scenes, red velvet lining **15.00**
Ladies Favorite Polish, paper label **10.00**
National Lead Co., paint chip samples **25.00**
Pine, worn orig brown graining, yellow ground, machine dovetails, 16-1/4" l **200.00**
Snuff, shoe shaped, curved toe, worn black lacquer, inlaid pewter trim, 3" l **225.00**
Ward Baking Co., wood **100.00**
Williams Brothers Valvriggans, men's long underwear **15.00**

❖ Boy Scouts

The Boy Scout pledge has been recited by millions of youngsters throughout the years. Collectibles relating to scouting troops, jamborees, etc., are eagerly sought and readily found at flea markets.

Reference: George Cuhaj, *Standard Price Guide to U. S. Scouting Collectibles 2nd Ed.*, Krause Publications, 2001.

Periodicals: *Fleur-de-Lis*, 5 Dawes Ct, Novato, CA, 94947; *Scout Memorabilia*, P.O. Box 1121, Manchester, NH 03105.

Collectors' Clubs: American Scouting Traders Assoc, P.O. Box 210013, San Francisco, CA 94121; National Scouting Collectors Soc, 803 E Scott St, Tuscola, IL 61953; World Scout Sealers, 509-1 Margaret Ave, Kitchener, Ontario N2H 6M4 Canada.

For additional listings, see *Warman's Americana & Collectibles.*

Axe, mkd Collins, oak handle, dated 1916, 12" l....................................**85.00**
Bank, cast iron **175.00**
Birthday card, "Happy Scout Birthday," recruitment nature, c1960s, unused with orig mailing enevelope, card 5-3/8" x 4-1/4" **5.00**

Boy Scouts, Cub scout hat, blue, yellow trim, yellow kerchief with printed blue Cub scout wolf logo, $15.

Bugle, Lexcraft, 17" l....................**250.00**
Calendar, 1946, "A Guiding Hand," Norman Rockwell illus, Michigan National Bank, Battle Creek, 34" l, 16" w...**40.00**
Canteen, Diamond Brand, canvas cover, c1950s...**12.00**
Card, 25-year veteran card, dated 1949, toning **8.50**
Coffee mug, "Blackhawk Area Council" and "Appreciation 72"..................**12.00**
Drum, all tin, litho scenes on sides, 5-1/4" h, 11" dia..........................**245.00**
Handbook, March 1963, Norman Rockwell cover, tears, binding loose **15.00**
Hat
  Scoutmasters, Boy Scouts of America insignia, felt, c1950s...............**125.00**
  Stetson, mkd "John B. Stetson Co. #1," leather chin strap, c1930s **65.00**
Mask, wolf head, tears, 7-1/2" w, 9-1/2" l **55.00**
Necktie, black tie with gold Boy Scout shields, orig box shows Boy Scout wearing tie, "Boy Scouts Of America Supply Division, New Brunswick, N.J. Melrose Park, San Francisco," worn and stained box...........................**70.00**
Patch
  15-year, c1930s-40s, 2" dia **35.00**
  1974 Third Jumpin' Joe Jamboree, Eastern Arkansas Area Council, 3" dia **13.00**
  Diamond Jubilee, 3" dia **18.00**
  St. Louis Council 1941 Camporee, 3-1/2" x 2" **34.00**
Pie bird, yellow uniform, brown hat, mkd "England," light stains **65.00**

Boy Scouts, Cub Scout Program Quarterly, dark blue and white cover, Fall, 1963, $5.

Pin, Jr. Scoutmaster, 3 pars, 1" w ...**55.00**
Triple-signal set, orig box, 1933 ..**125.00**
Trophy, round plastic base, copper-colored metal Boy Scout figure, 8-1/2" h **35.00**
Woody's Slide Carving Combination Pack, carving knife and 7 pre-printed basswood carving blanks, orig box yellowed **45.00**

❖ Boyd Crystal Art Glass

The Boyd Family of Cambridge, Ohio, has made some interesting colored glassware over the years. Many of their molds were purchased from leading glass companies, such as Imperial.

Reference: *Boyd's Crystal Art Glass, Boyd Crystal Art Glass: The Tradition Continues,* published by author.

Periodical: *Boyd's Crystal Art Glass Newsletter*, 1203 Morton Ave, P.O. Box 127, Cambridge, OH 43725.

Collectors' Club: Boyd Art Glass Collectors Guild, P.O. Box 52, Hatboro, PA 19040.

Box, cov, Candlewick, vaseline, sgd**35.00**
Doll, Louise, yellow slag..................**25.00**
Duckling, blue, 1-1/2" h **12.00**
Elephant, Zack, Mardi Gras, red and gold slag, 3-1/2" **35.00**
Hand, rubina, 4" l **20.00**
Horse, Joey, 4" h
  Amethyst, 1st logo........................**30.00**
  Delphinum **21.00**
  Furr Green......................................**20.00**
  Mardi Gras, orange slag...............**20.00**

Horse, Rocky, Black Beauty, 4" l.....**20.00**
Pickle dish, orange and yellow slag, yellow hob trim, sides emb "Love's request is Pickles," 9" l **45.00**
Pie vent, duck, yellow or blue **35.00**
Pig, Candyland, purple, 2" h **15.00**
Rabbit on scalloped nest, blue, 1983, mkd, 2-1/2" l, 2" w **37.50**
Salt
  Bird, orange and gold slag, 3" l....**26.00**
  Chick, Spring Surprise, red and gold slag, 2"......................................**10.00**
Shoe, Daisy and Button, bow on front, ribbed bottom, mkd, 5-1/2"
  Light blue......................................**40.00**
  Vaseline...**20.00**
Tomahawk, cobalt, 7" l...................**26.00**
Tractor, 1 blue irid, 1 carnival irid, 1 orange/red slag, 1 red carnival irid and 1 blue slag, each mkd "Boyd" on front, each 2-3/4" l, set of 5 ....**125.00**
Train, six cars, 1980s
  Iridescent milk glass....................**45.00**
  Lavender **40.00**
  Purple...**40.00**
Wine Glass, chocolate slag, lst logo, 4" h **20.00**

❖ Boyd's Bears & Friends

What's better than a teddy bear? How about collectible teddy bears with personality? Plus, Boyd's bears have companion figurines, magnets, and accessories, making them a popular collectible for the new millennium.

Alica R. Angel.................................**18.00**
Gary Bearenthal, bean bag construction, 16" h...**50.00**
Hemingway, fishing vest and hat, 14" h **32.00**
Lincoln B. Bearrington, golden brown mohair, 16" h.................................**85.00**
Miss Prissy Fussybuns, long haired white cat, dark blue hat with flowers, 16" h...**25.00**
Mrs. Trumball, fully jointed, hand-knit green sweater, matching hat, 10" h **28.00**
Mr. Trumball, mocha colored, dark brown sweater, plaid bowtie, 10" h **25.00**
Regena Haresford, white rabbit, blue checked dress, matching bow, 13" h **25.00**
Sally Quignapple & Annie, bear 10" h, doll 5" h **22.00**
Theodore **30.00**
Uncle Leo, hand-knit sweater, ball cap, 10" h...**32.00**
Vanessa R. Angel........................**15.00**

Boyd's Bears & Friends, Lula Quackenwaddle, #561930, orig tag, 3-1/2" h, $5.

❖ Brass

An alloy of copper and zinc, brass is an extremely durable yet malleable metal. It has long been favored for creating decorative and functional objects. Because it is so durable many brass items can be found at flea markets. Avoid pieces with unusual wear, those that are broken, or examples that are poorly polished.

Reproduction Alert

Ashtray, rope design on rim, 5" dia **12.00**
Bed warmer, pierced brass pan, long wooden handle, 40-1/2" l **150.00**
Brochure Holder, Elevated News-Take One, 5-1/2" sq, 15" h....................**35.00**
Candlestick, 5-1/2" d, 6-1/8" h, incised lines on socket and base, spiral twist stem, saucer base with few dents **110.00**
Chestnut roaster, heart-shaped, pierced lid, decorative handle, English, 19-1/2" l **300.00**
Cigar cutter, pocket type **40.00**
Door slot, mkd "Letters" on hinged flap, 2-3/4" h, 6-1/2" w **25.00**
Easel, late 19th/early 20th C, A-frame topped by girdled round finial, 61-5/8" h **500.00**
Letter Opener, 6-1/2" l, Union Station, St Louis...**25.00**
Mortar and pestle, 4-1/2" h...........**65.00**
Pail, iron bail with rat-tail ends, 8" h,

Brass Bowl, four-footed bowl, 22" dia, 6" h, $45.

12"dia **45.00**
Sleigh bells, set of 6, graduated, on leather strap, 24" l **145.00**
Steam Whistle, 2-1/2" d, 12" h, single chime, lever control **150.00**
Teapot, floral design on 1 side, Oriental lettering on other, swing handle, 9" x 7" **30.00**
Tray, stamped with Holland scenes, attached handles, 17" x 10" **45.00**

❖ Brastoff, Sascha

This internationally known designer and artist began producing ceramic artware in 1953. If a piece is marked with his full name, it was made by him. Pieces marked "Sascha B" indicate he supervised the production, but didn't necessarily make the item himself.

Ashtray
  Alaska pattern hooded ashtray, Eskimo face design, 5" h, 5" w..............**65.00**
  Igloo design, 4-1/2" h, 6" dia........**55.00**
  Rooftops, enameled copper.......**150.00**
Ashtray and cigarette set, Rooftops pattern, c1958, ashtray 13-1/2" x 5", lighter 3-3/4" h, cigarette container 2-5/8" w, 3 pcs.............................**150.00**
Bowl
  Mosaic pattern, 3 feet, minor paint chips, 14-1/2" l, 12" w.............**145.00**
  Star Steed pattern, sunfish design, 3 feet, 9-3/4" l, 8-1/2" w.............**110.00**
Box, cov, mosaic, figural dog finial, 6-1/2" sq **165.00**
Candy box, cov, gray mottled matte finish, seated figure with turban, sgd "Sascha B" on front in gold, gold rooster mark on lid int., 5-3/4" dia **150.00**
Charger, Star Steed, gray ground, Sascha B mark on front, rooster mark on back, 11-3/4" dia **150.00**
Cigarette lighter, Aztec or Mayan pattern, floral design, 1-1/4" h, 4-1/4" w **45.00**
Dish
  Alaska pattern, shell form, 11-1/2" l **85.00**
  Jewel Bird pattern, 10" dia **85.00**
  Star Steed pattern, sq.................**65.00**
Figure
  Horse, rearing, foam green, platinum spatter glaze **160.00**
  Polar bear, 9" l..........................**195.00**
Lamp, full signature......................**695.00**
Plate, ChiChi Bird pattern, sgd, 8-1/2" dia **195.00**
Platter, Alaska pattern, seal on white ground with blue sky, painted by Matt Adams, 13-3/4" x 8-1/4" **130.00**
Tobacco jar, Abstract pattern, stainless

steel lid, rust stains, glaze flaws, 6-1/2"
h **65.00**
Vase
Elk design, 8" h **75.00**
Eskimo man, base sgd "Sascha B" and
#047, 4" dia, 8-1/2" h..............**145.00**
Gold leaves design, white and
speckled yellow ground, rooster
mark, 9-1/4" h, pr...................**265.00**
Orange and Gold pattern, sgd, mkd "V-
3," l2" h...................................**155.00**
Vanity Fair pattern, rooster mark, 10" h
....**155.00**
Wall plaque, stylized fish, 1 turquoise, 1
maroon, 12" l, pr........................**110.00**
Wall pocket, Provincial Rooster pattern,
4" h, 5" w.....................................**95.00**

❖ Brayton Laguna Ceramics

Brayton Laguna Ceramics was founded by
Durline E. Brayton, a potter who produced
his wares in his home in South Laguna
Beach, Calif. Following Brayton's death in
1951, employees operated the company
until it closed in 1963.

Candleholders, Blackamoor, 4-3/4" h, pr
....**125.00**
Cookie jar, teal ground, golden brown
partridges, black branches, #V-11,
incised mark **260.00**
Creamer and sugar, Calico Cat and
Gingham Dog **90.00**
Figure
Begging Figaro, "B" carved in base, 3-
1/2" h **100.00**
Fox, from English Hunter with Fox and
Hound series, late 1930s, 4" h .**65.00**
Gay Nineties Bar, three men posing,
glaze flake on one shoe, 8-1/2" h, 7-
1/2" **110.00**
Lady with Wolfhounds, yellow dress,
red hair, 1943, 11" h...............**100.00**
Pluto, sniffing, 3-1/2" h...............**100.00**
Snow White's Deer, 6-1/2" h **125.00**
Flower ring **35.00**
Planter
Kneeling Blackamoor, holding
cornucopia, 10" h.....................**115.00**
Matilda, holding two planter baskets
held by strap across her shoulders,
yellow vest with wine and green
accents, wine colored skirt, incised
mark, c1930-37, 7-5/8" h..........**70.00**
Salt and pepper shakers, Mammy and
Chef, c1940, 5" h, pr **195.00**

❖ Breadboxes

Breadboxes were once a necessary item in
the all well-equipped kitchens. Today these

boxes are finding their way to flea markets.
Make sure the interior is clean and free of
rust if you're going to use this flea market
treasure.

Chrome, black Bakelite handle, rect**15.00**
Copper, Ransburg, enameled cream
color, rooster dec, 13-3/4" l, 12" w, 7-
1/2" h..**35.00**
Graniteware, gray, raised red handles
and letters "Bread," sq **35.00**
Metal
Painted green, scene of lady with
watering can, 13" l, 9" h **65.00**
Painted white, 1950s, 10-1/2" l, 17" w
....**30.00**
Plastic, turquoise, clear top, rounded
corners, 1940s, 11-3/4" l, 4-3/4" w, 5-
1/4" h..**24.00**
Porcelain, Blue Willow, roof-shaped lid,
13-1/2" l **80.00**
Tin
Bread & Cake, cast iron turn knob,
fading to letters, some rust, 12-1/2"
sq...**85.00**
Home Comfort Bread & Cake Cabinet,
patent #757282, 2 shelves, door, 13-
1/2" l, 11" w, 20" h **100.00**
Kreamer, painted white, decal, 13-1/2"
l, 11-1/2" w, 7-1/2" h **24.00**

❖ Breweriana

Collectors have always enjoyed finding new
examples of breweriana at their favorite flea
markets. Some specialize in items from a
particular brewery, while others collect only
one type of item, such as beer trays.
Whatever they enjoy, their collections are
bound to be colorful.

References: George Baley, *Back Bar Beer
Figurines,* Schiffer Publishing, 2002;
Michael A. Pollack and Richard A. Penn,
Mom and Pop Saloons, Pennyfield's
Publishing, 2002.

Periodicals: *All About Beer,* 1627 Marion
Ave, Durham, NC 27705; *Barley Corn
News,* P.O. Box 2328, Falls Church, VA
22042; *Suds 'n' Stuff,* 4765 Galacia Way,
Oceanside, CA 92056.

Collectors' Clubs: American Breweriana
Assoc, P.O. Box 11157, Pueblo, CO 81001;
East Coast Breweriana Assoc, P.O. Box 64,
Chapel Hill, NC 27514; National Assoc of
Breweriana Advertising, 2343 Met-To-Wee
Lane, Wauwatosa, WI 53226.

Reproduction Alert

Ashtray, A. Coors Co., Golden CO,
pottery **22.00**
Banner, Bud Light Beer, Welcome to the
Kemper Open, red and gold, plastic,
rope ties, 112" x 36"....................**35.00**

Bar light, Schlitz, logo on front and back,
gold-colored plastic, plaster goddess,
glass globe, 1976, 45" h **140.00**
Beer stein
Budweiser, Clydesdales, 1988, 6v h
....**25.00**
Miller, 1988, Great American
Achievements, 3rd in a series ..**22.50**
Beer tap, Schlitz, wood and ceramic,
worn **25.00**
Bottle opener
Blatz Milwaukee Beer.....................**8.00**
Wylre's Holland Brand Beer, wear .**5.00**
Coaster
Ballantine, 1967, set of 8, 3-1/2" d
....**10.00**
Fitzgerald's Beer, Troy, NY, octagonal
....**2.50**
Clock
Budweiser, pocket watch form, electric,
"Budweiser 1876, King of Beers, 15-
1/2" dia...................................**55.00**
Fort Pitt Special Beer, light-up, convex
glass, 15" dia **105.00**
Pabst Blue Ribbon, plastic, 17" dia
....**90.00**
Dexterity puzzle, Miller High Life, can-
shape, in orig plastic wrapper, 5" h
....**20.00**
Door push, Pabst Blue Ribbon Beer, 7-
1/4" h, 4-1/4" w..........................**125.00**
Lighter, miniature Miller Beer can shape,
out of butane, 1" w, 2-3/4" h.........**10.00**
Mug
Schlitz, brewery emblem on both sides,
scene of barrels brought by boat
being loaded on horse-drawn cart, 7"
h...**6.00**
Smith's Musty Ale, base mkd "WM
Brunt Pottery Co., E. Liverpool"**26.00**
Playing cards, Miller High Life, "The
Champagne of Bottle Beer," Girl on
Moon logo, 1950s, orig box, used**16.50**
Score pad, Falstaff Beer, for gin rummy,
8 sheets, 8-3/4" x 7-5/8"...............**13.00**
Sign
Ballentines Ale, stand-up type,
cardboard, 1951, 12" x 14".......**95.00**
Bavarian Beer, red, white, and gold, tin
over cardboard, 1950s, 6" x 10"**35.00**

*Breweriana, Tray, painted tin advertising, oval, Drink
20th Century Bottled Beer– The American Brewing
Co. of Pekin, Ills, U.S.A., $75.*

Breweriana, Paul Jones, black plastic base, bronze colored lettering, $5.

Budweiser, cardboard, "Custer's Last Stand," shows Battle of Little Big Horn, 20" h, 41" w **125.00**
Genesee Beer, doubled-sided window sign, late 1950s, 11" dia **18.00**
O'Keefe Canadian Ale, hard plastic, wooden easel for countertop display, 16" x 11" **14.00**
Pabst, red neon, blue ribbon border, plastic protector, 19" h, 21" w...**90.00**

Tray

Budweiser, tin, "St. Louis Levee In Early Seventies," shows paddlewheeler at busy dock, 1914 copyright **140.00**
Coors Light, gray and white, dated 1982, wear, 13" dia...................**10.00**
Falcon International Beer, Falcon logo, red, white, black, and gold, scratches **18.00**
Fitzgerald's Ale, Fitzgerald Bros. Brewing Co., Troy, T. Burgomaster Beer, 13" d, 1-1/4" h **80.00**
Schlitz, "The beer that made Milwaukee famous," 13" dia **75.00**
Window Sign, Genesee Beer, double-sided, round, late 1950s, 11" d.**18.00**

❖ Breyer

Founded in 1943, the Breyer Molding Company of Chicago has created some interesting radio and television cases. However, the company is best known for its animals, which were started as a sideline but had gained great popularity by 1958. The facility continued to develop new techniques, creating interesting new figures, primarily horses. The production operation was moved to New Jersey after the firm was acquired by Reeves International.

References: Felicia Browell, *Breyer Animal Collector's Guide*, 2nd ed, Collector Books; Nancy Atkinson Young, *Breyer Molds and Models: Horses, Riders and Animals*, rev and updated 5th ed, Schiffer Publishing.

Periodicals: *The Hobby Horse News,* 2053 Dryehaven Drive, Tallahassee, FL 32311; *The Model Horse Trader,* 143 Mercer Way, Upland, CA 91720; *TRR Pony Express,* 71 Aloha Circle, North Little Rock, AR 72120.

Collectors' Clubs: Breyer Collectors Club, 14 Industrial Rd, Pequannock, NJ 07440; North American Model Horse Show Association, P.O. Box 50508, Denton, TX 76206.

Web Site: www.breyerhorses.com

Accessories

Bucket, MIB...................................**3.00**
Crop **8.00**
Horse barn, pine, MIB................**270.00**
Leather saddlebag, MIB...............**16.00**
McClellan military saddle set, MIB **30.00**
Nylon halter with cotton lead rope, MIB **12.00**
Stable blanket, quilted, blue and yellow, MIB **7.00**
Tack box, blue, MIB......................**10.00**

Animals

Alpine Goat, 1999, MIB.................**6.00**
Collie, Honey, 1995-1996, MIB **55.00**
Elephant, re-release, 1992-1993, MIB **45.00**
Hawk, black, 1991-1992..............**25.00**
Jolly Cholly Basset Hound, tri-color, #325, 7" h **35.00**
Moose, 1966-1996 ....**35.00**
Texas Longhorn Bull, 1963-1990 .**30.00**

Horses

Arabian foal, black, 1999, MIB **15.00**
Black Stallion Returns set, 1983-1993 ....**65.00**
Chestnut Pinto Paint Western Prancing, chestnut and white, 9" h **35.00**
Chestnut Sorrel Belgian, red on yellow ribbon, #94, 9-1/2" h **40.00**
Dan Patch, limited edition, 1990, MIB **90.00**
Dapple Gray, mkd "Breyer Molding Co." **35.00**

Fighting Stallion

Alabaster, matte, 1973-1985........**40.00**
Bay, Toys R Us, 1993, MIB...........**50.00**
Little Bits scale (approx 4-1/2" to 5" h) Appaloosa, 1985-1988 ....**15.00**
Clydesdale, 1984-1988 ....**20.00**
Morganglanz, picture box............**35.00**
Palomino, grazing foal, 1965-1971 ....**25.00**
Polo pony, 1976-1981, damaged box **50.00**
Running mare, chestnut, 1963-1974 ....**35.00**
Secretariat, 1987-1996, MIB........**50.00**
Shetland Pony, alabaster, 1963-1973 ....**25.00**
Stablemate scale (approx 2-3/4" h) Citation, 1975-1990......................**10.00**
Thoroughbred mare, bay, 1989-1994 ....**15.00**

Western Prancing, with saddle and blanket, 9" l, 8-1/2" h....................**35.00**

❖ Bride's Baskets

The term *bride's basket* usually refers to a decorative glass bowl in a fancy silver or silver-plate holder. This traditional gift to brides was meant as a showpiece for the young couple's sideboard. Over time, bowls would be damaged, so it is not uncommon to find a bowl that is mismatched with a base.

Blue, ruffled, leaves, blossom, gold dec, no frame **150.00**
Cranberry, applied glass trim, SP holder, 6" dia................................**195.00**
Cranberry opalescent, no frame .**140.00**
Fenton, maize, amber and crystal crest, hp roses on int., white ext., SP holder, 10-1/2" dia................................**275.00**
Opalescent and colorless shading to lavender, applied flowers, looped thorn handle,7-3/4" dia **140.00**
Peachblow, shiny finish bowl, applied amber rim, SP Wilcox holder, 9" dia **215.00**
Satin glass, dark red satin glass shaded to cream, ruffled and crimped rim, SP stand, 11-1/2" dia **275.00**
Satin glass, shaded purple, white underside, purple and white enameled flowers, lacy foliage dec, 10-3/4" dia **225.00**
Silver plated, mkd "Middletown Plate Co., Quadruple Plate 1857," 9-1/2" dia, 5-1/2" h excluding handle..........**140.00**
Spiral white and turquoise dec, ruffled, colorless thorn handle, 8-1/2" dia **125.00**
Vasa Murrhina, outer amber layer, center layer with cream colored spots, random toffee colored spots, dark veins, gold mica flakes, mulberry pink lining, crossed thorn handles, 10" dia ..**635.00**

Bride's Baskets, Cranberry bowl with threaded ruffled rim, yellow-gold scrolling and ring of dots dec, semi-opaque white ground, silver-plated stand, 10" high, $150

❖ British Royalty

Generations of collectors have been fascinated by the British Royal family, and have saved memorabilia associated with the king's lineage. Quite an assortment survives from the past, in addition to the plethora of items associated with present-day royal weddings, births, and state visits.

Periodical: British Royalty Commemorative Collectors Newsletter, P.O. Box 294, Lititz, PA 17543.

Collectors' Club: Commemorative

Collector's Society, Lumless House, Gainsborough Rd, Winthrope, New Newark, Nottingham NG24 1NR UK.

For additional listings, see *Warman's Antiques & Collectibles*, as well as Princess Diana Collectibles in this edition.

Bell, Queen Elizabeth Coronation, 1953 ....**30.00**

Book, *The Princess Elizabeth Gift Book*, Cynthia Asquith and Eileen Bigland, four illus of fruit, worn...................**10.00**

Bottle opener and key fob, Queen Elizabeth II, color printing, 1-3/4" x 2-1/2" **7.50**

Box, cov, Elizabeth the Queen Mother, 1980, 80th Birthday, color portrait, Crown Staffordshire, 4" dia **75.00**

Cup and saucer, Elizabeth II, portrait flanked by flags, coronation, pairs of flags inside cup and saucer **45.00**

Goblet, Royal Wedding Commemorative, 6" h, MIB **70.00**

Loving cup, Elizabeth II and Philip, 1972 Silver Wedding Anniversary, Paragon, 3" h...**175.00**

Magic Lantern slide, Victoria and Albert **25.00**

Matchbook cover, Their Most Gracious Majesties, Canada, May 15-June 15, 1939 ....**18.00**

Mug, Queen Elizabeth Coronation, 1953 ....**24.00**

Pinback button

Queen Elizabeth, black and white cello, coronation portrait photo, red, white, and purple fabric ribbons, miniature gold luster finish metal replica crown pin, c1953, 1-3/4" dia...............**15.00**

Queen Elizabeth and Prince Philip, red, white, and blue cello, center black and white portraits, 1951 visit to Canada, waxed fabric red, white, and blue ribbons **20.00**

Plate, Queen Victoria, Jubilee Year, Royal Worcester, 10-1/2" dia................**275.00**

British Royalty, Plate, Queen Elizabeth II, Silver Jubilee, 1952-1977, $20.

British Royalty, Mug, Silver Jubilee, King George V, Queen Mary, 1910, $28.

Tin, Queen Elizabeth, Coronation, June, 1953, slight discoloration top, rust inside...**8.00**

View master reel set, Queen Elizabeth II coronation, 4-1/2" sq envelope, set of 3 color stereo view reels, orig fact leaflet for June 2, 1953 coronation **25.00**

❖ Bronze

An alloy of copper and tin, bronze is a sturdy metal that has been used to create functional and decorative objects for centuries. Collectors should be aware that some objects merely have a bronze coating and are not solid bronze. Those pieces are valued considerably less than if they were solid bronze.

Ashtray, round, leaf form, applied salamander, c1910, 7-1/2" dia ...**120.00**

Bookends, baby shoes, dated 1948 ....**25.00**

Bookrack, extending, Moffat, cast ends with Indian brave, polychrome paint, emb "9964," c1928, 14" l extended, 6-1/2" h.......................................**285.00**

Bust, Buddha, serene expression, draped covering, cloud tiara, verdigris finish, 9-1/2" h **195.00**

Charger, doré, deeply cast geometric designs on rim, stamped "Tiffany Studios New York #1746", 12" d, area of discoloration, minor edge dent **330.00**

Figure

Dog with game, dark patina, American School, 20th C, 6" h..................**90.00**

Donkey with gear, "Souvenir of Los Vegas, Nev.," made in Japan, 2-1/4" h, 2-1/4" l **5.00**

Low bowl, 4" d, shape no. 537, sterling applied geometric designs, imp Heintz logo and "Sterling", c1915............**45.00**

Sculpture, Startled Finch on a Perch, Ferdinand Pautrot, gold-green patina, sgd on base "F. Pautrot", 5" h.....**260.00**

Smoking tray, 6-1/4" d, Doré finish, applied scrolling on ash bowl, cigar

rests, matchbox holder, unmarked, c1910 ....**70.00**

Tray, 9" d, band of hammered designs, mkd "Apollo Studios, New York" c1910 ....**45.00**

Wall plaque, American Telephone and Telegraph Co., 9" dia.................**250.00**

❖ Bubblegum & Non-Sport Trading Cards

Bubblegum trading cards were big business in the late 1930s, especially for the Goudey Gum Company and National Chicle Company. They produced several series that had collectors clamoring for more. Bowman, Donruss, Topps, Fleer, and Upper Deck eventually joined the marketplace also. Today, companies omit the gum, concentrating solely on the trading cards.

Periodicals: *Non-Sport Update*, 4019 Green St, P.O. Box 5858, Harrisburg, PA 17110; *Non-Sports Illustrated*, P.O. Box 126, Lincoln, MA 01773; *Wrapper*, P.O. Box 227, Geneva, IL 60134.

Collectors' Club: United States Cartophilic Society, P.O. Box 4020, St Augustine, FL 32085.

The following listings are merely a sampling of the many bubblegum cards available. Prices are for complete sets in excellent condition.

Andy Griffth Show, 1990, set of 110 cards, mint...................................**25.00**

Batman, Topps, 1966, Riddle-Bback series, 38-card set **250.00**

Battlestar Galactica, Topps, 132 cards and 22 stickers to a set................**40.00**

Beatles, B-11 of 16, Revolver, lyrics of Eleanor Rigby on back...................**4.00**

Combat, series 2, Donruss, 1964, 66-card set **250.00**

Elvis Presley, Boxcar Enterprises, Inc., 1978, complete set....................**135.00**

Fabian, Topps, 1959, 115-card set**120.00**

Green Hornet, #29, 1966.................**5.00**

Bubble Gum Cards, Non-Sp Freedom's War, Topps, #65, Korea, Howitzer, $.75.

Mickey Mouse, #3 ....**30.00**
Rock Stars, Donruss, 1979, 66-card set
....**48.00**
Simpons, Radioactive Man, #412.....**5.00**
Tarzan, 1966, Philadelphia Chewing
Gum Co., 66-card set.................**185.00**

❖ Bunnykins

These charming bunny characters have delighted children for many years. But, did you know that they were created by a nun? Barbara Vernon Bailey submitted her designs from the convent. Many of her designs were inspired by stories she remembered her father telling. The Bunnykins line was introduced in 1934. A new series of figures was modeled by Albert Hallam in the 1970s.

Baby plate, Letter Box, Barbara Vernon
Bailey...**75.00**
Baby set, plate and 2 handled mug,
Royal Doulton.............................**55.00**
Bowl, Royal Doulton, Barbara Vernon
....**95.00**
Child's cup, two handles, mkd "English
Fine Bone China, Bunnykins, Royal
Doulton Tableware Ltd, 1936" **55.00**
Child's plate, Royal Doulton, 8" dia
Bunnykins at school **12.50**
Bunnykins camping **12.50**
Bunnykins filling car up **12.50**
Mother and father bunnykins........**15.00**
Christmas plate, 8" d **18.00**
Figure, Royal Dounton
Artist, DB13, 1975-82, 3-3/4" h..**250.00**
Bridesmaid, DB173, 3-3/4"...........**40.00**
Buntie Bunnykins helping Mother, DB2
....**85.00**

Bunnykins tote bag, cloth and vinyl, Bunnykin on rocking horse, mkd "© Royal Doulton Tablewares, 1984," $15.

Doctor Bunnykins, 4-1/2" h **40.00**
Easter Greetings **55.00**
Fisherman Bunny, DB170, 4" h....**50.00**
Jack and Jill Bunnykins, 4-1/2" h**120.00**
Little Jack Horner, 3-1/2" h...........**60.00**
Mother and Baby Bunnykins, DB167,
1997.......................................**45.00**
Mystic Bunnykins, DB197, 4-3/4" h
....**50.00**
Rocket Man,1982, 4" h..............**100.00**
Sailor Bunny, 1997, discontinued.**55.00**
Seaside, 1998 ....**55.00**
Uncle Sam, brown backstamp, 1985, 4-
1/2" h **45.00**

❖ Business & Office Machines

Folks who collect have always been fascinated with objects that are no longer in style or that technology has deemed obsolete. Early business and office machines fall into that category. Future generations will have fun pondering over some of these gadgets.

Collectors' Club: Early Typewriters Collectors Assoc, 2591 Military Ave, Los Angeles, CA 90064-1993.

Adding machine
Burroughs.....................................**17.50**
Star..**15.00**
Victor...**10.00**
Checkwriter, SafeGuard.................**25.00**
Dictaphone, Model 10 ....**50.00**
Notary seal, Stark County, Ohio, wear
....**90.00**
Typewriter
American Index, model 2, 1893 .**870.00**
L.C. Smith & Corona, Comet model
....**65.00**

Business & Office Machines, Victor, Champion adding machine, orig plastic cover, $15.

Royal, bookkeeper's model, wide
platen **40.00**
Underwood No. 5, 1930s............**225.00**
Typewriter ribbon tin
Pure Silk, woman in red dress, 2-1/2"
dia...**30.00**
Silhouette, woman typing at desk, 2-
1/2" dia.....................................**30.00**

❖ Buster Brown

R.F. (Richard Felton) Outcault first introduced the mischievous Buster Brown and his dog Tige in a New York Herald comic strip in 1902. During the St. Louis World's Fair Exposition of 1904, the characters were sold to merchants for use as trademarks. Outcault's idea to license rights to his comic figures was particularly innovative for the early 1900s. Subsequently, more than 50 different products incorporated the Buster Brown names and likenesses in their advertising and packaging.

Bank, cast iron, Buster Brown and Tige,
orig gold paint, 5-1/4" h.............**200.00**
Booklet, Quick Meal Gasoline Stoves,
Buster Brown cover....................**135.00**
Box, Buster Brown Shoes, empty ...**15.00**
Clicker, tin, Buster Brown Shoes **50.00**
Comics, premium, #40, issued by shoe
store **20.00**
Display, plaster Buster Brown and Tige,
mkd "Buena Park Calif. 1972," 17-1/2"
h, 11" w **395.00**
Lapel stud, 1-1/4" dia **45.00**
Fob, Buster Brown Blue Ribbon Shoes,
oval, silver, shows Buster Brown and
Tige **28.00**
Magazine tear sheet, Ladies Home
Journal, April, 1924, Buster Brown
Shoes ad, framed.........................**25.00**
Mask, die-cut paper, shows Buster
Brown, 8-1/2" h **13.00**
Pencil holder, wood and cardboard, tin
top, orig label, 10-1/2" l **85.00**
Pocket mirror, celluloid, Buster Brown
Vacation Days Carnival, 2-1/4" dia
....**45.00**
Ring, flicker ring, plastic, red............**8.00**
Shaving mug, shows Buster Brown with
blue-and-white teapot, Tige holds blue
cup, scalloped edge, Germany, 2-1/2" h
....**295.00**
Teacup, white with pink trim...........**72.50**
Toy, Buster Brown Brownbilt Shoes
cardboard gun and bullet disk,
unpunched **45.00**

❖ Busts

Decorative busts immortalized heroes and other special people. Made of durable materials such as marble, bronze, or alabaster, they are particularly long-lived. At one time, it was considered a sign of wealth to display a popular bust as part of your home decor. Values increase for examples with a plaque that identifies the subject, foundry or maker, and date.

Benjamin Franklin, carved oak, old brown alligatored finish, black carved base, sgd "Harris," 15" h.............**800.00**

Cavalier, porcelain, sepia colors, mkd "Teplitz," c1910, 8-1/2" h.............**185.00**

Cherub, bronze, winged, seated on broken column, playing hornpipe, pair of doves perched opposite, after Mathurin Moreau, dark brown patination, green marble socle, 9" h **250.00**

Child, bronze, gilt, green onyx base, mkd "S. Klaber & Co. Foundry N.Y.," 6-3/4" h **85.00**

Gentleman, Leo F. Nock, bronze, brown-green patina, sgd on base "Leo Nock Sc," dated 1919, stamped "Roman Bronze Works, NY," 22" h **320.00**

George Washington, cast plaster, orig bronze finish, 35" h **125.00**

John Locke, black basalt, raised base, imp title and mark, Wedgwood, c1865, 7-3/4" h.......................................**525.00**

Smiling Gypsy girl, plaster, Continental, 21-1/4" h.....................................**450.00**

Young woman, marble, head piece, cowl neck, 7-1/2" h **250.00**

Woman in lace headdress and bodice, alabaster, tapered alabaster socle, early 20th C, 17-1/4" h **450.00**

Busts, child, chalkware, gold highlights on drape, unmarked, 20th C, $25.

❖ Buttonhooks

Originally used for hooking tiny buttons on gloves, dresses, and shoes, these long narrow hooks are sometimes found hiding in vintage sewing baskets.

Bakelite handle, orange, 6" l..........**40.00**
Bone handle, folding, 3-3/4" l **20.00**
Celluloid handle
  6-1/8" l, mkd "Parisian Ivory," Loonen France trademark **25.00**
  7-1/8" l, black etched floral design**12.50**
Sterling
  3" l, folding, repousse...................**50.00**
  4-1/2" l, repousse, English hallmarks **125.00**
  6" l, floral and leaf design, mkd "Tiffany & Co. Pat'd '98" **800.00**
  6-1/8" l, feather paisley design.....**35.00**
  6-1/4" l, swirling design, mkd "Tiffany & Co." **100.00**
  7-1/4" l, Art Nouveau design **45.00**
  7-1/4" l, shield shaped handle, hallmark for Birmingham, England, 1907..**25.00**

Buttonhooks, Figural jockey handle, early molded mottled plastic, 5-3/4" l, $32.

❖ Buttons

Buttons are collected according to age,

material, and subject matter. The National Button Society, founded in 1939, has designated 1918 as the dividing line between old and modern buttons. Shanks and backmarks are important elements to consider when determining age.

References: There are many excellent button books available to collectors. Some of the standard reference books include Fink & Ditzler, *Buttons: The Collector's Guide To Selecting, Restoring and Enjoying New & Vintage Buttons*, 1993; Elizabeth Hughes and Marion Lester, *The Big Book of Buttons*, reprinted by New Leaf Publishers, 1981; Sally C. Luscomb, *The Collector's Encyclopedia of Buttons,* 4th ed, Schiffer Publishing, 1999; Florence Zacharie Nicholls, *Button Handbook, with three supplements, 1943-1949*, reprinted by New Leaf Publishers.

Periodical: *Button Bytes*, www.tias.com/articles/buttons (an internet magazine devoted to buttons).

Collectors' Clubs: National Button Society, 2733 Juno Place, Apt 4, Akron, OH 44313-4137; Pioneer Button Club, 102 Frederick St., Oshawa, Ontario L1G 2B3 Canada; The Button Club, P.O. Box 2274, Seal Beach, CA 90740.

Bakelite
  Log, carved, red **2.50**
  Round, maroon, two hole sew through, 1-1/8" dia **7.00**
  Tortoiseshell, large disc, 2-1/8" dia **5.00**
Black glass
  Gold luster, fabric-look, self shank, mkd "Le Mode," 1950s, 7/8" l..............**4.00**
  Silver luster, petal look, self shank with threaded groove, mkd "Le Chic," 1950s, 13/16"............................**4.00**
Brass, Picador, tinted, steel back, wire shank, 1-1/8" dia **10.00**
Carnival glass, purple
  Buckle & Scrolls, 5/8" dia.............**10.00**
  Frog...**12.00**
  Lazy Wheel, 5/8" dia **12.00**
  Windmill, 5/8" dia **14.00**
Celluloid, pink, cup shaped, gold painted deer escutcheon, celluloid shank, 1" dia **5.00**
Figural, plastic
  Apple, realistic coloring, metal shank **1.25**
  Flower basket, pastels, metal shank **1.50**
  Mouse, small, blue, self shank.......**3.00**
Lucite
  Clear, underside carved with wreath of leaves, pink highlights, 1-1/2" dia **10.00**
  Clear, red pansy inside, 1-1/8" dia **25.00**
  Yellow, carved grapes, two-hole sew through **15.00**
Moonglow (glass)

Great buttons might be hiding in this box full of vintage buttons.

Green flower, gold trim, 1/2" dia.....**2.00**
White, gold trim, four lobed, self shank,
1/2" dia.......................................**2.00**
Pewter, stamped, The Trumpeter of
Cracow, lead pewter mounted over
painted metal brass back with shelf
shank, 1-1/2" dia **12.50**
Plastic, metal insert of woman's head,
attached celluloid loop shank, 1-5/8"
dia **10.00**
Stenciled china
Black and white zebra stripes **1.00**
Blue and white flower....................**2.00**

✸✸ Byers' Choice

Joyce Byers started creating colorful
singing Christmas carolers in the late
1960s. By 1978 this home occupation
developed into a family business and
financial success. Today Byers' Choice
operates a stunning facility in Chalfont, PA,
where visitors can watch as Carolers,
Williamsburg figures, and other Byers'
Choice personalities are created.

Amish family, man, woman, boy, and
girl, 1999, each with an accessory,
each **90.00**
Baker, 1992.....................................**90.00**
Boy or girl with gingerbread man,
1996 or 1997 ....**65.00**
Butcher, 1995, with butcher block ..**70.00**
Flower girl, 2001, with orig box, sgd by
Joyce Byers.................................**80.00**
Gingerbread maker and oven, 1996
....**95.00**
Girl with teddy bear, in rocking horse,
1990 ....**110.00**
Mailman, 1993 ....**80.00**
Mother holding baby, 1991 ....**90.00**
Mrs Claus, with muff, 1990 ....**65.00**
Pilgrim boy with turkey, 1998.......**55.00**
Salvation Army man, with drum, 1996
....**50.00**
Salvation Army man, with trumpet, 1995
....**95.00**
Salvation Army man with tuba, 1998
....**55.00**

Byers' Choice, Salvation army figures, each figure $120, carolers to left and right, orig box in background.

Byers' Choice, Lady caroler, green jacket and hat, white skirt with plaid trim, same trim on hat, $100.

Salvation Army woman ringer, with
kettle and stand, 1998.................**95.00**
Salvation Army woman with tambourine,
1994 ....**55.00**

Byers' Choice, Carolers, children infront, $80, larger adult figures in back, $90.

Sandwich board man, 1997............**80.00**
Santa in sleigh, 1989.....................**300.00**
Santa with basket and cinnamon sticks,
white coat, 1987 ....**150.00**
Santa with tree, 1990 ....**80.00**
Schoolteacher and two children, 1993
....**195.00**

C

❖ Cake Collectibles

Here's a sweet collectible for you. In our recent trips to flea markets, we've seen more and more of these items. Doesn't anyone bake anymore? It certainly seems as if there are a lot of cake pans for sale! More and more collectors are also seeking out vintage bride and groom cake toppers.

Cake cutting set, Fagley Junior Card Party Cake Cutters, deck of cards, heart, diamond, spade and club, orig 3-1/2" x 3-1/2" box...........................**15.00**
Cake plate
 China, white ground, pink roses...**60.00**
 Depression-era glass, colorless, block type pattern, matching aluminum cover **65.00**
Candle holders for birthday cake, plastic, pink, c1950, set of 20 ....**2.00**
Cookie board, wood, metal top, 12 impressions **35.00**
Pan
 Bird shape, old **30.00**
 Child's building block shape.........**10.00**
 Christmas tree shape, Wilton.........**7.50**
 Garfield shape.............................**15.00**
 Santa shape **10.00**
Topper
 Bells, pink satin **25.00**
 Bride and Groom, tulle on base, orig flowers, c1945............................**65.00**
 Bugs Bunny, six matching birthday

Cake plate, red, pink, white, and yellow roses, green leaves, gold trim, scalloped, mkd in green "Imperial Crown (crown symbol) China Austria", 12" d, $25.

candle holders, Wilton, 1978 ....**24.00**
Disney **24.00**
Mickey & Minnie Mouse **28.00**
Snoopy **24.00**
Snow White **24.00**

❖ Calculators

What would we do without pocket calculators? Some of the first models are beginning to command steep prices; however, as with most other collectibles, condition is important. Collectors also want the original box and instruction sheet. Don't overlook examples with advertising.

References: Bruce Flamm and Guy Ball, *Collector's Guide to Pocket Calculators*, Wilson/Barnett Publishing, 1997.

Collectors' Club: International Assoc of Calculator Collectors, P.O. Box 70513, Riverside CA, 92513.

Addiator Duplex, brass **25.00**
Belltown Antique Car Club Show, 30th Anniversary, August 4, 1996, "A World of Thanks," 2-1/4" x 3-1/2" **5.00**
Bohn Instant...............................**30.00**
Bowmar 901B **70.00**
Burger King/Nickelodeon, 1999, 3-1/2" l **5.00**
Burroughs...................................**55.00**
Casio HL-809, 2-3/4" x 4-1/2", MIB **25.00**
Commodore MM1..........................**75.00**
Craig 4502..................................**55.00**
Crown CL 130..............................**150.00**
Donald Duck Calculator, Happy Birthday Donald Duck, 1934-84, Bradley Quartz Calculator, clock, 12" ruler, made in Hong King, mint in orig mailing box **35.00**
Keystone 390...............................**55.00**
Lloyds 303 ....**20.00**
National......................................**25.00**
Novus 650 Mathbox, 2-1/2" x 5" **18.00**
Radio Shack EC 425 ....**50.00**
Royal Digital 3 ....**110.00**
Wendy's, pen, pencil, and calculator set **6.00**

❖ Calendar Plates

Many of these interesting plates were made as giveaways for local merchants. They were often produced by popular manufacturers of the day, such as Homer Laughlin and Royal China. Many have fanciful gold trim and interesting scenes. Expect to pay more for a plate that is sold in the area where it originated.

Periodical: The Calendar, 710 N Lake Shore Dr, Barrington, IL 60010.

1909, flying bird with 1909 sash, "Souvenir of Centralia, Ill.," 8-1/4" dia **58.00**

Calendar Plates, 1913, center heart motif with holly, bells, and robin, calendar pages with blue forget-me-nots, worn gold trim on border, $15.

1910, children swimming, James Whitcomb Riley verse, Oriental Drug CO., Chanute, Kansas **60.00**
1910, Ye 1910 New Year, "Compliments of E. L. Dibble & Co., General Merchandising North Fork, PA, 8-1/2" dia, some crazing.........................**50.00**
1911, flower spray, "Compliments W. H. Greenwood," 7" d, hairlines on back **30.00**
1911, horseshoe with horse head center, adv for PA tinsmith, stove, roofing company, mkd "Taylor Smith Taylor," 7" dia, 1" hairline..............................**40.00**
1913, floral and holly designs, "Compliments of H. E. Yorks, Oriole, Pa.," cracks, 8-1/2" dia.................**32.00**
1920, multicolored flags of several nations, American flag in center, "Compliments of H. R. Sloan, Springfield, MO," back mkd "D. E. McNicol, East Liverpool, O 918," crazing..**60.00**
1955, floral wreath, Simplicity, Canonsburg, 10" dia **15.00**
1960, Zodiac figures, edge chip, 9-1/2" dia **6.50**
1961, English cottage and bridge, "God Bless This House Through All This Year," Royal Staffordshire, 9" dia..**18.50**
1964, montage of New Jersey map, capitol dome, state seal and Revolutionary War soldier, "The State of New Jersey 1664 Tercentenary 1964," Kettlesprings Kilns, Alliance, Ohio, 10-1/8" dia **28.00**
1966, Sabin, metallic gold dec, seasonal sports motif, 10" dia, light crazing to center **7.50**
1969, Currier & Ives, green, Royal China **40.00**
1971, cherubs playing and working, Wedgwood, 9-7/8" dia.................**32.00**
1973, Gaston's Mill, Beaver Creek State

Park (Columbiana County, Ohio), history of mill on back, 10-1/4" dia **25.00**

1974, God Bless Our House, maroon and white, mkd "Alfred Meakin Staffordshire England," 9" dia **7.50**

1980, Memory Plate by Alton Tobey, mural of memorable people and events, limited edition of 1,980 plates, Fairmont China, 12-1/4" dia **68.00**

1984, Columbia space shuttle, "Hail Columbia," Spencer Gifts, 9" dia **9.00**

1996, Wedgwood Peter Rabbit, 8" dia **32.50**

❖ Calendars

With a brand new century, what better thing to collect than calendars? They often contain artwork by the best illustrators of the day, in addition to advertising, household hints, and necessary telephone numbers.

Periodical: The Calendar, 710 N Lake Shore Dr, Barrington, IL 60010.

Collectors' Club: Calendar Collector Society, (send SASE to) American Resources, 18222 Flower Hill Way #299, Gaithersburg, MD 20879, www.collectors.org/ccs.

1909, American Clay Machinery Co., pocket size, bound in leather-type material, world maps, populations of US states, 2-1/2" w, 4-1/2" h **12.00**

1913, Swift's Premium, 4 pages, each with different scene, 17" x 9"........**20.00**

1918, Swift's Premium, The Girl I Leave Behind Me, soldier saying goodbye, illus by Haskell Coffin, sheets for January to March, pc missing, 15" x 8-1/4" **100.00**

1924, Red Goose Shoes, Getting His Goat, mountain goat hunter, H.C. Edwards, artist, ads for Red Goose Shoes, Friedman-Shelby Shoe Co, Atlantic Shoes, Pacific Shoes, 8" x 19" wall type **25.00**

Calendars, 1930, emb moon, winter scene with house, birds, flowers, trees, etc., orig calendar pad, $25.

1932, image of Betsy Ross sewing flag, George Washington looking on, full calendar pad, large size...............**35.00**

1935, Harmon Coal Co., Columbus, OH, weekly memo type **20.00**

1936, Seasons Greetings, Moss Grocery Store, Montpelier, MO, 8" w, 16" h, creases to cardboard **7.00**

1947, Illinois Bell Telephone, wallet size, adv on front, calendar on back **10.00**

1951, Coronet Kiddies, Butler's Sunoco adv **10.00**

1952, Myers Truck Lines, Knox City, Mo., cowgirl and horse, unused, 20-3/4" x 12" **22.50**

1958, Esso Family, Dec 1957 to Dec 1958 ....**10.00**

1959, Ramco Piston Rings, tin, stand-up type **12.00**

1963, Seattle World's Fair, linen towel, 30" x 15-1/4".............................**38.00**

1976, Mischief Makers, 3 puppies and a basket, full calendar pad, Leo's Shoe Store, Rehrersburg, Pa., 16-1/2" x 10" **12.00**

1977, Hunting scenes, advertises Weaver & Son Food Market, Merriam, Kansas, unused..**12.00**

1983, Chicago Cubs, by Jim Langford **9.50**

❖ California Potteries

This catchall category includes small studio potteries located in California.

Will & George Climes
Bluebird figurine, "Will & George, California" paper label, 3-1/4" h**40.00**
Robin figurine, "Will & George, California" paper label, 3" h......**40.00**
Freeman & McFarlin, elephant figurine, orig foil sticker, chips on ear and trunk, 6" h, 7-1/2" l **55.00**
Hedi Schoop
Planter, bridesmaids, ivory dress, yellow and mocha flowers, sgd "Hedi

California Potteries, bowl, leaf shape, red and white dec, gold trim, yellow ground, $8.

California Potteries, dinner plate, white, $5.

Schoop, Hollywood, Calif," 6-1/2" w, 9" h, pr......................................**65.00**
Tray, 8-1/2" x 7-3/4" x 4" h, ballerina, turquoise and white, gold trim, sgd "Hedi Schoop, California" **125.00**
Hollydale, chop plate, gold-yellow, swirled edges, 11-1/2" dia............**22.00**
Madeline Original, vase **35.00**
Maurice of California, covered cigarette and 2 ashtrays, white with gold trim, 3 pcs..**25.00**
Santa Rosa, L.A. Potteries, plate, hp plums, 10-1/8" dia **18.00**
Treasure Craft, ashtray..................**12.00**

❖ California Raisins

Savvy collectors began stashing California Raisins as soon as they appeared. So far, their investments haven't paid off, but hopefully they are enjoying their collections.

Bank, 1987 6-3/4" h **8.00**
Figure
Alotta Stile, purple boom box and pink boots, Hardee's, 1991, 2" h **10.00**
Anita Break, 1991 ....**10.00**
Bass player with gray slippers, 1988, MIP, 3" h **11.00**
Captain Toonz, blue radio, 1998.....**7.00**
Drummer with black hat and yellow feather, 1988, 3" h **10.00**
F.F. Strings, blue guitar and orange sneakers, 1988, 2" h...................**7.00**
Hands, hands touching head with fingers pointed up, Hardee's, 1987, 2" h **7.00**
Hands, left hand up, right hand down, Post Raisin Bran issue, 1987, 3" h **7.00**
Rollin' Rollo, yellow roller skates and hat marked H, Hardee's, 1988, 2" h **7.00**
Saxophone, gold sax, no hat, Hardee's, 1987, 2" h **7.00**
Sunglasses, orange sunglasses with index fingers touching face, 1987, 2" h...**7.00**

Lunchbox and thermos, "The California Raisins," plastic, blue ground........**24.00**

Pinback button, The California Raisins, 1-1/2" dia......................................**4.00**

Valentines, pack of 38 cards and teacher card, 1988, MIB.............................**6.00**

❖ Camark Pottery

Based in Camden, Arkansas, Camark Pottery was founded by Samuel Jack Carnes in 1926. The factory produced earthenware, art pottery, and decorative accessories. Several of the head potters had originally worked for Weller Pottery. The company remained in business until 1966.

Reference: David Edwin Gifford, *Collector's Guide to Camark Pottery*, Collector Books, 1997.

Collectors' Club: Arkansas Pottery Collectors Soc, P.O. Box 7617, Little Rock, AR 72217.

Basket, Iris pattern, hp in blue and green pastels, 9-1/2" h **185.00**

Console bowl, yellow Iris pattern, 14-1/2" l, 8" w, 5-5/8" h....................**75.00**

Console set, 15" d handled bowl, pr 5-1/2" h candlesticks, Iris pattern, incised marks, one orig sticker, one candlestick badly broken and repaired **150.00**

Dresser dish, blue, emb leaves and thistles, 11" l, 9" w, 3" h.................**40.00**

Ewer, pastel blue, spiral body and handle, 6-3/4" h **40.00**

Figure, burgundy pointer hound dog, hydrant, wood base, mkd "Souvenir of Lawton, Okla." **75.00**

Fruit dish, pedestal, lavender/purple glaze, scalloped edge, 8-1/2" d, 7" h **65.00**

Pitcher, #161, maroon, incised block style mark, orig paper label, 6" h .**75.00**

Strawberry planter, hanging, ribbed design, white, mkd N-50, 7" h **45.00**

Vase

Fan-shape, mottled rust, scarlet, and orange glazes, 1930s **55.00**

Glossy white, baluster shape, handles, 1930s, 6-1/2" h **50.00**

Water Lily pattern, mkd A10K, orig paper label, 7-1/2" h **195.00**

Yellow, sweeping cornucopia-type form **65.00**

Window box, green matte glaze, 2-3/4" h, 8" w **18.00**

❖ Cambridge Glass

Cambridge Glass Company of Cambridge, Ohio, was incorporated in 1901. Initially, the company made clear tableware, but they later expanded into colored, etched, and engraved glass. Over 40 different hues were produced in blown and pressed glass. Cambridge used five different marks, but not every piece was marked. The plant closed in 1954, with some of the molds being sold to the Imperial Glass Company in Bellaire, Ohio.

References: Gene Florence, *Elegant Glassware of the Depression Era*, 9th ed, Collector Books, 2000; National Cambridge Collectors, *Cambridge Glass Co., Cambridge, Ohio* (reprint of 1930 catalog and supplements through 1934), Collector Books, 1976 (1996 value update); ——, *Cambridge Glass Co., Cambridge, Ohio, 1949 thru 1953* (catalog reprint), Collector Books, 1976 (1996 value update); ——, *Colors in Cambridge Glass*, Collector Books, 1984 (1993 value update); Bill and Phyllis Smith, *Cambridge Glass 1927–1929* (1986) and *Identification Guide to Cambridge Glass 1927–1929* (updated prices 1996).

Collectors' Club: National Cambridge Collectors, P.O. Box 416, Cambridge, OH 43725.

For additional listings, see *Warman's Antiques & Collectibles* and *Warman's Glass*.

Banana Bowl, Inverted Thistle, 7" l, radium green, mkd "Near-cut" **95.00**

Bell, Rose Point.............................**150.00**

Bonbon, Diane, crystal, 8-1/2"........**25.00**

Bookends, pr, eagle, crystal...........**65.00**

Bowl and underplate, Wildflower, crystal, gold trim.........................**385.00**

Butter dish, cov, Gadroon, crystal..**45.00**

Candy dish, cov, Wildflower, crystal, 3 parts **20.00**

Champagne, Wildflower, crystal **24.00**

Cigarette Box, Caprice, blue, 3-1/2" x 4-1/2" **70.00**

Claret, Wildflower, crystal, 4-1/2 oz.**42.00**

Cocktail

Caprice, blue **48.00**

Diane, crystal **15.00**

Cordial, Caprice, blue **124.00**

Creamer and sugar

Caprice, crystal **35.00**

Cascade, emerald green.............**35.00**

Cambridge Glass, cake plate, wildflower pattern, crystal, gold trim, 1940-50, $85.

Cup and saucer

Decagon, pink **10.00**

Martha Washington **45.00**

Decanter Set, decanter, stopper, 6 handled 2-1/2 oz tumblers, Tally Ho, amethyst.....................................**185.00**

Finger bowl, Adam, yellow **25.00**

Flower frog, nude, crystal, 6-1/2" h **95.00**

Fruit Bowl, Decagon, pink, 5-1/2" dia **5.50**

Goblet, Rose Point, crystal, 10 oz ..**30.00**

Iced tea tumbler, Lexington...........**18.00**

Lemon plate, Caprice, blue, 5" dia .**15.00**

Mustard, cov, Farber Brothers, cobalt **50.00**

Plate

Decagon, pink, 8".........................**8.00**

Martha Washington, amber, lunch**15.00**

Relish, Mt. Vernon, 5-part, crystal...**35.00**

Server, center handle, Decagon, blue **20.00**

Swan, crystal, sgd, 7".....................**35.00**

Tumbler

Adam, yellow, ftd **25.00**

Caprice, blue, 12-oz, ftd..............**40.00**

Vase, Diane, crystal, keyhole, 12" h **110.00**

Wine, Diane, crystal, 2-1/2 oz **30.00**

❖ Cameo Glass

Antique cameo glass is actually several layers of glass that have been cut in a cameo technique. Look for examples that are aesthetically pleasing, free of damage, and have a signature or paper label.

For additional listings, see *Warman's Antiques & Collectibles* and *Warman's Glass*.

Reproduction Alert

Box, 3" h, triangular form sloping from

Cambridge Glass, candy dish, cov, pink milk glass, hp floral dec, 3 part int., $85.

Cameo Glass Vase, transparent crystal overlaid in yellow amber, cameo carved rubrum lilies on honeycomb ground, sgd "Webb" in script on pedestal foot, 8" h, $850.

round opening, cameo cut and etched mountain landscape in blues and greens, sterling silver lid, cameo-etched "Lamartine" on side, int. rim nicks **360.00**

Salt, bucket form, two upright handles, frosted clear ground, cameo etched and enameled black tree-lined shore, distant ruins, gilt rim, sgd "Daum (cross) Nancy" in gilt on base, small rim chips, 1-3/8" h **575.00**

Tray, 4-1/4" w, sq, translucent light amber ground, etched flowers and buds, pink, cream, deep red, and gilt enameling, cameo-etched "Galle" signature, light wear..**150.00**

Vase

3-3/8" h, ovoid, amber shading to cream, overlaid in orange and brown, cameo-etched pond plant life, cameo-etched "Galle" at side .**550.00**

4-1/4" h, conical, green ground, bands of stylized flower blossoms on etched and polished surfaces, gilt highlights, inscribed "Daum (cross) Nancy" on base, gilt wear.......**325.00**

4-1/2" h, conical rim, round body, overlaid in white on blue ground, cameo-cut rose blossom, leafy stems, borders, rim chips, 20th C **920.00**

5" h, gray ground internally dec with lavender and yellow mottling, overlaid in amethyst, cameo cut lattice and floral design, sgd "Charder" in cameo, c1925 .....**815.00**

6-5/8" h, slender neck on bulbous base, etched gold and black leafy fines and black enameled landscape scene, inscribed "Daum (cross) Nancy," rim nick.......................**350.00**

9-1/8" h, slender neck and bulbous

base, cameo-etched morning glory blossom on leafy vine, white cut to yellow, 20th C, rim chips.........**865.00**

9-3/4" h, oval, amber glass overlaid in orange and deep red, cameo cut and etched roses, sgd "Galle" **460.00**

10" h, cylindrical, colorless body overlaid in yellow, acid-etched palm trees and foliage, raised "Handel 4254" on base, sgd "Pamle" on side for Joseph Palme, Meriden, CT **500.00**

Whiskey jug, 10-1/2" h, textured translucent ground, cameo cut and enameled grapevine and leaves, metal lid and handle in form of knight's helmet, lion finial on flip lid, unsigned, c1895 ....**815.00**

❖ Cameos

Most jewelry collectors include a few cameos in their treasures. These carved beauties enchant buyers. When purchasing a shell-carved cameo, check that the settings are secure and original to the cameo. Hold the piece up to the light. If light passes through the carved layers, you're in luck, for if you can't see the image when held this way, it's probably a modern copy.

Bracelet, carved lava, various colored cameos, Victorian, 14k yg mounting **1,500.00**

Brooch

Rose, marquisette setting **125.00**

Scenic, house in center of oval plaque, white gold setting....................**900.00**

Woman, flapper style hair-do, off-shoulder dress, white gold setting **600.00**

Woman, head and shoulders, flowers in hair, Victorian, carved agate, gold beadwork frame, 18k yg setting **850.00**

Compact, onyx cameo, marcasite ring, yellow enamel............................**425.00**

Pendant

Diamond shaped frame, cameo with dancing figure, flowing dress and scarf, 14k yg setting **850.00**

Oval, woman's profile, flowers in her hair, 14k gold setting **250.00**

Ring, small woman's profile, diamond necklace ornament, white gold basket setting....................................**1,250.00**

Stickpin, carved shell with woman's profile, 14k yg mounting and pin **400.00**

❖ Cameras and Accessories

Many cameras and their accessories and ephemera find their way to flea markets. Carefully check completeness and condition. To some extent, value will be determined by the type of lens or the special features available on a particular model.

For additional listings, see *Warman's Antiques & Collectibles* and *Warman's Americana & Collectibles.*

Reference: James and Joan McKeown, *McKeown's Price Guide to Antique & Classic Cameras, 2001-2002*, Centennial Photo Service, 2001.

Periodicals: *Camera Shopper*, P.O. Box 1086, New Cannan, CT 06840; *Classic Camera*, P.O. Box 1270, New York, NY 10157-2078; *Shutterbug*, 5211 S Washington Ave, Titusville, FL 32780.

Collectors' Clubs: American Photographic Historical Soc, 1150 Avenue of the Americas, New York, NY 10036; American Society of Camera Collectors, 7952 Genesta Ave, Van Nuys, CA 91406; International Kodak Historical Soc, P.O. Box 21, Flourtown, PA 19301; Leica Historical Soc of America, 7611 Dornoch Ln, Dallas, TX 75248; Nikon Historical Soc, P.O. Box 3213, Munster, IN 46321; Zeiss Historical Soc, 300 Waxwing Dr, Cranbury, NJ 08512.

Accessories, Kodak Kodachrome box, bag and metal film can, 1959.......**12.00**

Beaker, clear glass, footed, "Use Only Kodak For Photography," 4" h.......**20.00**

Camera

Agfa Isolette **30.00**

Argus Argoflex 75.........................**10.00**

Cameras & Accessories, tripod, Majestic, large, adjustable, $65.

Ansco, Vest Pocket No. 1, c1915, strut-
type folding camera **30.00**
Canon Canonette **45.00**
CMC Camera **30.00**
Kodak Bantam f8, c1940, Bakelite body
....**25.00**
Kodak Brownie Hawkeye...............**5.00**
Kodak Duaflex **10.00**
Kodak Hawkeye No. 2C.................**5.00**
Kodak Tourist II...........................**15.00**
Minolta 16, 1960s.......................**35.00**
Pho-tak Corp., Marksman, 1950s **10.00**
Polaroid 95, 1948 ....**25.00**
Voigtlander Avus **60.00**
Trimming board, Kodak, No. 1, 5-x-6
wooden base...............................**20.00**

❖ Campbell's Soup

Joseph Campbell and Abram Anderson started a canning plant in Camden, New Jersey, in 1869, but it wasn't until 1897 that the facility began producing soup. The red-and-white Campbell's label was introduced in 1898, and the gold medallion that graced the company's cans until just recently was awarded in 1900. The pudgy, round-faced Campbell Kids were introduced in 1904, but their contemporary physiques are slimmer and trimmer.

Reference: David and Micki Young, *Campbell's Soup Collectibles from A to Z,* Krause Publications, 1998.

Collectors' Clubs: Campbell Kids Collectors, 649 Bayview Dr, Akron, OH 44319; Campbell's Soup Collector Club, 414 Country Lane Ct, Wauconda, IL 60084.

Baby dish, shows Campbell's Kids, 7-1/2" dia **55.00**
Bank, ceramic, 1970s.....................**70.00**
Book, *The Campbell's Kids at Home* by Alma S. Lach, Rand McNally Elf Book, 1954, story by Alma S. Lach, minor wear...**35.00**
Christmas Ornament **25.00**
Cookbook, *The Soup and Sandwich Handbook,* Campbell Soups, thermal mug on cover, 1971.....................**12.00**

Campbell's Soup, child's feeding plate, two Campbell kids, one holding doll behind back, Buffalo Pottery, $45.

Doll, boy and girl, vinyl, orig clothes, pr
....**145.00**
Novelty radio, tomato soup can shape, orig box **45.00**
Pennant, felt, "Campbell's Soups," white text, red ground, 1 shows child in rocker, 1 shows child with pail, 21" h, 8" w, pr **253.00**
Poster, Campbell's Kids behind board promoting weekly grocer's specials, can of soup in lower-left corner, tears, framed, 30" h, 23" w...................**121.00**
Watch, Campbell's Kid in green dress with hat and mirror, adult size, dated 1982 ....**61.00**

❖ Candlesticks

Designed to keep a burning candle upright, candlesticks can be found in all shapes and sizes at flea markets.

Reference: Gene Florence, *Glass Candlesticks of the Depression Era,* Collector Books, 2000; Paula Pendergrass and Sherry Riggs, *Elegant Glass CandleHolders,* Schiffer Publishing, 2002.

Brass
Chamberstick, side pushup, saucer handle, English, dents, 4-1/2" h**88.00**
Queen Anne, ring-turned base, boldly turned column, orig pushup, 12" h, pr
....**275.00**
Victorian, beehive, pushup, mkd England, 6" h, pr.....................**165.00**
Glass
Black, 2-handle, round base, 3-1/2" h, pr
....**35.00**
Crystal, L.E. Smith, 4-1/2" h, pr ...**32.50**
Milk glass, Dolphin pattern, Westmoreland, 4-1/2" h, pr.......**45.00**
Graniteware, white, saucer base, ring handle **20.00**
Porcelain, ivory, gold accents, Lenox, pr
....**75.00**
Pottery
Hull, Blossomtime, T11, pr **75.00**
Niloak, Mission Ware, pr **90.00**

Candlesticks, Graniteware, white, gold stripe dec, ring handle, saucer base, $15.

Sheet iron, hog scraper, round base, tubular shaft, ejector mechanism on side, ejector knob stamped "HYD," minor rust, 6-1/2" h **190.00**
Tin, Tindeco, orig stenciling, 6-3/4" h, pr
....**65.00**

❖ Candlewick

Imperial pattern No. 400, known as Candlewick, was introduced in 1936 and was an instant hit with American consumers. The line was continuously produced until 1982. After Imperial declared bankruptcy, several of the molds were sold, and other companies began producing this pattern, often in different colors.

References: Gene Florence, *Elegant Glassware of the Depression Era,* 8th ed, Collector Books, 1999; National Imperial Glass Collector's Soc, *Imperial Glass Encyclopedia, Vol. I: A–Cane,* The Glass Press, 1995; ——, *Imperial Glass Catalog Reprint,* Antique Publications, 1991; Virginia R. Scott, *Collector's Guide to Imperial Candlewick,* 4th ed, self-published, no date; Mary M. Wetzel-Tomalka, *Candlewick: The Jewel of Imperial, Book I,* and *Book II,* 1995; ——,*Candlewick, The Jewel of Imperial, Price Guide '99 and More,* 1998, self-published.

Periodicals: *Glasszette,* National Imperial Glass Collector's Soc, P.O. Box 534, Bellaire, OH 43528; *The Candlewick Collector Newsletter,* National Candlewick Collector's Club, 275 Milledge Terrace, Athens, GA 30606.

Collectors' Clubs: National Candlewick Collector's Club, 275 Milledge Terrace, Athens, GA 30606; National Imperial Glass Collector's Soc, P.O. Box 534, Bellaire, OH 43528. Check with these organizations for local clubs in your area.

For additional listings, see *Warman's Americana & Collectibles* and *Warman's Glass.*

Reproduction Alert

Ashtray, 400/176, large beads, 3-1/4" sq
....**12.00**
Atomizer, 400/247 shaker, atomizer top,

Candlewick, relish dish, curved open handle, $25.

amethyst....................................**150.00**
Baked Apple Dish, 6-1/2"..............**25.00**
Basket, turned-up sides, applied handle,
    6-1/2"....................................**35.00**
Bell, 400/108, 4-bead handle, 4" h..**60.00**
Bonbon, #51H, heart shape, handle, 6"
    ....**35.00**
Bowl, #106B, belled, 12" dia..........**70.00**
Bud vase, 400/25, 3-3/4" h, beaded foot,
    ball shape, crimped top................**35.00**
Butter dish, 1/4-pound **25.00**
Cake plate, sterling silver pedestal.**65.00**
Canape plate, #36 ....**12.00**
Candy dish, cov, 400/59, 5-1/2" d, 2-
    bead finial..................................**40.00**
Celery tray, #105, 13" **40.00**
Champagne, saucer **20.00**
Cigarette holder, eagle **95.00**
Coaster **12.00**
Cocktail set, 6" d plate with 2-1/2" off-
    center indent, #111 1-bead cocktail
    glass **35.00**
Compote, 4 bead stem, 8" dia........**65.00**
Cordial, flared belled top, 4 graduated
    beads in stem..............................**48.00**
Creamer and sugar, question mark
    handle **30.00**
Cup and saucer, #37, coffee..........**14.00**
Deviled egg tray, 11-1/2" dia..........**95.00**
Goblet, flared bell bowl, 4 graduated
    beads in stem, 9 oz......................**15.00**
Iced tea tumbler, 400/19, beaded base,
    straight sides...............................**15.00**
Jelly server, 1 bead stem, 2 bead cover
    ....**50.00**
Marmalade jar, cov.......................**60.00**
Mustard jar, 400/156, beaded foot,
    notched beaded cov with 2-bead finial,
    3-1/2" glass spoon, fleur-de-lis handle
    ....**40.00**
Pastry tray, #68D, floral cutting, 11-1/2" l
    ....**80.00**
Plate, beaded edge
    6" dia **8.00**
    8-1/2" dia....................................**12.00**
    10-1/4" dia..................................**35.00**
Relish, #55, 4 part **30.00**
Salt and pepper shakers, #247, pr**45.00**
Sherbet, low, #19, 5-oz **18.00**
Tidbit server, 2 tiers **55.00**
Tumbler, water, 400/19, beaded base,
    straight sides, 10 oz, 4-3/4" h **18.00**
Vase, 400/87F, fan, 8" h **30.00**
Wine, 400/190 line, belled bowl, hollow
    trumpet stem with beads, 5 oz.....**25.00**

❖ Candy Containers

Figural glass candy containers have been a part of childhood since 1876, when they were first introduced at the Centennial

Candy Containers, Santa-shaped glass candy container with plastic head, 6" high, $85.

Exposition in Philadelphia. These interesting glass containers often commemorated historical events. Candy containers were also made of papier-mache, cardboard, and tin. All are highly collectible and eagerly sought at flea markets.

References: *Candy Containers*, L-W Book Sales, 1996; Douglas M. Dezso, J. Lion Poirier & Rose D. Poirier, *Collector's Guide to Candy Containers*, Collector Books, 1997; George Eikelberner and Serge Agadjanian, *Complete American Glass Candy Containers Handbook*, revised and published by Adele L. Bowden, 1986; Jennie Long, *Album of Candy Containers*, vol. I (1978), vol. II (1983), self-published.

Collectors' Club: Candy Container Collectors of America, P.O. Box 352, Chelmsford, MA 01824-0352.

For additional listings, see *Warman's Antiques & Collectibles* and *Warman's Americana & Collectibles*.

Reproduction Alert

Battleship, glass, orig cardboard
    closure, printed "Victory Glass Inc."
    ....**48.00**
Black cat, with pumpkin, papier-mache,
    German **75.00**
Boat, clear glass, orig label, 5-1/4" l**40.00**
Boot, papier-mache, red and white.**24.00**
Bulldog, glass, orig paint **90.00**
Dog, glass, blue.............................**15.00**
Duck, cardboard, nodding head......**18.50**
Football, tin, German.....................**35.00**
Girl, two geese, orig closure **55.00**
Hen on nest, glass, 2-pc, Millstein..**15.00**
Irishman, top hat and pipe, papier-
    mâché **12.00**
Jeep, mkd "Jeanette Glass Co. & J. H.
    Millstein Co.," 4-1/2" l, chip..........**25.00**
Lantern, large, glass and metal **35.00**
Locomotive #888, clear glass, 4" l.**35.00**
Model T, glass **24.00**
Owl, glass, stylized feathers, painted,
    screw-on cap **90.00**
Pistol, glass....................................**30.00**
Pumpkin man, bisque **45.00**
Rabbit, papier-mache, pulling basket,
    pasteboard wheels **55.00**
Rooster, glass, screw-on cap **125.00**
Santa Claus

Cardboard, little girl carrying Christmas
    tree, round, cardboard, 3-1/4" d**30.00**
Plastic, standing, opening for candy in
    back, Rosbro Plastics, 5" h.......**30.00**
Suitcase Glass with wire handle, 2-3/8"
    h, 3-5/8" w **79.00**
Cardboard, The Leader Novelty Candy
    Co., 2-1/2" h, 2-3/4" w **35.00**
Telephone, glass, candlestick type
    ....**50.00**
Truck, Cherrydale Farms, metal, movable
    wheels, labeled "Nobel Hall Made in
    China," 7" l, 3-1/2" w, 4" h
    ....**5.00**
Turkey, chalk, metal feet, German..**35.00**

❖ Cap Guns

"Bang! Bang!" was the cry of many a youngster playing Cowboys and Indians. Whether you were the good guy or the bad guy, you needed a reliable six-shooter. The first toy cap gun was produced in the 1870s and was made of cast iron. It remained the material of choice until around World War II, when paper, rubber, glass, steel, tin, wood and even zinc were used. By the 1950s, diecast metal and plastic were being used.

References: Rudy D'Angelo, *Cowboy Hero Cap Pistols,* Antique Trader Books, 1997; James L. Dundas, *Cap Guns with Values,* Schiffer Publishing, 1996; Jerrell Little, *Price Guide to Cowboy Cap Guns and Guitars,* L-W Book Sales, 1996; Jim Schlever, *Backyard Buckaroos: Collecting Western Toy Guns,* Books Americana/Krause Publications, 1996.

Periodical: Toy Gun Collectors of America Newsletter, 312 Sterling Way, Anaheim, CA 92807.

Collectors' Club: Toy Gun Collectors of America, 3009 Oleander Ave., San Marcos, CA 92069.

Cap Gun, Daisy, white plastic handle, brown holster, $150.

Buck'n Bronc..............................115.00
Buffalo Bill, J.&E. Stevens, repeating,
   1920s, orig box......................320.00
Champion, Kilgore, brown grips, 1960s,
   11" l..70.00
Cheyenne Shooter, Hamilton.........70.00
Circle A, Oh Boy series 65.00
Derringer, Hubley, white plastic handle,
   worn, 3-1/4" l 7.50
Fanner 50, Mattel
   Impala grips, c1962, 10-1/2" l 55.00
   Stag grips, c1959, 10-1/2" l........210.00
Flintlock, double barrel, Hubley, amber
   color, 9" l 25.00
Gene Autry .44, Leslie-Hentry, 1950s,
   11" l 165.00
Hubley, white handle, 11" l............125.00
Invincible, Kilgore, cast iron, c1938, 5" l
   ....35.00
Kusan, #280.................................12.95
Maverick
   Long barrel, black and white grips,
   1960s, 11" l............................280.00
   Short barrel, nickel finish, new white
   grips, 1960s, 9" l.....................55.00
Pony Boy, orig black and white holster,
   1950s, 9-1/2" l............................45.00
Presto, 5" w, 3-1/4" h 40.00
Texan, Hubley, 1940s, black grips, 9-1/2"
   l 130.00
Wagon Trail, white grips, 9" l 175.00

❖ Cape Cod by Avon

This ruby red pattern was an instant hit with Avon lovers. Today, many pieces can be found at flea markets. Remember that this is a mass-produced pattern and examples in very good condition are available.

Butter dish, cov, MIB 65.00
Candleholder, MIB 27.50
Candy dish, MIB 40.00
Coffee cup 12.00
Creamer, orig scented candle, MIB 37.50
Cruet 20.00

Cape Cod, Avon Luncheon plate, $10.

Dessert plate 8.00
Dinner plate, 11" d, 1982, MIB......37.50
Goblet...8.00
Luncheon plate 10.00
Mug, ftd, 2 in orig box 30.00
Napkin rings, 1-3/4" d, set of 4 ......45.00
Platter, MIB 37.50
Salad plate...................................8.00
Salt and pepper shakers, pr, MIB .42.00
Saucer 6.00
Tumbler 18.00
Vase, ftd, 8" h 24.00
Water pitcher, 48-oz, 7-1/2" h 40.00
Wine goblet, MIB 18.00
Wine decanter 36.00

❖ Care Bears

Some people wear their hearts on their sleeves. Care Bears wear them (and other symbols representing personality traits) on their tummies. Kids of all ages have welcomed these lovable creatures into their homes—and their collections—since American Greetings Corp. first introduced them in 1982.

Book
   Caring is What Counts, hardcover,
   worn..1.50
   Bedtime Bears Book of Bedtime
   Poems, hardcover, loose binding0.50
Child's book with record, *Care Bears in*
   A Day in the Forest, color illus 2.00
Comb, folding, Tenderheart, MIP 3.00
Dolls, plush
   Baby Tugs Bear #2 ....10.00
   Bedtime Bear, 18" 12.50
   Birthday Bear, worn, 18" 6.00
   Braveheart Lion, 13" 9.00
   Champ Bear #2, 13".......................22.00
   Cheer Bear, 13"............................7.00
   Cousins Gentle Heart Lamb, 12-1/2" h
   ....9.00
   Friend Bear, wear, 13"....................9.00
   Love-A-Lot Bear, 13" 6.50
Dolls, poseable
   Baby Hugs #2...............................4.25
   Goodluck Bear 2.50
Game, On the Road to Care-A-Game,
   Parker Brothers, c1983 ....6.50
Glass, Tenderheart Bear, Pizza Hut..8.00
Lunch box, metal, orig thermos, Care
   Bear Cousins................................20.00
Mug, plastic, Cheer Bear with pink "hat"
   lid..3.25
Music box, Happy Birthday, American
   Greetings paper label, 1985, 6" h
   ....32.00
Rattle, clear ball with Tenderheart inside
   ....3.50
Sheet, flat, full bed size 10.00
Sticker book
   Brio, 28 stickers, dated 1994, marker
   on cover 3.00

Care Bears, child's desk, plastic, wood, and metal, blue, white lettering, $35.

   Caring and Sharing #1, Pizza Hut,
   stickers in place, some coloring .2.00
Swim ring, Coleco, "Splash Into Fun"
   ....4.50
Thermos, Aladdin.............................4.00

❖ Carlton Ware

Wiltshow and Robinson first manufactured this brightly colored pottery at their Charlton Works, Stoke-on-Trent, factory around 1890. In 1957, the company's name was changed to Carlton Ware, Ltd.

Collectors' Club: Carlton Ware Collectors International, P.O. Box 161, Sevenoaks, Kent, TN15 6GA, England.

Basket, Waterlily, green, 3-1/2" h
   ....125.00
Bowl, Hydrangea, blue, 9-3/4" dia
   ....125.00
Condiment set, Crinoline Lady.....225.00

Carlton Ware, egg cup or master salt, white container, blue and red striped socks, blue shoes, $42.

Carlton Ware, snack plate, white ground shading to pale blue rim, purple morning glories and leaves, $28.

Cream and sugar, Foxglove, green **65.00**

Cup and saucer, dark red luster, gilt int. rim and handle, 1920s **60.00**

Cup plate, leaf shape, green, 7" l ...**25.00**

Demitasse cup and saucer, quatrefoil shaped cup, gilt int.
   Lustre Ware, blue, gilt int., ear shaped handle.......................................**55.00**
   Lustre Ware, bright yellow, uniform crazing **48.00**
   Spiderweb dec, 2-1/2" x 2" cup, 4-1/4" dia saucer **195.00**
   Stork pattern, Rouge Royal luster, 2-1/2" x 2-1/2" cup, 4-1/4" dia saucer **115.00**

Dish
   Fish shape, green and purple, 4-1/4" dia..**50.00**
   Lettuce leaf shape, two red tomato accents, 5-1/2" w, 9" l **10.00**

Egg cup set, three yellow and white egg cups on 1-1/2" w, 7" l tray, 1930s **45.00**

Honey pot with lid, Wild Rose, yellow **89.00**

Jam dish with knife, Buttercup, pink, orig box, knife glued **125.00**

Jug, Shadow Bunny, orange ext., green int., 7" h **550.00**

Knife, Wild Rose, green **55.00**

Plate
   Buttercup, yellow, 7" x 6-1/2" **85.00**
   Hydrangea, green, 11-1/4" dia ...**165.00**

Reamer, Buttercup, yellow **195.00**

Sauceboat and stand, Buttercup, yellow **150.00**

Spoon
   Raspberry....................................**60.00**
   Wild Rose, green.........................**60.00**

Teapot, Waterlily, green, 2-cup......**395.00**

❖ Carnival Chalkware

Brightly painted plaster-of-Paris figures given away as prizes at carnivals continue to capture the eye of collectors. Most of

Carnival Chalkware, brown and white dog seated on red chair, $25.

these figures date from the 1920s through the 1960s.

Ashtray
   Collie, 8-3/4" h, ashtray 3-1/2" dia**22.00**
   German shepherd, dated 1936, paint loss, 8-1/2" h............................**20.00**

Bank, dog, long ears, yellow bow tie, wear, 12" h **32.00**

Figure
   Cocker spaniel, reclining **20.00**
   Collie, black and white, some glitter, base chips, 11-1/2" h................**40.00**
   Elephant by tree stump, 3 chips, 6" h **15.00**
   Horse, flat back side, 5-1/2" h......**15.00**
   Poodle, sitting, 3-1/2" h **10.00**
   Scottie, 2 dogs side by side, chips, 9-1/4" h **85.00**
   Superman, 1940s, 15-3/8" h **165.00**
   Tex, cowboy, 11" h........................**19.00**

❖ Carnival Glass

Carnival glass can be found in many different colors, including marigold, purples, greens, blues, reds, and pastels, all with a metallic-looking sheen or iridescence. Many different manufacturers created the hundreds of patterns

References: Carl O. Burns, *Collector's Guide to Northwood Carnival Glass*, L-W Book Sales, 1994; ——, *Dugan and Diamond Carnival Glass, 1909-1931*, Collector Books, 1998; ——, *Imperial Carnival Glass,* Collector Books, 1996 (1999 value update); Bill Edwards and Mike Carwile, *Standard Encyclopedia of Carnival Glass,* 7th ed, Collector Books, 2000; ——, *Standard Encyclopedia of Carnival Glass Price Guide,* 12th ed, Collector Books, 2000; Marion Quintin-Baxendale, *Collecting Carnival Glass,* 2nd ed., Francis Joseph, available from Krause Publications, 2002; Diane C. Rosington, *Carnival Glass Club Commemoratives, 1964-1999,* self-published, 2000; Glen and Steven Thistlewood, *Carnival Glass, The Magic & The Mystery,* Schiffer Publishing, 1998;

Carnival Glass, basket, rays, marigold int., white ext., applied clear handle, $50.

Margaret and Ken Whitmyer, *Fenton Art Glass: 1907-1939,* Collector Books, 1996 (1999 value update).

Periodical: *Network*, PageWorks, P.O. Box 2385, Mt. Pleasant, SC 29465.

Collectors' Clubs: American Carnival Glass Assoc, 9621 Springwater Ln, Miamisburg, OH 45342; Canadian Carnival Glass Assoc, 107 Montcalm Dr., Kitchner, Ontario N2B 2R4 Canada; Collectible Carnival Glass Assoc, 3103 Brentwood Circle, Grand Island, NE 68801; Heart of America Carnival Glass Assoc, 43-5 W 78th St, Prairie Village, KS 66208; International Carnival Glass Assoc, P.O. Box 306, Mentone, IN 46539. Many clubs have regional chapters. Contact the national organization for information about a club in your area.

For additional listings, see *Warman's Antiques & Collectibles* and *Warman's Glass.*

Reproduction Alert

Banana Boat, Grape and Cable, Northwood, purple.....................**185.00**

Berry Bowl, individual, Peacock at Fountain, Northwood, purple, 5" dia **35.00**

Berry Bowl, master, Grape and Cable, Northwood, emerald green **145.00**

Bonbon, Grape and Cable, Northwood, 2

Carnival Glass, ice cream bowl, Imperial Rose, purple, ruffled, $25.

handles, marigold **50.00**

Bowl

Fruits & Flowers, amethyst, 7-1/4" dia
....**70.00**

Grape, Imperial, 8-1/2" d, electric
purple, 8-1/2" dia **135.00**

Kittens, Fenton, six ruffles, marigold
....**135.00**

Peacock & Grape, marigold, 9" dia
....**50.00**

Peacock at Urn, green, 10-1/2" dia
....**250.00**

Raindrops, peach opalescent, 8-3/4"
dia...**85.00**

Strawberry, amethyst, 8-3/4" dia ..**85.00**

Vintage Leaf, green, 7-1/2" dia **72.00**

Bushel basket, white, Northwood
....**120.00**

Butter Dish, cov, Grape and Cable,
Northwood, green......................**175.00**

Calling card tray, Pond Lily, white
....**25.00**

Candy dish, Drapery, white **125.00**

Compote, Petals, amethyst, 7-1/2" x 3-
3/4" **45.00**

Cup and Saucer, Kittens, Fenton,
marigold **245.00**

Decanter, Grape, Imperial, electric
purple, stopper missing................**85.00**

Hat, Blackberry Spray, Fenton, green, 2
sides up, 6-1/2" h **95.00**

Hatpin Holder, Grape and Cable,
Northwood, purple......................**175.00**

Ice cream bowl, Daisy Wreath,
Westmoreland, moonstone, 8-1/2" dia
....**110.00**

Mug, 3-1/2" h

Orange Tree, aqua **60.00**

Singing Birds, amethyst **215.00**

Pickle dish, Poppy, blue.................**45.00**

Pitcher, 9" h, Butterfly & Berry, marigold
....**265.00**

Plate, Vintage, green, 7-1/2" dia ...**140.00**

Punch Cup, Peacock at Fountain,
Northwood, white **20.00**

Punch Set, Grape, Imperial, marigold
....**300.00**

Rose bowl

Double Stem, domed foot, peach
opalescent **160.00**

Fine Cut & Roses, Northwood, purple
....**135.00**

Frosted Block, Imperial, deep marigold
....**30.00**

Sweetmeat compote, cov, Grape and
Cable, Northwood, purple **170.00**

Tankard pitcher, Paneled Dandelion,
marigold **400.00**

Toothpick Holder, Kittens, Fenton,
ruffled, marigold, radium finish...**115.00**

Tumble-up, Smooth Rays, marigold
....**60.00**

Tumbler

Butterfly & Berry, marigold **30.00**

Concave Diamond, Celeste blue..**30.00**

Peacock at Fountain, Northwood,
amethyst **25.00**

Vase

Morning Glory, 6-1/2" h, olive green, 6-
1/2" h **60.00**

Ripple, amethyst, 11" h **110.00**

Thin Rib, Fenton, vase, 10" h, blue, 10"
h...**60.00**

Water Pitcher

Grape, Imperial, electric purple..**600.00**

Peacock at Fountain, Northwood,
amethyst **250.00**

❖ Cartoon Characters

They've entertained generations for decades and now collectors seek them out at flea markets. The charm and humor of cartoon characters light up collections across the country.

References: Ted Hake, *Hake's Price Guide To Character Toys*, Gemstone Publishing, 4th ed 2002; Jim Harmon, *Radio & TV Premiums*, Krause Publications, 1997.

Periodical: *Frostbite Falls Far-Flung Flier* (Rocky & Bullwinkle), P.O. Box 39, Macedonia, OH 44056.

Collectors' Clubs: Betty Boop Fan Club,

Cartoon Characters, lunch box, SS Popeye, Olive Oyl, Popeye, Sweetpea, and Wimpy in boat, Brutus swimming in front of shark, metal, $48.

Cartoon Characters, Fred Flintstone and Barney Rubble, plush and felt, 36" h, each, $20.

6025 Fullerton Ave, Apt 2, Buena Park, CA 90621; Peanuts Collector Club, 539 Sudden Valley, Bellingham, WA 98226; Pogo Fan Club, 6908 Wentworth Ave S, Richfield, MN 55423; Popeye Fan Club, Ste 151, 5995 Stage Rd, Barlette, TN 38184; R.F. Outcault Soc, 103 Doubloon Dr, Slidell, LA 70461.

Address Book, Peanuts, United Feature
Syndicate, Inc., 3-3/4" x 2-1/2".......**6.00**

Advertising Counter Display, Sunoco
promotion, six different 3-4" rubber
Looney Tunes figures, 1989, 17" x 15"
....**60.00**

Bank, Felix the Cat, tin....................**55.00**

Big Little Book, *Andy Panda and The
Mad Dog Mystery*, Whitman #1431
....**40.00**

Birthday card, Ziggy, unused **1.00**

Bubble gum wrapper, Popeye, 1981, 5-
1/2" x 5-1/2".............................**45.00**

Charm, Shmoo, bright silver-colored
plastic, 1940s **18.00**

Colorforms, Huckleberry Hound, 1960,
MIB..**75.00**

Coloring Book, *Flintstones Color by
Number*, Whitman **24.00**

Comic book, Popeye, large size format,
1972, 14" x 11"..........................**15.00**

Cookie jar

Bugs Bunny................................**40.00**

Felix the Cat **50.00**

Doll

Archie, cloth, 16" h **30.00**

Felix the Cat................................**8.00**

Drinking glass

Pepsi, Warner Brothers Looney Tunes,
copyright 1966 ....**8.00**

Welch's, 1971, Hot Dog Goes to
School......................................**5.00**

Egg cup, Betty Boop, figural, glazed
ceramic, stamped "Made in Japan,"
1930s, 1-5/8" dia, 2-3/8" h **250.00**

Figure

Archie, Sirocco, painted brown military
uniform and hat, 1944 ....**24.00**

Li'l Abner, plastic, hp, Marx, 1950s, 2-1/2" h **12.00**
Mammy and Pappy Yokum, plastic, hp, Marx, 1950s, 2" h, 1-1/2" w **20.00**
Popeye, jointed wood, 4-1/2" h, copyright K.F.S. **145.00**
Game
 Barney Google an' Snuffy Smith, Milton Bradley, 1963, orig box **42.00**
 Underdog, 1964, missing one decal **65.00**
Hand puppet, plush, tag "Bugs Bunny 50th Birthday Celebration," 1990, 14" h **12.00**
Lunch box, Woody Woodpecker and Buzz Buzzard, dark green leather, multicolored image of Woody stitched on front, holding hammer, copyright Walter Lantz Productions, c1970 **175.00**
Music box, Betty Boop, cowgirl **45.00**
Napkin holder, Popeye, ceramic **15.00**
Pencil holder, plastic, figural, Garfield **2.00**
Perfume set, Little Lulu **85.00**
Pinback button
 High Admiral Cigarettes, Yellow Kid **35.00**
 Member Archie Club, 1-1/2" dia ...**20.00**
Poster, The Sunday World, New York, 1896, pretty girl in bathing suit blowing smoke on beach at sun rise, newspaper on shoreline dated June 7, next to box labeled "Bathing Suit," artist sgd in text "F. Gilbert Edge," printed text "Municpal Baby Catchers Funny Cartoons, Coaching Paraide in Hogan's Alley, Major McKinley, Wood Sawyer Colored Cartoons, Eight Funny Pages And A Whole Magazine, How to Keep Your Temper Funny Cartoons, Zimmerman's Bicycle Pages" **125.00**
Push Puppet, Casper **100.00**
Ring, Betty Rubble, off-white plastic, expansion band, diecut portrait, c1960 ....**25.00**
Salt and pepper shakers, pr
 Bugs Bunny and Taz **15.00**
 Felix the Cat **20.00**
String holder, Betty Boop, hp, figural, plaster, 5-3/4" l **295.00**
Target set, Felix the Cat, 2-in-1, gun and orig stoppers, orig box **175.00**
Thermos, Casper the Friendly Ghost **75.00**
Vase, Betty Boop **30.00**
Viewmaster Reel, Andy Panda in Mystery Tracks, Sawyer, #822 ....**4.00**
Word Search puzzle book, The Jetsons, 1978, unused **10.00**
Wristwatch, Smitty, gray aged dial, black, white, red and green figure, New Haven Clock Co., orig case, c1935 ....**250.00**

❖ Cash Registers

One of the necessities of any store is a good cash register. However, with today's electronic gadgets, the large styles of yesterday have been cast aside. Collectors gather up these units, restore them, and then enjoy their purchase.

Collectors' Club: Cash Register Collectors Club of America, P.O. Box 20534, Dayton, OH 45420

National, candy store size, ornate cast detail, milk glass shelf on front, 21-1/4" x 10-1/4" x 16" **675.00**
National, Model 313, small, emb brass, marble ledge, 17" h, missing "Amount Purchased" marquee, restored ..**750.00**
Wooden, loose money in back **125.00**

❖ Cassidy, Hopalong

Hopalong Cassidy was a cowboy hero who successfully made the leap from movies to radio to television. Hoppy was also a master at self-promotion and did a lot of advertising, as did many other early cowboy heroes.

Collectors' Club: Friends of Hopalong Cassidy Fan Club, 6310 Friendship Dr, New Concord, OH 43762; Westerns & Serials Fan Club, Route 1, Box 103, Vernon Center, MN 56090-9744.

Bank, figural, blue plastic, 4-1/2" h **330.00**
Book, *Hopalong Cassidy Returns*, Clarence E. Mulford, Triangle Books, July 1943, front of dj partially missing **10.00**
Bread label, Bond Bread **100.00**
Calendar, 1952, sepia, white, and orange tinted photo for each month, 6" x 11-1/2" **175.00**
Cap pistol, Wyandotte, repeater, 8-1/2" l nickel finish white metal, ivory white incised grips with image **150.00**
Comic Book, *The Mad Barber*, Bond Bread **80.00**
Cookie jar, Hopalong and Topper, Happy Memories Collectibles **275.00**
Ear Muffs, red **175.00**
Little Golden Book, *Hopalong Cassidy & Bar 20* **25.00**

Hopalong Cassidy, night light, holster-shaped, original decal, $120.

Lunch Box, red, cloud decal, no thermos **150.00**
Magazine, Time **120.00**
Play set, Hopalong Cassidy Western Frontier Set, MIB **550.00**
Photograph, autographed, 5" x 7" ..**90.00**
Puzzle, frame tray **45.00**
Sign, Hopalong Cassidy Rides Again, Knickerbocker News, cardboard, 11" x 21" **150.00**
Soap, Topper, Castile **125.00**
Wristwatch, orig box with saddle, U.S. Time **260.00**

❖ Cast Iron

Cast iron has long been a favorite metal for creating durable goods, such as cooking utensils, farm implements, and tools.

Periodicals: *Cast Iron Cookware News*, 28 Angela Ave, San Anselmo, CA 94960; *Kettles n' Cookware*, Drawer B, Perrysburg, NY 14129.

Collectors' Club: Griswold & Cast Iron Cookware Assoc, 54 Macon Ave, Asheville, NC 28801.

> **Buyer beware!**
> A lot of people are seeing stars these days, reproduction stars that is. That's not a good thing!
> It seems these architectural minatures are everywhere. It only took a few showing up in illustrations in decorator magazines for people to go crazy for the things. Trouble is, many are being offered on the secondary market, where they're being represented as old. Your socks are probably older than these things.
> The original building stars were used on the outside of 19th-century structures, tying off the ends of metal supports that helped stabilize the structure.
> There's nothing wrong with buying the newer versions, providing you know what you're getting and the price is reasonable. How do you tell the new from the old? Most of the contemporary examples have been intentionally rusted. New rust has a bright-orange color, compared to the darker rust found on an object that has aged slowly over a long period of time.

Andirons, pr, faceted ball finials, knife blade, arched bases, penny feet, 20" h, rusted surface **325.00**
Boot scraper, scroll ends, green granite base **110.00**
Christmas tree stand, openwork base with trees and stars, orig green paint, 2-1/2" h, 7-3/4" sq **75.00**

Cast Iron, corn muffin pan, unmarked, slight rust, $95.

Dutch oven, #8, Griswold, painted black **55.00**

Egg beater, Dover, wooden knob, 10-1/4" l **25.00**

Hitching post, jockey, yellow, red, green, black, and white painted detail, wired for lantern, 31" h.........................**275.00**

Mirror, gilt, rococo scrolled acanthus frame, oval beveled mirror, Victorian, 22" h...**75.00**

Muffin tin, hearts motif, 8 cups.....**110.00**

Match safe, double holders, 4" h, 4" w **125.00**

Skillet, #8, Griswold **38.00**

Snow bird, 6" wingspan..................**40.00**

Trivet, horseshoe shape, "Good Luck To All Who Use This Stand," 1870 patent date, repainted, 8" l, 4-1/2" w.......**20.00**

❖ Catalina Pottery

Catalina Pottery is one of the California potteries that has begun attracting collector interest in recent years. The company was founded in 1927 on Santa Catalina Island. Dinnerware production was added in 1931. In 1937, Gladding, McBean & Co. bought the firm and closed the island plant.

Ashtray, fish, blue **60.00**

Bowl, light blue int., white ext. incised dec **65.00**

Cigarette box, covered, horse's head, ivory...**475.00**

Cup and saucer, green **60.00**

Demitasse cup, set of six, two shades of blue, yellow, mint green, ivory, burnt red, stamp mark, 2-3/4" h..........**225.00**

Head vase, terra cotta, turquoise head scarf **350.00**

Low bowl, light orange exterior, turquoise interior, 10" x 6"............**25.00**

Vase
Baluster, white, rim chip, 5" h.......**15.00**
Fan-shape, tan and green, 9" h .**125.00**
Fluted design, white, 10" h........**225.00**
Shell design, white ext., turquoise blue int...**85.00**

❖ Catalogs

Old trade and merchandise catalogs are sought by collectors. They are sometimes the best source of information about what a company produced.

Reference: Ron Barlow and Ray Reynolds, *Insider's Guide To Old Books, Magazines, Newspapers and Trade Catalogs,* Windmill Publishing, 1996.

For additional listings, see *Warman's Antiques & Collectibles* and *Warman's Americana & Collectibles.*

Avon, spiral-bound, 169 pgs, 1950s **30.00**

Bausch & Lomb Optical Co., Rochester, N.Y., 122 pgs, 1919 ...**55.00**

Big Gem Art Advertising Calendars, US, 1936, 10" x 16-1/2", salesman's demo kit, 10" x 16-1/2" folder with two 14" x 8-1/2" calendars laid down, green folder wraps, gold lettering...........**30.00**

Burgess Plant & Seed Co., Galesburg, Wis., 82 pgs, 1944 ....**10.00**

Butler Brothers, St. Louis, 50th anniversary catalog, May 1927, 420 pgs **40.00**

Century Furniture Co., Grand Rapids, Mich., 40 pgs, 1931.....................**50.00**

Chrysler Sales Division, Detroit, MI, 1950, 18 pgs, 8" x 10", 24" x 30" sheet folded as issued, color, shows 19 models..**24.00**

Eugene Dietzgen Co., Anabasis, NY, c1939, 56 pgs, 5-3/4" x 8-3/4" **22.00**

Frank & Son, Inc., New York, NY, c19128, 8 pgs, 3" x 6".................**10.00**

Geneva Wagon Co., Geneva, N.Y., 44 pgs, 1905, worn **75.00**

George Delker Co., Henderson, Ky., buggies catalog, 40 pgs, 1926.....**75.00**

Hartz Mountain Products, 32 pgs, 1933 ....**18.00**

Holtzman-Cabot Electric, Boston, MA, 1905, 4 pgs, 6-3/4" x 9-1/2" **15.00**

John Deere Co., Chicago, Ill., 24 pgs, 1970 ....**14.00**

Jordan, Marsh & Co., Boston, Mass., 254 pgs, 1895 ....**33.00**

Kirsch Manufacturing Co., Diturgis, Mich., 18 pgs, 1922.....................**13.00**

Milton Bradley Co., Boston, Mass., 124 pgs, 1923 ....**22.00**

Montgomery Ward & Co., Fall & Winter, 1,144 pgs, 1956 ....**32.00**

National Lumber Mfgrs, Washington, DC, 1929, 30 pgs, 8-1/4" x 11" **20.00**

Oakes Poultry and Hog Equipment Catalog, Tipton, Ind., 60 pgs, 1957 ....**7.50**

Reliable Incubators, Quincy, Ill., 1896 ....**28.00**

Safe Cabinet Co., Chicago, IL, c1931, 40 pgs, 6" x 9"...............................**15.00**

Schenfeld & Sons, New York, NY, no date, 1970s, 24 pgs, 6-3/4" x 9-1/2", 58 material swatches tipped in.........**24.00**

United States Rubber Co., New Orleans, LA, c1940, 12 pgs, 9" x 12",

Ked Catalog of Footwear **32.00**

Wanamaker, John, New York, NY, 1920s, 8 pgs, 4-3/4" x 6", March is the Month of China....................................**36.00**

Winchester Western, 31 pgs, 1962 ....**15.00**

❖ Cat Collectibles

It's purrfectly obvious—cat collectors love their cats, whether they are live and furry or an inanimate collectible. More often than not, collectors purchase objects that resemble their favorite furry friends.

> **Reproduction Alert**

For additional listings, see *Warman's Americana & Collectibles.*

Avon bottle, Kitten's Hideaway, white kitten in brown basket, 1974 ....**8.00**

Bookends, pr, ceramic, one with black and white cat stretching his paw through to other bookend, second bookend has gray mouse with mallet, ready to strike extended cat's paw, incised "© 1983" and ceramist's initials **35.00**

Bookmark, figural cat face, celluloid, reverse mkd "don't kiss me," 22" l green cord, c1920, 1-3/4" w x 1-3/4" h...**65.00**

Comic book, *Felix the Cat*, All Pictures Comics, 1945 ....**50.00**

Cup and saucer, child size, cat on pussy willow twig, mkd "Made in Japan"**12.00**

Figure
Siamese, ceramic, model #4693, paper label "Lefton Japan," 8" h **28.00**
Three pink kittens, attached and seated on blue Victorian-style sofa with gold trim, stamped "© 1959 Bradley Onimco," 4" h **25.00**

Handkerchief, embroidered.............**5.00**

Mug, 3-1/4" h, ceramic, cat face, white, dark blue floral collar and handle, incised "Avon"..............................**18.00**

Cat Collectibles, plate, decal of striped cat with blue bow, gold trim, white ground, faux Serves fleur-de-lis mark, 7" d, $10.

Seated Siamese cat with blue glass eyes, head swivels, 11-1/2" h, $185.

Nodder, 4-1/4" h, yellow, black stripes, fuzzy, blue rhinestone eyes, paper label "Made in Hong Kong" **8.50**

Pitcher, figural, tail forms handle, clear glass, incised "WMF Germany," 8-1/4" h **25.00**

Planter, brown and white cat, blue bow, standing upright, one paw raised .**12.00**

Puzzle, 10-1/2" x 14", cardboard, yellow cat in blue pants and white sailor hat, playing concertino **10.00**

Salt and pepper shakers, black and white figures, blue bows, porcelain, mkd "Czechoslovakia," pr **18.50**

Serving Tray, metal, painted gold, aqua border, two Siamese cats in center, sgd "Alexander," 15" x 21" **65.00**

Tape measure, celluloid case, pictures of playing cats, tape mkd "Made in U.S.A." **35.00**

Tea towel, linen **10.00**

Toy, tin, yellow and red cat, red ball and wheels, mkd "MAR Toys Made in USA," 6" l **115.00**

Wall plaque, chalkware, Tabby cat face, red ears and big bow, green eyes, 6-1/2" h **45.00**

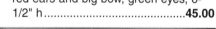

Ashtray, black cat, red highlights, Japan, $15.

❖ Celluloid

The first commercially successful form of plastic, celluloid has been a part of our world since the 1870s. Modern plastics have proved to be safer and easier to manufacture, so items made from celluloid are becoming quite collectible.

For additional information, see *Warman's Antiques & Collectibles,* and *Warman's Americana & Collectibles.*

Animal
Bear, cream, pink and gray highlights, VCO/USA, 5" w **20.00**
Horse, 7" l, cream, brown highlights, hp eyes, marked with VCO intertwined mark..**48.00**
Hound dog long tail, peach celluloid, gray highlights, crossed circle Japan mark, 5" l **18.00**

Bar pin, ivory-grained, orange and brown layered pearlescence, hp rose motif **15.00**

Bookmark, cream colored, diecut, poinsettia motif, Psalm 22 printed on front **15.00**

Brush and comb set, child's, orig box **20.00**

Cuff links, pr, matching stickpin, lever back links of silver tone metal, octagonal framework with circular imitation ivory set with rhinestone **75.00**

Doll, blue glass eyes, moveable arms and legs, dressed in fabric skirt, crochet top, bandana around head, earrings, 9" h.............................**90.00**

Dresser tray, imitation tortoiseshell rim, glass and lace center **35.00**

Hat pin, conical, imitation tortoiseshell, 12" l **20.00**

Ink Blotter, booklet of blotters with holiday lantern motif, "May this be your Merriest Christmas and 1929 your Happiest Year," The Charis Corp of Allentown, PA, 2-1/2" x 6" **45.00**

Picture frame, oval, ivory grained, easel back, 8" x 10" **20.00**

Pocket mirror, oval, woman with long red hair,, teal blue dress and cloche, holding bouquet of roses, 2-1/4" l**45.00**

Rattle, blue and white, egg shape, white handle **18.50**

Roly poly, chicken, weighted base, 2-1/2" dia **38.00**

Celluloid. Left to right: small hand mirror, yellow pearlized back, rect mirror, $28; hand mirror, tan and white streaked back, rect mirror, $20; hand mirror, ivory colored back, oval beveled mirror, $22; hair receiver, ivory colored, $5.

❖ Central Glass

In 1863, Central Glass Works of Wheeling, West Virginia, was established as a cooperative. A group of workmen from J.H. Hobbs, Brockunier and Company undertook the venture. It failed shortly thereafter and was reorganized as a stock company in 1867. Production continued until 1939, consisting of tableware and barware for commercial and domestic use.

Bowl, Frances, green, crimped, 11" dia **40.00**

Butter dish, cov, Chippendale pattern, colorless **20.00**

Candlestick, ribbed deep blue, silver trim, 9" h **42.00**

Cocktail, Balda, lavender **30.00**

Compote, Optic ribbing, amethyst, 12" dia, 8-1/2" h................................**250.00**

Creamer and sugar, Chippendale, 1909 ....**50.00**

Decanter, Brazen Shield, pattern #98, 1905, 10" h...............................**45.00**

Fruit bowl, Frances, 3 toes, green, 10" dia **35.00**

Goblet, water
Acorn, colorless **15.00**
Balda, lavender **30.00**
Veninga, colorless **15.00**

Hair receiver, cov, Chippendale, colorless **15.00**

Jug, Yodel, lotus etch, pink and crystal, 64-oz **300.00**

Mayonnaise, Morgan, ftd, 2 handles, matching ladle, rose **165.00**

Tumbler, Yodel, lotus etch, pink and crystal
2-3/4-oz, ftd **40.00**
7-oz, ftd **30.00**
12-oz, ftd **35.00**

Water pitcher, Acorn, colorless **35.00**

Water set, Greek, pitcher and six 7-oz tumblers, pink and crystal **500.00**

❖ Ceramic Arts Studio

Located in Madison, Wisconsin, Ceramic Arts Studio produced wheel-thrown ceramics. Founded in 1941 by Lawrence Rabbett and Ruben Sand, the studio turned out interesting ceramics until 1955.

Collectors' Club: Ceramic Art Studio Collectors Assoc, P.O. Box 46, Madison, WI 53701.

Aladdin's Lamp, 3" l **56.00**

Bank, Tony the Barber...................**125.00**

Creamer, kitten, head removes to fill, 5-1/2" h...**25.00**

Figure
Chinese children, 3" h..................**25.00**

Miscellaneous ashtray, Old Original Bookbinders, Philadelphia, white ground, red and black lettering, $5.

Cocker spaniel, sitting, black, 2-3/4" h
....**27.00**
Dutch boy and girl, 4" h................**55.00**
Gay nineties man, dog by side, green
 clothing, 7" h...............................**60.00**
Lamb, 3-1/2" h..............................**35.00**
Little Bo Peep, green clothing, 5-1/4" h
....**40.00**
Oriental children, 6" h **150.00**
 Wing-Sang and Lu Tang, 7" h **150.00**
Pitcher, miniature, emb bust of
 Washington circled by stars, 3" h.**55.00**
Salt and pepper shakers, pr, marked
 Brown bear and cub, nested **85.00**
 Cow and calf, snugglers, 5-1/4" h and
 2-1/4" h **190.00**
 Elephant, male 3-3/4" h, female 3-1/4"
 h..**70.00**
 Gingham Dog and Calico Cat, 2-7/8" h
 and 2-3/4" h **95.00**
Shelf sitter, Sun-li and Sun-lin, 7" h**75.00**

❖ Cereal Boxes

Cereal boxes have incorporated clever advertising, premiums, and activities for years. Early boxes were designed to appeal to the cook in the household, but as children began requesting their favorite brands and saving box tops to get a specific premium, the whole industry refocused on that group. By the 1970s, special promotional boxes were created, giving collectors even more opportunities to expand their collections.

Collectors' Club: Sugar-Charged Cereal Collectors, 5400 Cheshire Meadows Way, Fairfax, VA 22032.

Batman, Ralston, hologram t-shirt offer, 1989 ....**9.00**
Corn Kix, Rocket Space O-Gauge,

1950s **90.00**
Corn Pops, Kellogg's, Batman Forever
 with Batman, #1 in series of 4,
 copyright 1995...........................**10.00**
Froot Loops, Kellogg's, Mattel Fun on
 Wheels contest, 1970 ....**30.00**
Kaboom, flat/proof, no die-cut or scoring,
 border-signed by printers, stamped
 "Oct 9, 1979," 1 sheet..................**80.00**
Kellogg's, Star War C-3PO, 1984...**35.00**
Post Toasties Corn Flakes, sample,
 Mickey and Pluto on back panel, 5-5/8"
 h **195.00**
Puffa Puffa Rice, Kellogg's, H.R.
 Pufnstuf patch, 1970, unopened, 8-oz,
 6-1/4" x 8-3/4" **750.00**
Rice Chex, red check design, 1950s
 ....**65.00**
Sugar Smacks, seal balancing bowl of
 cereal on nose, Exploding Battleship
 offer on back, 1958, 9-oz, hole in
 bottom front, 7-1/2" x 9-1/2" **36.00**
Wheaties
 Muhammad Ali, 1960s picture, 1998
 ....**20.00**
 Lou Gehrig, flat **8.50**
 George Mikan, one oz size, c1953
 ....**125.00**
 Babe Ruth, flat **8.50**

Cereal Premiums

This category includes all of those fun things we saved after eating all that cereal. Sometimes these goodies were tucked into the box. Other premiums were things that you earned, through saving box tops, coupons, etc. Whatever the method, the treasure was the premium, and, at today's prices, collectors are having the most fun now.

Bowl sitter/pencil topper, Pinocchio
 ....**10.00**
Cereal bowl, Tom Mix, "Hot Ralston
 Cereal for Straight Shooters," white
 china, illus, copyright 1982, Ralston

Cereal Premiums, Cheerios, Wing-O-Ring, yellow sponge, red letters, $15.

Purina...**35.00**
Delivery truck, 1921 Model T, Matchbox,
 copyright 1989, Kellogg's Apple Jacks
 ....**8.00**
Figures, Snap, Crackle, and Pop, wood
 and fabric, mkd, dated, Kellogg's 1972
 ....**55.00**
Flashlight, Lurch, attached by
 cellophane to box of Addams Family
 Cereal, Ralston, copyright 1991.....**8.00**
Flicker ring, Frankenberry playing
 drums, early 1970s **100.00**
Magnet, Trix, Arjon Manufacturing Corp.,
 MOC..**8.00**
Military insignia button, Kellogg's Pep,
 complete set of 36, litho tin, insignia of
 U.S. Army, Air Force, Navy, or Marine
 unit, 1943 ....**375.00**
Ornament, Sugar Bear, spins inside
 glow-in-the-dark holder, MIP, 4" h, 2" w
 ....**10.00**
Premium button, Kellogg's Pep, litho tin,
 character portrait and name on front,
 "Kellogg's Pep" in blue on reverse
 B.O. Plenty **100.00**
 Felix..**110.00**
 Foxy Grandpa..............................**30.00**
 Lil Abner......................................**25.00**
 The Phamtom..............................**100.00**
Signal Light, Jack Armstrong Safety
 Signal-Light Kit, Wheaties, 1-5/8" x 2-
 1/4" cardboard box, orig bicycle light
 ....**195.00**
Wacky Wobbler, Count Chocula,
 bobbing head, made by Funko Inc.,
 orig box, 7" h **10.00**
Weather forecast ring, Howie Wing,
 Kellogg's, 1930s **250.00**

❖ Character and Promotional Drinking Glasses

Everybody's got one or two of these in the cupboard. However, there are also dedicated collectors who find flea markets are good hunting ground for the newer additions. Thanks to modern advertisers, such as Coca-Cola and McDonald's, there are many examples to find.

Periodical: *Collector Glass News*, P.O. Box 308, Slippery Rock, PA 16057.

Collectors' Club: Promotional Glass Collectors Assoc, 3001 Bethel Rd, New Wilmington, PA 16142.

Amazing Spider-Man, Marvel Comics, 1977 ....**5.00**
Aquaman, DC Comics, Pepsi, 1978**17.50**
Archie Takes The Gang For A Ride ..**4.50**
Batman, Pepsi, 16-oz, 1978...........**18.00**
BC Ice Age, riding on wheel, Arby's,

1981 ....**9.00**
Beaky Buzzard, Warner Bros., Pepsi,
1973 ....**17.50**
Big Mac, McVote, McDonald's, 1986 **5.00**
Bugs Bunny, Pepsi, 1973, copyright
Warner Bros. Inc. **9.00**
Bullwinkle, Crossing the Delaware,
Arby's, 1976 ....**12.00**
Charlie Tuna, 3-3/4" h, 3" dia, clear,
single image of Charlie in white, no
inscription, heavily fluted base, c1970,
pr **25.00**
Daffy Duck, Pepsi, Warner Bros., 1976
....**18.00**
Disney on Parade, Coca-Cola..........**5.00**
Empire Strikes Back, Luke Skywalker,
Burger King, 1980 ....**17.50**
Endangered Species, Bengal Tiger,
Burger Chef, 1978 ....**7.50**
Flash, Pepsi, 1976 ....**18.00**
Have It Your Way, two drummers, piper,
Burger King, 1976 ....**10.00**
Hot Air Balloon, Dr Pepper **9.00**
Little Bamm-Bamm, Flintstones,
Hardee's, 1991 ....**6.00**
Mayor McCheese taking pictures,
McDonald's.....................................**5.00**
Noid, beach chair, Domino's Pizza, 1988
....**2.50**
Popeye, Coca-Cola, Kollect-A-Set **6.00**
Santa and Elves, Coca-Cola **9.00**
Superman, Pepsi, 1975 ....**18.00**
Underdog, Brockway Glass Co., Pepsi,
16-oz, small logo **25.00**
Washington, Burger Chef.................**7.00**
Wonder Woman, National Periodical Pub
....**10.00**

❖ Character Banks

Banks that depict characters, whether they
are cartoon, fictional, or real, are popular
with collectors. Because so many of them
are figural, they create a colorful scene with
displayed.

Barney Rubble, vinyl, with bowling ball
....**45.00**
Batman, glazed ceramic, 1966, 7" h
....**24.00**
Bionic Man, plastic **40.00**
Bugs Bunny, pot metal...................**60.00**
Buster Brown and Tige, cast iron,
c1910 ....**165.00**
Captain Marvel, dime register type, litho
tin, Fawcett Publications, 1948.....**85.00**
Fred Loves Wilma, glazed ceramic, 8-
1/4" h...**150.00**
Garfield, ceramic, 1981, 6" h **50.00**
Humpty Dumpty, porcelain **70.00**
Lucy, Peppermint Patty and Linus,
baseball uniforms, 1973..............**50.00**
Laurel and Hardy, plastic, 14" h.....**45.00**
Old Dutch Cleanser, litho tin.........**25.00**

Peanuts, on dog house, Bank of
America, 1970s **50.00**
Popeye, multicolor litho metal, mkd
"Popeye Daily Quarter Bank," Kalon
Co., 1950s **115.00**
Snoopy, with Woodstock, 40th Anniv,
ceramic, orig hang-tag, unused ...**30.00**

❖ Character Clocks

Telling time is more fun when your favorite
character gives you a hand. Condition is
important when collecting clocks and
watches. Examples with original bands,
boxes, stands, and works will bring a higher
price.

Betty Boop......................................**45.00**
Davy Crockett, wall, pendulum.......**75.00**
Flintstones, wall clock, battery op ..**15.00**
Hello Kitty, alarm, MIB..................**65.00**
Howdy Doody, talking **65.00**
Mickey Mouse, Bradley animated hands
....**45.00**
Roy Rogers, alarm clock, color dial,
c1970 ....**30.00**
Sesame Street, schoolhouse shape
....**25.00**
Trix The Rabbit, alarm, c1960 ....**15.00**
Snoopy, alarm clock **30.00**
Star Wars, alarm clock, talking........**35.00**

*Character Clocks, Snoopy alarm clock, Schmid,
Snoopy in airplane, orig box, $20.*

❖ Character Collectibles

Some characters got their start on early
radio programs, some were popular
advertising spokesmen, and some were
permanent fixtures on the newspaper comic
page. As collectors become younger and
younger, so do the ages of the characters
they search for. Foxy Grandpa is giving way
to Gumby and now even Rugrats.

References: Bill Bruegman, *Cartoon
Friends of the Baby Boom Era*, Cap'n
Penny Productions, 1993; ——, *Superhero
Collectibles*, Toy Scouts, 1996; *Cartoon &
Character Toys of the 50s, 60s, & 70s*, L-W
Book Sales, 1995; Ted Hake, *Hake's Guide
to Cowboy Character Collectibles*, Wallace-
Homestead, 1994; ——, *Hakes Price Guide
to Character Toys 4th edition*, Gemstone
Publishing, 2002; Jim Harmon, *Radio & TV
Premiums,* Krause Publications, 1997; Jack
Koch, *Howdy Doody*, Collector Books,
1996; Cynthia Boris Liljeblad, *TV Toys and
the Shows That Inspired Them*, Krause
Publications, 1996; David Longest,
Character Toys and Collectibles (1984,
1992 value update), 2nd Series (1987, 1990
value update), Collector Books; Rex Miller,
*The Investor's Guide To Vintage
Collectibles,* Krause Publications, 1998; Ed.
Elizabeth Stephan, *O'Brien's Collecting
Toys*, 10th ed, Krause Publications, 2001;
and Micki Young, *Campbell's Soup
Collectibles from A to Z*, Krause
Publications, 1998.

Collectors' Clubs: Charlie Tuna Collectors
Club, 7812 NW Hampton Rd, Kansas City,
MO 64152; Dick Tracy Fan Club, P.O. Box
632, Manitou Springs, CO 80829; Howdy
Doody Memorabilia Collectors Club, 8 Hunt
Ct, Flemington, NJ 08822; Official Popeye
Fan Club, 1001 State St, Chester, IL 62233.

For additional listings, see *Warman's
Antiques & Collectibles* and *Warman's
Americana & Collectibles,* as well as
specific categories in this edition.

Andy Panda, view-master reel, Andy
Panda in Mystery Tracks, Sawyer, #822
....**4.00**
Barney Google, pep pin, Kellogg's, 1946
....**18.00**
Bugs Bunny, cookie jar **40.00**
Charlie Tuna, doll, vinyl.................**30.00**
Daffy Duck, character drinking glass,
Pepsi, Warner Brothers Looney Tunes,
copyright 1980................................**8.00**
Dennis the Menace
Book, *Dennis The Menace*, Hank
Ketchum, Holt & Co., 1952, 1st ed,
hardcover...............................**35.00**
Lamp, figural...............................**50.00**
Dick Tracy
Candy bar wrapper, premium offer,
1950s.......................................**10.00**
Toy, two-way radio set, 1950, MIB
....**40.00**
Flintstones, playset, #4672, copyright
1961, 15" x 24" x 4" orig box, played-
with condition **165.00**
Garfield, telephone, figural..............**48.00**
Heckle and Jeckle, premium ring, thin
copper luster metal band, circular
copper luster frame with convex metal
insert, color image, mkd "Copyright
Terrytoons," c1977, set of three....**18.00**
Jetsons
Colorforms Set, copyright Colorforms

and Hanna-Barbera, 1963........**40.00**
Record, "The Jetsons, First Family on the Moon," 33 RPM, 1977........**60.00**
Kayo and Moon Mullins
  Pinback button, black and white, *Los Angeles Evening Express* contest, 1-1/4" dia.....................**45.00**
  Salt and pepper shakers, chalkware, 3" h, flakes, pr.............................**60.00**
Pogo, poster, "The World of Pogo, Walt Kelly's menagerie of characters from Okefenokee Swamp," made for exhibit held at the Museum of Fine Arts, Springfield, MA, 1971, 17" x 11"..**55.00**
Popeye
  Flashlight, figural, King Features..**30.00**
  Pencil sharpener, figural, Bakelite, copyright 1929 King Features Syndicate, 1-3/4" h...................**75.00**
Tom and Jerry
  Puzzle, child's, copyright 1954.....**12.00**
  Pinback button, Tom and Jerry Go For Stroehmann's Bread, black, red and white litho, 1950s.....................**25.00**

❖ Character Watches

Having a favorite character tell you the correct time makes the day go better. Many collectors of character watches really do enjoy wearing their favorites. This is an added bonus as it keeps their collectibles in working order, adding extra value.

Betty Boop.....................**35.00**
Charlie Tuna, full-color image of Charlie on silver ground, copyright 1971 Star-Kist Foods, grained purple leather band **75.00**
Cinderella, Bradley, goldtone, white vinyl straps, 1973, orig case with full color case insert.....................**45.00**
Gene Autry **135.00**
Jetsons, lunch-box type, Fossil, MIB **80.00**
Lone Ranger, metal case, Lone Ranger on galloping Silver, orig tan strap, c1940 ....**165.00**
Mickey Mouse, Bradley, silvered metal case, 1970s, orig case **35.00**
Smitty, gray aged dial, white, red, and green figure, New Haven Clock Co., 1935, orig case **250.00**

❖ Chase Chrome and Brass

This American firm produced many interesting chrome and brass items. Their pieces are well marked and quite stylish.

Ashtray with matchbox holder, round, 2

cigarette holders, sq clip for matchbox **18.00**
Box, round, copper, leafy design around base, mkd, lid with shell-shaped handle, wear, 4-3/4" x 2" **8.00**
Candle snuffer, Puritan, MIB.........**85.00**
Cigarette urn, sq base, round container, mkd, 2-3/8" h, base 2-1/2" sq **45.00**
Cocktail ball, chromium, tray 6-1/4" dia, ball 3-1/4" dia **45.00**
Desk lamp, Half Moon, Art Deco, sgnd, replaced shade, ding on base....**225.00**
Humidor, round, mkd, large knob on lid, 6" dia, 6" h..................................**95.00**
Serving dish, polished chrome, 2 compartments, glass liner, stationary handle, with some wear **45.00**

❖ Chein Toys

An American toy company, Chein produced quality toys from the 1930s through the 1950s. Many of their playthings were lithographed on tin, and they are clearly marked.

Alligator, windup, native on back..**315.00**
Bear, litho tin wind-up, 1938, 4" h ...**65.00**
Cabin Cruiser motor boat, litho tin, 15" l, 4" w, sgd "Princess Pat," 1940s, MIB **275.00**
Carousel, litho tin wind-up **60.00**
Disney Top, litho tin, Walt Disney Productions, c1950, 5-1/2" d......**100.00**
Duck, litho tin wind-up, 1930, 4" h ..**45.00**
Ferris Wheel, Hercules, 1930s **350.00**
Handstand clown, 1940s, C-9 .....**135.00**
Hook and ladder, replaced ladders **750.00**
Motor boat, litho tin, sgd "Peggy Jane," 14" l, 3" w, 1930s, MIB..............**225.00**
Penguin, wind-up, played with condition **75.00**

Chein Toys, sand pail, dog and cat dec, sq, pink int., swivel handle, $145.

Playland Merry Go Round...........**575.00**
Roller Coaster, 2 cars, MIB.........**590.00**
Roly poly, monkey, 1930s.............**365.00**
Sand pail, litho tin, fish dec.............**35.00**
Sand shovel, litho tin **25.00**
Waddling duck, litho tin wind-up, c1935 ....**75.00**
Windmill, sand toy, litho tin **90.00**

❖ Chess Set

This game of kings has been played for centuries. Be certain that all of the playing pieces are present and that the age of the board matches the age of the pieces.

Bakelite, 1930s-1940s, box rough and hinge damaged **380.00**
Carved marble pieces, fitted case, no playing board..............................**40.00**
Civil War, Franklin Mint **365.00**
Football, hard plastic figures, green and white board, 1967, with *Official Football Chess Rule Book*, 22pgs, unplayed, figures 3" h, box 24" x 19" **78.00**
Lord of the Rings.........................**240.00**
Plastic, molded, black and white, cardboard board...........................**20.00**
Porcelain, blue and white, bases mkd "Royal Dux, Made in Czechoslovakia," early 20th C.............................**995.00**
Revolutionary War, Franklin Mint, issued 1986 ....**280.00**
Star Trek, 25th Anniversary Edition, authorized by Paramount Pictures **300.00**
Wood, hand carved, c1920 ....**80.00**

❖ Children's Collectibles

This category is a bit of a catchall, including things that children played with, as well as articles they used in their rooms.

Bib clips, sterling silver, clothespin type **75.00**
Blocks, wood, bright colors, c1950, some wear................................**20.00**

Children's Books, Primary Manual Work, A Suggestive Outline For A Years Course In First And Second Grades, 1911, $18.

Children's Books, train, plastic, baby-type book, $2.

Cloth book, handmade, buttons, zipper, etc. to teach children hand skills ..**10.00**
Crib, tapered high posts with incised line beading along edges, urn shaped supports on all sides, refinished, 38-3/4" d, 69-1/2" h, orig 48" l rails .**250.00**
Christening outfit, gown, slip, and cap, white cotton, c1920 ....**85.00**
Cup, Raggedy Ann, Johnny Gruelle, 1941, Crooksville China **65.00**
Diaper holder, fabric, clown face, striped body **10.00**
Kitchen cupboard, some old paint, some restoration **400.00**
Lamp, clown in rocking chair, music box base, orig shade **40.00**
Mug, white glass, red animal characters, Hazel Atlas, 1930-40, 3" h **25.00**
Night light, plug-in type, figural teddy bear, plastic **5.00**
Piano, "Concert," baby grand **110.00**
Print, Asleep & Awake, Bessie Gutmann, double matted, orig frame **150.00**
Rattle, Santa, celluloid, 5-1/2" l **75.00**

Chidren's Collectibles, Chalk board play center, revolving cylinder in top, sports image shown, oak frame, $35.

Children's Collectibles, chest of drawers, Victorian, cottage type, paint grained, red painted roses, green border, dated 1870, $225.

Scooter, steel frame and wheels, wooden platform and handle, worn orig red paint, black and yellow striping, partial label "...Arrow Deluxe" **150.00**
Sewing machine, Singer, cast iron and nickeled steel, 6-3/4" h **150.00**
Wagon, Roller Bearing Coaster, wood, metal fittings, black stenciled label, old red and brown paint, some touch-up to paint **385.00**
Walker, primitive, wood ring top, wood seat, replacement wrought iron ring base with wheels.......................**145.00**
Wall plaques, plaster of Paris, Jack and Jill on one, Humpty Dumpty other, self-framed, pr.....................................**20.00**
Wastebasket, tin, yellow ground, hp teddy bear on side, wear and dents **15.00**

❖ Children's Dishes

We've all made mud pies and other goodies. And, what better way to serve them to our dolls and teddies than on pretty, child-size dishes?

Children's Dishes, dinner set, rooster dec, pottery, green border, brown and red rooster, 15 pcs, $225.

Children's Dishes, tea set, white china, green, turquoise, and maroon leaf dec, orig red cardboard box, mkd "Japan," $58.

Collectors' Club: Toy Dish Collectors, P.O. Box 159, Bethlehem, CT 06751.

Baking set, tin, cookie tin, canister, bowl, pie pan, cake pans, angel food pan, muffin pan, etc.............................**25.00**
Bundt pan, aluminum, 3-3/4" w **4.00**
Candleholders, pr, Swirl pattern, opaque green milk glass **65.00**
Chocolate pot, china, decal with Model T and passengers **90.00**
Cup and saucer
   Blue Willow pattern **15.00**
   Holly, Napco, Japan, 2-1/4" dia saucer **7.00**
   Luster ware, Japan, floral dec........**4.50**
   Peach Luster, Fire-King...............**25.00**
Dinnerware set
   China, pink transferware Punch dec, mkd "Allerton & Sons," cup, saucer and three 5-1/2" d plates **150.00**
   Depression glass, My Little Hostess, orig box.................................**175.00**
   Plastic, Tinkerbell, Walt Disney, 9 pcs **25.00**
Mug
   Little Bo Peep, 3-1/2" h **22.00**
   Wee Branches, white milk glass ..**30.00**
Plate
   Hey Diddle Diddle, blue and white, 6-1/2" dia....................................**30.00**
   Moss Rose pattern, 2-1/2" dia **3.00**
Silverware set, aluminum, 4 spoons, 4 forks, knife, and pie server..........**15.00**
Strainer and meat grinder, Little Homemaker, Wirecraft Corp., NYC,

Children's Dishes Tea set, white china, delicate pink rose bud dec, $125.

MOC **18.00**
Sugar bowl, luster ware, Japan, 1-1/2" h
....**3.00**
Teapot
Aluminum, black wood knob, swing
handle **25.00**
China, Occupied Japan................**85.00**
Plastic, mkd "Eagle Toys, Made in
Canada," 4" x 6"..........................**3.00**
Tea set
Akro Agate, orig box mkd "The Little
American Maid, No. 3000"......**300.00**
China, transfer scene of Santa Claus in
balloon, dropping gifts to children,
pink trim, some damage, replaced
teapot lid, 7 pcs **210.00**

❖ Chintz Ware

Chintz ware is the general term for brightly
colored, multi-flower china patterns made
primarily in England. These popular
patterns resemble chintz fabrics and were
produced by many manufacturers. After
declining in popularity for years following
World War II, chintz has enjoyed a lively
comeback over the past several years.

References: Eileen Busby, *Royal Winton
Porcelain*, The Glass Press Inc.1998; Linda
Eberle and Susan Scott, *Charlton Standard
Catalogue of Chintz*, 3rd ed, Charlton
Press, 1999; Muriel Miller, *Collecting Royal
Winton Chintz*, Francis Joseph Publications,
1996, Jo Anne Welch, *Chintz Ceramics*, 3rd
ed, Schiffer Publishing, 2000.

Collectors' Clubs: Chintz Collectors Club,
P.O. Box 50888, Pasadena, CA 91115,
www. chintznet.com; Chintz Connection,
P.O. Box 222, Riverdale, MD 20738; Crazed
Collector P.O. Box 2635 Dublin, CA 94568;
Royal Winton International Collectors' Club,
Dancer's End, Northall, Bedfordshire,
England LU6 2EU; Royal Winton Collectors'
Club, 2 Kareela Road, Baulkham Hills,
Australia 2153

For additional listings, see *Warman's
Antiques & Collectibles* and *Warman's
English & Continental Pottery & Porcelain*.

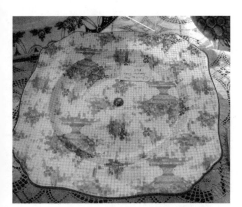

Chintz Ware, Sampler plate, shaped edges, $165.

Reproduction Alert

Bowl, Marguerite, Royal Winton, 9-1/2" x
10" **265.00**
Bread tray, Old Cottage, Royal Winton
....**200.00**
Breakfast set, Rosebud Iridescent,
green **250.00**
Bud vase, Royalty, Grimwades, Royal
Winton, 5-1/4" h **125.00**
Cake plate, three tiers, Brama, Midwinter
....**95.00**
Comport, Spring Blossom, A.G.
Richardson, 7" dia 195.00
Creamer and sugar, Queen Anne, Royal
Winton **285.00**
Cup and saucer
Marina pattern, Elijah Cotton **50.00**
Primrose, Oleander shape, Shelley
....**195.00**
Rosina **20.00**
Eggcup, double, Summertime,
Grimwades, Royal Winton **95.00**
Mustard pot, cov, underplate, Rosetime,
Lord Nelson................................**85.00**
Pin dish, Melody, Shelley, 4-1/2" l .**85.00**
Plate
Ascot, Majestic, Grimwades, Royal
Winton, 6" dia **75.00**
Melody, Royal Crown, 9" dia **195.00**
Old Cottage, Royal Winton, 8" dia**50.00**
Rosalynde pattern, James Kent, 9" dia
....**75.00**
Sweet Pea, Royal Winton, 5" sq **100.00**
Salt and pepper shakers, tray, Du Barry,
James Kent **95.00**
Sandwich tray, Crocus, Grimwades,
Royal Winton **125.00**
Soup bowl, two handles, underplate, Old
Cottage, Royal Winton **145.00**
Sugar shaker, Du Barry, James Kent
....**125.00**
Teapot, cov
Marina, Lord Nelson..................**325.00**
Primula, A.G. Richardson **275.00**
Tray, Old Cottage, Royal Winton ...**150.00**

❖ Chocolate Related

Many collectors suffer from a sweet tooth.
Happily there are wonderful examples of
items relating to chocolate that can satisfy
those cravings.

Box, Hershey's Milk Chocolate Candy
Bars, held 24 bars, cover has torn
corners, partial factory seal attached,
5" x 7" **15.00**
Can

Chocolate candy mold, standing dog, $95.

Cocomalt, food/drink powder, sample
size, orig contents....................**50.00**
Donald Duck Chocolate Syrup, Walt
Disney Productions, mint cond, 4-
1/2" h, 2-5/8" dia....................**190.00**
Comic book, *Major Inapak Space Ace*,
#1, 1951, Magazine Enterprises, N.Y.,
giveaway for "Inapak-The Best
Chocolate Drink in the World"......**10.00**
Cup and saucer, Johnston's Hot
Chocolate, mkd "Salem China" **35.00**
Milk shake glass, hard plastic, soda
fountain style, premium, Quik rabbit
and blue "Nestles Quik," 16-oz, 6-3/4"
h, pr..**12.00**
Mold
Egg, with divider........................**150.00**
Santa, #427, 2 small holes, 4-1/2" h
....**125.00**
Mug, plastic, Nestles Quik Bunny, 2
handles, 4" h **12.00**
Pitcher, hard plastic, Nestles Quik rabbit,
9" h...**22.00**
Tin
M & M's, diner, multicolored litho,
figural lid **4.00**
Nestle's, teal blue, litho Victorian
scene, rect..................................**2.00**
Toy truck, plastic, Hershey's Milk
Chocolate, two removable Hershey
kisses, Buddy L, 1982, mkd "Made in
Japan" **15.00**

*Chocolate Related, toothpick holder, red lettering
"Nestles Hot Fudge," Anchor-Hocking trademark in
base, $5.*

❖ Christmas and Easter Seals

The National Tuberculosis Association issued seals, pinback buttons, and other items in order to educate the public and raise funds for their work. The American Lung Association also issued seals.

Booklet, Christmas Seals, 200, thin paper between each sheet, 1939.**22.00**

Bottle, commemorative, Coca-Cola, Easter Seals, 1997......................**11.50**

Figurine, girl holding potted flower, "His Love will Shine on You," Easter Seals Limited Edition,............................**11.50**

Full sheet, 100
American Lung Assoc, Christmas, 1976..**5.00**
Christmas Seals, 1927 ....**8.00**
Christmas Seals, 1943 ....**5.00**
Easter Seals, 1957 ....**2.00**

Poster
"Fight the Big Bad Wolf 'Tuberculosis,' Buy Christmas Seals," paper, shows wolf and pigs, 1934, pinholes, 1" tear, 15" x 10-1/2" **160.00**
"Holiday Greetings, Sold Here, Christmas Seals, Protect your Home from Tuberculosis," hardstock, Santa Claus art by Walter Sasse, Official Post Office Dept. stamps, 1936, some soiling, 11" x 14" **45.00**

❖ Christmas

One of the most celebrated holidays of the year has provided us with many collectibles. Some collectors specialize in only one type of object or one character, such as Santa. Others just love Christmas and collect a wide variety of objects.

References: Beth Dees, *Santa's Guide to Contemporary Christmas Collectibles*, Krause Publications, 1997; Mary Morrison, *Christmas Jewelry*, 2nd ed., Schiffer Publishing, 2002; Lissa and Dick Smith, *Holiday Collectibles*, Krause Publications, 1998.

Christmas Items, Candle holders, set of 4, holding letters to spell out "Noel," orig box, mkd "Poinsettia Noel Angels," $15.

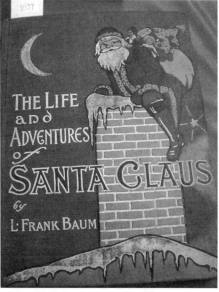

Christmas Items, child's book, The Life and Adventures of Santa Claus, *L. Frank Baum, Bowen-Merrill, illus by Mary Cowles Clark, 1902, red cloth cover, $25.*

Collectors' Club: Golden Glow of Christmas Past, 6401 Winsdale St, Golden Valley, MN 55427.

For additional listings, see *Warman's Antiques & Collectibles* and *Warman's Americana & Collectibles*.

Bank, 5" h, snowman, white, black bowler hat, red scarf, orig box......**15.00**

Book
A Christmas Carol, Dickens, Dana Estes & Co., 1902, 5 full color illus **28.00**
Christmas in Mexico, Jadwigo Lopez, World Book, 1976, 80 pgs..........**8.00**
Felicity's Surprise, A Christmas Story, Valerie Tripp, Pleasant Co., 1st ed **7.00**
Murder for Christmas, Thomas Godfrey, Wings Books, 1989, 1st ed., 465 pgs.....................................**12.00**
The Real Christmas, Pat Boone, Fleming M. Revell Co., 1961, 62 pgs **15.00**

Candy box, cardboard, string handle, Merry Christmas, Happy New Year, carolers in village, 1920s, 4-1/2" l..**8.00**

Candy cane, 6" l, chenille, red and white **4.00**

Candy container
Belsnickle style, faded felt outfit, 7" h **275.00**
Santa wearing snow shoes and holding Christmas tree, hard plastic, sack with opening for candy, Rosbro Plastics, 4-1/2" h......................**40.00**

Figure, choir boy, hard plastic, red and white, 3-1/2" h **4.50**

Icicles, metal, twisted, color or silver, 4"

h **1.00**

Light bulb, figural
Cluster of grapes, purple, mkd "15V Japan" on cap, minor paint loss, 2-3/4" h **9.00**
Lantern, hp, late 1940s-early 1950s, 2-1/2" x 4-1/2"............................**22.50**
Snowman, milk glass, mkd "120V Japan" on cap, minor paint loss, 3-1/2" h **12.50**

Nativity set, Precious Moments, "Prepare Ye The Way Of The Lord," #E-0508, angels preparing manger, 1983, from 1" to 6 1/2" h, 6 pcs **120.00**

Ornament
Angel, chromolithograph, tinsel trim, German 7" h **20.00**
Campbell Soup Kids, 1988, MIB..**12.50**
Heart, glass, red, 3-1/2" h............**15.00**
Mickey Mouse's 50th Birthday, Schmid, limited edition, 1978, orig box...**15.00**
Santa Claus, red plastic, painted white trim, black eyes, 1940s-1950s, 3-1/4" h...**16.00**
Turkey, Great Gobbles, Christopher Radko, retired, hang tag attached, 6" h...**60.00**

Pinback button, celluloid cover, metal back, Santa, "Merry Christmas & Happy New Year," 1-1/4" dia.........**35.00**

Plate
Cherubs surrounding Nativity scene, Wedgwood, 1997.....................**19.00**
Mickey Mouse as Santa, Schmid, limited edition, 5th in a series, 1977 ....**60.00**

Postcard, A Hearty Christmas Greeting, sledding Victorian children **4.00**

Sheet music, Rudolph the Red-Nosed Reindeer by Johnny Mark, copyright 1949, with lyrics and music as recorded by Gene Autry, some foxing **6.00**

Snow dome, Nativity scene, #833, made in Hong Kong, 2-1/4" h................**10.00**

Stocking, red flannel
Mr. & Mrs. Frosty, white flannel top cuff, "Wes" written in glitter box on cuff, 1950s.....................................**12.00**
Santa, stenciled Santa and sleigh, 12" l **15.00**

Tag, 2-3/4" l, Christmas Greetings, dog in wrapped box, made in USA....**2.00**

Christmas Items, Sixty-one early glass Christmas tree ornaments, including seven figural Santas, $300.

Christmas Items, Santa mug, red and white, black stroke eyes, gold foil label, Made in China, $2.

Tree

3" h, brush, green, mica trim, red wood base **5.00**

12" h, feather, white sq red base, mkd "West Germany" **72.00**

Tree stand, cast iron, Christmas scenes, 3 diamond-shape screws, sgd "Gesetzl-Gesch," 6" h, 11-1/2" sq **100.00**

Tree Topper, silvered glass, multicolored, 9" h..**20.00**

❖ Cigar Collectibles

The late 1990s certainly revived the fine art of cigar smoking. And, along with this newfound interest, collectors are enjoying an increase in the number cigar-related collectibles to add to their collections.

Periodical: *The Cigar Label Gazette,* P.O. Box 3, Lake Forest, CA 92630; *Tobacco Antiques and Collectibles Market*, Box 11652, Houston, TX 77293.

Collectors' Clubs: Cigar Label Collectors International, P.O. Box 66, Sharon Center, OH 44274; International Lighter Collectors, P.O. Box 536, Quitman, TX 75783; International Seal, Label and Cigar Band Soc, 8915 E. Bellevue St., Tucson, AZ 85715; Pocket Lighter Preservation Guild, P.O. Box 1054, Addison, IL 60101.

Box, wood and litho paper, c1920, 5" x 8"

Kenwood Club, full color.................**5.00**

Little Chancellor, blue and gold labels **4.00**

Seal of Minneapolis/Lafayette, full color **5.00**

Cigar Collectibles, Cigar mold, cast iron, slight rust, $45.

Cigar Collectibles, tray, decorated with cigar bands and cutouts from labels, two small handles, $65.

Can, El Paxo, litho tin, Indian princess, 5" dia **187.00**

Cigar case, silver color, holds 3 cigars, 5-1/2" **11.00**

Counter display, litho tin, "Kennebec" in silver oval over portrait of Indian flanked by tomahawks, image repeated inside lid, 2-1/4" h, 8-1/2" w, 5" d .**32.00**

Dish, 7-1/8" d, all over multicolored cigar bands, diecut beautiful woman in center, green felt back...................**35.00**

Jar, amber glass, fired-on text, tin lid, "Mercantile Cigars, 5 Cents," 5-1/2" h, 4-1/2" dia **16.50**

Label

Oceanic Steamer **3.00**

Old Soldier, Union soldier shown, c1920...**5.00**

Our Kitties, white cat and black cat **10.00**

Quaker Cigar...................................**7.00**

Pinback button

Dutch Masters, blue lettering, white ground, "President" in red letters, 1950s...**8.00**

Enjoy A Cigar, brown on yellow, slogan "Join The Cigar Enjoyment Parade," c1930..**30.00**

Premium coupon, United Cigar Stores Company of America, set of 4 ....**8.00**

Sign, cardboard, "Smoke Jennie Lind, Hand Made Havana, 5 Cents," 8-1/4" x 14-1/2".......................................**132.00**

Sign, paper, "Golden's Blue Ribbon Cigars," blue and white, 5-1/2" x 10"..............**8.00**

Sign, tin, Charles The Great Cigars, tin, shows full box of cigars, ashtray, fancy match safe, c1910, framed, 17-1/2" l **275.00**

Tin

Old Abe Cigars, round, paper label **65.00**

Reichard's Cadet Cigar **85.00**

❖ Cigarette Collectibles

During the 1990s, the cigarette industry took a beating in regards to its product and its advertising methods. However, collecting interest in the topic is hot! Whether this politically incorrect habit will be snuffed out is anyone's guess.

Periodical: *Tobacco Antiques and Collectibles Market*, Box 11652, Houston, TX 77293.

Collectors' Clubs: Ashtray Collectors Club, P.O. Box 11652, Houston, TX 77293; Camel Joe & Friends, 2205 Hess Drive, Cresthill, IL 60435; Cigarette Pack Collectors Assoc, 61 Searle St, Georgetown, MA 01833; International Lighter Collectors, P.O. Box 536, Quitman, TX 75783; International Seal, Label & Cigar Band Soc, 8915 E. Bellevue St, Tuscon, AZ 85715; Pocket Lighter Preservation Guild, P.O. Box 1054, Addison, IL 60101.

Ashtray, metal, figural, Mt. Rushmore, made in Japan.............................**17.50**

Banner, Old Gold Cigarettes, Not A Cough In The Car Load, 42" x 120" **95.00**

Box, cardboard, flat 50, cardboard case shows 3 guards holding cards saying "Season's Greetings," **92.50**

Cigarette case, enameled, woman's, black, envelope style, red stone dec, 3" x 4" **35.00**

Cigarette Holder, aluminum top, brown Bakelite mouth piece, stamped "Denicotea Cunni," 4" l **55.00**

Cigarette silk

Duckbill, New South Wales, yellowed, 2" x 3" **7.50**

Goat, Italy, slight fraying 2" x 3" **9.00**

Gorilla, French Congo, 2" x 3" **9.00**

Dexterity puzzle, Camel Lights, clear styrene plastic key chain case, miniature replica of cigarette pack, small square opening in top to capture nine miniature filter tip cigarettes in filter ends up, c1980....................**25.00**

Display, litho tin, "They're so Refreshing! Kool Cigarettes," 8" h, 7 1/8" w, 4-1/8" d **25.00**

Game, Camels, The Game, MIB, 1992 ....**10.00**

Ashtray Souvenir of NY, showing Empire State building in on left, Statue of Liberty in center, Rockfeller Center on right, blue and white porcelain, mkd "Fine Staffordshire Ware, Enco, Made in England," with history of landmarks, $25

Money Clip, Chesterfield Cigarettes, white enamel and chrome, Liggit & Myers Tobacco Co., made by Robbins Co., c1950s **20.00**

Pinback button

Perfection Cigarettes, multicolored image of lady, back paper with list of tobacco products **20.00**

Philip Morris Cigarettes, black, white, and fleshtones, c1930 ....**50.00**

Sign, paper, model in negligee, glamour pose, Brown & Williamson Co., c1940s, 12" x 18", two archival tape repairs on back...**65.00**

Sign, tin, Smoke Kools, emb penguin with pack of Kools, 16-3/4" x 8-1/2" **83.00**

Thermometer, litho tin, "Chesterfield, More Than Ever, They Satisfy," emb cigarette pack, 13-1/2" h, 5-3/4" w **121.00**

Tin, vertical, litho tin

Ardath Cigarettes Splendo, Mild Natural Egyptian Blend.............**37.50**

Pall Mall, Christmas dec **15.00**

❖ Circus Collectibles

Whether it's the allure of the big tent or the dazzling acts, circuses have delighted kids of all ages since the 18th century. Of course this has helped to generate lots of collectibles, advertising, schedules, etc.

Periodical: *Circus Report,* 525 Oak St. El Cerrito, CA 94530.

Collectors' Clubs: Circus Fans Assoc of America, P.O. Box 59710, Potomac, MD 20859; Circus Historical Soc, 3477 Vienna Court, Westerville, OH 43081; Circus Model Builders International, 347 Lonsdale Ave., Dayton, OH 45419.

Circus pass, Circus Hall of Fame, Sarasota, Fla.................................**3.50**

Circus Items, Poster, Ringling Bros. World's Greatest Shows–Army of 50 Clowns–Logansport Friday, July 29, 17-1/4" x 19-3/4", $175.

Circus Items, noisemaker, tin, black, white, and red clown, gray ground, red wood handle, $5.

Clown, celluloid figure riding fuzzy horse, mkd "M.M.," orig box.....................**75.00**

Doll, clown, cloth body, painted plaster head, celluloid hand (1 missing), Ringling Bros., 1936, crazing and flaking to head, stain and hole to fabric **175.00**

Little Golden Book, *Howdy Doody's Circus,* 1st ed, 1950 ....**16.00**

Magazine/program, Ringling Bros. and Barnum & Bailey Circus, 1949, cover illus by E. McKnight Kauffer, water stains...**30.00**

Pinback button, "Souvenir of the Circus," shows clown, 1-3/4" dia **9.50**

Pop-Up Book, *Circus,* 1979............**15.00**

Poster

Al G. Kelly & Miller Bros. giraffe, 28" h, 21" w...............................**60.00**

Hunt Bros. Circus, shows saber tooth tiger..................................**95.00**

Tom Mix Circus and Wild West, white linen backing, professional mounted paper poster, 28" x 42"..........**115.00**

Press-out book, *Tiny Circus,* Whitman, 1972, 8" x 11-1/2" **9.00**

Ring, grey metal, circus giant Al Tomaini **35.00**

Stuffed toy, elephant, King Tusk, gold blanket with silver trim, plastic tusks 5" l, Ringling Bros. Barnum and Bailey Combined Shows, made in Korea, 11" h, 21" l **48.00**

Wade figurine, circus elephant, sitting, 1-1/4" h..**8.00**

❖ Civil War

This sad time in American history has led to an interesting range of collectibles, including weapons, uniforms, flags, and ephemera.

Periodicals: *Military Collector Magazine,* PO ox 245, Lyon Station, PA 19536; *Military*

Collector News, P.O. Box 702073, Tulsa, OK 74170; *North South Trader's Civil War,* PO Drawer 631, Orange, VA 22960.

Reference: John F. Graf, *Warman's Civil War Collectibles,* Krause Publications, 2003.

Collectors' Clubs: American Soc of Military Insignia Collectors, 526 Lafayette Ave, Palmerton, PA 18071; Assoc of Military Uniform Collectors, P.O. Box 1876, Elyria, OH 44036; Company of Military Historians, North Main St, Westbrook, CT 06498; Military Collectors Soc, 137 S. Almar Dr, Fort Lauderdale, FL 33334; Orders and Medals Soc of America, P.O. Box 484, Glassboro, NJ 08028.

Reproduction Alert

Badge, Delegate, G.A.R., Indiana, metal hanger bar, cello pendant joined by red, white, and blue striped ribbon, inscribed in gold, dark bronze luster hanger with IN state seal, view of "Entrance to Soldier's Home, Marion, Ind.," 36th annual encampment, May, 1915, ribbon worn **25.00**

Belt, enlisted man's, black leather, brass retaining clips, oval brass "U.S." buckle **175.00**

Book, *The Gettysburg Campaign and the Campaigns of 1864 & 1965 in Virginia by A Lieutenant in Confederat Artillery,* Stribling, 1905, illus, 308 pgs.......**45.00**

Button, brass, U.S. eagle imprint....**10.00**

Cartridge box plate, lead filled die-struck brass, iron wire fasteners, Maryland, mkd "E. Gaylord" on back **3,600.00**

Fife, 17-1/2" l, rosewood, nickel silver ends, 8 bands, orig dark finish, faint signature "W. Crosby, Boston"....**125.00**

Frock coat, swallowtail, boy's, inked "Robert Beecher" on inner pocket label, dark blue with 2 rows of U.S. Army staff officer's buttons, post-war button

Stereoscope card, The War for the Union, pr, $20.

maker **950.00**
Newspaper, Cincinnati Gazette, for year
    of 1863, fold lines and minor damage,
    group of 19 newspapers **150.00**
Print, *Battles of the Rebellion, 1863*,
    Charles Magnus lithographer, hand-
    colored, framed **400.00**
Recruiting broadside, woodcut, "One
    More Rally, Boys!" and eagle with "The
    Union Forever" ribbon, New York,
    matted, verso repaired with archival
    tape, 2 light stains, 17" x 11" ...**2250.00**
Tintype, unidentified Union soldier .**30.00**

❖ Clarice Cliff

To some collectors the name Clarice Cliff
means Art Deco. To others, it's the bright
ceramics created by this talented English
woman. Cliff's work is becoming very
popular and very expensive.

Collectors' Club: Clarice Cliff Collector's
Club, Fantasque House, Tennis Dr, The
Park, Nottingham, NG7, 1AE, England.

For additional information and listings, see
Warman's Antique & Collectibles and
*Warman's English & Continental Pottery &
Porcelain.*

Reproduction Alert

Biscuit barrel, Celtic Harvest, hp floral
    dec, 6-1/2" h **395.00**
Bowl, Bizarre, Blue Chintz, 4" h, 8" dia
    ....**750.00**
Cup and Saucer, Bizarre, conical shape,
    Orange Autumn, printed factory marks
    ....**425.00**
Fruit bowl, Lily Pad, blues and greens,
    5" h, 8" l.....................................**300.00**
Honey pot, Beehive, Crocus, printed
    factory marks, 4" h **595.00**
Jam pot, Melon, band of overlapping

Clarice Cliff, pitcher, Fantasque, bizarre, $525.

fruit, orange, yellow, blue, and green,
    brown outline, stamped on base in
    black ink, c1930, 4" h, restoration to
    rim and side **690.00**
Plate, Crocus, center scratched, 8-3/4"
    dia **185.00**
Salt and pepper shakers, Bizarre, Blue
    Chintz, pepper 3" h, salt 3-1/4" h, pr
    ....**550.00**
Sugar sifter, conical, Autumn Crocus, 5-
    1/2" h..**600.00**
Teapot, Cotswold, slight crazing, 5" h
    ....**145.00**
Vegetable dish, cov, Duvivier **75.00**
Wall vase, cloud shape with flying
    swallow **200.00**

❖ Cleminson Pottery

This California pottery is known for its hand-
decorated pieces. Started by Betty
Cleminson in her El Monte, California,
home, the business grew to the point of
expansion in 1943.

Reproduction Alert

Bowl, cov, hand painted "Gram's Bowl,"
    2-1/2" h.......................................**30.00**
Child's cup, clown head, conical hat
    cover, rough spots **80.00**
Clothes sprinkler
    Chinese man, 8" h........................**90.00**
    Kate, 6-1/2" h **36.00**
Creamer, rooster, 5-1/2" h **62.50**
Flour canister, 6-1/2" x 7-1/2"........**35.00**
Hors d'oeuvre set, 7 dishes and wooden
    lazy Susan base, 16" dia **72.00**
Marmalade set, hand painted, flower pot
    base, lid with strawberry finial, 4" h
    ....**15.00**
Pie bird, rooster, 4-1/2" h...............**95.00**
Plate, girl in center with bonnet, blue
    border, 2 holes for hanging on back, 7-
    1/2" d..**30.00**
Razor bank, green, sgd "Betty
    Cleminson, 8/12/95" **65.00**
Ring holder, bulldog, white and peach,
    tails hold rings **30.00**
Salt and pepper shakers, pr
    Pixies, 1 with 5 holes, 1 with 7 holes,
    orig corks, crazing, wear to bottoms,
    pr **75.00**
    Sailors, male "Old Salt" and female
    "Hot Stuff," 5-1/4" h **75.00**
String holder, ceramic, heart shape, lid
    lettered "You'll Always Have Pull with
    Me," 5" h **110.00**
Wall pocket, clock...........................**24.00**

❖ Clickers

These little giveaways were popular with
early advertisers and children, too.

Clickers, also known as crickets,
have long been an inexpensive child's
toy that became popular with
merchants, who emblazoned the small
metal items with graphics and
advertising. One type of clicker,
however, was of a much more serious
nature.
    Plain-looking clickers were issued
to paratroopers before the D-Day
invasion during World War II. The
crickets were used to identify friendly
troops in the dark or behind obstacles.
    Reproductions exist, so be careful
when buying a clicker said to have been
used on D-Day. The best course of
action is to purchase such historical
items from a well-established militaria
dealer who offers a written money-back
guarantee of authenticity.

Buster Brown Shoes, round, "Extra
    Wear in Every Pair," shows Buster and
    Tige, 1-1/4" dia **225.00**
Cowboy playing guitar, Japan.........**13.00**
Frog, frog-shaped, Life of the Party
    Products, Kirchhof, 1-1/2" x 3" x 1"
    ....**38.00**
Golliwogg, with clown, 4" l...........**320.00**
Halloween, frog-shaped, shows witch on
    broom, haunted house and flying bats,
    T. Cohn, 1940s, tin, 3" l **30.00**
OshKosh, "Clicks Everywhere with
    Everyone, Buy 'em at Armstrong's"
    ....**65.00**
Poll Parrot Shoes, shows parrot on tree
    limb, 4-1/4" x 1-3/4".....................**90.00**
Quaker State, 1-7/8" l **68.00**
Red Goose Shoes
    Goose head form, 1-7/8" x 5/8" .**165.00**
    Standing goose, dark blue ground,
    image off-center, 1-7/8" x 7/8"**110.00**
Smile, "Drink Smile, It's So Good" ..**54.00**
WeatherBird Shoes
    "They're Weatherized, For Boys, For
    Girls" **30.00**
    "All Leather For All Weather"........**55.00**

❖ Clocks

Tick-tock. Most clock collectors specialize
and seek particular manufacturers or
certain types of clocks. Buyers should
carefully examine a clock to determine if it's
in working order. Missing parts may result in
considerable expense after the sale when
it's time to pay for repairs.

Reference: Robert W.D. Ball, *American*

Waterbury china case mantel clock, decorated with flowers and leaves, porcelain dial, open escapement, time and strike, 12" h, $200.

Shelf & Wall Clocks, 2nd ed, Schiffer Publishing, 1999; Robert and Harriet Swedberg, *Price Guide to Antique Clocks*, Krause Publications, 1998.

Periodicals: *Clocks*, 4314 W 238th St, Torrance, CA 90505.

Collectors' Club: National Association of Watch and Clock Collectors, Inc, 514 Poplar St, Columbia, PA 17512.

For additional listings, see *Warman's Antiques & Collectibles* and *Warman's Americana & Collectibles*.

Advertising
Hire's Root Beer, "Drink Hires Root Beer with Root Barks, Herbs," 15" dia **250.00**
None Such Mincemeat, pumpkin face, 8-1/2" w, some wear **300.00**
Alarm, Bradley, brass, double bells, Germany **40.00**
Animated
Ballerina, music box, United **150.00**
Fireplace, Mastercrafter's...........**125.00**
Grandmother, rocking chair, Haddon **190.00**
Spinning Wheel, Lux **85.00**
Ansonia
China, white scrolled case, painted cherry blossom design, paw feet, works mkd "June 14, '81, Ansonia Clock Co., New York," 10-1/4" w, 11-1/2" h, minor imperfections on case **350.00**
Shelf, gingerbread, carved and pressed walnut case, paper on zinc dial, silver dec glass, 8-day time and strike movement with pendulum, 22" h...**185.00**
Atkins and Downs, 8-day triple, reverse-painted glass with buildings, pendulum

Mantel clock, gray marble, open escapement, time & strike, 16" l, 10" h, $175.

Ansonia brass framed clock with beveled glass panels, time & strike, 9" h, $195.

window, and split columns, middle section with mirror and full columns, top section with dec dial, split columns, top crest with spread eagle, most of orig label remains, 38" h, 17" w, 6" d **450.00**
Carriage, New Haven Clock Co., gilded brass case, beveled glass, gold repaint to case, orig pendulum and key, 11-1/2" h **315.00**
Desk, American, shaped rect, brass case, white enamel bordering cobalt blue, stylized applied monogram, decorative brass corners, central dial with Arabic numerals, 4-3/4" h ...**150.00**
Empire, shelf, mahogany veneer, ebonized and stencil gilded pilasters and crest, wooden works with weights, key and pendulum, worn paper label "William Orion & Co.," door with mirror in base, replaced reverse-painted panel, finials missing, some veneer damage and repair **350.00**
Germany, mantel, white onyx, amber and brown striations, ormolu mounts with shells, paw feet, porcelain dial with chased ormolu center with rampant lions, works mkd "Germany," no key, dial damaged, 13" l, 10-3/4" h....**275.00**
Seth Thomas, Cambridge, textured oak case, 8-day movement, 23-3/4" h, 15" w..**315.00**
Unknown maker, attributed to New England area, wall, c1825, giltwood and mahogany, eagle and shield finial above mahogany and giltwood case, brass bezel, convex painted dial, eight-day weight-driven movement, glass throat panel with gilt scroll, lower panel showing sea battle, both framed by gilt spiral moldings, flanked by brass side arms, 33-3/4" h, restorations...**1,550.00**
Weatherstation, L.L. Bean, clock, thermometer, hygrometer and moonphase, oak jointed round case, 11-3/4" dia, bezel **75.00**

❖ Cloisonné

Cloisonné is an interesting decorative technique in which small wires are adhered to a metal surface, and then the design is filled in with enamel, creating a very colorful pattern. The more intricate the design and the enameling, or the older the piece, the

higher the price can be.

Collectors' Club: Cloisonné Collectors Club, P.O. Box 96, Rockport, MA 01966.

For additional listings, see *Warman's Antiques & Collectibles Price Guide*.

Reproduction Alert

Box, 2" x 3"....................................**100.00**
Candlesticks, pr, figural, blue mythical animals seated on round dark red base with open work sides, 3 feet, each animal holds flower in mouth, red candle socket on back, 7-1/8" h.**200.00**
Charger, roosters and floral dec, black ground, Chinese, late 19th C, surface scratches, 14" dia......................**190.00**
Cigarette case, green, 3 dragons, Chinese **175.00**
Cross pendant, blue ground, rose and white dec, Russian hallmarks **150.00**
Desk set, brush pot, pen, pen tray, blotter and paper holder, Japan .**130.00**
Jardiniere, bronze, bands of cloisonné designs, golden yellow and blue triangles, polychrome geometric designs on dark blue, chrysanthemums on light blue, cast relief scene of water lily, turtle, and flowering branches on int., 13" dia, 10" h, soldered repair at foot **220.00**
Planter, classical symbol and scroll dec, blue ground, Chinese, 11" dia....**100.00**
Tea kettle, multicolor scrolling lotus flowers, medium blue ground, double handles, Chinese, 19th C...........**690.00**
Vase, finely enameled geometric designs, stylized florals, turquoise ground, Oriental, 20th C, 16" h, price for pr...**230.00**

❖ Clothes Sprinklers

Here's a part of the flea market world that has taken off. Who would have ever thought that Grandma's way of preparing ironing would become so popular with collectors? Because many of these handy sprinklers are figural, they make great display pieces.

Chinese man, Cleminson, 8" h.......**90.00**
Dutch boy, ceramic, 8-1/4" h **295.00**
Elephant, ceramic
Pink and gray **165.00**
White **110.00**
Glass, clear recycled bottle, black rubber and tin stopper top **5.00**
Iron shape, white ceramic, green ivy dec **25.00**
Kate, Cleminson, 6-1/2" h **36.00**

Mammy, ceramic, white dress, 7" h
....**495.00**
Merry Maid, plastic, mkd "Made in USA"
....**15.00**
Rooster, ceramic, some paint missing,
10" h...**165.00**
Siamese cat, ceramic, 8-1/4" h.....**195.00**
Sprinkle Plenty, 8" h **85.00**

❖ Clothing

As fashions change from year to year, collecting vintage clothing never seems to go out of style. Many clothing collectors look for prestigious labels as well as garments that are in good condition.

References: Blanche Cirker (ed.), *1920s Fashions From B. Altman & Company,* Dover, 1999; Paula Jean Darnell, *Victorian to Vamp, Women's Clothing 1900-1929,* Fabric Fancies, 2000; Chet Gadsby, *Victorian Paisley Shawls,* Schiffer Publishing, 2002; Carol Belanger Grafton, *Fashions of the Thirties,* Dover Publications, 1993; —, *Shoes, Hats and Fashion Accessories,* Dover Publications, 1998; ——, *Victorian Fashion: A Pictorial Archive,* Dover Publications, 1999; Kristina Harris, *Authentic Victorian Dressmaking Techniques,* Dover Publications, 1999; —, *Collector's Guide to Vintage Fashions,* Collector Books, 1999; Erhard Klepper, *Costume Through The Ages,* Dover Publications, 1999; Elizabeth Kurella, *The Complete Guide to Vintage Textiles,* Krause Publications, 1999; Ellie Laubner, *Fashions of the Roaring '20s,* Schiffer Publishing, 1996; —, *Fashions of the Turbulent 1930s,* Schiffer Publishing, 2000; Tina Skinner, *Fashionable Clothing from the Sears Catalogs, Mid 1950s,* Schiffer Publishing, 2002.

Periodicals: *Glass Slipper,* 653 S Orange Ave, Sarasota, FL 34236; *Lady's Gallery,* P.O. Box 1761, Independence, MO 64055; *Lill's Vintage Clothing Newsletter,* 19 Jamestown Dr, Cincinnati, OH 45241; *Vintage Clothing Newsletter,* P.O. Box 88892, Seattle, WA 98138; *Vintage Connection,* 904 N 65th St, Springfield, OR 97478; *Vintage Gazette,* 194 Amity St, Amherst, MA 01002.

Japanese silk kimono, navy blue with embroidered decoration, $195.

Collectors' Clubs: The Costume Soc of America, P.O. Box 73, Earleville, MD 21919; Vintage Fashion and Costume Jewelry Club, P.O. Box 265, Glen Oaks, NY 11004.

For additional listings, see *Warman's Antiques & Collectibles* and *Warman's Americana & Collectibles.*

Bathing suit, girl's, cotton print, ruffles, 1950s **15.00**
Bed jacket, satin, pink, ecru lace trim, labeled "B. Altman & Co. NY," 1930s
....**35.00**
Blouse
Beaded taffeta, black, black glass beads at yoke, hand sewn........**90.00**
Cotton, white, Victorian cutwork...**25.00**
White lawn, embroidery and lace insertion, c1890, minor edge damage to collar **30.00**
Bridesmaid's gown, pink chiffon, satin ribbon trim, size 10......................**50.00**
Cape, black velvet, modified Napoleon collar, single button closure, lined with black quilted satin, c1930.............**60.00**
Chemine, linen, ruffles and lace at cuffs, late 18th/early 19th C...................**25.00**
Christening gown, cotton, white, lace trim, matching bonnet, 47" l **115.00**
Coat
Boy's, linen, hand stitched, dec cuffs
....**35.00**
Lady's, Persian lamb, black, matching hat and muff.............................**95.00**
Dress, girl's, georgette and chiffon, pink, c1920 ....**75.00**
Dress, lady's
Beige lace, light tan silk crepe, lace belt with brass buckle, pleated lace skirt, lace tunic with ruffles at neckline, three-quarter length lace jacket with long sleeves, pin tucks, collar, c1925, some damage to dress shoulder **65.00**
Navy blue silk and silk chiffon, pin tucks at hipline, beige silk crepe and lace trim, c1930 ....**45.00**
Pale lilac silk, sq cut steel buttons, cream lace collar, bubble-effect skirt, draped back, c1900, wear **60.00**
Lingerie dress, white batiste, embroidery and lace insertion on bodice, and skirt, ruching below waistline, c1910............................**45.00**
Nightgown, white cotton, elaborate yoke of ruched white lawn alternating with lace, long lace trimmed sleeves, placket with lace trim, c1910........**20.00**
Pajamas, lady's, silk, red, 1920s.....**75.00**
Pant suit, top and palazzo pants, Andrea Gayle, bright green, orange, yellow, pink, gray and purple satiny material, 2 pcs...**65.00**
Petticoat, cream organdy, pin tucks, lace,

ruffles at hem, train, c1890 ....**35.00**
Robe, printed green, tan, gray, yellow, and ivory silk, swirls, floral, and feather shapes, c1945......................**60.00**
Skirt, lady's, black wool, Victorian...**45.00**
Suit
Boy's, navy wool blazer, short pants, orig Tom Sawyer brand.............**45.00**
Lady's, linen, straight skirt, jacket with shoulder pads and fitted waist, English.....................................**70.00**
Man's, black gabardine, jacket, vest, trousers, size 42, c1940 ....**50.00**
Waistcoat, gentleman's, English, 18th C, embroidered on front with feather and boat motif, floral and dotted border, buttons embroidered with floral sprigs
....**550.00**
Wedding gown, satin, ivory, padded shoulders, sweetheart neckline, waist swag, self train, c1945 ....**150.00**

❖ Clothing Accessories

Clothing accents and accessories are even more collectible than vintage clothing. Perhaps this is because many of these accessories are just as fun to use today as when they were originally created. And, as with vintage clothing, with proper care and handling, it's perfectly acceptable to use these collectibles.

References: LaRue Johnson Bruton, *Ladies' Vintage Accessories,* Collector Books, 2000; Roseann Ettinger, *Handbags,* 3rd ed, Schiffer Publishing, 1999; Roselyn Gerson, *Vintage & Contemporary Purse Accessories,* Collector Books, 1997; ——, *Vintage & Vogue Ladies Compacts,* 2nd ed, Collector Books, 2000; ——, *Vintage Vanity Bags and Purses,* Collector Books, 1994 (1997 value update); Michael Jay Goldberg, *The Ties That Blind,* Schiffer Publishing, 1997; Richard Holiner, *Antique Purses,* Collector Books, 1999; Susan Langley, *Vintage Hats & Bonnets, 1770-1970,* Collector Books, 1997 (1999 value update); Rosanna Mihalick, *Collecting Handkerchiefs,* Schiffer Publishing, 2000; Laura M. Mueller, *Collector's Encyclopedia of Compacts, Carryalls & Face Powder Boxes,* Collector Books, Vol. I (1999 values), Vol. II (1997 values); Leslie Piña, Lorita Winfield, and Constance Korosec, *Beads in Fashion, 1900-2000,* Schiffer Publishing, 1999; Maureen Reilly, *Hot Shoes, 100 Years,* Schiffer Publishing, 1998; Desire Smith, *Fashion Footwear, 1800-1970,* Schiffer Publishing, 2000; ——, *Hats,* Schiffer Publishing, 1996; ——, *Vintage Styles: 1920-1960,* Schiffer Publishing, 1997; Jeffrey B. Snyder, *Stetson Hats & The John B. Stetson Company 1865-1970,* Schiffer Publishing, 1997; Lorita Winfield, Leslie Pina, and Constance Korosec, *Beads on Bags, 1880s to 2000;* Schiffer Publishing, 2000.

Clothing Accessories, ear muffs, child size, Cabbage Patch Kids, yellow yarn pigtails, slight wear, $3.

Periodicals: *Glass Slipper*, 653 S Orange Ave, Sarasota, FL 34236; *Lady's Gallery*, P.O. Box 1761, Independence, MO 64055; *Lill's Vintage Clothing Newsletter*, 19 Jamestown Dr, Cincinnati, OH 45241; *The Vintage Connection*, 904 N. 65th St., Springfield, OR 97478; *Vintage Clothing Newsletter*, P.O. Box 88892, Seattle, WA 98138; *Vintage Gazette*, 194 Amity St, Amherst, MA 01002.

Collectors' Clubs: The Costume Society of America, P.O. Box 73, Earleville, MD 21919; Vintage Fashion and Costume Jewelry Club, P.O. Box 265, Glen Oaks, NY 11004.

For additional listings, see *Warman's Antiques & Collectibles* and *Warman's Americana & Collectibles*.

Apron
Gingham, green, embroidered design,

Clothing Accessories, book, To Have and To Hold, 135 Years of Wedding Fashions, *Mint Museum of Art, sepia toned cover, $15.*

Clothing Accessories, spats, $15, pearl collars, $5 each.

pockets **10.00**
Printed cotton, Christmas train motif, patch pockets, slight wear **15.00**
Baby bonnet, white cotton, pink ribbon ties, c1960.................................**10.00**
Collar
Beaded and fur, white, early 1950s **10.00**
Black silk and velvet, steel beading, c1890 ....**25.00**
Gloves, pr
Girl's, white nylon, ruffled cuff **10.00**
Lady's, satin, long, white **20.00**
Handbag
Alligator, brown, brass clasp, brown leather lining, c1945 ....**45.00**
Black velvet, lined with cream silk with rosettes, pierced ivory frame, c1930 ....**45.00**
Floral tapestry, rose, green, and blue on cream ground, black border, brass frame with chain handle, c1940, 8-1/2" x 5-1/2" **30.00**
Handkerchief, printed, Christmas poinsettia design, red stitched edge **10.00**
Hat
Beanie (Beanie & Cecil), propeller top **55.00**
Indiana Jones, "Official," size XL ..**50.00**
Muff
Child's, white rabbit fur **25.00**
Lady's, mink **45.00**
Shawl
Paisley, dark ground, long fringe, small holes **70.00**
Silk, floral ivory satin embroidery on ivory background, knotted satin fringe, Spanish, c1900, 44" sq .**75.00**
Stole, marabou, white **50.00**
Sweater, child's, hand-knit, train on back **30.00**
Teddy, yellow, pink emb trim on bodice, 1920s **25.00**
Tie, hp scene of New York harbor, 1940s **12.00**
Vest, white cotton, mother-of-pearl buttons, c1910............................**65.00**
Yoke, crocheted, ribbon trim **15.00**

❖ Cobalt Blue Glassware Items

Blue has always been a favorite color for interior decorating. There has been a resurgence in the popularity of cobalt blue glassware items. A quick tip for telling the age of cobalt glass is the "greasy fingers test"—try rubbing your fingertips over the surface of a piece. If you get a slightly greasy feeling or leave streaks on the glass, it's a modern creation.

Animal dish, cov, hen on nest, Kemple Glass **15.00**
Barber bottle, 7" h **85.00**
Basket, white dot dec, applied clear handle with large medallion at side connections, 11" h.....................**150.00**
Bottle, violin shape **12.00**
Paperweight, apple shape, cobalt blue crackle glass body, hand-blown, hand-applied crystal stem and leaf, Blenko Glass Co., 6" h, 3-1/2" w.............**65.00**
Plate, 3 bunnies at top, Westmoreland Glass Co......................................**15.00**
Rose bowl, white stripes and white edging **20.00**
Salt and pepper shakers, range size, 6" h, pr..**80.00**
Tumbler, 5" h, "Atlantic City," white frosted design with skyline, ocean and hotels...**45.00**
Vase, cone, applied glass flower, clear pedestal base, 8-1/4" h **45.00**

❖ Coca-Cola

An Atlanta pharmacist, John S. Pemberton, is credited with first developing the syrup base used for Coca-Cola. He was attempting to formulate a patent medicine for those experiencing headaches, nervousness, or stomach upsets. In 1887, Willis E. Venable mixed the syrup with carbonated water, and the rest was history. The *Atlanta Journal* carried the first print ad for Coca-Cola on May 29, 1886. In 1893, a trademark was granted for Coca-Cola written in script, and in 1945, the term Coke was registered.

References: Allan Petretti, *Petretti's Coca-Cola Collectibles Price Guide*, 11th ed, Antique Trader Books, 2001; Bob and Debra Henrich, *Cola-Cola Commemorative Bottles,* Collector Books, 1998; Allan Petretti and Chris Beyer, *Classic Coca-Cola Calendars*, Antique Trader Books, 1999; —, *Classic Coca-Cola Serving Trays,* Antique Trader Books, 1998; B.J. Summers, *B.J. Summers' Guide to Coca-Cola*, 4th ed., Collector Books, 2003; Al and Helen Wilson, *Wilson's Coca-Cola Guide*, Schiffer Publishing, 1997.

Collectors' Club: Cavanagh's Coca-Cola Christmas Collector's Soc, 1000 Holcomb Woods Parkway, Suite 440B, Roswell, GA

30076; Coca-Cola Collectors Club, 400 Monemar Ave, Baltimore, MD 21228-5213; Coca-Cola Collectors Club International, P.O. Box 49166, Atlanta, GA 30359-1166.

For additional listings, see *Warman's Advertising, Warman's Antiques & Collectibles* and *Warman's Americana & Collectibles*.

Reproduction Alert

Coca-cola items are often sold with a condition grade designation, like C 8.5. This coding gives collectors valuable information. Of course, the higher the grade, the higher the price.

10 = mint, unused, no wear or fading
9.5 = near mint, very minor imperfections
8.5 = outstanding, few minor imperfections
8 = excellent, light scratches, minor dents, light edge wear
7.5 = fine-plus, some scratches, fading
7 = fine, noticeable scratches, light dents
6.5 = fine-minus (good), noticeable slight damage, slight rust
6 = poor, noticeable damage, discoloration

Badge, hat, bronze, circa 1940s, "Drink Coca-Cola," C 8.5+, 3-1/2" **38.50**
Banner, silk, white with gold fringe, "things go better with Coke" in red text, 1960s, light soiling, 46" h, 23-1/2" w **55.00**
Blotter, 3-1/2" x 7-1/2", cardboard, full-color ski scene, copyright 1947, unused.......................................**20.00**
Bookmark, Romance of Coca-Cola, 1916 ....**30.00**
Calendar, paper
1958 ....**145.00**
1960 ....**24.00**
Card table, 1930s, bottle logos in corners, Coke tag on back **55.00**
Carrier, 6-pack
Aluminum, 1940s, embossed "Coca-Cola" **72.00**
Wooden, early 1940s, lift handle, "Drink Coca-Cola in Bottles, Pause... Go refreshed" logo with wings, mkd "new consumer case," red on yellow ground.....................................**245.00**
Change tray
1914, Betty **150.00**
1941, girl with skates **48.00**
1970, Santa Claus **85.00**
Clock, light-up, metal and glass, rectangular, "Drink Coca-Cola," clock

Coca-Cola Items, sign, red and white, worn, $20.

face over red text, white ground, 11" h, 12" w **165.00**
Coasters, colored aluminum, 1950s, boxed set of 8, orig box................**65.00**
Cooler, Cavalier picnic cooler, 1950s, "Drink Coca-Cola in Bottles," orig box, 18" h, 18" w, 13" d.....................**440.00**
Dish, pretzel, circa 1935, 3 miniature Coke bottles hold central round dish **187.00**
Dispenser, syrup, countertop, metal, 1940s, "Drink Coca-Cola, Ice Cold" in oval, end has "Have A Coke" in circle, with glass stand/mounting hardware, 14" h, 8" w, 18" d.....................**110.00**
Doll, Santa Claus, 1950s-1960s, stuffed body, black boots, 18" h **110.00**
b, 8" h, plastic and metal, bottle shape, orig instructions and screws, C-9.3-9.5...**275.00**
Game board, 11-1/4" x 26-1/2", Steps to Health, prepared and distributed by Coca-Cola Co. of Canada, Ltd., copyright 1938, orig unmarked brown paper envelope............................**60.00**
Insignia button, 24 of 25 set, 1" celluloid multicolored pinbacks, Army, Air Force, Navy, and Marines, orig back papers, c1943 ....**350.00**
Magazine advertisement
1914, "Delicious Coca-Cola, Pure and Wholesome," portrait of woman drinking glass of Coke, back cover of The National Sunday Magazine,

Coca-Cola Items, cooler, red metal, aluminum carrying handle, white int., white lettering, $65.

Coca-Cola Items, salt and pepper shakers, red and white vending machine shaped shakers, white plastic stand, mkd "Made in Japan," $10.

framed......................................**38.50**
1936, "Thru 50 Years...the pause that refreshes," color image of 2 women in bathing suits **44.00**
Menu sign, tin, 1960s, "Enjoy Coca-Cola" in red circle logo beside "things go better with Coke" slogan, red/white top over green board, 28" h, 20" w **330.00**
Paperweight, girl in white swimsuit **80.00**
Prize chance card, 4-1/4" x 5-1/4", printed in red and black on white, c1940, unused...........................**12.00**
Service pin, 10 Years, 10K gold, raised image of bottle, c1930.................**65.00**
Sign, cardboard cutout, 1951, "Be refreshed" in banner by button sign, 3 women at table drinking glasses of Coke 16" h, 24" w **165.00**
Sign, celluloid
Circa 1940s, "Coca-Cola, Delicious, Refreshing," orig envelope, 9" dia **330.00**
1940s-1950s, "Coca-Cola" in script over hobbleskirt bottle, 9" dia .**275.00**
Sign, paper, "Take Along Coke in 12 oz. Cans, Buy a Case," large-diamond can and dock scene, framed, 20" h, 36" w **365.00**
Sign, tin, embossed, 1961, "Drink Coca-Cola, Enjoy That Refreshing New Feeling," white text on red fish tail ground on white, clean-cut ends, rolled top/bottom border, 24" h, 36" w .**150.00**
Thermometer, tin, 5" x 17" diecut emb tin, figural Pat'd Dec 25, 1923 bottle, 1930s **150.00**
Toy
Car, litho tin, Ford taxi, friction, made by Taiyo, 1960s, orig box, 3" h, 10-

1/2" w...........................**315.00**
Truck, Buddy L, model 5426, pressed
    steel, yellow with 5 cases and 2
    hand trucks, orig box cond. 7, truck
    C 9-9.25+, 15" l **550.00**
Van, Corgi, 5" l diecast metal and
    plastic replica, copyright 1978, 2-3/4"
    x 6" x 3-1/2" color box with display
    window.......................................**35.00**

Tray
1907, large oval, "Drink Coca-Cola,
    Relieves Fatigue, 5¢," woman in
    green dress with white trim, glass in
    right hand, gold border, C 7.5-7.75,
    16-1/2" h, 13-1/2" w.............**5,000.00**
1914, Betty, woman in white shawl and
    bonnet, "Drink Coca-Cola, Delicious
    and Refreshing," "Ward Gayden"
    engraved above bonnet, possibly a
    presentation tray, chips, C 8.5-8.75
    ....**550.00**
1922, Summer Girl, woman in wide-
    brim hat, C 8.5........................**935.00**
1928, Soda Jerk..........................**367.50**
1935, Madge Evans, C-7.5 ....**165.00**
1940, Sailor Girl, girl in sailor outfit
    sitting on dock..........................**615.00**
1941, Skater Girl, woman in skates
    sitting on log **425.00**

❖ Cocktail Shakers

"Make mine a dry martini" was the plea of
many well-heeled party guests we gazed at
in the movies. To make that perfect drink, a
clever device called the cocktail shaker was
used. Today these shakers are finding their
way to flea markets and collectors.

Reference: Stephen Visakay, *Vintage Bar
Ware,* Collector Books, 1997.

Aluminum, gold color, shaker top has
    insert with holes, Mirro, 1950s, 8-1/2" h
    ....**18.00**
Chrome
    Farberware, 1950s, 12" h.............**30.00**
    Mr Bartender, measuring jigger, glass
        insert, 8" h **25.00**
Farber Bros., Bakelite handle, 12-1/2" h
    ....**85.00**
Glass
    Cobalt blue, barbell, 3-pc chrome top
        ....**595.00**
    Clear, silver-plate top, 9" h...........**48.00**
    Clear with recipes, metal lid, 1950s, 8-
        1/4" h **35.00**
    Clear with yellow circles of varying
        sizes, chrome pour top with
        removable lid, 11-1/4" h............**22.00**
    Ruby, gold rooster on side, 2 gold
        bands, chrome strainer and top,
        bands worn, dent in lid, 11" h...**85.00**
Plastic and metal, traffic light shape,
    battery op, orig swizzle stick, 1950s

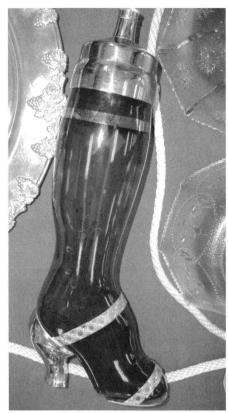

*Cocktail Shakers, leg shaped, amber glass body,
chromed lid, decorative bands, and shoe, $95.*

    ....**50.00**
Pottery, green, Rookwood, mkd on base,
    1951, 12" h.............................**700.00**
Set, clear glass, ribbed, chrome top, six
    matching glasses **60.00**
Silver, repousse, scenes of woman,
    cottage, windmill, scrolled shield,
    hallmarks, wear, 12" h...............**195.00**

❖ Coffee Mills

The secret to a really great cup of coffee
has always been freshly ground coffee
beans. Today's collectors are discovering
this is still the case. With the current
popularity of coffee, perhaps we'll see an
increase in coffee mills.

Collectors' Club: Assoc of Coffee Mill
Enthusiasts, 657 Old Mountain Road,
Marietta, GA 30064.

Arcade, wall style, top jar emb "Crystal,"
    tin twist lid mkd Arcade, lower glass
    container on adjustable platform,
    overall 17" h **185.00**
Crown Coffee Mill, cast iron, mounted n
    wood base, decal "Crown Coffee Mill
    Made By Landers, Frary, & Clark, New
    Britain, Conn, U.S.A.," number 11 emb
    on top lid **525.00**
Enterprise, #00, two wheel, store type,
    orig paint, orig decals, 12-1/2" x 7-1/2"
    x 8-3/4", C 8+.........................**1,450.00**
Enterprise, #0 ....**100.00**

*Coffee Mills, wooden, brass fittings, marked 1896,
$120.*

Imperial No. 705, long cast iron crank
    handle, domed cast iron top, molded
    scrolls above dovetailed case, small
    drawers, remnants f label above
    drawer, 11" h **65.00**
Kitchen Aid, electric, white metal base
    with glass jar, 14" h **145.00**
Olde Thompson, wooden, drawer,
    handle with wooden knob, 6-3/4" sq
    ....**95.00**
Parker's Union Coffee Mill, wood, label
    on front, 9-1/4" h **145.00**
Rossenhaus, wooden, German or
    Dutch, 3-3/4" x 4-1/4", 8" h **48.00**
Sun Manufacturing, Greenfield, Ohio,
    worn orig label, round wooden sides,
    cast iron hardware, directions for use,
    12" h.......................................**300.00**
Wood, drawer, metal cup to hold beans,
    iron handle, 7-1/4" sq **125.00**

❖ Coffee Tins

Here's an advertising categories that has
only gotten hotter over the past few years.
Collected for their colorful labels, these tins
are found in many sizes and shapes.

Anchor Coffee, 1-lb **25.00**
Blanke's Portonilla Coffee, green and
    gold, bail handle, dome lid, c1900, 10"
    h **80.00**
Elmwood Coffee, tin top and bottom,
    paper label with country club image, 3-
    lb, 5-1/2" d, 9-5/8" h **190.00**
Folger's Coffee, 5-lb, keywind........**50.00**
Gold Bond Coffee, 1-lb, screw top.**35.00**
Hersh's Best **70.00**
Honeymoon Coffee, paper label over tin,
    image of couple cuddling on crescent
    moon, red ground, 1-lb, 3-5/8" x 5-3/8",
    C.8+...**275.00**
King Cole, 1-lb, 5-3/4" x 4-1/4" **300.00**
Luzianne Coffee, small size, Mammy
    illus **95.00**

57350; *Gameroom Magazine*, 1014 Mt Tabor Rd, New Albany, IN 47150; *Jukebox Collector*, 2545 SE 60th Street, Des Moines, IA 50317; *Pin Game Journal*, 31937 Olde Franklin Dr, Farmington, MI, 48334; *Scopitone Newsletter*, 810 Courtland Dr, Ballwin, MO 63021.

Collectors' Club: Coin Operated Collectors Assoc, 1511 Holliston Trail, Ft. Wayne, IN 46825.

Duck Hunter, 1¢, arcade, shoots penny at target for gum ball, ABT Silver King, c1949 ....**250.00**
Ford, c1950, round globe, gum balls, large, organizational use, 12" h....**75.00**
Fortune Telling, Waitling, scale, #400, 1948 ....**400.00**
Marklin Phillies, cigars, 1930s **150.00**
Marvel, 1 cent, cigarette/gumball/ 3-reel trade simulator slot machine, Bakelite knob, paper cigarette labels on reels, 11" h, 8" w, 11" d......................**550.00**
Master, c1923, 1 cent, confection, 16" h **200.00**
Mercury, 1 cent, cigarette trade stimulator slot machine, blue-green color, wear, paintchipped along top, 11" h, 9" w, 10-1/2" d......................**550.00**
Pete's Penny Ante trade stimulator, 1920s **400.00**
Photo Viewing Machine, American Mutoscope, NY, c1920, 1 cent, metal, orig photos and paper marquee **1,100.00**
Skill Game, Kicker/Catcher, 5¢, 3 balls, Baker Mfg., c1940 ....**400.00**
Stamp Machine, Shipman, 1960 ....**35.00**
Tally-Ho, 5¢, wood rail pinball machine **250.00**
Zeno Gum, 1¢, wooden case dispensed

Coke machine, Vendo, red, white logo, working condition, some wear, $300.

Coffee Tins, Pantry Pride, drip grind, plastic lid, $1.

Mammy Coffee, 4-lb size, Mammy illus **500.00**
National's Best Blend, 1-lb, screw top **60.00**
Red Rose, 1-lb, keywind **45.00**
Sears Coffee Pail **200.00**
Yale Coffee, Steinwender Stoffregen, navy, red, white, and gold, 1-lb, 5-7/8" x 4-1/8"......................................**200.00**
White House Coffee, 1-lb, tin vacuum pack, keywind.............................**400.00**

❖ Coin Ops & Trade Stimulators

Because many of these machines have seen a lot of use, expect to find wear and maybe even a repair or two. Look for a reputable dealer and ask him to explain the machine's history and operating techniques.

References: Richard M. Bueschel, *Collector's Guide to Vintage Coin Machines*, Schiffer Publishing, 1995; ——, *Guide to Vintage Trade Stimulators & Counter Games*, Schiffer Publishing, 1997; ——, *Lemons, Cherries and Bell-Fruit-Gum*, Royal Bell Books, 1995; ——, *Pinball 1*, Hoflin Publishing, 1988; ——, *Slots 1*, Hoflin Publishing, 1989.

Periodicals: *Always Jukin'*, 221 Yesler Way, Seattle, WA 98104; *Antique Amusements Slot Machines & Jukebox Gazette*, 909 26th St NW, Washington, DC 20037; *Around the Vending Wheel*, 5417 Castana Ave, Lakewood, CA 90712; *Coin Drop International*, 5815 W 52nd Ave, Denver, CO 80212; *Coin Machine Trader*, 569 Kansas SE, P. O. Box 602, Huron, SD

sticks of gum, c1910 ....**600.00**

❖ Coins, American and Foreign

Coin collecting has been a favorite pastime for generations. Coin collectors are very particular about the grading of their coins, and they have established very specific guidelines. Many coin collectors find treasures at flea markets, partly because they are dedicated lookers, but also because they are usually very knowledgeable about their field   For more information about this fascinating hobby, check the following references and periodicals.

References: Krause Publications is the country's premier publisher of books on coins. The following are all excellent references by this publisher. Colin Bruce, *Standard Catalog of World Coins 1901 to Present 31st ed*; Colin Bruce and George Cuhaj, *Standard Catalog of World Coins 1601-1700 2nd ed*; Richard Doty, *America's Money-America's Story;* Dave Harper, *2003 North American Coins & Prices,* 12th ed; Chester Krause and Clifford Mishler, ed by Colin Bruce, *Standard Catalog of World Coins, 1801-1900 3rd ed*; Richard Lobel, Mark Davidson, Alan Hallistone and Eleni Caligas, *Coincraft's 1998 Standard Catalog of English & UK Coins, 1066 to Date;* N. Douglas Nicol, ed by Colin Bruce, *Standard Catalog of German Coins, 1601-Present,* 2nd ed; Jules Reiver, *The United States Early Silver Dollars, 1794 to 1804*; Wayne G. Sayles, *Ancient Coin Collecting 2nd ed*; Bob Wilhite, *1998 Auction Prices Realized,* 17th ed

Periodicals: *Coin Prices,* Krause Publications, 700 E State St, Iola, WI 54990; *Numismatic News,* Krause Publications, 700 E State St, Iola, WI 54990.

❖ College Collectibles

Flea markets are great places to look for college items. Most collectors concentrate on memorabilia from their alma mater.

Book, *The University of Minnesota 1851-1951,* Minnesota Press, sgd by author, 609 pgs, maps.............................**10.00**
Coloring book, Univ. of Florida Gators, 1982, unused **15.00**
Compact, Roanoke Univ, gold tone ...**28.00**
Cuff links, Vassar, gold colored, pr.**50.00**
Final exam, science, Yale, 1905, folded **25.00**
Handbook, Harbrace College, 1951, hardcover **4.00**
Lunch box, oval, graphics of colorful college pennants **16.00**

College Collectibles, suitcase, blue and white Franklin and Marshall college pennant, brown and yellow suitcase, $15.

Mascot, Baylor Univ., bear, hard rubber, 1950s **20.00**

Pennant, Iowa State, maroon and gold felt, 23" l **12.00**

Photograph, Colorado Agricultural College, black-and-white photo of track team, 1904 ....**65.00**

Pinback button, Texas Bowl, 1960s, red and white......................................**4.00**

Plate

Alma College, Alma, Mich., Vernon Kilns

....**30.00**

Robinson Hall, Albion College, Albion, Mich., Wedgwood, 10-1/4" dia..**45.00**

Postcard

A and M College, campus scene, unused......................................**1.00**

Campus, Univ. of Chicago, Ill., 1926, unused......................................**2.50**

Main Hall, Rutgers Univ., N.J., 1946, unused......................................**2.00**

Meridian Senior High School-Junior College, Meridian, Miss., unused**4.00**

The Student Center, Douglass College, New Brunswick, N.J., used.........**2.00**

Program, Rice Univ. vs Univ. of Houston, Sept. 11, 1971 ....**100.00**

Record, College Marching Songs, Russ Morgan & His Band, 45 rpm, Decca, 4-record set **65.00**

Ring, man's, 10kt yg
Lafayette Univ, PA **200.00**
Pace Univ, NY, 1951..................**325.00**

Souvenir plate, Alma College, Mich., Vernon Kilns **30.00**

Souvenir spoon, St. Mary's College
....**35.00**

Textbook, *Food for the Family*, Wilmot and Batter, hardcover, 1938, some writing inside **30.00**

Yearbook, Oregon Agricultural College, 1920 ....**50.00**

❖ Coloring & Activity Books

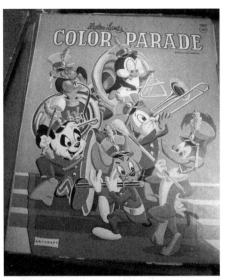

Coloring Books, Walter Lantz Color Parade, Woody leading band of popular Lantz characters, unused, $10.

Remember how much fun it was to color and paint? Today's collectors are still trying to "stay in the lines" as they accumulate interesting coloring books. Coloring and paint books were introduced in the early 1900s, but they didn't really catch on until the 1930s, when manufacturers began printing coloring books based on child stars, such as Shirley Temple. Most collectors look for uncolored books, but some will buy books with neatly executed work.

Africa, A Missionary Color Book for Children, Paul Hubartt, 10-3/4" x 7-1/2," few pgs colored....................**12.00**

A-Team New Adventures Coloring and Activity Book, Modern Promotions, 1984, 24 pgs, binding tears and activities completed.......................**5.00**

Ballerina, Merrill, 1953, 10-1/2" x 14"
....**16.00**

Bullwinkle & Dudley Do Right, Saalfield, copyright 1971, unused................**30.00**

Bunny, Southfield Publishing, 7" x 8-1/4", 1950, unused **10.00**

Christmas Cut-Out and Coloring Book, illus by Florence Sarah Winship, flocked hat on cover Santa, 1954, 15" x

Coloring Books, Robin Hood, Color and Color, orig crayons, wipe off book, $4.

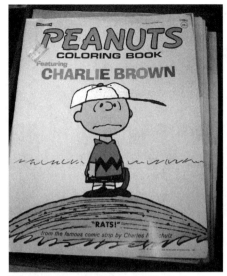

Coloring Books, Peanuts, featuring Charlie Brown, Rats, Saalfield, authorized edition, unused, $10.

11", unused **35.00**

Dumbo Press-Out Book....................**6.00**

Elsie's My Family and Friends, 10 pgs, 4" x 6" **22.00**

E. T. Coloring Book, Wanderer Book, Simon & Schuster, Universal Studios, 1982, 8" x 11"..............................**15.00**

G.I. Joe, 1982, few pages colored ...**10.00**

Henry, 1956, one page colored.......**30.00**

JFK, 1962, unused.........................**15.00**

Lady and the Tramp Sticker Activity Book, unused..**6.00**

Lone Ranger, 1959, unused **50.00**

Mask, 8" x 10-3/4" **12.00**

Mister Magoo, Whitman, 1965, few pages colored **45.00**

Monkey Shines, 1953, 8-1/4" x 11-3/8", few pages colored, some yellowing
....**12.00**

Mr T, #2814, green cover, unused.....**8.50**

Pinocchio **20.00**

Planet of the Apes, Artcraft, authorized ed, Apjac Productions, Twentieth Century Fox Film Corp., some pages colored **20.00**

School Days Coloring Book, 1956, 6 pgs colored **9.50**

Surprise! Whitman, drawings by Mary Alice Stoddard.................................**3.00**

The Love Bug, Hunt's Food promotional, 1969, full page promo on back cover, unused.......................................**20.00**

Thundercats, red cover, 1989, unused
....**15.00**

Wizard of Oz, Waldman Publishing Corp., N.Y., 1966, 8" x 11", unused **10.00**

❖ Comedian Collectibles

Those who can make us laugh seem to find

their way into our hearts. Some collectors are now choosing to concentrate on these folks and are having a great time doing it.

Also see Autographs, Character Collectibles, and Movie Collectibles in this edition.

Book, *Don't Shoot, It's Only Me: Bob Hope's Comedy History of the United States*, Bob Hope, Putnam, 1990, 315 pgs, used..................................**7.50**
Colorforms set, Three Stooges, 1959, MIB..**270.00**
Coloring book, Bob Hope, Saalfield, unused..**18.00**
Comic book
  Get Smart, #5.................................**5.00**
  Jackie Gleason & The Honeymooners, #2...**35.00**
  Laurel & Hardy 3-D Comic Book, #2, 1987..**7.00**
Cookie jar, I Love Lucy................**100.00**
Game, Laurel and Hardy, Transogram, 1962 copyright............................**42.50**
Magazine
  Life, Feb. 4, 1946, Bob Hope and Bing Crosby cover............................**10.00**
  Pet Milk Magazine, 1958, Red Skelton cover..**15.00**
  Time, April 7, 1947, Fred Allen cover story...**25.00**
  TV Guide, Feb. 25-March 3, 1967, Phyllis Diller cover...................**15.00**
Matchbook, Comedian Series, 1975
  Fields, W.C. **5.00**
  Lewis, Jerry...................................**5.00**
  Marx, Groucho...........................**21.00**
Notebook binder, Laugh-In, 1969..**20.00**
Photo, sgd, 8" x 10"
  Hope, Bob **35.00**
  Jones, Spike................................**25.00**
  Seinfeld, Jerry **20.00**
  Skelton, Red................................**45.00**
Press kit, George Carlin, 1977 ....**10.00**

Mug, Archie Bunker, Mr. American, red, white, and blue, photo image center, $10.

Diecut, Laurel, barrel reads "This End Up, from Stan Laurel to Oliver Hardy, Rush," holding hammer in hand, arms move, masonite, $95.

Puppet, Jerry Lewis, 9" h, fabric, soft vinyl head, c1950 ....**55.00**
Salt and pepper shakers, Three Stooges, pr...................................**20.00**
Tobacco card, Jimmy Durante, 1930s **10.00**
T-shirt, Carrot Top, black, XL..........**10.00**
Waste basket, Laugh-In, litho show characters....................................**45.00**

❖ Comic Books

Comic books date back to the 1890s when newspapers started to print their popular funny-strips in book form. By the late 1930s, comic book manufacturers were producing all kinds of tales to delight young readers. Through the years, the artwork found in comic books has gotten more and more sophisticated, and many collectors now specialize in a particular artist or maker. This is one of those area in which collectors have learned to rely on good reference books. We've listed a few of the current publications here, but more exist.

References: Maggie Thompson, Brent Frankenhoff, et.al., *Comic Book Checklist & Price Guide*, 9th ed, Krause Publications, 2003. Maggie Thompson, Brent Frankenhoff, et. al., *The Standard Catalog of Comic Books*, 2nd ed, 2003. *All in Color for a Dime,* Krause Publications, 1997; Alex G. Malloy, *Comics Values Annual 2003*, Antique Trader Books, 2003; Robert M. Overstreet, *Overstreet Comic Book Price Guide*, 32nd ed, Avon Books, 2002.

Periodical: *Comics Buyer's Guide*, 700 E State St, Iola, WI 54990.

Collectors' Clubs: American Comics Exchange, 351-T Baldwin Rd, Hempstead, NY 11550; Fawcett Collectors of America & Magazine Enterprise, too!, 301 E Buena Vista Ave, North Augusta, SC 29841.

Reproduction Alert

Comic Books, Marvel's Greatest Comics featuring the Fantastic Four #50, Cocoon, July, 02468, $5.

Action Comics, #35, April 1941 ....**95.00**
All-American Comics, #26, May, 1941
  ....**295.00**
Atom, #35 ....**26.00**
Battlestar Galactica, 1978, 10" x 13-1/2"
  ....**15.00**
Blondie, 1972, 14" x 11" **15.00**
Blue Beetle, #26, Oct, 1943...........**145.00**
Crime Reporter, #2 ....**68.00**
Daredevil, Oct, #114 ....**10.00**
DC Super Spectacular, #20 ....**80.00**
Detective Comics, #105, Nov, 1945
  ....**155.00**
Famous Crimes, #4 ....**100.00**
Fightin' Marines, #15 ....**5.00**
Flash Gordon, #16...........................**18.00**
GI Joe I Battle, #1...........................**60.00**
Henry, 1971, 14" x 11"....................**15.00**
Jungle Adventures, #3 ....**2.00**
Katy Keene, #45 ....**12.50**
Mister Miracle, June, #2....................**9.00**
Moon Girl Fights Crime, EC Comic, #7
  ....**150.00**
Oliver Twist, Classics Illustrated, #17 **2.00**
Red Ryder, Frame-Up, Dell, #133, August, 1954, slight wear.............**18.00**
Sherlock Holmes, Classics Illustrated, #2
  ....**40.00**
Six Gun Heroes, #81 ....**12.00**
Sleeping Beauty, Walt Disney, #1 ....**20.00**
Spiderman, 1974, 14" x 11".............**15.00**
Strange Adventures, #7 ....**45.00**
Super Heroes, #4..............................**2.50**
The Phantom, Feature Book #20, 1939, large size...................................**290.00**
Woody Woodpecker, #194, copyright 1981, some wear............................**4.00**
Zebra Jungle Empress, #1...............**22.00**

❖ Commemorative Glasses

Decorative drinking glasses have always been a popular way to commemorate a special event or place. When sold at a flea market near the location being commemorated, they will command a slightly higher price.

Airplane, single propeller, green images of early planes, 1940s **16.00**
Florida, flamingo dec, hard plastic, hand-painted, c1950, 2-1/2" h **8.00**
Gettysburg Address, etched on clear glass **20.00**
Lord's Prayer, etched on clear glass**20.00**
Midwinter Fair, 1894, ruby stained, etched "Edward Doyle" **110.00**
Niagara Falls, Prospect Point, gold rim **20.00**
The Alamo, San Antonio, Tx., three portraits **18.00**
Whittier's Birthplace, etched, waisted tumbler **60.00**

❖ Commemorative Medals

Commemorative medals are collected according to type, subject matter, and maker. Collectors look for unusual examples and prefer those in very good condition. Information on medal collecting is often found in coin reference books, and many coin dealers also handle medals.

American Legion
Circular, bronze and enamel, 1-1/4" dia **8.00**
With attached pinback button, "12th Grand Promenade, Camden, N.J., 1932" **12.00**
American Red Cross, Military Welfare, cap, enamel **20.00**
Junior Baseball District Champs, American Legion, 1-1/4" dia........**35.00**
Knights of Pythias, medal with bar pin, "Conn. Lodge 37," name on back.**38.00**
Kodak Movie Awards, bronze, by Medallic Art Co., N.Y., "Sponsored in Cooperation with UFF/UFPA and CINE," 3" dia................................**19.00**
Military
Armed Forces Reserve, ribbon bar and pin, 1-1/4" dia medal, MOC **28.00**
Canada, 1939-45 Victory Medal, ribbon **38.00**
Drill Corps 1944 on bar pin, medal reads "York Comy, New York, S.J. Ecker," sterling **28.00**
Efficiency, Honor, Fidelity, back reads "For Good Conduct," name inscribed

....**16.00**
For Merit, Army Air Forces, bar pin with medal, sterling **35.00**
For Merit, 500 Hours, Army Air Forces, bar pin with medal, sterling **38.00**
For Merit, 1000 Hours, Army Air Forces, bar pin with medal, sterling
....**38.00**
French, white and green fabric with stripes, reverse with long metal vertical pin, small brass top suspends brass medallion accented by white, surrounding center area showing Vietnam outlined against dark green, 4" h **20.00**
Heroic or Meritorious Achievement, no name, ribbon.........................**12.00**
Merit Cross, 1st Class, Nazi, orig box
....**165.00**
Nazi Police Service, 18 years **150.00**
Waffen SS Army Infantry Assault Badge **50.00**

❖ Compacts & Purse Accessories

Ladies have been powdering their noses for years and using interesting compacts to perform this task. Today's collectors have a variety of shapes, materials, and makers to search for at flea markets.

References: Roselyn Gerson, *Ladies Compacts,* Wallace-Homestead, 1996; ——, *The Estee Lauder Solid Perfume Compact Collection,* Collector Books, 2002; ——, *Vintage and Contemporary Purse Accessories, Solid Perfumes, Lipsticks, & Mirrors,* Collector Books, 1997; ——, *Vintage Ladies Compacts,* Collector Books, 1996; ——, *Vintage Vanity Bags and Purses: An Identification and Value Guide,* 1994, 1997 value update, Collector Books; Laura M. Mueller, *Collector's Encyclopedia of Compacts, Carryalls & Face Powder Boxes* (1994, 1999 value update), vol. II (1997), Collector Books.

Collectors' Club: Compact Collectors Club, P.O. Box 40, Lynbrook, NY 11563.

For additional listings, see *Warman's Antiques & Collectibles* and *Warman's Americana & Collectibles.*

Avon, oval, lid dec with blue and green checkerboard pattern **35.00**
BOAC, British Overseas Airways Corp, 3" d, gold, black leatherette, gold metal logo, framed mirror, BOAC puff, royal blue felt cover **70.00**
Celluloid, orange compact studded with floral rhinestone motif, 3" dia........**45.00**
Coty, #405, envelope box **65.00**
Daniel, black leather, portrait of lady

encased in plastic dome, Paris **90.00**
Djer Kiss, with fairy **95.00**
Dorset, 3-1/8" sq, white, gold birds, flowers, and leaves, mkd "Dorset, Fifth Avenue," slight discoloration around edges **15.00**
Dunhill, Mary, rouge........................**28.00**
Elgin, I Love You in different languages, cupids and hearts on front **48.00**
Estee Lauder, compact necklace, oval silvertone engraved pendant suspended from ornate silvertone ball and tube chain, orig solid fragrance **55.00**
Evans, goldtone and mother-of-pearl, compact and lipstick combination **45.00**
German, 2-7/8" dia, double mirror, couple in colonial dress, mkd "Made in West Germany", slight discoloration **10.00**
Halston, silver plated, name on puff, used **150.00**
Kigu, lady swinging **45.00**
Lampi, light blue enamel, five colorful three-dimensional scenes from Alice in Wonderland enclosed in plastic domes on lid..**180.00**
Mondane Beauty Box, goldtone, rhinestone basket, 3 reservoirs ..**125.00**
Petit Point, 2-1/4" x 2-3/4", gold metal edge, red and yellow roses, blue flowers, green leaves, plain black petit point on back.............................**15.00**
Princess Pat, rouge and large puff, orig package......................................**20.00**
Rowanta, brown enamel, oval petit-point compact......................................**65.00**
Schildraut, seed-pearl design **55.00**
Timepact, enamel, black, elongated horseshoe shape, case and watch **190.00**
Volupte, Adam and Eve under apple tree **55.00**
Whiting & Davis, vanity bag, silvered mesh, etched and engraved lid, braided carrying chain, 1920s....**425.00**

Heart shaped, gold filled case, English, $39.

❖ Computers & Computer Games

Technology is improving so rapidly that your computer is almost outdated before you've even had a chance to remove it from the box. With our increasing reliance on computers and our continual quest for the biggest and the fastest, it's a sure bet that more computers will find their way to flea markets. Make sure you've got all the parts and as many original documents as possible when buying a computer on the secondary market. Because this is a relatively new segment of the flea market scene for many dealers, firm pricing is not yet established.

AOL giveaway disk, Windows Version 3.0, Canadian, 1998, MSP **18.00**

Apple
    Macintosh, 128K, 1st ed, standard keyboard and mouse **325.00**
    Macintosh Plus, 1MB, beige **50.00**
    IIc, 128K RAM, 1st "portable" computer made by Apple, includes power supply **65.00**

Atari XL 800, additional modem ... **125.00**

Compaq, typical PC, heavily used .. **50.00**

Epson HX-40, laptop, 4MB RAM, 1987 .... **125.00**

Fujitshu, laptop, needs new battery, 1989 .... **20.00**

IBM, typical PC, 5-1/4" floppy drive, heavily used **75.00**

Packard Bell, typical PC, 3-1/4" disc drive, moderate use **75.00**

Zenith, PC, 5-1/4" floppy drive, 28K hard drive, working condition **25.00**

❖ Condiment Sets

Condiment or castor sets are useful tableware containers. Usually they contain salt and pepper shakers as well as mustard pots, and perhaps bottles for vinegar, oil, etc. Early castor sets are found with pressed or cut glass bottles held in a silver frame with matching tops and stoppers.

Omni entertainment center, Milton Bradley, game in C-8 condition, box worn, with two extra game cartridges, $10.

Condiment Set, salt and pepper shakers, center mustard container, silver plated frame, mustard cov missing, $10.

China condiment sets have a more whimsical flavor.

Bavarian china, blue band, floral trim, salt and pepper shakers, cov mustard, matching tray **65.00**

Chintz, James Kent, salt and pepper, jam with spoon, matching tray **100.00**

Condiment dish, cobalt, silverplate holder, 5"h, 8-1/8" x 3-1/4" **116.00**

Hobnail, white milk glass, salt and pepper shakers, creamer, sugar and mustard, matching round tray with chrome loop handle **95.00**

Holt Howard
    Cozy Kittens, Meow Oil and Vinegar **175.00**
    Cozy Kittens, mustard jar **180.00**
    Jeeves, olives **135.00**
    Pixieware, Cocktail Cherries, 1958 .... **135.00**
    Pixieware, Cocktail Olives, 1958 **130.00**
    Pixieware, Mayonnaise, 1959 .... **180.00**

Plastic, 4 red pots with yellow lids, relish, mustard, jam and 1 unlabeled, mkd Aladdin, each 3-1/2" h **38.00**

Pressed glass, clear
    2 glass cruets, dry mustard with spoon, salt and pepper, metal holder, 1 stopper damaged, silverplating worn **125.00**
    Salt and pepper shakers, mustard, silverplate holder **125.00**

Porcelain, Strawberry pattern, 8 pcs (plate, 3 triangular bowls, 3 spoons, lid) **45.00**

❖ Consolidated Glass Co.

Formed in 1893, Consolidated Glass produced interesting glassware and lamps until 1964, when a fire destroyed the plant. Some of the Consolidated patterns, such as Ruba Rombic and Dancing Nymph, are highly sought by collectors. However, don't overlook some of the other interesting color combinations and shapes produced by this firm.

Collectors' Club: Phoenix and Consolidated Glass Collectors, P.O. Box 81974, Chicago, IL 60681.

For additional listings, see *Warman's Antiques & Collectibles* and *Warman's Glass.*

Berry bowl, master, Cone, pink, glossy, SP rim **115.00**

Bowl, Catalonian, yellow, 9-1/2" dia **48.00**

Butter dish, cov, Cosmos pattern, pink bands **200.00**

Candlestick, Five Fruits, Martele, green **32.00**

Cigarette box, Catalonian, ruby flashed lid, crystal base **65.00**

Cologne Bottle, orig stopper, 4-1/2" h, Cosmos **120.00**

Cruet, orig stopper, Florette, pink satin **225.00**

Cup and Saucer, Dancing Nymph, ruby flashed **265.00**

Goblet, Dancing Nymph, French Crystal **90.00**

Jug, Spanish Knobs, pink, 5-1/2" h **125.00**

Lamp, Dogwood, brown and white **140.00**

Old Fashioned Tumbler, 3-7/8" h, Catalonian, yellow **20.00**

Pitcher, Cosmos pattern, 9" h **265.00**

Plate
    Catalonian, yellow, 10-1/4" dia **40.00**
    Five Fruits, green, 8-1/2" dia **40.00**

Puff box, cov, Lovebirds, blue **115.00**

Sherbet, Catalonian, green **20.00**

Snack Set, Martelé Fruits, pink **45.00**

Spooner, Criss-Cross, cranberry opalescent **75.00**

Toothpick holder, Florette, cased pink **75.00**

Tumbler, Catalonian, ftd, green, 5-1/4" h **30.00**

Consolidated Glass Co., butter dish, cov, Cosmos pattern, 6" h, $200.

Vase

Floral pattern, sea foam green, lavender, and tan, floral pattern, 6-1/2" h **150.00**

Regent Line, #3758, cased blue stretch over white opal, 6" h **175.00**

❖ Construction Toys

Building toys have delighted children for many years. Today's collectors look for sets in original boxes with all the tools, vehicles, instructions, etc.

A.C. Gilbert

Chemistry Experiment Lab, 3 pc metal box **35.00**

Erector Set, No. 4, complete, orig instructions **285.00**

Erector Set No. 10181, Action Helicopter **80.00**

American National Building Box, The White House, wood pieces, landscaping, orig wood box **120.00**

Auburn Rubber, Building Bricks, 1940s **25.00**

Embossing Company, No. 408, Jonnyville Blocks, deluxe edition, blocks, trees, hook and ladder, village plan **65.00**

Halsman, American Plastic Bricks, #717 ....**45.00**

Lego, Main Street Set, orig box and pcs, unused..**120.00**

Lincoln Logs, #25 ....**75.00**

Tinkertoy, box with odd parts and pieces **10.00**

Construction Toys, Lego, builders set, orig cardboard, booklets, etc., $15.

❖ Cookbooks and Recipe Leaflets

What's for supper? The answer to this perplexing question might be as close as your nearest flea market—perhaps you might want to try something daring and different—something that catches your eye while browsing through a nifty cookbook. Collectors have long treasured these books and leaflets promoting different household

products. Collectors are eager to find those with advertising or displays that show vintage china patterns, accessories, etc.

Periodicals: *Cook Book,* P.O. Box 88, Steuben, ME 04680; *Cookbook Collector Exchange,* P.O. Box 32369, San Jose, CA 95152-2369; *Cook Book Gossip,* P.O. Box 56, St. James, MO 65559; *Old Cookbook News & Views,* 4756 Terrace Dr, San Diego, CA 92116-2514.

Collectors' Club: Cook Book Collectors Club of America, P.O. Box 56, St. James, MO 65559.

A General's Diary of Treasured Recipes, Brigadier General Frank Dorn, 1953 ....**10.00**

Any One Can Bake, Royal Baking Powder, 1929, 100 pgs **10.00**

Arm & Hammer Good Things to Eat, Church & Dwight Co., 3" x 5", 1925, 32 pgs **5.00**

Baker's Chocolate Cookbook, 1926, 64 pgs **15.00**

Betty Crocker's Picture Cook Book, McGraw-Hill, 1950, 1st ed, 9th printing, 463 pgs **18.50**

Carnation Cookbook, Mary Blake, 1943, softcover......................................**10.00**

Classic Cooking with Coca-Cola **5.00**

Favorite Recipes From Our Best Cooks Cookbook, Women's Club of Batavia, Ohio, Circulation Service, 1981 .....**4.00**

Forty Delightful Ways to Serve, Green & Green Co., Dayton, OH, 1928, 16 pgs, 5" x 7".......................................**9.00**

From Amish and Mennonite Kitchens, Phyllis Pell, Good & Rachel Pellman, 1984, 420 pgs **10.00**

Game Cookery, E.N. & Edith Sturdivant, Outdoor Life, 1967, 166 pgs **6.00**

Hershey's Index Recipe Book, 1934**12.00**

Holiday Food Fun: Creative Ideas for Halloween, Thanksgiving, Christmas, and More, Pub. Int., Ltd., 1993, 4th ed, 96 pgs **8.00**

Knox Gelatine Cookbook, 1933, 71 pgs **12.00**

Louisiana Kitchen, Chef Paul Prudhomme, 1984, 351 pgs.........**11.00**

Magic in Herbs, Leonie de Sounin, Gramercy, 1941 ....**9.50**

Martha Washington Log Cabin Cookbook, Philadelphia, 1924, 132 pgs **38.00**

McCormack Cookbook, 1924, 32 pgs **34.00**

Monarch Range Cook Book, shows gas and electric ranges, 72 pgs..........**10.00**

My Better Homes & Gardens Cook Book, Meredith Publishing, 1935, 10th printing, tabs..............................**18.00**

Pillsbury Family Cookbook, 1863 ....**12.00**

Rawleigh's Good Health Guide Almanac

Cookbooks & Recipes, The Great American Tomato Book, orig dj, $5.

Cookbook, 1951, 31 pgs **12.00**

Royal Cookbook, 1939, 64 pgs **10.00**

Ryzon Baking Powder Cookbook, Marion Harris Neil, 1916, hardcover, 81 pgs **25.00**

Shumway's Canning Recipes, booklet form **5.00**

Southern Sideboards Recipe Book, Junior League of Jackson, MS, 1980, 5th printing, spiral bound, 414 pgs.**9.00**

The Cookbook of the Stars, 1941, hardcover, 394 pgs......................**35.00**

The Cookie Cookbook, Deloris K Clem, Castle Books, 1966, slight edge wear **11.50**

The Vegetarian Cook Book, E. P. Dutton, Pacific Press, 1914, 271 pgs **50.00**

Your Frigidaire Recipes, 1937...........**3.50**

❖ Cookie Cutters

Cookie cutters are found in various metals and plastics. Look for cutters in good condition and that are free of rust and crumbs.

Tin, club, spade, diamond, and duck, $20.

Horse, tin, two finger holes, 7-1/2" l, 5-1/2" h, $28.

Periodicals: *Around Ohio,* 508 N Clinton, Defiance, OH 43512; *Cookie Crumbs,* 1167 Teal Rd SW, Dellroy, OH 44620; *Cookies,* 9610 Greenview Ln, Manassas, VA 20109-3320.

Collectors' Club: Cookie Cutters Club, 1167 Teal Rd, SW, Dellroy, OH 44620.

The following are tin or aluminum figural cookie cutters.

Bird, hand-made, 3-1/2" x 4"...........**15.00**
Biscuit, red wood handle, 2-3/4" dia **10.50**
Bunny, rolled edge, spot soldered, 5" h **3.50**
Chicken, 2" w, 2" h, 1920s.............**22.50**
Club, green wood handle **7.50**
Cowboy, gingerbread type, 6" h, stamped design, aluminum **15.00**
Elephant, orig box mkd "Campaign Cookie Cutter-Vote Republican"...**50.00**
Flower, red wood handle, 2-1/2" dia**10.00**
Gingerbread man, rolled edge, spot soldered, 5" h **4.00**
Horse, aluminum, 1-3/4" **10.00**
Lion, aluminum, 1-3/4" **10.00**
Rabbit, green wood handle, 4" l......**12.50**
Reindeer, tin, 3" **12.00**
Santa, hard red plastic **4.00**
Set
  Alumode, stainless steel, reindeer, lamp, star, Christmas tree, Santa and snowman, orig box **15.00**
  Aunt Chick Flower Garden Cookie Cutters, red plastic, strawberry, morning glory, daisy, crocus, wild rose, tulip, holly and poinsettia, 1950s, orig box, cutters show slight use **32.00**
  Hallmark, Peanuts Gang, Christmas Cutters, four plastic cutters, orig box **35.00**
Squirrel, soldered handle, used......**10.00**
Star, tin, 2"....................................**6.50**
Turkey, tin, 2" **8.50**

❖ Cookie Jars

Cookie jars have been a highly desirable collectible for years. Today more and more cookie jars are appearing at flea markets, some new, some vintage. If you're looking for new jars, check for a signature by the artist or company's mark and the original box will add to the value. If vintage jars are more your style, check carefully for signs of use and damage.

Periodicals: *Cookie Jar Collectors Express,* P.O. Box 221, Mayview, MO 64071-0221; *Cookie Jarrin',* RR2, Box 504, Walterboro, SC 29488-9278; *Crazed Over Cookie Jars,* P.O. Box 254, Savanna, IL 61074.

Collectors' Club: Cookie Jar Club, P.O. Box 451005, Miami, FL 33245-1005.

For additional listings, see *Warman's Americana & Collectibles.*

TIAS Top 10
The following list ranks the most highly sought collectibles on the Internet during 2002.
1. China
2. Cookie jars
3. Dolls
4. Furniture
5. Lamps
6. Carnival glass
7. Books
8. Plates
9. Depression glass
10. Roseville
Source: www.tias.com

African Village, Avon **35.00**
Apple Barrel, Metlox.......................**75.00**
Ballerina Bear, Metlox **120.00**
Bear, Avon, California Originals, 1979 ....**90.00**
Bird House, Treasure Craft **45.00**
Blue Bonnet Sue **40.00**
Bugs Bunny...................................**40.00**
Cactus, wearing bandana and cowboy hat, Treasure Craft........................**50.00**
Cathy, Papel..................................**75.00**
Cat in a Basket, American Bisque .**50.00**
Chef, American Bisque **90.00**

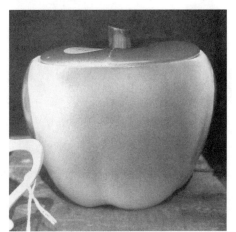

Cookie Jars, Apple, $45.

Cookie Jars, Strawberry, McCoy, $95.

Clock, Brush..................................**185.00**
Cookie Jug, brown stoneware, 11" h **30.00**
Curious George.............................**50.00**
Elvis, in car **100.00**
Felix...**50.00**
Flintstones.....................................**50.00**
Friendship Space Ship, McCoy...**165.00**
I Love Lucy **100.00**
King Corn, Shawnee, 10-1/2" h....**355.00**
Magilla Gorilla, Twin Winton **275.00**
Maxine..**60.00**
Mickey Mouse, mkd "Walt Disney Productions" **250.00**
Mr. Rabbit, American Bisque **185.00**
Nanna, Mammy-type, Treasure Craft, USA, 1989.................................**95.00**
Olympics, Warner Bros., 1996 ....**75.00**
Quaker Oats, 120th Anniversary **70.00**
Panda, black and white, Brush......**325.00**
Pepper, yellow................................**95.00**
Pillsbury Funfetti **45.00**
Pink Panther, Treasure Craft **125.00**
Rocking Horse, Fitz & Floyd **265.00**
Santa's Magic Workshop.............**165.00**
Smokey Bear, 50th Anniversary...**275.00**
Sugar Town General Store **60.00**
Superman **85.00**
Sylvester and Tweety, Applause....**55.00**
Television Set, young Indian and teepee image on front **120.00**
Troll, Norlin.....................................**55.00**
Uncle Sam, American Cookie Jar Co. **150.00**
Yosemite Sam................................**40.00**
Wally Walrus, Metlox, 1976 ....**200.00**

❖ Cooper, Susie

This English designer founded her own pottery in 1932. Her designs were bright and innovative.

Collectors' Club: Susie Cooper Collectors

Group, P.O. Box 7436, London, N12 7GF, UK.

For additional listings, see *Waman's English & Continental Pottery & Porcelain.*

Berry set, Nosegay, 8-1/2" d master bowl, six 5-1/2" individual bowls.**500.00**
Bowl, Longleaf, 7-1/2" dia **60.00**
Breakfast set, Concentric Circles, two each: 6-1/2" d cereal bowl, cups and saucers, 9" plates, 5" side dishes
....**500.00**
Coffeepot
Crescent Sgraffito, Kestrel shape, dusty pink, 7" h, damage to rim
....**300.00**
Green Dresden, Rex shape **320.00**
Patricia Rose pattern, Kestrel shape, light green with pink rose, 7-1/2" h
....**550.00**
Nosegay pattern, Kestrel shape, 7" h
....**450.00**
Swansea Spray, 7" h, hairline on lid
....**400.00**
Cup and saucer, Swansea Spray, set of four **320.00**
Cup, saucer and plate
Romance Pink, rim wear..............**45.00**
Tigerlily...**80.00**
Demitasse cup and saucer
Endon...**60.00**
Swansea Spray, pink...................**50.00**
Gravy pitcher and plate, Floral Spray, crazing..**70.00**
Pitcher
Crescent Sgraffito, inner lip damage, 7" h...**300.00**
Dresden Spray, 4-1/2" h **95.00**
Susan's Red, 4" h **80.00**
Plate, Apple **42.00**
Soup Bowl, Dresden Spray **18.00**
Teapot, Dresden Spray, Kestrel shape, 1932, 7" l, 5" h.........................**250.00**
Tea set
Leaf Spray, one cup teapot, cup and saucer, individual size milk jug and sugar.....................................**595.00**
Rex shape, two cup teapot, two cups and saucers, small milk jug and sugar.....................................**425.00**

❖ Coors Pottery

Founded in Golden, Colorado, Coors Pottery produced industrial, chemical, and scientific porcelain wares. They then developed a household cooking ware and, later, six dinnerware lines. The company went out of business in the early 1940s, having lasted only 30 years.

Periodical: *Coors Pottery Newsletter*, 3808 Carr Place, N Seattle, WA 98103.

Ashtray, green **15.00**
Baker, brown glaze, #111, 5-1/2" dia, 2-

1/2" h..**4.00**
Cake knife, Rosebud, maroon, yellow rosebud, green leaves.................**37.50**
Cake plate, Rosebud, 11" dia **110.00**
Creamer, individual, Chefsware, purple, 5" h...**14.50**
Cup and saucer, Rosebud
Blue **35.00**
White **50.00**
Mortar and pestle, white, 3" h, 5" w
....**110.00**
Pie plate, orange, handles, 10" dia .**75.00**
Pitcher, Rosebud, 6-1/2" h...........**135.00**
Platter, Mello-Tone, oval, canary yellow
....**24.00**
Teapot, Chefsware, 3-1/2" h, chip on spout **20.00**
Tray, green, 5" sq **12.00**
Vase
Urn shape, 2 handles, green ext, white int, 5-3/4" h, 7" w **55.00**
Round body, matte blue ext, white int, 10" h **100.00**

❖ Copper

Copper has long been a favored metal with craftsmen as it is relatively easy to work with and is durable. Copper culinary items are lined with a thin protective coating of tin to prevent poisoning. It is not uncommon to find these items relined. Care should be taken to make sure the protective lining is intact before using any copper pots, etc. for domestic use.

Ashtray, sombrero shape, painted design of trees and water, 4" dia .**12.00**
Blowtorch, Bernz, red wood handle, 10" h **30.00**
Breadbox, 12" l, 7-1/2" w, 11" h, chamfered oblong rect form, hinged cov, paneled domical form, brass finial raising from lozenge-shaped plaque over brass ring handles, brass bottom, Neoclassical, possibly Dutch, c1800
....**165.00**
Carpenter's pot, 11" l, 8" h, globular,

Copper, Food mold, $125.

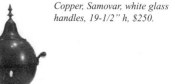

Copper, Samovar, white glass handles, 19-1/2" h, $250.

dovetailed body, raised on 3 plain strap work iron legs, conforming handle**70.00**
Colander, punched star design, 10-3/4" d **80.00**
Funnel, 4" h.....................................**12.00**
Ladle, 6" dia copper bowl with rounded bottom, wrought-iron handle, 20-3/8" l
....**45.00**
Lighter, cowboy boot form, 5-1/2" h**12.00**
Measure, round with flat bottom, straight sides, broad flared tapering spout, C-shaped handle, wear, dents, 10" h, 6-5/8" dia **25.00**
Pan
Frying, metal handle, 5-1/4" dia, 9-1/4" l...**35.00**
Young & Co., East Boston, Mass., brass handle, copper pan 1-3/4" h, 3-1/4" dia **25.00**
Teakettle, dovetailed, hinged cover on spout, scrolled finial, stamped initials, 10" h...**165.00**
Teapot, Paul Revereware, wooden grip on handle **30.00**
Vacuum washer, conical copper head, wooden handle, British Vacuum Washer Co., 1921 patent date, 24" l
....**95.00**
Wash tub.......................................**75.00**
Water urn, 14" h, copper body, int. with capped warming tube, applied brass ram's head handles, urn finial, brass spout, sq base with four ball feet, unmarked, repairs to lid **125.00**

❖ Corporate Collectibles

2002 is going to be remembered for the year the stock market reacted negatively to many corporate scandals. As soon as some of the big corporations filed for bankruptcy, collectibles bearing their logos began to appear at flea markets. When the big "E" from in front of the former Enron building was sold, it made the evening news.

Ashtray, Xerox **1.00**
Cap, khaki, Enron...........................**10.00**
Cigarette lighter, Seagrams............**2.00**
Cufflinks, Enron, gold plated.........**15.00**
Door mat, rubber, white lettering "Bucks County Bank & Trust" **10.00**

Teddy Bear, Summit Bank, orig flag "Reach Higher Summit Bank," hiking outfit with backpack, Vermont Teddy Bear tag on ear, 12" h, $20.

Golf ball, Enron.................................**1.00**
Golf tee, Philip Morris, 3 in orig package
....**3.00**
Mouse pad, Enron **2.00**
Mug, Bell Telephone.........................**4.00**
Pen, Worldcom **1.00**
Pocket knife, Enron **8.00**
Sign, big "E" from Enron headquarters
....**44,000.00**
Stock certificate, Enron **2.00**
Tie tac, Champion Spark Plugs, silver
tone **5.00**
Travel Mug, Mobil Oil **4.00**

❖ Costumes

Playing dress-up has always been fun for children. Collectors today enjoy finding vintage Halloween and other type of costumes. It's possible to find some very interesting costumes and accessories at flea markets.

Costumes, Witch, Collegeville, costume and orig mask, orig box, $10.

Costumes, Deputy Dog, Wonderland Masquerade Costume, size medium, orig box, wear, $10.

Costumes, Rin-Tin-Tin, Ben Cooper, orig box, slight wear, $15.

Costumes, Bluebird, various blue fabric feathers hand sewn, 1940s, $59.

Collectors' Club: The Costume Soc of America, P.O. Box 73, Earleville, MD 21919.

Banana Splits, orig costume, mask, box
....**80.00**
Bat Masterson, orig box **140.00**
Batman, display bag, vinyl cape, mask, cuffs and badge, copyright 1966 National Periodical Publications.**120.00**
Captain Action, cloth outfit, mask, knife, 2 pistols, skull, brass knuckles, holster, belt, rifle and boots, orig box, copyright 1966 Ideal Toy Corp. **225.00**
Captain Kangaroo, orig costume, mask, box..**85.00**
Cowboy, child size
Boots, Acme **85.00**
Chaps...**90.00**
Outfit, 4 pcs, 1960s **200.00**
Vest and chaps, hide rosettes....**150.00**
E.T., orig costume, mask, box **15.00**
Fred Flintstone, vinyl mask and outfit, Ben Cooper, copyright 1973 Hanna-Barbera, orig box.........................**40.00**
Matador, adult size, heavily embroidered, sequins and gold metallic thread, minor wear...**120.00**
Miss Piggy, orig costume, mask, box
....**15.00**
Red Riding Hood, red cotton cape and skirt, yellow yarn braids sewn on hood, home made, c1950 ....**35.00**
Rosey the Robot, orig costume, mask, box...**350.00**
Star Wars, R2D2, plastic mask, vinyl costume, Ben Cooper, copyright 1977, orig box **40.00**
Superman, Ben Cooper, orig box ...**50.00**
Winky Dink, orig costume, mask, box
....**200.00**
Zorro, orig costume, mask, box **90.00**

❖ Cottage Ware

Cottage ware is the name given to charming English tea items that are shaped like a cottage. It is possible to complete a set of all the pieces necessary for serving a proper tea.

Biscuit jar, wicker handle, Price Bros., 7-1/2" h...**95.00**
Butter dish, cov, Fox and Hounds pattern, Kensington Cottage Ware
....**165.00**
Creamer and sugar, brown, yellow, green and pink Keele Street Potteries
....**45.00**
Ye Old Cottage, Made in England, ink stamp in wreath "Price Bros. Made in England, Cottage Ware, Reg. No. 845007" **120.00**
Cup and saucer, Price Bros..........**35.00**
Jam jar, cov, mkd "Kensington, England"
....**35.00**

Milk pitcher, mkd "Price Brothers, England," 7-1/4" h **75.00**

Set, creamer, cov sugar, cov jam jar, mkd "Keele Street Potteries" **95.00**

Teapot, brown, yellow, green and pink, Ye Old Cottage, ink stamp in wreath "Price Bros. Made in England, Cottage Ware, Reg. No. 845007" **100.00**

❖ Counter Culture

"Cool, man!" Whether you lived through the 1960s or just fantasize about that era of hippies and beatniks, you should know that collectors are actively seeking those love beads and psychedelic things.

Bolo tie medallion, star design, pink star, circles and checks shading from gray to light tan in background, Peter Max **15.00**

Book, *Psychedelic Pscounds*, Alan Vorde, interviews with psychedelic bands **30.00**

Bumper sticker, Save the Whales ...**1.00**

Cigarette holder, Beatnik, figural man or woman, orig cardboard and plastic pkg, Hong Kong, 1950s **40.00**

Hat, suede, wide floppy brim, 1970s, 23" d **24.00**

Medallion, peace sign, bronzed metal **10.00**

Mood ring, adjustable band **12.00**

Pet rock, MIB **35.00**

Pinback button

Feed Twiggy, black-and-white center photo, mkd "1967 Design Unlimited 1896 Pacific, S.F." **20.00**

Go Mod, white lettering, deep pink background, 1970s, 2-1/4" dia..**10.00**

❖ Country Store Collectibles

Today we tend to think of old time store items as "Country Store." In reality, much of the memorabilia we collect was from small stores located in cities as well as country locales. These stores offered people a place to meet, stock up on supplies, and catch up on the latest gossip. They were filled with advertising, cases, cabinets, and all kinds of consumer goods.

Reference: Richard A. Penn, *Mom and Pop Stores*, R.S. Pennyfield's, 1998.

Broom display, hanging, metal, round with ring for holding brooms by handles **100.00**

Coffee barrel, BAR Special Blend, R.A. Railton Co., Chicago, 75 lbs, 25-1/2" h, 17-1/2" dia **175.00**

Coffee grinder, double wheel, Enterprise, cast iron, old red and blue

Seed packet, Bachelor Buttons, W. Atlee Burpee, $2.

repaint, yellow details, finial replaced **357.50**

Cracker box lid, tin with glass insert "Purity Pretzel Co., Stuber & Kuck Co., Peoria, Ill." **27.00**

"Uneeda Bakers" **30.00**

Crate, Rumford Baking Powder, held 1 dozen cans, 5-3/4" h, 13" w, 10" d **25.00**

Continental Cane rack, red and white enameled sign, circular metal base, $20.

Box, Kennedy's Sunflower Biscuits, paper label with blue ground, wooden box, top missing, $35.

Display, Beechnut Gum, tin, 27-1/2" x 15-1/2", c1950, 3 tiers **130.00**

Scoop, 5", tin, wood handle **28.00**

Seed box

"Choice Flower Seeds From D.M. Ferry & Co., Detroit, Mich.," shows 3 children in flower garden, oak, litho paper label under lid, 6-3/4" h, 11-1/2" w, 9-3/4" d **440.00**

"Reliable Seeds, From the Sioux City Nursery & Seed Co. Sioux City, Iowa," wood, machine dovetails, paper labels on front and inside lid, chipping to labels....................**200.00**

Seed packet, Ruppert's Seeds, Washington, D.C., orig 10 cents, color picture of the vegetable or fruit **1.00**

Spool cabinet, "Clark's Mile-End Spool," wood, 5 drawers with reverse-painted glass fronts advertising product, paint loss to glass, 19" h, 30" w..........**495.00**

Store jar

Clear, swirl lid with ground stopper, 11" h, 4-1/2" dia **125.00**

Necco Candies, clear, orig lid, 10-1/2" h..**55.00**

String holder, cast iron

Beehive form, 6" h, 7-1/4 dia **150.00**

Inverted J-shaped arm, 11" h.......**45.00**

Tobacco cutter, cast iron, "Griffin Goodner Grocer Co., Tulsa, Okla," 1914 patent date, 8-1/2" h, 12-3/4" l...**195.00**

❖ Country Western

Even if you've never been to Nashville, you've probably tapped your foot to a few country western tunes. Country Western collectors know their favorite stars and eagerly search for memorabilia, autographs, records, and other items related to their singing career.

Periodical: *Goldmine*, 700 E State St, Iola, WI 54990.

Book

Johnny Cash: Man in Black, Johnny Cash, Zondervan Books, 1975, 1st ed, 244 pgs, edges nicked **8.75**

Tray, Loretta Lynn, Coal Miner's Daughter, photo vignettes of her home and ranch, red lettering, simulated wood grain background, tin, $12.

Kentucky Stand, Jere Wheelwright, 1951, 279 pgs **6.00**
Movie poster, Your Cheatin Heart, Hank Williams story, 1964, folded **85.00**
Paper dolls, Built Rite, 1965, unused **45.00**
Photo, black and white, 8" x 10" Cliffie Stone, auto pen sgd, 1950s **25.00**
   Dolly Parton, sgd **38.00**
Program, Grand Ole Opry **5.00**
Ring, cowboy hat form, sterling silver, c1940 ....**85.00**
Scrapbook, Hillbilly and Western Stars, 22 pcs **65.00**
Sheet music
   Chattanoogie Shoe Shine Boy **5.00**
   San Antonia Rose **4.50**
   Sioux City Sue **4.50**
Straw hat, Dale Evans model **180.00**
T-shirt, Garth Brooks, "The Hits," promo, face image and "Garth" on front ...**35.00**

❖ Cowan Pottery

Cowan Pottery encompasses both utilitarian ware and artistic ware. R. Guy Cowan began making pottery in Ohio around 1915 and continued until 1931. Most pieces are marked with an incised name. Later a black stamp mark and initials were used.

Bookends, pr, Sunbonnet Girl, antique green crystalline glaze **375.00**
Bowl, irid blue luster glaze, ink mark, 12" dia **70.00**
Candleholders, pr, 8-1/2" h, Ming Green glaze, c1928 ....**80.00**
Card holder, green, chip, 3-1/2" h ..**50.00**
Cigarette holder, sea horse, aqua .**42.00**
Compote, diamond shape, tan ext., green int., 2" h **38.00**
Console set, oval bowl, 2 short candlesticks, white **200.00**
Lamp base, molded leaves, gray and ivory semi-gloss glaze, orig fittings, 19" h **100.00**
Match holder, cream color, 3-1/2" h **60.00**

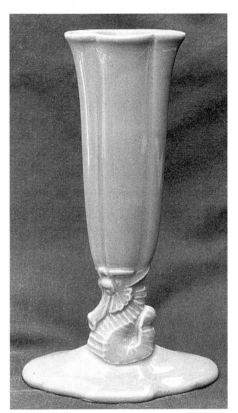

Cowan Pottery Vase, Seahorse, light green, white int., imp mark, 7-1/2" h, $72.

Trivet, scalloped rim, bust of young girl framed by flowers **325.00**
Vase
   5" h, shouldered form, pink and maroon high glaze, imp mark ...**70.00**
   10-3/4" h, irid blue, c1925 ....**90.00**

❖ Cowboy Heroes

Although most cowboy heroes were matinee idols, there were some cowboy heroes who were popular radio and/or television personalities. Many of today's collectors specialize in one character or show, but some are fascinated with all kinds of cowboy memorabilia.

Periodicals: *Collecting Hollywood,* American Collectors Exchange, 2401 Broad St., Chattanooga, TN 37408; *Cowboy Collector Newsletter,* P.O. Box 7486, Long Beach, CA 90807; *Westerner,* Box 5232-32, Vienna, WV 26105; *Westerns & Serials,* Route 1, Box 103, Vernon Center, MN 56090.

Collectors' Clubs: Cowboy Collector Network, P.O. Box 7486, Long Beach, CA 90807,

Print, black & white lithograph, rodeo cowboy on horse, signed lower left "Frederic Remington," 23" x 19", $575.

www.hopalong.com; Cowboy Collector Soc, 4248 Burningtown Rd, Franklin, NC 28734

For additional listings, see *Warman's Americana & Collectibles* and categories covering specific cowboys in this edition.

Arcade card
   Bob Baker, on rearing horse, black-and-white **12.00**
   John Mack Brown, green tones ...**12.00**
   Sunset Carson, red tones **12.00**
   Charles Starrett, full color **15.00**
Better Little Book, *Buck Jones and The Two-Gun Kid*, Whitman, #1404, 1937 ....**30.00**
Big Little Book, *Bobby Benson on the H-Bar-O Ranch*, Whtiman, 1934 ..**42.00**
Chaps and vest, Tom Mix Ralston Straight Shooters, Ralston premium, 11" x 24" pr brown suede chaps, nickel accents, red, white, and blue cloth patch, 14" x 16" brown suede vest with matching patch, c1935 ....**200.00**
Comic book, *Red Ryder Comics*, #102, Dell, 1952 ....**18.50**
Dixie Cup picture, color, Bill Elliott and Gabby Hayes **50.00**
Game, board, Annie Oakley, Milton Bradley **45.00**
Guitar, Buck Jones, 37" l **250.00**
Magazine, Parade, cover and story about Bonanza **25.00**
Movie, *Zane Gray Adventure Stories Action-Packed Thrillers*, 16mm, orig box...**40.00**
Photograph, William S. Hart, 1980s re-release **5.50**
Poster, Ponderosa, c1967, facsimile autographs of cast, 22-1/2" x 17".**18.00**
Puzzle, frame tray, Fess Parker **35.00**
Record, Bobby Benson's B-Bar-B Riders, 10-1/8" x 10-1/8" illus picture sleeve, 78 rpm record, white and white label, "The Story of the Golden Palomino," Decca #88036, copyright 1950 ....**12.00**

Bookend, bronzed, cowboy on horse, $20.

Sheet music, *You Two-Timed Me One Time Too Often* by Jenny Lou Carson, recorded by Tex Ritter, 1945, Ritter on cover..**15.00**

Snack set, plate and mug, Cisco Kid **50.00**

Target game, Straight Arrow, litho tin board, 3 magnetic feather-tipped arrows, National Biscuit Co., c1950 ....**75.00**

❖ Cow Collectibles

Cows have been a part of the folk art and country decorating schemes for years. But cow collectors will be the first to tell you that they are also popular themes for advertising and even children's items.

Periodical: *Moosletter*, 240 Wahl Ave., Evans City, PA 16033.

Bank, Nestle Nespray, figural, vinyl.**40.00**

Blotter, Cow Brand Baking Soda, 4" x 9-1/4" **15.00**

Butter crock, ink stamp of cows, large chip on lid **225.00**

Butter stamp, 1-pc, cow with tree, 3-5/8" dia **170.00**

Charm, 1" d, Swift's Brookfield, brass, emb cow on award base, inscribed "June Dairy Month Award," early 1900s **17.50**

Cookie jar
Brush-McCoy, mouse on cow, early

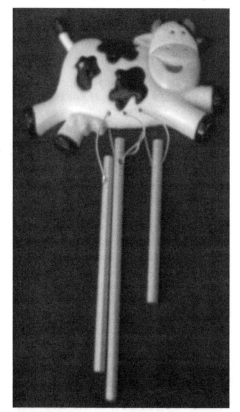

Cow Collectibles, wind chime, black and white cow, plastic, $1.

1950s...**200.00**
Elsie the Cow in barrel, 11-1/2" h **400.00**

Creamer
"Fairway, Made in Japan," 1950s, 4-1/2" h, 6-1/2" l **38.00**
Royal Bayreuth, unmkd, c1920, 6-1/2" h, 10" l **395.00**
Souvenir of Washington, D.C., mkd "Hand Painted, Japan," 1940s, 3-1/4" h, 5-1/4" l **45.00**

Pinback button, Guernsey-The Only Breed Increasing in Every State, multicolored portrait of cow's head, blue award ribbon, c1930.............**18.00**

Poster, Evaporated Milk-Pure Cow's Milk, black and white illus of cows, green ground, c1940 ....**25.00**

Sign, flange "Slow, Cattle Crossing," porcelain, 2-sided, 18" h, 14" w .**115.00**

Sugar, cov, figural, Elmer, c1940 ....**40.00**

Toy, ramp walker, plastic, brown and white, 1950s, mkd "Made in Hong Kong," orig sealed cellophane **18.00**

❖ Cracker Jack

When Frederick William Rueckheim added molasses to popcorn in1896, the concoction became known as Cracker Jack. Beginning in 1910, each box contained a coupon that could be redeemed for a prize. It wasn't until 1912 that the prizes themselves were placed in the boxes.

The Cracker Jack sailor boy and his little dog Bingo first appeared in the company's advertisements in 1916 and debuted on the boxes in 1919. Early toy prizes were made of paper, wood, and even lead, with plastic toys introduced after 1948.

References: Alex Jaramillo, *Cracker Jack Prizes*, Abbeville Press, 1989; Larry White, *Cracker Jack Toys: The Complete Unofficial Guide for Collectors*, Schiffer Publishing, 1997.

Collectors' Club: Cracker Jack Collectors Assoc, 5469 S Dorchester Ave, Chicago, IL 60616.

Cracker Jack Top, litho tin, wooden center peg, $24.

Cracker Jack Puzzle, Springbok, 1000 pcs, unopened, $5.

Activity book, *Cracker Jack Painting & Drawing Book*, Saalfield, 1917, 24 pgs **35.00**

Booklet, *Cracker Jack Riddles*, red, white and blue cover, 42 pgs, 1920s **60.00**

Charm, owl, 1920s, 7/8" h................**9.00**

Doll, Cracker Jack boy, fabric, 8" h **16.00**

Prize
Auto Race spin toy, one crease ...**13.00**
Chair, 1920s **9.00**
Fire truck, tin litho, 1930s, 1-3/4" l**45.00**
Horse & wagon, tin, red, white and blue, 1930's, 2-1/4" l **65.00**
Rocking horse, 1920s, 11/16" **9.00**
Rooster, 1920s, 3/4" h....................**9.00**
Spinner, blue and white, "Always on Top"...**95.00**
Spoon and fork, tin, 1930s, 2" l....**10.00**

Telescope, 1920s, 1-1/16" l **9.00**

Watch, litho, 1940s..........................**85.00**

Whistle, mkd "Close Ends with Fingers," 1930s, 1-15/16" **10.00**

❖ Crackle Glass

Crackle glass can be identified by the web-like system of light cracks that covers the surface of the glass. These cracks are an intentional part of the design, but since they are random, no two pieces are alike. From the late 1930s to the early 1970s, crackle glass was quite popular in the West Virginia glass houses, including Pilgrim, Blenko, Kanawha, and Viking.

References: Judy Alford, *Collecting Crackle Glass with Values,* Schiffer, 1997; Stan and Arlene Weiman, *Crackle Glass Identification and Value Guide, Book I (1996), Book II (1998),* Collector Books.

Collectors' Club: Collectors of Crackle Glass, P.O. Box 1186, N Massapequa, NY 11758.

For additional listings, see *Warman's Glass.*

Bottle, stopper, 16" h, crackled, crystal, sgd, Blenko Glass, price for pr, 16" h **385.00**

Bowl, crystal bowl, amethyst foot, Blenko Glass, 5-1/4" dia, 8-1/4" h **85.00**

Cranberry Glass Vase, oval portrait panel, 13" h, $350.

For additional listings, see *Warman's Antiques & Collectibles* and *Warman's Glass.*

Reproduction Alert

Basket, star shaped top, ruffled edge, colorless thorn loop handle, c1890, 6" w, 5-1/2" h **195.00**

Bottle, gold mid-band, white enameled trim, colorless faceted stopper, 3" d, 8" h **145.00**

Brandy Jug, Inverted Thumbprint pattern, applied colorless handle, colorless hollow stopper, pontil, 8" h **90.00**

Butter Dish, cov, round, Hobnail pattern **125.00**

Candlestick, applied yellow eel dec, 10-1/2" h.....................................**125.00**

Cologne Bottle, gold scrolls, small gold flowers, matching sq cranberry bubble stopper, 2-3/8" dia, 8-5/8" h **185.00**

Creamer, Optic pattern, fluted top, applied clear handle.....................**90.00**

Finger Bowl, scalloped, matching underplate **145.00**

Muffineer, Parian Swirl pattern.....**125.00**

Perfume Bottle, ball form body, white enamel floral dec, orig clear ball stopper, 3-1/2" h..........................**80.00**

Pitcher, Ripple and Thumbprint pattern, bulbous, round mouth, applied clear handle, 6-1/2" h.........................**125.00**

Rose Bowl, six-crimp top, worn gold rim, 3-3/4" dia, 3-3/4" h **95.00**

Sauce dish, Hobb's Hobnail pattern**45.00**

Toothpick holder, crystal prunts **48.00**

Tumble-up, Inverted Thumbprint pattern **75.00**

Vase
7-1/2" h, emb ribs, applied colorless feet, 3 swirled applied colorless leaves around base **110.00**
8" h, vertical bands of ribbed thumbprints cut to colorless, ground pontil **110.00**

❖ Crockett, Davy

"King of the Wild Frontier" was used to described Walt Disney's version of this popular American character.

Crackle Glass Vase, jug shape, blue, applied clear handle, attributed to West Virginia area, 4" h, $24.

Brandy Snifter, crystal, turquoise foot, Blenko Glass, 8" h.........................**35.00**

Bud vase, amberina, Kanawha, orig label, 7-1/4" h **60.00**

Candy dish, cov, amberina, Kanawha, 3" h **45.00**

Creamer, emerald green body, clear handle, Pilgrim **35.00**

Lemonade set, 8-1/4" h pitcher, applied reeded handle, 6 glasses 4-3/4" h, topaz **295.00**

Nappy, heart shaped, amberina, hand-blown, pontil scar, Blenko Glass, 5" x 5-1/4" x 2" h **65.00**

Paperweight, apple, red, applied crystal stem and leaf, Blenko Glass, 6" h**55.00**

Pitcher, blue, applied colorless handle, c1950, Blenko Glass, 6" h............**40.00**

Punch bowl set, large punch bowl with clear cover, four glasses, clear, orig German manufacturer's stickers, 9-3/4" h **500.00**

Punch cup, emerald green body, clear handle, Pilgrim **20.00**

Vase
4" h, 4" w, double neck, Blenko Glass **35.00**
5-1/2" h, smoke gray **65.00**
9" h, blue, Blenko Glass..............**55.00**

❖ Cranberry Glass

When a glassmaker mixes a small amount of powdered gold in a warm blob of molten glass, the glass changes to a rich cranberry color, hence the name. Because glassmakers used slightly different formulas, there are slight differences in shade between examples of cranberry glass.

Bib, paper, large **6.00**

Carrying case, paper covering with snakeskin pattern, felt likeness of Davy Crockett glued to side **55.00**

Comic book, *Davy Crockett, Indian Fighter*, #631, Dell, 1955..............**35.00**

Cookie jar, Brush, unmkd, 1956, 10-1/4" h **425.00**

Friction toy, stagecoach, rubber tires off wheels, 5-1/4" l, 3-1/4" h............**250.00**

Fringe jacket, 1950s, some stains .**55.00**

Game, Davy Crockett Rescue Game, compass, 1955............................**45.00**

Moccasins, suede leather, child's size 3, imprinted with Davy Crockett insignia, slight wear **32.00**

Mug, white milk glass, green image**28.00**

Paper plate, "Walt Disney's Official Davy Crockett Indian Fighter," shows 4 movie scenes in each corner, c1955, 6-1/4" sq **18.00**

Record and book, *Disneyland Davy Crockett Record Story Book*, 24-pg book and long-playing record, Walt Disney Productions, 1971, 7-1/4" sq **29.00**

Ring, plastic....................................**60.00**

Shirt, boy's, unused, orig tags.........**40.00**

Tie clip, coppertone metal, 1950s, mint cond **18.00**

❖ Crooksville Pottery

Crooksville Pottery in Crooksville, Ohio made semi-porcelain dinnerware and housewares from 1902 until 1959. Some pieces were marked.

Bowl, Petit Point House, 11" d **60.00**

Casserole, cov, La Grande, 1-1/2 qt **35.00**

Cup and saucer
Iva Lure **25.00**
Sun Lure......................................**22.00**

Crooksville Pottery, dinnerware set, blue, yellow, and pink flowers, green foliage, trellis dec, emb border, service for 4 and serving pcs, $35.

Gravy boat, Hibiscus **35.00**
Pitcher and cover, Petit Point House, 6"
  h **90.00**
Plate, bread and butter
  Iva Lure **9.00**
  Petit Point House...........................**6.50**
Plate, dinner
  Apple Blossom **12.00**
  Flamingo **15.00**
  Goldenrod **30.00**
  Iva Lure **30.00**
  Petit Point House..........................**37.50**
  Sun Lure..**22.00**
Plate, salad, Iva Lure **15.00**
Platter
  Goldenrod **35.00**
  Petit Point House, 13-1/4" dia **40.00**
  Wildflowers, oval, 13" l **25.00**
Set, Spring Blossom.......................**150.00**
Sugar, cov, Petit Point House..........**25.00**
Vegetable, Wildflowers, 8-3/4" dia ..**25.00**

❖ Crown Devon

Crown Devon is an English pottery dating from 1870 to 1982. The factory was located at Stoke-on-Trent and produced a wide range of pottery, from majolica, luster wares, figurines, souvenir wares, etc.

For additional listings, see *Warman's English & Continental Pottery & Porcelain.*

Ashtray, Hot Scent...........................**25.00**
Bowl, oval, pedestal base, painted green, orange and black, geometric banding, gilt accents, paper label, 11" l......**90.00**
Cheese dish, Spring pattern, red and blue flowers and urn, scattered ivy, tan shaded ground, slant top **85.00**
Cup and saucer, Coaching Days, 5" dia **8.00**
Jug, musical
  Auld Lang Syne, dec of men in tavern, 4-1/2" h **85.00**
  Here's A Health Unto Her Majesty, raised tinted portraits of Queen Elizabeth II, colored bands, gold trim **145.00**
Tidbit, floral form, orange enameled highlights, 6" l, 4-1/2" w, 1" h **25.00**
Toby jug
  Chelsea Pensioner, 1950s, 4" h...**60.00**
  Guardsman, 1960s, 8-1/4" h........**90.00**
Vase, two geese in flight, patch of cat-o-nine tails, mkd with crown over "Crown

Crown Devon, biscuit barrel, stylized decoration, silver plated lid, rim and handle, $95.

Devon, Fieldings, Made in England 5785," impressed 1183, 11" h **95.00**

❖ Cuff Links

Certain fashion styles dictated long sleeves that needed to be fastened with a decorative cuff link. These little jewelry treasures have been making colorful statements for years. Look for backs and closures in different styles.

References: Most jewelry books will contain information about cuff links, including Christie Romero's *Warman's Jewelry.*

Collectors' Club: National Cuff Link Society, P.O. Box 346, Prospect Heights, IL 60070.

Brushed and textured goldtone metal, smoky black center stone, 1970s...**6.00**
Cameo, hematite-type stone, silvertone setting..**8.00**
Gold filled, Christian Dior, textured ovals, orig box, c1960.............................**40.00**
Gold, 10k yellow, hexagon shape, engine turned engraved design on front, sgd "NJSC" in four leaf clover, c1920**125.00**
Gold, 14k rose, cushion shape top, inlaid turquoise, crescent shape back, late 19th C, wear and some cracking to turquoise **175.00**
Gold, 14k yellow, round, engine turned design on front and back, sgd "C" in arrowhead, c1920 ....**225.00**
Gold, 18k yellow, Art Deco style, little diamonds in center of MOP plaques, set in platinum bezels **350.00**
Goldtone, Retro, opposed goldtone swirls set with colorless rhinestones, sgd "Coro Duette," 1931 patent no., 2-1/2" w x 1-1/2" **75.00**
Silver colored, prong-set yellow stones **12.00**
Silverplated, mkd "Correct Links".....**4.00**
Silvertone
  Knight riding horse **8.00**
  Mother-of-pearl disks **10.00**
  White around smoky gray center, Victorian....................................**18.00**
Snappers, enameled black and white, 1/2" dia **15.00**
Sterling silver, Georg Jensen, rect

Cuff Links, Swank, silver-plated, initial "W" on black field, $18.

Cuff Links, Silvertone, three small black stars, $12.

checkerboard pattern, c1950, sgd "Georg Jensen" in dotted oval, mkd "sterling Denmark, #113" **170.00**

❖ Cupids

Cute little cupids have been charming our hearts since Victorian times. They can be found on many types of objects, just watch out for those arrows. They might be pointing at you.

Collectors' Club: Cupid Collectors Club, 2116 Lincoln St, Cedar Falls, IA 50613, www.net-ins.net/showcase/cupidclub.

Bookends, pr, bronze, Frolic, cupid playing with frog, kneeling down, leaning against foliage cov boulder, sgd "S. Morani," Armor Bronze shopmark, c1914, 5-1/2" x 5-1/4" x 7-3/4" **325.00**
Box, cov, porcelain, yellow glazed ground, cupids on base and top, flower finial, green "Hand Painted, Made in Japan" mark, 4-1/4" l....................**30.00**
Bud vase, amber shading to clear, white enameled cupid, in the style of Mary Gregory, 8-5/8" h, some wear, slight gold loss at top rim....................**175.00**
Dresser box, ceramic, heart shaped,

Dish, pressed glass, intaglio center with cupid, green trim on center and scalloped edges, price for pr, $15.

Two-handled serving tray decorated with cupid playing lute, flowers, bird, metal frame and handles, 18-1/2" w, $125.

cupids on top, bow pattern on base
....**35.00**

Dresser set, beveled mirror with red cupids, brass handles with filigree
....**250.00**

Easter card, postcard type, pair of Cupids with Easter egg, unused **5.00**

Figure, bisque, 4-1/2" h....................**20.00**

Jar, cov, porcelain, orange and gold, center scene of Victorian woman and cupid, 4-1/2" dia **35.00**

Limited edition plate, Wedgwood, Mother's Day, 1984, musical cupids under tree......................................**40.00**

Pin, shooting arrow
Brass, Coro, lavender and white rhinestones, c1940, 2" x 2".......**42.00**
Sterling silver, intent expression, stamped "Sterling" on back, c1940, 2" l, 2-1/2" w **110.00**

Postcard, Cupid sharpening arrow, holding bow, unused **5.00**

Print, Cupid Asleep or Cupid Awake, orig frame **115.00**

Valentine, postcard type
Biplane with cupid, "To My Valentine, Cupid's stolen my heart which he is bringing to you".........................**15.00**
Cupid with heart in wheelbarrow, "It's all for You," leather postcard, postmarked Indianapolis............**6.00**
Man and woman in floral heart wreath with cupid, "A Token of My True Love," used **7.50**

Vase, Bristol Glass, transfer dec of woman and cupids, English, c1880, 8" h **295.00**

❖ Cups and Saucers

Cup and saucer collecting is a hobby that many different generations have enjoyed. Some porcelain makers have created special cups and saucers for collectors. Other collectors prefer collecting cups and saucers that were made as dinnerware or even Depression glass patterns.

Fortune telling cup, multicolored designs, white ground, black script "Perchance this cup Woulds't Thy Fortune Tell," Royal Kendal, Made in England, Fine Bone China, © H & M, 1985, $25.

Bavaria, blue luster ext, MOP int, black handle and rim, mkd "Bavaria".....**10.00**

Belleek, Limpet pattern, 3rd black mark **100.00**

Bone china, purple thistles, green leaves and pods, brown stems, gold trim **17.50**

Buffalo Pottery, Deldare, Coaching Days scene...**275.00**

Coronation, George and Elizabeth, sepia portraits, multicolor royal crest on saucer, gold trim, Aynsley **95.00**

Creamware, handleless, blue bands, gaudy foliage dec, minor wear, pinpoint flake on cup rim.........................**175.00**

Fiesta, turquoise.............................**35.00**

Flow Blue, Hamilton pattern **45.00**

Forget Me Not, white shaded to cobalt blue ground, gold int, gold striped handle and rim, mkd "Made in Germany" **12.00**

Johnson Bros, Albany pattern, flow blue **85.00**

Moss Rose, gold trim, mkd "H & Co. Limoges" **30.00**

Pratt, Indian pattern, flow blue **135.00**

Quimper, hex shape, male peasant on panel, scattered red and blue florals, blue outlined rims, gold outlined wishbone handle with blue dashes, "HenRiot Quimper France" marks **50.00**

Remember Me, brown and pink flowers, scalloped saucer, mustache guard in cup **35.00**

Roses dec, gold handle, mkd "Germany" **30.00**

Woods, handleless, Woods Rose ...**65.00**

❖ Cuspidors

Cupsidors, Bennington, emb cupids on sides, brown rockingham glaze, $95.

Called cuspidors or spittoons, these functional items can be found in metal or ceramic. They were common elements in bars, on trains, and even in homes.

Brass, small dents **95.00**

Cast iron, turtle form, copper shell and bowl, mkd "Golden Novelty Co., Chicago, Ill.," 1901 patent date, orig paint, 13-1/2" l **485.00**

Graniteware
Cobalt/white swirl, white int., 4-1/4" h, 7-1/2" dia **300.00**
Columbian, 1-pc............................**275.00**

Ironstone, warrior and lion transfer, copper luster **265.00**

Pewter, bulbous body, flared rim, handle, 4-3/4" h................................**85.00**

Pottery/stoneware
Albany glaze, incised "L.J. Underwood. Barberton, Ohio. July 24, '09" and "L.J.U., 7-24-1909," 4-1/2" dia...**93.50**
Blue and white, butterfly and shield pattern, 6" h, 7-1/2" dia **85.00**
Brown glaze, embossed vines **35.00**
Green and cream, stylized floral design **85.00**

Romantic Staffordshire, blue transfer, molded basketweave pattern **260.00**

Spongeware, circular sponged dabs around body, blue bands at rim and shoulder, 4-1/2" h **120.00**

Yellowware, green, blue and tan sponging, 7-1/2" dia **85.00**

❖ Custard Glass

Custard glass is a yellowish opaque glass. Its color is derived from the uranium salts that are added to the hot molten glass. Because different manufacturers used slightly different formulas, you can expect variations in color from maker to maker. The term "nutmeg stain" refers to a rust or brown colored stain applied to highlight the design.

Collectors' Club: Custard Glass Collectors Soc, 14312 SE 111th St, Oklahoma City, OK 73165.

For additional listings, see *Warman's Antiques & Collectibles* and *Warman's Glass.*

Berry bowl, master, Louis XV, good gold

....**110.00**
Bonbon, Fruits and Flowers, nutmeg stain..**225.00**
Bowl, Grape and Cable, 7-1/2" d, basketweave ext., nutmeg stain ...**65.00**
Butter dish, cov, Georgia Gem, enamel dec **300.00**
Compote, Argonaut Shell **80.00**
Creamer, Fluted Scrolls **90.00**
Goblet, Grape and Gothic Arches, nutmeg stain................................**80.00**
Hair Receiver, Winged Scroll........**125.00**
Nappy, Prayer Rug.........................**65.00**
Plate, Grape and Cable...................**55.00**
Punch cup, Northwood Grape........**50.00**
Sauce, ftd, Intaglio **90.00**
Spooner, Intaglio............................**95.00**
Sugar, cov, Georgia Gem, pink floral dec **185.00**
Table set, cov butter, creamer, cov sugar and spooner, Argonaut Shell......**425.00**
Toothpick holder, Louis XV **200.00**
Tumbler
   Cherry Scale **50.00**
   Vermont.......................................**90.00**
   Wild Bouquet..............................**45.00**

❖ Cut Glass

Cut glass should sparkle and feel sharp to the touch. It has been made by American and European companies for many years. Most companies didn't sign their work, but collectors can identify different makers by their intricate patterns. Minor flakes can be ground away and such small repairs do not affect the value negatively.

Collectors' Club: American Cut Glass Assoc, P.O. Box 482, Ramona, CA 92065.

For additional listings, see Warman's Antiques & Collectibles and Warman's Glass.

Banana Bowl, 11" d, 6-1/2" d, Harvard pattern, hobstar bottom **210.00**
Basket, diamond miters, diamond points, small stars, 6" x 4-1/4" x 6" h, pinhead nick **55.00**
Bowl
   8" dia, brilliant cut pinwheels, hobstars, and miters.............................**145.00**
   8-1/4" dia, heavy blank, serrated rim, two rows of vertical rays, star bottom **45.00**
   9" dia, deep cut, medallions, large pointed ovals, arches, and base **110.00**
Butter Dish, cov, hobstar **250.00**
Candlesticks, pr, hobstars, teardrop stem, hobstar base, 9-1/2" h......**250.00**
Carafe, 2-1/2" floral leaf band, star, file, fan, and criss-cross cutting, molded neck, 8" h **70.00**
Champagne, Kalana Lily, pattern,

Dorflinger..............................**75.00**
Champagne pitcher, hobstars and cane, double thumbprint handle, 10" h **210.00**
Cider Pitcher, 7" h, hobstars, zippers, fine diamonds, honeycomb cut handle, 7" h..**175.00**
Compote, hobstar and arches, flared pedestal, 6" h **150.00**
Creamer and sugar, hobstar, American Brilliant Period, 3" h......................**50.00**
Decanter, stopper, large hobstars, deep miters, fan, file, hallmarked silver neck and rim, 11" h, 3" sq **130.00**
Dish, heart shaped, handle, American Brilliant Period, 5"........................**45.00**
Goblet, strawberry diamond, pinwheel, and fan, notched stem, 7-pc set **350.00**
Ice Bucket, Harvard pattern, floral cutting, eight sided form , 6-1/2" h, minor edge flaking on handles ...**100.00**
Nappy, 9" d, deep cut arches, pointed sunbursts and medallions, ...**135.00**
Perfume bottle, 6-sided, alternating panels of Harvard pattern and engraved florals, rayed base, matching faceted stopper, American Brilliant Period..**175.00**
Pickle tray, checkerboard, hobstar, 7" x 3"..**45.00**
Plate, alternating hobstars and, large graduated circles and fans, notched miters, hobstars, 15-3/4" h, Higgins & Seiter..**250.00**
Punch Ladle, 11-1/2" l, silver plated emb shell bowl, cut and notched prism handle **165.00**
Relish, two handles, divided, Jupiter pattern, Meriden, 8" l.................**120.00**
Salt Shaker, Notched prism columns **30.00**
Tumbler
   Harvard, rayed base.....................**45.00**
   Hobstars.....................................**40.00**
Vase
   12" h, three cartouches of roses, star and hobstar cut ground **225.00**
   12" h, 5-1/2" w, triangular, three large and three small hobstars, double notched pedestal and flaring base **150.00**
Water pitcher, Keystone Rose pattern, 10" h...**190.00**

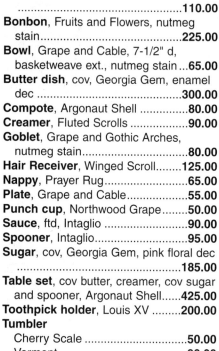

Cut Glass Vase, 13-3/4" h, $350.

❖ Cybis

Opened as an artists' studio by Polish immigrants, Boleslaw Cybis and his wife Marja, this enterprise turned out porcelain sculptures. Cybis porcelains are exquisitely detailed.

Bluebirds, nesting, 1978..............**250.00**
Boy riding stick horse **170.00**
Buffalo, 1968 ....**200.00**
Cat, white, blue ribbon...................**150.00**
Dandy Dancing Dog, 1977 ....**300.00**
Easter Egg Hunt, 1972................**220.00**
Eskimo child, bust, wood base **195.00**
Girl
   Holding doll **175.00**
   Holding panda **190.00**
   Seated, reading book.................**190.00**
   Wearing white cape, red trim **175.00**
Independence Celebration, 1972 **210.00**
Kitten Chantilly, 1984 ....**215.00**
Lullaby Pink, 1986.......................**195.00**
Merry Christmas, 1982 ....**315.00**
Owl, white....................................**130.00**
Pinto, 1972..................................**225.00**
Recital, 1985 ....**300.00**
Sebastian Seal, 1976 ....**250.00**
Sheep, white................................**130.00**
Snail, 1968, 4" l, 2-3/4" h **125.00**
Summer, 1982 ....**210.00**
Windy Day, 1972 ....**215.00**

Cybis Porcelain rose, white, delicate pink shading, brown stem with thorns, green leaves, blurred mark, $20.

❖ Czechoslovakian Collectibles

Finding an object marked "Made in Czechoslovakia" assures you that it was made after 1918, when the country proclaimed it's independence. Marks that also include other names, such as Bohemia or Austria, indicate that the piece pre-dates the country's independence. Expect to find good quality workmanship and bright colors.

Periodical: *New Glass Review*, Bardounova 2140 149 00 Praha 4, Prague, Czech Republic.

Collectors' Club: Czechoslovakian Collectors Guild International, P.O. Box

901395, Kansas City, MO 64190.

For additional listings, see *Warman's Antiques & Collectibles* and *Warman's Glass.*

Belt buckle, metal, 4 amber rhinestones, mkd "Czechoslovakia 81-Ges Gesch" **18.00**

Bowl, brightly colored dec, incised mark, 9" dia **60.00**

Box, cov, blue glass, sterling rosary **120.00**

Cologne Bottle, 4" h, porcelain, glossy blue, bow front.............................**40.00**

Flower frog, bird on stump, pottery **35.00**

Lemonade set, 13" h blown glass pitcher, 4 matching glasses, bright orange, black silhouettes of children at play, trees, birds and animals, applied handle **225.00**

Necklace

Fringed, multicolor, 2 baroque pearls, 4" w, 20" l................................**110.00**

Glass, red center pendant, brass setting, red glass and brass filigree beads, 13" l, mkd.....................**95.00**

Marbleized green stone, set in brass, small green spacer beads, clear rhinestones set at top **80.00**

Perfume bottle, small, heavily cut Amethyst **125.00**

Czechoslovakianv Teapot, lusterous light blue, black finial and angular handle, Victoria Czecho-slovakia mark, $25.

Crystal, large faceted stopper **60.00**

Pitcher, crackled, irid marigold flashing, hp underwater scene of fish and coral, polished pontil, 6" h...................**150.00**

Place card holders, glass, set of 6, orig box...**80.00**

Powder box, cov, yellow glass, black knob finial on lid **75.00**

Vase

6-1/4" h, glass, cylindrical, mottled white and purple, cased to clear, enameled stylized vignette of woman fishing, silver mounted rim with English hallmarks, c1930 ....**275.00**

9-1/4" h, 4" w, pottery, 6 sides, 3 legs, glaze flake..............................**225.00**

10" h, pottery, brightly painted, incised numbers..................................**118.00**

Czechoslovakian Atomizer, enameled floral dec on gold ground, blue glass base, orig sprayer and bulb, $175.

❖ Dairy Collectibles

Collecting items pertaining to dairies is a popular segment of the antiques and collectibles marketplace. Some collectors specialize in examples from local dairies, while others concentrate on specific items such as milk bottles or milk bottle caps.

Periodicals: *Creamers*, P.O. Box 11, Lake Villa, IL 60046; *Cream Separator and Dairy Collectors Newsletter*, Route 3, P.O. Box 488, Arcadia, WI 54612; *Fiz Biz*, P.O. Box 115, Omaha, NE, 68101; *The Milk Route*, 4 Ox Bow Rd, Westport, CT 06880.

Collectors' Clubs: Cream Separator and Dairy Collectors, Rt 3, P.O. Box 488, Arcadia, WI, 54612; National Assoc of Milk Bottle Collectors, 4 Ox Bow Rd, Westport, CT 06880.

Cookbook
1001 Dairy Dishes from the Sealtest Kitchens, softcover, 1963, 288 pgs **5.00**
Dairy-Best Desserts, softcover, 1960s, 18 pg, 5-1/4" x 7-1/2"..................**2.00**
Drinking glass
King Quality Dairy, St. Louis, red text, 5-1/4" h **45.00**
Little pig playing fiddle, red image, copyright Walt Disney, 2nd Dairy Series, 1936-37, 4-1/4" h..........**70.00**
Milk box, galvanized
Property of Homestead Dairy, painted white, insulated, 10" x 11" x 13-1/2" **20.00**
Hedlins Richer Milk, 10" x 10" x 12-1/2" **45.00**

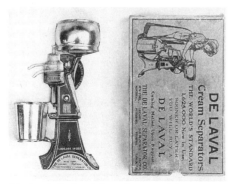

Match safe, De Laval Cream Separator, litho tin, orig box, $185.

Model train car, HO scale, Dairymen's League billboard refrigerator car, missing brake wheel....................**10.00**
Paperweight, white-veined marble, embedded emblem, Dixie Dairy 75th Anniversary **25.00**
Sand pail, litho tin, smiling Mickey Mouse on desert island, Donald dressed as commander on homemade warship, "Farm Crest" text around bottom, copyright Walt Disney Enterprises, Ohio Art Co., c1937**250.00**
Spinner, plastic with paper inlay, Dellwood Milk & Dairy Products...**30.00**
Thermometer, silhouette image of baby in highchair, "Compliments of Barry's Dairy Products, Phone 1062, New Ulm, Minn.," 4" x 5" **45.00**
Trade card, diecut, Borden milk wagon pulled by horse..........................**25.00**
Whistle, plastic, bugle shape, red and white, Foremost Dairy, 1950s, 5" l**32.00**

❖ Dakin

Dakin collectibles are cuddly and fun to collect. Look for original tags to help identify genuine Dakin.

Bamboo and baby.........................**28.00**
Bulldog **12.00**
Coca-Cola polar bear, white, red scarf, 1993, no tag, 14" h......................**20.00**
Daffy Duck, vinyl.............................**20.00**
Doll, cloth, three faces **55.00**
Donald Duck, articulated, orig string tag, 1972, 9" h......................................**37.50**
Garfield the College Cat, United Feature Syndicate, Inc., Dakin, Inc. San Francisco, Calif. tags, 1981...**18.00**
Little Koala, 1981 ....**30.00**
Lassie, 10", jointed, 1978 ....**100.00**
Mouse, tagged "Dream Pets, R. Dakin Company, Japan" **10.00**
Opus, 1984, 11-1/2" h....................**18.00**
Seal, 1960s...................................**30.00**
Smokey Bear, orig tags, c1970, 8" h **40.00**
Store display, Dakin Dreams, 4 orig pets, 13-1/2" x 21".......................**75.00**

❖ Decorative Accessories

Call it "kitsch" or "bric-a-brac," but decorative accessories make a statement about who we are as we decorate our living spaces. Decorators have been using objects d'art for years. Now that many of these objects are coming onto the flea market scene, collectors get a second chance to add some of these decorative objects to their domain.

Bird house, snow covered, DeForest **110.00**
Bust, Sheherazade, chalkware painted to resemble bronze........................**250.00**
Carousel horse, Allen Herschell, metal, restored **800.00**
Compote, alabaster, four white birds perched on edge **10.00**
Cricket cage, brass.........................**35.00**
Crocus pot, ceramic, white ground, purple floral design, unmkd............**2.00**
Figure
Charging elephant, brass, antique bronze finish, 29" h, 30" l **300.00**
Rooster, 5-1/4" h, pine, cross-hatched wing detail, orange, red, yellow, pink and green, standing on grassy mound, Carl Snavely, Lititz, Pa., 20th C **400.00**
Fruit, alabaster, apple, pear or orange, each **45.00**
Immigrants Totem, 2-1/2" w, 3" d, 26" h, attributed to Canada, late 19th/early 20th C, polychrome, carved pine, four seated male figures all wearing hats, one cross-legged, one in kilt, lowest with head of dog at his feet, stand **815.00**
Inkwell
Figural, rose, brass, color wash, pink and red petals, green stem.....**250.00**
Paperweight, multicolor concentric millefiori base, dated 1848 cane, Whitefriars **190.00**
Lamp, traffic meter base, cloth shade **50.00**
Magnifier, 8" l, silver-plated bronze, Faux Bamboo, c1960-65, made for and retailed by Bonwit Teller, N.Y., mkd as such, also "Made in Italy"...........**100.00**
Mantel ornaments, 12-1/2" h, fruit and foliage design, chalkware, American, made in 19th C, some paint wear, pr **475.00**
Schierschnitt, 12-7/8" x 13-7/8", bouquet in vase, bright green, c1840, framed **350.00**
Theorem, watercolor on velvet, basket of fruit, unidentified maker, framed.**200.00**
Urn, Capo-di-Monte, ovoid, central molded frieze with figures and cupids, molded floral garlands, multicolor dec, pedestal base...........................**450.00**

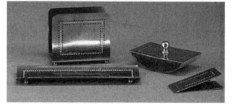

Desk set, brass, stamped geometric band, pen tray, roller, clip, and letter holder, stamped Bradley & Hubbard mark, $115.

Globe, wood and cast iron stand, damage and losses to base of globe, $15.

Wall plaque, Masks, Comedy and Tragedy, white ceramic, unmkd....**70.00**

❖ Decoys

Designed to coax waterfowl into target range, decoys have been made of wood, papier-mache, canvas, and metal. These hand-carved and even machine-made decoys have been recognized as an indigenous American art form. Signed examples are quite desirable, as are decoys made by noted regional artists.

References: Loy S. Harrell Jr., *Decoys: North America's One Hundred Greatest*, Krause Publications, 2000; Bob and Sharon Huxford, *The Collector's Guide to Decoys*, vol. I (1990), vol. II (1992), Collector Books; Carl F. Luckey, *Collecting Antique Bird Decoys and Duck Calls*, 2nd ed, Books Americana, 1992; Donald J. Peterson, *Folk Art Fish Decoys*, Schiffer Publishing, 1996.

Periodicals: *Decoy Magazine*, P.O. Box 787, Lewes, DE, 19558; *North America Decoys*, P.O. Box 246, Spanish Fork, UT 84660; *Wildfowl Carving & Collecting*, 500 Vaughn St, Harrisburg, PA 17110.

Collectors' Clubs: Midwest Decoy Collectors Assoc, P.O. Box 4110, St. Charles, Il 60174; Minnesota Decoy Collectors Assoc, P.O. Box 130084, St. Paul, MN 55113; Ohio Decoy Collectors and Carvers Assoc, P.O. Box 499, Richfield, OH 44286.

For additional listings, see *Warman's Antiques & Collectibles.*

> **Reproduction Alert**

Black Bellied Bustard, miniature, H. Gills, initialed "H. G. 1957," identified in pencil, natural wood base, 3-1/2" x 4" **230.00**

Black Duck, A. Elmer Crowell, East Harwich, MA, orig paint, glass eyes, stamped mark in oval on base, minor paint wear and wear to tip of beak, 7" h **460.00**

Bluebill Hen, Irving Miller, Monroe, MI, carved wood, glass eyes, orig paint, 11-1/2" l......................................**165.00**

Canada Goose, folding, waterproof wax-coated graphics, W.R. Johnson Co., Seattle, WA, 1940s......................**75.00**

Canvasback Drake, attributed to VA, stamped "W. O & G. H.," old worn working repaint, glass eyes, 14-1/2" l, 7-1/2" h......................................**300.00**

Dove, papier mache, clothespin on bottom to hold decoy in place, 9" l **35.00**

Ear of corn
Papier mache, Carry-Lite Decoy Co., Milwaukee, Wisc., 1940s, unused **45.00**
Wooden, painted yellow, 9" l........**25.00**

Goldeneye drake, tack eyes, lead weight inset in bottom, hollow construction held together with pegs, by Stanley Grant, Barnegat Bay, New Jersey, c1880, old repaint, bill repaired..**225.00**

Hooded Merganser Drake, miniature, H. Gibbs, 1965, sgd in pencil on base, 2-1/2" x 2-3/4"..............................**290.00**

Merganser, red breast, carved late 20th C, Maine or Nova Scotia, 19" l...**335.00**

Pintail Drake, Zeke McDonald, MI, high head, hollow body, glass eyes, orig paint, c1910..............................**550.00**

Red Head, Eastern Shore of Maryland, 13" l...**135.00**

Ruddy Duck Drake, Len Carmeghi, Mt Clemens, MI, hollow body, glass eyes, orig paint, sgd and dated, 10-3/4" l **250.00**

Sickle Bill Curlew, unknown maker, carved wood, glass eyes, pitchfork tine beak, orig paint, 22" l.................**150.00**

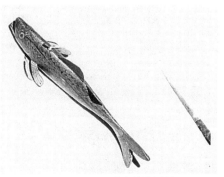

Fish, contemporary, unsigned, 8-1/4" l, $50.

❖ Deeds and Documents

Collectors seek out interesting vintage deeds and other documents from which to glean historical information. When purchasing a deed, check for authentic signatures, revenue stamps, seals, etc. Prices for deeds vary according to age, size, and location. Expect to pay $10 and upward for a common deed, more if a famous person's name appears. Documents also vary in price, with value being determined by content, date, signature, etc.

Appointment of Gideon Mumford Deputy Postmaster at East Greenwich, RI, dated April 19, 1796, foxing, fold weakness, 12-1/2" x 7-1/2" **75.00**

Bill of Exchange, written for Robert Robson, London, March 2, 1796, in Charleston, SC, 2 pgs, concerns exchange for 160 pounds sterling, 8-1/2" x 7"......................................**50.00**

Help Wanted Poster, W. R. Parsons, Chicago, IL, c1900, "Agents Wanted by Manufacturers of the Daisy Stair Corner"..**18.00**

Land indenture, Pennsylvania
Bucks County, signed by John Penn, sale of 1,000 acres, seal with some chipping, 15" h, 32" w.............**220.00**
Lancaster County, 24-1/4" h, 29-5/8" w **330.00**

Land transfer, "Lot four in block two in the town of Heppner, Oregon," July 20, 1882, slight staining **5.00**

Letterhead
Arkansas State Penitentiary, 1949, discusses purchase of fishing equipment................................**10.00**
The Bennett House, Augustine, Fla., c1915, 2 pages both with letterhead, 6" x 9-1/2" **6.00**
Geo. Spalt Soda Fountains & Drug Store Fixtures, 1911 ....**5.50**
United States Senate, letter from Robert F. Kennedy to constituent, Sept 20, 1966, with envelope with printed postal facsimile signature of RFK **135.00**
Jimmy Carter, letter to constituent, March 1980, sgd Jimmy (Not authentic) but Walter Mondale autograph across bottom..........**48.00**
New Tifft House, John Hood & Co., Pan American Exposition, Buffalo 1901, writing both sides, May 4, 1900, 6" x 9-1/2"......................**15.00**

Ship paper, issued by port of Charleston, SC, for brig *Mary*, March 10, 1812, 8" x 11"....................**80.00**

Warranty deed, The Red Man Land Company, Anadarko, Okla., 1954,

Deeds and Documents, Letter, Treasury Department, Sept 27, 1838, Sir: You will please inform the Department whether the public property cannot be stored in the Custom House Building at your port, and the charge for the storage dispensed with. Sgd Nowell Cobb, Secretary of the Treasury, John Cousens, Esq, Collector, Kennebunk, Maine, $20.

grants for the sum of 1 dollar, 2 sq. inches of an orig Indian reservation, edges rough **40.00**

❖ Degenhart Glass

Operating from 1947 until 1978, John and Elizabeth Degenhart created glass novelties under the name of Crystal Art Glass. They created some unusual colors. When Crystal Art Glass went out of business, many of the molds were purchased by Boyd Crystal Art Glass, also located in Cambridge, Ohio.

Collectors' Club: Friends of Degenhart, Degenhart Paperweight and Glass Museum, Inc, 65323 Highland Hills Rd, P.O. Box 186, Cambridge, OH 43725.

Reproduction Alert

Animal covered dish
Hen, mint green, 3" **22.00**
Turkey, custard **60.00**
Bell, Bicentennial, Vaseline **15.50**
Boot, 2-1/2" h, black slag, "D" in heart mark **25.00**
Candy dish, cov, Wildflower, twilight blue **32.00**
Coaster, intro 1974, mkd 1975, crystal **9.00**
Creamer and Sugar, Daisy and Button, carnival **45.00**
Cup plate, heart and lyre, mulberry **15.00**
Hand, pink **25.00**
Hat, daisy and button, milk blue **10.00**
Jewel Box, heart shape, blue **38.00**
Owl
Chad's blue **45.00**

Degenhart Glass, Goblet, dark chocolate slag, $45.

Cobalt blue **35.00**
Emerald green..............................**45.00**
Midnight sun.................................**30.00**
Purple slag **35.00**
Paperweight
Multicolor floral bouquet, 3-1/2" dia **250.00**
Single blue flower, 3" dia...........**250.00**
Pooch
Amethyst **40.00**
Bittersweet....................................**15.50**
Brown **15.00**
Robin, covered dish, blue, 5-1/2" w **40.00**
Salt, bird, amber **12.00**
Tomahawk, 2" w, 3-3/4" l, "D" in heart mark
Amethyst carnival.........................**18.00**
Chocolate slag **15.00**
Cobalt blue carnival......................**15.00**
Toothpick holder
Basket, milk white **20.00**
Elephant's head, jade...................**24.00**
Forget-Me-Not, Bloody Mary........**24.00**
Wine Glass, Buzz Saw, milk glass, blue **22.00**

❖ Delftware

Traditional Dutch motifs of windmills and tulips often decorate these wares, which are white with blue decorations.

Delftware Tile, blue windmill design, white background, unmarked, $20.

For additional listings, see *Warman's Antiques & Collectibles* and *Warman's English & Continental Pottery & Porcelain.*

Reproduction Alert

Ashtray, windmill scene, applied Dutch shoes on rim, mkd, 4-1/4" dia **15.00**
Charger, blue and white, floral rim, landscape, 12" dia, edge chips ..**200.00**
Coffee grinder, wall mount, orig decal "Made in Holland, DEVE, 1921," 13" l **300.00**
Creamer, cow shape, windmill on one side, floral deco on the other, 3-1/4" h, 5-1/2" l **25.00**
Decanter, windmill scene, bottom mkd "Delft, Blaauw, Ram, made in Holland," missing cork **68.00**
Figurine, Dutch girl, Japan, 4-1/4" h **18.00**
Pin, floral, sterling framing and clasp, mkd, 1-1/8" dia **90.00**
Plate
Blue and white floral dec, Dutch inscription on front, another on back, 9" dia, edge chips **200.00**
Manganese, iron red, yellow, and underglaze blue floral design, 8-3/4" dia, chips **200.00**
Urn, 3-1/4" h, windmill on front, bottom mkd "4107, Delft Blue, Holland" ...**25.00**
Wall pocket, Dutch shoe, windmill scene, mkd, hole in heel to hang, 8" l **20.00**

❖ Depression Glass

Depression glass was made from 1920 to 1940. It was inexpensive machine-made glass and was produced by numerous companies in various patterns and colors.

References: There are many excellent reference books on Depression glass. Gene

Florence, Carl Luckey, Kent G. Washburn and others have all authored books on Depression glass. Hazel Marie Weatherman wrote the first and most referred to editions, titled *Colored Glassware of the Depression Era*, Books 1 and 2, plus several supplements.

Periodicals: *Depression Glass Shopper On-Line Magazine*, www.dgshopper.com; *Glasstown USA*, 5216 63rd St, Kenosha, WI 53142.

Collectors' Clubs: Canadian Depression Glass Club, 1026 Forestwood Dr, Mississauga, Ontario L5C 1G8, Canada; National Depression Glass Assoc, Inc, P.O. Box 8264, Wichita, KS 67209; 20-30-40 Society, Inc, P.O. Box 856, LaGrange, IL 60525.

For additional listings, see *Warman's Depression Glass*.

The following listings are a mere sampling of the current Depression glass market.

Reproduction Alert

Ashtray
Adam, green, 4-1/2" dia **25.00**
Diana, pink **4.00**
Early American Prescut, crystal, 4" dia
....**3.00**
Forest Green, 4-5/8" sq.................**5.50**
Manhattan, 4" dia **11.00**
Moderntone, cobalt blue............**235.00**
Moroccan Amethyst, 3-1/2" dia **5.75**
Windsor, pink, 5-3/4" dia **35.00**

Berry bowl, individual
Anniversary, irid, 4-7/8" dia **4.50**
Bowknot, green **16.00**
Bubble, blue **30.00**
Cloverleaf, green **52.00**
Fortune, pink **6.00**
Iris, crystal, ruffled......................**11.00**
Normandie, irid, 5" dia **5.00**
Old Cafe, ruby **6.00**
Patrician, amber **12.00**
Sharon, pink.................................**10.00**

Berry bowl, master
Aunt Polly, blue............................**45.00**

Depression Glass, dinner set, Christmas Candy, teal green, $400.

Depression Glass, salt and pepper shakers, pr, Floragold, irid, white plastic tops, $45.

Cameo, pink **150.00**
Daisy, amber **25.00**
Heritage, pink **42.00**
Indiana Custard, French Ivory......**32.00**
Pretzel, crystal............................**18.00**
Raindrops, green..........................**45.00**
Ribbon, green...............................**30.00**
Strawberry, green or pink.............**20.00**

Bowl
American Pioneer, crystal, 9" dia.**24.00**
Bamboo Optic, green, 4-1/4" dia....**6.00**
Carolyn, 11" dia, topaz................**36.00**
Early American Prescut, crystal,
ruffled, 8-3/4" dia **9.00**
Iris, irid, 9-1/2" dia **10.00**
Jody, oval, topaz, 12" l **35.00**
Jubilee, pink, 8" dia **265.00**
Moonstone, cloverleaf, opal **13.00**
Oyster and Pearl, heart shape, ruby, 5-
1/4" w.....................................**15.00**
Roxana, golden topaz **12.00**

Butter dish, cov
Anniversary, pink.........................**60.00**
Block Optic green.........................**50.00**
Cameo, green.............................**250.00**
Doric, green.................................**90.00**
Lace Edge **85.00**
Madrid, amber **80.00**
Moderntone, cobalt, metal cov...**100.00**
Royal Lace, pink.........................**150.00**
Windsor pink **60.00**

Cake plate
Adam, green.................................**32.00**
American Sweetheart, monax.......**24.00**
Anniversary, crystal, round............**7.50**
Block Optic, crystal......................**18.00**
Cameo, green, 10" dia **27.00**
Holiday, pink, 10-1/2" dia............**100.00**
Miss America...............................**25.00**
Primo, green or yellow **23.50**
Thistle, Macbeth-Evans, green...**150.00**

Cake stand, Harp, crystal **25.00**
Candleholders, pr, Iris, crystal **42.00**

Candy dish, cov
Cloverleaf, green **45.00**
Floragold, irid **15.00**
Moroccan Amethyst, tall..............**32.00**
Ribbon, black...............................**38.00**

Celery tray, Pretzel, crystal **8.00**

Cereal bowl
Bubble, green, 5-1/4" dia **19.00**
Dogwood, pink **32.00**
Horseshoe, green or yellow **25.00**
Old Cafe, crystal or pink................**8.00**
Ribbon, green...............................**25.00**
Royal Ruby...................................**12.00**

Chop plate, American Sweetheart,
monax **24.00**

Coaster
Adam, pink **32.00**
Cherry Blossom, green or pink **15.00**
Manhattan, crystal.......................**18.00**

Cocktail
Iris, crystal...................................**25.00**
Manhattan, crystal.........................**4.00**
Royal Ruby.....................................**8.50**

Comport
Anniversary, crystal, ruffled...........**6.50**
Windsor, crystal.............................**6.00**

Console set, Block Optic, amber, bowl
11-3/4" dia, 2 candlesticks 1-3/4" h, 3-
pc set......................................**160.00**

Cookie jar, cov
Mayfair, green **575.00**
Princess, blue...........................**875.00**

Creamer
Adam, green................................**22.00**
Bamboo Optic, Liberty, ftd, green **10.00**
Bubble, green...............................**14.00**
Colonial Knife & Fork, crystal.......**18.00**
Cube, green **10.00**
Holiday, pink................................**12.50**
Newport, cobalt **20.00**
Ovide, Hazel Atlas, black **7.00**
Royal Ruby, flat.............................**8.00**
Sunflower, green or pink **20.00**

Cream soup
American Sweetheart, monax....**120.00**

Depression Glass, Salver, Petalware, Florette pattern, red flower, $25.

Daisy, amber **10.00**
Madrid, amber.............................**16.00**
Mayfair, Federal Glass Co., amber
....**18.00**
Patrician (Spoke), Federal Glass Co.,
amber **16.00**

Cup and saucer
American Sweetheart, red **160.00**
Bubble, red **15.00**
Cameo, crystal **14.00**
Dogwood, pink, thin......................**20.00**
Iris, crystal...................................**29.00**
Lorain, crystal or green **15.00**
Miss America, pink.......................**36.00**
Parrot green **55.00**

Decanter, Cameo, green...............**215.00**

Demitasse cup and saucer, Iris, crystal
....**215.00**

Fruit bowl
Bubble, crystal, 4-1/2" dia **5.00**
Floragold, irid **8.50**
Oyster and Pearls, pink................**10.00**
Raindrops, green...........................**11.00**

Goblet
Block Optic, green........................**24.00**
Bubble, forest green **15.00**
Colonial Block, crystal....................**9.00**
Diamond Point, ruby stained, 7-1/2" h
....**35.00**
Miss America, pink.......................**69.00**
Moroccan Amethyst **10.00**
Old English amber, green, or pink**30.00**
Ring, crystal **7.00**

Iced tea tumbler, ftd, 12-oz
Circle, green or pink.....................**17.50**
Dewdrop, crystal **17.50**
Floral & Diamond Band, pink **50.00**
Hobnail, crystal **8.50**
Homespun, crystal or pink **32.00**
Ships, cobalt blue........................**18.00**

Juice tumbler, ftd
Cameo, green..............................**42.00**

Madrid, amber..............................**15.00**
Old Cafe, crystal or pink..............**10.00**
Royal Ruby, ruby **5.00**

Mayonnaise set, underplate, orig ladle
Diamond Quilted, blue..................**65.00**
Patrick, yellow **80.00**

Mug
Block Optic, green........................**35.00**
Moderntone, white.........................**8.50**

Parfait, Harp, crystal **18.00**

Pitcher
Adam, pink, 32-oz **125.00**
Floragold, irid **40.00**
Forest Green, 22-oz **22.50**
Fruits, green **85.00**
New Century, ice lip, 80-oz, cobalt
....**45.00**
Ring, decorated or green, 60-oz ..**25.00**
Royal Lace, green **160.00**

Plate
Adam, pink, salad, 7-3/4" dia **18.00**

American Pioneer, crystal, 6" dia.**12.50**
American Sweetheart, monax, 9" dia
....**10.00**
Aurora, cobalt, 6-1/2" dia **12.00**
Bowknot, green, 7" dia.................**12.50**
Bubble, crystal, 6-3/4" dia **3.50**
Cherry Blossom, grill, green or pink, 9"
dia...**22.00**
Circle, green or pink, 8-1/4" dia ...**11.00**
Cloverleaf, green, 6" dia...............**32.00**
Columbia, pink, 9-1/2" dia............**32.00**
Dogwood, pink, 9-1/4" dia............**36.00**
Doric, green or pink, 6" dia **6.50**
Doric & Pansy, dinner, ultramarine
....**35.00**
Early American Prescut, crystal, 11"
dia...**10.00**
Egg Harbor, luncheon, green or pink
....**9.00**
Floragold, dinner, irid, 8-1/2" dia ..**35.00**
Floral, green, 9" dia......................**30.00**
Floral and Diamond Band, luncheon,
green or pink, 8" dia **40.00**
Florentine No. 1, dinner, green, 10" dia
....**16.00**
Florentine No. 2, dinner, yellow, 10" dia
....**15.00**
Fortune, luncheon, crystal or pink, 8"
dia...**17.50**
Georgian, luncheon, green, 8" dia**10.00**
Hobnail, luncheon, crystal, 8-1/2" dia
....**5.50**
Holiday, sherbet, pink, 6" dia..........**6.00**
Homespun, dinner, crystal or pink, 9-
1/2" dia...................................**17.00**
Horseshoe, salad, green or yellow, 8-
3/8" dia...................................**10.00**
Iris, dinner, irid, 9" dia **45.00**
Jubilee, luncheon, 9-3/4" dia........**16.50**
Lace Edge, blue, 10" dia..............**90.00**
Lorain, yellow **90.00**
Madrid, amber, 8-7/8" dia...............**8.00**
Manhattan, crystal, 10-1/4" dia **23.00**
Mayfair, pink, 8-1/2" dia...............**25.00**
Miss America, dinner, crystal **15.00**
Moderntone, Hazel Atlas, cobalt, 7-3/4"
dia...**12.50**
Moroccan Amethyst, dinner, amethyst,
9-3/4" dia **7.00**
Newport, dinner, fired-on color, 8-1/2"
dia...**15.00**
Normandie, irid, 6" dia **3.00**
Old Cafe, crystal or pink, sherbet, 6"
dia...**4.00**
Parrot, dinner, green, 9" dia **38.00**
Patrician, amber, 7-1/2" dia..........**15.00**
Patrick, luncheon, pink, 8" dia.....**45.00**
Peanut Butter, luncheon, crystal, 8" dia
....**5.00**
Petalware, dinner, monax, 9" dia **10.00**
Pineapple & Floral, sherbet, amber, 6"
dia...**6.00**
Pretzel, dinner, crystal, 9-3/4" dia **10.00**

Primo, dinner, green, 10" dia........**22.50**
Princess, grill, green or pink, 9-1/2" dia
....**15.00**
Queen Mary, crystal, 6" dia...........**4.00**
Romansque, octagonal, gold, 8" dia
....**8.00**
Rose Cameo, salad, green, 7" dia**16.00**
Rosemary, dinner, green, 9-1/2" dia
....**15.00**
Roulette, luncheon, crystal, 8-1/2" dia
....**7.00**
Round Robin, sherbet, irid or green, 6"
dia...**7.00**
Roxana, sherbet, crystal, 6" dia.....**4.00**
Royal Lace, luncheon, cobalt, 8-1/2"
dia...**30.00**
Royal Ruby, salad, ruby, 7" dia **3.00**
Sandwich, crystal, 9" dia..............**20.00**
Ships, dinner, cobalt, 9" dia **32.00**
Sierra Pinwheel, dinner, green, 9" dia
....**18.00**
Starlight, dinner, crystal, 9-1/2" dia**7.00**
Tea Room, luncheon, green, 8-1/4" dia
....**37.50**
Thistle, luncheon, green, 8" dia ...**22.00**
Vernon, luncheon, green or yellow,
8"dia..**10.00**
Waterforddinner, crystal **10.00**
Windsor, dinner, green or pink, 9" dia
....**25.00**

Platter
Cherry Blossom, green **48.00**
Lace Edge, blue, 13" l **165.00**
Royal Lace, pink..........................**40.00**
Windsor, green, oval, 11-1/2" l.....**25.00**

Punch bowl set, Royal Ruby, bowl, 12
cups..**110.00**

Relish
Doric, green.................................**32.00**
Early American Prescut, crystal, 4-part,
11" dia.....................................**10.00**
Lorain, 4-part, crystal or green, 8" dia
....**17.50**
Miss America, 4-part, crystal **11.00**
Pretzel, 3-part, crystal **9.00**
Princess, 4-part, apricot.............**100.00**
Tea Room, divided, green **30.00**

Salt and pepper shakers, pr
Adam, green..............................**100.00**
American Sweetheart, monax....**325.00**
Florentine No. 2, Hazel Atlas, green
....**40.00**
Hex Optic, green or pink **30.00**
Ribbon, green...............................**25.00**
Waterford, crystal, tall **7.00**

Sandwich server, center handle
Landrum, topaz **55.00**
Old English, amber **60.00**
Spiral, green.................................**30.00**
Twisted Optic, canary...................**35.00**

Sherbet
Adam, green................................**40.00**
April, ftd, pink, 4" h......................**15.00**

Cameo, green..............................35.00
Cherry Blossom, pink..................17.00
Daisy, amber 7.00
Florentine No. 2, yellow.................8.00
Forest Green, Boopie, green..........7.00
Hex Optic, green or pink 5.00
Lace Edge 125.00
Old English, green.......................20.00
Parrot, cone shape, green...........24.00
Raindrops, crystal 4.50
Sunflower, green 13.50
Thumbprint, green.........................7.00
Windsor, pink 13.00
Snack set, Harp, crystal..............48.00
Soup plate, Iris, irid, 7-1/2" dia 75.00
Sugar, cov
  Adam, pink 45.00
  Bamboo Optic, ftd, green 10.00
  Cameo, pink, 3-1/4" h 100.00
  Holiday, pink 25.00
  Madrid, amber 7.00
  Ring, dec 10.00
  Sierra Pinwheel, pink 20.00
  Tulip, blue 20.00
Tumbler
  Bamboo Optic, ftd, pink, 8-oz, 5-1/2" h
  ....15.00
  Bubble, crystal..............................5.00
  Cloverleaf, green, 10 oz, ftd.........50.00
  Dogwood, pink, 10 oz 45.00
  Fortune, pink 10.00
  Hex Optic, green or pink, 7-oz, 4-3/4" h
  ....8.00
  Horseshoe, green, 9-oz, ftd 22.00
  Madrid, amber, 5-1/2" h 18.00
  Mayfair, ftd, pink, 6-1/2" h 40.00
  Manhattan, 10 oz, ftd 19.00
  Moderntone, cone, white...............4.00
  Peanut Butter, crystal 7.00
  Princess, green, 9-oz 28.00
  Pyramid, ftd, crystal or pink, 8-oz 50.00
  Rose Cameo, green 22.50
  Ships, cobalt, 9-oz.......................14.00
  Vernon, yellow 35.00
Vase
  Cameo, green, 8" h 70.00
  Iris, crystal..................................32.00
Vegetable, open
  Cameo, green...............................30.00
  Daisy, amber 13.00
  Florentine No. 2, cov, yellow.........55.00
  Sharon, oval, amber.....................20.00
  Star, amber.................................10.00
  Tea Room, green..........................75.00
Wall vase, Anniversary, pink 90.00
Whiskey
  Diamond Quilted, pink..................12.00
  Hex Optic, green or pink 8.50
  Hobnail, crystal 5.00
Wine
  Manhattan 5.00
  Miss America, pink 115.00

Desert Storm magazine, Life, Special Investigation Edition, *cover story "Has Our Country Abandoned Them," other articles about Desert Storm, $7.50.*

❖ Desert Storm

Collectibles from this historical event are making their way to flea markets. Because these items are relatively new, expect to find them in very good condition.

Commemorative plate, Hamilton Collection, 8-1/2" dia, MIB............**38.00**
Comic book, *Desert Storm Journal*, #7
....**8.00**
Flag, white, yellow center ribbon, slight fading from use **5.00**
Key chain, "Operation Desert Storm, Come Home," with yellow ribbon, 2"
....**8.00**
Lighter, butane, "Desert Storm"........**5.00**
Medallion, ceramic, "Protecting World Peace," 1991, MIB **12.00**
Pin, "Support Our Troops, Desert Storm," shows yellow ribbon and American flag
....**3.00**
Pinback button
  "Operation Desert Storm, Support Our Troops," stars & stripes shield and planes, 2-1/4" dia........................**7.50**
  "Support Desert Storm, Free Kuwait," flags of Kuwait and the U.S., 1-3/4" dia..**8.50**
Soda bottle, Jolt, painted "Jolt salutes the US Armed Forces of Operation Desert Storm," 12 oz **5.00**

❖ Dexterity Puzzles

Small enough to hold in the palm of your hand, these little puzzles have provided hours of enjoyment for kids and collectors alike. From inauspicious beginnings as premiums or giveaways, these tiny playthings have certainly increased in value over the years.

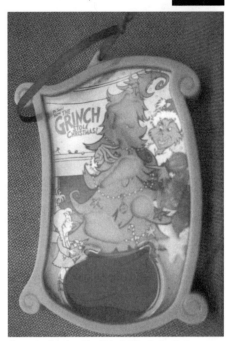

Dexterity Puzzles, The Grinch Who Stole Christmas, plastic, candy cane magnetic wand, $5.

Harlequin Puzzle, cardboard, paper and glass, by Journet, directions on bottom, 3-1/4" x 4-1/4" **30.00**
Hungry Pup, cardboard and glass, A.C. Gilbert Co., c1940, 3-1/4" x 4-1/4"**40.00**
Indian, tin and glass, "Nabisco Shredded Wheat Juniors" on back, 1-1/4" dia
....**15.00**
Lone Ranger, 5" x 3-1/2" **60.00**
Lucky Horseshoe, cardboard and glass, A.C. Gilbert Co., c1940, 3-1/4" x 4-1/4"
....**40.00**
New York-Paris Aero Race **65.00**
Pin U Ring It, cardboard, paper and glass, by Journet, directions on bottom, 3-1/4" x 4-1/4" **20.00**
Reddy Killowatt.............................**15.00**
Sgt. Biff O'Hara, "Nabisco Shredded Wheat Juniors" on back, 1-1/4" dia
....**30.00**
Turnstyle Puzzle, cardboard, paper and glass, by Journet, directions on bottom, 5" x 4"..**25.00**
Witch, flying on broomstick, orange background, round, early **45.00**

❖ Dick Tracy

Here's a comic strip character that made it to the big-time—movies! And, he and his pals generated some great collectibles along the way.

Badge, brass, pinback, Dick Tracy Detective Club **35.00**
Camera, 127mnm, 1950s, 5-1/2" l, 2-1/4" w, 3" h **75.00**
Cap gun, small..............................**35.00**
Coloring book, *Dick Tracy Movie*

Dick Tracy No. 1 Police car, Marx, painted tin wind-up, 11-1/4" l, $395.

Coloring Book, collector card photos on back cover, 1990, unused **5.00**
Comic book, *Motorola Presents Dick Tracy Comics*, 1953......................**15.00**
Film, 8mm, "Brain Game," black-and-white, silent, Republic Pictures, orig box 5-1/4" sq **22.00**
Game, Dick Tracy, Selchow & Righter, 1961 ....**25.00**
Little Golden Book, *Dick Tracy*, 1962, minor wear to cover.....................**15.00**
Magazine ad, Kraft caramels, 1958, 10" x 13" **16.00**
Marbles, Dick Tracy Straight Shooters, orig bag **15.00**
Ring, metal, adjustable, enameled deco, mkd "Copyright Wendy Gell, Disney Co." **49.00**
Trading cards, Willard's Chocolates, 56 cards, 1930s, complete set **90.00**
Transfer, "Official Member Dick Tracy Crime Stoppers," blue and red graphics, 1940s, 10" x 8" **15.00**
Water pistol, Luger style, 1971 ......**40.00**

❖ Dinnerware

Complete sets of dinnerware frequently appear at flea markets. They are usually priced considerably less than what you'd expect to pay for a comparable new set, unless, of course, it's manufactured by one of the more desirable names in dinnerware, such as Royal or Stangl. It's not unusual for a few pieces to be missing or damaged, but they are easily replaced with today's replacement services.

❖ Dionne Quints

Born in Ontario, Canada, on May 28, 1934, these 5 little girls excited everyone. They led an interesting yet sheltered life, attracting attention from around the world. Of course, all of this adoration resulted in a wide variety of collectibles and souvenirs.

Collectors' Club: Dionne Quint Collectors, P.O. Box 2527, Woburn, MA 01888.

Booklet
The Dionne Quintuplets: We're Two Years Old, Willis Thornton, Whitman Publishing Co., 1936, softcover, 40 pgs..**50.00**
The Story of the Dionne Quintuplets, Whitman Publishing Co., 1935,

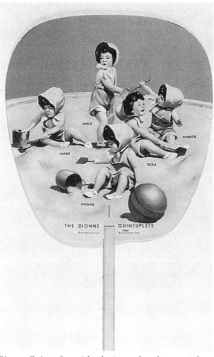

Dionne Quints, fan, girls playing at beach, copyright 1936, adv on back, cardboard, wooden handle, $45.

authorized edition, 40 pgs, 9-1/2" x 10" **25.00**
Calendar, 1945, Armstrong Lumber, features Dionne Quints, 8-1/2" x 11" **35.00**
Child's feeding dish, names on outside of rim, emb faces in center, 6" dia **85.00**
Dexterity puzzle, 1930s.................**90.00**
Fan, cardboard, wooden handle, beach scene, San Fernando Laundry, "Don't Kill Your Wife, Let Us Do the Dirty Work," 14" l **18.00**
Figurines, 3 with baskets, 1 with basket of flowers, 1 with Scottie dog, bottoms mkd "Dresden," 2 chips, each 5-1/2" h, set of 5 ....**850.00**
Magazine cover, *Woman's World*, Feb, 1937 ....**12.00**
Paper dolls, *Let's Play House with the Dionne Quints*, unused.................**55.00**
Photo, one year old babies in basket, 1936 ....**30.00**
Postcard, Dr. Dafoe and babies......**18.00**
Print, Nea Services, Inc., 1936, framed, 23-1/4" x 19-1/2" **60.00**

❖ Disneyana

Walt Disney was the impetus for a wonderful cast of characters that still delights children of all ages. Through the many Disney movies and television shows, many collectibles are available. Check for the official "Walt Disney Enterprises" logo.

References: Ted Hake, *Hake's Guide to Character Toys*, 4th ed, Gemstone

Publishing, 2002; Rex Miller, *The Investor's Guide to Vintage Character Collectibles*, Krause Publications, 1999.

Periodicals: *Mouse Rap Monthly*, P.O. Box 1064, Ojai, CA 93024; *Tomart's Disneyana Digest*, 3300 Encrete Ln, Dayton, OH 45439; *Tomart's Disneyana Update*, 3300 Encrete Ln, Dayton, OH 45439.

Collectors' Clubs: Imagination Guild, P.O. Box 907, Boulder Creek, CA 95006; Mouse Club East, P.O. Box 3195, Wakefield, MA 01880; National Fantasy Fan Club for Disneyana Collectors and Enthusiasts, P.O. Box 19212, Irvine, CA 92713.

> Buyer beware!
> Antiques & Collectors Reproduction News reports that all Mickey Mouse 1933 Worlds Fair pocket knives are fantasy items. This has been confirmed by several experts.

Bank, Cinderella.............................**35.00**
Bell, Tinkerbell handle, bronze colored metal, emb "Copyright Walt Disney Productions," 3-1/4" h **55.00**
Big Little Book, *Mickey Mouse The Mail Pilot*, Whitman, copyright 1933, softcover, 3-1/2" x 4-3/4", some wear **60.00**
Bobbing head, Dumbo, composition, seated, 1960s, Japan paper label **145.00**
Book
Donald Duck Sees South America, D. C. Heath & Co., Walt Disney Storybooks, hardcover, 6-1/4" x 5-1/2" **40.00**
Thumper, Grosset & Dunlap, 1942, 32 pgs...**30.00**
Bookends, Donald Duck carrying school books, chalkware, pr **25.00**

Disneyana, Hallmark Christmas ornament, Mickey snow angel, Mickey & Co., MIB, $15.

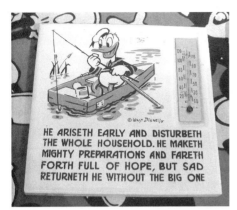

Disneyana, Donald Duck tile, ceramic, copyright Walt Disney, thermometer, white ground, black lettering "He ariseth early and disturbeth the whole household, he maketh mighty preparations and fareth forth full of hope, but sad returneth he without the big one," $30.

Bubble gum card, Mickey Mouse, #23 ....**8.00**
Card Game, Pluto, Whitman, 1939 copyright, black, white, and red illus, 35 playing cards **50.00**
Cup, Mickey Mouse, glazed ceramic, Paragon China, 1930s, 2-7/8" dia **195.00**
Doll, Pollyanna, 30" h **100.00**
Drinking glass, Donald Duck, "Full, Going, Going, Gone!," 1940s, 4-3/4" h **40.00**
Earrings, clip-on, Mickey Mouse.....**35.00**
Figure
　Alice, plastic, hp, Marx, 1950s, 2-1/2" h **10.00**
　Daisy, plastic, hp, Marx, 1950s, 2-1/2" h..**12.00**
　Donald Duck, accordian, bisque, 1930s, 4" h **195.00**
　Dumbo...**35.00**
　Mickey Mouse, plastic, hp, Marx, 1950s, 2-1/2" h **15.00**
　Minnie Mouse, plastic, hp, Marx, 1950s, 2-1/2" h **12.00**
　Pinocchio, bisque, 1940s, 3" h...**110.00**
　Thumper, painted and glazed ceramic, tan, brown and pink, Hagen-Renaker, 1940s **50.00**
　Unicorn, Fantasia, gray glazed ceramic, mkd "Vernon Kilns," 1940 ....**350.00**
Film, Donald the Skater, 1935, black-

Disneyana, Snow White and 7 dwarfs rug, red or yellow jackets, green pants or gold, white ground, $165.

and-white, 16mm, orig box...........**24.00**
Flasher pin, I Like Disneyland/Mickey Mouse, 1950s.............................**40.00**
Greeting card, get well, diecut Mickey, Hallmark, 1930s **35.00**
Hair brush, Mickey Mouse, Walt Disney Enterprises, 1930, orig box..........**45.00**
Iron-on patch, 3 images of Mickey, dated 1946, orig package **24.00**
Labels, stick-on, English, 1940s, full sheet **85.00**
Magazine
　Mickey Mouse Magazine, Vol 2, #1, Oct 1936, Kay Kamen Ltd., 36 pgs **195.00**
　Newsweek, Feb 13, 1950, 3 pg article about Cinderella, color cover....**25.00**
Mask, diecut stiff paper, Doc, premium from Stroehmann's Bread, ad for Snow White Cake, marked "Part-T-Mask/Eison-Freeman Co, Inc.," poem on back, 1937 copyright..............**25.00**
Music box, Happy, figural **30.00**
Napkin holder with salt and pepper shakers, Snow White, Enesco, copyright Walt Disney Productions 1964, 6" h, set..........................**400.00**
Paper dolls, Mary Poppins Cut-Out Book, Watkins-Strathmore Co., 1964, Jane and Michael on front, 8 pgs, uncut **40.00**
Pencil, red, white, and blue, Donald Duck Bread, loaf of bread, imprint of Ungles Baking Co, 5-1/2" l, 1950s **25.00**
Pinback button
　Mickey Mouse Club, copyright 1928, 1-1/4", some wear and rust **40.00**
　Official Mickey Mouse Store, Kay Kamen Ltd., yellowed paper insert, 1937..**35.00**
Record, Mickey Mouse Club March, 7 x 7" colorful stiff paper sleeve, 45 rpm record, Disneyland label, 1962 copyright.....................................**20.00**
Ring, brass, thin expansion band, diecut brass figure of black, white, and red Mickey in Santa suit, green gloves, copyright "Walt Disney Productions," 1970s **12.00**
Rug, Uncle Scrooge McDuck, woven, 1950s, slight wear, 34" x 21"......**175.00**
Salt and pepper shakers, pr
　Ludwig Von Drake, 1961, MIP....**285.00**
　Mickey and Minnie, glazed ceramic, cork stoppers **375.00**
　Pluto, glazed white china, over glaze black and red paint dec, Leeds China, unmarked, 1947 ....**30.00**
Stamp, Mickey Mouse, Walt Disney Enterprises.....................................**40.00**
Teapot, cov, large, Mickey Mouse ...**95.00**
Television, Build Your Own TV, 6 Walt Disney full-color films, punched out

Disneyana, Mickey Mouse and Walt Disney Viewer, pink box with viewer, 12 boxes with film strips, $135.

parts, Tower Press Product, Made in England, 1950s, 9-1/2" x 7" **125.00**
Thermometer, 6" x 6" ceramic Sportsman plaque, Donald as bowler, black text, Kemper-Thomas Co., 1940s **35.00**
Toothbrush holder, Three Pigs, glazed ceramic, Disney copyright, English, 1930s, set of 3 ....**375.00**
Toy
　Climbing Mickey Mouse, Dolly Toy Co., Dayton, OH, copyright Walt Disney Enterprises, mid 1930s, 8-3/4" h diecut, orig 9-3/8" h box **575.00**
　Mickey Mouse Racing Car, Donald Duck 415, side box panels show Minnie, Pluto, and Donald racing in cars, 1935 Walt Disney Enterprises copyright, orig box **495.00**
Tray, Mickey and Minnie, Ohio Art, 1930s, tin, 7-1/2" l, shows wear ...**95.00**
Valentine, Jiminy Cricket, diecut, movable arms, 1939....................**27.50**
Wall plaque, Mickey Mouse as band leader, mkd "Ceramica De Cuernavaca," 1970s **95.00**
Wristwatch, silvered metal case, white dial, Mickey with red gloves, c1970, working.......................................**50.00**

Disneyana, Mickey Mouse and Donald Duck, chalk board, other Disney characters across top, wooden frame, $20.

❖ Disneyland and Disney World

From celebrities to kids of all ages, lots of folks enjoy Disneyland and Disney World. Collectibles from these wonderful amusement parks are eagerly sought.

References: Ted Hake, *Hake's Guide to Character Toys*, 3rd ed, Gemstone Publishing, 2000; Rex Miller, *The Investor's Guide to Vintage Character Collectibles*, Krause Publications, 1999.

Periodicals: *Mouse Rap Monthly*, P.O. Box 1064, Ojai, CA 93024; *Tomart's Disneyana Digest*, 3300 Encrete Ln, Dayton, OH 45439; *Tomart's Disneyana Update*, 3300 Encrete Ln, Dayton, OH 45439.

Collectors' Clubs: Imagination Guild, P.O. Box 907, Boulder Creek, CA 95006; Mouse Club East, P.O. Box 3195, Wakefield, MA 01880; National Fantasy Fan Club for Disneyana Collectors and Enthusiasts, P.O. Box 19212, Irvine, CA 92713.

Book, Disneyland The First Quarter Century, hardcover **45.00**

Box, cov, porcelain, Castle, white, mkd "Disneyland copyright Walt Disney Productions," 4-5/8" l, 3-1/4" w, 2" h **40.00**

Coke cans, Toon Town, 6-pack, Mickey, Roger Rabbit, Donald, Goofy.......**20.00**

Guide book, 32 pgs, 1965..............**65.00**

Invitation, 25th Anniv, cast members open house, 1-5/8" dia silver medallion attached **30.00**

Little Golden Book, Donald Duck in Disneyland, 1955 ....**15.00**

Locket, brass, heart shape, raised castle on front, pink and blue accents, late 1950s **28.00**

Map, Welcome to Disneyland, fold-out, 1958, 12" x 8-1/2" **80.00**

Pin, Tokyo, "First Day Last Day," Mickey, millennium **30.00**

Pinback button, Main Street Commemorative, blue text, 3000th Performance, Sept 4, 1991, color photo **37.50**

Plate, Disneyland, Mark Twain, palette mark with "Eleanore Welborn Art Productions, Monterey, California," 1950s, 6" dia **85.00**

Poster, Family Fun Night, 1971, copyright Walt Disney Productions, 9" x 12" **45.00**

Puzzle, Tea Party, Tower Press, copyright 1960 Walt Disney Productions **30.00**

Record story book, Disneyland Davy Crockett, 1971, 7-1/4" sq **35.00**

Salt and pepper shakers, pr, one shows Main Street, other shows Sleeping Beauty castle.............................**30.00**

Sign, Studio One and Tavern Guild Private Party, May 25, 1978 ....**35.00**

Thermos, Disney's Wonderful World, Aladdin, 6-1/2" h..........................**10.00**

Tray, metal, white designs around rim, 1960s **15.00**

Wrist watch, 35 Years of Magic-Disneyland, Mickey's face, band with relief of Fantasy Land Castle, the Matterhorn and Ferris wheel, Japan, MIB..**25.00**

❖ Dog Collectibles

Collecting dog-related items is a fun sport for many collectors. Some specialize in collectibles showing a certain breed; others look for items with canines that resemble a favorite pet. Those who are celebrity-minded search for famous dog characters, such as Tige, Rin Tin Tin, and Lassie.

Collectors' Clubs: Canine Collectors Club, 736 N Western Ave, Suite 314, Lake Forest, IL 60045; Wee Scots, P.O. Box 1597, Winchester, VA 22604.

Bank, St. Bernard, cast iron, painted black and gold **130.00**

Book

Huskies in Action, The Fascination of Sled Dog Racing, Rico Pfirstinger, 1995, color photos **15.00**

Lassie & The Mystery of Blackberry Bog, Dorothea Snow, Whitman, illus by Ken Sawyer, 1946.................**5.00**

The Rin Tin Tin Book of Dog Care, Lee Duncan, Prentice Hall, 1958, dj**40.00**

Bottle opener, wall-mount, cast iron, bulldog, 4" h, 3-1/2" w **75.00**

Calendar Plate, 1910, black and white Bulldog, white china, gold trim **45.00**

Cocktail glasses, Scottie dec, set of 6 ....**55.00**

Cookie jar, McCoy, Mac Dog, mkd "208 USA"...**160.00**

Costume jewelry, poodle pin, Trifari, sits begging, goldtone metal, gray rhinestone accents, mother-of-pearl body, collar with 3 gray baguettes, red cabachon eye, 2-1/4" h, 7/8" w **45.00**

Framed print, On Guard, landscape with young sleeping girl and dog, ornate oak and gold painted frame, 30"x 33-1/2", $175.

Hallmark Christmas Ornament, Dog of the Year, 1994, rolled up newspaper titled Canine Edition, place for dog's photo, $5.

Dresser jar, cov, satin glass, dog finial **45.00**

Figure

Beagle, #1072, Llardo **140.00**

Bonzo Dog, 3" h, bisque, mkd "Germany," c1920 ....**45.00**

Collie, bisque, black and brown ...**40.00**

Dachshund, Beswick, #1469........**50.00**

Magazine ad, Gaines dog food, shows Rin Tin Tin, 1947 ....**9.00**

Pinback Button, Duke the Peters Dog, multicolored, black Labrador clenching Peters shotgun shell carton in mouth, white lettering on black rim **12.00**

Ramp Walker, 3-1/2" l dachshund, brown hard plastic, black and yellow accents, Marx, 1950s **15.00**

Salt and pepper shakers, pr

Poodle, heads, Rosemeade.......**165.00**

RCA Nipper, Lenox **75.00**

Stuffed toy, Lassie, vinyl collar.......**75.00**

Toothbrush holder, dog holds toothbrush in mouth, Japan, 5-1/8" h **95.00**

Wall plaque, Collie, Mortens Studio **24.00**

❖ Dollhouse Furniture

Dollhouse furnishings are those tiny articles used to finish and accessorize a dollhouse. Materials and methods of production range from fine handmade wooden pieces to molded plastic items. Several toy manufacturers, such as Tootsietoy, Petite Princess, and Renwal, made dollhouse furnishings.

Reference: Nora Earnshaw, *Collecting Dolls' Houses and Miniatures*, Pincushion Press, 1993; Dian Zillner with Patty Cooper, *Furnished Dollhouses 1880s-1980s*, Schiffer Publishing, 2001.

Periodicals: *Doll Castle News*, P.O. Box 247, Washington, NJ 07882; *Miniature Collector*, 30595 Eight Mile, Livonia, MI 48152; *Nutshell News*, P.O. Box 1612, Waukesha, WI 53187.

Collectors' Clubs: Dollhouse & Miniature Collectors, P.O. Box 16, Bellaire, MI 49615;

National Assoc of Miniature Enthusiasts,
P.O. Box 69, Carmel, IN 46032.

Arm chair, Petite Princess, matching
ottoman **27.50**
Bathroom set, Tootsietoy, 10 pcs, orig
box...**85.00**
Bear rug, white, purple velvet lining,
glass eyes **35.00**
Bed, Renwal, twin size **9.00**
Bedroom suite, Tootsietoy, 6 pcs, orig
box...**65.00**
Candelabra, Petite Princess, MOC.**12.00**
Chaise lounge, Petite Princess, one
pillow missing **10.00**
Chest of drawers, walnut, handmade
....**65.00**
Cradle, Renwal, turquoise..............**16.00**
Desk, maple, hinged front, royal blue and
black int **115.00**
Fireplace, Renwal, brown plastic....**37.50**
Garbage can, cylindrical, lid lifts with foot
pedal, red body, yellow pedal and lid,
Renwal **15.00**
Kitchen set, Allied, hard plastic, orig box
....**30.00**
Living room suite
Arcade, cast iron, sofa and chair**185.00**
Tootsietoy, sofa, two chairs, library
table, 2 lamps, phonograph stand, 7
pcs **90.00**
Piano, Ideal, plastic, litho, mirror.....**30.00**
Plant stand, Petite Princess **1.00**
Server, woodtone plastic, Renwal, one
drawer opens..................................**5.00**
Slide, silver and blue, Renwal.........**20.00**
Treasure trove cabinet, Ideal, MIB **15.00**
Wing chair, Petite Princess, MIB....**15.00**

❖ Dollhouses

Early dollhouses were reserved for the
wealthy and were designed primarily as
display cabinets for collections of valuable
miniatures rather than as playthings for
children. The first American doll houses
were made in the late 18th century, but it
wasn't until 1860, with the development of
chromolithography, that they were mass-
produced.

Reference: Dian Zillner with Patty Cooper,
Furnished Dollhouses 1880s-1980s,
Schiffer Publishing, 2001.

Periodicals: *Doll Castle News*, P.O. Box
247, Washington, NJ 07882.

Collectors' Clubs: Dollhouse & Miniature
Collectors, P.O. Box 16, Bellaire, MI 49615.

Bing, Germany, garage, litho tin, double
doors, complete with 2 orig cars **600.00**
Bliss, chromolith on wood
Stable, 2-story, red shingle roof,
painted green and red cupola,
painted red base, single opening
door on 2nd floor, brown papier-

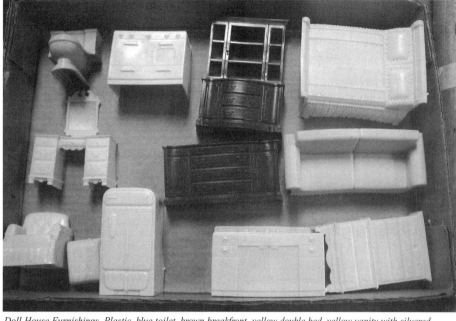

Doll House Furnishings, Plastic, blue toilet, brown breakfront, yellow double bed, yellow vanity with silvered mirror, brown chest of drawers, yellow sofa, yellow stuffed chair and ottoman, ivory sink, ivory refrigerator, ivory sink unit, yellow chest on chest, sold as lot, $40.

mache horse, mkd "R. Bliss" ..**900.00**
Victorian, 2 rooms, 2-story, high
steeple roof, dormer windows,
spindled porch railing, second floor
balcony **1,400.00**
Converse, cottage, red and green litho
on redwood, printed bay windows, roof
dormer......................................**550.00**
Ideal
Colonial style, 3 rooms up, 3 rooms
down, balcony, back open **300.00**
Fantasy Room, Petite Princess, red,
MIB **45.00**
Marx, litho tin, 2 story house, detailed
living room with fireplace, kitchen
cupboard with dishes, toy soldier motif
in nursery, 19" l, 8" d, 16" h, front door
missing, some rust damage, some play

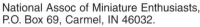

Doll Houses, Barn, wood, 2 story, stables on ground level, papier-mâché animals and accessories, orig paint, gray walls, blue trim, red roof, late 19th/early 20th C, second floor cracked, roof door missing, 23" w, 10" d, 17" h, $275.

wear...**45.00**
McLoughlin, folding, 2 rooms, dec int,
orig box **925.00**
Tootsietoy, printed Masonite, half
timbered style, 4 rooms, removable
roof **200.00**
Wolverine, litho tin, 2 story house, 5
rooms, bay windows, 10 pcs of period
plastic furniture, 22" l, 12" deep, 15" h,
chimney missing, some play wear
....**45.00**

❖ Doll Accessories

Collectors are just finding out what little girls
have always known—you can't really play
dolls unless you also have the beds, cribs,
bassinets, and other necessary items found
in a real nursery. Barbie has her own
furniture and accessories, plus an extensive
wardrobe. But, she wasn't the first doll to be
so fortunate. Many early dolls came
complete with trunks of clothes, shoes, and
other fine accessories.

References: Charles F. Donovan, Jr.,
*Renwal: World's Finest Toys, Dollhouse
Furniture*, L-W Book Sales, 1999; Jean
Mahan, *Doll Furniture, 1950s-1980s*, Hobby
House Press, 1997.

Bassinet, fold-up type, holds water **65.00**
Blanket chest, pine, old worn repaint, 6-
board type **450.00**
Bottle sterlizer, granitewate **35.00**
Bunk beds, wood, orig bedding, c1960
....**80.00**
Chair, Queen Anne style, upholstered
seat **90.00**
Chest of drawers, Empire style,

Doll Accessories, cupboard, painted wood, 3 shelves, 2 doors, home made, $20.

mahogany and mahogany veneer, 3 dovetailed drawers, scrolled feet, some veneer damage **500.00**

Clothespins, plastic, set of 20 ....**5.00**

Cradle, pine, bell rings when rocked back and forth **45.00**

Crib, light oak, movable side rails, orig hand made bedding, c1955 ....**70.00**

Cupboard, 2 open shelves over 2 cupboard doors, Strawberry Shortcake dec, litho tin, wear **10.00**

Doll bed, high scrolled Victorian-style headboard, matching footboard, mahogany, new quilt and bedding **250.00**

Fainting couch, professionally restored **130.00**

Kitchen set, metal, sink, stove and refrigerator, colorful litho dec......**175.00**

Rocker, pierced pressed board back and seat, scrolled arms.....................**125.00**

Stroller, red plaid seat, white metal frame, c1960, played-with condition **20.00**

Trunk, dome-top, lined with wallpaper,

Doll Accessories, dish, divided, red plastic, "cat, dog, fish, bird, and pig" in words and symbols on edge, mkd "Amsco," orig spoons. $3.50.

orig handles....................................**75.00**
Wash tub, aluminum, 5" dia............**15.00**

❖ Dolls

Made from a wide variety of materials, dolls have always been favorite playthings of the young and the young at heart. Doll collectors are a very dedicated group. Some specialize in a particular style of doll or company, while others simply love them all. There are hundreds of examples for collectors to consider. Condition, age, markings, and original clothing all help to determine a doll's value.

References: Jan Foulke, *14th Blue Book Dolls and Values*, Hobby House Press, 2000; Dawn Herlocher, *Antique Trader's Doll Makers & Marks*, Antique Trader Books, 1999; —, *200 Years of Dolls 2nd ed*, Antique Trader Books, 2002; Patsy Moyer, *Doll Values, Antique to Modern*, 4th ed, Collector Books, 2000; —, *Modern Collectible Dolls*, vol. IV, Collector Books, 2000; Cindy Cabulis, *Collector's Guide to Dolls of the 1960s and 1970s,* Collector Books, 2000.

Periodicals: *Antique & Collectible Dolls*, 218 W Woodin Blvd, Dallas, TX 75224; *Antique Doll Collector*, 6 Woodside Ave, Suite 300, Northport, NY 11768; *Doll Collector's Price Guide*, 306 E Parr Rd, Berne, IN 46711; *Doll-E-Gram,* P.O. Box1212, Bellevue, WA 98009-1212; *Doll Life*, 243 Newton-Sparta Rd, Newton, NJ 07860; *Doll Reader*, 741 Miller Drive, SE, Harrisburg, PA 20175; *Doll Times*, 218 W Woodin Blvd, Dallas, TX 75224; *Doll World*, 306 East Parr Rd, Berne, IN 46711;

Effanbee, witch, orig box, orig basket with apples, $35.

"Ruth," Amish Doll, Knowles, limited edition, MIB, $45.

Dollmasters, P.O. Box 151, Annapolis, MD 21404; *Dolls: The Collector's Magazine*, 170 Fifth Ave, 12th Floor, New York, NY 10010.

Collectors' Clubs: Annalee Doll Society, P.O. Box708, Meredith, NH 03253; Doll Collector International, P.O. Box 2761, Oshkosh, WI 54903; Doll Costumers Guild, 7112 W Grovers Ave, Glendale, AZ 85308; Doll Doctor's Assoc, 6204 Ocean Front Ave, Virginia Beach, VA 23451; Ginny Doll Club, P.O. Box 338, Oakdale, CA 95361; Madame Alexander Doll Fan Club, P.O. Box 330, Mundeline, IL 60060; United Federation of Doll Clubs, 10920 N Ambassador Dr, Suite 130, Kansas City, MO 64153.

Artist type

Dianna Effner, Sweetness, christening dress, 1988............................**125.00**

Lee Middleton, Alexis, skating outfit **350.00**

Bed doll, silk face, painted bangs, gray wig, sewn shoes, undressed......**100.00**

Boudoir type, French, cloth face..**160.00**

Celebrity or character

Bert, Sesame Street, Knickerbocker, 1981, MIB **25.00**

Brooke Shields, MIB....................**30.00**

Captain Caveman, stuffed, 30" h .**65.00**

Carrie, Little House on the Prairie, © 1975, Knickerbocker, MIB.........**50.00**

Charlie McCarthy, composition, movable mouth, 1930s **185.00**

Cher, © 1975 Mego, MIB **50.00**

Kate Jackson, Mattel, 12" h **70.00**

Mary Poppins, Horsman, 1964.....**55.00**

Spider-Man, Mego, 8" NRFP, orig price sticker **85.00**

Sunbonnet Baby, Molly, Mandy or May, © 1975, Knickerbocker, MIB, each **25.00**

Cloth

Heather, Knickerbocker, painted features, calico dress and hat, MIB
....**20.00**

Raggedy Ann, Christmas box **35.00**

Composition

Anne Shirley, Effanbee, orig clothes, 18" h **195.00**

Baby Dear, Vogue, bent baby limbs, 1961, 12" h **40.00**

Barbara Lou, Effanbee, orig clothes, 21" h **350.00**

Deanna Durbin, orig box, 15" h..**245.00**

Dream Baby, Arranbee, redressed, 20" h..**115.00**

Judy Garland, Wizard of Oz costume, Ideal, 18" h **675.00**

Nancy, Arranbee, orig outfit, 21" h
....**410.00**

Plastic

Betsy McCall, jointed knees, brunette rooted hair, orig red and white striped skirt, white organdy top, c1960, 8" h **45.00**

Karne Ballerina, Eegee, jointed at knees, ankles, neck, shoulders, and

Mattel, Morton Salt Girl, yellow dress, orig blue salt box, orig red and white box, $12.50.

"Skipper" and "Skooter" dolls # 950 & # 1040, 9" high, in original boxes, $85 each.

hips, ballet shoes, satin and net ballet dress, c1958, 21" h, MIB.**45.00**

Mary Ellen, Madame Alexander, orig clothes, 31" h..........................**225.00**

Penny Brite, orig clothes **45.00**

Sweet Sue, blond wig, blue sleep eyes, rose dec white taffeta dress, pearl pin, silver dance shoes, all orig, 15" h..**200.00**

Tammy, Ideal, orig clothes............**45.00**

Tiny Terri Lee, Terri Lee Dolls, trunk with 6 orig outfits, 10" h..........**450.00**

Toni, American Character, collegiate outfit, orig booklet, 10" h..........**70.00**

Rubber, 11" h, Sun Rubber Co., molded features Betty Bows, drinks and wets, c1953 ....**35.00**

Gerber Baby, open nurser mouth, dimples, crossed baby legs **45.00**

Vinyl

Baby Linda, Terri Lee, molded painted hair, black eyes, c1951, 9" h....**95.00**

Butterball, Effanbee, all orig.........**65.00**

Cheerful Tearful, Mattel, orig clothes, 1966, 12" h **35.00**

Ginny, Girl Scout outfit, 8" h.......**115.00**

Little Dear, Arranbee, c1956, 8" h**80.00**

Mary Poppins, Horsman, extra clothes
....**70.00**

Ruthie, Horsman, Oriental hair style, 12-1/2" h **30.00**

Shirley Temple, Ideal, c1962, orig dress, orig box, 15" h,.............**275.00**

Truly Scrumptious, Mattel, 11-1/2" h
....**95.00**

Vinyl and hard plastic

Andy, Eegee, 12" h.......................**25.00**

Brenda Star, Madame Alexander, played with, 12" h **450.00**

Chatty Cathy, Mattel, talking, MIB**85.00**

Littlest Angel, Arranbee, 11" h **45.00**

❖ Doorknobs

If a man's home is his castle, it's no wonder that collectors have latched on to the idea of collecting ornamental doorknobs and other types of hardware. A special doorknob can give a house personality and a bit of pizzazz.

Reference: Web Wilson, *Antique Hardware Price Guide*, Krause Publications, 1999.

Collectors' Club: Antique Doorknob

Doorknocker, parrot on branch, pink and rose body, cast iron, 4-1/2" l, $40.

Collectors of America, P.O. Box 126, Eola, IL 60519.

Doorknob

Arts and Crafts, stamped metal, rose motif, 1 nickel-plated, 1 copper-plated, knobs 2" dia, matching plates 9" h x 1-1/2" w, pr **50.00**

Brass, emb, with plate, pr............**45.00**

Eastlake style, brass **40.00**

Glass, clear, pr **25.00**

Glass, mercury, 2-1/4" dia, pr.......**80.00**

Porcelain, Limoges, floral deco, gold accents, pr **150.00**

Doorknob plate, china, oval, rose pattern, 6-3/8" h, 3-1/2" w, set of 4
....**55.00**

Door knocker, dog, cast iron, old tan paint **235.00**

Mail slot cover, brass, emb "Letters," Victorian **48.00**

❖ Doorstops

Functional figural doorstops became popular in the late 19th century. Examples could be either flat-backed or three-dimensional. The doorstop's condition is critical to determining value, and collectors prefer doorstops with as much original paint as possible. The following listings are for examples that retain at least 80% of their original paint

Collectors' Club: Doorstop Collectors of America, 1881-G Spring Rd, Vineland, NJ 08630.

Doorstop, kittens, dressed as boy and girl, cast iron, some orig paint, 7-1/4" h, $65.

Reproduction Alert

All listings are cast iron unless otherwise noted.

Bellhop, blue uniform, with orange markings, brown base, 8-7/8" h .**300.00**

Boston terrier, 9-1/2" h **85.00**

Cat, black, red ribbon and bow around neck, on pillow, 8" h **155.00**

Clipper ship, mkd "Copyright Creation Co. 1930," 10-1/2" h, 11-1/4" w **75.00**

Cottage, Cape type, blue roof, flowers, fenced garden, bath, sgd "Eastern Specialty Mfg Co. 14", 8-5/8" l, 5-3/4" h **150.00**

Drum Major, ivory uniform, red hat with feather, yellow baton, left hand on waist, sq base, 12-5/8" h............**225.00**

Flower basket
   Marigolds, Hubley, mkd "Made in USA" and "315," 7-1/2" x 8" **175.00**
   Petunias & Daisies, Hubley........**115.00**

Frog, sitting, yellow and green, 3" h**50.00**

Golfer, 10" h................................**475.00**

Owl, sitting on books, sgd "Eastern Spec Co.," 9-1/2" h **285.00**

Pan, sitting on mushroom, green outfit, red hat and sleeves, flute, green grass base, 7" h **165.00**

Pointer dog, 8" h, 14" w **495.00**

Show horse, Chestnut, Hubley, slight retouch to nose **150.00**

Windmill, ivory, red roof, house at side, green base, 6-3/4" h...................**115.00**

❖ Dr. Seuss

Remember reading *Green Eggs and Ham* and *The Cat In The Hat*? Both of those titles are dear to Dr. Seuss collectors. This is a field in which collectors are still establishing fair market values, primarily because so many of the items are just now entering the secondary market. Adding to the thrill of the hunt is the fact that this favorite author also wrote under several pseudonyms.

Books

Dr. Seuss's ABC, Beginner Book, hard cover, 1963, book club edition..**10.00**
Green Eggs and Ham, 1966 ....**2.00**
Happy Birthday To You!, 1959 ......**26.00**
The Cat in the Hat, Random House, 1957..**7.50**
The Hat Comes Back, Random House, 1958..**7.50**
You're Only Old Once, 1986........**12.00**

Cereal bowl, plastic, "The Wubbulous World of Dr. Seuss" **6.00**

Christmas decoration, Dept 56. How The Grinch Stole Christmas series Christmas countdown tree, 24 resin ornaments................................**50.00**
   Cindy Lou Who's House...............**75.00**
   Musical Sleigh **45.00**
   Town Hall....................................**75.00**

Christmas ornament, Horton Hatches the Egg, Hallmark, MIB **14.00**

Doll, Cat in the Hat, 1983, 26" h **65.00**

Figure, Horton the Elephant, china, 4" l, 5-1/4" h...**55.00**

Growth chart, The Cat in the Hat Growth Chart, paper, orig packaging........**17.50**

Jelly glass, No. 1, The Cat In The Hat and the Zubbie Wump, "The Wubbulous World of Dr Seuss," 1996,

Dr Seuss Book, I Can Lick 30 Tigers Today, wear, $15.

4" h...**2.00**

Lunchbox, metal, Aladdin, 1970, matching plastic thermos **200.00**

Pin, pewter, figural, Cat in the Hat ..**12.00**

❖ Drinking Glasses

Many drinking glasses start out life as part of a set, but due to breakage and other tragedies, they are sometimes orphaned and end up at flea markets, just waiting for a new home.

Bohemian glass, ruby flashed, cut design, gold dec, 4-pc set **150.00**

Carnival glass
   Acorn Burrs, marigold **60.00**
   Orange Tree, blue.........................**60.00**
   Peacock at Fountain, amethyst **25.00**
   Tiger Lily, marigold **75.00**

Cut glass
   Clear Button Russian pattern.......**95.00**
   Hobstars.....................................**40.00**

Depression era
   Flowers, yellow and green **12.00**
   Madrid, amber **9.00**
   Princess, yellow, ftd.....................**30.00**
   Stars, white **10.00**
   Sunbonnet Girl, red, white and blue **15.00**

Fostoria
   American, ftd...............................**11.00**
   Colony, flat..................................**27.00**

Heisey, Rose Etch, 12-oz, ftd **50.00**

Libbey Glass, green, slight swirl pattern, mkd, set of 5 ....**72.00**

Northwood, blue, 1" opalescent white band at top, mkd **10.00**

Pattern glass
   Broken Column, ruby trim **65.00**
   Bull's Eye and Diamond Panels ...**50.00**
   Cherry and Cable, color trim........**20.00**
   Cranes and Herons, etched.........**30.00**
   Croesus, amethyst **90.00**
   Dakota, etched fern and berry dec **35.00**
   Esther, green, gold trim...............**45.00**
   Festoon **20.00**
   Yale **25.00**

❖ Drug Store Collectibles

Aacchhoo! Here is another collecting field where the collectors are beginning to really specialize. Whether they collect paper epherma relating to drug stores, or perhaps collect items related to a favorite local drug store, or perhaps bottles or old packaging, this is a fun category. However, please don't try any of the remedies you might find. Those old compounds might not be stable any more.

Periodical: *The Drug Store Collector,* 3851

Gable Lane Drive, #513, Indianapolis, IN 46208.

For additional listings, see *Warman's Americana & Collectibles.*

Almanac, 1937, *The Ladies Birthday Almanac*, Medlock's Drug Store, Roscoe, Texas **12.00**

Bottle
Bromo-Seltzer, The Emerson Company, Baltimore cobalt, 2-1/2" dia..................................**10.00**
Leitsch's Drugstore, light aqua.....**20.00**
Sodium Phosphate, United Drug Company, corked, aluminum screw-top, 4-oz..................................**30.00**

Calendar, 1901, Colgate, miniature, flower...............................**20.00**

Fan, cardboard with wooden handle
"666 Quartette" laxative, Hill's Pharmacy, Tampa, Fla., cardboard, chipped wooden handle, creases, 11-1/4" h **16.00**
Tums for the Tummy, hand screen type, young boy beckons to girl leaving drugstore **35.00**

Glass, ice cream soda
Clear, ribbed stems, 8" h, set of 5**30.00**
Light amber, 7" h, set of 6............**55.00**

Jar, glass, Ramon's, countertop, blue metal lid, Ramon's character in 2 places...**150.00**

Matchbook, "Humphrey Drug Store, Home Store of Vice President Hubert H. Humprey," shows Liberty Bell.....**7.50**

Needle book, Rexall - Make A Point of Saving At Our Rexall Drug Store, 3 needle packets and threader........**16.00**

Ornament, Hallmark, Neighborhood Drugstore, Nostalgic Houses and Shops series, MIB, 1994 ....**25.00**

Postcard, interior of Harry Neamand's drugstore, Perkasie, PA, c1940....**15.00**

Scale, chemist's, General Scientific Co., milk glass platforms, 2 weights, 8" h, 13" w **150.00**

Tin
Doan's, tin and cardboard, 40-count **7.00**
Dr. Scholl's Foot Powder, cylindrical, green, black and gold, 6-1/4" h **20.00**
Men-Tho-Lo, Leighton Supply Co., orig box and instruction sheet, 2-1/2" dia **12.50**
Nyal Cold Capsules, Nyal Co., Detroit, black and orange, 3" x 2" x 1/2"**12.50**

Trade card, Hood's Latest Tooth Powder, Emlet's Drug Store, Havover, Pa., shows woman's face breaking through newspaper....................................**15.00**

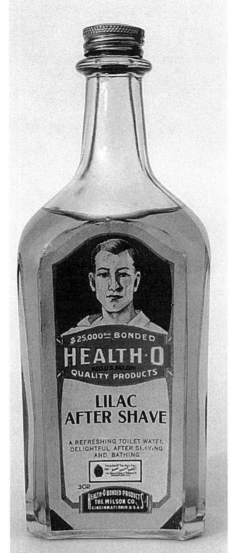

Drugstore Collectibles, Health-O Lilac After Shave, Milson Co., orig contents, orig paper label, $15.

❖ Duncan and Miller Glassware

The glass company known as Duncan & Sons and, later, Duncan and Miller, was founded in 1865 and continued through 1956. Their slogan was "The Loveliest Glassware in America," and many collectors will certainly agree with that sentiment.

Collectors Club: National Duncan Glass Soc, P.O. Box 965, Washington, PA 15301.

For additional listings, see *Warman's Antiques & Collectibles* and *Warman's Glass.*

Animal
Heron **100.00**
Swan, red bowl, 7-1/2" h..............**45.00**

Ashtray, Terrace, red, sq.................**35.00**

Bowl, First Love, crystal, 9" dia.......**75.00**

Candelabra, First Love, crystal, 2-light,

pr...**75.00**

Candy jar, cov, Sandwich, chartreuse, 8-1/2" h..**95.00**

Champagne, Tear Drop, 5 oz.........**10.00**

Coaster, Sandwich, crystal **15.00**

Cocktail glass, Caribbean, blue, 3-3/4 oz **48.00**

Console Bowl, 11" d, Rose etch, crystal **37.50**

Creamer and sugar, Passion Flower, crystal..**42.00**

Cup and saucer, Radiance, light blue **24.00**

Goblet
Caribbean, blue...........................**40.00**
Festival of Flowers, crystal...........**30.00**
Plaza, cobalt................................**40.00**

Ice cream dish, Sandwich, crystal, ftd **12.00**

Juice Tumbler, Sandwich, crystal, 3-3/4" h, ftd **12.00**

Nappy, Sandwich, crystal, 2 part, divided, handle **14.00**

Oyster cocktail, First Love, crystal.**24.00**

Plate
Canterbury, crystal, 8" dia.............**8.00**
Radiance, light blue, 8-1/2" dia **12.00**
Sandwich, green, 8" dia **24.00**
Spiral Flute, crystal, 10-3/8" dia ...**15.00**

Relish dish
Caribbean, blue, divided **30.00**
Terrace, 5-part, hammered aluminum center lid, 12" w **50.00**

Sherbet, Sandwich, green...............**12.00**

Sugar, Caribbean, crystal **12.00**

Tumbler, Terrace, red **40.00**

Whiskey, Seahorse, etch #502, red and crystal..**48.00**

Wine glass, Sandwich, crystal........**20.00**

❖ Earp, Wyatt

Hugh O'Brian starred when Wyatt Earp's character got his own television show. Western collectors search for this cowboy hero at many flea markets.

Bowl, cereal, Hazel Atlas, set of 5 ....**200.00**

Calendar plate, 1982, Wild West, Wedgwood, 10-1/8" dia **60.00**

Color and stencil set, Hugh O'Brian, MIB **145.00**

Comic book, *Wyatt Earp*, #21, 1958 ....**10.00**

Gun set, Hubley, black and white leather double holster, "Marshal Wyatt Earp" logo, 2 No. 247 Wyatt Earp Buntline Specials, purple swirl grips, 10-3/4" l, set **175.00**

Magazine, *Look,* Hugh O'Brien **15.00**

Mug, Wild West Collection, mkd "D6711," 1985-89, handle is a gun and sheriff's badge, 5-1/2" h **200.00**

Puzzle, frame tray, full-color portrait, Whitman, 1958 ....**25.00**

Statue, Hartland **125.00**

❖ Easter Collectibles

Here's a holiday that's always hoppy to be collected. From chicks to bunnies, this one is fun and whimsical, in addition to having a serious, religious side.

Book, *The Easter Story*, 1904 ....**32.50**

Candle, rabbit, sitting, off-white, mkd "Tavern Novelty Co." 5" h, 4" dia .**10.00**

Candy container

Easter Bunny dressed like cowboy, hard plastic, pulling "wood-look" cart, 1950s, yellow and blue, 13" l....**22.00**

Candy mold, makes eggs, bunnies, peanuts, chicks, and bells, $45.

Banner, dark green top panel, pink lower panel with embroidered white lilies, green leaves, gold trim and tassels, $70.

Rabbit, crouching on all fours, papier-mâché, removable head for storage of candy, mkd "Made in Germany, U.S. Zone, 4" x 4" **45.00**

Decoration, cardboard and tissue paper honeycomb, unfolds to set-up, rabbit sitting among lilacs, surrounded by

honeycomb eggs and basket, USA, 8-1/2" l **20.00**

Easter egg

Milk glass, white, gilded lettering "Easter Greetings," painted purple spring flowers, 6" **45.00**

Papier-mâché, 2 baby chicks on front, Easter basket filled with lily of the valley flowers, flowered paper int., 3" w, 4-1/2" l **75.00**

Greeting Card, stand-up, girl, "To Wish you a Happy Easter," yellow tissue paper honeycomb skirt, USA, 7" h **5.00**

Plate

Ceramic, Easter Morning Visitor, Recco, from the "Hearts & Flowers" collection by Sandra Kuck, 2 girls with bunny and basket of flowers, #2474A, 7th in series, 1992, 8-1/2" dia...**25.00**

Paper, Easter bunny, eggs, and spring flowers, 8-3/4" sq **4.00**

Sterling silver, "Easter Christ," Salvador Dali, Lincoln Mint, 1972, 1st ed, orig box, 9" dia..............................**225.00**

Postcard

A Peaceful Easter, girl and rabbit looking at Easter eggs, 1911......**5.00**

Best Easter Wishes, 2 roosters, April 1908 postmark............................**6.00**

Rattle, dancing rabbit, pink, blue jacket and holding a blue carrot, dancing,

Bunny, yellow plastic, clear Lucite ears and tail, black and white eyes, $15.

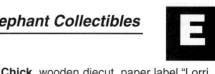

hard plastic, mkd "Irwin" 4" h..........**4.00**
Sheet music, "Easter Dawn" by A. Fieldhouse, 1904, edges rough ...**15.00**
Snowbunnies figures, Dept. 56
Counting the Days Til Easter, 1997, MIB **24.00**
I'll Color the Easter Egg, MIB.......**18.00**
Wishing You a Happy Easter, MIB**32.50**
Toy, musical Easter basket, cardboard, plastic handle, orig box, mkd "Mattel, 1952," 4" x 6" **65.00**

❖ Eggbeaters

Before modern kitchens were outfitted with electric appliances, eggbeaters were powered by hand. More than 1,000 patents were issued for items designed to beat eggs, and most of them were granted prior to the 1900s.

Reference: Linda Campbell Franklin, *300 Years of Kitchen Collectibles*, 5th ed, Krause Publications, 2003; Don Thornton, *Beat This: The Eggbeater Chronicles*, Off Beat Books, 1994.

A & J, center drive, blue and white painted wood handle, 1923..........**30.00**
Aluminum Beauty, Made in USA, Pat. Apr 20, 1920 ....**12.00**
Baby Bingo, tin, 5-1/2" l **8.00**
Dover, cast iron, 1904....................**35.00**
Ekco
A & J High Speed Beater, red Bakelite handle, wooden knob, 12" l **40.00**
Best, 2 arrowheads mark, turquoise plastic handle and knob, 12" l **8.00**
Ladd, blue handle, 11" l **18.00**
High Speed Beaker, stainless, butterscotch Bakelite handles, 12" l **75.00**
H-L Beater, Tarrytown, NY, No. 0, cast wheel, gears, loop type handle, wood knob, wavy beaters, 9" l **40.00**
Ladd Beater No. 1, United Royalties Corp, NY, patent July 7, 1908, Feb 24, 1915, coiled wire knob, 11" l **35.00**
Taplin Light Running Eggbeater, metal, 1908 patent date, 10-1/2" l...........**35.00**
Turbine Egg Beater, metal, wooden knob, Cassady-Fairbank Mfg. Co., Chicago, 1912 patent date, 10-1/2" l **32.50**
Ullman, wooden handle, 11" l **18.00**
Unmarked, child-size, red wooden handle, 4-1/4" l **9.50**

❖ Eggcups

Delicate eggcups make a wonderful collection, both useful and pretty to look at. Some were made as part of dinner services, and others were simply novelty items.

Collectors' Club: Eggcup Collectors' Corner, 67 Stevens Ave, Old Bridge, NJ 08857.

Advertising, Fanny Farmer, rabbit standing nest to egg shell, 2-1/2" h **65.00**
Ceramic or porcelain
Child's, Indian motif, gold trim, blue Japan stamp, 2-1/4" h..............**18.00**
Figural, lady with hat, salt shaker in red hat, mkd "Italy C22," 5-1/2" h....**65.00**
Hand-painted, mkd "Japan," 1950s, 4" h..**12.00**
Hen on nest, mkd "Worcester Royal Porcelain Co., Ltd., Worcester, England," 4-5/8" h **30.00**
Limoges, white, gold trim **30.00**
Mickey Mouse, mkd "Walt Disney Productions," 3-3/4" h **85.00**
Organdie, Vernon Kilns **15.00**
Rabbit leaning against eggshell house, incised "Germany 6458" on back, red stamped "69" on bottom, 3-1/4" h, 2-1/2" w..**50.00**
Rabbit with cane, incised "Germany 6450" on back, red stamped "76" on base, 3-1/4" h, 2-1/2" w...........**50.00**
Rooster, mkd "Made in Japan", 2-1/4" h **15.00**
Glass, figural
Bunny with eggcup on back, hp, Fenton, sgd by artist, orig box, 3-1/2" h..**28.00**
Chick, white milk glass, mkd "Made in France/Opalex" **18.00**
Hand holding cup, blue milk glass**25.00**
Jasper, blue, white dec, Wedgwood, Portland base mark, 1910............**85.00**
Silverplate, holds 4 eggs, ftd base with swags, mkd "C & Co, E.P.," castle mark **235.00**
Sterling silver, hallmarked Chester, 1911-12, maker SB **35.00**
Wood
Chick, bright yellow, child size, 1-3/4" dia, 2-3/4" h **25.00**
Little boy's head, hp, mkd "Made in Italy"..**20.00**

❖ Egg Timers

Figural egg timers are really catching on with collectors. They are colorful, cute, and useful, too.

Bellhop, kneeling, earthenware, 3" h, worn **85.00**
Building, emb details, plastic, glass timer, emb "Casdon" 4" h **40.00**
Chef, porcelain, red "Germany" mark, incised numbers on back, 3-3/4" h **110.00**
Chef, standing, porcelain, mkd "Made in Germany," 3-1/2" h **85.00**

Chick, wooden diecut, paper label "Lorri Design," 3-3/4" h..........................**50.00**
Dutch boy, mkd "Made in Japan" ...**75.00**
Elf with mushroom, plastic, back emb "A. Casdon Product, Made in England," 3" h, 5" w..**50.00**
Hour glass shape, wood and glass, 4" h **3.00**
Humpty Dumpty, hard plastic, mkd "A. Casdon Product, Made in England," 4" h **95.00**
Jenny Jones, hard plastic, apron emb "Jenny Jones," back emb "A. Casdon Product, Made in England," 4-1/4" h **45.00**
Kitchen Pixie, Enesco, recipe clip on back, 5-1/2" h **45.00**
Maid, mkd "Occupied Japan" **45.00**
Mauchline Ware, New Suspension Bridge dec....................................**85.00**
Milk bottle shape, People Dairy Co., 5-1/8" x 2-1/4", orig box..................**85.00**
Mr. Micawber, ceramic, mkd "Made in Germany," 4" h...........................**65.00**
Peasant woman, porcelain, script sgd "Germany," 4-1/2" h **80.00**
Pine bark, pinecone decal dec, 3-1/4" h **30.00**
Sailor boy, white suit, blue details, stamped "Germany," 3-1/4" h **110.00**
Sea captain, 5-1/2" h **25.00**
Telephone, candlestick-type, wooden, mkd "Cornwall Wood Products, Paris, Maine," 5" h **30.00**
Tommie, Black Cat, 1940s **50.00**
Windmill with bird, earthenware, mkd "Germany" and incised "Germany 825," 3-3/4" h **95.00**
Woman with shawl, porcelain, incised lettering on front "Cymru am byth," stamped "Foreign" in red ink on bottom, incised "Germany" and numbers on back, 4-1/4" h **110.00**

❖ Elephant Collectibles

Many folks consider elephants to be a symbol of luck. Particularly lucky are those elephants with their trunks raised. Whether due to their size or the fact that they are exotic, people just seem to enjoy them.

Periodical: *Jumbo Jargon*, 1002 W 25th St, Erie, PA 16502.

Advertising Trade Card, 4-7/8" x 3", Clark's Spool Cotton, Jumbo's Arrival, sepia, white, adv on back..............**7.50**
Bank, chalk, orig paint, c1930, 12" h **125.00**
Book, Edward Allen, *Fun By The Ton* **20.00**
Bottle opener, figural, cast iron, sitting,

trunk raised

Elephant, gray mohair, tusks, 12" l, 8" h, $110.

Brown, pink eyes and tongue, 3-1/2" h
....**55.00**
Pink, "GOP" on base, 3-1/4" h **55.00**
Christmas ornament, blown glass, gray
body, red blanket, 3-1/2" l.............**95.00**
Cigarette dispenser, cast iron **95.00**
Creamer and sugar, lusterware, red
blankets, black riding on sugar, mkd
"Made in Japan," c1940.............**195.00**
Figure
Brass, bronze finish, trunk in air, 29" h,
30" l.......................................**300.00**
Glass, trunk raised, 2-1/2" l, 3" h .**12.00**
Porcelain, Armani......................**280.00**
Teak, carved adult and baby, 20th C,
one tusk missing, 23-1/2" h **140.00**
Lamp, elephant with girl, hand painted,
Japan, 14" h **45.00**
Letter opener, celluloid, marked
"Depose-Germany," c1900 ....**40.00**
Mug, Frankoma, 1970s....................**20.00**
Napkin ring, Bakelite, navy blue, c1940
....**65.00**
Pie bird, dark gray, mkd "Nutbrown Pie
Funnel, Made in England," c1940
....**195.00**
Pin, gold tone, figural **25.00**
Pitcher, white, orange and blue trim, tail
forms handle, 2-1/2" h.................**20.00**
Planter, figural, pottery, unmkd
5" h, glossy finish **18.00**
8" x 5-1/2".....................................**20.00**
Postcard, Elephant Hotel, Margate City,
N.J., 1953.......................................**7.50**
Salt and pepper shakers, figural, mkd
"Japan," pr **24.00**
Toy, Jumbo, litho tin wind, mkd "U. S.
Zone Germany," 3-1/2" h **85.00**

❖ Enesco

Enesco has made quality limited editions for
years. Some are marked with a stamp,
while others have foil labels or paper tags.
The company's Precious Moments line is a
favorite of collectors.

Reference: Kathleen Deel, *Enesco, Then &
Now,* Schiffer Publishing, 2002.

Also see Precious Moments in this edition.

*Enesco Mug, Merry Christmas, green ground with
white dots, gold stripe, red edged frame, black
lettering, copyright 1985, Sonrise Creations,
Enesco, Made in Korea, $2.50.*

Bank, Garfield, arms folded, 6" h....**60.00**
Christmas ornament, John Deere,
Model B, Mrs. Claus driving, 1998, MIB
....**60.00**
Cookie jar
Garfield.......................................**90.00**
Sugar Town General Store...........**60.00**
Dealer sign, "The Rose O'Neill Kewpie
Collection by Enesco," 3-3/4" h, 1991
....**45.00**
Egg timer, Prayer Lady, pink, 6" h**125.00**
Figure
Athena, mermaid, 6" h **70.00**
Betsy Ross and Friend, 4-1/2" h ..**18.00**
Blot, Dalmatian, 1960s, 3-3/4" h**125.00**
Irish Mouse, hard plastic, 2-1/2" h .**5.00**
Pluto, 1960s, copyright Walt Disney
Productions, 6-1/4" h **60.00**
Shaggy Dog, copyright Walt Disney
Productions, orig paper tag, foil
sticker, 5" h **65.00**

Snow White and Seven Dwarfs, Walt
Disney Productions Japan, 1960s
....**275.00**
Mug, Mouseketeers, emb Mickey Mouse
face, foil label, c1960 ....**50.00**
Music box, Love Story, Mickey and
Minnie Mouse, plays "Love Makes The
World Go Round," 6" h, orig paper label
....**75.00**
Powder shaker, winking cat **15.00**
Salt and pepper shakers, pr
Blue Birds, orig paper labels, 4" h**24.00**
Christmas Presents, white, green dots,
red ribbon, paper label, 2-1/2" h
....**16.00**
Colonial America, orig box, 4" h....**24.00**
Piggy Chef, yellow base, clear plastic
pig, white plastic chef hat, paper
label, orig box **18.00**
Squirrels, holding large green acorn,
orig gold foil labels....................**22.00**

❖ Ertl

Although Ertl has produced a wide range of
toys and figures, the company is perhaps
best known as a manufacturer of farm toys.
Ertl also specializes in promotional and
commemorative trucks and banks, the sale
of which has most certainly assisted a
number of volunteer fire companies and
other civic groups.

Collectors' Club: Ertl Collectors Club, PO
Box 500, Dyersville, IA 52040.

Airplane
American Airlines **40.00**
Shell Oil, tri-motor **50.00**
U.S. Navy Air Express.................**30.00**
Bank
Ford Van, 1932, Anheuser Busch logo,
1991, 6-1/2" l **40.00**

Ertl Bank, Quakertown National Bank, 1951 Ford pickup, blue and white, orig box, $15.

Jewel Tea, 1905 truck, orig packaging
....**65.00**
Kodak, replica of Ford's first delivery
car, MIB **75.00**
Car
Batmobile, 1989, paint worn, 3-3/4" l
....**5.00**
Cale Yarborough, Nascar stock car,
Pow-R-Pull, 3" l, MOC **30.00**
Dick Tracy, Microsize set, 1990,
crayons and cars, MIB...............**8.50**
Ken Schrader Budweiser Monte Carlo,
1995, MIB **75.00**
Combine, International Harvester, 1974
....**110.00**
Figure, diecast
Daffy Duck, driving fire engine, Looney
Tunes, 1980s, MOC..................**40.00**
Wondergirl, 1990, MOC, 2" h.......**15.00**
Pedal tractor, International Harvester, rip
in metal seat, metal emblems painted
red, chain-driven **750.00**
Semi-trailer
John Deere, 1980s, MIB **75.00**
US Express, 1986, MIB...............**75.00**
Tractor
International, play wear, 9-1/2" l...**35.00**
John Deere, utility tractor, 1993, 1/16th
scale **36.00**
Tractor and wagon set, "Campbell's" on
tractor, "Campbell's Harvest of Good
Foods" on wagon, box mkd
"September-October 1985" **300.00**
Trailer, farm, movable tailgate, paint
chips, 3-3/4" h, 12" l.....................**12.00**
Watch, service premium for Ertl
employees, orig box **75.00**

❖ Ethnic Collectibles

All men were created equal, but they
haven't always been treated that way. Many
of today's collectibles reflect the stereotypes
of a bygone era.

Ancestor board, Papua, New Guinea,
96" l..**150.00**
Bank, Indian chief, porcelain, Japan, 4" h
....**87.50**
Brooch, Chinaman, holding pole with 7
beads, enameled, C-clasp, 3" h ...**65.00**
Chest, Afghanistan..........................**50.00**
Helmet mask, long protruding nose,
attached horns, small...................**20.00**
Lamp, sleeping Mexican, pink glass, no
shade, 7-3/4" h.............................**65.00**
Nodder, Chinaman, composition, Japan,
6-1/2" h...**65.00**
Perfume bottle, sleeping Mexican, chip
on hat, 1-1/4" h.............................**45.00**
Salt and pepper shakers, Indian chief
and brave, 3-1/4" h, pr **30.00**

*Ethnic Collectibles,
Picture, man playing
drum, created from
different hides, gray,
black, white, and tan,
unframed, $15.*

Shield, tan, Cameroon **90.00**
Statue, Beji, twin figure, Yoruba tribe,
Nigeria..**70.00**
String holder, Indian chief, chalkware,
1950s, 8-3/4" h............................**275.00**
Toothbrush holder, sleeping Mexican,
Japan, 6" h **120.00**
Trade card, Chinaman, "New Process
Starch, Firmenich Mfg. Co., Peoria, Ill.,"
2-3/4" x 4"......................................**20.00**

❖ Eyeglasses

Some collectors are always on the lookout
for vintage eyeglasses. Spectacles are great
decorator accents. Other flea market buyers
look for period eyeglasses that they can use
for theatrical purposes or that can be worn
during historical reenactments.

Reference: Nancy N. Schiffer, *Eyeglass
Retrospective*, Schiffer Publishing, 2000.

Bakelite, honey colored, round lenses,
1940s **12.00**
Jewelry, scarf holder, eyeglasses design,
rhinestone-studded, 1" dia **4.50**
Lorgnette, cream colored cat's eye
plastic, rhinestone dec, side handle
....**55.00**
Monocle, gold frame **25.00**
Plastic
8-sided lenses **20.00**

Mauritius, red with rhinestones and
leopard......................................**32.00**
Miniature cat's-eye, champagne color,
accented with rhinestones on the
eye piece and temples............**105.00**
Swank, black with glitter..............**32.00**
Vogue, cat's-eye, gold and taupe, silver
and gold accents **32.00**
Tortoiseshell, oval lenses, 1900s...**75.00**
Wire rim, gold, case mkd "Henderson
Jeweler and Optometrist, Delhi, N.Y."
....**35.00**

*Eyeglasses, Pinch nose type, orig leather carrying
case, mkd "Frank Muller, Mf'g, Optician, 1721
Chestnut St, Philada, PA," $20.*

❖ 4-H

Pledging head, heart, hands and health, 4-H club members have been awarded (and have made) a multitude of 4-H collectibles since the organization's inception around 1902. Expect renewed interest in this field as the centennial of the 4-H Youth Development Program is 2002. While pins, ribbons and trophies are the traditional finds, don't overlook 4-H projects themselves. Entomology collections—those small display boxes filled with bugs and butterflies—are especially attracting attention for their folk art nature.

Calendar, 1957, front shows boy and prize pig, black-and-white photos, F.W. Bosworth Co., Plymouth, Ind., 7" x 9-1/2" **8.00**
Cookbook, *Prize Winning Recipes: 4-H and F.H.A. Favorite Food Shows*, Suburban Propane Gas, 1957, paperback, 62 pages, worn spine, 8-1/2" x 5-1/2".....................................**2.00**
Fruit jar rings, full box, mkd "4-H"....**5.00**
Magazine, *National Geographic*, November 1948, feature on 4-H clubs, worn spine......................................**6.50**
Paperweight, gold plated metal, round base, clover finial, 2 1/2" h.............**9.00**
Pin
1st Year, 1950s.............................**2.50**
3rd Year, mkd "Presented by N.Y. State Bankers Assn,"...........................**3.00**
4th Year, green, black and silver, clover logo, mkd "sterling," orig card **5.00**
1987 Ohio State Fair Participant, shaped like state of Ohio............**3.50**
Junior Leadership, gold, enameled clover logo, 1960s........................**4.25**
Membership Pin, Guernsey 4-H Club, full color, plastic, c1940 ....**15.00**
Songbook, *National 4-H Club Songbook*, 1954, softcover, 65 pgs.................**6.00**
Tie tac, gold, green enamel clover logo **3.25**
U.S. postage stamps, SC1005, 4-H club issue, 1952, full sheet of 50, unused **14.50**

❖ Farber Brothers/Krome Kraft

Farber Brothers was located in New York City, from 1919 to 1965. Their principal business derived from the sale of fine table accessories. Some of these items had ceramic or glass inserts by such quality manufacturers as Lenox and Cambridge. The bases were of chrome, silver plate, or mosaic gold. Most of their output was marked Farber Brothers, and they did use some paper labels with the Krome Kraft name.

Candlesticks, Cambridge nude stem, one with cracked base, 8-1/2" h, pr **125.00**
Cocktail shaker, Bakelite handle, 12-1/2" h **85.00**
Compote, Cambridge amber bowl, chrome holder, 7-1/4" h................**50.00**
Cordial set, figural woman center, 6 different colored 2-1/8" h glasses, chrome tray **125.00**
Decanter, Cambridge, Duchess, filigree, amber, 12" h................................**75.00**
Goblet, amber glass bowl, chrome stem, 5-7/8" h, set of 4........................**125.00**
Mustard, cov, cobalt Cambridge bowl, chrome lid...................................**50.00**
Percolator set, hammered chrome, Bakelite handles, electric percolator, creamer, sugar and tray **45.00**
Salt and pepper shakers, Cambridge, amber, 2-1/2" h, pr **30.00**
Shaker, textured surface, Bakelite handle, stamped "Krome Kraft by Farber Bros."................................**45.00**
Tray, crystal and chrome, 9-1/2" l ...**42.00**
Tumbler, 12-oz, varied colors, Cambridge #5633, set of 6 ....**150.00**
Wine, Cambridge, amethyst, 6-1/2" h, set of 6 ....**150.00**

Farber Bros/Krome Kraft, decanter and glasses set, gold Cambridge glass inserts, $245.

❖ Fans, Electric

Summer heat often melts other collectors, but such is not the case for those who specialize in electric fans. Almost every manufacturer has made electric fans, and there are many varieties to collect. Look for clever designs, well-made fans, and well-known names. Visually check the wiring and other mechanics before plugging in any electrical appliance. Then sit back and enjoy the breeze!

References: John M. Witt, *Collector's Guide to Electric Fans*, Collector Books, 1997; ——, *Witt's Field Guide to Electric Desk Fans*, self-published, 1993.

Collectors' Club: American Fan Collector Assoc, P.O. Box 5473, Sarasota, FL 34277.

Ceiling, Emerson CF28, 2-blade, restored **3,000.00**
Desk, oscillating, brass cage and blades, orig tags **125.00**
Floor model, Westinghouse, adjustable, quatrefoil metal standard, cast iron base, metal "Westinghouse" tag, mid 20th C, 58" h **175.00**
Tabletop
Emerson, #444A, black, gold painted blades, 2-speed, 1926, 8" **35.00**
General Electric, #2364327, Whiz, polished brass blades, glossy hunter green finish, 1924, 9"...............**40.00**
Knapp-Monarch, brown finish, 1940, 9" **18.00**
Polar Cub, black metal base, mkd "A.C. Gilbert, New Haven, Conn.," 8-1/2" dia, 11" h **65.00**
Robbins & Meyers, 4 blades, oscillating, cast iron base **150.00**
Westinghouse, mkd "USA Cat. N 12LAH, Part No. Y-35258".........**28.00**

❖ Fans, Hand-Held, Advertising

Fans, hand (back), Back of fan, showing advertising for Helms & Son, Funeral Home, Lewisville, Indiana, A Sympathetic Courteous Service, 24 Hour Ambulance Service, North American Cal. Co., Chicago, Il, patent number at bottom, $15.

Today we tend to think of fans as decorative accessories, but for our ancestors, they were the primary means of cooling themselves. Collectors can find a wide range of advertising fans, usually with a decorative image on one side and advertising on the back. The highest value usually is achieved when the fan is sold near where the original advertiser was located.

For additional listings, see *Warman's Antiques & Collectible.*

> Buyer beware!
> If it looks old, it must be old, right? WRONG! When it comes to the antiques and collectibles market, looks can be deceiving—and costly.
> Among the many reproductions and fantasy items found at flea markets are a number of cardboard fans with wooden handles. Having been aged to look old, these reproductions can easily fool unsuspecting buyers, who think they're acquiring an authentic antique.
> The following is a partial listing of the fans available. We spotted these for sale on the Internet, where they were offered as new collectibles for $8 apiece. Unfortunately, many of these fans are finding their way onto the secondary market, where they are passed off as originals and priced accordingly.
>
> Cherub with mandolin
> Darkie Toothpaste
> Lou's Diner and Rib Shack, Mobile, Ala.
> Null's Dairy Fan
> Pickaninny Restaurant
> Shirley Temple RC Cola
> Smoking Joe's Restaurant
> Sozodont "National Dentifrice"
> Uncle Remus Syrup
> Wegman Piano

Burke Drug Co., The Real Drug Store, Morganton, N.C., cardboard, wooden handle, 14-3/4" h, 9-1/2" w...........**16.00**

Independent Life and Accident Insurance Co., Jacksonville, Fla., "Cooling Off," shows naked child walking toward river, Scheer, #3183, cardboard, wooden handle.............**8.00**

M-F-A, Mutual Insurance Co., Little Rock, Ark., cardboard, wooden handle, creases, tear, 12" h **7.00**

Moxie, Eileen Perry, copyright 1925, all paper, edge wear, 8-3/8" x 5-1/4" **95.00**

Southern belles in cypress garden, 3 panels, funeral home adv on back **15.00**

Tip-Top Bread, diecut cardboard, full color stars artwork, reverse with six red, white, and blue illus of suggested

snacks using bread, c1930, 7-1/4" x 9-1/4" **25.00**

Wallace's Farmer and Iowa Homestead Newspaper, little girl standing in front of school, holding book and blue metal lunch box, 1955, 10" w, 10-1/2" h **35.00**

❖ Farm Collectibles

Farm collectors are saving an important part of our American heritage. Collecting and protecting the items related to or used on a farm will give future generations insights into the amount of work farming entailed.

References: C.H. Wendel, *Encyclopedia of American Farm Implements & Antiques,* Krause Publications, 1997; ——, *Unusual Vintage Tractors,* Krause Publications, 1996.

Periodicals: *Antique Power,* P.O. Box 1000, Westerville, OH 43081; *Belt Pulley,* P.O. Box 83, Nokomis, IL 62075; *Country Wagon Journal,* P.O. Box 331, W Milford, NJ 07480; *Farm Antiques News,* 812 N 3rd St, Tarkio, MO 64491; *Farm Collector,* 1503 SW 42nd St, Topeka, KS 66609; *Rusty Iron Monthly,* P.O. Box 342, Sandwich, IL 60548; *Tractor Classics,* P.O. Box 191, Listowel, Ontario N4H 3HE Canada; *Turtle River Toy News & Oliver Collector's News,* RR1, Box 44, Manvel, ND 58256.

Collectors' Clubs: Antique Engine, Tractor & Toy Club, 5731 Paradise Rd, Slatington, PA 18080; Cast Iron Seat Collectors Assoc, P.O. Box 14, Ionia, MO 65335; Early American Steam Engine & Old Equipment Soc, P.O. Box 652, Red Lion, PA 17356; Farm Machinery Advertising Collectors, 10108 Tamarack Dr., Vienna, VA 22182; The Feedsack Club, 25 S Starr Ave, Apt. 16, Pittsburgh, PA 15202-3424; International Harvester Collectibles, 310 Busse Hwy., Suite 250, Park Ridge, IL 60068-3251.

Advertisement, 1948 Oliver Model 88 industrial tractor, black-and-white, 10-1/4" x 7-1/2"..................................**20.00**

Book, *Farm Life on The South Plains Of Texas* **18.50**

Booklet, International Harvester, *Make Soil Productive,* 64 pgs, 1931 ....**8.50**

Farm Collectibles Sign, painted tin, advertising, "Best at the Price The Ebbert Owensboro, Ky and always the same," young man and lady picking apples, horse drawn cart, chickens in foreground "In The Shade of the Old Apple Tree", 23-1/2" x 34-1/2" $275.

Farm Collectibles Six early farming pamphlets: Moline Plow Co.; John Deere, Moline, Ill.; Pattee Plow Company, Monmouth, Illinois; David Bradley Mafg. Co., Chicago, Ill; Avery Mfg. Co., Peoria, Ill. And Grand Detour Plow Company, Dixon, Illinois, $250.

Bridle rosette, heart shape **38.50**
Cider press, oak and other hardwoods, old refinish, mortised and pegged, base with 4 legs, threaded wooden shaft missing its handle, 44" h, 26" w, 15" d..**220.00**
Feed sack, printed cloth
   Advertising type...........................**18.00**
   All over floral dec..........................**15.00**
Feed chest, smoke-decor, white ground with black smoke, slant-lid, 3 interior compartments, turned legs with ball feet, wear, mouse holes, 35-1/2" h, 53-1/4" w, 24" d **375.00**
Flour sack, printed paper, Harvest Queen Improved Roller Flour, Red Mills, shows woman in bonnet, Centre Hill, Pa., framed, soiled, stains, 20" h, 14" w **50.00**
Goat yoke, single, wood, bentwood bow **60.00**
Hay fork, wooden, 4-prong, 3 wooden prongs on front with 4th mounted on handle with iron bracket, 84" l......**60.00**
Hay hook, cast iron with wood handle, 14" l...**15.00**
Magazine, *Farm Journal,* Feb. 1963, chickens on cover..........................**4.00**
Medallion, John Deere, front shows bust of John Deere and "He gave the world the steel plow," back shows wagon train and plow with "John Deere Quality Farm Equipment, since 1837".....**35.00**
Memo book, Agrico Fertilizer, 1947 calendar **3.50**
Milking stool, wooden, crescent-shaped seat, 3 round splayed stake legs, primitive, refinished, 8" h, 17" w, 7" d **35.00**
Operator's manual
   Allis-Chalmers, model B front-mounted planter, 600 series, soiling..........**8.25**
   Ford, model 8N tractor, 1948 ....**50.00**
   John Deere, horse-drawn cultivator, 7 pgs, stains, folds......................**40.00**

Farm Collectibles, chicken house, double decker, steel, wooden slat perches, maker's name emb on top, $125.

Tractor, International, red, white accents, black steering wheel, $195.

Fast Food Collectibles, Pizza Hut Play-Doh Make-A-Meal playset, played with condition, orig box with wear, $5.

John Deere, sweep-type planting and fertilizing attachments for tractor cultivators, light soiling...............**5.25**

Pinback button, celluloid, Purina Chicken Chowder, red and white checkered feed sack, blue ground, white slogan "If Chicken Chowder Won't Make Your Hens Lay They Must Be Roosters," 1920s.....................**10.00**

Sickle, 21" l, wooden frame, iron blade **25.00**

Sign, paper, Buckeye, Our New Low Down Drills, They Are Endorsed And Demanded, central scene of man driving 2-horse team pulling drill, 4 smaller images of horse-drawn equipment, 30" h, 21-1/4" w.......**715.00**

Tape measure, metal, Kent Feeds, Nichols (Iowa) Grain and Feed, 2-digit phone number, scratches, 2" dia..**25.00**

❖ Farm Toys

Toy and farm machinery manufacturers have provided young farmers with wonderfully detailed farm toys. Today's collectors are eager to find good examples and can find additions to their collections ranging from toys from the 1920s to the present.

Periodicals: *Toy Tractor Times*, P.O. Box 156, Osage, IA 50461; *Turtle River Toy News & Oliver Collector's News*, RR1, Box 44, Manvel, ND 58256. *Toy Farmer*, 7496 106th Ave. SE, LaMoure, ND 58458-9404 www.toyfarmer.com.

Collectors' Clubs: Antique Engine, Tractor & Toy Club, 5731 Paradise Rd, Slatington, PA 18080; CTM Farm Toy & Collectors Club, P.O. Box 489, Rocanville, Saskatchewan S0A 3L0 Canada; Ertl Replicas Collectors' Club, Hwys 136 and 20, Dyersville, IA 52040; Farm Toy Collectors Club, P.O. Box 38, Boxholm, IA 50040.

Combine

Claas, Matchbox, #65C, red body, yellow head, 1967, orig box with wear..**9.50**

Co-op, litho tin, friction, Marx, 6" l **30.00**

Matchbox, #51, 1978, MIB **8.00**

Corn picker, John Deere, steel, Ertl **55.00**

Delivery wagon, Heffield Farms, articulated horse, 21-1/2" l, considerable wear and paint loss **320.00**

Harrow, tandem disc, Corgi, 1967 ..**15.00**

Hay rack, Arcade, 7" l **85.00**

Manure spreader, McCormick-Deering, team of horses, Arcade...............**65.00**

Plow, Case, Ertl **10.00**

Steam engine, Mamod, English, c1965, 6-3/4" h, 10" l **275.00**

Set, Corgi, No. 55 Fordson Tractor, No. 51 Tipping Trailer, No. 438 Land Rover, No. 101 Flat Trailer, 1962-64 .....**280.00**

Thresher, McCormick-Deering, Arcade, gray and cream wheels, red lining, chromed chute and stacker, 12" l **320.00**

Tractor

Auburn Rubber, blue, 1930s, 1 tire losing rubber, 4-3/4" l **45.00**

Farmall, 1991 National Farm Toy Show, Ertl, 9" l.....................................**40.00**

Fordson, No. 273, Arcade, 1928, 3-7/8" l...**95.00**

International, Tootsietoy **10.00**

John Deere, Matchbox, #50, green body, 1964 ....**15.00**

Tru-Scale, 4-1/2" h, 8" l **125.00**

Truck

Chevrolet livestock truck, Smith-Miller, unpainted cab and trailer, 1946 ....**175.00**

Farm stake truck, Tonka, #0404, 1963 ....**60.00**

Farm truck, battery-op, litho tin, Japan, 1950s, 9-1/4" l **150.00**

❖ Fast Food Collectibles

The hamburger has long been a popular American food, and fast food restaurants have certainly done their best to convince us that they hold the secret to the perfect sandwich. And, in an effort to increase

sales and generate future purchases, they've added toys and premiums. These special extras have become an interesting part of the collectibles marketplace.

Reference: Robert J. Sodaro, *Kiddie Meal Collectibles*, Krause Publications, 2001. Elizabeth A. Stephan, *Ultimate Guide to Fast Food Collectibles*, Krause Publications, 1999. Gail Pope and Keith Hammond, *Fast Food Toys*, 2nd ed, Schiffer Publishing, 1998.

Periodicals: *The Fast Food Collectors Express*, P.O. Box 221, Mayview, MO 64071-0221.

For additional listings, see *Warman's Americana & Collectibles* and McDonald's in this edition.

Ashtray, Big Boy, heavy glass, orange image and inscription "Frisch's Big Boy," 1968, 3-1/2" dia **12.00**

Bowl, plastic, Dairy Queen, yellow, Schroeder Paper Co., Cincinnati....**9.00**

Box, Kentucky Fried Chicken, 1969 **35.00**

Building

Bob's Big Boy Restaurant, Lefton, NRFB, 6" h, 8" w **45.00**

McDonald's, Dept 56 ....**55.00**

Calendar, Burger King, Olympic games theme, 1980 ....**4.00**

Coloring book, *Sambo's Restaurant Family Funbook Activity Book*, 1978, unused **42.00**

Doll, Burger King, molded plastic head and hands, 1980, 22" h...............**35.00**

Glider, King Glider, Burger King, Styrofoam, 1978.............................**2.50**

Menu, Denny's, plastic coated, c1960 ....**2.50**

Mug

Hardees Breakfast Club, 1993.......**3.00**

Hardees Rise and Shine Homemade Biscuits, ceramic, 1984...............**6.00**

Lendy's Hamburgers, ftd, ceramic, shows character in Lendy's hat carrying a double hamburger ...**44.00**

Paperweight, Wendy's, "Decade II," metal and celluloid **29.00**

Pen, pencil and calculator set, Wendy's
....**6.00**
Pinback button
Big Boy Club, red, white, blue, and
brown hair, c1950 ....**65.00**
Vote for Col. Sanders, KFC, blue and
white, 1972, 1-1/2" dia..............**24.00**
Puppet, hand, A & W Root Beer bear,
cloth...**12.00**
Salad Plate, Archie's Lobster House at
top, Roanoke, VA at bottom, mkd
"Sterling Vertified China, East
Liverpool, Ohio, USA," 7-1/4" dia .**35.00**
Spoon, red plastic, long handle, ice
cream cone top **1.00**
Teddy bear, Burger King, Crayola blue
bear, 1986, 7" h..............................**8.00**
Trading Cards, Burger King, The Empire
Strikes Back, complete set of 36 .**37.50**
Whistle, Dairy Queen, white plastic ice
cream on tan cone **4.00**

❖ Fenton Glass

Founded by Frank L. Fenton in 1905 in
Martin's Ferry, Ohio, Fenton first decorated
glassware for other makers. By 1907, the
company was making its own glass and had
relocated to Williamstown, West Virginia.
Today the company is still producing quality
glass, and collectors are encouraged to visit
the factory site and museum in
Williamstown. Fenton family members and
their decorators frequently sign pieces. The
Dec, 2002, passing of Bill Fenton, may
cause pieces with his signature to increase.

References: There are several very good
older reference books about Fenton Glass.

Periodicals: *Butterfly Net*, 302 Pheasant
Run, Kaukauna, WI 54130; *Glass
Messenger*, 700 Elizabeth St, Williamstown,
WV 26187.

Collectors' Clubs: Fenton Art Glass
Collectors of America, P.O. Box 384,
Williamstown, WV 26187; National Fenton
Glass Soc, P.O. Box 4008, Marietta, OH
45750.

For additional listings and a detailed list of
reference books, see *Warman's Antiques &
Collectibles* and *Warman's Glass*.

Ashtray, Hobnail, topaz opalescent, fan
shape **15.00**
Banana bowl, Silver Crest, low, ftd.**50.00**
Basket, Silver Crest, crystal handle
....**45.00**
Bell, Christmas Morn.......................**45.00**
Bicentennial Plate, white milk glass, orig
box and wrappings **25.00**
Bonbon
Dolphin, handle, green **32.50**
Rosalene Butterfly, 2 handles **35.00**
Bowl
Gold Crest, 8" dia.........................**40.00**
Peach Crest, shell shape, 10" dia **75.00**

Rosalene, basketweave **32.00**

Fenton Glass, cat, opaque white ground, hand painted dec, $24.

Cake dish, Pink Pastel, ftd, 12-1/2" dia
....**65.00**
Candlesticks, pr
Ming, cornucopia, 5" h, pr **50.00**
Silvertone, Sheffield, blue **24.00**
Candy dish, cov
Custard, hp pink daffodils, sgd "Louise
Piper" **165.00**
Teardrop, white............................**55.00**
Cocktail Shaker, #6120 Plymouth,
Crystal **55.00**
Compote, Waterlily, Rosalene.........**30.00**
Condiment set, Teardrop, white **55.00**
Creamer
Coin Dot, Cranberry Opalescent, 4"
....**65.00**
Diamond Optic, ruby **30.00**
Cruet, Coin Dot, cranberry opalescent
....**120.00**
Epergne, Petite French Opal, 4" h ..**40.00**
Fairy Light, Colonial Amber, Hobnail, 3
pcs..**25.00**
Float bowl, Silver Crest, 13" dia **45.00**
Flower frog, Nymph, blue opalescent, 6-
3/4" h, 2-3/4" w...........................**48.00**
Goblet, Lincoln Inn, red..................**24.00**
Hat, Coin Dot, French Opal **45.00**
Hurricane Lamp, five petal blue
dogwood dec................................**75.00**
Perfume bottle, Peach Crest, DeVilbiss
....**75.00**
Pitcher, Coin Dot, cranberry opalescent
....**65.00**
Plate
Fenton Rose, dolphin handles, #1621,
6" dia.......................................**27.50**
Ming Rose, #107, 8" dia.............**32.00**

Fenton Glass, punch bowl, pedestal, Silver Crest, $275.

Powder Box, Wave Crest, blue overlay
....**120.00**
Rose bowl, Black Rose, 6-1/2" dia.**40.00**
Salt and pepper shakers, Hobnail,
cranberry opalescent, flat, #3806, pr
....**50.00**
Sherbet, Plymouth, amber **15.00**
Tumbler, ftd, Lincoln Inn, red, 5-oz.**25.00**
Vase
5" h, Rose Crest, triangle............**55.00**
6-3/4" h, Silver Crest, jack-in-the-pulpit
....**45.00**
7" h, Burmese, roses, sgd "Sue Foster"
....**120.00**
10" h, Apple Tree, milk glass........**95.00**
11" h, cranberry Snow Crest, swirl
....**60.00**

❖ Fiesta

Frederick Rhead designed this popular
Homer Laughlin pattern. It was first
introduced in 1936 and became a real hit
after a vigorous marketing campaign in the
early 1940s. Original colors were red, dark
blue, light green, brilliant yellow, and ivory.
Turquoise was added in 1937. Red was
removed in 1943, but brought back in 1959.
Light green, dark blue, and ivory were
retired in 1951 and replaced by forest
green, rose, chartreuse, and gray. Medium
green was added in the late 1950s. By
1969, the popular pattern was redesigned
and finally discontinued in 1972. However,
by 1986, Homer Laughlin had reintroduced
the pattern, but in a new formula and with
new colors, including a darker blue, black,
white, apricot, rose, and even pastels some
years later.

Reference: Jeffrey B. Snyder, *Fiesta:
Homer Laughlin China Company's Colorful
Dinnerware,* 4th ed., Schiffer Publishing,
2002.

Collectors' Clubs: Fiesta Club of America,
P.O. Box 15383, Loves Park, IL 61132;
Fiesta Collectors Club, 19238 Dorchester
Circle, Strongsville, OH 44136.

For additional listings, see *Warman's Antiques & Collectibles,* *Warman's Americana & Collectibles,* and *Warman's American Pottery & Porcelain.*

Ashtray
Forest green	60.00
Red	60.00
Turquoise	50.00
Yellow	40.00

Bud vase, ivory, 6-1/2" h 65.00
Candleholders, pr
Bulb, turquoise	115.00
Bulb, yellow	110.00
Tripod, red	357.50
Tripod, light green	330.00

Carafe
Light green	185.00
Red	275.00

Casserole
Ivory	88.00
Yellow, large	175.00

Chop Plate, 14-1/4" d
Chartreuse	65.00
Gray	70.00

Coffeepot, cov
Green	225.00
Ivory	245.00

Creamer
Chartreuse	40.00
Cobalt blue, stick handle	50.00
Medium Green	80.00
Rose	35.00

Cream soup
Cobalt blue	110.00
Red	55.00
Turquoise	165.00
Yellow	100.00

Cup and saucer, pair
Cobalt blue	155.00
Medium green	255.00
Red	100.00
Turquoise	155.00

Egg cup
Cobaltblue	88.00
Forest green	105.00
Gray	125.00
Red	145.00
Rose	110.00

Fruit bowl, 11-3/4" dia
Cobalt blue	275.00
Ivory	250.00
Red	330.00
Yellow	195.00

Juice Pitcher, disc, 5-1/2" h
Cobalt blue	135.00
Yellow	60.00

Juice Tumbler, 4-1/2" h
Cobalt blue	45.00
Light green	55.00

Rose	60.00

Mixing Bowl
#1, red	180.00
#2, cobalt blue	200.00
#3, ivory	80.00
#4, light green	85.00
#5, turquoise	85.00
#6, light green	110.00
#7, cobalt blue	200.00

Mug
Chartreuse	80.00
Cobalt blue	55.00
Gray	72.00
Ivory	72.00
Medium green	140.00
Red	75.00

Nappy, 8-1/2" dia
Cobalt blue	35.00
Medium green	125.00
Red	33.00

Nappy, 9-1/2" dia
Cobalt blue	45.00
Light green	40.00
Turquoise	24.00

Plate, 6" dia
Ivory	35.00
Medium green	145.00
Turquoise	40.00

Plate, 7" dia
Green	6.50
Turquoise	7.50

Plate, 9" dia
Gray	35.00
Medium green	100.00
Red	55.00
Turquoise	60.00
Yellow	45.00

Platter
Medium green	165.00
Turquoise	24.00
Red	50.00
Rose	40.00

Relish, yellow base, cobalt blue center, four yellow inserts, gold trim 135.00
Salad Bowl, 9-3/8" d, yellow 100.00
Salt and Pepper Shakers, pr
Cobalt blue	24.00
Yellow	40.00

Stack set, cobalt and green bowls, orange lid 140.00
Sugar bowl, cov
Gray	80.00
Rose	70.00

Sweets compote, light green 75.00
Syrup, ivory 275.00
Teapot, medium
Cobalt blue	145.00
Red	100.00
Yellow	100.00

Teapot, large

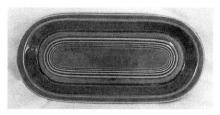

Fiesta, utility tray, turquoise, $28.

Light green	180.00
Red	195.00

Utility Tray
Cobalt blue	17.50
Light green	25.00
Red	70.00
Turquoise	20.00

Vase, 8" h
Ivory	440.00
Light green	475.00
Turquoise	415.00
Yellow	470.00

Vase, 10" h
Light green	525.00
Red	660.00
Yellow	635.00

Vase, 12" h
Ivory	660.00
Yellow	770.00

Water pitcher, disc
Chartreuse	165.00
Cobalt blue	145.00
Forest green	150.00
Light green	100.00
Red	120.00
Turquoise	135.00

Water tumbler
Cobalt blue	80.00
Ivory	72.00
Red	75.00

❖ Figurines

Collectors will usually find an assortment of figurines to pick from while browsing at their favorite flea market. Some specialize in certain types of figurines, while others concentrate on specific makers

Aloha, Treasure Craft, 1959 ....45.00
Angel Fish, green "Japan" mark, 2" h
..............7.00
Blue jar, mkd "Homco" 25.00
Dove, Artesania Rinconada, retired 1987
..............90.00
Friar, holding sausages, pewter and ceramic, 3-1/4" h 50.00
Girl with watering can, Japan 35.00
Graduate, Pen Delflin, hp stonecraft
..............85.00
Lion and child, porcelain, mkd "Japan" on bottom, 5" w, 4" h 38.00

Girl, standing, pink sunbonnet, green dress, white cat at feet, cork on base, orig paper label "Coventry Ware, 2121C" $5.

Man, glass, blue head, hands, and shows, applied bushy hair, 4" h....**12.00**
Oriental girl, 6" h **15.00**
Parrot, chip on tail **15.00**
Polar Pal, paddling kayak, with Malamute puppy, icy blue pool base, Westland Resin, retired.............................**35.00**
Ram, small chip on base, 6-1/4" h ..**10.00**
Rottweiler, Beswick, 5-3/4" h..........**95.00**
Snowbunny, "I'll Love You Forever," Dept 56, 4-3/4" h...............................**15.00**
Wild Rabbit, Artesania Rinconada, retired 1995 ....**100.00**
Woman, wearing evening gown, holding feather fan **12.00**

❖ Finch, Kay

Kay Finch started her pottery in her California home around 1935. She was eventually joined by her husband, Braden, and son, George—artists and sculptors in their own right. Together, they produced interesting figures and tableware until 1963.

Angel, white and blue, 4-1/2" h.......**95.00**
Bank, Sassy Pig.............................**165.00**
Bowl, egg shape, daisies at top, pink ext, Kay Finch pink int., mkd, 5-1/2" l, 3-3/4" h...**95.00**
Candleholder, white flower, 14" h ..**35.00**
Dish, shell, chartreuse, mkd, 12" x 10" **42.00**
Figure
   Ambrosia Persian Cat, 10-3/4" h**600.00**
   Bunny, 3" h **160.00**
   Cherub **160.00**
   Godey Lady, chip, 8-7/8" h..........**45.00**
   Lamb, pink, standing on rear legs, 5-1/2" h **95.00**

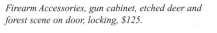

Kay Finch, plate, cat face, pink, $65.

   Muff the Cat, 3-1/2" h.................**75.00**
   Owl, Tootsie, 3-3/4" h **75.00**
   Pheasant Boy, chip.......................**35.00**
   Pheasant Girl **50.00**
   Smiley Pig, 6-3/4" h, 8" l **350.00**
Mug, Santa, #4950 ....**145.00**
Planter
   Baby block and bear **100.00**
   Jezzy the kitten, 7" h.................**185.00**
Soup tureen, turkey **500.00**
Wall pocket, Santa **90.00**

❖ Firearms Accessories

Collectors of firearm accessories and related memorabilia have found that flea markets are great sources for adding to their collections. Collectors of firearms are well advised to ask to see any required licenses on the part of vendors hey are dealing with. Some states are getting strict about this collecting area. For that reason, we've decided not to include firearms prices in this edition, as fewer quality dealers are choosing to use flea markets to sell guns. Memorabilia, advertising, and related items are still sold at general flea markets, and those items are covered here.

References: Ned Schwing, *2003 Standard Catalog of Firearms*, 13th ed, Krause Publications, 2003; John Ogle, *Colt Memorabilia Price Guide*, Krause Publications, 1998; John Walter, *Rifles of the World*, Krause Publications, 1998.

Periodicals: *Gun List,* 700 E State St, Iola, WI 54990; *Military Trader*, P.O. Box 1050, Dubuque, IA 52004; *The Gun Report*, P.O. Box 38, Aledo, IL 61231.

Collectors' Club: The Winchester Arms Collectors Assoc, P.O. Box 6754, Great Falls, MT 59406.

Firearm Accessories, gun cabinet, etched deer and forest scene on door, locking, $125.

Box
   Federal Hi-Power Rifled Slugs, shotgun shells, 5-count **22.00**
   Hoppe's Gun Cleaning Patches, 1940, wear...**22.00**
   Monark, 16-gauge shotgun shells, Federal Cartridge Corp., Minneapolis **45.00**
   Wards Red Head, 12-gauge shotgun shells, shows goose **25.00**
Bullet mold, Winchester, cast iron with wooden handle............................**65.00**
Check
   Colt firearms founder Sam Colt, Phoenix Bank, Hartford **125.00**
   Sharps Rifle Co., Bridgeport, Conn., 1878...**75.00**
Folder, diecut, shotgun shape, Winchester New Rival Shells, blue, yellow and red stiff paper, 1930s, 2" x 6-1/4"...**85.00**
Pinback button
   Peters Ammunition, red, white and blue, gold letters, c1910 ....**50.00**
   Shoot Peters Shells, brass and red shell on white ground, Pulver Co., early 1900s...............................**40.00**
   Winchester Products, red and white "W" on blue and silver design, early 1900s......................................**40.00**
Tin, Dupont Superfine Gun Powder, paper label shows animals, 6" h ..**79.00**
Trophy cup, Pennsylvania Gun Club, 1902, wood, pewter trim and handle, mkd "Smith Patterson & Co., Boston" **150.00**

❖ Firefighters

Hats off to firefighters, those brave men and women who help others in time of need. Many of them also collect fire memorabilia.

Periodical: *Fire Apparatus Journal*, P.O. Box 121205, Staten Island, NY 10314.

Collectors' Clubs: Antique Fire Apparatus Club of America, 5420 S Kedvale Ave, Chicago, IL 60632; Fire Collectors Club, P.O. Box 992, Milwaukee, WI 53201; Fire Mark Circle of the Americas, 2859 Marlin Dr, Chamblee, GA 30341; Great Lakes International Antique Fire Apparatus Assoc, 4457 285th St, Toledo, OH 43611; International Fire Buff Associates, 7509 Chesapeake Ave, Baltimore, MD 21219; Society for the Preservation & Appreciation of Motor Fire Apparatus in America, P.O. Box 2005, Syracuse, NY 13320.

Advertising button, Knox's Gelatine Running Team, Johnstown, text around bottom "Compliments of Tryon Hook & Ladder Co.," Johnstown, NY, young Black cook, large bowl of gelatin, and cookbook, blue text letters "Taint Nun Too Much Cos It's Knox's," orig back Pulver paper, 2" dia....................**250.00**
Badge, Mineola Fire Dept, relief image of fire hydrant on 1 side, hook and ladder on other, c1950, 2" x 2"................**10.00**
Bucket, galvanized tin, red lettering, "Fire Only"...**35.00**
Commemorative Mug, glass, Roslyn Fire Company, Roslyn, PA, May 21, 1983, Mack Aerialscope Fire Truck **15.00**
Dress hat, front reads "Fire Dept Chicago," black, red piping **25.00**
Figurine, Real Heroes Top Jake Firefighter, firefighter in full gear, Ertl, 1998, 12" h, NRFB........................**35.00**
Fire Engine Name Plate
   Ahrens-Fox....................................**15.00**
   LaFrance **17.50**
   Mack Trucks, bulldog....................**25.00**
Fire extinguisher, Fyr Fyter Fire Fighter Model A, brass **45.00**
Helmet, Quakertown Fire Dept, No. 1, black, leather shield, orig liner **75.00**
Hose nozzle, brass **50.00**
Liquor decanter, Fireman's Thirst Extinguisher **20.00**
Patch, Texas State Fireman's Assoc, 3-7/8" dia **7.50**
Pinback button, celluloid, "Firemen's Celebration," on ribbon, shows fireman, 1958, 1-1/4" dia, 3-3/4" l **18.00**
Post Card, real photo, unused
   Firemen searching for victims of 1906 fire, unused...............................**10.00**
   Main Fire Station, Water Street, Piqua, OH, unused **5.00**

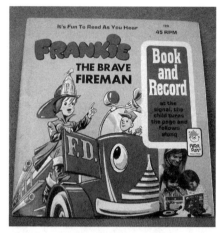
Child's storybook record, Frankie the Brave Fireman, *Peter Pan Records, 45 rpm, 1959, $15.*

   Quakertown, PA, firehouse and borough hall, unused **8.00**
Ribbon, 1958, Firemen's Celebration, multicolored pinback, some wear to 3-3/4" l ribbon **18.00**
Stein, Tribute to American Firefighters, Avon, 1989, 8" h............................**40.00**
Tie Tac, 1/2" d, "Member, County Firemen's Ass'n", 10K gold mounting, keystone shape, blue and rust colored enamel, center white enamel "6"..**30.00**
Toy
   Chief's car, litho tin, battery op, Linemar, Japan, 1950s, MIB...**225.00**
   Helmet, Emergency 51, wear.......**40.00**
   Rampwalker, fireman with hose, Marx **110.00**
Watch Fob, 1-1/4" d, aluminum, accepted by small red fire helmet, New Kensington, PA, firehouse, inscription "1928 Wet Penna. Volunteer Fireman's Assn," back reads "33rd Annual Convention/The Aluminum City/Aug 1926," black leather strap **15.00**
Wrench, brass, 7-function, polished, lacquered, 12-3/4" x 3-1/4" **98.00**

❖ Fire-King

Made by Anchor Hocking Glass Co., Fire-King is currently one of the hottest segments of the glass market. Production of ovenproof Fire-King glass began in 1942 and continued until 1972. Dinnerware was made in several patterns, and a variety of colors, including azurite, forest green, gray, ivory, jade-ite, peach luster, pink, ruby red, sapphire blue, opaque turquoise, and white. Some pieces were also decorated with decals. Jade-ite items, a light green opaque color, are currently the most popular and command high prices. Fire-King also manufactured utilitarian kitchenware that is also quite popular with collectors.

References: Gene Florence, *Anchor Hocking's Fire King & More*, 2nd ed, Collector Books, 2000; ——, *Collectible Glassware from the 40's, 50's, 60's*, 5th ed, Collector Books, 2000; ——, *Kitchen Glassware of the Depression Years*, 6th ed, Collector Books, 1995 (2001 value update); Joe Keller and David Ross, *Jadite*, 2nd ed, Schiffer Publishing, 2000; Gary & Dale Kilgo and Jerry & Gail Wilkins, *Collectors Guide to Anchor Hocking's Fire-King Glassware*, K&W Collectibles Publisher, 1991; ——, *Collectors Guide to Anchor Hocking's Fire-King Glassware*, vol 2, K&W Collectibles Publisher, 1998.

Periodicals: *Fire-King Monthly*, P.O. Box 70594, Tuscaloosa, AL 35407; *Fire-King News*, K&W Collectibles, P.O. Box 374, Addison, AL 35540.

Fire-King, saucer, Swirl, jade-ite, 5-3/4" dia, $4.

Collectors' Club: Fire-King Collectors Club, 1161 Woodrow St, #3, Redwood City, CA 94061.

For additional listings, see *Warman's Americana & Collectibles*, *Warman's Glass*, and *Warman's Depression Glass*.

Dinnerware

Alice, Jade-ite
   Cup and saucer............................**12.00**
   Dinner plate..................................**70.00**
   Salad plate **14.00**
Charm, Azurite
   Bowl, 4-3/4 dia **5.00**
   Cereal bowl, 6" dia **18.00**
   Cup and saucer.............................**4.00**
   Luncheon plate..............................**5.00**
   Salad plate **15.00**
Golden Anniversary, white
   Bowl, 8" dia **6.00**
   Creamer **3.50**
   Cup and saucer.............................**5.00**
   Dinner plate..................................**3.00**
   Fruit bowl, 4-7/8" d **4.00**
   Plate, 7-1/2" d **2.00**
   Platter, oval..................................**10.00**
   Soup bowl **7.50**
   Sugar, open...................................**3.50**

Jane Ray

Berry bowl, ivory **55.00**
Cup and saucer.............................**15.00**
Demitasse cup and saucer, jade-ite
....**85.00**
Dinner plate, 9" dia, ivory.............**55.00**
Soup bowl, 7-5/8" dia **30.00**

Laurel Gray

Bowl, 4-1/2" dia **6.00**
Creamer and sugar **7.00**
Cup and saucer.............................**5.00**
Dinner plate...................................**8.00**
Serving plate, 11".........................**40.00**

Peach Luster

Bowl, 4-7/8" dia **4.50**
Creamer **4.50**
Cup and Saucer **6.00**
Custard Cup, ruffled.......................**1.00**
Dessert Bowl, 4-7/8" dia **4.00**
Dinner Plate, 9" dia **6.50**
Salad Plate, 7-1/2" dia **3.00**
Serving Plate, 11" dia **14.00**
Soup Bowl, 7-5/8" dia....................**9.50**
Sugar, cov **10.00**

Restaurant ware, Jade-ite, heavy

Bowl, 4-3/4" dia **15.00**
Cereal bowl, 5" dia **35.00**
Chili bowl......................................**15.00**
Creamer and sugar, cov...............**35.00**
Cup and saucer.............................**18.00**
Dinner plate, 9" dia.......................**32.00**
Grill plate **35.00**
Luncheon plate..............................**85.00**
Mug **15.00**
Platter, 9-1/4" l.............................**60.00**
Platter, 11-1/2" l...........................**65.00**
Salad plate **15.00**

Swirl, Azurite

Cup and saucer.............................**8.00**
Dinner plate..................................**8.50**
Platter, oval.................................**20.00**
Salad plate **7.00**

Swirl, Ivory

Cup and saucer.............................**7.00**
Dinner plate, orig label **11.00**
Soup, flat, orig label **12.00**
Starter set, orig pictorial box, 4 dinner
plates, 4 cups and saucers......**60.00**

Turquoise

Child's plate, divided, 7-1/2" dia ...**40.00**
Starter set, orig box **75.00**

Kitchenware

Red Dots

Grease jar, white **35.00**
Mixing bowl set, white, 7", 8" and 9"
dia **70.00**
Salt and pepper shakers, white, pr
....**45.00**

Stripes

Grease jar **35.00**
Salt and pepper shakers, pr........**37.50**

Swirl

Pie pan, orig label **15.00**
Range shaker, orig tulip top **24.00**

Tulip

Bowl, 9-1/2" dia **35.00**
Grease jar, ivory..........................**35.00**
Grease jar, white **35.00**

Turquoise, bowl, splashproof, 3-qt..**25.00**

Ovenware

Baker, Sapphire Blue, individual serving
size..**4.50**
Casserole, cov, Sapphire Blue, 1-pint
....**14.00**
Custard cup, crystal, orig label **3.00**
Loaf pan, Sapphire Blue.................**17.50**
Pie plate, crystal, 10-oz **4.00**
Utility bowl, Sapphire Blue, 7" dia..**14.00**

❖ Fireplace Collectibles

In addition to providing a place to hang your stocking at Christmas, fireplaces also serve as important decorative and functional elements. And, as such, they need to be accessorized. Flea markets are wonderful places to find interesting objects to accomplish this goal.

Andiron

Bulldog, cast iron, 16" h, pr........**880.00**
Woman, cast iron, 14" h, pr **165.00**

Fireplace andirons and matching tool set, brass, urn shaped finials, baluster shaped standards, spur feet, c1950, $50.

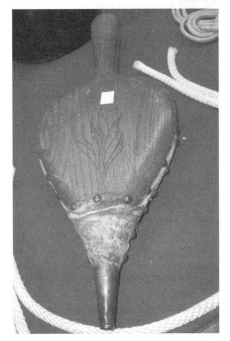

Fireplace bellows, wood with incised dec, leather sides, copper nozzle, studded sides, wear, $15.

Bellows, fruit and foliage decor, yellow
paint, green banding, 18" l........**330.00**
Broom, wooden handle, 49-1/4" l ...**35.00**
Coal hod, hammered brass, emb tavern
scenes, 25" h **90.00**
Fender, brass, reticulated front **245.00**
Fireback, cast iron, figures in relief, floral
garland border, floral basket cartouche
flanked by sphinx, dated 1663,
cracked, 26" x 16-1/2" **110.00**
Fire lighter, gun shape, Dunhill **90.00**
Fireplace, artificial, cast iron, electric,
Arts & Crafts style, 2 bulbs with
porcelain sockets, 21" w.............**375.00**
Fire screen
Oak, medallion decor, beadwork
molding, 27" h, 20" w...............**90.00**
Walnut frame, Persian embroidered
panel in center, c1930, 24" w, 39" h
....**225.00**
Log fork, wrought iron, long round
handle, cast-brass ovoid finial, some
rust, 44" l **25.00**
Mantle
Cast iron, late 19th C., 40" h, 43" w
....**1,200.00**
Oak, full columns, beveled mirror, 82"
h, 60" w..............................**1,400.00**
Shovel and tongs, wrought iron, brass
finials, 30" l, pr.............................**55.00**

❖ Fishbowl Ornaments

Fishbowl Ornaments, Oriental temple, bridge, and tea house, blues, tan, green, and cobalt blue, mkd "Japan", $5.

Perhaps you want to give Goldie a little company or a place to play hide and seek with her friends. Imaginative collectors can find an interesting assortment of aquatic ornaments to brighten their aquariums. Check that the paint is non-toxic and the item is waterproof.

Aquarium background panel, blues, greens **2.00**
Castle, ceramic
  4" h, 3-3/4" w, white and brown ...**16.00**
  4" h, 4-1/4" w, mkd Zenith, 1968..**12.00**
Ferns, flowers, vines, plastic, each **50**
Figure
  Deep Sea Diver..............................**2.00**
  Goldfish, ceramic, 3-1/2" l, pr.......**22.00**
  Mermaid, seated **3.00**
Pagoda, ceramic, blue, yellow, burgundy and green, 3-1/4" h, 3-1/2" w, Japan
  ....**16.00**

❖ Fisher, Harrison

Harrison Fisher was a well-known illustrator and portraitist of the 19th century. Many collectors search for illustrations that bear his signature.

Magazine cover
  Cosmopolitan, May 1919, Salvation Army Girl....................................**30.00**
  Ladies Home Journal, Oct, 1909, American Girls Abroad series, footer reads "The American Girl in the Netherlands," 9-1/2" x 14-3/4"...**25.00**
Postcard, typical view of American Girl series..**15.00**
Poster, "I Summon You to Comradeship in the Red Cross," WWI, heavy edge wear, 40" x 28" **335.00**
Print, framed
  "Fair Exhibitor", lady with bulldog, collie and Pekingese, copyright 1910,

Crowell Publishing, 8-1/2" x 11-3/4" **220.00**
"In Suspense," woman having tea, seated gentleman, copyright Charles Scribner & Sons, 12" x 17-1/2" **295.00**
Woman holding locket, c1910, 8" x 10" **125.00**
Watercolor, "Moonlit Romance," sgd, dated 1910, 9-1/2" x 14-1/2" ...**1,500.00**

❖ Fisher-Price Toys

What kid didn't play with Fisher-Price toys as a child? Founded in East Aurora, New York, in 1930, the company eventually became one of the leading producers of children's toys. Collectors still search for, and sometimes play with, all types of Fisher-Price items. Flea markets are prime hunting ground in the hunt for both old and new examples.

Fisher-Price Toys, ferris wheel, wind-up, orig riders missing, some play wear, $4.

Reference: Brad Cassity, *Fisher-Price Toys*, Collector Books, 2000; John J. Murray and Bruce Fox, *Fisher-Price, 1931-1963*, 2nd ed, Books Americana/Krause Publications, 1991.

Collectors' Club: Fisher-Price Collector's Club, 1442 N Ogden, Mesa, AZ 85205.

Bunny Cart, #311, mint **100.00**
Circus Train set, 4 pcs, 30" l **48.00**
Dollhouse, furniture, 1969, orig box **225.00**
Donald Duck Xylophone **65.00**
Dr. Doodle, #132, 1940, 10" h **95.00**
Hickory Dickory Dock, radio and clock **30.00**

Little People Farm Play Set, #2501, 1986, played-with cond, orig box .**55.00**
Little Snoopy, wood and plastic.....**18.50**

Fisher-Price Toys, Bingo, toddler walker, figural dog play center, plays "Bingo," color lights up, blue plastic walker with red handle, foldable, 1990s, $7.50.

Magic Key Mansion, six rooms, furnishings, 125 pc set..............**245.00**
Mickey Mouse Drummer **60.00**
Molly Mop, #190 ....**250.00**
Music Box, #795..........................**10.00**
Play Family Village, #997, 1973, most pcs included, played-with cond **65.00**
School House, 1971, played-with cond **55.00**
Windup Clock, #998, played-with cond **75.00**
Woodsey Squirrel **50.00**

❖ Fishing

Perhaps the only thing better than meandering through a flea market on a lazy summer afternoon is going to the waterhole to do a little fishing. Recently, several auction houses have established record-setting prices for lures, ephemera, and other related fishing items.

References: Arlan Carter, *19th Century Fishing Lures*, Collector Books, 2000; Dudley Murphy and Rick Edmisten, *Fishing Lure Collectibles*, 2nd ed, Collector Books, 2001.

Periodicals: *American Fly Fisher*, P.O. Box 42, Manchester, VT 05254; *Antique Angler Newsletter*, P.O. Box K, Stockton, NJ 08559; *Fishing Collectibles Magazine*, 2005 Tree

House Ln, Plano, TX 75023; *The Fisherman's Trader*, P.O. Box 203, Gillette, NJ 07933.

Collectors' Club: American Fish Decoy Assoc, 624 Merritt St, Fife Lake, MI 49633; National Fishing Lure Collectors Club, Box 4012, Reed Spring, MO 65737; Old Reel Collectors Assoc, 849 NE 70th Ave, Portland, OR 97213.

Badge, 1-3/4" d, Fishing, Trapping, Hunting License, NY, 1930...........**55.00**
Bobber
  Panfish float, hp, black, red and white stripes, 5" l...............**12.00**
  Pike float, hp, yellow, green and red stripes, 12" l...............**27.50**
Book
  Lures: The Guide to Sport Fishing, Keith C. Schuyler, 1955, dj.......**20.00**
  Practical Black Bass Fishing, Mark Sosin and Bill Dance, 1977, illus...............**10.00**
Creel, wicker, rear hinged door, 9-1/2" w, 8" d, 8" h, repairs.......**110.00**
Decoy, Ice King, perch, wood, painted, Bear Creek Co., 7" l.......**70.00**
Fishing License
  Connecticut, 1935, for resident use, yellow, black, and white.......**65.00**
  Pennsylvania, 1945, blue and white, black serial number.......**18.00**
Lure
  Carters Bestever, 3" l, white and red, pressed eyes.......**9.00**
  Creek Chub Co., Baby Beetle, yellow and green wings.......**40.00**
  Heddon, King Bassor, red, gold spot, glass eyes.......**35.00**
  Meadow Brook, rainbow, 1-1/4" l, orig box.......**120.00**
  Paw Paw, underwater minnow, green, and black, tack eyes, 3 hooks..**18.00**
  Pfleuger, polished nickel minnow, glass eyes, 5 hooks, 3-5/8" l.......**250.00**
  Shakespeare, mouse, white and red, thin body, glass eyes, 3-5/8" l...**30.00**
  South Bend, Panatella, green crackleback finish, glass eyes, orig box.......**50.00**
  Souvenir, Lucky Lure, Souv of Indian Lake, OH, 3-1/2" l, nude black female, MOC.......**130.00**
Reel
  Ambassador 5500C Silver, counter balance, handle, high speed gear rates.......**120.00**
  Hardy, Perfect Fly Reel, English, 3-3/8" x 1-1/4".......**150.00**
  Horton, #3, suede bag.......**425.00**
  Meek 33, Bluegrass, suede bag **425.00**
  Penn-Jic Master No. 500, 3" d.....**65.00**
  Pflueger 1420 1/2 templar, lightly scratched owner's name.......**175.00**

Keep your eyes open for this reel, it's one of the all time American classic reels, made by Edw Vom Hofe, c1920, in German silver and hard rubber, this one brought $6,820 at Lang's Auction.

  Shakespeare, tournament.......**110.00**
  Union Hardware Co., raised pillar type, nickel and brass.......**30.00**
Rod
  Bamboo, fly fishing, orig reel, wear.......**125.00**
  Hardy, split-bamboo fly, English, 2-pc, 1 tip, 7' l.......**250.00**
  Heddon Co., casting, nickel silver fittings, split-bamboo fly, fish decal brown wraps, bag and tube, 5-1/2' l.......**50.00**
  Montaque, bamboo, 2 tips, orig case.......**135.00**
  Shakespeare Co., premier model, 3-pc, 2 tips, split-bamboo fly, dark brown wraps, 7-1/2' l.......**35.00**
Tackle box, leather.......**470.00**
Trophy, large mouth bass, mounted on 13" x 9" wood.......**115.00**

❖ Fitz & Floyd

Fitz & Floyd is a true American success story. In the late 1950s the company served as a distributor for other company's products. After Pat Fitzpatrick died, Bob Floyd went on to establish a colorful niche in the dinnerware and table accessories business by introducing the mix-and-match philosophy. Most Fitz & Floyd is sold through the company's own stores. Some items are marked "Fitz & Floyd," while others bear the "OCI" mark of their Omnibus subsidiary.

Candy jar and candle holder, Old World Santa, incised "Copyright F, 1993," 9-1/2" h.......**95.00**
Coffee pot
  Montpelier, blue and gold.......**130.00**
  Roanoke, gold encrusted border**165.00**
Cookie jar
  Daisy the Cow, sgd OCI.......**125.00**
  Hampshire Pig, incised "Copyright F &

F 1992".......**195.00**
  Mama Bear, 1991, 11" h.......**165.00**
  Pig Waiter, incised "Copyright FF 1987".......**165.00**
  Prunella Pig, orig paper label.....**150.00**
  Queen of Hearts, incised "Copyright F & F 1992," 10-1/2" h.......**245.00**
  Rio Rita, designed by Vicki Balcou, 10-3/4" h.......**195.00**
  Russian Santa, incised "Copyright OCI, 1991," 10-1/4" h.......**145.00**
Creamer and sugar, cov
  Palais, white.......**130.00**
  Renaissance, dark green.......**140.00**
Figure
  Cinderella and Godmother.......**75.00**
  Giraffe.......**45.00**
  Night Before Christmas.......**175.00**
Gravy boat
  Christmas Wonderland.......**140.00**
  Renaissance, cinnabar.......**140.00**
Mug, Saint Nicholas, 4" h.......**160.00**
Pitcher, Damask Christmas, angel**150.00**
Place setting, 5 pcs
  Cherub.......**125.00**
  Eastchester.......**135.00**
  Lake Charles.......**140.00**
  Richmond.......**130.00**
  Roanoke.......**135.00**
Platter
  Holly, medium.......**190.00**
  Palais, white, round.......**135.00**
  Regatta, blue, white, yellow, and red.......**128.00**
  White Classic, medium.......**124.00**
Rabbit series figure
  Ballooning Bunnies.......**85.00**
  Bustles & Beaus.......**85.00**
  Busy Bunnies.......**85.00**
  Floral Rabbit.......**60.00**
  Hat Box.......**85.00**
  Mayfair.......**85.00**
  Mother.......**65.00**
Salt and pepper shakers, pr
  Cat and Ball of Twine, 3-3/4" h.....**25.00**
  Ham & Eggs, 4" h.......**30.00**
  Kittens, 3-1/2" h.......**27.50**
  Mama Bunny and Baby Bunny, 4" h.......**22.50**
  Policeman and Patrol Car, 4-5/8" h.......**22.50**
Serving plate, Renaissance, peach.......**130.00**
Teapot, Renaissance, cinnabar.....**150.00**
Vase, white and green, black details, 8" h.......**48.00**

❖ Flag-Related

It's a grand old flag, indeed. Not only are flags collectible, but so are countless items having a flag motif.

Collectors' Club: North American Vexillological Assoc, Suite 225, 1977 N Olden Ave, Trenton, NJ 08618.

Booklet, *Our Flag*, Department of Defense, 1960, 24 pgs **7.50**

Cigar felt, American flag, 48 stars, 10-1/2" x 8-1/2" **4.00**

Flag
36-star, 1908-12, stars sewn on, 4" x 5" **70.00**
38-star, coarse muslin, mounted on stick, 12-1/2" x 22" **50.00**
44-star, tacked to 50" wooden pole, stains, tears, 19-3/4" x 34-1/2"**145.00**
45-star, painted stars, tear, 11" x 16" **85.00**

Flag pole stand, lion-paw feet, mkd "Loyalty," "Fraternity," "Charity" and "1883," 3-1/2" h, 8" sq **175.00**

Jewelry, costume, flag pin
Ciner, enameled stripes, raised gold lines, 50 stars, 1-1/2" x 1-3/4" ..**32.00**
Coro, red, white and blue enameling, clear rhinestones, 1-1/4" x 1-1/2" **88.00**
Unmarked, rhinestones, 2" h........**18.00**

Lapel pin, plastic flag with 50 stars, Reddy Kilowatt, "Reddy Says Thanks for Voting," orig card, set of 5 ....**22.00**

License plate attachment, 48-star flag, 6" x 5 1/2" **35.00**

Pinback button, celluloid, shows American flag, 7/8" dia **18.00**

Postcard, flag and poem, "Our country stands for Humanity...," unused, 1920s **8.00**

Trivet, Frankoma, sand glaze, America's Stars & Stripes, Flag of Freedom, 1776-1976, commemorative backstamp, 6-1/2" dia...................**20.00**

Poster, "Give It Your Best," World War II, shows 48-star flag, 1942 office of War Information, fold lines, 28-1/2" x 20" **60.00**

Flag Collectibles, booklet, This Wonderful Country of Ours, *$10.*

❖ Flamingos

Long-legged and bright pink, these feathered friends bring smiles to the faces of collectors. Pink flamingos as yard ornaments have passed their golden anniversary, attesting to the lasting appeal of these birds.

Console bowl, figural 14" h flamingo in center, 14-1/2" l bowl, 2-1/2" deep, incised "Made in USA, Maddux," artist sgd "E", 1940s **375.00**

Cookie jar, copyright "Lotus, China," pink and green **115.00**

Desk calendar, metal, shows month, day and date, Japan **145.00**

Figurine
Ceramic, Will George, 7-3/4" h...**245.00**
Plastic, souvenir of Sunken Gardens, Fla., 1 flamingo with head down, 1 with head up, 4-1/2" h..............**15.00**

Glass, "Wesley Johnson's Club Flamingo, 1836 Fillmore St., San Francisco, The Texas Playhouse," 4-3/4" h...**15.00**

Jewelry, costume
Plastic flamingo pin, "Hialeah, 1967," 3" h..**5.00**
Enamel and rhinestone flying flamingo, Coro, 3" x 4-1/2" **525.00**

Lawn ornament, plastic, white, orig legs **35.00**

Napkin ring, c1980, 3" h, set of 4...**20.00**

Nodder, Standing Ovations, 1987, 7" h **39.00**

Paint by number, neatly painted, gold frame, 1950s, 24" x 22"................**45.00**

Paperweight, bronze, "The Lakeeny Malleable Co., Cleveland, Ohio," 5-3/4" h **68.00**

Photograph album, wooden, "Our Honeymoon" cut in relief, Silver Springs, Fla., 9" x 6" **36.00**

Planter
9" h, 8" l, 4-1/2" w, 9" h, pink and white seated bird, black beak and highlights, mkd "Made in USA, #508, Maddux"...................................**185.00**
10" l, 7-1/4" h, attributed to American Bisque......................................**65.00**

Thermometer
Ceramic, "Souvenir of Florida," 6" h **57.50**
Wooden, embossed wall plaque, "Silver Springs, Fla." 5" dia **19.00**

Tray, plastic, 2 flamingos flying across inlet at Marineland, Fla., 11-3/4" dia **42.00**

TV lamp/planter combination, Lane & Co., Van Nuys, Calif., 1957, 14-1/2" h, 16" w **495.00**

Vase, Sunglow, Hull, 8-3/4" h **75.00**

❖ Flashlights

Shall we shed a little light on an interesting collectible topic? Flashlights actually evolved from early bicycle lights. Conrad Hubert invented the first tubular hand-held flashlight in 1899.

Collectors' Club: Flashlight Collectors of America, P.O. Box 4095, Tustin, CA 92781.

Candle, Eveready, #1643, cast metal base, cream-colored painted candle, 1932 ....**40.00**

Lantern
Delta Lantern, Buddy model, 1919 ....**15.00**
Eveready, #4707, nickel-plated case, large bull's eye lens, 1912 ....**25.00**

Novelty
Flintstones, 1975, MOC, 3" h.......**15.00**
Frankenstein, c1960, 9-1/2" l **48.00**
Hulk Hogan, WWF Wrestling, 1991 ....**12.00**
Peter Pan, McDonald's premium, MIB **4.00**

Railroad, Jenks, brass, patent July 25, 1911 ....**90.00**

Tubular
Aurora, all nickel case **20.00**
Bond Electric Co., Jersey City, N.J., 1940s, 5-1/4" l **10.00**
Homart, all metal, 1930s, 10-1/2" l **35.00**
Ray-O-Vac, Space Patrol **40.00**
Winchester, marble lens, gold-colored body, 1919-26, 5-1/2" l **100.00**
Yale, #3302, double-ended, flood lens and spot lens **30.00**

Vest pocket
Eveready, Masterlight, #6662, nickel-plated, ruby push-button switch, 1904..**30.00**
Franco, glass button switch..........**25.00**

❖ Flatware

Whether you're setting an elegant table or striving for an informal look, great looking flatware is a must. There are many many patterns to choose from, and the price range reflects the age, maker, and composition of the service being considered. In addition to a number of excellent reference books, there are many matching services that can help you complete a flatware set. But, many of us enjoy the hunt and prefer to scout flea markets for those additional place settings and unique serving pieces.

References: Frances M. Bones and Lee Roy Fisher, *Standard Encyclopedia of American Silverplate*, Collector Books, 1998; Tere Hagan, *Silverplated Flatware*, rev 4th ed, Collector Books, 1990 (1998 value update).

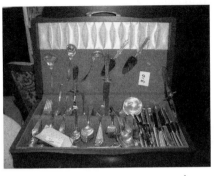

Flatware, service for 20, serving pieces, wooden chest with red lining, $250.

Bacon server, Old Maryland, Kirk-Steiff **90.00**
Bonbon, Princess Patricia, Gorham**18.50**
Butter knife
   Bridal Rose, Alvin..........................**30.00**
   Celeste, Gorham **12.00**
   Silver Wheat, Reed & Barton **15.00**
Carving set, Cactus, Jensen **325.00**
Cheese knife, Allure, Rogers, 1939..**8.00**
Cocktail fork
   Contour, Towle...............................**24.00**
   Empress, International **10.00**
Cold meat fork
   Moselle, American Silver Co. **60.00**
   Silver Spray, Towle **32.00**
   Woodwind, Reed & Barton...........**53.00**
Cream soup spoon
   Bridal Rose, Alvin..........................**65.00**
   Castle Rose, Royal Crest.............**15.00**
   Fleetwood, Manchester...............**30.00**
   Pointed Antique, Reed & Barton ..**24.00**
Demitasse spoon, Virginia Carvel, Towle **12.00**
Dessert spoon, Bridal Rose, Alvin .**60.00**
Dinner fork
   Bridal Rose, Alvin..........................**55.00**
   Celeste, Gorham **22.00**
   Concord, Whiting............................**25.00**
   Fleetwood, Manchester...............**30.00**
Dinner knife
   Colonial Fiddle, Tuttle **25.00**
   King George, Gorham **40.00**
   Lily of the Valley, Gorham............**27.50**
Fish knife, Acorn, Jensen..............**38.00**
Grapefruit spoon, Fleetwood,
   Manchester **20.00**
Gravy ladle
   Continental, Tuttle........................**70.00**
   Horizon, Easterling.......................**40.00**
   Silver Spray, Towle **34.00**
   Silver Wheat, Reed & Barton.......**40.00**
Iced tea spoon
   Lily of the Valley, Gorham............**30.00**
   Romansque, Alvin **20.00**
Lemon fork
   Celeste, Gorham **13.00**
   Silver Spray, Towle **16.00**

Flatware, Cheese spreaders, figural Father Christmas gold plated handles, silver plated blades, The Bombay Co., orig velvet lined box, $20.

Letter Opener, King Edward, Gorham **25.00**
Luncheon fork
   King Albert, Whiting **20.00**
   King Edward, Gorham...................**27.00**
   Pointed Antique, Reed & Barton,
     engraved...................................**24.00**
Luncheon knife
   King Edward, Gorham..................**24.00**
   King George, Gorham...................**35.00**
Meat fork, DuBarry, International....**90.00**
Olive fork, Chippendale, Alvin **25.00**
Pasta scoop, Beauvoir, Tuttle **25.00**
Pickle fork, Celeste, Gorham **14.00**
Pie server, Acorn, Jensen **135.00**
Place setting
   Contour, Towle...............................**95.00**
   Prelude, International....................**60.00**
Salad fork
   Castle Rose, Royal Crest.............**20.00**
   Chapel Bells, Alvin **20.00**
Salt spoon, Old Master, Towle........**11.00**
Sardine fork, Cambridge, Gorham .**50.00**
Soup spoon, oval
   Celeste, Gorham **17.00**
   Elegante, Reed & Barton **21.00**
Strawberry fork, King Edward, Gorham **21.00**
Sugar spoon
   Copenhagen, Manchester............**24.00**
   Fairfax, Dugan...............................**28.00**
   Tara, Reed & Barton **21.00**
   Windsor, Towle **12.00**
Sugar tongs, Bridal Rose, Alvin, large **90.00**
Tablespoon
   Colonial Fiddle, Tuttle, pierced **55.00**
   Elegante, Reed & Barton **21.00**

   King Albert, Whiting **30.00**
   Rambler Rose, Towle **30.00**
Teaspoon
   Bridal Rose, Alvin.........................**24.00**
   Castle Rose, Royal Crest.............**12.00**
   Celeste, Gorham **11.00**
   Fairfax, Dugan...............................**18.00**
   Old Master, Towle.........................**17.00**
   Rambler Rose, Towle **15.00**
   Rose Solitaire, Towle....................**10.00**
   Wildflower, Royal Crest **10.00**
Tomato server, King Edward, Gorham **68.00**

❖ Florence Ceramics

Florence Ward began producing decorative ceramic items in her Pasadena, California, work shop in 1939. By 1946 her business had grown to the point that it occupied a full-size plant, and her husband and son joined the company to help keep up with demand. Semi-porcelain figurines and other decorative accessories were produced until 1977 when operations ceased.

Reference: Barbara S. Kline, Margaret C. Wehrspaun, and Jerry Kline, *The Complete Book of Florence Ceramics,* Schiffer Publishing 2002.

Collectors' Club: Florence Collector's Club, P.O. Box 122, Richland, WA 99352.

Bust, white, choir boy, 9-1/2" h **75.00**
Cigarette box, cov, winter.............**245.00**
Dealer sign **395.00**
Figure
   Abigail **165.00**
   Bea..**150.00**
   Blue Boy, 12" h............................**295.00**
   Delia **135.00**
   Douglas **240.00**
   Irene...**55.00**
   Matilda, 8-1/2" h..........................**145.00**
   Melanie, gray dress, red trim......**120.00**
   Pinkie, 11-1/2" h..........................**295.00**
   Rhett, white, 9" h.........................**385.00**
   Scarlett, beige dress **180.00**
   Sue Ellen, 8-1/4" h **150.00**
   Suzette, 6" h..................................**85.00**
   Vivian, 10" h **245.00**
Wall plaque, figural lady in center, 6" w,
   7" h...**100.00**

❖ Flow Blue

The name of this pretty china is derived from the blue design that is flowed or blurred on a white background to create a distinctive look. Flow blue china was first produced in 1830 in the Staffordshire district of England. Many potteries manufactured flow blue, including some American firms.

Flow Blue, chocolate pot, cov, Acme pattern, gold trim, $650.

References: Susan and Al Bagdade, *Warman's English & Continental Pottery & Porcelain*, 3rd ed, Krause Publications, 1998; Mary F. Gaston, *Collector's Encyclopedia of Flow Blue China*, Collector Books, 1983 (1993 value update); Jeffrey B. Snyder, *Fascinating Flow Blue*, Schiffer Publishing, 1997; ——, *Flow Blue: A Closer Look*, Schiffer Publishing, 2000; ——, *Flow Blue: A Collector's Guide to Pattern, History, and Values*, Schiffer Publishing, 1992; ——, *Historic Flow Blue*, Schiffer Publishing, 1994; Petra Williams, *Flow Blue China and Mulberry Ware: Similarity and Value Guide*, rev ed, Fountain House East, 1993.

Collectors' Club: Flow Blue International Collectors' Club, 1048 Llano, Pasadena, TX 77504.

Reproduction Alert

For additional listings, see *Warman's Antiques & Collectibles*, *Warman's Americana & Collectibles*, and *Warman's English & Continental Pottery & Porcelain*.

Bacon platter, Touraine, 10" l.......**245.00**
Bone dish, Argyle, J & E Mayer **55.00**
Butter dish, cov, insert, Chapoo, Wedgwood **525.00**
Butter pat, 3" dia
  Argyle, J & E Mayer **40.00**
  Delph, Sebring **35.00**
  Windmill, The French China Co. ..**40.00**
Cake plate, Cracked Ice, International Pottery **120.00**
Coffee cup and saucer, Arcadia, large **85.00**
Creamer, Fairy Villas, 5" h **275.00**
Cup, handleless, Amoy **250.00**
Cup and saucer
  Colonial, Homer Laughlin............**85.00**

Flow Blue, plate, LaBelle pattern, 8-3/4" d, $35.

Touraine......................................**90.00**
Winona, French China Co..............**65.00**
Dessert bowl, Poppy, Warwick **30.00**
Gravy boat, Chapoo, Wedgwood..**275.00**
Jardiniere, Autumn Leaves, Warwick, 8" x 7-1/2" **550.00**
Milk pitcher, Argyle, J & E Mayer, 7" h **150.00**
Plate
  Argyle, J & E Mayer, 8" dia **60.00**
  Autumn Leaves, Warwick, 10-1/2" d **135.00**
  Colonial, Homer Laughlin, 10" dia **65.00**
  Dundee, Ridgways, 10" dia........**125.00**
  Eclipse, Johnson Bros., 7" dia **65.00**
  Royal Blue, Burgess & Campbell, 9-7/8" dia....................................**75.00**
  Touraine, Stanley Pottery, 8-3/4" dia **60.00**
Platter, Windmill, The French China Co., 13" l **125.00**
Relish
  Autumn Leaves, Warwick, 8" l....**110.00**
  Windmill, The French China Co., oval, 10" l...**55.00**
Serving bowl, Conway, 9" dia.......**135.00**

Flow Blue, cup and saucer, "Love the Giver" in gold lettering, bead trim, $35.

Soup plate
  Alaska, Grindley **75.00**
  Royal Blue, Burgess & Campbell.**55.00**
  Touraine, Stanley Pottery, 7-1/2" dia **75.00**
  Windmill, The French China Co., 8" dia **45.00**
Syrup pitcher, Autumn Leaves, Warwick, silver plate lid **275.00**
Teapot, cov, Strawberry **200.00**
Toothbrush holder, Alaska, Grindley **145.00**

❖ Flower Frogs

Flower frogs are those neat holders that were sometimes designed to complement a bowl or vase. Others were made to be purely functional and had holes to insert flower stems, making flower arranging a little easier.

Art Deco lady
  6" h, white porcelain, dancing nude **90.00**
  7-1/2" h, mkd "3941 Germany," c1930 ....**195.00**
Bird, figural, bright colors, mkd "Made in Japan," 5-1/2" h, chipped **50.00**
California Pottery, candle holder type, made to hold fresh flowers around candle, mkd "Calif USA V17," 3-1/2" h, 4" w **20.00**
Cambridge Glass
  Draped Lady, amber, 8-1/2" h **200.00**
  Rose Lady, green **250.00**
  Two Kids, crystal **155.00**
German, nude, lavender scarf, porcelain, 9-1/2" h................................**135.00**
Rookwood, figural nude, porcelain glaze, c1930 ....**325.00**
Silver deposit glass, clear glass frog with candleholder, 4" dia **45.00**
Van Briggle, light blue, mkd "Van Briggle/Colo. Spgs," 4-1/2" dia.....**82.00**
Weller, Brighton Woodpecker, 6" h, 3-1/2" w, 3" l **520.00**

❖ Folk Art

Folk art remains one area of collecting that doesn't have clearly defined boundaries. Some people confine folk art to non-academic, handmade objects. Others include manufactured material. When referring to artwork, the term encompasses everything from crude drawings by untalented children to works by academically trained artists that depict common people and scenery. The following listings illustrate the diversity of this category.

References: Wendy Lavitt, *Animals in American Folk Art*, Knopf, 1990; George H. Meyer, *American Folk Art Canes*, Sandringham Press, 1992; Donald J.

Petersen, *Folk Art Fish Decoys*, Schiffer Publishing, 1996; Beatrix Rumford and Carolyn Weekly, *Treasures in American Folk Art from the Abby Aldrich Rockefeller Folk Art Center*, Little, Brown Co., 1989.

Periodical: *Folk Art Finder*, One River, Essex, CT 06426; *Folk Art Illustrated*, P.O. Box 906, Marietta, OH 45750.

Collectors' Club: Folk Art Society of America, P.O. Box 17041, Richmond, VA 23226.

Museums: Abby Aldrich Rockefeller Folk Art Center, Williamsburg, VA; Museum of American Folk Art, New York, NY; Museum of Early Southern Decorative Arts, Winston-Salem, NC.

Bank, 3-1/4" h, gourd form, paint decorated with face **115.00**
Bookends, pr, sculpted sandstone, seated figures of Adam and Eve, mkd "E. Reed 1976 A.D.," 11" h, pr....**495.00**
Cane, wooden
Dog handle, dark-brown paint, root-carved, worn **165.00**
Lion's head, glass eyes, gold metal band with presentation engraving dated 1924, Malacca shaft, horn ferrule.......................................**485.00**
Snake, 1 spiraling snake, black bead eyes, salmon repair, mushroom cap handle, 31-1/2" l **375.00**
Carving
Hat, smoke-deco, mustard-painted carved walnut burl, stars around band and top, 19th C, minor wear, 4-1/2" h, 12-1/4" dia..................**920.00**
Grouping, painted wood 2-story house and carved and painted figures celebrating the 4th of July, includes band members and croquet players, 14 figures, house 10" h, base 14" sq **1,430.00**
Face jug
Abraham Lincoln, green running glaze, incised inscription on back "Abraham Lincoln, Shyster Lawyer from Illonois (sic) Also Was President Of The North," sgd "Cleater Meaders, 1993," 12-1/2" h **475.00**
Burlon Craig, glossy black-brown Albany slip, large ears, pop-eyed, 1-pc eyebrow, china plate teeth, pierced nostrils, mkd "B.B Craig, Vale, N.C.," c1980-82, 6" h **275.00**
Marie Rogers, glossy Albany slip with multicolor drippings, tongue sticking out, white teeth, blue pupils, incised beard and eyelashes, script and impressed marks, early 1980s, 9-1/8" h **165.00**
Indian club, red and black grained, 18" h, pr..**185.00**

Folk Art, hand carved Noah's Ark with animals, artist signed, dated 12/94, $95.

Painting, watercolor on paper, flowers and heart, yellow roses and snowdrops in corners, heart formed of multicolor vining flowers, "Forget Me Not" with verse, name and 1866, molded wooden frame, glued down, foxing, edge damage, 11" h, 12-1/4" w .**110.00**
Sculpture, limestone
Bust, Indian, mkd "E.R." (Popeye Reed), 9-1/2" h **275.00**
Indian in canoe, mkd "E. Reed 1976 A.D.," 5-1/2" h, 7-3/4" l **660.00**
Theorem, watercolor on velvet, American School, early 19th C, unsigned, flowers, shades of blue, gold, green, and brown, ivory ground, period gilt frame, 6" x 6-1/2", toning, losses to frame **440.00**
Tinsel Picture, flower arrangement, reverse-painted glass backed with foil and paper, American School, late 19th C, Victorian frame, 22" x 17", repaired **180.00**

❖ Food Molds

Flea markets are great places to find food molds. Originally intended for creating cakes, ice cream, chocolate, etc. in interesting shapes, many of these molds are now collected for their decorative appeal.

Cast iron
Lamb, seated................................**95.00**
Rabbit, Griswold.........................**225.00**
Graniteware
Strawberry, gray, 1-3/4" h, 5" l, 4" w **235.00**
Turk's head, blue/white swirl **115.00**
Ironstone
Corn, mkd "Made in USA," chips, hairline **35.00**
Grapes, oval with flat bottom, rounded fluted sides **175.00**
Pewter, ice cream mold
Floral wreath, "E. & Co., 1142," 3-3/4" dia...**40.00**
Heart, mkd "E. & Co., N.Y., 902," 4-1/8" h...**38.50**
Redware, Turk's head, scalloped and fluted, hairlines, 8" dia..................**85.00**
Yellowware, pudding mold

Food Molds, left to right: melon shaped pudding mold, tin, $35; copper turk's head jelly mold, $25; copper round mold with circle motif, $30.

Ear of corn, scalloped designs on interior sides, simple gallery-like foot, oval, 4-3/8" h, 7-3/8" x 9-1/4" .**170.00**
Pear, deep bowl shape, ribbed sides, dark-brown glaze, roughness on rim, hairline, 4" h, 7" dia **49.50**
Sheath of wheat, minor rim chips, 3-1/4" h, 7-5/8" l **110.00**
Tin
Melon, two mark, marked "Kraemer" **48.00**
Pear, oval, deep ruffled sides, design stamped in top, framed by raised rim band, 3-1/2" x 5-1/2".................**90.00**

❖ Football Cards

Trading cards for this sport are readily found at flea markets. As with baseball cards and other sports trading cards, it is relatively easy for collectors to check values and scarcity.

References: *Tuff Stuff Standard Catalog of Football Cards 2003*, 6th ed, Krause Publications, 2003.

Periodicals: *Sports Cards Magazine & Price Guide*, 700 E State St, Iola, WI 54990; *Sports Collectors Digest*, 700 E State St, Iola, WI 54990.

Note: The following listings are merely a sampling of the thousands of cards readily available to collectors. For detailed information, we recommend the *Standard Catalog of Football Cards* by the editors of Sports Collectors Digest, Krause Publications.

Bowman, complete set
1992, 573 cards **160.00**
1995, 357 cards **125.00**
1998, 220 cards **100.00**
Bowman, individual cards
1995, Kordell Stewart, #105.........**20.00**
1995, Curtis Martin, #301 ....**10.00**
1998, Randy Moss, #182 ....**30.00**
Pro Set, 1990
Factory sealed set.........................**5.00**
Hand collated set **17.00**
Score
1989, complete set (330) **220.00**
1990, factory sealed set..............**10.00**
Stadium Club, 1991, complete set (500) **90.00**

Topps, complete set

1980, 528 cards **65.00**
1985, 396 cards **80.00**
1990, 528 cards **10.00**
1995, 468 cards **45.00**
1996, 165 cards, chrome **160.00**
1997, 165 cards, chrome **180.00**
Topps, individual cards
1984, John Elway, #63 ....**125.00**
1989, Chris Carter, #121................**2.00**
1993, Drew Bledsoe, #130............**3.00**
1998, Troy Aikman, #75..................**1.10**
Upper Deck, complete set
1991, factory sealed set..............**17.00**
1998, Super Powers, 30 cards.....**45.00**

❖ Football Memorabilia

Every collector has a favorite team or player. Most can tell you more about their collection and the game of football than you'll ever need to know. This dedicated fan truly enjoys the sport and the collectibles it generates every year.

Reference: John Carpentier, *Price Guide to Packers Memorabilia*, Krause Publications, 1998.

Periodical: *Sports Collectors Digest*, 700 E State St, Iola, WI 54990.

Autographed NFL Footballs
Allen, Marcus **190.00**
Culpepper, Daunte **180.00**
Dent, Richard, Super Bowl 20....**200.00**
Elway, John **250.00**
Favre, Brett...............................**200.00**
Autographed Jersey
Aikman, Troy, pro-cut, Nike.........**285.00**
Csonka, Larry, Dolphins, aqua, Wilson
....**250.00**
Farve, Brett, Packers, green, Nike
....**300.00**
Griese, Bob, Dolphins, Champion
....**250.00**
Autographed photo, 8" x 10"
Crockett, Ray, Detroit **5.00**
Eliss, Luther, Detroit.....................**5.00**
Howard, Desmond, Washington...**10.00**
Bobbing Head
Cleveland Browns, sq brown wood base..**75.00**
St. Louis Cardinal, 6-1/2" h **130.00**
Book, The Big One, Michigan vs Ohio State, A History of America's Greatest Football Rivalry, Bill Cromartie, Rutledge Press, Nashville, 1988, 399 pgs, dj....................................**10.00**
Doll, rubber face, plush body, Charm Toy Co., 1960s....................................**35.00**
Football, Wilson, "Official Intercollegiate Wilson TD," some lacings broken, labels faded **95.00**
Game

TV Football, Coleco, 1974...........**30.00**
Football Bag-A-Telle, orig box, 6" x 11"
....**20.00**
Hartland Figurine
Browns, orig box **95.00**
Giants, orig box **150.00**
Key chain, Super Bowl XXX, NRFP .**6.00**
Pajama bottoms, football print, cotton
....**15.00**
Pennant, felt
Chicago Bears, black ground, orange "Bears," orange, green and red football art, orange felt trim, late 1940s.......................................**25.00**
Cincinnati Bengals Super Bowl 16 AFC Champions, orange **65.00**
Denver Broncos World Championship, 1977.......................................**45.00**
Philadelphia Eagles, 1940s-1950s, 28" l...**35.00**
Program
Notre Dame v USC, Nov 21, 1931
....**100.00**
Super Bowl XXII, 1988.................**20.00**
Salt and pepper shakers, Football Hall of Fame, porcelain, 2-3/4" h.........**20.00**
Ticket stub
NFC Division, 1977, Minnesota and LA Rams **12.00**
Notre Dame vs Stanford, 1964 ....**15.00**
TV Guide, Super Bowl Preview, Jan 28-Feb 3, 1995 ....**6.00**
Yearbook, Green Bay Packers, 1974, autographed by coaches and players
....**40.00**

❖ Fostoria Glass

The Fostoria Glass Company was initially located in Fostoria, Ohio, but in 1891 it was relocated to Moundsville, West Virginia. Their fine glass tableware included delicate engraved patterns and also pressed patterns. Like many other American glass manufacturers of that era, several of their lines were also produced in various colors.

References: Milbra Long and Emily Seate, *Fostoria Stemware*, Collector Books, 1995, 1998 value update, ——, *Fostoria Tableware, 1924-1943*, Collector Books, 1999; ——, *Fostoria Tableware 1944-1986*, Collector Books, 1999; ——, *Fostoria, Useful and Ornamental: The Crystal for America*, Collector Books, 2000; Leslie Pina, *Fostoria American Line 2056*, 2nd ed., Schiffer Publishing, 2002.

Collectors' Clubs: Fostoria Glass Collectors, P.O. Box 1625 Orange, CA 92856; Fostoria Glass Soc of America, P.O. Box 826, Moundsville, WV 26041.

Reproduction Alert

Fostoria Glass Goblet, Jamestown pattern, pink, $15.

For additional listings and a detailed list of reference books, see *Warman's Antiques & Collectibles* and *Warman's Glass*.

After Dinner Cup and Saucer, Queen Anne...**45.00**
Almond, Grape Leaf, Regal Blue....**55.00**
Ashtray, Century, individual size.....**12.00**
Berry bowl, June, blue...................**50.00**
Bookends, Lyre, pr **145.00**
Bowl
Coronet, handle, 11" dia **60.00**
Flame, oval, 12-1/2" l, oval..........**45.00**
Butter, cov, America, round **125.00**
Cake plate
Baroque, crystal, handle **65.00**
Fern, ebony, gold trim, two handles, 10" dia....................................**85.00**
Candelabra, pr, Baroque, crystal, 2-lite, #2484 ....**295.00**
Candy dish, cov, Coin, amber, round
....**35.00**
Celery vase, Double Greek Key ...**140.00**
Champagne
Distinction, red **14.00**
Fern, #5298, pink **55.00**
Heraldry, #6012 ....**10.00**
Cheese and cracker, Chintz **70.00**
Cigarette holder with ashtray, Two Tone, #5092, amethyst and crystal
....**75.00**
Claret, June, blue **95.00**
Comport, Baroque, flared, gold tint **68.00**
Creamer and sugar
Alexis, hotel size, cut dec...........**115.00**
Fairfax, green, ftd **35.00**
Cream soup, American...................**47.50**
Cruet, Coin, olive green **50.00**
Demitasse cup and saucer, June, topaz
....**60.00**

Fostoria Glass Relish, American pattern, oval, divided into 3 parts, 9-1/2" l, $20.

Goblet, water

  American, 7" h.............................**17.50**
  Baroque, blue...............................**25.00**
  Chintz...**25.00**
  Colonial Dame, 11-oz..................**15.00**
Ice tub, American, 6-1/2" dia **60.00**
Jug, Baroque, crystal **225.00**
Juice tumbler, Navarre...................**24.00**
Mayonnaise, underplate

  Baroque......................................**65.00**
  Colony **25.00**
Nut Bowl, Baroque, 3 toes, topaz yellow

  ....**35.00**
Pitcher

  Beverly, amber **125.00**
  Jamestown, green......................**115.00**
  Meadow Rose **195.00**
Plate

  Baroque, blue, salad **14.00**
  Colony, dinner **35.00**
  Fairfax, green, salad.....................**6.50**
  Lafayette, luncheon **24.00**
Platter, American, 12" l **60.00**
Relish

  American, 2-part **18.00**
  Chintz, 2-part **30.00**
  Silver Spruce, 3-part **35.00**
Salad bowl, Fairfax, green **27.50**
Sherbet

  Colonial Dame, 6-1/2 oz **10.00**
  Fairfax, yellow.............................**12.00**
  Jamestown, medium blue **15.00**
  Versailles, topaz **18.00**
Sugar, cov, Coin, olive green **30.00**
Syrup, glass lid, American **135.00**
Top Hat, American, 4" h.................**50.00**
Tumbler

  Chintz, ftd **24.00**
  Vernon, etched **17.50**
Tumbler, old-fashioned (cocktail), Coin,

  crystal..**30.00**
Vase

  American, flared, 9-1/2" h **200.00**
  Two Tone, #2470, red and crystal, 10"

  h..**150.00**
Water pitcher, Coin, olive green.....**55.00**
Wedding bowl, Coin, red...............**65.00**
Whiskey, American **17.50**
Wine

  American **15.00**
  Argus, ruby.................................**25.00**

Chintz **38.00**
Laurel **35.00**
Jamestown, green..........................**20.00**
Oriental..**25.00**

❖ Franciscan Ware

Gladding, McBean and Co., of Los Angeles, California, first produced this popular dinnerware around 1934. Their use of primary colors and simple shapes was met with much enthusiasm. Production was finally halted in 1986.

Reference: Jeffrey B. Snyder, *Franciscan Dining Services,* 2nd ed., Schiffer Publishing, 2002.

Collectors' Club: Franciscan Collectors Club, 8412 5th Ave NE, Seattle, WA 98115.

For additional listings, see *Warman's Americana & Collectibles* and *Warman's American Pottery & Porcelain.*

Ashtray, Starburst **25.00**
Baker, Apple, apple shape, 5-1/4" x 4-3/4" **400.00**
Bowl

  Apple, ftd **22.00**
  Coronado, turquoise, 7-1/2" dia ...**17.50**
  Ivy, buffet **370.00**
Butter dish, cov, Starburst.............**42.00**
Casserole, cov

  Ivy, 1-1/2 qt...............................**350.00**
  October **420.00**
  Starburst, 9-5/8" dia **365.00**
Cereal bowl, Meadow Rose **22.00**
Coffeepot

  Denmark, blue...........................**100.00**
  Heritage......................................**80.00**
Chop plate

  Apple, 14" dia............................**125.00**
  Starburst......................................**62.00**
Creamer and sugar

  Apple **60.00**
  Magnolia......................................**75.00**

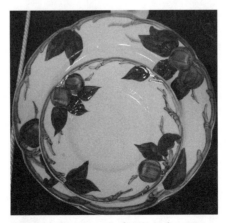

Franciscan Dinnerware Apple pattern, 2 saucers, $7.50 each, 6 dinner plates, $20 each.

Franciscan Dinnerware, sugar bowl, Desert Rose, lid missing, $25.

Cup and saucer

  Apple **16.00**
  Poppy **32.00**
Demitasse cup and saucer

  Desert Rose.................................**48.00**
  Rosemore....................................**45.00**
Dinner plate

  Apple **20.00**
  Poppy **37.50**
Eggcup, Desert Rose **35.00**
Fruit bowl, Poppy...........................**30.00**
Gravy boat

  Arcadia, green, gold trim............**145.00**
  Fremont **145.00**
  Granville **120.00**
  Huntingdon, attached underplate

  ....**450.00**
  Mesa, gold trim **110.00**
  Woodside **140.00**
Grill plate, Apple...........................**140.00**
Jam jar, Apple...............................**135.00**
Mixing bowls, nested 3 pc set, Apple

  ....**400.00**
Oil and vinegar cruet set, Starburst

  ....**335.00**
Pepper mill, Starburst...................**350.00**
Platter

  Fremont, large **175.00**
  Olympic, white, violets, gold trim, large

  ....**165.00**
  Renaissance, gray border, gold trim,

  medium **150.00**
Relish

  Coronado, 12" l **70.00**
  Ivy, 11" l......................................**60.00**
Salad plate, Apple **18.00**
Salt and pepper shakers, pr

  Apple, small.................................**36.00**
  Mariposa **98.00**
Side salad plate, Starburst, crescent

  shape **27.50**
Soup bowl, Desert Rose **20.00**
Sugar bowl, cov

  Canton, gray, black and rose floral,

  cream ground **75.00**
  Del Monte....................................**82.00**
  Olympic, white, violets, gold trim..**90.00**
Teapot, cov

Ivy	430.00
Mariposa	165.00
Meadow Rose	200.00
Tray, 3 tiers, Starburst	335.00
Turkey platter, Apple	320.00
Vegetable bowl, cov, Palomar, Jasper	190.00
Vegetable bowl, oval	
Carmel, platinum trim	86.00
Fremont	98.00
Woodside	90.00

❖ Frankart

Frankart is the name used by artist Arthur Von Frankenberg, who achieved his goal of mass producing "art objects" in the mid 1920s. Most of his creations were stylized forms, particularly ashtrays, bookends, lamps, vases, etc. The pieces were cast in white metal, and one of several popular metallic finishes was then applied. Finishes ranged in color from copper to gold to gunmetal gray, in addition to several iridescent pastel colors.

Note: The following listings have a bronzoid finish (bronze colored).

Ashtray

Duck, outstretched wings support green glass ash receiver **145.00**
Nude, kneeling on cushions, holding 3" dia removable pottery ashtray **250.00**
Scottie and frog, 8-3/4" l, 5-1/2" h, paint loss **65.00**

Bookends, pr

Cocker Spaniels, c1934, 6-1/4" h **165.00**
Gazelles, 7-1/4" l, 6-1/4" h **225.00**
Owls, 6" h....................................**225.00**
Scotties, 5" l, 5" h, one repaired ..**60.00**

Cigarette box, back-to-back nudes supporting green glass box........**475.00**
Lamp, standing nude holding 6" round crackle glass globe shade..........**450.00**

Frankart ashtray, chrome Scottie, black enamel base, mkd "Frank Art Inc., Pat Appld For," $80.

❖ Frankoma Pottery

John N. Frank founded Frankoma Pottery in Oklahoma in 1933. Prior to 1954, the pottery used a honey-tan colored clay from Ada, Oklahoma. Brick-red clay from Sapulpa has also been used, and pink clay is in use currently. The plant has suffered several disastrous fires over the years, including one that destroyed all of the molds that had been used prior to 1983.

Reference: Phyllis and Tom Bess, *Frankoma and Other Oklahoma Potteries*, Schiffer Publishing, 2000.

Collectors' Club: Frankoma Family Collectors Assoc, P.O. Box 32571, Oklahoma City, OK 73123.

For additional listings, see *Warman's Antiques & Collectibles* and *Warman's American Pottery & Porcelain*.

Ashtray, Texas shape, pink, mkd 459, 6-1/4" l **17.50**
Butter dish, cov, Aztec, green **25.00**
Canister set, Desert Gold, Ring Band design, flour, sugar, coffee, and tea, 4 pc **110.00**
Casserole, Aztec, #7W, 10" w **40.00**
Christmas plate, 8-1/2" dia
1967, Gifts for the Christ Child.....**65.00**
1970, Joy to the World **80.00**
Deviled egg tray, green glaze, mkd "Frankoma #819," 12" dia.............**35.00**
Dish, leaf-shape, green and brown, mkd 225, 9-1/4" x 4 1/2" **18.00**

Frankoma Pottery, Will Rogers boot, green and brown, 4-1/2" h, $50.

Frankoma Pottery, ashtray, wagon wheel pattern, green and brown, $6.

Figurine

Indian maiden, brown glaze, 12-1/2" h **75.00**
Woman, brown, 14-1/2" h **45.00**
Masks, pr, black glaze, 6-3/4" h happy face, 8-3/4" sad face **130.00**
Mug
Republican elephant, maroon, 1984, 4" h...**20.00**
U.S. Postal Service, "National Maintenance Training Center, Norman, Okla.," black, 4" h.......**24.00**
Pitcher, ice lip, green and brown, 6" dia, 8" h..**85.00**
Planter, duck, brown, 4-3/4" h.........**39.00**
Plate
1974 Battles for Independence, 3rd in series of 5, sand color, 8-1/4" dia **40.00**
Kansas Centennial, 1861-1961, 9" dia **25.00**
Soup tureen, cov, Plainsman Gold, orig ladle...**65.00**
Teapot, brown glaze, 6-3/4" h **50.00**
Trivet
2 birds in a tree, brown, leaf pattern around edge **25.00**
Oklahoma, Prairie Green, 6-1/2" dia **28.00**
Wall pocket
Boot, brown, mkd 133, slight chip, 7" h **35.00**
Phoebe head, white, 1973-1975 re-issue, 7" h, 5" w.......................**75.00**

❖ Fraternal and Service Collectibles

Folks have often saved family items relating to benevolent societies and service clubs. Today, many of these articles are entering the flea market scene. These items tell interesting stories about how past generations spent some of their leisure time.

Attendee pin, Lion, 1954-55.............**7.00**
Belt Buckle, Rotary Club, cog emblem, silvertone, 2-1/2" dia **20.00**
Cream and sugar, Eastern Star, Lefton **50.00**
Cufflinks, pr, Lions...........................**30.00**
Cufflinks and tie clip, Masonic, cameo-type carving...............................**150.00**
Fez, Knights of Columbus **20.00**
Letter opener, Masonic, "Jordan Lodge No. 247, F&AM, Robert Rogove-WN. 1967," in plastic case, worn lettering **20.00**
Medal
  Loyal Order of Moose, heavily oxidized (green), 3-1/2" dia.....................**13.00**
  Salvation Army, "With Heart to God and Hand to Man 1880-1955," 1-1/4" dia..**18.00**
  Shriner, Amarillo, Texas...............**90.00**
Medal with bar pin, Knights of Pythias, "Conn Lodge 37," name on back..**38.00**
Mug, Rotary Club, Tulsa, OK, mkd "Frankoma Pottery," 3" dia **10.00**
Paperweight, Lions International, brass, figural lion, 2" w, 3" l....................**15.00**
Pinback button, BPOE, celluloid, "Dedication, New Home, Dunellen Lodge No. 1488, October 27, 1927" on torn ribbon, 1-1/2" dia, 2-1/2" l.....**38.00**
Plate, Masonic, Shenango China....**85.00**
Ring, Osiris, sterling silver, synthetic ruby, sides show horses and chariot, Chicago **75.00**

Chocolate pot, Masonic, New Jersey lodge, very dark mulberry dec, silver luster trim, base mkd "Theo Maddock, Trenton, NJ" $125.

Fez, tan felt, maroon tassel, orig cardboard tube container mkd "J. W. L. & Co.," size 7-1/8, $10.

Salt & pepper shakers, Lions International, "Iowa" in blue, Milford Pottery by KlayKraft, 1-3/4" h.......**12.00**
Service Pin, 50 Years, Lions **7.00**
Shaving mug, Odd Fellows, traditional IOOF symbols, with owner's name, 3-3/4" h..**80.00**
Vest, Cousin Jacks Lions Breakfast Club, Grass Valley, 1970s.....................**15.00**
Watch fob, Osiris, sterling silver, enameled in red-brown, green and yellow, "Osiris Temple Boosters Club," back mkd "Robbins Co., Attleboro, Mass.," 1-3/8" dia.........................**75.00**

❖ Frog Collectibles

Ribbit, ribbit! From Kermit to Frogger, frogs have been popular advertising characters in our culture.

Collectors' Club: The Frog Pond, P.O. Box 193, Beach Grove, IN 46107.

Advertising trade card, Pond's Extract **7.50**
Band, Lefton Pottery trio, saxophone, accordion and banjo players, 3" h**75.00**
Bank, porcelain, mkd "Made in Japan," 3-3/4" h..**110.00**
Beanie Baby
  Legs the Frog, retired Oct 97, protector **55.00**
  Smoochy the Frog, protector........**16.00**
Candy mold, tin **48.00**
Clicker, Life of the Party Products, Kirchhof, Newark, N.J...................**18.00**
Condiment set, figural salt and pepper shakers on tray, stamped "Hand Decorated, Shafford, Japan".......**48.00**
Cookie jar, green frog with yellow bow tie **55.00**
Figure
  Bisque, German, 1" h..................**15.00**
  Ceramic, Josef, 5-3/4" x 4"..........**40.00**
Netsuke, ivory, sgd, silver stand with turquoise lady bug, 1-1/4" h.......**145.00**
Pin, figural
  Enamel, black, green eyes, Ciner, 1-1/2" x 2" **200.00**

Weller Coppertone lilypad bowl with applied frog and flower bud, Weller half kiln stamp mark, minor flake to bud. 4" x 11", $495.

  Goldtone, clear rhinestones, emerald green cabochon eyes, 2" h.......**45.00**
  Rhinestones, 43 clear stones, green stones for eyes, 3" l.................**50.00**
  Sterling silver, amethyst colored glass eyes, Taxco, 1-1/2" h **45.00**
Planter, Niloak, dark brown swirls, 4-1/2" h **55.00**
Sculpture, The Frog Prince, Franklin Mint, 1986 ....**40.00**
Stein, Budweiser, frog posing with bottle, another on handle, mkd "Handcrafted by Ceramate," 6" h.....................**28.00**
Toothbrush holder, frog playing mandolin, mkd "Goldcastle, Made in Japan," 6" h **145.00**

❖ Fruit Jars

People in some areas of the country refer to these utilitarian glass jars as "canning jars," while others refer to them as "fruit jars" or "preserving jars." In any event, the first machine-made jar of this type was promoted by Thomas W. Dyott in 1829, and the screw-lid jar was patented in November of 1858.

Reference: Bill Schroeder, *1000 Fruit Jars Priced and Illustrated*, 5th ed, Collector Books, 1987 (1996 value update).

Periodical: *Fruit Jar Newsletter*, 364 Gregory Ave., West Orange, NJ 07052.

Collectors' Clubs: Ball Collectors Club, 22203 Doncaster, Riverview, MI 48192; Midwest Antique Fruit Jar & Bottle Club, P.O. Box 38, Flat Rock, IN 47234; Northwest Fruit Jar Collectors' Club, 12713 142nd Ave., Pulallup, WA 98374.

Amazon Swift Seal, clear, glass lid, wire bail **6.00**
Atlas E-Z Seal, green, pint.............**15.00**
Atlas Mason's Patent, apple green, pint **25.00**
Ball Ideal, aqua, pint, glass lid, wire bail **3.00**
Ball Mason, apple green, 1/2-gal....**30.00**
Bosco Double Seat, clear, quart....**43.00**
Brighton, clear, 1/2-gal **145.00**
Commonwealth Fruit Jar, clear, quart **98.00**
Everlasting Jar, light green, quart..**30.00**

Fruit Keeper, GCC Co. monogram, aqua, quart **50.00**
Gimball's Brothers Pure Food Store Philadelphia, clear, pint **48.00**
Hamilton, clear, 1/2-gal..................**90.00**
Hero over a cross, aqua, quart......**38.00**
The Ideal Imperial, aqua, quart......**35.00**
Mason Fruit Jar (2 lines), amber, pint **125.00**
Mason Improved, 2 dots below Mason, apple green, quart.......................**30.00**
Mason's Patent, teal, 1/2-gal..........**25.00**
Mason's Patent, Nov. 30th 1858, amber, quart..**325.00**
Mason's 20 Patent, Nov. 30th 1858, aqua, quart..................................**30.00**
Michigan Mason, beaded neck seal, clear, pint...................................**30.00**
Presto Wide Mouth, clear, glass lid, wire bail, 1/2-pint.............................**3.50**
Trademark Lightning Putnam, aqua, tall quart...**100.00**

❖ Fry Glass

The H.C. Fry Glass Co. of Rochester, Pennsylvania, is a sterling example of how a company must adapt in order to stay alive. Fry first produced brilliant cut glass, but by the Depression they had switched to making patented heat-resistant ovenware known as Pearl Oven Glass. In 1926 and 1927, the company also produced an art glass line known as Foval.

Reference: The H.C. Fry Glass Soc, *The Collector's Encyclopedia of Fry Glassware*, Collector Books, 1990 (1998 value update).

Collectors' Club: The H.C. Fry Glass Society, P.O. Box 41, Beaver, PA 15009.

Reproduction Alert

For additional listings, see *Warman's Antiques & Collectible* and *Warman's Glass*.

Bread maker, Pearl Oven Ware, 9" l **25.00**
Butter dish, cov, Pearl Oven Ware.**80.00**
Canape plate, Foval, cobalt center handle **175.00**
Cup and saucer, Foval, cobalt handles **68.00**
Hot water server, cov, Foval, green handle and finial.........................**275.00**
Nappy, brilliant period cut glass, pinwheel and fan with hobstar center, sgd **65.00**
Plate, pearl white, Delft blue rim, 9-1/2" dia **75.00**
Platter, Pearl Oven Ware, 17" l.......**65.00**
Trivet, Pearl Oven Ware, 8" dia.......**24.00**
Tumbler, Wild Rose etch, #51, 3-1/2" h, 8 oz, cut fluted base....................**24.00**
Vase

7-1/2", Foval, jade green............**210.00**
9" h, trumpet, pearl white, jade green foot..**395.00**

❖ Fulper

Fulper Pottery, located in Flemington, New Jersey, manufactured stoneware and pottery from the early 1800s until 1935. Their pieces are usually well-marked.

Collectors' Club: Stangl/Fulper Collectors Club, P.O. Box 583, Flemington, NJ 08822.

For additional listings, see *Warman's Antiques & Collectibles* and *Warman's American Pottery & Porcelain*.

Bowl
Chinese style, ftd, dark-green leopard-skin glaze, shape #447, flared, 7-1/2" dia..**525.00**
Scalloped rim, shades of tan, green, gray, blue and rust, 3-1/2" h, 8" dia **345.00**
Bud vase, baluster, butterscotch flambé glaze, ink racetrack mark, 9" h...**275.00**
Console set, 7-3/4" d floriform bowl, pr 4-1/4" h candlesticks, cov in turquoise and clear crystalline flambé glaze, ink racetrack mark, touch-up on one candlestick rim **100.00**
Flower frog
Lily pad, matte green, 4" dia **135.00**
Mushroom form, wisteria, 1-1/2" h, 2-1/2" dia.....................................**75.00**
Low bowl, blue with brown drip glaze, 11" dia **250.00**
Mug, Prang, green crystalline over brown, 4" x 5".............................**225.00**
Pitcher, blended, ringed, 6-1/2" h, 5-1/2" w..**135.00**
Plate, Oriental style, oatmeal color with blue freckles, 9-1/8" dia.............**185.00**
Trivet, lavender blue, 6-1/2" dia **145.00**
Urn, indigo and light blue glaze, incised racetrack mark, 11-3/4" h, stilt-pull bruise **865.00**
Vase
Blue and green mirror glaze, bulbous, flaring rim, raised racetrack mark, 7" h...**290.00**
Cat's Eye flambé glaze, pillow, ink racetrack mark, 6-1/4" h **175.00**

Fulper Pottery, low bowl, faceted, leaf-shaped flower frog, both covered in ivory flambé over mustard matte glaze, incised racetrack marks, 9" dia., $225.

Chinese Blue flambé glaze, speckled blue glaze, rect ink mark, 5" h**230.00**
Vessel
Frothy blue flambé glaze, squatty, 2 angular handles, ink racetrack mark, 6" dia, 5" h, restoration to one handle.....................................**195.00**
Nirrored Cat's Eye flambé glaze, spherical, 2 buttressed handles, ink racetrack mark, 7-1/2" dia, 6-1/4" h **435.00**

❖ Funeral

Morbid as it may seem, death- and funeral-related items are popular collectibles with some people. Postmortem photographs and casket hardware are a few of the items they look for.

Bottle, Frigid embalming fluid, emb, full, 8-1/2" h................................**90.00**
Cane, 4-1/2" l x 1-1/2" h staghorn handle, 1/2" dec gold filled collar, opens with straight pull to reveal long brass internal measuring stick, when locked in place graduated inches allow undertaker to measure deceased for coffin, briarwood shaft, 1" brass ferrule, English, c1890, 35" l **1,350.00**
Casket, child's, cypress, Birmingham Casket Co., Birmingham, Ala., 1930s, 46" l.......................................**115.00**
Casket plate, "Our Darling" in banner over lamb, Victorian......................**20.00**
Casket stands, sawhorse-type, turned wood, painted black, pr **70.00**
Fan, cardboard, 3-section, shows family in church, "Presented for your comfort by Wm. J. Schlup Funeral Home, The Home of Sincerity in Service, Akron, Ohio" **15.00**
Hand truck, used for moving caskets, brass plate for "C.W. Price, Greenfield, Ohio," 1897 patent, brass-plated steel, spoked wheels in 2 sizes, rubber tires, 19-1/2" h, 45" l, 20-1/2" w, collapses to 8" h...**200.00**
Photograph
Cabinet card, memorial floral arrangements, imprint of Clifford & Son, Muscatine, Iowa **6.00**
Memorial, 1890s, man's portrait in gilded frame sitting on a stool surrounded by funeral sprays, mounted, image size 7-1/2" x 9-1/2" **18.50**
Military funeral, postcard size **12.00**

❖ Furniture

Flea markets are great places to look for furniture. And, you can expect to find furniture from almost every time period and in all kinds of condition. When shopping for furniture, make sure you take a measuring tape, know your room sizes, and have a way to get your treasures home.

References: There are many excellent reference books available. Please contact a bookseller or library.

For additional listings and a detailed list of reference books, see *Warman's American Furniture* and *Warman's Antiques & Collectible.*

TIAS Top 10
The following list ranks the most highly sought collectibles on the Internet during 2001.
1. China
2. Cookie jars
3. Dolls
4. Furniture
5. Lamps
6. Carnival glass
7. Books
8. Plates
9. Depression glass
10. Roseville
Source: www.tias.com

Bed, rope
  Federal, wear to blue paint.........**215.00**
  Jenny Lind, stripped...................**100.00**
Blanket chest
  New England, pine, lift top, two drawers **300.00**
  Oriental carving, brass lock plate **150.00**
Bookcase, barrister type, stacking, glass front, 4 sections, removable top and base **395.00**

Rocking chair made to look as though it's made from spinning wheel parts, $150.

Corner cupboard, leaded glass doors top and bottom, open section, oak, Arts & Crafts style, $250.

Bureau, molded crest over rect mirror, candle holders at side, 2 lidded boxes, 3 drawers, orig dark brown paint, gold striping, floral dec **500.00**
Butler's tray table, mahogany......**125.00**
Chair
  Queen Anne, ladderback, five back slats, rush seat **200.00**
  Oak, pressed back **100.00**
  Windsor, high comb back, 1920s.**95.00**
Chest of drawers
  Chippendale style, walnut with inlay, molded cornice arched to accommodate 3 arched top drawers, 3 long drawers with stringing. 3 overlapping drawers in base, cabriole legs, small feet, shaped apron, refinished, base later construction, 67-3/4" h.........**1,750.00**
  Country style, solid cherry, 4 large drawers, scrolled front piece, scrolled feet, refinished, old glass knobs **750.00**
Church bench
  23" l, oak **135.00**
  61" l, primitive, solid ends **165.00**
Clothes tree, oak, sq center posts, all orig hooks...................................**150.00**
Corner chair, New England, maple, turned stretcher base **175.00**
Cupboard, step back, painted blue-gray, 19th C..**500.00**

Morris chair, rose covered cushions, carved dec on arms and skirt, finish worn, $50.

Desk, 36" x 72-1/2" x 29-1/2" h, oak, light natural finish, traces of white, carved horseshoe detail, plate glass top, matching desk chair with cowhide back, Brandt Company...............**500.00**
Desk chair, Arts & Crafts, Charles Limbert, horizontal H-back, orig leather seat, branded mark, c1912, 35" h **550.00**
Dining room chairs, Chippendale-style, 1 arm chair, 5 side chairs, veneered, pierced splat, slip seat, cabriole legs, paw feet...................................**950.00**
Filing cabinet, oak, 4 drawers, worn finish...**400.00**
Glider, metal, repainted turquoise, working condition **500.00**
Hall bench, Colonial Revival, Baroque-style, cherry, shell carved crest over cartouche and griffin carved panel back, lift seat, high arms, mask carved base, paw feet, c1910, 51" h......**700.00**

Kitchen table, painted white, tapered legs, top possibly replaced, $45.

Wardrobe, cedar, two doors on top, orig hardware and locks, $150.

Highboy, Chippendale style,
Philadelphia, some period elements,
some hardware missing **650.00**
Jelly cupboard, 2 doors, stripped **350.00**
Kitchen cabinet, painted surface,
agateware sliding work surface, some
wear...**350.00**
Loveseat, Sheraton style, mahogany,
reupholstered in dusty rose and tan
stripe fabric................................**200.00**
Music cabinet, Art Nouveau, hardwood,
cherry finish, crest with beveled glass,
paneled door, applied dec, 49" h**200.00**
Night stand, sq top, slightly splayed legs,
small drawer, refinished **200.00**
Pie safe, poplar and white pine, light
brown paint dec, 2 drawers over 2
paneled doors, 2 circular vents on each
side, 54-1/2" h **600.00**
Plant stand, cast iron, worn orig gilding
with red and green dec, onyx inset top,
bottom shelf, 14" x 14" x 30" h...**165.00**
Morris chair, as found cond, very worn
orig cushions **200.00**
Rocking chair
Boston style, maple seat, worn..**250.00**
Cane seat and back, newly caned
....**300.00**
Wicker, painted, upholstered seat
....**215.00**
Shelf
Empire, oak, beveled mirror **125.00**
Shaker style, cherry, double row of
pegs, 84" l................................**95.00**
Stool, primitive, pine, stretcher base
....**95.00**
Table
Coffee table, blue glass top, curving
sides, lower shelf **120.00**

Dining, rect, extra leaves, mahogany
colored, c1940 ....**115.00**
Drop leaf, cherry, refinished, burn mark
on one leaf.............................**400.00**
Kitchen, oak, drop leaf, some wear,
c1890 ....**200.00**
Side, half moon top painted yellow,
natural straight legs **200.00**
Tilt top, painted blue, Chinoiserie dec
top...**425.00**
Trestle base, three board top, 64" l
....**425.00**
Wash stand
Federal, painted, wear to paint ..**285.00**
Hepplewhite, painted pine, one board
top painted yellow...................**195.00**
Sheraton, mahogany.................**210.00**
Welsh dresser, walnut, molded cornice,
3 open shelves with hooks, base with 3
drawers, lower shelf **3,700.00**

❖ Gambling

Some of us buy lottery tickets, chances, etc. and are willing to take a chance on "winning it big." Others prefer to seek out memorabilia that is related to gambling, lotteries, and other games of chance.

Collectors' Club: Casino Chips & Gaming Tokens Collectors Club, P.O. Box 63, Brick, NJ 08723.

Advertisement, 2-sided card, promotes Rol-A-Top Bell Twin Jack Pot from Watling Mfg Co., Chicago, 1941...**45.00**
Ashtray, Fabulous Las Vegas, copper-coated with glass bottom with working roulette wheel, embossed scenes, lever spins wheel and ball, 1950s, 5" dia **27.50**
Book
　Blackjack, Winner's Handbook, Patterson **12.00**
　Card Tricks, Magic, Gambling Guidebook, 1st ed. **18.00**
Card Counter, plated, imitation ivory face, black lettering **20.00**
Catalog, H.C. Evans & Co., Secret Blue Book, Gambling Supply, 1936, 72 pgs **55.00**
Chip
　Crest and seal, Choctaw Club, Louisiana **175.00**
　New Southport Club of New Orleans, terra cotta and ivory................**20.00**
　Top hat design, burgundy, 1-1/2" dia **14.00**

Gambling Collectibles, tray, tin, decorated with hand of playing cards "The Skat Players Dream – issued by the Leisy Brewing Co. Peoria, Ill.," 5" dia, $300.

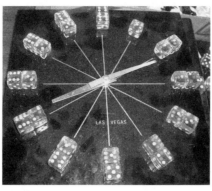

Gambling Collectibles, clock, black Lucite ground, red dice as numerals, gold handles, gold trim, mkd "Las Vegas," $8.

Chuck-a-luck, red Bakelite **75.00**
Faro cards, sq corners, Samuel Hart & Co., NY, complete......................**125.00**
Keno cards, 136, wood, paper and material covering, H.C. Evans & Co., Chicago **250.00**
Matchbook, Golden Nugget, gambling hall on cover..................................**1.50**
Roulette wheel, wood and metal, single and double zero decals, 4-prong spinner **45.00**
Shot Glass, ribbed dec, porcelain dice in bottom **25.00**
Token, casino, $1
　Majestic **2.00**
Trump................................**2.25**
Wheel of Fortune, 30 numbers, hand decorated yellow and white, cut-out paneled center, red ground........**150.00**

❖ Games

Kids of all ages have enjoyed games for decades. Some played hard, but those who carefully preserved the pieces and the instructions, and who took very good care of the box, are loved by today's collectors. Flea markets are great sources for vintage games as well as for those that feature popular television and movie characters.

References: Alex G. Malloy, *American Games Comprehensive Collector's Guide*, Antique Trader Books, 2000; Desi Scarpone, *More Board Games*, Schiffer Publishing, 2000. Sharon Korbeck and Dan Stearns, *Toys & Prices 2003*, Krause Publications.

Periodicals: *The Games Annual*, 5575 Arapahoe Rd, Suite D, Boulder, CO 80303; *Toy Shop*, 700 E State St, Iola, WI 54990; *Toy Trader*, P.O. Box 1050, Dubuque, IA 52004.

Collectors' Clubs: American Game Collectors Assoc, P.O. Box 44, Dresler, PA, 19025; Gamers Alliance, P.O. Box 197, East Meadow, NY 11554.

Acquire, Avalon................................**25.00**

Peg Solitaire, A Sherm's Creation, $20.

All Star Hockey, metal figures, 1960s **90.00**
Ally Oop Game, cylinder-shaped container **75.00**
Anagrams Game, Milton Bradley, 1930s **35.00**
Apple's Way, Milton Bradley, 1974 ...**25.00**
Beetle Bailey **25.00**
Bozo the Clown Circus Game, Transogram **15.00**
Candyland, Milton Bradley, 1960s ...**10.00**
Captain Video **125.00**
Charge Account, Lowell, 1961.........**12.00**
Clue, Parker Bros., 1949, 1st ed. **35.00**
Dream House....................................**25.00**
Dukes of Hazzard, Ideal, 1981 ....**10.00**
Easy Money, Milton Bradley.............**7.50**
Family Ties......................................**20.00**
Finance and Fortune, Parker Bros., 1930s **45.00**
General Hospital, Cardinal, 1982 ....**18.00**
Giggles Game, Rosebud Art Co., 1950s **45.00**
Hardy Boys, 1959 ....**35.00**
Huckleberry Hound Bumps, Transogram, 1961 ....**50.00**
I Spy..**50.00**
Knight Rider **25.00**
Little House on the Prairie..............**25.00**

Perry Mason, Case of the Missing Suspect Game, Transogram, all pcs present, box worn and torn, $5.

The Original Radio Game, Evryn Novelty Co., Philadelphia, bingo game, orig cards, $15.

Section of weathered fence, Spring Thyme sign, flower posts attached to 2 pickets, $12.

Statue, concrete, eagle, 23" h, $45.

Mystery Date **75.00**
Name That Tune, Milton Bradley, 1959
....**20.00**
Password, Milton Bradley, 1963.......**15.00**
Ruff and Ready, Transogram, 1962 .**35.00**
Silly Sidney, Transogram, 1963........**55.00**
Terry Toons, Ideal **45.00**
Twilight Zone....................................**195.00**
Uncle Wiggily, 1930s.......................**45.00**
Woody Woodpecker..........................**25.00**
You're Out, Corey Game Co., 1941 .**40.00**
Zorro, Whitman, 1958 ....**30.00**

❖ Gardening

There's something therapeutic about gardening. And, when the weather is bad, why not collect gardening items to soothe your spirit? Many landscapers use antique elements to enhance garden areas, so dig around flea markets for interesting gates, garden benches, etc.

Bird bath
    Cast iron, some rust.....................**95.00**
    Concrete, 2-pc.............................**35.00**
Book
    Crockett's Tool Shed, Gardening Equipment, James Crockett, photos by Lou Jones, 1989 ....**7.00**
    Daylilies and How to Grow Them, Ben Arthur Davis, 1954, 1st ed, some wear to dj **8.00**

Flea market buyers could choose any tin sap bucket they wanted for $25.

Successful Gardening with Perennials, Helen Van Pelt Wilson, 1976, 1st edition, worn dj **12.00**
Taylor's Guide to Gardening, Techniques, Planning, Planting & Caring For Your Garden, Houghton Mifflin Co., 1991, 1st ed.............**7.00**
Brooch, 1-3/8" h, watering can, goldtone watering can, flowers, faux pearls on handle **22.00**
Child's Watering Can, Mistress Mary, Cohn Toys, Brooklyn, NY, 8" w, 6-1/2" h, wear **115.00**
Flowerpot, clay, typical **1.00**
Garden bench, precast concrete **45.00**
Gardening gloves, well worn **2.00**
Harvester, R.C. Kingmaker, Carlisle, Ky., orig red and black paint, handle shows some wear, 16" h, 10-1/2" w **165.00**
Harvesting basket, woven splint **65.00**
Hoe, heart shaped blade, worn wooden handle **20.00**
Panel, wrought iron, climbing vine dec, some orig gilt dec, slight rust **300.00**
Planter, cement, painted green, white Viking ship and lion dec, 1930s, 15" sq, 10" h, pr.....................................**155.00**
Seed box, litho label, wooden box with lid..**30.00**
Seedling bell, glass dome, knob top **35.00**
Seed packet
    Shaker...**7.50**
    Typical **3.00**
Shears, wooden handles................**25.00**
Shovel, worn wood handle..............**15.00**
Sprayer, Gulf Space, small dent in tank, 18" l......................................**65.00**
Sundial, brass, mounted on marble base **125.00**
Urns, pr, concrete..........................**85.00**
Watering can
    Brass, 9-1/2" l, 4-3/8" h, few small dents..**8.00**
    Metal, painted black, orig sprinkler attachment, 12" h **25.00**
    Porcelain, painted flowers, 8-1/2" h **17.50**

Tin, wide brass head....................**25.00**
Watering pot, patent April 17, 1894, mkd "Imported for R & J Farquatlar & Co., Boston, Reliable Seeds, Market Street," 22" l, 9" w, 9-1/4" h.....................**225.00**
Wheel barrow, wood wheel and body, removable sides, old green paint, 62" l, 27" h, 23" w..............................**225.00**

❖ Garfield

Who's the coolest cat around the cartoon pages these days? Garfield! Flea markets are favorite hangouts for this lasagna-loving feline and his buddies.

Reference: Robert Gipson, *The Unauthorized Collector's Guide to Garfield and the Gang*, Schiffer Publishing, 2000.

Alarm clock, Sunbeam, 1978.......**115.00**
Bank
    Ceramic, bowling, mkd "Garfield Copyright 1981, United Feature Syndicate, Inc.," orig stopper **60.00**
    Ceramic, wearing graduation gown and cap, 5-1/2" h, mkd "Enesco" **60.00**
    Plastic, gum ball type, "Can I Borrow A Penny," orig plastic key, 6-1/2" h**20.00**
Beach towel, Franco design, 28" x 51" **18.00**
Bookends, pr, lounging Garfield, white base, Enesco, 1981, 4-1/2" w, 5-1/2" h **50.00**
Clock, battery operated, 1978, 6-1/2" h **32.00**
Lunch box, plastic **5.00**

Garfield Game, Parker Brothers, all pcs present, box slightly worn, $7.50.

Garfield Bank, plastic, light caramel colored, red hat lid, 14" h, $8.

Mug

Ceramic, "I am A Redskins Fan-atic"
....**15.00**

Glass, McDonald's **10.00**

Nodder, MIB, 7-1/2" h **27.00**

Pez...**6.50**

Statue, boxing, United Feature
Syndicate, Inc., 1981, 4-1/4" h **35.00**

Telephone, Tyco Industries Model #1207
....**40.00**

Thimble, dressed as Santa.............**14.00**

Tie, blue background **12.00**

Trophy, Garfield leaning towards Arlene,
captioned "Where have you been all
my life?" 4-1/4" h **25.00**

Window sticker, stuffed figure, four
suction cups, faded body, 6-1/2" h .**4.00**

❖ Gas Station Collectibles

Whether you refer to this category as Gas Station Collectibles, Service Station Memorabilia, or Petroliana isn't important. What does matter is that there are plenty of advertising items, premiums, and related materials from those places that sell us gas so we can drive to flea markets!

Texaco Toy Tanker Truck, 1994, MIB, $15.

Reference: Jack Sim, *An Illustrated Guide to Gas Pumps*, Krause Publications, 2002; Mark Anderton, *Encyclopedia of Petroliana*, Krause Publications, 1999; Scott Benjamin and Wayne Henderson, *Gas Globes: Pennzoil to Union and Affiliates*, Schiffer Publishing, 1999; ——, *Sinclair Collectibles*, Schiffer Publishing, 1997; J. Sam McIntyre, *The Esso Collectibles Handbook: Memorabilia from Standard Oil of New Jersey*, Schiffer Publishing, 1998; Rick Pease, *Petroleum Collectibles*, Schiffer Publishing, 1997; ——, *A Tour with Texaco: Antique Advertising and Memorabilia*, Schiffer Publishing, 1997; Charles Whitworth, *Gulf Oil Collectibles*, Schiffer Publishing, 1998.

Periodical: *Check the Oil!*, 30 W Olentangy St, Powell, OH 43065, www.oldgas.com/info/cto.htm; *Petroleum Collectibles Monthly*, 411 Forest St., La Grange, OH 43065, www.pcmpublishing.com.

Collectors' Club: International Petroliana Collectors Assoc, P.O. Box 937, Powell, OH 43065; Oil Can Collectors Club, 4213 Derby Ln, Evansville, IN 47715, www.oilcancollectors.com.

Banner, Texaco Havoline, plastic, 8" l
....**65.00**

Blotter, Nu-Blue Sunoco Gas, Donald Duck, M. C. Sparks & Son, Ronton, OH, 1948, 4" x 7", slight use........**24.00**

Calendar, 1959, Sinclair, shows attendant cleaning windshield, slight tear, 7-1/2" x 8-1/2" **28.50**

Car attachment, Shell Oil, 3-3/4" x 5-1/2" metal domed image of Shell symbol, three colorful International Code Flags, late 1930s...................................**190.00**

Coaster/ashtray, Mobil Safe Driving Award, 1953, metal, shield logo, 4"dia
....**25.00**

Coloring book, Esso Happy Motoring, unused...**25.00**

Dashboard Memo, Harry's Auto Service, Auto Repairing of All Kinds, Bernard, OH, use to record dates, car servicing info...**55.00**

Drinking glass, Phillips 66, Deem Oil Co., St. Louis, 5-1/4" h **48.00**

Fan, 10-1/2" l, 7-5/8" w, Sinclair Opaline Motor Oil, adv on back **75.00**

Gas pump, electric, orig hose, nozzle missing, 16" w, 10" d, 36" h **325.00**

Key chain, flicker, Amoco, As You Travel Ask Us, back side has place for name and address with please return to**12.00**

License plate tag, Shell Motor Oil, 1930s, wear and rust, 5-1/4" h, 3" w **38.00**

Measuring can, Be-Sure Gasoline, side pouring spout **12.00**

Oil can, D-A Speed Sport Oil, yellow full quart with old cars, checkered flags logo, "Racing Division," D-A Lubricant, Indianapolis, Indiana, C9+ **50.00**

Hess Recreation Van, MIB, $10.

Pencil, lead, Gulf Oil, unused **5.00**

Pinback Button

Amoco, celluloid, 1" d...................**15.00**

Mobil Oil, 1932 ....**35.00**

Puzzle, Sohio Ethyl Gasoline, Mickey Mouse, plastic, 1950s, adv on back
....**72.00**

Sign

Fisk Tires, porcelain, 1930s **425.00**

Sinclair Gas, porcelain **100.00**

Thermometer, Shell Anti-Freeze **85.00**

❖ Geisha Girl

Geisha girl porcelain consists of over 150 different patterns. It was made during the last quarter of the 19th century and again during the 1940s, primarily for export to western markets. All of the items show at least one elaborately dressed Geisha, and they are hand-painted with many bright colors. Because over 100 different manufacturers produced Geisha Girl wares, many marks can be found.

Bowl, petal design, 7" dia **20.00**

Celery set, Porch, Torii Nippon mark, 5 pcs...**40.00**

Chocolate pot, Child Reaching for Butterfly pattern, Japan, 9-3/8" h .**65.00**

Chocolate set, pot and 8 cups, Japan, pot 9-3/4" h...............................**125.00**

Creamer **20.00**

Cup and saucer, Nippon **25.00**

Eggcup, Japan, 2-1/4" h **18.00**

Hatpin holder, 4" h **55.00**

Mug, Bamboo Trellis......................**20.00**

Plate, 7-1/2" dia.............................**10.00**

Geisha Girl tea cup, Bicycle pattern, wavy red-orange border, int. border of gold lacing, bamboo style handle, unmarked, $10.

Ring tree, figural hand in center **25.00**
Salt and pepper shakers, pr, Japan, 2-
 1/4" h...**14.00**
Sugar bowl, cov, handles, Japan....**20.00**
Toothpick holder, Parasol Modern, 2" h
 ....**12.00**

❖ GI Joe

Billed as "A Real American Hero," Hasbro's GI Joe has been a favorite for years. Collectors search for GI Joe action figures, accessories, vehicles, etc. Over the years, GI Joe has undergone changes in size and even attitude, resulting in a variety of items to collect.

References: Vincent Santelmo, *The Complete Encyclopedia of GI Joe*, 3rd ed, Krause Publications, 2001; ———,.*GI Joe Identification & Price Guide, 1964-1998*, Krause Publications, 1999.

Periodicals: *GI Joe Patrol*, P.O. Box 2362, Hot Springs, AR 71914.

Collectors' Clubs: GI Joe Collectors Club, 225 Cattle Baron Parc Dr. Fort Worth, TX 76108, (800) 772-6673; GI Joe: Street Brigade Club, 8362 Lornay Ave, Westminster, CA 92683.

For additional listings, see *Warman's Americana & Collectibles*.

Accessories

 Ammo belt...................................**18.00**
 Bullet proof vest, secret agent **8.00**
 Heavy Artillery Laser, MIB **45.00**
 Goggles, orange..........................**14.00**
 Jet pack, Jump **25.00**
 Life ring **1.00**
 Machine gun, played-with, orig box
 ....**20.00**
 Navy flag **28.00**
 Sand bag.......................................**5.00**
 Ski Patrol Set **95.00**
 Snowshoes..................................**15.00**
 Sleeping bag **24.00**
 Tent, poles missing......................**20.00**

Brochure, fold-out, shows different toy series, 1986, $2.

Action figure, 3-3/4"
 Armadillo, 1988, loose................**12.00**
 Blizzard, 1988, MOC...................**35.00**
 Breaker, 1982, loose **20.00**
 Buzzer, 1985, MOC.....................**45.00**
 Clutch, 1982, loose **15.00**
 Cobra, 1982, loose......................**40.00**
 Crystal Ball, 1987, loose **12.00**
 Dee-Jay, 1985, MOC...................**12.00**
 Desert Camo Savage, 1994, mail-in,
 loose **6.00**
 Grunt, 1982, loose **22.00**
 Iceberg, 1986, loose **10.00**
 Muskrat, 1988, loose...................**12.00**
 Snow Job, 1983, loose.................**25.00**
 Spirit, 1984, loose **19.00**
 Torch, 1985, MOC.......................**60.00**
 Torpedo, 1983, MOC....................**50.00**
 Wild Bill, 1991, MOC...................**50.00**
 Windmill, 1988, loose **7.00**
 Zandor, 1986, Canadian, MOC **25.00**
Action figure, posable, Hall of Fame, Hasbro, 12" h, NRFB
 Combat Camo Duke, 1993...........**40.00**
 Rapid Deployment Force, Marine, 1994
 ....**45.00**
 Rapid-Fire Ultimate Commano, 1993
 ....**45.00**
 Surveillance Specialist, 1995 ....**40.00**

Cobra Flight Pod, Trubble Bubble, MIB, $28.

Four GI Joe dolls, early 1990s, new in original boxes, each $35.

Clothing
 Beret, green **85.00**
 Boots, short, black.........................**4.00**
 Boots, tall, brown...........................**8.00**
 Hat, Army **28.00**
 Helmet, dark blue **18.00**
 Jacket, dress, Marine **30.00**
 Jacket, Russian **12.00**
 Pants, dress, Marine **6.00**
 Pants, ski patrol...........................**22.00**
 Set, secret agent, trench coat, bullet
 proof vest.................................**28.00**
 Shirt, Navy, 1 pocket **4.00**
 Shirt, soldier, no pockets...............**8.00**
Coloring book, 48 pgs, Spanish text, 1989 ....**15.00**
Playset, Atomic Man Secret Outpost, good box **85.00**
Vehicle
 Amphibious Personnel Carrier, MIB
 ....**150.00**
 Armored Missile Vehicle Wolverine,
 orig, box, card missing **90.00**
 Flying Submarine, orig box, card
 missing **40.00**
 Tank Car, motorized, MOC..........**12.00**
Weapon
 Bayonet **15.00**
 Flare pistol...................................**2.00**
 M-16 ....**30.00**
 Night stick...................................**20.00**

❖ Girl Scouts

It's easy to identify Girl Scouts during their cookie campaigns, but they are as dedicated to community service and education as are their male counterparts. Flea market finds might include clothing, badges, and camping equipment.

Reference: George Cuhaj, *Standard Price Guide to U.S. Scouting Collectibles 2nd ed.*, Krause Publications, 1998.

Periodicals: *Scout Memorabilia*, P.O. Box 1121, Manchester, NH 03105; *Scouting Collectors Quarterly*, 806 E Scott St, Tuscola, IL 61953.

Girl Scouts Patch, Camp Hibucks, $3.

Collectors' Clubs: American Scouting Traders Assoc, P.O. Box 92, Kentfield, CA 94914; International Badgers Club, 7760 NW 50th St, Lauder Hill, FL 33351; National Scouting Collectors Soc, 806 E Scott S., Tuscola, IL 61953; Scouts on Stamps Soc International, 7406 Park Dr, Tampa, FL 33610.

Appreciation statue, copper coated spelter figure, recipient's name on front, designed by Marjorie Daingerfield, 1953, 6" h.............**125.00**
Belt, elasticized, 31" l.......................**14.00**
Calendar
 1947, 8" x 11"..............................**48.00**
 1967, orig envelope, 10" x 17".....**22.00**
Canteen, aluminum, cloth jacket, Girl Scout insignia, 7-1/4" dia.............**25.00**
Charter, tan textured paper, dated Jan 1921, dark brown inscription and design, inked signatures.............**30.00**
Doll, cloth mask face, 14" h.........**115.00**
Handbook, 1953, 510 pgs..............**18.00**
Handkerchief, 12" sq......................**21.00**
Hat, Brownie, wool, orig tag............**18.00**
Invitation, "Sister Scout," white and green, cartoon fishes, 1980 ....**5.00**
Leader book, *Leadership of Girl Scout Troops, Intermediate Program,* 1943, 365 pgs **15.00**
Magazine, *The American Girl*, June, 1934 ....**10.00**
Mug, white ground, red insignia........**7.00**
Pin, gold plated metal, 7/8" w, 7/8" h
 ....**16.00**
Pinback button
 Boone Brownie Olympics, brown and orange, early 1980s..................**12.00**
 Brownie Day, brown and orange, cartoon clown image, 1981 ......**10.00**
 Girl Scouts Audubon Project, green and white, blue lettering, 1980s **10.00**

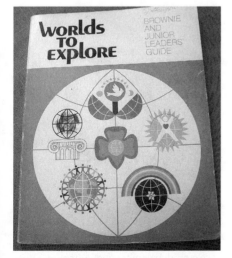

Girl Scouts Worlds to Explore, *Brownie and Junior Girl Scout Leaders Guide, copyright 1981, $15.*

Pinback button, The Girl Comes First in Girl Scouting, $2.

 Girl Scouts Meet the Challenge, green and yellow, 1980s.......................**8.00**
Ring, Brownie, sterling silver, adjustable, center image of dancing Brownie, 1930s **35.00**
Sash, Lake Erie Council Troop #1007, badges, gold star pin....................**25.00**
Sewing kit, Brownies, red case, 1940s
 ....**15.00**
Shirt, size 7 ....**5.00**
Tin, Peanut Crunchies, 5" h **20.00**

❖ Glass Knives

Most glass knives date to the Depression, produced by many of the glass manufacturers who dominated the market at that period. They vary in color and design, and, as with most collectibles, a premium is paid for examples with the original box.

Block pattern, pink **45.00**
Flower handle, pink, inscribed "Nettie," mkd "Made in USA"......................**40.00**
Plain, green, 9-1/8" l........................**42.00**
Three Leaf pattern, crystal.............**18.00**

Glass knives in orig box, top: green cardboard, green glass knife, box mkd "Glass Fruit & Cake Knife, Always Clean and Sanitary," $20; bottom box, pink cardboard, "The New Vitex-Glass Knife, Always Sharp, Sanitary, Stainless," orig pink glass knife, $25.

Three Star pattern, Barry Importing Co., Broadway, N.Y.
 Blue **42.00**
 Crystal, orig box **40.00**
 Pink **38.00**
Vitex, crystal, orig box, 9" l.............**40.00**

❖ Goebel

Many dealers and collectors associate the name "Goebel" with Hummels, but the company has also produced many other figures, animals, and accessories. Look for Hummel-type markings and well-made porcelain.

Collectors' Clubs: Friar Tuck Collectors Club, P.O. Box 262, Oswego, NY 13827; Goebel Networkers, P.O. Box 396, Lemoyne, PA 17043.

Animal figure
 Buffalo, 6" h.................................**70.00**
 Fish, incised mark, 3"...................**45.00**
 Irish Setter, 10" h **90.00**
 Spaniel Dog, 8" h.........................**80.00**
Decanter, Friar Tuck, large...........**130.00**
Figure
 Bellhop, Sheraton, orig suitcases
 ....**425.00**
 Betsey Clark..............................**100.00**
 Eleanor, mkd "Made in West Germany," incised numbers, 8-3/4" h.........**75.00**
 Elisabeth, gold trim, mkd "Made in West Germany," incised numbers, 8-3/4" h **75.00**
 Woody, 6" h **350.00**
Flower pot, Oriental man attached to side, crown mark.........................**90.00**
Perfume lamp, Bambi, stylized bee mark, foil paper label, 6-1/2" h ...**275.00**
Salt and pepper shakers, pr
 Friar Tuck, full bee mark, "Made in West Germany," 4" h...............**145.00**
 Frog and toadstool **35.00**
 Peppers, one red, other green, full bee mark, black "Germany" stamp, 2" w
 ....**30.00**
Vase, Figaro the Cat.........................**90.00**

Goebel bank, yellow duck, $40.

❖ Goldschneider Porcelain

Friedrich Goldschneider established a porcelain and faience factory in Vienna, Austria, in 1885. Production continued there until the early 1940s, when the family fled war-torn Europe for the United States. The Goldschneider Everlast Corporation was located in Trenton, New Jersey from 1943 until 1950, producing traditional figures and accessories.

Bust, black woman, blue hair, orange highlights, pedestal base...........**400.00**
Figure
Lady with parasol, 8-1/2" h **85.00**
Madonna and Child, orig label, 4-1/2" h **60.00**
Southern Belle, 10-1/2" h.............**90.00**
Music box, Colonial Girl **120.00**
Plate, mermaid pattern..................**175.00**
Wall mask, Art Deco, curly brown haired girl, aqua scarf **450.00**

❖ Golf Collectibles

"Fore!" When you consider that the game of golf has been played since the 15th century, you begin to understand how many golf collectibles are available to collectors. Flea markets are great sources for interesting clubs, paper ephemera, and other related items.

Reference: Chuck Furjanic, *Antique Golf Collectibles*, 2nd ed, Krause Publications, 1999.

Periodicals: *Golfiana Magazine*, 222 Levette Ln #4, Edwardsville, IL 62025; *US Golf Classics & Heritage Hickories*, 5207 Pennock Point Rd, Jupiter, FL 33458.

Collectors' Clubs: Golf Collectors Soc, P.O. Box 20546, Dayton, OH 45420; Logo Golf Ball Collector's Assoc, 2552 Barclay Fairway, Lake Worth, FL 33467; The Golf Club Collectors Assoc, 640 E Liberty St, Girard, OH 44420.

Ashtray, Senior PGA Golf Tour, ceramic, figural sand trap, green golf flag missing **7.00**
Ball
Gutta percha, made in Great Britain, c1895, 60% to 70% paint, numerous iron marks...............................**440.00**
Lynx, rubber core **18.00**
Book
Golf My Way, Jack Nicklaus with Ken Bowden, Simon & Schuster, 1974, softcover, 265 pgs **8.00**
The Golfers Companion, Peter Lawless, 1st ed, 1937, 512 pgs.........
150.00
Cigarette card, A. Padgham, British Sporting Personalities series, issued by W.D. & H.O. Wills, 1937, photo of 1936 British Open champion, 3" x 2" **5.00**

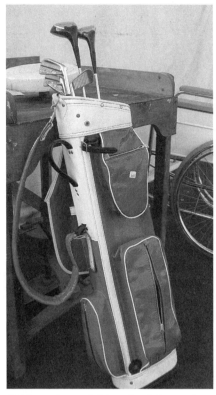

Golf bag with several clubs, red and white vinyl, $15.

Club
Fleetwood, Draper Maynard Co., Plymouth, NH, #10 ....**25.00**
Hagen, iron-man sand wedge, wood shaft.......................................**170.00**
Lady Diana, Mashie 5 iron **50.00**
Wilson, wedge, staff model, 1959, steel shaft.......................................**60.00**
Medallion, 14k yg, inscribed "G. V. C. Golf Chairman 1973," intaglio snowflake design, 1" dia **75.00**
Paperweight, U.S. Open, 1980 ....**32.00**
Plate, crossed golf clubs under "D," Syracuse China, scalloped edge, 9-3/4" dia **35.00**
Program, Bob Hope Desert Classic, 1967 ....**20.00**

Golf plaque, brass, black and red lettering, "Behold the Golfer, he riseth up early in the morning & disturbeth the whole household. Mighty are his preparations. He goeth forth full of hope and when the day is spent, he returnith, smelling of strong drink and the Truth is not in him." $15.

Putter, The Spaulding, gooseneck blade, period replacement grip, 32-3/4" l **140.00**
Tee, wooden, 1920s, two Rite Hite, 1 Carrot, set of 3 ....**20.00**
Trading cards, Golf Card Set, 1981**59.00**

❖ Gonder Pottery

Established in 1941 by Lawton Gonder, this Gonder Pottery was located in Zanesville, Ohio, until it closed in 1957. Gonder pieces are clearly marked and many have interesting glazes.

Collectors' Club: Gonder Collectors Club, 917 Hurl Dr, Pittsburgh, PA 15236.

Bookends, pr, 10-1/2" h, horses, yellow, brown glaze..............................**135.00**
Bowl, white, crackle glaze, 8" dia....**15.00**
Bulb bowl, light blue, 6" d..............**15.00**
Candlestick, cornucopia-shape, light gray, pink accents, #552, 5" h **32.00**
Cornucopia, blue and gray, 7-1/4" l**15.00**
Ewer, Shell and Star pattern, green, 13" h **60.00**
Lamp, Flying Ducks, chartreuse and dark green, 10" w, 12" h.......................**75.00**
Pitcher, twist motif, red and white...**65.00**
Planter
Feather, pale blue, 12" h, 10" w ...**90.00**
Flower-shape, yellow....................**15.00**
Shell-shape, gray **58.00**
Swan, light blue, E-44, 5-1/2" h, 5" l **25.00**
Teapot, cov, brown and yellow glaze, mkd "Gonder USA P-31," 7" x 11"**85.00**
Urn, handled, gray, H-49 ....**45.00**
Vase, light gray shading to pink, mkd "Gonder, E-5," 7" h **30.00**

Gonder Pottery, bulb bowl, green exterior, mottled pink and white int., marked "E-12 Gonder USA," $12.

❖ Goofus Glass

Whether collectors identify it as goofus glass, Mexican ware, or hooligan glass, there's no denying its unique beauty. Goofus glass is actually clear pressed glass that has been painted, usually on the back, with a metallic gold ground and colored highlights. Because the colorful decoration is not fired, it is very susceptible to flaking. Most goofus glass was produced from 1890 to about 1920.

Periodical: *Goofus Glass Gazette*, 9 Lindenwood Ct, Sterling, VA 20165.

Bowl, Roses, 8" dia.........................**35.00**
Cake plate, Dahlia and Fan, red flowers, gold ground **45.00**
Child's plate, "This Little Pig Went to Market," 6-1/2" d.........................**125.00**
Coaster, Grapes, red grapes, gold ground **4.00**

Goofus Glass, bowl, red roses, emb fern-type foliage, gold ground, scalloped edge, $25.

Dish, Chrysanthemum Sprays, red flowers, gold ground, scalloped rim, 11" dia **85.00**
Oil lamp, banquet type, gold ground, 21" h **180.00**
Plate
   Advertising, Old Rose Distilling Co., Chicago, 8-1/4" dia **75.00**
   Apples, red fruit, gold ground, 7-1/2" dia..**28.00**
   Double Roses, red roses, gold ground, 10-1/2" dia **30.00**
Vase, Cabbage Rose, gold ground, red roses, 7" h **25.00**

Goofus Glass, bowls, left: gold and red hops band dec, clear center, 9" d, $45; right: gold background, red grapes, 10" d, $65.

❖ Graniteware

Graniteware is the name given to metal kitchen and dinnerwares that have an interesting speckled or swirled paint decoration. The first graniteware was made in Germany in the 1830s. By World War I, American manufacturers were taking over the market. Common colors include gray and white, but savvy collectors will tell you

that graniteware comes in a variety of colors. Graniteware is still being produced.

Adhering single or multiple layers of enamel to metal items through the use of high temperatures resulted in a product with a glass-like finish that was referred to as graniteware. Although such pieces were advertised as quite durable, they do in fact chip rather easily. Pattern and color are extremely important when determining value.

References: Helen Greguire, *Collector's Encyclopedia of Granite Ware: Colors, Shapes and Values, Book I* (1990, 1994 value update), *Book II* (1993, 1998 value update), Collector Books; David T. Pikul and Ellen M. Plante, *Collectible Enameled Ware: American & European*, Schiffer Publishing, 1998.

Collectors' Club: National Graniteware Society, P.O. Box 9248, Cedar Rapids, IA 52409-9248.

Graniteware, hanging utensil rack, gray, hand painted pink flower with green leaves, chip on front tray lip, $165.

Baking Pan, white, black trim, 9" x 13" x 2-1/2" h, some wear **15.00**
Berry bucket, brown mottled, tin lid, wooden knob, bail handle, 4-1/4" h, 6-1/4" dia **85.00**
Bowl
   Blue and white, medium swirl, black trim, c1960, 6-1/8" dia **35.00**
   Red and white stripes, 8" dia, 3-1/4" h **32.00**
Bread Box, white, lavender tulip dec, brass handle and latch, 13" l, 6" h **95.00**
Bucket, black and white swirl........**265.00**

Graniteware, hanging utensil rack, bright red, black and white checkerboard trim, $145.

Graniteware, canister set, gold names in French, slight use wear, $240.

Chamberstick
Blue and white swirl, 5-1/4" dia, 2-1/4" h, chips, rust **135.00**
Gray, 6-1/4" dia..........................**95.00**

Coffeepot
Blue and white swirl, black handle and finial, 10-1/8" h.........................**140.00**
Gray, gooseneck spout, pewter-decor engraved Victorian design, 9-3/4" h **150.00**

Colander, gray **35.00**

Cream can, gray, tin lid, wire bail, 4-1/2" high, 3-1/4" dia **225.00**

Cup, cream and green, rolled rim, one ding on edge, wear to edge of handle **45.00**

Dipper, gray.................................**40.00**

Dustpan, gray mottled....................**35.00**

Graniteware, pitcher, tall, gray and white, $195.

Food mold, blue/white swirl, turk's head **115.00**

Funnel, white, cobalt blue trim, 4" l, wear, scuff marks on handle and tip of spout **25.00**

Frying pan, blue and white speckled, 7-1/4" w, some wear and rust..........**45.00**

Ladle, white, 14" l, heavy wear, dings, rust **10.00**

Match safe, gray, double pockets, 5-1/8" h **225.00**

Mending Kit, Mendets, directions on back, 2 missing **9.50**

Milk Pail, orange, blue, black, and white Art Deco design, 8" h, chips around base and lid.................................**70.00**

Mixing Bowl, green, black trim, 11" dia, dull int., some wear **30.00**

Mold, 9" d, 3" d, gray, some wear and chipping.......................................**35.00**

Muffin pan, 8-hole, gray, wire frame**60.00**

Mug, white, black trim, 2-1/4" h, some wear..**12.50**

Pie pan, cobalt blue and white swirl**65.00**

Pitcher, blue and white, swirl dec, French, 1920s, 15" h, some damage **225.00**

Plate, gray and white, 9" dia............**20.00**

Roaster, gray mottled, metal rack, indented handle, 17" l, 13" w, 7-1/2" h, some wear....................................**35.00**

Sauce Pan, gray mottled, 8-1/4" dia **20.00**

Strainer, blue and white, double handles **50.00**

Teapot, solid blue, chrome lid with clear glass insert knob, 10" h, slight wear and rust **150.00**

Tray, blue and white swirl, white back, 17" x 13-1/2"..............................**90.00**

Utensils on rack, hanging
Green, 3 utensils, emb diamond design, 18" l...........................**250.00**
Red shading to orange, 4 utensils, 12" h...**280.00**

✪ Gray's Pottery

This Stoke-on-Trent English pottery is starting to catch on with collectors. Many pieces have luster trim or gold, silver, or copper banding. Look for the distinctive sailing ship mark.

Creamer, copper luster, floral trim, 3-1/4" h **40.00**

Cup and saucer
Copper fluster, pink floral dec, sailing ship mark..................................**22.00**
Purple luster, Dickens ware dec...**30.00**

Jar, cov, turquoise blue ext., white int **20.00**

Jewel box, cov, copper luster, hand painted sailing ship on lid, Sailor's Poem inside, 1934-61, 4" x 5"......**45.00**

Pin dish, Isle of Amble souvenir, 4" w **12.00**

Pitcher

Gaudy Welsh type floral dec, pink and green, pink band.......................**35.00**
Mariner's Compass, multicolored compass on one side, poem on other **45.00**
Silver luster trim, silver band, grapes dec..**40.00**

Gray's Pottery, creamer, bronze luster grapes and vine design, 4-3/8" h, $25.

❖ Greentown Glass

The term Greentown glass generally refers to items made by the Indiana Tumbler and Goblet Co., which was located in Greentown, Indiana. Starting in 1894, the company produced pressed pattern glass and bar wares. By 1900, the factory had expanded several times, and Jacob Rosenthal developed an opaque brown glass the company referred to as chocolate glass. This color innovation would save the struggling company. Rosenthal went on to develop other opaque colors, including Golden Agate and Rose Agate. The factory closed in 1903 after a fire destroyed the operation.

Collectors' Clubs: National Greentown Glass Assoc, 19596 Glendale Ave, South Bend, IN 46637.

Gray's Pottery, pitcher, Mariner's Compass, multicolored decal, copper luster band and handle, poem on reverse, ship mark, $45.

Greentown Glass, mug, Serenade pattern, chocolate, 4-1/2" h, $225.

Reproduction Alert

For additional listings, see *Warman's Antiques & Collectible* and *Warman's Glass.*

Bowl, Herringbone Buttress, green, 7-1/4" dia **135.00**
Celery vase, Beaded Panel, clear **100.00**
Cordial, Austria, canary yellow **125.00**
Creamer, Shuttle, chocolate, tankard style **95.00**
Goblet, Overall Lattice, clear...........**45.00**
Mug, 5" h, Nile Green, chip.............**35.00**
Nappy, Masonic, chocolate **115.00**
Salt and pepper shakers, pr, Cactus, chocolate....................................**275.00**
Tumbler, Cactus, chocolate **30.00**
Wine, Cord Drapery, amber **280.00**

❖ Greeting Cards

From "Merry Christmas" to "Happy Birthday," we've grown up sending and receiving greeting cards. Some folks save these remembrances, and many find their way to flea markets. Some collectors look for examples with colorful images or witty sayings, while others search for interesting autographs. This is one area in which prices for the secondary market are still being established.

Birthday
Amos & Andy, brown portraits, message includes song title "Check and Double Check," Rust Craft, inked birthday note.............................**28.00**
Ballerina, A Birthday Message, Sunshine Card............................**2.00**
Blondie, Dagwood illus, full color, Hallmark, ©1939......................**20.00**
First Lady, card sgd "Mrs. Eisenhower,

Nov 14, 1965, Dear Delores, May we celebrate many more mutual birthdays together," orig envelope **70.00**
Golliwogg, "Say! What's Cookin?," mammy with young boy and pie **28.00**
Space Patrol Man, diecut, full-color, transparent green helmet, orig envelope **25.00**
Superman, Quality Cards, 1940s **125.00**

Christmas
A Christmas Wish for Someone Very Nice!, little girl playing toy piano, Christmas tree, wrapped presents, Pollyanna Cards, 1950s..............**3.00**
Christmas Cheer, red poinsettias with glitter trim, mkd "Made in U.S.A.," late 1940s **2.50**
Hello There! Merry Christmas, diecut Santa, toys in pack on back, Rust Craft, 1950s **3.00**
Hi! It's Christmas, triangular shaped card, Norcross, New York, 1950s**3.50**
Seasons Greetings, winter stage coach scene, glitter, Candlelight Card ..**2.50**
Snow people, Best wishes for Christmas and the New Year, Plastichrome, Made in USA **1.50**
Get Well, Amos n' Andy, black-and-white photo, Hall Bros., ©1951 ....**30.00**

"Merry Christmas, A wish for joys enough to fill a hundred Christmas days and all the years between them too, in countless pleasant ways!" Illus by two snow people, mkd "Made in U.S.A.," c1950, $.50.

❖ Griswold

Here's a name that evokes thoughts of cast-iron skillets and kitchen implements. Griswold items are frequently found at flea markets. The company based in Erie, Pennsylvania, originally produced hardware.

By 1914, they had begun making the cast-iron cookware that many people associate with their name. In 1946, the company was sold to a group of New York investors, and in the late 1950s the trade name Griswold was sold to their major competitor, the Wagner Manufacturing Co. Wagner continued operations, but dropped the words "Erie, Pa" from the trademark.

Griswold, patty mold set, MIB, $85.

Ashtray, #00 ....**43.00**
Corn stick pan
    #28, Wheat and Corn.................**310.00**
    #262, miniature **125.00**
    #273 ....**50.00**
Damper, mkd New American **15.00**
Dutch oven, #8 ....**55.00**
Famous Patty Molds, orig box.......**85.00**
Food mold
Lamb, 7-3/4" h, 12" w...................**175.00**
    Rabbit, 11" h, 8" l **355.00**
Hotplate, 3-burner.........................**145.00**
Plet pan #34, slight rust, 9-1/2" d ...**70.00**
Popover pan, #10 ....**38.50**
Sad iron, top mkd "Erie" and "Griswold" **135.00**
Skillet
    #3 ....**22.00**
    #5 ....**80.00**
    #6, large logo **38.00**
    #7 ....**65.00**
    #8 ....**90.00**
    #10 ....**60.00**
Teakettle, Colonial, 5-qt **40.00**
Trivet, #7, 7-1/4" dia......................**45.00**
Waffle iron
    #8, American **50.00**
    #18, Heart & Star **175.00**

❖ Guardian Ware

Before aluminum came into its own as a great material for soft drink cans, it was put to use in making pots and pans. Light and versatile, aluminum became the cookware of choice for many years. Among the leading lines was Guardian Ware, with its distinctive symbol of a knight.

Cleaner, Guardian Service Cleaner,

paper can, unopened, 8 oz **22.50**
Coffeepot, 2-pc bottom, glass top **130.00**
Cookbook, *Guardian Service Tested Recipes*, softcover, 72 pgs, shelf wear **24.00**
Fryer, glass lid, 9-1/4" dia **50.00**
Griddle, octagonal, 13" w...............**51.00**
Ice bucket, glass lid **36.00**
Omelet pan, plastic handles, 16" x 6" **35.00**
Pan, triangular, domed metal lid......**55.00**
Platter, 10" x 13" **20.00**
Roaster, domed metal lid, 15" x 10" **115.00**
Salt and pepper shakers, pr, teapot form, glass bases, aluminum tops, 3" h **72.00**
Skillet, glass lid, 2 handle covers, clip-on handle **90.00**
Tray, round, 15-1/2" d....................**40.00**
Turkey roaster with lid, 19" x 10"**155.00**
Water pitcher, tilted ball shape, plastic handle **430.00**

❖ Guitars

Guitars do occasionally show up at flea markets. And, if you're the strumming type, ask to try it out before agreeing on a purchase price. Interest in vintage guitars has increased during the last few years, spirited on by record setting prices at auction.

Periodicals: *Twentieth Century Guitar*, 135 Oser Ave, Hauppauge, NY 11788; *Vintage*

Guitar Classics, P.O. Box 7301, Bismarck, ND 58507.

Gibson, J45, 1980 ....**1,300.00**
Singing Cowboy, wooden, 1941, red and yellow stenciled campfire scene **155.00**
Stanford, imitation rosewood finish.**95.00**
University, rosewood back and sides, vine and leaf pattern, spruce top, ebony guard plate, mahogany neck, MOP trim, c1905-10 ....**250.00**

❖ Gunderson

In the late 1930s, Robert Gunderson took over the old Pairpoint Glass operations. Using the name Gundersen Glass Works, the new company manufactured tableware until 1952. One of the most distinctive glass colors made by Gunderson is Peach Blow. Their interpretation of this antique glass shades from a faint opaque pink to white to deep rose.

Bottle, peachblow, pink shading to white, 2-1/2" w, 6" h..............................**110.00**
Cornucopia, white shading to light pink to dark pink base, ruffled, etched mark, 6-1/4" h......................................**395.00**
Cup and saucer, peachblow, glossy finish, c1953 ....**325.00**
Goblet, glossy finish, deep peachblow color, applied Burmese glass base **295.00**
Jug, burgundy, applied handle, c1910, 5-1/2" w, 7-3/4" h..........................**125.00**

Paperweight, white rose, green leaves **425.00**
Vase, crystal, controlled bubble paperweight base, c1950, 10" h **185.00**

Guitar, electric, black and brown body, jack on front for amplifier, orig carrying case, ready to pick up and play, $65.

❖ Haeger Potteries

Haeger Pottery has an interesting history. Established as a brickyard in Dundee, Illinois, in 1871, the company began producing an art pottery line in 1914. Their high quality luster glazes and soft pastels met with success. A line named "Royal Haeger" was introduced in 1938. Members of the Haeger family are still involved with the pottery.

Collectors' Club: Haeger Pottery Collectors of America, 5021 Toyon Way, Antioch, CA 94509.

Bowl, shell form, 18" l **18.00**
Candy dish, cov, textured white, sgd "Royal Haeger".............................**12.00**
Console set, Mauve Agate glaze, pink glaze with powder blue and aqua blue splotches, 14-3/4" l asymmetrical bowl with scalloped rim, pr 9" h fan shaped leafy vases, mkd Haeger R-476 USA on bowl, R-301 on vase, minor wear, chip on one vase..........................**75.00**
Ewer, long thin neck, 18-1/2" h **70.00**
Figurine
    Cat, orange, #1792, 21" h..........**190.00**
    Cocker spaniel puppy, reclining, 2-3/4" h...**25.00**
    Hound, brown, 4" h **40.00**
    Swan with uplifted wings, light gray and brown, 9" l.................................**48.00**
    Warlord, pink, 12" h, 12" w.........**125.00**
Flower pot, 4-1/4" h, 5-1/2" dia **20.00**
Lavabo, white, light blue, 19" h top, 7" h base **75.00**

Haegar group, all marked: vase, two shaped bowls, shell-shaped planter, low bowl, small dish, variety of glazes, nicks, $50.

Haeger Potteries, ashtray, light green, S. A. F. 1968, orig silver foil label for 75th anniversary, carnation dec, mkd "Haegar, USA," $15.

Planter
    Bassinet, blue, 5" h, 7" l...............**12.00**
    It's A Boy, light blue, 3-3/4" h, 4-1/4" sq **16.00**
    Madonna with Cherub, blue, 11" h **35.00**
    Wheelbarrow, 7" l **15.00**
Vase
    Cylinder, white, R670, 9" h..........**12.00**
    Deer, amber, mkd, orig sticker, 15" h **40.00**
    Lily, blue, green and pink, R-446, 1930-40s, 14" h **100.00**
Wash bowl and pitcher, white, pale blue flowers, mkd "Haeger #4060".......**75.00**

❖ Hagen Renaker

The Hagen Renaker name is recognized for producing quality miniature figurines and other accessories.

Figure
    Appaloosa and Colt, 3" h **18.00**
    Buckskin Mare, 2-1/2" h **12.50**
    Duck, female lying down, male standing, Studio Line, male 6-3/4" h, pr **175.00**
    Pedro the Chihuahua, Walt Disney's Lady and the Tramp................**125.00**
    Pegasus, standing figure 2" h, reclining figure 1" h, 1995 ....**15.00**
    Saddlebred Horse, Honora, 8" h**600.00**
    Snow White, orig Walt Disney label **250.00**
    Tramp, Walt Disney's Lady and the Tramp, 2-1/4" h **195.00**
    Trusty, Walt Disney's Lady and the Tramp, 1-7/8" h **75.00**
Wall plaque, irregular shape, high glaze
    Butterfly, 14" x 9".........................**250.00**
    Fawn, 10-1/2" x 5" **175.00**
    Fish, 7" x 12" **250.00**

Fish, 19" x 8" **350.00**
Reindeer, 10-1/2" x 15" **250.00**

❖ Hair Related

Today we've got a commodity the Victorians couldn't get enough—hair. And to think that we pay barbers and beauticians to cut it off! During the Victorian era, people saved every loose strand of hair in dresser jars called hair receivers. When enough hair had been accumulated, it was used to make jewelry and ornate flower wreaths. Of course, all of the voluminous hair that was so popular during that time had to be brushed and tucked in place with hair combs, barrettes, etc.

Reference: Mary Bachman, *Collector's Guide to Hair Combs*, Collector Books, 1998; Christie Romero, *Warman's Jewelry*, 2nd ed, Krause Publications, 1998.

Collectors' Club: Antique Comb Collectors Club International, 8712 Pleasant View Rd, Bangor, PA 18013; Antique Fancy Comb Collectors Club, 3291 N River Rd, Libertyville, IL 60048; National Antique Comb Collectors Club, 3748 Sunray Dr, Holiday, FL 34691.

Hair brush, sterling silver, Art Nouveau style, wear to bristles **125.00**
Hair comb
    Celluloid, engraved grapes, tortoise shell look....................................**12.00**
    Celluloid, rhinestone trim **45.00**
    Gutta percha, French jet, Victorian **95.00**
    Mexican silver, mkd "Made en Mexico, 925" **15.00**
    Sterling silver, 3 turquoise stones, wave shape..............................**45.00**
Hair pick, single-prong hair ornament, imitation ivory, gracefully twisted top, diecut filigree, 7" l.........................**35.00**
Hair pin, silver twisted work, two-pronged comb, Victorian, c1890, 5" l **75.00**
Hair receiver, top with center hole, porcelain, roses dec.....................**85.00**
Jewelry
    Brooch, central oval glazed compartment with braided light brown hair, scrolled frame, convex back, 10k yg, c1840 ....**195.00**
    Locket, oval, beveled-edge glass front and back, braided knot of gray hair, plain gold filled frame, c1850..**200.00**
Wreath, ornate flowers made from hair, paper leaves, other period decorations, 19" x 23" shadow box **145.00**

❖ Hall China

Hall China Company was located in East Liverpool, Ohio, and produced semi-porcelain dinnerware. By 1911, Robert T.

Hall had perfected a non-crazing vitrified china, allowing the body and the glaze to be fired at one time. Initially, Hall's basic product was dinnerware for hotels and restaurants. Eventually, the line was extended to include premiums and retail wares, such as Autumn Leaf for the Jewel Tea. An extensive line of teapots was introduced around 1920, and kitchenware was introduced in 1931. The company is still in business today.

Collectors' Club: Hall China Collector's Club, P.O. Box 360488, Cleveland, OH 44136.

For additional listings, see *Warman's Antiques & Collectible*, *Warman's Americana & Collectibles*, *Warman's American Pottery & Porcelain*, and *Autumn Leaf* in this edition.

Bean pot, Orange Poppy **95.00**
Bowl, Orange Poppy, silver rim, 9" dia
....**35.00**
Casserole, cov, Rose White...........**30.00**
Cereal bowl, Pastel Morning Glory.**17.50**
Coffeepot, Orange Poppy, Great
American **85.00**
Creamer, Lazy Daisies, Kraft **15.00**
Cup and saucer
Blue Bouquet.............................**25.00**
Red Poppy..................................**10.00**
Taverne.......................................**20.00**
Custard cup, Orange Poppy.............**6.50**
Drip jar, Red Poppy **30.00**
Gravy boat, Serenade **40.00**
Jug
Radiance **48.00**
Rose White, 7-3/4" h **48.00**
Mixing bowl, Crocus, 7-1/2" dia **55.00**
Onion soup, cov, Red Dot **48.00**
Pie plate, Pastel Morning Glory **32.00**
Platter, Cameo Rose, medium........**40.00**
Pretzel jar, cov, Taverne................**195.00**
Refrigerator container, Hotpoint, yellow,
4-1/4" h...**80.00**
Refrigerator jug, Hotpoint, Chinese blue,
7" h...**70.00**
Silverware caddy, Red Poppy, 1940s, 9"
l **75.00**
Sugar bowl, cov, Mount Vernon......**20.00**

Hall China, salt and pepper shakers, large size, handle, red flower, black leaves, $30.

Hall China, Silhouette pattern, dinner plate, $20.

Sugar shaker, handle, Crocus......**150.00**
Stack set, Red Poppy **75.00**
Teapot
Airflow, cobalt blue **200.00**
Morning, Chinese Red **200.00**
Ohio, pink, gold dot trim **430.00**
Radiance and Wheat..................**390.00**
Ribbed Rutherford, Chinese Red
....**390.00**
Tom and Jerry set, bowl, 12 mugs,
black, gold lettering **65.00**
Vegetable bowl
Cameo Rose **30.00**
Red Poppy...................................**25.00**

❖ Hallmark

Hallmark is an American success story. In 1913, brothers Joyce and Rollie Hall established their company to sell Christmas cards. Through purchases of printing and engraving plants, they developed into a nationwide company. After World War II, they expanded and attracted famous artists to the company. One of Hallmark's most popular lines, the Keepsake Ornament series, was started in 1973.

"For your birthday, two little bunnies are coming, you see, with two little wishes as glad as can be, for a whole lot of fun while your birthday is here, and a whole lot of happy days all through the year," early 1950s, $.50.

Reference: Rosie Wells, ed, *The Ornament Collector's Official Price Guide for Past Years' Hallmark Ornaments and Kiddie Car Classics*, 12th ed, Rosie Wells Enterprises, 1998.

Periodicals: *Hallmarkers*, P.O. Box 97172, Pittsburgh, PA 15229; *The Ornament Collector*, 22341 E Wells Rd, Canton, IL 61520.

Collectors' Club: Hallmark Keepsake Ornament Collectors Club, P.O. Box 412734, Kansas City, MO 64141.

Cookie cutter, Peanuts, Lucy holding package, Snoopy in a Santa hat, Linus holding lights and Charlie Brown holding ornament, set of 4 ....**100.00**
Greeting card, birthday, black characters, copyright Hall Brothers, Inc., c1940s, 4" x 5" **25.00**
Jewelry, Valentine pin **10.00**
Magazine advertisement, Thanksgiving cards adv, 1959..............................**5.00**
Ornament,
Barbie, 1993, 1st in series, orig box
....**125.00**
Calico Mouse, Merry Miniatures, 1977,
2-1/4" h **100.00**
Enterprise, 1991, MIB **225.00**
From Our House To Yours, 1992 ..**10.00**
Frosty Friends, Eskimo and Husky in igloo, 2nd in series, 1981, no box, 2"
h..**350.00**
Heavenly Angel, 1992, MIB, 3" h .**32.00**
Mustang, Classic Car series, 1992,
MIB **48.00**
Noel Railroad, Coal Car, miniature, 1990, 2nd in series **24.50**
Puppy's Best Friend, 1986, worn orig box **28.00**

Hallmark Christmas ornament, Bugs Bunny, Looney Tunes Collection, MIB, $9.50.

Snowman, Merry Miniatures, 1976, 2-1/4" h **70.00**
Superman lunchbox, 1998, tin, 3-1/4" x 2-1/2" **13.50**
World-Class Teacher, 1992, 3-1/4" h, MIB **9.00**

❖ Halloween

Among holiday collectibles, Halloween is second only to Christmas. Early Halloween items have a distinctive look that appeal to many collectors.

References: Mark B. Ledenbach, *Vintage Halloween Collectibles*, Krause Publications, 2003; Pamela Apkarian-Russell, *Collectible Halloween*, Schiffer Publishing, 1997; ----, *Halloween: Collectible Decorations and Games*, Schiffer Publishing, 2000; ----, *More Halloween Collectibles: Anthropomorphic Vegetables and Fruits of Halloween*, Schiffer Publishing, 1998.

Periodicals: *BooNews*, P.O. Box 143, Brookfield, IL 60513; *Trick or Treat Trader*, P.O. Box 499, Winchester, NH 03470.

Reproduction Alert

Candle, jack-o-lantern, 4" h **15.00**
Cookie cutter
    Aluminum, startled cat, 3-1/4" w **7.00**
    Tin, witch on broom, Foose..........**15.00**
Costume, child's
    Dr. Kildare.....................................**45.00**
    Fred Flintstone **25.00**
    Howard the Duck, Collegeville, 1986, orig box **60.00**
    I Dream of Jeannie, 1960s.........**125.00**
    Indiana Jones..............................**80.00**
    Pac Man **40.00**
    The Fonz, Happy Days, Ben Cooper, 1976, orig box..........................**35.00**
Cup, paper with handle, orange with black cats, bats, trees and full moon, C.A. Reed & Co., Williamsport, Pa., 3-3/4" h...**5.00**
Hat, cardboard and crepe paper, black and orange, Germany, 4" h..........**17.50**

Halloween Decoration, pumpkin, orange, black, and white, green stem, mkd "Made in U.S.A.," $35.

Halloween Mask, pair of jester masks, one with orig label "Luminous, Glows in the Dark, Masklite, Made in U.S.A.," orange, white, and black, unused, each $18.

Horn, litho tin with plastic end, witch on broom, spider webs and stars, Kirchhof, 6-1/2" l............................**20.00**
Jack-o-lantern
    Black cat, cardboard, mouth insert with small tear, Western Germany.**475.00**
    Devil, compressed paper, face restored, 6-3/4" h....................**500.00**
    Pumpkin, cardboard, worn paper inserts in eyes and mouth, Germany, 3-1/2" h **225.00**
    Pumpkin, tin, nose doubles as a horn, U.S. Metal Toy Co., wear, 5" h, 6" dia **155.00**
Mask
    Deputy Dawg, 1960s....................**32.00**
    Esso Tiger, 1960s **16.00**
    I Dream of Jeannie, 1970s.............**3.00**
    Mork from Ork **3.00**
    Rabbit, 1960s **10.00**
    Yogi Bear, 1950s **15.00**
    Zorro, large brim, 1960s..............**35.00**
Napkin, shows black cat, jack-o-lantern man & woman, bats and moon......**5.00**
Nodder, skeleton, papier-mache, gray with black, green and white accents, 1930s-1940s, Japan, 5-3/4" h......**90.00**
Noisemaker
    Skillet-shape, litho tin with wooden clappers, shows witches, cats, skeletons, etc., U.S. Metal Toys, 8" l, 4" w..**45.00**
    Twirl-type, litho tin with wooden handle, shows witch, black cat and owl, scratches, 5" l **45.00**
Party favor, cardboard paper face, plastic disc, eyes move, Japan.....**45.00**
Table decoration, black cat, tissue-paper construction, H.E. Luhr, 9-1/4" h, 6" w **32.00**
Tambourine, litho tin
    Black cat motif, 7-1/4" dia **195.00**
    Jack-o-lantern motif, 6-1/4" dia ..**175.00**

Halloween Mask, tiger, cardboard, orange, black, and white, unused, $24.

Toothpick holder, papier-mache, 1940s, Japan, 1" x 1-1/2"
    Jack-o-lantern, papier-mache, 1940s, Japan, 1" x 1-1/2" **20.00**
    Skull **18.00**
    Witch **24.00**
Trick-or-Treat bag, cloth, orange with black ghost chasing man and woman, black vinyl handles, stains............**16.00**

❖ Handkerchiefs

Aaacchhooo! Today we grab for a box of disposable tissues, but that's not what our grandmothers did. Vintage etiquette called for well-dressed folks to carry a well-pressed handkerchief, just in case a sneeze was waiting. Remember those gallant gestures in the movies where the gent would whip out his handkerchief for the damsel in distress? And, of course, grandma had to have the proper place to store her hankies.

Reference: Rosanna Mihalick, *Collecting Handkerchiefs*, Schiffer Publishing, 2000.

> Flea market dealers have come up with a neat way of displaying their handkerchiefs for sale. They take a 3-hole notebook and put in clear sleeve pages. A handkerchief is carefully tucked into each side. Some dealers take time to add colored construction paper dividers, which really show off the colors and design of the vintage handkerchiefs.

Appliqued
    Cocktail, 5" l embroidered orange flowers, cutwork, orig label "Cocktail Sixe, 100% Cotton Made in Switzerland," 12" sq **9.00**
    Flowers, scalloped edge, orig label "Made in Switzerland, All Cotton," 12-1/2" sq.....................................**10.00**

Handkerchiefs, Christmas design, printed in red and green, each $6.

Hanna-Barbera Parade, Charlton Comics, showing many characters on train, Nov, $2.

Handkerchiefs, Left: lady's, pink, blue, and purple trim, floral embroidery, $30 for set of 3; right: child's, Humpty Dumpty, silk, $25.

Handkerchiefs, Left: New York, graphic, maroon, tan, and turquoise, orig Herrmann silver foil label, Irish linen, $45; right: Marriage Game, $42.

Embroidered, "A" monogram, crocheted
edges, 11" sq **12.00**

Florals
Bouquet of flowers, white waffle border,
hand-rolled hem, 13" sq **12.50**
Chrysanthemums, deep rust blossoms,
dark brown ground, polished cotton,
machine hem, 13" sq................**10.00**
Gladiolas, scalloped hem, cotton, 15-
1/2" sq.......................................**15.00**
Gray flowers, orange background,
scalloped hem, 13" sq **10.00**
Morning glories, red flowers on white
background, black border, machine
hem, 11-1/2" sq **11.50**
Pink roses, black ground, hand-rolled
hem, 13-1/2" sq **12.50**
Poppies, red and white flowers, blue
background, hand-rolled hem, 12-
1/2" sq.......................................**10.00**
Roses, white and deep brown petals,
medium brown shading to darker
brown border, machine hem, 13-1/2"
sq **12.50**

Handkerchief box, pink silk lining, lace
and floral trim, sq **45.00**

Humorous, Pekingese, hand-rolled hem,
cotton, by Burmel, small stains, 14-1/2"
sq **15.00**

Souvenir type
London, rayon, 13-1/2" sq............**17.50**
Montana, scalloped edge, cotton, 14"
sq...**22.00**
Texas, hand-rolled hem, cotton, some
fading, 13" sq...........................**15.00**

Handkerchiefs Left: Valentine's Day theme, red hearts, white ground, orig gold foil label reads "Nylon," gives washing instructions, $7; right: embroidered Valentine's Day theme, red hearts, red and pink roses, $6.

❖ Hanna-Barbera

The partnership of William Denby Hanna and Joseph Roland Barbera developed slowly. They both worked for MGM, and, when a new cartoon division was started in 1937, they were teamed together. For twenty years they worked under this arrangement, creating such classics as Tom and Jerry. After striking out on their own, they began producing cartoons for television and created such great characters as Huckleberry Hound and the Flintstones. In 1966, Taft Communications purchased the company.

Animation cel, Yogi Bear, late
1970s/early 1980s, single 5-1/2" image
of Yogi on laser background, 13" x 11"
....**85.00**
Ashtray, Barney bowling, pottery, Arrow
Houseware Products, Chicago, 5-14" x
8"..**90.00**
Book, *Jetsons' Word Search Puzzles*,
1978, 64 pgs, unused **10.00**
Camera, Fred Flintstone, 1976, 3-1/4" x
3-3/4"..**20.00**
Charm bracelet, Huckleberry Hound,
Pixie, Dixie, Boo Boo, Huck, Yogi, Mr.
Jims, Tom Tom, 1959, orig card ...**80.00**
Comic book
The Flintstones at the New York
World's Fair, official fair souvenir
....**25.00**
Space Ghost, Comico, 1987, 48 pgs
....**7.00**
Cookie jar
Barney Rubble, Certified International
Corp, 12" h **60.00**
Yogi Bear, American Bisque.......**450.00**
Doll, plush, Barney Rubble, Nanco, 1989,
14" h..**22.00**

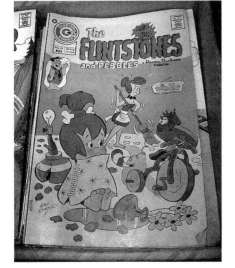

The Flintstones and Pebbles, comic book, Charlton Comics, Nov, $3.50.

Figure, Quick Draw McGraw.........**100.00**
Flashlight, interchangeable faces, Fred Flintstone, Huckleberry Hound and Yogi Bear, 1975, MOC **15.00**
Lamp, Quick Draw McGraw, plastic, 22" h **20.00**
Lunchbox
Flintstones, Aladdin, metal, 1971.**95.00**
Sky Commanders, plastic, 1987 ..**25.00**
Mug, Fred Flintstone, Flintstone Multiple brand Vitamins, 1968, 3 1/4" h.......**8.00**
Pinback button, Tom and Jerry Go For Stoehmann's Bread, 1950s, 1-1/8" dia **27.50**
Soakie, Barney Rubble, 7-3/4" h.....**30.00**

❖ Hardware

Decorative and ornate hardware has graced our homes for decades. Vintage hardware items are popular with those who are restoring antique homes, those who want to add a unique touch to a newer home, or collectors who simply appreciate the beauty of the object. Some collectors have discovered that mounting these vintage hardware beauties on a wall or board creates a neat place to hang their hat as well as an interesting display of their collection.

Reference: H. Weber Wilson, *Antique Hardware Price Guide*, Krause Publications, 1999.

For additional listings, also see Doorknobs in this edition.

Door knocker, figural fox head, cast iron **85.00**
Door push plate, bronze, Windsor pattern, Sargent, c1885, 16" h...**150.00**
Knob, 6-sided, 1" h, 1" dia
Black glass **12.50**

Clear glass **7.50**
Mail slot and receiver, "Letters"
Cast iron, Gothic pattern, 2-1/2" h, 8" w **195.00**
Nickel-plated cast brass, 2-1/2" h, 7" w **195.00**
Cast brass, 2-1/2" h, 7-1/2" w **165.00**
Outlet plate, copper, ivy design, 4-3/4" h, 3-1/4" w **31.00**
Shelf bracket, wrought iron, ornate scrolling pattern, pr **20.00**
Switch plate
Brass, for double pushbuttons......**32.00**
Copper, gingko design, 5" h, 3" w**30.00**

❖ Harker Pottery

The Harker Company was one of several East Liverpool, Ohio, firms. Founded by Benjamin Harker around 1840, the company produced yellow ware items using the natural clay deposits from the surrounding area. White ware was first made about 1879. Dinnerware and table accessories were the order of the day until the plant was destroyed by fired in 1975.

For additional listings, see *Warman's Americana & Collectibles* and *Warman's American Pottery & Porcelain*.

Batter bowl, Petit Point Rose..........**65.00**
Cake server, Petit Point Rose.........**20.00**
Casserole, cov, Petit Point Rose.....**65.00**
Cheese plate, Cactus Blooms, 11" dia **60.00**
Cookie jar, cov, Modern Tulip **85.00**
Creamer, Kriebel's Dairy, Hereford, Pa. **50.00**
Cup and saucer, Cameo, Shell Ware, blue...............................**17.50**
Dinner plate, Petit Point Rose **15.00**
Pie plate, Cameo, Dainty Flower, blue **75.00**
Platter, Ivy, large **75.00**
Rolling pin, Petitpoint **140.00**
Salad bowl, Red Apple **27.50**
Spoon and fork
Kelvinator **160.00**
Petit Point **140.00**
Silhouette, platinum trim.............**170.00**
Teapot, cov
Hallow, some flakes **75.00**
Ivy...............................**200.00**
Vegetable bowl, Red Apple............**32.00**

❖ Harlequin China

This bright and cheery pattern was made by Homer Laughlin and originally sold by F.W. Woolworth Co. When it was introduced in the 1930s it was available in bright yellow, spruce green, maroon, and mauve blue. Eventually, the line was produced in all of the Fiesta colors except ivory and cobalt blue. The line was discontinued in 1964 and then reissued in 1979. The reissued pieces were made in turquoise, yellow, medium green, and coral. Look for the Homer Laughlin back stamp on most pieces.

Dinnerware

After-dinner cup, chartreuse..........**95.00**
After-dinner cup and saucer
Maroon **100.00**
Red...**130.00**
Spruce.......................................**195.00**
Ashtray, saucer, red.......................**90.00**
Casserole, cov
Chartreuse **240.00**
Maroon **200.00**
Spruce.......................................**195.00**
Yellow.......................................**165.00**
Creamer, individual, green.............**125.00**
Deep plate, medium green **125.00**
Eggcup, double
Gray...**40.00**
Mauve...**30.00**
Red...**40.00**
Rose...**38.00**
Spruce..**42.00**
Turquoise.....................................**25.00**
Marmalade, maroon.......................**325.00**
Nappy, medium green....................**195.00**
Nut dish, rose...............................**95.00**
Pitcher, ball, Spruce **95.00**

Harlequin China, pie plate, orange, $18.

Plate
7" dia, medium green....................**45.00**
10" dia, medium green...............**135.00**
10" dia, red...................................**25.00**
Spoon rest, yellow **295.00**
Sugar, cov, gray or maroon.............**45.00**
Teapot, cov
Gray...**185.00**
Red...**95.00**
Rose...**100.00**
Tumbler, red or yellow **65.00**

Figure

Cat

Mauve................................**175.00**
Spruce...............................**275.00**
Yellow................................**175.00**
White and gold
b

Donkey

Gold trim...............................**80.00**
Mauve..................................**225.00**
Spruce.................................**325.00**
Yellow and gold **250.00**

Duck

Maroon **275.00**
Spruce.................................**175.00**
Yellow **245.00**

Fish

Gold trim...............................**80.00**
Maroon **350.00**
Yellow **250.00**

Lamb

Gold.....................................**125.00**
Mauve..................................**325.00**
White and gold **125.00**

Penguin

Maroon **285.00**
Yellow **250.00**
White and gold **125.00**

❖ Harmonica and Related

Harmonicas used to be the musical choice of those who couldn't afford fancy instruments. Their rich sounds are still enjoyed today. Flea markets are a wonderful place to look for vintage harmonicas, many of which will still be in their original boxes.

Figurine, Precious Moments, "Lord Give Me A Song," girl with harmonica, 5" h **35.00**

Harmonica

American Ace Harmonica, Hohner-Panarmonic, orig box...............**28.00**
Bell Bird, orig box.........................**18.00**
Hohner Chrometta 12, 6-1/2" l.....**68.00**
Hohner Chromonica Deluxe #440, orig box **100.00**
Hohner, Herb Shriner's Hoosier Boy Harmonica, orig box **95.00**
Hohner Little Lady #39, orig box, 1-1/2" l... **50.00**
Hohner Marine Band, #1896, orig box **95.00**
Horner Super Chromonica, green case **75.00**
Woody Woodpecker Harmonica, nodding head, red plastic, 5-1/2" h **25.00**

Key chain, Harmonica for the Musically Hopeless, small plastic harmonica, orig blister pack **3.50**
Political novelty, peanut shaped plastic

harmonica, Musical Fun for Kids of All Ages, by Jimmy Peanut, 1977, caricatures of boy and girl playing harmonicas, MOC **48.00**

❖ Hartland Plastics

Hartland Plastics, a small midwestern company based in Hartland, Wisconsin, produced a wide variety of plastic models. Their detailed, finely molded figures included horses, dogs, gunfighters and baseball players, as well as religious statuettes and cake-top decorations. The company was founded in 1939, but it wasn't until the late 1940s that the first of their famous horses was released.

References: Gail Fitch, *Hartland Horses and Dogs*, Schiffer Publishing, 2000.

Baseball

Yogi Berra, 1960s, mask missing **250.00**
Roberto Clemente, limited edition, orig box, 7" h.................................**150.00**
Whitey Ford, orig box, 6-1/2" h ..**125.00**
Babe Ruth, 1960s **275.00**
Warren Spahn, 1959-63, freestanding version **159.00**
Ted Williams, 1960s **350.00**

Character

Cochise, Ring Eye horse............**200.00**
Dale Evans.................................**75.00**
Lone Ranger, rearing Trigger **225.00**
Sgt Preston **100.00**
Tonto and horse **70.00**
Wyatt Earp, with horse **70.00**

Horse

Bay Draft, Tinymite, 2" h **12.00**
Bay Foal, mahogany **12.00**
Chestnut, Arabian, 11" scale, 9-3/4" h **50.00**
Chestnut, semi-rearing, 8-1/2" h ..**75.00**
Mustang, rearing, woodgrain........**30.00**

❖ Hatpin Holders and Hatpins

Hatpins are coming back into vogue with collectors. Perhaps it's the renaissance of large hats, or maybe it's the romance that hatpins evoke. Whatever the reason, more and more hatpins are entering the flea market scene, and prices are rising. Of course, if you're going to collect hatpins, you've got to have a few hatpin holders to display your treasures.

Collectors Clubs: American Hatpin Soc, 20 Monticello Dr, Palos Veres Peninsula, CA 90274; International Club for Collectors of Hatpins and Hatpin Holders, 15237 Chanera Ave, Gardena, CA 90249.

For additional listings, see *Warman's Antiques & Collectibles* and *Warman's Jewelry.*

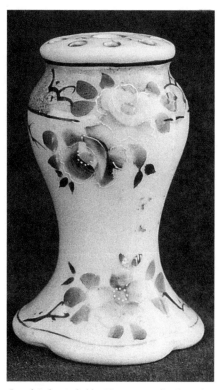

Porcelain hatpin holder, Nippon, rose floral motif, gold line highlights, marked, 4" h, $50.

Doll, porcelain half doll, arms folded, satin dress as cushion for hatpins, 9" h **125.00**

Hatpin

Ball, rhinestones, 8-1/4" l **48.00**
Beaded and sequined head, black, 2-3/8" x 1-1/4" dia, 6-1/4" l...........**75.00**
Embossed copper top, bezel set coral colored stone, 8" l....................**95.00**
Faceted glass, black, 2-1/4" x 1-1/4" dia, 5-5/8" l **150.00**
Filigree, teardrop, 3/4" l head, 7-5/8" l **65.00**
Gold lustered metal, screw-type, 1920, 6-1/2" l **20.00**
Iridized metal head, faceted dome, 1-3/4" dia, 11-1/4" l....................**125.00**
Military insignia, 2" dia, 9-1/2" l..**125.00**
Wood, black ebonized head, metal separator, 11-1/2" l **100.00**

Hatpin holder, porcelain

Austrian, hp blue flowers, 5" h **45.00**
Bavarian, hexagonal, pastel florals, mkd "Z.S. & Co.," 4-3/4" h.........**45.00**
Germany, yellow roses, 6-1/2" h ..**90.00**
Nippon, pink roses, green leaves, gold trim, 4" h **100.00**
Souvenir, Capitol Building, Washington, D.C., 4-1/2" h **125.00**

Rhinestone hatpin dec circular top, 1-1/4" dia, $15.

Display with several hats, black straw on right, $10; top left mink, $30; fake fur leopard print, $15; white wool with ribbon trim, $10; black velvet, $12; brown fake fur at base, $5.

❖ Hats, Lady's (Vintage)

A well-groomed lady used her hat to complete her ensemble. Some vintage hats are large and colorful, while others are a little more demure. There has been a resurgence of hat collecting, perhaps due to popular movies featuring stars in large bonnets. Whatever the reason, our hats are off to those who enjoy this field of collecting.

Reference: Susan Langley, *Vintage Hats and Bonnets, 1770-1970*, Collector Books, 1997.

Beaded, black, evening type, orig Hess Bros label **35.00**

This display has several summer hats; wide brims ranged from $15 to $20, smaller brims ranged from $10 to $20.

Brown velvet hood-type hat, fur trim, brown ribbon ties, $45.

Felt

Black, small bowl crown, short back brim, trimmed in black ostrich feathers, black ribbon with bow in back, orig label "Yowell Drew Ivey Co., Daytona Beach" **125.00**

Brown, wide brim, beige feathers, green netting, 1930s...............**125.00**

Brown, wide brim, dark brown underbrim, light brown felt on top, felt bowl, color colored embroidery, wooden button dec, black silk lining, marker's mark "H & I," Los Angeles, San Francisco, 15-1/2" w........**150.00**

Sapphire blue, Art Deco style, small matching bow and netting **40.00**

Fur

Fox, dyed black, Winkelman's label, 1950s.....................................**125.00**

Hat, purple felt, rows of tan and pink stitching, matching cord band, sold with clear round hatbox, $20.

Haviland China, set of dishes, Plaisance pattern, pink flowers, tiny green and gold leaves, service for 8, red Haviland Limoges mark with castle, green Haviland France Limoges mark, $200; shown with gold rimmed iced tea tumblers, valued at $85 for the set.

Hats Lady's, black velvet, wide brim, feather trim, $65.

Natural mink, pillbox style **40.00**
Wide brim, white feather dec, pink
  rose, Victorian..........................**175.00**
Lace and wire, Edwardian, dark gray,
  medium brim **130.00**
Sport, rose colored silk flowers on top,
  horsehair brim, 1920s, 10" from front to
  back, 4-1/2" h **225.00**
Straw
  Black, large brim, fabric crown, orig
    label "Schiparallei Jr. Paris" **70.00**
  Black, flowers in pink, rose and white,
    green leaves, orig label "Neiman
    Marcus"....................................**40.00**
  Navy, feathers and veil, small turned up
    brim, orig label "Gage Brothers &
    Co., Chicago, New York, Since 1856"
    ....**70.00**
Velvet, black, red poppies, fully lined,
  wire in brim, narrow back brim.....**60.00**
Wool, black, close fitting, orig label.**45.00**

❖ Haviland China

Haviland China has an interesting history in that it was founded in America by importer David Haviland, who then moved to Limoges, France, to begin manufacturing. He was quite successful. His sons, Charles and Theodore, split the company in 1892. Theodore went on to open an American division in 1936 and continued to make produce dinnerware. The Haviland family sold the firm in 1981.

Reference: Nora Travis, *Evolution of Haviland China Design*, Schiffer Publishing, 2000.

Collectors' Club: Haviland Collectors International Foundation, P.O. Box 802462, Santa Clarita, CA 91380.

For additional listings, see *Warman's Antiques & Collectibles* and *Warman's American Pottery & Porcelain*.

Bone dish, turtle dec **65.00**
Bowl, hp yellow roses, 8" dia **37.50**
Butter dish, cov, Gold Band, mkd "Theo
  Haviland" **48.00**
Cake plate, Baltimore Rose, #1151, #1
  blank, gold trim..........................**145.00**
Chop plate, Chrysanthemum, #88, 11"
  dia **80.00**
Coffee cup, Marseille....................**25.00**
Compote, ftd, reticulated, gold trim
  ....**175.00**
Cream Soup, underplate, cranberry and
  blue scroll border..........................**30.00**
Creamer and sugar, small pink flowers,
  scalloped, gold trim **65.00**
Cup and saucer, deep pink flowers,
  scalloped gold edge **30.00**
Demitasse Cup and Saucer, 1885
  ....**30.00**
Milk Pitcher, pink flowers, green
  branches, underglaze green Haviland
  mark, red "Haviland & Co., Limoges for

PDG, Indianapolis, Ind.," 8" h **450.00**
Oyster Plate, blue and pink flowers, mkd
  "Haviland & Co.," 9" dia **120.00**
Plate
  Blue flowers, green leaves, 7-1/2" dia
    ....**15.00**
  Princess, 9-1/2" dia **24.00**
  Rajah, mkd "Theo Haviland," 6" dia**8.00**
Platter, Athena pattern, 14" l........**195.00**
Relish dish, Marseilles, #48, 8-1/2" dia
  ....**30.00**
Sandwich plate, Drop Rose pattern, 11-
  1/2" dia **275.00**
Tea cup and saucer, small blue flowers,
  green leaves....................................**28.00**
Teapot, Baltimore Rose, #1151, #1 blank
  ....**215.00**
Vegetable dish, open, Golden Quail
  ....**435.00**

❖ Hawaiiana

Aloha. Some collectors are just naturally drawn to colorful Hawaiian objects. Perhaps it's the smiles of the hula girls or their alluring dance. Prices are beginning to escalate for items in this category. Be aware that objects actually made in Hawaii tend to cost more than items imported from Japan.

Bell, Hula Girl, ceramic, "Hawaii" written
  across skirt, "Made in Japan" sticker, 4-
  1/2" h..**36.00**
Dress, lounging, 1960s, Honolulu
  designer Pomare Tahiti.................**60.00**
Figurine, hula girl, Josef Originals,
  International Series, orig Hawaii Poem
  string tag, 4" h **80.00**
Handkerchief, "Aloha Hawaii,"
  embroidered hula girl, MIB, set of 4
  ....**30.00**
Magazine ad, "Take A Trip," Hawaii
  Tourist Bureau, 1934, from *Fortune
  Magazine*.......................................**8.00**
Menu
  Royal Hawaiian Hotel, Hula Dancer
    cover by John Kelly, 1949, 10" x 14"
    ....**90.00**
  Metropolitan Hotel, 4 pgs, c1974 .**35.00**
  S.S. Lurline, Matson Lines, "Hawaii's
    Decisive Hour" print by Savage,
    1956, 21" x 13-1/2"..................**60.00**
Pillow cover, Honolulu, tropic themes
  and poem to mother, 17-1/4" sq plus
  fringe **50.00**
Plate, Aloha from Hawaii, Hula maids
  and other colorful scenes, gold trim, 8"
  dia **25.00**
Postcard, real-photo
  Mauna Kea, unused **12.00**
  Pineapples at Harvest Time- Hawaiian
    Islands, unused **12.00**
Quilt, pieced, nine pineapple medallions,
  meandering floral vines, green and

Hawaiian Stereograph, Keystone View #315 10156T, titled, "Native hula girls in characteristic attire near Honolulu, Terrority of Hawaii," $10.

orange, white ground, quilted floral rosettes in corners, 64" sq **600.00**

Record, "Hawaii, Melodies from Paradise," Longines Symphonetee Recording Society, presentation set, cover scuffed **13.00**

Salt and pepper shakers, figural suitcases, pr **24.00**

Sheet music, *Hawaii Will Be Paradise Once More*, 1947 ....**5.00**

Scarf, Hawaiian Hula, silk, faded, 35" sq **19.00**

Shirt, man's
1960s, Islander.............................**45.00**
1970s, Royal Hawaiian.................**40.00**

Stereoview, *Royal School, Honolulu, Hawaii*, Keystone View Co., #10161 ....**12.00**

Swizzle stick
Hale Koa Hotel on the Beach, Waikiki, 6" l..**1.00**
Kahala Hilton, Honolulu, 6" l **1.00**
Spencecliff Restaurants, 5-1/2" l....**1.00**

Tin, Hawaiian Coconut Snow, Lihue Kauai, Hawaii, 10-oz **35.00**

Travel brochure, Hawaii Tourist Bureau, Honolulu, 1942, wear, 11" x 8-1/2" **15.50**

View-Master reel, Hawaii Five-O, 1973, pack of 3 reels, booklet **22.00**

❖ Hazel Atlas

Hazel Glass Company merged with the Atlas Glass & Metal Company in 1902 to form Hazel Atlas. The company, based in Washington, Pennsylvania, aggressively developed ways to automate the glassware industry. Their primary output consisted of tableware, kitchen items, and tumblers.

References: Gene Florence, *Collectible Glassware from the 40s, 50s, 60s*, 5th ed, Collector Books, 2000; ——, *Kitchen Glaswsare of the Depression Years*, 6th ed, Collector Books, 1995 (2001 value update).

Bowl, cobalt blue, metal holder.......**60.00**
Cereal bowl, Cowboy, white opaque glass, black cowboy scenes **25.00**
Custard cup, green...........................**5.00**
Berry bowl, mkd "Hazel Atlas," 4-1/4" dia **4.50**

Child's mug, animal characters, bottom mkd "H/A," some wear to dec, 3" h **22.00**
Creamer, Aurora, blue, 4-1/4" h **25.00**
Dinner plate, Moderntone, pink, 1940s, 9" dia **7.50**
Drinking glass, frosted, Florida souvenir, yellow state image, sailfish, alligator, palm tree and flamingo, 5" h **12.00**
Gravy boat, Florentine #2, yellow...**65.00**
Mixing bowl, Ivy, nested set of 4 ....**80.00**
Old Fashioned tumbler, Moroccan Amethyst, 3-1/4" h........................**15.00**

Hazel Atlas, Royal Lace, stack of four pink plates, each $30.

Orange reamer, Criss-Cross, pink **295.00**
Platter, Royal Lace, pink **40.00**
Salad plate, Moderntone, mint green, 1940s, 6-3/4" dia **5.50**
Salt and pepper shakers, pr, grapes, Hazel Atlas symbol on bottom **15.00**
Sherbet, Moderntone, pink, early 1950s **5.00**
Snack set, cup and oblong plate with cup ring
Capri Seashell, light blue **18.00**
Seashell, crystal...........................**22.50**
Sugar bowl, cov, Ovide, black, 2 handles **5.00**
Syrup pitcher, green, tin lid, 6" h ...**70.00**
Tom and Jerry set, 2-qt punchbowl, six 6-oz mugs **75.00**

❖ Heisey Glass

Heisey Glass is a name most collectors recognize. That H in a diamond logo is easy to spot. But, did you know that Heisey didn't mark any glass until 1901 and then used paper labels for years before starting to use the diamond mark. The Heisey Glass Company was known for it's brilliant colors and excellent quality crystal.

References: Neila Bredehoft, *Collector's Encyclopedia of Heisey Glass, 1925–1938*, Collector Books, 1986 (1997 value update); Shirley Dunbar, *Heisey Glass, The Early Years: 1896-1924*, Krause Publications, 2000; Gene Florence, *Elegant Glassware of the Depression Era*, 7th ed, Collector Books, 1997.

Periodicals: Heisey Herald, P.O. Box 23,

Clinton, MD 20735; The Heisey News, 169 W Church St, Newark, OH, 43055; The Newscaster, P.O. Box 102, Plymouth, OH 44865.

Collectors' Clubs: Bay State Heisey Collectors Club, 354 Washington St, East Walpole, MA 02032; Heisey Collectors of America, 169 W Church St, Newark, OH, 43055; National Capital Heisey Collectors, P.O. Box 23, Clinton, MD 20735; Southern Illinois Diamond H Seekers, 1203 N Yale, O'Fallon, IL 62269.

Heisey Glass, tankard pitcher, Orchid etch, applied clear handle, $500.

Reproduction Alert

For additional listings, see *Warman's Antiques & Collectibles* and *Warman's Glass*.

Animal
Goose, wings half up **90.00**
Plug horse, Oscar **115.00**
Sparrow.....................................**140.00**
Ashtray, Crystolite, zircon...............**65.00**
Basket
Bow Tie, flamingo......................**125.00**
Crystolite, 6" h **175.00**
Daisy **140.00**
Beer Mug, fisherman etching........**275.00**
Berry Bowl, Beaded Swag, opalescent, metal foot **25.00**
Cake plate
Crystolite **325.00**
Rose, pedestal **325.00**

Heisey Glass salt, individual, tub shape, crystal, $25.

Candelabra, Ridgleigh, bobeches and prisms, 7" h, pr....140.00
Candle Block, Crystolite, sq....20.00
Candlesticks, pr
Cascade, #142, 3-lite, crystal....75.00
Tea Rose, 2-lite, fern blank....120.00
Thumbprint and Panel, #1433....140.00
Candy Dish, cov, Empress, silver overlay, ftd....75.00
Card Box, cov, Windsor, Royal Sensation cutting....125.00
Champagne
Minuet....35.00
Tudor....20.00
Cheese plate, Crystolite, 2 handles, 8" dia....45.00
Coaster, Crystolite, Zircon....45.00
Cocktail
Lariat, moonglo cutting....15.00
Rosalie....12.00
Cocktail Shaker, Cobel, two quart .55.00
Creamer, Crystolite....25.00
Cruet
Crystolite....55.00
Old Sandwich....60.00
Pleat and Panel, flamingo....65.00
Cup, Crystolite....22.50
Cup and saucer, Empress, yellow .42.00
Floater bowl, Crystolite, 12" l, oval.48.00
Floral bowl, Tear Drop, pink....90.00
Goblet
Delaware, flamingo, diamond optic....20.00
Galaxy....25.00
Narrow Flute....30.00
Provincial....19.50
Tudor....17.50
Iced tea tumbler, ftd
Fred Harvey, amber....45.00
Plantation....75.00
Jug, Queen Anne, dolphin ftd, silver overlay....125.00
Lamp, Dolphin, candlestick type ...180.00
Madonna, 9" h, frosted....110.00
Mustard, cov, Flat Panel, #352....48.50
Nappy, Prison Stripe, #357, 4-1/2" d....22.00
Plate
Colonial, 4-3/4" dia....6.50
Empress, yellow, 8" dia....24.00
Orchid Etch, 7-1/4" dia....24.00
Yeoman, #1184, Sahara, 7" d....8.50
Punch cup, Crystolite....10.00
Salad plate, Impromptu, 7" d....12.00
Sandwich plate, center handle, Rose....225.00
Sherbet, Orchid Etch....24.00
Sherry, Renaissance, Old Glory stem, 2 oz....24.00
Soda Tumbler
Coronation, #4054, 10 oz....9.50
Gascony, #3397 line, Ambassador, #452, etching, 12 oz, 5-1/2" h ..35.00
Sugar cube tray, Narrow Flute, flower and leaf cutting....45.00
Tankard, Greek Key....265.00
Toothpick holder, Waldorf Astoria115.00
Tumbler, ftd, Rose Etch....50.00
Vase
Pineapple and Fan, 6" h, green, worn gold trim....40.00
Rooster, crystal....70.00
Wine
Gascony, 2 oz, Sportsman etch...60.00
Orchid Etch....75.00

❖ Hess Trucks and Oil Company Promos

We've got Hess Gas to thank for starting a wonderful line of collectible gas-related vehicles. Remember to save the orig boxes and packaging for these collectible toys.

1971, Hess....800.00
1980, Hess....300.00
1984, 1986, and 1987, Hess....150.00
1990, Hess....55.00
1992, BP Oil, tanker....30.00
1992, Exxon, tanker....95.00
1993, BP Oil, car carrier....30.00
1993, Exxon, Mack truck....25.00
1993, Phillips 66, Marx tanker bank 30.00
1993, Sunoco, Marx tanker bank....40.00
1994, Citgo, tanker, orig card....150.00
1994, Mobil, Marx tanker bank....45.00
1994, Texaco, tanker....50.00
1995, BP Oil, transporter and cars..35.00
1995, Exxon, transporter and cars..45.00
1995, Hess, MIB....65.00
1995, Texaco, tanker....30.00
1996, Crown Petroleum, fire truck...25.00
1996, Texaco, tanker, Olympics....30.00
1997, Exxon, tanker, chrome....25.00
1997, Gate, wrecker....25.00
1997, Texaco, 95th Anniversary train set....300.00
1998, Crown Petroleum, tanker....30.00
1998, Marathon, tractor trailer....45.00
1998, Texaco, Fire Chief Tank....55.00
1999, Exxon, wrecker, gold....35.00
1999, Hess....40.00
1999, Texaco, Millennium Tanker....40.00
2000, Hess....35.00
2000, Mobil, car carrier....40.00
2000, Texaco, Center Tanker....40.00
2001, Hess....20.00
2002, Hess, airplane transporter....40.00

❖ Historic Sites & Recreations

Most of us were introduced to historic sites and recreations such as Mount Vernon during field trips and family vacations. The products made at these sites, along with the souvenirs these attractions spawned, are finding new life in the collections of historic-minded individuals.

Booklet
Edison Institute Museum & Greenfield Village, 1940s, 68 pgs....2.50
Handbook, Mount Vernon Ladies Assoc, 1985....10.00
Boyd's Bear, Sturbridge Q. Patriot, retired....15.00
Brochure, *Jamestown, Virginia*, 2-fold, published by National Park Service & Assoc for the Preservation of Virginia Antiquities, 1957, 8-1/2" x 24"....1.00
Handkerchief, Old Sturbridge Village, blue and white, 14-3/4" x 15"....25.00
Magazine, *Antiques,* Oct 1979, cover story about Old Sturbridge Village .5.00
Pipe, red clay, Jamestown Colony, mkd "1607 Jamestown 1907" and "Patented July 31, 1906," 2" h....75.00
Souvenir plate
Jamestown, Capt John Smith and Princess Pocahontas, mulberry and white, Adams Co. for Assoc for the Preservation of Virginia Antiquities, 7" dia....135.00
Monticello, pink and white, Charlottesville Hardware Co., 10-3/8" dia....85.00
Mount Vernon, black and white, Conrad Crafters, Wheeling, VA, 9" dia ..18.00
Mount Vernon, blue and white, Old Staffordshire, Jonroth Importers, 10" dia....40.00
Souvenir ring, Monticello, silver tone....10.00
Tie, Mount Vernon, blue background, embroidered cupola design, orig label reads "Mount Vernon Ladies Assoc"....15.00

Steiff hobby horse, mohair, leather, iron, and wood, c1900, 20" h, $600.

❖ Hobby Horses

Children love hobby horses. From primitive homemade wooden creations to exquisite professionally made examples, these stick-and-head toys were loved and ridden for hours.

Also see Rocking Horses in this edition.

Cisco Kid, played-with cond **30.00**
Colt 45, vinyl head, wood stick, played-with cond **5.00**
Mobo, c1920 ....**475.00**
Rich Toys, played-with cond **15.00**
Snoopy, vinyl head, 36" l wood stick, played-with cond **5.00**
Zebra, stuffed white and black striped plush fur head, white mane, plastic eyes, red cord, wood stick, played-with cond **7.50**

❖ Hockey Cards

As with baseball, basketball, and football trading cards, hockey cards are plentiful. A good price guide is essential to understanding the sporting card market.

Reference: James Beckett et. al., *Beckett Hockey Card Price Guide & Alphabetical Checklist*, Beckett Publications, 2002; *Standard Catalog of Football, Basketball and Hockey Cards*, 2nd ed, Krause Publications, 1996.

Periodicals: *Sports Cards Magazine & Price Guide*, 700 E State St, Iola, WI 54990; *Sports Collectors Digest*, 700 E State St, Iola, WI 54990.

Donruss, 1997, complete set..........**20.00**
Fleer Ultra Series I, 1992-93, set of 250 cards **11.00**
McDonald's, 1991, set of 31 cards.**11.50**
Parkhurst, 1963-64
  #44, MacDonald **60.00**
  #45, Pronovost **60.00**
#49, Cushenan.............................**40.00**
Score, 1990-91, set of 440 cards......**8.00**
Stadium Card, 1991/92 ....**12.00**
Topps
  1961-62, #24, Pilote...................**125.00**
  1961-62, #25, Vasko **60.00**
  1987, complete set....................**115.00**
  1990-91, set of 396 cards **7.00**
  1992-93, set of 396 cards **7.00**
Upper Deck
  1993-94, set I **15.00**
  1995, complete............................**55.00**

❖ Hockey Memorabilia

Whether you're into field hockey or ice hockey, flea markets are a great place to score a goal with this collectible.

Book, *Hockey's Great Rivalries*, Stan Fischler, Random House, 1974, hardcover, 151 pgs........................**6.00**
Figurine, Rod Gilbert, by Sports Impressions, 1994, limited edition of 3,950 pcs, NRFB, 6" h **35.00**

Hockey Puck, autographed
  Belfour, Ed, Chicago **12.00**
  Burr, Shawn.................................**3.00**
  Draper, Kris **15.00**
  Gadsby, Bill **10.00**
Jersey, game-worn, NHL
  Bouchard, Joel, Calgary Flames, #6, red, 96-97 ....**250.00**
  Cirella, Joe, Florida Panthes, #2, white, 94-95 ....**375.00**
  Crowder, Troy, Vancouver Vanucks, #18, white, 96-97 ....**200.00**
  Holzinger, Brian, Tampa Bay Lighting, #9, black, 99-00 ....**475.00**
  Laflamme, Christian, Chicago Blackhawks, #3, red, 98-99 ....**350.00**
Mask, PCI, autographed by Patrick Roy **70.00**
Patch, 2"
  Detroit Red Wings **5.00**
  Montreal Canadiens **5.00**
  New York Rangers.........................**6.00**
  Oilers...**4.50**
  Quebec Nordiques **5.00**
Photograph, 8" x 10", autographed
  Bucyk, John.................................**8.00**
  DelVecchio, Alex..........................**7.00**
  Flemming, Reggie **8.00**
Starting Linuep figure
  Ed Belfour, 1998.........................**12.50**
  Dominik Hasek, 1998 ....**16.50**
  Gordie Howe, 1995, Timeless Legends **10.00**
  Brian Leetch, 1994.......................**15.00**
  Mark Messier, 1996.....................**12.50**
  Felix Potvin, 1998.......................**12.50**
  Joe Sakic, 1996...........................**17.50**
  Brendan Shanahan, 1996 ....**10.00**

❖ Holiday Collectibles

Holidays have long been commemorated through a variety of collectibles, from postcards to cookie cutters. Today collectors enjoy searching through their favorite flea markets for more interesting items and then incorporating them with their décor. Here's a sampling of what's available.

For additional listings, see Christmas, Easter, and Halloween in this edition.

Bank, turkey, chalkware, tan, red and yellow, 1950s, USA, 11" h............**85.00**
Calendar, framed, November, 1933, from *St. Nicholas Magazine*, 8" x 12"...**25.00**
Candles, pr, figural boy and girl pilgrims **5.00**
Candy box, shamrock shape, cardboard, green, litho shamrocks on top, 8-1/2" h **17.50**
Candy Container
  Hat, green and gold cardboard hat,

base label "Loft Candy Corp" ...**25.00**
Turkey, wax, white, Fanny Farmer
  Candy, orig box.......................**25.00**
Decoration, honeycomb tissue paper,
  table top decoration, 2 sided
  lithographed cardboard turkey, mkd
  USA, 8-1/2" h **15.00**
Greeting Card, The Mayflower, With
  Joyful Thanksgiving Wishes **8.00**
Magazine Cover, *Life,* March 15, 1923,
  cherub wearing Irish hat, playing harp
  ....**15.00**
Noisemaker, crepe paper and cardboard
  ....**10.00**
Pinback button, Labor Day March for
  Human and Labor Rights, Sept 6,
  1976, Raleigh, North Carolina, black
  and white sketch of people with signs,
  3" dia **14.00**
Place Card Holder, 2-1/2" h, standing
  celluloid turkey, holder at base of metal
  spring legs....................................**20.00**
Plate, Fourth of July, Americana Holidays
  Collection, 1st in series, 1978, Edwin
  M. Knowles China Co., Bradford
  Exchange, 8-1/2" dia....................**30.00**
Postcard
  Independence Day, 2 Victorian children
    with firecrackers, 1910 postmark**8.00**
  New Year, elves and clock, 1910....**3.50**
  New Year, calendar design, angels,
    1911...**18.00**
  Thanksgiving, Pilgrim child, by Whitney,
    1919 postmark............................**6.00**
Puzzle, "First Thanksgiving," Big Star
  Picture Puzzle, orig box, 10" x 13-1/2"
  ....**15.00**
Tip tray, litho tin, Thanksgiving motif of
  boy with turkey, C.D. Kenny, Baltimore
  ....**90.00**

❖ Holly Hobbie

This cute country gal first appeared on the
scene in the late 1970s, spreading her
special brand of sunshine for several years
thereafter. Holly Hobbie and her friends
often had inspirational messages.

Bell, annual, bisque.........................**40.00**
Brunch bag, vinyl, zipper closure,
  Aladdin Industries, 1978, orig thermos
  ....**65.00**
Children's play dishes, plastic, large
  plate, 7 smaller plates, 2 mugs, mkd
  "Aluminum Specialty, Chilton Toys,
  Manitowoc, Wis.," 10 pcs..............**25.00**
Christmas plate, 1972...................**25.00**
Coffeepot, 1973, 8" h....................**70.00**
Cradle, doll size............................**40.00**
Creamer **25.00**
Doll, Amy, 15" h.............................**30.00**
Figure
  Holly's Little Friend, 1971, MIB **50.00**

Robbie, seated with toy train........**25.00**
Halloween Costume, Ben Cooper,
  American Greetings, small child size,
  worn **15.00**
Limited edition plate, Mother's Day, 10-
  1/2" dia **40.00**

*Holly Hobbie doll, stuffed, large, blue bonnet,
multicolored dress, and pinafore, play wear, soiling,
$3.50.*

Lunch box, metal, several different
  scenes, 1979................................**40.00**
Plaque, "Love is a Way of Smiling with
  Your Heart," ceramic, 1973..........**18.00**
Platter, oval, 14-1/2" l.....................**45.00**
Sugar bowl, cov.............................**35.00**
Teapot, white porcelain, green trim,
  green and brown Holly, "Tea for two is
  twice as nice," 5-3/4" h **32.00**

❖ Holt-Howard

The partnership of brothers John and
Robert J. Howard with A. Grant Holt created
an import company in 1948 in Stamford,
Connecticut. Robert designed some novelty
ceramic containers that proved to be very
successful.

Reference: Walter Dworkin, *Price Guide to
Holt-Howard Collectibles and Related
Ceramic Wares of the '50s and '60s*, Krause
Publications, 1998.

Air Freshner, Girl Christmas Tree ..**65.00**
Ashtray
  Golfer Image **110.00**
  Li'l Old Lace **50.00**
  Merry Mouse, corner....................**55.00**
Bank, bobbing
  Coin Clown.................................**135.00**
  Dandy Lion.................................**135.00**
Bells, Elf Girls, pr...........................**55.00**
Bud vase, Daisy Dorable **70.00**
Butter dish, cov, Red Rooster........**65.00**

Candelabra, Li'l Old Lace, spiral.....**50.00**
Candle climbers, set
  Honey Bunnies **85.00**
  Ole Snowy....................................**48.00**
Candleholders, pr
  Ermine Angels with snowflake rings,
    set...**48.00**
  Red Rooster **30.00**
  Reindeer, pr.................................**38.00**
Candle rings, Ballerina, set...........**48.00**
Cereal bowl, Red Rooster **15.00**
Coffee mug, Red Rooster...............**14.00**
Coffee server, Red Rooster **65.00**
Condiment Jar, Pixieware, 1958
  Cherries......................................**115.00**
  Cocktail Cherries........................**135.00**
  Cocktail Olives............................**130.00**
  Cocktail Onions **155.00**
Cookie jar
  Clown, pop-up **225.00**
  Red Rooster **100.00**
Creamer and sugar, Red Rooster .**55.00**
Crock, Merry Mouse, Stinky Cheese
  ....**50.00**
Dinner plate, Red Rooster.............**18.00**
Egg cup, Red Rooster **20.00**
Head Vase, My Fair Lady **75.00**
Letter and pen holder, Santa **55.00**
Mug, Cozy Kittens **35.00**
Napkin holder, Santa, 4"...............**25.00**
Oil and vinegar, Cozy Kittens **175.00**
Salad dressing jar, Pixieware, 1959
  Flat head, French, Italian, or Russian
    Pixie...**140.00**
  Round head, French, Italian or Russian
    Pixie...**125.00**
Salt and pepper shakers, pr
  Bell Bottom Gobs (sailors) **50.00**
  Bunnies in baskets.......................**32.00**
  Chattercoons, Peppy and Salty....**38.00**
  Cloud Santa **38.00**
  Holly Girls....................................**20.00**
  Rock' N' Roll Santas, on springs ..**75.00**
  Snow Babies **35.00**

❖ Home Front Collectibles

While the "boys" were off to World War II,
there was a real effort here at home to
influence those left behind to contribute to
the war effort. Today, these items and their
powerful messages are becoming choice
collectibles.

Reference: Martin Jacobs, *World War II
Homefront Collectibles*, Krause
Publications, 2000.

Bookmark, "Prevent Forest Fires," stiff
  orange paper, Hitler and Hirohito at top
  with blazing forest fire in background,
  U.S. Dept of Agriculture, black and
  white reverse with text, 2-1/2" x 7"

....**45.00**
Game, "V for Victory" **40.00**
Jewelry
   V-shaped victory pin, sterling silver with
     30 rhinestones, 1-1/2" h, 1-1/4"**60.00**
   "Sweetheart" in script, sterling silver,
     gold-plated and red/white/blue
     Bakelite, orig box, 1-1/2" sq....**102.50**
Matchbook, V for Victory, War Bond
   promotion, Diamond Match Co.,
   unused, 1-1/2" x 3-3/4" **12.00**
Puzzle, "Keep 'Em Flying," fighter planes,
   Perfect Picture Puzzle, "For Victory Buy
   United States Savings Bonds and
   Stamps" logo, 19-1/2" x 15-1/2" ...**50.00**
Sticker, "Salvage Will Win The War,"
   cartoon image of Japanese soldier
   choking on "v" of word "salvage," 1-1/2"
   x 2" **25.00**
Window banner, fabric panel, printed in
   red, white, blue and bright gold, loop
   for hanging, 8-1/2" x 12" **35.00**

❖ Homer Laughlin

The Homer Laughlin Company is another
dinnerware manufacturer that helped make
East Liverpool, Ohio, a busy place. This
company was producing white ware by the
late 1880s. When the firm was sold to a
group of investors from Pittsburgh,
expansion soon followed. New plants were
built in Ohio and West Virginia, and the
dinnerware lines increased. Besides giving
us such interesting patterns as Fiesta, and
Harlequin, the firm also designed Kitchen
Kraft and Riviera, plus thousands of others
designs.

Reference: Jo Cunningham and Darlene
Nossaman, *Homer Laughlin China: Guide
to Shakes and Patterns,* Schiffer Publishing,
2002.

Periodical: *The Laughlin Eagle,* 1270 63rd
Terrace S., St. Petersburg, FL 33705.

For additional listings, see *Warman's
Americana & Collectibles* and *Warman's
American Pottery & Porcelain.*

*Homer Laughlin, cereal bowl, green dec, mkd
"Pastoral, Homer Laughlin," hairline, $1.*

*Homer Laughlin, set of dishes, Georgian pattern,
service for 6 plus serving pieces, green mark
"Eggshell, Georgian, Homer Laughlin, Made in
USA", some chips and wear, $80.*

Baker, Mexicana, oval **25.00**
Bowl, Cavalier, egg shell, numbered, set
   of 4 ....**20.00**
Butter, cov, Virginia Rose, jade.......**80.00**
Casserole, cov, individual, Conchita
....**225.00**
Casserole, cov, large
   Conchita **125.00**
   Mexicana **145.00**
Cereal bowl, ftd, Rhythm, chartreuse, 5-
   1/2" dia **5.00**
Cup, Rhythm, forest green or gray **7.00**
Deep plate, Mexicana **45.00**
Dessert bowl, Rhythm, yellow, 5-1/4" dia
....**3.00**
Dinner set, service for 8
   Century.......................................**835.00**
   Eggshell Nautilus **380.00**
   Virginia Rose............................**425.00**
Fruit bowl, Mexicana **15.00**
Nappy, Rhythm, yellow, 8-3/4" dia ..**18.00**
Pie baker, Mexicana **37.50**
Plate, Virginia Rose, 9" dia..............**7.50**
Platter, Rhythm, yellow, 11-1/2" l **12.00**
Soup bowl, Rhythm, yellow **9.00**

Homer Laughlin, plate, Rhythm Scene, green border, $22.

Tea service, Riviera, red, yellow, mauve,
   green, and ivory cups and saucers,
   yellow tea pot **500.00**
Tray, Virginia Rose **30.00**

☆ Hooked Rugs

Once thought only as something to put on
the floor, hooked rugs are now gaining folk
art status. Collectors recognize the
interesting designs and colors, plus the
many hours of artistry involved in each
piece. When cleaned, put on a stretcher
frame, a vintage hooked rug can make a
lovely decorating statement.

*Hooked Rugs, cottage, white house, red roof, green
shrubs and trees, white picket fence, light tan sky,
worn, stain on border, $35.*

Baskets of colorful flowers, black, dark
   brown, and gray ground, flower and
   leaves in each corner divided by
   multicolored borders, 37" x 19-1/2",
   light overall wear **990.00**
Chickens, central reserve with eight
   black and gray chickens surrounded by
   red and pink flower blossoms on top
   sides, brown and black horse below,
   36" x 27-1/2", stretched on wooden
   frame, fading, wear....................**690.00**
Country village with train in center,
   church and houses on the green, horse
   drawn carriages, people, and farm
   animals, flowering trees and shrubs,
   blue and purple border, 35" x 75",
   losses to center and border **1,530.00**
Deer, running, multicolored scalloped
   border, blue edge binding, 34" x 21-
   1/2" **75.00**
Geometric, multicolored, 40" x 25", some
   edge fraying..................................**65.00**
Dog, oblong central panel, surrounded by
   line and floral borders, dark orange,
   tan, dark purple, red, green, and blue-
   gray, Frost, 37" x 19-1/2", minor edge
   wear..**275.00**
Hearts, two center hearts, star in each
   corner, multicolored striped field,
   mounted on cotton backing, stretched
   onto wood frame, 30-3/4" x 40-1/8",
   minor losses **2,115.00**
   Black horse on blue oval medallion,
   four lions and four red flowers
   spaced evenly around outside, dark
   gray braid border, hooked by PA
   woman, c1940-50, 42" x 46" ..**975.00**

Red horse, black bridle, striped mane and tail, tan medallion, two tone brown with gold background, blue and ivory corner leaves, wreath around medallion with red berries, black cloth binding, minor wear and small hole at horse's back, 24-1/2" x 41" **315.00**

House flanked by two trees, worked in shades of green, blue, red, and brown, mottled blue and tan ground, 16-1/2" x 26-1/2", mounted on wood frame **725.00**

Lighthouse, red and white striped lighthouse in coastal setting, light blue sky with clouds, 22" x 34-1/2" **200.00**

Parcheesi board design, multicolored, 37-1/2" x 24"................................**50.00**

Hooked Rugs, eagle, holding E Pluribus Unum banner, golds, tans, olive green, wear, $45.

❖ Horse Collectibles

Bookend, black painted back and base, silvered figural horse, $25.

Clock, United Self Starting, gilt case and figural saddled horse, variegated marble base, $35.

Some collectors specialize in items related to the care of horses, others search for items used for riding, and some prefer items with images of horses.

Bank, Beauty, cast iron, 4-1/2" h...**300.00**
Bells, worn leather strap with over 40 nickel bells, tug hook.................**225.00**
Bit, eagle, mkd "G. S. Garcia" **775.00**
Book
    Horse Power_A History of the Horse and Donkey in Human Societies, Brock...**38.00**
    The Black Stallion, Walter Farley, 1st ed., dust jacket **25.00**
Bridle, Calvary, mule bridle, brass "US" spots...**225.00**
Bridle rosette, glass with rose motif inside, mkd "Chapman" **40.00**
Clock, brass horse standing next to western saddle, wood base, United **170.00**
Contest flyer, Dan Patch, illus........**28.00**
Cookie jar, McCoy, Circus Horse, McCoy **50.00**
Curry comb, tin back, leather handle, early 1900s.................................**45.00**
Decanter, Man O'War, Ezra Brooks **25.00**
Fruit Crate label, Bronco, bucking horse **25.00**
Game, Pony Express, cast-metal horses, 1940s **85.00**
Lasso, horsehair **135.00**
Magazine, *Western Horseman*, vol 1, #1, 1935 ....**30.00**
Men's brush, horse head figural handle **10.00**

Tile, octagonal, white ground, brown horse illus, $8.

Mug, Clydesdales, Budweiser, Christmas, Ceramarte, 1985........**50.00**
Newspaper, Horse & Stable Weekly, Boston, Jan. 2, 1891 ....**35.00**
Postcard, bucking bronco, cowboy flying off, rodeo in Prescott, Ariz., 1920s **15.00**
Rosette, brass, Civil War................**25.00**
Saddle, McClellan type, large fenders for leg protection, early 1900s.........**900.00**
Saddle blanket, Navajo, early 1900s **950.00**
Snowdome, Budweiser Clydesdales, 1988 limited edition **75.00**
Spurs, Crockett, arrow shank........**700.00**

Tray, Genessee Twelve Horse Ale, horse team illus, 12" dia......................**115.00**

❖ Horse Racing

Man's love for competition has long been reflected in horse racing. Here's a sample of some collectibles on today's market.

Collectors' Club: Sport of Kings Soc, 1406 Annen Ln, Madison, WI 53711.

Also see Kentucky Derby Glasses in this edition.

Ashtray
Count Fleet, sgd by Lynn Bogue Hunt, ceramic, 5-1/4" sq......................**30.00**
Kentucky Derby, 1976, Galt House, Louisville, smoke glass, 7" dia..**30.00**
Festival pin, Kentucky Derby
1974, blue and silver.....................**85.00**
1976, blue and silver....................**65.00**
1977, green and gold...................**65.00**
1978, red and gold......................**65.00**
1992, gold tone...........................**85.00**
1993, gold tone...........................**85.00**
Gambling device, chrome stop watch case, glass cover, diecut celluloid grandstand in center, surrounded by 8 openings, each with numbered running horse, early 1900s, 1-5/8" dia....**150.00**
Pegasus parade pin, 1997.............**85.00**
Pinback button
Silky Sullivan Winner, multicolor, white ground, blue letters, c1950.......**20.00**
Topeka Derby Day, Sept 13, 1904, sepia...**20.00**
Print, Currier & Ives, "The Grand Racer Kington, by Spendthrift," 1891, unmatted, unframed...................**475.00**
Sheet music, *Dan Patch March*......**40.00**
Soup cup, china, "Beautiful Wheeling Downs," mkd "Shenango Restaurant China Soup Cup," 3-1/2" h, 3-1/4" dia **30.00**
Souvenir book, 1941, 67th running, 12-3/4" x 9-3/4"................................**85.00**
Souvenir plate, Jorge Velasquez, Meadowlands jockey, Belcrest Fine China, copyright 1983 by Daily Racing Form, Inc, 8-1/2" dia....................**25.00**
Tray, Reynolds Aluminum, 1956, 14" x 18", some wear.........................**225.00**
Trophy, silver, typical.......................**50.00**

❖ Hot Wheels

Harry Bradley, an automotive designer; Howard Newman, a Mattel designer; Elliot Handler, chairman of Mattel; and Jack Ryan, also of Mattel, joined forces to produce the first diecast Hot Wheels cars in 1968.

Hot Wheels Vintage collection, #5708, California Custom Miniatures, dark pink hot rod, collector's button, MOC, $10.

References: Michael Zarnock, *Hot Wheels Field Guide: Redlines and Blackwalls 1968-1988*, Krause Publications, 2003; Michael Zarnock, *The Ultimate Guide to Hot Wheels Variations*, Krause Publications, 2002; Elizabeth A. Stephan, *O'Brien's Collecting Toy Cars & Trucks*, 3rd ed., Krause Publications, 2000; Dan Stearns, *Standard Catalog of Die-Cast Vehicles,* Krause Publications, 2002.

Periodicals: *Hot Wheels Newsletter*, 26 Madera Ave, San Carlos, CA 94070; *Toy Cars & Vehicles*, 700 E State St, Iola, WI 54900; *Toy Shop*, 700 E State St, Iola, WI 54900.

Accessories

Case, Sizzlers Race.........................**75.00**
Full Curve Accessory Pak...............**12.00**
Gas Pumper, Mattel........................**12.00**
Snake Mountain Challenge.............**20.00**

Cars and Trucks

Baja Bruiser, #8258, orange, 1974..**75.00**
Beach Bomb, green.........................**75.00**
Boss Hoss, #6406, 1971................**75.00**
Buzz Off, #6976, blue, 1974............**90.00**
Camaro Z28, #33, red, chrome base **46.00**
Captain America, #2879, white, 1979 ....**175.00**
Cement Miser, #6452, 1970...........**60.00**
Chevy, '57, Ultra Hots, #47...........**110.00**
Circus Cats, #3303, white, 1975......**75.00**
Corvette, billionth............................**10.00**
Custom Firebird, blue.....................**40.00**
Datsun 200XS, #3255, maroon, Canada, 1982...**175.00**
Delivery Truck, #52.........................**32.00**
Designer Dreams............................**17.50**
Dump Truck, #38, steel bed.............**7.00**
Dune Daddy, #6967, light green, 1975 ....**75.00**

Hot Wheels Vintage collection, #5714, California Custom Miniatures, purple hot rod, collector's button, MOC, $10.

Earthmover, #16 ....**85.00**
Emergency Squad, #7650, red, 1975 ....**65.00**
Ferrari, #312, red enamel...............**50.00**
Fire Truck, 1980.............................**2.00**
Fireworks.......................................**20.00**
Fleetside, purple............................**35.00**
Ford Bronco, #56, turquoise...........**18.00**
Golden Knights VW Bug.................**20.00**
GT Racer, #598, 1995, NRFP..........**3.00**
Hard Rock Café I............................**25.00**
Hot Heap, #6219, 1968...................**65.00**
Jet Threat, #6179, 1976..................**60.00**
Jiffy Lube, milk truck, red...............**10.00**
Marrow Foundation.........................**30.00**
McDonald's, Tattoo Machine, 1993, NRFP...**3.00**
Mercedes 500 SL, 1997, NRFP......**26.00**
Motorcross Team Van, #2853, red, 1979 ....**125.00**
Neet Streeter, #9510, chrome, 1976 ....**40.00**
Penske 70 Mustang Mach 1...........**15.00**
Penske S'Cool bus, silver...............**13.00**
Poison Pinto, #9240, green, blackwall, 1977..**30.00**
Porsche 911, #6972, orange, 1975 ....**65.00**
Race Ace, #2620, white, 1968........**75.00**
Red Baron, #6963, red, blackwall, 1977 ....**25.00**
Rock Buster, #9088, yellow, blackwall, 1977..**15.00**
Sand Crab, #6403, 1970.................**60.00**
Silhouette, #6209, 1979..................**90.00**
Super Van, #9205, chrome, 1976....**40.00**
Tail Gunner, #29.............................**75.00**
Tractor Trailer, 1979.........................**1.00**
Van de Kamps, mail in premium, NRFP, Hiway Hauler Truck, 1996...........**24.00**
Set
25th anniversary, 1993, NRFP, 5 cars **38.00**

30th anniversary, 30 cars..............**150.00**
Christmas, 1999...........................**55.00**
Christmas, 2000...........................**55.00**
Drive-In, 3 cars **30.00**
Holiday, 1995 ....**80.00**
Lowrider **25.00**
Muscle Cars, Set #1, 2 cars **15.00**
Night at the Races **18.00**

❖ Howdy Doody

"What time is it kids? Howdy Doody Time!" Every Howdy Doody Show started with Buffalo Bob Smith asking the Peanut Gallery that question. It was a great kids show, and today's collectors are happily searching for items relating to Howdy, Mr. Bluster, Clarabelle, and the other characters.

Collectors Club: Doodyville Historical Society, 8 Hunt Ct, Flemington, NJ 08822.

Book

Howdy Doody's Circus Book, Little Golden Book, 1950...................**35.00**
Howdy Doody & Santa Claus, Little Golden Book, 1955, 1st ed.......**38.00**
Comic book, *Howdy Doody*, #3 1950, cover damage................................**8.00**
Cookie jar, Purinton Pottery, 9-3/4" h **900.00**
Cup, yellow plastic, Howdy Doody's face at top, Gotham Ware **30.00**
Fork and spoon, Kagran, Crown Silverplate, 4-1/2" l **95.00**
Game, Howdy Doody Card Game, Russell Mfg. Co., orig box **71.00**
Jelly glass, "Here Comes Music for Doodyville Circus," Welch's, variation with no animals in circus wagon, early 1950s **35.00**
Key chain, 3-dimensional, NRFP......**4.50**
Marionette

Howdy Doody, composition, 14" h **475.00**
Clarabelle, new strings, 14" h **300.00**
Princess Winter, Spring, Summer, Fall, composition, cracked, 14".......**500.00**
Night light, head moves, wear, 6" h **275.00**
Pinback button, It's Howdy Doody Time!, orange and white **18.00**
Record spindle spinner, 4" h **275.00**
Ring, Poll Parrot, adjustable..........**125.00**
Toy, Howdy Doody Flub-A-Dub push-up toy, #177, Kohner, tail missing, 5-1/4" h **245.00**
Ventriloquist dummy, composition and cloth, Reliable, Canada, 1950s, 21" h **450.00**

❖ Hubley Toys

Hubley Manufacturing was founded in Lancaster, Pennsylvania, in 1894. The company's first toys were made of cast iron. By 1940, cast iron had been phased out and replaced with other metals and plastic.

Periodicals: *Toy Cars & Models*, 700 E State St, Iola, WI 54900; *Toy Shop*, 700 E State St, Iola, WI 54900.

Bookends, Hunting Dog, bronze, orig paint, c1925, 4-1/2" h, pr............**195.00**
Cap gun

Army .45-caliber pistol, nickel-plated, brown checkered grips, finish, 1945, 6-1/2" l **75.00**
Hawk .45-caliber automatic, plastic pearlized grip, 5-1/4" l...............**45.00**
Pet **15.00**
Doorstop, Lilies of the Valley, cast iron, mkd 146, 10-1/2" h, 7-1/2" w **250.00**
Duck, very worn orig paint, rust, 9-1/2" l **110.00**
Toy, airplane

Single prop, die-cast, orange and yellow, folding wings, 11" wingspan **145.00**
U.S. Army, retractable wheels, paint chips, tires cracked, 7-1/2" wingspan, 6" l...**75.00**
P-38, paint chips, 7-1/2" x 8 1/2" **50.00**
Toy, cars and trucks

Coupe, very worn orig paint, deteriorated white rubber tires, 6-1/4" l...**300.00**
Delivery Truck, worn old repaint, label on side of panel, deteriorated white rubber tires, 4-3/4" l................**100.00**
Fire Truck, ladder wagon, worn old paint, some touch-up repair, mismatched driver, accessories missing, 13-1/2" l.....................**80.00**
Kiddie Toy Race Car, metal, nickel plated driver, red, black rubber tires, 1950s, 7" l................................**30.00**
Milk Cream Truck, 1930s, 1 tire missing, paint chips, 3-3/4" l...**365.00**
Racer, driver, old worn paint, some rust, labeled inside body, 7" l..**165.00**

Hubley Toys, Huber cast metal steam roller, 7-1/4" l, $395.

Surf 'n' Sand, jeep and boat with trailer, blue and white, orig window box, 15" l..**95.00**
Toy, motorcycle

Cast iron, replaced handle bars, 60% orig paint................................**200.00**
Police Department Motorcycle, Kiddietoy, 5" l, 1950s **165.00**

❖ Hull Pottery

In 1905, Addis E. Hull purchased the Acme Pottery Company in Crooksville, Ohio. In 1917, the A.E. Hull Pottery Company commenced producing art pottery, novelties, stoneware and kitchenware, including the Little Red Riding Hood line that would become one of their best sellers. Most items had a matte finish with shades of pink and blue or brown as the dominant colors.

Following a disastrous flood and fire in 1950, J. Brandon Hull reopened the factory in 1952 as the Hull Pottery Company. These newer pieces usually have a glossy finish and tend to have a more modern look. The company currently produces items for florists, e.g. the Regal and Floraline lines.

References: Susan and Al Bagdade, *Warman's American Pottery and Porcelain*, Wallace-Homestead, 1994; Barbara Loveless Gick-Burke, *Collector's Guide to Hull Pottery*, Collector Books, 1993; Joan Hull, *Hull, The Heavenly Pottery*, 6th ed, self-published, 1999; Brenda Roberts, *The Ultimate Encyclopedia of Hull Pottery*, Collector Books, 1995; Mark and Ellen Supnick, *Collecting Hull Pottery's Little Red Riding Hood*, rev ed, L-W Books, 1998.

Periodical: *Hull Pottery Newsletter*, 7768 Meadow Dr, Hillsboro, MO 60350.

Collectors' Club: Hull Pottery Assoc, 11023 Tunnel Hill NE, New Lexington, OH 43764

For additional listings, also see *Warman's Americana & Collectibles*.

Hull Pottery, planter, green, mkd Hull, USA, $15.

Coaster/ashtray, gingerbread man **20.00**
Cornucopia

Blossom Flite, pink and black, 12" l **115.00**

Hull Pottery, vase, Magnolia, matte, 1946-47, 10-1/2" h, $200.

Ebbtide, Mermaid on Shell, rose and turquoise glaze, 7-1/2" h, 9" w
....**200.00**
Creamer, Waterlily, L-19, 5" h **75.00**
Head vase, Newborn, #92, 5-3/4" h
....**65.00**
Jardiniere, Dogwood, 514, 4" h....**110.00**
Pitcher, Magnolia, yellow matte glaze, #5, 7" h...**185.00**
Planter, Parrot................................**60.00**
Salt and pepper shakers, pr
Apple **25.00**
Mushroom, 3-3/4" h.....................**20.00**
Tea set, Blossom Flite, teapot with lid, creamer, sugar with lid...............**200.00**
Teapot
Dogwood, 507, 5-1/2" h **350.00**
Waterlily, L-18, 6" h **225.00**
Tray, gingerbread man, brown **65.00**
Vase
Bow-Knot, B10, 10-1/2" h..........**495.00**
Dogwood, 504, 8-1/2" h **150.00**

Magnolia, H5, 6-1/2" h **45.00**
Magnolia, H17, 12-1/2" h **250.00**
Waterlily, L-8, 8-1/4" h................**165.00**
Wall pocket, cup and saucer, yellow background, pink flower **40.00**
Window box, Woodland Gloss, rose shading to lime-green, W14, 4" h, 10" l
....**80.00**

❖ Hummels

Based on original drawings by Berta Hummel, these charming children have delighted collectors for generations. Production of her figurines started in 1935.

References: Carl F. Luckey and Dean Genth, *Luckey's Hummel Figurines and Plates*, 12th ed, Krause Publications, 2003; Robert L. Miller, *Hummels 1978-1998: 20 Years of "Miller on Hummel" Columns*, Collector News, 1998.

Collectors' Clubs: Hummel Collector's

Club, 1261 University Dr, Yardley, PA 19067; M.I. Hummel Club, Goebel Plaza, Rte 31, P.O. Box 11, Pennington, NJ 08534.

Annual plate, Singing Lesson, 1979
....**50.00**
Annual Bell, bas relief, 3rd ed, 1980, MIB...**70.00**
Ashtray
Happy Pastime, #62, trade mark 1, c1935-50................................**400.00**
Joyful, #33, trade mark 2, c1950-57
....**285.00**
Singing Lesson, #34, trade mark 1, c1935-50................................**440.00**
Bank, Little Thrifty, #118, stylized bee, 1958-64 ....**230.00**
Bell, 1975, orig box **65.00**
Bookends, pr, Apple Tree, trademark 5, 1972-79 ....**320.00**
Calendar, 1955, 12 illus **15.00**
Candleholder, Herald Angels, #37, full bee mark, c1950-57 ....**300.00**
Christmas plate, 1st ed, 1971, orig box, 7-1/2" dia **650.00**
Figure
Apple Tree Girl, #141/I, 6" h.......**290.00**
Artist, #304, trademark 6 ....**90.00**
Barnyard Hero, #195/2/0, trademark 2
....**115.00**
Builder, #305, trademark 4...........**82.00**
Carnival, #328, trademark 6.........**80.00**
Crossroads, #331, 6-3/4" h **360.00**
Doll Mother, stylized bee mark...**135.00**
Farewell **325.00**
Friend or Foe, #434....................**285.00**
Good Shepherd, #42/0, incised crown mark, full bee, 6-1/4" h **600.00**
Happy Birthday, #176/0, 6" h **245.00**
Just Resting **175.00**

Hummel, Apple Tree Boy and Apple Tree Girl, both trademark 5, 6" h, $250.

Letter To Santa Claus, #340.......**350.00**
Little girl, #475..............................**45.00**
Mischief Maker **290.00**
Sensitive Hunter.........................**240.00**
She Loves Me, She Loves Me Not
....**225.00**
Strolling Along, #5, full bee mark, 5-
3/4" h **550.00**
Tuneful Angel, #359, trademark 6
....**45.00**
Village Boy, #51/2/0, trademark 1
....**115.00**
Waiter, #154/0, trademark 2.......**130.00**

❖ Hummel Look-Alikes

A number of companies have produced figures that resemble the more-expensive, popular Hummels. Always check for the familiar Hummel mark, but don't be surprised to find another maker's identification mark or label.

Boy, standing
Hands behind back **15.00**
Next to fence **20.00**
Girl, standing
Holding basket **17.50**
Reading book.............................**15.00**
With cat, 1973, Avon **10.00**

Hummel-look alikes, boy playing fiddle, dog at feet, unmarked, 6" h, $3.50.

❖ Hunting

Flea markets make great hunting, whether you're looking for big game or small treasures. Substitute a camera for the usual rifle or trap, and bring along a bag to tote your catch in.

Periodicals: *Sporting Collector's Monthly,*

P.O. Box 305, Camden Wyoming, DE 19934.

Collectors' Clubs: Call & Whistle Collectors Assoc, 2839 E 26th Place, Tulsa, OK 74114; Callmakers & Collectors Assoc of America, 137 Kingswood Dr, Clarksville, TN 37043.

Book
Handling Your Hunting Dog, 3rd ed, by J. Earl Bufkin, Purina Mills, 1942, 64 pgs..**15.00**
The Complete Book of Hunting, Clyde Ormond, 1962, 467 pgs, illus ...**11.50**
The Sportsman's Almanac: A Guide to the Recreational Uses of America's Public Lands, with Special Emphasis on Hunting and Fishing, Carley Farquhar, 1963, 1st ed., 453 pgs, small tear to dj **9.50**
Broadside, litho, DuPont Powders, two anxious duck hunters pecking out of camp, "Just look at 'em," image by Edmund Osthaus, c1910, 12" w, 14-1/2" h **50.00**
Call
Duck, Herter's orig box................**40.00**
Turkey, orig box **35.00**
Catalog
Kirtland Bros Sporting Goods, 16 pgs, 1924..**15.00**
Winchester Rifle, John Wayne cover, 16 pgs, 1982..............................**8.50**
Counter Felt, Dead Shot Powder, "Kill Your Bird Not Your Shoulder," multicolored on black, trimmed **90.00**
Handbook, Winchester Ammunition, 112 pgs, 1951 ....**13.50**
License
Deer, New York State, 1936, pinback style **35.00**
Game, New York State, 1918, red and white, serial number in blue, brass lapel stud fastener, 1-1/2" dia...**75.00**
Guide, Ontario, 1935, black and white, red numerals, worn...................**20.00**
Magazine, *Hunting and Fishing*, April 1935 ....**24.00**
Photograph
Hunter with ducks, hand-tinted, dated 1930, framed, 12-1/8" x 19-1/4"**20.00**
Hunting club members posing with shotguns, 6" x 8" **145.00**
Pinback button
Dupont Smokeless Powder, multicolored, fall hunting scene, pair of black and white pointer dogs, black lettering "Dupont Smokeless-The Champion's Powder" **100.00**
Peters Cartridges, multicolored, silver bullet in brass casing, pale green ground, black letters **45.00**
Remington UMC Bears, blue and white cartoon art, red rim, white letters

Hummel-look alikes, Pair, boy holding watering can, girl sweeping, white geese at feet, mkd "Made in Japan" on blue sticker, faint fake blue Goebel mark, $6.50.

Mounted deer head, $35.

"Shoot Remington UMC Steel Lined
Shells," **140.00**
Poster, "Remington Game Load Game,"
shows various wildlife, 26" x 18-1/2"
....**200.00**
Stickpin, Smith Guns, celluloid,
multicolored, oval, brass insert back,
inscribed "The Hunter Arms Co, Fulton,
NY" **120.00**
Watch fob, Dead Shot, brass rim,
multicolor celluloid insert, reverse
inscribed "Dead Shot Smokeless
Powder Manufactured by American
Powder Mills, Boston, Mass.," 1920s
....**175.00**

❖ Ice Cream Collectibles

Cold and creamy, ice cream can be the perfect accompaniment to a few hours at the flea market. But, if your tastes run to ice cream collectibles instead, some great examples may be waiting for you, too.

Collectors' Club: National Association of Soda Jerks, P.O. Box 115, Omaha, NE 68101; The Ice Screamers, P.O. Box 465, Warrington, PA 18976.

Ashtray, glass, "Carnation Ice Cream," stains **10.00**
Booklet, Eckels Ice Cream Co., Baltimore, 23 pgs **11.00**
Box, Sclater's Superior Ice Cream, Marion Drug Co., Marion, Va........**12.00**
Cone holder, Sealtest Ice Cream, "Get the best - Get Sealtest," red with white lettering, paper with a metal rim, 5" h **12.00**
Mold
   Flag on a shield, E.&Co., N.Y., 3-1/2" x 4" **195.00**
   George Washington on shield, mkd 456, 4-1/2" x 4" **195.00**
   George Washington on hatchet, E.&Co., N.Y., 1092, 3-1/2" x 3-3/4" **195.00**
   Liberty Bell, mkd 605, 3-1/2" X 4"**52.00**
   Wishbone, mkd 322, 5-1/2" x 4" **145.00**
Pinback button, celluloid, Arctic Rainbow Ice Cream Cones, 1912**30.00**
Salt and pepper shakers, Safe-T Cup ice cream cone, 3-1/2" h, pr.........**35.00**
Scoop
   Gilchrist #12, 11" l.......................**55.00**
   Gilchrist #31, wooden handle, 10-1/2" l **58.00**
   Kingerly # 12, dated Sept. 4, 1894 ....**325.00**
Top, litho tin with wooden shaft, "Ask for Jersey Maid Milk and Ice Cream" and "Can You Spin It-80 Seconds," red on cream ground, 1915 patent date..**20.00**
Towel, linen, embroidered ice cream sundae, 15" x 26" **12.00**
Toy, ice cream truck, tin, friction, Japan, 1960 on license plate, wear, 3-1/2" h, 8" l **85.00**

Trade card, The Crown Ice Cream Freezer, shows cherubs, American Machine Co., Philadelphia, 2-7/8" x 4-3/8" **15.00**
Tray, "Southern Dairies, Sealtest Ice Cream," paint loss, scratches, rust **115.00**
Whistle, plastic, Dairy Queen, ice cream cone shape, 3-1/4" h **10.00**

❖ Ice Picks

An ice pick was once a necessary household utensil. Today collectors search for examples with interesting shapes and advertising slogans. Most ice picks consist of a wooden handle with a metal pick. Expect to find examples with wear and minor rusting.

1939 World's Fair, San Francisco...**23.00**
Clarkson Peoples Coal & Ice **12.50**
"Drink Coca-Cola, Delicious and Refreshing," wooden handle, 8" l **25.00**
Dr. Pepper **5.00**
Keystone Ice Co., "Markley & Oak Sts. Phone 2684," all metal **18.00**
Maretta Ice Co., "Phone 7," worn wooden handle, 8-1/4" l **7.00**
Seaboard Ice Co., "Coolerator," all metal, 8-1/2" l **18.00**
Standard Ice Co., "Use Kris Kleer Ice, Ice for All Purposes," wooden handle, 8-1/2" l **10.00**
Union Ice Company **10.00**
"Use The Year Round, Dependable Ice Service, Those Who Really Know Prefer ICE, Save With Ice," wooden handle **4.00**

❖ Ice Skating

Ice skating is actually an old past time, going back to a time when skates where hand made and much cruder than today's finely shaped skates. Collecting ephemera related to skating is also quite popular with today's generation.

Animation cel, Mickey and Minnie Mouse on ice pond, from 1930s short, laser background, 10" x 12" **60.00**
Christmas ornament, Hallmark, Kristi Yamaguchi, 2000, MIB **12.50**
Costume, girl's, So-Fine label, 1950s Green wool, white rayon lining, white criss-cross lacing in front..........**35.00**
   Navy wool, embroidered flower trim **35.00**
Doll
   Ideal, Dorothy Hamill, 1970s, with rink, orig box **35.00**
   Mattel, Skipper, red skating outfit, 1963 ....**95.00**
Figurine, Precious Moments, "Dropping

In For Christmas," boy skating, 1982, 5-1/2" h, MIB **45.00**
Ice skates
   Child's, aluminum, leather straps, beginner's type, double runners, c1950......................................**20.00**
   Figure, white leather uppers, metal blades, worn, c1960 ....**10.00**
   Hockey, brown leather uppers, wide blades, c1960 ....**25.00**
Magazine cover, *The Associated*, Jan. 18, 1914, cover art of couple walking with ice skaters in background.....**90.00**
Pin, enamel sweater, pearl fringed skirt, pearl on hat, 1-3/4" h **15.00**
Program
   Holiday On Ice, 30th anniversary, 1975 ....**20.00**
   Ice Follies, Philadelphia, 1960 ....**5.00**
Tray, Coca-Cola, 1941, woman with skates.......................................**185.00**

❖ Illustrators

Many flea market adventurers are starting to specialize in one or more specific illustrators. You'll see them scouring through magazines for illustrations and advertisements by their favorites. Other collectors of illustrated items devote their search to prints, calendars, books, and other types of ephemera.

Periodicals: *Calendar Art Collector' Newsletter*, 45 Brown's Ln, Old Lyme, CT 06371; *The Illustrator Collector's News*, P.O. Box 1958, Sequim, WA 98232; *The Philip Boileau Collectors' Society Newsletter*, 1025 Redwood Blvd, Redding, CA 96003.

Book
   Chandler, Howard, *An Old Sweetheart of Mine* by James Whitcomb Riley, 1903 ....**65.00**
   Fisher, Harrison, *Love Finds the Way* by Paul Leicester Ford, Dodd Mead & Co., 1904............................**75.00**
   Peat, Fern Bisel, *The Sugar-Plum Tree and Other Verses* by Eugene Field **45.00**
Magazine cover
   Fisher, Harrison, *Saturday Evening Post*, May 18, 1907, "The Man Hunt" **80.00**
   Fisher, Harrison, *Saturday Evening Post*, June 19, 1915, "Horse Woman" **75.00**
   Fisher, Harrison, *Ladies Home Journal*, September 1909 ....**50.00**
Postcard
   Atwell, Mabel Lucie **9.00**
   Clapsaddle, Ellen Hattie..............**25.00**
   Outcault, R. **17.50**
Print
   Smith, Jessee Wilcox, "Goldilocks and

the Three Bears," 1907 copyright, 16"
x 10-3/4" **90.00**
Leyendecker, J.C., "Pay Day," 1906
copyright, P.F. Collier and Son, 16" x
10-3/4" **80.00**
Remington, Frederic, "Shadows at the
Water Hole," 1907 copyright, P.F.
Collier and Son, 16" x 10-3/4" ..**70.00**

❖ Imari

Imari is a Japanese porcelain that dates
back to the late 1770s. Early Imari has a
simple decoration, unlike later renditions
that are also known as Imari. As the
Chinese and, later, the English copied and
interpreted this pattern, it developed into a
rich brocade design.

Bowl, blue and white, scalloped rim,
early 20th C, 15" dia **225.00**
Charger, underglaze blue and enamel
dec, central reserve of planter with
flowers, grape and brocade borders,
late 19th/early 20th C, 14-1/2" d
.................................**250.00**
Dish, shaped rim, all-over flowering vine
dec, gilt highlights, 9-1/2" dia **150.00**
Jardiniere, hexagonal, bulbous, short
flared foot, alternating figures and
symbols, stylized ground, 10" h
.................................**265.00**
Plate, scalloped edge, rib banding,
polychrome dec, floral panels,
surrounding floral medallions, bats on
reverse, character mark
8-1/2" dia, gilt loss.....................**55.00**
10-1/4" dia, rim chip **65.00**
Sauce tureen, Boston retailer's mark,
imp "Ashworth Real Ironstone," 6-1/8"
h, 5-1/4" w, 9-1/4" l.....................**325.00**
Teabowl and saucer, floral spray dec
.................................**215.00**
Urn, all over hexagonal panels with gold
pheasants and orange drawings,
flowers, and plant, orange, tomato red,
yellow, green, and cobalt blue, old
shield shaped "U.S. Customs" label
underneath, 25" h.....................**550.00**

❖ Imperial Glass

Bellaire, Ohio, was the home of Imperial
Glass Company, founded in 1901. Through
the years they have produced pressed
glass in patterns that imitate cut glass, art
glass, animals figures, as well as elegant
tableware.

Collectors' Club: National Imperial Glass
Collectors Soc, P.O. Box 534, Bellaire, OH
43906.

Baked apple, Cape Cod, 6" dia........**9.00**
Bowl, Diamond Quilted, black, crimped,
7" dia **20.00**
Bread and butter plate, Cape Cod ..**7.00**

*Imperial Glass, creamer, Beaded Block pattern,
green, $20.*

Cake stand, pressed imitation cut glass
pattern, orig label **35.00**
Candlesticks, pr, Laced Edge, 2-lite,
green **180.00**
Candy box, cov, ftd, Grape, milk glass,
satin finish **40.00**
Cocktail, Cape Cod.........................**12.00**
Console set, Diamond Quilted, 10-1/2" d
bowl, pr candlesticks, green.........**55.00**
Cracker jar, cov, Americana, milk glass
....**60.00**
Creamer and sugar, Cape Cod **15.00**
Cup and saucer, Cape Cod **7.50**
Figure, pony stallion, caramel, c1970
....**65.00**
Goblet, Traditional **15.00**
Juice tumbler, Cape Cod, 6 oz **10.00**
Jug, Doeskin, milk glass, 36-oz, 8" h
....**50.00**
Parfait, Cape Cod **11.00**
Plate
Cape Cod, Verdi, 8" dia................**15.00**
Diamond Quilted, black, 8" dia.....**15.00**
Platter, Laced Edge, blue, 13" l **165.00**
Punch bowl set, Mount Vernon, 15 pcs
....**90.00**
Relish
Candlewick, 2-part, 6-1/2"............**25.00**
Cape Cod, 3-part **35.00**
Tea cup, #400/35 ....**8.00**
Tray, Cape Cod, 12" l, 7" w.............**75.00**
Tumbler, Katy Blue, opalescent, 10-oz
....**65.00**
Vase, bottle shape, cased, orange ext,
white int., 6-1/2" h, 4-1/2" dia.....**275.00**

❖ Indiana Glass

The good news is that Indiana Glass
Company has a colorful history, dating back
to 1907, when it was founded in Dunkirk,
Ind. The bad news is that some of the
company's more popular patterns have

been reproduced over the years. Flea
market shoppers can distinguish vintage
Indiana Glass from newer pieces by
examining color and the detail of the
pattern.

Bowl, Daisy, amber, 9-1/4" dia........**35.00**
Butter dish, cov, Sandwich, amber
dome, crystal base.....................**55.00**
Candlesticks, pr, Tea Room, green
....**48.00**
Cereal bowl, Horseshoe (No. 612), green
or yellow **25.00**
Cup
Pineapple & Floral, (No. 618), amber or
red **10.00**
Pretzel (No. 622), crystal...............**6.00**
Fairy lamp, Sandwich pattern, amber, 7"
h **20.00**
Mayonnaise Set, underplate, Christmas
Candy (No. 624), crystal, orig ladle
....**24.00**
Pitcher, Pear pattern, amber, Tiara,
c1970, 9-1/4" h.............................**75.00**
Plate
Christmas Candy (No. 624), crystal, 9-
5/8" dia......................................**12.00**
Daisy (No. 620), amber, 6" dia.......**3.00**
Horseshoe (No. 612), green, 9-3/8" dia
....**13.00**
Vernon (No. 616), green or yellow, 8"
dia..**10.00**
Platter, Indiana Custard, French Ivory
....**30.00**
Sherbet, clear, 3-1/2" h.....................**9.00**
Tumbler, Lorain, yellow, c1929, 5" h
....**38.00**

❖ Indian Jewelry

Indian jewelry is abundant at most flea
markets. Bargains can be found in
collectible Indian jewelry, but vintage Indian
jewelry is getting quite pricey. Buy pieces
because they appeal to you. Make sure the
craftsmanship is good, and the stones are
secure in the settings. Watch for signs of
heat-stabilized turquoise when considering
collectible Indian jewelry.

Barrette, silver...............................**45.00**
Beads, turquoise, from Sleeping Beauty
mine, graduated disks, leaf design
pendant 2-1/2" l, overall 20" l.....**225.00**
Bolo tie, Navajo, hand-made, woven
leather tie, tipped in sterling silver, sgd
"Sterling," mkd by artist **112.00**
Bracelet
Navajo, silver leaf design on matte
black ground, ten Kingman turquoise
stones, engraved "D" on back, by J.
Delgarito **200.00**
Squash blossom design, Morenci
turquoise nugget and coral accent,
silver, drop style, stamped "MLS,"
attributed to Loren Begay **55.00**

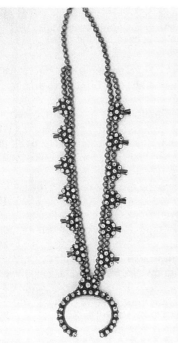

Indian Jewelry, squash blossom necklace, silver and turquoise, 24" l, $550.

Zuni, silver, hummingbird and flower, turquoise, coral, mother-of-pearl and tortoise shell, engraved on back "Made by Bobby & Corraine, Zuni, N.M." **220.00**

Fetish necklace
Santo Domingo, shell, turquoise and coral triangle pieces, bird pendant with upraised wings, c1940, shortened..................................**55.00**
Zuni, silver beads, inlaid pendant with silver leaves and inlaid basket center figure in turquoise, coral and jet, mother-of-pearl background, stamped artist's mark on back, beads have some dents, by Wylie Hill, 14-1/4" l **275.00**
Zuni, 1 strand, silver, birds, bears, frogs and turtles, tubular silver rain spacers, 28" l......................**250.00**
Zuni, 3 strands, tortoise shell, silver cones at clasp, 26" l **315.00**

Necklace
22" l, Sand Cast Naja, sterling, 1-7/8" w x 2-7/8" medallion with bezel set turquoise **250.00**
24" l, spiderweb 2-1/4" l, turquoise center, Navajo......................**465.00**
24" l, beaded medallion with bird motif 3-1/2", white, yellow, green, black, blue and red............................**15.00**
24-1/2" l, silver and inlaid red coral, 13 graduated dec silver beads with large red coral inlaid center 26.7 mm bead flanked by two 20.8 mm beads,

46 chased smaller beads, sgd "MW" **325.00**
26-1/2" l, Heishi, 38 turquoise nuggets, silver beads and cones............**90.00**
Ring, man's, Navajo
Silver and turquoise, feathers around cabochon **120.00**
Silver, coral, and turquoise........**110.00**
Squash blossom necklace
Hopi, shadowbox style, silver, 15 blue diamond turquoise stones, 13" l **275.00**
Naja, 16 crushed turquoise eagles, 23" l...**400.00**
Navajo, 2 strands of silver beads, 20 turquoise nuggets, 13" l.........**275.00**
Suite, squash blossom necklace, bracelet and ring, Navajo, Royston turquoise settings, silver beads, rope twist details, 20 stones in necklace, 16-1/2" l
....**715.00**

❖ Ink Bottles

Before the invention of the ballpoint pen, ink was sold in bottles. Because most examples date to the 1800s, they can be quite expensive if found in good condition.

Periodical: *Antique Bottle and Glass Collector*, P.O. Box 187, East Greenville, PA 18041.

Barrel shape, blue-green, rim chips, 4" h, 2-1/2" dia................................**95.00**
Bourne Benby, stoneware, English, c1860, 4-7/8" h, 2-3/8" dia **15.00**
Cardinals Ink, amber bottle, raised lettering, 3-1/2" h, 1-3/4" dia **25.00**
Carter's, cobalt, cathedral shape, 6-sided, master ink.......................**225.00**
Empire Ink, "Williams Black Empire Ink, New York," lime green, tooled mouth, smooth base, some damage to label **200.00**
Harrison's Columbia Ink, octagonal, light green **75.00**
Sawyer's Crystal Blue Ink, 6-1/4" h **10.00**
Senate Ink Co., house shape, "Bank of Writing Fluid, Manuf by Senate Ink Co., Philadelphia," aquamarine, tooled sq collared mouth, some fading to label, 2-5/8" h.....................................**325.00**
Umbrella shape, New England, 1840-60, octagonal, golden amber, sheared mouth, 2-1/4" h..........................**160.00**

❖ Inkwells

Small receptacles designed to hold ink were a necessity in the days of quill pens and steel dip pens. Inkwells were most commonly made of glass and pottery,

because the ink would not adversely affect those substances. Inkwells have become quite popular with collectors, who search for examples made of glass, bronze, pewter, pottery, and even wood. Particularly fascinating are the miniature wells designed for children's desks.

References: Veldon Badders, *Collector's Guide to Inkwells, Book I* (1995), *Book II* (1997), Collector Books; Jean and Franklin Hunting, *The Collector's World of Inkwells*, Schiffer Publishing, 2000; Ray and Bevy Jaegers, *The Write Stuff: Collector's Guide to Inkwells, Fountain Pens, and Desk Accessories*, Krause Publications, 2000.

Collectors' Clubs: St. Louis Inkwell Collectors Soc, Box 29396, St. Louis, MO 63126; The Society of Inkwell Collectors, 5136 Thomas Ave S, Minneapolis, MN 55410, www.soic.com.

Brass, embossed, double, two porcelain inserts, late 19th/early 20th C, 10-1/2" l, 6-1/2" w **150.00**
Bronze, figural, Robert Burns, 19th C, 5-1/2" h...**775.00**
Delft, square with round lid, c1910 ....**295.00**
Glass
Clear, 2" h, 1-7/8" dia...................**25.00**
Freeblown, sq, opaque electric blue, flared mouth, pontil scar, attributed to America, 1840-60, 1-3/4" h **120.00**
Olive-amber, blown, some wear, 1-1/2" h, 2-3/8" dia **165.00**
Hoof, animal hoof, English, Birmingham hallmarks on silver fitting...........**295.00**
Paperweight, multicolored concentric millefiore, base with 1848 date canes, Whitefriars, 6-1/4" h **175.00**
Porcelain, rose/leaves decor, hinged lid, 2-1/2" h.....................................**22.50**
Snail, clear glass, ground mouth, 1830-70, flat chip...............................**150.00**
Teakettle shape, glass, brick red and burgundy slag, ground mouth, brass cap, 1830-60, two small chips....**115.00**

Inkwells, gilt metal kneeling woman, oval marble base, $125.

Treen, sponge-decor, brown and yellow, gilt stenciling, glass insert, "Manufactured by S. Silliman & Co...Conn.," wear to top, 2-1/2" h, 4-1/4"dia **192.50**

❖ Insulators

Insulators date to 1837, when the telegraph was developed. Styles have been modified over the years, and collectors have a wide variety of shapes and colors to choose from.

Reference: Mike Bruner, *The Definitive Guide to Colorful Insulators*, Schiffer Publishing, 2000.

Periodicals: *Canadian Insulator Magazine*, Mayne Island, British Columbia, V0N 2J0 Canada; *Crown Jewels of the Wire*, P.O. Box 1003, St Charles, IL 60174.

Collectors' Clubs: National Insulator Assoc, 1315 Old Mill Path, Broadview Heights, OH 44147. In addition, there are many local clubs devoted to this hobby.

Armstrong, clear.............................**2.00**
Brookfield
    Olive green, chip **15.00**
    No. 20, emerald green.................**20.00**
    W. Brookfield B., aqua...................**2.00**
B.T.C., aqua.......................................**5.00**
Ceramic, 3-1/2" h, small chip..........**10.00**
Harlow Trade Mark, aqua **4.00**
Hemingray
    E1 B, light lemon.........................**90.00**
    No. 4, 1893 patent, aqua...............**8.00**
    No. 12, aqua..................................**8.25**
    No. 14, aqua, crack **5.00**
    No. 15, aqua, chip **5.00**
    No. 53B, clear................................**2.00**
H.G. Co., aqua.................................**12.00**
Gayner, No. 90, aqua **7.00**
Lynchburg, No. 31, aqua **7.00**
McLaughlin, No. 9, aqua **2.00**
Pyrex, double threaded, clear, 4" h...**7.50**
Star, aqua..**15.00**
Whitall Tatum
    Light aqua, #1 ....**8.00**
    Yellow, 4" h **12.00**

Insulators, Hemingray, #60, aqua, 5" h, $8.

❖ Irons

Folks have been trying to keep their clothes pressed neatly since the 12th century. Of course, irons from those days are vastly different than the streamlined appliances we use today.

References: Dave Irons, *Irons by Irons*, self-published, 1994; ——, *More Irons by Irons*, self-published, 1997; ——, *Pressing Iron Patents*, self-published, 1994.

Periodical: *Iron Talk*, P.O. Box 68, Waelder, TX 78959.

Collectors' Clubs: Club of the Friends of Ancient Smoothing Irons, P.O. Box 215, Carlsbad, CA 92008; The Midwest Sad Iron Collectors Club, 24 Nob Hill Dr, St. Louis, MO 63138-4171.

Electric
    American Beauty No. 66A, American Electrical Heater Co., Detroit....**10.00**
    Singer model 820476, Singer Sewing Machine Co...............................**40.00**
Flat iron
    Enterprise, Star, holes in handle..**40.00**
    Griswold #2, wooden handle......**120.00**
    Simmons Special, detachable handle
    ....**90.00**
Fluter, American Machine, wood handle, roller type **125.00**
Gasoline, ball-shaped tank, Diamond Iron, Akron Lamp Co., Akron, Ohio, ...**35.00**
Natural gas, Humphrey, General Specialty Co. **160.00**
Slug
    Bless-Drake, salamander box iron
    ....**160.00**
    Swedish, Husquarna, box **125.00**
Travel, Universal, electric, cloth cord, wooden handle, made by Landers, Frary & Clark, New Britain, 7-3/4" l
    ....**35.00**

Two small smoothing irons, detailed cast handle on one on left, other typical iron, resting on larger iron trivet, mkd "...New York, NY...," all three cast iron, oval based iron, $20, typical, $15, base, $15.

❖ Ironstone

Charles Mason first patented ironstone in England in 1813. The dense, durable, white stoneware was named "Mason's Patent Ironstone China," even though the reference to china was misleading since the items were actually earthenware. Ironstone derives its name from the fact that iron slag was mixed with the clay used to produce dinnerware and the like. Manufactured throughout the 19th century, ironstone was available in plain white as well as decorated versions.

Collectors' Club: Mason's Ironstone Collectors' Club, 2011 E Main St, Medford, OR 97504.

Bowl, Tamerlane pattern, Oriental design, J.&M.P. Bell, 9-3/4" dia ..**165.00**
Coffee set, white ironstone, yellow and orange daffodils, mkd "Nikko Ironstone, Dishwasher - Oven Safe, Made in Japan," coffee pot 11-1/4" h, creamer and sugar 3-1/4" h, set.................**40.00**
Dessert set, white ground, 8 decals representing different countries, mkd "Kaysons Fine Ironstone China, Japan, 1966," cake plate 12" dia, 8 plates 7-3/4" dia, set **30.00**
Dinner plate, Stratford Stage, mkd "Royal Staffordshire Ironstone" **6.00**
Jug, white, Strathmore, #30, mkd "Mason's," wear, 5-1/4" h **100.00**
Ladle, white
    Flower and fern dec, gray transfer, worn gold edging, 6" l...............**45.00**
    Lavender daisies, gold trim, c1895
    ....**50.00**
    Plain, crazed, 10-1/2" l................**48.00**
Pitcher, Wheat, Furnival, 12" h.....**165.00**

Ironstone pitcher, wash bowl type, Burgess & Campbell, gold linear design, $65, non-matching plain white ironstone bowl, $35, filled with dried hydrangea to show how lovely these older pitchers can be.

Ironstone Comb box, cov, oval, figural pear finial, $45.

Place setting, Royal Mail, brown and white, mkd "Fine Staffordshire Ironstone…Made in England," 4 pcs **25.00**

Plate
Corn & Oats, mkd "J. Wedgwood," c1841, 8-3/4" dia **45.00**
Forget-Me-Not, mkd "E&C Challinor," c1862, 8-3/4" dia **45.00**

Platter, plain white
14" x 10", mkd "Royal Ironstone China, Alfred Meakin, England" **65.00**
15" x 20", illegible maker's mark **220.00**

Salad plate, Stratford Stage, mkd "Royal Staffordshire Ironstone"..................**4.00**

Soup tureen, cov, underplate, mkd "Bridgewood Porcelaine Opaque" **300.00**

Tea set, child's, painted pansies, faded gold trim, worn paint, 15 pcs........**75.00**

Toothbrush holder, mulberry variant, c1890, 5-1/2" h..............................**75.00**

Vegetable bowl, American Hurrah, mkd "J&G Meakin," 8-1/2" l **45.00**

❖ Italian Glass

Italian glassblowers have been crafting functional items and whimsical glass novelties for generations. There is strong interest in modern Italian glass. Look for bright colors and flowing forms.

Ashtray, free-form, swirling blues, reds, and purple **20.00**

Basket, Hobnail, blue, applied handle **32.00**

Bottle, clear, silver overlay, orig sticker, 6" h..**32.00**

Italian Glass Dish, triangular, amber base with white swirled feathery dec, one corner turned up, $15.

Cordials, etched vining leaves, blue, pink, yellow and green, set of 4 ...**50.00**

Decanter set, green, gold floral dec, decanter 10" h, 4 glasses 3" h, set **40.00**

Earrings, pr, clip, millefiori **28.00**

Figure
Donald Duck, made by Cristallerie Antonio Imperatore, copyright Walt Disney Productions, MIB, 4-3/4" h **50.00**
Fish, multicolored, bulging eyes...**25.00**

Vase
5-1/2" h, irid, green waves **125.00**
8" h, orange, white swirls **95.00**

❖ Ivory

Ivory is derived from the teeth or tusks of animals. Yellow-white in color, the substance is quite durable and lends itself to carving. Some ivory objects have been highlighted with ink, metal, or stones.

Chess set, 3" to 7" h natural and tea stained pieces, each carved with Oriental figures standing on mystery ball bases, inlaid box with brass clasp **700.00**

Earrings, pr, pierced, hand carved, drops suspended from gold filled leaves, c1910, 1-1/4" l...........................**180.00**

Figure
Eagle attacking monkey, Japan, 3" h **475.00**
Laughing monk, carrying turtle, staff with palm frond, bat on head, dark yellow stain, sgd, 6-1/4" h.......**200.00**

Letter Opener, oblong blade carved to end with writhing dragon, Chinese, early 20th C, 9-3/4" l **115.00**

Measure, whalebone, ivory and exotic wood, American shield inlay, inscribed "WH," 19th C, minor imperfections, 14-7/8" l **200.00**

Necklace, hand-carved beads, c1910, pendant 1-1/2" x 1-1/4", overall 15" l, ...**165.00**

Rolling pin, exotic wood, baleen spacers, 19th C, cracks, 13-5/8" l **245.00**

Seal, intaglio, handle, 19th C, cracks, 3-7/8" l **400.00**

Snuff bottle, elephant ivory, carved bird on one side, carved rose on other, gold-tone neck chain, sgd "LRS," orig wand.......................................**125.00**

Top, carved, sealing wax inlaid scribed lines, 19th C, minor cracks and chips, 2-7/8" l **365.00**

Walking stick, elephant ivory handle, raised basketweave carving halfway down length, plain silver collar, cherrywood shaft, 1-1/3" white metal

and iron ferrule, American, c1880, 34-1/4" l **400.00**

❖ Jade-ite Glassware

Jade-ite is currently one of the hottest colors in glassware. The name is derived from the jade-like hue of the glass, with the color varying from manufacturer to manufacturer. Anchor-Hocking and McKee are perhaps the best known makers of jade-ite. First produced around 1920, jade-ite items are still being made today.

Bowl, 4-1/2" dia **20.00**
Bud vase, Jeannette **20.00**
Butter dish, cov, 1-lb size **140.00**
Canister, dark, Jeannette **90.00**
Measuring cup, Jeannette, 2-oz **50.00**
Pitcher, sunflower in base...............**60.00**
Range shaker, sq, mkd "Flour,"
    Jeannette **45.00**
Reamer...**60.00**
Refrigerator dish, cov, 4" x 8" **65.00**
Salt and pepper shakers, Ribbed,
    Jeannette, 4-1/2" h, pr...............**180.00**
Skillet, 2 spouts **35.00**
Tea canister, sq, light jade-ite, 48-oz
    ....**165.00**
Water dispenser, metal spigot **160.00**

Jade-ite Glassware Candy dish, leaf shape, $18.

❖ Japanese Ceramics

The term Japanese ceramics covers the entire spectrum of porcelain and ceramic items made in Japan throughout the centuries. As the western world became interested in Oriental things, Japanese ceramics were imported in greater numbers, and they remain treasured objects.

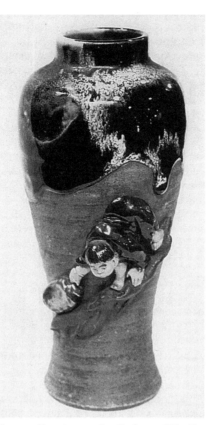

Japanese Ceramics vase, Sumida Guwa, child with pitcher, green robe, redware ground, black glazed top, sgd in cartouche, 7" h, $225.

Charger, 2 large iron oxide carp, underglaze blue ground, peonies, stylized waves, flowering branches, Meiji period, 13-1/4" dia **350.00**
Ewer, red and gilt motif, riverscape and figure dec, loop handle, dragon finial, Kaga, late 19th C **570.00**
Incense burner, Hirado ware, basketweave design, underglaze blue floral sprays, late 19th C, 4-1/4" h
    ....**300.00**
Jar, Mizusahi, blue phoenixes and dragon, white ground, agate set wooden cov, 19th C, 8-1/2" h **690.00**
Plate, Nabeschima style, relief and underglaze blue hibiscus dec, c1900, 8-1/2" dia **225.00**
Sake bottle, Arita ware, Ko-imari dec, three friends pine, bamboo, and prunus, gray underglaze blue, crackled ground, 18th C, 11-1/4" h...........**300.00**
Tea bowl, Raku, hand modeled, irreg straight sides, small recessed ring foot, central well of flower heads, peach glaze, double crackle pattern **190.00**
Teapot, Seven Gods of Wisdom, glazed and unglazed clay, polychrome dec, Banko, 5" h **450.00**
Vase, flowing blue dec, fan shape, 20th C
    ....**20.00**

❖ Japanese Toys

Some of our favorite childhood toys were inexpensive imports from Japan. We loved the colors, the action, and the fact that we could afford them on our pitiful allowances. Now that we're all grown up, many collectors are busy buying back their happy childhood memories. Before making a purchase, check for the original box and make sure all the accessories are present. Top dollar is often paid for toys in excellent working order.

Air Defense Pom-Pom Gun Truck, tin, friction, Linemar, 1950s, 16" l.....**155.00**
Boat, Great Swanee Paddle Wheeler, friction powered tinplate, whistle mechanism, T.N., orig maker's box
    ....**175.00**
Car, tin friction, 6" l.........................**45.00**
Crazy Clown in Crazy Car, litho tin wind-up, MIB **175.00**
Douglas Sky Rocket, 20" l...........**140.00**
Dump truck, friction powered tinplate, red and cream, automatic side dump action, T.N., orig maker's box **150.00**
Fire Chief Car, tin friction, MIB, 9" l**70.00**
Ford Taurus, blue litho tin friction car, Bandai, c1960, wear **18.00**
Harley Davidson, TN, 1950s, 9" l.**170.00**
Jeep and trailer, battery operated, Bandai, 1970s, MIB.....................**45.00**
Jet racer, friction, red.....................**95.00**
Lotus racer, battery op, 1960s, 12" l
    ....**140.00**
Mercedes Convertible 300, friction
    ....**75.00**
Planet Explorer, battery op, Modern Toys, 1960s, 9-1/2" l...................**160.00**
Reading Bear, turns page of tin book, MIB..**145.00**

Japanese Toys, Clown, white suit with red polka dots, wind-up tumbling action, mkd "Made in Japan," orig box, $10.

Japanese Toys, girl, red dress, white trim, wind-up and plays xylophone, no box, $5.

Speed Race Car #20, lavender, Modern Toys, 1950s, 6-1/2" l **155.00**
Telephone Bear, tin and cloth, phone rings, picks up phone and places it back on stand, MIB **145.00**
Tugboat, 12-1/2" l, battery operated tinplate, red, cream, yellow, and blue, smoking mechanism, San, orig maker's box..**200.00**

❖ Jeannette Glass

Jeanette Glass Company was located in Jeannette, Pennsylvania, and produced mainly depression era glassware. Many of the items they produced from 1900 to 1983 are marked with a "J" inside a square.

For additional listings, see *Warman's Depression Glass*.

Ashtray
  Adam, pink **32.00**
  Cowboy hat, Delphite **22.75**
Banana split dish, oval, clear **5.00**
Beverage set, Willow pattern, c1950, five 5-oz tumblers, 5 plastic coasters, 5 plastic stirring spoons, 6 juice glasses 3-3/4" h, pitcher 9-1/2" h, 22 pcs
  ....**195.00**
Butter dish, cov, Anniversary, pink
  ....**60.00**
Candy dish, cov, Stippled Acorn, light marigold **65.00**
Canister, cov
  3" h, jade-ite, Allspice, Ginger, Nutmeg or Pepper, each **72.00**
  5-1/2" h, sq, Delphite, Coffee......**85.00**
Compote, pink milk glass...............**18.00**
Creamer, Cubist, pink **7.00**
Drippings jar, cov, jade-ite **35.00**

Iced tea tumbler, Dewdrop, crystal, ftd, 12 oz **17.50**
Mixing bowl, clear, 6" dia **16.00**
Plate, Doric & Pansy, ultramarine, dinner
  ....**35.00**
Platter, Cherry Blossom, green.......**48.00**
Reamer, Delphite **90.00**
Refrigerator dish, cov
  4-1/2" h, sq, jade-ite **20.00**
  8-1/2" x 4-1/2", clear **20.00**
Salt and pepper shakers, ribbed, jade-ite, pr **30.00**
Sherbet, Sunflower, green **13.50**
Snack set, plate and cup, Dewdrop, crystal..**9.00**
Tumbler, Cubist, green, 9-oz..........**75.00**

❖ Jelly Glasses

The concept of putting jelly into a glass container with colorful or whimsical decorations no doubt helped boost sales. Collectors today eagerly look for vintage and contemporary jelly glasses.

Archie, Betty and Veronica, 1971 ...**10.00**
BAMA Racing Collection, Bobby Allison, 4" h **1.00**
Flintstones, Fred And His Pals At Work, Welch's, 4-1/2" h **10.00**
Howdy Doody, "Dilly Dally is Circus Big Shot," Welch's, 4-1/4" h **18.00**
Jack & Jill, nursery rhyme, 4-3/4" h .**8.00**
Pooh's Grand Adventure: The Search for Christopher Robin, 4" h **3.00**
Spacemen, 2 yellow spacemen, planets, rockets, 1960s, 5" h...................**18.00**
Speedy Gonzales, "Speedy Snaps Up the Cheese," 1974 ....**3.00**
Tom and Jerry, Tom roller skating toward open manhole **10.00**
"World's Fair Seattle 1962, America's Space Age World's Fair, Century 21 Exposition, Seattle, USA 1962," 4-3/8" h **12.00**

❖ Jensen, Georg

This designer hailed from Denmark, but he is known worldwide for his jewelry, flatware, and decorative accessories. Most of his creations were produced in sterling silver. Expect to find pieces that are well marked.

Bar pin, sterling silver, mkd "GI #136 Sterling, Denmark," 3-3/4" x 1-1/4"
  ....**775.00**
Berry spoon, Acanthus, 8-7/8" l ...**350.00**
Bread knife, Bernadotte pattern, stainless steel blade...................**650.00**
Brooch, sterling silver, tulips, post-1945 mark, 1-7/8" x 1-1/4" **400.00**
Carving knife and fork, Acanthus, stainless blades, 11-1/4" l and 12-1/2" l
  ....**325.00**

Cuff links, pr, oval, design #75A, post-1945 mark, mkd "Sterling, Made in Denmark" **300.00**
Earrings, pr, 18kt yg, circle mark, screw backs...**550.00**
Key ring, design #208, pineapple decorative ends, sgd "Sterling, Denmark, Georg Jensen" in dotted circle, 1-7/16" dia **225.00**
Meat fork, Acanthus, two tines, 8-1/8" l
  ....**250.00**
Ring, sterling silver, mkd "#130 925 Denmark," c1915-27, size 6 ....**775.00**
Soup spoon, Acanthus, 6-7/8" l **95.00**
Sugar tongs, mkd "925 Sterling," 4-1/4" h
  ....**175.00**
Tie bar, design #64, post-1945 mark
  ....**125.00**
Youth knife and fork, Acanthus, 6-3/4" l and 5-5/8" l **180.00**

❖ Jewel Tea Company

Most flea market browsers picture the Autumn Leaf pattern when they hear the name Jewel Tea, but the company was actually responsible for a diverse selection of products. The Jewel Tea Company, headquartered in Barrington, Illinois, has been supplying household necessities for years.

References: C.L. Miller, *Jewel Tea Grocery Products*, Schiffer Publishing, 1996.

Bank, 1905 truck, Ertl, orig box.......**65.00**
Beverage coaster set, Autumn Leaf pattern, orig box, 9 pcs **235.00**
Christmas ornament, pewter, Oh Come All Ye Faithful, 1980s, orig box **12.00**
Cookbook, *476 Tested Recipes*, cover missing corners **2.00**
Flour canister, tin body, white plastic lid, Autumn Leaf dec, 5-3/4" h, 5" dia
  ....**10.00**
Laundry soap, Jewel T Jetco Bead Bluing, 8-3/4" x 5-3/4" **85.00**
Jar, peanut butter, 3-3/4" h..............**45.00**
Playing cards, Pinochle deck, orig box
  ....**225.00**
Soap, Shure, 3 bars in box, unused**85.00**
Spice tin, nutmeg, some minor dents, 3-7/8" sq **145.00**
Tin
  Fruitcake, 1981...........................**20.00**
  Ginger, 2-oz, 3" x 2-1/4"..............**95.00**
Truck
  1926 delivery truck, 100th anniversary, Tootsietoy, MIB **16.00**
  Banner truck, replica of 1950s delivery truck......................................**325.00**
Urn, Jewel Best Coffee, made by West Bend, orig box...........................**525.00**

❖ Jewelry, Costume

Jewelry with faux stones became fashionable in the 1920s, thanks to Coco Chanel. Initially, designers were copying real gemstone jewelry, but soon they began creating their own exciting pieces.

References: C. Jeanenne Bell, *Antique Jewelry Field Guide*, Krause Publications, 2002; Marcia Brown, *Signed Beauties of Costume Jewelry*, Collector Books, 2002; Maryanne Dolan, *Collecting Rhinestone & Colored Jewelry*, 4th ed, Krause Publications, 1998; Karen L. Edeen, *Vintage Jewelry for Investment and Causal Wear*, Collector Books, 2002; Leigh Leshner, *Vintage Jewelry*, Krause Publications, 2002; Mary Morrison, *Christmas Jewelry*, 2nd ed., Schiffer Publishing, 2002; Christie Romero, *Warman's Jewelry*, 3rd ed, Krause Publications, 2002.

Collectors' Clubs: Leaping Frog Antique Jewelry and Collectable Club, 4841 Martin Luther Blvd, Sacramento, CA 95820; National Cuff Link Soc, P.O. Box 346, Prospect Heights, IL 60070; Vintage Fashion & Costume Jewelry Club, P.O. Box 265, Glen Oaks, NY 11004.

Reproduction Alert

Bracelet

Ciner, rhinestones, panther, black enamel trim, sgd.....................**215.00**

Corocraft, 8 charms, gold-tone links, sgd..**40.00**

Eisenberg, linked clusters of marquise-cut colorless rhinestones, v-spring and box clasp, block letters mark, safety chain, c1950, 7-1/2" l.....**70.00**

Hollycraft, large multi-colored emerald-cut rhinestones flanked by white metal S-scrolls set with multi-colored circ-cut rhinestones, fold-over clasp, safety chain, sgd, "Hollycraft COPR 1957", 7" l.................................**85.00**

Jewelry, costume Cross, pewter, silvertone link chain, $15.

Jewelry, costume earrings, top: daisies, white, yellow centers, goldtone wire backs, $15; bottom: crystal beads, clear, silvertone wire backs, $18.

Kenneth Jay Lane, bangle, snake, hinged goldtone, rhinestones, green glass cabochon eyes, sgd "KJL".**155.00**

Brooch

Avon, acorn, gold wash, pearl trim, sgd, 1-1/2" x 1-1/2"...................**20.00**

B.S.K., sunflowers, pale yellow double layer flower petals, amber colored faceted stones in center, green enameled leaf, gold washed metal, 2-1/2" x 2-1/2"...........................**45.00**

Corocraft, rose, sterling vermeil, rhinestone accents, 2-1/2" x 2"...**195.00**

Florenza, starfish, gold-tone, green, brown and gold rhinestones, Florenza.....................................**65.00**

Haskell, fan, Oriental design, gold-tone, bamboo handle, sgd "Haskell"..**50.00**

Hollycraft, floral wreath design, large center circ red rhinestone encircled by goldtone floral and foliate motifs set with small red rhinestones, sgd "Hollycraft, Copr 1954," 1-1/2" w x 3/8"...**40.00**

Kramer of New York, rhodium, bar pin with criss-cross clear rhinestone dangles ending in emerald stones, 2-3/4" w, 1" h................................**95.00**

Kenneth Jay Lane, Maltese cross of large green oval cabochons and circ green rhinestones around center circ blue rhinestone, outlined in marquise and sq-cut colorless rhinestones, sgd "KJL," c1965, 3" x 3"..........**35.00**

Unknown maker, airplane, ivory Bakelite, USAF decals (scuffed), 3" w...**110.00**

Weiss, bow, two layers, rhinestones prong set in large and small marquise, round, and baguette shaped stones, imp mark, 2-3/8" w, 1-1/2" h...................................**175.00**

Jewelry, costume pin, rose motif, silvered metal, $8.

Weiss, triangle, three layers, rhinestones prong set in sq, small round, large round, baguette, and teardrop shaped stones, sgd, 2-1/2" w, 2-1/4" l...............................**175.00**

Cameo, faux carnelian surrounded by clear rhinestones, scrolled mounting, Coro...**32.00**

Choker, pavé faux turquoise links, center aurora borealis rhinestones, gold-tone casting, Kramer, late 1950s, sgd **45.00**

Clip

Eisenberg Original, Retro Modern, goldtone floral spray with large emerald-cut green rhinestone at base, smaller emerald-cut green rhinestone encircled by circ-cut green rhinestones forming flowerhead, marquise-cut green rhinestones in center of second flowerhead, sgd "Eisenberg Original," c1940-45, 3-1/4" w x 2-1/2"....**155.00**

A great way to display costume jewelry, is to stuff a glove and add rings and bracelets. Having price tags on the items is appreciated by shoppers.

A jewelry dealer has her wares displayed in small boxes, trays, on stands, and in open jewelry boxes, on this table at Renninger's Flea Market, Adamstown, PA.

Trifari, painted enamel floral spray, red flowers, colorless rhinestone centers and accents, green leaves, brown stems on rhodium-plated white metal, c1935-40, sgd "Trifari," 1-1/2" w x 2-1/2"..................................**90.00**

Cross, filigree, 18k yg, 3 large pearls **120.00**

Cuff links and tie clip set
LaMode Originals, black stone and goldtone, orig box **25.00**
Mask shape, unmkd....................**12.00**
Square, gold-plated, inset MOP disk **18.00**
Swank, gold- and silver-plated, orig box **25.00**

Cuff links, pr, Duette, Coro, "Jelly belly" fish, sterling vermeil, Lucite centers, colorless rhinestone accents, red glass cab eyes, blue glass cab mouths, c1940, sgd "Coro Duette," mkd "sterling," 1931 pat no., 2-1/2" w x 1-3/4" **300.00**

Earrings, pr, clip
Carnegie, Dangling, chandelier type, crystal and rhinestone, Carnegie **60.00**
Ciner, textured goldtone circ domes, small faux pearls in star-cut settings, c1960, sgd "Ciner," 1" dia **32.50**
Eisenberg, clusters of prong-set cobalt blue marquise and circ rhinestones, small colorless rhinestone accents, c1950, block letter mark, 3/4" w x 1-1/4...**55.00**
Kramer, Turquoise egg-shaped glass dangles, gold tops, mkd "Kramer" **35.00**

Necklace
Carnegie, Hattie, goldtone, double strand, peridot green aurora borealis crystals, 20" l **40.00**
Caslecliff, three strands, red glass beads, goldtone leaf closure, 22" l **45.00**
Coro, heat style links, small spacers, gold tone, Francois, Coro, 15" l, 1937 ....**27.50**
Coventry, Sarah, goldtone links, 11 faceted aurora borealis crystals, 16" l **18.00**
Trifari, X design with rhinestones, Crown Trifari, 14" l **65.00**

Pendant
Sarah Coventry, teardrop, polished faux coral, plastic, gold trimmed open center, Sarah Coventry, gold-tone chain 28" l.........................**20.00**
Joseff of Hollywood, stamped gold-plated brass in a design of three overlapping circ disks with open scroll and geometric motif, suspending by two outside and two inside crossing chains a large circ disk with geo design, c1950, hook and ring clasp on gold-plated brass foxtail chain, pendant 3" w x 5", chain 16" l.............................**200.00**
Unknown maker, lucite "ice cube" held by rhodium-plated tongs on matching large curb link chain, pendant 1-3/4" w x 4", chain 30" l....................**75.00**

Ring, Vogue, triangular cluster, one large half-round faux pearl, two flowerheads, each center set with five colorless rhinestones encircled by glass cabs, one streaked turquoise colored and other mottled green, c1960, mkd "VOGUE", adjustable shank, 1-7/8" w x 1-5/8"..**50.00**

Stickpin, Anson, owl, sterling, white opal cabochon, 2-1/2" l **25.00**

Suite (Parure)
Hattie Carnegie, 17-1/2" l necklace, 1-3/4" chip earrings, goldtone, leaf design, white dangling beads and cabs, snake chain, hook and chain closure, all signed..................**195.00**
Hobe, 15-1/4" necklace, simulated pearls and coral, each prong set into goldtone metal, decorative gold link chains applied to top row of beads, set in 3 graduating strands, 1" dia round earrings, hallmark........**185.00**
Selro, 18" l necklace, 1" w x 7" l bracelet, and 1-1/2" earrings, silvertone, marquise shaped blue Lucite transparent cabs, with marquis shaped settings of prong set light blue rhinestones, all signed **250.00**

Tie bar, gold-plated, abstract design.**2.00**
Tie tack
Car, gold-plated, Sarah Coventry...**4.00**
Initial, "G", silver-plated **2.00**

❖ Johnson Brothers

Three English brothers founded Johnson Brothers in 1883. Their dinnerware business flourished, and a fourth brother joined the firm in 1896. He was charged with establishing a stronghold in the American market. Ultimately, this venture was so successful that additional factories were established in England, Canada, and Australia. By 1968, Johnson Brothers had become part of the Wedgwood Group.

Bread and butter plate, Old Britain Castles, blue dec on white **12.00**
Breakfast set, Lily of the Valley, 5 pcs **155.00**
Butter dish, cov, Eternal Beau **72.00**
Cereal bowl, Old Britain Castles, blue dec on white................................**18.00**
Coffeepot, Hearts & Flowers **200.00**
Creamer and sugar, Friendly Village **35.00**
Cup and saucer
Brooklyn pattern, flow blue, mkd "Royal Semi Porcelain, Johnson Brothers, England," c1900 ....**100.00**
Countryside, cup 3" h, saucer 7" dia **55.00**
Harvest Time, cup 3" h, saucer 7" dia **55.00**
Old Britain Castles, blue dec on white **20.00**
Dinner plate
Brooklyn pattern, flow blue, mkd "Royal Semi Porcelain, Johnson Brothers, England," c1900, 8-3/4" dia **100.00**
Old Britain Castles, blue dec on white **22.00**
Fruit bowl, Old Britain Castles, blue dec on white......................................**10.00**
Gravy boat, attached underplate
English Chippendale, red...........**250.00**
Old Britain Castles, pink.............**185.00**
Plate, Mt Rushmore, imported for Sunset Supply, Keystone, 10-3/4" dia **15.00**
Platter
Albany, 12-3/4" l **225.00**
Hearts & Flowers, 14" l **200.00**
Historic America, large...............**265.00**
Lindsey, small............................**250.00**
Old Britain Castles, brown, 12" l **165.00**
Relish, Friendly Village, 3-part........**38.50**
Salad plate, Old Britain Castles, blue dec on white **15.00**

Johnson Brothers, bowl, Sheraton pattern, red, yellow, blue, and tan flowers, green leaves, mkd "Johnson Brothers, Made in England, A Genuine Hand Engraving, all decoration under the glaze, pat. pending," $12.

Saucer, Cherry Thieves, mkd "Staffordshire Old Granite Made in England by Johnson Brothers".......**5.00**
Soup bowl, Old Britain Castles, blue dec on white.......................................**22.00**
Soup tureen, Friendly Village, 10" x 7-1/2" **235.00**
Teapot
 Hearts & Flowers, 5 cup **270.00**
 Old Britain Castles, pink.............**250.00**
Turkey platter, Friendly Village, 20" l
 ....**190.00**
Vegetable, cov, Hearts & Flowers.**185.00**
Vegetable, open, Lindsey, oval, 10-1/4" l
 ....**250.00**

❖ Jordan, Michael

Can you believe it? This basketball legend retired on January 13, 1999 and then came back to the game. He is scheduled to retire at the end of the 2002-2003 season. As a result, values for collectibles relating to this sports legend will most certainly increase.

Reference: Dennis Tuttle and Dennis Thornton, eds., *Standard Catalog of Sports Memorabilia 2nd ed.*, Krause Publications, 2001; Tom Mortenson, *Warman's Sports Collectibles*, Krause Publications, 2001.

Advertising display, life size, Ball Park Hot Dogs, cardboard, slight damage
 ....**125.00**
Book, *For the Love of the Game,* Michael Jordan, 1st ed, paperback **10.00**
Comic book, *Sports Superstars, #1, Michael Jordan*, 1992, Revolutionary Comics **8.00**
Cup, McDonald's NBA Looney Tunes All Star Showdown, 1995, Michael Jordan and Bugs Bunny, scratched **1.00**
Figure, Upper Deck, 16" h **55.00**

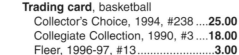

Michael Jordan tumbler, plastic, blue, multicolored scenes with Bugs Bunny, from Space Jam, mkd "TM & © 1996 Warner Bros.," 4" h, $1.

Magazine, *Sports Illustrated*, March 13, 1989, "Chicago's Indomitable Michael Jordan" **5.00**
Movie poster, *Come Fly with Me* ...**45.00**
Photograph, wire service, 1989, Chicago Bulls Michael Jordan and Cleveland Cavaliers Horace Grant..................**3.50**
Pinback button, "Me and Michael are Madly for Bradley 2000," red and blue lettering, 2-1/4" dia **7.50**
Trading card, baseball, Upper Deck, 1994, #661 ....**50.00**
Trading card, basketball
 Collector's Choice, 1994, #238 ....**25.00**
 Collegiate Collection, 1990, #3 ....**18.00**
 Fleer, 1996-97, #13 ....**3.00**
 NBA Hoops, 1991, #30 ....**3.00**
 Skybox, 1992, #41 ....**2.00**
 Topps, All Star Team, 1994 ....**25.00**
 Topps, Gold Topps, 1994, #384 ...**25.00**
 Upper Deck Hologram, 1992, AW4
 ....**12.00**

❖ Josef Originals

Even though a printer originally misspelled the name of this company, Tom and Muriel Joseph George had success on their hands shortly after they started in 1946. Eventually, production was moved to a Japanese factory, with Muriel continuing to create the designs. The company was sold to Applause, Inc. in 1985.

Reference: Jim and Kaye Whitaker, *Josef Originals*, Schiffer Publishing, 2000.

Josef Originals, Birthday girl, 15 years, holding white present, pink dress, gold trim, $40.

Periodical: *Josef Original Newsletter*, P.O. Box 475, Lynnwood, WA 98046.

Bank, owl, 5-3/8" h **15.00**
Bell, angel, white, orig sticker, 3-7/8" h
 ....**20.00**
Cat, white Persian, paper label **115.00**
Doll, California January **80.00**
Figure
 Angel Kitty, 4" h...........................**15.00**
 April, 4-1/2" h **85.00**
 At Home, 6-1/2" h.......................**115.00**
 Black Native Girl, orig spear **85.00**
 Birthday Girl, 10th birthday **40.00**
 Dress Up Like Dad......................**45.00**
 Elephant, orig foil label...............**40.00**
 Frog, 1" h....................................**16.00**
 Girl with flower, foil label, 4-3/4" h**45.00**
 Hawaiian Hula Girl **80.00**
 Hippo Mama, 3" h **22.00**
 January girl, orig tag, 4" h............**40.00**
 Pa Duck, orig foil label, 3-5/8" h...**22.00**
 September girl, orig foil label, 4" h
 ....**45.00**
 Singing mouse **25.00**
 Teddy...**35.00**
 Wee Folks **25.00**
Music box, Happy Birthday series, girl with pale blue dress, orig tag, 4-1/4" h
 ....**55.00**
Night light, Persian kitten, 5-3/4" h **35.00**
Pie bird, yellow chick, 3-1/4" h........**90.00**

❖ Jugtown Pottery

Jugtown Pottery, bowl, pedestal foot, turquoise and maroon glazes, 6-1/2" dia, 4" h, $185.

Although serious about their craft of pottery making, Jugtown founders Jacques and Juliana Busbee were noted for their offbeat operation. The pottery was established in 1920 and was in business until 1958. Ben Owens was one of their most talented potters, Jacques did most of the designing, and Julie took care of promotion.

Bowl, domed lid, orange glaze, minor glaze flakes, 4-1/4" h, 5-1/2" dia
....**85.00**

Candlesticks, pr, 3" h, Chinese Translation, Chinese blue and red, mkd
....**85.00**

Creamer, cov, 43/4" h, yellow **60.00**

Figurine, pedestal chicken, salt-glazed, "Jugtown Pottery A.P.," made by Al Powers, 1960-62, 7" h................**315.00**

Jug
    Frogskin green glaze, incised bands, 5" h...**35.00**
    Salt-glazed, incised wheat on shoulder, 1977, 10" h **110.00**

Pitcher, orange-yellow swirlware, 1940s-50s, small chip **935.00**

Vase
    Vernon Owens sig, 1988, 6-1/4" h, 5" dia...**75.00**
    Oriental style, Chinese blue, early 1930s, 5" h **770.00**
    Oriental style, frogskin glaze, late 1920s, 2 handles, 5-1/2" h......**935.00**

❖ Jukeboxes

Let's spin those tunes! Jukeboxes provided many hours of musical entertainment, and, with the proper care and maintenance, these early entertainment centers can still delight.

Periodicals: *Always Jukin'*, 221 Yesler Way, Seattle, WA 98104; *Antique Amusements, Slot Machines & Jukebox Gazette*, 909 26th St NW, Washington, DC 20037; *Coin-Op Classics*, 17844 Toiyable St, Fountain Valley, CA 92708; *Gameroom Magazine*, P.O. Box 41, Keyport, NJ 07735; *Jukebox Collector*, 2545 WE 60th Court, Des Moines, IA 50317.

Note: All prices are for fully restored machines.

AMI
    Continental II, 1962 ....**6,500.00**

Rock-ola
    Model 1422 ....**6,000.00**
    Tempo....................................**4,500.00**
    Tempo II **3,300.00**

Seeburg
    Entertainer..............................**2,000.00**
    Mardi Gras, 1977 ....**2,000.00**
    Matador, 1973 ....**1,800.00**
    Model 201 ....**5,700.00**
    Model 202 ....**5,700.00**
    Model B **6,000.00**
    Model C **7,000.00**
    Model G **6,600.00**
    Model LPC, 1963 ....**1,700.00**
    Model Q-160, 1959 ....**1,800.00**
    Sunstar..................................**2,000.00**

Wurlitzer
    Model 2610, 1962 ....**2,400.00**

Zodiac, 1971 ....**1,800.00**

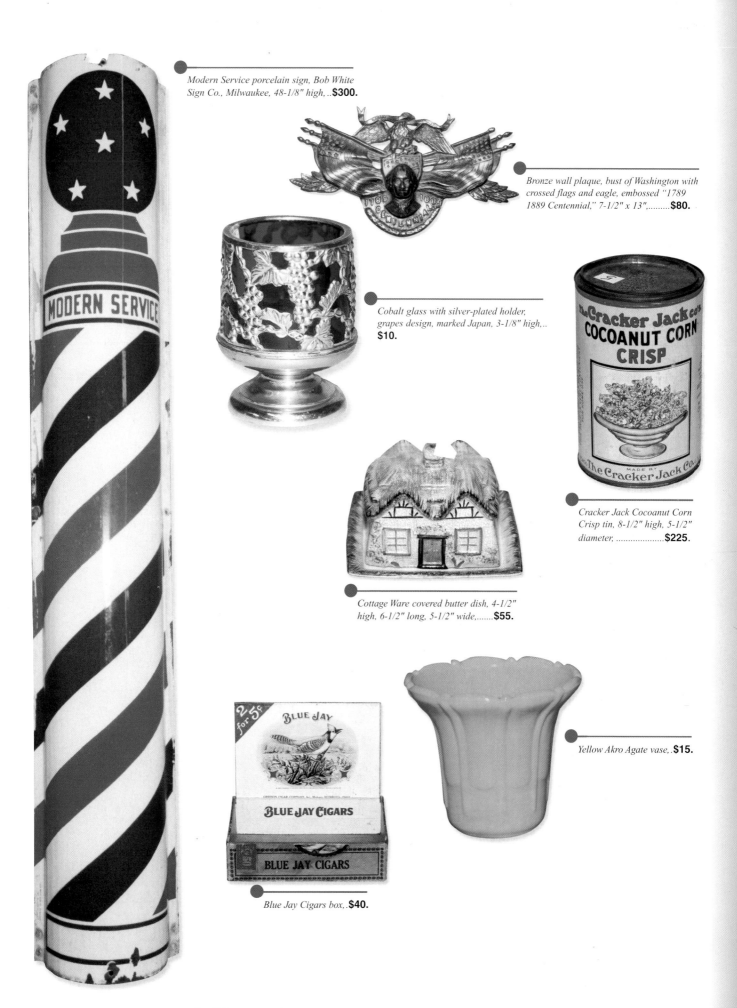

Modern Service porcelain sign, Bob White Sign Co., Milwaukee, 48-1/8" high,.. **$300.**

Bronze wall plaque, bust of Washington with crossed flags and eagle, embossed "1789 1889 Centennial," 7-1/2" x 13",........ **$80.**

Cobalt glass with silver-plated holder, grapes design, marked Japan, 3-1/8" high,.. **$10.**

Cracker Jack Cocoanut Corn Crisp tin, 8-1/2" high, 5-1/2" diameter, ... **$225.**

Cottage Ware covered butter dish, 4-1/2" high, 6-1/2" long, 5-1/2" wide,........ **$55.**

Yellow Akro Agate vase, .. **$15.**

Blue Jay Cigars box, .. **$40.**

*Figural lady's head, Christmas theme, 1959, 4-1/8" high, ..***$20.**

*Occupied Japan figurine, reclining Oriental girl, 4-1/2" long,........***$12.**

*Harlequin blue eggcup, 3-7/8" high,........***$28.**

*Goebel figurine, ...***$60.**

*Hummel figurine, Postman, 110, 5-1/4" high, ...***$125.**

*Oak plant stand,.....***$225.**

*Cast-iron oversized jack, 6-1/2" x 7-1/2",......***$35.**

Keen Kutter No. 12 knife and fork set, oak dovetailed box, ...**$100.**

Josef Originals musical figurine, 5-3/4" high, ...**$55.**

Tea Leaf ironstone coffeepot, ...**$200.**

Hydrox Ice Cream sign, celluloid over cardboard, 4-5/8" x 6-5/8",..........**$90.**

Flour sifter, "The State Bank of Carson City, Mich.,". **$45.**

Cast-iron child's sad iron, 3-5/8" long,..............**$38.**

Kitchen Kraft salad fork, green, slight nick to one tine, 10" long, ...$85.

Keen Kutter advertising lock,..................$125.

Tin #12 Marx windup race car, metal wheels, 16" long, $225.

Mork & Mindy tin lunch box and thermos, Thermos brand, ...$30.

Onion marble, 1-1/4" diameter,......$190.

Lady's head vase, .$75.

Vel detergent box, Colgate-Palmolive-Peet Co., unopened, 12-ounce, ...$20.

Chalkware King Kong,..**$60.**

Lotus Leaf flowerpot, McCoy, 5" high, .**$60.**

Chopped Mini model kit, Model Products Corp.,**$15.**

Hour of Charm Paper Dolls, The Saalfeld Publishing Co., 1943, uncut, ...**$25.**

You're Not Elected, Charlie Brown, World Publishing, 1973, 1st printing, ...**$15.**

Covered jar, O.&E.G., Royal Austria, 3-1/2" diameter, ...**$35.**

McKee covered "Butter" dish, green, 3-1/4" x 6-5/8",....**$65.**

Royal Copley bluebird planter,
5-1/4" diameter, ...$20.

Rookwood 1929 fox ashtray, blue glaze,
6-3/4" diameter, chipped ear, ...$90.

California Raisin ramp walker,
4-3/4" high,......................$3.

"The 500 Hats of Bartholomew
Cubbins," RCA Victor, ...$40.

Roseville Silhouette vase, browns,
11-1/2" high,....................$600.

Paneled bowl with red and blue sponging,
Red Wing, 10-1/4" diameter, $150.

Scotties cast-iron doorstop,
6" high, 9" wide, ...**$115.**

Jetsons mug, back side
advertises Carnation Hot
Cocoa Mix, ...**$3.**

Ladies' brown high-top shoes,
scuffed toes, ...**$85.**

Whistle chalkware thermometer,
12-1/2" square, ...**$170.**

Star Trek Color & Activity Book,
1982, Merrigold Press, ...**$5.**

"There's A Gold Mine In The Sky,"
Bing Crosby cover, ...**$10.**

Steve Sax, 1991 edition,
Starting Lineup, ...**$12.**

GAF View-Master reel No. J23, Godzilla in "Godzilla's Rampage," 1978, ...**$12.50.**

Traveler, used for measuring barrels and other round objects, cast iron, ...**$25.**

Milk glass wedding bowl, 8" high ....**$75.**

Yellow ware batter bowl, embossed design,..**$125.**

Dragnet / Official Jack Webb Whistle, black plastic, 2" long,...............**$15.**

AC Spark Plugs tin thermometer, 21" x 7-1/2",...................**$450.**

Manoil boxers,..**$60 each.**

❖ Kaleidoscopes

Changing colors and patterns as they turn, kaleidoscopes date to a time when entertainment didn't involve a remote or a computer screen. Scottish scientist David Brewster is created with inventing the first kaleidoscope in 1816. The name is taken from Greek *kalos* (beautiful) and *eidos* (form) and *scopos* (viewer). Look for examples with interesting designs and colorful elements.

Brass case, multicolor crystals, leather carrying case, English, c1910 ....**400.00**
Brass-colored metal, 5" l **100.00**
Paper case, child's, multicolor bits of paper, c1950 ....**5.00**
Paper case, child's, Hallmark, decorated with Peanuts characters, rainbow colors on turning cylinder, 9" l......**10.00**
Paper case, multicolor bits of glass, Corning Glass Museum, c1980, 8-3/4" l **15.00**
Tin case, tin screw caps for ends, multicolor crystals......................**200.00**
Von Cort, 12 gauge, 2-1/2" l **65.00**

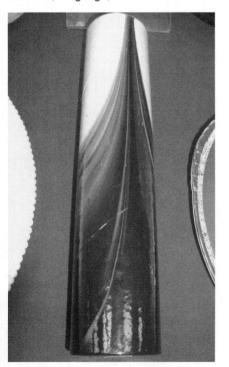

Kaleidoscopes, coated cardboard tube, white shading to brown, wooden ends, glass eye piece, mkd, $15.

❖ Kanawha

West Virginia was home to this glass company that produced colored glass and crackle glass. Kanawha Glass marked its wares with paper labels.

Basket, amberina crackle, 5-1/4" h .**35.00**
Creamer, amberina crackle, milk white int., ruffled spout, amber glass handle, 4" h...**30.00**
Pitcher
  Amberina crackle, long neck, applied amber handle, 8-1/4" h **70.00**
  Orange crackle, elongated spout, applied handle, 14-1/2" h..........**75.00**
Shoe, Colonial Slipper, white milk glass, 1968, 6" l, 2-1/2" h **35.00**
Syrup pitcher, ruby crackle, applied amber handle, cork stopper, stainless steel top, 6-3/4" h **65.00**
Vase
  Aqua blue, crackle, orig paper sticker, 3-1/2" h **26.50**
  White, blue hand painted flowers, cornflower blue satin in., orig label, 5" h **45.00**
  White, diamond and dot pressed pattern, red int., ruffled, 5-1/2" h **50.00**
  White, hand painted grapes and pears, green satin int., ruffled, 5-1/2" h**40.00**
  White, hand painted roses and green leaves, red satin int., ruffled, orig label, 5-1/2" h **45.00**
  White, raised grapevine dec, mint green int., ruffled rim, 9" h........**60.00**
Vinegar cruet, red crackle, applied yellow handle, 6" h **48.00**

❖ Keeler, Brad

Brad Keeler got his start making flamingo figurines that he sold to various California department stores. Once his business expanded, Keeler continued to design the pieces himself, but other individuals created the molds and glazes. Keeler died in 1952, ending a promising career at an early age.

Figure
  Cockatoo, #30, mkd, 10-3/4" h...**125.00**
  Cocker puppy, #748, black and white, 4-1/2" h **60.00**
  Deer family, 5-1/4" h....................**90.00**
  Flamingo, #1, head up, male, light crazing, 12" h..........................**215.00**
  Flamingo, #3, head down, female, 7-1/2" h **145.00**
  Oriole, #39, apricot and black, 7-1/2" h **75.00**
  Pheasant, female, #21, 6-1/2" h...**80.00**
  Rose colored, #17, 6" h **70.00**
Lobster dish
  3 compartments, gray tone, 12-1/2" l,

12-1/2" w...............................**125.00**
  5 compartments, deep red, mkd "rad Keeler Made in USA 872," 7" l, 12" w **125.00**
Planter, Pride & Joy, dog **50.00**
Serving dish, crab, 11" **80.00**
Tray, figural lettuce leaf, figural tomato relish container............................**85.00**

❖ Keen Kutter

Keen Kutter was the brand sold by the E.C. Simmons Hardware Company. Their fine tools were welcome in the workshop and the garden as well as in the kitchen.

Reference: Jerry and Elaine Heuring, *Collector's Guide to Keen Kutter*, Collector Books, 2000.

Collectors' Club: Hardware Companies Kollectors' Club, 715 W 20th Ave, Hutchinson, KS 67502.

Can opener, patent Sept 20, 93 .....**25.00**
Food chopper, orig booklet............**15.00**
Hatchet...**30.00**
Letterhead, 1911 ....**12.00**
Lock, brass, 3-3/4" h **75.00**
Pencil clip, 1950s, ...**17.50**
Pinback button, celluloid, red logo, 3/4" dia **58.00**
Pocketknife, pearl..........................**28.00**
Scissors, 6-3/4" l **20.00**
Razor, red Bakelite, 4" l...................**19.00**
Waffle iron **90.00**

Keen Kutter padlock, cast iron, bale marked "E. G. Simmons," orig key, $25.

❖ Kennedy, John F.

Many people were fascinated with JFK and his family during his life. Since his tragic death, collectors have continued to keep his memory alive.

Collectors' Club: Kennedy Political Items Collectors, P.O. Box 922, Clark, NJ 07066-0922.

Autograph, signed letter, as Senator in 1957 ....**1,200.00**
Bank, "John F. Kennedy 1917-1963," plaster bust painted bronze, 7" h .**25.00**
Book
  John F. Kennedy: War Hero by Richard Tregaskis, paperback................**15.00**
  The Living JFK, Robert N Webb, 1964, Grosset & Dunlap, 93 pgs **18.00**
Bottle, Wheaton, "Ask not what your country can do for you..."..............**25.00**
Cigar band, set of 4 different JFK bands **250.00**
Coloring book, unused, 1962 ....**15.00**
Comic book, *John F. Kennedy, Champion of Freedom,* 1964............................**8.00**
Magazine, *Life*
  Nov. 29, 1963, devoted to assassination...........................**25.00**
  Dec. 6, 1963, devoted to funeral ..**25.00**
Paperweight, sulphide, cameo set against translucent green ground, Baccarat, 1963, 2-3/4" dia **165.00**
Plate, pewter, Hamilton Mint, 9" dia **110.00**
Record, "The Voice of President John F. Kennedy, highlights from Nomination Acceptance Speech and Inaugural Address," Golden Memorial Record, photos labeled "Wide World Photos," printed in USA, yellow label **125.00**

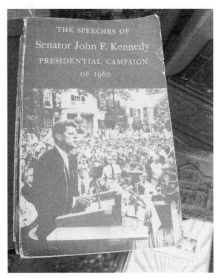

Paperback book, The Speeches of Senator John F. Kennedy, Presidential Campaign, 1960, *wear, $5.*

Record, Bob Booker and Earle Doud Present The First Family, John F. Kennedy spoof, some wear to jacket, orig record, $5.

Salt and pepper shakers, pr
  Figural, JFK seated in rocking chair, "Copyright Arrow 1962" **75.00**
  Porcelain, JFK decal on 1, Jackie on other, gold trim.........................**40.00**
Spoon, silver-plated, bust of JFK, "35th President 1961-1963," bowl emb "Friendship 7," Wm. Rogers Mfg. Co. **25.00**

❖ Kentucky Derby Glasses

The Run for the Roses is perhaps the best-known horse race in the world. Collectors are equally excited about the fact that this event signals the arrival of a new commemorative drinking glass each year. Examples from the 1940s through the 1960s are comparatively scarce at flea markets, but Derby glasses from later decades are available and affordable.

1945	500.00
1948	220.00
1951	600.00
1953	150.00
1954	120.00
1960	60.00
1970	45.00
1973	40.00
1974	30.00
1975	16.00
1976	16.00
1979	22.00
1980	18.00
1981	10.00
1983	15.00
1985	14.00
1986	12.00
1987	12.00
1990	20.00
1993	10.00
1994	9.00

❖ Kewpies

Rose O'Neill's Kewpies made their first appearance in art form in a 1909 issue of *Ladies Home Journal.* These charming characters caught the attention of Joseph Kallus, whose Cameo Doll Company produced the first Kewpie dolls in 1913. In the intervening years, several different companies have produced O'Neill's designs, including Lefton and Enesco.

Periodical: *Traveler,* P.O. Box 4032, Portland, OR 92708.

Collectors' Club: International Rose O'Neill Club, P.O. Box 668, Branson, MO 65616.

Bank, bisque, Lefton, orig foil label, 1950s, 7-1/4" h..........................**145.00**
Blanket, felt fabric, fleshtone images, blue sky, tan buildings, red stitched border, 1914 Rose O'Neill copyright **8.00**
Candy container, glass, patent date on base **100.00**
Doll
  2-1/2" h, celluloid, some paint missing **20.00**
  8" h, chalk, black skin tone **65.00**
  10" h, vinyl, head turns, mkd "Cameo" **75.00**
  13" h, vinyl, orig tag, mkd "Cameo" **95.00**
Figure, Lefton
  Bewildered...................................**12.00**
  Content, 5" h **27.50**
  Holding foot, 3" h.........................**12.00**
  On belly, 3-3/4" l..........................**12.00**
  Puzzled, 5" h **27.50**
  Winking, 5" h **30.00**
Night light, figural, orig foil sticker "Lefton Trade Mark Exclusives Japan," 6-1/2" h..**75.00**
Pendant, small **10.00**

Celluloid carnival type Kewpie, pink and purple feather dec, silver hair, $95.

Postcard, "Can't think of an earthly thing to say, 'Cept I hope you are happy Valentine's Day," Kewpie writing valentines, © Rosie O'Neill, postmarked Feb 12, 1925, published by Gibson Art Co...........................**20.00**

❖ Key Chains

Everybody has a couple of key chains saved, whether in a desk drawer, a pocket, or even a collection. Key chains are wonderful collectibles for children—relatively easy to find and usually inexpensive.

Collectors' Club: License Plate Key Chain & Mini License Plate Collectors, 888 Eighth Ave, New York, NY 10019-5704.

Ballantine Light Lager Beer, 3-ring motif, plastic, red and white, 3" h .**10.00**
Batman, PVC head, Funatics, MOC .**2.00**
Bob Hope, silhouette, goldtone, 1-1/2" d **85.00**
Coca-Cola, Spanish version, 1960s, 1-1/2" dia **8.00**
Curious George, pewter, Danforth .**16.00**
Elephant, wood, 3" l **3.00**
Flicker, pinup, 1-1/4" x 2" **6.00**
Ford, metal, mkd "Karriers USA".......**4.00**
Good Luck Penny, circular, "Keep me and never go broke," penny dated 1957 ....**12.00**
Horse, key chain in mouth, 5" h **30.00**
Johnson Feed Service, Feeding Grinding & Mixing On Your Farm, Griffin, Ga., flicker **12.00**
License plate, Missouri, 1968 ....**10.00**
Minnie Mouse, plastic, 4" l **5.00**
Puzzle, two sided, plastic **6.00**
Super Bowl XXX, 1996, NRFP.........**6.00**
Vincent System, Exterminators— Fumigators, Tampa, Florida, flicker **12.00**
Western Auto, Over 50 Years of Service, metal **15.00**

❖ Keys

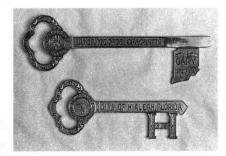
Keys Presentation, top: Mayor George Chacharis, Gary, Indiana, $12; bottom: City of Hialeah, Florida, $10.

Bed key, used to tighten ropes on rope beds, carved wood, $75.

We've all got some keys saved—keys from our first car or first house, the key to a diary or a bicycle lock. Flea markets almost always have a selection you can choose from when seeking to add to a collection.

Collectors' Clubs: Key Collectors International, 1427 Lincoln Blvd, Santa Monica, CA 90401.

Cabinet
　Brass, decorative bow **12.00**
　Nickel-plated, lyre design bow **6.50**
Car
　Ford, Model T, diamond mark **3.50**
　MGB, 1973, orig leather fob...........**7.50**
　Packard, logo key **8.00**
Door
　Bronze, Keen Kutter bow, 4" l **8.00**
　Steel, standard bow and bit **4.50**
Folding, bronze and steel, jack knife **17.50**
Hotel
　Bit type, steel, bronze tag **4.50**
　Pin tumbler, plastic tag..................**2.50**
Jewelers, brass, 6-point **22.00**
Padlock, Yale, 2-1/4" h **5.00**
Railroad
　C & O **18.50**
　IC RR **15.00**
　TT RR..**22.00**
Watch, brass and steel, loop bow, folds **7.50**

❖ Kitchen Collectibles

The kitchen is probably the one room in the house that generates more collectibles than any other room. When one considers all the equipment needed to prepare food and the dishes required to serve and store food, it isn't surprising. Somehow, many gadgets make their way to the back of the cupboard when the latest and greatest contraption arrives on the scene. Often, it's those old timers that become the basis for a collection of kitchen items.

References: Linda Campbell Franklin, *300 Years of Kitchen Collectibles*, 5th ed, Krause Publications, 2003; ——, *300 Years of Housekeeping Collectibles*, Books Americana, 1992; Linda Fields, *Four & Twenty Blackbirds: A Pictorial Identification and Value Guide for Pie Birds*, self-published; Don Thornton, *Apple Parers*, Off Beat Books, 1997; ——, *Beat This: The Eggbeater Chronicles*, Off Beat Books, 1994. Don Thornton.

Periodicals: *Cast Iron Cookware News*, 28 Angela Ave, San Anselmo, CA 94960; *Cookies*, 9610 Greenview Ln, Manassas, VA 20109; *Griswold Cast Iron Collectors' News & Marketplace*, P.O. Box 521, North East, PA 16428; *Kettles 'n Cookware*, P.O. Box B, Perrysville, NY 14129; *Kitchen Antiques & Collectibles News*, 4645 Laurel Ridge Dr, Harrisburg, PA 17110; *Piebirds Unlimited*, 14 Harmony School Rd, Flemington, NJ 08822.

Collectors' Clubs: Assoc of Coffee Mill Enthusiasts, 5941 Wilkerson Rd, Rex, GA 30273; Cookie Cutter Collectors Club, 1167 Teal Rd, SW, Dellroy, OH 44620; Corn Items Collectors Assoc, 613 N Long St, Shelbyville, IL 62565; Eggcup Collectors' Corner, 67 Stevens Ave, Old Bridge, NJ 08857; Griswold & Cast Iron Cookware Assoc, 54 Macon Ave, Asheville, NC 28801; International Soc for Apple Parer Enthusiasts, 735 Cedarwood Terr, Apt 735B, Rochester, NY 14609; Jelly Jammers Club, 110 White Oak Dr, Butler, PA 16001; Kollectors of Old Kitchen Stuff, 501 Market St, Mifflinburg, PA 17844; National Reamer Collectors Assoc, 47 Midline Ct, Gaithersburg, MD 20878-1996; Pie Bird Collectors Club, 158 Bagsby Hill Lane, Dover, TN 37058.

For additional listings, see *Warman's Antiques & Collectible* and *Warman's Americana & Collectibles*.

Apple corer, White Mountain, orig box **30.00**
Basting spoon, granite, cobalt blue handle **15.00**
Biscuit cutter, 1-12" d, tin, bail.......**10.00**
Bundt pan, iron, scalloped, 4-1/2 x 10-1/2" **45.00**
Cake carrier, aluminum, copper brushed color **27.50**
Canister, house shape, roof as lid, Avon, set of 4 ....**55.00**
Can opener, metal, red wood handle **15.00**
Cheese crock, Kraft, ceramic, name emb on top, 3-1/2" dia, 2-3/4" h **15.00**
Chopping knife, Henry Disston & Sons, curved steel blade, wood handle, 6-

Kitchen Collectibles, wall plaques, red and white gingham roosters, silver foil label, pr, $16.

1/2" l **20.00**

Double boiler, cov, Porcelier, Sprig, pink, orange, and blue flowers, white ground **40.00**

Egg poacher, red enamel, gray enamel insert, 3-3/4" x 8" **24.00**

Egg separator, aluminum, 9" l..........**7.00**

Flour sifter, Bromweld's, side crank, red wood knob **15.00**

Food chopper, aluminum shaft and blades, red wooden handle, Hazel Atlas measuring cup base............**20.00**

Hot pad holder, black boy, chalkware, 1940s, chips, 8" h........................**55.00**

Lemon squeezer, tin-plated iron, 6-1/2" l **20.00**

Mayonnaise maker, 8-1/4" h, Wesson, glass base, aluminum top and mixer, orig directions............................**60.00**

Meat grinder, Sargent & Co, Patent March 8, 1892 ....**40.00**

Mouli-Julienne, rotary cutter, 3 interchangeable cutting and shredding discs, c1950, orig box **30.00**

Platter, Kraft, ceramic, 10" x 12-3/4" **18.00**

Potato masher, 9" h, zig zag wire end, red catalin handle......................**10.00**

Rolling pin, 10" l, 3-1/2" handles, aluminum....................................**40.00**

Set, cookie cutter, biscuit cutter, donut cutter and pastry cutter, mkd "Calumet," Wear-Ever Aluminum, made in USA, set of 4 ....**14.00**

Spoon rest, pear shape, red plastic, mkd "Fuller Brush Co." **5.00**

Strawberry huller, Nip-It, 1906 ....**4.00**

Teapot and salt and pepper shakers, aluminum, 4-cup teapot, cov with red finial, orig strainer with red handle, mkd "Highly Polished Aluminum, Made in Japan," orig box **25.00**

Tin, rect, Krispy Crackers **35.00**

Vegetable grater, tin, iron back, wood handle, old blue paint, Schroeter .**40.00**

Wall plaque
   Fruit, 1950s, paint scuffed..............**8.00**

Parrot, chalkware, chips, 10" x 6" **12.00**

❖ Kitchen Glassware

One area of kitchen collection that is brightly colored and durable is kitchen glassware. What started as a few manufacturers who were determined to create glass ware that could go from the stove to the table to the refrigerator has given us products few of us could live without, such as Pyrex and Corningware.

Reference: Gene Florence, *Kitchen Glassware of the Depression Years*, 5th ed, Collector Books, 1995 (2001 value update).

Collectors' Club: National Reamer Collectors Assoc, 47 Midline Ct, Gaithersburg, MD 20878-1996.

For additional listings, see *Warman's Americana & Collectibles* and *Warman's Glass.*

Batter bowl, black ships dec **25.00**

Bowl
   Kellogg's, green............................**75.00**
   Orange Dot, custard, 8" dia **32.00**

Butter dish, cov
   Criss-Cross, blue, 1/4-lb size **125.00**
   Federal, amber, 1-lb size..............**35.00**

Canister, cov, round, Seville Yellow, coffee, sugar or tea, 48-oz **135.00**

Cheese dish, cov, slicer, opaque white **90.00**

Flour shaker
   Deco, ivory, black lettering **45.00**
   Roman Arch, ivory **45.00**

Fruit bowl, Sunkist, pink **335.00**

Grease jar
   Red Dots, white............................**30.00**
   Seville Yellow, black trim..............**35.00**

Measuring cup
   Crystal, Kellogg's............................**8.00**
   Green, Kellogg's............................**22.00**
   Seville Yellow, 4-cup **125.00**

Mixing bowl, Criss-Cross, blue
   7-1/2" dia **85.00**
   8-1/2" dia **100.00**

Refrigerator bowl, cov, round, Jennyware, pink, 16-oz **48.00**

Four bowls, fired on turquoise, orange, red, and yellow, three honey jars with fired-on turquoise, yellow, and red bases, lids marked "Walkers Honey Spread," each $5.

Refrigerator dish, cov
   4" x 4", Criss-Cross, blue **35.00**
   4" x 8", Criss-Cross, blue **100.00**

Salt and pepper shakers, pr
   Jennyware, ftd, pink **55.00**
   Ships, red trim, red lids **55.00**

Salt box, crystal, 4-1/2" x 3-3/4" **25.00**

Spice set, green lids, Scotty Dog dec, green tiered holder, cinnamon, ginger, red pepper, paprika, mustard, cloves, allspice, set of 7 ....**325.00**

Sugar bowl, Roman Arch, custard, red dot **60.00**

Tom & Jerry set, custard, bowl and 12 mugs..**135.00**

❖ Kitchen Kraft

Kitchen Kraft, platter, silver plated holder, blue mark, $35.

Kitchen Kraft is a line of kitchenware that was produced by Homer Laughlin during the early 1930s. The pieces feature floral decals, and most of the items are marked "Kitchen Kraft" and/or "Oven-Serve."

Canister, cov, yellow, 7-1/4" h.......**290.00**

Casserole, cov
   Cobalt blue, 8-1/2" dia...............**110.00**
   Yellow, individual size...................**90.00**

Cream soup bowl, double handles, pink **7.50**

Jar, cov
   Cobalt blue, small......................**500.00**
   Green, large **390.00**

Mixing bowl, Mexicana, 10-1/4" dia **170.00**

Pie plate, yellow, 9" dia **20.00**

Platter, oval, yellow **50.00**

Salad fork
   Green..**115.00**
   Yellow..**245.00**

Salad spoon, red **200.00**

Salt and pepper shakers, red, pr ..**95.00**

❖ Kitchen Prayer Ladies

These pretty ladies entered the kitchen scene in the 1970s and gently reminded us of the power of prayer as we bustled about.

Bank, pink 275.00
Bud vase....................................160.00
Canister, Instant Coffee
    Blue 175.00
    Pink 130.00
Coffee mug, blue 325.00
Cookie jar
    Blue 350.00
    Pink 350.00
Crumb pan.....................................60.00
Salt and pepper shakers, pr, pink .35.00
String holder, pink.......................350.00
Teapot, pink..................................325.00

❖ Kliban

Who is that black and white cool cat? Kliban! He's available in many shapes and sizes, on almost any type of object imaginable. The one constant, however, is his trademark sly smile.

Bank, Sigma, 1997, 8-1/2" l 65.00
Candle, votive type, cinnamon scent,
    unused, 2-3/4" h 4.00
Candlestick....................................50.00
Checkbook cover, rollerskating 15.00
Mug, "Eat Them Mousies," English origin
    ....27.50
Pin, pewter, flying, 2" l 27.50
Placemat, woven, rect, red and white,
    unused, pr 20.00
Plate, wearing sneakers, Kiln Craft, 9"
    dia 22.00
Poster, Top Cat 6.00
Pot holder 5.00
Sleeping bag, light use.................22.00
Teapot, Sigma Trend Setter 47.50
Tumbler, plastic, 4-1/4" h 30.00
Wastebasket, 12" h.........................65.00

❖ Knowles, Edwin M. China Company

Some collectors associate the name Edwin M. Knowles China Co. with fine dinnerware. Others correlate it with limited edition collector plates. The firm was founded in West Virginia in 1900 and continued producing quality wares until 1963. The company used several different marks, and should not be confused with Knowles, Taylor, & Knowles, another manufacturer of fine dinnerware.

Berry bowl, Yorktown, wheat dec 8.00
Bread and butter plate, Beverly.......4.00
Bowl, Mexican motif 35.00
Cake plate, Yorktown, white ground, blue
    daisies 7.50
Cookie jar, Tulip pattern, 7-1/2" h ...65.00

Edwin M. Knowles plate, wheat and flower motif, red rim band, $8.

Doll, Little Red Riding Hood, MIB ...30.00
Gravy boat, attached underplate,
    Williamsburg.................................40.00
Mixing bowls, nesting, white, tulip
    design..125.00
Mother's Day plate, Norman Rockwell,
    1988 ....35.00
Plate, Ebonette..............................38.00
Platter
    Buttercup......................................50.00
    Carlton...38.00
    Carolina 45.00
    Leaf Dance...................................40.00
Sauceboat, stand, Mayflower 35.00
Soup bowl, Yorktown, floral dec........8.50
Souvenir plate, San Francisco Bay,
    Alcatraz, Treasure Island, 10" dia 75.00
Water pitcher, Tulip pattern, ice lip.60.00

Edwin M. Knowles limited edition plate, The Mallards, by Bart Jerner, numbered on back, second issue in series, 1986, $8.

❖ Knowles, Taylor & Knowles

Knowles, Taylor & Knowles was located in

East Liverpool, Ohio. In business from 1854 to 1931, their production included ironstone, yellowware, and fine dinnerware, as well as translucent china known as Lotus Ware. Knowles, Taylor & Knowles used as many as nine different marks.

Baker, Victory, rose medallion, c1925, 9-
    1/2" l 20.00
Butter dish, cov, round, gold band, orig
    drainer insert 45.00
Casserole, cov, Victory, 10" l 35.00
Chamber pot, white ground, gold
    medallions and dec 45.00
Chamber set, blue floral transfer print,
    gold trim, 5 pcs...........................130.00
Dinner plate, Grapevine, 10-1/4" dia
    ....10.00
Milk pitcher, white, 1891-93 mark, 7" h
    ....250.00
Platter
    Bittersweet, 15" l 25.00
    Coronado, 14-3/4" l 20.00
    Plymouth, 13" l 20.00
Tier, Ebonnette, 3 snack plates, black
    and white......................................12.00
Vegetable bowl, roosters in center, hens
    around edge 15.00
Wash bowl and pitcher set, large bowl
    and pitcher, small pitcher, soap dish,
    toothbrush holder, white, blue floral
    transfer 250.00

❖ Korean War

This sad time in the world's history is remembered by veterans and collectors. Flea markets are starting to see more items relating to the Korean War as well as later conflicts.

Cigarette lighter, engraved...............25.00
Decanter, "Korean War Statue Dedicated
    1984," base mkd "Mount Hope,
    American Legion, Limited Edition,
    1984," 12-1/4" h 130.00
Helmet, aviator, gold dome helmet with
    goggles and electronics, with liner and
    earphones 255.00
Medal, Bronze Star, 1953, with
    documentation.............................47.50
Newspaper, *Record Herald*, Korean War
    news 5.00
Pass, Safe Conduct, UN 35.00
Patch
    Foxy Few, 12th Fighter Squadron
    ....355.00
    Utron Five, Navy...........................85.00
Pin, veteran 9.50
Postcard
    Battleship, 1952 postmark.............3.00
    Sailor's prayer, 1951 postmark.......4.00
Tour jacket..................................155.00

❖ Labels

Labels are colorful, plentiful, and usually inexpensive. Used to identify an almost endless variety of products, they make wonderful collectibles.

References: Joe Davidson, *Fruit Crate Art*, Wellfleet Press, 1990; Lynn Johnson and Michael O'Leary, *En Route: Label Art from the Golden Age of Air Travel*, Chronicle Books, 1993; Ralph and Terry Kovel, *The Label Made Me Buy It*, Crown Publishers, 1998; Gordon T. McClelland and Jay T. Last, *Fruit Box Labels: An Illustrated Guide to Citrus Labels*, Hillcrest Press, 1995; Gerard S. Petrone, *Cigar Box Labels: Portraits of Life, Mirrors of History*, Schiffer Publishing, 1998.

Periodical: *Banana Label Times*, P.O. Box 159, Old Town, FL 32860.

Collectors' Clubs: The Citrus Label Soc, 131 Miramonte Dr, Fullerton, CA 92365; Fruit Crate Label Soc, Rte 2, Box 695, Chelan, WA 98816; International Seal, Label and Cigar Band Soc, 8915 E Bellevue St, Tucson, AZ 85715; Soc of Antique Label Collectors, P.O. Box 24811, Tampa, FL 33623.

Cigar box
Club House, 6-1/2" x 8"................**12.00**
Mark Twain, inner box label..........**15.00**
Quaker Cigar.................................**7.00**
White Cat, 7" x 8-3/4".................**15.00**

Fruit and vegetable
Avenue, palm and eucalyptus tree lined shady avenue, early auto, Riverside **4.00**

Basket, golden basket holding 5 lemons, blue ground, Lemon Cove **2.00**

Black Bear, comical black bear operating wine press, red ground..**75**
California Beauty, bunch of roses, bunch of grapes...........................**25**
Desert Glow, red shading into yellow letters, blue ground, Highgrove, tangerines....................................**50**
Don't Worry, little boy holding apple with bite taken out of it, black ground **2.00**
El Merito, lemons, blue, green, yellows, Santa Paula **1.00**
Full O'Juice, partially peeled orange, glass, lavender ground, Redlands **2.00**

Gilbert Orchards, snowy mountain peaks, two big red apples..........**3.00**
Golden State, four lemons, leaves, map of California, Lemon Cove..........**2.00**
Hill Beauty, orchard scene, purple mountains, yellow and blue sky, orange with leaves and blossoms, aqua ground, Porterville **2.00**
Jersey Jerry, cute laughing little boy holding red apple, black ground .**6.00**
Lake Wenatchee Pears, lake scene, framed, 12-1/8" x 14-3/4" **35.00**
La Paloma, gentle dove, bunches of green and red grapes, red and yellow ground................................**25**
Mary Agnes, little pigtailed blond girl holding big straw hat full of yams **2.00**
Mr. Pear, cartoon pear with top hat and cane, blue ground......................**2.00**
Og-Na Tomatoes, Ogna Indian, framed, 9-1/2" x 18-1/2" **32.00**
"Oh Yes! We grow the Best California Pears" **4.00**
Pride of Venice Cove, crowing rooster, two oranges, leaves, blossom, maroon ground, Ivanhoe **3.00**
Rose Apples, two big pink roses, blue ground..**3.00**
Shamrock Navels, Placentia, Calif., shows shamrock, mountains and orange grove..............................**7.00**
Yuba Orchard, two yellow pears, blue ground..**50**

Hotel luggage
Hotel California, Paris, swan and Champs-Elysees, 1920s-30s, 4" sq **14.00**
Hotel Quirinal, Rome, Italy, green, white and red, 2-1/2" x 4", varnished **8.00**
Oriental Hotel, Kobe, Japan, "Operated by Toyo Kisen Kaisha - Kent W. Clark, Manager," pre-World War II, varnished **14.00**

Center: Lulu, label, drum major costume, round $20, upper right: King Pelican CA peas, oval, $5.

❖ Labino

Keep your eyes open for studio glass by Dominick Labino. Prices are rising quickly for marked items.

Creamer, light green, mkd "Labino 6-1975," 4-3/8" h **220.00**
Vase
4-1/2" h, bulbous, opaque white, brownish red flames, cased in clear, mkd "Labino 11-1974" **275.00**
4-3/4" h, sculpture type, f4-bubble design in pink veiling, gold flecks, cased in clear, mkd "Labino 11-1978" **470.00**
4-3/4" h, unsymmetrical, irid light green, mkd "Labino 1968" **250.00**
4-7/8" h, opaque black, subtle ruby swags, mkd "Labino 1969"......**350.00**
5-1/4" h, sculpture type, clear, amber center, hour glass opening, red and black flames, mkd "Labino 9-1974" **485.00**
6" h, bulbous, opaque metallic irid green, purple highlights, mkd "Labino 1964" **385.00**

❖ Lace

Collecting lace became a hobby for the wealthy around 1940. Collectors were dedicated to their hobby and devoted a great deal of time and effort to acquiring and studying various examples. As time passed, some of these collections were sent to museums, and others were dispersed. Now, once again, collectors are eagerly searching for antique lace.

References: Elizabeth Kurella, Guide To Lace and Linens, Antique Trader Books, 1998; ——, Secrets of Real Lace, The Lace Merchant, 1994; ——, Pocket Guide to Valuable Old Lace and Lacy Linens, The Lace Merchant, 1996; ——, The Complete Guide To Vintage Textiles, Krause Publications, 1999.

Periodical: The Lace Collector, P.O. Box 222, Plainview, MI 49080.

Collectors' Club: International Old Lacers, P.O. Box 554, Flanders, NJ 07836.

Bridal veil, cathedral length, white lace trim, 1950s **90.00**
Collar, Duchesse bobbin lace, roses, daisies and scrollwork design, c1870, 5" at center back, 32" l..............**125.00**
Curtain, machine-made lace, ecru, 36" x 72"...**75.00**
Doily, round, needle lace, rose design, 6" dia **20.00**
Shawl, machine made lace, ecru, rect, fringed on ends **65.00**
Yardage, machine-made Valenciennes lace, cotton, floral and scrollwork

design, 4", 1-yard **10.00**

❖ Ladders

Flea markets are good places to find used ladders, often at bargain prices. Those examples that are aged and weathered are being snatched up for their decorative appeal. If you're more concerned with functionality, be sure to check for sturdiness. It will save you from any nasty surprises if called upon to rescue a neighbor's kitten in distress.

Aluminum, extension type, working cond
....**20.00**
Wood, painting type, paint spatters.**15.00**
Wood, primitive, some wear
 3-foot, narrow **18.00**
 6-foot **12.00**
 10-foot **5.00**

❖ Lady's Head Vases

Planters and vases in the shape of a lady's head are common sights at any flea market. But, did you ever notice how many variations and styles there are? These holders were popular with florists from the 1940s through the early 1960s.

Reference: Maddy Gordon, *Head Vases: The Artistry of Betty Lou Nichols,* Schiffer Publishing, 2002.

Collectors' Club: Head Vase Society, P.O. Box 83H, Scarsdale, NY 10583.

Ardco, blond, green dress, 7-1/2" h
....**295.00**
Baby, blond hair, open mouth, pink ruffled bonnet tied under chin, pink dress, unmkd, 5-3/4" h **20.00**

Lady's Head Vases, green hat and dress, white blouse and ribbon on hat, orig pearl necklace, earrings missing, $85.

Lady's Head Vases, Napco, green bonnet and dress, blond, mkd on base, c1959, $20.

Carmen Miranda............................**125.00**
Cowboy, brown hair, blue eyes, yellow hat and neckerchief, yellow star-shaped badge, unmkd, 6" h **35.00**
German Shepherd, mkd Japan, 6" h
....**125.00**
Howdy Doody **45.00**
Jackie Kennedy, orig foil label, mkd "#E-1852, INARCO," 6" h **650.00**
Napcoware
 #C3307, red hat and dress, orig foil label, 6" h...............................**185.00**
 #C6428, blue dress, orig paper sticker, 6" h **195.00**
 #C6429, blue dress, white collar, 7-1/2" h..**265.00**
 #C7495, green hat and dress, 7-1/2" h
....**325.00**
National Potteries Co., #C5047, wide brimmed hat, orig foil label, 6-1/2" h
....**250.00**
Relpo, Japan, #K1633, green dress with white trim, 7-1/4" h **290.00**

❖ Lalique

Many collectors associate the name Lalique with French glass, but did you know that Rene Lalique started his artistic career as a jewelry designer? His early molded glass brooches and pendants were highlighted with semiprecious stones and are eagerly sought by Lalique collectors today. By 1905, he had devoted himself to making glass tableware, and, by 1908, he had begun designing packaging for cosmetics and perfumes. Most of his glass was marked.

Collectors' Club: Lalique Collectors Society, 400 Veterans Blvd, Carlstadt, NJ 07072.

Reproduction Alert

Ashtray, Vezelay, c1928, deep amber glass, molded "R. LALIQUE" and engraved "R. Lalique France no. 481," $350.

For additional listings, see *Warman's Antiques & Collectibles* and *Warman's Glass.*

Ashtray, inscribed "Lalique France"
....**75.00**
Bookends, pr, perched birds, upraised tails and wings, press-molded, acid finished, polished colorless glass, paper label, bases inscribed "Lalique France," Shreve, Crump & Low Co. paper retailer's labels, 6-1/8" h ..**175.00**
Bowl, Fleurons, press-molded opalescent, six wavy line swirl designs in relief, acid etched "R. LALIQUE FRANCE" on base, 8" dia **215.00**
Box, cov, Emiliane, clear and frosted, engraved "R. Lalique France," 3-1/2" dia
....**350.00**
Cigarette box, Fouad I, clear and frosted, sepia patina, molded "R. LALIQUE," presentation inscription, 4" sq **120.00**
Medallion, Chose Promise, for Fioret Fragrances, clear and frosted, c1920, silk-lined box, molded "R. LALIQUE," 1-1/4" dia **520.00**
Pendant, Gui, yellow, modern beaded cord, c1920, molded "LALIQUE," 2" l
....**415.00**
Perfume bottle, Deux Fleurs, double flower blossom bottle, press molded flower center stopper, acid-etched "R. LALIQUE, FRANCE" on base, 3-3/4" h, minor nicks on stopper...............**175.00**
Powder box, cov, Trois Figurines, clear and frosted, for D'Orsay, c1920, molded "R. LALIQUE," 4" dia......**210.00**
Tumbler, molded with 8 recessed full-length figures, engraved "Lalique France" on base, modern, 4" h ..**175.00**
Urn, Marc Lalique design, Dampierre, 5-1/4" h...**195.00**

Finding great pieces of early Lalique glass is hard at flea markets, but do keep your eyes open for something of this quality: letter seal, Aigle, c1912, clear and frosted glass with gray patina, engraved "Lalique," $1,850.

Vase
Eglantines, frosted oval, polished thorny branches and rose blossoms, center base inscribed "R. Lalique," 4-1/2" h **400.00**
Meudon, clear, c1933, stenciled "R. LALIQUE France," 5" h **380.00**

❖ Lamps

Flea markets are great places to find all kind of lamps and replacement parts. When considering a purchase, check to see that all necessary parts are included. As a precautionary measure, any vintage lamp should be rewired before placed into service.

Periodical: *Light Revival*, 35 W Elm Ave, Quincy, MA 02170.

For additional listings, see *Warman's Antiques & Collectibles*, *Warman's Americana & Collectibles*, and *Warman's Glass*.

Bedroom, Southern Belle, blue, orig shade **80.00**
Character
Football Player, 14-1/2" h, hollow plaster, football player standing next to figural football standard, linen over cardboard shade, WK, Japan, Sears, Roebuck, 1978.........................**25.00**
Fred Flintstone, 13-1/4" h, painted vinyl, black metal base, missing shade..**45.00**
Mickey Mouse, 4" d, 6-1/2" h, globular metal base, beige ground, three Mickey decals around sides, Soreng-Manegold Co **85.00**
Children's
ABC blocks, wood and plastic, linen-

over-cardboard shade...............**25.00**
Hobby horse, wood, tail missing, no shade..**2.00**
Sesame Street characters, plastic and wood **15.00**
Dresser, Porcelair, black cameo, silhouette of young woman, surrounded by ribbon **48.00**
Floor, brass, adjustable arm **25.00**
Headboard, pink shade, chrome.....**65.00**
Lava, red flakes move when heated**70.00**
Motion
Antique cars, Econolite, 1957, 11" h **150.00**
Fountain of Youth.......................**130.00**
Niagara Falls, Goodman, extra wide style **150.00**
Snow scene, bridge, Econolite...**175.00**
Table
Milk can, metal base, repainted, decals added, no shade........................**10.00**
Porcelain, white, baluster shaped base, painted floral dec, orig silk shade **40.00**
Small stoneware crock, brown-and-white linen shade......................**35.00**
Wicker, latticework panels, round base, c1920, 24" h **595.00**
Television
Gondola, ceramic, brown with gold trim, marked "Copyright Premco Mfg Co, Chicago, IL, 1954," 16" w, 7" h **45.00**
Horse Head, ceramic, 12 x 10-3/4" **25.00**
Panther, black, 8-1/2 x 6-1/2".......**35.00**
Wall, tole, peach ground, white floral trim **10.00**

Motion lamp, locomotive dec, multicolored scenic background, $95.

❖ Lap Desks

Because they were portable, lap desks (or folding desks as they were sometimes called) were the laptop computers of the 18th and 19th centuries. They also provided a firm writing surface as well as a place to store papers and writing instruments. Some examples are quite ornate, having locks, drawers, and even secret compartments.

Black lacquer, mother of pearl inlay of flowers, leaves and grape clusters, 4" h, 14" w, 10" d **600.00**
Cherry, replaced felt writing surface, ink stains in base **75.00**
Mahogany, brass bands, green leather writing surface, 6-1/2" h, 17" w, 9-3/8" d **650.00**
Mahogany, satinwood inlay, Victorian, replaced leather writing surface, repairs to underlying wood....................**395.00**
Rosewood, mother-of-pearl inlay, velvet writing surface, 4-1/2" h, 13" w, 10-1/4" d **760.00**
Walnut, velvet writing surface, 8-1/2" d x 12" x 5-1/2" **295.00**

Walnut hinged-lidded traveling lap desk, brass corner mounts, brass handles, interior with ink bottles and secret drawer, $225.

❖ Laundry

It's Monday; must be wash day. Somewhere between pounding clothes against a rock along the creek and tossing them into a Maytag washer came the washboard. Most washboards had a galvanized metal scrubbing surface in a wooden frame; however, glass and pottery inserts were also made, with the latter being especially valuable. A number of other items were also used to assist in early laundry duties, including sprinklers, dryers, and a whole host of cleaning agents.

Also see Clothes Sprinklers, Irons, and Soap in this edition.

Bag, cloth
2 black laundresses, 29" x 20".....**35.00**
Embroidered "Laundry" and with flowers, stains **10.00**

Sunny Suzy, tin toy washing machine with wringer and wash tub, $150.

Booklet, *Washee Washee Laundry List*, The Really & Britton Co., Chicago, 1905, 11" x 5" **26.00**

Box, Cook's Washing and Blueing, 5" h **30.00**

Calendar, 1959, Schulberger's Appliances......................................**5.00**

Crate, Gold Dust Soap, embossed with images of Gold Dust Twins, paper label on ends, no lid, 8-1/4" h, 29-3/4" w, 16-1/2" d **295.00**

Figurine
Precious Moments, "Be Not Weary In Well Doing," laundry girl, 6" h ...**70.00**
Napco, "Washday," girl doing laundry, 5-1/4" h **39.00**

Ruler, folding, 3-section, celluloid, "Quaker City Laundry, Souvenir of the National Export Exposition, Fall 1899" **25.00**

Sprinkler, metal, Jack and Jill decal **20.00**

Trade card, "Higgins' German Laundry Soap," shows sailors and young lady, removed from scrapbook **5.00**

Washboard
Glass insert, wooden frame, National Washboard Co., No. 860 ....**30.00**
Graniteware, blue scrubbing surface, wooden frame, National Washboard Co., Soap Saver, 24" h, 12-1/2" w **115.00**
Mother Hubbard, wooden rollers, 1 dowel cracked, 22-1/4" h, 12-1/4" w **105.00**

❖ Law Enforcement Collectibles

Collectors actively investigate flea markets for items to add to their collections of law enforcement memorabilia. Some have a desire to honor those who risk their lives to keep the peace, while others enjoy the sense of history that's attached to these items.

Police bullet proof vest, olive green, white lettering, $15.

References: Matthew G. Forte, *American Police Equipment*, Turn of the Century Publishers, 2000; Monty McCord, *Law Enforcement Memorabilia*, Krause Publications, 1999.

Periodical: *Police Collectors News*, RR1, Box 14, Baldwin, WI 54002.

Button, uniform, brass-tone, 3/4" dia
Toledo Police **9.00**
Cincinnati Police, scales of justice .**9.00**
Philadelphia Police **9.00**

Envelope, D.A. Farrell, Sheriff of Mills County, Glenwood, Iowa, late 1800s **12.00**

Magazine, *National Police Gazette*, December 1947............................**15.00**

Patch, uniform, Correction Department, City of New York, shield shape, 4-1/4" x 3-1/2"..**6.00**

Photograph, Police & Shore Patrol, 1940s, small tears, 11" x 14" **13.00**

Plate, Royal Canadian Mounted Police, shows 3 Mounties on horseback, Wood & Son, Burslem, England, 10" dia**12.00**

Postcard, Mounted Police Squad on Parade in Manhattan, hand-tinted, unused..**9.00**

Toy
Patrol, battery-op, remote control, twin propellers, litho tin and plastic, late 1960s/early 1970s, Japan, 6-1/2" l **36.50**
Motorcycle, Marx, litho tin with siren **400.00**
Volkwagen police car, tin, Taiwan, 1970s, MIB, 9" l **67.00**

❖ Lefton China

Founded by George Zoltan Lefton, this company has created china, porcelain, and ceramic tableware, animals, and figurines. Lefton wares are well marked, and some also include a Japanese factory mark.

Reference: Loretta DeLozier, *Collector's Encyclopedia of Lefton China*, vol. 1 (1995), vol. 2 (1997), v. 3 (1999), Collector Books; Ruth McCarthy, More Lefton China, Schiffer Publishing, 2000.

Lefton China, plate, Christmas dec, green ground, red poinsettias, green and white holly leaves, red berries, gold trim, self handles, orig red and gold foil label, green mark "Lefton China, (crown) Hand Painted, Reg US Pat Off, Limited Edition, 4393," $20.

For additional listings, see *Warman's Antiques & Collectibles.*

Bookends, tigers, #6663................**35.00**
Cake plate, Hollyberry, matching server **45.00**
Candy box, cov, heart-shaped, red and white, doves, #5597 ....**22.00**
Cigarette set, Elegant Rose, 5 pcs **200.00**
Cup and saucer
Christmas Cardinal......................**25.00**
Roses **45.00**
Egg, roosters and chick on lid, paper label, #3429................................**25.00**
Figure
Birthday Boys **30.00**
Madonna and Child, #543...........**75.00**
January Angel, #3332 ....**22.00**
Pixie on mushroom watching frog, 4" h **20.00**
Rock A Bye Baby in the Treetop, 8" h **100.00**
Siamese Dancers, pr, 6-1/2" h ...**120.00**
Mug
Elf handle, green, #4284..............**15.00**
Grant **35.00**
Jackson **35.00**
Music box, Nativity, plays O Holy Night, 1980s, 8" h **65.00**
Planter
Angel, on cloud **40.00**
Calico Donkey **35.00**
Salt and pepper shakers, pr, fruit baskets, 2-3/4" **24.00**
Snack set, Fleur de Lis **50.00**
Teapot, To A Wild Rose, #2561.....**165.00**
Wall plaque, rose, black background, 5" **24.00**

❖ Lenox

Seven pieces of Lenox Blue-Dot china, pre-1932: a bouillon cup in sterling silver frame; a covered cheese dish; three dessert coupes monogrammed TLB; and 9-1/2" dia faceted serving plate monogrammed S, green stamp marks, $200.

Walter Scott Lenox opened his porcelain factory in 1906, employing potters and decorators, whom he lured from Belleek. Fine Lenox is almost translucent in appearance. The firm is still in business and many factory outlet stores sell their products.

For additional listings, see *Warman's Antiques & Collectible* and *Warman's American Pottery & Porcelain*.

Bowl, 2 handles, etched gold trim, M-139, pre-1930.............................**45.00**
Chocolate Set, cov chocolate pot, 6 cups and saucers, Golden Wheat pattern, cobalt blue ground, 13 pc set **275.00**
Christmas ornament, inn, gold trim, orig box..**35.00**
Cigarette Box, white apple blossoms, green ground, wreath mark..........**40.00**
Coffeepot, Cretan #0316 ....**165.00**
Compote, brown rim, white ground, black hp insignia, pre-1930, 5" dia **40.00**

Three-piece Lenox tea set, hand-painted pink roses over a green body, gilded handles, green stamp marks, c1910, 9-1/2" x 9" teapot, $500.

Cup and saucer
  Alden................................**25.00**
  Golden Wheat **35.00**
Figure
  Snow Queen **70.00**
  Stardust..**70.00**
Honey Pot, 5" h, 6-1/4" d underplate, ivory beehive, gold bee and trim ..**85.00**
Platter, Oak Leaf, platinum trim, 13-1/2" l **75.00**
Salt, molded seashells and coral, green wreath mark, 3" dia **35.00**
Shoe, white, bow trim....................**190.00**
Tea strainer, hp small pink flowers .**72.00**
Vase, ivory ground, pale pink roses dec, gold trim, gold mark **55.00**

❖ Letter Openers

These knife-like collectibles are also handy little desk accessories. Constructed of almost any type of material, early manufacturers found them to be wonderful tools for advertising.

Reference: Everett Grist, *Collecto's Guide to Letter Openers*, Collector Books, 1998.

Advertising
  The Empire Varnish Co., Cleveland, Ohio, metal, 8" l **7.00**
  Fuller Brush Man, plastic **8.00**
  Martin Mfg. Co., Pick Up Beaner, Keck-Gonnerman's Bean Thresher, Phone 325, Bad Axe, Mich., celluloid handle, 8-1/2" l **20.00**
  Pennsylvania Independent Telephone Association, 50th Anniversary, 1902-1952, plastic handle, 8-1/8" l **10.00**
Brass, emb florals on handle **15.00**
Celluloid, metal blade, 6-1/2" l........**28.00**
Political, "Republican Convention 1976 Kansas City, Missouri," black plastic **22.00**
Silver, monogrammed, English hallmarks **125.00**
Souvenir
  Chicago's World's Fair, Federal Building, marble handle, metal blade **95.00**
  Florida, alligator shape, celluloid..**10.00**
  Toledo, brass-colored cross, 6-5/8" l **10.00**

❖ Libbey Glass

Libbey Glass is a true American success story. Established in Toledo, Ohio, in 1888, Libbey Glass Company produced quality cut glass. Eventually, the company added art glass and pressed wares. Libbey Glass was a frequent exhibitor at World's Fairs, allowing them to advertise their products and promote future lines. Some of their glassware is marked, but not all of it.

Bowl
  Amberina, ruffled, flared rim, sgd, 7" dia...**350.00**
  Cut glass, hobstar, bands of strawberry diamond and fans, sgd, 8" dia**110.00**
Candlestick, Flute pattern, sgd, 6" h **100.00**
Candy dish, cov, cut glass, divided, clover shape, hobstar and prism dec, sgd, 7" dia **90.00**
Champagne, Talisman pattern, colorless, ruby threading, 6" h...................**135.00**
Cordial, cut glass, American Prestige, c1930 ....**50.00**
Goblet, clear, Liberty Bell pattern, 7" h **25.00**
Plate, Optic Swirl pattern, green **45.00**
Sherbet, silhouette stem, black rabbit, sgd **165.00**
Spooner, Maize pattern, creamy opaque kernels of corn, blue husks, gold trim **190.00**
Tumbler, light green, lightly swirled ribs, mkd, set of 6 ....**60.00**
Vase, cylindrical, slightly flaring, light vertical ribbing, blue threaded dec, opal ground, c1933, 8" h...................**275.00**
Wine, Silhouette, clear bowl, black cat silhouette in stem, sgd, 7" h.......**200.00**

✪ Liberty Blue Dinnerware

Flea markets are buzzing with this blue and white dinnerware. Nicknamed Liberty Blue by dealers and collectors, the correct name is "Staffordshire Liberty Blue." Enoch Wedgwood in the Staffordshire district in England made it in 1976. The style is based on the traditional blue and white designs made in the Staffordshire district in the 19th century. The scenes reflect important times in Colonial history. Used as a promotional premium, it was eagerly acquired as a tie in to the American Bicentennial. Many mint examples are appearing on flea market tables, so collectors can afford to be choosey about condition as they build their collections of this interesting pattern.

Reference: Debbie and Randy Coe, *Liberty Blue Dinnerware,* Schiffer Publishing, 2002.

Baker, Minute Men, oval **50.00**
Berry bowl, Betsy Ross, 5-1/2" dia **14.00**
Bread and butter plate, Monticello, 6" dia **9.00**
Cereal bowl, Mount Vernon, 6-1/2" dia **22.00**
Cream pitcher, Paul Revere..........**35.00**
Cup and saucer, Paul Revere and Old North Church..............................**16.00**
Dinner plate, Independence Hall, 10" dia **30.00**

Liberty Blue Dinnerware platter, blue and white, scene of Colonial Williamsburg Governor's Palace, floral border, $35.

Gravy boat underplate, Governors House, Williamsburg **14.00**
Pie plate, Washington Leaving Christ Church, 7" dia **20.00**
Platter
  Governor's Palace, Williamsburg, 12" l **65.00**
  Washington crossing Delaware, 14" l **85.00**
Soup Plate, flat rim, North Church, 8-1/2" d...**30.00**
Sugar bowl, cov, Betsy Ross..........**40.00**
Teapot, cov, Minute Men, 8-7/8" w, 6-1/2" h **170.00**
Tureen, cov, Boston tea party **250.00**
Vegetable bowl, Fraunces Tavern, round **50.00**

❖ License Plates

As a driver, you won't get far without one of these. And, few of us can throw them out when new plates are issued. So, many of these humble identifiers find their way to flea markets, much to the delight of collectors. Since many states and organizations now issue specialty license plates, watch for those to increase in value too. Beginning license plate collectors should seek out a flea market devoted to automobiles, where common examples range from $2 to $5. Look for examples in good condition, but expect to find some wear.

Attachments
  48-star U.S. flag, 6" x 5-1/2".........**35.00**
  Shell Motor Oil, metal, 1930s, wear, rust, 5-1/4" x 3"..........................**39.00**
Political
  "Al Smith," metal, green and white**60.00**
  "All the Way with LBJ," red letters on white ground, 1964 ....**22.50**
  "Hoover," white on black ground, rust, 60% paint..................................**25.00**
States
  California, 1935 ....**40.00**
  Colorado, 1972, rust.......................**4.00**

Illinois, 1916, rust **30.00**
Illinois, 1933 ....**25.00**
Illinois, 1961 ....**18.00**
Kansas, 1971 ....**5.00**
Maine, 1914, porcelain.................**95.00**
Massachusetts, 1915, porcelain...**95.00**
North Dakota, 1970.......................**5.00**
South Dakota, 1934 ....**5.00**
Walt Disney
  Disneyland Paris, Mickey Mouse **30.00**
  Disney Surprise 20th Birthday, AAA **50.00**
  Disney Wilderness Lodge Resort **17.00**

❖ Liddle Kiddles

Introduced by Mattel in 1965, these half-pint dolls drew a big response from little girls. But that was nothing when compared to the reaction of adult collectors today that eagerly search for these reminders of their childhood. While the dolls themselves constitute the main attraction, accessories and go-withs are also on many want lists.

Beauty Parlor Purse Playset, 1996, MIB...**5.00**
Collector's case, vinyl, holds 8 dolls, minor wear, 14-1/2" x 10".............**15.00**
Colorforms, Dress-Up Kit, trays missing, incomplete, box damaged **24.00**
Coloring book, unused, 1966 ....**43.00**
Doll
  Beatnik **30.00**
  Belinda Little, kitchen chairs, MOC **28.00**
  Blond, red dress..........................**10.00**
  Brunette, white lace dress, green ribbon.......................................**7.50**
  Family dolls, MOC **30.00**
  Robin Hood **10.00**
Play outfit, "Cook 'N," Totsy Corp., orig box...**45.00**
Pop-Up Playhouse, 1967 ....**45.00**
Sink, accessories, MOC.................**28.00**
Stove, diecast metal, MOC **28.00**

❖ Light Bulbs and Sockets

Because light bulbs were usually thrown away when no longer needed, finding vintage examples—especially those in working condition—can be a real challenge.

Christmas
  Grape cluster, minor paint loss, 2-3/4" h...**9.00**
  Pear, paint loss, 2-1/8" h **36.00**
  Santa Claus, 2-faced, 3-1/4" h **40.00**
  Snowman carrying umbrella, milk glass, paint loss, 3-3/4" h **35.00**

Snowman with shawl, milk glass, paint loss, 3-3/4" h............................**35.00**
Rose bud, point loss, 2-1/4" h......**30.00**
Edison, early 1900s, mkd "SAC JAC" and "Property of NY Edison Company - Not to be sold," double curl, classic filament.....................................**32.00**
Edison, Mazda flood light, paper lights, works, 5-1/2" h **28.00**
Westinghouse, Edison base, sharp tip, double anchored filament with 3 loops, red patent label with yellow cotton insulation **32.00**

❖ Lighters

Cigarette lighters have attracted collectors for years. Watch for examples with figural forms or with interesting advertising. Look for examples in good condition, but exercise caution when trying to determine if a lighter is in working order.

Collectors' Clubs: International Lighter Collectors, P.O. Box 3536, Quitman, TX 75783; Pocket Lighter Preservation Guild & Historical Society, 380 Brooks Dr, Suite 209A, Hazelwood, MO 63042.

Advertising
  Amoco, Barlow **50.00**
  CBC Radio, Bowers, Canada, 3-5/8" h **85.00**
  Loretto Casket Co., enameled on both sides, Japan............................**88.00**
  Mutual Metal Products, Zippo, orig box **75.00**
Alligator, ceramic, made in Japan, 1-3/4" h, 5" l...**28.00**
Boat, Occupied Japan, Bakelite and chrome **148.00**

Zippo lighter, slim chrome case with chased panel, orig box, $25.

Silverplated lighter, barber bottle shape, emb dec, mkd, $10.

Bowling, Zippo **85.00**
Donkey, ceramic, "Japan" on side,
  Amico, 2" h, 2-1/2" l **35.00**
Lucite, dark pink, 1940s, 4" h **85.00**
Royal Crown Derby, Imari pattern,
  Ronson **100.00**
Space Needle, chrome **180.00**
Spaniel, ceramic, 3-1/2" h, 4-3/4" l .**25.00**
Stein, nautical motif, pewter, made in
  Japan, 5" h **20.00**
Trichette Rhinestones, Wiesner, faceted
  prong set rhinestones **85.00**
Tuxedo stripe, gold filled, Dunhill .**275.00**
Wedgwood, jasper, light blue, white
  classical design **65.00**
Zippo, ship and a lighthouse design,
  white on chrome **15.00**

❖ Lightning Rod Balls

If you're reading this and wondering just what on earth we're talking about, take a gander at the roof of an old barn the next time you're out in the country. We'll bet you'll spot a colored glass ball up on top of that lightning rod. Lightning rods used on homes and other structures in rural America were often embellished with decorative glass ornaments. Although some were odd shapes, most were round with embossed star or swirl designs. Dark blue and amber

were fairly common, but other rare colors such as red can also be found.

References: Russell Barnes, *Lightning Rod Collectibles Price Guide*, self-published; Michael Bruner and Rod Krupka, *The Complete Book of Lightning Rod Balls.*

Periodical: *The Crown Point*, 2615 Echo Ln, Ortonville, MI 48862.

Collectors' Club: Weather or Knot Antiques, 15832S CR 900W, Wanatah, IN 46390.

Classic round shape, amethyst, copper
  caps, 3-1/2" dia **60.00**
Diamond quilted, white, short rod and
  stand **125.00**
D&S
  Blue milk glass, 10-sided, with short
    rod and stand **100.00**
  White milk glass, 10-sided, copper
    caps, 4" dia **85.00**
Electra round, white milk glass, copper
  caps, 5-1/8" h, 4-1/8" dia..............**75.00**
Hawkeye, blue milk glass, rounded top
  with starbursts, tapering bottom,
  copper caps, 5-1/8" h, 4-3/8" dia
  ....**175.00**
Moon & Stars, white milk glass, copper
  caps, 5-1/8" h, 4-3/8" dia..............**75.00**
Ribbed grape
  Blue milk glass, copper caps, 5-1/8" h,
    4-3/8" dia **100.00**
  White milk glass, copper caps, 5-1/8"
    h, 4-3/8" dia **90.00**
Round pleat (Barnett Ball), cobalt,
  copper caps, 5" h, 4-3/8" dia......**175.00**
Sharp pleated, sun-colored amethyst
  (orig white milk glass), copper caps, 5"
  h, 4-1/2" dia.................................**75.00**
Shinn System, white milk glass, copper
  caps, 4-1/2" dia **32.00**
Smooth round, sun-colored lavender
  (orig white milk glass), copper caps, 4-
  1/2" dia **50.00**

Lightning rod ball, white milk glass, Moon and Star pattern, 4-1/2" dia, 5" h, $65.

❖ Limited Edition Collectibles

Limited Editions plate, Norman Rockwell, New Arrivals, 1979, Continental Mint, first edition, no box, $5.

You're guaranteed to find limited edition collectibles at any flea market you visit. This multi-million dollar market includes many types of objects, with some very dedicated artists and companies offering their wares. Please remember that much of the value of a limited edition object lies with the original box, packaging, etc.

References: Jay Brown, *The Complete Guide to Limited Edition Art Prints*, Krause Publications, 1999; Collector's Information Bureau, *Collectibles Price Guide & Directory to Secondary Market Retailers*, 9th ed, Krause Publications, 1999.

Periodicals: *Collector Editions*, 170 Fifth Ave, 12th Floor, New York, NY 10010; *Collector's Bulletin*, 22341 East Wells Rd, Canton, IL 61520; *Collectors Mart Magazine*, 700 E State St, Iola, WI 54990; *The Treasure Trunk*, P.O. Box 13554, Arlington, TX 76094.

Collectors' Clubs: International Plate Collectors Guide, P.O. Box 487, Artesia, CA 90702. There are also many company-sponsored clubs, as well as local groups.

For additional listings, see *Warman's Antiques & Collectibles* and *Warman's Americana & Collectibles*. Also see specific makers, such as Bing & Grondahl in this edition.

Christmas ornament
  Angel, Danbury Mint, 4" h **48.00**
  Angel Bear, Enesco, 1992 ....**6.00**
  Bailey and Matthew, Boyds, 1996 **10.00**
  Camille, Christopher Radko, 1994**20.00**
  Candy cane, Wallace Silversmiths,
    1986...**35.00**
  Choir Boy, Christopher Radko, 1992
  ....**12.00**
  Christmas Castle, Reed & Barton,
    1980...**80.00**
  Christmas is Love, Coca-Coloa, 1995
  ....**5.00**
  Hearts & Flowers, Christopher Radko,

1990.................................**10.00**
Holly Ball, Christopher Radko, 1991
.................................**12.00**
Holy Family, Hallmark, 1998 ....**12.00**
Sleigh bell, silver-plated, Wallace
    Silversmiths, 1992 ....**30.00**
Snowflake, sterling silver, Gorham,
    1973...**95.00**
Stewart at Play, Charming Tails, 1995
    ....**5.00**

Cottage
Aurora Rainbow Row, Shelia's
    Collectibles, 1993 ....**10.00**
Conway Scenic Railroad Station,
    Shelia's Collectibles, 1994........**18.00**
Green Gables, Anne, Hawthorne .**40.00**
Portland Head Lighthouse, Spencer
    Collins, 1984 ....**60.00**
Rhett and Scarlett, Hawthorne, 1995
    ....**20.00**

Figure
Bedtime, Sarah Kay, 1983............**20.00**
Budweiser Frogs, 1996 ....**20.00**
Can I Help Too?, Dept 56 Snowbaby
    1991...**30.00**
Chocolate Factory, Dave Grossman,
    1999 ....**15.00**
For My Sweetheart, Anri, 1987 ....**90.00**
Good Friends are Forever, Enesco,
    1989 ....**15.00**
Our Puppy, Anri, 1985 ....**70.00**
Out of Step, Schmid, 1985 ....**25.00**
Sagebrush Kids, Leading the Way, G.
    Perillo, 1987 ....**25.00**

Plate
A Christmas Welcome, T. Kinkade,
    Bradford Exchange, 1997 ....**15.00**
Ashley, Gone with the Wind Series,
    Edwin M. Knowles, MIB **100.00**
Cardinal, Audubon Society, 1973.**50.00**
Caroling, Disney, Schmid, 1975 ...**15.00**
Christmas in Mexico, Royal Doulton,
    1973...**10.00**
Down the Alps, Schmid, 1987 ......**60.00**
Easter, 1980, Edwin M. Knowles, MIB
    ....**30.00**
Flowers for Mother, Schmid, 1974
    ....**85.00**
Good Catch, Hamilton, 1992........**15.00**
Hopes and Dreams, Edwin M.
    Knowles, 1987, MIB..................**20.00**
Just Married, Franklin Mint, 1994.**15.00**
Sunday Best, Reco, 1983 ....**50.00**
Valentine's Day, Edwin M. Knowles,
    1981, MIB **20.00**

❖ Lincoln, Abraham

This famous American president is a
favorite among collectors. Lincoln
memorabilia is also a favorite with many

Hotel Abraham Lincoln, "A Robert Meyer Hotel," A. B. Moody, Res. Mgr, Reading, PA, black ground, portrait medallion and lettering in orange, orig cardboard box, $95.

museums, and genuine vintage articles can
be prohibitively expensive. Contemporary
items bearing Lincoln's likeness are more
reasonably priced, however.

Bank, cast metal, bronze finish, 5-1/2" h
    ....**75.00**
Bust, bronze, c1900, 15" h.............**98.00**
Calendar plate, 1911, Lincoln portrait,
    "Compliments of Chas. Seepe & Sons,
    Peru, Ill.," 9" dia **95.00**
Face jug, green running glaze, incised
    inscription on back "Abraham Lincoln,
    Shyster Lawyer from Illonois (sic) Also
    Was President Of The North," sgd
    "Cleater Meaders, 1993," 12-1/2" h
    ....**475.00**
Newspaper, *Harper's Weekly*, March 2,
    1861, "Abraham Lincoln, the President-
    Elect, addressing the people from the
    Astor House balcony"..................**40.00**
Plate, commemorative, 150th
    anniversary of Lincoln's birth, Lincoln
    image, floral border, Enoch & Ralph
    Woods, 1959, 10" dia **40.00**
Stereoptican card, The Birthplace of
    Abraham Lincoln, Keystone View Co.,
    back stained **4.00**
Tobacco silk, image of Lincoln with
    facsimile signature, black on white, 3" h
    ....**100.00**

❖ Lindbergh, Charles

Collectors are fascinated with this early
aviator and his adventures. Look for printed
items, commemorative pieces, and even
textiles that pertain to his many flights.

Autograph, book *We*, one of 1,000
    numbered copies signed by Lindbergh,
    New York, 1927, worn, backstrip
    defection **435.00**
Bank, G&T, 1928 ....**300.00**

Charles Lindbergh doll, jointed, cloth body, orig clothing and tag, one arm missing, wear, $55.

Book
The Lone Eagle: Lindbergh, Blakely
    Printing Co., Chicago, 1929, color
    portrait photo, 20 pgs, stiff paper 8" x
    9" **35.00**
War Within and Without, diaries and
    letters of Anne Morrow Lindbergh,
    Harcourt Brace Jovanovich, 1980, dj
    ....**8.50**
Children's book, *Boy's Story of
    Lindbergh, Lone Eagle*, by Richard J.
    Beamish, hardcover **35.00**
Commemorative coin, issued for golden
    anniversary of flight, bust portrait,
    bronze **25.00**
First day cover **2.25**
Magazine, *Time*, June 13, 1938, color
    cover of Lindbergh and scientist
    working on Fountain of Age, 76 black-
    and-white pages, 8-1/2" x 11" **15.00**
Newspaper, Nebraska State Journal,
    May, 1927, covering Atlantic flight
    ....**55.00**
Pin, Lucky Lindbergh........................**22.00**
Plate, yellow glazed china, color graphics
    of smiling Lindy, plane over ocean
    between Statue of Liberty and Eiffel
    Tower, "First To Navigate The Air In
    Continuous Flight From New York To
    Paris-1927," Limoges China Co., 8-1/2"
    dia **24.00**
Postcard, 3-1/2" x 5-1/2"
    Red-tinted, Lindbergh in cockpit of
        Spirit of St. Louis **15.00**
    Sepia-tone photo of Lindbergh with
        unidentified gentleman on ornate
        balcony, Underwood copyright,
        unused.....................................**25.00**
Sheet music, Like An Angel You Flew
    Into Everyone's Heart, 1927 ....**35.00**

Charles Lindbergh memorabilia: Collector's silver ring, "New York-Paris," complete with original box, unmarked; Patinated metal "Spirit of St. Louis" bookends, "We," by Charles A. Lindbergh, G.P. Putnam's Sons, 1927, blue cloth with gilt lettering, good condition; "Lindbergh, The Lone Eagle," by Richard J. Beamish, The John C. Winston Company, 1928, foxing, wear to corners; and an etching,"Wings or the Morning May 21, 1927," pencil signed illegibly, darkened, losses, matted, unframed, plate: 9-3/4 x 12-3/4"; and June 12, 1927 Boston Sunday Post Extra with headlines "Lindberg Comes Home in Matchless Triumph.", $250.

Silhouette, 4-1/8" w, 5-1/2" h, black silhouette, black and gold border, orig label reads "Hand Painted Silhouette of Col. Charles A. Lindbergh, Copyrighted," 1927, orig wood frame **85.00**
Tapestry, New York to Paris..........**115.00**

❖ Linens

No dining room or bedroom is properly dressed without an assortment of linens. Today's collectors treasure these textiles. Some pieces were hand-made and exhibit exquisite craftsmanship, although machine-made examples have a beauty all their own. Enjoy them, but use them with care.

Reference: Elizabeth Kurella, *Guide to Lace and Linens*, Antique Trader Books, 1998.

Periodical: *The Lace Collector*, P.O. Box 222, Plainview, MI 49080.

Collectors' Club: International Old Lacers, P.O. Box 554, Flanders, NJ 07836.

A table full of "Better Linens" at the Lititz, PA, September flea market.

Calendar towel, 1967, birds dec on turquoise ground, $5.

Doily
Crocheted, pink and cream, 7" sq..**5.00**
Embroidered, oval, shaped scalloped edge, scrolled design, 10" x 7"...**6.50**
Embroidered, round, holly dec, scalloped edge **12.00**
Dresser scarf, white cotton, flower basket embroidered in bright colors, white crochet edging, c1930, 24" x 38" **12.00**
Handkerchief
Oriental motif, orig silver tag "Hermann Irish Linen," 15" sq **17.50**
Purple petunias and green crocuses, orig label "Pure Linen, Hand Rolled," 12" sq.......................................**17.50**
Napkin, linen, 25" sq, set of 6........**20.00**
Pillowcases, pr
Cotton, embroidered multicolored flower-basket design, crochet edge, c1930.......................................**15.00**
Maderia, white cotton, flower silhouetted in cutwork, embroidered with satin stitch **18.00**
Tablecloth and napkins
Damask, light blue, some minor stains, 79-1/2" x 60", 4 napkins 15-1/2" sq **50.00**
Irish linen, 4 matching napkins, orig box, never used, 54" sq............**30.00**
Table runner
Blue and white weave, winter cabin scene at each end......................**5.00**

Place mats and matching napkins, cream colored linen, light gray floral embroidery, six each, $35.

Dark green tapestry type, rabbit in garden setting, with fancy script alphabet, solid dark green cotton back **12.00**
Tea towel, printed, unused mint condition
Calendar, 1972.............................**5.00**
Cats..**7.50**
State birds....................................**6.50**
Teapots, teacups and saucers **10.00**

❖ Little Golden Books

Little Golden Books, Three Little Kittens, c1950, wear to cover, $2.

Read me a story! From the time Simon & Schuster publisher the first Little Golden Book in 1942 until today, millions of stories have been read. Collectors have many fun titles to choose from, and everyone is sure to have a childhood favorite.

Reference: Steve Santi, *Collecting Little Golden Books*, 4th ed, Krause Publications, 2000.

Collectors' Club: Golden Book Club, 19626 Ricardo Ave, Hayward, CA 94541.

Bedtime Stories, 1942 ....**40.00**
Brownie Scouts, 1961 ....**15.00**
Bugs Bunny's Birthday, 1950...........**15.00**
A Day at the Zoo, 1950 ....**8.00**
Dinosaurs, 1959...............................**6.00**
Farmyard Friends, 1956....................**7.00**
Exploring Space, 1958 ....**7.00**
Five Little Firemen, 1948 ....**15.00**
Gunsmoke, 1958 ....**20.00**
Heidi, 1954......................................**8.00**
Little Golden Giant Golden Book Farm Stories, illus by Gustaf Tenggren and K & B Jackson, 1946, some damage to cover...**15.00**
Little Golden Book of Dogs, #131, Nita Jones, 1952...............................**20.00**
Little Golden Paper Dolls, #113, Hilda Milouche and Wilma Kane, 1951, paper dolls removed **15.00**

Little Lulu and Her Magic Tricks, #203, Kleenex wrapper, 1954 ....**28.00**
Mother Goose, #4, Phyllis Fraser, illus by Gertude Elliott, 1950 ....**15.00**
Noel, 1991 ....**2.00**
Rudolph the Red-Nosed Reindeer, 1958 ....**7.00**
Supercar, #492, Geroge Sherman, illus by Mel Craford............................**25.00**
Tarzan, 1964 ....**20.00**
Tootie, #21, Gertrude Crampton, illus by Tibor Gergely, 1950......................**10.00**
Walt Disney's Mother Goose, A Mickey Mouse Club Book, D51, 2nd ed., 1951 ....**14.00**

❖ Little Orphan Annie

Two Little Orphan Annie Ovaltine mugs with lids in center, four bisque figurines: two "Orphan Annie & Sandy", "Andy & Min," and "Uncle Walt & Skeezix", $200.

Little Orphan Annie has been the subject of comic strips, books, radio shows, and even a modern musical.

Big little book, *Little Orphan Annie in the Den of the Thieves*, 1948 ....**25.00**
Book, *Little Orphan Annie in Cosmic City*, 1933, spine missing, wear **15.00**
Doll, plastic, Knickerbocker, 1982 ...**15.00**
Glass, Sunday Funnies, 1976, 5-1/2" h **15.00**
Mug, ceramic, Annie holding an Ovaltine mug, The Wonder Co., Chicago, 3" h **100.00**

Plate, "Daddy Warbucks," Knowles, 1982, 8-1/2" dia.......................................**37.50**
Shaker with lid, plastic, Ovaltine....**80.00**
Toothbrush holder, bisque, "Orphan Annie and Sandy," mkd Japan, 4" h **145.00**
Toy stove, orig green paint, 1930s, 4-1/2" x 5"......................................**125.00**

❖ Little Red Riding Hood

This storybook character has been portrayed on all manner of items, the most popular of which are the pottery pieces sold by Hull. Some people feel that Hull manufactured the blanks and sent them to Royal China and Novelty Company in Chicago for decorating. Others think that Hull contracted with Royal China for both production and decoration. In any event, prices have escalated for these charming figures.

Reproduction Alert

Allspice jar.....................................**375.00**
Bank, standing **575.00**
Canister
   Cereal...**950.00**
   Coffee...**750.00**
   Sugar..**600.00**
   Tea..**750.00**
Cookie jar
   Gold stars, red shoes.................**300.00**
   Poinsettia trim............................**300.00**
Creamer, tab handle **275.00**
Flour canister **375.00**
Match holder, Little Red Riding Hood and Wolf, striker, Staffordshire **75.00**
Milk pitcher...................................**400.00**
Mustard, orig spoon......................**250.00**
Salt and pepper shakers, pr 3-1/4" h, incised "135889," gold trim **140.00**
   5-1/2" h......................................**150.00**
Sugar bowl, cov, crawling............**275.00**
Teapot, cov...................................**325.00**

❖ Little Tikes

When it comes to toys, many surges in collectibility begin as adults start buying back the items they remember from their childhoods. With that being the case, expect Little Likes items to continue to grow in popularity. Flea markets are excellent sources for these plastic playthings. Because the items were mass-produced, look for examples in prime condition.

Doll house, with family, furniture, horse and car, blue roof, 21" h, 28" w, 17" d **95.00**
Grandma's House, with grandma, girl and accessories **32.00**
Mansion dollhouse, 3-story, 32" h, 44" w, 18"d....................................**65.00**
Noah's Ark, with Noah, lion, giraffe and sheep **15.00**
Pirate, 4" h **4.00**
Roadway set, 68 pcs, with train, people, station, bridge and accessories ...**26.50**

Little Tikes Noah's Ark, orig animals, $15.

School bus, 9 figures **9.00**
Stable set, with swinging doors, fence, horses and accessories **73.00**

❖ Lladro Porcelain

Brothers José, Juan, and Vincente Lladro established this Spanish ceramics business in 1951. The company produces ceramic figurines and flowers. This segment of the collectibles market underwent a period of speculation several years ago. It remains to be seen whether the high prices realized at that time will remain in place when those items return to the marketplace.

Collectors' Club: Lladro Collectors Society, 1 Lladro Dr, Moonachie, NJ 07074.

August Moon, 1982......................**175.00**
Boy with lamps, 1989 ....**30.00**
Girl in nightgown, pigtails, puppy on lap, 7" h...**125.00**
Girl with lamb, 10-3/4" h **65.00**
New Beginning, 1999...................**200.00**
Painter, 1969.................................**40.00**
Pepita, sombrero **175.00**
Puppy, butterfly on tail, 4" h..........**250.00**
Riding the Waves, 1997 ....**300.00**
Sea Captain, 1969 ....**45.00**
Sewing Circle, 1986 ....**200.00**

Llardo Porcelain, pair of white doves, 4-1/2" high, $155.

Spanish Policeman 100.00
Today's Lesson, 2000 .... 250.00
Watching the Pigs, 1974.............. 150.00
Wedding Couple.......................... 45.00
Woman with umbrella................... 90.00

❖ Locks and Padlocks

Locks and padlocks have been around since the 1600s, so collectors have much to choose from. Many will specialize in a particular type of lock or will focus on products produced by a particular manufacturer.

Collectors' Club: American Lock Collectors Assoc, 36076 Grenada, Livonia, MI 48154.

Reproduction Alert

Ames Sword Co., Chicopee, Mass., bronze, no key............................ 150.00
Champion 6 Lever, brass, no key .. 28.00
Dragons, embossed steel 15.00
Good Luck, brass, 2-3/4" h........... 40.00
Hurd, brass case, 3-1/8" h 5.00
J.B. Miller Keyless Lock Co., combination 5.00
Junkunc Bros, combination, 2-5/8" h
.... 10.00
Leader, no key, some rust, 2-7/8" h .. 5.00
New Champion 6 Lever, brass 4.00
Railroad
  L&N, Yale, pink tumbler 25.00
  NC&StL, switch type, Yale, figure-8 back 30.00
  Union Pacific, switch type, brass lever
  .... 45.00
U S N 10.00
Wilson Bohannan, 3-1/4" h........... 15.00
Yale Junior, 2-3/4" h 32.00

❖ Loetz Glass

This pretty Austrian glass often features bright iridescent colors, threading, or interesting oil spot finishes. Base colors tend to be deep purple or dark green. Some examples can be found with metal ornamentation. Some pieces are signed, but not all. Beware of later added script signatures.

For additional listings, see *Warman's Antiques & Collectibles* and *Warman's Glass.*

Basket, brilliant green mottled on clear ground, irid blue and purple finish, 6-1/2" h, 5" w 100.00
Bowl, oyster white ground, diamond quilted design, applied deep black-green edge, highly irid surface, 10" dia

.... 120.00
Bowl and stand, irid deep ruby shading to irid pale green, 5 crimps, 3 chased metal studs, reticulated 4-ftd stand, 8" x 4" 400.00
Candlesticks, slender baluster form, raised circular foot, gold irid, 9-1/2" h, pr 300.00
Compote, bright orange int., deep black ext., white flaring circular rim, 3 ball feet, c1920, 5-1/4" h 310.00
Dish, 3 applied pulled-out handles, gold base, sgd in pontil with monogram "M" and "L," 8-1/2" dia 200.00
Inkwell, amethyst, sq, irid, web design, bronze mouth, 3-1/2" h.............. 125.00
Rose bowl, ruffled purple, irid raindrop dec, 6-1/2" dia 265.00
Vase
  3-3/4" h, bulbous stick, lustrous Papillon design, cobalt blue ground, internal rim nicks, possibly trimmed, unmarked................................ 180.00
  4-3/4" h, green, oilspot dec, crimped edge, large polished pontil, fake LCT signature 230.00
  7-1/4" h, green, oilspot dec, turned-down rim, large polished pontil
  .... 150.00
  8" h, 4-5/8" dia, amethyst, eggshell irid, bulbous bottom 235.00

❖ Lone Ranger

The Lone Ranger and his Indian pal Tonto rode into our lives on the silver screen, over the radio waves, and through the television. For those wishing to collect, there is a plethora of items from which to choose.

Periodical: *The Silver Bullet,* P.O. Box 553, Forks, WA 98331-0553.

Collectors' Club: Lone Ranger Fan Club, 19205 Seneca Ridge Ct, Gaithersburg, MD 20879-3135.

Badge, masked cowboy, sheriff and gun, metal, orig package, 1960s, mkd "Made in Japan" 8.00
Big little book, *Lone Ranger and the Black Shirt Highwayman,* 1939 .... 20.00
Book, *The Lone Ranger and the Warhorse,* 1951 .... 30.00
Cap gun, "The Lone Ranger, Hi-Yo Silver," trigger missing, 9-1/4" l..... 65.00
Cereal premium, National Defenders Club, Kix Cereal, danger warning siren, 7-1/8" l plastic tube, wooden mouthpiece, slight wear 195.00
Club button and card, Lone Ranger Safety Club, WFIL Radio and Philadelphia Daily News, 2-3/4" x 4-1/2" membership card, 1-1/4" celluloid pinback button, late 1930s 145.00
Coloring book, 1959 .... 50.00

Parker Brothers 1938 board game "The Lone Ranger Game, Hi-Yo Silver," original box, chalkware figure, copyright 1938, 4" h, $85.

Comic book, *Lone Ranger and Silver,* #369, Dell, 1951 .... 22.00
Game, Lone Ranger Game, Parker Brothers, 1938, faded cover, wear
.... 75.00
Hair brush, wooden 25.00
Halloween mask, 1960s 30.00
Holster, 2-gun set, no guns, 1976, Gabriel.. 45.00
Squirt gun, plastic, figural, hat broken
.... 50.00
Target game and gun, target 27" x 16"
.... 300.00
Toy, Lone Ranger Hi-Yo Silver, tin windup, Marx, 8" h 295.00

❖ Longaberger Baskets

Made in Dresden, Ohio, these baskets attract a lot of attention and have a huge following. Sold mostly through home shows, baskets have begun entering the secondary market. To achieve high prices, baskets must be in mint condition. Liners and protectors add to the value, as does a maker's signature.

All-American Candle, liner, protector, 1994 .... 50.00
All-American Sparkler, liner, protector, 2000 .... 60.00
All-Star Trio, liner, protector, 1993 .. 35.00
Booking basket
  Chives, liner, protector, 1992 .... 20.00
  Lavender, liner, protector, 1994.... 25.00
  Parsley, 2000.............................. 25.00
  Sweet Basil, liner, protector, 1993 15.00
Baking basket, Crisco American, napkin liner, protector, non-Longaberger wooden lid, 1993 .... 95.00
Bee basket, protector, 1996, 8-1/2" x 8-1/2" x 5" 95.00
Cake basket, swing handles, fabric liner, protector, 1993 .... 50.00
Easter basket, fabric liner, protector
  1993, large 45.00
  1993, orig J.W., sgd 70.00
  1996 .... 35.00

Longaberger Baskets, Sweet pea basket, orig liner, ceramic tie-in, $55.

Longaberger Baskets, Collector's Club Century basket, 2000, orig liner, protector, and box, $45.

Father's Day, address, liner, protector, card holder, orig cards **45.00**
Heartland, medium chore, protector, 1994 ....**45.00**
Hostess basket
   Appreciation, 1996 ....**35.00**
   Christmas Evergreen, fabric liner, protector, 1995.........................**90.00**

Sleigh bell, fabric liner, protector, wooden lid, 1994 ....**85.00**
Wildflower, protector, 1994...........**75.00**
Horizon of Hope, liner, protector
   1995 ....**50.00**
   1996 ....**40.00**
   1997 ....**35.00**
   1998, with tie-on, sgd by Judy, Carmen, and Mary Longaberger **85.00**
Key basket
   Medium, fabric liner, 1989............**25.00**
   Small, red accent weaving, protector, 1995..**20.00**
   Tall, 1993..................................**20.00**
Lilac basket, fabric liner, protector, tie-on, 1994 ....**40.00**
May series, liner, protector
   Tulip, tie-on and handle gripper, 1995 ....**165.00**
   Violet, 1990 ....**150.00**
Measuring, Holiday, protector, 1990, 13" **80.00**
Mother's Day, liner, protector, 1993...**30.00**
Petunia basket, fabric liner, protector, 1997 ....**35.00**
Pumpkin basket, swing handle, orange and black trim..............................**50.00**
Season's Greetings, fabric liner, 1992 ....**55.00**
Sentiments Basket, red trim, artist sgd and dated, 3" d, 4" sq **85.00**

❖ Lotton, Charles

A contemporary studio glass maker, Charles Lotton started out in a small studio at his home in Sauk Village, Illinois. His exquisite glass creations are sold to select retailers and at some antique shows. Several of the Lotton children are now part of the business. Expect to find pieces signed by Charles or by his son David.

Atomizer, selenium red...................**85.00**
Bottle, long neck, flared lip, mandarin red **250.00**
Bowl, Leaf & Vine, red ground, sgd "David Lotton"...........................**145.00**
Chalice, ftd, mandarin red............**160.00**
Paperweight, Dana Flora, pink flower, green leaves, sgd, 1982.............**150.00**
Rose bowl, cobalt ground, gold zipper-style pattern **150.00**
Vase, irid selenium red, blue luster draped web pattern, sgd, 8" h, 7" dia **795.00**

❖ Luggage

Interior decorators have been known to frequent flea markets looking for interesting old suitcases and other travel bags. What they have discovered is that luggage can serve as a wonderful storage container at

---

the same time that it is decorative.

Reference: Helenka Gulshan, *Vintage Luggage*, Phillip Wilson Publishers, 1998.

Child's, round, pink vinyl, black and white poodle dec, zipper closure, pink carrying loop, wear.....................**20.00**
Hatbox, Louis Vuitton, wood, leather, cloth and brass, painted with stripes and initials, minor damage, 18" x 18" x 9"...**995.00**
Suitcase
   Belber, gray, shows black porter, 6"h, 20-3/4" w, 16" d **35.00**
   Samsonite #4635, scorch marks, 6-1/2" h, 24" w, 17-1/4" d **40.00**
Train case, brown, light beige stripes, fitted int. with mirror, molded plastic handle, 1940s..............................**35.00**
Valise, dark brown leather, padded leather handles, some wear.......**150.00**

❖ Lunch Boxes

As a kid, it was always easier to remember your lunch if it was packed in a brightly colored lunch box. And, although the term conjures up images of a plastic container with cartoon characters on the sides, lunch boxes or kits have been around since the mid 1930s.

Periodical: *Paileontologist's Report*, P.O. Box 3255, Burbank, CA 91508.

Note: Prices include lunch box and thermos.

Plastic
   Beetlejuice, 1980, Thermos **14.00**
   Ewoks, 1983, Thermos **25.00**
   Hot Wheels, 1984, Thermos **70.00**
   Los Angeles Olympics, 1984, Thermos **25.00**
   Mr. T, 1984, Aladdin.....................**30.00**
   Rocketeer, 1990, Aladdin **15.00**
   Scooby Doo, 1984, Aladdin..........**60.00**
   Smurfs Fishing, 1984, Thermos...**20.00**
   Wayne Gretzky, 1980, Aladdin...**130.00**
Steel
   Astronaut, dome-top, 1960, King Seeley Thermos.....................**310.00**
   Batman, 1966, Aladdin..............**230.00**
   Beverly Hillbillies, 1963, Aladdin **260.00**
   Bionic Woman, with car, 1977......**55.00**
   Care Bear Cousins, 1985, Aladdin **25.00**
   Dr. Seuss, 1970, Aladdin............**200.00**
   Flipper, 1966, Thermos **235.00**
   Happy Days, 1977, Thermos........**60.00**
   Hogan's Heroes dome-top, 1966, Aladdin..................................**390.00**
   Indiana Jones, 1984, King Seeley Thermos **35.00**
   Jonathan Livingston Seagull, 1973, Aladdin....................................**75.00**

Pelé lunch box, soccer field background, green, $45.

Little House on the Prairie, 1978, King
Seeley Thermos.....................**115.00**
Muppet Babies, 1985, King Seeley
Thermos **17.00**
Pele, 1975, King Seeley Thermos
....**120.00**
Supercar, 1960s...........................**15.00**
U.S. Mail, dome-top, 1969, Aladdin
....**85.00**

Vinyl
Alvin and the Chipmunks, 1963, King
Seeley Thermos.....................**540.00**
Barbie Softy, 1988, King Seeley
Thermos **60.00**
Deputy Dawg, Deputy reading book in
front of hen house, Thermos, 1961
Terrytoons copyright **195.00**
Monkees, 1967, King Seeley Thermos
....**500.00**
Peanuts, 1965, Charles Schultz, King
Seeley Thermos.......................**35.00**

Sesame Street, 1977, Aladdin, orange
....**45.00**
Tinker Bell, Disney, 1969, Aladdin
....**350.00**
Yogi Bear, Aladdin, Hanna Barbera
copyright **250.00**

❖ Lu-Ray Dinnerware

This pretty pattern was introduced by Taylor,
Smith, & Taylor in the late 1930s, and
production continued until the early 1950s.
The pastel shades were made in Chatham
Gray, Pesian Cream, Sharon Pink, Surf
Green, and Windsor Blue.

Bowl
Fruit, green, 5-1/2" dia **10.00**
Vegetable, pink, 9" dia..................**22.50**

Lu-Ray Dinnerware, stack of dinner plates, each $10.

Calendar plate, 1951 ....**50.00**
Casserole, cov, pink.....................**155.00**
Creamer, yellow **22.50**
Cream soup, underplate, pink **135.00**
Cup, green, 2-1/2" h **8.00**
Eggcup, blue..................................**20.00**
Fruit bowl, 5-1/2" dia **2.00**
Gravy boat, attached undertray, yellow,
chip...**25.00**
Plate
Blue, 10" dia................................**28.00**
Yellow, 9" dia **10.00**
Platter, pink, 9-1/2" x 13-1/2" **22.50**
Salt shaker, yellow.........................**12.00**
Teapot, pink....................................**65.00**
Tumbler, juice, cream.....................**70.00**

*Lu-Ray Dinnerware, pink vegetable bowl, blue
platter, each $10.*

❖ MAD Collectibles

Look for Alfred E. Neuman's smug mug on any number of items, from games to timepieces.

Bookends, pr, Alfred E. Neuman, gold plastic, black relief **35.00**
Card game, Parker Brothers, 1980, boxed..**3.50**
Game, Screwball, The MAD MAD MAD Game, 1960, Transogram.............**75.00**
Magazine
MAD Magazine, December 1973...**3.00**
MAD Magazine, March 1976 ....**3.00**
Mad Star Wars Spectacular, 1996 .**2.00**
Model, Alfred E. Neuman, Aurora, 1965, unassembled, orig box, complete **145.00**
Paperback book, *The Bedside Mad* by William M. Gaines, 1959, 21st printing **1.50**
Skateboard, Alfred E. Neuman **120.00**

❖ Maddux of California

Maddux of California was founded in 1938 in Los Angeles. The company produced and distributed novelties, figurines, planters, lamps, and other decorative accessories until 1974.

Ashtray, triangular, gunmetal gray, #731, each side 10-1/2" l **20.00**
Bowl, off-white, squares and circles on rim, mkd "Maddux of Calif. 3093 USA," 5-1/2" dia **16.00**
Figurine
Bull, blue and white, ...**140.00**
Flamingo, 6-1/2" h......................**40.00**
Planter
Bird, spread wings, 9-1/8" l, 3" w **20.00**
Flamingo, mkd "Maddux of Calif, #445, copyright 1959, Made in USA," 6" h **165.00**
Low bowl, 6" h figural flamingo, head down, pink and green, 13" l, 6-1/4" w, 2" h....................................**195.00**
Pheasant, white, #527, 11-1/4" h, 7-1/4" w..**38.00**
Ribbed, brown, 6-1/2" l, 4-1/2" w ...**8.00**
Swan, taupe, 1959, 9-1/2" l, 3-3/4" w,

4" h **35.00**
Television lamp, swan, white, #828, 9" w, 12" h **50.00**
Vegetable bowl, cov, white and turquoise, mkd "Maddux of California, 3066B USA," 7-3/4" w, 4-1/2" h **25.00**

❖ Magazines

Magazine collecting offers a unique perspective on American life. By reading the old issues, you can get a clearer idea of what life was like, what products were being advertised, who was making news, etc. Some collectors buy magazines that they can take apart and sell as individual advertisements or articles.

Amateur Photographer's Weekly, June 6, 1919 ....**3.00**
American Heritage, 1958, Oct, Pocahontas cover...........................**6.00**
Better Homes and Gardens, 1942, Dec **6.00**
Car Toons, December 1969...............**3.00**
Child's Life, 1930 ....**4.00**
Delineator, 1904 ....**20.00**
Ellery Queen Mystery Magazine, 1950s **5.00**
Family Health, September, 1976, John Wayne cover and article..............**10.00**
Farm Life, 1923, Sept, cows in pasture cover..**6.00**
Fortune, March 1974 ....**3.00**
Good Housekeeping, 1965 ....**4.00**
Horticulture, 1959, Dec, poinsettia cover **3.50**
Iron Man, December 1962.................**7.50**
Jack & Jill, 1961.............................**10.00**
Life
1941, Dec 8, Douglas MacArthur...**9.00**
1961, July 7, Ike Down on the Farm cover **10.00**
1964, March 13, series on World War I **7.00**

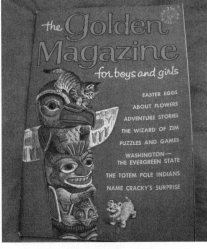

The Golden Magazine for Boys and Girls, April, 1963, $.50.

The Golden Magazine for Boys and Girls, April, 1965, $.50.

Look, Gary Cooper as Lou Gehrig cover **45.00**
McCall's, 1961, Christmas Make-It Ideas **5.00**
National Geographic
1901, September.......................**200.00**
1923, 12 issues...........................**55.00**
1958, 12 issues...........................**12.00**
Popular Sports, Fall, 1943 ....**4.00**
Quick Magazine, April 13, 1953, Lucille Ball cover,....................................**32.50**
Redbook, June, 1925.......................**5.00**
Seventeen Magazine, June, 1970, Susan Dey cover **45.00**
The Magazine Antiques, June, 1972 ....**22.75**
Time
1933, Dec 11, 1933, General Chiang **75.00**
1944, June 19, Eisenhower cover..**8.00**
Vogue, Dec 1986, Paloma Picasso on cover..**19.00**
Wee Wisdom, 1939, July **7.50**

Farm Journal, April, 1938, $1.

❖ Magic Collectibles

Abracadabra! Magic collectibles can be found at flea markets, but you have to be careful that they don't disappear before your eyes!

Book

Al Baker's Pet Secrets, Al Baker, illus, 1951, sgd by author................**125.00**
Elusive Magical Secrets, Will Goldston, illus, London, 1912, lock and key, cover badly worn **250.00**
Fifty TV Magic Tricks, Marshall Brodien, 1960s...**10.00**

Catalog, Magical Place of Conjuring Wonders, Price List of Mr. J. Bland's Best and Cheapest Conjuring Tricks, London, 1895 ....**450.00**

Lobby card

Carter Beats the Devil, Carter the Great, color litho, turbaned Carter playing cards with the devil, Cleveland, c1930 ....**400.00**
World's Super Magician, Harry Blackstone, RKO Orpheum Theatre, Davenport, 1950s **125.00**

Photograph, Harry Blackstone, bust portrait, inscribed by Blackstone, 1939, 8" x 10"...**75.00**

Poster

El Saba, 3-color, photo of acts, 1937, 24" x 36" **175.00**
The Great Virgil, full color, 1940s, 40" x 80" **375.00**
Virgil, 3-color, Cheating the Gallows, 1940s, 28" x 41" **250.00**

Program, B. F. Keith's Theatre Program, Boston, Dec 19, 1921, including a performance by Houdini, 10-1/2" x 4" **95.00**

Set, Master Magic Set, "A Sherms Creation," 1937, MIB **160.00**

Shaving mug, detailed hand painted image of man in suit holding top hat while flying through cloud filled moon lit sky, light wear to gold lettering and trim, 3-7/8" d, 3-7/8" h.................**275.00**

Toy, Mickey Magician Magic Show, Durham, 1976, NRFB **150.00**

Window card, Mind Reading Abilities of Joseph Dunninger, 1926 ....**75.00**

❖ Magic Lanterns

Here's one of the first types of home entertainment equipment. With a magic lantern, images could be projected and shared for all to see. These do occasionally surface at flea markets. Check to see if the original slides are included with the lantern.

Lantern

Brass, attached alcohol burner ..**295.00**
Delineascope, Spencer Lens Co., Buffalo, 350 slides, orig box ...**600.00**
Germany, orig kerosene burner, 17 glass slides, orig instructions and box **1,890.00**
Laterna Magica, orig box and slides **190.00**
Optimus, converted to electric **90.00**

Slide

Auction scene, Civil War era **15.00**
Bearded man...............................**6.00**
Berkeley Univ, 1920 ....**4.00**
Christmas scenes........................**10.00**
Holiday scenes **8.00**
Hunt scene, horses, Victorian **2.00**
Marching troops **6.00**
Travel scenes **7.50**
War scenes **8.50**

❖ Magnifying Glasses

Did you ever play detective and scour the house with a magnifying glass in your hand? Most of us did at one time or another. And, as baby boomers age, perhaps a few of us will be looking for them to help read that fine print in the local newspaper.

Brass and rosewood, matching letter opener, 10" l **50.00**
Cracker Jack prize **10.00**
Ivory handle, large round glass lens **125.00**
Jade handle, large oval glass lens .**35.00**
Plastic handle, rect lens................**10.00**
Porcelain handle, floral dec, large round glass lens **75.00**
Sterling silver, emb floral dec, large round glass lens..........................**95.00**
Wood handle, large round glass lens **27.50**

❖ Majolica

Majolica is defined as an opaque tin glazed pottery. Made for centuries, most majolica pieces consist of designs with naturalistic elements such as flowers, leaves, insects, and shells. Few majolica pieces are marked. Many pieces show wear, chips, repairs, or some sort of damage. Take any defects into consideration, remembering that a damaged piece will always bring a lower price than a perfect one.

Collectors' Club: Majolica International Society, 1275 First Ave, Suite 103, New York, NY 10021.

Reproduction Alert

Majolica, Left: cake plate, pink geranium dec, green leaves, 11-1/2" d, $95; plate, dog and deer dec, slight hairline, 8-1/4" d, $75.

For additional listings, see *Warman's Antiques & Collectible, Warman's American Pottery & Porcelain*, and *Warman's English & Continental Pottery & Porcelain.*

Butter dish, cov, insert, Shell and Seaweed, Etruscan, minor rim nicks to lid...**660.00**

Butter pat
Butterfly, Fielding, stains **220.00**
Grape, Clifton, rim nick **145.00**
Horseshoe, Wedgwood **300.00**

Cake stand, Pond Lily pattern, unmarked, 9" dia, 5-1/2" h, wear on rim and base **150.00**

Cheese keeper, Raspberry pattern, unmarked, pink raspberries, foliate, mottled green, gold, and brown ground, 11-3/4" dia, 9" h, hairline on lid, chips on base plate **425.00**

Creamer, Shell and Seaweed pattern, Griffin, Smith & Hill, 5-1/2" h, rim roughness **200.00**

Cup and saucer, Shell and Seaweed pattern, Griffin, Smith & Hill, 2-1/4" h cup, 6" d saucer, roughness on cup **100.00**

Deep dish, oval, Argenta Ware, molded floral designs, imp Wedgwood mark, star-form frame with imp mark, c1882, 11-7/8" l.....................................**420.00**

Dish, figural, boy pulling rect cart, 4 wheels, English, c1885, slight foot rim hairline, 9-3/8" l **750.00**

Jardiniere, Magnolia pattern, pink and yellow glazes, Wedgwood, England, imp mark, c1887, 12-1/4" h........**230.00**

Pitcher, Shell and Seaweed pattern, Griffin, Smith & Hill, 4-3/4" x 5-1/2" h, minor flake................................**400.00**

Plate
Pond Lily, unmarked, 8-1/4" dia, price for pr, one with small glaze flake **200.00**
Shell and Seaweed pattern, Griffin, Smith & Hill, 7" dia, set of 7, one with hairline, minor flakes **350.00**

Sugar, open, Shell and Seaweed pattern, Griffin, Smith & Hill, 3-1/2" h, rim roughness **125.00**

Majolica, leaf dish, Etruscan, brown, green, and yellow center, purple edge, $95.

Teapot, cov, Shell and Seaweed pattern, Griffin, Smith & Hill, crooked spout, 6" h, chips on lid int. **350.00**

Tea trivet, round, multicolor **155.00**

Tile, red rose center, shaded blue ground, mkd "Made in England, H & R Johnson, Ltd.," 6" sq.....................**45.00**

Umbrella stand, relief iris, streaked brown, green and ochre, 18-1/2" h, 9-3/4" dia **350.00**

Vase, applied duck, full-relief bamboo and water plants, cream glossy cylinder, gold trim, 11" h.............**270.00**

Waste bowl, 5" d, 3" h, Shell and Seaweed pattern, Griffin, Smith & Hill, in-the-making flake.....................**175.00**

❖ Marbles

Playing the game of marbles may not be as popular as it once was, but collectors are still able to find great examples at flea markets. Many collectors specialize in a particular type of marble, such as agates, clambroths, clay, or end-of-day examples. Contemporary studio glass blowers are creating some interesting specimens also.

Reference: Paul Baumann, *Collecting Antique Marbles*, 3rd ed, Krause Publications, 1999.

Collectors' Clubs: Marble Collectors Unlimited, P.O. Box 206, Northboro, MA 01532; Marble Collectors Soc of America, P.O. Box 222, Trumbull, CT 06611; National Marble Club of America, 440 Eaton Rd, Drexel Hill, PA 19026.

Akro Agate Co., machine-made
  Blue oxblood.................................**65.00**
  Helmet patch **2.50**
  Lemonade corkscrew **15.00**
  Slag **1.00**
Benningtons....................................**1.00**
Clays ....**.10**
End-of-day onionskin, 3/4" dia......**35.00**
Glazed painted china....................**10.00**
Lutz
  Banded, 1" dia.............................**250.00**

  Clear, 7/8" dia..............................**200.00**
  End-of-day onionskin, 3/4" dia ...**300.00**
  Ribbon, 1" dia..............................**800.00**
Marble King Co., machine-made
  Bumblebee **1.75**
  Cub scout.......................................**5.00**
  Wasp **5.00**
Mica, 1-1/2" dia **200.00**
Oxblood
  5/8" dia, limeade **140.00**
  3/4" dia **105.00**
Peltier Glass Co.
  Peerless patch...............................**5.00**
  Slag **20.00**
  Two-color, Rainbow, old type..........**1.50**
Sulphide
  Bear, 1-1/2" dia **95.00**
  Sheep, 1-3/4" dia........................**125.00**
Swirl
  Banded, 1" dia..............................**65.00**
  Divided core, 3/4" dia **18.00**
  Latticino core, 1-1/2" dia **75.00**
  Ribbon core, 3/4" dia...................**75.00**
  Solid core, 3/4" dia......................**25.00**
Unglazed painted china **5.00**

❖ Marx Toys

Louis Marx founded the Marx Toy Co. in 1921. He stressed high quality at the lowest possible price. Marx toys tend to be very colorful, and many can be found with their original box, which greatly enhances the price.

Reference: Michelle L. Smith, *Marx Toys Sampler: A History & Price Guide*, Krause Publications, 2000. Tom Heaton, *The Encyclopedia of Marx Action Figures*, Krause Publications, 1998.

Periodical: *Toy Shop*, 700 E State St, Iola, WI 54990.

Army car, battery operated.............**65.00**
Astronaut figure, white plastic, 5-1/2" h **10.00**
Bagatelle
  Combat, 1950s, NMIB..................**50.00**
  Pop A Puppet, 1950s, orig box..**25.00**
Falcon, plastic bubble top, black rubber tires **50.00**
Fireman ramp walker with hose.**110.00**
Gravel Gertie figure, white plastic, 2" h **12.00**
Jalopy pickup, litho tin wind-up, 7" l **60.00**
Hangar with one plane, 1940s **150.00**
Honeymoon Express, litho tin wind-up, orig box **350.00**
Midget Road Building Set, litho tin wind-up, 1939, 5-1/2" l tractor......**30.00**
Royal Bus Lines, litho tin wind-up, 1930s, 10-1/4" l **135.00**
Scottie Dog, tin wind-up, orig box **215.00**

Marx-Atomic Cape Canaveral Missile Base, slightly played-with condition, orig box, $125.

Stake bed truck, pressed steel, wooden wheels, 1936, 7" l........................**65.00**
Train set, #532, 4 cars, 10 pcs of track, box torn **200.00**
Tricky Taxi, tin windup, 4-1/2" l **85.00**
Zippo the climbing monkey, multicolored litho tinplate, pull-string mechanism, 10" l........................**60.00**

❖ Matchbox Toys

Matchbox toys were developed by Lesney in 1953. The name reflected the idea that there was a miniature toy packed in a box that resembled a matchbox. The toys were first exported to America from England in 1958 and were an instant success.

Collectors' Clubs: Matchbox Collectors Club, P.O. Box 977, Newfield, NJ 08344; Matchbox U.S.A., 62 Saw Mill Rd, Durham, CT 06422; The Matchbox International Collectors Assoc, P.O. Box 28072, Waterloo, Ontario, Canada N2L6J8.

Atlantic Trailer, tan body, six metal wheels, 1956 ....**15.00**
Big Tipper, MIB.............................**24.00**
Case Tractor Bulldozer, red body, yellow base, 1969 ....**5.00**
Dodge Daytona Turbo, 1994............**1.50**
Ford Customline Station Wagon, yellow body, 1957....................................**20.00**
Ford Escort.....................................**2.00**
Hillman Minx, 1958 ....**15.00**
International Ltd. Trailer, 1979 ....**2.00**
Jaguar...**50.00**
Jennings Cattle Truck, no back gate, 4-1/2" l..**30.00**

Matchbox Official Collector's Case, 48 vintage Matchbox vehicles, all in played-with condition.

Korean Airlines Airbus, Sky Busters, 1988, MOC, 4-1/4" l **35.00**
Land Rover Fire Truck, 1966 ....**10.00**
Maserati, 1958 ....**10.00**
Nissan 300 ZX Turbo, 1986.............**1.00**
Plymouth Grand Fury police car, white body, black detailing, 1979 ....**5.00**
Rig, 1993, NRFP **6.00**
Setra Coach, #12, 1970...................**5.00**
Train car, green, 1978.....................**28.00**
Wells Fargo truck, #69, 1978.........**24.00**

❖ Matchcovers

Matchcovers have been on the scene since the early 1900s, but any examples from before the 1930s are considered scarce.

Collectors' Clubs: Rathkamp Matchcover Society, 1359 Surrey Rd, Vandalia, OH 45377; American Matchcover Collecting Club, P.O. Box 18481, Asheville, NC 28814, www.matchcovers.com.

Benetz Inn, gold and maroon **1.25**
Bucks County Bank & Trust Co.......**2.50**
Champion Spark Plugs, 1930s **2.00**
Lion Match Co., N.Y. **32.00**
Dr. Pepper, 1930s **25.00**
Dutch Boy Paint, Ulrich Paint & Glass **3.00**
Enron..**1.00**
Howard Johnson.............................**7.00**
Military design, shows barracks and flagpole, World War II vintage, Universal Match Corp., San Francisco **6.00**
Nu-Grape **9.00**
Patriotic, World War II, "Buy More War Bonds, We Must Win, Our First Duty," cover only **3.00**
R & S Diner, 50th Anniv......................**50**
San Diego, souvenir type.................**4.00**

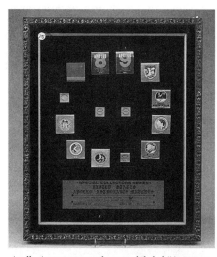

Apollo Astronauts matchcovers, labeled "Astronaut Specialties, Inc.," c1971, windowbox frame, 23 1/2" x 19 1/2", $25.

❖ Match Holders and Match Safes

Matches were precious commodities many years ago. Care had to be taken to keep matches dry, but still handy. Match holders can be found in almost every medium, ranging from table or mantle top containers to wall containers. Match safes, on the other hand, are small containers used to safely carry matches in a pocket. Many are figural and can be found in many metals. Some match safes will also have a striking surface.

Collectors' Club: International Match Safe Assoc, P.O. Box 791, Malaga, NJ 08328.

Agate, black, brown, white banded agate, brass trim, engine turned design, push button lid release, abrasive striker inside lid, 2-3/4" x 1" **75.00**
Art Nouveau, sterling silver, 2-1/2" x 1-1/8" **135.00**
Biscuit, figural, adv for Huntley & Palmer, orig paint on brass, 2-1/8" d.......**125.00**
BPOE, fob type, red, white, and blue enameled clock, by Simons Bros. & Co., sterling, 2-5/8" x 1-1/2" **275.00**
Channel Fleet at Blackpool, nickel plated, enameled lettering, 1-7/8" x 1-1/2" **75.00**
Cherry tree motif, by Wallace, silver plate, 2-1/2" x 1-1/2" **150.00**
Flask, figural, top nickel plated brass, bottom glass, 2-3/4" x 1-3/8"......**150.00**
Hunter Baltimore Rye, multicolored graphics, celluloid wrapped, by Whitehead & Hoag, 2-3/4" x 1-1/2" **135.00**
Leonardt & Co., pen points, book shape, gold lacquered tin, 2-1/8" x 2-5/8" x 3/4" **85.00**
Red Top Rye, orig white and red highlights, thermoplastic, 2-7/8" x 1-1/8" **115.00**
Stoneware, Whites Utica, salt-glazed Plain, tooled pattern, minor surface roughness, mold mark #1, 3" h **44.00**
"American Brew Co., Rochester, N.Y.," eagle inside badge, small impact fracture on rim, 2-3/4" h..........**220.00**

Bronze matchbox holder and ashtray, marked "Rock Island," base stamped "Reiffer & Husted Makers Chicago," 5" l, 3-1/4" h, $145.

"Westcott & Parker, Dealers in Coal & Wood, Utica, N.Y.," 3" h **275.00**
Wooden, barrel-form, brown and tan sponge-painted, 2-1/8" h...........**115.00**
World's Fair, 1904 Exposition, Palace of Manufacturing & Palace of Mines & Metallurgy, metal **65.00**

❖ McCoy

The J.W. McCoy Pottery was established in Roseville, Ohio, in 1899. Initially, the company produced stoneware and some art pottery. In 1911, three area potteries (Brush Pottery Company, J.W. McCoy Pottery Company, and Nelson McCoy Sanitary Stoneware Company) merged to create the Brush-McCoy Pottery Co. The new company produced all kinds of utilitarian ware, including cookie jars, garden items, and kitchenware.

References: Sharon and Bob Huxford, *Collector's Encyclopedia of Brush-McCoy Pottery*, Collector Books, 1996; ææ, *Collectors Encyclopedia of McCoy Pottery*, Collector Books, 1980 (1997 value update); Martha and Steve Sanford, *Sanfords' Guide to Brush-McCoy Pottery, Book 2*, Adelmore Press, 1996; ææ, *Sanfords' Guide to McCoy Pottery,* Adelmore Press, 1997.

Reproduction Alert

For additional listings see, *Warman's Antique & Collectibles*, *Warman's Americana & Collectibles*, and *Warman's American Pottery & Porcelain*.

Brush-McCoy

Bowl and flower frog, Onyx pattern in greens, blues, black and rust, bowl 7" dia..**127.50**
Flower frog
Duck form, 2" h, 4" l **175.00**
Jardiniere, swallows, brown and green matte glaze, 7" dia **85.00**
Jug, Onyx, brown, with stopper, 10" h **150.00**
Lantern, cat, patio type, 12-1/2" h **125.00**
Mug, Davy Crockett, cream and brown glaze...**65.00**
Pitcher
Keg shape, brown glaze..............**70.00**
Kolor Kraft, #331, dark-green glaze, 6-1/2" h **85.00**
Planter
Duck, yellow, 3" h........................**15.00**
Frog, green, 5-1/2" l **40.00**
House and Garden, green glaze, 5" h, 11" l...**50.00**
Peanut, matte glaze **50.00**
Vase

McCoy Pottery vase, swan emerging from swirled foliage, yellow glaze, mkd, $25.

Art Vellum Fawn, red glaze, 5" h, 6" dia **100.00**
Onyx, green.................................**70.00**
Ringed, #508, white, 8" h.............**40.00**
Wall pocket, dog and doghouse, chip, 8" h, 7" w **80.00**

McCoy

Ashtray, Seagram's VO, Imported Canadian Whiskey, black, gold letters **15.00**
Bank, Centennial Bear, sgd, numbered **110.00**
Basket, black and white, emb weave ext., double handle..............................**25.00**
Cookie jar
 Cottage......................................**120.00**
 Rooster......................................**225.00**
 Cornucopia, yellow **20.00**
Decanter, Apollo Mission **45.00**
Jardiniere, green **185.00**
Lamp, Cowboy Boots, replaced shade, 14" h..**150.00**
Mixing bowl, medium and large, tan, blue/pink/blue stripes **60.00**
Planter
 Bird, double cache pot **45.00**
 Duck, 1940s, 57.50
 Gondola, black, 11-1/2" l.............**45.00**
Spoon Rest, butterfly, dark green, 1953 ....**15.00**
Tankard, Buccaneer, green, 8-1/2" h **110.00**
Teapot, Grecian, 1958....................**30.00**
Vase
 Bird of Paradise, green, 8" h........**45.00**

Brown Onyx, 7" h **45.00**
Green Onyx, 7" h **45.00**
Lily, single flower, three leaves, 7-1/2" h **48.00**
Sailboat, pedestal, blue...............**50.00**
Wall pocket, trivet **50.00**
Wash bowl and pitcher, blue, medium size.....................................**95.00**

❖ McDonald's

It might be the sight of those golden arches, or it might be the growling of your tummy that convinces you to head to McDonald's. In any event, if you've got children with you when you go, you'll most certainly go home with a fast-food collectible.

Periodical: *Collecting Tips Newsletter*, P.O. Box 633, Joplin, MO 64802.

Collectors' Club: McDonald's Collectors Club, 255 New Lenox Rd, Lenox, MA 01240.

Ashtray, 3-1/2" x 6", metal, green, 1970 logo in yellow, street address in silver **18.00**
Bank, 1953 Ford delivery van, Ertl, 1/25 diecast, copyright 1996, orig box and key **25.00**
Building, Dept 56, orig box............**15.00**
Cup, Hamburglar, yellow plastic, copyright 1978...........................**12.00**
Doll, Hamburglar, played-with cond **15.00**
Employee cap, flattened service cap, blue cardboard headband with yellow arch symbol on each side, white mesh open crown, mid-1960s, unused, 12-1/2" x 11-1/2"..............................**15.00**
Glass Tumbler, 5-3/4" h, set with Ronald, Mayor McCheese, Grimace, Hamburglar, Big Mac, and Captain Cook, bright graphics, 1977 copyright, price for set of six.........................**20.00**

Here is an example of what one very clever crafter did with McDonald toys, the mirror sold for $125 at Shupp's Grove Flea Market in Pennsylvania.

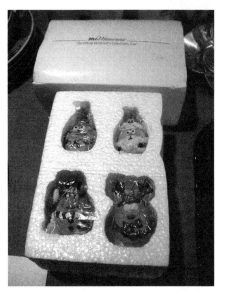

Christmas ornaments, McMemories, The Official McDonald's Club, four ornaments in orig wrapping, all with golden arches trademark, MIB, $24.

Happy Meal Prize, Genie and Building 5, from Aladdin and the King of Thieves, MIB...**4.00**
Lunch box, Sheriff of Cactus Canyon, Aladdin, 1982, orig thermos, orig hang tag **175.00**
Map, Ronald McDonald Map of the Moon, 1969 ....**7.50**
Mug, Garfield, c1987, set of 4.........**12.00**
Patch, cloth, Ronald McDonald, red, white, blue and yellow stitching......**2.00**
Puppet, hand, plastic, Ronald McDonald, c1977 ....**2.00**
Ruler, Ronald McDonald, cardboard, early 1970s...................................**12.00**
Salt and pepper shakers, pr
Snow globe, 101 Dalmatians, MIB .**25.00**
Teeny Beanie Babies, from 1998 series, Pinchers, Happy, Bongo, Mel, Inch and Twigs, set of 6 ....**50.00**
Valentines, strip of 6 different valentines, 1978 ....**3.00**

❖ McKee Glass

Founded by the McKee Brothers in 1853, this glassware company remained in production until 1961. Their output included pattern glass, depression-era glass, kitchenware, and household wares.

Batter bowl, jade-ite **45.00**
Bottoms up tumbler, light emerald, patent #77725, orig coaster **175.00**
Butter dish, cov, Seville Yellow, sgd on lid and base, flake on bottom, 1-lb size **80.00**
Creamer, custard **24.00**
Dresser tray, milk glass.................**35.00**
Egg cup, custard.............................**8.50**

McKee Glass, ashtray, clear, two cigarette holders on each side, $2.

Pitcher, Wild Rose and Bowknot, frosted, gilt dec...**75.00**

Range shakers, Roman Arch, custard, blue dots, salt, pepper, flour and sugar **135.00**

Refrigerator box, cov, white, 8" x 5" x 2-1/2" **95.00**

Salt and pepper shakers, pr

Sandwich server, center handle, Rock Crystal, red.................................**165.00**

Tom and Jerry set, punch bowl and 10 cups, red and green dec............**150.00**

Tumbler, Seville Yellow....................**17.50**

❖ Medals

One way to honor a hero was to present him with a medal. Many of these awards were passed down through families as treasured mementos. Other medals include those that are commemorative in nature.

Iron Cross, 2nd class, ribbon, Nazi issue, $35.

Commemorative

Dwight D. Eisenhower Inauguration, 1953, bronze, Medallic Art Co., 2-3/4" dia...**80.00**

Mercedes Benz, South American dealerships, shows airplane, auto and boat, mkd 1885-1913 ....**17.50**

Pan American Games, Sao Paulo, Brazil, 1963, bronze, in Portuguese, 2" dia.......................................**14.50**

Military

American Legion, 1-1/4" dia...........**8.00**

Bronze Star, engraved name, with ribbon bar and lapel pin, 1960s, in presentation case **40.00**

Connecticut Foot Guard, 1st Company of Foot Guards, 5 years of service **25.00**

U.S.S. Puget Sound, orig box **35.00**

Religious

St. Dominic Pray for Us, shows Virgin Mary with infant Jesus, mkd Italy, 1" x 5/8"..**2.00**

St. Jude Thaddeus Intercede for Us, Infant of Prague Shrine New Haven, Conn., brass-colored, 5/8" dia **2.00**

Sports, 1-1/8" dia

Basketball....................................**12.00**

Rowing **9.00**

Swimming.....................................**10.00**

Tennis...**8.50**

❖ Medical Items

Ouch! Collectors of medical items certainly aren't squeamish as they search flea markets for new items to add to their collections. Some folks concentrate on medical apparatus and instruments, while others focus on other aspects of the profession.

Bleeder, 3 folding blades, copper and brass, 18th C, 3-3/4" l **225.00**

Book

Allergy in Adults, Med Clinics of N. America, 1974 ....**7.50**

Anatomy & Physiology, C. Gray, and D. Dimber, 1931, 8th ed., 629 pgs **25.00**

Diseases of the Blood, Roy R. Kracke, 1941, 2nd ed., 54 color plates, 46 illus, 692 pgs............................**25.00**

Box, Red Cross Sterilized Gauze, Johnson & Johnson **8.00**

Dental Sterilizer, 11-3/4" x 7" x 8", paneled mahogany case, nickeled brass fittings, compartment with alcohol burner, steam boiler fitted in large zinc copper cavity, 3 removable wood slat racks, 19th C.............**230.00**

Doctor's bag, leather **33.00**

Letterhead, Reinle-Salmon Co., maker of druggist fixtures, 1912...................**3.50**

Mortar and pestle

Brass **70.00**

Wooden **200.00**

Mug, plastic, purple, adv **1.25**

Order form, mentions opium, Crawford's Drug Store, Atlantic City, N.J. 8-1/2" x 10-1/2"..**20.00**

Paperweight, oversized aspirin, orig box **10.00**

Pinback button

Dental Manufacturers Club, red on white celluloid, oval, early 1900s **12.00**

Luden Cough Drops, black and white celluloid, center package of Luden's Menthol Cough Drops, two gold fabric 1-1/2" unmarked ribbons on back **2.00**

Tooth extractor, bronze, 4-1/2" l .**130.00**

❖ Meissen

Meissen is a fine porcelain with a long and interesting history. Briefly, the original factory dates to 1710 in Saxony, Germany. Over the years, decorating techniques were developed that led to the creation of beautiful pieces that are eagerly sought by collectors today. Each period of the Meissen story features different styles, colors, and influences. The factory is still in business today.

Many marks have been used by Meissen over the years. Learning to read those marks and ascertain the time period they represent will enhance a collector's knowledge of this lovely porcelain.

Reproduction Alert

For additional listings and background information, see *Warman's English & Continental Pottery & Porcelain* and *Warman's Antiques & Collectibles.*

Ashtray, Onion pattern, blue crossed swords mark, 5" dia.....................**80.00**

Bread and butter plate, Onion pattern, 6-1/2" dia.....................................**75.00**

Cup and saucer, flower filled basket dec **90.00**

Dessert dish, painted red rose and foliage center, bouquets at corners, c1770 ....**225.00**

Figure, young man and woman gathering eggs from under tree, white glaze, blue crossed swords mark, late 19th C **275.00**

Hot plate, Onion pattern, handles.**125.00**

Teabowl and saucer, 3 purple flowers, green leaves, early 19th C, chip **325.00**

Urn, white, gilt trim, 2 delicate snake-form handles, pr **500.00**

Tray, 17-3/8" l, oval, enameled floral sprays, gilt trim, 20th C **400.00**

Vase, floral dec, 20th C, 3" h...........**80.00**
Vegetable dish, cov, Onion pattern, 10" sq **150.00**

❖ Melmac

Melmac is a trade name associated with thermoset plastic dinnerware made by American Cyanamid. Although first introduced for commercial use, Melmac became popular with housewives in the 1950s. Collectors today search for pieces in very good condition with interesting colors and shapes.

Collectors' Club: Melmac Collectors Club, 6802 Glenkirk Rd, Baltimore, MD 21239.

Child's set, bunny dec, Oneida, used, plate 8-1/4" dia, cereal bowl 6-1/2" dia, dessert bowl 4-3/4" dia **8.00**
Creamer and sugar, blue, mkd "Made in Canada," 3" h...............................**17.50**
Magazine advertisement, Boonton Ware, Melmac Dishes Guaranteed Against Breakage, 8-1/2" x 11"......**2.00**
Platter, pink, N416, 13-3/4" x 9-3/4" .**8.00**

Melmac plate, light yellow, scalloped corners, square, $2.

Set
Avocado fruit bowls, bread plates and cups, white saucers, service for 8 ....**20.00**
Shasta Daisy, dinner plates, salad plates, cereal bowls, cups and saucers, Texas Ware, service for 6.............**60.00**
Wall pocket, sq gray saucer as backplate, green cup as pocket, mkd "Maherware, 2, Made in USA" **10.00**

★ Menus

What's for lunch? While browsing at flea markets, finding vintage menus can make you even hungrier. Look for ones with interesting graphics and from restaurants in your home town. Many collectors enjoy finding menus that cross over into their other collections, such as Coca-Cola.

Air France, Buenos Aires to Paris, 1955 ....**25.00**

Banquet To The Western Michigan Press, Reed City, 1883, fold-over, Robison Engraving Co., 1882, printed, black and white **15.00**
Columbian Line, Get Together Dinner, July 10, 1936................................**18.00**
Denny's, plastic coated, 1990s **4.00**
El Mirador Hotel, Palm Springs, night scene of hotel, color photo litho, dinner menu on back, 1954, 8" x 10"......**32.00**
Elvis, from Sahara Tahoe, 1972......**72.00**
Hotel Oakland, luncheon menu, 1929, honoring Japanese hotel men's delegation, front gold engraved hotel, tipped in real photo of Wild Ducks at Lakeside Park, 5" x 8" **20.00**
Hotel Vancouver, Canadian Pacific Railroad Alaskan service dinner menu, 9-1/2" x 6-3/4" **22.00**
Illinois Room, St. Clair Hotel, Indian motif, 9" x 12" **45.00**

Menu, The Order of the Day, Hull's Beer-Ale, Hull Brewing Co., New Haven, CT, 8-1/4" x 11", $5.

Japan Airlines, fan shaped, 1950s, opens to 11" x 7-1/4"....................**75.00**
Los Angeles Turf Club, insert for San Francisco Chronicle Harry B. Smith 6" Annual Santa Anita Handicap Tour Luncheon, March 1, 1941, engraving of Turf Club on front, 5 pgs, 7" x 10" **27.50**
Pendavis House, Mineral Point, WI, 1950s **22.00**
7-Up, New York World's Fair, 1964 ..**15.00**
SS City of Omaha, Christmas, 1940 ....**10.00**
Swiss Air, 1966, 5-pgs **25.00**
Trainers, Quakertown, PA, black printing on green cover, red and black printing on white inside, attached children's menu and specials **40.00**
United States Hotel, Saratoga Springs,

NY, 1892, 7" x 10" **15.00**
U.S. Forces in Thailand, Thanksgiving, 1963, 4 pgs **12.00**

❖ Metlox Pottery

After its formation in 1927, Metlox manufactured outdoor ceramic signs. During the Depression, the company reorganized and began producing dinnerware. During World War II, the factory was again retooled so that workers could make machine parts and parts for B-25 bombers. After the war, dinnerware production resumed along with the creation of some art ware. The factory finally closed in 1989.

For additional listings and history, see *Warman's Americana & Collectibles* and *Warman's American Pottery & Porcelain*.

Bowl
Ivy, 5-1/2" dia.............................**20.00**
Sculptured Grape, 8-1/2" dia........**16.00**
Bread tray, Poppytrail **35.00**

Metlox Pottery, milk pitcher in foreground, $30; canisters on right, $115, all Poppytrail pattern, mkd on bases.

Canisters, cov, Poppytrail, tea, sugar, flour, cookies **225.00**
Casserole, cov, Sculptured Grape, 1-qt **50.00**
Cereal bowl, Sculptured Daisy **12.00**
Chop plate
Cookie jar, Clown **200.00**
Creamer, Poppytrail.........................**40.00**
Cup and saucer
Sculptured Grape **10.00**
Dinner plate, Della Robbia **8.00**
Dinner service, California Ivy, 47-pc set **330.00**
Figure, Dobbin horse and buggy, repaired leg **120.00**
Gravy, attached underplate, Sculptured Grape **27.50**
Milk pitcher, Poppytrail, shaped green handle **50.00**
Miniature, White House, orig sticker

....**175.00**
Mustard jar, Red Rooster **48.00**
Place setting, Liberty Blue, 5 pcs ..**35.00**
Platter, Provincial Rose...................**70.00**
Salad bowl, California Strawberry ..**55.00**
Salad plate, Sculptured Grape, 7-1/2" dia
....**8.00**
Salt and pepper shakers, Sammy Seal,
pr **75.00**
Soup bowl, Camellia California **17.50**
Sugar, cov, Sculptured Grape.........**22.00**
Vegetable bowl, cov, Poppytrail....**100.00**
Vegetable bowl, divided, Poppytrail**40.00**

❖ Mettlach

Most collectors think of steins when they hear the name "Mettlach," but this German company also produced very fine pottery, including plates, plaques, bowls, and teapots. One of their hallmarks is underglaze printing on earthenware, achieved by using transfers from copper plates. Relief decorations, etched decorations, and cameos were also used. Individual pieces of Mettlach are well marked.

Periodical: *Beer stein Journal*, P.O. Box 8807, Coral Springs, FL 33075.

Collectors' Clubs: Stein Collectors International, 281 Shore Dr, Burr Ridge, IL 60521; Sun Steiners, P.O. Box 11782, Fort Lauderdale, FL 33339.

Coaster, drinking scene, print under glaze, mkd "Mettlach, Villeroy & Boch," 4-7/8" dia.....................................**150.00**
Loving Cup, 7-3/8" w, 6-3/4" h, three handles, musicians dec..............**185.00**
Plaque
#1044-542, portrait of man, blue delft dec, 12" dia............................**125.00**
#1108, incised castle, gilt rim, c1902, 17" dia...................................**230.00**
Stein
#1027, relief, face and floral dec, beige, rust and green, inlaid lid, 1/2-liter
....**215.00**
#2057, etched, festive dancing scene, inlaid lid, 1/2-liter **325.00**
#2755, cameo and etched, 3 scenes of people, Art Nouveau design between scenes, inlaid lid, 1/4-liter.......**560.00**
#2833B, 1/2-liter.........................**350.00**
Teapot, 3-1/2" h, #3051, etched, Art Deco repeating design, lid missing
....**95.00**
Vase, #1808, stoneware, incised foliage dec, 10" h, pr.............................**230.00**

❖ Microscopes

Microscopes are included in the field of scientific instrument collecting, a category that has really taken off recently. If

considering a purchase of a microscope, check to see that all the necessary parts are included. And remember, value is enhanced by original documentation, boxes, slides, etc.

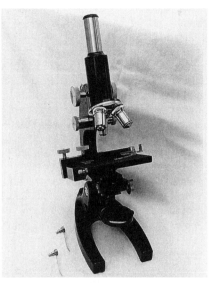

Bausch & Lomb microscope, three-lens turret, mechanical stage, orig box, $295.

Collectors' Club: Maryland Microscopical Society, 8261 Polk St, McLean VA 22102.

Booklet, Gilbert microscope, 1960, 75 pgs **5.00**
Catalog, Biological and Chemical Supplies and Apparatus, 1930s, microscope cover, 24 pgs **24.00**
Microscope
Gilbert, toy, 1956, orig box **59.00**
New Gem Microscope, Bausch & Lomb Optical Co, Rochester, 75-300x. 7-1/4" h **80.00**
Regency, 100-400x, dovetailed wooden box, 7-7/8" h **75.00**
Spencer, mkd "CENCO/Spencer/USA," double optical turret, orig case, 11"
....**175.00**
Unknown maker, compound monocular, 3-1/2" d stage with condenser and diaphragm, double mirror on calibrated rotating arm, japanned and lacquered brass, case, mkd "3373," c1885, 12" h
....**575.00**

❖ Militaria

Throughout history, men have marched off to war. Those who return often bring mementoes of their travels. Years later these treasures end up at flea markets where eager collectors find them.

References: Many good reference books are available that cover all periods of military history.

Military uniform jacket, woman's, rank and service corp patches, medium, $40.

Periodicals: *Men at Arms*, 222 W Exchange St, Providence, RI 02903; *Militaria Magazine*, P.O. Box 995, Southbury, CT 06488; *Military Collector Magazine*, P.O. Box 245, Lyon Station, PA 19536; *Military Collector News*, P.O. Box 702073, Tulsa, OK 74170; *Military Images*, RD1 Box 99A, Henryville, PA 18332; *Military Trader*, P.O. Box 1050, Dubuque, IA 52004; *North South Trader's Civil War*, PO Drawer 631, Orange, VA 22960; *Wildcat Collectors Journal*, 15158 NE 6th Ave, Miami, FL 33162; *WWII Military Journal*, P.O. Box 28906, San Diego, CA 92198.

Collectors' Clubs: American Society of Military Insignia Collectors, 526 Lafayette Ave, Palmerton, PA 18071; Assoc of American Military Uniform Collectors, P.O. Box 1876, Elyria, OH 44036; Company of Military Historians, North Main St, Westbrook, CT, 06498; Imperial German Military Collectors Assoc, 82 Atlantic St, Keyport, NJ 07735; Militaria Collectors Society, 137 S Almar Dr, Ft Lauderdale, FL 33334; Orders and Medals Society of America, P.O. Box 484, Glassboro, NJ 08028.

Reproduction Alert

For additional listings, see *Warman's Antiques & Collectibles* and specific topics in this edition.

Autograph Album, GAR, 4-1/2" x 7", most pages signed at Milwaukee Reunion, Aug 29, 1889, maroon velvet cover...**110.00**
Book
Regimental History of the 316 Infantry
....**25.00**
Cartridge Box, leather, white cloth strap, very worn, missing plate **70.00**
Fife, 15-1/2" l, sgd "Firth, Pond & Co.," Broadway, NY," large "C" below signature, brass ends, nickel silver and

pewter mouth piece....................**175.00**
Handkerchief, machine-stitched emblem of Strategic Air Command............**22.00**
Hat Badge, infantry, brass, crossed krag rifles, 2" l **55.00**
Map, Pacific Theater, Esso premium
....**18.00**
Newspaper, *The Wardial*, April 14, 1945, military base newspaper for Ward Island, Corpus Christie, Texas, 16 pgs
....**15.00**
Paperweight, West Point, sulphide, marching cadets holding 2 flags, 3" dia
....**35.00**
Pennant, felt
   Admiral Farragut Academy, eagle, buoy with anchor and cadet, 28" l.....**25.00**
   Camp Pickett, Va., red background with eagle, 25" l...............................**25.00**
Photograph, black and white, 5" x 7", slightly faded
   U.S.S. Arizona **15.00**
   U.S.S. Los Angeles **12.50**
Pin, Naval officer insignia, eagle over shield and pair of anchors, sterling silver with gold wash, 1" dia.........**32.00**
Poster, World War I, "Join the Red Cross," Howard Chandler Christy, creases, edge wear 25-1/2" x 19-1/2"
....**250.00**
Shoes, leather, pegged sole, brass buckle, stitching reads "H.S. Shawner, CT" **150.00**
Tie tack, R.C.A.F. Reserves, 3/4" sq
....**26.00**
Token, U.S. Marine Corp, Third Battalion, brass...**10.00**
Wings, Army Air Force, AWS, 1-1/8" l
....**28.00**

❖ Milk Bottles

Before the advent of paper and plastic containers, milk was sold in glass bottles. Today's flea markets often contain great examples of different sizes and designs. Keep your eyes open for interesting slogans.

Reference: John Tutton, *Udderly Beautiful*, self-published, no date.

Periodical: *The Udder Collectibles*, HC73 Box 1, Smithville Flats, NY 13841.

Collectors' Club: National Assoc of Milk Bottle Collectors, 4 Ox Bow Rd, Westport, CT 06880.

Bonfoey's Dairy, Three Rivers, Mich., pyro label, 1/2-gal........................**15.00**
Borden, in script above Elsie, quart, squat, red pyro **18.00**
Capital Dairy, North Dartmouth, MA, quart, round, clear, emb capital dome emb on front slug plate **15.00**

Country Delights, 2-tone green pyro label, 1-gal....................................**32.00**
Dairylea, quart, square, red, Miss Dairylea, picture of fruit and vegetables
....**18.00**
Empire State Dairy Co, Brooklyn, half pint, round, emb, state seal in frame
....**10.00**
Farm Fresh, Grade A Dairy Products, Chester, Ill., orange pyro label, 1/2-pt
....**5.00**
Foremost Dairy, embossed, 1-qt ...**28.00**
Handy's Putnam Gold Dairy Products, Greencastle, Ind., red pyro label, 1-qt
....**15.00**
Hoods, quart, round, cow in framed log, red pyro **12.00**
Newport Dairy, quart, squat, round, emb
....**10.00**
Palmerton Sanitary Dairy, Palmerton, PA, quart, sq, emb, cream top **12.00**
Sanitary Dairy, Chisholm, Maine, 1/2-pt
....**5.00**
Sheffield Farms, Slawson Decker, NY, quart, logo, round, emb...................**8.00**
University of Connecticut, Storrs, CT, one half pint, round, clear, emb name
....**8.00**
White Springs Farm Dairy, Geneva, quart, orange pyro........................**12.00**

❖ Milk Glass

Milk glass is an opaque white-bodied glass that was produced by many manufacturers. Early in the 20th century it was a popular choice for tableware and accessories. By the early 1960s, preferences had cycled again, and milk glass was fashionable once more.

References: Several older reference books are wonderful tools for determining makers and pattern names.

Collectors' Club: National Milk Glass Collectors Society, 46 Almond Dr, Hershey, PA 17033.

Milk Glass plates, heart lacy border, price for pr, $7.50.

Animal covered dish
   Dolphin **145.00**
   Duck, white................................**145.00**
   Fish, flat, white.........................**120.00**
   Hen, basketweave base **175.00**
   Kitten, ribbed base, Westmoreland
....**130.00**
   Lion, reclining, white, criss-cross base
....**135.00**
   Robin on nest, medium blue **165.00**
   Setter dog, blue.........................**195.00**
Bowl, Daisy, all-over leaves and flower dec, open scalloped edge, 8-1/4" dia
....**85.00**
Candy container, cat in boot, goofus dec **80.00**
Child's mug
   Elephant handle **60.00**
   Fish dec......................................**40.00**
Creamer and sugar, Trumpet Vine, fire-painted dec, sgd "SV"................**135.00**
Ink blotter, Scottie, chips to ear **65.00**
Match safe, smiling boy **170.00**
Plate
   Donkey **50.00**
   Easter, bunny, basket of eggs **35.00**
   Easter, gold hen and peeps, gold border, some orig paint.............**30.00**
   Fort Necessity, Indian chief, some orig paint, edge chip **40.00**
Soap dish, cov, orig drainer, Wheat
....**125.00**
Spooner, Monkey, scalloped rim...**140.00**
Sugar Shaker, Forget-me-not, green, orig top **150.00**
Syrup, plain, hp red flowers, damage to pewter top **165.00**
Tumbler, Royal Oak, fire-painted dec, green band **50.00**

❖ Miniature Bottles

Flea markets are great places to find these clever bottles. Often they are samples, or they were designed to provide single servings for restaurant or commercial use.

Acme Beer, stubby, decal **6.50**
Budweiser, stubby, paper label.......**17.50**
Carstairs, lipstick shaped, 1950s......**8.00**
Fort Pitt Beer, stubby **3.00**
Gold Bond Beer **20.00**
Hamms Preferred...........................**5.00**
J & B Scotch **10.00**
Maple Farms, Vt., maple syrup.........**1.00**
Old Dutch, stubby **24.00**
Tavern Pale **12.00**

❖ Miniatures

The world of tiny objects is truly a fascinating one. Some collectors are attracted to the craftsmanship shown by these tiny treasures, while others are more interested in finding examples to display. Keep scale in mind when purchasing miniatures for use in a doll house.

Periodicals: *Doll Castle News*, P.O. Box 247, Washington, NJ 07882; *Miniature Collector*, Scott Publications, 30595 Eight Mile Rd, Livonia, MI 48152; *Nutshell News*, 21027 Crossroads Circle, P.O. Box 1612, Waukesha, WI 53187.

Collectors' Clubs: International Guild Miniature Artisans, P.O. Box 71, Bridgeport, NY 18080; National Association of Miniature Enthusiasts, 2621 Anaheim, CA 92804-3883.

Armoire, tin litho, purple and black **35.00**
Bed, 4-poster, mahogany stain, hand-made **40.00**
Bench, wood, rush seat **25.00**
Bird cage, brass, bird, stand, 7" h ..**65.00**
Blanket chest, 6-board construction, old worn paint dec..........................**200.00**
Chair, golden oak, center splat, upholstered seat, German, c1875, pr **75.00**
Christmas tree, decorated..............**50.00**
Clock, metal **40.00**
Decanter, 2 matching tumblers, Venetian, c1920 ....**35.00**
Desk, Chippendale style, slant front, working drawers **65.00**
Fireplace, Britannia metal fretwork, draped mantel, carved grate **65.00**
Living room set, Empire style, sofa, fainting couch, two chairs, 4pcs .**350.00**
Piano, grand, wood, 8 keys, 5" h **35.00**
Sewing Table, golden oak, drawer, c1880 ....**100.00**
Sofa, porcelain and metal **35.00**
Stove, Royal, complete **120.00**
Table, tin, painted brown, white top, floral design...**35.00**
Umbrella stand, brass, ormolu, emb palm fronds, sq..............................**65.00**
Urn, silver, handled, ornate **100.00**
Vanity, Biedermeier........................**90.00**
Wash bowl and pitcher, cobalt glass, minor chips.................................**275.00**

❖ Mirrors

"Mirror, mirror, on the wall ..." Mirrors are something we all depend on, and many of us use them as decorative accents in our homes and offices. Flea markets are great sources for interesting examples in almost every decorating style.

Hand mirror
   Bakelite with rhinestones, butterfly design **40.00**
   Celluloid, Art Deco design **37.00**
   Celluloid, plain, beveled glass......**23.00**
Hanging
   Chippendale style, mahogany, molded

frame, gilt phoenix, loss to crest **300.00**
   Curly maple, frame and liner, 20th C, 17-1/2" h, 27-1/2" w **220.00**
   Gold leaf, carved florals and scrolls, beveled mirror........................**300.00**
   Mahogany veneer frame, rect, some loss to silvering **200.00**
   Reverse painted scene over beveled mirror, architectural pediment frame **250.00**
   Tramp art frame, dark finish over varnish, stepped sawtooth border, stacked geometric designs, 15" h, 17-1/2" w.............................**275.00**
Pocket mirror, advertising
   Bee Hive Overalls Best Maid, 1-3/4" w, 2-3/4" h, made by Whitehead & Hoag, Newark, NJ, c1910, bright image of girl modeling blue overalls, mirror broken **260.00**
   Berry Bros. Varnishes, 2-3/4" l, 1-3/4" h, little boy in overalls, straw hat, pulling dog in wagon..............**140.00**

Mennen's Violet Talcum Toilet Powder mirror, picture of Mennen, purple violets, oval, not orig box, $95.

   Lava Soap, celluloid centered by image of gray soap bar, opened container box, yellow ground, early 1900s **35.00**
   Mascot Tobacco, multicolored portrait of dog, red rim, white lettering..**85.00**
   National Life Insurance, pink and white celluloid centered by replica of policy certificate, inscriptions for representatives located in Kansas City **25.00**
   Tydol Veedol Petroleum Products, celluloid, birthstones, 2" d **80.00**
Shaving mirror, mahogany veneer on pine, line inlay, bowfront case, turned feet, 2 drawers, adjustable mirror with turned posts, repairs, 23-1/2" h, 18-1/2" w, 7-1/2" d **145.00**
Vanity mirror, three sections, folding, delicate engraving at top............**150.00**

❖ Model Kits

Plastic scale models were introduced in England in the mid 1930s. The popularity of these kits reached a high in the 1960s, but the oil crisis of the 1970s caused a setback in the industry. Understand that the character the model is based on has more to do with determining value than does the kit itself.

Model Kits, '32 Ford Vicky, AMT, Matchbox, unassembled, orig box, $12.

Reference: Bill Coulter, *Stock Car Model Kit Encyclopedia and Price Guide*, Krause Publications, 1999.

Collectors' Club: International Figure Kit Club, P.O. Box 201, Sharon Center, OH, 44274; Kit Collectors International, P.O. Box 38, Stanton, CA 90680.

Apollo spacecraft, Revell, unbuilt ..**58.00**
Corvette, 1989, AMT Ertl, MIB **10.00**
Cutty Sark, Scientific Model Airplane Co., carved wood hull, cast metal fittings **65.00**
Jet fighter, Guillows, unbuilt **10.00**
Klingon Battle Cruiser, Star Trek: The Next Generation, AMT Ertl, MIB ..**35.00**
Mercedes-Benz 500K roadster, 1935, paperboard, Wrebbit, MIB **30.00**
Metaluna Mutant, Jumbo Series Model #20, built, 15" h **125.00**
Model T, 1909, Gabriel, unbuilt.......**45.00**
Robin, The Boy Wonder, Revell, 1999 rerelease, MIB............................**15.00**
Sense of Taste, Lindbergh Line, 1973, instructions, unbuilt **35.00**

Model Kits, VW Pickup with ATW, Revell, snap-together kit, 1:32 scale, unassembled, orig box, $15.

Star Trek Vulcan Shuttle, AMT/Ertl, 1984, sealed..................................**55.00**
U.S.S. Constitution, Revell, 1966, unbuilt, some damage to orig box **80.00**
Visible Man, Revell, dated 1977, unbuilt **15.00**
Vostol, first Russian spacecraft, Revell, unbuilt..............................**70.00**
Wells Fargo Stagecoach, Marx, 1953, MIB...**295.00**

❖ Monroe, Marilyn

Marilyn Monroe was a model turned actress who captured the hearts of moviegoers in the 1950s. Her tragic life has been the subject of numerous books, magazine articles, television shows, etc.

Reference: Clark Kidder, *Marilyn Monroe Cover to Cover 2nd edition*, Krause Publications, 2003; Clark Kidder, Marilyn Memorabilia, Krause Publications, 2002.

Collectors' Club: All About Marilyn, P.O. Box 291176, Los Angeles, CA 90029.

Book, *Strange Death of Marilyn Monroe*, 1964 ....**95.00**
Calendar, 1974, orig envelope........**30.00**
Christmas Ornament
　Carlton, 1998, MIB **13.00**
　Hallmark, 1999, 3rd in series, orig box **25.00**
Commemorative coin, Marilyn on one side, Joe DiMaggio on other, 1-1/2" dia **10.00**
Cookie jar **50.00**
Doll, emerald evening gown, Collector's Series, MIB.................................**25.00**
Figurine, Royal Orleans Porcelain ..**40.00**
Magazine
　Look, July 5, 1960 ....**25.00**
　Tempo, July 1953 ....**10.00**
　Stare Magazine, June 1953 ....**20.00**
Plate, Lady in Red, Up Close and Personal series, 3rd issue, Bradford Exchange, 8-1/8" dia....................**35.00**

❖ Monsters

Perhaps it was those Saturday afternoon matinees, or those science-fiction books we read as kids that caused so many collectors to seek out monster related memorabilia. And, those lucky folks are finding plenty of their favorite demons at flea markets.

Reference: Dana Cain, *Collecting Monsters of Film and TV*, Krause Publications, 1997; John Marshall, *Collecting Monster Toys*, Schiffer Publishing, 1999.

Periodical: *Toy Shop*, 700 E State St, Iola, WI 54990.

Beer Bottle, Elvira, Night Brew, 1996 ....**5.00**

Book, *Frankenstein Or The Modern Promethus,* Mary W. Shelley, illus by Nino Carbe, Halycon House, dj clipped **15.00**
Figure, Dracula, hard rubber, 1986, 8" h **30.00**
Film, 8mm, black-and-white, "Doom of Dracula" with Boris Karloff, orig box **22.00**
Flashlight/key chain, Wolfman, Universal, MOC.........................**15.00**
Game, Monster Madness, Pressman, MIB...**30.00**
Inflatable, Giant Godzilla Toho, Imperial, 6', with orig box, mint **35.00**
Magazine
　Fangoria, #1, August 1979...........**50.00**
　Horror Monsters, #9, Fall 1964 ....**22.00**
　Life, Sept. 1964 Boris Karloff cover, mint......................................**10.00**
　Monster World, #6, 1965..............**10.00**
　World Famous Creatures, #1, one corner missing **45.00**
Model kit, Frankenstein, Horizon, unbuilt **75.00**

Wolf Man monster model, Universal Pictures Presents, completed, orig box, $5.

Pinback button, Dracula, black and white picture, color background, 1960s **15.00**
Poster, Frankenstein and the Monster from Hell, 1-sheet, 27" x 41" **10.00**

Pressbook, Horror of Dracula, 1958, near mint **95.00**
Record, The Thing, soundtrack, John Carpenter's...................................**15.00**
Toy
　Dracula, made by Telco, battery-op, 1992, MIB **75.00**
　Monster Machine, Gabriel, orig molds, 1970, C-9................................**80.00**
Wax Pack, Creature from the Black Lagoon, Feature, Topps Gum, 1980 ....**13.00**

❖ Moon & Star Pattern

Moon & Star pattern, Front: green cov candy dish, $18; next is blue open compote, $12; rear, clear cov candy dish, $15.

This popular glassware pattern has its origins in America's pattern glass industry. Adams & Co. of Pittsburgh, Pennsylvania manufactured an extensive line called Palace. The L.G. Wright Co. began reproducing that pattern in a broad spectrum of colors and called the design Moon & Star. The molds have changed hands several times since then, but the pattern is still being made.

For additional Adams listings, see *Warman's Pattern Glass Price and Identification Guide.*

Moon and Star, clear
Bowl, small, flat, clear **7.50**
Compote, clear **10.00**
Ashtray, amberina **20.00**
Banana boat, ruby, 12-1/2" l, 5-1/2" h **80.00**
Basket, green, LE Smith **55.00**

Moon & Star pattern ashtray, bright orange, thick, $12.

Bowl, low pedestal, clear **7.50**
Canister, green, LE Smith, 9-1/2" h....**35.00**
Celery vase, clear............................**25.00**
Compote, cov, clear **50.00**
Compote, open, green, LE Smith ...**42.50**
Cookie Jar, blue, roughness on lid, late
    color **5.00**
Creamer and sugar, amber............**40.00**
Cruet, clear.....................................**30.00**
Dinner plate, clear, Weishar **15.00**
Goblets, clear, set of 8....................**20.00**
Relish, 2 part, clear..........................**2.50**
Sauce bowl, clear **2.50**
Sherbet, clear, Weishar....................**15.00**
Toothpick holder, green, L.E. Smith **9.00**
Tumbler, blue, Weishar **17.50**
Vase, amber....................................**20.00**
Water set, L.E. Smith, pitcher, four 13-oz
    tumblers.......................................**185.00**

❖ Morgantown Glass

Founded in Morgantown, West Virginia, this manufacturer of hand-made glass created lovely household items and tableware. The colors produced by Morgantown are bright and clear, and the company introduced several innovative techniques and forms to the industry.

Collectors' Club: Old Morgantown Glass Collectors' Guild, P.O. Box 894, Morgantown, WV 26507.

For additional listings, see *Warman's Antiques & Collectibles* and *Warman's Glass.*

Bowl, Fantasia, Bristol Blue, 5-1/2" dia
    ....**75.00**
Bud vase, Lara, Thistle, 10" h........**95.00**
Candlesticks, pr, Rhoda, Bristol Blue
    ....**80.00**
Candy jar, Jupiter, Steel Blue, 6" h.**95.00**
Champagne
    Jockey, crystal **50.00**
    Monroe, red and crystal **35.00**

Morgantown Glass, goblet, Golf Ball, cobalt blue, $60.

Claret, Golf Ball, red.......................**75.00**
Cocktail
    Stiegel Green **35.00**
    Majestic Chanticleer, Copen blue **35.00**
    Golf Ball, red and crystal.............**32.50**
Compote
    Stella, Peacock Blue, 4" **48.00**
    Withers, Bristol Blue....................**38.00**
Cordial
    Mayfair, crystal **35.00**
    Plantation, cobalt.......................**145.00**
Flower light, Vesta, Gypsy Fire, with
    candle frog **65.00**
Goblet
    Astrid, #734 American Beauty etch,
       punty cut stem **65.00**
    Golf Ball, cobalt...........................**60.00**
    Hanover, Virginia etch **30.00**
Guest set, Trudy, Baby Blue, 6-3/8" h
    ....**85.00**
High ball, Mexicana, 5" h..............**115.00**
Ivy ball, Golf Ball, red, 4" w **95.00**
Oyster cocktail, Sunrise Medallion, blue,
    slight wear **190.00**
Parfait, Versailles, Callahan stem ...**65.00**
Plate, Mexicana, Ice, 6" dia.............**18.00**
Tumbler
    Old English, Ritz Blue, ftd, 6-1/4" h
    ....**40.00**
    Ringling Red, 3" d, 4-1/2" h **35.00**
Vase
    Donna, India Black, 6" h **65.00**
    Lara, Burgundy, slant top, 10" h...**28.00**
    Serenade, Anna Rose...............**125.00**
Wine, Old English, Spanish red **35.00**

❖ Mortens Studio

Collectors identify the name Mortens Studios with finely crafted porcelain dog figurines.

Airedale, #742, 4-1/4" h..................**85.00**
Borzoi, #749.................................**145.00**
Boston Terrier, 3" h **50.00**
Chihuahua, chips on ears, 1-3/4" h
    ....**55.00**
Cocker spaniel, nose chip, 2-3/4" h**47.50**
Collie **175.00**
Dachshund **65.00**
English setter **150.00**
Fox terrier **185.00**
Mustang, 7-1/2" h **45.00**
Palomino, ear damaged, 8" h.........**85.00**
Plaque, frame type back, center horse
    figure, mkd #651, 7" x 8-1/2" **125.00**
Pomeranian, #739, 4" h..................**55.00**
Spaniel...**80.00**
Spaniel puppy, 2-1/2" h.................**24.00**
Wild Stallion, #718 ....**95.00**

❖ Morton Potteries

Morton Pottery Works was established in Morton, Illinois, in 1922. Production of dinnerware, earthenware, and table accessories continued until 1976. The company also specialized in kitchenware and novelties for chain stores and gift shops.

Cookie jar
    Basket of fruit **55.00**
    Panda **85.00**
Drip-o-lator, brown Rockingham glaze, 4
    pcs...**135.00**
Figurine
    Elephant, mkd "GOP, Martin," 1940s, 2"
       h..**30.00**
    Lamb, green, 2-3/8" h **12.00**
    Kangaroo, white, 2-5/8" h............**15.00**
    Squirrel, 2" h **10.00**
Nightlight
    Old woman in a shoe, yellow and red
    ....**45.00**
    Teddy bear, brown, hand-painted.**50.00**
Pie bird, 5" h **75.00**
Planter
    Duck, white...................................**20.00**
    Rabbit, umbrella, blue egg **20.00**

❖ Moss Rose Pattern

Several English and American pottery companies made this pretty pattern. The pink rose bud with leaves makes it easy to identify this pattern. Some pieces also have gold trim.

Moss Rose Pattern, cup and saucer, $30.

Butter pat, mkd "Meakin," sq...........**25.00**
Cake plate, 2 emb handles.............**40.00**
Coaster, mkd "Nasco" **12.95**
Creamer and sugar, mkd "Haviland, Limoges" **150.00**
Cup and saucer, mkd "Haviland, Limoges" **30.00**
Dinner plate, mkd "Haviland," 9-1/2" dia **25.00**
Gravy boat, matching underplate, mkd "Green Co., England" **35.00**
Luncheon plate, mkd "Haviland" **20.00**
Nappy, mkd "Edwards," 4-1/2" dia...**18.50**
Sauce dish, mkd "Haviland," 4-1/2" dia **20.00**
Sugar bowl, cov, mkd "Rosenthal"..**35.00**
Teapot, bulbous, gooseneck spout, basketweave trim, mkd "T&V" **95.00**

❖ Mother's Day Collectibles

The first Mother's Day celebration was held in Philadelphia, Pennsylvania, in 1907, but it wasn't until 1914 that it became a national observance. Most of us think of cards, flowers, and candy as the traditional Mother's Day gifts, but there is also a wide selection of items to commemorate the day, including ornaments and limited edition collector plates.

Greeting card, Hallmark, sgd, 1975 .**2.00**
Limited edition plate
    Bing and Grondahl, Hare and Young, H. Thelander, 1971, 6" dia **40.00**
    Precious Moments, "Mother's Day 1990," Samuel J. Butcher, 4" dia.**7.00**
    Schmid, "Devotion for Mother," Sister Berta Hummel, 1976 ....**32.50**
Magazine, *MAD*, #79, June, 1963, Special Mother's Day Issue..........**15.00**
Magazine ad, Western Union, "Remember Your Mother," 1955......**6.00**
Ornament for mother-to-be, hen nesting on bowed wrapped egg, mkd "Hallmark Handcrafted," 1992, orig box **20.00**
Planter, ceramic, white, swans, FTD **3.50**

Table decoration, tissue paper type, image of Victorian Mother, "Remember your mother on Mother's Day. Second Sunday in May," 11" x 14".............**15.00**

❖ Motorcycle Collectibles

Most people who are interested in motorcycle collectibles either ride this unique form of transportation or did so in the past. Whatever their motivation, it's a field that is growing, and these collectibles are sure to increase in value.

Collectors' Clubs: American Motorcycle Assoc, P.O. Box 6114, Westerville, OH 43081; Antique Motorcycle Club of America, P.O. Box 300, Sweetser, IN 46987-0300; Women on Wheels, P.O. Box 546, Sparta, WI 54656-9546.

Catalog, Harley-Davidson Motorcycles, accessories catalog, blue and yellow accents, 1954, 36 pgs, 8-1/2" h, 11" w **25.00**

Motorcycle Collectibles, door bell, metal, repainted gold, $30.

Flyer, Harley-Davidson Motorcycles, Christmas, accessories, Baltimore, Md. dealer imprint, some inked notations, 6" x 9"..**10.00**
Magazine tear sheet
    Harley-Davidson, *Farm Life*, 1919 .**2.00**
    Honda Mini Trail, 1969, large sheet **2.50**

Member card and patch, card 2-1/4" x 4", buff paper with orange accents, American Motorcycle Association, typewritten member identification, 1952 expiration date, fabric patch 2" x 2-1/4", green, red and yellow on blue ground **35.00**
Patch, Harley-Davidson Motorcycles, embroidered, gold trademark in center, flanked by silver wings on black felt ground, early 1950s, 7-1/2"..........**75.00**
Stationery, white sheet, 2" red, pink and gray logo, Indian Motorcycles Dealer, profile of Indian head at left, text "Motorcycles for Sport, Business, and Police," wheel and wing design across top, Alabama dealer imprint, 3-digit phone number, c1920, 8-1/2" x 11" **20.00**
Toy, cast iron, Hubley, replaced handle bars, 60% orig paint.................**200.00**

❖ Movie Memorabilia

Scarf, blue and white, facsimile signatures of movie stars including Norma Shearer, Clark Gable, Dick Powell, Joel McCrea, Sonja Henji, and Bing Crosby, $35.

Going to the movies has always been a fun event. Today's collectors actively seek memorabilia from their favorite flicks or items that are related to a particular star or studio.

Periodicals: *Big Reel*, P.O. Box 1050, Dubuque, IA 52004; *Collecting Hollywood Magazine*, P.O. Box 2512, Chattanooga, TN 37409; *Goldmine*, 700 E State St, Iola, WI 54990; *Movie Advertising Collector*, P.O. Box 28587, Philadelphia, PA, 19149.

Almanac, Yvonne DeCarlo on cover, Rexall **15.00**
Book
    Crime Movies: An Illustrated History, 1980, softcover **9.00**
    Encyclopedia of Western Movies, 1984 ....**25.00**
    Ginger Rogers and the Riddle of the Scarlet Cloak, Lela E. Rogers, Whitman 2378, 1942 ....**15.00**
    James Bond Show Book, Purnell &

Sons, Ltd., London, c1960 ....**20.00**

King Kong, Grosset & Dunlap, 1932, dj, photos of Fay Wray, Robert Armstrong, and King Kong **200.00**

Chair, War of the Worlds, director's chair, Gene Barry..............................**150.00**

Christmas Stocking, *ET*, cotton **15.00**

Cookbook, Gone With The Wind, 5-1/2" x 7-1/4", soft cover, 48 pgs, Pebeco Toothpaste premium, c1939........**45.00**

Dish, 10-1/4" d, white china, blue dec with facsimile signatures of over 25 movie stars around rim, images of Hollywood Bowl, Ciro's Sunset Strip, Grauman's Chinese Theatre, Earl Carroll's Theatre Restaurant, Brown Derby Restaurant, NBC Studios, mkd "Vernon Kilns," 1940s **120.00**

Handbill

Men Are Not Gods, Miriam Hopkins, 6" x 9", 1930s.............................**20.00**

Spellbound, Gregory Peck and I Bergmann, 8" x 11", 4 pgs **25.00**

Handkerchief, Gone With The Wind, Scarlet O'Hara, floral design, yellow, rose, green, black, white, and gold, black diecut foil sticker, early 1940s, 13" sq **60.00**

Lobby Card

Chick Carter, Detective, 11" x 14", bluetone photo, Chapter 1, Chick Carter Takes Over, 1948 Columbia Pictures serial **25.00**

Gone with the Wind, set of 6, first Italian release, 1948 ....**130.00**

Lost Horizon, Mexican release, 12-1/2" x 16-1/2" **35.00**

Miss Tatlock's Millions, Robert Stack, Dorothy Wood, 1948, framed....**45.00**

Rawhide Rangers, Johnny Mack Brown, Universal.......................**20.00**

Pinback Button, Beau James, Bob Hope, 1957, 2-1/2" d **38.00**

Press book, Mary Poppins, Julie Andrews **15.00**

Sheet music, As Time Goes By, Casablanca, 1942, cover shows Humphrey Bogart, Ingrid Bergman and Paul Henreid.................................**65.00**

❖ Movie Posters

Posters are a specialized area of movie collectibles. Created by the studios to promote their movies, posters are usually brightly colored and make wonderful display pieces. One of the most common types of poster measures 27" x 41" and is called a "one sheet."

Periodicals: *Collecting Hollywood,* American Collectors Exchange, 2401 Broad St., Chattanooga, TN 37408; *Hollywood Collectibles,* 4099 McEwen Drive, Suite 350, Dallas, TX 75244; *Movie Poster*

Update, American Collectors Exchange, 2401 Broad St., Chattanooga, TN 37408.

Note: The following listings are all full-color one sheets, unless otherwise noted.

Background to Danger, George Raft and Sidney Greenstreet, 1943 movie **85.00**

Bomba and the Jungle Girl, six-sheet, 80 x 80", 1953 Monogram Pictures, folded to 11" x 14" **90.00**

Cinderalla, full color, 1920s, 20" x 30" **150.00**

Every Which Way But Loose.......**150.00**

Guys and Dolls **600.00**

Love Story **500.00**

Melody Time, Walt Disney, 1948, margin deterioration from dampness, 60" x 40" **150.00**

New York, New York....................**200.00**

Patton, 20th Century Fox, George S. Scott, full color image, folded, 27" x 41 ....**12.00**

Tangier Incident, one sheet, Allied Artists, 1953, George Brent, full color portraits, folded, 27" x 41"............**10.00**

The Bells of St Mary's, 1945, Bing Crosby, folded............................**150.00**

The Searchers, oversized............ **350.00**

Utah Wagon Train, Republic Picture, 1951, margin damage, tear, 58" x 40" **150.00**

Prison Train *movie poster, Fred Keating, Linda Winters, Malcom-Browne Production, $45.*

❖ Moxie

Originally called Moxie Nerve Food and intended to be taken with a spoon, Moxie was first sold in Salem, Massachusetts, in 1876. Created by Augustin Thompson, the

mixture was one of a number of patent medicines he sold to supplement the income from his medical practice. Several years later, wanting to capitalize on the popularity of soft drinks, Thompson modified his medicine. By 1884, Moxie was being sold in carbonated form, and it is still sold today.

Collectors' Club: Moxie Enthusiasts Collectors Club of America, Route 375, Box 164, Woodstock, NY 12498; New England Moxie Congress, 445 Wyoming Ave., Millburn, NJ 07041.

Bag, paper, 1932 copyright, stain, tear, 11" x 9-1/4"...............................**45.00**

Bottle, Moxie embossed on shoulders, pale green, 7-oz, 7-3/4" h **10.00**

Fan

Eileen Pery, all paper, 5-1/4" x 8-3/8" **95.00**

Pinback button, litho tin, diecut

Moxie man, face shot **125.00**

Moxie woman, orig card, 2" h, 1-3/4" w **550.00**

Sign

Tin over cardboard, "Drink Moxie," 2-1/2" x 10" **325.00**

Tip tray, litho tin, woman with glass of Moxie, 6" dia..............................**140.00**

❖ Mugs

While no one is sure when the first mug was produced, many early pottery manufacturers did include mugs in their patterns. Collectors tend to focus on advertising mugs or those related to a particular character.

Beer, pink, New Martinsville Glass..**25.00**

British commemorative, Royal Silver Jubilee, 1952-1977, mkd Royal Grafton **28.00**

Carnival glass, Beaded Shell, Dugan, blue..**115.00**

Glass, root beer type........................**5.00**

Lusterware, emb "Present," violets deco, base mkd "J.C.S. Co., Germany" .**55.00**

Milk glass, Yum-Yum Donuts **6.00**

Pattern glass

Arched Fleur-De-Lis, ruby stained**30.00**

Beaded Swirl **15.00**

Bird and Owl **80.00**

Cupid and Venus **30.00**

Cut Log, 3-1/4" h **32.00**

Plastic, advertising

Hires, scratches **1.50**

Mr. Peanut, yellow, 1970s.............**12.00**

Nestles Quick bunny, 4" h **12.00**

Pottery

Bennington, brown Rockingham glaze, double ring handle....................**25.00**

Unmarked, cobalt blue mirror glaze, oop handle, set of four..............**40.00**

❖ Mulberry China

Mulberry china is similar to flow blue, but the design is a dark purple that appears almost black in some cases. The name derives from the resemblance of the color to crushed mulberries. Many of the same factories that produced flow blue also manufactured mulberry items.

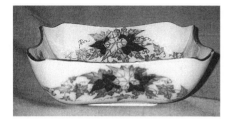

Mulberry China bowl, Bryonia pattern, 9" w, $265.

Creamer
Corean **120.00**
Marble, Wedgwood....................**90.00**
Nankin, Davenport **75.00**
Creamer and sugar, Ning Po, Hall set
....**350.00**
Cup plate, Ning Po, Hall **75.00**
Dessert/individual vegetable dish,
Bryonia **30.00**
Gravy boat, Calcutta....................**110.00**
Honey dish, Nankin, Davenport **60.00**
Milk pitcher, Ning Po, Hall, restored
spout **175.00**
Plate
Avon, 9-3/4" dia...........................**40.00**
Berry, Ridgways, 10" dia **145.00**
Blackberry Lustre, Mellor Venables, 9"
dia...**95.00**
Calcutta, Edward Challinor, 8-1/2" dia
....**95.00.**
Corean, Podmore Walker & Co, 7-3/4"
dia...**50.00**
Ning Po, Hall, 7-1/2" dia...............**40.00**
Pelew, E. Challinor, 8-1/2" dia **115.00**
Strawberry, Walker, 9" dia **110.00**
Washington Vase, Podmore Walker &
Co., 8-3/4" dia..........................**100.00**
Platter
Foliage, A. Walley, 15-1/4" l........**275.00**
Washington Vase, Podmore Walker &
Co., 17-3/4" l.............................**300.00**
Teacup and saucer, handleless
Cyprus.......................................**100.00**
Floral **80.00**
Teapot, 7" h.................................**395.00**

❖ Music Boxes, Novelty Types

Music boxes were invented by the Swiss around 1825. They can now be found in many shapes, sizes, and materials. When buying a music box at a flea market, ask the dealer if it works properly and perhaps you'll hear the pretty tune.

Collectors' Club: Musical Box Society International, 12140 Anchor Ln SW, Moore Haven, FL 33471.

Ballerina, pink, metal base, some wear
....**50.00**
Birdcage, singing bird, German....**250.00**
Children on merry-go-round, wood,
figures move, plays "Around the World
in 80 Days," 7-3/4" h....................**30.00**
Christmas tree, revolving, German **65.00**
Cuff links, pr, gold plated, one plays
Brahms Lullaby **125.00**
Dancing dude................................**90.00**
Evening in Paris, illus of different
cosmetics, velvet and silver box.**125.00**
Hummel
Joyful, #IV/53, trademark 6 ....**150.00**
Playmates, #IV/58, trademark 6.**150.00**
Jewelry box, celluloid, French music
box, red velvet lining, 3-1/2" w, 6-1/2" h
....**180.00**
Nativity, bisque, O Holy Night, Lefton
....**65.00**
Piano, silver-plated, red velvet lining
....**45.00**
Snowball, glass, Frosty the Snowman,
red wooden base, 5" h **12.00**
South of the Border......................**35.00**
Windmill, Delft blue and white porcelain,
5-1/4" h......................................**175.00**

Music Box, jewelry box, red lacquer, painted Oriental motif, int. with Geisha girl on mirror, red velvet lining, two small drawers, $20.

❖ Music Related

Perhaps you're the type who likes to whistle while browsing at a flea market. Bet you'll find some music-related collectibles while you regale your fellow shoppers with a happy tune.

Periodical: *Goldmine*, 700 E State St, Iola, WI 54990

Also see Sheet Music and related categories in this edition.

Player piano rolls, Duo-Art, each $1.

Book
History of English Music, London, 1895
....**20.00**
Songs for the Family, yellow hardcover,
c1960...**10.00**
Bookmark, figural grand piano, celluloid,
printed adv **25.00**
Calendar print, dogs playing piano ..**5.00**
Catalog
Hamilton Piano Co., Chicago Heights,
IL, c1910, 8" x 10-1/2".............**45.00**
Kohler & Campbell, New York, NY,
1920, 5-1/2" x 8", pianos **32.00**
Guitar case, canvas, brown, leather
bound edges, strap, buckle, and
handle, 1890 ....**20.00**
Guitar pick, used **1.00**
Hat, marching band, blue and white,
white plume, worn **10.00**
Music stand, chrome, folding type ...**2.00**
Piano instruction book, beginner, green
cover, worn.....................................**2.00**
Piano roll cabinet, Adam style,
mahogany veneer, painted panels on
doors, incomplete applied ornament,
English, 38-1/4" h, 40" w, 16" d .**330.00**
Sign, emb tin, Mason & Hamlin Grands &
Upright Pianos, Boston, New York,
Chicago, shows grand piano, framed,
19-1/2" x 27".............................**300.00**

❖ Musical Instruments

The musical instruments generally found at flea markets have been used as practice instruments, or have been under the ownership of children. Expect to find wear, and understand that your purchase will probably need some repairs before it can make music again.

Periodicals: *Concertina & Squeezebox*, P.O. Box 6706, Ithaca, NY 14851; *Jerry's Musical Newsletter*, 4624 W Woodland Rd, Minneapolis, MN 55424.

Collectors' Clubs: American Musical Instrument Society, RD 3, Box 205-B, Franklin, PA 16323; Automatic Musical Instrument Collectors Assoc, 919 Lantern

Drum set, light blue marbleized, chrome fittings, chimes in background, $175.

Glow Trail, Dayton, OH 45431; Fretted Instrument Guild of America, 2344 S Oakley Ave, Chicago, IL 60608; Musical Box Society International, 887 Orange Ave. E, St. Paul, MN 55106; Reed Organ Society, Inc., P.O. Box 901, Deansboro, NY 13328.

Accordion, black lacquer, brass, silver and abalone inlay, keys and decorative valve covers with carved mother-of-pearl, needs repair, some damage **95.00**

Banjo, Bacon Banjo Co., Style C, 17 fret neck, hard-shell case **185.00**

Bassoon, 15-keyed, maple, brass mounts and keys, c1900, 50-1/4" l **460.00**

Bugle, nickel-plated, minor dents, wooden case with black paint **100.00**

Clarinet, 10-keyed boxwood, key of C, brass mountings, brass keys with round covers, c1860, orig mouthpiece, 21-1/2" l.....................................**400.00**

Cornet, silver-plated brass tubing, engraved at the bell, three piston valves with pearl buttons, Lyric, The Rudolph Wurlitzer Co. USA, stamped "P21766," fitted case, 2 period mouthpieces, turning crook and mute **150.00**

Cymbals, leather handles, American, c1900, 10" dia **90.00**

Drum, worn orig varnish and transfer dec of eagle and shield, labeled "Carl Fischer, New York," 16-1/2" dia, replaced ropes and leather, old heads, two drum sticks **330.00**

Flute, Firth Hall and Pond, 8 keys, crocuswood and nickel silver mounts, inlaid lip plate, nickel-silver keys with salt spoon cup cover, adjustable stopper c1855, stamped "Firth, Hall & Pond, Franklin Sq, New York, 1242," fitted mahogany case, 26-1/4" l..**230.00**

Melodeon, rosewood veneer, lyre shaped ends, ivory and ebony keyboard, 4-1/2 octaves, mkd "Carhart & Needham, New York," wear and veneer damage, lyre and bench mismatched, one bellows rod is missing, 28" h, 32-1/2" w, 16-1/4" d **175.00**

Orguinette, "Mechanical Orguinette Co., New York," small roller organ, walnut case, silver stenciled label and dec, working cond, paper rolls, 10" h, 12" w, 9-1/4" d.....................................**500.00**

Pianola, Aeolian, quartersawn oak, foot pedals, repairs required to bellows, 60 orig rolls, 36" h, 45" w **400.00**

Pitch pipe, walnut, book form, paper label on int, "WN," crack, 6" l......**200.00**

Trombone, Concertone, SP, gold plated bell, satin finish **300.00**

Ukulele, The Serenader, B.&G., N.Y., double binding, celluloid fingerboard and head **250.00**

Zither, Columbia, 47 strings, c1900 ....**275.00**

❖ My Little Pony

It is said that the idea for My Little Pony came about when research by Hasbro discovered that young girls see horses when they close their eyes at night. The result: ponies that even city kids can keep. My Little Pony memorabilia has been putting smiles on the faces of girls, young and old, since 1982.

Reference: Debra L. Birge, *The World of My Little Pony*, Schiffer Publishing, 2000.

Alarm clock, Bubbles......................**45.00**
Carrying case, 1983......................**22.00**
Figurine, bisque, First Born by Extra Special, 4" l **19.50**
Key chain, Morning Glory, detachable with rainbow-colored comb **4.00**
Pony
 Baby in sand box, pink, blue mane, 1987..**15.00**
 Baby unicorn, 1984, 5" h.............**12.00**
 Firefly, with brush and ribbon, orig card **9.00**
 Merry Treat, 2nd of 3 Christmas ponies, 1984 ....**13.50**
 Morning Glory, Birthflower Ponies, September 1982 ....**26.00**
 Nightglider, 1984 ....**35.00**
 Pink, hot pink mane and tail, 1984 ....**12.00**
 Turquoise, 1998............................**5.00**

❖ Napkin Rings

Figural napkin rings are useful collectibles. Victorian silver and silver plate napkin rings, including examples having a whimsical nature, often are available at flea markets.

Aluminum, souv of Washington DC, 3 scenes..**10.00**

Bakelite
  Angelfish, marbled blue, c1940....**70.00**
  Bird, butterscotch **40.00**
  Elephant, navy blue, c1940..........**95.00**
  Rocking Horse, red **225.00**

Pewter, turtle, 2-1/2" h **28.00**

Plastic, clear, oval, carved floral dec **5.00**

Porcelain, sunbonnet girl, mkd "Erphila Czechoslovakian," 2" x 4" **72.00**

Silver
  Beaded edge, plain center **95.00**
  Eagle, Meriden, 2" h..................**125.00**

Leaf and barrel, tarnished.............**45.00**

Silvered Metal, cuff style, double band **20.00**

Silver-plated, flowers on lily pad, top emb with fan and flowers, sgd "Middletown Quad Plate #97" **100.00**

Silver plate napkin ring, engraves florals and leaves, no mark, $15.

❖ NASCAR

It's a pretty cool sport when you think about—guys racing cars that, except for the abundance of colorful advertisements, look like they could have come out of your driveway. When it comes to racing collectibles, nothing's hotter. Are you racing off to a flea market? You should find plenty of good NASCAR collectibles to choose from.

Also see: Racing Collectibles, Auto

NASCAR Toy trucks, MIB, top: Kodak, Morgan McClure Motorsports, yellow, $15; middle: McDonald's Racing Team, racing team transporter, $18; bottom: Racing Champions, Inc., racing team transporter, 1992 Winston Cup Champion, $15.

Bank
  1991, Jeff Gordon, Carolina Ford Dealers, NASCAR Club Bank ..**68.00**
  1998, Terry Labonte, Monte Carlo, Kellogg's Corny Bank, 1:24, MIB **65.00**

Barbie, 50th Anniversary Nascar Barbie, MIB..**30.00**

Book, *NASCAR, The Thunder of America* **40.00**

Comic book, NASCAR Christmas 100, 1991, unused **5.00**

Curtains, pinch pleated, 1960s Dodge Charger, Champion Spark Plus, Coca-Cola, Sears, STP and Union 76 advertising, 72" w 34" l **80.00**

Die-Cast
  1992, Pit Stop Showcase, Ford #98 and 6 pit crew figures, 1:43 scale, Racing Champions **15.00**
  1994, Rusty Wallace #2, Premier Edition, 1:64 scale, Racing Champions, MIB **45.00**

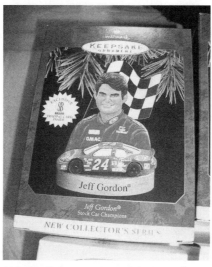

NASCAR Christmas ornament, Jeff Gordon, Stock Car Champion, Hallmark, MIB, $8.

NASCAR Bottle of Coca-Cola, #3, orig contents, never opened, $2.50.

  1997, Transporter Truck, 1:64 scale, Racing Champions, MIB...........**25.00**
  1998, Todd Bodine, #35 ....**20.00**
  2000, Winner's Circle, Dale Earnhardt **20.00**

Program, 1927 Official Indy 500, slight wear..**300.00**

Watch, men's, Jeff Gordon, #24....**125.00**

❖ Nautical

Anchors Away! Nautical items can encompass things with a nautical theme or items that were actually used on a ship.

Periodicals: *Nautical Brass,* P.O. Box 3966, North Ft. Myers, FL 33918; *Nautical Collector,* P.O. Box 949, New London, CT 06320.

Collectors' Club: Nautical Research Guild, 62 Marlboro St., Newburyport, MA 01950.

For additional listings, see *Warman's Antiques and Collectibles Price Guide.*

Book, D. Arnott, *Design and Construction of Steel Merchant Ships,* Society of Marine Archives, 1955, 1st ed **35.00**

Model sailing ships: Whaling Ship Clipper 1846, 15" h, $200; America, 22" h, $145; Gorch Fock, 17" h, $200.

Framed oil on canvas, seascape, signed "Rosati" lower left, 31" x 56", $275.

Bookends, pr
Anchors, brass, mounted on faux stone base, 8" h **47.50**
Whale's Heads, bronze verdigris finish, 5-1/2" h **50.00**
Chart, Boston Harbor, George W. Eldridge, 1876, 17" x 24" **195.00**
Diorama, ship, old paint dec, c1920 ....**585.00**
Diving helmet, Russian, 3-bolt ..**1,295.00**
Folk art, carved fish, wood plaque, c1940, life size
Pickerel......................................**265.00**
Rainbow Trout **295.00**
Salmon **345.00**
Key chain, ship's wheel, leather attached to medallion, "VN Balboa," 1" dia .**25.00**
Lifeboat compass, 8" sq, 7-1/4" h, boxed, 20th C **175.00**
Model, English motor launch, steam powered, c1950, 44" l, 7-1/2" w .**850.00**
Plaque, White Star Line, thick brass plate, engraved words, mounted on varnished mahogany board, 18" x 7" **375.00**
Porthole, hinged brass, rect, WWII era **975.00**
Print
Clippers *Ariel & Taiping*, M. Dawson, 26" x 31" **65.00**
Cutty Sark, Racing Home, M. Dawson, 20" x 28" **65.00**
Ship *Triumphant*, Frank Vining Smith, 22" x 32" **38.50**
Ship Compass, 10" d magnetic compass, teakwood box, polished brass gimball ring, U.S. Navy, World War II era, made by John E. Hand & Co...**750.00**
Ship's bell, 8" d, *Alister Hardy,* brass, dated 1953 ....**145.00**
Table Lamp, brass boat cleat-ships wheel, sea navigation chart lamp shade, 15" h **235.00**

❖ New Martinsville Glass

Founded in 1901, the New Martinsville Glass Manufacturing Company was located in West Virginia. Its glassware products ranged from pressed utilitarian wares to some innovative designs and colors.

Animal
Baby bear, head straight **60.00**
Seal, holding ball, light lavender, candle holder **75.00**
Rooster, crooked tail **95.00**
Ashtray, Moondrops, red **35.00**
Basket, Janice, black, 12" l, 7" w, 9-1/2" h **190.00**
Bitters bottle, Hostmaster, cobalt blue **75.00**
Bookends, pr, clipper chips **95.00**
Bowl, Teardrop, crystal, 3 ftd, 11" dia, 4" h **45.00**
Cake plate
Janice, 40th Anniversary silver overlay **45.00**
Prelude, pedestal foot **10.00**
Candlesticks, pr
Janice, red..................................**200.00**
Radiance, 2-lite **230.00**
Candy box, Radiance, 3 part, amber, etch #26 ....**160.00**
Champagne, Moondrops, red **40.00**
Celery dish, swan, 8" l neck, 6" h...**25.00**
Cigarette holder, cart shaped **20.00**
Console bowl, Janice, ftd, crystal ..**38.00**
Console set, Radiance, crystal, 12" bowl pr 2-lite candlesticks...................**125.00**
Cordial, Janice, red, silver trim **40.00**
Creamer and sugar, Janice, red **48.00**
Cup and saucer
Janice, red...................................**30.00**
Radiance, amber.........................**30.00**
Decanter, Moondrops, amber **80.00**
Figure, crystal
Baby Bear, 3-1/2" h **65.00**
Polar Bear, 4" h **95.00**
Squirrel, 5" h **55.00**
Goblet, Diamond Thumbprint..........**12.00**
Ivy ball, Janice, light blue...............**95.00**
Lamp, 10" h, Art Deco style, pink satin, black enamel accents.....................**45.00**
Mug, Georgian, ruby.......................**18.00**
Nappy, Prelude, 5" d, heart shaped, handle **20.00**
Pitcher, Oscar, red.......................**100.00**

New Martinsville, sandwich server, Prelude pattern, clear glass, etched design, 1930-50, 13" d, $40.

Punch cup, Radiance **15.00**
Punch ladle, Radiance, red **125.00**
Relish, Radiance, amber, 3 part **15.00**
Swan, Janice, crystal......................**38.00**
Tumbler
Amy, #34, ftd **22.50**
Janice, red, 10 oz, ftd..................**35.00**
Moondrops, cobalt blue, 5 oz.......**24.00**
Oscar, red **20.00**
Vanity set, 3 pc, Judy, green and crystal or pink and crystal.....................**100.00**
Vase, Radiance, #4232, 10" h, crimped, etch #26 ....**140.00**

❖ Newspapers

Saving a newspaper about a historic event or memorable occasion seems like such an easy thing to do. Happily for newspaper collectors, folks have been doing that for centuries. Flea markets are a great place to find these interesting publications.

Collectors Club: Newspaper Collectors Society of America, 6031 Winterset, Lansing, MI 48911.

Cincinnati Weekly Herald and Philanthropist, Nov. 22, 1843, feature on "Mr. Adams and the Colored People" **45.00**
Hagerstown Daily Mail, Hagerstown, Md., April 6, 1964, "Hero's Homage Paid MacArthur" **25.00**
Havanna Post, Cuba, Oct 7, 1926, "National Foreign Trade Committee" **25.00**
Metropolis Planet, Metropolis, Ill., June 28, 1973, Superman souvenir edition **35.00**
New York Times, July 21, 1969, Man Worlks on the Moon **30.00**
The Fiery Cross, Indianapolis, IN, Feb 14, 1924 ....**20.00**
The Washington Daily News, July 12, 1972, "FAREWELL" headline, final edition of publication **30.00**
The Youths Medallion, Boston April 17, 1841 ....**40.00**
Wilmington Home Weekly, May 2, 1886 ....**10.00**

❖ Nicodemus Pottery

Made in Ohio by Chester Nicodemus, this pottery is especially noted for a variety of charming animal figurines. The company name is usually found impressed in a semi-circular form.

Bud vase, figural girl, 6-1/4" h **295.00**
Cabinet jug, yellow and brown on ferrostone, 4-1/4" h.......................**65.00**
Cornucopia, 6-1/2" h, 14" l **360.00**

Figurine
  Fox terrier, 4-1/2" h, 9" l **425.00**
  Owl, 4-1/2" h **125.00**
  Robin, 4-1/2" h **100.00**
Flower frog, Madonna, 10-1/2" h..**210.00**
Plaque, Orange Johnson House Quilt, 2-
  7/8" h...**100.00**
Salt and pepper shakers, pr, green and
  brown, 3-1/2" h............................**75.00**
Vase, turquoise, 5-1/2" h **180.00**

❖ Niloak Pottery

Niloak Pottery was located near Benton, Ark. The founder of the company, Charles Dean Hyten, experimented with native clays and tried to preserve their natural colors. By 1911, he had perfected a method that gave this effect, a product he named Mission Ware. The pottery burned but was rebuilt. It reopened under the name Eagle pottery and by 1929 was producing novelties. Several different marks were used, helping to determine the dates of pieces. By 1946 the company went out of business.

Collectors' Club: Arkansas Pottery Collectors Society, 12 Normandy Road, Little Rock, AR 72007.

For additional listings, see *Warman's Antiques and Collectibles Price Guide, Warman's Americana & Collectibles,* and *Warman's American Pottery and Porcelain.*

Ashtray, blue glaze, hat shape **12.00**
Bud vase, Ozark Dawn glaze, 7-1/4" h
  ....**65.00**
Candlestick, Mission Ware, 10" h.**245.00**
Creamer, Ozark Dawn **35.00**
Ewer, Ozark Dawn, 16-1/2" h........**150.00**
Figure
  Frog, matte green..........................**30.00**
  Polar Bear, matte white................**45.00**
Planter
  Deer, blue, 4-1/2" h **35.00**
  Dutch shoe, tan.............................**40.00**
  Elephant, pink **30.00**
  Fox, red **27.50**
Squirrel, white................................**65.00**
Swan, blue, 7-1/2" h **65.00**
Strawberry vase, pink, gray-green glaze,
  opening with turkey, tail feathers
  spread out, orig paper label, sgd .**65.00**
Vase
  4" h, Mission Ware, flared lip **110.00**
  5-1/2" h, Mission Ware, hourglass form
  ....**175.00**
  6" h, Mission Ware, inverted bell shape
  ....**150.00**
  6" h, Ozark Dawn, twisted handle
  ....**155.00**
  6-1/2" h, pink, twisted design **30.00**
  8-3/4" h, Ozark Dawn.................**200.00**

❖ Nippon China

From 1891 until 1921, *Nippon* was the mark Japan used on hand-painted porcelain made for export. However, in 1921, the United States required all imported Japanese wares to be marked *Japan.*

There are more than 200 documented marks or backstamps for Nippon. For some makers, the color of the mark helps determine the quality of the piece. Green was used for first-grade porcelain, blue for second-grade, and magenta for third-grade. Other types of marks were also used.

Sadly, today there are marked reproductions that can be very deceiving. Carefully examine any piece, study the workmanship, and thoroughly investigate any marks.

References: There are several older reference books that provide information about marks and various makers.

Collectors' Club: Contact the International Nippon Collectors Club, 112 Oak Lane, N., Owatonna, MN 55060 to find a chapter in your local area.

Reproduction Alert.

For additional listings, see *Warman's Antiques and Collectibles Price Guide.*

Buyer beware!

  Don't believe everything you see.

  That's good advice when it comes to buying antiques and collectibles. It's not that a person should be a cynical. However, the existence of reproductions, fakes, forgeries and fantasy items have led collectors to approach the marketplace knowledgeably and with caution.

  The phrase "caveat emptor" — let the buyer beware — is especially true for anyone interested in Nippon porcelain. Fewer areas of the antiques market have been plagued by more reproductions bearing more fake marks than Nippon.

  This hatpin holder is a prime example. An unsuspecting buyer might assume it's an authentic piece of Nippon, since it's marked. However, the mark is a fake—one of many. Therefore, his hatpin holder has no value as an antique.

  One of the best resources providing information about such bogus items is Antique & Collectors Reproduction News, a monthly newsletter. For information, phone (515) 274-5886 or write to ACRN, P.O. Box 12130, Des Moines, IA 50312.

Ashtray, black cat on roof **125.00**
Biscuit jar, ftd, hp roses, gold beading,
  deep teal background, 7" h, 6" dia
  ....**395.00**
Bowl, scalloped edge, floral and gold
  border, green "M" in wreath mark, 7-
  1/2" dia **20.00**
Cake plate, floral design, gold trim,
  green "M" in wreath mark, 11" dia
  ....**40.00**
Candlestick, hand painted gold
  highlights, light green ground pedestal
  base, green maple leaf mark, 11" h
  ....**115.00**
Candy dish, divided, scenic design, blue
  rising sun mark..............................**50.00**
Celery tray, pink flowers **60.00**
Child's cup and bowl, pulled out face,
  googlie eyes, red bow tie **175.00**
Cup and saucer, Orange Blossom
  pattern, gold trim, blue mark........**30.00**
Dresser Tray, delicate hp pink floral
  design, gold trim, closed handles,
  green M in wreath mark, 18" l, minor
  gold wear.....................................**50.00**
Hatpin Holder, shaped, raised beading
  ....**65.00**
Mayonnaise set, underplate, spoon,
  floral border, magenta "M" in wreath
  mark **50.00**
Mustard pot, scenic design, green "M" in
  wreath mark, 3-1/2" h...................**40.00**
Nut bowl, raised nut design, ftd, green
  "M" in wreath mark, 7" dia **85.00**
Plaque, Waiting by Shore, Dutch mother
  and two children looking over bay, dec
  rim, blue M in wreath mark, 10" dia
  ....**100.00**
Plate, two handles, floral and gold
  border, red and green mark, 10-1/2"
  dia **35.00**
Relish, cov, scenic design, gold trim,
  matching spoon, green "M" in wreath
  mark, 4" h....................................**50.00**
Serving tray, center handle, floral dec,
  magenta "M" in wreath mark **20.00**
Sugar shaker, ecru and white ground,
  blue and yellow butterfly..............**80.00**
Tea Set, 6" h cov teapot, creamer, sugar,
  six cups and saucers, hp swans in
  pond, mill in background, gold
  highlighted beading, green "M" in
  wreath mark, wear to gold **150.00**
Vase
  Double handles, double handles, Lilac
  pattern, gold trim, blue maple leaf
  mark, 8-1/2" h **150.00**
  Florals, gold trim, 11" h **450.00**
  House and trees scene, ivory ground,
  gold painted grape leaves, green
  Morimura mark, 8" h..............**375.00**

❖ Nodders and Bobbin' Heads

Here's a collecting category that folks never seem to tire of. Perhaps it's the whimsical nature of these pieces or the idea that there is constant motion. Whatever, there are plenty of examples to be found at flea markets.

Reference: Tim Hunter, *Bobbing Head Dolls 1960-2000*, Krause Publications, 1999.

Collectors' Club: Bobbin' Head National Club, P.O. Box 9297, Daytona Beach, FL 32120.

Nodder

Alligator, mkd "Made in Japan," c1940, 4-1/2" h **95.00**

American League umpire, 8-1/2" h **45.00**

Cowboy, Japan, 5" h **65.00**

Chinaman, Japan, 6-1/2" h **65.00**

Elephant, celluloid, S.A. Reider & Co., Germany **65.00**

Elephant, in green overalls, Hong Kong, 4" h **35.00**

Goose, S.A. Reider & Co., U.S. Zone, Germany, 1-1/2" h, 3-1/2" l **65.00**

Hawaiian boy,"Let's Kiss," Japan, 5-1/2" h...**85.00**

Hawaiian girl, "Let's Kiss," Japan, 5-1/4" h...**85.00**

Lion, fleece, plastic teeth **22.00**

Mickey Mantle, 1962 ....**700.00**

Oakland Athletics, 1988, 8-1/2" h **45.00**

Raggedy Ann, 5-1/2" h **175.00**

Robin Hood, Japan, 6" h **85.00**

Scottie, celluloid, windup, Occupied Japan **125.00**

St. Louis Cardinals football player, plaster, 6-1/2" h **130.00**

Nodder/bank

Black policeman, Nassau, black pants, white hat and jacket, doubles as bank................................**145.00**

Colonel Sanders, plaster, 7-1/2" h **165.00**

Oriental girl....................................**57.50**

Nodder/clock, flamingo, pink and green, quartz clock, mkd "Japan," 1985, 10" w, 6-1/2" h.................................**195.00**

❖ Norcrest

Not a lot of information has been printed about this porcelain maker, but many folks are finding their products to be charming and worth collecting.

Anniversary plate, 45th, 10-1/2" d.**10.00**

Bank, wishing well, blue bird and bucket at edge, 7" h............................**14.50**

Bowl, Merry Christmas to You, 4-3/4" dia

....**18.00**

Creamer, Sweet Violet **20.00**

Cup and saucer

Apple blossoms, gold design on white ground..**20.00**

Pine Cone pattern **7.50**

Figure

Chihuahua, mkd "A583," 4" h **22.00**

Dalmation, 1960s, 6-1/4" l............**15.00**

Giraffe...**35.00**

Rooster and hen, hand painted, 1940s

....**225.00**

Tumbling elephants, pr, mkd "A148," 2-1/2" h **20.00**

Zebras, pr, flirty eyes, orig stickers, 6-1/4" h and 8" h.........................**85.00**

Goblet, 50th Anniversary, gold, colonial couple, 4-3/4" h **15.00**

Miniature cup and saucer, hand painted floral dec, foil label "Norcrest Fine China Japan," orig 2-1/8" h stand, 1-1/4" dia **30.00**

Mug, Psycho Klone, toothy grin, "You're The Greatest," pink shading to white, orig label, 4-1/2" h....................**35.00**

Salt and pepper shakers, pr

Hula Girl and Ukelele Boy, paper label, 3-1/2" h **45.00**

Sad Sack, George Baker, black ink stamp, 4-1/2" h **350.00**

Wall pocket, clock, orig label, 6" h .**25.00**

❖ Noritake China

Noritake China was founded by the Morimura Brothers in Nagoya, Japan, about 1904. The company produced high-quality dinnerware for export and also some blanks for hand painting. Although the factory was heavily damaged during World War II, production resumed and continues today. There are more than 100 different marks to help determine the pattern and date of production.

Reference: David Spain, *Noritake Fancyware A to Z: A Pictorial Record and Guide to Values,* Schiffer Publishing, 2002.

Collectors' Club: Noritake Collectors' Society, 145 Andover Place, West Hempstead, NY 11552.

Bowl, autumn leaves, molded filbert nuts, ftd, turned-in sides, 7" sq **80.00**

Bread Plate, ear of corn dec, 12" l.**50.00**

Candlesticks, pr, gold flowers and bird, blue luster ground, wreath with "M" mark, 8-1/4" h............................**125.00**

Celery set, celery holder, six matching salts, gold trim, green wreath marks

....**85.00**

Compote, blue, gold, and white, fruit dec, 2 pcs...**175.00**

Creamer, Chandon, #7306 ....**42.00**

Cup and saucer

Chelsea pattern............................**30.00**

Noritake China, tray, two small handles, pearlized luster, pink and yellow roses, green leaves, gold trim, $20.

Margarita pattern.........................**12.00**

Roanne, #6794.............................**18.00**

Dinner plate, Margarita pattern, 9-7/8" dia **18.00**

Dish, handle, red and gold flower border, gold trim, red wreath mark, 5-1/2" w **28.00**

Easter egg, yellow hat with blue trim, blue and pink flowers, dated 1976, satin lined box, 3" h......................**26.00**

Gravy boat, Carolyn.......................**105.00**

Hair receiver, Art Deco geometric designs, gold luster, wreath with "M" mark, 3-1/4" h............................**50.00**

Jam jar, cov, basket style, figural applied cherries on notched lid.................**55.00**

Platter

Asian Song, medium....................**85.00**

Candice, large **85.00**

Carolyn, small **82.00**

Potpourri jar, blue and white, pierced cov with red and yellow rosebud finial, 6" h...**85.00**

Salt, swan, white, orange luster **12.00**

Soup bowl, Margarita pattern.........**18.00**

Sugar bowl, cov, Margarita pattern **18.00**

Vase, medallion with landscape scene on one side, florals on reverse, gold moriage, black background covered with tiny gold roses, gold edge at bottom, some wear to gold, green M" in wreath mark, c1920, 6" h.............**90.00**

Vegetable bowl, cov, Bamboo......**115.00**

Wall Pocket, orange luster, figural bird peering over top **180.00**

❖ Noritake China, Azalea Pattern

In the 1920s, the Larkin Company of Buffalo, N.Y., became a prime distributor of Noritake China. Two of the most popular patterns they promoted were Azalea and Tree in the Meadow, causing them to be the most popular with collectors today. The design of Azalea pattern includes delicate pink flowers, green leaves on a white background. Many pieces have gold trim, especially on handles and finials.

Noritake, Azalea Pattern platter, oval, 2 handles, $20.

Bon bon	48.00
Cake plate	40.00
Casserole, cov	75.00
Creamer	25.00
Dinner plate	24.00
Egg cup	55.00
Lemon tray	30.00
Luncheon plate	15.00
Platter, oval	20.00
Salad bowl, 10" dia	37.50
Teapot	100.00
Vase, fan	150.00
Vegetable dish, cov	75.00

❖ Noritake China, Tree in the Meadow Pattern

This popular pattern was also sold by the Larkin Company. The pattern shows a scene with a meadow, sky, buildings, and, of course, trees. It's a more colorful pattern than Azalea.

Ashtray, green backstamp, 5-1/4" dia 35.00
Bowl, green backstamp, 6-3/4" l, 6" dia 30.00
Butter dish, cov, orig insert 65.00
Cake plate, 7-1/2" sq 38.00
Creamer and sugar, red wreath mark 45.00
Demitasse cup and saucer 48.00

Noritake, Tree in the Meadow pattern, Heart shaped tray and small heart shaped dish, $25.

Lemon dish, 5-1/2" dia 35.00
Plate, red-brown backstamp, 7-3/4" dia 30.00
Platter, two handles 45.00
Relish tray, 8-1/2" l, red mark.........40.00
Teapot 100.00
Vase, fan shape, green backstamp, 5" w 35.00

❖ Northwood Glass

Northwood Glass is a term used to describe the glassware made by both the Northwood Glass Company and Northwood & Company, two distinct glass makers. The histories of these companies are quite interesting and involved. Between them, fine pressed pattern glass, opalescent glass, and Carnival glass was made. The name Northwood has again surfaced as a glass manufacturer as Northwood family descendants are beginning to issue new pieces. Contemporary wares have a different mark than the familiar N or script signature found on vintage pieces. Like many glass manufacturers, not every piece was marked.

Basket, white carnival, basketweave, open handles, ftd, sgd, 4" h 125.00
Bon bon, Stippled Rays pattern, blue carnival 60.00
Butter dish, cov, Cherry and Lattice, ruby and gold flashing, wear, roughness 90.00
Candlestick, 3" h, 5-1/4" dia, Chinese Coral...85.00
Candy dish, cov
  Ruffles and Bows, blue opalescent 45.00
  Stretch, blue iridescent, #636 ......70.00
Compote, Chrysanthemum Sprig, custard, 5" h, 3" dia......................80.00
Creamer
  Lustre Flute, green carnival 50.00
  Regal, blue opalescent................60.00
Cruet, Leaf Umbrella, Mauve, heat check, no stopper.......................500.00
Goblet
  Grape and Gothic Arches, custard, nutmeg stain 75.00
  Nearcut, colorless 40.00
Jelly compote, Poppy pattern, green 35.00
Nut bowl, Leaf and Beads pattern, purple carnival.............................65.00
Pitcher, Ribbed Opal, blue.........1,450.00
Salt and pepper shakers, pr, orig tops
  Bow and Tassel pattern, milk glass 65.00
  Leaf Umbrella, mauve, cased 165.00
Sugar, cov
  Cherry and Plum pattern, clear, ruby and green trim 85.00

Paneled Spring, milk glass, green and gold dec.................................125.00
Tumbler, Acorn Burrs, green..........75.00
Water set, Regent, amethyst, pitcher and six tumblers 800.00

❖ Nutcrackers

Mug, nutcracker face, modern resin, $1.

Clever devises to release the tasty part of a nut were invented as far back as the 19th century. Collectors today seek out interesting examples in various metals and wood.

Collectors' Club: Nutcracker Collectors' Club, 12204 Fox Run Drive, Chesterland, OH 44026.

Nutcrackers Soldier, wooden, fleece beard and hair, painted facial features and jacket, natural wood hat, pants and stand, 1" h, $20.

Nutcrackers Soldier, wooden, red painted jacket, black hat with gold trim, white pants, black boots, fur hair and beard, green base, 8" h, $15.

Bear, wooden, Black Forest, glass eyes, curved tail with lever that operates the mouth, 4-1/2" h, 8" l **165.00**

Crocodile, wooden, full-figure, Swiss or German, screw press in belly, 8" l **585.00**

Dog, graniteware over cast iron, white on black base, black tail and lower jar, 5-3/4" h, 10-1/2" l **115.00**

Dog's head, wooden, Black Forest style, glass eyes, levered jaw, mkd "Chalet Minerve & Chalet Suisse Egger & Bruger...," oval base, 3-1/2" h, 7" l **520.00**

Eagle's head, wooden, Swiss, glass eyes, levered beak, 6-1/2" l **310.00**

Elephant's head, wooden, glass eyes, levered mouth, 10-1/2" l **650.00**

Man with umbrella, bearded, smoking a pipe, wooden, German, 1 foot reattached, 8-1/2" h...................**570.00**

Squirrel, cast iron, 4-1/2" h, 5-1/2" l **100.00**

St. Bernard, metal, advertises L.A. Althoff Makers of Headlight Stoves and Ranges Chicago, Ill., 5-3/4" h, 11" l **275.00**

Nutcrackers Mailman, wooden, blue uniform, letter pouch, 6" h, $20.

❖ Nutting, Wallace

The story of Wallace Nutting is a fascinating tale of enterprising American. Born in 1861, he attended Harvard University and several theological seminaries. In 1904 he opened a photography studio in New York, later other branch studios. By the time he moved to Framingham, Mass., in 1913, he was employing more than 200 colorists, framers, and support staff. Nutting photographed the images that were to be hand colored under his specific directions. Nutting died in 1941, but his wife continued the business. After her death, the business continued until 1971, when the last owner ordered the glass negatives destroyed.

Although the listing below is devoted to his pictures, remember that he also published several books and sold silhouettes and furniture.

References: Michael Ivankovich, *Alphabetical & Numerical Index to Wallace Nutting Pictures*, Diamond Press, 1988; ——, *Collector's Guide to Wallace Nutting Pictures*, Collector Books, 1997.

Collectors' Club: Wallace Nutting Collectors Club, P.O. Box 2458, Doylestown, PA 18901.

Among the Ferns, 14" x 17" **165.00**
Between the Spruces, 10" x 14"..**200.00**
By the Stone Fence, The Swimming Pool, 10" x 12"..........................**160.00**
California Hilltops, 11" x 14" **185.00**
Dell Dale Road, 16" x 20".............**235.00**
The Goose Chase Quilt, 10" z 18" **375.0**
Harmony, 14" x 17".......................**375.00**
The Home Hearth, 10" x 16" **325.00**
Honeymoon Blossoms, 12" x 16"**185.00**
June Beautiful, 13" z 16" **195.00**
Lingering Waters, 9" x 11" **185.00**
Pennsylvania Arches, 14" x 17'...**300.00**
Shadowy Orchard Curves, 11" x 14"
....**85.00**
Village Spires, 10" x 12"...............**125.00**
Wilton Waters, 13" x 16"...............**155.00**

❖ Nutting-Like Pictures

Because Wallace Nutting's pictures were so successful, copycats soon appeared on the scene. Some artists had worked for Nutting and learned the techniques. These pictures are starting to catch the eye of collectors.

Davidson, David
   Berkshire Sunset.........................**80.00**
   Christmas Day............................**160.00**
   Over the Hills, 7" z 9" **75.00**
   Rivers of Peace, 7" x 9" **65.00**
   The Road Home, 6" z 8" **75.00**

Haynes, F. Jay
   Old Faithful, 8" x 10" **95.00**
   Great Falls, Yellowstone Park, 13" x 18"
....**150.00**

Sawyer
   At the Bend of the Road **35.00**
   Crystal Lake **65.00**
   Echo Lake, 7" x 9".......................**65.00**
   Upper-Flame Falls, 14" x 16" **150.00**
   Willoughby Lake, 5" x 6" **110.00**

Thompson, Fred
   Apple Tree Road **45.00**
   Blossom Dale...............................**75.00**
   Deep Hole Brook, 5" x 13"...........**75.00**
   Fireside Fancy Work, 7" x 9"......**110.00**

❖ Occupied Japan

To help repair their devastated economy after World War II, the Japanese made items to export, including porcelain, toys, and all kinds of knickknacks. Today savvy collectors know that items made during the occupation time period might be marked "Japan," "Made in Japan," or "Occupied Japan" as well as "Made in Occupied Japan."

Referenc: Florence Archambault, *Occupied Japan For the Home*, Schiffer Publishing, 2000.

Collectors' Club: The Occupied Japan Club, 29 Freeborn St., Newport, RI 02840.

Ashtray, china, souvenir from Florida, shaped like state, black letters, gold trim 15.00
Basket, china, small figural roses and leaves 7.50
Bell, chef holding wine bottle and glass 27.50
Demitasse cup and saucers, Dragonware, yellow and white, brown, green, and white enameled dragons, stamp mark, 2" dia cup, 4" dia saucers, price for set of four 175.00
Dinner plate, Damara Tajimi, mkd, 10" dia 6.50
Doll, bisque, Black, painted eyes and mouth, fabric hair, arms and legs slightly loose, imp "Made in Occupied Japan," 4" h 75.00
Egg timer, maid, mkd 45.00
Figurine
  Couple, 7" x 4-1/2" 35.00
  Cowboy on rearing horse, metal ..18.00
  Lady holding musical instrument, mkd, 7" h 55.00
  Man and woman, 18th C costume, mkd, 6" h 60.00
  Santa, 7-1/2" h 60.00
Flower frog, bisque, girl with bird on shoulder, pastel highlights, gold trim 48.00
Mug, boy-shaped handle 15.00
Opera glasses, metal, mkd "3X," slight wear, 4" l 90.00
Planter, black cat, red ribbon 15.00
Reamer, strawberry shape, red, green

leaves and handle, mkd "Occupied Japan", 3-3/4" h 90.00
Rice bowl, hand painted, bright orange and yellow flowers, budding orange flower on back, mkd "Made in Occupied Japan," and ISCO in red triangle, 4-1/2" dia 30.00
Tape measure, pig, stamped "Occupied Japan" 45.00
Teapot, figural, squirrel on corn, yellow kernels, green foliage, brown squirrel handle and finial, mkd, 7" w, 5-1/4" h 120.00
Tea set, 5" h cov teapot, 3-1/4" h creamer, 3-1/2" h cov sugar, glossy black luster with open rose, gold dec, mkd "Made in Occupied Japan," M and T superimposed over mark in circle 125.00
Toy, boy on sled, litho tin wind-up, MIB 150.00
Vase, facing pair, man on one, lady on other, light blue cylindrical vase, white base, 5" h, mkd 55.00
Wall pocket, lady with hat, 5" h 45.00

❖ Ocean Liner Memorabilia

The thought of a leisurely ocean cruise has enticed many to try this mode of travel. Of course they brought back souvenirs. Today collectors are glad they did as they discover these mementoes at flea markets.

Collectors' Club: Steamship Historical Society of America, Inc., 300 Ray Drive, Suite 4, Providence, RI 02906.

Ashtray, *Normandie*, Opalex Glass, France, 1945, 3-3/8" x 2-3/4" 55.00
Baggage tag, French Line, first class, unused 7.50
Book, *USS Triton SSRN 586 First Submerged Circumnavigation*, Government Printing Office, Washington, DC, 1960, 1st printing 50.00
Brochure
  Cunard Line, Getting There is Half the Fun, 16 pgs, 1952 ....7.50
  French Line, Sunshine Trail to Europe, 12 pgs, 1930s 55.00
Deck plan, *RMS Queen Elizabeth*, Cunard, plan of first class accommodation, cream colored folder, gold and brown lettering, 1952 ....50.00
Dish, Cunard *RMS Queen Mary*, ceramic, oval, color portrait, gold edge, Staffordshire, 5" l 37.50
Fan, Cie Galen Transatlantique French Line, chromolithograph of Spanish style

lady overlooking Mediterranean, watching ocean liner sail past, paper on wood, orig tassel, artist sgd, 1919 ....85.00
Magazine illus, framed, *SS Normandie* being escorted by the E.J. Moran tug into slip in NY harbor, 12" x 15".125.00
Map, Norwegian Cruise Lines, *M/S Southward*, map of West Indies and Caribbean Sea, routes, antiquities images, 1970s, framed, 18" x 24" 40.00
Menu
  SS Leonardo Da Vinci, January, 1973 ....6.00
  SS Lurline, Matson Lines, Commodore's Dinner, March 3, 1959, 12" x 9" 22.00
Newspaper Supplement, *Queen Mary, the World's Wonder Ship*, 20" x 24", acid free mat 125.00
Passport cover, Red Star Line, fabric, ship illus 27.50
Pencil, *S/S Oceanic*, Caran D'ache lead pencil, plastic case 25.00
Pennant, *R.M.S. Queen Elizabeth*, gray felt, blue, red, white, and black, some fading, 26-1/2" l 25.00
Playing cards, Eastern Steamship Corp., 3/4" x 2-1/4" x 3-1/2" gold foil box, red, and black accents, full color deck, showing ship at sea, yellow and white border, revenue stamp attached to edge flap, c1950 ....15.00
Poster, *Nord-Lloyd Bremen* and *Europa*, marketed for American transatlantic travel, conservation framed, 6-1/2" x 9-1/2" 150.00
Program, Charity Fete, *De La Salle*, French Lines, benefiting Central Lifeboat Society, Marine Welfare Society, Society Aid to Families of French Shipwrecked Mariners, and Transatlantique Maternity Fund, 5 color images by Jean Droit, Dec 24, 1927 ....50.00
Souvenir Spoon, Cunard *White Star*, demitasse, silver plated 20.00
Tie clasp, Cunard Line *RMS Queen Mary*, gold tone, red, white, and blue enameled ship 18.00
Track Chart, Anchor Line, *SS Anchoria*, voyage from New York to Glasgow, 10-1/2" x 6" 75.00

❖ Old Sleepy Eye

Old Sleepy Eye, Minn., was the home of the Old Sleepy Eye Flour Mill. The company used an Indian as its. Collectors can also find his image on stoneware premiums that were issued by the mill.

Old Sleepy Eye Butter crock, blue and gray stoneware, 6-1/2" dia, 4-3/4" h, hairline crack, $185.

Collectors' Club: Old Sleepy Eye Collectors Club, P.O. Box 12, Monmouth, IL 61462.

Reproduction Alert

Advertising premium card, full-color Indian lore illus. 5-1/2" x 9" **65.00**
Bowl, rounded bottom, 4" h, 6-1/2" dia **355.00**
Butter crock, straight-sided, 5" h, 6-1/2" dia **375.00**
Cookbook, shaped like a loaf of bread, 4-7/8" x 4-1/4" **175.00**
Mug, 4-1/2" d, 4-1/2" h, attributed to Brush/McCoy.............................**250.00**
Pillow top, Chief Sleepy Eye before the Great Father, known as the Monroe top, 1901 ....**500.00**
Pitcher, blue and white
No.1, blue rim, 4-1/8" h **275.00**
No. 1, plain rim, 4-1/8" h **180.00**
No. 2, 5-1/4" h **275.00**
No. 4, blue rim **410.00**
Salt crock, hanging, blue and white, 5-1/2" h, 5-1/4" dia **1,650.00**
Vase, cylindrical, 8-1/2" h **350.00**

❖ Olympic Collectibles

Most of us are familiar with the Olympic rings logo. Watching for those is a great way to spot Olympic collectibles. It's usually easier to find fresh examples at flea markets during years the Olympics are held.

Periodical: *Sports Collectors Digest,* 700 E State St., Iola, WI 54990.

Collectors' Club: Olympic Pin Collector's Club, 1386 Fifth St., Schenectady, NY 12303.

Barbie, Olympic Gymnast Barbie, 1995, NRFB **20.00**
Booklet, viewers guide, 1992 Olympic Winter Games, Albertville **10.00**
Bottle opener, 1996, Atlanta, American flag design on one side, 4-1/2" l ..**12.00**

Coca-Cola bottle, 1984, 23rd Olympiad, Los Angeles, 10" h **12.00**
Figurine, Hallmark, Atlanta Centennial Games, 1996
Swimming, sculpted by Robert Chad **65.00**
Track and Field............................**65.00**
Key chain, 1984, Olympic rings........**4.00**
License plate, 1996, Atlanta............**4.00**
Pennant, 1996, Atlanta, Olympic Baseball **6.00**
Photo, U.S. Olympic Tumbling Team, coaches, Los Angeles, 1932, name written on......................................**90.00**
Pin, enameled brass
1984, Official Olympic International flag series, Los Angeles, sponsored by Coca-Cola, three sets of 50 each, mounted on black velvet in shadow box wood frame **480.00**
1988, Annheuser-Busch, set of 4 pins **45.00**
Plate
1972 Olympics, Bing & Grondahl, 7-1/8" dia...............................**50.00**
1992, Winter Olympics Skating, Albertville, France, Budweiser, orig box, 8-1/2" dia........................**28.00**
Platter, 1984, features Olympians, McDonald's, tin, 8" x 11" **9.00**
Program
1948, "Olympic Games London 1948 Official Souvenir," 176 pgs **50.00**
1996, "The Games of the XXVI Olympiad Centennial Olympic Games," 196 pgs **32.00**
Warm-up jacket and pants, red, white, and blue, Levi's, insignia patch "1984 USA Olympics, Los Angeles," USA on back of jacket **125.00**

❖ Orrefors, Kosta Boda

Here's interesting glassware to start collecting. Made in Sweden since 1898, current pieces often reflect their historical antecedents. The crystal used is high quality and the designers certainly develop some interesting shapes and color combinations.

Bowl, crystal
Cornelia, 8-1/4" d **38.00**
Hand painted yellow and green floral dec, sgd Kosta Boda, 5-1/2" d..**45.00**
Bucket, heavy walled cylinder, transparent teal blue, base inscribed "Orrefors Esp. PA 245-62 Sven Palmqvist"..................................**200.00**
Candlesticks, pr, 3" h, 5" dia, crystal, sgd **115.00**

Orrefors, Kosta Boda Bowl, colorless, swirls, sgd, $35.

Decanter, 12-1/2" h, squared crystal bottle, Romeo serenading Juliet on balcony, base engraved "Orrefors No. 880" **350.00**
Figurine
Lemon, yellow and green, orig label, 5-1/2" l..**22.00**
Scottie, crystal, 4" h **60.00**
Jar, cov, 1000 Windows, sgd and numbered **450.00**
Perfume bottle, crystal, orig label, 4-1/4" h **32.00**
Rose bowl, round, layered, sgd "Orrefors H 7 48" **200.00**
Scent bottle, octagonal, engraved fish and bubbles, 9-1/4" h **180.00**
Vase
3" h, spherical, white spatter, blue, green, black, and rust stripe on one side, green, yellow, blue, and turquoise stripe on other side, paper label **55.00**
6-1/2" h, engraved fish dec, orig label **125.00**
7-1/2" h, pulled white loops, sgd "Boda B Valdine" **200.00**

❖ Owl Collectibles

Whoo, whoo, who collects owl items - lots of folks! Some are enchanted with the wisdom of this regal bird, while others find owls fun and whimsical. Lucky for them, artists and designers have been incorporating the owl's image into items for years.

Owl Collectibles Cast iron owl mechanical bank with glass eyes, no paint, 7-1/4" h, $250.

Ashtray, ceramic, 3 cut owls, figural **30.00**

Blotter, "Whoo? Oswald, I told you we couldn't get away with that bone!", 2 puppies under a tree, owl sitting on branch, Harry N. Johnson, Real Estate & Insurance, Highlands, NJ..........**10.00**

Book rack, expandable, owl on each end **55.00**

Brooch, Mandle, japanned mounting, clear rhinestones for the body and head, dark greet eyes and ears, 2-1/4" h, 1" w **50.00**

Candy container, owl on branch **50.00**

Figurine, glass, alpine blue, Boyd, 3-1/2" h **12.00**

Letter opener, brass **25.00**

Napkin ring, standing owl, silver plated **150.00**

Notepad holder, chalkware, figural, 1970, 7" sq **29.00**

Pin, Avon, solid perfume sachet, goldtone, 2" h **10.00**

Print, Mottled Owl, hand-colored, Beverly Robinson Morris, from *Birds of Great Britain*, 1895, slight stain, foxing, 10" x

6-3/4: **20.00**

Salt and pepper shakers, Shawnee Pottery, 3-3/8" h, pr **35.00**

Spoon rest, ceramic, souvenir of San Francisco, shows cable car, has kitchen prayer, 7" x 4-1/2" **20.00**

Tape measure, brass, glass eyes, mkd "Germany" **40.00**

Tin, Red Owl allspice, Red Owl Stores **17.00**

✿ Paden City Glass

Founded in Paden City, W.Va., in 1916, this company made glassware until 1951. Paden City's wares were all hand made until 1948. The glass was not marked, nor was it heavily advertised. Much of their success laid with blanks supplied to others to decorate. Many of their wares were sold to institutional facilities, restaurants, etc. Paden City is known for rich colors in many shades.

Reference: O.O. Brown, *Paden City Glass Mfg. Co., Catalogue Reprints From the 1920s*, Glass Press, 2000; Paul and Debbie Torsiello and Tom and Arlene Stillman, *Paden City Glassware,* Schiffer Publishing, 2002.

Animal
Bunny, ears down, cotton dispenser **95.00**
Goose..**60.00**
Pheasant, light blue....................**170.00**
Pony, tall **100.00**
Bowl, #440 Nerva, 8" d, silver overlay, mkd "Sterling"..............................**95.00**
Cake plate, ftd
#411 Mrs. B., Ardith etch, yellow .**55.00**
#412 Crow's Foot Square, Orchid etch, yellow......................................**95.00**
Candleholders, pr
#191 Party Line, dome foot, Gypsy cutting, medium blue **25.00**
#210 Regina, Black Forest etch.**140.00**
Candy box, cov, #191 Party Line, pink **50.00**
Compote
#191 Party Line, pink, ftd, 11"......**35.00**
#411 Mrs B, Ardith etch, yellow ...**75.00**
Console bowl, #881 Gadroon, Frost etch **65.00**
Creamer and sugar
#411 Mrs B, Gothic Garden etch, crystal **45.00**
#412 Crow's Foot Square, mulberry **42.00**
Cup and saucer, Largo, red **32.50**
Goblet
#991 Penny Line, mulberry, low foot **18.50**
#994 Popeye & Olive, 6-1/8" h, cobalt blue **35.00**
Iced tea tumbler, #991 Penny Line, 12 oz, amethyst...............................**22.50**
Marmalade, cov, Emerald Glo,

coppertone lid **40.00**
Napkin rings, Party Line, set of 6...**60.00**
Parfait, #191 Party Line, ftd, green.**20.00**
Plate
#411 Mrs. B, 8-1/2" d, amber **6.00**
#412 Crow's Foot Square, 6" w sq, ruby...**5.00**
#890 Crow's Foot Round, 6-1/2" d, blue **6.00**
Relish, #890 Crow's Foot Round, 3-part, 11" l oblong, crystal, star cut........**35.00**
Sherbet
#69 Line, Georgian, ruby **12.50**
#191 Party Line, pink **8.50**
Tumbler
#191 Party Line, 5-3/4" h, cone shape, pink..**9.75**
#210 Regina, 5-1/2" h, Black Forest etch, pink **80.00**
#890 Crow's Foot Round, amber .**35.00**
#991 Penny Line, 3 1/4" h, ruby.....**8.00**
Vase
#182, 8" h, elliptical, crystal, Trumpet Flower etch **115.00**
#184, 10" h, bulbous, Peacock and Rose etch, Cheriglo **165.00**
#210 Regina, 6-1/2" h, Harvesters etch, ebony **145.00**
#513 Black Forest etch, 10" h, crystal..**195.00**

❖ Paden City Pottery

Located near Sisterville, W.Va., Paden City Pottery was founded in 1914 and ceased operation in 1963. They produced semi-porcelain dinnerware with high-quality decal decoration.

Cup and saucer
Rose..**12.50**
Yellow Rose.................................**14.50**
Gravy boat, Minion, dark green **35.00**

Paden City china cup and saucer, yellow tulips, red roses, white daisies, blue forget-me-nots, green foliage dec inside cup, gold trim on cup ext., matching saucer, green Paden City factory mark, also mkd "Warranted 22 K Gold," $15.

Plate
Far East, 10-1/2" dia **20.00**
Modern Orchid, 9-3/8" dia...........**11.75**

Pink Roses, 9-3/4" dia.................**12.00**
Rose, 10" dia...............................**12.00**
Shell Crest, tab handle, 10-1/2" dia **20.00**
Yellow Rose, 9-1/4" dia **10.00**
Platter
American Rose, 13-3/4" l **30.00**
Jonquils, yellow and pink **45.00**
Minion, charteuse........................**30.00**
Modern Orchid, 12-1/4" sq..........**25.00**
Patio, 12" l **30.00**
Petit Point Bouquet, 13-3/4" l **35.00**
Rose, oval, 13-3/4" l....................**35.00**
Shell Crest, 16" l **30.00**
Touch of Black, 14" l....................**25.00**
Yellow Roses, 14" l......................**25.00**
Wild Grasses, 12" l......................**30.00**
Salt and pepper shakers, Modern Orchid...**16.50**
Teapot, Bak-Serv, stains, spot chip.**95.00**
Tureen, cov, rose dec, mkd "A-50," 7-1/2" dia **65.00**
Vegetable bowl, Jonquil, 8-1/2" dia.**30.00**

❖ Paint-by-Number Sets

For those of us who aren't artistically inclined, paint-by-number sets open a world that turns anyone into a first-class artist. Popular-culture figures are favorite subjects. Collectors look for sets that are mint in box. However, buyers are also snapping up many finished products, especially those with unusual subjects.

Autumn mill, 19-1/4" x 15-1/2" **22.50**
Barbie and Rockers, unused, MIP.**15.00**
Blue jays, framed, 13" x 10-1/2" **20.00**
Deer scene, 24" x 18" **24.50**
Desert scene with prospector, 15-1/2" x 11-1/2" **28.00**
Hunting dogs, 1950s/60s, 16-1/2" x 20-1/2" **17.50**
Impalas drinking at African water hole, framed, 12" x 16" **32.00**

Paint by Number Sets, mountainous seaside scene, unsigned, well done, $5.

Jesus and children, framed, 21-1/2" x 27-1/2" **7.50**

Little boy praying, beagle by his side, Simpson's order label on back, 12-1/2" x 6-1/2" **10.00**
Lighthouse, framed, 10" x 14" **16.50**
Nude, woman sitting on rocks on beach, 12" x 16" **55.00**
Roses, still life, 1958, PP Corp, 2 paintings, MIB **7.50**
Ship, 15-1/2" x 19-1/2" **15.00**
Winter landscape, 13" x 17" **15.00**

❖ Pairpoint

Here's a name that can confuse flea market dealers. Some associate Pairpoint with the Pairpoint Manufacturing Company or Pairpoint Corporation, a leader in silver-plated wares. Others associate it with National Pairpoint Company, a company that made glassware and aluminum products such as windows, and other commercial glassware. Today lead crystal glassware is still made by Pairpoint.

Basket, silver plated, 12-5/8" l, 9-1/4' w, 9-1/4" h, mkd "Pat applied for 12/1904," some wear to plating **295.00**
Bowl, amethyst glass silver label, unused **75.00**
Bride's basket holder, silver plated, figural berries dec, mkd..............**325.00**
Compote, peachblow, hp florals, paper label, 6-3/4" dia **160.00**
Dish, fish shape, teal blue, controlled bubbles dec, late **275.00**
Epergne, center glass vase etched with roses, silver plate holder with matching roses, mkd "Pairpoint Mfg Co., New Bedford, Mass," 11" h **675.00**
Fruit tray, silver plated, birds, cherries, and leaves, 11" x 14" **195.00**

Pairpoint, bride's basket, peppermint stick rim, frosted bowl, silver plated frame with six medallions of Roman warriors, four feet, $195.

Mustache cup, silver plated, elaborate

floral design, mkd "Pairpoint Mfg Co., New Bedford, Mass, Quadruple Plate, 2060," 3-1/4" h **45.00**
Perfume bottle, amethyst, painted butterfly, teardrop stopper, "P" in diamond mark, 6-3/4" h..............**375.00**
Tea set, silver plated **300.00**
Trophy, copper, 2 fancy handles with feather design, plaque "New Bedford Yacht Club, Ocean Race, won by Nutmeg for fastest time, Aug 5th, 1909," base mkd and numbered, 8-1/2" h, 7" dia **400.00**
Tray, silver plated, designer Albert Steffin, 14" l, patented June 28, 1904 ....**195.00**

❖ Paper Dolls

Paper dolls date to the 1880s. Several early magazines, including *McCall's*, used to include paper dolls in every issue. The book form of paper dolls came into favor in the 1950s. Look for interesting characters and vintage clothing styles.

Periodicals: *Celebrity Doll Journal*, 5 Court Pl, Puyallup, WA 98372; *Cornerstones*, 2216 S. Autumn Lane, Diamond Bar, CA 91789; *Golden Paper Doll & Toy Opportunities*, P.O. Box 252, Golden CO, 80402-0252; *Loretta's Place Paper Doll Newsletter*, 808 Lee Ave., Tifton, GA 3194-4134; *Midwest Paper Dolls & Toys Quarterly*, P.O. Box 131, Galesburg, KS 66740; *Northern Lights Paperdoll News*, P.O. Box 871189, Wasilla, AK 99687; *Now & Then*, 67-40 Yellowstone Blvd., Flushing, NY 11375-2614; *Paper Doll & Doll Diary*, P.O. Box 12146, Lake Park, FL 33403; *Paper Doll Circle*, 5 Jackson Mews, Immingham, NR, Grimsby, S Hubs DN40 2HQ, UK; *Paper Doll Gazette*, Route #2, Box 52, Princeton, IN 47670; *Paper Doll News*, P.O. Box 807, Vivian, LA 71082; *Paperdoll Review*, P.O. Box 584, Princeton, IN 47670; *PD Pal*, 5341 Gawain #883, San Antonio, TX 78218.

Collectors' Clubs: Original Paper Doll Artist Guild, P.O. Box 14, Kingsfield, ME 04947; Paper Doll Queens & Kings of Metro Detroit, 685 Canyon Road, Rochester, MI 48306; United Federation of Doll Clubs, 10920 N Ambassador, Kansas City, MO 64153.

Annie Oakley, 1956, uncut.............**65.00**
Ballet Cut-Out, Whitman #1962, uncut **65.00**
Barbie, Peck Aubrey, 1994, MIP **15.00**
Betsy McCall Cut-Out/Punch-Out Paper Dolls, Saalfield #1370, 8-1/4" x 11-1/2", copyright 1965, 1966 McCall Corp., USA, 16 full color pages ...**24.00**
Big n Little Sister, Merrill, #1549-15, 1951, uncut **125.00**
Cinderella, Saalfield Publishing Co., 4 dolls, 4 pgs, uncut **20.00**
Elizabeth Taylor, Whitman, #1954, uncut

....**95.00**
Heart Family, Golden Book, 1985, uncut **15.00**
Madeline, Viking, 1994, uncut..........**5.00**
Miss America Magic Doll, Parker Bros, 1953, uncut **24.00**
Nanny and the Professor, Artcraft, 1971 ....**24.00**
Opera Stars of the Golden Age, Tom Tierney, 1984, uncut....................**15.00**
Our Gang, Whitman, 1931, clothes uncut **65.00**
Pony Tail, Samuel Gabriel & Sons, uncut **24.00**
Sparkle Plenty, uncut **60.00**
Stand-Up, National Syndicate Display, 1942, 16" h, uncut.......................**45.00**
The Wedding Party, Samuel Gabriel & Sons, uncut **35.00**

❖ Paperback Books

Mass-marketed paperback books date to the late 1930s. Collectors tend to focus on one type of book or a favorite author.

Periodicals: *Books Are Everything*, 302 Martin Drive, Richmond, KY 40475; *Dime Novel Round-Up*, P.O. Box 226, Dundas, MN 55019; *Echoes*, 504 E. Morris Street, Seymour, TX 76380; *Golden Perils*, 5 Milliken Mills Road, Scarboro, ME 04074; *Paperback Parade*, P.O. Box 209, Brooklyn, NY 11228.

A Little Princess, Frances Hodgson Burnett, Apple, 1987 ....**4.00**
Favorite Christmas Carols, Firestone Tire and Rubber Co., 1955....................**5.00**
First Lady, Charlotte Curtis, Pyramid Book, 1962, 1st printing **12.00**

Paperback Books, 11th Antiques and Their Current Prices with Golden Treasury, *Edwin G. Warman*, Warman Publishing Co., 1972, $24.

Flying Saucers in Fact and Fiction, Hans Stefan Santesson, 1968................**6.00**

Folk Medicine, D. C. Jarvis, MD, Crest Book, 4th printing **3.00**

For Your Eyes Only, James Bond, 1st ed., 1981 ....**5.00**

Growing Up, Karl de Schweinitz, Collier Books, 1965 ....**5.00**

John F. Kennedy: War Hero, Richard Tregaskis **15.00**

Little Women, Louisa May Alcott, Apple, 248 pgs, book club edition **4.00**

Number 1, Billy Martin (autographed) and Peter Goldenbock, Dell, 1st printing, 1981 ....**20.00**

Putting People First, How We Can All Change America, Governor Bill Clinton and Senator Al Gore, Times Books, 1992, first edition..........................**7.50**

Saddle Man, Matt Stuart, Bantam, Sept. 1951, 1st printing **8.00**

Super Eye Adventure Treasure Hunt, Jay Leibold, Ray zone and Chuck Roblin illus, Bantam Skylar Books, 1995 ..**5.00**

U-Boats In Action, Robert C. Stern, 1977 ....**10.00**

They Were Expendable, W.L. White, 1941 ....**15.00**

Wings of Joy, Joan Winmill Brown, World Wide Publications, 1977.................**5.00**

❖ Paper Money

Paper Money, frame on right small frame with Continental Currency $7 bill, Philadelphia 1775 and National Currency $5 bill issued by the Commercial-German National Bank of Peoria, January 2, 1904, $145.

Here's another one of those topics where thousands of examples exist, and collectors should to critical of condition. There are many good reference books to help with both issues.

References, all from Krause Publications: Neil Shafer and George S. Cuhaj, eds., *Standard Catalog of World Paper Money, Specialized Issues,* Volume I, 9th ed. 2002; Chester Krause, *Wisconsin Obsolete Bank Notes and Scrip;* Eric P. Newman, *Early Paper Money of America,* 4th ed. 1997; Dean Oates & John Schwartz, *Standard Guide to Small Size U. S. Paper Money,* 4th ed. 2002; Neil Shafer and Colin R. Bruce II, *Standard Catalog of World Paper Money, General Issues,* Volume II, 9th ed. 2000; Arlie Slabaugh, *Confederate States Paper Money,* 10th ed. 2000; Chester L. Krause and Robert F. Lemke, Joel T. Edler, ed.,

Standard Catalog of U. S. Paper Money, 21st ed., 2002.

Periodical: *Bank Note Reporter,* 700 E State St., Iola, WI 54990.

> **It's a record!**
> As noted in the Bank Note Reporter, an auction record was set when an 1890 $1,000 treasury note sold for $792,000. The note is commonly known as the Levitan Grand Watermelon. Only three Grand Watermelons are known to be in private hands.

Bank of State of Georgia, 1857 ....**20.00**
Bank of Tennessee, 1861, 5 cents.**10.00**
Consecutive Numbers, set of five, $1, CU FRNS, 1995 Star, District B ...**20.00**
Continental Note, Philadelphia, Feb 17, 1776, 2$, decorative border, woodcuts **85.00**
Djibouti, 20 francs..........................**65.00**
Egypt, 10 pounds, 1958.................**48.00**
First Reserve Bank Knot, 1929, 5$ **150.00**
State of Florida, 1$ **26.00**
State of North Carolina, 2$ note, 1861 ....**21.00**
Tecumseh, Michigan, 1$...............**30.00**

❖ Paperweights

Kosta paperweight, controlled white bubbles, mkd "Kosta 96099 Lindstrnd," 4" h, $35.

About the same time folks invented paper, they needed something to hold it down, so along came the paperweight. They can be highly decorative or purely practical. Look for ones of interesting advertising, perhaps a unique shape, or showing an interesting location.

References: For high end priced antique and modern glass paperweights, consult one of the many standard paperweight reference books.

Collectors' Clubs: Caithness Collectors Club, 141 Lanza Ave., Building 12, Garfield,

NJ 07026; International Paperweight Society, 761 Chestnut St., Santa Cruz, CA 95060; Paperweight Collectors Association, Inc., P.O. Box 1263, Beltsville, MD 20704.

For additional listings of traditional glass paperweights, see *Warman's Antiques and Collectibles Price Guide* and *Warman's Glass.*

> **Slimy critter**
> Salamander paperweights—so called because they contain a glass replica of the amphibian—are among the most desirable of all 19th-century French paperweights? The proof is in the price.
> In 1998, Sotheby's sold one for $156,500. In 2000, Lawrence Selman of Santa Cruz, Calif., set the bar up another notch when he sold a salamander paperweight for $169,400.
> Think you might have one? Don't start digging through the desk drawers quite so quickly. Only 12 examples are known.

Cast iron, 7-1/2" l, skeleton hand, realistic **125.00**
Glass, rect, advertising
  Coutes Clipper Mfg., Worcester, MA, illus of pair of clippers, 2-1/2" w, 4" l **75.00**
  Donnelly Machine Co., Brockton, MA, scalloped edge, illus of vintage factory, 3" w, 4-1/2" l **50.00**
  Heywood Shoes, shoe illus, titled "Heywood is in it," 2-1/2" w, 4" l**40.00**
  J.R. Leeson & Co., Boston, Linen Thread importers, spinning wheel image **80.00**
  Oscar R. Boehne & Co., gold scale, 2-1/2" w, 4" l **60.00**
Glass, antique
  Clichy, millefiori, complex millefiori canes set in colorless crystal, 1-3/4" dia, 1-3/8" h **375.00**
  Sandwich Glass, dahlia, c1870, red petaled flower, millefiori cane center, bright green leafy stem, highlighted by trapped bubble dec, white latticino ground, 2-1/2" dia, 1-3/4" h, ...**650.00**
  St Louis, Queen Victoria, c1840, sulfide portrait sgd "Victoria" in blue at base, 3-1/2" dia, 2-1/2" h, few small inclusions **750.00**
Glass, modern
  Ayotte, Rick, yellow finch, perched on branch, faceted, sgd, and dated, 1979.......................................**750.00**
  Baccarat, Peace on Earth, sgd ..**130.00**
  Banford, Bob, Iris and rose, purple, blue, and pink irises, center pink roe, recessed diamond-cut base, "B" cane at stem, 3" dia...............**250.00**

Paperweights, Unknown maker, red, white, green, and blue canes, 3" w, $35.

Caithness, Chai, gold symbol,
  translucent blue background, faceted
  front window, 3-1/4" dia **210.00**
Gunderson, rose, white petals, green
  leaves **425.00**
Kaziun, Charles, millefiori spider lily,
  green ground, pedestal..........**365.00**
Lundberg Studios, Art Nouveau design,
  irid orange, gray, and black flower,
  central millefiori star canes, irid dark
  green ground, sgd "Lundburg 73," 2-
  3/4" dia..................................**225.00**
Murano, cluster of green and white
  daisies, pink and white cushion,
  signature cane "Fili Tosi," 2-3/4" dia
  ....**300.00**
Perthshire, miniature bouquet, yellow
  flowers, pink buds, basket of deep
  blue canes, green and pink millefiori
  canes cut to form base, orig box and
  certificate, 2-1/2" dia..............**160.00**
Whittemore, Francis, two green and
  brown acorns on branch with 3
  brown and yellow oak leaves,
  translucent cobalt blue ground,
  circular top facet five oval punties on
  sides, 2-3/8" dia......................**300.00**
Souvenir
  Acrylic, torch inside made from
    materials from Statue of Liberty,
    1886-1996, round, 4-1/2" dia....**20.00**
  Glass, Gillinder, Memorial Hall,
    Philadelphia Exposition, 1876, 5-1/4"
    l, scratches **350.00**

❖ Parrish, Maxfield

Like many illustrators, Maxfield Parrish did
commercial work. Today, some of those
commercial illustrations are highly sought
by collectors.

Bookplate print, 8" x 10"
  The City of Brass **65.00**
  The Fisherman and the Genie **65.00**
  Wynken, Blyken & Nod **65.00**
  With Trumpet and Drum **65.00**

Calendar top, Edison Mazda Reveries,
  1927, framed, 6-3/4" x 10-1/4" ...**175.00**
Magazine cover
  American Heritage, December 1970
  ....**25.00**
  Scribner Magazine, 1902 ....**55.00**
  Matchbook, Old King Cole, St. Regis
    Hotel, Newy Ork, wooden matches
    ....**25.00**
Playing cards, The Waterfall, advertise
  Edison Mazda Lamps, boxed single
  deck...**127.50**

❖ Patriotic Collectibles

Three cheers for the red, white, and blue!
And three cheers for the collectors who
thrive on this type of material. There are lots
of great examples just waiting to be found
at America's flea markets.

Collectors' Club: Statue of Liberty
Collectors' Club, 26601 Bernwood Rd.,
Cleveland, OH 44122.

Bank, Uncle Sam, Puriton...............**32.00**
Button, Liberty Bell, plastic shelf shank,
  3/4" dia **2.50**
Change Tray, 4" d, Hebbrun House Coal,
  eagle in center, holding banner, wood
  grain ground **50.00**
Costume jewelry
  Flag pin, Coro, sterling silver, enamel
    and rhinestones, 1-1/2" h **88.00**
  "USA" pin, red, clear and blue
    rhinestones, 1-3/8" h **15.00**
Eagle, pot metal, gold paint, 6" h **35.00**
Envelope, Civil War, 2-3/4" x 5-1/8"**22.00**
Fan, "America First," die-cut shield, red,
  white and blue cardboard, sailor raising
  deck flag, warships in background,
  biplanes overhead, 7" x 9" **45.00**
Magic lantern slide, American flag, 3-
  1/4" x 4"..**48.00**
Medal, Victory Liberty Loan, U.S.
  Treasury Dept...............................**15.00**
Needle book, World's Best, Statue of
  Liberty, airplane, ship, world, 6 needle
  packets **20.00**

Yard ornament, flag shape, painted red, white, and blue, wood, c2002, $45.

Candle sconces, pr, cast iron spread wing eagles, $20.

Postcard
  Betsy Ross sewing flag..................**5.00**
  Santa Claus toasting the holidays with
    Uncle Sam, "Christmas Greetings,"
    early 1900s..............................**40.00**
Sash, Mexican War era, patriotic seal,
  39" l **625.00**
Sheet music, *Liberty Bell Time To Ring
  Again*, 1918 ....**10.00**
Statue of Liberty, Avon, 7-1/2" h ...**10.00**
Tumbler, red, white and blue bands, gold
  eagle, 1970s, 4" h **2.00**

❖ Pattern Glass

Pattern glass can best be defined as
tableware made in a wide range of patterns
and colors. Early manufacturers developed
machinery to create glassware and as the
years went by, the patterns became more
intricate. Most pattern glass is clear, but
some pieces came in translucent colors.
The mass-produced glassware came in
hundreds of patterns and a variety of
shapes and sizes.

References: There are many older
reference books that are good sources for
identifying a pattern name, maker, and
pieces available. There are also several
good resources giving solid information
about the reproductions found in today's
marketplace.

Collectors' Clubs: Early American Pattern
Glass Society, P.O. Box 266, Colesburg, IA
52035; Moon and Star Collectors Club,
4207 Fox Creek, Mount Vernon, IL 62864;
The National American Glass Club, Ltd.,
P.O. Box 9489, Silver Spring, MD 20907.

┌─────────────────────────────┐
│   **Reproduction Alert**   │
└─────────────────────────────┘

For additional listings, see *Warman's
Antiques and Collectibles Price Guide,
Warman's Pattern Glass, Warman's Glass,*
and *Early American Pattern Glass,* 2nd ed.

Items listed are clear unless otherwise noted.

Banana boat, Heart with Thumbprint, ruby stained..............................**155.00**

Berry bowl, Daisy and Button, oval, amber..**45.00**

Berry Set, Cord Drapery.................**75.00**

Biscuit jar, cov, Minnesota.............**55.00**

Bowl
Buckle, flint, 10" dia......................**65.00**
Delaware, green, oval..................**65.00**
Utah..**20.00**

Bread plate, Horseshoe, double horseshoe handles.....................**70.00**

Butter, cov
Beaded Loop.............................**75.00**
Crystal Wedding.........................**65.00**
Finecut & Panel, vaseline..........**115.00**
Loop and Jewel.........................**95.00**

Pattern Glass, Frosted Lion oval bread plates, 13" dia, round two handled plate "Give Us This Day Our Daily Bread," 12" dia, each $75.

Pattern glass, covered jar, Daisy and Button pattern, amber, $85.

Cake stand
Button Arches, ruby stained, high standard.................................**185.00**
Festoon **48.00**
Holly **175.00**
Loop and Dart **40.00**
Pogo Stick **45.00**
Thousand Eye, apple green........**60.00**

Castor set, King's Crown, 4 bottles, glass stand.............................**175.00**

Celery tray, Nail, etched................**45.00**

Celery vase
Chandelier................................**25.00**
Honeycomb **45.00**

Champagne
Lily of the Valley.......................**165.00**
Mardi Gras **26.00**

Cheese dish, cov
Flamingo Habitat.......................**150.00**
Illinois **75.00**
Thumbprint, etched **145.00**

Compote, cov, high standard
Dakota, 5" dia...........................**50.00**
Frosted Circle, 7" h...................**125.00**
Pleat and Panel, 8" dia..............**145.00**

Compote, cov, low standard, Loop and Dart, 8" dia **65.00**

Compote, open
Brilliant, Royal's, 6" dia..............**20.00**
Grape Band...............................**35.00**
New England Pineapple, 8" dia....**70.00**
Thousand Eye, amber, 6" dia.......**45.00**

Pattern glass, Beaded Grape, relish, green, $15.

Pattern glass, milk pitcher, Thistle pattern, $70.

Creamer
Bird in Ring **25.00**
Flowerpot **32.00**
King's Crown **50.00**
Paneled Diamond Point, applied handle **35.00**
Stippled Chain...........................**25.00**
Thousand Eye, blue **45.00**

Cruet
Dakota, clear, etched dec **125.00**
Paneled Thistle..........................**25.00**
Tacoma, orig stopper **40.00**
Zenith, blue, replaced stopper, 7" h **50.00**

Eggcup
Ashburton..................................**25.00**
Loop and Dart **25.00**
Thousand Eye, vaseline............**100.00**
Viking **40.00**

Finger Bowl, Heart with Thumbprint **45.00**

Goblet
Argus, barrel, flint......................**40.00**
Basketweave, amber..................**16.00**
Chain and Shield **28.00**
Curtain Tie Back.........................**20.00**
Dewdrop **20.00**
Frazier **20.00**
Greek Key **20.00**
Heart with Thumbprint.................**65.00**
King's Crown **35.00**
Late Paneled Grape **20.00**
Loop and Dart **25.00**
Minnesota.................................**35.00**
New Hampshire **20.00**
Rose in Snow.............................**20.00**
Star in Bull's Eye **32.00**
Thousand Eye, amber.................**50.00**
Wheat & Barley, amber **38.00**

Hair receiver, Heart with Thumbprint, emerald green **100.00**

Honey dish, Bleeding Heart **25.00**

Jelly compote, Reverse Torpedo....**35.00**

Pattern glass, goblet, Jersey Swirl, $15.

Lamp, oil
Crystal Wedding **245.00**
One-O-One, finger **95.00**
Marmalade jar, cov, Illinois **145.00**
Nappy, handle
Crystal Wedding **25.00**
Lily of the Valley **25.00**
Thousand Eye, blue **45.00**
Pitcher
Crystal Wedding, square............**120.00**
Feathered Points **85.00**
Flowerpot **65.00**
Peacock Feather **85.00**
Plate
Beautiful Lady, 8" dia **20.00**
Egyptian, tab handle, 10" dia **95.00**
Loop and Dart, 6" dia **35.00**
Stippled Cherry, 6" dia **12.00**
Wheat & Barley, 7" dia **35.00**
Punch bowl set, Manhattan, bowl, 12
cups..**80.00**
Punch cup
Hickman **10.00**
Iowa, gold trim.............................**15.00**
Kentucky......................................**8.00**
King's Crown, ruby stained **30.00**
Relish
Currier and Ives...........................**20.00**
Dewey, flower flange, serpentine,
amber **45.00**
Loop and Dart **20.00**
Minnesota....................................**20.00**
Oregon #1 ....**18.00**
Wisconsin **25.00**
Salt, master, Royal Lady **30.00**
Salt shaker
Diamond Ridge **45.00**
Minnesota....................................**25.00**
Three Face...................................**75.00**
Willow Oak, blue **40.00**
Spooner
Berry Cluster **28.00**
Cable, flint **55.00**
Cathedral.....................................**25.00**
Fine Rib, flint **45.00**
Sugar, cov
Flowerpot **48.00**

Hidalgo **65.00**
Rose Point Band **65.00**
Syrup Pitcher
Knobby Bull's Eye **85.00**
Louise..**75.00**
Toothpick holder
Bull's Eye and Fan **40.00**
Colonial, blue, 2 handles.............**35.00**
U.S. Sheraton **35.00**
Tumbler
Broken Column, ruby stained.......**55.00**
Eyewinker.....................................**45.00**
Maine **30.00**
Red Block.....................................**40.00**
Wisconsin **45.00**
X-Ray, amethyst, gold trim **65.00**
Vase
Michigan **18.00**
New Hampshire, amethyst stain ..**30.00**
Paneled Thistle, 9-1/4" h **25.00**
Water set, pitcher and 6 tumblers
Anthemion, green.......................**345.00**
Beaumont's Floral, emerald green, gold
trim...**285.00**
Inverted Thistle, green, gold trim**280.00**
Peerless, flint.............................**355.00**
Red Block, ruby stained **330.00**
Whiskey
Argus, applied handle **75.00**
Bull's Eye....................................**85.00**
Comet, flint, 3" h.......................**180.00**
Diamond Point, flint, applied handle
....**85.00**
Wine
Ashburton, flint **40.00**
Bridal Rosette..............................**15.00**
Currier and Ives, blue..................**55.00**
Cut Log..**20.00**
Iowa...**30.00**
Maine **50.00**
Manhattan **15.00**
Nailhead **15.00**
Two Panel, green.........................**35.00**

❖ Peachblow Glass

Taking its name from its peach color and
shading, this glassware has differences in
color and texture from one major
glassmaker to another.

Reference: Sean and Johanna Billings,
*Peachblow, Collector's Identification & Price
Guide,* Krause Publications, 2000.

> **Reproduction Alert**

For additional listings, see *Warman's
Antiques and Collectibles Price Guide* and
Warman's Glass.

Bowl, peachblow ext., ivory int., applied
crystal feet, flower prunt over pontil
mark, English, 8-1/2" dia............**425.00**

Bride's bowl, wavy ruffled rim, cased
int., New Martinsville, 11" dia.....**125.00**
Candlesticks, pr, Gundersen........**275.00**
Celery vase, 5" sq, glossy, Wheeling
....**300.00**
Compote, 5" h, Pairpoint..............**250.00**
Creamer and sugar, satin finish, ribbed,
applied white handles, New England
....**500.00**
Darner, New England...................**175.00**
Dish, wavy ruffled rim, New Martinsville,
5" dia **100.00**
Finger bowl, cased, Webb, 4-1/2" dia
....**195.00**
Hat, Diamond Quilted pattern, satin
finish, Gunderson, 3-1/4" h **150.00**
Lamp shade, light pink shading to dark
pink, gold trim, fluted, undulating rim,
small chips **295.00**
Rose bowl, Wheeling, 4" dia........**225.00**
Toothpick holder, bulbous, deep color,
glossy finish, Wheeling, two cracks in
outer casing................................**70.00**
Tumbler, Hobbs, Brockunier, 3-1/2" h, 2-
3/4" dia **450.00**
Vase
Cased, shaded pink, white opal casing,
enameled gold pendant blossoming
branches, Webb, 10" h **300.00**
Lily form, shading near white to dark
pink, New England, 7-3/4" h...**975.00**
Trumpet form, deep rose tricorn rim,
New England, 9-1/2" h...........**375.00**
Whimsey, figural pear, attributed to New
England, roughness at stem, 5" l
....**125.00**

❖ Peanuts

The comic strip Peanuts has been bringing
smiles to faces since 1950. Snoopy, Charlie
Brown, Lucy and the rest of the gang are all
creations of Charles M. Schulz. Peanuts
collectibles are licensed by Charles M.
Schulz Creative Associates and United
Features Syndicate.

Collectors' Club: Peanuts Collector Club,
539 Sudden Valley, Bellingham, WA 98226.

Book, Here's To You, Charlie Brown,
Fawcett Crest Books, 1962, 21st
printing **4.50**
Cookbook
Peanuts Cook Book, Scholastic Books,
1970, cartoon illus by Charles
Schultz....................................**5.00**
Peanuts Lunch Bag Cook Book,
Scholastic Books, 1974, cartoon illus
by Charles Schultz....................**5.00**
Cookie cutters, Hallmark, set of 4, Lucy
holding package, Snoopy in a Santa
hat, Linus holding lights and Charlie
Brown holding ornament **100.00**

Peanuts lunch box, metal, "Have Lunch With Snoopy," 1970, $65.

Commemorative coin, The Great Pumpkin, 30th anniversary, silver **70.00**

Dishes, tin, tray, 3 plates, 3 saucers **115.00**

Figurine, porcelain, Life with Peanuts collection
Schroeder, 4-3/4" h **20.00**
Snoopy, 4-1/2" h..........................**20.00**

Game, Charlie Brown's All-Star Baseball Game, Parker Brothers, 1965 .....**30.00**

Lunch box, Have Lunch with Snoopy, domed, 1968, King Seeley Thermos **50.00**

Musical figurine, ceramic, Charlie Brown, Lucy, Linus, Sally, Snoopy and Woodstock at Christmas Tree, Schmid, 1984, plays Joy to the World, 8" h **200.00**

Pez, Charlie Brown, frown, MIP........**8.00**

Pinback button, Charlie Brown, celluloid, 1-1/4" dia......................................**20.00**

Soap dish, Avon, Snoopy, 7" l **10.00**

Telephone, Snoopy And Woodstock, 13-1/2" h..**82.50**

Thermos, Charlie Brown, 1969, 3-1/2" h **5.00**

View-Master reel, It's a Bird, Charlie Brown, GAF, 1973, 3 reels, top flap detached **25.00**

Peanuts curtains, pinch pleated, pr with matching bedspread, cream colored background, black and red design, black edge binding, © United Features Syndicate 1966, $85.

❖ Pedal Cars

Pedal cars date to about 1915, when they were made to closely resemble automobiles of the day. War-time material supplies curbed growth for a few years, but these popular toys gained popularity again, just in time for special cars issued to tie into television programs of the 1950s and 1960s.

Periodical: *The Wheel Goods Trader,* P.O. Box 435, Fraser, MI 48026.

Collectors' Club: National Pedal Vehicle Association, 1720 Rupert NE, Grand Rapids, MI 49505.

Airplane, gray body, blue and white decals, red seat, restored **195.00**

Blue Streak, blue and white, BMC **450.00**

Coca-Cola Truck, red and white, AMF **500.00**

Comet, Murray..............................**775.00**

Earthmover, Murray...................**1,100.00**

Fire truck, orig ladders **325.00**

Junior Trac, AMF **250.00**

Mustang, AMF **800.00**

Safari wagon, AMF......................**50.00**

Studebaker, Midwest Industries, restored **950.00**

Tin Lizzy, green, Garton **500.00**

Oscar Mayer Wienermobile pedal car, plastic, faded, $95.

Pedal Car, red body, black and silver wheels, completely rebuilt, repainted, red and yellow kazoo for hood ornament, $95.

❖ Pencil Clips and Paper Clips

Companies developed a clever way to help folks remember their names, advertising on both paper clips and pencil clips. Most advertising was on a metal or celluloid disk.

Diamond Crystal Salt, celluloid **18.00**

Morton's Salt, It Pours....................**10.00**

The Page Milk Co., celluloid..........**48.00**

Red Goose Shoes.........................**12.00**

Reddy Kilowatt Power, V, patrioitc, 1942 ....**10.00**

7-Up..**10.00**

Use Victor Flower, red and yellow on white design **15.00**

Worcester Iodized Salt, cello on silvered tin, inscription in white letters outlined in black, orange ground.................**8.00**

❖ Pencil Sharpeners

Figural pencil sharpeners are starting to catch on with collectors. Look for examples in good condition.

Cannon on wheels, bronzed metal, 3" l **6.50**

Coffee grinder, double-wheel, metal, painted red, Hong Kong, 3" h.........**7.50**

Covered wagon, metal and plastic, Hong Kong, 3-1/4" l................................**4.50**

Dallas Cowboy helmet, plastic, 1-1/2" h **10.00**

Farm lantern, metal, blue paint, clear plastic globe, Hong Kong, 2-3/4" h **6.00**

Franklin Roosevelt, 32nd President, 1882-1945, bronzed metal bust, 3" h **10.00**

Hep Cats, decal, Bakelite, Walt Disney, crack, 1-1/4" dia **45.00**

John Kennedy, 35th President, 1917-1963, bronzed metal bust, 3" h **12.50**

Popeye, figural, Bakelite, 1929, 1-3/4" h **75.00**

Porky Pig, waving, orig bog.............**3.25**

Ronald McDonald, August 1984 Happy Meals, 2" h **4.00**

Sewing machine, figural, plastic, Germany, 1970s, 2" sq.................**19.00**

Stagecoach, bronzed metal, 2-1/2" l **6.50**

Submarine, bronzed metal, 5" l **7.50**

Tweety Bird, orig bag **3.25**

Volkswagen Beetle, bronzed metal, 3-1/2" l **7.50**

❖ Pennants

Rah Rah! Pennants used to be the flag of choice for sporting events and parades. Today they have become colorful collectibles.

1933 Chicago World's Fair, 25" l ...**42.00**

1957 Eisenhower-Nixon Inauguration, Washington, D.C., 25-1/2" l **60.00**

1996 Olympic Baseball, Atlanta 1996 ....**6.00**

Atlantic City, scenes Steel Pier, Convention Hall and bathing, 27" l **45.00**

Cincinnati Redlegs, 1 tassel missing, 29" l **55.00**

Cleveland Indians American League Champions.................**140.00**

Democratic National Convention, Atlantic City, 1964, black and white picture of Linden Johnson in shield, 29" l **30.00**

Empire State Building, "The tallest man-made structure in the world, 102 floors, 1,472 ft. high, Souvenir of Empire State Building, New York City," 26-1/4" l **15.00**

Gettypsburg, Pa., dated 1938, shows Virginia State Monument, 17-1/2" l **18.00**

Howe Caverns, dated 1958, shows pagoda, 17-1/4" l **18.00**

Lumbermen's Memorial, image of lumberjacks, 1940s, 26" l **27.00**

Meramec Caverns, Jesse James' Hideout, Stanton, Mo., 26" l **29.00**

Mt. Washington, White Mountains, N.H., dated 1957, shows World's First Cog Railway, 17-1/4" l **18.00**

Navy, yellow and blue, 5-1/2" l **15.00**

New Jersey Turnpike, 25" l **22.00**

Newark Airport, airplane in clouds, 25" l **25.00**

Pennsylvania Turnpike, 25" l **25.00**

Philadelphia Eagles, 1940/50, 28" l **35.00**

South Carolina, black boy sitting on bales of cotton, 27" l **45.00**

Souvenir of Gettysburg Battlefield, panorama of the Gettysburg Battlefield and monuments, 1930s/40s, 28" l **26.00**

Univ of Wisconsin.........................**20.00**

❖ Pennsbury Pottery

Taking its name from the close proximity of William Penn's estate, Pennsbury, in Bucks County, Pa., this small pottery lasted from 1950 until 1970. Several of the owners had formerly worked for Stangl, which helps explain some of the similarities of design and forms between Pennsbury and Stangl.

Ashtray, Doylestown Trust **30.00**
Bird
 Bird on Nest **300.00**
 Goldfinch, #102 ....**200.00**
Creamer, Rooster, 4-1/2" h **45.00**
Cup and saucer, Black Rooster pattern

................**20.00**
Dinner plate, Hex pattern **17.50**
Eggcup, Red Rooster pattern.........**25.00**
Milk pitcher
 Amish Family, 6-1/2" h **175.00**
 Yellow Rooster, 7-1/2" h **150.00**
Mug, Schiaraflia Filadelfia, owl and seal **30.00**
Pie plate, Rooster, 8" dia **65.00**
Plaque
 Amish Family, 8" dia....................**55.00**
 B & O Railroad, 5-3/4" x 7-3/4" **65.00**
Teapot, Red Rooster pattern...........**65.00**
Tea tile, 6" dia, skunk "Why Be Disagreeable" **60.00**
Tray, Yellow Rooster, 8" l **50.00**

Pennsbury Pottery, dinner plate, Rooster pattern, gold, green, red, and black, green border, brown rim, marked, $20.

❖ Pens and Pencils

Before computers, folks actually wrote letters with pens and pencils! Today some collectors find interesting examples at flea markets.

References: Paul Evans, *Fountain Pens Past & Present*, Collector Books, 1999; Stuart Schneider and George Fischler, *The Illustrated Guide to Antique Writing Instruments*, 3rd ed, Schiffer Publishing, 2000.

Periodical: *Pen World Magazine*, P.O. Box 6007, Kingwood, TX 77325.

Collectors' Clubs: American Pencil Collectors Society, RR North, Wilmore, KS 67155; Pen Collectors of America, P.O. Box 821449, Houston, TX 77282.

Pen
 Cartier, 14k, large, 2 dents.........**260.00**
 Conklin, Endura Model, desk set, 2 pens, side-lever fill, black marble base......................................**135.00**
 Dunn, black, red barrel, gold filled trim, c1920......................................**45.00**
 Moore, lady's, black, 3 narrow gold bands on cap, lever fill..............**75.00**

Sheaffer Lifetime Stylist, gold filled metal, professionally engraved clip, 1960s......................................**35.00**

Two Shaeffer Lifetime standard fountain pens, c1935, a Balance in black and cream pearl plastic with gold filled trim and lever-filler with two-tone Shaeffer nib; other red and pearl striped plastic with two-tone Shaeffer nib and vacuum filler, jammed mechanism, both marked, $75.

 Wahl, lady's, ribbon pen, double narrow band on cap, 14k #2 nib, lever fill, 1928......................................**80.00**
 Waterman's, black, gold trim, clip, unused......................................**50.00**
Pencil
 Brown-McLaren MFG. Co., Hamburg, Mich., Detroit Office-7340 Puritan Ave., Phone UNiversity 3-3520, Redipoint, USA, celluloid..........**10.00**
 Conklin, rolled gold, initials engraved on clip **85.00**
 Electric Café, Detroit, Michigan, clip mkd "Wearever," some paint missing **9.00**
 Mr. Peanut, engraved on both sides of clip, some paint missing from top hat **12.00**
Set, Cross, Ertl emblem, service premium for 10 years of service, MIB **75.00**

❖ Pepsi-Cola

"Pepsi Cola Hits The Spot!" That was part of a popular jingle the 1950s. Pepsi collectibles today are hot, just as the beverage itself has remained popular since first it was introduced in the late 1890s.

Reference: Phil Dillman and Larry Woestman, *Pepsi Memorabilia...Then and Now*, Schiffer Publishing, 2000.

Collectors' Club: Pepsi-Cola Collectors Club, P.O. Box 1275, Covina, CA 91722.

Advertisement, Pepsi, 1956, woman and man carving turkey in very 1950s setting, 11" x 14" **10.00**
Bottle cap, green, c1910 ....**50.00**

Pepsi bottles in collector carrier, mkd "1992 Collector, Richard Petty," 8 bottles, orig contents, $40.

Bottle opener, metal, bottle shape, "America's Biggest Nickel's Worth," rust, 2 3/4" l **45.00**

Carrier, 6-pack, wooden, "Buy Pepsi-Cola," red and blue, 1930/40 ....**95.00**

Clock, bottlecap shape, plastic, "Drink Pepsi-Cola, Ice Cold," white ground, 11" dia **165.00**

Clock, lightup, glass face, metal case, "Say Pepsi please" 16" sq **209.00**

Cooler, metal, "Drink Pepsi-Cola" in white, blue ground, 18-1/2" h, 18" w, 13" d **88.00**

Glass, clear with syrup line, 1930/40, two-color decor, 10 oz **13.00**

Menu sign, "Have a Pepsi" beside bottlecap, "Pepsi-Cola, the Light Refreshment" at bottom, black chalkboard area, yellow/white striped ground, 1950s, 30" h, 20" w **75.00**

Salt and pepper shakers, plastic, 1-pc, "The Light refreshment" under bottlecap logo, 1950s, orig box **60.00**

Sign
Celluloid, button-type, "Ice Cold Pepsi-Cola Sold Here," red name, white text, blue/white/blue ground, 1940s, 9" dia **330.00**
Tin, die-cut, bottlecap shape, "Pepsi-Cola," crazing, 14" d **140.00**

Thermometer, tin
"Have a Pepsi" at top, bottle cap "The Light refreshment" at bottom, yellow with V-shaped white area, 1950s, 27" h **235.00**
"Pepsi-Cola" bottlecap logo at top, "More Bounce To The Ounce" at bottle with red, white, and blue ribbon, white ground, rounded top and bottom, 27" h, 8" w **275.00**

❖ Perfume Bottles

Decorative and figural perfume bottles have remained a popular area of collecting for generations. Perfume bottles can be found

in a variety of sizes, shapes, and colors, as well as price ranges. Look for examples with matching stoppers and original labels.

Collectors' Clubs: International Perfume Bottle Association, P.O. Box 529, Vienna, VA 22180; Miniature Perfume Bottle Collectors, 28227 Paseo El Siena, Laguna Niguel, CA 92677.

Amber glass perfume bottle, Art Deco style triangular motif, intaglio cutting on stopper, brass collar, 3-3/4" h, $85.

Atomizer
Cambridge, stippled gold, opaque jade, orig silk lined box, 6-1/4" h **150.00**
Czechoslovakian, cobalt blue, large enameled and faceted crystal stopper, c1930, 8" h **80.00**
Devilbiss, clear, threaded dec, 4" h, #127 ....**45.00**

Boxed set
Evening In Paris **135.00**
Hudnut, Sweet Orchid, 3" h, 1920s **45.00**
L'Heure Bleue, fluted and scrolled design, Guerlain fitted box **90.00**

Cut glass, Button and Star pattern, rayed base, faceted stopper, 6-1/2" h ..**125.00**

Figural
Decanter shape, glass, opaque blue ground, enameled white leaves and grape garlands, dragonfly in center, three gold applied ball feet, clear ground stopper **125.00**
Genie slippers, glass, cork stoppers, paper labels, "Rose Oil and Cologne by H. P. & C. R. Taylor, Phila," some damage to orig labels, pr........**125.00**
Purse shape, sterling silver, gilded int., mkd "John Turner, Birmingham," 1792 ....**250.00**

Glass
Cobalt blue, sheared top, c1890, 3" h **65.00**

Melon ribbed body, emb, lacy gold enameled fern leaves, colorless cut faceted stopper, 4-1/2" h **165.00**

Lay-down type, satin glass, Diamond Quilted pattern, shading yellow to white, 6" l **415.00**

Mary Gregory, cranberry ground, white enameled girl dec, colorless ball stopper **175.00**

❖ Pet Equipment

One new area that was very apparent during this past summer's flea market season was the increasing number of pet related items. Most are slightly used, but might be good enough for a new pet owner to start with. And, prices at a flea market are probably much less than those charged at a pet store.

Aquarium, 10 gallon, complete with heater, air filtration system **15.00**

Bird cage, white metal, white glass watering and feeding dishes, removable bottom tray **20.00**

Brush, dog grooming, wood handle, sturdy bristles **5.00**

Car seat for small dog...................**5.00**

Cat carrier
Cardboard, folding..........................**1.00**
Plastic, metal door, carrying handle on top...**15.00**

Cat lounger to fit at windowsill, sheepskin-type fabric, plastic supports **2.00**

Clothing
Dog boots, set of 4 ....**6.00**
Dog coat, felt, small dog **8.00**
Dog coat, polar fleece, greyhound size **12.00**
Halloween costume, small dog, coat, hat, bowtie with elastic **15.00**

Collar
Choke-chain type **2.00**
Leather, large dog **12.00**
Leather, small dog, rhinestone trim **15.00**

Crate
Folding, metal, medium dog size .**20.00**
Stationary, wood and metal, large dog size **45.00**

Dog bed, sheepskin lined, for small dog **15.00**

Dog house, wood, home made, for medium sized dog **45.00**

Dog igloo, plastic, for medium sized dog **35.00**

Feeding station, plastic platform on legs, chrome or plastic feeding bowls **20.00**

Grooming items
Grooming platform, collapsible.....**40.00**

Large dog feeding station, chrome bowls, maroon plastic base, gray plastic legs, $20.

Nail clippers.................................15.00
Hamster cage, metal 5.00
Hamster habitat, plastic, action and
   exercise elements 5.00
Leash
   Cat type, braided harness..............3.00
   Leather, hand tooled, for small dog
   ....12.00
   Woven nylon...............................10.00
Training video 2.00
Vehicle harness................................4.00
Water dish, continuous feed, plastic.2.00

❖ Pez

Pez was invented in Austria as a cigarette substitute. Eduard Haas hoped his mints would catch on when he named it PEZ, an abbreviation for *Pfefferminz*. By 1952, a tabletop model arrived in America, but it was not until the container was redesigned for children that the candy caught on. Many popular characters get periodic design updates, giving collectors variations to search for. The dispensers are highly collectible today and several PEZ conventions are held annually around the country.

Reference: Shawn Peterson, *Collector's Guide To PEZ: Identification & Price Guide*, 2nd ed., Krause Publications, 2003.

Goofy Pez dispenser, white, black, and flesh colored face, green hat, red base, with feet, $4.

Pez dispensers, 2 unopened w/bubble gum at top, pink pig and penguin, Fly from Bugz series, Bugs (yellow base, feet), Daffy, lower row: Regular, Santa, Bugs (yellow base, no feet) $12, Mickey Mouse, Peter Pez, octopus, Daffy, Dino, Garfield.

Periodicals: *PEZ Collector's News,* P.O. Box 14956, Surfside Beach, SC 29587 www.pezcollectorsnews.com; *Toy Shop,* 700 E State St., Iola, WI 54990.

Aardvark, orange stem, loose.........10.00
Ant, green stem, loose 8.00
Aral, Gas, blue hat and shoes, loose6.00
Barney Bear, 1970s........................12.00
Boy with hat, Pez Pal, 1960 ....12.00
Clown, Merry Melody Maker, MOC...5.00
Donald Duck, no feet, MIP 27.50
Fozzie Bear, 1991............................3.00
Icee...5.50
Inspector Clouseu, yellow stem, loose
 ....6.00
Kermit, mkd "Made in Hungry"..........7.50
Lamb, mkd "Made in Yuglosavia" 6.00
Mariner, blue hat, black shoes, loose7.50
Muselix, orange stem, loose...........12.00
Parrot, Merry Melody Maker, MOC ...8.50
Penguin, Melody Maker, MOC........12.00
Pilot, white hat, black shoes, loose...6.00
Pink Panther, pink stem, loose.......12.00
Rabbit...7.50
RD-D2...5.00
Santa, mkd "Made in Yuglosavia" 8.00
Shell Gas, yellow hat, red shoes, loose
 ....7.00
Smurf, Papa, red stem 3.00
Tom..6.00
Tuffy 7.50
Whistle, 1960s 2.50

❖ Pfaltzgraff

Here's a name most flea marketers associate with dinnerware. However, Pfaltzgraff originally started as a stoneware company. By the early 1950s, company officials realized their future was in dinnerware production, and production successfully shifted toward that goal.

Pfaltzgraff Mustard, cov, Yorktown pattern, slotted lid, $25.

Pfaltzgraff has announced a new series of miniature replicas. The series will continue through 2011 as a celebration of the founding of the first Pfaltzgraff pottery in 1811 in York, PA. The first replica will be a stoneware jug with a simulated Bristol glaze. The miniatures will be issued in a gift box which contains a certificate of authenticity.

This dealer at Shupps' Grove, Adamstown, Penn., usually has a wide range of Pfaltzgraff patterns.

Butter dish, Village 10.50
Canister, Coffee, Yorktowne...........12.00
Casserole, Aura, 12" x 8"...............14.00
Child's mug, bear faces..................10.00
Cup and saucer
   Christmas Heirloom 7.50
   Yorktowne.....................................5.00
Custard, Village, set of 4.................12.00
Dinner plate
   Gazebo.......................................10.00
   Gourmet 12.00
   Windsong 12.00
   Yorktowne....................................10.00
Goblet, Village, set of 4...................14.00
Honey pot, cov, Village, 5-1/4" h.....21.00
Platter, Folk Art, oval, 14" l 10.00
Salad bowl, Village, set of 8 ....10.50
Teapot, Yorktowne 15.00
Vegetable dish, divided, Yorktowne12.00

Pfaltzgraff bread tray, motto emb on sides, Yorktown pattern, $20.

❖ Phoenix Bird China

Phoenix Bird china plate, 7-1/4" dia, $15.

Phoenix Bird China a blue-and-white dinnerware made from the late 19th century through the 1940s. The china was imported to America, where it was retailed by several firms, including Woolworth's, and wholesalers such as Butler Brothers.

Collectors' Club: Phoenix Bird Collectors of America, 685 S. Washington, Constantine, MI 49042.

For additional listings and a detailed history, see *Warman's Americana & Collectibles.*

Bread and butter plate, 6" d **8.00**
Celery tray, 13-1/2" l.....................**145.00**
Cup and saucer...........................**10.00**
Dessert plate, 7-1/4" dia................**12.00**
Dinner plate, 9-3/4" dia..................**40.00**
Eggcup, double cup **15.00**
Luncheon plate, 8-1/2" dia............**17.50**
Platter, oval, 14" l...........................**95.00**
Salt dip, scalloped, 3 footed **16.00**
Soup dish, 7-1/4" d.......................**35.00**
Teapot, squatty.............................**42.00**
Tea tile, 6" d **28.00**

❖ Phoenix Glass

Phoenix Glass Company, founded in Beaver, Pa., in 1880, was initially made commercial products but later shifted to art glass. The company's molded and sculptured wares are what most dealers think of as "Phoenix" glass.

Phoenix Glass vase, sculpted nudes, light blue ground, cream figures, orig paper label, 11-1/2" h, $395.

Collectors' Club: Phoenix & Consolidated Glass Collectors Club, P.O. Box 3847, Edmond, OK 73083.

Ashtray, Phlox, large, white, frosted **90.00**
Basket, pink ground, relief molded dogwood dec, 4-1/2" h **65.00**
Bowl, Swallows, purple wash........**150.00**
Candlesticks, pr, blue ground, bubbles and swirls, 3-1/4" h.....................**65.00**
Canoe, 8" l, white ground, sculptured green lemons and foliage.............**95.00**
Charger, blue ground, relief molded white daffodils **100.00**
Cigarette Box, Phlox, white milk glass, cocoa brown.............................**140.00**
Ginger jar, cov, frosted ground, bird finial **80.00**
Lamp, boudoir, Wild Rose, brown highlights, milk glass ground......**150.00**
Planter, white ground, relief molded green lion, 8-1/2" l........................**95.00**
Vase
 Bellflower, burgundy pearlized ground **95.00**
 Bluebell, brown, 7" h **125.00**
 Philodendron, Wedgwood blue, white ground...................................**160.00**
 Wild Geese, pearlized white birds, light green ground **195.00**

❖ Photographs

Photograph collecting certainly is one way to add "instant ancestors" to those picture frames you'd like to hang. Many photographs are found at flea markets. The market for vintage photos has received increased attention, in part because they are easy to sell over the Internet. Look for photographs that have interesting composition or those that give some perspective to the way an area once looked.

Reference: O. Henry Mace, *Collector's Guide to Early Photographs,* Krause Publications, 1999.

Collectors' Clubs: American Photographic Historical Society, 1150 Avenue of the Americas, New York, NY 10036; National Stereoscopic Association, P.O. Box 14801, Columbus, OH 43214; The Photographic Historical Society, P.O. Box 39563, Rochester, NY 14604.

Albumen print
 Baseball game, mounted, 5-1/4" sq **125.00**
 Buffalo Bill, cabinet card **360.00**
 Cowboy on horse with dog doing a trick on back of the horse, 1920-1930s, mounted, 5" x 7" **48.00**
 Man with horse-drawn moving van in front of building with sign for "Pacific Transfer Company," dated 1913, identified in pencil as Portland, Ore., mounted, 5" x 7" **60.00**
 New Jersey shorebird, Arthur Dill, 1983, framed, presentation documentation attached **15.00**
Cabinet card, 6-1/4" x 4-1/2"
 Identical twins, Willow City, ND **30.00**
 Jefferson Davis, President of Confederacy **80.00**
 Memorial floral arrangements, Massillon, Ohio, imprint, mounted on cream stock **6.00**
 Main Street, Dorchester, Wisc., 1890s, mounted on cream stock **15.00**
Carte de viste (CDV)
 Boy on toy rocking horse, Louisana, Mo., imprint..............................**45.00**
 Girl with bisque doll.....................**14.00**
 Postmortem, baby **42.00**
Tintype
 Civil war era soldier, unidentified .**45.00**
 Young woman, swatch of twill from jacket, 1-5/8" gold filled engraved locket case..............................**85.00**

❖ Pickard China

Wilder Pickard founded this company in 1897 in Chicago. China blanks imported from Europe were hand-painted by company artists. Signed pieces are especially sought.

Collectors' Club: Pickard Collectors Club, 300 E Grove St., Bloomington, IL 67101.

For additional listings, see *Warman's Antiques and Collectibles Price Guide* and *Warman's American Pottery & Porcelain.*

Bon bon, basket style, four sided, gold **45.00**
Bowl, pink and blue flowers, gilding, unsigned, 1912-18 mark, 10" dia .**70.00**
Cake plate, open gold handles, Desert Garden pattern **185.00**

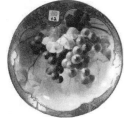

Pickard China plate decorated with grapes and leaves, etched gilded border, signed "Coufall," 1903-05 mark, 8-1/2" dia, $200.

Celery Set, two handled oval dish, five matching salts, allover gold dec, 1925-30 mark **125.00**

Creamer, red and yellow currants, green leaves, unsigned, 1905-10 mark **165.00**

Demitasse cup and saucer, Gold Tracery Rose & Daisy pattern, green band, 1925-30 mark **40.00**

Hatpin holder, allover gold design of etched flowers, c1925 ....**50.00**

Mug, poinsettia flowers, gold banding and trim, sgd "N. R. Clifford".......**275.00**

Perfume bottle, yellow primroses, shaded ground, artist sgd and dated 1905, gold stopper **200.00**

Plate

Blackberries and leaves, sgd "Beitler" (Joseph Beitler), 1903-15, 8-1/2" dia **90.00**

Currants, 7-1/2" dia **75.00**

Gooseberries dec, sgd "P. G." (Paul Gasper), 1912-18 mark, 8-1/4" dia **45.00**

Peaches, gilded and molded border, sgd "S. Heap," 9-1/8" dia.........**110.00**

Platter, roses, gilded border, sgd "Seidel," 12" dia **275.00**

Tea set, teapot, creamer, sugar, and cake plate, pink apple blossoms and green leaves, gilded trim, artist sgd **550.00**

Vase

8-1/4" h, scenic, sgd "E. Challinor" (Edward Challinor), 1912-18...**425.00**

9-1/4" h, three large dark poppies, gold, rust, and brown dec, sgd "Gasper" **365.00**

❖ Picture Frames

Here's a topic few people admit to collecting, but most of us have many of these in our homes. Flea markets are a good place to find interesting frames. Make sure you take measurements if you're looking for a certain size frame.

Celluloid, 8" x 6-1/4" **70.00**

Curly maple, good curl, 16-1/4" x 16" **385.00**

Grain-decor, pine, 17" x 14" **385.00**

Horseshoe-form, white paint, gilt liner, 17-1/4" x 13-1/2" **95.00**

Mahogany, gilt and black liner, 12" x 16" **75.00**

Speckled picture frames, brown, rust, yellow, white, tan, and orange, thin black liner, sold with vintage bird prints, price for pr, $85.

Oak

Cross-corner, leaves in corners, 17" x 15" **45.00**

Gesso border in gold, 30" x 25-1/2" **132.50**

Shells, 8-1/2" x 6-1/2" **65.00**

Silver, sterling, easel back, holds 6" x 8" **45.00**

Tramp art

Cross-corner, 7" x 6" **115.00**

Divided for 2 photos, gold paint, minor damage, 13-1/2" h, 26-1/2" w **250.00**

Walnut

Cross-corner, gilt liner, 8" x 7"....**125.00**

Oval, deep, 13-1/2" x 11-1/2" **40.00**

Shadowbox type, gilt liner, 14-1/2" h, 12" w.................................**75.00**

Chip carved wood picture frame, unmarked, 6" l, 4" w, $35.

❖ Pie Birds

These little birds with their beaks wide open are a bit unusual looking when found out of their natural habitat. Designed to act as a vent for a pie with a top crust, they work well, but many collectors won't think of using them for baking. New examples abound.

Reproduction Alert
Baby Chick, English **85.00**
Bird, Shawnee, 5-1/2" h **85.00**
Bluebird **75.00**
Eagle, Boyd **45.00**
Elephant, mkd "Nutbrown Pie Funnel, Made in England," trunk raised ..**185.00**
First Day of Spring, baby chick in egg **40.00**
Lady, blue dress, pink apron, holding cherry pie, flowers at base, 4" h ..**25.00**
Mama bear, blue dress, English **95.00**
Mammy, black **245.00**
Pirate, English **85.00**
Rooster
Art Deco, 5-1/4" h......................**175.00**
Cleminson, 4-1/2" h.....................**95.00**

❖ Pierce, Howard

Howard Pierce was a California potter who designed and created interesting figurines, dinnerware, and some accessories.

Dealer sign **75.00**

Dish, brown and white, 1950s, 13" l **24.00**

Figure

Bulldog, Marine Corps, U.S.M.C. on base, 5" h **200.00**

Giraffe trio, brown matte finish, largest stamped................................**200.00**

Mouse **27.50**

Owls, pr **48.00**

Penguin, 7" h..............................**85.00**

Raccoon **75.00**

Robin **46.00**

Sparrows, trio **55.00**

St Francis of Assisi, holding bird, 12" h **195.00**

Vase, Wedgwood jasper style, light green ground, white cameo of Oriental boy on one, girl on other, 5-3/4" h, pr **48.00**

❖ Pig Collectibles

"This little piggie went to market ... " Actually lots of piggies are heading to flea markets so that collectors can give them a new home. Some collectors specialize in famous characters, like Babe or Porky Pig, while others prefer figurines.

Collectors' Club: The Happy Pig Collectors Club, P.O. Box 17, Oneida, IL 61467.

Advertising trade card, Try Wright's Little Liver Pills, shows 5 pigs **12.00**

Ashtray, green ceramic base, figural pink pig **5.00**

Bank, pig shape, ceramic, pink and white, multicolored flowers, curly tail, 1950s **30.00**

Crock, orange pig along side, 3" h..**85.00**
Cutting board, pig shape, home made,
    well used **2.00**
Figure
    Black bisque pig jumping over fence, 4-
        1/2" l, 3-1/2" h...........................**80.00**
    Lobster pulling leg of red pig......**115.00**
    Pig riding in canoe, c1930 ....**65.00**
    Purse, black bisque pig sitting on top of
        green purse, 2-1/4" h...............**80.00**
    Well, gold pig, orange roof, mkd
        "Souvenir of Chicago, Made in
        Germany," 1930s......................**65.00**
Inkwell, pink pig sitting on top of green
    inkwell, 3" h **100.00**
Match holder, pair of pink bisque pigs,
    "Scratch My Back" and "Me Too"
    ....**120.00**
Pinback button, Swift's, multicolored
    carton of smiling pig wearing rope
    noose while seated in frying pan,
    c1901 ....**45.00**
Pocket mirror, Newtown Collins Short
    Order Restaurant, St. Joe, MO, yellow
    and orange, 2-1/8" d **55.00**
Shoe, two pigs inside looking out....**85.00**
Toaster cover, padded fabric, white
    background, pink pigs, Ulster Weavers,
    Ireland, 12" w, 9" h **15.00**
Toothpick holder, Lawn Tennis, pig with
    racquet, 3-3/4" h...........................**85.00**

*Jones Dairy Farm Circus, paper toys, top: circus
tent with sign "World's Greatest Aerialist" showing
two performing pigs, other dressed pigs waiting to
go into tent; bottom: sausage stand, two pigs
serving sausage to dressed pig buyers, $15 each.*

❖ Pigeon Forge Pottery

Among the array of regional pottery
commonly found at flea markets is Pigeon
Forge Pottery, made in the Tennessee town
of the same name. Capitalizing on the
popularity of the tourist trade, many pieces
were sold as souvenirs. The market is still
being established for Pigeon Forge Pottery.
Look for artist-signed pieces and unusual
glazes.

Bear, figurine, 4-1/4" h **17.50**
Bowl, tan exterior, blue interior, 5-1/4" dia
    ....**20.00**
Butter molds, mustard color, set of 4,
    snowflake, flower, 2 swans, impressed
    designs, 4"...................................**15.50**
Cream pitcher, Dogwood pattern, 4" h
    ....**9.00**
Jug, miniature, 5" h **12.50**
Mug, tan, brown owl, blue interior ...**10.00**
Racoon, D. Ferguson, 5-1/4" h   44.00
Teapot, brown, squatty form, 3-1/2" h
    ....**6.00**
Tile, aqua, 3 yellow flowers, D. Ferguson,
    5-3/4" sq...................................**114.50**
Vase, blue, Dogwood pattern, 3-1/2" h
    ....**6.00**

❖ Pinback Buttons

Here's a form of advertising that was an
instant hit and is still popular. Look for
interesting pinback buttons with advertising
and political slogans of all types. Many early
manufacturers included a paper insert
which further exclaimed the virtues of the
product. An insert adds value to a pin.
Bright colors and good condition are also
important.

Amoco, Join The American Party,
    American Gas, litho tin **18.00**
Batman and Robin Fan Club, 1960s
    ....**10.00**
Big Chef White Bread, black, white, and
    red, white lettering, 1930s............**12.00**
Buster Brown Bread, multicolored, red
    rim lettering, Buster as sign painter,
    "Resolved that the Best Bre(a)d People
    eat Buster Brown Bread...............**24.00**
Chocolate Mason Mints, blue on silver,
    slogan "Soothing Cooling Flavor,"
    1940s **8.00**
Cinderella Rubberetts, red, white, and
    blue litho, "Replacable At Knees/No
    Sewing," c1930s **8.00**
Cinderella Stoves and Ranges,
    multicolored, red, white, blue, and gold
    accents..**15.00**
Dakota Gold Turkey, blue and yellow
    design, red lettering, 1940s..........**12.00**

*"My Band Leader Deserves Me" pinback button,
turquoise background, black lettering and note, $1.*

*"I A M Solidarity Days, AFL CIO, Washington, DC,
Aug 31" pinback button, white background, blue
lettering, $5.*

Diamond C Hams, celluloid, 1-1/2" dia
    ....**95.00**
Gore '88 ....**9.50**
I'm a Beech-Nut, Wearer Qualified to
    Win **15.00**
Lucky Strikes Again, 2-1/2" dia   25.00
Meet Me At The Bon-Ton, shows Santa
    Claus, 1-1/4" dia.........................**28.00**
Mickey Mouse Club, black and white,
    7/8" dia **50.00**
Official Mickey Mouse Store, 1-1/4" dia
    ....**18.00**
Ritz Crackers **14.00**
Super Hero Hornet Society, Green
    Hornet memberbership, 3-1/2" dia
    ....**25.00**
Vote for Betty Crocker, red, white, and
    blue, 1970s...................................**8.00**
White Rose Bread..........................**10.00**
Yale Bread Wins, blue and white image
    of pennant, yellow ground, blue
    lettering, solid tin reverse **18.00**

❖ Pin-Up Art

Charles Dana Gibson is credited with
creating the first pin-up girl with his famous
Gibson Girls in the early 1900s. Other
famous artists followed, creating pretty girls
for calendars, magazines, advertisements,
etc. It wasn't until the 1920s, when the film
industry got involved, that their clothes
seemed to be less important. Later pin-up
artists, including Vargas, Elvgren, and
Moran, helped create the modern image of
pin-up art.

Periodicals: *Glamour Girls: Then and Now,*
P.O. Box 34501, Washington, DC 20043;
The Illustrator Collector's News, P.O. Box
1958, Sequim, WA 98382.

Calendar
    Devorss, 1944 ....**45.00**
    MacPherson, 1953, Models
        Sketchbook, 9-1/2" x 12-1/2", spiral
        bound paper, wall type, 12 monthly
        pages, sgd full color art...........**75.00**

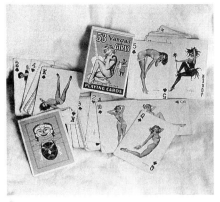

Pin-Up Art, Playing cards, 53 Vargas Girls, Albert Varga artist, Creative Playing Card Co., Inc., St. Louis, MO, plastic coated, $150.

Petty, Esquire, 1955, desk, 5-3/4" x 6-1/4", white cardboard eagle frame, dark red diecut opening around 12 monthly cardboard sheets **45.00**

Petty, Fawcett, 1947 ....**70.00**

Greeting Card

Bettie Page, artist Olivia.................**7.00**

Bride, Varga......................................**9.00**

Cowboy, artist Olivia.......................**6.00**

Gum card, 2-1/2" x 3", Gum Inc., American Beauties, Elvgren art, full color, unsigned artwork, titled captions, 1940s **15.00**

Magazine, Esquire, Christmas, 1943, Varga fold-out, 10" x 13", 320 pgs **45.00**

Pocket knife, 3-3/4" l, silvered steel, two blade, black and white cello insert, one side with standing nude, hands held discreetly over mid-torso, wearing high heels, similar dec on other side, c1940 ....**30.00**

Poster, Hollywood Peep Show, burlesque strip revue, c1950, 27" x 41" **150.00**

Print

Elgren, Two Cushion, sultry girl in red dress playing billiards, 5" x 7", matted.......................................**55.00**

Rubens, Fox and Wolf Hunt, 1937, published by U.S. Government Art Committee, headed by Eleanor Roosevelt, heavy paper, 9" x 13" **25.00**

Vargas Girl, 1960s Playboy, captioned "Mr. Farnsworth, ..." 8-1/4" x 11" **12.00**

Stand-up card, 4-3/4" x 10" diecut cardboard, perforations for folding to form model figure standing on triangular display, full color Moran art, titled "Aiming To Please," pretty redhead archer, mini skirt, red high heels, c1950, unused **15.00**

❖ Pisgah Forest

Pisgah Forest vase, bulbous, ivory and celadon crystalline glaze, pink int., raised potter's mark, 3-1/2" dia, 5-1/4" h, $300.

This American potter has made interesting wares. They used a layered or cameo technique, giving an interesting texture to their work. Most of their wares are clearly marked and dated.

Dish, cov, blue-green, 1935, 4" h, 4-1/2" dia **135.00**

Jar, cov, aqua, 4" h, 2-1/2" dia **110.00**

Mug, cameo, clog dancers, Walter Stephen.......................................**115.00**

Teapot, white cameo relief of pioneering scene, light blue ground, 1951/Stephen **225.00**

Vase

Cameo, covered wagon and riders on horseback, blue ground, 1953, Walter Stephen, 5-1/2" h **302.50**

Crystalline, 1943, 6-1/2" h..........**395.00**

Green, 11" h...............................**325.00**

Green, 5" h...................................**90.00**

❖ Planters

Flea markets are great places to find planters of every type. Unfortunately, many of us have brown thumbs and are soon left with a pretty container and little foliage. However, with careful inspection, you just might find out that your favorite planter is a piece of Westmoreland glass or McCoy pottery.

Additional listings for planters can be found throughout this book; look under specific companies and also Lady's Head Vases.

ABC block, pastels **8.00**

Bambi, mkd "Walt Disney Productions" **65.00**

Bootie, blue, unmarked.....................**4.00**

Butterfly on log, brown and white, glossy glaze, mkd "Shawnee USA 524" **12.00**

Cactus and cowboy, natural colors, Morton **17.50**

Dog planter, pottery, yellow glaze, unmarked, 7" h, $10.

Cat, coral glaze, green box, McCoy, 1950 ....**12.00**

Fawns, standing pair, McCoy, 1957 ....**35.00**

Flamingos, facing pair, 10" l **150.00**

Gondola, yellow, McCoy **20.00**

Mallard, head down, Royal Copley **22.00**

Oriental style, green floral design, gold fish, white ground, large..............**25.00**

Parrot, white, orange accents **15.00**

Pheasant, mkd "Napcoware," small chip **10.00**

Pink, rect, unmarked **5.00**

Pipe, brown, black stem **9.00**

Springer spaniel, black and white, unmarked **10.00**

Straw hat, yellow, blue ribbon.........**17.50**

Swan, ceramic, white glaze..............**5.00**

Telephone **8.00**

Turkey, brown, Morton **15.00**

Wishing Well, McCoy, orig chain **30.00**

Swan planter, pottery, white glaze, unmarked, 3-1/4" h, $6.

❖ Planters Peanuts

The Planters Nut and Chocolate Co. was founded in Wilkes-Barre, Pa., in 1906. In 1916 the company held a contest to find a mascot, and Mr. Peanut came to life by 1916. He has remained a popular advertising icon.

Reference: Jan Lindenberger, *Planters Peanut Collectibles Since 1961*, Schiffer Publishing, 1995

Collector's Club: Peanut Pals, P.O. Box 652, St. Clairsville, OH 43950

Planters Peanuts Counter jars, clear glass, peanut finials on two, one with lid missing, one repaired, $75.

Reproduction Alert

For additional listings, see *Warman's Americana & Collectibles.*

Bank, plastic, set of 4, solid colors, red, cobalt, green, tan **175.00**
Beach ball, 13" dia..........................**22.00**
Bobbing head figure, Mr. Peanut, composition, smiling, waving, plastic cane, 5-1/4" h **150.00**
Box, cardboard
  "Planters Roasted Peanuts," oval red medallion shows peanut lettered "The Peanut Store," 10" h, 6-1/4" sq **143.00**
  "Planters Salted Nuts, fresh, Roaster To You," shows bowl of peanuts, 1940s-1950s **11.00**
Can, litho tin, Planters Pennant Brand Salted Peanuts, red pennant with Mr. Peanut, 5 lb, 8" h, 6-1/4" dia **55.00**
Coloring book
  50 States, 1970s **15.00**
  American Ecology, 1970s **15.00**
  Presidents of the United States, unused **20.00**
Coin, Mr. Peanut, Olympics, 1980...**14.00**
Costume, Halloween, Mr. Peanut, plastic mask, plastic/cloth peanut-body, orig shipping box, 1960s, mint **99.00**
Jar, glass, countertop
  4 Corners Peanut jar, bottom mkd "Made in U.S.A." **215.00**
  6-Sided jar, yellow printing on all sides, bottom mkd "Made in U.S.A."..**266.00**
  8-Sided jar, embossed on all sides **125.00**
  Fired-on enamel label, "Planters Peanuts 5¢," and Mr. Peanut, red and blue, embossed back, orig red tin lid, c1940, 7-5/8" dia, 9" h...........**200.00**
Lighter, Bic, 1970s.......................**15.00**
Mask, cardboard, unused, smiling peanut face with monocle, 7-3/4" x 8-1/4" **200.00**
Mechanical pencil, 1970s **15.00**
Post card, Planters Peanuts at Times

Square, 1940s scene, unused **20.00**
Radio, transistor, plastic, yellow Mr. Peanut design, unused, orig box/mailing carton, mint, 10" h, 5" w **110.00**
Tennis balls, Dunlop, can of 3........**24.00**
Toy, plastic, windup, Mr. Peanut figure walker, 1950s, 8-1/2" h Tan body, black arms/legs/hat, works **420.00**
  Green, works............................**440.00**
  Red, works **550.00**
  Yellow, works **600.00**
Whistle, figural, 1970s **5.00**

❖ Plastic

It's hard to imagine life without plastics. Today collectors actively search for early plastics, including acrylics, Bakelite, and celluloid.

For a more detailed history and additional listings of plastics, see *Warman's Americana & Collectibles* and Bakelite and Celluloid in this edition.

Alarm clock, key wind, Black Forest works, octagonal translucent green case..**30.00**
Bag handle, Blue Cross, white, blue lettering **50**
Business card holder, sea shells suspended in rect acrylic base **6.50**
Dress clip, green opaque Lucite, triangular, chevron design, rhinestone trim **20.00**
Mirror, hand, beveled acrylic handle and frame, U-shaped mirror, sterling silver floral ornament, c1946 ....**55.00**
Mug
  Clear, Wiedner University in blue letters **5.00**
  Purple, Nexium advertising............**4.00**
Napkin ring, translucent Lucite, sq shape, rounded edges, circular center, c1960, 4 pc set............................**12.00**
Paperweight, translucent Lucite cube, suspended JFK half dollar, c1965**10.00**
Pen, Karlene's Hairstyling....................**50**
Pin, figural Santa face, American Greeting Cards..............................**1.00**
Push puppet, Santa, holding bell, mkd "Made in Hong Kong for Kohner".**60.00**
Wall shelf, translucent neon pink, 30" l, 6" d, 1970s **25.00**

Plastic canister set, sugar, coffee, tea, yellow, white lettering and lids, $18.

Clock, Session "Mastercrafters" hard plastic case electric clock with girl on swing, lighted scenic background, 10-1/2" h, $95.

⋆ Playboy

Everyone smiles when someone tries to convince them that they really only read *Playboy* for the articles since we all know this enterprise has grown into a mega business. Dedicated Playboy collectors know there is more than a magazine to this interesting collectible as they scour the flea market landscape for that distinctive bunny logo.

The first *Playboy* magazine was released in December of 1953. Owner and publisher Hugh M. (Marston) Hefner did not put a date on the cover because he was not sure if there would be another copy. The popular Femlin was introduced into Party Jokes section of the August, 1955 magazine.

The first Playboy club opened in 1960. In just over a year it had become the most visited night club in the world. After yielding a seemingly endless supply of ashtrays, mugs, swizzle sticks, and other collectibles, the last state side club closed in 1988.

Ashtray, smoked black glass, Femlin logo in center, 3-3/4" x 3-3/4".......**12.00**
Book, *Playboy's Host & Bar Book,* Thomas Mario, Playboy, 1971, hard cover, 339 pages.........................**25.00**
Crock, stoneware, beige, red logo, 3" dia **32.00**
Earrings, pr, clip, goldtone, 1" dia   **65.00**
Eggcup, Jackson China, tan ext., white int., logo on front, Playboy Club around rim in black lettering, mkd "Jackson China, HMH Publishing Co., Inc," 1960s **22.00**
Key charm, goldtone, black logo, 3-3/4" l **45.00**
Magazine, *Playboy,* with centerfold intact
  1955, September **180.00**
  1955, November.........................**130.00**
  1957, March **175.00**
  1968, November, with centerfold, fine **9.00**
  1985, September, Madonna on cover, last stapled issue.....................**15.00**
  1994, November, Pamela Anderson on cover, autographed, mint **50.00**
Money clip, Playboy Casino, 1-1/2" d **75.00**

Playboy Magazine, Dec, 1967, Gala Christmas Issue, psychedelic cover, orange, hot pink, neon green, $5.

Mug, clear, black rabbit head logo, 9-3/4" h, mint **12.00**
Pin, gold plated, rhinestone eyes, 1-1/4" h **85.00**
Puzzle, 1968, centerfold, Playmate Jean Bell, canister, opened...................**15.00**
Ring, 14kg yg, logo in center **85.00**
Shot Glass, 2" x 3", Femlin.............**18.00**
Swizzle Stick, black or white, Playboy on side, each......................................**1.00**
Wall calendar, 1963, Playmate, orig envelope, mint **55.00**

❖ Playing Cards

What we know today as playing cards were developed in 1885 by the U.S. Playing Card Company of Cincinnati. However, Americans had been using cards for games and entertainment since they first arrived in the 1700s. Look for interesting designs, complete sets, and original boxes.

Collectors' Clubs: Chicago Playing Card Collectors, 1826 Mallard Lake Drive, Mariette, GA 30068; 52 Plus Joker, 204 Gorham Ave., Hamden, CT 06514; International Playing Card Society, 3570 Delaware Common, Indianapolis, IN 46220.

1965 New York World's Fair, "52 Outstanding World's Fair Exhibits, Memorable Illustrations In Color," Stancraft, 2-part plastic box, promotional sleeve, sealed...........**55.00**
American Airlines **10.00**
Boys Town Souvenir Paying Cards, double deck, shows the famous "He ain't heavy, Father, he's my brother" scene, Brown & Bigelow, mint......**60.00**
Chessie System, double deck, sealed **40.00**

Playing Cards 400 Smart Set, Russell Playing Card Co., New York, NY, $18.

Frisco Railroad, sealed **22.00**
Jeff Gordon, double deck, in collector's tin, 1999, NRFB **12.00**
Quilt design, "Patchwork," double deck, Hallmark, 1 joker missing, plastic box **8.00**
Raggedy Ann, Hallmark, orig box ..**25.00**
Texas souvenir deck, "Historical facts about Texas," features "Home of the President of the United States" mid-1960s, sealed..............................**24.00**
U.S. Military Vertical Vehicles, double deck, Vertol Aircraft Corp., Morton, Pa., plastic holder **40.00**
Woman with dogs, double set, Congress.....................................**28.00**

❖ Playsets

Marx dominated the market for playsets in the 1950s and 1960s, producing a wide variety of the multi-piece toys. Other makers and newer sets have followed, including some contemporary reproductions of popular vintage playsets. However, collectors remain most keenly interested in early examples.

Values are for playsets in excellent condition.

Adventures of Robin Hood, Marx, 1956 ....**750.00**
Battleground, Montgomery Ward, 1971 ....**275.00**
Cape Canaveral, Sears, 1959 ......**325.00**
Daniel Boone Frontier, Marx **230.00**
Fort Apache, Sears, 1972 ....**90.00**
Galaxy Command, Marx, 1976 ......**30.00**
Johnny Apollo Moon Launch Center, Marx, 1970 ....**135.00**

Fisher-Price nursery school playset, orig plastic accessories, some play wear, $5.

Lone Ranger Ranch, Marx...........**250.00**
Modern Service Center, Marx, 1962 ....**210.00**
Rin Tin Tin at Fort Apache, Series 500, Sears, 1956..............................**475.00**
Roy Rogers Double R Bar Ranch, March, 1962 ....**300.00**
Strategic Air Command, Marx.....**520.00**
Untouchables, Marx, 1961 ....**975.00**
Walt Disney's Zorro, Series 1000, Sears, 1972..............................**500.00**

❖ Playskool

Remember Mr. Potato Head? How about wooden Lincoln Logs and Tinkertoys. Does anyone recall Weebles, which wobble but don't fall down? Those are some of the most popular toys made by Plaskool, which was founded in 1928. Playskool products are still largely designed for children 6 years old and under. Flea markets are a prime hunting ground for all manner of Playskool toys, both vintage and contemporary.

Colored blocks, cardboard canister, 1972 ....**22.00**
Doll
  Dressy Bessy, 1970, stuffed cloth, 1 button missing, 18" h...............**48.50**
  Raggedy Ann, Christmas dress ...**65.00**
Magazine advertisement, black and white, 1952, shows round block stack, Peggy ball pull, Nok-out bench, etc., 11" x 14".......................................**6.00**
Play set
  Gilligans Island, 12" w x 8" h island, raft, row boat, orig figures, mkd "Filmation," 1977 ....**60.00**
  Sleep Dolly Sleep, Pullman A-756, tin, 1920s....................................**400.00**

Playskool Mailbox, red and blue, $9.

Pounding bench, wooden, solid colored
pegs, some play wear **10.00**
Puzzle
Airplane, #330-16, 15 pcs............**12.00**
Bird, wood, 9-1/2" x 11-1/2" **18.00**
Cookie's Sesame Street Number,
Sesame Street, train motif, #105, 5
pc..**15.00**
Dipsy and La La, Teletubbies, wooden
....**3.00**
Mary had a little lamp, wood **6.00**
Po and Winky, Teletubbies, wooden
....**3.00**
Steam Shovel, #360-29, 18 pcs...**12.00**
Skaneateles Train, Track and Blocks set,
1960s, orig box, #S950, 55 pcs .**102.50**
Zoo, late 1960s/early 1970s, complete
with animals **95.00**

❖ Pokémon

This big collecting phase at the end of the
millennium attracted much interest with
youngsters. As with most flash-type
collectible phenomenon, reproductions
arrived on the scene early and have caused
confusion and frustration. Unless you're
buying for the sheer pleasure of collecting,
know your dealer's reputation well.

Action Flipz cards, ten packs of four
unopened cards, premier edition .**13.00**
Toy
Mew, #151, comes with Pokeball, light-
up, Burger King premium, battery
needs to be replaced................**40.00**
Togepi, bean bag, Burger King
premium.....................................**9.50**
Trading card
Dark Blastoise, non-holo, 1st edition
....**30.00**
Dark Dragonite, non-holo.............**15.00**
Flareon, holo foil, #3 ....**16.00**
Hitmonchan, holographic **9.00**
Kangaskhan, holo foil, #5.............**18.00**
Meowth Common, #62 ....**62.00**
Misty's Poliwrath, non-holo...........**15.00**
Pokemon Chansey, holographic...**13.00**
Pokemon Clefairy, holographic.....**13.00**
Vaporeon, holo foil, #12 ....**15.00**

❖ Pocketknives

Pocketknives have been made in various
forms and with different types of handles
and blade materials. Some collectors
search out pocketknives from specific
makers, while others specialize in certain
handles or advertising knives.

References: Joe Kertzman, *Knives 2003*,
23rd ed., Krause Publications, 2003;
Bernard Levine, *Levine's Guide to Knives
and Their Values*, 5th ed. Krause
Publications, 2001; Jack Lewis and Roger
Combs, *The Gun Digest Book of Knives*,
5th ed., Krause Publications, 1997; Jim

Sargent, *American Premium Guide to
Pocket Knives & Razors*, 5th ed., Krause
Publications 1999; Ron Stewart and Roy
Ritchie, Big Book of Pocket Knives,
Collector Books, 2000; J. Bruce Voyles,
IBCA Price Guide To Antique Knives, 2nd
ed., Krause Publications; —, *IBCA Price
Guide to Commemorative Knives, 1960-
1990*, Krause Publications.

Periodicals: *Blade*, 700 E State St., Iola,
WI 54990; *Knife World*, P.O. Box 3395,
Knoxville, TN 37927.

Collectors' Clubs: American Blade
Collectors, P.O. Box 22007, Chattanooga,
TN 37422; Canadian Knife Collectors Club,
Route 1, Milton, Ontario L9T 2X5 Canada;
National Knife Collectors Association, P.O.
Box 21070, Chattanooga, TN 37421.

Advertising, "Canadian Club, Best in the
House," mkd "Stainless Steel, Japan,"
normal wear **20.00**
Barlow, blade mkd "Colonial Prov. USA,"
2 blades, 3-1/2" l folded **95.00**
Camillus
Babe Ruth, facsimile signature on side,
2-1/2"..**125.00**
#702, stainless **17.50**
4 line stamp, black composition handle,
mkd "Camillus Cutlery, Camillus, NY,
USA," 3 blades, pre 1942..........**18.00**
Case
XX #799, single blade **15.00**
XX USA, 3 dots, #31048, single blade
....**18.00**
Forestmaster, blade mkd "Colonial," 4
blades, used, some rust, 3-3/4" l folded
....**25.00**
Hammer Brand, loop missing, 2-1/4" l
....**10.00**
Hoffritz, Switzerland, stainless, 2 blades
and scissors, adv "American
Greetings," 2-1/4" d **25.00**
Remington, 2 blade, one blade missing,
rusted, bone handle, 3-1/4" l........**15.00**
Schrade Cutlery, Captain DL-2, Dura
Lens diamond nail file, precision
scissors, pen blade, mkd "Snap On"
....**12.00**
Thornton, red handle, 2 blades, well
used, 3-1/2" l................................**55.00**
Zippo, 2 blades, adv "Trio Mfg Co., Inc.,"
2" l **18.00**

❖ Pocket Watches

Pocket watches never go out of style and
currently are quite fashionable. When
shopping for a pocket watch at a flea
market, ask a lot of questions as you
carefully examine the watch—who made it,
when, where, has it been repaired or
cleaned recently, does it keep the proper
time, etc.

Periodical: *Watch & Clock Review*, 2403
Champa St., Denver, CO 80205.

Collectors' Clubs: American Watchmakers
Institute, Chapter 102, 3 Washington St.,
Apt 3C, Larchmont, NY 10538; Early
American Watch Club Chapter 149, P.O.
Box 5499, Beverly Hills, CA 90210; National
Association of Watch & Clock Collectors,
514 Poplar St., Columbia, PA 17512.

American Waltham Watch Co.
14K yellow gold, model 1890
movement, size 6, fancy hunting
case, scalloped edges, engraved and
dated 1897 on front cover **700.00**
Gold filled case, size 16, Roman
numeral dial, elk on back, c1891,
open face..................................**250.00**
Silver, Deuber coin silver, model 1883
movement, size 18, open face,
c1891, small chip and ding to case
....**295.00**
Bautte, Jq Fd. Geneve, 18k yg, white
dial, Roman numerals, chased case
with bi-color floral bouquet on one side,
mixed meal and enamel dec on other,
scalloped edges, enamel damage
....**260.00**
Champney, S. P., Worcester, MA, 18k yg,
openface, gilt movement, #8063, key
wind, white dial, Roman numerals,
subsidiary seconds dial, hallmarks, orig
key, c1850, dial cracked, nicks to
crystal......................................**250.00**
Elgin National Watch Co.
Gold tone, open face..................**325.00**
White metal, 16 size, fancy edges and
back, c1906, open face, replaced
crystal **250.00**
Yellow gold filled, model 2 movement,
12 size, three-quarter plate, hunter
case, pendant set, c1916 ......**395.00**
Eterna, pendant, 18K yg, rect form, black
line indicators, hallmark **230.00**
Hampden, nickel, large, open face**475.00**
Howard, 14K white gold, 17 jewels,
matching chain, open face **450.00**
Vacheron & Constantin, 18kt gold,
hunting case, white enamel dial,
Roman numerals, gilt bar movement,
cylinder escapement, sgd on cuvette,
engraved case, 10 size **350.00**
U.S. Watch Co., 14K yg, hunter, size 6,
white dial, black Roman numerals,
subsidiary seconds dial, engraved floral
and scroll motifs on case **245.00**
Waltham, lady's, 14kt yg, hunting case,
white enamel dial, Arabic numeral
indicators, subsidiary seconds dial,
Lady Waltham jeweled nickel
movement by A.W.W. Co., floral
engraved case no. 224709, 0 size, gold
ropetwist chain **300.00**

❖ Political and Campaign Items

As the cost of getting elected to political office continues to spiral upward, we can thank our forefathers for establishing the practice of creating items with their image or slogan. Intended to passively generate votes, these political items are now eagerly sought by collectors.

Periodicals: *The Political Bandwagon,* P.O. Box 348, Leola, PA 17540; *Political Collector,* P.O. Box 5171, York, PA 17405.

Collectors' Club: American Political Items Collectors, P.O. Box 340339, San Antonio, TX 78234; Third Party & Hopefuls, 503 Kings Canyon Blvd., Galesburg, IL 61401.

> **Reproduction Alert**

For additional listings, see *Warman's Antiques and Collectibles Price Guide* and *Warman's Americana & Collectibles,* as well as specific topics in this edition, including John F. Kennedy, Abraham Lincoln, and Presidential.

Book
  Balance, Senator Al Gore, Houghton, Mifflin Co., 1992, first edition, du **15.00**
  Blind Ambition, The White House Years, John Dean, Simon and Schuster, orig shrinkwrap **5.00**
  Clinton, Portrait of Victory, Warner Books, photographs by P.F. Bentley, 1993, dj.....................................**20.00**
  Kennedy and Roosevelt, The Uneasy Alliance, Michael R. Meschloss, W.W. Norton and Co., 1980, first edition **10.00**
  Lyndon's Legacy, A Candid Look at The President's Policymakers, Frank L. Kluckhorn, Davin-Adair Co., 1964, first edition, dj **5.00**
Cuff Links, pr, McKinley, real photo, brass frame, clear celluloid over sepia portrait, c1896 ....**18.00**
Dress, Humbert Humphrey, red, white, and blue, 8-1/2" l black and white facial photo of Humphrey on front and back, 32" l..**85.00**
Earrings, clip back, red, white, and blue oval shaped stones, gold tone metal backings **25.00**
Golf tee, Eisenhower, 1-1/2" x 2" red, white, and blue pack of three Ike golf tees **18.00**
Jugate
  Ford-Reagan, black and white photos, white background, red top lettering, blue bottom lettering, red stars, pre-convention, 1976 ....**35.00**

Political & Campaign Items, pinback button, Roosevelt, red, white, and blue, $18.

  Goldwater/Miller, black and white photos in center, white background, red, white, and blue lettering......................................**5.00**
  Johnson-Humphrey, bluetone photos, red, white, and blue background, blue stars **8.00**
Lapel Stud
  Eisenhower, 3/4" h, brass, blue enamel background, "I Like Ike," needle post and clutch fastener **5.00**
  Harrison, 1/18", white and blue enamel flag, white enamel background, blue enamel ribbon design with brass letters "R.L.U.S," c1888.............**12.00**
  McKinley, diecut, white metal, black finish, cut-out circle surrounding portrait, c1896 ....**10.00**
Matchbook, Nixon's The One, red lettering, white background, unused **5.00**
Pinback button
  Bush 1992, 2" sq, center multicolored photo of Bush, red, white, and blue flag in background, red and blue lettering and stars on outer white background..............................**12.00**
  Carter Inauguration, black and white photos, red, white, and blue background **8.00**
  Dewey, 1-5/8" d, God Bless America, 1944-1948, litho, red rim, black and white photo on pale gray **24.00**
  Nixon's The One, orig wrapper, 1" dia **125.00**
Poster
  Humphrey/Muskie, name in big letters, birds, fish, trees, stars, and rising sun, numbered 30 of 115, sgd and dated by artist DI Stovall 1/9/71, stiff poster board stock **125.00**
  Reagan/Bush, Vote Republican, Palm Beach, framed, 22" x 27".........**75.00**
Tab, unbent, Nixon, yellow and dark blue, 1962 Governor, 1-1/2" h..................**8.00**
Thimble, Sew It Up For Nixon-Lodge/Experience Counts, 1" h, white plastic, red and blue lettering.........**8.00**
Watch fob, Young Democratic Clubs of America/First National Convention Kansas City, 1933, brass, raised lettering **10.00**

❖ Poodles

In the 1950s, poodles were supreme! From poodle skirts to television lamps, they were the favorites of many kids. Collectors enjoy reliving some of that nostalgia at flea markets by finding those friendly pink, white, or black poodles they loved as a kid.

Ashtray, black, some wear to ear and face, 4-1/2" **5.00**
Autograph dog, white vinyl, signatures, 1950s, 4-1/2" x 7".........................**18.00**
Beanie Baby, Gigi, MWBT and protector **18.00**
Jewelry Box, wood, white, poodle dec, sgd "Kellerman Jewel Case, Japan," 1960s, 10" x 6"...........................**25.00**
Figure, Paulette.............................**30.00**
Lamp, television type, poodle and puppy, mkd "Kron," 1950s, 13" h............**160.00**
Pin
  Beau, sterling, 1-1/2" x 1-3/4" **35.00**
  Stein, Parisian Poodle, orange body, ivory pom-poms, purple hair bow, mkd "Lea Stein, Paris" on clasp, 1-1/2" x 1-1/2" **95.00**
  Tortolani, gold-tone, faux pearls, and red rhinestone eye, 1-1/2" x 2-1/4" **85.00**
Pillow, poodle design, tiny rhinestone accents, tassels on each corner, 16" sq **165.00**
Pincushion, metal and fabric, nodding head and tail **35.00**
Planter, ceramic, pink, c1940, 6-1/2" h, 8-1/2" w, 3-1/2" d.......................**45.00**
Playing cards, yellow and blue backgrounds, Congress Playing Cards, Cell-U-Tone Finish, used..............**35.00**
Purse, wool, gold embellishment, large **56.00**
Salt and pepper shakers, pr, egg shape, one with yellow poodle, other with blue poodle, flowers, butterfly, raised relief, orig plastic stoppers and Enesco stickers **25.00**
Wall plaque, chalk, white head, illegible imp mark, 4-1/2", 4-1/4" w **30.00**

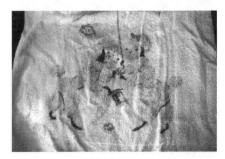

Poodles towel, white terry cloth, two blue poodles holding umbrella, c1960, wear, stains, $2.

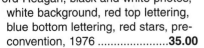

❖ Porcelier

Porcelain light fixtures, small appliances and a variety of tableware were some of the items produced by Porcelier Manufacturing Company, which was in business between 1926 and 1954. Collectors look for flawless items, wanting any gold trim to be unworn and items such as light fixtures to have their original pulls.

References: Susan E. Grindberg, *Collector's Guide to Porcelier China*, Collector Books, 1996.

Collectors' Clubs: Porcelier Collectors Club, 21 Tamarac Swamp Rd., Wallingford, CT 06492-5529,

Coffee set, percolator, sugar and creamer, lavender-blue bell platinum design..**130.00**
Coffeepot, Dutch couple, 4 pcs, 12-3/4" h **85.00**
Cream and sugar, Field Flowers, platinum......................................**22.50**
Light fixture
Ceiling-mount, 2 sockets, white with pink lilacs, needs rewired, no mounting hardware, 11" x 6-1/4" **30.00**
Wall-mount, circular back, socket arm, white with red roses, gold accents, rewired, replaced socket,........**129.00**
Teapot
Nautical, shows sailboats, 8" h **48.00**
Hearthside, rim chip, 6-3/4" h **25.00**
Waffle iron, Barock-Colonia, gold dots variation......................................**187.50**

Porcelier Coffee set, urn, matching creamer and sugar, pastel flowers, luster and gold trim, $130.

❖ Portrait Plates

Portrait plates and other types of wares with portraits of prominent people were made as decorations. Displays of American leaders could subtly express a political affiliation. Other portrait plates were made with busts of lovely women and were intended only for decorative display.

Napoleon portrait plate, green border, gold tracery, multicolored portrait, $60.

Gibson Girl, brown hair, blue-green ground, shaded purple to pink ground, shaped gold rim, artist sgd, mkd "Austria"..**50.00**
Marie Antoinette, sgd "Johner," dark green border, gilt scrolled and leaf dec, blue Austrian beehive mark, 14" dia **275.00**
Mrs. Lincoln, 6" d, Imperial China ..**85.00**
Napoleon, Louisiana Purchase souvenir, fair buildings on rim, blue and white earthenware, high glaze, Victoria Art Company, NY, 10" d **300.00**
Queen Louise, white dress, pink sash, gold rim, sgd "Mme A-K, France," 8-1/2" d..**180.00**
Traumerci, sgd "Wagner," young woman seated on trunk, boughs of flowers, heavily gilt border with urns and garlands, pale green ground, blue Austrian beehive mark, 9-1/2" dia, hairline, gilt loss **790.00**
Woman, brown hair, pale purple fringed lavender shawl on shoulder, gold stenciled inner rim, green border, blue "Victoria Austria" mark...............**125.00**

❖ Postcards

Ever wonder what happened to all those postcards tourists have sent over the decades? Postcard collectors are searching flea markets for them. Some buyers specialize in local history cards, while others seek a specific maker or artist. Most are reasonably priced, but recently some rare postcards have sold for record prices.

Periodical: *Postcard Collector*, Krause Publications, 700 E. State St., Iola, WI 54990.

Reference: Ron Menchine, *Tuff Stuff's Baseball Postcard Collection*, Tuff Stuff Books, 1999; Robert Reed, *Advertising Postcards*, Schiffer Publishing, 2001.

Collectors' Clubs: There are many regional collectors clubs. Contact one of these national organizations to find out about a chapter near you. Deltiologists of America, P.O. Box 8, Norwood, PA 19074; Postcard History Society, P.O. Box 1765, Manassas, VA 22110.

Advertising
Case Stem Tractor, salesroom, Columbus, OH **60.00**
Kellogg's, Tony the Tiger, Tony with camper's gear, pointing to sign post, mid-1960s, 3-5/8" x 5-5/8" **15.00**
Airline, issued by airline, unused
Pluna, Uruguay, Boeing 737 ....**6.00**
Trans-Canada Airlines, Viscount at Windsor Airport, Windsor, Ontario, Canada **8.00**
Bank, Buffalo, NY, Buffalo Savings Bank, Buffalo Square, 1900s....................**6.50**
Baseball, Palace of Fans Ballpark, Cincinatti, stamped "Sept 18 1908" **125.00**
Cats, four kittens, "Greetings from the Kills," early 1900s **6.00**
Christmas, little girl and doll, silk insert, Wolf and Co., NY, writing on back**10.00**
Dogs
Happy Birthday, "We're sending these puppies to say, Have a Happy Birthday," photo of beagles by Roberts......................................**6.00**
Pekingese, "Just a Few Lines," B B London, Series No. G 53, printed in Germany....................................**9.00**
Scottish Terriers, sgd "M. Gear," published by Valentine & Sons, Ltd., Dundee and London, unused ...**30.00**
Easter, Easter angel, early 1900, never used **9.00**
Hold to light, used
Art Nouveau couple dancing........**35.00**
Cat and Mouse, kissing couple....**15.00**
Cinderella, 1900, Belgium............**85.00**
Girl with Umbrella........................**30.00**
U.S. Treasury Building, Washington, DC **25.00**
Interior, real photo type
Bakery interior.............................**85.00**
Will Roger's house in Pacific Palisades, CA...**5.00**
Pretty Lady
Cowgirl on horseback, The Belle of the Plain, traces of glue....................**8.00**
Dear Heart, pretty lady wearing large hat, copyright 1908, previously glued into album **10.00**
Railroad, chrome
Erie Railroad **3.50**
Milwaukee Railroad **3.00**
Southern Pacific Limited **3.00**
Southern Pacific Railroad..............**3.00**
Steam Town USA **2.00**
Vista-Dome Zephyr **3.50**
Restaurant, Hollywood Cabaret

Restaurant, Broadway, 48th, NYC**10.00**
School scene, children posed in front of
    brick building, names identified on
    back, 1910, real photo **20.00**
Street scene
    Red Lion Inn, Quakertown, PA, trolley,
        passengers **30.00**
    Santa Fe, chrome...........................**3.00**
Valentine
    Cupid with arrows, "You stole a heart!
        Love's law is plain, that bids you
        part, with one again"..................**6.00**
    Two cupids tending love fire, 1900.**8.75**

❖ Posters

Posters have long been an effective
communication tool. Their size, bright
colors, and great illustrations caught the
attention of many passersby. Today they are
treasured and becoming more available at
flea markets.

Periodicals: *Biblio,* 845 Willamette St,
Eugene, OR 87401; *Collecting Hollywood*,
American Collectors Exchange, 2401 Broad
St, Chattanooga, TN 37408; *Movie Poster
Update*, American Collectors Exchange,
2401 Broad St, Chattanooga, TN 37408.

For additional listings, see *Warman's
Antiques and Collectibles Price Guide* and
Warman's Americana & Collectibles, as well
as Movie Posters in this edition.

Air France - North Africa, Villemot,
    stylized imagery of mosques and
    minarets, lave3nders, yellow, and blues
    against sky blue background, plane
    and Pegasus logo, c1950, 24" x 39"
    ....**225.00**
Bridge of Peace, Venette Willard
    Shearer, anti-war poster from American
    Friends Service Committee, National
    Council to Prevent War, children of all
    nations play beneath text of song of
    peace, c1936, 16" x 22" **125.00**
Buddha and Heartstone, Polish
    magician performing tricks, English and
    Polish text, c1914, 14" x 26" **100.00**
Carry On With Franklin D. Roosevelt,
    portrait in gravure, black letters against
    white ground, framed, 1936, 9" x 11"
    ....**15.00**
Central Hudson Line,
    Newburgh/Poughkeepsie/Kingston,
    shows man and woman with binoculars
    at railing, "B.B. Odell" on life preserver,
    with trip dates, 45-1/2" x 29-1/2"**715.00**
Clyde, Beatty-Cole Bros Combined
    Circus, the World's Largest Circus,
    "Clyde Beatty in Person," Roland
    Butler, Lion tamer, 19" x 26" **90.00**
Ediswan Electric Home Iron, full color,
    showing 1930s electric iron, c1935, 11"
    x 18" **60.00**

*Poster, Highlights of the Jazz Story in USA,
Peter Von Bartkowski edition, framed, $20.*

Family Fun Night, Disneyland, May 16,
    1971, 12" x 9"...............................**45.00**
Give It Your Best, 48-star U.S. flag,
    World War II, 28-1/2" x 20"...........**60.00**
**"I Summon You to Comradeship in the
    Red Cross,"** Harrison Fisher
    illustration, World War I, heavy wear at
    edges, tears, creases, 40" x 28"
    ....**335.00**
I Want You, Uncle Sam Army recruiting
    poster, 1975, 14" x 11".................**80.00**
Post Toasties, "Sweet Memories," 1909,
    framed, 21-3/4" x 16-1/2" **575.00**
Tin Cans Going to War, World War II,
    orig wooden frame, 36" x 30".....**150.00**
Wings Cigarette, Piper Cub giveaway,
    1940s, cardboard, 30" x 20".......**145.00**
Which? Soldier Or Mechanic, L.H.,
    "Enlist in the 57th Engineers (Inlaid
    Waterways) and Be Both… Camp
    Laurel, Maryland," 1918, 18" x 23"
    ....**200.00**

❖ Powder Jars

Containers to hold powder were a staple of
a lady's dressing table. The boxes were
often decorative or whimsical. Today
collectors are charmed by them.

Celluloid lid, frosted green glass jar
    base, wear to emb black design on top,
    3-1/2" h, 4-1/4" w **28.00**
Glass
    Clear, elephant on top, raised trunk
    ....**28.00**
    Clear, lady sitting in front of beveled
        mirror **55.00**
    Clear, lady's portrait under lid, reverse
        painted highlights, box shape, wear
        to paint, 3" x 4" **85.00**

Clear, My Pet..............................**40.00**
Clear, woman with child, 9" h, inside
    nick **145.00**
Frosted, green, Art Deco lady **250.00**
Frosted, green, Cameo lady.......**225.00**
Frosted, green, Crinoline Girl.....**145.00**
Frosted, green, hand painted flowers
    ....**30.00**
Frosted, green, Scottie **85.00**
Frosted, pink, elephant, trunk down
    ....**65.00**
Frosted, pink, lovebirds **60.00**
Hobnail, clear, opalescent white
    hobnails, 4-3/8" d.....................**25.00**
Iridescent, marigold, figural poodle on
    top...**32.00**
Pink, Annette...............................**75.00**
Musical, dresser jar, 8-1/2" h **60.00**

❖ Precious Moments Figurines

Created by Samuel J. Butcher in 1978 and
produced by Enesco, Precious Moments
are now in their third decade of production.
This popular line of collectibles features
cute kids with inspiring messages. The
collectibles include figurines, mugs,
ornaments, and plates. Collectors should
enjoy their Precious Moments, but not hope
to reap great rewards on the re-sale of
these objects.

References: Rosie Wells, *Rosie's
Secondary Market Price Guide for Enesco's
Precious Moments Collection*, 16th ed,
Rosie Wells Enterprises, 1998; *Precious
Collectibles*, 22341 E. Wells Rd., Canton, IL
61520.

*Precious Moments September, little girl balancing
books on her head, 1988, $7.50.*

Precious Moments Abbey, vinyl doll, purple dress, orig accessories, NRFB, $15.

Collectors' Clubs: Enesco Precious Moments Collectors' Club, P.O. Box 99 Itasca, IL 60143.

Bookmark, brass, Your Love is So Uplifting, 2-1/2" h, MOC **6.00**

Cake top, Lord Bless You and Keep You, bride and groom, 6" h **65.00**

Figurine
Birthday Club, Clown Drummer, B-0001, Charter Member figure, 3-3/4" h..**80.00**
God's Speed, little boy jogging with dog, base dated and mkd "Jonathon & David" **85.00**
God Understands, triangle mark, string tag, no box.............................**125.00**
Healer of Broken Hearts, 6" h......**55.00**
Love Lifted Me, older boy helping younger friend tumbling from wagon, 5-1/2" h **80.00**
Peacemaker, 1979, 5" h..............**55.00**
This Is Your Day To shine, little girl being helped by kitten and puppy, 6" h..**80.00**
Thou Art Mine, little boy and girl with turtle, writing in sand, 5-1/4" h..**70.00**

Stationery, note cards and envelopes, assorted designs, orig box.............**5.00**

❖ Premiums

Saving box tops and barcodes has been a way to get a promotional item from a favorite company. Many early premiums promoted radio and cowboy heroes. Some of these vintage treasures have become quite valuable.

Periodicals: *Box Top Bonanza,* 3403 46th Ave., Moline, IL 61265; *Premium Collectors Magazine,* 1125 Redman Ave., St. Louis, MO 63138; *The Premium Watch Watch,* 24 San Rafael Drive, Rochester, NY 14618; *The Toy Ring Journal,* P.O. Box 544, Birmingham, MI 48012.

Autographed Photo
Captain Tim Healy, 5" x 7" still paper

black and white fan card, issued by Ivory Soap, c1938, dark blue inscription **28.00**
Lyman, Abe, 8" x 10" glossy black and white fan photo, printed text at bottom "The World's Biggest 15 Minute Show," sgd in black ink, 1934 ....**15.00**

Book, *The Friskies Book of Dog Care,* Gracie Allen signature, 5-1/2" x 7-1/4" color cover, 1955..........................**15.00**

Catalog
Kellogg's Funny Jungleland Moving-Pictures, 1932...........................**48.00**
Octagon Soap Premium List, 1930 edition **38.00**

Decoder, Lil Orphan Annie Secret Society Decoder, 1935, brass with silver outer rim..............................**65.00**

Mask, Cisco Kid, paper, Schulze Butter-nut White Bread. 1949, 12-1/2" w **30.00**

Premium dial, Uncle Don, 40 Wonders/Great Inventions of the World, stiff paper diecut wheel, Compliments of Uncle Don and Silver Wings, copyright 1931 Knapp, New York, 10" dia **24.00**

Premium letter, The Cruise of the Blue Dart, vignettes of various pirate scenes, 3" x 4-1/2" gray mailer with Maltex Co., Inc. Vermont, return address, late 1930s, folded as issued **15.00**

Puzzle, Just Plain Bill, Kolynos Dental Cream, 150 pcs, orig envelope **32.00**

Ring, Cap'n Crunch, plastic, blue figure on red base **295.00**

Sign, Squirt doll, paper banner offering 18" h vinyl doll with fabric outfit through participating store of direct mail, 1962, Squirt Co. **40.00**

Spoon, Charlie McCarthy, orig mailer **50.00**

Thank You card, orange and black illus, message to broadcasters, Art Deco style art of jazz band, copyright 1924 Exclusive Co., Philadelphia, orig envelope, unused **10.00**

❖ Presidential

Collectors who follow the winners to the White House have additional collectibles to gather. Tried-and-true presidential collectors will add to their campaign paraphernalia by gathering inaugural and other collectibles generated by the office holder. Other presidential memorabilia might deal with family members.

Periodical: *The Political Bandwagon,* P.O. Box 348, Leola, PA 17540; *Political Collector,* P.O. Box 5171, York, PA 17405.

Box showing Mount Rushmore, $15.

Collectors' Club: American Political Items Collectors, P.O. Box 340339, San Antonio, TX 78234.

First-day cover, autographed by Gerald Ford **60.00**

Inaugural program
Bill Clinton, glossy content, full color photos, 24 pgs **15.00**
Lyndon Johnson, gold presidential seal, Jan 20, 1965, full color and black and white photos and text**20.00**

Inaugural Souvenir, 1-1/4" d black and white button with 1-3/4" x 3-1/4" attached gold type on red, white, and blue ribbon which reads "Inauguration Franklin D. Roosevelt , Our First Third Term President/January 2, 1941/Washington, D.C."...............**50.00**

Magazine cover, *Time*
Johnson and Goldwater collage, Sept. 25, 1964...................................**5.00**
Johnson and Humphrey, Sept. 4, 1964 ....**8.00**
President Clinton, December 1998 ...**50**
President Johnson, Man of the Year, Jan. 1, 1965 ....**8.00**

Newspaper, "F.D.R. Is Laid To Rest," Daily Mirror, 11-1/2" x 15", 20 pg section, April 18, 1945, large 10" x 10" black and white photo on cover, follow-up stories...................................**25.00**

Nodder, Dwight Eisenhower, composition, brown hat, blue coat, c1956, 6" h **100.00**

Paperweight
Dwight D. Eisenhower, sulphide, Baccarat, cameo, grid-cut base, 1963, 2-3/4" dia **325.00**
Franklin D. Roosevelt dime motif, made for Imperial Glass by Lenox, 1977 ....**15.00**

Plate, ceramic
President and Mrs. Dwight D. Eisenhower, America's First Family, 9" dia..**8.00**
U.S. presidents, ending with John F. Kennedy...................................**15.00**

Postcard
President and Mrs. Taft, 1909 inauguration **25.00**

President Roosevelt and Family...**10.00**

Print, sepia portraits of President and Mrs. Harrison, brown card mount, c1888, 4-1/4" x 6-1/2" **20.00**

Sheet Music, *Teddy You're A Bear*, credits to Ring H. Larder for worlds, music by Lee S. Robert, published by Jerome h. Remick & Co., 1916, 4 pgs **25.00**

Stereoview

The President and Mrs. McKinley, floral border **15.00**

Tomb of Late President McKinley, Canton, Ohio, tinted...................**6.00**

Transit pass, brown, red, and yellow, weekly pass for Inauguration Week, Jan 19-25, 1941, 1-1/2" h oval black and white portrait of FDR on left side, 2" x 4-1/2"......................................**25.00**

❖ Presley, Elvis

"You ain't nothin' but a hound dog…" Elvis was quite a hit in his day. Even after his death in 1977, memorabilia sales remain strong. Fans still flock to his home and swoon when they hear his songs.

Collectors' Club: Elvis Forever TCB Fan Club, P.O. Box 1066, Pinellas Park, FL 33281; Graceland News Fan Club, P.O. Box 452, Rutherford, NJ 07070.

Album, LP

Our Memories of Elvis, black label, DNT **75.00**

Personally Elvis, blue label, double pocket, silhouette......................**50.00**

Spinout, black label, DOT, RCA, white top..**35.00**

Welcome to My World, black label, DNT **30.00**

Barbie, Barbie Loves Elvis, 1996, MIB **130.00**

Book, *Meet Elvis Presley,* Favius Friedman, © 1971, 1973, 1977, paperback, 128 pgs, includes epilogue written after Presley's death, 7-3/4" x 5-1/4"...**10.00**

Elvis Presley assorted gum cards and Gracelands brochure, $5.

Elvis Presley doll, wearing black, white, and silver outfit, microphone and other accessories in orig box, $20.

Calendar, 1977, Tribute to Elvis, Boxcar Enterprises, 12" x 13" **50.00**

Cookie jar, riding in car **100.00**

Decanter, McCormick Distillery, porcelain

Music box base plays "Blue Hawaii," Aloha Elvis, shows Arizona Memorial, 16" h **295.00**

Music box base plays "Loving You," mkd "Young Elvis '55," 16" h, MIB **275.00**

Portrait bust, orig booklet titled "1935-1977, The End of an Era," 15" h, MIB **275.00**

Singing pose, 14" h, MIB **275.00**

Flicker button, black and white photos of Elvis playing guitar, titled "Love Me Tender," © 1958 Elvis Presley Enterprises, 2-1/4" dia..................**25.00**

Magazine, Saturday Evening Post, July/August, 1985, "Legends that Won't Die"..**10.00**

Paperback book, *Elvis Presley: The King is Dead*, Martin A. Grove, 1977 ....**6.00**

Portrait, sgd by artist Ivan Jesse Curtin, mounted on wooden frame, c1960 ....**125.00**

Puzzle, The King, Springbok, 1992, 1000 pieces...**50.00**

Sheet music, 1954, Love Me.........**35.00**

Tab, litho tin, blue, gold lettering, "I Love Elvis," metallic gold background, 1970s, 2" dia **15.00**

❖ Princess Diana

Princess Diana plate, oval, wearing crown and black gown, orig box and certificate, $20.

Her tragic death in 1997 stopped the world for a brief time. Collectibles ranging from things made during her lifetime, such as wedding commemoratives, and later memorial pieces are readily available at flea markets.

Ale glass, Royal Wedding...............**32.00**

Beanie baby, purple bear **32.00**

Beer can, Felinfoel Brewery, Wales, 1981, official Royal Wedding commemorative, bottom opened..**15.00**

Brooch, memorial heart pin, orig card **50.00**

Calendar, 1998, still sealed **10.00**

Coach replica, Matchbox, replica of coach used in wedding, made for Her Majesty's 40th Anniversary, limited edition, MIB **65.00**

Doll, porcelain, flower girl, pastel yellow dress, white roses, Danbury Mint, 11" h **195.00**

First-day cover, Marshall Islands **3.00**

Postcard, birthday card type, photo of Diana and Charles, unused **10.00**

Slippers, figural head of sleeping Diana and Charles, c1980, unused, orig tags **48.00**

Tea towel, Irish linen, portraits of Diana and Charles, Prince of Wales plumes, 28-1/2" x 18-1/2" **20.00**

Thimble, HRH Prince William of Wales, to commemorate his 1st birthday, portrait of Prince and Mother, June, 1983 ....**27.00**

Tin, engagement photo, banner on top "Royal Wedding, July 1981," mkd "Regent Ware, Made in England," minor dent **22.00**

Trade card set, full unopened package, Press Pass **95.00**

❖ Prints

Prints are a great way for the common folk to have copies of fine artwork for their homes or offices. Currier & Ives was one of numerous publishers that reproduced a variety of artwork. Today's limited-edition prints compete for the same collector dollars.

References: Jay Brown, *The Complete Guide to Limited Edition Art Prints,* Krause Publications, 1999; Michael Ivankovich, *Collector's Value Guide to Early 20th Century American Prints,* Collector Books, 1998. Plus there are many other excellent reference books available about prints, fine arts, and artists.

Periodicals: *Journal of the Print World,* 1008 Winona Road, Meredith, NH 03253; *On Paper,* 39 E. 78th St., #601, New York, NY 10021.

Reproduction Alert

For additional listings, see *Warman's Antiques and Collectibles Price Guide.*

Baille, James, publisher, colored lithograph, period frame
The Marriage, 1849, 12" x 8-1/2"
....**115.00**
The Young Bride, 1848, 17" x 13"
....**75.00**

Currier & Ives
James Polk, Eleventh President of the United States, period decor frame, light water stains, top margin worn, 14" x 9-7/8" **220.00**
Jay Eye See, Record 2:10, cherry frame, stains, minor damage, edge repair, 13-3/8" x 17-5/8"..........**165.00**
Lady Washington, period veneer frame with chips, slight stains, 1 small pc missing from margin **275.00**

Fox, R. Adkinson, The Westwinds,
....**75.00**

Kellogg & Comstock
The Angler, girl reading letter to man fishing, grain-decor frame, margin tear, stains, fold line, 9-3/4" x 14"
....**137.50**
The Fruit, light stains, walnut cross-corner frame, short margin tear, 10" x 14"..**88.00**
Napoleon, hand-colored, 1870, 17" x 13" **225.00**

Leighton, Clare, *The Lovers,* woodcut on paper, 1940, edition of 30, sgd "Clare Leighton" in pencil lower right, numbered and titled "26/30..." in pencil lower left, 7" x 4-7/8" image size, matted, unframed, margins over 1", scattered foxing, annotations to margins **325.00**

Soyer, Raphael, *Bust of a Girl,* lithograph in black, red and blue on paper, edition of 300, sgd "Raphael Soyer" in pencil lower right, numbered "86/300" in

pencil lower left, image size 18-3/8" x 13-5/8", framed, over 1" margins
....**210.00**

Walker, George H. and Co., publisher, Joe L. Jones, lithographer, *Deacon Jones' One Hoss Shay, No. 2,* lithograph in blue and black, hand coloring, on paper, identified in inscriptions in matrix, 22-1/2" x 29-5/8"
....**490.00**

❖ Pull Toys

Simple toys made to delight young children have been collected for decades. Many are home made and those often contain a certain charm that appeals to collectors. Look for examples that are in good condition and have all their parts. Don't be surprised if the favorite little one in your life wants to play with these colorful toys.

Bouncing Buggy, Fisher-Price, c1973
....**10.00**
Bunny, pink plastic bunny, wooden wheels, 7" h, 5" l **15.00**
Chiming Turtle, Fisher-Price **22.00**
Dump truck, Fisher-Price, 12-1/2" l**16.00**
Elephant, wooden, mkd "Montgomery Schoolhouse, Inc., Vermont," orig tail and pull cord, some wear to edges, 7-1/4" l **20.00**
Mary Had A Little Lamb, hand painted plaster, wooden wheels................**85.00**
Mickey Mouse Locomotive, Mickey as conductor, Pluto and Donald Duck on stickers on one side, Minnie and Goofy on other, red, green, orange, and yellow popping balls in globe, worn paint **12.00**
Mickey Mouse Piano, Arco Kubler, 7" h
....**20.00**
Pegs, wood, Holgate, 1940s, 10-3/4" l
....**28.00**
Pixie Face, green hat and mouth, red, green, and blue face, Bakelite and wood, mkd "Cinderella Mfg Co., Jackson, Mich," 1940s................**120.00**
Slinky Dog, from Toy Story, fair condition, 8" l..............................**10.00**
Suzy Seal, Fisher-Price, all wood, applied decals **35.00**
Timmy Turtle, Fisher-Price, 1962, 8" l
....**35.00**
Tractor, Fisher-Price, red plastic wheels, 1960 ....**40.00**

❖ Punch Boards

Feel like taking a chance? For those lucky collectors who enjoy finding punch boards, flea markets often offer several choices.

Ace High, deck of cards for jackpot, 13" x 17" **90.00**

Western Saddle Horses punchboard, pay what you punch, 25 cents maximum, cardboard, 6-1/2" x 7-1/4", $15.

Barrel of Cigarettes, Lucky Strike Green, 10" x 10"..........................**44.00**
Candy Special, penny candy board, 4-1/2" x 7-1/2",................................**24.00**
Elvgren's Flashy, 11-7/8" x 9-5/8" .**50.00**
Fancy Fives, 11-7/8" x 9-5/8" **50.00**
Five Tens..**24.00**
Good Punching, cowboy motif, 9-1/2" x 10" **36.00**
Jackpot Bingo, thick card jackpot, 10" x 8"..**10.00**
Nickel Special, shows Lucky Strike pack, pre-World War II, 500 punches at 5 cents each..................................**45.00**
Odd Pennies, small change, 2¢ and 3¢ board, 6-3/4" x 11" **45.00**
Pick A Cherry, fruit seal **24.00**
Professor Charley, 1946, Superior Mfg. Typical 25¢ cash board **18.00**
Speedy Tens, 10" x 13"..................**18.00**
Three Sure Hits, 10" x 13" **24.00**

❖ Puppets

Puppets come in all shapes and sizes, from hand operated to elaborate marionettes to ventriloquist dummies and little push puppets, giving collectors a real variety. The fun part about collecting puppets is that all probably have made people laugh and smile, and probably still have lots of smiles left to share with their new owners.

Hand, all used condition
Boglin, purple, yellow eyes, 1980s, 8" h
....**16.00**
Donkey, Kamar............................**10.00**
Goofy, Gabriel, 1977 ....**10.00**
Pinocchio, Gund, soft plastic head, printed cotton body..................**50.00**
Snuggle Bear **8.75**
Tweety Bird, 10" h **13.50**
Marionette, all used condition

Small Fry Club marionette, character from late 1950s children's television show, yellow hat, hands, and feet, multicolored outfit, $125.

Clown	**42.00**
Mr. Bluster	**635.00**

Howdy Doody, cloth body, vinyl head and hands, body mkd "Goldberger Doll Co., Made in Hong Kong," head mkd "Eegee," one arm and hand damaged, 12" l **30.00**

McCarthy, Charlie, composition, 12" h **125.00**

Pinocchio, Walt Disney Enterprises, composition, 12" h.................**125.00**

Princess Winter, Spring, Summer, Fall, cracks to composition head, 14" l **500.00**

Siamese Temple Dancer **130.00**

Push puppet, used condition

Atom Ant	**25.00**

Cowboy on White Horse, by Kohner, Socko label **45.00**

Donald Duck	**30.00**
Mickey Mouse	**30.00**
Olive Oyl	**35.00**
Pluto	**25.00**
Popeye	**35.00**
Santa Mouse	**35.00**
Terry the Tiger	**30.00**

Ventriloquist dummy, all used condition

Bozo	**42.00**
Jerry Mahoney	**60.00**
Three Stooges	**100.00**
Willie Talk, Horsman	**42.00**

❖ Purinton Pottery

Purinton Pottery is another Ohio pottery company that made dinnerware and some table wares. Founded in Wellsville, the company was in business from 1936 to 1959.

Periodical: *Puritan Pastimes*, P.O. Box 9394, Arlington, VA 22219.

Bank, Raggedy Andy, 6-1/2" h	**80.00**
Casserole, cov, Apple, oval	**25.00**
Cereal bowl, Pennsylvania Dutch	**15.00**
Chop plate, Apple	**20.00**
Creamer, miniature, Apple, 2" h	**15.00**
Cruet set, Intaglio	**36.00**

Cup and saucer

Estate	**12.00**
Normandy Plaid	**17.50**

Dinner plate

Fruits	**15.00**
Normandy Plaid	**20.00**
Plaid	**15.00**
Dutch jug, Apple, 6" h, 8" w	**35.00**
Grill plate, Apple, 12" d	**25.00**
Honey jug, Red Ivy	**35.00**
Marmalade, cov, Maywood	**32.00**
Pitcher, Fruit, qt, 5-1/2" h	**55.00**
Platter, Intaglio, 12-1/2"	**22.00**

Relish dish, Fruits, divided, three parts, handle **18.50**

Salt and pepper shakers, pr, Apple, jug-style, 2-1/2" h **25.00**

Serving dish, Intaglio, 11-1/4"	**22.00**
Snack set, Apple	**32.50**
Sugar, cov, Apple, 5" h	**38.50**
Teapot, Red Ivy, crack, 5" h	**25.00**
Tumbler, Apple	**20.00**

Vegetable

Intaglio, brown, 8-1/2" d	**25.00**

Normandy Plaid, 10-1/2" l, divided **50.00**

Wall pocket, Apple, 4" h **130.00**

❖ Purses

Here's an item most ladies wouldn't be without. Collectors are intrigued with the styles, colors, and different textures of purses from bygone eras.

Alligator, brown, designer type.......**50.00**

Bamboo, boxy style, 13" x 14", one small red knob missing..........................**65.00**

Beaded

Enameled pink, blue, and yellow, frame stamped "Whiting and Davis" .**200.00**

White with pastel colored beaded flowers, mkd "Made in Hong Kong," 9" x 5" **40.00**

Evening

Brocade, Art Deco, engraved gold filled frame.......................................**75.00**

Faille, black, marcasite set mounting, gold onyx monogram, c1930 ....**70.00**

Satin, pink, silver bugle beads, ivory colored seed pearls, silver frame and clasp, trimmed in white rhinestones, silver chain handle, Jolle Original, 9" x 7-1/2" x 1" **110.00**

Leather, Mexican, tooled leather, brown, white inserts **45.00**

Evening bag, red, orange, yellow, and purple flowers, green stylized bows, white scrolling beaded trim, tan ground, snap closure, $10.

Lucite, trapezoid, cream colored, gold-tone frame, rigid handle, snap clasp, navy lining and side gussets, c1950, 8" w..**185.00**

Macramé, yellow twine, olive colored wooden beads, shoulder type, hand made **5.00**

Mesh, silver and enamel, R. Blackington & Co., mesh link bag, frame enameled with white geometric pattern, green squares, lavender border, interior engraved with name, silk cord strap, early 20th C, 6" w.......................**250.00**

Plastic, white opaque, applied pink rose, green leaves, goldtone fittings **25.00**

Straw, two handles, gold-tone ball type clasp, c1950 ....**20.00**

❖ Puzzles

What's got lots of pieces and hours of fun? Puzzles. Puzzles have been around about as long as the America, starting as ways to keep children occupied. By the 1890s, adults wanted to have some fun too, leading the creation of more intricate examples. Ask the dealer if the puzzle is complete and if any pieces are damaged. Missing pieces can drastically reduce the price.

Collectors' Clubs: American Game Collectors Association, P.O. Box 44, Dresher, PA 19025.

For additional listings, see *Warman's Antiques and Collectibles Price Guide.*

Walt Disney's Lady & The Tramp puzzle, Jaymar, complete, wear to box, $12.

Popeye, Interlocking Picture Puzzle, complete, wear to box, $10.

A Puzzler Picture, Le Petit Jean, A. T. Crosby, 1930-40s, 324 pcs, 7 figural pcs, orig box, 12" x 15" **80.00**

Cunard Line, Queen Mary in Trafalgar Square, Chad Valley, W. McDowell artist, 1936, 300 pcs, replaced box, 11-1/2" x 16" **65.00**

Dumbo, Jaymar Specialty 11" x 14" **15.00**

Evening on Grand Canal, Venice, #2, Pastime Puzzles, Parker Brothers, plywood, c1930, 150 pcs, 20 figural pcs, orig box, 9-3/4" x 10" **60.00**

First In The Heart Of His Countrymen, Corker Picture Puzzle, Whitman Publishing Co. **15.00**

Game of Chess, Pickwick, Hoadley House, 1930s, 365 pcs, 4 replaced, replaced box, 17-3/4" x 13-3/4"....**75.00**

Land of the Midnight Sun, W.E. Bryant, 160 pcs, 1 figural pcs, "B" signature pc, orig box, mail lending library, 12" x 10" **50.00**

Lending Library, Painting the Vase, Goddard artist, Eugene Sexton, orig box, 16" x 21-3/4"......................**150.00**

Mother Goose, 1954, Sifco Co., 10" x 8" **16.00**

Premier, Kidnapped (bear), Milton Bradley, 200 pcs, 8 figural pcs, orig box, 12" x 9", ...**50.00**

Sunset, #7, Pastime Puzzles, Parker Brothers, plywood, c1928, 126 pcs, 12 figural pcs, orig box, 7" x 9" **55.00**

❖ Pyrex

Pyrex was developed by the researchers at Corning Glass in the early 1910s. By 1915, Corning launched its Pyrex line with a 12-piece set. Fry Glass Company was granted permission to produce Pyrex under its Fry Oven Glass label in 1920. Cooks today still use many Pyrex products. This kitchenware collectible is just starting to become popular with many people. Don't overlook advertising and paper ephemera dealing with Pyrex.

Reference: Barbara Mauzy, *Pyrex*, 2nd ed., Schiffer Publishing, 2002.

Baker, cov, delphite blue, 6-3/4" x 4-1/4" **22.00**

Bowl, tab handles, bright red ext., gold pinecone dec................................**45.00**

Bean pot, cov, clear, 2 qt **12.00**

Casserole, cov, 2 qt, round, robin's egg blue base, clear cover, light use...**15.00**

Double boiler, mkd "Flameware"....**17.50**

Freezer server, Butterprint **12.00**

Mixing bowl Set, four nested bowls, solid colored exterior, white int., one yellow, green, orange/red, and blue **40.00**

Percolator, Flameware, Deluxe, 4 cup size **45.00**

Pie plate, clear, 10" **10.00**

Refrigerator set, Butterprint pattern, 8 pc set...**45.00**

Serving dish, Bluebelle **20.00**

Vegetable dish, divided, red ext. **20.00**

❖ Pyrography

It's an interesting concept—give someone a hot tool and tell him to go burn a design on a piece of wood. That is essentially what pyrography was all about. Skilled artisans introduced the form to America in the mid 1800s, but it became a hobby for the masses around the turn of the century, when several companies began offering items with designs stamped on them for burning. The Flemish Art Company of New York was the largest producer of pyrography products, and the term Flemish Art has become synonymous with burnt wood pieces of that era. The hobby was most popular from 1890 to 1915.

Reference: Frank L. Hahn, *Collector's Guide to Burnt Wood Antiques*, Golden Era Publications, 1994.

Bench, small child holding ball, another child in high chair, red poinsettia flowers, lift seat **75.00**

Book rack, folding, 18" l.................**80.00**

Pyrography Box, geometric dec, $22.

Pyrography Glove box, roses dec, $25.

Box

Book-shaped, woman wearing crown, 2 pcs, 1905, 4" x 3-1/2" x 1-1/2" **45.00**

Hand-painted, cherries design **42.00**

Chair-table, floral and other decor, sides with 2 large oval cutouts, 47" h ..**495.00**

Utensil box, 3" h, 12" w, 9" d........**135.00**

Gameboard, triangle-design surface, owl on reverse, 11" x 14" **110.00**

Handkerchief box, hand-painted, 9" sq **65.00**

Plaque

Dutch girl with cookie jar, painted floral border, 12" x 9" **65.00**

Gibson Girl, 10" dia **165.00**

Indian maiden in headdress, oval **85.00**

Plate, pyrography design highlighted by red flowers, illegible signature on back **18.00**

Plate rack, fruit motif, 12" h, 42" l **220.00**

Spoon holder, 3 dancing Dutch girls, slots for 8 spoons **55.00**

Wastebasket, woman's bust and grapes decor, square, scalloped top, 14" h **71.50**

❖ Quilts

Colorful bits and pieces of material sewn together make up quilts. Wonderful examples can be found at flea markets, from vintage, handmade, one-of-a-kind quilts to newer designer quilts. Carefully examine any quilt before purchasing, look at the design for it's aesthetic quality as well as colors. Make sure the fabrics are stable. Check the binding and the back. Feel how heavy the inner layer is to help determine warmth. And don't be afraid to give it a sniff test too. Depending on the age, design, and fabrics, you probably can't toss an antique quilt into the washer and dryer, so make sure your potential purchase is appealing to all your senses. Remember fabrics may age differently, making some more fragile than others, sometimes in the same quilt. Do consider using quilts for more than bed coverings, they make great wall hangings, informal slipcovers and table coverings, as well as cuddly throws to snuggle under.

References: There are many excellent quilt identification books available to collectors. Many collectors are also quilt makers and may find the quilt books by Krause Publications of interest, including Patricia J. Morris and Jeannette T. Muir's *Worth Doing Twice, New Quilts from Old Tops.*

Periodical: *Quilters Newsletter,* P.O. Box 4101, Golden, CO 80401.

Collectors' Club: American Quilter's Society, P.O. Box 3290, Paducah, KY 42001; The National Quilting Association, P.O. Box 393, Ellicott City, MD 21043.

Broken Star, orange, yellow, green, red, brown, blue, and white painted calico patches, red and white calico Flying Geese border, PA, 19th C **475.00**

Crazy patch, pieced velvet and cotton, multicolored, some embroidery, 1920s, wear and loss to fabrics **65.00**

Cross and Crown, yellow, red, and olive patches, yellow borders, red backing, 84" x 83"....................................**450.00**

Eight patch star, red and black bandanna prints, yellow ground .**130.00**

Floral Medallions, pastel pink, green and yellow appliques, swag border, minor stains, 82" x 90" **420.00**

Flying Geese variant....................**190.00**

Four Patch, green, brown, red, and blue printed calico horizontal panels, diamond and zigzag quilting, Mennonite, PA, 19th C **230.00**

Grandmother's Fan, pinks and greens, some fading, staining **45.00**

Grandmother's Flower Garden, blue, pink, yellow, and green, 20th C..**500.00**

Irish Chain, pink, green, and peach calico, straight green and pink borders, brown calico backing, embroidered with red "B" in lower left hand corner, 6'10" x 6'11", very minor staining........**225.00**

Log Cabin, yellow, brown, red, green, brown, pink, and white bars, broad red and black borders, rope quilting, red, yellow, and green calico backing, 81" x 81"..**250.00**

Nine Patch variation, blue, gray, and tan, white background and backing, 73" x 72" **365.00**

Oak leaf, red and green printed fabric vine border, white ground, late 19th C, 72" x 88", minor stains, marker lines **300.00**

Pineapple Medallion, pink calico and white, 76-1/2" x 94 ....**395.00**

Pinwheel, red and white **115.00**

Serrated Square, pink and green calico, shell and diamond quilted, 82" x 84" **325.00**

Shoofly variant, pink calico, green zigzag..**125.00**

Star of Bethlehem, yellow, pink, purple, green, gray, and blue, white ground, pink, and green borders, c1940, 85" x 85" **725.00**

Sunbonnet Sue, some wear, 1930s **125.00**

Tulip medallions and potted tulips, red, green, and goldenrod calico, white ground, zigzags, tulips, stars, and circles border, hand quilted with tulips hearts, stars, and moons, 88" sq **800.00**

Windmill, blues and white...............**90.00**

❖ Quimper

Known for its colorful peasant design, Quimper is a French faience that dates to the 17th century. As times and styles changed, patterns were also influenced but still continued to have a certain charm that is special to Quimper.

Reference: Sue and Al Bagdade, *Warman's English & Continental Pottery & Porcelain,* 3rd ed, Krause Publications, 1998; Barbara Walker and David Williamson, *The Quest for Quimper,* Schiffer Publishing, 2002.

For additional listings, see *Warman's Antiques and Collectibles Price Guide.*

Bookends, pr, 5-1/2 h, Modern Movement, standing figural child with cobalt blue dress, white cap, red striped yellow or red striped pink apron, leaning on brown wall, brown base, mkd "HenRiot Quimper J. E. Sevellec"....................................**450.00**

Bowl, cov, band of single stroke red and green florals on bowl, female peasant vertical florals and border band of single stroke florals, yellow and blue lined rim, blue knob, blue dash and yellow outlined scroll handles, mkd "HenRiot Quimper, France, " 9" w **195.00**

Quilts were displayed on metal racks as well as old wooden drying racks at the Lititz, PA, September flea market.

Quimper tray, 3 sections, peasant woman, multicolored florals, blue and orange rim, blue dash handle with orange trim, mkd "HenRiot Quimper France 96," hairline, $235.

Butter dish, cov, 2 small chips **350.00**
Cake plate, pedestal base, black haired male peasant playing bagpipes, surrounded by floral sprays and floral garland border, pattern repeated on underside and base, mkd "HR Quimper" on front **385.00**
Cider jug, cov, 7" h, male peasant on front under spout, blue sponged trees and vertical rushes, scattered 4 blue dot designs, single stroke florals, blue sponged overhead handle, spout, and knob, mkd "HB Quimper" under spout **210.00**
Cup and saucer, male peasant on cup, green and red horizontal single stroke foliage, yellow-centered blue dot flowers, scattered 4 blue dot designs, blue banded rim, green sponged handle, mkd "HR Quimper" **85.00**
Knife rest, 3-1/2" l, triangle shape, male or female peasant and foliage, blue dash edges, blue sponged ends, mkd "HenRiot Quimper France" on front, price for pr **90.00**
Plate
Center crowing rooster, red and green single stroke floral and yellow-centered blue dot florals in center, border band of single stroke red,

green, and blue florals and foliate, mkd "HB Quimper," 9-3/8" dia **195.00**
Male peasant, green, yellow, blue and rust florals, green and rust border with blue dots, yellow, green, and blue lined rim, "HB" mark, 9" d **300.00**
Salt, figural, double swans, blue wings, blue dotted breasts and heads, yellow bills, orange outlined blue dash center loop handle, female peasant on one int., floral sprig on other, mkd "HenRiot Quimper France," 2" h **50.00**
Tray, Breton Broderie pattern, male and female portraits facing each other in center, wide cobalt blue border with raised orange dashes and dots, scalloped rim, "HB Quimper" mark **325.00**
Wall pocket, open umbrella, male and female peasant, floral sprays, orange outlined blue acanthus border, brown umbrella handle with tied cord, mkd "HenRiot Quimper 141," 13" l **475.00**

❖ Racing Collectibles, Auto

"Start your engines" is music to the ears of racing collectors. Auto racing has become one of the hottest spectator sports of the 1990s. This category looks at some of the collectibles spawned by motor sports.

Collectors' Club: National Indy 500 Collectors Club, 10505 N. Delaware St., Indianapolis, IN 46280.

Also see Nascar

Bank, Robert Yates, diecast, 1994 ....**7.50**
Banner, Coors Light, slight wear.....**10.00**
Book, *The Speed Merchants, The World of Road Racing, The Men, The Machines, The Tracks,* Michael Keyser, 1973, 1st edition, dj **15.00**
Bottle, Jim Beam, Indianapolis 500, 1970 ....**50.00**
Coca-Cola Bottle, commemorative, honoring Jeff Burton, Nascar series **10.00**
Display, Pepsi Racing, Jeff Gordon, life size **325.00**
Drinking Cup, 6-1/4" h, plastic, racing car theme, Pepsi 89 Car, "Pepsi Official Soft Drink of the Daytona 500," red plastic cap, reverse side with racing flags and their meanings.................**1.00**
Indianapolis 500 program, 1964 ...**36.00**
Jacket, Racing Team, dark blue, yellow lining, Mr. Peanut on front, larger one on back, unworn...........................**30.00**
Lighter, Zippo, Indianapolis 500
1994 ....**50.00**
1997 ....**30.00**
Magazine Tear Sheet, MGB, British Racing Green **12.00**
Photograph, color, titled "One Last Lap, A Final Tribute to Davey & Alan, November 14, 1993, Atlanta Motor Speedway," 11" x 13" **15.00**
Pinback Button, Gilmore, celluloid, Souvenir of Gilmore Auto Races, some discoloration, 1930s **25.00**
Playing cards, Dale Earnhardt **4.50**
Press kit
Kenny Schrader Kodak, 1991 ......**15.00**
Ricky Rudd Tide, 1994 ....**12.00**

Stock certificate, Western Racing, Inc., 1958 ....**5.00**
Toy
Diecast, Jeff Gordon Car, #24, 3 pack, MOC **25.00**
Hot Wheel, Winner's Circle Nascar #24, Jeff Gordon, collectible tin with two decks of playing cards, diecast replica race car, 1999 Motorsports, Inc., unopened..........................**25.00**
Trading cards
1992 Grid Formula 1, Premier Edition, factory sealed, 200 cards **5.00**
1996, Indy 500 Racing League inaugural season card set and Racing Champions die-cast pace car, box opened, cards sealed .**16.00**

❖ Racing Collectibles, Other

If you're not into auto racing, there are other racing collectibles that can be found at flea markets. Keep your eyes open for air racing, dog racing, and other fast-paced collectibles.

Collectors' Club: Sport of Kings Society, 1406 Annen Lane, Madison, WI 53711.

Ashtray, Kentucky Derby, 1976, glass **32.00**
Badge, Budweiser Million, Second Running, Aug 29, 1982, full color illus, 3" dia **10.00**
Book, Tactics Strategy Yacht Racing, Joachim Schult, 1970, Dodd Mead **10.00**
Cigarette card, World's Marathon Record Set by W. Kolehmainen of Finland, 1925 ....**8.00**
Cup, restaurant china, Beautiful Wheeling Downs, Shenango, 3-1/4" h **29.00**
Needle book, Steep Chase, cardboard, full color art, 1930s, 4-1/2" x 4-3/4" **30.00**
Pinback button
American Air Races, mechanic, red and cream, 1923 ....**50.00**
Dan Patch Days, brown horse, white ground, 1967, Savage, MN commemorative celebration......**25.00**
Jockey portrait, American Pepsin Gum **30.00**
Los Angeles National Air Races, red and white, 1928 ....**75.00**
Post card
Dog racing, Hialeah, Miami, Fla.....**7.00**
Greyhound track, Derby Lane, St. Petersburg, Fla. **4.00**
Stickpin, brass, jockey cap over

entwined initials, green and white enamel accents, 1906 ....**30.00**
Toy, Racing Motorcycle, litho tin, friction, Japan, 1960s, 3-3/4" l **18.00**
Tray, tin litho, running greyhounds ..**15.00**

❖ Radio Characters and Personalities

The golden age of radio created a whole cadre of heroes and characters for the listeners. Like the stars of today, these folks had fan clubs and created premiums and memorabilia to meet the demands of the earliest collectors.

Periodicals: *Friends of Old Time Radio,* PO Box 4321, Hamden, CT 06514; *Hello Again,* PO Box 4321, Hamden, CT 06514; *Nostalgia Digest and Radio Guide,* PO Box 421, Morton Grove, IL 60053; *Old Time Radio Digest,* 10280 Gunpowder Road, Florence, KY 41042.

Collectors' Clubs: National Lum & Abner Society, #81 Sharon Blvd, Dora, AL 35062; North American Radio Archives, 134 Vincewood Drive, Nicholasville, KY 40356; Radio Collectors of America, 8 Ardsley Circle, Brockton, MA 02402.

Bank, Uncle Don's Earnest Saver Club, oval, paper label, photo and cartoon illus, Greenwich Savings Bank, New York City, 1930s, 2-1/4" h **40.00**
Blotter, The Shadow, orange, blue, and white, red silhouette, 1940s **28.00**
Book
All About Amos 'n' Andy and Their Creators Correl & Gosden, 1929, 128 pgs, illus.............................**55.00**
'R' You Listening? Tony Wons, radio scrapbook, CBS, Reilly & Lee, 1931, 1st ed., dj.....................................**9.00**
Booklet, Zenith Radios, Burns & Allen, Boswells, 1930s **45.00**
Flashlight, Jack Armstrong, cardboard, red metal ends, c1939 ....**25.00**
Game, Charlie McCarthy Radio Party Game, orig envelope....................**65.00**

Jack Armstrong Ped-O-Meter, Wheaties premium, aluminum, enameled metal center, belt clip, 2-5/8" d, $25.

Greeting card, get well Card, black and white photo of Amos n' Andy, Hall Brothers, 1931, 4-1/2" x 5-1/2".....**32.00**

Magazine, *Post*
Arthur Godfrey, 1955....................**10.00**
Jack Benny article, 1963..............**15.00**

Map, Jimmy Allen, full color, printed letter on back, 1934............................**125.00**

Membership badge, Pilot Patrol, Phantom...................................**32.00**

Menu, Brown Derby, autographed by Fibber McGee and Molly............**120.00**

Newsletter, Jimmy Allen, red, white, and green holiday design and signatures on front cover, black and white photos on back, 4 pgs.....................................**65.00**

Patch
Captain Midnight **30.00**
Jack Armstrong, Future Champions of America, 1943 ....**22.00**

Pencil Sharpener, figural, Charlie McCarthy, diecut plastic, color decal, 1930s..**72.00**

Photo, Fiber McGee and Molly, black and white glossy, cast members, late 1930s, 8-1/4" x 12"......................**40.00**

Pinback Button
Adventurers Club, Frank Buck, 1936 ....**20.00**
Magic Club, Mandrake the Magician **60.00**
Uncle Don, Taystee Bread............**55.00**

Puzzle, Amos n' Andy, Pepsodent premium, 1931 ....**42.00**

Ring, Jack Armstrong, Dragon's Eye, crocodile design, green stone, 1940 ....**150.00**

Stamp album, Jimmie Allen Flying Club Stamp Album, stamps mounted inside, 1936 ....**85.00**

Valentine, Joe Penner, mechanical diecut, Joe holding duck on shoulder, inscribed "I'll Gladly Buy A Duck," c1935 ....**30.00**

Whistle, Jimmie Allen, brass, c1936 ....**30.00**

Whistle ring, Jack Armstrong, Egyptian symbols, orig mailing envelope, c1938 ....**135.00**

❖ Radios

Today a radio brings us news, weather, and some tunes. But to generations past, it brought all those things plus laughter, companionship, and entertainment. The mechanical device that allowed connection to this new exciting world was developed and refined at the beginning of the 20th century. New technology caused changes in the shapes and materials of early radio receivers.

References: There are many older reference books to help identify radios.

Periodicals: *Antique Radio Classified*, PO Box 2, Carlisle, MA, 01741; *Antique radio Topics*, PO Box 28572, Dallas, TX 75228; *Horn Speaker*, PO Box 1193, Mabank, TX 75147; *Radio Age*, 636 Cambridge Road, Augusta, GA 30909; *Transistor Network*, RR1, Box 36, Bradford, NH 03221.

Collectors' Clubs: Antique Radio Club of America, 300 Washington Trails, Washington, PA 15301; Antique Wireless Assoc., 59 Main St., Bloomfield, NY 14469; New England Antique Radio Club, RR1, Box 36, Bradford, NH 03221; Vintage Radio & Phonograph Society, Inc., PO Box 165345, Irving, TX 75016.

Also see: Transistor Radios

Arvin, #522A, ivory metal case, 1941 ....**65.00**

Atwater Kent, Cathedral, 80, c1931 ....**200.00**

Bulova, clock radio
#100 ....**30.00**
110 ....**25.00**

Crosley
Bandbox, #600, 1927 ....**80.00**
Liftella, 1-N, cathedral **185.00**
Super Buddy Boy **125.00**

Dumont, RA346, table, scroll work, 1938 ....**110.00**

Emerson
274, brown Bakelite..................**165.00**
#888 Vanguard **80.00**

General Electric
#410 ....**30.00**
#515, clock radio **25.00**

Thomas Collector's Edition Radio, wood case, $20.

Motorola
Jet Plane **55.00**
Jewel Box **80.00**
Pixie **45.00**
Ranger, portable **60.00**

Novelty
Green Giant...................................**30.00**
Pet evaporated milk can...............**48.00**
Radio Shack D-cell battery **38.00**

Twix candy bar, orig box..............**60.00**

Philco
T1000, clock radio.......................**80.00**
#20, cathedral **200.00**

RCA Victor, Radiola, #18, with speaker **125.00**

Silvertone - Sears
#1, table **75.00**
#1582, cathedral - wood **225.00**
#1955, tombstone **135.00**

Stromberg-Carlson, The Dynatomic, #1500-H, Bakelite.........................**65.00**

Zenith
Table, #6D2615, boomerang dial .**95.00**
Trans-Oceanic **90.00**
Zephyr, multiband.........................**95.00**

❖ Raggedy Ann

Who's always got a smile? Of course, it's Raggedy Ann. This happy creation of Johnny Gruelle has lived on for decades. You can find her, Andy, their dog and friends in children's literature and all kinds of decorative accessories.

Reference: Susan Ann Garrison, *The Raggedy Ann & Andy Family Album*, 3rd ed., Schiffer Publishing, 2000,

Children's book
Raggedy Ann & Hoppy Toad, McLoughlin, 1940 ....**95.00**
Raggedy Ann & Laughing Book, Perks, 1946...**30.00**
Raggedy Ann & Marcella's First Day At School, Wonder Book, #588 ....**22.00**
Raggedy Ann Stories, Volland, 1918, 1st ed., Johnny Gruelle, color pictures, light use.....................**65.00**
Sweet and Dandy Sugar Candy Scratch and Sniff Book, Golden Press, 1976, well read.............**15.00**

Raggedy Andy doll seated in child's striped lawn chair, $65 for Raggedy Andy, $45 for chair.

Cookie jar
California Originals, incised mark on lid and "859 USA," 13-3/4" h........**175.00**
Certified International, 11" h **125.00**
Creamer, figural, foil label, Royal Sealy,
4-1/2" h..**35.00**
Doll
Georgene Novelties, 1947, 19" h**265.00**
Hasbro Commemorative Edition, 1996, 12" h **40.00**
Knickerbocker, Raggedy Ann and Andy, 1960s, 30" h..................**250.00**
Game, Raggedy Ann's Magic Pebble
Game, Milton Bradley, copyright 1941 Johnny Gruelle Co., orig box **95.00**
Lunch box, plastic, Raggedy Ann and
Andy on front, orig thermos **75.00**
Music box, ceramic, Raggedy Andy,
plays Do-Re-Me, Schmid **75.00**
Nodder, 5" dia head, 5-1/2" h **175.00**
Paint by number canvas, 1988, unused
....**18.00**
Print, copy of orig Johnny Gruelle
drawing, 6" x 9" **35.00**
Pop-up book
Raggedy Ann and Andy, 45 rpm record, 1974, played with **5.00**
Raggedy Ann & the Daffy Taffy Pull, 1972..**15.00**

❖ Railroad Collectibles

All Aboard! Transportation of goods and passengers across this great country was a dream of the early railroad men. Today, we take it for granted that these giants will keep moving along tracks laid so many years ago. Collectors can tell you about their favorite rail lines or types of collectibles.

Periodicals: *Key, Lock and Lantern,* 3 Berkeley Heights Park, Bloomfield, NJ 07003; *Main Line Journal,* PO Box 121, Streamwood, IL 60107; *Railfan & Railroad,* PO Box 700, Newton, NJ 07860-0700; *Trains,* PO Box 1612, Waukesha, WI 53187; *US Rail News,* PO Box 7007, Huntingdon Woods, MI 48070.

Collectors' Clubs: Canadian Railroad Historical Association, 120 Rue St. Pierre, St. Constant, Quebec J5A 2G9 Canada; Chesapeake & Ohio Historical Society Inc., PO Box 79, Clifton Forge, VA 24422; Illinois Central Railroad Historical Society 14818 Clifton Park, Midlothian, IL 60445; New York Central System Historical Society, Inc., PO Box 58994, Philadelphia, PA 19102-8994; Railroad Enthusiasts, 102 Dean Rd, Brookline, MA 02146; Railroad Club of America, Inc., PO Box 8292, Chicago, IL 60680; Railroadiana Collectors Association, 795 Aspen Drive, Buffalo Grove, IL 60089; Railway and Locomotive Historical Society PO Box 1418, Westford, MA 01886; Twentieth Century Railroad Club, 329 West 18th St., Suite 902, Chicago, IL 60616.

Spittoon, brass, "Union Pacific" emb under locomotive, some corrosion, $45.

Baggage Check, Texas Central RR, 1-
5/8 x 2", brass, Poole Bros, Chicago **38.50**
Blanket, Canadian Pacific...............**85.00**
Booklet
By The Way Of The Canyons, Soo Line, 1907......................................**20.00**
Union Pacific RR, 1926 ....**15.00**
Box, tin, black, paper attached to handle
reads "Pittsburgh, Cincinnati, Chicago, St. Louis Railway Co., June 15, 1901" **40.00**
Brochure
Eastern Summer Trips, B & O......**12.00**
Holiday Haunts, Adirondacks & 1,000 Islands, NYC, 1940, 63 pgs......**20.00**
Button, uniform, "Baggage Master,"
silvertone, 3/4" dia..........................**8.00**
Caboose marker, Atlantic Coast Line RR
Co., 1900, 4-way lamp **385.00**
Calendar, Burlington Zephyr, 1943.**90.00**
Car inspector's record, D & RGW,
Ridway, filled in, 1928...................**10.00**
Catalog, Erie Railroad, Co., New York,
NY, 32 pgs, 1918..........................**42.00**

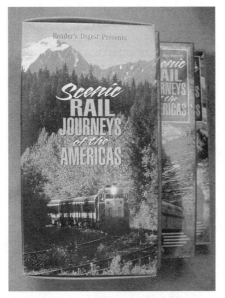

VCR tape, Scenic Rail Journeys of the Americas, Readers Digest, boxed set of 3 tapes, $15.

China
Creamer, B & O, Centenary pattern, Scammell's Lamberton China, 3-1/2" d, 3-3/4" h **210.00**
Cup and Saucer, B & O, Capital.**60.00**
Demitasse Cup and Saucer, CMSTP & P, Traveler, Syracuse, backstamped **85.00**
Dinner Plate, B & O, Shenango, 10-1/2" d **120.00**
Coaster, Central RR, New Jersey, Statue of Liberty logo, set of 6 ....**15.00**
Coloring book, Union Pacific RR giveaway, 29 pgs, 1954 ....**20.00**
Freight receipt, NY, Lake Erie & Western RR, dated 1883............................**4.00**
Funnel, Pennsylvania RR, metal, 9" h **40.00**
Hat rack, overhead type, coach, wood and bras, 6 brass double-sided hooks **200.00**
Head rest cover, PRR, tan ground, brown logo, 15" x 18" **15.00**
Lantern
Dietz, Nightwatch, deep red globe, some wear **60.00**
Penn Central RR, red globe with logo, Adlake, 10" h **95.00**
Magazine, *Railway Age*.....................**5.00**
Membership card, American Association Railroad Ticket Agents, 1931 ....**10.00**
Menu, Amtrak, Good Morning, single card, 7" x 11".................................**3.50**
Napkin, linen
Burlington Route, 20" sq, white, woven logo..**10.00**
C & O, blue monogram **8.50**
Padlock, Rock Island, orig key........**35.00**
Pass
Ft Wayne, Cincinnati & Louisville and White Water, 2-1/2" x 3-3/4" white card, green accents, purple ink stamp facsimile signature of president, 1889........................**12.00**
Ohio, Indiana, and Western, 2-1/4" x 3-3/4", black and white, ornately printed, signed in ink by general manager, 1889......................**12.00**
Patch, South Shore Line, embroidered, 3-3/8" x 1-1/2" **9.00**
Playing Cards
Chessie **20.00**
Denver & Rio Grande Railways ...**35.00**
EJ & ERR.....................................**20.00**
Post Card
Fresh Air Pullman, C-4, giant grasshopper in open cargo car, Multrakrom Postcard Co., Dodge City, Kansas, c1950..................**10.00**
White River at Sharon, VT, New England States Limited, scenic, 5-3/4" x 3-3/4" **22.00**

Dish, pottery, figural train, coggled edge, front marked "East Broad Top RR, Rockhill Furnace, PA," dark brown glaze with white highlights, $15.

Ribbon, Brotherhood of Railroad Men, Grand Union Picnic, Harrisburg, PA, June 27, 1901, 1-7/8" x 3-3/4", beige, gold accent lettering.......................**10.00**
Sign, Seaboard RR, "Explosives," 1948 ....**20.00**
Spike, chromed, Chesapeake & Ohio RR, engrave 1944-1970, retirement presentation, 6" l **25.00**
Step, Pullman RR Station, wood, hand cut out on top, 21" w, 10" h..........**25.00**
Sugar tongs, Canadian Pacific, SP, mkd "England".....................................**20.00**
Timetable
Atchison, Topeka & Santa Fe, 1954 ....**12.50**
Erie Railroad, 1907 ....**32.00**

L&N Kansas City Southern, 1955..**8.50**
Southern Pacific RR, 1915...........**22.00**

❖ Ramp Walkers

Here's a collectible where the prices might be a surprise to you. Remember those little plastic toys we all played with as a kid, no batteries required, just a sturdy surface that we could tilt so the little critter could walk away. Well, today collectors are walking all over flea markets to find them.

Cow, plastic, 2-1/4" h **45.00**
Cowgirl, plastic, c1945, 6-1/2" h.....**95.00**
Donald Duck, pushing wheelbarrow, Marx, plastic, 1950s **120.00**
Elephant, plastic, Hong Kong, 2-1/4" h **65.00**
Farmer, plastic, 2-5/8" h.................**60.00**
Hop and Hop, marching soldiers, Marx, 2-3/4" h..**20.00**
Little Girl, plastic, orig weight ball, 6-1/2" h **115.00**
Nanny pushing carriage................**22.00**
Penguin Ramp, plastic, Hong Kong, 2-5/8" h......................................**60.00**
Popeye and Wimpy, plastic, Marx, © 1964, orig box, never played with **80.00**
Soldier, wood and cloth, c1920, 4-3/4" h **65.00**

❖ Razor Blade Banks

Razor blade banks were designed as a safe place to deposit used razor blades, hence the name. Just because they were useful, they didn't have to be ordinary. Many ceramic manufacturers created whimsical figural banks, which nicely compliment the tin and advertising razor blade banks also found at flea markets. The listing below are all for ceramic or pottery banks.

Barber head, Ceramic Arts Studio .**80.00**
Barber pole....................................**80.00**
Frog..**15.50**
Happy shaver, Cleminson **18.00**
Hobo...**20.00**
Mule, adv for Listerine on bottom....**25.00**

❖ Reamers

Feel like putting the squeeze on something? How about an orange, lemon, or grapefruit? Reamer collectors know just how to make their favorite juice and end up sweetly smiling when making a new purchase to add to their collection. They will tell you that reamers can be found in all types of materials, shapes, and sizes.

Collectors' Club: National Reamer Collectors Association, 47 Midline Court, Gaithersburg, MD 20878.

China
Bavaria, white, red, yellow, and green flowers dec, gold trim, 2 pc type **60.00**
Czechoslovakia, orange shape, white, green leaves, mkd "Erphila", 2 pc, 6" h...**60.00**
England, white, orange, and yellow flowers, 3-1/2" h **68.00**
Germany, Goebel, yellow, 5" dia......**60.00**
Japan, lemon, yellow, white flowers, green leaves, 4-3/4" h **60.00**
United States, Ade-O-Matic Genuine, 8" h, green **135.00**
Glass
Crystal, Criss-Cross, Hazel Atlas, tab handle, small **25.00**
Pink, Jennyware, Jeanette **135.00**
Transparent green, pointed cone, tab handle, Federal.........................**30.00**
White, embossed "Sunkist," McKee **15.00**
Metal
Aluminum, Pat, 8" l, 161609, Minneapolis, MN.........................**5.00**
Dunlap's Improved, iron hinge, 9-1/2" l **35.00**
Gem Squeezer, aluminum crank handle, table model 2 pc (M-100) **12.00**
Kwicky Juicer, aluminum, pan style,

Quam Nicholas Co. **10.00**
Nasco-Royal, scissors type, 6" l...**10.00**
Wagner Ware, cast aluminum, skillet shape, long red seed dams beneath cone, 2 spouts **20.00**

❖ Records

Spin me a tune! Records have evolved from early cylinders for Thomas Edison's first phonographs to the vinyl disks of today. This music can cross into other collecting areas devoted to specific artists such as Elvis or because of the subject matter on the record's album sleeve or protective box. Quickly gaining in popularity are children's records having an image imprinted on the vinyl.

Periodical: *Goldmine,* 700 E State St., Iola, WI 54990.

Reference: Tim Neely, *Goldmine Price Guide to 45 RPM Records,* 4th ed., Krause Publications, 2003; — *Goldmine Jazz Album Price Guide,* Krause Publications, 2000; — *Goldmine Country & Western Record Price Guide,* 2nd ed., Krause Publications, 2001; Les Docks, American Premium Record Guide, 1900-1965, 6th ed., Krause Publications, 2001.

Allen Brothers, *Glorious Night Blues*, Victor **50.00**
Belafonte, Harry, LP, *Streets I Have Walked*, 1963 ....**35.00**
Berry, Chuck, *Johnny Bgoode*, 78 RPM, Chess **10.00**
Blue Ridge Mountain Girls, *She Came Rolling Down The Mountain*, Champion **12.00**
Brooklyn Tabernacle Choir, *Rejoice* **15.00**
Bye Bye Birdy, Columbia, orig cast, 1980 ....**17.50**
Campbell, Glen, *Christmas with Glen Campbell*, Capitol, SL 6699, black label with pink colorband **8.00**
Checker, Chubby, *Limbo Party*, Parkway, LP, 1962 ....**20.00**
Cline, Patsy, *Crazy, Who Can I Count On*, Decca 31317, 1961, 45...........**3.00**

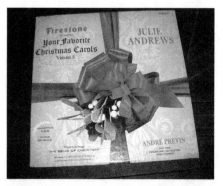

Firestone Presents, Your Favorite Christmas Carols, Volume 5, Julie Andrews, Andre Previn and the Firestone Orchestra and Chorus, $15.

Crosby, Bing, *The Songs I Love*, six long play records, mint in orig case **75.00**

Danny Davis & Nashville Brass, *Movin On*, RCA, LSP 4232, orange label, 1969 ....**8.00**

Day, Doris, *Wonderful Day*, Columbia Records XTV 82022, 1960s...........**8.00**

Dragnet, 78 rpm, Jack Webb cover **30.00**

Eastwood, Clint, *Rawhide*, Cameo #C-1056, autographed **245.00**

Ellington, Duke, *Jubilee Stomp*, Okeh, 41013, 1938 ....**15.00**

Fountain, Pete, *Those Were The Days*, Coral, CRL 757505, black label with multicolored band through center **15.00**

Griffith, Andy, *Goober Sings*..........**35.00**

Lennon, John, *Roots*, Adam Vii-A-80180, orig, LP............................**200.00**

Liverpool Five, *Out of Sight*, RCA LSP-33682, German imp, LP **8.00**

Lulu, *To Sir with Love*, Epic LN 24339, LP, mono, 1967 ....**6.25**

Miller, Glenn, *Glenn Miller Story*, Unbreakable, LP, Decca, 1954 .....**22.00**

Oklahoma, Decca, orig cast, 1953 .**42.00**

Presley, E., *Touch of Gold*, Volume 2, EPA-5101, maroon label **85.00**

Superman, the Movie, 1978, 2 record set, LP **24.00**

Teardrops, *The Stars Are Out Tonight*, Josie..**30.00**

Welling & McGhee, *Ring the Bells of Heaven*, Champion, 16660 ....**17.50**

Wells, Kitty, *Country Music Time*, Decca DL 74554, black label with rainbow band through center **8.00**

Williams, Hank, *Reflections of Those Who Loved Him*, MGM-Pro-912, 3 LPs, promotional box set, 1975............**60.00**

Wynette, Tammy, *Your Good Girl's Gonna Go Bad*, Epic LN 26305, LP, stereo, 1967 ....**5.00**

❖ Records, Children

Do you remember the tunes you enjoyed as a child? Most of us do, and with a little encouragement, you probably can even remember most of the words, right? Today, children's records represent a collecting area that's becoming hot. The graphics of the covers are usually great. Records associated with famous personalities and characters command a slightly higher price.

Archies, The, *Sugar Sugar*, Melody Hill, Calender 63-1008, 1969, 45 ....**2.50**

Banana Splits, The, *Tra-La-La Song*, Toy Piano Medley, Decca 32429, 45, 1968, picture sleeve **9.25**

Bond, James, Hanna-Barbera........**40.00**

Brady Bunch, membership application **38.00**

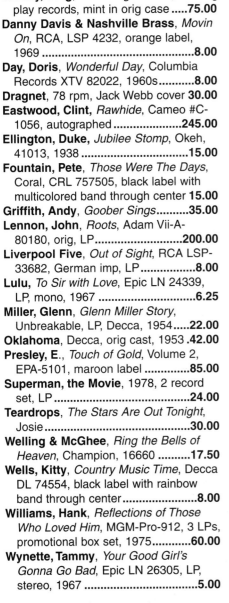

Teddy Bears' Picnic and Songs We All Like, Cricket Records, 45 rpm, $15.

DiMaggio, Joe, *Little Johnny Strikeout*, double, 78 rpm **135.00**

Disneyland Davy Crockett, record storybook, copyright 1971, 24 pgs **35.00**

Doody, Howdy
Christmas **24.00**
Clowns with Jazz, Normal Paris Trio, Golden Crest, 1950s **50.00**

Dumbo, *Disneyland*, record and book, 1968, some wear...........................**7.60**

Higitus Figitus, Walt Disney Productions, Little Golden Record, 1938 ....**8.00**

Hot Rod Granny, Hanna-Barbera...**50.00**

Johnny Quest, Hanna-Barbera, 45 rpm **28.00**

Knight Rider, record storybook **15.00**

Lewis, Shari, *Party Record*, 6" sq black and white thin cardboard vinyl-coated sheet, 5-3/4" d vinyl record with black and white photo of Shari, 2 puppets, Allied Creative Services, Inc., c1950 ....**25.00**

Night Before Christmas, The, Golden Record, R33, 78 RPM, as told by Peter Donald, full orchestra directed by Mitchell Miller, c1950, some scratches and wear **5.50**

Return of the Pink Panther, United Artists, 1970s, 45 rpm..................**30.00**

Rogers, Roy, Dale Evans, *Jesus Loves Me*, Camden, 1960, LP **30.00**

Secret Squirrel, Hanna-Barbera, 45 rpm **30.00**

Squiddly Diddly, Hanna-Barbera, 45 rpm..**35.00**

Star Wars, 24-page read-along book, 33-1/3 rpm record, Buena Vista **5.00**

Strawberry Shortcake, 1980, LP ...**20.00**

The Big Gun, blue and white record jacket, 33-1/3" rpm, from Revell model kit..**4.00**

Bunny Hop, Peter Pan Records, 45 rpm, $10.

Winnie the Pooh and Christopher Robin Songs, 1948, 78 rpm, Decca Record...**40.00**

❖ Red Wing Pottery

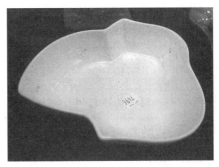

Red Wing Pottery bowl, leaf shape, yellow, mkd, $10.

Red Wing is a generic term that covers several manufacturers that produced utilitarian stoneware and ceramic dinnerware in Red Wing, Minn. The trademark red wing is the most recognizable symbol used in Red Wing, but other marks also identify the pottery.

Collectors' Clubs: Red Wing Collectors Society, PO Box 50, Red Wing, MN 55066; The RumRill Society, PO Box 2161, Hudson, OH 44326.

For additional listings, see *Warman's Americana & Collectibles* and *Warman's American Pottery & Porcelain*.

Bean Pot, cov, stoneware, adv........**85.00**

Casserole, cov, 8" d, sponge band, chip on handle **165.00**

Celery dish, Lotus pattern, Concord shape, 11-1/4" l.............................**35.00**

Cookie jar, Chef Pierre, rim chip, discoloration **40.00**

Crock, 2-gallon, large wing **100.00**

Figure
Cowboy, rust...............................**175.00**
Cowgirl, #B1414, white **175.00**
Floor vase, embossed designs, bronze-like glaze, Red Wing Union Stoneware Co., hairline, 22" h.................**330.00**
Pitcher, Bobwhite, 12" h **65.00**
Platter, Random Harvest, 13" l **30.00**
Salt and Pepper Shakers, pr, Town and Country, dark green.....................**65.00**
Soup bowl, Lotus pattern, Concord shape, 6-3/8" dia, set of 6............**70.00**
Teapot, Town & Country, rust color**195.00**
Water cooler, 3-gal., no lid **400.00**

❂ Redware

American colonists began making redware in the late 17th century, using the same clay as for bricks and roof tiles. Ready availability of the clay meant that items could be produced in large quantities. The lead-glazed items retained their reddish color, hence the name redware, although various colors could be obtained by adding different metals to the glaze. Modern craftsmen have kept the redware tradition alive and can be found working in several parts of the country today

References: Susan and Al Bagdade, *Warman's American Pottery and Porcelain*, 2nd ed., Krause Publications, 2000; William C. Ketchum Jr., *American Redware*, Henry Holt and Company, 1991; Kevin McConnell, *Redware: America's Folk Art Pottery*, Schiffer Publishing, 1988.

Bank, apple shape, red and yellow paint, 3-1/4" h.....................................**160.00**
Bowl, Foltz Pottery, bowl, tulip sgraffito decor in cobalt, 1980, 14-1/2" dia
....**145.00**
Canning jar, John Bell, orange glaze, cylindrical shape, impressed "J. Bell" on bottom, side repairs, chips, 5-5/8" h, 4-5/8" dia **425.00**
Charger, large, sgraffitto, eagle dec, Lester Breininger........................**300.00**
Compote, int. with black glaze, bird dec, Lester Breininger, 1986..............**100.00**
Crock, John Bell, light greenish-brown glaze, slightly rounded sides, impressed "John Bell" below collar, cracks, 4-3/8" dia........................**270.00**
Dog figure, Lester Breininger
Basket in mouth **275.00**
Basket by paw, 1988 ....**275.00**
Fish mold
Stahl Pottery, mottled brown glaze, dated 1939, glaze imperfections, 3" h, 11" l **165.00**
Unmarked, vintage, spiraled flutes, scalloped rim, brown sponging on pinkish-amber ground, wear, slight hairline, 8" dia.........................**137.50**

Redware Tumbler, mkd "LB" for Lester Breininger, 1979, 4" h, $20.

Jar, Stahl Pottery, dark reddish-brown glaze, ovoid, shoulder handles, mkd "Made in Stahl Pottery by Thomas Stahl, April 16, 1936," chips, hairline, 3-3/4" h..**82.50**
Jug, ovoid, dark-brown glaze, black running spots around shoulder and strap handle, tooled foot and neck, old edge chips, 8" h **550.00**
Pie plate
2-line swag decor, yellow slip, imperfections, 11-1/2" dia.......**247.50**
3-line, yellow slip, wavy decor, wear, hairlines, 8-1/2" dia.................**440.00**
Turk's head mold, mottled red and dark brown glaze, c1830, 10" dia.......**150.00**

❖ Regal China Corporation

Here's a chinaware maker that was owned by Jim Beam Distilleries. Their wares include those wonderful decanters you think of as Beam bottles, plus several types of advertising wares and items made for clients including Quaker Oats and Kraft Foods.

Canister, Old McDonald's Farm, gold trim
Coffee, horse lid **235.00**
Flour, Grandpa lid........................**225.00**
Pretzels, Grandma lid..................**300.00**
Sugar, Grandma lid **225.00**
Cookie jar, cov
Kraft Teddy Bear...........................**95.00**
Quaker Oats.................................**85.00**
Creamer, Old McDonald, rooster ..**135.00**
Decanter, Jim Beam, empty
Antique Trader, 1968 ....**10.00**
Cat, 1967......................................**10.00**
Cherubs, 1974..............................**12.00**
Ford, 1978.....................................**25.00**
Hawaii, 50th State **15.00**
Ohio...**10.00**
Sailfish, 1957, 14" h **10.00**
Telephone, 1979............................**10.00**
Lamp base, 12-3/4" h, Davy Crockett

....**125.00**
Salt and pepper shakers, pr, Old McDonald's Farm, barrels, gold trim, 4" h **125.00**
Teapot, Old McDonald's Farm, duck, 7-1/2" h..**300.00**
Tobacco jar, Fox, Jim Beam...........**60.00**

❖ Religious Collectibles

Fan, Where there is Faith, There is love, center panel with Christ, American flag, open Bible, Where there is Love, there is peace, cardboard, adv on back for Shelly Funeral Home, Elmer S. Shelly, Lansdale, Pennsylvania, © 1934, Messenger Corp. Pat. 1655229, $10.

Hunting for religious collectibles at flea markets is a great idea, but not in lieu of going to church services. (Well, perhaps before or after Sunday services.) However, no matter when you shop, you're likely to find something of interest.

Collectors' Clubs: Foundation International for Restorers of Religious Medals, PO Box 2652, Worcester, MA 01608; Judaica Collectors Society, PO Box 854, Van Nuys, CA 91408.

Alms Box, oak, old brown grained repaint, Gothic style, English, 16" h, wear and one incomplete scalloped bracket.....................................**145.00**
Book, Jesus Lover of My Soul by C. Wesley, 1907, 20 pgs, spine damage, mildew **10.00**
Chalice, sterling silver and gold-washed base metal, Ecclesiastical, silver bowl with gold-washed lip and int., stem with central gothic-style knop, plain hexafoil foot with emb cross, 9-1/4" h **150.00**
Doorstop, church door, painted cast iron, 6" h..**165.00**
Figurine
Plastic, Madonna, blue rhinestone halo, paint peeling, 3-3/4" h.................**4.00**
Precious Moments, "Jesus Loves Me," 1976, 1 of orig 21 ....**55.00**
Precious Moments, "Jesus Is The Answer," cross mark, 4-1/2" h.**105.00**
Menorah, porcelain, Lenox, 6" h, 12" l
....**100.00**

Paperweight, Star of David design, white stardust canes, millefiori garland, cobalt ground, Perthshire, 2-1/2" dia **110.00**
Pinback button, Vacation Bible School, tin, 3/4" dia **3.00**
Santos, carved wood, polychrome and gesso, Spanish
Crucified Christ, 14" h **200.00**
Infantata, 7-3/4" h......................**375.00**
St. Mary in Glory, standing on cloudwork with seraphim, 10" h
....**115.00**

❖ Riviera

This popular Homer Laughlin pattern was introduced in 1938 and sold by the Murphy Company. Not all pieces were marked, but some have gold backstamp. Riviera was produced in Laughlin's Century shape in dark blue (considered rare), light green, ivory, mauve blue, red, and yellow.

Periodical: *Laughlin Eagle,* 1270 63rd Terrace, South, St. Petersburg, FL 33705.

Butter dish, 1/2 lb, red..................**150.00**
Casserole, cov
Light green **95.00**
Mauve blue................................**110.00**
Creamer, light green or red.............**18.00**
Cup and saucer, ivory **125.00**
Juice pitcher, mauve blue **350.00**
Juice tumbler, light green..............**85.00**
Nappy, yellow...............................**50.00**
Oatmeal bowl
Ivory **95.00**
Light green **85.00**
Mauve blue................................**85.00**
Red..**95.00**
Yellow **85.00**
Sugar bowl, cov
Light green **30.00**
Mauve blue................................**45.00**
Red..**45.00**
Teapot, light green **185.00**
Tumbler, handle
Light green **55.00**
Red..**95.00**

❖ Road Maps

Today's road maps are a far cry from the early guide books that provided written descriptions of how to get from Point A to Point B. While most maps are readily affordable, earlier examples, especially those with colorful covers, have taken the hobby to a new price level. Using old road maps as decorative elements has taken off recently. Look for inexpensively priced ones to use as a colorful addition to a plain desk—spread the maps out, then top with a piece of glass the size of the desk top. Other ideas to decorate with maps would include making lamp shades, boxes, etc. out of them.

Virginia road map, 1994-95, "Virginia is for Lovers," $2.

Central & Western United States, Deep Rock Gasoline, 1960s **10.00**
Georgia, Texaco, 1965 ....**5.00**
Hawaii, Shell Oil Co., 1961, 1/4" tear**8.00**
Illinios, Sinclair, 1962....................**3.00**
Indiana Official Highway Map, 1970-71
....**3.00**
Mid-Atlantic Region, Delaware, Maryland, Virginia and West Virginia Road Map with **Pictorial Guide**, Esso, 1952 ....**7.50**
New Jersey, shore points on reverse**2.50**
Ohio, AAA triptik...............................**4.00**
Pennsylvania Official Highway Map, 1972-73 ....**3.00**
South Dakota Official Highway Map
....**4.00**
USGS Quadrangle, Norristown, PA, framed **20.00**
Wyoming, Mobil Oil Co. **5.00**

❖ Robots

These mechanical marvels have delighted moviegoers and science fiction buffs for years. The first documented robot is Atomic Robot Man, created in 1948. The Japanese dominated the robot market. By the 1970s, production had moved to Hong Kong and other foreign countries. Some older Japanese robots are commanding big prices (see boxed story).

Reference: Jim Bunte, Dave Hallman and Heinz Mueller, *Vintage Toys: Robots and Space Toys*, Antique Trader Books, 1999; Karen O'Brien, *Toys & Prices 2004*, Krause Publications, 2003; — *O'Brien's Collecting Toys* 11th ed., 2003.

Periodical: *Robot World & Price Guide*, PO Box 184, Lenox Hill Station, New York, NY 10021; *Toy Shop*, 700 E State Street, Iola, WI 54990.

For additional listings, see *Warman's Americana & Collectibles*.

Action figure, Robot Zone, five 2-1/2" h figures, 1985, mkd "Made in British Colony of Hong Kong," MOC........**25.00**
Bank, wind-up, plastic, dumps coin in slots when revolving, mkd "Made in Hong Kong," orig box....................**25.00**
Cookie jar, Plantery Pal, Sigma, 1984, 11-1/2" h................................**265.00**
Figure
Lost in Space, chrome version, Trendmasters Classic **60.00**
Rosie, Jetson's, plastic, Applause, orig sticker, 1990............................**25.00**
Top, Shogun Rocket, plastic, Mattel, 1978, MIP.................................**15.00**
Toy
Biliken Ultra 7, tin litho wind-up, Japan, MIB **300.00**
Cosmos Robot, battery-op, plastic, Kamco, China, 1980s, MIB, 12-1/2" h
....**38.00**
Fighting Robot, tin litho, battery operated, Japan, 1960s, C-8.5
....**245.00**
Lost in Space, battery operated, Remco, C-9....................................**685.00**
Moon Stroller, wind-up, arms swing, moving radar, mkd "Made in Hong Kong," 3-1/4" h, orig box with slight wear...**35.00**
Rascal, wind-up, mkd "1978, Tomy Corp., Made in Taiwan," MIP, 2" h
....**20.00**
Robot Sentinel, battery operated, walks, arms move, lights, 4 shooting missiles, plastic, mkd "Made in China by Kamco," 1980s, 13" h, MIB ..**55.00**

Poster, Forbidden Planet, MGM, starring Walter Pigeon, Anne Francis, Leslie Neilson, Robbie the Robot, $750.

Saturn, battery operated, walks, lights up eyes, mkd "Made in Hong Kong by Kamco," missiles missing, 13" h
....**38.00**
Sentinel Robot, plastic, made by Kamco, China, 1980s, MIB, 13" h
....**31.00**
Silver colored, wind-up, mkd "Made in Hong Kong," 4" h, orig box........**35.00**
SP-1, friction, blue and red space ship, Japan, 1950s, 6-1/2" l.............**330.00**
Sparky Robot, wind-up, silver and red, flashes, 1950s, Japan, 8" h, C-9
....**355.00**
Tang, General Foods, 7-1/4" h.....**30.00**
TR2 Talking, mkd "Made in Hong Kong," orig box.........................**65.00**
Ultra 7, windup, made by Biliken, Japan, orig box, 8-1/2" h **300.00**

❖ Rock 'n' Roll

"Rock, Rock, Rock Around the Clock!" Remember the good ol' days with American Bandstand and the great singers Dick Clark introduced us to? No matter what kind of music you associate with rock 'n' roll, chances are good that some neat collectibles will be rocking at your favorite flea market.

Reference: Joe Hilton and Greg Moore, *Rock-n-Roll Treasures*, Collector Books, 1999.

Belt, Michael Jackson, metal buckle, Lee, 1984, 29" l.....................................**30.00**
Book
 Mike Jagger: Primitiv Cool, Christopher Sanford, St. Martin's, 1994 ....**12.00**
 Rock Elvis, 1994, 240 pgs **24.00**
 Picture Life of Stevie Wonder, A. Edwards and G. Wohl, 1977.......**7.00**
Book cover, orange and red title paper, 3 black and white book covers, one with Pat Boone, one with Sal Mineo, third generic signer, 1958 Cooga Mooga Products, Inc., NY, unused in clear plastic bag **18.00**
Bracelet, gold chain link, burnished gold disc with raised Monkees guitar symbol, orig retail card, © 1967 ...**27.50**
Colorforms, KISS, MIB...................**27.50**
Comic book
 AC/CD, early 1990s.....................**15.00**
 Frank Zappa, #32, 1991................**20.00**
 Jane's Addiction, early 1990s **15.00**
 Janis Joplin, #63 ....**15.00**
 Queensryche, early 1990s...........**20.00**
Cuff Links, pr, Dick Clark, MIB.......**35.00**
Figure, Dave Clark Five, Remco, Rick, Mike, Dennis.............................**95.00**
Game, Duran Duran into the Arena, Milton Bradley, 1985....................**18.00**

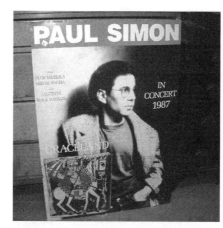

Rock 'N Roll Poster, Paul Simon, in concert, 1987, Graceland, $15.

Lunch box, The Osmonds, metal, orig thermos, unused, 1973..................**95.00**
Magazine, *Hit Parader*, February 1960, Paul Anka cover **5.00**
Nodder, twisting man, gold base, "Let's Twist" decal, Japan sticker, c1960**75.00**
Pinback button, black and white photo Bob-a-Loo, WABC, disc jockey.....**70.00**
 Dick Clark, dark green ground **15.00**
 Frankie Avalon-Venus, bright pink ground.....................................**25.00**
Puzzle, frame tray
 Bee Gees **20.00**
 KISS, 1964 ....**25.00**
Record case, cardboard, full color photo and signature of Dick Clark, blue, white plastic handle, brass closure, holds 45 RPM records **45.00**
Salt and pepper shakers, pr, ceramic feet, mkd "Rock-N-Roll Indiana," mkd "Japan", 2-3/4" l.............................**6.00**
Scarf, AC/DC, EuroTour, 1980-81 ...**60.00**
Tie clip, Dick Clark American Bandstand, gold-tone metal **15.00**
Window Card, 22" x 14", Rolling Stones, *Gimme Shelter,* blue, yellow, and white
....**165.00**

❖ Rockwell, Norman

One of America's most beloved artists, Norman Rockwell was born 1894. By the time he died in 1978, he had created more than 2,000 paintings. Many of these paintings were reproduced as magazine covers, illustrations, calendars, etc. Rockwell's ability to capture the essence of everyday life has attracted people to his work for generations. Besides the artwork, many of Rockwell's illustrations have been used in designs of limited-edition collectibles.

Collectors' Club: Rockwell Society of America, PO Box 705, Ardsley, NY 10502.

For additional listings, see *Warman's Antiques and Collectibles Price Guide* and *Warman's Americana & Collectibles.*

Bell, Love's Harmony, 1976, wooden handle, 9" h **45.00**
Dealer sign, porcelain figure standing next to plaque, c1980, 5-1/4" h ..**125.00**
Figure
 Dave Grossman Designs, Inc., The Graduate, 1983....................**35.00**
 Gorham, Jolly Coachman, 1982 ..**50.00**
 Lynell Studios, Cradle of Love, 1980
....**85.00**
 Rockwell Museum, Bride and Groom, 1979....................................**95.00**
Ignot, Franklin Mint, Spirit of Scouting, 1972, 12 pc set **295.00**
Magazine cover
 Boys' Life, June, 1947 ....**45.00**
 Family Circle, Dec, 1967 ....**15.00**
 Red Cross, April, 1918................**25.00**
 Saturday Evening Post, April 19, 1950
....**85.00**
 Saturday Evening Post, Sept 7, 1957
....**35.00**
 Saturday Evening Post, Jan 13, 1962
....**20.00**
 Scouting, Dec, 1944....................**15.00**
Plate
 Dave Grossman Designs, Huckleberry Finn, 1980................................**45.00**
 Franklin Mint, The Carolers, 1972
....**175.00**
 Gorham, Boy Scout, 1975............**65.00**
 Knowles, Grandma's Courting Dress, 1984, MIB **35.00**
 Lynell studios, Mother's Day, 1980
....**45.00**
 River Shore, Jennie & Tina, 1982 **45.00**
 Rockwell Museum, First Prom, 1979
....**35.00**
 Rockwell Society, A Mother's Love, first edition, 1976 ....**38.00**
 Royal Devon, One Present Too Many, 1979....................................**30.00**
 Royal Manor Porcelain, Scotty's Stowaway, 10" dia....................**35.00**

❖ Rogers, Roy

This popular cowboy hero made a positive impression on many young minds. Today collectors are drawn to Roy Rogers' memorabilia to remember and commemorate the morals and honesty he stressed.

Reference: Lenius, Ron. *The Ultimate Roy Rogers Collection*, Krause Publications, 2001. P. Allan Coyle, *Roy Rogers and Dale Evans Toys & Memorabilia*, Collector Books, 2000.

Collectors' Club: Roy Rogers-Dale Evans Collectors Association, PO Box 1166, Portsmouth, OH 45662-1166.

Two painted tin lunch boxes: Roy Rogers and Dale Evans Double R Bar Ranch, and Gene Autry, with Thermos flask, each $175.

Autographed photo, Roy Rogers and Dale Evans, 8" x 10" 65.00

Cereal Kit, Roy Rogers Riders Club, Post Cereals, orig mailing envelope, 1951-52, orig unused contents ..195.00

Child's Book

Roy Rogers and the Desert Treasure, Alice Sankey, color ills by Paul Souza, Whitman Cozy Corner Book, 1954...20.00

Roy Rogers and the Outlaws of Sundown Valley, Snowden Miller, Whitman Pub., 1950, 250 pgs ..13.50

Comic book

Roy Rogers #5, May 1948, Dell, wear 100.00

Roy Rogers #20, 1949, wear 20.00

Roy Rogers #72, 1953, wear 25.00

Gloves, pr..150.00

Guitar, orig box, 1950s 140.00

Horseshoe game, hard rubber horseshoes..190.00

Lantern, cracked, incomplete, 8" h .75.00

Raincoat, cap, child's oilcloth over canvas fabric, mid 1950s 150.00

Ring, branding iron, brass, 1948, Quaker 195.00

Tie slide, metal, 2" l, 1950s 30.00

Watch, Roy and Dale 120.00

❖ Rookwood

Founded in 1880, Rookwood Pottery underwent a metamorphosis as produced a varying line of wares that ranged from highly detailed artist-decorated vases to production-line figural paperweights. The distinctive mark used indicates the clay or body mark, the size, the decorator mark, a date mark, and the factory mark. Learning to accurately read these marks will enhance your understanding and appreciation for Rookwood Pottery.

Ashtray, owl, green high glaze, 1950, 4-1/4" h..125.00

Bowl, standard glaze, almond husk shape, by Grace Young, 1899, incised golden flowers, brown ground, flame mark/279A-Y/G.M.Y., 6" dia, crack and several nicks..............................100.00

Chamberstick, standard glaze, painted by Jeannette Swing, yellow violets, flame mark, artist's cipher, 1894, 3" h 350.00

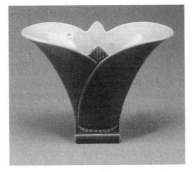

Rookwood vase, floriform, flaring lobes, yellow interior and glossy green exterior, flame mark, no date, 8" h, $115.

Cocktail shaker, green glaze, 1951, 12" h, 8" w 700.00

Paperweight

Canary, white, 1946, 3-5/8" h.....145.00

Cocker spaniel, 24K gold, 1985, 4" h 95.00

Gazelle, white, 1934, 4-1/2" h....250.00

Rooster, 1946, 5" h 350.00

Pitcher, light standard glaze, squatty, leaf handle, painted by Constance Baker, daisies dec, flame mark and "CAB," c1890, 3-3/4" h.............................265.00

Vase

High glaze, hand-painted floral decor by E.T. Hurley, 7-1/4" h...........895.00

Standard glaze, red poppies, green leaves, dec by Mary Luella Perkins, c1896, 5" h 350.00

Vellum glaze, grape decor, Margaret McDonald, 1912, 6-7/8" h.......660.00

❖ Rose Bowls

A rose bowl is defined as a round or ovoid bowl with a small opening. Crimped, pinched, scalloped, petaled, and pleated designs are common. They held potpourri or rose petals.

Blenko, transparent amethyst, free blown, 30 tight rolled crimps, rough pontil, 3-5/8" h 25.00

Bohemian, amber stained cut to clear, grape and vine dec, 3-1/2" h........20.00

Carnival glass, Northwood Drapery, marigold 325.00

Custard glass, ovoid, rose and swag dec, nutmeg stain highlights, ftd, chips on one foot 20.00

Dugan, Japanese line, light yellowish green, three crimps, three indentations on side, decorated with vertical rows of frit, collar base, c1907, 4" h 45.00

Fenton, Beaded Melon, white with yellow interior, eight crimps, collar base, 3-1/2" dia 45.00

Pattern glass, Puritan pattern, 2-1/4" h 50.00

Rose Bowls, Imperial glass, 5" dia, 3-1/2" h, $25.

Porcelain, blue glaze over white base, white int., oval scene captioned "Water St., Shullsburg, Vt," gold outline ...40.00

Satin

Light green, embossed apple blossoms in glass, eight crimps, ground pontil, 3-3/4" dia 150.00

Shaded pink to white, soft white interior, undecorated, eight crimps, ground pontil, 3-1/2" dia 45.00

❖ Roselane Pottery

This California pottery was founded in 1938 in Pasadena. Production included dinnerware and accessories. Roselane Pottery is perhaps best known for its figures, many of which have jeweled eyes and are known as "Sparklers" to collectors.

Bust, Oriental, pearl luster glaze, 9" h, pr 30.00

Candy dish, pink and gray, paper tag, imp mark 25.00

Console bowl, black matte ext., turquoise glaze int., 1950s, 13-3/4" l 25.00

Figure, Sparklers

Bird, pale yellow and pink, 8" w wingspan, 5" h 32.00

Bulldog, 3" h...............................45.00

Cat, 6" h 24.00

Chihuahua....................................57.00

Cocker spaniel, glossy finish, 3" h 22.00

Deer, green glaze, 8" h 30.00

Dog family 42.00

Elephant, round amber rhinestones, 3 pink rhinestones head piece, 5" h 75.00

Fox, 3" h.......................................22.00

Giraffe...22.00

Owl...22.00

Pheasant, 4-3/4" h.......................26.00

Quail, 6" h 45.00

Road runner, 4-1/4" h...................25.00

Swimming duck 50.00

❖ Rosemeade Pottery

Located in Whapeton, N.D., from 1940 to 1961, this pottery created many figures and novelties. They are known for their accurate wildlife designs.

Ashtray
Bear, emb "Breckenridge, Minnesota" 315.00
Duck 50.00
Bell, elephant 300.00
Boot, orig label "Rosemeade No. Dak.," 3-7/8" h...30.00
Figure, Chinese Ringneck Pheasant, 11-1/2" l..195.00
Flower frog, rust colored, script mark, 3" h...25.00
Flower pot, tulip design, light green, 3" h 45.00
Pansy ring, white, 8-1/2" d, 2" h.....35.00
Range shaker, Paul Bunyan...........60.00
Salt and pepper shakers, pr
Bears, 3" h 80.00
Gopher, large 145.00
Mice...35.00
Pheasants 35.00
Running Rabbits........................145.00
White Duck, orig paper label........50.00
Vase, creamy green with pink highlights, Arts and Crafts style, orig sticker, 1940, 5" h..125.00

❖ Rosenthal China

Rosenthal China has been made in Selb, Bavaria, since 1880. Major production centers around dinnerware and some accessories.

Cake plate, grape dec, scalloped ruffled edge, ruffled handles, 12" w 75.00
Creamer and sugar, pate-sur-pate type blue cherries dec.......................125.00
Cup and saucer, Chippendale pattern, c1945 ....50.00
Demitasse cup and saucer, Marie pattern..25.00
Figure, clown, 6" h 225.00
Lemon plate, handles, hp, peacock, early 1920s, sgd "Knapp"...........300.00
Plate, girl and lamb dec, multicolored, 10" dia 40.00
Vase, hexagonal bulbous form, stepped flared base, burnt orange, cream colored egg shaped raised medallions on shoulder and flared rim, silver overlay of stylized floral and leaf motif 290.00

❖ Roseville Pottery

In 1892 the J.B. Owens Pottery was renamed Roseville Pottery Co., taking its name from the Ohio town where the manufacturer was based. From the late 19th century until the business was sold to Mosiac Tile Co. in 1854, Roseville produce a vast quantity of art pottery and dinnerware.

In the 1930s and 1940s the company hit full stride with numerous lines of mass-produced pottery that remain highly popular with collectors today. Unfortunately, reproductions of many of those designs were reproduced in the 1990s. Although those imported reproductions can be easily detected by knowledgeable collectors, the fakes continue to fool many people who see the name Roseville and think they're buying a vintage piece of pottery.

References: Mark Bassett, *Introducing Roseville Pottery*, Schiffer Publishing, 1999.

Collectors' Club: Roseville's of the Past, PO Box 656, Clarcona, FL 32710.

Reproduction Alert.
For additional listings, see *Warman's Antiques and Collectibles Price Guide, Warman's Americana & Collectibles,* and *Warman's American Pottery & Porcelain.*

Basket
Bleeding Heart, #360, 9-1/2" h ..395.00
Clematis, #389, 10" h.................275.00
Mock Orange, No. 911-10, white blossoms, green leaves, green ground, 10" h 180.00
Bookends, pr
Burmese, green, raised marks, 4-3/4" w, 6-3/4" h...............................255.00
Iris, book shape, blue, raised mark, No. 5, 5-1/4" w, 5-1/4" h................290.00
Bowl, Rosecraft Panel, rolled rim, orange floral dec, brown ground, c1920, 8" d, 2-3/8" h..140.00
Candlesticks, pr
Columbine, blue, #1145 ....90.00
Ixia, #1125, green 75.00
Snowberry, mauve, #1CS1..........75.00
Console bowl, Cremona, oval, pink, 11" dia, 2-1/4" h..95.00
Cookie jar
Freesia, No. 4-8, terra cotta ground 440.00
Magnolia, No. 2-8, blue ground ..425.00
Cornucopia, #190, 6" h 220.00
Flowerpot and saucer, Zephyr Lily, green, #672, 5" h.......................255.00
Hanging basket, Zephyr Lily, green, small chip 245.00
Jardiniere
Florentine, cream and green, 8" h, 12" dia..325.00
Fuchsia, bulbous, blue, imp mark, No. 645-8" 350.00

Roseville Pottery, hanging basket, Waterlily, pink, with hanging chains, mkd "81", 5-1/2", $225.

Planter
Florentine, brown, rect, 11-1/4" l, 5-1/4" h, few base chips...............290.00
Matte Green, bulbous, four buttresses, unmarked, 5-3/4" h 400.00
Vase
Blackberry, #572, 6" h 635.00
Dahlrose, bulbous, black paper label, 5" d, 8-1/4" h.........................290.00
Fuschia, brown, #898, 8" h 325.00
Gardenia, gray, raised mark, No. 689-14" 320.00
Ming Tree, green, #581, 6" h......175.00
Pine Cone, gold and brown, #838, 6" h 265.00
Rosecraft Vintage, RV ink mark, small tip chip, 8-1/2" l......................265.00
Wall pocket
Apple Blossom, green................550.00
Gardenia, brown, 8" h 150.00
Maple Leaf, 8-1/2" h 75.00
Snowberry, blue, 8" h 180.00
Window box, Zephyr Lily, green, #1393, 3" h, 10" l.. 210.00

❖ Royal Bayreuth

Royal Bayreuth bowl, molded, four portraits, central panel decorated with flowers, pearlized finish, 10-1/2" dia, $225.

Another Bavarian firm, Royal Bayreuth traces its history to the late 1790s. The company is still in business, producing dinnerware. Royal Bayreuth is well known to collectors for its figural lines that were popular in the late 1880s. One interesting type of porcelain Royal Bayreuth introduced is Tapestry Ware. Placing a piece in fabric,

then decorating and glazing and firing the item caused the texture of this ware.
Reference: Mary J. McCaslin, *Royal Bayreath: A Collector's Guide, Book II*, Glass Press, 2000.

Collectors' Clubs: Royal Bayreuth Collectors Club, 926 Essex Circle, Kalamazoo, MI 49008; Royal Bayreuth International Collectors' Society, PO Box 325, Orrville, OH 44667.

For additional listings, see *Warman's Antiques and Collectibles Price Guide* and *Warman's English &Continental Pottery and Porcelain.*

Ashtray
Devil and Cards	500.00
Elk	225.00

Bell, peacock dec, 3" h...**275.00**
Bowl, Snow Babies, 6" dia...**325.00**
Candy dish, Lobster...**140.00**
Celery tray, Tomato pattern...**95.00**
Chamberstick, Corinthian, enameled Grecian figures, black ground, 4-1/2" h
...**60.00**

Creamer, figural
Bird of Paradise	225.00
Clown, red	275.00
Eagle	200.00
Elk	55.00
Frog, green	250.00
Lamplighter, green	250.00
Pear	290.00

Creamer, tapestry
Brittany women, double handle, 4" h
...**125.00**
Mountain sheep, hunt scene, 4" h
...**110.00**

Cup and saucer
Boy with turkey	125.00
Man in boat fishing	125.00

Hatpin holder, courting couple, cutout base, gold dec, blue mark...**400.00**
Match holder, tapestry, Arab scene
...**100.00**
Milk pitcher, 3-1/2" h, pinched spout, mountain sheep...**125.00**

Mustard, cov
Sunbonnet Babies	395.00
Tomato, figural leaf underplate	125.00

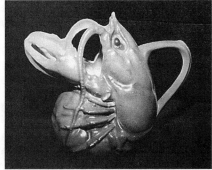
Royal Bayreuth creamer, Lobster, $95.

Pitcher, turkey and cock fighting, 7" h
...**375.00**
Plate, 7-1/2" dia
Man and dogs	95.00
Man in boat fishing	95.00

Plate, boy and donkeys, 8-1/2" dia..**95.00**
Ring Box, cov, pheasant scene, glossy finish...**85.00**
Salt and pepper shakers, pr
Elk	165.00
Rose Tapestry, pink roses	375.00

Vase, peasant women and sheep, silver rim, 3 handles, blue mark...**60.00**
Wall pocket, Strawberry...**265.00**

❖ Royal China

Manufactured in Sebring, Ohio, from 1924 to 1986, Royal China made a large variety of dinnerware patterns. Collectors today are particular fond of several patterns, including Currier & Ives, Bucks County, Colonial Homestead, Fair Oaks, Memory Lane, Old Curiosity Shop, and Willow Ware.

Collectors' Club: Currier & Ives Dinnerware Collectors Club, RD 2, Box 394, Hollidaysburg, PA 16648.

For additional listings and more detailed history, see *Warman's Americana & Collectibles*.

Ashtray, Old Curiosity Shop...**12.00**
Bread and butter plate
Bucks County	3.00
Old Curiosity Shop	3.50

Breakfast plate, Currier and Ives...**15.00**
Butter dish, cov
Colonial Homestead	30.00
Memory Lane	35.00
Willow Ware	27.50

Casserole, cov
Bucks County	75.00
Old Curiosity Shop, tab handles	100.00

Cereal bowl
Currier and Ives	12.00
Memory Lane	10.00

Coffee mug
Colonial Homestead	20.00
Old Curiosity Shop	30.00
Willow Ware	22.00

Creamer
Currier and Ives	7.50
Willow Ware	5.00

Cup and saucer
Bucks County	4.00
Colonial Homestead	3.00
Currier and Ives	6.50
Memory Lane	5.00
Willow Ware	4.50

Dinner plate
Bucks County	4.50
Colonial Homestead	5.00
Currier and Ives	6.00

Royal China Co. plate, Currier & Ives, blue, white ground, 10-1/4" dia, $4.50.

Memory Lane...**4.00**
Old Curiosity Shop	4.50
Willow Ware	4.00

Fruit bowl
Bucks County	3.00
Currier and Ives	3.50
Old Curiosity Shop	3.00

Gravy boat, underplate, Old Curiosity Shop...**28.00**
Pie plate, 10" dia
Currier and Ives	25.00
Willow	25.00

Platter
Colonial Homestead, 11-1/2" l	20.00
Currier and Ives, 10" x 13"	25.00
Willow Ware, 11" l	25.00

Salad plate
Bucks County	8.25
Willow Ware	10.00

Salt and pepper shakers, pr
Bucks County	20.00
Old Curiosity Shop	20.00

Soup bowl
Colonial Homestead	8.50
Willow Ware	10.00

Sugar bowl, cov
Bucks County, tab handles	20.00
Currier and Ives, angled handles	17.50
Memory Lane, angled handles	12.00

Teapot, Old Curiosity Shop...**100.00**
Vegetable dish, 9" d
Old Curiosity Shop	20.00
Willow	20.00

❖ Royal Copenhagen

Many collectors think of Royal Copenhagen as making blue-and-white Christmas plates. However, this Danish firm has also made dinnerware, figurines, and other tablewares.

Bowl, reticulated blue and white, round
...**125.00**
Butter Pat, Symphony pattern, 6 pc set
...**35.00**

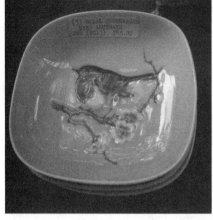

Royal Copenhagen ashtrays, bird motif, set of 3, $45.

Candlesticks, pr, blue floral design,
white ground, bisque lion heads, floral
garlands, 9" h **160.00**

Christmas plate
1976 ....**40.00**
1981 ....**35.00**

Cup and saucer, #1870..................**75.00**

Figure
Girl knitting, No. 1314, 6-3/4" h ..**350.00**
Lady with deer, 9-3/4" h **350.00**

Inkwell, Blue Fluted pattern, matching
tray **165.00**

Plate, #1624, 8" dia **50.00**

Tray
Blue Fluted pattern, 10" l **65.00**
Half Lace pattern, blue triple wave
mark, 9" l **70.00**

Vase, sage green and gray crackled
glaze, 7" h **150.00**

*Royal Copenhagen plate, narcissus dec, blue
ground, $25.*

❖ Royal Copley

Royal Copley was a trade name used by
the Spaulding China Company of Sebring,
Ohio. Concentrating on the table ware and
novelty market, Royal Copley was sold
through retail stores to consumers who
wanted a knick-knack or perhaps something
pretty to use on their table.

*Royal Copley china vase, cream colored ground,
green ivy leaves, ftd, 7-1/4" h, $35.*

Reference: Joe Devine and Leslie C. &
Marjorie A. Wolfe, *Collector's Guide to
Royal Copley, Book II*, Collector Books,
1999.

Periodical: *The Copley Courier,* 1639 N.
Catalina St., Burbank, CA 91505.

Bank, rooster
Green, gold trim **70.00**
Multicolored..................................**50.00**

Dish, bluebird **15.00**

Figure
Blackamoor Woman **45.00**
Parrot, 8" h **55.00**
Rooster and hen **95.00**

Lamp, Flower Tree........................**70.00**

Pitcher, pink, blue flowers, partial paper
label, 7-1/4" h **45.00**

Planter
Blackamoor princess, 1950s........**50.00**
Blossom, large **8.00**
Boy and girl leaning on barrels, deep
blue and yellow, 6" h..................**55.00**
Cow **20.00**
Deer head, 9-1/4" h......................**50.00**
Kitten with yarn, c1942-57 ....**42.00**
Mallard Duck **30.00**
Puppy and mailbox......................**15.00**

Wall pocket
Angels, blond, blue gown, 6-1/4" h
....**25.00**
Pirate, raised lettering mark **50.00**

❖ Royal Doulton

This English firm has had a long and
interesting history. The company produced a
variety of figurines, character jugs, toby
jugs, dinnerware, Beswick, Bunnykins, and
stoneware. One popular dinnerware line is
known as Dicken Ware, named for the
Dickens characters included in the design.

The listings below are a sampling of Royal
Doulton found at flea markets.

References: Susan and Al Bagdade,
*Warman's English & Continental Pottery &
Porcelain*, 3rd Edition, Krause Publications,
1998; Jean Dale, *Charlton Standard
Catalogue of Royal Doulton Animals*, 2nd
ed., Charlton Press, 1998; ——, *Charlton
Standard Catalogue of Royal Doulton
Beswick Figurines*, 6th ed., Charlton Press,
1998.

Periodicals: *Collecting Doulton*, BBR
Publishing, 2 Strattford Ave, Elsecar, Nr
Barnsley, S Yorkshire, S74 8AA, England;
Doulton Divvy, PO Box 2434, Joliet, IL
60434.

Collectors' Clubs: Heartland Doulton
Collectors, PO Box 2434, Joliet, IL 60434;
Mid-America Doulton Collectors, PO Box
483, McHenry, IL 60050; Royal Doulton
International Collectors Club, PO Box 6705,
Somerset, NJ 08873; Royal Doulton
International Collectors Club, 850 Progress
Ave, Scarborough Ontario M1H 3C4
Canada.

Animal
Brown Bear, HN2659 ....**175.00**
Bunnykins, Aerobic **150.00**
Cat with Bandaged Paw, 3-1/4" h
....**45.00**
Dalmatian, HN1113....................**250.00**
Elephant, Flambe, HN489A **200.00**
Fox Terrier, HN1068 ....**1,750.00**
Pine Martin, HN2656...................**275.00**
Stalking Tiger, Flambe, HN809 ..**700.00**
Winnie The Pooh, boxed set of Poof,
Kanga, Piglet, Eeyore, Owl, Rabbit,
and Tigger, Beswick...............**650.00**

Character jug
Cardinal, large...........................**150.00**
Pickwick, miniature.......................**85.00**

Christmas Carol plate
#1, 1982 ....**35.00**
#2, 1983 ....**35.00**

Figure
Alice, girl reading book.................**95.00**
Balloon Seller, HN 1743.............**135.00**
Bedtime Stories...........................**185.00**
Biddy Penny Farthing.................**150.00**
Blythe Morning **190.00**
David Cooperfield, small **90.00**
Daydreams **275.00**
Diana...**95.00**

Falstaff.......................................**120.00**
Fat Boy, small..............................**60.00**
Fionna, maroon skirt **90.00**
Gentleman from Williamsburg, foot
repaired **30.00**
Invitation **95.00**
Jack **120.00**
Jill **145.00**
Lady Charmain, pink skirt, green shawl
....**165.00**
Little Boy Blue **120.00**

Royal Doulton figures, left to right: Stephanie, HN 2807, 7-1/2" h, $175; Christmas Morn, HN 1992, 7" h, $165; The Last Waltz, HN 2315, 8" h, $150.

Little Bridesmaid 170.00
   Master, HN 2325 ....195.00
   Premier, green dress, opera glasses
   ....175.00
   Southern Belle, pink dress 180.00
   Sweet & 20, pink dress, seated on gray
     sofa 350.00
Mug, mermaid handle 65.00
Plate
   Alfred Jingle 145.00
   Bottom from Mid Summer's Night
     Dream....................................185.00
   General store 30.00
   Gullivers 95.00
   Henry VIII 135.00
   Orchids..85.00
   Skater...90.00
   Toxophilite 95.00
Sign, white, gold letters..................20.00
Toby jug, small, Farmer John 50.00

❖ Royal Dux

Royal Dux dog, shaded brown to cream, gold foil label, 12" l, $65.

Here's lovely porcelain, made in Bohemia starting about 1860. Some of the most popular designs are the Art Nouveau inspired wares. Look for a distinctive raised triangle mark or acorn mark to help identify genuine Royal Dux.

Bust, female portrait, raised leaves and berries on base, Czechoslovakia, early 20th C, unmarked, 14" h, chips...290.00
Figure
   Boy with accordion 65.00
   Bulldog, pink triangle mark, blue
     stamped circle "Czech Republic"
     ....110.00
   Elephant, pastel blue, white, and beige,

triangular gold mark, stick, oval "Made in Czech Republic" sticker, 4-1/4" h 50.00
   Poodle, 7-1/2" l..............................75.00
   Sheepherder, #2261, and Peasant Girl, #2262, 9" h, price for pr..........250.00
Jardiniere, rect, large molded flower handles, center Art Nouveau maiden in flowing robes, 7-5/8" h 850.00
Vase
   Art Deco, gold sticker, back stamp "Royal Dux Bohemia, Hand Painted, Made in Czech Republic," raised pink triangle, incised numbers, 6-1/2" h
   ....60.00
   Art Nouveau style female to one side of leaf and floral molded body, bisque, imp mark, early 20th C, 19-1/4" h 290.00

❖ Royal Winton

Known best for its chintz patterns, Royal Winton also made other dinnerware and tablewares. The firm was started by the Grimwade brothers and some marks bear their name in additional to Royal Winton and other information.

For additional listings, see *Warman's English & Continental Pottery & Porcelain* as well as Chintz in this edition.

Cake plate, Hazel, chrome and Bakelite handle 220.00
Candlesticks, pr, Delphinium, hand painted, octagonal......................80.00
Cup and saucer, Spring, #2506 ...125.00
Dinner plate, Sweet Pea...............245.00
Figure, Dickens character, Sam Weller, red jacket.................................155.00
Jug, 8-1/2" h, Fish, gurgles when pours 45.00
Place setting, Ivory, mkd "Wye," black Art Deco design with multicolored flowers 12.00
Snack set, plate and cup, Tiger Lily pattern 85.00
Soup plate, Rosebud pattern, 8-1/4" d 15.00
Tea cup
   Eversham pattern, 2-3/4" h 95.00
   Hibiscus, gold trim, 2-3/4" h 28.50
Teapot, cov
   Chanticleer 350.00
   Mayfair.......................................285.00
   Tiger Lily, 5-3/4" h 350.00
Vase, Royalty, 3-3/4" h 220.00

❖ Royal Worcester

Here's another venerable English pottery that's a favorite with collectors. Some of the porcelains are hand decorated while others take advantage of a transfer print decoration technique, which Royal

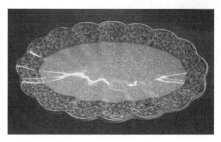

Royal Worcester dish, black and white transfer printed floral border scalloped, brown and white transfer printed int., gold trim, black crown mark, $45.

Worcester perfected. Look for a mark, which will help date the piece, give clues as to the decorator, etc.

For additional listings, see *Warman's Antiques and Collectibles Price Guide* and *Warman's English & Continental Pottery and Porcelain*.

Bud vase, bulbous, triangular handle, reticulated leaf design, ivory ground, hp floral trim, gold accents, purple crown mark, registration mark 75.00
Centerpiece, oval, ftd, Royal Lily pattern, first period, c1800, 6-1/4" h, repaired 125.00
Cup and saucer, Imari pattern, c1910 ....48.00
Egg coddler, silver lid with ring on top 3" h, peach on front, leaf with berries on back 20.00
   3 1/4" h, two different bird scenes on each coddler, mkd "Royal Worcester Porcelain, Made in England", pr 30.00
Figure
   Politician, white glaze, hat rim restored, minor staining 300.00
   Saturday's Child, boy 130.00
   The Thief 225.00
Mustard pot, cylindrical, blue and white transfer, floral clusters, floral finial, first period, mid 18th C, 4" h 325.00
Plate, diaper pattern border surrounding floral spray, blue and white transfer dec, first period, mid 19th C, 8" dia 220.00

Royal Worcester mark, Black crown mark, stamped on bottom of dish, incised numerals.

Tea bowl and saucer, painted chinoisiere vignette, blue border, first period, c1865 ....**185.00**

Urn, cov, pierced dome top, painted floral sprays, basketweave molded base, early 20th C, 11-1/2" h **200.00**

Vase, floral dec, gilt trim, reticulated, 3-1/4" h **115.00**

Waste bowl, floral molded ext., floral spray int., lambrequin border, c1765, 5" dia **200.00**

❖ Roycroft

Roycroft is a familiar name to Arts and Crafts collectors. The Roycrofters were founded by Elbert Hubbard in East Aurora, New York. He was a talented author, lecturer, and manufacturer. Perhaps his greatest contribution was the campus he created with shops to teach and create furniture, metals, leather working, and printing.

Collectors' Clubs: Foundation for the Study of Arts & Crafts Movement, Roycroft Campus, 31 S. Grove St., East Aurora, NY 14052; Roycrofters-At-Large Association, PO Box 417, East Aurora, NY 14052.

Bookends, pr, 4-1/8" w, 3-1/4" d, 5-1/4" h, model no. 309, hammered copper, rect, riveted center band suspending ring, dark brown patina, imp Roycroft orb, minor wear **225.00**

Book, *Elbert Hubbard's Scrapbook,* emb leather cov, orig glassine dust jacket, fitted box, c1923, 228 pgs, 7" x 10" **90.00**

Bracelet, hammered sterling silver **225.00**

Etching, Elbert Hubbard **65.00**

Humidor, brass, 5" h, acid-etched finish, discoloration **200.00**

Jug, stoneware, brown glaze, 5" h ..**15.00**

Letter holder/perpetual calendar, 3-1/2" x 4-3/4" x 2-1/4", copper, acid-etched border, orb and cross mark with "Roycroft," normal wear to patina **150.00**

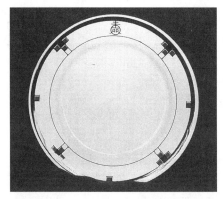

Roycroft dinner plate, Roycroft orb mark at top, Buffalo China, 9-1/4" dia, $40.

Stand, Little Journey's stand, oak, orig finish, 26" h, 26" w, 14" d **1,150.00**

Tray, 17" d, octagonal, hammered copper, 2 handles, orb and cross mark, cleaned patina, slight bend to one edge **290.00**

Vase, model no. 212, copper, tall cylindrical form, rim border of stylized dogwood flowers within diamonds, brass wash with green accents around rim, imp "Roycroft" orb on base, all over wear to brass wash, 10-1/4" h **460.00**

❖ R.S. Germany

R.S. Germany wares are also known as Schlegelmilch porcelain, in reference to the brothers whose potteries in the Thuringia and Upper Silesia region of Poland/Germany produced wares from the 1860s until the 1950s. Generally R.S. Germany porcelain is decorated with florals and detailed backgrounds. Handles and finials tend to be fancy.

Biscuit jar, cov, roses dec, satin finish, loop handles, gold knob, 6" h **95.00**

Bread plate, Iris variant edge mold, blue and white, gold outlines, steeple mark **115.00**

Bride's bowl, floral center, ornate ftd stand **95.00**

Chocolate pot, white rose florals, blue mark **95.00**

Demitasse cup and saucer, pink roses, gold stenciled dec, satin finish, blue mark **95.00**

Lemon plate, cutout handle shaped as colorful parrot, white ground, gold trim, artist sgd "B. Hunter" **60.00**

Nut bowl, cream and yellow roses, green scalloped edge, 5-1/4" dia............**65.00**

Plate, white flowers, gold leaves, green ground, gilded edge, dark green mark, gold script signature, 9-3/4" dia ...**45.00**

Tea tile, peach and tan, green-white snowballs, RM over faint blue mark **165.00**

❖ R.S. Prussia

Like R.S. Germany, R.S. Prussia was porcelain made by Reinhold Schlegelmilch in the same region. Designed for export, the wares are mostly table accessories or dinnerware. Pieces of R.S. Prussia tend to be more expensive than R.S. Germany, primarily because of better molds and decoration.

Reference: Leland and Carol Maple, *R. S. Prussia: The Formative Years,* Schiffer Publishing, 2002.

Collectors' Club: International Association of R. S. Prussia Collectors, Inc., 212 Wooded Falls Road, Louisville, KY 40243.

Reproduction Alert.

Pitcher, hand painted pink flowers, gold scrolls, artist sgd "D. Kent," red wreath mark, 5-1/8" h, $250.

Bowl, cov, delicate handles, white ground, pink roses, gold tracery **190.00**

Bowl, open, 11" d, white satin finish, swans, red mark..........................**350.00**

Cake plate, floral with 3 medallions of cherubs **500.00**

Cake plate, turkey and evergreens**500.00**

Celery dish, green florals **175.00**

Chocolate pot, cov, green and yellow luster, pink flowers......................**325.00**

Ferner, mold 876, florals on purple and green ground, unsigned **175.00**

Hair receiver, green lilies of the valley flowers, white ground, red mark ...**95.00**

Plate, poppies dec, raised molded edge and gilt trim, 8-3/4" dia **75.00**

Spoon holder, pink and white roses, 14" l **200.00**

Syrup, cov, underplate, green and yellow luster, pink flowers......................**125.00**

Toothpick holder, pink and white roses, green shadows, jeweled, six small feet, red mark......................................**250.00**

❖ Ruby Stained Glass

Pattern glass with ruby stained highlights can be a great find at flea markets. Look for examples that are in good condition with little wear to the ruby staining and gold trim. Many pieces of ruby stained glass were used as souvenirs and are engraved with names, places, and dates.

Berry set, Tacoma pattern 7 pc **310.00**

Compote, Tacoma pattern **110.00**

Dish, canoe shape, Tacoma pattern **75.00**

Mug
Button Arches pattern, engraved "Mother" **35.00**

Heart Band pattern 30.00
Rose bowl, Tacoma pattern 85.00
Spooner, Royal Crystal pattern 75.00
Syrup
   Late Block Pattern, orig top........300.00
   Pioneer's Victoria pattern, orig top
   ....350.00
   Prize pattern, orig top 325.00
   Truncated Cube pattern 250.00
Toothpick holder
   Double Arch pattern 195.00
   Harvard pattern 80.00
   Pleating pattern.........................85.00
   Prize pattern..............................135.00
Tumbler, Riverside's Victoria pattern
   ....85.00
Water set, water pitcher and six tumblers
   Art Novo pattern.........................425.00
   Hexagon Block pattern..............325.00
   Loop and Block pattern 465.00
   Pioneer's Victoria pattern 350.00

❖ Rugs

Rug styles and the techniques for making them have changed greatly over the years. Embroidered rugs date to the early 19th century. Braided rugs, made from strips of fabric that were braided and then sewn together to form a circular or oval shape, were first popular in second quarter of the 19th century. Hooked rugs, which were introduced about 1830 and came into vogue in the 1850s, were crafted from homemade designs as well as from commercial patterns.

Most rugs found at flea markets are later examples of those styles, with many being machine-made. Especially popular today are hooked rugs with bold graphic designs or pictorials with a folkish flair. Never buy a rug without carefully examining the piece beforehand, checking for damage and repairs.

Reference: Joel and Kate Kopp, *American Hooked and Sewn Rugs: Folk Art Underfoot*, E.P. Dutton, 1975; Mildred Cole Peladeau, *Art Underfoot: The Story of Waldoboro Hooked Rugs*, American Textile History Museum, 1999; Jessie A. Turbayne, *Hooked Rug Treasury*, Schiffer Publishing, 1997.

Collectors' Club: RugNotes, 12700 Ardennes Ave., Rockville, MD 20851.

Bambi and Thumper, Belgium, 22" x 36"
   ....60.00
Hooked
   Collie, landscape ground, birds in air, border in stripes of red, blue and white, 30" x 48"......................495.00
   Lighthouse 34-1/2" x 22"............200.00
   Horse, running, impressionistic multicolor ground, 24" x 34" ...192.50
   Cabin scene, 29" x 50"...............275.00
   Tulips, daffodils, lilies and iris, white

central oval ground, gray border, 54" x 35"...357.50
Indian, Navajo, Stunning Storm pattern, woven by Alice Yazzie, 41" x 26"**875.00**
Mickey and Minnie Mouse on flying broom, 21" x 41"......................200.00
Penny, 6-sided, tan, orange, blue, dark- and light-green circles on tan ground, staining, minor damage, 19-1/4" x 33"
   ....220.00
Rag
   Oval, gray, green, tan, blue and red, 23" x 30" 148.00
   Runner, stripes of red, green, white and black, 33" w, 120" l 220.00
Uncle Scrooge McDuck, 21" x 34"
   ....175.00

❖ RumRill Pottery

This American art pottery has been around, literally. At different times, RumRill Pottery has been made by the Red Wing potteries (and sold by a sales force located in Little Rock, Ark), Florence Pottery in Ohio, and Shawnee Pottery, also in Ohio. Knowledgeable collectors can identify when and where a piece of RumRill was made.

Bulb bowl, Class pattern, chartreuse exterior, olive-green interior, 9" dia
   ....40.00
Figure, seal, glass bowl on nose, black glaze, 12" h 250.00
Jug, ball shape, matte dark cornflower blue with light blue sponged dec, mkd "Rumrill, 547", 7-1/2" h...............400.00
Planter
   Log 60.00
   Scalloped, pink, E12, 7" dia 15.00
Vase
   4-1/2" h, 7-1/2" dia, three swan handles, blended green glaze 250.00
   8-1/8" h, white shading to lavender- mauve, two swans at base, mkd "Rumrill K47 Made in USA" 155.00
   9" h, 5-1/2" dia, urn shape, off-white, pink speckled overlay, mkd "Rumrill H-4" on bottom.........................150.00

❖ Russian Items

Flea markets are great places to find Russian collectibles. From beautiful amber from the Baltic region to pieces commemorating events, there is a lot of variety. Russian craftsmen were known for the exquisite work in silver, enamels, and lacquer.

Beads, amber, graduated, screw closure, 28" l 375.00
Belt, turquoise cloisonné links spaced with silver gilt links, large turquoise clasp, hallmarks 185.00

Box, lacquer, Fedoskino, Tzar surveying wonders of Dvidon's Country 575.00
Commemorative coin, Russian scientist A.C. Popov, 1984, 1 Rubl 25.00
Compact, sterling, Catherine the Great on front, puff missing..................175.00
Egg, porcelain, floral and foliate polychrome dec, gilt highlights, 4-1/2" l
   ....50.00
Match safe, patinated, applied plaque with Russian characters, 3" l......125.00
Plate
   Double-headed eagle crest, hand- painted, 12" dia..........................95.00
   St. Petersburg Palace, 1991, 7-3/4" sq
   ....22.00
   Tianex, Bradford Exchange, 1988, 7-3/4" dia......................................15.00
Stool, painted, top with geometric strapwork dec, turned tapered legs, early 20th C, 13-1/2" w, 9-1/4" d, 8-7/8" h 125.00
Wine cup, silver, Slavic flowers decor, 19th C., 2-1/2" h 125.00

Russian box, black lacquer background, yellow, and red florals, gold scrolls, green foliage, 4" x 6", $25.

❖ Salt and Pepper Shakers

What table would be complete without a pair of salt and pepper shakers? Flea markets are great places to spot novelty and decorative sets. Most can add a smile to even a sleepy head! Generally the salt shaker has larger or more holes than the pepper.

Reference: Irene Thornburg, *The Big Book of Salt & Pepper Shaker Series*, Schiffer Publishing, 1999.

Collectors' Club: Novelty Salt & Pepper Shakers Club, PO Box 3617, Lantana, FL 33465.

For additional listings, see *Warman's Antiques and Collectibles Price Guide* and *Warman's Antiques & Collectibles.*

Barn and silo	**10.00**
Baseball and glove	**12.00**
Birds on nest	**10.00**
Chicks, emerging from egg-shaped cups, script mark "Japan," 4-1/2" h	**60.00**
Cowboys, Vandor	**10.00**
Dachshund and tire	**18.00**
Donald Duck and BBQ	**15.00**
Duck and egg, 3-1/4" h	**27.50**
Feet	**5.00**
Frogs	**7.00**
Indian chief and squaw, 3-1/4" h, composition wood, both mkd "1947 copyright, Multi Products"	**18.00**

Salt & Pepper Shakers Pearls, blue plastic shell, white plastic pearl shakers, $12.

Salt & Pepper Shakers, cats, green plastic, green plastic holder, painted black and white details, $45.

Lawn Mower, moving wheels and pistons, 1950s	**30.00**
Lemons	**5.00**
Milk cans, copper	**20.00**
Minnie Mouse and vanity	**15.00**
Penguins, black and white body, orange bill and webbed feet, mkd "Japan," c1930s, 3" h	**10.00**
Pluto and doghouse	**15.00**
Poodles	**40.00**
Rabbits, yellow, snuggle type, Van Telligen	**42.00**
Refrigerators, GE, 1930 style refrigerator, milk glass	**30.00**
Skunks, Enesco	**12.00**
Thermos and lunch pail	**35.00**

❖ Salts, Open

Before the advent of salt shakers, open salt containers were used on tables. Frequently there was a master salt to hold this precious condiment. Another way of dispensing salt was individual salts, often called salt cellars, one per place setting, along with a tiny spoon. The individual salts were originally sold as sets and can be found in silver, silver plate, and various types of glassware. Today collectors can be found searching flea markets for individual examples to add to their growing collections.

Salts, open Porcelain, white, yellow flowers, gold trim, pedestal base, mkd "Made in Japan," $5.

Salts, open, Pattern glass, amber, fan shape, 3" w, 3" l, $7.50.

Periodical: *Salty Comments,* 401 Nottingham Road, Newark, DE 19711.

Collectors' Clubs: Central Mid-West Open Salt Society, 10386 Fox River Drive, Walnut Springs, Newark, IL 60541; Mid-West Open Salt Society, 9123 S Linden Rd, Swartz Creek, MI 48473-9125; New England Society of Open Salt Collectors, 6-2 Clear Pond Drive, Walpole, MA 02081; Open Salt Collectors of the Atlantic Region, 71 Clearview Lane, Biglerville, PA 17307-9407; Open Salt Seekers of the West (Northern Chapter), 84 Margaret Drive, Walnut Creek, CA 94596; Open Salt Seekers of the West (Southern Chapter), 2525 East Vassar Drive, Visalia, CA 93292; Salt Collector's South East, 1405 N Amanda Circle, Atlanta, GA 30329-3317.

Bavaria, lavender ext., gold int., mkd "Bavaria", 1-1/2" dia	**18.00**
Cut glass, master, green cut to clear, silver plated holder, 2" h	**120.00**
Intaglio, individual, bronze basket frame with "jewels", burnished gold scene on body, 8-sided	**80.00**
Limoges, peach flowers, white ground, gold trim, three small feet	**30.00**
Lusterware, swan, mkd "Made in Japan by Noritake," 2" h	**27.50**
Milk glass, top hat, Daisy and Button pattern	**20.00**
Pattern glass, individual	
Fine Rib, flint	**35.00**
Hawaiian Lei	**35.00**
Three Face	**42.00**
Pattern glass, master	
Barberry, pedestal	**45.00**
Jacob's Ladder, pedestal base	**40.00**
Snail, ruby stained	**75.00**
Pewter, master, cobalt blue liner, pedestal	**70.00**
Porcelain, octagonal, master, blue and white paisley design	**10.00**
Royal Bayreuth, individual, lobster claw	**85.00**
Silver plated, cobalt blue glass liner, 2-1/2" dia	**22.00**
Sterling silver, whale, crystal salt, mkd "Sterling, Germany," 3-1/2" h	**60.00**

❖ Sand Pails

Sand pail, white cat, $225.

Bright lithographed metal sand pails have gained in popularity in recent years. Made by several of the major toy manufacturers, they were designed with all types of characters and childhood scenes. Look for ones with bright colors. Most collectors prefer very good examples, but will tolerate some dents and signs of use.

Beach scene, German, 1950s......**115.00**
Cowboy chased by Indian, Ohio Art, with shovel..................................**100.00**
Easter scene, bunnies and chicks, 6" h **85.00**
Flowers, metallic blue, Ohio Art, 1960s, 9-1/2" h...**40.00**
Humpty Dumpty, Ohio Art, some wear **25.00**
Man selling flower from cart, 6" h **32.00**
Mecki Hedgehog, German **35.00**
Red Riding Hood, Ohio Art, 7-7/8" h **75.00**
Under the Sea design, Ohio Art, 9-1/2" h **42.00**

Sand Pails, Front: King-Kup, Hershey, ducks dec, round, $195; back: Chein, dog and cat dec, sq, $145.

❖ Sarreguemines

This porcelain is another example of tin-glazed earthware, like majolica. It was made in France and can be found in all types of design, some quite whimsical. Some have the name impressed on the back.

Basket, quilted green body, heavy leopard skin crystallization, 9" h.**250.00**
Character jug, lawyer **125.00**
Cup and saucer, Orange, majolica **50.00**
Demitasse cup and saucer, cup dec inside and out..............................**40.00**
Dinnerware Service, white china, multicolored scenes, 6 luncheon plates, 6 bread and butter plates, 6 demitasse cups, 6 porringers, 2 platters, divided dish..............................**150.00**
Dish, cov, majolica, 6-1/2" l...........**300.00**
Ewer, tall, cylindrical, 13" h **150.00**
Humidor, man with top hat **175.00**
Pitcher, ugly man's head, blue int., majolica **275.00**
Stein, high relief dec, mkd "Sarreguemines/1237/215/Y," 8-1/4" h **195.00**

❖ Scales

Whether it's the scales of justice or a candy scale, collectors like to find interesting examples to add to weight their collections.

Reference: Bill and Jan Berning, *Scales*, Schiffer Publishing, 1999.

Collectors' Club: International Society of Antique Scale Collectors, 300 W. Adams, Suite 821, Chicago, IL 60606.

Balance, V.W. Brinckerhoff, New York, cast iron, scroll designs, brass pans, 7-1/4" h, 14-3/4" w..........................**85.00**
Candy scale, white enamel, 2-lb capacity, Eureka Automatic Scales, No. 35864, with pan, 20" h, 13" w **195.00**
Kitchen scale
Montgomery Wards Family Scale, 25-lb capacity **35.00**
Universal Family Scale, 24-lb. capacity, 1865 patent date **40.00**
Platform, Peerless Junior, Peerless Weighing Machine Co., porcelainized steel, tiled platform, gold lettering, 63" h **350.00**
Postal, Nolan Scale Co., Boston, nickel plated, sq pan, dial graduated 0-7, 1889 patent date, desk clamp, 4-1/2" h **175.00**
Spring
Fray's Improved Spring Balance, brass and iron, 48 lb, 14-3/8" l...........**30.00**
Penn Scale Mfg. Co., brass and iron, 100 lb., 17-1/2" l, wear..............**35.00**

Bathroom scale, chrome body, c1950, $10.

Morton & Bremner, iron, brass face, 24 lb., 9-1/4" dia round tin pan, 11" l **35.00**
Store, Hanson Weightmaster, cast iron, gold case with ground, black lettering and indicator, 6" x 14" x 10".........**60.00**

❖ Schafer & Vater

The first of Schafer and Vater was located in Rudolstadt, Thuringia, from about 1890 to 1962. They made porcelain dolls, figurines, and novelty wares of all types.

For additional listings, see *Warman's English & Continental Pottery & Porcelain.*

Bottle, figural, One of the Boys.....**150.00**
Box, cov, olive green bisque, gold and bronze accents, white glazed emb cameo of lady and cupid on lid, chip on lid, 5" x 3" **225.00**
Cup and saucer, pale blue rose as cup, petal form saucer, minor wear to gilt **75.00**
Mug, figural, elk.............................**50.00**
Pin tray, figural, lady golfer **235.00**
Pitcher, figural
Lady with cape, blue **130.00**
Man, hat and cane, blue and white **125.00**
Plaque, jasperware, dark green, white dec, mkd #2870, artist #18, 12" h **275.00**
Rose bowl, cherubs, two rams head handles, mkd "5660," 3-1/4" h **230.00**
Shaving mug, raised relief elk, tan, shades of brown, light tan, rusty-orange, glossy white int. **115.00**
Urn, jasperware, blue and white, man and woman planting tree, 2-1/2" h**50.00**
Vase, jasperware, lilac, raised Art Nouveau dec, large cobalt blue jewels, iridized and crystallized glaze, c1900-20, 6-1/4" h................................**225.00**

❖ Schoop, Hedi

Hedi Schoop Art Creations represents another California pottery. This one was located in North Hollywood from 1942 to 1958. The company is well known for its detailed figures and other tablewares.

Bowl, 8" w, 4-1/4" h, hand crafted, mkd **75.00**
Figure
Dutch Boy and Girl, 11" h, missing one pail **95.00**
Lady, seated, holding bowl, tinted bisque, high glaze turquoise, 12" h **300.00**
Oriental Couple, carrying pottery buckets with rope handles, white, blue, and black, 12" h and 13" h **300.00**
Planter
Butterfly, green and gold, pr.......**175.00**
Lady, full skirt, 7" w, 9" h, minor chips, cracks, water damage to back..**30.00**
Vase
8" h, feather design **110.00**
8-1/2" h, 8-1/4" d, c1940 ....**90.00**

❖ Schuco

Founded by Heinrich Muller and Herr Schreyer in 1912, Schreyer and Co adopted the name Schuco for its line of toys. Often having ingenious mechanisms, Schuco toys were made from the 1930s to 1950. Originals are makred "Germany" or "U.S. Zone Germany." Other markings indicate a reissued toy.

Beach Buggy, worn orig box **195.00**
Curvo 1000 Motorcycle, red shirt, brown pants, green cycle, orig box, missing end flap **680.00**
Car
Akustico 2002, 5-5/8" l **185.00**
Examico 4001, 5-3/4" l **300.00**
Clown Fiddler, made in U.S. Zone Germany, 1950s, box with restored flaps, 4-1/2" h **275.00**
Motorcycle, Motodrill 1006, windup, 1960s, 5-1/2" l **485.00**
Pig musicians, fife, violin and drums, set of 3 ....**990.00**
Sedan, red, wind-up with key, 6-1/2" l, near mint **135.00**
Teddy bear, gold mohair, bead eyes, embroidered nose, perfume vial hidden in body, 3-1/2" h **425.00**

❖ Scotties

Scotties are one of the most recognizable dog breeds. Some attribute this to President Franklin Roosevelt and his dog, Fala. Others identify Scotties with Jock from Lady and the Tramp. Many Scottie collectibles are found with black dogs and red and white accents. Scottie images can be found on every type of item, and they bring a smile with their cheerful attitude.

Reference: Candace Sten Davis and Patricia Baugh, *A Treasury of Scottie Dog Collectibles, Vol. II,* Collector Books, 2000.

Collectors' Clubs: Wee Scots, PO Box 1597, Winchester, VA 22604.

Bank, cast iron, Hubley **115.00**
Bowl, running Scotties design, red on white ground, faded......................**18.00**
Calendar, 1959, Texaco, Scottie and girl on telephone **20.00**
Christmas card, 2 black Scotties on front, single-sided, 1930s...............**6.00**
Cocktail shaker, glass, black Scottie, red checkered border **15.00**
Doorstop, cast iron, 2 dogs, orig paint, 6" h, 8-3/4" l **225.00**
Glass, red and black design, 1940s, 6-1/4" h, set of 4..............................**42.00**
Ice tub, glass, 8 black Scotties around outside, red checker border, 1940s, 4-1/4" h..**55.00**
Pin, gold filled, rhinestone eye and collar **25.00**
Salt and pepper shakers, figural, pr
Black and white **32.00**
Orange Scotties playing instruments **75.00**
String holder, figural....................**125.00**
Toothbrush holder, porcelain, 3 dogs, Japan, 4" h **125.00**

❖ Sebastian Miniatures

Marblehead, Mass., was the home for Prescott Baston's Sebastian figurines. He started production in 1938 and created detailed historical figurines or characters from literature. Finding a figure with the original label adds to the value of these little charmers.

Collectors' Clubs: The Sebastian Exchange Collector Association, PO Box 10905, Lancaster, PA 17605; Sebastian Miniature Collectors Society, 321 Central St., Hudson, MA 01749.

Abraham Lincoln **18.00**
Aunt Betsy Trotwood, wear **20.00**
Building Days Boy, blue label........**35.00**
Colonial Carriage **80.00**
Confederate soldier **22.00**
Ezra, yellow label...........................**30.00**
Gibson Girl **90.00**
House of Seven Gables..............**100.00**
In the Candy Store, green and silver Marblehead label......................**135.00**
Mrs. Cratchit, light blue label, 2-1/2" h, wear to paint, chip........................**20.00**

Sebastian Miniatures, Priscilla, woman sitting at spinning wheel, $185.

New England Town Crier, figure standing next to dealer's plaque, base nick **20.00**
Pecksniff, red label **20.00**
Peggoty, blue label **20.00**
Sailing Days Girl, red label **35.00**
Sea Captain, #132 ....**30.00**
Snow Days Girl, #6253, orig box ...**35.00**
Mark Twain...................................**120.00**
William and Hannah Penn..........**200.00**

❖ Sesame Street

"Sunny day, everything's A-Ok!" That's the song Sesame Street collectors sing as they gleefully search through flea markets for the growing number of items related to Big Bird, Elmo, and the rest of the Sesame Street gang. Wise collectors know to watch for knockoffs—cheap, unlicensed imitations of Sesame Street products. Most of the copycats aren't worth adding to a collection.

Bank, Cookie Monster, MIB **24.00**
Book, *Sesame Street L & M Book,* Funk & Wagnalls, copyright 1978, hardcover **4.00**
Candy box, tin, Sesame Street Friends for Life, 7" d **4.00**

Sesame Street Train, Big Bird engineer, Cookie Monster, and Ernie, plastic, wind-up, cars separate, Big Bird head turns, $12.

Sesame Street Car, Big Bird driving, teddy in rumble seat, plastic, red and yellow body, blue wheels, white hubcaps, blue rumble seat cover, copyright 2000 Mattel, Inc., © Sesame Street Muppets, © Henson, Made in China, $1.

Cookie jar, Big Bird, pale yellow, 11-1/2" h **55.00**

Cup, plastic, Cookie Monster **5.00**

Game, Walk Along Sesame Street, Milton Bradley, orig box, c1975...............**20.00**

Halloween costume, child's, Big Bird, orig costume, mask, box **10.00**

Lamp, child's, Big Bird....................**15.00**

Little Golden Book, *Sesame Street The Together Book*, #1978 ....**5.00**

Lunch box, metal, Aladdin, orig thermos, 1979 ....**45.00**

Record, Hits from Sesame Street, Vol. III, Peter Pan Records, 45 rpm............**4.00**

Plush toy
    Baby Piggy, 1987 ....**8.00**
    Christmas Elmo, Tyco, 1997.........**18.00**
    Cookie Monster, laughs, says "Oh Boy Oh Boy," 1996 ....**18.00**
    Grover, Tyco **5.00**
    Kermit the Frog, Fisher-Price, 1976, some wear **15.00**
    Kermit the Frog, NHL, McDonald's, 1995..**10.00**
    The Count, Tyco, 1997 ....**6.00**

Pop-up book, *Grover's Superprise*, 1978 ....**12.00**

Puzzle, wooden tray, Hen Pen Men, Playskool, 1973..............................**8.00**

TV Guide, Cookie Monster on cover, July, 1971 ....**15.00**

Toy, car, Big Bird driving, © Mattel Inc., Sesame Street Muppets, © Henson, Made in China..................................**1.00**

Sesame Street Pez dispenser, Gonzo, blue, yellow bowtie, $3.

❖ Sevres and Sevres-Type China

Sevres porcelain at a flea market—sure, not every dealer carries it, but some pieces of this fine French porcelain show up at flea markets. Just like today, when Sevres porcelain became so popular, imitations were made. Those are often considered "Sevres type" and are also found at flea markets. Carefully check the mark and decoration of an item before buying it. Many reproduction Sevres pieces exist, including some older fakes.

For additional listings, see *Warman's Antiques and Collectibles Price Guide* and *Warman's English & Continental Pottery & Porcelain.*

Bowl, genre dec top panel, landscape face panel, turquoise blue ground, gilt floral ornamentation, bun feet, entwined "L" mark, date mark "L", 3-1/2" l, 2" w, wear to gilt **180.00**

Compote, polychrome transfer printed figural landscapes, bronze mounts, 20th C, 5-1/4" h, price for matched pr **175.00**

Luncheon plate, central gilt six-pointed star, border with hunt scenes, 9-3/4" d, price for 6 pc set **325.00**

Patch box, cov, 3-1/4" l, shaped ovoid, green ground, hinged lid with hand painted scene of Napoleon on horseback, sgd lower right "Morin" **250.00**

Pin box, cov, cartouche of romantic couple on cover, blue ground, oval, 6-1/2" l **275.00**

Portrait plate, Mme Duchatelet, sgd "G. Perlex," cobalt blue border with floral panels and gilt accents, scalloped rim, entwined "L" mark, dated "BB"....**125.00**

Salt, hp roses, paneled blue and white ground **58.00**

Vase, gilt ground, enamel Art Nouveau stylized leaf and flower design, printed mark, 6" h.................................**645.00**

❖ Sewer Tile

Also called sewer pipe, sewer tile was produced from about 1880 through the early 20th century. Draining tiles and sewer tiles were produced at the factories, but the workers often spent their spare time creating other items of utilitarian or whimsical nature. Although some molded pieces were made, much of the production was one-of-a-kind items. Pieces that are signed and/or dated are especially prized.

Ohio is recognized as the leading producer of sewer tile, but other states, including New York, Pennsylvania, and Indiana, all had a strong presence in the sewer tile market.

For additional listings, see *Warman's Country Price Guide.*

Alligator, Ohio, 15" l **440.00**

Bank, dog, seated Spaniel, probably Tuscarawas County, Ohio, 10-1/2" h, minor glaze flakes **220.00**

Cat, seated, glaze with copper speckles, small chips, 1 front foot missing, 7" h **330.00**

Dog, seated, spaniel
    5-1/2" h, minor edge chips **195.00**
    8-1/4" h, incised detail up the back, over the head and down the front leg, incised collar and chain, deep-brownish red glaze, oval base, minor base chips **275.00**
    10-1/2" h, light-brown glaze **330.00**

Owl, perched on log, 20th C., 8-1/2" h **165.00**

Planter, stump, 3 branches, hand tooled bark, 9" dia, 26" h **225.00**

Umbrella stand, tree trunk design, applied roses, chips on flowers, 25-1/2" h **330.00**

❖ Sewing Collectibles

"A stitch in time saves nine," or so thought Ben Franklin. Today collectors find lots of sewing memorabilia at flea markets. From tiny needle holders to interesting sewing machines, it just takes a little hunting, like finding a needle in a haystack.

Collectors Clubs: International Sewing Machine Collectors Society, 1000 E. Charlston Blvd., Las Vegas, NV 89104; National Button Society, 2730 Juno Place, Apt 4, Akron, OH 44313; Toy Stitchers, 623 Santa Florita Ave., Milbrae, CA 94030.

For additional listings, see *Warman's Antiques and Collectibles Price Guide* and *Warman's Americana and Collectibles.*

Advertising trade card, Clark's Thread **7.50**

Basket, wicker, round, beaded lid ..**27.50**

Book
    American Needlework, 1776-1976, Leslie Tillett, NY Graphic Society, 1975...**15.00**
    Terrace Hill Needlepoint Designs, Orig Designs from Iowa Governor's Mansion, Billie Ray, 1980, sgd .**10.00**

Catalog
    Davis Sewing Machine Co., Watertown, NY, 1881, 64 pgs, 5-1/2" x 8-3/4", cover wear **24.00**
    New Home Sewing machine, New York, NY, c1900, 12 pgs, 3-3/4" x 6-1/4" **12.00**

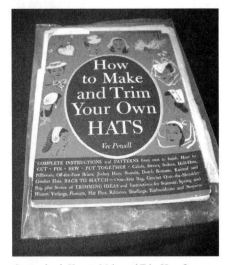

Sewing book, How to Make and Trim Your Own Hats, *Vee Powell, $10.*

United Thread Mills, New York, NY, c1930, 7 pgs, 6-3/4" x 10" **18.00**
Crochet Hook, metal, capped **15.00**
Darning egg
   Ebony, sterling handle **100.00**
   Porcelain, marbleized finish, one piece, 5-1/2" l **12.50**
   Wood, 5-1/2" l, age crack **10.00**
Dress form, wire and cloth **50.00**
Embroidery hoop, clamp for table, wood **85.00**
Instruction manual
   Domestic Sewing Machine, model 725 ....**10.00**
   Singer Sewing Machine 400w, 106, 107, 108, 109 and 110, dated 1948 ....**10.00**
Machine
   Chasige, blue body, child's **35.00**
   Singer Featherweight, Model 221, black case, attachments, c1941 ....**400.00**
Needle Book
   Sears Roebuck and Co, "A Gift to you from Kenmore - Fine Needlework", Japan **9.00**
   Sewing Circle, 4 ladies sewing, 6 needle packets and threader **10.00**
Needle case, egg shape, wood, mkd "The Columbian Egg," Germany, orig needles **155.00**
Pincushion
   Apple, satin, red and yellow, green leaves and stem, 2-1/2" h, 3" d **65.00**
   Calico Dog, holding flower pin cushion, mkd "Made in Japan," 3" l, 2-1/4" h **30.00**
   Chinese figures surrounding cushion **35.00**
   Victorian, velvet, fruits and flowers **35.00**
Quilt frame, large, fancy scroll work ends **150.00**

Sewing machine, Household *brand, orig cabinet with some updating, "Household" spelled out in wrought iron sides and on lift-off cover, $85.*

Scissors, emb florals on handle, German **30.00**
Sewing bird, gilt finish, pin cushion **180.00**
Sign, Coats & Clark's Quality Threads, porcelain **900.00**
Spool, woolen, mill type, 8-1/2" h, old blue paint **10.00**
Tape Measure, figural
   Apple, hard plastic, red, leaf pull ..**24.00**
   Dress form **50.00**
Thimble holder, carved acorn **70.00**
Tracing Paper, Singer, unopened back, c1960 ....**4.00**

❖ Shaving Mugs

"Shave and a hair cut, 2 bits!" Oh how we'd love to pay those prices again. And probably finding a barber who still uses old-fashioned shaving mugs might just be harder than finding vintage shaving mugs at a flea market. There are several different types of shaving mugs, fraternal, generic, scuttles. By far the most popular are the occupational style mugs, made exclusively for use in barbershops in the United States. Introduced shortly after the Civil War, they were still being made into the 1930s. Unlike shaving mugs used at home, these mugs typically had the owner's name in gilt. The mug was kept in a rack at the barbershop, and it was used only when the owner came in for a shave. Occupational shaving mugs, which have a hand-painted scene depicting the owner's line of work, are especially prized.

References: Ronald S. Barlow, *Vanishing American Barber Shop*, Windmill Publishing, 1993; Keith E. Estep, *The Best of Shaving Mugs*, Schiffer Publishing, 2001; —, *Shaving Mug and Barber Bottle Book*, Schiffer Publishing, 1995.

Shaving Mug, C.F. Shaeffer, black background, white china, worn gold trim, mkd "T & V Limoges," $40.

Collectors' Club: National Shaving Mug Collectors Assoc., 1608 Mineral Spring Rd., Reading, PA 19602-2229.

Museums: Atwater Kent History Museum, Philadelphia, PA; Barber Museum, Canal Winchester, OH; Lightner Museum, Saint Augustine, FL.

For additional listings, see *Warman's Antiques and Collectibles Price Guide* and *Warman's English & Continental Pottery & Porcelain.*

Floral and scrolls, transfer design, late 19th C., 3-3/4" h **45.00**
Forget Me Not, transfer design, Germany, 3" h **45.00**
Fraternal
   Loyal Order of the Moose, gold circle with gray moose head, purple and green floral dec, gilt rim and base, mkd "Germany" **220.00**
   United Mine Workers, clasped hands emblem flanked by crossed picks and shovels, floral dec, rose garland around top, mkd "Germany" ...**125.00**
Milk glass, 1927 Mercedes, mkd Surrey, with shaving brush, 3-1/4" h **8.00**
Occupational, hand-painted
   Finish carpenter, man planing a board, name above, floral sprigs on sides, handle crack, 3-3/4" h **357.50**
   Hotel Clerk, clerk at desk, guest signing register **375.00**
   Shoemaker, hp, scene of shoemaker in shop, gilt foot and swags around name **195.00**
   Writer, black desk inkwell with sander, pen, and brass handle **350.00**
Patriotic, flying bald eagle with U.S. flag and leaves/berries in claws, gilt ribbon across flag with name, wear, 3-1/2" h **220.00**
Scuttle
   Coronation of H M King Edward VII, 18th May 1937, British seal with monarch, flags on reverse **40.00**

Fish shape, green and brown **75.00**

❖ Shawnee Pottery

From 1937 until 1961, Shawnee Pottery operated in Zanesville, Ohio. The company made kitchenwares, dinnerware, and some art pottery. Two of their most recognized patterns are Corn Queen and Corn King.

References: Susan and Al Bagdade, *Warman's American Pottery and Porcelain*, Wallace-Homestead, 1994; Jim and Bev Mangus, *Shawnee Pottery*, Collector Books, 1994, 1998 value update; Mark Supnick, *Collecting Shawnee Pottery*, L-W Book Sales, 2000.

Collectors' Club: Shawnee Pottery Collectors Club, PO Box 713, New Smyrna Beach, FL 32170.

Bookends, pr, cattails and ducks....**75.00**
Bowl, 8-3/4" l, oval, Corn King, #95 **45.00**
Butter Dish, cov, 7" l, Corn King, mkd "#72, Oven Proof" **165.00**
Cookie jar
   Happy, Dutch boy **385.00**
   Mugsey, blue scarf, 11-3/4" h.....**600.00**
   Smiley Pig, tulip decor, 11-1/4" h
   ....**400.00**
Creamer
   Cat, yellow and green **55.00**
   Corn King, #70 ....**25.00**
   Puss-n-Boots...............................**85.00**
Figurine
   Goldfish, 3-1/4" h **16.00**
   Elephant, yellow, 3-1/4" h............**18.00**
   Frog, chip, 2-1/4" h **13.00**
Fruit Dish, 6" d, Corn King, #92 .....**40.00**
Incense Burner, 5" h, Chinaman, blue base, mkd "USA".........................**30.00**
Pie bird, Pillsbury, 5-1/2" h.............**85.00**

Shawnee Pottery cookie jar, Puss n' Boots, ivory, red bow, yellow bird, blue trim, $95.

Pitcher
   Bo Peep, 1940s, mkd "Patented Bo Peep USA".............................**195.00**
   Chanticleer **250.00**
Planter
   Deer and Fawn, 6" h, 6-1/2" w **27.50**
   Old Mill **25.00**
   Pixie Boot, green, gold trim..........**15.00**
   Polynesian Girl, 5-3/4" h, #896 ....**35.00**
Salt and pepper shakers, pr
   Corn King, tall **35.00**
   Milk Can, 3-1/4" h.......................**24.00**
   Puss-n-Boots...............................**75.00**
   Smiley Pig, 3-1/4" h......................**75.00**
Spoon Holder, flower pot, mkd "patent pending" **15.00**
Sugar Shaker, White Corn **55.00**
Teapot, Granny Ann **175.00**
Wall pocket, Wheat.......................**35.00**

❖ Sheet Music

Here's a topic that might get you humming along. Sheet music is especially popular today, perhaps because the nostalgic appeal of the old tunes or the interesting cover art. You might want to check that old piano bench to see what titles are stored there.

Periodical: *The Rag Times*, 15522 Ricky Court, Grass Valley, CA 95949.

Collectors' Clubs: City of Roses Sheet Music Collectors Club, 13447 Bush St. SE, Portland, OR 97236; National Sheet Music Society, 1597 Fair Park Ave., Los Angeles, CA 90041; New York Sheet Music Society, PO Box 354, Hewlett, NY 11557; Remember That Song, 5623 N 64th St., Glendale, AZ 85301; Sonneck Society for American Music & Music in America, PO Box 476, Canton, MA 02021.

Sheet Music, France We Have Not Forgotten You, words by Grant Clarke and Howard E. Rogers, music by Milton Ager, published by Leo. Feist, Inc., $10.

Any Bonds Today, Irving Berlin **16.00**
A Woman In Love, Guys & Dolls, photo of Brandy & Sinatra **25.00**
Blue Christmas, 1964 ....**2.50**
Coast Guard Forever **15.00**
Couldn't Sleep A Wink Last Night....**12.50**
Down Yonder, Spade Copley **10.00**
Father of the Land We Love, 1931 ....**8.00**
Five Minutes More **12.50**
Gone With The Wind.......................**12.50**
Heart of My Heart, 1926 ....**3.75**
It's Always You **12.50**
Keep 'Em Flying **15.00**
Lady Madonna, Beatles **18.00**
Love & Marriage **12.50**
No Orchids For My Lady.................**15.00**
Now Is The Hour, Bing Crosby **12.00**
One Zy, Two-Zy, 1964 ....**12.00**
Paper Doll, Sinatra.........................**15.00**
Sleigh Ride in June, 1944.................**4.50**
The Marines' Hymn, 1942...............**15.00**
Thicker than Water, Andy Gibbs **4.00**
Welcome Back, John Sebastian........**4.00**
White Christmas, 1942 ....**4.50**

❖ Shelley China

The Shelley China Company has been in business in Longton, England, since the mid 18th century, producing figurines and dinnerware. Many of the dinnerware patterns are known for interesting shapes. Expect to find a variety of decoration and marks since this firm has been around for so long.

Collectors' Club: National Shelley China Club, 5585 NW 164th Ave., Portland, OR 97229.

Bowl, 10" d, 3" h, satin glaze, abstract design...**150.00**
Bread and Butter Plate, Rock Garden
   ....**115.00**
Cake Plate, Charm, Richmond shape, tab handles trimmed in gold.........**90.00**
Creamer and sugar, Meisenette **95.00**
Cup and saucer
   Country Garden, pattern #2500, Ludlow shape **85.00**
   Maytime, pattern #13452, Henley shape, beige trim....................**155.00**
   Morning Glory, Dainty shape........**85.00**
   Orange pattern **170.00**
   Scilla, pattern #2511 ....**85.00**
   Shamrock pattern........................**85.00**
   Syringa pattern...........................**85.00**
Demitasse cup and saucer
   Begonia, pattern #13427.............**85.00**
   Red Rose & Daisy, pattern #12425
   ....**85.00**
   Rosebud, pattern #13291 ....**85.00**
Dinner Plate
   Harebell, 10-3/4" d **70.00**
   Rose Spray, #13545 ....**190.00**

Eggcup, Rose **18.00**
Gravy boat and underplate, Dainty Blue
....**525.00**
Luncheon plate, Blue Rock, 8-1/4" d
....**75.00**
Pin dish, Regency, Dainty shape, sq, tab
handle, gold trim **65.00**
Place setting, Block pattern, #11787,
yellow, black, and silver, 3 pcs ...**380.00**
Platter, medium, Dainty, blue **350.00**
Teapot, cov, Rosebud pattern, Dainty
shape **395.00**
Teaset, Woodlands pattern, teapot, plate,
two cups and saucers, milk jug, sugar
....**750.00**
Toothpick holder, Stocks, 2-1/8" h, 2-
1/8" d...**70.00**
Vase, Japanese Lake Scene, #4142, 3-
1/2" h...**150.00**

❖ Shoe-Related Collectibles

Perhaps you know the old woman who lives in a shoe, or just like to buy shoes! Whatever the reason, flea markets can be a great place to find nifty additions to a shoe collection.

Bronzed baby shoe, c1955............**10.00**
Charm, baby shoe, silvertone, 1/2" l.**3.50**
Comic book, shoe store give away,
Porky Pig, Lobel's Shoe Store imprint
on back cover, #71, 1951 copyright
....**24.00**
Cookie jar, Old Woman in a Shoe, Fitz &
Floyd, 1986 ....**165.00**
Ink blotter, Culliman Shoe Hospital, J.L.
Vick, Prop, 1930s, unused, 3" x 6".**4.00**
Miniature, man's cordovan wingtip,
French Shriner & Urner Men's Shoes,
5-1/4" l..**65.00**
Pinback button, Dottie Dimple, D.P.
Ramsdell Sweet & Co., celluloid, wear,
1-1/8" dia....................................**50.00**

Pair of child's shoes, worn brown leather uppers with 6 black buttons, black bottoms, $35.

Planter, ceramic, wooden shoe shape,
white, red tulips dec, gold trim **12.50**
Shoe
Fenton, milk glass, 4-1/4" h..........**33.00**
Occupied Japan, porcelain, 2-1/2" l**4.00**
Porcelain, red roses decor, 8" l....**28.00**
Wright, L.G., amber glass **25.00**
Trade card, Tappan's Shoes, motif of 2
bare feet **15.00**

❖ Shot Glasses

Here's a flea market collectible that's almost always available. Watch for interesting sets of shot glasses with their original decanter or those boxed in an unusual way. Souvenir shot glasses have always been a popular memento to take home. They are usually plentiful and reasonably priced.

Adam's Rodeo, blue lettering, 2-1/2" h
....**15.00**
Baltimore Orioles, clear glass, orange
and black lettering **4.50**
Crackle glass, 3-1/8" h **15.00**
Frosted, flamenco dancers and drink
recipes, Federal, 2 oz....................**5.00**
Glass, etched floral design..............**8.00**
Harvard, red lettering **5.00**
Hotel Dupont, Wilmington, DE, clear
glass, white lettering **4.50**
Mug, ring handle **1.50**
Say When!, frosted, 4 humorous
illustrations, Anchor Hocking..........**7.50**
Souvenir of Detroit, shows Model T,
frosted, Anchor Hocking, 2 oz........**5.00**
Sterling sliver, 1930s **80.00**
Traveling set, four silver plated shot
glasses, fitted leather case with snap
....**35.00**

❖ Signs

Advertising signs have been a staple of flea markets for many years. With the many signs available, great examples can be found in all price ranges and made from different types of materials. Bright colors and appealing graphics are important, but condition is always critical.

For additional listings, see *Warman's Advertising Price Guide.*

Atlantic, pump sign, porcelain, white
letters on red ground, 9" x 13" **90.00**
Barber Shop, porcelain flange, 12" x 24"
....**260.00**
Bell System, Public Telephone, bell logo
in center, porcelain flange, 18" sq
....**275.00**
Cetacolor, "Not a Soap, Prevents Wash
Good from Fading, 10 cents Package,"
graphic of Gibson style girl, linen,
framed, 36" x 12" **125.00**

Sign, The Leading Line, Shell Motor Oil, early auto race, tin litho, some damage, $65.

Columbia Records, cardboard,
Columbia Phonograph cylinder
packages on either side of highly emb
American eagle standing stop stars
and stripes shield, 11" x 14-1/2" **200.00**
Columbian Rope, linen, seaman
carrying coil of rope, 49" x 29-1/2"
....**325.00**
Edgemont Tobacco, linen, shows two
colorful packages, framed, 36" x 12"
....**70.00**
Entrance, reverse-painted glass, 3-3/4" x
18" **22.00**
Helmar Turkish Cigarettes, porcelain,
24" x 12".......................................**80.00**
Independence Indemnity Insurance, tin
litho, 15" x 18" **55.00**
Masury's House Paints, reverse glass,
corner sign, "Masury's Pure Linseed
Oil House Paints," wood frame, 21" x
16-1/2"..**275.00**
"Men" and "Women," porcelain, 2-
sided, red on white ground, each 7" x
20"...**110.00**
**Nu-Wood Insulating Wall Board and
Lath**, porcelain, house among trees,
mfg. by Veribrite Signs, 22-1/2" x 35"
....**100.00**
Red Coon, Sun Cured Chewing Tobacco,
heavy paper, red and black raccoon,
yellow ground, black lettering, 18" x 22"
....**60.00**
Segal Key, double sided, diecut tin litho,
key shape, 31" l..........................**170.00**
Street sign
Dead end, yellow and black, bullet
holes **5.00**
Stop, red and white **45.00**
Vienna Pudding, paper, comical dinner
guests looking as family dog runs
between butler's legs, spilling the
Vienna Pudding, border trimmed, 12-
1/4" x 9".......................................**80.00**

❖ Silhouette Pictures

Silhouette of lady in full skirt raking leaves, young boy carrying basket, fall trees in golden background, rect, convex glass covering, gold and brown herringbone border on edges, $15.

Silhouette pictures are decorative plaques with rounded or convex frames over a black image. Having foil or colored backgrounds, they were a later generation's answer to the old hand-cut silhouettes, thus the name.

Dresser box, wood, red metal trim, large heart shaped cut-out on top with dancing silhouettes, lined int. with mirror, 8-1/2" x 6-1/2", wear **50.00**

Picture, convex glass type
Equestrian jumping fence.............**40.00**
Fairies, painted background, 1929
....**35.00**
Girl with doll **30.00**
Hearts, shows suitor, mkd "Deltex"
....**24.00**
Lady, seated at vanity, hairbrush in hand...**40.00**
Lady with bird in cage, pale pink background, silver stars, 8-3/4" x 10-1/2" **60.00**
Lovebirds, boy courting girl, 2 lovebirds watching, foil accents on dress and boy's suit..................................**30.00**
Victorian couple..........................**40.00**

❖ Silver, Plated and Sterling

Every flea market has great examples of silver in sterling and also silver plate. Look for hallmarks and maker's mark to determine the age of a piece, its silver content, and perhaps the country of origin. Also check for signs of silver polish hidden in crevices, often an indication that a piece has been polished for years. When examining plated silver, some wear is acceptable if it doesn't detract from the overall appearance.

For additional listings, see *Warman's Antiques and Collectibles Price Guide.*

Silver Plate

Bank, clown with umbrella **35.00**

Candelabra, pr, 3-light, tapering stem issuing central urn-form candle-cup and two scrolling branches supporting wax pan and conforming candle-cup, oval foot with reeded border, vertical flutes, Continental, 12" h **150.00**
Champagne bucket, cylindrical, bracket handles, applied scroll border band, monogram, Simpson, Hall, Miller & Co., 9" h **275.00**
Child's mug, two handles, engraved
....**30.00**
Entree Dish, oval, gadrooned rim, detachable foliage handles, monogrammed, American, 11-1/2" l
....**80.00**
Meat dome, Victorian, bright cut with panel of foliage swags and roses, beaded base edge, twisted branch handle, monogram, maker's mark, 18" x 10-1/2" **250.00**
Punch bowl, cylindrical, reeded circular foot, applied flowers at rim, International Silver, 12" d **200.00**
Toast rack **45.00**
Tray, rectangular, center chased with scrolls, trellis, and foliage, gadrooned and foliate handles, English, 27" l
....**150.00**

Sterling silver candlesticks, pr, English silver, Crighton Bros., London, & New York," 1916, $825

Notice how the hallmarks are on impressed into the sterling silver base, along with the maker's name, "Crichton Bros, London, & New York," "K. F. Merle-Smith" is engraved.

Wine cooler stand, Art Deco, Reed & Barton......................................**200.00**

Silver, Sterling

Baby spoon, ornate curled handle
Cupid...**65.00**
Mother Goose **60.00**
Basket, reticulated, sides with scrolls and diapering, scroll rim, three scroll feet, fluted base, monogrammed, Whiting Mfg Co., 9" dia **460.00**
Child's mug, single handle, engraved bands, monogram **45.00**
Cigarette/dompact case, chain, allover scrolling **110.00**
Creamer, tapered cylindrical, short spout, scroll handle with shell terminal, applied stepped base, monogrammed, Paul Storr, London, 1831, side mkd "Storr & Mortimer," 2-7/8" h **200.00**
Glove hook, ornate handle **30.00**
Grape shears, grape motif dec.......**90.00**
Nail file, head of woman as handle, 6-1/2" l **30.00**
Punch Ladle, scrolling foliage, monogrammed, 9-1/2" l.............**100.00**
Salad serving fork and spoon, Chambord pattern, Reed & Barton, monogrammed, 9" l....................**200.00**
Teapot, Kingston pattern, Wallace **250.00**
Travel Clock, plain rect case with rounded corners, eight-day movement, oct goldtone engine-turned face, black Roman numerals, silver surround with engine turning, engraved scrolls and floral sprays, monogrammed cover, Wm Kerr & Co., 3-5/8" l.............**200.00**
Whistle, chain, Reed and Barton, sterling, MIB **45.00**

Sterling silver sugar spoon, engraving in bowl, handle engraved flowers and foliage, monogrammed, mkd "Sterling," English hallmarks, $35.

❖ Skateboards

Whooosh, skateboarding around a flea market would be too fast to spot all the great buys. However, if you're in the market for a vintage skateboard, you'll want to slow down, so you don't miss a good buy. Look for early wooden boards with bold graphics.

Reference: Ryhn Noll, *Skateboard Retrospective, A Collector's Guide,* Schiffer Publishing, 2000.

Black Night, wood, graphic of Black Night, clay wheels, 1960s, 22" l, 5-3/4" w.................................**55.00**
Butcher block style, wood, Power Paw red plastic wheels, 23-1/2" l, 6-1/2" w **32.00**
Charlie's Angels, Jill, 1977 ....**45.00**
Hawaii Super Surfer, wood, graphics of Hawaii Islands and "Hawaii" painted on top, clay wheels...........................**50.00**
Pro-Line 66-99, see-thru gold plastic, Jacksonville, FL...........................**65.00**
Roller Derby, Mustang 15, blue, gold trim, horse graphic, ball bearing wheels, 21" l, 5" w.......................**55.00**
Valterra Dragon, wood, 27" l, 8" w .**20.00**

❖ Sleds

You won't find the infamous "Rose Bud" sled at a flea market, but you might be able to find some other interesting examples. There are many variations of sleds, some made for boys, girls, singles, doubles, and even some with wheels for those who lived in "snowless" climates. Don't overlook sled-related collectibles.

Inkstand, brass, sled figural, glass well **195.00**
Pencil box, sled shape, wooden, 8-1/2" l **200.00**
Postcard, Christmas Greetings, 2 children on sled, 1915 postmark..**15.00**
Sled, wooden
  Dog oval decal and "Wagner Make," 30-1/2" l **300.00**
  Flexible Flyer, No. 60J, 1960s, 60" l **40.00**

A great selection of wood sleds, imported from Germany, they were tagged at $35 each or 2 for $80.

Rocket Plane, Flexible Flyer type, 51" l **55.00**
"Hustler" painted on red ground .**360.00**
Running horse design, 19th C., 26" l **150.00**

❖ Slot Machines

The first slot machine, the Liberty Bell, was developed by Charles Fey in San Francisco in 1905. Advancements were made through the years by several of the manufacturers. Some were enhancements to the playing action, others to prevent players from cheating.

Periodicals: *Antique Amusements Slot Machines & Jukebox Gazette*, 909 26th St NW, Washington, DC 20037; *C.O.C.A. Times*, 3712 W Scenic Ave, Mequon, WI 539092; *Co-Op Newsletter*, 909 26th St, NW, Washington, DC 20037.

Groetchen, Columbia, c1936, three reel, high maintenance, 25 cent.........**500.00**
Jennings
  Little Duke, 1933, orig cond. ...**3,500.00**
  Standard Chief, 10 cent **1,2100.00**
Mills
  Lion Head, 1932, 25 cent, restored **3,000.00**
  Puritan Bell, c1925, cash register design, 5 cent, 8" h, 8" w........**700.00**
  War Eagle, 1931, 25-cent, restored **3,200.00**
Pace, All Star Comet, c1936, three reel, side mint vendor, 5 cent..........**1,400.00**
Wattling, Rol-A-Top, twin jackpot, back doesn't open............................**2,420.00**

❖ Smokey Bear Collectibles

Since 1947, Smokey Bear has been telling us, "Remember, only you can prevent forest fires." The character was created by the U.S. Forest Service in 1944, when he appeared on a poster warning of the dangers of forest fires, which threatened the country's lumber supply during World War II. The lovable character, always seen with his campaign hat, starred in an animated television show from 1969 to 1971.

Shopping bag, plastic, "Prevent Forest Fires, Smokey Has For Fifty Years," $.50.

Ashtray set, aluminum, 4 pc, embossed image of Smokey, 4" dia..............**20.00**
Bank, ceramic, Norcrest, Japan **195.00**
Coloring book, *Smokey Bear's Story of the Forest*, Florida Forest Service, 1959, 15 pgs, unused **25.00**
Comic book, *The True Story of Smokey Bear*, 1969..................................**25.00**
Hand puppet, plush, Ideal, 1965 ..**195.00**
Pinback button, I'm Smokey's Helper, 2-3/4" dia **4.50**
Plush figure, hard plastic hat, Dakin tag, 1985 ....**65.00**
Salt and pepper shakers, figural, Norcrest, Japan, 3-3/4" h, pr........**55.00**
Sign, "Prevent Forest Fires," 1960s, 18" x 24"..**195.00**

Smokey Bear bookmark, Smokey holding sign in front of boy and girl, heavy paper, yellow and brown, $2.

❖ Smurf

Smurfs made their debut in 1958, as secondary characters for a story illustrated by Pierre Culliford, better known as Peyo. It wasn't long for these little blue guys and gals were taking center stage. Collectors know to watch for figurines, toys, records, and other Smurf memorabilia at flea markets.

Collectors' Club: Smurf Collectors Club International 24 Cabot Road W. Massapequa, NY 11758.

Web site: www.smurf.com

Smurfs Mug, Super Smurf, white, red, black, yellow, and turquoise dec, $5.

Animation cel, matted, mkd "#240 21 65," 11" x 14" **95.00**
Card game, 1982, MIB..................**12.00**
Dexterity puzzle, Smurf girl shooting Pez into Papa Smurf's mouth, green case, European, 1980s.....................**10.00**
Figure
    Olympic Smurf.............................**40.00**
    Smurf with Go-Cart, MIB.............**15.00**
    Super Smurf, with hobby horse, MIB **15.00**
Key chain, figural, 2-1/4" h **5.00**
Lunch box, plastic, Thermos Co., 1987, no thermos **32.00**
Mushroom cottage, Peyo Schleich, orig box, description in English, French and German, 1970s, MIB..................**55.00**
Ornament, wearing red hat, 1978.....**1.25**
Pez
    Boy, blue stem................................**3.00**
    Papa, red stem **3.00**
    Smurfeette, yellow stem **14.00**
Puppet, hand, Pecor, 1981 ....**12.00**
Stuffed toy
    Amour Smurf **12.00**
    Baby Smurf, pink, 16" l.................**25.00**
    Baseball Smurf, baseball shirt, baseball in hand, orig side tag, 1982 ....**12.00**
    Blue, 1979, 16" h.........................**20.00**
    Papa, sitting, 10" h, soiled..............**6.00**
    Smurfette......................................**12.00**
    St. Patrick's Day **14.00**
    Sweetheart Valentine **12.00**
Telephone, mkd "H.G. Toys," 1982, numbers faded, slight wear **20.00**
Wind-up toy, blue and white, mkd "Wallace Berry Co., Hong Kong," 1980 ....**12.00**

❖ Snack Sets

A snack set is the combination of a plate or tray with an indent to hold a cup. Perfect for a snack in front of that new invention, television, or perhaps just the item to serve refreshments on the patio. Many glass and

Snack set bridge motif, 2 snack plates, 3 cups, teapot, orange luster ground, mkd "Occupied Japan," $45.

dinnerware services included these items in the 1950s. Whole sets can be found in original boxes, perhaps attesting to the fact that although they were a great wedding present, the idea never really caught on.

Periodical: *Snack Set Searchers,* PO Box 158, Hallock, MN 56728.

Anchor Hocking
    Fleurette, 8 pcs in orig box, some damage to box..........................**18.00**
    Grape, clear, grape and leaf design, orig box.....................................**26.50**
    Primrose, Anchorglass, milk glass, 11" l plate, 8 pc set **25.00**
Bavaria, bone china, purple roses dec, 7-1/2" d plate...............................**15.00**
California Pottery, bright orange, 1960s, 4 pcs, orig sticker "Cal-Style Ceramics Torrance Calif #2433"...................**40.00**
Federal, Yorktown, orig boxed set ...**16.00**
Fire-King, Soreno, green, 9-3/4" d plate, 2-1/2" h cup **5.00**
Hand painted, pink flowers with yellow centers, green leaves, gold edge, artist sgd "G. H. T. 1940," 8-1/2" x 7-1/4" plate, 3-1/2" d x 1-7/8" h cup **27.50**
Hazel Atlas
    Capri Sea Shell pattern, light blue**18.00**
    Sea Shell, crystal, 10" x 6-1/2" tray, 3-1/2" d x 2-1/2" h cup................**22.50**
Lefton, Golden Wheat, 8" snack plate with tab handle, low scalloped ftd cub, gold trim **12.50**
Noritake, kidney shaped plate, white, blue luster trim, black lines, black floral dec, green mark, 8-1/2" x 7" plate, 3-1/4" h cup **35.00**
Porcelain, Oriental design, purple, red, gold, light blue, yellow, and olive green, 8" d plate **15.00**
Shelley, Flowers of Gold, pattern #141287, Dainty shape **130.00**

Paneled Grape pattern snack set, white milk glass, four cups and snack plates, $40.

Steubenville, Woodfield pattern, 2 Tropic Green, 2 Salmon Pink, 4 Dove Gray, 9" plate, 4-1/4" w x 2-1/2" h cup, 16 pc set, one chipped plate..................**60.00**

❖ Snow Globes

Some folks refer to these as snow globes, others prefer the name snowdomes. Whatever you call them, the fun is to shake the paperweight-type ball and see the snow fly through the water and swirl around the featured character. Many companies created snow globes over the years. The objects remain a popular souvenir for tourists.

Periodical: *Roadside Attractions,* 7553 Norton Ave., Apt 4., Los Angeles, CA 90046.

Collectors' Club: Snowdome Collectors Club, PO Box 53262, Washington, DC 20009.

For additional listings, see *Warman's Americana & Collectibles.*

Berta Hummel, Tree Trimming Time**68.00**
Betty Boop, musical, plays "Red Roses for a Blue Lady," 1995 ....**55.00**
Chevrolet 1958 Corvette, musical, plays "Little Red Corvette," white base with Chevy logo, Westland, MIB..........**45.00**
Cherub kneels in prayer, licensed by Kristen Haynes, Westland **15.00**
Christmas ornament, penguin with top hat and scarf standing on top of ball **7.50**
Coca-Cola, Heritage Collection, polar bear scene, authorized seal, plays Coke theme, retired 1996.............**60.00**
Disney 75th Anniversary, fiber optics **75.00**
Easter Bunny train, Glama, retired, 4" l **10.00**
Happy bunny with chick, Glama, 3" h **10.00**
Little girl gazing at rose, resin pedestal base, Westland, MIB **20.00**
Little Mermaid, Ursula....................**48.00**
Make Your Own, plastic **5.00**
Santa, toyshop background.............**20.00**
Souvenir, Florida, coral, tethered fish, rect **6.00**

Teletubbies 36.00
Winnie the Pooh............................30.00
Yogi Bear 3.00

❖ Soakies

These character soakies were for sale at Renninger's Flea Market, Adamstown, PA, all valued at $10.

Remember those great figural plastic bottles we got bubble bath in when we were kids? Collectors happily relive those days as they search flea markets for those bottles, now called "soakies."

Alvin Chipmunk, red 20.00
Beauty and the Beast....................5.00
Bozo Clown 35.00
Bugs Bunny, some paint loss 25.00
Casper Ghost 35.00
Chewbacca 10.00
Cinderella, movable arms.............25.00
Deputy Dawg, small......................20.00
Dick Tracy, crack at neck 25.00
Dopey Dwarf.................................25.00
Dum Dum......................................65.00
Elmer Fudd 35.00
Frankenstein 95.00
Mickey Mouse, lots of wear to paint.5.00
Might Mouse, small 25.00
Pinocchio......................................25.00
Pluto, with hat 25.00
Santa Claus 10.00
Squiddly Diddly............................75.00

Left to right: Woody, Bugs, Deputy Dog, Alvin, Goofy, Pluto, Mighty Mouse at top, each $8.

Sylvester Cat, some paint loss.......35.00

Tennessee Tuxedo 45.00
Topcat, red or blue vest 45.00
Wendy Witch................................45.00
Woody Woodpecker 25.00

❖ Soap Collectibles

If you're not into cleaning up with soakies, how about some soap collectibles. Again, flea markets are a great place to find all kinds of ephemera relating to soap, as well as some great examples of vintage soap. Don't overlook vintage illustrations used in advertising.

Box
  Aristocat Kitten Soap, 1970s, Avon
  ....65.00
  Peets Washing Machine Soap, goat
  image, 6" x 5 3/8" 125.00
  White King, lg, 1933.....................25.00
Brochure, Larkin Soap, 1885..........17.50
Door push, Crystal White Soap, metal, white lettering on dark blue ground, 3-1/2" w, 8-3/4" h..........................235.00
Pocket mirror, Lava Soap, celluloid centered by image of gray soap bar, opened container box, yellow ground, early 1900s.................................35.00
Ruler, Glory Soap Chips, folding, celluloid, Swift & Co., trademark, 1919 calendar, 5-1/2" l 35.00
Shipping crate, Castile Soap, Chicago, 1900, wooden, paper label..........10.00
Soap, Goblin Soap, wrapped bar, orig box, graphics both sides 30.00
Tin, Pax Soap, rooster, Packwood Mfg. Co., St Louis, 1940, 5-1/2" x 3-1/4" 28.00
Trade card, Babbitts Soap, "A Thing of Worth is a Joy Forever," Uncle Sam among men comparing Babbitts Soap to gold 9.00

❖ Social Cause Collectibles

Here's a topic where a collectors find memorabilia related to their favorite cause. Feel free to interpret this area as you see fit, for isn't that what social causes are all about?

Reference: William A. Sievert, *All For the Cause: Campaign Buttons For Social Change, 1960s-1990s*, Decoy Magazine, 1997.

Badge, "Old Newsboys Day Globe-Democrat Fund For Children," attached purple ribbon, gold lettered text "Old Newsboy," c1960 ....7.50
Flicker card, "The Tin Woodman," Heart

Assn premium, colorful image pointing to his heart "Take Care Of Your Heart," Heart Assn inscription on back, c1960, 2-1/4" x 3-1/4", ...35.00
Key chain, Good Will 2.50
Lapel pin, gold, drop shape, Red Cross
....5.00
Pinback button
  Eat Grapes, purple grapes, white
  ground, c1970............................8.00
  Flowers for Peace, orange psychedelic
  lettering, yellow background, 1-3/4" d
  ....40.00
  Keep the Faith Baby, Adam Clayton
  Powell, c1960 ....12.00
  I Support Lesbian and gay Rights,
  black and white, dark pink heart,
  Texas, c1960.............................10.00
  Support the Equal Rights amendment,
  dark blue n white 10.00
  Take a Hippie to Lunch, black lettering,
  bright yellow ground, 1-1/2" d...15.00

❖ Soda

Getting thirsty? Collectors from around the country tend to call carbonated beverages by different names—it's "soda" to some, "soda pop" to others, and "pop" in other regions. Whatever your passion, flea markets are a great place to find collectibles that will "wet your whistle."

Periodical: *Club Soda,* PO Box 489, Troy, IN 83871.

Collectors Clubs: Dr. Pepper 10-2-4 Collectors Club, 3508 Mockingbird, Dallas, TX 75205; Grapette Collectors Club, 2240 Highway 27N, Nashville, AR 71852; National Pop Can Collectors, PO Box 7862, Rockford, IL 61126; Painted Soda Bottle Collectors Association, 9418 Hilmer Drive, La Mesa, CA 91942; Root Beer Float, PO Box 571, Lake Geneva, WI 53167.

For additional listings, see *Warman's Advertising Price Guide.*

Blackboard, Frostie Root Beer, tin, 1950s 75.00
Calendar, 1947, Squirt, 25" h 300.00

Soft Drink Collectibles, cooler, Canada Dry, metal, white enamel, navy trim, red logo, orig handle, rust and wear, $25.

  Can, Dad's Root Beer, tin, conetop,

1940s-50s, qt **155.00**
Cooler, Drink Dr. Pepper, airline style, 16" h, 18" w, 9" d....................**190.00**
Counter Bin, 9" x 13-3/4" x 4-1/4", Quaker Brand Salted Peanuts **42.00**
Coupon, Hires Root Beer, druggist stamp on front, 1-3/4" x 3" **95.00**
Door pull, Enjoy Kist Beverages, Here's Refreshment, litho tin **66.00**
Fan, 75 Years Good, Dr. Pepper, Good For Life, cardboard....................**143.00**
Mug, Buckeye Root Beer, cearmic, figural handle, cracks, chips, 6-1/4" h **22.00**
Playing cards, Dr. Pepper, 1946, woman in red dress, 10-2-4 logo in corner, orig box....................................**385.00**
Sidewalk marker, Enjoy Grapette, Walk Safely, brass, round, 1940s-50s...**50.00**
Sign
    Ask For Orange-Crush Carbonated Beverage, embossed tin, 1940s, 12" x 20"......................................**165.00**
    Drink Barq's, It's Good, embossed tin, 12" x 30" **100.00**
    Drink Canada Dry, metal flange, white shield with crown, chips, scratches, 14-1/2" x 17-1/2"....................**100.00**
    Drink Orange-Crush, Naturally - It Tastes Better, orange ground, 1940s-50s, 40" sq............................**250.00**
    Drink Sun Spot, tin, 9-3/4" x 12" **185.00**
    Dr. Pepper, tin, bottle-cap shape, 10-2-4 logo, 24" dia........................**410.00**
    Enjoy Orange Crush, celluloid, 9" dia **75.00**
Thermometer
    Cheer Up by bottle, round with dial, 12" dia..**495.00**
    Drink NuGrape Soda, A Flavor You Can't Forget, tin, rounded top and bottom, shows 6 bottles, 16" x 6-3/4" **100.00**

❖ Soda Fountain

Soda fountains are another icon of a bygone era. However, a variety of soda fountain collectibles draw keen interest on today's collectibles market.

Collectors' Club: National Association of Soda Jerks, PO Box 115, Omaha, NE 68101; The Ice Screamers, PO Box 465, Warrington, PA 18976.

Ashtray, Breyers, 90th Anniversary, 1866-1956 ....**22.00**
Barbie, Soda Fountain Sweetheart Barbie, Coca-Cola, 1st in series, MIB **250.00**
Can, Abbott's Ice Cream, half gallon, Amish girl, c1940 ....**15.00**
Dispenser, Buckeye Root Beer, tree trunk shape, minor chips............**375.00**

Soda Fountain Collectibles, hat, paper, Showalter's Ice Cream and Dairy Products, green lettering, $5.

Display Card, 5" x 8-1/2", 7-Up, diecut cardboard, full color image of infant in red playsuit, copyright 1950 ....**15.00**
Glass, Hershey's, clear, 5-3/4" h, pr**22.00**
Jar, Borden's Malted Milk, glass ...**175.00**
Magazine Cover, *Saturday Evening Post,* young soda jerk talking to girls at counter, Norman Rockwell, Aug 22, 1953 ....**15.00**
Menu, Rush's Luncheonette, 1955....**5.00**
Milkshake machine, Hamilton Beach, triple head, green **75.00**
Paper cone dispenser, glass tube, metal holder, "Soda Fountain Drinks & Ice Cream Served in Vortex," gold label, wall mount, 11" l **40.00**
Pinback button, Sanderson's Drug Store, blue and white, soda fountain glass illus, "Ice Cream, Soda/Choice Cigars/Fine Candies," 1901-12, 1" dia **28.00**
Seltzer bottle, cobalt, Babad's Miami Seltzer Co.................................**100.00**
Sign, Orange County Fountain, porcelain on steel, yellow oval center, blue and white lettering, dark blue ground**110.00**
Straw holder, pressed glass, clear Cradle shape, 1910s **250.00**
    Cylindrical, red metal lid, 1950s.**175.00**
Syrup jar, white porcelain, metal lid/pump, set of 4........................**125.00**
Tray, 13" x 11", Schuller's Ice Cream, ice cream sodas and cones.............**200.00**

❖ Souvenirs

Vacations are always too short. Maybe that's what compels us to bring home momentos of those days. Flea markets are a good place to look for souvenirs.

Ashtray
    Souvenir of New York City, metal, Statue of Liberty in the center, other landmarks around the edge, oval, 4-3/4" x 3-3/4" **15.00**
    Souvenir of Queen Elizabeth, metal, shows ship..............................**15.00**
Bank, Souvenir of Florida, ceramic, black boy on pig, 1940s-50s................**155.00**
Basket, Souvenir of Crosby, Minn.,

frosted, gold accents, 4-3/4" h **28.00**
Bathtub, Souvenir of Craig, Iowa, milk glass, molded legs, 5-1/4" l.........**27.50**
Candy Box, Steel Pier, Atlantic City, NJ **5.00**
Creamer and sugar, San Francisco, shows Golden Gate Bridge, dragonware, 2-3/4" h...................**35.00**
Handkerchief, Ocean City, NJ, printed seaside scene **5.00**
Pennant, Hershey Park, brown ground, white letters, c1950 ....**25.00**
Pillow cover
    Souvenir of Cheyenne, cowboy motif **20.00**
    Washington, D.C., verse, fringe, 12" sq **8.50**
Teabag holder, Souvenir of Florida, ceramic, teapot shape, chips, 4-1/4" x 3-1/4"..**4.00**
Tumbler, ruby stained, engraved "Gettysburg" **45.00**
Trade card, Souvenir of the Virginia Exposition, With Compliments of Walter A. Wood, shows log cabin with black banjo player, farm machinery.......**45.00**
View Master reel
    Alaska, 49th State, Sawyers **15.00**
    Beautiful Cypress Gardens, FL, Sawyer, #A961, 1958 ....**20.00**
    Brooklyn USA, 3 reels.................**40.00**
    France, Sawyers, sealed pack **15.00**
    Mexico, 1973, GAF, sealed pack..**15.00**

❖ Souvenir China

These porcelain souvenirs have images of the places or events. Early examples were hand-painted in England and Germany, specially made for merchants in the United States. Souvenir china can be found in a variety of forms, from ashtrays to plates to pitchers to vases.

Periodical: *Antique Souvenir Collectors News,* PO Box 562, Great Barrington, MA 01230.

For additional listings, see *Warman's Americana & Collectibles* and *Warman's Antiques and Collectibles Price Guide.*

Bank, Marion, VA, Smith County Courthouse, barrel shape, 3" h **80.00**
Box, cov, Rushville, IL, Wester School, black transfer, made by Wheelock ..**76.00**
Chamberstick, Brant Rock, MA, National Electric Signalling Co., From Bluefish Rock, Aladdin style, 2-1/4" h, 6-3/4" l **160.00**
Condiment Set, Gettysburg, 1863, hp, salt and pepper shakers, condiment jar with lid and spoon, 5-1/4" x 5-1/2" base, orange, yellow flowers, green leaves, gold, irid slate blue, and white accents, mkd "Nippon," 1930s......**28.00**

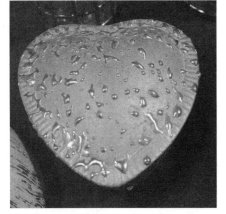

Souvenir China Box, heart shape, porcelain, gold texture, bottom mkd for 50th anniversary of Reading, PA, dept store, 1926-1964, $15.

Cup and Saucer, Niagara Falls, marked "Carlsbad, Austria" **18.00**

Demitasse Cup and Saucer, Hotel Roosevelt, New Orleans...............**35.00**

Plate

Along 101 The Redwood Highway, maroon, Vernon Kilns **25.00**

Baltimore & Ohio Railroad, Harpers Ferry, blue and white, 10-1/2" d...**95.00**

Birmingham, AL, The Industrial City, maroon, Vernon Kilns **22.00**

Boston, MA, Filene's, brown, Vernon Kilns...**22.00**

Carlsbad Caverns, White's City, New Mexico **25.00**

Delaware Tercentenary Celebration, 1938, black and white, Spode ..**35.00**

Denver, CO, state capital in center, blue, Vernon Kilns.....................**22.00**

Greenville, SC, blue, Vernon Kilns**22.00**

Luray Caverns, colorful center, gold rim **28.00**

Nevada, The Silver State, Hoover Dam in center, brown, Vernon Kilns..**22.00**

New Mexico, picture map **22.00**

San Diego County Fair, Delmar, CA, Don Diego Welcomes You, blue**35.00**

West Virginia, state capital in center, brown.......................................**22.00**

Williamsport, PA, The River And Market Street Bridge, made by Wheelock, 7-1/2" dia.....................................**60.00**

Match holder, Grand Falls, NE, cobalt, Germany **50.00**

Teapot, Little Falls, NY, High School, 5-1/2" h...**100.00**

Tip Tray, Hotel Coronado **15.00**

Toothpick holder, Alexandria, VA, Christ Church, 2-1/2" h **50.00**

Tumbler, Bridgton, ME, views of Public Library, Sunrise Rock and Scene From Ingalls Grove, 3-5/8" h...............**110.00**

Souvenir China Plate, Arizona, green dec on white ground, unmarked, $5.

Vase

Cripple Creek District, CO, The Independence Mine, cobalt, 2 handles, Germany, 3" h..........**130.00**

Lapeer, MI, Nepessing Street, 4-7/8" h **68.00**

❖ Souvenir Spoons

Collecting souvenir spoons has become more popular in the past few years. Collectors are starting to admire the tiny treasures often for their colorful decoration as well as the place they honor. The following is a sampling of sterling silver souvenir spoons.

Periodicals: *Spooners Forum*, c/o Bill Boyd, 7408 Englewood Lane, Raytown, MO 64133

Collectors' Club: American Spoon Collectors, 7408 Englewood Lane, Kansas City, MO 64133; Northeastern Spoon Collectors Guild, 52 Hillcrest Ave., Morristown, NJ 07960.

For additional listings, see *Warman's Americana & Collectibles*.

Souvenir spoon, Lancaster, PA, sterling, name in bowl, figural floral and sheaf handle, $15.

Souvenir spoon, Ocean City, NJ, sterling, demitasse size, enameled plaque with name, fish, $12.

Alaska Yukon Pacific Expo, emb "Alaska" on front, dog tem, huskies, and skagway on back, emb "A.Y.P. Expo, 1907," 5-1/2" l..................**115.00**

Atlantic City, oar shape, shows sailing ship and lighthouse, Codding Bros. & Heilborn, 4" l..............................**18.00**

Colorado Springs, script name in bowl, handle of columbine flowers, prospector, Balance Rock, state capitol crest, Federal post office and Mining Exchange on back.......................**55.00**

Houston, engraved in bowl, mkd "Wallace Silversmiths, Watson Co., Texas"...**45.00**

Lookout Mountain, Chattanooga, TN, Incline Railroad in bowl, floral pattern handle, 4" l **20.00**

Mormon Temple, Salt Lake City, engraved in bowl, block letters handle, 5-1/8" l...**45.00**

New York City, Statue of Liberty, city seal in bowl, Shiebler, 4-1/4" l......**75.00**

New York City skyline, Metropolitan Building engraved in bowl, Statue of Liberty, **Grants Tomb**, and Flat Iron building on back, mkd "Sterling," 3 hallmarks, 5-1/2" l **115.00**

San Diego Skyline, mission, fruit, Paye & Baker, Old Palms, 5-5/8" **59.00**

St Louis, Missouri, corn stalks, hay, "United We Stand, Divided We Fall," St. Louis engraved in bowl, American eagle and Justice on back, 5-1/2" l **85.00**

Summerville, SC, double-sided full-figured black man holding melon, engraved bowl **110.00**

Tacoma, WA, Old Church, gold-washed bowl, state handle, Mayer Bros., 5-3/8" l **29.00**

Vermillion, SD, gold-washed bowl, view of the university building, Whiting, 5" l **24.00**

❖ Space Adventurers, Fictional

Space adventurers have always fascinated folks, from Buck Rogers in 1929 to the eagerly awaited sequels to Star Trek. We're spellbound by their adventures—taken to new places and returned safely at the journey's end.

References: Karen O'Brien, *Toys & Prices 2004*, Krause Publications, 2003; Dana Cain, *UFO & Alien Collectibles Price Guide*, Krause Publications, 1999; Rex Miller, *The Investor's Guide to Vintage Character Collectibles*, Krause Publications, 1999; Stuart W. Wells, III, *Science Fiction*

Collectibles Identification & Price Guide, Krause Publications, 1998.

Collectors' Club: Galaxy Patrol, 22 Colton St., Worcester, MA 01610.

For additional listings, see *Warman's Americana & Collectibles.*

Activity Book, Battlestar Galactica, Wonder Books, Universal City Studios, Inc., unused **10.00**

Book

Buck Rogers, 25th Century A. D., Big Little Book, Whitman, 1938, Cocomalt premium **48.00**

Buck Rogers in the 25th Century, Kellogg's, 1932, 32 pgs **300.00**

Buck Rogers in the 25th Century, Big Little Book, 1933.....................**35.00**

Major Matt Mason- Moon Mission, George S. Elrick, Little Big Book, 1968, worn cover **26.00**

Tom Corbett's Wonder Book of Space, Marcia Martin, Wonder Books, 1953 ....**12.00**

Booklet, *Meet Major Matt Mason- Mattel's Man in Space Mattel's Man In Space*, 1965 ....**18.00**

Code wheel, Captain Midnight........**20.00**

Coloring book, Rocky Jones, Space Ranger, Whitman, cockpit cov, 1951 ....**40.00**

Comic book

Space Family Robinson/Lost In Space, 1965, World Distributors **20.00**

Space Ghost, 1987, Hanna-Barbera **7.00**

Lost in Space, #13, Voyage to the Bottom of the Soul, 1993, Innovation, sealed in orig plastic with poster **8.00**

Cookie jar, space capsule, decal "A Lasting Reminder of the Space Age," and "Gateway to the Stars, Cape Kennedy," Capitol Pottery, 1965, 8-1/2" h **225.00**

Crayon box, Buck Rogers Crayon Ship, cardboard, 6 colored pencils, c. 1930 ....**175.00**

Die-cast, Lost in Space Jupiter 2, with bonus film clip, MOC **5.00**

Figure, Buck Rogers, Buck, Dr. Huer, Dale, Friend, Monster, painted lead, each **42.00**

Flashlight, Captain Astro, wrist type, Bantamalite, c1967, MOC **45.00**

Game, battery operated, space ship saves the world, plastic and cardboard, 1970s **115.00**

Gun, Captain Video Secret Ray Gun, red plastic flashlight, secret message instructions, Power House Candy premium **90.00**

Lunch box

Buck Rogers in the 25th Century,

metal, with plastic thermos, 1979, Aladdin................................**55.00**
Space 1999, metal, with thermos **58.00**

Match cover, Buck Rogers, Popsicle adv **17.50**

Movie poster, 2001: A Space Odyssey, 1968 ....**175.00**

Pinback button, Rocky Jones, Space Ranger, membership type............**45.00**

Pop gun, Buck Rogers, XZ-31 Rocket Pistol, cardboard, full color, Cocomalt premium, 1934, 9-1/2" l.............**350.00**

Wallet, Battlestar Galactica, vinyl, 1971, Larami, MOC...............................**18.00**

Wings, Rocky Jones, Space Ranger, pin **40.00**

Star Trek lunch box, orig thermos, metal, $95.

❖ Space Exploration

In a day when space shuttle flights are commonplace, we've lost the excitement associated with early space flights. Nonetheless, space-related memorabilia, from the days of Sputnik to today's missions to Mars, is available to collectors. Flea markets are a great place to find such items.

Periodical: *Space Autograph News,* 862 Thomas Ave., San Diego, CA 92109.

For additional listings, see *Warman's Americana & Collectibles.*

Autograph, full color photo of Apollo XIII, matted with autograph of Jim Lovell, Commander, cloth patch from flight, 16-1/4" x 20-1/2" frame **250.00**

Book, Neal Armstrong: Space Pioneer, Paul Westman, 1980, hardcover, 64 pgs **15.00**

Clock, Apollo 11, animated windup, ivory case, Lux Clock Co. **145.00**

Drinking glass, Apollo 13, 4-1/8" h ..**2.00**

Jewelry, pin, Apollo 11, 1969, dated 7-20-69, 1-1/2" h **29.00**

Magazine, Life, July, 4, 1969, Apollo, "Off to the Moon"................................**15.00**

Newspaper, The Washington Evening Star, Washington, D.C., July 21, 1969, Apollo Edition **45.00**

Plate, "John H. Glenn Jr., Feb 20, 1962, First American to Orbit the World," 9-1/4" dia **25.00**

Paperweight, glass, Apollo 11, 1969, "One small step for man, one giant leap for mankind" around border, Fenton, 4" dia............................**160.00**

Photograph, Space Shuttle Orbiter 101 crew, Official NASA photo..............**4.00**

Record, *The First Man On The Moon,* Apollo 11 flight, 45 rpm **20.00**

Stamp, Mercury Space Exhibit cover, 1962, 14th National Postage Stamp Show labels.................................**10.00**

Token, Apollo 13, Shell Oil, 1970, 1-1/8" dia **12.00**

NASA plaque, circular center Apollo mission patch in black, gray, white, gold and yellow sun, blue and green earth, white stars, surrounded by 11 bronze medallions, green felt background, framed, $45.

❖ Space Toys

Now that we've done some imagining about space adventurers and real space heroes, how about some toys to round out our experience? Flea markets are sure to yield some out-of-this-world treasures.

References: Karen O'Brien, *Toys & Prices 2004*, Krause Publications, 2003; Jim Bunte, Dave Hallman and Heinz Mueller, *Vintage Toys: Robots and Space Toys*, Antique Trader Books, 1999; Dana Cain, *UFO & Alien Collectibles Price Guide*, Krause Publications, 1999; Stuart W. Wells, III, *Science Fiction Collectibles Identification & Price Guide,* Krause Publications, 1998.

Periodical: *Toy Shop*, 700 E. State St., Iola, WI 54990.

Also see Robots.

Action figure, Commander Sisko, Deep Space Nine, 1994, MIB, 5" h..........**8.00**

Astronaut, Mark Apollo Astronaut, Marx, jointed plastic, orange space suit, white helmet, plastic accessories, orig instructions and box, 7-1/2" h **175.00**

Bagatelle game, space theme, rockets and moon graphics, 14" x 8"........**25.00**

Bendee, Close Encounter of the Third Kind, Alien, MOC **45.00**
Card Game, Space-O **30.00**
Colorforms, Battlestar Galactica **35.00**
Eagle Lunar Module, Daishin, Japan, battery operated, 1969, MIB **300.00**
Flying saucer, litho tin, space pilot, revolving antenna, swivel lighted engine **395.00**
Game
Moon Blastoff, Schaper, unused, sealed, MIB.......................**48.00**
Planet Patrol, 1950s.....................**75.00**
Space Faces, Pressman Toys, 1950s, unplayed with condition, C-8 box **340.00**
Gun
Jet Space Gun, KO, Japan, tin litho, 1960s, 10" l.....................**55.00**
Junior Jet Play Gun, open faced box with Space Girl graphics...........**45.00**
Rocket Jet Space Gun, silver plastic, 7" l.....................................**45.00**
Space Fazer, Kusan, 12" l............**65.00**
Space Flash, battery operated, plastic, 6" l, MIB **65.00**
Helmet, Space Patrol, cardboard, 1950s **235.00**
Kite, Gayla Space Craft, unused, MIP **35.00**
Model kit, Vostol, Russian space ship, Revell, 1969 ....**70.00**
Play set, Space Shuttle Space Set, plastic, 11 pcs, 1984, Hong Kong, unsealed......................................**25.00**
Space ships
Apollo, battery-op, Japan, MIB...**275.00**
Gemini, litho tin, plastic windshield broken, 6" h **100.00**

Flying Saucer with pilot, orange body, turquoise int., multicolored space pilot, Cragston, battery powered, orig box, $35.

Liddle Kiddles Kozmic Space Ship, red with lime green wheels, clear dome, Mattel, c1969-70, 5-1/2" h **80.00**
Top, Space Top, litho tin, 1950s **45.00**
Yo-Yo, Orbit, small white plastic satellite, green plastic ball used to represent Earth, string, copyright 1969 Tom Boy Inc., blue, white, and orange blister card **10.00**

❖ Spark Plugs

Spark plug collectors are quite at home at flea markets devoted to automobiles. They look for interesting spark plugs, boxes, and other ephemera.

Champion
J-9 14 MM, 13/16" hex, MIB **10.00**
V-3, airplane **15.50**
W-18, oversized.............................**6.00**
Red Head, 1-1/2" pipe thread, unused **40.00**
Western Auto
Endurance Red Seal, box only, 1950s **2.00**
Wizard, orig box, MIB.....................**3.00**

❖ Spatter Glass

This colorful glassware is so named because of the spatters found in the clear glass body. The misnomer "end of day glass" has been associated with spatter glass for years. These colorful combinations weren't unplanned; instead, many are terrific examples of a glass blower showing off his craft.

Basket, multicolored spatter, white int., cased, applied crystal thorn handle, polished pontil, Stourbridge, England, c1880
7" h, 6" w triangular body...........**285.00**
8" h, 6-1/4" w, sides pinched to form ruffled top...............................**295.00**
Creamer, 4" h, multicolored spatter, white int., cased, applied crystal handle, English...........................**125.00**
Darner, multicolored spatter on egg shaped bulb, white handle **165.00**
Pitcher, aqua colored body, maroon, tan, and blue spatter streaks, applied aqua handle **295.00**
Vase
4-1/4" h, multicolored spatter, cased, Stourbridge, c1880 ....**75.00**
5" h, silver and multicolored spatter, mica flecks, white int., cased, attributed to Stevens & Williams **195.00**
7-1/4" h, white, yellow, and pink spatter, cased, applied crystal handles, English, c1880 ....**325.00**
Water set, Leaf Mold, cased cranberry

spatter, pitcher and 6 tumblers...**900.00**

❖ Spongeware

Ever see pottery that looked like someone had taken paint and just sponged all over the piece—well that's spongeware. Extensively produced in England and America, spongeware items were most commonly blue and white, but yellowware with mottled tans, browns, and greens was also popular. The design was achieved by sponging, spattering, or daubing on the color, and it was generally applied in an overall pattern. Care should be taken when examining a piece of spongeware, as modern craftsmen are making some examples that rival their antique ancestors.

References: William C. Ketchum Jr., *American Country Pottery: Yellowware and Spongeware*, Alfred A. Knopf, 1987; Kevin McConnell, *Spongeware and Spatterware*, 2nd ed., Schiffer Publishing, 1999.

Reproduction Alert: Reproductions and contemporary examples are quite common.

Note: All listings are blue-and-white unless otherwise noted.

For additional listings, see *Warman's Antiques and Collectibles Price Guide* and *Warman's Country Price Guide.*

Bank, pig, brown and green sponging, pierced eyes and coin slot, 6" l..**220.00**
Bowl
11-1/2" dia, green and brown sponging, glaze flakes.............................**330.00**
12" dia, blue sponging above and below blue stripe.....................**275.00**
12" dia, blue sponging overall **415.00**
Bowl, mixing
4" h, scalloped panels on sides, glaze wear in bottom, rim hairline **165.00**
10" dia, 4-3/4" h, blue, heart panels, large glaze imperfection on interior **120.00**
12" dia, 5-1/2" h, molded arched panels **275.00**
Butter crock, Good Luck pattern, 5" h, 7-1/2" dia **225.00**
Carpet Ball, 3-1/4" d
Brown **85.00**
Green **75.00**
Red and white plaid **90.00**
Chamber pot with handle, overall sponging, 5-1/2" h, 10" dia.........**125.00**
Custard, minor surface wear, hairline, 2-3/4" h..**45.00**
Mush cup and saucer, worn gilt trim, slight hairline in cup base **85.00**
Pitcher
Bulbous form, double bands around top and base, sponged body, 9-3/4" h..**635.00**
Lattice design, brown and green sponging, yellow body, rim chips, 9-

1/4" h **85.00**
Wild Rose, roses highlighted in cobalt, upper and lower part of pitcher sponged, small surface chip, 9" h **400.00**
Spittoon, blue bands, imperfections, 5" h, 7-1/2" dia.............................**100.00**
Teapot, chips on lid and spout......**700.00**
Wash pitcher, bulbous base, 3 blue lines around body **310.00**
Whimsy, figural cowboy hat, dark blue sponging, c1900, some glaze crazing, 5-1/2" l...**45.00**

❖ Sporting Collectibles

Whatever sport is your passion, you're bound to find some interesting examples of ephemera and other collectibles while browsing a flea market.

Reference: Sports Collectors Digest Editors, *Sports Collectors Almanac*, Krause Publications, 1998; Tom Mortenson, *2000 Standard Catalog of Sports Memorabilia*, Krause Publications, 1999.

For additional listings, see *Warman's Antiques and Collectibles Price Guide, Warman's Americana & Collectibles,* and specific categories in this edition.

Autograph, photo, sgd, Mike Tyson **60.00**

Badge, Larry Holmes, black and white photo, red and black inscriptions, 1979 copyright Don King Productions, 4" dia **25.00**

Bumper Sticker, Kentucky Colonels, ABA ball, team logo, name in blue and white, unused, 1974-75, 15" l **20.00**

Charm, male archer, sterling silver .**28.00**

Magazine, *The Sporting News*, Oct. 24,1970, Johnny Bench cover......**10.00**

Noisemaker, 2-3/4" d, 6-1/2" l, litho tin, full color image of male golfer, mkd "Germany" on handle, 1930s **35.00**

Pendant, metal, crossed arrows, attached to ribbon safety pin, "Class A, 1942" on back, 3/4" sq **22.00**

Pinback button
American Bowling Congress 1932, 32nd Annual Tournament, Detroit **82.00**
Devil's Lake Regatta, blue and white, 1934...**15.00**
U.S. Open Tennis Championship, 1975 ....**18.50**

Plate, hunter walking in brook with 5 dogs, Royal Bayreuth, chip, 7-1/2" dia......**65.00**

Program, Fort Worth Open Golf Championship, Glen Garden Country Club, Ft Worth, TX, 1945............**100.00**

Record, ABC Wide World of Sports, 33 rpm, 1970, narrated by Jim McKay **25.00**
Tie tack, male archer, sterling silver**22.00**
Tobacco card
Jackie Brown, boxer, 1935, Sporting Events & Stars series, J.A. Pattreioux, yellowing...................**5.00**
E.W. Higgins, cycler, 1935, Sporting Events & Stars series, J.A. Pattreioux................**5.00**

❖ Sporting Goods

So, you'd rather participate sports than watch? Needing some kitschy decor items for your family room? Well, head for the flea market and look for some of these neat collectibles.

See specific listings for fishing, skateboards, etc.

> Shoeless Joe Jackson's favorite bat, affectionately referred to as "Black Betsy" was auctioned in August, 2001, for $525,100. The historically significant bat, used for 13 seasons by Jackson, was auctioned by eBay for Real Legends. The hand carved hickory bat had it's one leather carrying case and is engraved with the Spaulding logo and the words "Old Hickory No. 150." The bat was kept in the Jackson family since Jackson's death in 1951.

Baseball cap, autographed, game used
Jackson, Bo, 1994 CA Angels......**85.00**
Walker, Larry, 1995 Colorado Rockies **165.00**
Baseball glove, professional model
Del Ennis, Wilson **60.00**
Draper Maynard, D&M **110.00**
Grover Alexander **130.00**
Joe Dimaggio, Spalding **50.00**
Pee Wee Reese, pre-World War II**75.00**
Basketball, autographed
Archibald, Nate..........................**100.00**
Bird, Larry **200.00**
Bradley, Bill................................**150.00**
Catalog
Horrocks-Ibbotson Co., Utica, NY, 1940, 30 pgs, *Fishing Tackle & Tackling Fish*............................**36.00**
Melrose Boat Works, Melrose Park, IL, c1930, 19 pgs, *You Won't Go Wrong With the Melrose Boat Way! Build Your Own Boat with Our Blue Prints*, cuts of cabin cruisers, sail boat, etc **40.00**
Old Town Canoe Co., Old Town, ME, 1973, 28 pgs, *Old Town Discovery, The Finest in Canoes, Kayaks & Power Boats* **35.00**

These snow shoes are all ready for a new owner, priced at $90.

Spaulding, A. G., & Bros., Chicopee, MA, 1911, 52 pgs, *Catalog X*, steel playground apparatus **55.00**
Football, autographed
Bergey, Bill **70.00**
Ditka, Mike **125.00**
Flaherty, Ray **150.00**
Hockey stick, game used, autographed
Cashman, Wayne, Sher-wood, uncracked **175.00**
LeBlanc, J.B., Koho, cracked **50.00**
Minnow bucket, green canvas, collapsible, No. 08, Mfd. by the Planet Co., West Field, Mass., 7-1/2" h.**155.00**
Roller skates, Glove Roller Skates No. 197, Marvel Beginners Ages 2-5, orig box, 1 leather strap missing **35.00**
Shot holder, James Dixon & Son...**35.00**
Skis, pr, wood, early, hand made, leather straps...**150.00**

❖ Staffordshire Items

The Staffordshire district of England is well known for the quality porcelain produced there through the centuries. This region was home to many potteries that supplied dinnerware, table items, and novelties such as mantel figures and toby jugs.

For additional listings, see *Warman's Antiques and Collectibles Price Guide* and *Warman's English & Continental Pottery & Porcelain.*

Bank, cottage shape, 5-1/4" h, repairs **195.00**
Chamber pot, cov, 9" h, Columbia, mkd "W. Adams," short hairline in bottom **80.00**

Plate, Winter View of Pittsfield, Mass., dark blue transfer, Clews, 7-3/4" d, $325.

Plate, Park Theater, New York, medium blue transfer, acorn and leaf border, R.W.S. mark, $185.

Creamer, cow, blue and dark red splotch polychrome dec, pearlware, early 19th C, 7" l..**235.00**

Cup and saucer, handleless, dark blue transfer of vase with flowers, imp "Clews," small chips, wear............**95.00**

Figure
Gentleman, seated, book and spectacles, polychrome enamel, damaged, old repairs..............**275.00**
Rabbit, black and white, green and brown base, 3-1/4" h, wear and enamel flaking **315.00**
Squirrel, sitting upright, holding nut, naturalistic stump base, ear repaired **125.00**

Mantel ornament, cottage, Potash Farm, hairlines, 9" h **175.00**

Mug, pearlware, black transfer print of Hope in landscape scene, silver luster highlights, minor imperfections, 3-3/4" h **60.00**

Plate, Dr. Syntax Disputing his Bill with the Landlady, blue and white transfer, James and Ralph Clews, Cobridge, 1819-36, 10-1/2" d **125.00**

Staffordshire, pair of cats, white ground, rust spots, dark green bows, yellow eyes, black highlights, damage to one, $85.

Teapot, cov, black basalt, oval form, scalloped rim and classical relief centering columns with floral festoons, banded drapery on shoulder, incised brick banded lower body, unmarked, early 19th C, 9-3/4" l, restored spout **360.00**

Undertray, Death of Punch, Dr. Syntax literary series, blue and white transfer, James and Ralph Clews, Cobridge, 1819-36, 10" x 5-3/4", crazing on reverse **85.00**

Waste bowl, Forget-Me-Not, red transfer, edge roughness, 5-5/8" d.............**60.00**

❖ Stamps

Stamp collecting has long been one of the most popular hobbies. Like many other hobbies, it is crucial that participants spend time reading and researching stamps and their values. Stamps sold at flea markets are generally of limited value, head for a Stamps show and sale for really quality investment grade stamps.

References: George Cuhaj, ed., *Krause-Minkus Standard Catalog of Canadian & United Nations Stamps,* Krause Publications, 1998; Arlene Dunn, ed., *Brookman Price Guide for Disney Stamps, 2nd edition,* Krause Publications, 1998; Robert Furman, *The 1999 Comprehensive Catalogue of United States Stamp Booklets, Postage and Airmail,* Krause Publications, 1998, plus many others.

Periodical: *Stamp Collector,* 700 E. State St., Iola, WI 54990, plus others.

Collectors' Clubs: American Philatelic Society, PO Box 8000, State College, PA 16803; International Stamp Collectors Society, PO Box 854, Van Nuys, CA 91408. Contact either one of these to inquire about local chapters.

❖ Stangl

Stangl Pottery was an active pottery in the Flemington, N.J., area. They produced colorful dinnerware, table wares and are well known for their interesting bird figurines.

Reference: Robert C. Runge Jr., *Collector's Guide to Stangl Dinnerware,* Collector Books, 2000.

Collectors' Club: Stangl/Fulper Collectors Club, PO Box 538, Flemington, NJ 08822.

For additional listings, see *Warman's Antiques and Collectibles Price Guide* (Stangl Birds) and *Warman's Americana & Collectibles* (dinnerware).

Basket, #3414 ....**20.00**
Butter dish, cov, Country Garden...**42.00**
Casserole, Fruit, 8" d **85.00**
Cigarette box, cov, goldfinch **55.00**
Coffeepot, Blueberry....................**100.00**
Creamer
Blueberry.....................................**15.00**
Blue Rooster **27.50**
Fruit **25.00**
Cup and saucer
Country Garden **20.00**
Fruit **18.00**
Harvest.......................................**22.00**
Terra Rose..................................**24.00**
Town and Country, brown............**20.00**
Dinner plate
Country Garden **40.00**
Fruit **25.00**
Terra Rose..................................**15.00**
Thistle..**19.50**
Eggcup, Country Garden...............**15.00**
Gravy boat, Thistle........................**24.00**
Mug, Town and Country, blue **22.00**
Platter
Blueberry, 14" dia.......................**75.00**
Fruit,12-1/2" dia.........................**35.00**
Salt and Pepper Shakers, pr, Blueberry
....**24.00**

Stangl Pottery, candleholders, pr, gold dec, orig gold foil label, $20.

Teapot
Fruit **100.00**
Harvest **80.00**
Tidbit tray, Bittersweet, 10" d **45.00**
Vegetable bowl
Blueberry...................................**50.00**
Fruit, divided..............................**38.00**

❖ Stanhope

Remember those Easter Eggs that you peaked in one end to see an Easter scene at the other end? That's a large form of a Stanhope. Stanhopes are little scenes tucked in miniature holders. Sometimes the cases are shaped like cameras and the viewer sees different images when holding the camera up to the light. Other stanhopes are shaped like tiny binoculars.

Disney 40th Anniversary, a scene from "Aladdin's Oasis" at Disneyland **4.00**
Easter egg, composition and plastic, blue egg, multicolored scene, c1950 ....**5.00**
Eiffel Tower, binoculars shape, bone, brass ring, c1900, 1-1/2" l **55.00**
Garfield, General James A., scenes and incidents from his life, 1831-1881 ....**100.00**
Lord's Prayer, cross shape, silver-tone, baguettes dec, 1950s, 1-1/2" l, 1" w **35.00**
Napoleon, figure, 2" h, bronzed......**80.00**
Rock City, plastic camera with 15 views, mkd "Brownie Mfg Co., West Germany," 2-1/4" x 1-1/4" **10.00**
Rome, Coliseum, St. Peters, binoculars shape, 1-1/8" l **35.00**
Rosary......................................**21.50**

❖ Stanley Tools

Some of the finest tools were created by the Stanley Tool Co. Today they are increasingly collectible. Look for examples free of rust and damage, but expect to find some wear from usage.

Periodical: *Stanley Tool Collectors News,* 208 Front St., PO Box 227, Marietta, OH 45750.

Adjustable scraper, wooden handle **65.00**
Brace, #923, 8" l..........................**45.00**
Doweling jig, No. 59, nickel-plated, orig box..**30.00**
Folding measure
No. 27, 24".................................**10.00**
No. 38, 24" **20.00**
Jointer, No. 7, 22" l **85.00**
Level
No. 27, 9" l.................................**10.00**
No. 104 ....**40.00**
Pick, No. 7 ....**45.00**

Plane
No. 25, block, 9-1/2" l **250.00**
No. 45 ....**150.00**
No. 48, tongue and grove...........**120.00**
No. 62 ....**400.00**
No. 90 rabbet plane, orig box.....**165.00**
Pocket level, patent date June 23 '96, 3" l **75.00**
Router, No. 71-1/2 ....**60.00**
Vise, No. 700 ....**45.00**

❖ Star Trek

"Beam Me Up Scottie" certainly is a phrase many collectors associate with Star Trek. The adventures of this space team started on television in September 1966 and lasted until June 1969. By 1978 syndicated broadcasts were reaching 51 countries, while the number of Star Trek fan clubs kept growing. *Star Trek, the Motion Picture* was released in 1979, followed by additional movies.

Collectors' Clubs: International Federation of Trekkers, PO Box 84, Groveport, OH, 43125; Starfleet, 200 Hiawatha Blvd., Oakland, NJ 07436; Star Trek: The Official Fan Club, PO Box 111000, Aurora, CO 80042.

Action figures
Captain Kirk, Mego, 8" mid-1970s**45.00**
Gowron, ritual Klingon attire, *Star Trek the Next Generation*, 1994 series, second set, MIB, 5" h **45.00**
Montgomery Scott, 1994, MIB, 5" h **30.00**
Mordock the Benzite, *Star Trek the Next Generation*, 1994 reissue, MIB **26.00**
Children's dishes, *Star Trek The Motion Picture*, bowl, cup and tumbler, hard plastic **35.00**
Dress, mid-1980s, mint **160.00**
Game, Star Trek Game, 1983 copyright **30.00**
Matchbook, *Star Trek, The Motion Picture*, 1977, cover only...............**9.00**
Micro Machine, U.S.S. Enterprise, fold-out ship with 4 figures, 10" l.........**25.00**
Model Kit, U.S.S. Enterprise, Star Trek the Motion Picture, #S970 1979...**50.00**
Pin, Star Trek Deep Space Nine, 1993, Paramount Pictures, 1-1/2" h **4.00**
Plate, All Good Things, 1994, Star Trek Next Generation, no box **17.50**
Premium ring, McDonald's, set of four, copyright 1979..............................**95.00**
Trading card
Star Trek, 1993, Skybox, factory-sealed box of 36 packs **35.00**
Star Trek - The Original Series, 1996, 30th anniversary set, meal cards, set of 6, factory-sealed box **11.00**

❖ Star Wars

"May The Force Be With You" as you search for collectibles from this series of science-fiction movies. George Lucas brought such special effects to the screen that fans of all ages were mesmerized. Twentieth Century Fox was clever enough to give Kenner a broad license to produce movie-related toys and items, creating a wealth of Star Wars materials for collectors.

References: Stuart W. Wells, III, *A Universe of Star Wars Collectibles*, Krause Publications, 2002; — *Science Fiction Collectibles Identification & Price Guide,* Krause Publications, 1998; James T. McCallum, *Irwin Toys: The Canadian Star Wars Connection,* Collector's Guide Publishing, Inc., 2000; Karen O'Brien, *Toys & Prices 2004*, Krause Publications, 2003.

Periodical: *The Star Wars Collector,* 20982 Homecrest Court, Ashburn, VA 22011.

Collectors' Club: Official Star Wars Fan Club, PO Box 111000, Aurora, Co 80042.

Action figures
Chewbacco, 1978, with weapon, pouch and ammunition belt, mint, 12".**70.00**
Chief Chirpa, Return of the Jedi, MOC **35.00**
Darth Vader, 12" h, Kaybees Exclusive, MISB......................................**60.00**
Hoth Snowtropper, *Empire Strikes Back*, MOC **150.00**
Imperial Commander, loose **8.00**
Luke Skywalker, 1996, MIB..........**60.00**

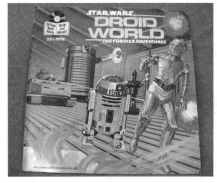

Child's book with record, Star Wars Droid World, The Further Adventure, *Lucasfilms copyright, 24 pgs, orig record, $20.*

Star Wars set, classic figurines, including Boba Fett, mint in sealed package, mid-1990s, $45.

Bank, Yoda, litho tin, combination dials
....**25.00**

Book, *Star Wars: A Pop-up Book*,
Random House, 1978, 1 section
missing **25.00**

Clock, Bradley, 1980-84 ....**45.00**

Game

Escape from Death Star Game, 1977
....**35.00**

Ewoks Save the Trees, 1984, sealed
....**25.00**

Mug

Luke Skywalker, Sigma **24.00**
Obi-Wan Kanobi, Rumph, 1977 .**135.00**

Pencil tray, C-3PO, Sigma..............**50.00**

Play set, Rebel Pilot/Hoth, Micro
Machines, MIP **15.00**

Postcard, Greetings Earthlings, Droids
....**25**

Poster, Luke Skywalker, Coca-Cola, 24"
x 18" **18.00**

Radio, child's, Ewoks, MIB..............**35.00**

Shampoo, Yoda, 6-1/2" h **35.00**

String Dispenser, R2-D2, Sigma ...**45.00**

Vehicle

Cloud Car, MIB............................**95.00**

Darth Vader's TIE Fighter, Kenner,
1978, played with......................**60.00**

Empire Rebel Transport, MIB.....**150.00**

Landspeeder, Kenner, 1978, MIP **75.00**

❖ St. Clair Glass

Molds from defunct glass companies were
used by St. Clair, which produced items in
new colors as well as pieces in colors
similar to the originals. The glass is usually
marked and is eagerly sought by collectors.

Bell, Rosette pattern, chocolate glass, 6-
1/4" h...**55.00**

Bicentennial plate, blue carnival, 5-1/2"
dia **40.00**

Candleholder, paperweight base, red
florals, applied glass handle, sgd, 11-
1/2" dia **55.00**

Figure, buffalo, caramel slag...........**40.00**

Paperweight

Apple, red....................................**82.00**
Bell shape, turquoise, sgd............**55.00**
Bird, yellow, sgd **50.00**
Blue flowers.................................**40.00**
Pear, green..................................**100.00**
Turtle, clear and brown, sgd "Maude
and Bob," 1982.......................**155.00**
Yellow flowers, 10" dia.................**70.00**

Salt, open, wheelbarrow, caramel slag
....**15.00**

Toothpick holder, Indian, yellow, 2-3/4"
h **30.00**

Tumbler, Cactus, cobalt blue **28.00**

❖ Steiff

Steiff bears and toys are recognized by
their button ear tag. Steiff's first teddy bear
appeared in 1903 and was an instant hit.
The company remains in business, and
collectors know the name means quality
and a well-made toy.

Reference: Dee Hockenberry, *Steiff Bears
& Other Playthings*, Schiffer Publishing,
2000.

Collectors' Clubs: Steiff Club USA, 225
Fifth Ave., Suite 1033, New York, NY 10010;
Steiff Collectors Club, PO Box 798, Holland,
OH 43528.

Beaver, Nagy, mohair, chest tag, post
WWII, 6" l **95.00**

Boxer, beige mohair coat, black trim,
glass eyes, leather collar mkd "Steiff,"
head turns, minor wear, straw stuffing,
16-1/2" l.......................................**165.00**

Bunny, Manni, button.......................**85.00**

Circus seal, with ball, on stand **85.00**

Frog, 3-3/4" l, velveteen, glass eyes,
green, sitting, button and chest tag
....**125.00**

Goat, 6-1/2" h, ear button..............**150.00**

Hen, gold and black spotted feathers,
yellow plush head, felt tail, black button
eyes, c1949 ....**85.00**

Kangaroo, plush, glass eyes, 2 plastic
Joeys in pouch **70.00**

Koala, glass eyes, ear button, chest tag,
post WWII....................................**135.00**

Leopard...**90.00**

Llama, standing, white, brown spots
....**110.00**

Owl, 10" h.......................................**75.00**

Parakeet, Hansi, bright lime green and
yellow, airbrushed black details, plastic
eyes, button tag, chest tag, plastic
beak and feet **115.00**

Penguin, Peggy, glass eyes, ear button,
chest tag, post WWII **95.00**

Rabbit, jointed, mohair, 6-1/2" h ...**110.00**

Squirrel, Perri, plush **45.00**

Teddy bear

Blond mohair, glass eyes, ear button,
brown embroidered nose, mouth and
claws, excelsior stuffed, felt pads,
c1930, 13" h **150.00**

Light brown plush, glass eyes, jointed,
c1950.....................................**350.00**

One Hundredth Anniversary Bear, ear
button, gold mohair, fully jointed,
plastic eyes, orig box, 17" h
....**230.00**

Tan mohair, ear button, chest tag,
jointed, c1980 ....**75.00**

✪ ✭ Stein, Lea

A French lady by the name of Lea Stein is
taking over the jewelry market! Her
creations use a secret method of layering
colored sheets of plastic, then cutting
fanciful shapes. She started her jewelry
business in Paris in 1969 and continues
today, releasing a new design every year.
Look for her signature on the closure to
make sure it's a genuine piece of Lea Stein
jewelry.

Bracelet, bangle, dark green and red
swirled peppermint stick swirls.....**75.00**

Earrings, pr, clip, bright green swirls on
pearly white, stamped on back, 1-3/8"
dia **75.00**

Pin, with signature Lea Stein-Paris v-
shaped pin back

Bacchus, cat, pearly silver and black,
2-3/8" w, 1-1/8" h **65.00**

Bee, transparent wings with gold edge,
faux ivory body and head, topaz
colored glass edge eye, 2-3/8"
wingspan **70.00**

Blueberries, peach lace, 2-7/8" l ..**65.00**

Cat, standing, magenta lace, faux-
mother-of-pearl ears and eyes, 3-
3/4" l, 1-3/4" h **75.00**

Cicada, irid red wings, striped body
and head, 3-3/8" l, 1-1/4" w......**75.00**

Flamingo, pink, 1-7/8" w, 2-3/8" h **55.00**

Flower pot, two flowers, one aqua lacy
turquoise, other purple lacy, dark
blue leaves, turquoise lacy pot, 1-
1/2" w, 2-1/2" h **65.00**

Mistigri Kitty, caramel, 4" 2, 3-7/8" h
....**70.00**

Oriental girl, shades of blue and white,
transparent light blue hat, faux-ivory
face, transparent light blue eye, 2" w,
2-1/8" h **90.00**

Panther, pearly ivory harlequin,
medium faux tortoiseshell, 4-1/4" l,
1-3/4" h **65.00**

Swallow, pink and white lace wings, 2-
3/4" w, 1-3/8" h **60.00**

❖ Steins

Finding steins at flea markets is great fun.
Look for advertising or novelty steins, and
don't overlook the limited ones made to
commemorate a special event, such as a
fire truck housing.

Periodical: *Regimental Quarterly,* PO Box
793, Frederick, MD 21705.

Collectors' Club: Stein Collectors
International, PO box 5005, Laurel, MD
20726; Sun Steiners, PO Box 11782, Fort
Lauderdale, FL 33339.

For additional listings, see *Warman's
Antiques and Collectibles Price Guide.*

Avon, vintage automobiles, 1979, no box, 8-1/2" h.................................**19.50**

Budweiser

50th Anniversary, 1933-1983, 3rd in Holiday series, Clydesdales on snow scene with cabin.....................**100.00**

Basketball, 1991, orig box............**15.00**

Frog, Albert Stahl and Co., 9-1/2" h **210.00**

Figural

Ape, dressed in hobo tuxedo jacket, top hat, drinking from stein, smoking pipe, pewter thumbrest, 9-1/2" h **100.00**

Jolly Man, sitting on stump, playing accordion, pewter thumbrest and lid rim, 9-1/2" h............................**150.00**

Monk, #3, fat monk with book, pewter handle, by Gertiz, West Germany, 7" h...**125.00**

Skull, 1/3 liter, porcelain, large jaw, inlaid lid, E. Bohne & Sohn, pewter slightly bent..........................**550.00**

McCoy, Spirit of '76, 8" h **35.00**

Mekelbach, half liter, Hassfurt Township, pewter lid and thumbrest, raised lettering and seal on lid, German inscription on front, blue and whtie border and green wreath, 5-1/2" h **100.00**

Mettlach

#171, half liter, figures representing monthly activities, blue background, inlaid top, pewter rim and thumbrest, 9-1/2" h, minor rubbing **90.00**

2-1/4 liter, PUG, pewter lid and thumbrest, print of musical cherubs, man and woman performing ceremony, 17" h......................**250.00**

Oakland Radiers, National Football League Collector's Stein 7-1/2" h.**15.00**

Oktoberfest, German beer garden scene, Ceramarte, 1996, 5-3/4" h**20.00**

Olympics, deep relief, full color, official logo, Atlanta, 1996, mkd "Made in Brazil, Ceramarte," 5-3/4" h..........**25.00**

Regimental, 1/2 liter, porcelain

11 Armee Corps, Mainz 1899, names to Res. Doring, 2 side scenes, plain thumblift, strap tear repaired, lines in lithophane, 10" h.....................**485.00**

30 Field Artillery, Rastatt 1897-99, named to Freund Hilfstromp, 2 side scenes, roster, thumblift missing **375.00**

61 Field Artillery, Dartmstadt 1910-12, named to Kanonier Boxheimer, 4 side sides, roster worn, lion thumblift **415.00**

❖ Stereoptican and Cards

Aluminum stereoptican with emb dec, Sun Sculpture trademark, wood handle, $35.

Here's another way to bring antiques into your family entertainment area. Think of a stereoptican as the pre-cursor of the modern View-Master. Stereopticans were made as tabletop and handheld model. Stereoviews covered many topics, from comedy to disasters, and from everyday scenes to tourist sites.

Collectors' Club: National Stereoscopic Association, PO Box 14801, Columbus, OH 43214.

Stereoview

Birthplace of Abraham Lincoln, Keystone.....................................**4.00**

Bristol, steamship scene..............**18.50**

Civil War, Libby Prison, Anthony #3365, yellow mount.................**45.00**

Crystal Palace, yellow mount.......**27.50**

Deer hunting, Keystone #26396.....**8.50**

Eskimo Dog Team on Trail, Hopedale, Labrador, Keystone...................**10.00**

Fishing in the Pool, copyright 1903, T. W. Ingersoll, No. 499...................**6.00**

Fireman, steam pumper, 1870.....**50.00**

Panoramic View of Washington, D.C., Underwood & Underwood **15.00**

Princess Gray Paws, Keystone #34467 ....**10.00**

Portland Fire, 1866, Soule #469 ..**12.00**

Savannah, Bonaventura cemetery **10.00**

Viewer

Handheld, aluminum hood, wooden folding handle **125.00**

Handheld, Sears Roebuck, with 56 cards.......................................**125.00**

Handheld, walnut, screw on handle, velvet hood **115.00**

Tabletop, Bates-Holmes, paper or wood hood...**195.00**

Tabletop, Bowstills Graphoscope**695.00**

Tabletop, Keystone, school and library type, black crinkle metal finish..**95.00**

❖ Steuben Glass

The Steuben Glass Works was established in Corning, N.Y., in 1904. The company produced many types of glass, from crystal to art glass. A trip to the Corning Museum is always a treat that includes seeing the glass made. Look for the traditional fleur-de-lis mark on Steuben Glass, although not all pieces are marked. Beware of faked signatures.

For additional listings, see *Warman's Antiques and Collectibles Price Guide* and *Warman's Glass.*

Bowl, blue Aurene, 6" d **275.00**

Bud vase, crystal, elongated neck on swollen base, applied ball and scroll dec, base inscribed "Steuben," designed by Don Wier, 1947, 6-3/4" h, light staining **200.00**

Champagne, ruby, crystal stem, catalog #6521, set of 8 ....**500.00**

Cologne, 5" h, catalog #6887

Flemish Blue, ...**225.00**

Wisteria **300.00**

Compote, Cerise, ruby and crystal, twisted stem, catalog #6043 ......**325.00**

Goblet, Rosaline, crystal foot..........**90.00**

Perfume, Verre de Soie, green jade stopper, catalog #1455...............**300.00**

Puff box, Green Jade, catalog #2910 ....**325.00**

Rose Bowl, smooth jade crystal, 7" d **350.00**

Salt, gold Aurene on calcite, pedestal foot, 1-1/2" h..............................**375.00**

Serving Plate, Bristol Yellow, folded rim, slight optic ribbing, wear scratches, 14-1/4" d...**200.00**

Sherbet set, catalog #2960, gold Aurene stemmed bowl, calcite stem, matching undertray, sgd "F. Carder Aurene" on base **300.00**

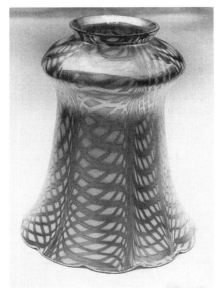

Steuben Glass lamp shade, green, purple, and irid gold, opal ground, fish net pattern, irid gold interior, 2-1/2" d fitter ring, 5-1/2" h, $175.

Vase

Celeste Blue, catalog #6298, fan shape, optic ribbed version, triple wafer stem, pedestal base stamped with fleur-de-lis mark **320.00**

Rosaline, catalog #345..............**300.00**

❖ Stocks and Bonds

Stocks & Bonds, State of New York, Canal Department, Draper, Tappan & Co., NY, engravers, 1842, 10-1/2" x 8", $15.

Just as today's Wall Street stocks and bonds fluctuate, so do the prices of vintage stocks and bonds, just not as quickly. Many collectors enjoy researching the companies that issued stock; some enjoy the intricate vignettes.

Periodical: *Bank Note Reporter*, 700 E State Street, Iola, WI 54990.

Collectors' Clubs: Bond and Share Society, 26 Broadway at Bowling Green, Room 200, New York, NY 10004; Old Certificates Collector's Club, 4761 W. Waterbuck Drive, Tucson, AZ 85742.

American Locomotive Co., 50 shares, canceled, 1947.............................**20.00**

Ben-Hur Motor Car, globe vignette, issued by not canceled, 1917 ......**85.00**

California Street Cable RR Co., San Francisco, CA, 1884, unissued, cable car vignette...................................**35.00**

Carson City Controller's Office Warrant, March 8, 1888, Carson Gas Co...**40.00**

Ford International Capital Corporation, $1000 bond, 1968 ....**15.00**

Fruit of the Loom, script certificate for fractional share of common stock, 1938 ....**7.50**

F.W. Woolworth Co., eagle over two hemispheres vignette, brown **8.00**

Hornell Airways Inc., issued and canceled, NY, two women and sun rising over mountains vignette, 1920s **65.00**

International Business Machines Corp, issued, brown **5.00**

Milwaukee Street Railway, incorporated under the laws of New Jersey, c1880 ....**50.00**

New York City Revenue Bond, 1858 ....**45.00**

Nickel Plated Railway, June 4, 1957 ....**40.00**

Packard Motor Car Company, August 7, 1951, one share **30.00**

Pennsylvania New York Central Transportation Co., 100 shares, blue on white, black vignette, Sept 11, 1968 ....**50.00**

Pepsi-Cola United Bottlers, vignette of goddess holding world globe and Pepsi bottle, issued **15.00**

Rochelle & Southern, Illinois, 1900, unissued, black and white............**12.00**

Sentinel Radio Corp, issued and canceled, green, goddess and two radio towers vignette **5.00**

United Airlines, $1000 share, 1970s...**9.50**

Western Union Telegraph Co., 100 shares, 1969 ....**15.00**

❖ Stoneware

Crocks and jugs are forms of stoneware. Early potters boasted of its durability and added cobalt blue lettering to advertise their location, or perhaps a flower or bird as decoration. Pieces which exhibit slightly pitted surfaces are referred to as having an "orange peel" glaze. Stoneware items are impervious to liquid and extremely durable, making them ideal for food preparation and storage. The most desirable pieces are those with unusual cobalt decorations.

References: Georgeanna H. Greer, *American Stonewares: The Art and Craft of Utilitarian Potters*, Schiffer Publishing, 1999; Kathryn McNerney, *Blue & White Stoneware*, Collector Books, 1996; Terry Taylor and Terry & Kay Lawrence, *Collector's Encyclopedia of Salt Glaze Stoneware*, Collector Books, 1997.

Collectors' Clubs: American Stoneware Association, 208 Crescent Ct., Mars, PA 16066-3308; American Stoneware Collectors Society, P.O. Box 281, Bay Head, NJ 08742; Blue & White Pottery Club, 224 12th St., N.W., Cedar Rapids, IA 52405; Collectors of Illinois Pottery & Stoneware, 308 N. Jackson St., Clinton, IL 61727; Red Wing Collectors Society, Inc., P.O. Box 14, Galesburg, IL 61401; Southern Folk Pottery Collectors Society, 1828 N. Howard Mill Rd., Robbins, NC 27325-7477; Uhl Collectors' Society, 80 Tidewater Rd., Hagerstown, IN 47346.

Museums: Bennington Museum, VT; Brooklyn Museum, NY; DAR Museum, Washington, DC; Henry Ford Museum, Dearborn, MI; Henry Francis DuPont Winterthur Museum, DE; Museum of Ceramics at East Liverpool, OH; Shelburne Museum, VT.

For additional listings, see *Warman's Country Price Guide*.

Batter pail, unsigned, attributed to White's, Utica, 6 qt, imp "6", oak leaf design under spout, orig bale handle, c1865, 6" h, short tight hairline ..**330.00**

Bottle, imp and blue accented "C. F. Washburn," minor crow's foot at shoulder, 9-1/2" h **35.00**

Canning jar

Hamilton & Jones, Greensboro, Pa., salt-glazed, cobalt stencil, minor chips, 8-1/2" h.........................**132.00**

Mason Fruit Jar, Union Stoneware Co., Red Wing, Minn., 1/2-gal, bristol glaze, blue ink-stamp mark.....**220.00**

Churn

Uhl Pottery Co., Acorn Wares ink stamp, 2-gal, bristol glaze.......**150.00**

Unmarked, 2 gallon, table top type, fitted carved wooden guide, brushed double plume design repeated front and back, c1870, 13" h..........**275.00**

Cream pot

Brady & Ryan, Ellenville, NY, 6 qt, singing bird on dotted branch, imp "6" below maker's name, c1885, 8-1/2" h, extensive glaze flaking at rim and spots on back **180.00**

Unsigned, attributed to NJ, 1 gallon, Bristol glaze, slip blue bird design, c1880, 8" h, full length hairline on back, some surface chipping at rim **220.00**

Crock

John Burger, Rochester, 2 gallon, unusual accents around gallon designation, c1855, 9" h.........**315.00**

J. Fisher, Lyons, NY, 10 gallon, brushed tulips cover entire front, brushed blue accent under applied ears, cobalt blue gallon designation, c1880, 16" h, professional restoration to three full-length through lines **470.00**

A. & C. W. Underwood, Fort Edward, NY, 2 gallon, stylized floral spray dec, blue at name, c1865, 9" h, some surface design fry, stone ping at base on side **200.00**

Unmarked, double handles, incised lines, imp "3" with freehand spray of flowers below dark cobalt blue, int. with Albany slip glaze, 8-1/4" h, shallow chips and flakes on rim and handles **330.00**

N.A. White & Son, Utica, NY, 1-1/2 gallon, blue paddle tail running bird, looking backward, c1870, 7-1/2" h, tight freeze line around base ..**360.00**

Jug

John Burger, Rochester, 2-gal, salt-glazed, poppy decor **440.00**

Cowden & Wilcox, 1-gal, salt-glazed, freehand cobalt flower with petals and scrolled leaves, chip **450.00**

A.P. Donaghho, Parkersburg, W.Va., 2-gal, salt-glazed, beehive shape, stenciled "2" in circle motif above name, minor spout chips **245.00**

Hamilton & Jones, Greensboro, 2-gal, salt-glazed, ovoid, cobalt stencil and freehand decor, minor chips on neck **300.00**

T. Harrington, Lyons, 4-gal, salt-glazed, ovoid, brushed leaf, stains......**250.00**

C.W. Weaver, Stoneware Depot, Cincinnati, O., 2-gal, salt-glazed, cobalt stencil, handle cracked, small chips **110.00**

Unmarked, bee-sting decor, 3-gal, salt-glazed, beehive shape, handle cracked **250.00**

Mug, applied handle, two brushed cobalt bands with incised edging, 4-3/4" h **250.00**

Pitcher

J. Burger, Rochester, NY, 1 gallon, blue accents at handle and imp name, bow tie dec, c1880, 11" h **600.00**

Lyons, 1 gallon, brushed tulip, blue imp name, c1860, 10" h, minor kiln burns at top occurred in making, professional restoration to chip at spout **550.00**

Preserve jar

Fulper Bros, Flemington, NJ, 1-1/2 gallon, fitted stoneware lid, chicken pecking corn dec, c1885, 10" h, hairlines extending from rim, stone ping, glaze drip in front at base, overall dry glaze in the making.............**800.00**

Little West, 12th St. N. Pottery Works, 1-1/2 gallon, double dropping flower design, c1870, 10" h, two short clay separation lines at rim probably occurred in making **495.00**

Lyons, blue leaf and double blue "I's" for gallon designation, orig lid, c1860, 9-1/2" h, few minor glaze spots on side **330.00**

E. & L. P. Norton, 1-1/2 gallon, stylized dotted floral design, c1880, 10-1/2" h, very minor stone ping on side **275.00**

❖ Strawberry Shortcake

Who's that freckle-faced kind in the puffy bonnet? It's Strawberry Shortcake, of course. Strawberry Shortcake memorabilia is both available and affordable, meaning it's perfect flea market material as well as a great collectible for children and adults.

Collectors' Clubs: Strawberry Shortcake Collectors' Club, 1409 72nd St., North Bergen, NJ 07047-3827; Strawberry Shortcake Doll Club, 405 E Main Cross, Greenville, KY 42345.

Carrying case, strawberry shape ...**15.00**

Jewelry

Charm Set, Apricot, Lemon, Custard, some wear **100.00**

Necklace, Strawberry Shortcake, hand over mouth **25.00**

Ring, Strawberry Shortcake **20.00**

Comforter, Strawberry Shortcake, some wear...**15.00**

Doll

Angel Cake with Souffle, MIB **45.00**

Apricot with Hopsalot, MIB...........**65.00**

Lem & Ada with Sugar Woofer, MIB **90.00**

Mint Tulip with Marsh Mallard, MIB **80.00**

Strawberry Shortcake, 1st ed., MIB **75.00**

Game, board, slight play wear

Berries to Market Game, American Greetings Corporation, copyright 1979.....................................**35.00**

Strawberry Shortcake Berry-Go-Round, Parker Brothers, copyright 1981.....................................**25.00**

Lunch box, Aladdin, thermos missing, C-8 ....**25.00**

Pillow panel, Strawberry Shortcake train, uncut **27.00**

Playset

Lime Chiffon, Dance n' Berry-cise, 1991, MIP **35.00**

Strawberry Shortcake, Berry Beach Park, 1991, MIP.......................**45.00**

Sleeping bag, Strawberry Shortcake, some wear...................................**15.00**

❖ String Holders

The string holder developed as a useful tool to assist the merchant or manufacturer who needed tangle-free string or twine to tie packages. The early holders were made of cast-iron, with some patents dating to the 1860s. Among the variations to evolve were the hanging lithographed-tin examples with advertising and decorative chalkware examples. In the home, string holders remained a useful kitchen element until the early 1950s.

Look for examples that are bright and colorful, free of chips or damage, and include the original hanger.

Apple, chalkware, 7-3/4" h **95.00**

Black man and woman, chalkware, matched pair **275.00**

Boy, top hat and pipe, chalkware, 9" h **125.00**

Cast iron, ball shape, designed to be hung from ceiling.........................**75.00**

Cat, ball of twine, white cat, red/orange ball, chalkware, 7" h **75.00**

Cat, ball of twine and bow, black cat, white face, green bow, chalkware, 6-1/2" h...**100.00**

Chef

Black, chalkware, 8" h................**165.00**

White, chalkware, 7-1/4" h **145.00**

Dutch girl, chalkware, 7" h **100.00**

Mammy, holding flowers, chalkware, 6-1/2" h...**185.00**

Pear, chalkware, 7-3/4" h **85.00**

Pineapple, face, chalkware, 7" h ...**165.00**

Senor, chalkware, bright colors, 8-1/4" h **90.00**

Strawberry, chalkware, 6-1/2" h ...**115.00**

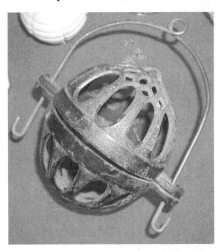

String holder, hanging type, cast iron, some rust, $25.

❖ Structo

Founded in 1909 in Freeport, Ill., this company's earliest products were construction toys. Sturdy metal toy vehicles were added to the line about 1919. Ertl bought Structo's toy patents and designs in 1975.

Army Cub Jeep, #200, pressed steel, orig box **75.00**

Cargo truck, steel, #702................**75.00**

Cattle Farms truck and trailer, metal **220.00**

Cement mixer truck, 18-1/2" l, 9" h **150.00**

Dump truck, diecast, painted white, red sheet metal body, extension frame, dual rubber tires, side decals, 12" l, MIB..**225.00**

Structo dump truck, red, $85.

Fire truck, hydraulic hook and ladder, pressed steel, red, 3" l **175.00**
Fix-It tow truck, #910, pressed steel, MIB...**200.00**
Overland freight truck, #704 ....**90.00**

❖ Stuffed Toys

Steiff was the originator of stuffed toys. By the middle of the 20th century, stuffed toys of every type, color, and animal were made. Some were sold in stores, others used for carnival prizes. Today many of these animals find their way to flea markets, hoping someone will give them a new home.

Periodical: *Soft Dolls & Animals,* 30595 Eight Mile, Livonia, MI 48152.

Bear, blue, red, white, and blue Union Pacific shield logo on chest..........**20.00**
Bucky Badger, University of Wisconsin mascot, Animal Fair, 1960s, 23" h**36.00**
Cat, tiger-striped, Purrfection, Gund, 1985 Collectors Classic Limited Edition #1174, 15" h................................**16.00**
Dinosaur, Animal Fair, late 1970s, 26" l **15.00**
Dumbo, Character Novelty Co., 14" h **88.00**
Fozzie Bear, tan hat with felt holly trim, Tyco...**15.00**
Lion, standing, Animal Fair, 1979, 15" h **24.00**
Paddington Bear, Holiden Eden, 16" h **16.00**
Parrot, plush, glass eyes, Merrythought, 16" h...**325.00**
Penguin, black and white, orange beak, button eyes..................................**35.00**
Polar bear, Always Coca-Cola emblem ... 7" h..**10.00**
Winnie the Pooh, Japan, 4-1/2" h **1.50**

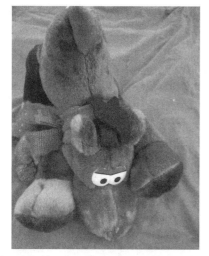

Reindeer, felt antlers, browns, and golds, red and green knit scarf, battery pack activates red flashing nose, $5.

❖ Sugar Packets

Here's a sweet topic. Collectors used to find many of their most interesting examples while traveling and enjoying diners and restaurants. Many sugar packets have interesting scenes or advertising, and some were made in sets. Today some sugar packets are finding their ways to flea markets. Because the collecting interest is relatively small, expect to find sugar packets for as little as 25 cents.

❖ Sugar Shakers

Two sweet categories in a row! Sugar shakers, also called muffineers, were designed to sprinkle powdered sugar, so the holes in their tops tend to be large. When looking for sugar shakers, check to see that the top and bottom started life together. Like salt shakers, tops do wear out. Replacement tops detract slightly from the value.

Bristol glass, tapering cylinder, pink, blue flowers and green leaves dec, 6-1/4" h..**75.00**
Cranberry glass, Parian Swirl mold **185.00**
Custard glass, Paneled Teardrop .**110.00**
Mt. Washington, opaque white ground, flowers dec, orig top **350.00**
Nippon, white, gold beading **65.00**
R.S. Prussia, pearl finish, shaded roses and green leaves, scalloped base, red mark **250.00**
Spanish Lace
Blue opalescent, light blue color **275.00**
Vaseline opalescent **300.00**
Tomato shape, Mt. Washington **410.00**
Wedgwood, jasperware, white classical design, dark blue ground **50.00**

❖ Sunbonnet Babies

These cute little gals did everything in their large-brimmed sunbonnets. They washed and ironed and played on all types of material, from postcards to Royal Bayreuth china.

Book, *Sunbonnet Babies,* 1902 ......**90.00**
Cake plate, babies washing, Royal Bayreuth, 10-1/4" d **400.00**
Cup and saucer, babies fishing, Royal Bayreuth **250.00**
Dish, babies ironing, ruffled edge, blue Royal Bayreuth mark, 8" dia **175.00**
Fruit Bowl, babies washing and hanging wash, blue Royal Bayreuth mark, 9-3/4" dia **95.00**
Picture, watercolor, professionally framed, 13-1/2" x 9-3/4", pr........**160.00**

Sunbonnet Babies plate, babies sweeping, $60.

Plate, babies ironing, Royal Bayreuth **110.00**
Postcard, Weekly series, set of 7 ...**85.00**
Quilt, Sunbonnet Sue and Sam, summer weight, c1910, some wear **45.00**

❖ Sunday School

Jesus loves me, this I know. Anyone who's sat through Sunday school has probably sung that song. Sunday school items can be readily found at flea markets. Looking to start a collection on a budget? This is one area where most items remain readily affordable. Anyone who's looking for Sunday school items really does have a prayer of finding them.

Book
International Sunday School Lessons, 1918...**15.00**
Sunday School is Fun, 1948, with dustjacket..................................**7.50**
Cards, lesson cards, 1901-05, set of 47, 3" x 4"..**26.00**
Felt storyboard, cutouts, background, c1960 ....**35.00**
Magazine, *Sunday School Magazine*, November 1881, Southern Methodist Publishing House **3.50**
Pin
Christian, brass and enameled **12.50**
Lutheran Sunday School, 8-year pin, 10K gold 1" dia **5.00**
Postcard, Rally Day, 1924 ....**3.50**
Record, Little Marcy Sings Sunday School Songs **22.50**
Songbook
Bradbury's Golden Shower of Sunday School Melodies, 1862 ....**18.00**
Sunday School Songbook, 1870..**15.00**

❖ Super Heroes

Shazam! Super heroes have been influencing the minds and checkbooks of collectors for decades. Batman, Green

Hornet, Captain Midnight, Superman, etc., and all kinds of villains have come to life from comic books, radio, television, and movie tales.

Reference: Ted Hake, *Hake's Price Guide to Character Toys,* 3rd ed, Gemstone Publishing; Rex Miller, *The Investor's Guide to Vintage Character Collectibles,* Krause Publications, 1999.

Periodical: *The Adventures Continue,* 935 Fruitsville Pike, #105, Lancaster, PA 17601.

Collectors' Club: Air Heroes Fan Club, 19205 Seneca Ridge Club, Gaithersburg, MD 20879; Batman TV Series Fan Club, PO Box 107, Venice, CA 90291; Rocketeer Fan Club, 10 Halick Court, East Brunswick, NJ 08816.

For additional listings, see *Warman's Americana & Collectibles* and related topics in this edition.

Action Figure, Aquaman, MOC......**35.00**
Bank, Batman, plastic, full color, arms
    crossed...**75.00**
Big little book, *Flash Gordon*.........**55.00**
Coloring book
    Flash Gordon, 1958, unused **30.00**
    Six Million Dollar Man, Saalfield,
       unused.....................................**20.00**
    Spiderman, 16 pgs, unused.........**12.00**
Comic book
    The Amazing World of Superman,
       1973, map of Krypton.................**8.50**
    Aquaman #4, August 1962 ....**34.50**
    Superman #30, Sept-Oct 1944 ..**295.00**
    Wonder Woman #9, Summer, 1944
    ....**395.00**
Costume
    Aquaman, Ben Cooper, 1967.....**210.00**
    Wonder Woman, 1980s................**15.50**
Cape, Superman, home made, c1975
    ....**20.00**
Doll, Wonder Woman, MIB..............**90.00**
Drinking glass, Aquaman, 1973 ....**15.00**
Figure
    Captain America, wind-up, 5-1/2" h,
       MIB **90.00**

Comic book, DC Comics, Superman in Action Comics, No. 471, $5.

    Thor, wind-up, 5-1/2" h, MIB **110.00**
Gun
    Batman escape gun, 1966, MOC..**45.00**
    Superman Krypton Ray Gun......**475.00**
License Plate, Captain America, metal,
    full color graphics, © 1967 Marvel
    Comics Group, Louis Marx & Co,
    Japan, 2-1/4" x 4" **28.00**
Pez Dispenser, European, Dark Knight,
    TAS, MOC **20.00**
Pinback, Green Hornet Society
    membership pin, 3-1/2" dia **25.00**
Puzzle
    Aquaman, action scene, Whitman,
       1967...**45.00**
    Wonder Woman puzzle, 130 pcs ...**9.50**
Ring, Incredible Hulk face, 1977 .....**15.00**
Spoon, Green Hornet figure on handle,
    1955 ....**20.00**
Toy, Spiderman Helicopter, NRFB **115.00**
Wallet, Superman, leather and plastic,
    made in Hong Kong, 1976 ....**27.50**
Watch, Batman, Fossil, MIB............**60.00**

Super heroes action figure, Superman, Mego, 1970s, 12-1/2" h, some box damage, $40.

❖ Surveyor's Equipment

Keep your eyes open while out surveying at your favorite flea market. Perhaps you'll spot an interesting piece of used surveying equipment. With today's electronics and computers, many old rods and transits are being sold. Instruments with original cases are worth more. Time will tell whether collectors like their instruments brightly polished or with the original patina.

For additional listings, see *Warman's Antiques and Collectibles Price Guide.*

Alidade, Keuffel & Esser Co., Model No
    5093A, high post plane table, 10"
    telescope, one beveled edge, strider
    level, orig case, c1940 ....**360.00**

Surveyors equipment, tripod base, chrome and aluminum, adjustable, $70. Also shown are small braided rug, box of factory made decoys, PA RR license plate.

Compass, W. Davenport, Phila.,
    detachable brass sight vanes, worn
    fitted dovetailed mahogany case with
    brass fittings **920.00**
Level, Worth, 12', plumb, brass top.**35.00**
Sight level, Dieterich, leather case ..**80.00**
Military level, Berger & Sons, Boston, 9-
    1/4" l telescope with high precision vial,
    c1950 ....**375.00**
Tape measure, English land surveyor
    measuring tape, 30'......................**78.00**
Transit, Bostrom, orig box..............**50.00**

Surveyors equipment, tape measure, red trimmed chrome case, Evans, National White Tape, 100 feet, $25.

❖ Swankyswigs

Collectors never seem to tire of finding these little glasses. Kraft Cheese Spreads were originally packed in these colorful juice glasses as early as the 1930s. Over the years many variations and new patterns have been introduced.

Collectors' Club: Swankyswig's Unlimited, 201 Alvena, Wichita, KS 67203.

Antique, brown coal bucket and clock, 3-3/4" h..............................**5.00**
Bands, red and black **3.00**
Bustlin' Betsy **5.00**
Checkerboard, green, red, and dark blue, 3-1/2" h **25.00**
Deer and squirrels, brown, 3-3/4" h.**8.00**
Dots and circles, black, blue, green, or red **4.50**
Elephants and birds, red, 3-3/4" h ..**8.00**
KiddieCup, pig and bear, blue..........**2.00**
Modern flowers, dark and light blue, red or yellow
   Cornflower.....................................**3.25**
   Forget-me-not................................**3.25**
   Jonquil...**3.00**
Roosters, red, 3-1/4" h **6.00**
Sailboat, red, green, or dark blue, racing or sailing.....................................**25.00**

❖ Swarovski Crystal

The Swarovski family traces its glassmaking tradition to Austria in 1895. Today, the company is still identified with high-quality crystal. Look for a swan logo on most pieces. The original box and packaging add to an items value.

Periodicals: *Swan Seekers News,* 9740 Campo Road, Suite 134, Spring Valley, CA 91977; *The Crystal Report,* 1322 N. Barron St., Eaton, OH 45320.

Collectors' Clubs: Swan Seekers, 9740 Campo Road, Suite 134, Spring Valley, CA 91977; Swarovski Collectors Society, 2 Slater Road, Cranston, RI 02920.

Charm, musical clef note, enamel and crystal, 1-3/4" h **15.00**
Christmas ornament, snowflake, MIB
   1992 ....**250.00**
   1996 ....**195.00**
   1997 ....**160.00**
Crystal City, retired Dec, 1994
   Cathedral......................................**215.00**
   City Gates **215.00**
   Poplar trees **175.00**
   Town Hall......................................**215.00**
Figure
   Bear, miniature, 1-1/8" h **200.00**
   Butterfly, miniature, 1" h **125.00**
   Dachshund, large, 3" l................**125.00**
   Dragon, Society member, "Fabulous Creatures," 1997 ....**595.00**
   Elephant, large, frosted tail **115.00**
   Harp, #74477, MIB.....................**295.00**
   Kiwi, 1956, 1-3/4" h....................**200.00**
   Mouse, spring tail, #7631, 2-1/2" h **195.00**
   Rabbit, large...............................**250.00**
   Squirrel, 10th anniversary **275.00**
Fur clip, gold-tone, crystal stones,

sterling silver setting, sgd "Eisenberg Original, Sterling," 2-1/2" h, pr....**695.00**
Paperweight, pyramid, helio, small, 1990, orig box and certificate.....**595.00**
Pendant, red and black enameled child's sled, crystal on top, 2" h..............**35.00**
Star
   1994, MIB....................................**225.00**
   1995, MIB....................................**275.00**
   1999, MIB....................................**235.00**

❖ Swizzle Sticks

Radish swizzle stick, red and green glass, clear glass stirrer, 8-1/4" l, $15.

Here's another example of something people tend to save as a souvenir. Who hasn't tucked one into their pocket? After awhile you've got a collection started, so why not search for some more examples during your next trip to a flea market.

Aluminum, golf club shape, "O'Donnell's Sea Grill" on shaft, "Stolen in Washington, D.C." on other side, pr **15.00**
Commemorative, plastic
   Alaska Airlines, white, gold lettering "Gold Coast Alaska Airlines," 5-1/2" l **3.00**
   American Airlines, blue, 6" l **5.00**
   Continental Airlines, Continental to Hawaii, yellow **4.50**
   Hard Rock Café, guitar at top, 9" l.**2.00**
   Howard Johnson's, 5-1/2" l **1.00**
   Lawrence Welk Welkome Inn, 6" l..**1.00**
   Mirage, Las Vegas, 6" l **1.00**
   Playboy, 8" l.................................**5.00**
   SAS, light blue, 6" l **4.50**
   San Francisco, white, cable car on one side, "San Francisco, the Friendly Skies" on other, 5" l **3.50**
   S.S. Independence, 5-1/2" l...........**1.00**
   The Sands, Las Vegas **1.00**
   TWA, airplane on top **10.00**
Glass
   Amber, 6" l....................................**3.00**
   Christmas Tree **7.00**
   Manny Wolf's Chop House, New York City, cobalt blue **9.00**
   Rosoff's, Times Square, c1950, 6" l **8.00**
Plastic
   Hawaiian girl...................................**1.00**
   Mr. Peanut, Everybody Loves A Nut **5.00**
   Sword **25**

❖ Syracuse China

Founded in Syracuse, N.Y., in the mid 1800s, this china company is still in operation. Along with the many dinnerware patterns produced over the years are pieces for commercial accounts, such as the C&O Railroad. The company's restaurant wares are especially popular with collectors.

Ashtray, Irish setter in center, front mkd "Stuart Bruce," some hairline cracks from use, 4-1/2" dia.....................**10.00**
Cake cover, Santa Fe RR, California Poppy, 6" dia **200.00**
Coffeepot, cov
   Diane, cobalt blue trim **300.00**
   Lilac Rose **195.00**
Creamer, Chessie, C & O Railroad.**20.00**
Cup and saucer, Adobe Ware, Rodeo Cowboy, stenciled "Adobe Ware, Syracuse China, 5-EE USA," c1950 ....**38.00**
Place setting, Chicken in the Rough, golfing rooster, 4 pc set...............**95.00**
Plate
   AAA, 50th Anniversary, Oct 4, 1950, mkd "Iroquois China, Syracuse, NY" **55.00**
   Black Waiter, Homestead Hotel, Hot Springs, VA, 10-1/2" dia..........**110.00**
   Caprice, 10-1/2" dia **5.00**
   George Washington Hotel, Jacksonville, FL, 1959, 10" dia **20.00**
Platter
   Corabel, Winchester shape, 15-3/4" l **255.00**
   Sabella, fish chef logo, green mark, 12" x 9-1/2" **35.00**
Soup bowl, Anderdsen Restaurant, Pea Soup Characters, Hap-Pea and Pea-Wee, 9" dia..............................**45.00**
Sugar bowl, cov, Coralbel, Winchester shape **240.00**

Syracuse China creamer, white, turquoise dec, mkd "Syralite by Syracuse," 3" h, $5.

Teapot, cov

Coralbel, Virginia shape **275.00**

Sante Fe RR, California Poppy, 4" dia
....**200.00**

Vegetable, cov

Bracelet, gold rim **200.00**

Coralbel, Virginia shape, 8-1/4" dia
....**300.00**

❖ Syrup Pitchers

Here's another specialized type of glassware for your table or sideboard. It was designed to hold syrup. Look for metal tops to be in good condition, but some use-related wear is acceptable.

Coin Spot & Swirl, blue opalescent
....**185.00**

Cord Drapery, chocolate **350.00**

Currier and Ives, clear **95.00**

Dahlia, amber..................................**85.00**

Daisy & Fern, cranberry opalescent
....**210.00**

Hazel Atlas, clear body, plastic top.**90.00**

Hercules Pillar, amber, 8-1/2" h ...**110.00**

Inverted Thumbprint, pinched base, blue, 6-7/8" h **80.00**

Inverted Thumbprint, tapered, apple green, 7" h.................................**100.00**

Lattice, blue opalescent **335.00**

Medallion Sprig, blue fading to clear, 8" h, crack in top of handle, missing thumb tab **90.00**

Patee Cross, clear **65.00**

Robin's Nest, amber, 7-1/4" h, thumb tab missing **50.00**

Rope and Thumbprint, amber, mkd inside lid "Pat. Jan 29, 84"............**60.00**

Waffle Variant, clear, reeded pressed handle, 6" h **60.00**

❖ Taylor, Smith & Taylor

Taylor, Smith & Taylor was started by W.L. Smith, John N. Taylor, W.L. Taylor, Homer J. Taylor, and Joseph G. Lee in Chester, W.Va., in 1899. By 1903 the firm reorganized and the Taylors bought out Lee. By 1906 Smith bought out the Taylors. The company continued making dinnerware and table wares until 1981, when the plant closed. The Smith family sold its interest to Anchor Hocking in 1973.

For additional listings, see *Warman's Americana & Collectibles* and LuRay pattern in this edition.

Bowl
Autumn Harvest 40.00
Vistosa, cobalt blue, 8" dia...........65.00
Butter dish, cov, Empire.................20.00
Cake plate, Laurel, 10-1/4" d..........12.00
Casserole, cov
Autumn Harvest 38.00
Sea Shell, 8" dia...........................50.00
Chop plate
Plymouth 20.00
Vistosa, light green, 11" dia 85.00
Coffeepot, cov
Autumn Leaves, stain on handle..65.00
Boutonniere, 10" h 70.00
Creamer and sugar, Vistosa, light green
....45.00
Cup and saucer
Marvel 6.00
Vogue 6.50
Dinner plate
Empire, 10" d 12.00
Fairway, 9-1/2" dia 8.50
Pebbleford, 10" dia 10.00
Dish, Autumn Harvest, 12-1/2" l, 9-7/8" w
....60.00
Gravy boat, English Abbey.............60.00
Pan, cov, Chateau Buffet, Pebbleford,
blue int.......................................62.00
Platter
Autumn Harvest, 13-1/2" l...........45.00
Cathay, 13-1/2" l, light scratches..36.00
Golden Jubilee 42.00
Salad bowl, Marvel 17.50
Salt and pepper shakers, pr, Versatile
....6.00
Sauce boat, underplate, Pattern #1377
....45.00

Platter, Dandelion pattern, Delphian shape, oval, emb floral border, gold trim, 13-1/2" l, $28.

Soup bowl, Vistosa, deep yellow....**24.00**
Sugar bowl, cov
Dwarf Pine, yellow.....................**125.00**
Golden Jubilee **40.00**
Teapot, Vistosa, deep yellow..........**85.00**
Vegetable dish, cov
Autumn Harvest **40.00**
Silhouette **95.00**

❖ Teapots

To devoted tea drinkers, the only way to properly brew a cup of tea is in a teapot. Thankfully there are many wonderful examples of teapots available to collectors. From decorative porcelain teapots to whimsical figural teapots, the array is endless.

Reference: Tina M. Carter, *Collectible Teapots*, Krause Publications, 2000.

Periodicals: *Tea Talk,* PO Box 860, Sausalito, CA 94966; *Tea Time Gazette,* PO Box 40276, St. Paul, MN 55104.

For additional listings, see specific companies, such as Hall China, in this edition.

Figural
Betty Boop...................................**35.00**
Dickens character, Beswick, English
....**85.00**
Doc...**35.00**
Lucy..**50.00**
McCormick, black........................**35.00**
Minnie Mouse..............................**35.00**

Teapot, cream colored background, cobalt blue, orange, and gold trim, green stamp mark "Made in England," decorators hand painted initials on base, $20.

Teapot, Chelsea pattern, white ground, blue sprig dec, minor chips, handle repaired, $50.

Porcelain
English, Abrams, cosy pot, pitcher
shape, patents **50.00**
English, James Kent, Du Barry, some
int. staining.............................**550.00**
English, Wade, paisley chintz pattern,
c1925......................................**650.00**
German, Royal Hanover, hand painted
....**75.00**
Homer Laughlin, Rhythum, 5" h...**45.00**
Japan, hand painted scene..........**40.00**
Royal Albert, Old English Rose, 5-3/4"
h...**350.00**
Shawnee, Granny Ann **250.00**

❖ Teddy Bears

Everybody has loved one of these at some time in their lives, and many collectors start by buying one or two that reminds them of a childhood companion. Whatever the motivation, teddy bears are still one of the hottest collectibles. Look for teddy bears that are in good condition, perhaps showing a sign or two of a little loving. Some collectors are more discriminating about condition and know they may pay a premium.

References: Shawn Brecka, *Big Book of Little Bears*, Krause Publications, 2000; Ken Yenke, *Bing Bears and Toys*, Schiffer Publishing, 2000.

Periodicals: *National Doll & Teddy Bear Collector*, PO Box 4032, Portland, OR 97208; *Teddy Bear & Friends*, PO Box 420235, II Commerce Blvd., Palm Coast, FL 32142; *Teddy Bear Review*, 170 Fifth Ave., 12th Floor, New York, NY 10010.

Collectors' Clubs: Good Bears of the World, PO Box 13097, Toledo, OH 43613; My Favorite Bear: Collectors Club for Classic Winnie the Pooh, 468 W Alpine #10, Upland, CA 91786; Teddy Bear Boosters Club, 19750 SW Peavine Mountain Road, McMinnville, OR 97128.

For additional listings, see *Warman's Antiques and Collectibles Price Guide,* as well as Steiff and other categories in this edition.

A special bear
Black isn't a traditional color for teddy bears. However, 600 black Steiff bears made in May 1912 were of special significance. They were made by Steiff in Germany and exported to England as a symbol of mourning after the sinking of the Titanic.

When one of the bears was offered at Christie's South Kensington in December 2000, it drew considerable attention. The consignor's great uncle was among the more than 1,500 who perished when the Titanic sank in the icy waters of the North Atlantic.

The child who originally owned the bear took a dislike to the toy, and it was put away—for the next 88 years. When it returned to the light of day, it drew great enthusiasm from collectors and sold for $136,000.

Anker, mohair, mkd "Plustchtiere Aus Muchen," 16" h **215.00**
Brooklyn Doll and Toy Co., brown plush, plastic eyes and nose, 1982 ....**25.00**
Campbell's cheerleader bear........**70.00**
Campbell's Super Chief bear........**25.00**
Hershey's Cocoa...........................**85.00**
Jeane Steele Original, 11-1/2" h, straw hat, felt collar, big fabric bow, jointed, tag "Kent Collectibles/Jeane Steele Originals/©1985" **48.00**
Koala Me, store display, 10" h.........**75.00**

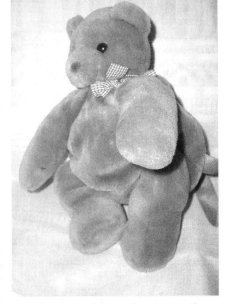

Teddy bear backpack, zippered compartment in back, tan mesh adjustable shoulder straps, int. tag reads "Made in Indonesia," $4.

Large Gund black jointed bear "Blackbeard" #90/350, with black leather paws & feet, signed, 26" h, $90.

Laveen bear, Shug, long gray fur, blue corduroy vest, large blue marble eyes, leather snot and paw pads, orig hang tag, 18" h.....................................**165.00**
Merrythought, curly cream mohair, fully jointed, glass eyes, shaved muzzle, yellow embroidered nose, mouth, and claws, "I Growl" chest tag, cream felt pads, 1930s, 15" h, slight fur matting, muzzle soiled **635.00**
Musical, Swiss, 16" h, mohair.......**350.00**
Petsey, Steiff, blond, button **95.00**
Tara Toys, Ireland, light gold mohair, fully jointed, plastic eyes, Rexine pads, mouth opens and closes by squeezing knobs on back of head, early 1950s, cloth label sewn in foot seam, pads worn, fur loss around mechanism, replaced nose, 16" h **175.00**
Teddy Ruxpin, orig box, 2 tapes, orig books..**100.00**
This Bear, Possum Trot, brown plush, orig tags **75.00**
Yes-No bear, Schuco, mohair, 20" h, 1950s **1,200.00**
Westinghouse, adv, 1983..............**15.00**

❖ Telephones & Related

Talk, talk, talk, that's what we've been doing since this wonderful invention caught on with our ancestors. As technology changes, some folks are starting to notice that perhaps telephones are something to collect. Add to that some interesting ephemera, and you've got a great collecting area.

Collectors' Clubs: Antique Telephone Collectors Association, PO Box 94, Abilene, KS 67410; Mini-Phone Exchange, 5412 Tilden Road, Bladensburg, MD 20710; Telephone Collectors International, 19 N. Cherry Drive, Oswego, IL 60543.

Candy container, Miniature Dial Telephone, glass candlestick telephone, 4-1/4" h......................**55.00**
Lighter, desk phone motif, Occupied Japan..**248.00**

Candlestick-style telephone, Western Electric Co., Aug 04 and Jan 15 patent dates, $90.

Postcard
 Bell Telephone Co. Building, Kansas City, MO, 1924 ....**5.00**
 Christmas, girl using candlestick telephone, 1913 postmark..........**3.50**
 Christmas, girl using wall telephone, 1911 postmark............................**4.00**
Salt and pepper shakers, pink wall telephone, orig box mkd "Party Line," c1950 ....**25.00**
Sheet music, *Hello Central Give Me Heaven*, cover shows girl with phone **15.00**
Sign
 New York Telephone Co., porcelain, trademark bell, 8" dia **150.00**
 United Utilities System, Public Telephone, porcelain, 2-sided, L-shape, flange **200.00**
Telephone
 Candlestick, Kellogg...................**300.00**
 Co-pay, gray, box with key............**95.00**
 Desk, rotary, blue plastic, Bell System **30.00**
 Figural, Bozo, no lights when rings, Telemania, 12-1/2" h.................**60.00**
 Figural, '57 Chevy, red, push-button, modular plugs, unused **37.50**
 Figural, Mickey Mouse, 1978, Western Electric....................................**150.00**
 Figural, Pizza Inn, cartoon figure of mustache-wearing pizza maker, touch-tone, Taiwan, late 1970s, 10" h **25.00**
 Figural, Snoopy, push button dial.**75.00**
 Wall, Chicago Telephone Supply Company, receiver missing, 26" h **200.00**
 Wall, single box, Kellogg, refinished **200.00**

Wall single box, Kellogg, oak case, mouth base mkd "Kellogg," 25-1/2" h **200.00**

Wall, single box, Western Electric **190.00**

Stock certificate, Associated Telephone Co, 1945...........................**10.00**

Telephone Almanac

1940, Bell System Telephone Subscribers, American Telephone & Telegraph **5.00**

1959, Michigan Bell Telephone Co., slight discoloration **2.50**

Telephone Book

Beloit, WI, 1954..............................**5.00**

Villisca, Iowa, 1962 ....**17.50**

Washington, D.C. March, 1948, Yellow Pages Directory, slight use **55.00**

Toy

Fisher-Price telephone pull toy, # 2251, 1993...**6.00**

Junior Phone, battery operated, Modern Toys, Japan, 1950s, 2 large hard plastic phones, orig wiring, instructions, and fold-out display box **60.00**

Yellow Pages, Washington, D.C., March 1948 ....**55.00**

❖ Television Characters and Personalities

"Now on with the show" was Ed Sullivan's promise to the audience waited to be entertained. Today's flea markets are a great place to find vintage items relating to early television and the many characters who became stars.

Reference: Rex Miller, *The Investor's Guide to Vintage Character Collectibles,* Krause Publications, 1999, plus many others on specific stars and character memorabilia.

Periodicals: *Big Reel,* PO Box 1050, Dubuque, IA 52004; *Television Chronicles,* 10061 Riverside Drive, #171, North Hollywood, CA 91602; *The TV Collector,* PO Box 1088, Easton, MA 02334.

For additional listings, see *Warman's Americana & Collectibles,* plus other categories in this edition.

Activity book, paste type

Blondie, 1968 ....**14.00**

Rowan & Martin Laugh-in, Fun Book, 1989...**20.00**

Activity set, Captain Kangaroo, shoe box size, c1956, unused **75.00**

Advertisement, Red Skelton Pledge of Allegiance, 1969.........................**20.00**

Bank, Romper Room, Do-Bee, Hasbro **55.00**

Bart Simpson doll, vinyl, fabric clothing, $10.

Big Little Book, *Lassie Adventure in Alaska,* Whitman, 1967 ....**15.00**

Card game

Beverly Hillbillies, Milton Bradley, complete **24.00**

Howdy Doody, orig slide-out box..**45.00**

Cigar band, Hawaii Five-O, full color **2.50**

Colorforms, Daniel Boone, Fess parker, 1964, unused **85.00**

Coloring book, unused

Beverly Hillbillies, Whitman, 1963 **24.00**

Dennis the Menace, 1973............**15.00**

Gilligan's Island, Whitman, 1965 **135.00**

Comic book, *I Love Lucy,* Dell, #3, 1954 ....**135.00**

Cookbook, *Buffy's Cookbook,* Jody Cameron, Family Affair.................**15.00**

Doll

Cher, Mego, 12" h **50.00**

Honey West, Gilbert, 12" h, MIB **375.00**

Six Million Dollar Man, 1973, MIB ...**35.00**

Game

Down You Go, Selchow & Righter Co., copyright 1954 ....**18.00**

Lost in Space **180.00**

Mister Ed, Parker Brothers, copyright 1962, missing dice and markers **45.00**

Road Runner, Milton Bradley, Warner Bros, 1968 ....**65.00**

Gum card wrapper, Beverly Hillbillies, Topps, 1963.................................**65.00**

Halloween costume, child's, orig costume, mask, box

I Love Lucy **325.00**

Mr. Ed..**115.00**

Hat box, Buffy, Family Affair, pink plastic, 1969, 10-1/2"dia..........................**45.00**

Lunch box

Andy Griffith, labeled "Barney Fife Security," 8" x 6".........................**18.00**

Child's storybook record, Knight Rider, Highway to Danger, *Universal Studios, 1984, $5.*

Bewitched....................................**18.00**

I Dream of Jeannie.......................**18.00**

Munsters, 1965, lunch box and thermos...................................**375.00**

Magazine, *TV Junior,* March 1959 ..**20.00**

Medic set, M*A*S*H, Ja-Ru, copyright 1981, 20th Century Fox Film Corp, 6" x 10" blister card, MOC...................**18.00**

Mirror, Miss Piggy, Sigma, glazed ceramic, easel back and hook for hanging, early 1980s....................**80.00**

Night light, Flintstones, Fred and Barney **25.00**

Nodder, Dr. Kildare, Lego **125.00**

Paint set, Winky Dink, licensed by CBS, 16" x 12", c1950, MIB **100.00**

Photograph, Robert Redford in "Jeremiah Johnson," ABC Sunday Night Movie, Dec 19, 1976...........**10.00**

Pinback button

Ben Casey, white, blue letters......**15.00**

Bullwinkle for President, red, white, and blue flag, 1972 copyright, 2-1/4" d..**40.00**

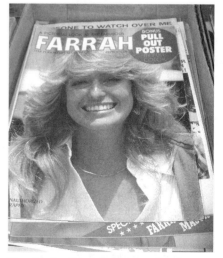

Magazine, Star Personality, featuring Farrah, $3.00.

Puppet, hand
    Captain Kangaroo 3.00
    Gumby..28.00
Push puppet
    Huckleberry Hound 45.00
    Pebbles..50.00
Ring, Sky King, adjustable, sq red plastic
    television box................................98.00
Toy
    Flying Nun, Ray Plastic Inc., copyright
        1970 Screen Gems, Inc., color photo
        of Sally Fields, plastic figure,
        launching unit, some wear to orig
        box 50.00
    Starsky & Hutch, diecast car, 3" l,
        metal and plastic, 1970s...........35.00
Wallet, CHIPS, orig display card, MGM,
    MOC..20.00
Waste can, Laugh-In, litho metal 45.00
Whistle, Dragnet 15.00

❖ Television Sets

Used television sets are something that occasionally show up at flea markets. Often their size and bulk finds them still sitting on the truck or in the back of a booth. Before plugging in a vintage television set, have someone knowledgeable check over the circuits and old tubes.

Collectors' Clubs: Antique Wireless Association, 59 Main St., Holcomb, NY 14469-9336; Mid-Atlantic Radio Club, PO Box 67, Upperco, MD 21155.

AC/DC, white case, black and white,
    working condition, 1992, 7" h.......**65.00**
GE, portable, cream colored plastic case,
    black and white, working condition, one
    knob chipped..................................**25.00**
Hallicrafters, T-54, c1950 ....**250.00**
Philco, reconditioned, floor model **325.00**
Pilot, TV-37, magnifier model........**120.00**
RCA, CT-100, first RCA color set ..**550.00**
Zenith, portable, black plastic case, black
    and white, working condition........**35.00**

Motorola television, portable, black and white, c1970, $25.

❖ Temple, Shirley

Her smile and curly hair were her trademarks as she stole the hearts of moviegoers in the 1940s. Her mother carefully licensed items with her image, including dolls, glassware, jewelry, and soap. More recently, several companies have revived interest in Shirley Temple by creating new collectibles with vintage images. Beware of reproductions, especially copies of cobalt glassware.

Reproduction Alert

Book, *Story of Shirley Temple,* 1934 **28.00**
Clothing tag, "Just Like Mine, Shirley
    Temple," Christmas design, holly leaves
    and berries, facsimile autograph, diecut
    sleeve **15.00**
Doll, Ideal, 1982, Captain January, 1982
    ....**60.00**
Doll dress, 1930s, for 18" or 20" doll,
    orig tags **90.00**
Figure, limited edition, Nostalgia
    Collectibles, made in Japan
    Curly Top **60.00**
    Standup and Cheer......................**60.00**
Movie book, *The Little Colonel,*
    Saalfield, hard cover, black and white
    movie scenes, full color front cover
    ....**40.00**
Movie poster, *I'll Be Seeing You,* Ginger
    Rogers, Joseph Cotton, and Shirley
    Temple, United Artists 1945, 27" x 41"
    ....**150.00**
Pinback button, Ideal Dolls............**75.00**
Plate, limited edition, Nostalgia
    Collectibles, made in Japan
    Baby Take A Bow **65.00**
    Standup and Cheer......................**65.00**
Pocket mirror, 1937 Fox Film Corp. ..**35.00**

Shirley Temple paper dolls, cut-out, c1935-36, $38.

Shirley Temple doll, composition, sleep eyes, open mouth, orig red polka-dot dress, white shoes and socks, pin with photo "The World's Darling, Genuine Shirley Temple Doll, 13" h, $700.

Scrapbook, Saalfield #1722, copyright
    1936, full color front and back covers,
    Shirley wearing pink dress, white
    bonnet, spiral binding, used **40.00**
Sheet music, *Goodnight My Love,* name
    written in pencil on front..............**21.00**

❖ Tennis Collectibles

Tennis anyone? Here's another sport where the collectibles are starting to command increased attention. Look for ephemera and equipment with endorsements by famous players.

Autograph, Billie Jean King, 8" x 10"
    photo **22.00**
Book, *How to Improve Your Tennis*, Harry
    "Cap" Leighton..............................**7.50**
Cigarette card, 1931 Lawn Tennis series
    Lakeman, Jan Fry **10.00**
    Wilmer Allison **10.00**
    Jacques Brugnon **7.00**
Cuff links, pr, sterling, mkd "Fenwick &
    Sailor"...**135.00**
Decanter, Erza Brooks, tennis player,
    1973, 14" h....................................**20.00**
Figurine
    Armani, tennis star, 8" h.............**275.00**
    Goebel, rabbit with tennis rackets
    ....**125.00**
    Precious Moments, boy tennis player,
        olive branch mark, 1985, 5-1/2" h
        ....**35.00**
Pin, tennis racket, green enamel, mkd
    Gerry's, 2-1/2" l **4.00**
Swizzle stick, tennis racket shape, blue
    plastic **1.00**
Tennis balls
    Dunlop, Mr. Peanut.........................**9.00**
    Dunlop, Vinnie Richards..............**25.00**
    MacGregor, red and white plaid can
    ....**25.00**
    Spaulding, Pancho Gonzales, blue
        label **20.00**
    Wilson, Jack Kramer illus, red and
        white **55.00**
Tennis racket
    Dayton, 1923 patent.....................**70.00**
    Knickerbocker, wood **45.00**
    Spaulding, needs restringing **10.00**

Wilson Sporting Goods, Maureen Connolly, full color portrait on handle, 1950s...**25.00**

Wright & Ditson Championship, 26" l **50.00**

Valentine, German, honeycomb tissue type, girl with tennis racket and bag of balls, 1920s, 5" h.........................**26.00**

❖ Thermometers

We've got Galileo to thank for the first practical thermometer. There have certainly been a few advances since that 1593 start. One of the most collectible types of thermometers are those used as advertising. Look for examples that are free of rust or damage. You might also want to check the accuracy of the reading.

Reference: Curtis Merritt, *Advertising, Thermometers*, Collector Books, 2001.

Collectors' Club: Thermometer Collectors Club of America, 6130 Rampart Drive, Carmichael, CA 96508.

> **Reproduction Alert**

For additional information, see *Warman's Americana & Collectibles* and *Warman's Advertising.*

Advertising

The Baltimore Tank and Tower Co., celluloid, 6-1/4" x 2" **95.00**

Chesterfield, They Satisfy, tin, 13" h **132.00**

Drink Double Cola, You'll Like It Better, tin, 1960s, 17" h......................**165.00**

For Best Results Feed Your Dog Ken-L-Ration, tin, 26-3/4" x 7-1/4" **175.00**

Phillips 66, plastic, 14" l **16.00**

Salem, triangular..........................**75.00**

Sylvania Radio Tubes, tin, rounded top and bottom, 39" x 8" **75.00**

Winstons, 5-3/4" x 13-1/2" **75.00**

Figural

Cat, Enesco, 5" h **20.00**

Flamingo, Souvenir of Florida, c1940-50, 6" h **60.00**

Wishing well, chalkware, 6-3/4" h....**22.00**

Thermometers Large metal advertising thermometer, Chew Mail Pouch Tobacco–Treat Yourself to the Best, 38-1/2" h, $135.

❖ Thimbles

Thimble, thimble, who's got the thimble? Collectors do! And, they enjoy their tiny treasures. Finding thimbles at flea markets is probably easier than it sounds since there are so many different kinds of thimbles—advertising, commemorative, political, porcelain, and metal.

Periodical: *Thimbletter,* 93 Walnut Hill Road, Newton Highlands, MA 02161.

Collectors' Clubs: The Thimble Guild, PO Box 381807, Duncanville, TX 75138; Thimble Collectors International, 8289 Northgate Drive, Rome, NY 13440.

Aluminum, plain................................**4.00**

Commemorative

California, gold-tone, white background with bear, 3/4" l.........................**10.00**

Mackinaw Bridge, copper-tone, showing bridge **10.00**

Virginia Beach, silver-tone, seagull **10.00**

Figural, ceramic, 2-1/4" h

Donald Duck..............................**15.00**

Goofy..**15.00**

Minnie Mouse.............................**17.50**

Miniature, Arcadia, gold thimble, gold thread **30.00**

Porcelain

Anniversary, violet flower, gold band, mkd "Fine Bone China, Ashleydale, England" **8.00**

Blue and red flowers, mkd "Avon" ..**6.00**

Bird..**5.50**

Orange flowers.............................**5.00**

Queen Mother **12.00**

Pink and blue flowers....................**6.00**

Silver, plain, 5/8" l **5.00**

❖ Ticket Stubs

The Grateful Dead, Pittsburgh Civic Arena, April, 1989, $2.

Here's another collectible that most of us have tucked in a drawer and probably have almost forgotten. However, there are dedicated collectors of tickets for all kinds of events—charities, sporting event, theatrical shows, expositions, fairs, etc. Most tickets are small in size and easy to display in an album.

Airplane, Cedar Rapids Airways, biplane illus, 3-1/4" x 2-1/8" **12.00**

Children's Day, March 31, 1894, San Francisco Chronicle, coupons attached, unused......................................**135.00**

Disneyland

Fantasyland and Adventureland...**20.00**

River Packet, 1955 ....**25.00**

Snow White, 50th Anniversary, bronze medallion, July 17, 1987..........**25.00**

Led Zepplin, Arizona State Univ, ticket dated March 6, 1977, concert actually held July 20, 1977 ....**50.00**

Political

Inaugural Ball, 1981, Reagan/Bush, John F. Kennedy Center for the Performing Arts, red, white, and blue, gold inauguration seal **10.00**

Republican Convention, 1964, San Francisco, elephant, and shield logo, "Entertainer" Pass.......................**6.00**

Stevenson Rally, Memorial Auditorium, Thursday, Nov 1 (1956), red, white and blue **17.50**

Railroad

PA RR...**50**

Pitt & Lake Erie, passenger, 1918 .**2.00**

Rock Island, Rand McNally & Co., Chicago **14.00**

Rose Bowl, 1952 ....**55.00**

Ship, *Italia Societa Di Navigazione Marco Polo,* from Valparaiso to La Guaira...**6.00**

World's Fair

Panama-Pacific International Exposition, tan and brown, Nov 2, 1915, used..............................**45.00**

Souvenir of the California Midwinter International Exposition, Souvenir San Francisco Day, July 4, 1894, four fair buildings on back, 4-3/4" x 3-1/2" **85.00**

❖ Tiffany Studios

Louis Comfort Tiffany was an interesting man. While he was a patron of arts and crafts, he was also a skilled craftsman. Although he worked in many mediums, he is most acclaimed for his glass creations and designs. Flea market shoppers should be aware that most "signed" Tiffany glass pieces were not signed by Louis Tiffany. Never buy a piece of Tiffany glass based solely on the signature.

> **Reproduction Alert**

For additional listings, see *Warman's Antiques and Collectibles Price Guide* and *Warman's Glass.*

Bowl, squared dimpled form, transparent aquamarine, foot inscribed "L.C. Tiffany Favrile," 4-1/4" d, 2-1/2" h, price for pair **490.00**

Calling card receiver, bronze, mkd "Tiffany Studios" **75.00**

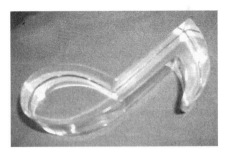

Tiffany Studios, musical note paperweight, crystal, mkd "Tiffany & Co." on side, $20.

Candlestick, heavy walled amber glass stick, 10 prominent swirled ribs, fine gold luster, inscribed "L. C. T.," labeled, 6-3/4" h.........................**400.00**

Champagne flute, Favrile, pale yellow with deep green yellow opalescent finish, highly irid, sgd "L. C. T. Favrile #1806," 5" h **350.00**

Desk accessories, Zodiac pattern, bronze
  Calendar Holder **95.00**
  Rocker Blotter...........................**120.00**

Paper rack, bronze, Chinese pattern, dark patina, some green wash in pattern recesses, three-tier, imp "Tiffany Studios New York 1756," some metal corrosion...........................**260.00**

Salt, open, ruffled rim, shallow bowl, amber glass, irid gold, polished pontil, initialed "L.C.T." on base, 2-1/2" dia
  ....**250.00**

Serving fork, sterling silver, Wave Edge pattern **150.00**

Tile, pressed molded irid blue glass, stylized blossom motif, imp "Patent Applied For," small chip, 4" sq **375.00**

Vase
  Elongated bulbous body, 10 prominent ribs below flattened rim, gold irid, inscribed "L. C. Tiffany Favrile," and number, 7-1/4" h **525.00**
  Oval body, teal blue, lined in opal white glass, smooth matte lustrous surface, inscribed "L. C. Tiffany Favrile 1753E," 5-3/4" h **750.00**

❖ Tiffin Glass

Found around 1888, A.J. Beatty & Sons made Glass in Tiffin, Ohio. The factory became part of the United States Glass conglomerate and continued to provide high-quality glassware. The company closed in 1980, ending a long tradition that included many types of glassware produced in brilliant colors.

Reference: Ed Goshe, Ruth Hemminger, Leslie Pina, *'40s, '50s & '60s Stemware by Tiffin*, Schiffer Publishing, 1999.

Collectors' Club: Tiffin Glass Collectors' Club, PO Box 554, Tiffin, OH 44883.

Tiffin Glass, poppy vase, very dark amethyst, raised flowers, $22.

Bud vase, Cherokee Rose, 6" h **38.00**

Candy Dish, cov
  Canterbury, #115, 9-1/4", Desert Red
  ....**60.00**
  Oneida, crystal **50.00**
  Satin, #330, crystal, cone, enameled flowers on lid...........................**48.00**

Celery Tray
  Cherokee Rose, 10-1/2" l, crystal **35.00**
  Fuchsia, crystal **48.00**

Champagne
  Athens Diana, crystal...................**25.00**
  Barber, #14196, blue...................**28.00**
  Charlton.....................................**22.00**
  Mystic **26.00**
  Rosalind **20.00**

Cigarette Holder, Killarney Green, 3-1/2" h...**55.00**

Cocktail, Cherokee Rose...............**16.00**

Compote, Wisteria, Cellini foot **400.00**

Console set, Fuschia, console bowl and pr matching candlesticks............**190.00**

Cordial
  June Night **40.00**
  Rambling Rose...........................**28.00**

Goblet
  Byzantine, yellow........................**38.00**
  Cadena, pink..............................**35.00**
  Cherokee Rose **32.00**
  Mystic **28.00**
  Rosalind **30.00**

Iced Tea Tumbler, 12 oz, ftd
  Cadena, yellow...........................**44.00**
  Chardonay, crystal......................**40.00**
  Cherokee Rose, crystal...............**35.00**
  Classic, crystal **40.00**

Mayonnaise Set, 3 pc
  Cadena, yellow...........................**30.00**
  Cerise, crystal **35.00**
  Cherokee Rose, crystal...............**45.00**

Parfait, Mystic **27.00**

Plate
  Blue Satin, luncheon **15.00**
  Byzantine, crystal, 8-1/2" dia **7.50**
  Cerise, crystal, 8" dia..................**15.00**
  Cherokee Rose, 8" dia **30.00**

  First Love, crystal, 6" dia.............**16.00**
Sherbet, Cordelia, crystal, high type
  ....**15.00**

Tumbler
  Rambling Rose, flat.....................**13.00**
  Rosalind, ftd **20.00**

Vase
  Black satin, red poppies dec, #16255
  ....**125.00**
  Crystal, #83, lily, four openings **65.00**
  Emerald Satin, #16261 8-1/2" h...**85.00**

Water pitcher, Dolores, 9" h **250.00**

Wine
  Rosalind **25.00**
  Thistle..**17.00**

❖ Tiles

Tiles have been used as a functional design element for decades. Collectors have also recognized the beauty of tiles and search them out. Examples range from inexpensive souvenirs to more pricey art pottery examples.

American Encaustic Tiling Co., white, black design of horseman riding through brush, 4-1/4" sq **48.00**

Batchelder, imp bird design, blue ground, imp mark, 6" sq, price for pair **175.00**

Cambridge Art Tile, Goddess and Cherub, amber, 6" x 18", price for pair **250.00**

California Art, landscape, tan and green, 5-3/4" sq......................................**65.00**

Evangel Pottery, Alburquerque, NM, cream ground, brown, blue, and gold hand-painted dec, 5-1/4" ss **6.00**

J. & J. G. Low, Chelsea, MA
  4-1/4" sq, putti carrying grapes, blue, pr **75.00**
  6" d, circular, yellow, minor edge nicks and glaze wear **35.00**
  6" sq, woman wearing hood, brown **95.00**

Jane Tallman, Miami, FL, Tile Art Originals, colorful hand-painted parrot, 7" sq..**5.00**

Mercer tile, redware body, blue glaze, tulip motif, imp mark, 8" sq, $20.

Marblehead, blue and white ships, 4-5/8" sq, price for pair **125.00**

Minton Hollins & Co., urn and floral relief, green ground, 6" sq............**48.00**

Mosaic Tile Co., Delft windmill, blue and white, framed, 8" sq **55.00**

Pardee, C., portrait of Grover Cleveland, gray-lavender, 6" sq....................**125.00**

Souvenir

Mount Vernon, multicolored **6.00**

Myrtle Beach, S.C., boating and beach scene, blue on white...................**6.00**

Old Deerfield, Massachusetts, black on white **5.00**

Washington, D.C., Bicentennial, 1776-1976, 200 Years of Progress **6.00**

West Dennis, Mass., The Lighthouse Inn...**6.00**

U.S. Encaustic Tile Works, flowered wreath, light green, 6" sq **20.00**

Wedgwood, Tally Ho, man riding horse, blue and white, 8" sq...................**85.00**

❖ Tins

One of the most decorative aspects of collecting vintage advertising is to collect tins. They were designed to catch the consumer's eye with interesting graphics and/or colors. Today collectors seek them out for many of the same reasons.

For addition listings, see *Warman's Advertising.*

A & P Peanuts, 7 ozs, red, white, and yellow label, "Made for the Great Atlantic & Pacific Tea Company, New York, NY," 3-1/2" dia, 3" h, C.8+ ...**38.00**

Blanke's Portonilla Coffee, green and gold, bail handle, dome lid, c1900, 10" h, some losses **60.00**

Buster Popcorn, 10 lb, 9-1/2" h **75.00**

Campfire Marshmallows, Campfire Kitchens, 7-1/4" d, 2" h **70.00**

Capitol Mills, Lincoln, Seyms & Co., 5-1/2" h..**60.00**

Colgate Talc for Men, Invisible, Soothing, Refreshing, blue on white, 3-1/4" h..**27.50**

Constans Brand Coffee, slid lid, 9-1/2" h **22.00**

Donald Duck Coffee, keywind, 1 lb **742.50**

Elite Powder, A Perfect Foot Powder, 4-1/8" h..**34.00**

Evening In Paris, round, 5" h **10.00**

Frozen Mints, hinged, satin pebbly finish litho, 1-3/8" x 4" x 2-5/8," C.8.....**150.00**

Hershey's, A Kiss for You................**55.00**

Italina Antacid, 1930s **30.00**

Jack Sprat, black-eye peas, paper label, unopened, 12 oz, 7" h..................**50.00**

Johnson & Johnson Baby Talc.....**60.00**

Libbey's Miniature Asparagus......**95.00**

Log Cabin Syrup, blacksmith scene, 5" h **330.00**

Mammy Salted Peanuts, pictures Mammy, some wear **2,500.00**

Monarch Cocoa, 3" h **50.00**

Mount Cross Coffee, J. S. Brown Mercantile Co., 3 lb, 7-1/2" h........**70.00**

National Biscuit.............................**15.00**

Old Berma Coffee, Grand Union Co., 1 lb, 6-1/4" h, minor blemishes........**50.00**

Omar Cigarettes............................**15.00**

O-So-Easy Mop, 1920s **50.00**

Plee-zing, no graphics **7.00**

Rawleigh's Cocoa, sample, 2-1/4" h **60.00**

Red Rooster Coffee, keywind, 1 lb **72.00**

Red Wolf Coffee, keywind, 1 lb **144.00**

Royal Violet Talc, image of young girl, 1-3/4" w, 4-1/8" h, some spots and small dent **90.00**

Rose Kist Popcorn.........................**48.00**

Runkel's Cocoa, sample, 1-1/4" h..**66.00**

Shur-Fine, no graphics **7.00**

Sovereign Toffees, hinged, full color American Indian scene, c1950, 3" x 3-1/2" x 5-3/4"..............................**38.00**

Sudan Spice, graphics......................**9.00**

Tom Thumb Crescent Crackers, blue and silver litho, red ground, two pound size, 7" h..**60.00**

Whitman's Salmagundi, hinged, Art Nouveau design of young lady, copyright S. F. W. & S. Inc., 1920s, 4-1/4" x 7-1/2" x 2", scattered nicks and scratches....................................**20.00**

Widlar's Spice, no graphics.............**7.00**

❖ Tinware

Edward and William Pattison settled in Berlin, Conn., in 1738, becoming America's first tinsmiths. Before that time, the pieces of tinware used in the Colonies were expensive imports. It wasn't until the discovery of tin near Goshen, Conn., in 1829 that tinplate was produced in America. The industrial revolution ushered in machine-made, mass-produced tinware, and, by the late 19th century, the handmade era had ended. Tinware with painted decorations is known as toleware.

References: Marilyn E. Dragowick, ed., *Metalwares Price Guide*, Antique Trader Books, 1995; John Player, *Origins and Craft of Antique Tin & Tole*, Norwood Publishing, 1995.

Periodical: *Let's Talk Tin Newsletter*, 1 S. Beaver Ln., Greenville, SC 29605.

Museum: Cooper-Hewitt Museum, New York, NY.

Book Box, remnants of painted design, 9-1/4" l **125.00**

Candle Sconces, pr, semicircular, candle socket and tall back with crimped crest, later white and green flowers, yellowed varnish, 12-7/8" h **250.00**

Coffeepot

Gooseneck, flared gallery foot, inverted conical top, stamped banding, arched tapered ribbon handle with handle brace, rounded hinged lid, wooden turned finial, 10" h.....**250.00**

Punched heart and floral motif, V-shaped spout, 10" h **550.00**

Comb holder, hanging, mirrored **95.00**

Cookie cutter, cat, 4" h **145.00**

Cream pail, stamped banding around sides, arched bail handle, early solder repair, 8-3/4" h, 5-3/8" dia **60.00**

Flour bin from Hoosier cabinet, 31" h **125.00**

Food mold, 3 fruits, tin and copper **135.00**

Lunch kettle, hinged lid, 2 hinged brass handles, mkd "Champion," 1917 patent date, interior with removable tray and insulated container, minor rust, 5-7/8" h, 9-3/4" w, 6-1/4" d.....................**75.00**

Grouping of spice tins, prices range from $2 to $14.

Tin, Cresca Fancy Cluster Raisins, hinged lid, $35.

Tinware magazine holder, green ground, hand painted pink and white roses, green foliage, white ribbon, rolled reticulated edge trim, $45.

Quilt Template
4-5/8" d, star.................................**30.00**
7" d, flower **35.00**
Skater's lantern, light teal-green globe,
6-3/8" h......................................**225.00**
Tray, painted village scene, "Concord
1839," copper-painted rim with flowers,
15" x 18-1/2"...............................**195.00**
Wall pocket, large arched top with
crimped rim, flanked by 2 small circular
elements, full-width rect pocket, some
rust, 5-1/8" w, 7-5/8" h **200.00**

❖ Tip Trays

Tip trays are small colorful trays left on a table so that a patron could live a tip for the wait staff. Their colorful lithographed decoration makes them an interesting collectible to many collectors. Because these little beauties saw a lot of use, carried coins, etc., expect to find signs of wear, perhaps some denting.

For additional listings, see *Warman's Advertising.*

Reproduction Alert

Bull Brand Feeds, Maritime Milling Co.,
Buffalo, NY, rect...........................**185.00**
C.D. Kenny, Baltimore, boy with turkey,
round **90.00**
Cleveland and Buffalo Line, shows
ship, 4-1/8" dia **400.00**
Clysmic, King of the Table Waters,
woman with bottle, oval................**80.00**
El Verso Cigar, man smoking in den
....**60.00**
Fraternal Life & Accident Insurance,
rect, 4-7/8" x 4-1/4" **135.00**
Jap Rose Soap, James S. Kirk & Co.,
Chicago, back worn, 4-1/4" dia ..**250.00**
National Cigar Stands Company,
beautiful lady in center, 6" d.......**195.00**
Prudential Insurance, The Prudential, 2-
1/2" x 3-1/2"................................**20.00**
Quick Meal Ranges, oval, 4-1/2" x 3-3/8"
....**255.00**

Tip tray, small painted tin advertising tray decorated with young girl seated on bar of soap "Have You A Little FAIRY in Your Home", 4" dia, $90.

Success Manure Spreader, side
margins name sponsor Kemp &
Burpee Mfg. Co., Syracuse, early
1900s, 3-1/4" x 4-3/4" **140.00**
World's Best Table Water, White Rock,
scantly clad female kneeling, looking
into water, rect, 6-1/8" x 4-1/8"...**100.00**

❖ Tire ashtrays

Miniature tires and round ashtrays were a marriage just waiting to happen. When the two came together, they created tire ashtrays—a perfect advertising medium. These interesting items are becoming harder to find, especially the earlier examples.

Firestone
Clear glass insert, 6-1/2" dia........**50.00**
Red and black swirled plastic insert
....**82.00**
Goodrich, clear glass insert with white
advertising for Amarillo, Texas,
merchant **50.00**
Goodrich Silvertowns, green glass
insert, early 1920s **125.00**
U.S. Royal Master, clear glass insert, 5-
7/8" dia **30.00**
U.S. Tire, blue slag glass insert.......**88.00**
Vogue Tyre, clear glass insert, 2-1/2" dia
....**28.00**
Western Auto, marbelized Bakelite
insert, 6" dia **33.00**

❖ Titanic Collectibles

There are two types of Titanic collectibles. The older are those that were generated when the great ship was built and first launched. The public then was eager for news about this disaster just as we would be today. There were newspaper reports, books written, and other memorabilia. The second classification of Titanic memorabilia relates to the recent movie and its popularity.

Collectors' Clubs: Titanic Historical Society, 208 Main Street, Indian Orchard, MA 01151; Titanic International, Inc., PO Box 7007, Freehold, NJ 07728-7007.

Book, *Wreck & Sinking of the Titanic,*
Marshall Everett, 1912, worn condition
....**150.00**
Key chain, Titanic, White Star Line, MOC
....**3.95**
Magazine, National Geographic,
December, 1985............................**2.25**
Model kit, Minicraft 350 scale, Japan,
30" l, MIB......................................**55.00**
Movie prop, certificate of authenticity
Oar Lock, brass..........................**450.00**
Passageway Lamp, brass **250.00**

Newspaper, Daily Mirror **35.00**
Photograph, movie set, set of 27 4" x 6"
photos, showing film crews, actors,
1977 ....**35.00**
Print, 6" d round sealed bubble frame,
shells and seaweed dec on frame
....**250.00**

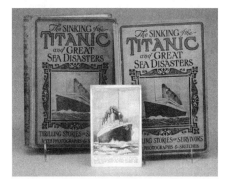

Three TITANIC items: "The Sinking of the Titanic and Great Sea Disasters," 1912, Logan Marshall, ed., the salesman sample for same, and a black and white postcard "Ocean Liner Titanic–Largest Steamer in the World," minor water damage, $145.

❖ Toasters

You need a good breakfast to help you get through a hard day at the flea market. Better include some toast in that feast. That breakfast staple has been around for generations, and the toaster has been evolving too. Watch for interesting designs and shapes in toasters. However, like other electrical appliances, be careful if you try to use any vintage toaster.

Periodical: A Toast To You, 26245 Calle Cresta, Temecula, CA 92590.

Collectors' Clubs: Electric Breakfast Club, PO Box 306, White Mills, PA 18473-0306; Upper Crust, PO Box 529, Temecula, CA 92593.

Capitol Products, #50, tin and chrome,
1930s **45.00**
Cornet-CGNN Appliance Co., Winsted,
CT, Art Deco styling, orig cord **40.00**
Edison Appliance Co., #214-T-5, open
nickel body, free-swinging tab closures
at top, single side knob, removable
toast warming rack, c1918 ....**95.00**
General Mills, 2 slice pop-up, chrome
body, wheat dec, black Bakelite base,
early 1940s..................................**38.00**
Knapp Monach Reverso, light weight
nickel plated body, rounded corners,
black painted base, flip-flop doors with
tab handles...................................**35.00**
Landers, Fray & Clarke, EE-947, 1915,
orig cord **75.00**
Montgomery Ward & Co., #94-KW2298-
B, flip-flop type, solid nickel-chrome
body, Bakelite handle, mid-1930s,**50.00**

Swinger, electric, two wooden handles, $150.

Radiant Roast................................**65.00**
Steel Craft, painted green wire
  construction, flip-flop type, red painted
  wood knobs and feet, late 1920s .**65.00**
Sunbeam, Model B, flat, chrome body,
  round reeded legs, hexagonal Bakelite
  feet, double wire cages flip over
  horizontally, small drop bail handles for
  carrying, 1920s, 5" x 9" **145.00**
Toast-A-Lator, conveyor belt toaster
  ....**125.00**

❖ Tobaccoania

Tobaccoania is a term coined to reflect the
joys of smoking, and includes cigar,
cigarette, and pipe smoking. As a
collectible, tobaccoania seems to be as
strong today as it was several years ago.

Collectors' Club: Society of Tobacco Jar
Collectors, 3011 Falstaff Road, #307,
Baltimore, MD 21209-2960.

For additional listings, see *Warman's
Advertising.*

Folder, Mail Pouch Chewing Tobacco,
  black and white, diecut of baby laying
  on blanket next to Mail Pouch tobacco
  package, copyright 1938 ....**15.00**
Humidor, cov, figural, Devil head,
  majolica, 6" h................................**85.00**
Lunch box, Central Union Cut Plug, The
  United States Tobacco Co., Richmond,
  VA, 4-1/4" x 7" x 4-5/8", grade C.9
  ....**210.00**
Plate, tin, Havana Post, Morning English,
  La Tarde-Castello, woman holding jug
  ....**150.00**

Pouch, orig contents
  Arrow **15.00**
  Bigger Hair, 5" h.........................**30.00**
  Buckeye, Mellow Chewing Tobacco, 5"
    h...**5.00**
  Harp **15.00**
  Star, empty..................................**10.00**
  Sure Shot, 5" h............................**20.00**
  Uncle Daniel, 3-1/2" h **15.00**

Sign
  Red Coon Tobacco, cardboard...**278.00**
  Edgeworth Tobacco, metal over
    cardboard, 9-1/4" x 13-1/4" **475.00**
Tobacco cutter
  Enterprise Mfg. Co., Philadelphia, April
    13,1875 patent........................**195.00**
  Drummond's Good Luck Tobacco
    Cutter, American Machine Co., 16" l
    ....**185.00**
  Griswold, Erie, PA **70.00**
Tobacco Jar
  Crystal, hammered copper top, Roman
    coin dec, sgd "Benedict Studios"
    ....**250.00**
  Fisherman **275.00**
  Mandarin, papier-mâché **95.00**
  Scotsman **295.00**
Tobacco silk, zebra, 2" x 3"............**10.00**

❖ Tobacco Tags

The colorful tags used to identify bundles of
tobacco that were sold at country tobacco
auctions have become collectible. Watch for
interesting shapes, names or places to help
identify the original locale of the tag.

Collectors' Club: Tobacco Tin Tag
Collectors Club, Route 2, Box 55, Pittsburg,
TX 75686-9516.

Battle Axe **9.00**
Bull of the Woods..............................**6.00**
Brown & Williamson, Sun Cured **10.00**
Close Figures...................................**28.00**
Favorite **28.00**
Flat Iron...**13.50**
Golden Slipper **6.00**
Gravely's Second **10.00**
Harvey's Nat'leaf **8.00**
Legal Tender **9.50**
Little Henry **11.50**
Little Mattie **9.50**
New Coon **28.00**
New Moon...**10.00**
Old Bob **28.00**
Old Lorillard Climax Plug, 5/8" d **3.00**
Old Navy, Zahm **5.00**
Penn's Red J.....................................**6.00**
Ram's Horn Sun Cured **10.00**
Rich and Ripe **13.00**
Scotten's Brown Slag........................**10.00**
Spur **22.50**
Sun Cured..**10.00**
Taylor Made **6.00**
Uncle Sam **14.00**

❖ Tobacco Tins

Everybody remembers the old joke about
letting Prince Albert out of the can. Today's
collectors of tobacco tins search for Prince
Albert and many other colorful characters
who grace the front of tobacco tins.

For additional listings, see *Warman's
Advertising.*
Bowl of Roses, vertical pocket tin, short
  version, man smoking in chair, 3-5/8" h
  ....**245.00**
Century, horizontal, 1-1/4" x 2-1/8" x
  3/8", C.8 ....**170.00**
Dill's Best, vertical pocket tin, 4-1/2" h
  ....**44.00**
Edgeworth Junior, Extra High Grade
  Tobacco, vertical pocket tin **72.00**
Fashion Cut Plug Tobacco, lunch box,
  4-1/2" h, 7-1/2" w **385.00**
Golden Rod Plug Cut, 1-3/8" h, 4-3/8"
  w, 3-3/8" d **40.00**
Golden Sceptre, vertical pocket tin,
  rounded corners.......................**250.00**
Guide, vertical pocket tin, outdoorsman,
  4-1/4" h **335.00**
Hi-Plane Smooth Cut Tobacco, round,
  6-1/4" h **220.00**
J.G. Dill's Best Cube Cut Plug, 4 oz, 2-
  3/4" h..**55.00**
Lucky Strike Roll Cut, vertical pocket
  tin, 4-1/4" h.................................**92.00**
Picoback, The Pick of Tobacco, screw
  lid, 1/2-lb, round, 4-1/2" h............**35.00**
Qboid Cube Cut, vertical, plantation
  illus, 4" x 3-1/2" x 1", C.8+ **190.00**

❖ Tokens

Tokens are small medallion or coin-like
objects. Some tokens were used in lieu of
currency for transportation, such as a
railroad token. Other tokens were forms of
advertising or perhaps were used for
admission to an event. Look for tokens
where you tend to find coins and medals.

References: Many coin reference books
also contain information about tokens.

Collectors' Clubs: Active Token Collectors
Organization, PO Box 1573, Sioux Falls, SD
57101-1573; American Numismatic
Association, 818 N. Cascade Ave, Colorado
Springs, CO 80903-3279; American
Vecturist Association, PO Box 1204,
Boston, MA 02104-1204; National Token
Collector's Association, PO Box 5596, Elko,
NV 98902; Token & Medal Society, PO Box
366, Brayntown, MD 20617-0366.

Chief Of The Sixes, Product Of General
  Motors **25.00**
Chuck E. Cheese Pizza Time Theatre,
  Ogden, Utah / In Pizza We Trust, 1980,
  1" dia **1.00**
General Motors Motorama, 1956 ..**20.00**
Houston Transit Authority, Houston
  skyline, 7/8" dia **2.00**
Ford, 30th Anniversary, 1933, copper
  ....**30.00**
Green River Whiskey, goldtone 1-1/4"
  dia **45.00**

Washington token, Member of Friendship Fire Co., portrait of Washington on obverse, bronze, $25.

North Shore Animal League, 1945-1975, gilded bronze......................**20.00**
Pierce-Arrow, brass, 1-3/4" dia **60.00**
Union Pacific, "A sample of the aluminum in the new Union Pacific Train built by Pullman Car & Mfg. Corp., ALCOA Aluminum Co. of America," 1-1/4" dia......................**10.00**
Washington, Member Friendship Fire Co., bronze..................................**25.00**
World's Fair and Expositions
1939 New York World's Fair, brass, Communications Building...........**9.00**
Expo '74, Spokane, Wash., U.S. Pavilion, silver, 1-1/2: dia............**8.00**

❖ Tonka

Tonka Toys were built to last, and many a male flea market shopper has been known to get weak in the knees over seeing vintage Tonka Toys. Remembering all those hours of happily building roads and playing with cars and trucks can make a fella real nostalgic, especially when you realize Tonka first introduced it's full line of trucks in 1949 and is still in business today—that's a lot of trucks—all built for hours of play.

References: Karen O'Brien, *Toys & Prices 2004*, 11th ed, Krause Publications, 2003; --, *O'Brien's Collecting Toys*, 11th ed, Krause Publications, 2003.

Army Jeep **45.00**
Baggage tractor, trailer **50.00**
Camper, #1070, purple metal, white plastic camper top, mini, 1970s, MIB..........**90.00**

Tonka truck, pressed steel, "Allied Van Lines" moving truck and trailer, 24" l, $195.

Cement Mixer, 1970s **150.00**
Construction Set, #3109, red and black box art, sealed in orig box..........**600.00**
Crawler, 1970s............................**150.00**
Dump Truck, 1970s......................**150.00**
Dump Truck, red and green, Tonka, 1955 ....**100.00**
Dune Buggy, #2445, bumper chain, 1970s, MIB **90.00**
Pickup, red body, white roof.........**225.00**
Sportsman Pick-Up.......................**75.00**
Stables Set, #1104, light blue metal, mini, 1970s, MIB **450.00**
Universal Jeep, MIB....................**125.00**

Tonka Jeep, olive green, white seats and trim, $25.

❖ Tools

Plane, painted green, red wooden handle knob, $25.

Considering this great country was built from the ground up, tools have been with us for a long time. Treated properly, good tools last for years, many eventually making their way to flea markets. Tool collectors tend to find flea markets to be like gold mines when they are searching for something new to add to their collections.

Collectors' Clubs: Collectors of Rare & Familiar Tools Society of New Jersey, 38 Colony Court, New Providence, NJ 07974-2332; Early American Industries Association, 167 Bakersville Road, South Dartsmouth, MA 02748; New England Tool Collectors Association, 11-1/2 Concord Ave., Saint Johnsbury, VT 05819; Tool Group of Canada, 7 Tottenham Road, Ontario MC3 2J3 Canada, plus many regional and specialized groups.

Anvil, 4" l, "Compliments of John Fink Metal Works, San Francisco and Seattle Wash".............................**30.00**
Archimedian Drill, bit, c1915 ....**50.00**
Axe head, single bit, Black Raven ..**20.00**

Book
Delta Power Tools 1940 Catalog, Delta Mfg. Co., Milwaukee, 48 pgs **25.00**
Working Wood, A Guide for the Country Carpenter, Mike & Nancy Rubel, Rodale Press, 1977 ......**24.00**
Broad ax, W. Hunt, 6" h, orig handle **50.00**
Buck saw, wood, worn varnish finish, mkd "W. T. Banres," 30" **45.00**
Carving chisels, S. J. Addis Cast Steel, Masonic hallmark, set of 12 ....**125.00**
Draw knife, D.R. Barton 1882, 22" l, orig finish...**85.00**
File, half round, 20" l **15.00**
Foot measure, Korrecto, directions on back..**32.00**
Hammer, claw type, Winchester **55.00**
Ice saw, 78" l.................................**85.00**
Measuring tape, Lufkin. 100' **65.00**
Plane, Doscher Plane & Tool Co., Saugatuck, Conn., 9-1/2" l..........**55.00**
Router, unmarked, wrought iron, 1/2", wood handles, needs cleaning.....**25.00**
Saddle maker's knife, H. G. Comph & Co., Albany, NY, crescent shape, rosewood handle, orig tooled leather scabbard..**45.00**
Screwdriver, flat wood handle, round sides, 9" blade............................**35.00**
Socket chisel
9/16" gouge, mkd "Lakeside" **15.00**
1-1/4" gouge, mkd "Butcher Cast Steel," handle split **15.00**
2", heavy, needs handle..............**17.00**
Woodworking plane, "The Cincinnati Tool Co. Hargrove" on blade, spoke shave, 10-1/2" l **45.00**
Wrench
John Deere JD 50, 6" l.................**19.00**
Morrison #260 multi-wrench, 10-1/4" l **9.00**
Unmkd, twisted handle................**45.00**

❖ Toothbrush Holders

Getting kids to brush their teeth has been a challenge for decades. One way to help this activity was a character to hold toothbrushes. They certainly make a neat collectible. Because many were made of plaster or bisque, expect to find some damage and loss to the paint.

Collectors' Club: Toothbrush Holder Collectors Club, PO Box 371, Barnesville, MD 20838-0371.

Drum major, tube tray....................**90.00**
Girl with dog, tube tray...................**80.00**
Lone Ranger, plaster, painted, 4" h**75.00**
Mickey and Minnie Mouse, bisque **350.00**

Mickey Mouse, bisque, one arm moveable, other connected to body, string tail missing, paint worn, late 1930s **225.00**
Soldier..**85.00**
Three Pigs **155.00**

❖ Toothpick Holders

Here's another accessory that has been present on the table or sideboard since Victorian times. Typically they are high enough for a toothpick to stand on end and large enough to hold many toothpicks. Over the years, toothpick holders have been made in all different types of materials.

Collectors' Club: National Toothpick Holders Collectors Society, PO Box 417, Safety Harbor, FL 34695-0417.

Bisque, skull, blue anchor shape mark
....**65.00**
China
　Japan, pig, basket along side, wearing top hat.......................................**65.00**
　Royal Bayreuth, elk **120.00**
　R.S. Germany, white mother-of-pearl luster **40.00**
　R.S. Prussia, pink and green luster ground, floral trim.....................**45.00**
Glass
　Cut Glass, pedestal, chain of hobstars dec..**150.00**
　Milk Glass, parrot and top hat, c1895
....**45.00**
Pattern glass
　Daisy and Button, blue.................**75.00**
　Jewel with Dewdrop **55.00**
　Paneled 44, Reverse, platinum stain
....**75.00**
　Texas, gold trim...........................**50.00**

Toothpick holder, roller skate, amber, dated 1886, $65.

Silver plate, chick standing next to egg, engraved "Just Picked Out," Victorian, plate very worn............................**25.00**

❖ Torquay Pottery

This English pottery is often called Motto Ware because it usually contains a motto written into the clay. Some of the sayings are quite humorous. The pieces were hand decorated and usually well marked.

Collectors' Clubs: North American Torquay Society, 12 Stanton, Madison, CT 06443; Torquay Pottery Collectors Society, 23 Holland Ave., Cheam, Sutton, Surrey SM2 6HW UK.

Bowl, Allervale, "Du'ee mak yerzel at 'ome," 3-3/4" d **18.00**
Candlestick, "Many are called but few get up," 3-1/2" h..........................**100.00**
Cheese dish, "Cheese" on one side, "Comfort is better than pride" on other, 6-1/2" x 5-1/4" x 3-1/2" h............**175.00**
Console bowl, Kingfisher, 9-1/2" dia, 3" h **195.00**
Creamer, house dec, "Don't make a fool of pleasure" **26.00**
Finger bowl, "Time Ripens All Things," 4-1/4" d..**27.00**
Jug, cov, "Kind words are the music of the world," 5-3/4" h **180.00**
Jug, open, cottage dec, 4" h
　"Better to sit still than rise to fall" .**85.00**
　"Time ripens all things"................**85.00**
Planter, mottled black and brown ext., blue flowers, green leaves, 6-1/2" d
....**80.00**
Plate, cottage, "To thine own self be true"
....**75.00**
Shaving mug, scuttle, "The nearer the razor, the closer the shave," Dad on back, 6-1/2" l **215.00**
Teapot, small, house dec, 4" h......**120.00**
Tulip vase, hand painted, cobalt blue ground, hummingbird and floral design, black mark and #32, 7-1/2" h **98.00**
Vase, peacock, raised details, 3 handles, 9-1/2" h.....................................**125.00**

❖ Tortoiseshell Items

The mottled brown design known as tortoiseshell was so popular with Victorians that many items were made of actual tortoise shells as well as being imitated in glassware and pottery. With the invention of celluloid and plastics, imitations saw a revival. Today, real tortoiseshell falls under the protection of the Endangered Species Act. But, remember when many vintage tortoiseshell items were made, the entire tortoise was being used for food and other purposes, so the shell was also used.

Box, cov, circular, painted figure by riverscape, French, late 19th C, minor losses, 3" d................................**495.00**
Calling card case, mother-of-pearl and ivory inlaid dec, c1825, 4" x 3"...**225.00**
Cigarette case, domed oval, applied central carved monogram, Continental, late 19th/early 20th C, 4-1/4" l ...**325.00**
Glove box, domed lid, ornate ivory strapping, sandalwood int., 3-1/2" h
....**375.00**
Snuff box, oval, silver dec, 1-1/2" x 3"
....**325.00**
Tea caddy, rect, hinged lid, small brass plate and escutcheon, int. fitted with tortoise shell veneered cover, English, late 18th/early 19th C, some small losses, 4-3/4" w, 3-3/8" d, 4-3/8" h
....**885.00**
Travel set, case, comb, nail file, hand mirror, shoe horn, hair brush, soap box, toothpaste box, toothbrush box, powder box, nail buff, monogrammed "B.M.A," case worn **40.00**

❖ Toys

Every toy at a flea market is collectible, although some are worth more than others. Factors that influence price include age, condition, the original box, desirability, and maker. Probably the most deciding factor in the purchase of an antique toy is the one that makes the heart of the collector skip a beat, something that says that toy is important. The sampling below is just a mere peak into the giant toy box that many flea markets represent to collectors.

References: Karen O'Brien, *Toys & Prices 2004*, 11th ed, Krause Publications, 2003; --
-, *O'Brien's Collecting Toys*, 11th ed, Krause Publications, 2003; Ted Hake, *Hake's Price Guide to Character Toys*, 4th ed. Gemstone Publishing, 2003; Sharon and Bob Huxford, *Schroeder's Collectible Toys*, 8th ed., Collector Books, 2002; Dana Johnson, *Collector's Guide to Diecast Toys & Scale Models*, 2nd ed., Collector Books, 1998; Mike and Sue Richardson, *Diecast Toy Aircraft*, New Cavendish, 1998; Elizabeth Stephan, *O'Brien's Collecting Toy Cars & Trucks*, 3rd ed, Krause Publications, 2000;.

Periodicals: *Antique Toy World*, PO Box 34509, Chicago, IL 60634; *Model and Toy Collector Magazine*, PO Box 347240, Cleveland, OH 44134; *Toy Farmer*, 7496 106th Ave., SE, Lamoure, ND 58458; *Toy Shop*, 700 E. State St, Iola, WI 54990.

Collectors' Clubs: American Game Collectors Association, PO Box 44, Dresher, PA, 19025; Antique Toy Collectors of America, 2 Wall Street, 13th Floor, New York, NY, 10005; Canadian Toy Collectors Society, 67 Alpine Ave., Hamilton, Ontario L9A 1A7 Canada; Gamers Alliance, PO Box 197, East Meadow, NY 11554; plus many regional and specialized clubs.

School bus, yellow plastic, mkd "Metro School District No. 18," paper inserts in windows with smiling driver, children, battery operated, $5.

For additional listings, see *Warman's Antiques and Collectibles Price Guide* and *Warman's Americana & Collectibles,* as well as specific company listings in this edition.

Airplane, 1940s, 9" wingspan, blue and red, white wooden wheels, metal propeller, wings fold at hinges, Wyandotte **145.00**

Bristol helicopter, Dinky, #715, MIB **65.00**

Bunny, three-wheeler bike, litho tin wind-up, mkd "MTU, China" **65.00**

Camper truck, all tin, litho, friction, 8" l, MIB.. **175.00**

Charleston Trio, litho tin wind-up, 1921, C-8 .... **700.00**

Child in stroller, litho tin, converts from stroller to high chair, 2-1/4" h **150.00**

Coney Island Roller Coaster, 22" w, 15" deep, two large bus type cars, bright graphics, Techonix, Germany, MIB **395.00**

Coupe, rumble seat, A. C. Williams, 4-3/4" l, c1930, small chip on bottom of seat **195.00**

Dancing black men, litho tin wind-up, built-in key, two dapper Black men wearing 3-pc suits, hat, lapel flower, jointed legs, mkd "Made in U.S.A.," 1930s **275.00**

Dipper Bug, pull toy, 1950s, MIB....**85.00**

Dairy Transport Truck, Duo-Tone slant design paint, red and white, opens in back, orig decal, Buddy L, 26" l **75.00**

Dump truck, litho tin wind-up, mkd "England," C-8 .... **200.00**

Easy Bake Oven, Kenner's, 1960, orig mixes and box **140.00**

Easy Show, Kenner's, 1960, six movies, orig box **140.00**

Express Parcels Delivery, litho tin wind-up, separate tin driver figure, built-in key, 1-3/4" h.............................. **195.00**

Auburn rubber, red painted hard rubber racing car with driver, 10-1/4" l, $90.

Evel Knievel Skycycle, Ideal Toys, diecast, MIB **125.00**

Farm Produce Wagon, Dinky, #343, MIB **75.00**

Ferris wheel, colorful seats and graphics, Ohio Art **295.00**

Fire Chief Car, pull toy, metal, clanging bell, T. Cohen, 1940s, MIB **275.00**

Fire Truck, red, rubber, Auburn **25.00**

Flat Tire Wrecker, yellow, Buddy L**125.00**

Flying Patrol Set, Tootsietoy, MIB **175.00**

Gibbs Teeter Totter, painted tin, c1905, C-9 .... **350.00**

Give A Show Projector, Kenner, boxed **35.00**

Go-Go Turtle, plastic wind-up, Daito, 1960s, MIB **35.00**

Grand Prix Special, racer and trailer, Nylint **50.00**

Greyhound Coast to Coast Bus, Arcade, 8" l..................................**80.00**

Hansom Limo, 6" l, cast iron, Kenton **300.00**

Horse Van, yellow, red, Sun Rubber, 1935 .... **40.00**

Incredible Edibles, Mattel, 1966 ....**35.00**

Jack in the box, Beanie & Cecil...**160.00**

Jet Roller Coaster, Wolverine, orig box **145.00**

Jumpy Rudolph, Asahi Toys, cable, 6" **155.00**

Lincoln Van Lines Trans Canada Service Truck, 18 wheeler, 23" l**150.00**

Merry Grinder, litho tin wind-up, sandpaper grinding wheel, paper label on lid, 1920s, 4" h **175.00**

Musical clown, Mattel, MIB **210.00**

Outdraw the Outlaw, Mattel, C-9 toy, C-8 box **165.00**

Policeman on motorcycle, tin, friction, MIB..**75.00**

Race car
  Auburn Rubber.............................**65.00**
  Buffalo Toys, Red Streak, C-7.5 .**200.00**
  Schuco, green, key wind, MIB....**190.00**

Roadster, red and black, Wyandotte, 7" l **175.00**

Buddy L, horse trailer, red pick-up cab, tan and red body, orig horse, orig box, $115.

Shooting gallery, litho tin wind-up, tin target, orig darts, Wyandotte......**290.00**

Scooter, Radio Flyer, orig emblem present, but very worn, late 1930s **75.00**

Shark Race Car, Remco, 19" l **70.00**

Stake truck, cast iron, Kenton **350.00**

Trombone, 10" l, tin, brass-color.....**60.00**

UPS package car, brown hard plastic truck, orig brown and white box, copyright UPS 1977, friction, 2" x 5-1/2" x 2-1/2" box.......................... **45.00**

UPS truck, hard plastic, clicker on front tiers, copyright UPS, Made in China, 1977, 5-1/2" l............................. **45.00**

Whirlybird, 25 men attack team, Remco, 1960s, orig box.......................... **275.00**

❖ Toy Dimestore Soldiers

Dimestore soldiers, set of frontiersmen, yellow, red, green, or blue jackets, brown pants, standing on green bases, tied in later red box, $65, with miscellaneous group of Barclay figures in front, Indian $15, Cowboy, $12.

Children have been fascinated with three-dimensional lead, iron, rubber, and plastic toy soldiers for many years. About the time of World War II, dimestores started to carry soldiers, which immediately became popular with youngsters. The toys could be purchased one at a time, making each set unique, unlike the English lead soldiers, which were sold in sets.

References: Richard O'Brien, *Collecting American-Made Toy Soldiers*, 3rd ed., Krause Publications, 1997. —, *Collecting Foreign-Made Toy Soldiers*, Krause Publications, 1998.

Periodicals: *Old Toy Soldier,* 209 N. Lombard, Oak Park, IL 60302; *Plastic Figure & Playset Collector,* PO Box 1355, LaCrosse, WI 54602; *Plastic Warrior,* 905 Harrison St., Allentown, PA 18103; *Toy Shop,* 700 E. State St., Iola, WI 54490; *Toy Soldier Review,* 127 74th St., North Bergen, NJ 07047.

Aircraft spotter, Manoil **27.50**

Army motorcycle with sidecar, Barclay **50.00**

Bandit, hands up, Grey Iron...........**42.00**

Baseball player, Auburn Rubber **35.00**

Bicycle dispatch rider, soldier, Manoil
....**25.00**
Bomb thrower, 2 grenades in pouch,
Manoil..**20.00**
Boy in travel suit, Grey Iron...........**10.00**
Bugler, pre-war, tin helmet, Barclay ...**20.00**
Cadet officer, Grey Iron..................**20.00**
Charging soldier with tommy gun,
Auburn Rubber...............................**12.00**
Colonial soldier, Grey Iron............**17.50**
Cowboy, mounted, firing pistol, Barclay
....**24.00**
Crawling soldier, Barclay..............**15.00**
Deep sea diver, 65 on chest, Manoil
....**18.00**
Farmer, sowing grain, Manoil..........**20.00**
Flag bearer, post-war, Manoil.........**24.00**
Football player, Auburn Rubber.....**35.00**
Indian chief, Barclay......................**12.00**
Knight with pennant, Barclay........**15.00**
Lineman, football player, Auburn Rubber
....**25.00**
Machine gunner, kneeling, Auburn
Rubber...**15.00**
Marine officer, pre-war, marching,
sword, blue uniform, tin hat..........**27.50**
Navy doctor, in white, Barclay, flat
underbase **15.00**
Nurse, white uniform, Barclay **24.00**
Officer, post war, pot helmet, Barclay,
orig sword...................................**175.00**
Pirate, Barclay................................**15.00**
Policeman, raised arm, Barclay......**15.00**
Red Cross nurse, Auburn Rubber..**30.00**
Sailor, blue uniform, Barclay...........**15.00**
**Soldier in gas mask and with flare
gun**, Manoil..................................**20.00**
Wounded soldier, Manoil **17.50**

❖ Toy Train Accessories

Toy train accessories, like Plasticville houses, tunnels, miniature figures and fences, are often found at flea markets. Look for these tiny treasures to add to your train set-up.

Airport Hanger, Lionel...................**36.00**
Bachman Hotel, Plasticville, HO **6.00**
Barnyard animals set, Plasticville,
1940s, MIB....................................**26.00**
Billboard, Plasticville **10.00**
Diner, Plasticville, orig box, some wear
....**25.00**
Fence and gate, Plasticville..............**3.25**
Foot bridge, Plasticville, #1051 ....**7.00**
Gas station, Esso/Shell, Plasticville**15.00**
Green house, Plasticville, MIB **65.00**
House, Plasticville
   Brick-look......................................**8.00**
   Cape Cod **10.00**
   Ranch..**5.00**

Moving and storage van, Plasticville,
NRFB **35.00**
Outhouse, Plasticville, O or S gauge
....**10.00**
People kit, #2809-149 Citizens,
Plasticville, orig paint missing **15.00**
Spruce trees, pr, Plasticville............**9.00**
Switch control box, Atlas, custom line
....**19.00**
Train signal, cast metal, 10-1/2" h ...**20.00**
Trestle set
   American Flyer, #780 ....**42.00**
   Lionel, #111................................**24.00**
Union Station, Plasticville **18.00**
Waiting room, American Flyer, metal
....**30.00**
Water tower
   American Flyer, red and white
   checkerboard sides, bubbling type
....**100.00**
   Lionel......................................**82.00**
   Plasticville **6.00**

❖ Toy Trains

Toy trains are one of the most popular types of toys that collectors invest in today. Early toy trains were cast iron and quickly progressed to well-crafted examples using different types of metals and materials. American Flyer, Ives, and Lionel are among the most recognized makers. The prices listed below are for sets of trains.

References: Excellent references exist for every kind of toy train. Elizabeth Stephan, *O'Brien's Collecting Toy Trains*, 5th ed., Krause Publications, 1999.

Periodicals: *Classic Toy Trains*, PO Box 1612, Waukesha, WI 53187; *LGB Telegram*, 1573 Landvater, Hummelstown, PA 17036; *Lionel Collector Series Marketmaker, Trainmaster*, 3224 NW 47th Terrace, Gainesville, FL 32606; *O Scale Railroading*, PO Box 239, Nazareth, PA 18064; *S. Gaugian*, 7236 Madison Ave., Forest Park, IL 60130.

Collectors' Clubs: American Flyer Collectors Club, PO Box 13269, Pittsburgh, PA 15234; LGB Model Railroad Club, 1854 Erin Drive, Altoona, PA 16602; Lionel Collectors Club of America, PO Box 479, LaSalle, IL 61301; Lionel Operating Train Society, 18 Eland Ct, Fairfield, OH 45014; Marklin Club-North America, PO Box 51559, New Berlin, WI 53151; Marklin Digital Special Interest Group, PO Box 51319, New Berlin, WI 53151; The National Model Railroad Association, 4121 Cromwell Road, Chattanooga, TN 37421; The Toy Train Operating Society, Inc., Suite 308, 25 West Walnut St., Pasadena, CA 91103; Train Collector's Association, PO Box 248, Strasburg, PA 17579.

Tracking the market

Mention "John Deere," and most people think of tractors. However, a variety of collectible items have been made to promote the popular farm equipment manufacturer, including this train set. Oddly enough, there was little interest when this John Deere HO Scale Train Set was first made available at a John Deere parts meeting in 1985. Accordingly, few sets were ordered. Enter the supply-and-demand factor, and as interest climbed, so did prices on the secondary market. Having originally sold for $69.95, the train jumped to as high as $500 within a year. As the initial frenzy subsided, the value readjusted to its current level of $400. Made by Athearn, Inc., of Compton, Cal., the electric train consists of an engine, tanker, boxcar, flatbed with two John Deere tractors, caboose and track. Other John Deere train sets have also been made.

American Flyer
   Burlington Zephyr Streamliner,
   passenger, O gauge **725.00**
   Minnie Ha-Ha, locomotive, 3 coaches,
   orange and gray, minor wear..**295.00**
   Passenger, #253 locomotive, two #610
   cars, #612 dark green, maroon
   inserts, 1924, O gauge...........**295.00**
Bachmann, N gauge, Spirit of 1776
commemorative set, diesel locomotive,
caboose, and three box cards, MIB
....**135.00**
Ives, passenger set, locomotive, tender,
3 cars, S gauge.........................**150.00**
LBG Lehman
   Baggage car, Rhaetian railway, MIB
....**150.00**
   Coach 111 Rhaetian railway, LB &
   BRHB, composite, large scale**225.00**
   Street car, Sieman, 1914, battery
   operated, MIB **550.00**
Lionel
   Freight, #33, #35, #36, olive green, S
   gauge, 1920..........................**350.00**
   Passenger, #352E, #10# locomotive,
   #332 baggage car, #339, coach,
   #341 observation car, 1926, S
   gauge, orig box, minor wear to
   locomotive..............................**550.00**
Marx, black locomotive, #551 Union
Pacific tender, #91257 Seaboard
gondola, #3724 Union Pacific caboose,
track, battery operated, orig box, c1955
....**125.00**

❖ Tramp Art

Tramp Art, box, covered, pyramid style construction, one hinge broken, some loss, $20.

Here's a hot part of the flea market scene! Now considered to be folk art by some, these pieces were crafted by someone with limited materials, tools, and sometimes skill. By adding bits and pieces together, layers became objects such as picture frames, boxes of all kinds, etc.

References: Michael Cornish and Clifford Wallach, *They Call It Tramp Art*, Columbia University Press, 1996; Helaine Fendelman and Jonathan Taylor, *Tramp Art: A Folk Art Phenomenon*, Stewart, Tabori & Chang, 1999; Clifford A. Wallach and Michael Cornish, *Tramp Art: One Notch at a Time*, Wallach-Irons Publishing, 1998.

For additional listings, see *Warman's Country*.

Box, hinged cover, dove, heart, and anchor dec, 4-1/4" w, 1-3/4" h....**200.00**
Comb box, hanging, arched scalloped back with layered notch-carved rosette in center accented with small round white porcelain knobs, front of open box slopes forward and has scalloped top edge, double dart-shaped ornament on front, dark-red paint, 10-1/8" h, 8-3/4" w..........**110.00**
Crucifix, wooden pedestal base, wooden carved figure, 16" h....**185.00**
Doll dresser, 3 drawers, old white repaint, gold trim, worn, age cracks, 21-1/2" h, 15-1/2" w, 8-3/4" d.....**357.50**
Frame
12-1/2" h, 10-1/8" w, applied notch-carved molding with hearts and X's around sides, stained finish.......**110.00**
14" x 12", hearts and diamonds, painted gold............**255.00**
Jewelry box, hinged lid, 4 square layered notch-carved feet, 1 back foot missing, 6" h, 14" w, 8-1/4" d, 140.00
Match Safe, strike surface, open holder for matches..................**75.00**
Mirror, frame with dark finish over varnish, stepped sawtooth border, stacked geometric designs, 15" h, 17-

1/2" w............**275.00**
Sewing stand, dark orig finish, 4 molded legs, applied sawtooth trim, shelf in base, well at top with handles on each side, large rectangular pincushions on front and back, lid missing, 27" h, 18-1/4" w, 13-1/4" d........**412.50**
Wall pocket, open work and porcelain buttons, 9" w, 7" h........**95.00**

❖ Transformer Toys

The first generation of Transformers were released in 1984 and introduced GenX children to good-guy Autobots fighting bad-guy Decepticons. These toys transform from robot to vehicle and featured cars and trucks before expanding to include planes, motorcycles, cassettes, and even the space shuttle. Transformers mint-on-the card or mint-in-sealed box command the highest prices. The Marvel comics series, television series, and even Transformers the Movie established well-know characters, like Autobot, leader Optimus Prime, that hold even higher values.

Air Hammer, MOC, C-9.........**15.00**
Bone Crusher, MOC, C-9........**60.00**
Buzzsaz, MOC, C-9.........**50.00**
Claw Jaw, MOC, C-9.........**30.00**
Devastator, 1985, loose.........**85.00**
Grimlock, 1985, sword missing, loose........**70.00**
Inferno, MISB, C-9.........**15.00**
Injector, MOC, C-8.........**10.00**
Omega Supreme, 1985, C-9, loose..**85.00**
Optimus Prime, 1984, MIB, C-7, decals unopened.........**225.00**
Overdrive, 1985, C-8, loose.........**25.00**
Polar Claw, MISB, C-9.........**60.00**
Scraper, 1984, gun missing, loose...**8.00**
Sky Shadow, MOC, C-8.........**10.00**
Sunstreaker, 1984, C-9, C-7 box.**150.00**
Swoop, 1985, loose, C-9.........**110.00**

Transformers, Optimal Optimus, complete, $9.

Tigatron, MOC, C-8.........**40.00**
Trailbreaker, 1984, C-9, C-8 box..**140.00**
Tripredacus, MISB, C-8.........**30.00**
Wheeljack, 1984, C-9, C-6 box.....**120.00**
Wolfgang, MOC, C-8.........**45.00**

❖ Transistor Radios

Remember how cool it was to walk around as a teenager, holding your radio up so only you could hear it! Those transistor radios spelled freedom from electrical cords and sometimes were even in funky shapes and colors. Most of us didn't care that they only got AM stations, it was the "old folks" that listened to FM anyway. Today collectors like to find transistor radios with original cases, instructions, and little wear.

Admiral, AM, #PR290, red, white, and blue stripe.........**20.00**
Binotone, binocular and radio combo, burgundy leather case, crown seal, orig box stamped "Made in Japan"......**45.00**
Bulova, transistor, orig case..........**45.00**
Channel Master, leather carrying case.........**45.00**
Emerson, #888, Vanguard, transistor, portable, 1958.........**65.00**
GE, P-910C, aqua.........**12.50**
Guild Radio, telephone shape, crank changes stations, 18" h.........**95.00**
Juilette, solid state full eight, circuit model AK-8, orig carrying case and box.........**35.00**
Panasonic, 1950s, blue.........**55.00**
Radio Shack, shaped like D-cell battery.........**38.00**
Realtone 6.........**48.00**
Silvertone, #9205, transistor, plastic, 1959.........**42.00**
Snoopy, Joe Cool, white plastic case, AM FM, 2 television stations and weather, mkd "United Features Syndicate, Inc., Salton/Maxim Housewares, Inc., Mt Prospect, IL, Made in China".........**50.00**
Sony, TFM-151, transistor, 1960.....**60.00**
Toy telephone and cigarette lighter, plastic, 1950s, 5-1/2" h.........**20.00**
Tropicana.........**15.00**
Zenith
RG 47J, Hong Kong.........**4.00**
Royal 500 Deluxe.........**45.00**
Royal 710.........**30.00**

❖ Transportation

Memorabilia relating to the transportation of goods and people has long been a favorite with collectors. Perhaps it's the romance of the open road or the fun of finding out about faraway places. Whatever the mode of transportation, you'll find some ephemera relating to it.

Reference: Barbara J. Conroy, *Restaurant China: Identification & Value Guide For Restaurant, Airline, Ship & Railroad Dinnerware*, Collector Books, 1998.

Periodical: *Airliners*, PO Box 52-1238, Miami, FL 33152.

Collectors' Clubs: Bus History Association, 965 McEwan, Windsor Ontario N9B 2G1 Canada; Central Electric Railfans' Association, PO Box 503, Chicago, IL 60690; International Bus Collectors Club, 1518 "C" Trailee Drive, Charleston, SC 29407; Steamship Historical Society of America, Inc, Ste #4, 300 Ray Drive, Providence, RI 02906; Transport Ticket Society, 4 Gladridge Close, Earley, Reading Berks RG6 2DL England.

Blotter, Firestone Bicycle Tires, black, white, orange, and blue, 1920s, unused **20.00**
Booklet, St. Lawrence route to Europe, Canadian Pacific, 1930, 16 pgs, 8" x 11" **25.00**
Bus calendar, Greyhound, 1940 ....**80.00**
Fan, Air India, adv **4.00**
Game, Pirates & Travelers, 1911, tri-fold board, boxed pcs........................**120.00**
Map, Greyhound Routes, folded......**10.00**
Luggage tag, Canadian Pacific, stringed cardstock, red, white, and blue ship signs, c1930, 5" x 3" **15.00**
Stickpin, brass, bug pedaling bicycle, mkd "Compliments of United States Tire Co.," 1920s **27.50**
Ticket holder, blue plastic, TWA logo **2.00**
Tourist guide, Cannes, sgd by Hotel Martinez director, Italian, 1956, 8" x 10-1/2" **15.00**
Traffic light, rewired........................**85.00**

❖ Traps

Snap! Gotcha! Hunters have been trapping since the old days when fur traders trapped and traded goods. Today many traps are considered to be collectible. Be careful if you test one of these!

Collectors' Clubs: National Trappers Association, PO Box 3667, Bloomington, IL 61701; North American Trap Collectors Association, PO Box 94, Galloway, OH 43119-0094.

Blake & Lamb model #21, Hawkins Co. **15.00**
Jump #13, beaver **46.00**
Mousetrap, wire and wood, domed, 4-1/2" h, 4-3/4" sq **55.00**
Minnow, Orvis..............................**225.00**
Newhouse #15, bear....................**400.00**
Oneida, painted black, welded in open position......................................**25.00**

Sargent & Co. #1, muskrat **22.50**
Triumph
   #4, painted black, 18" l, 30" chain ...**30.00**
   Ranger #42, 18-1/2" l.................**130.00**

❖ Trays

Trays are another type of advertising collectible. Like tip trays, expect to find interesting lithographed scenes and advertising for all types of products. Also expect to find some signs of usage.

Reproduction Alert

For additional listings, see *Warman's Advertising*.

Jim Beam, plastic, 17" x 11" **9.00**
Bartlett Spring Mineral Water, 13" d **150.00**
Beamer Shoes, Victorian woman, c1900 ....**75.00**
Bozo, TV tray, some rust **30.00**
Buffalo Brewing Co., scratches and soiling, 13" d..............................**100.00**
C.D. Kenny Co., Christmas motif of girl with doll, holly border, 10" dia **230.00**
Golden West Brewing Co., factory scene, early trolleys and horse drawn carts, American Art Works, some chipping and soiling **300.00**
Happy Birthday Mickey Mouse, Cheinco, 1978, 14" dia................**45.00**
Knickerbocker beer, metal, 13" dia**15.00**
Maier Brewing, woman in orange outfit, Maier trademark on side, © 1909, Kaufmann & Strauss Co. litho, some overall scratching **100.00**
Moerlein Beer, trademark "Crowned Wherever Exhibited" in fancy filigree, rim shows different expositions, Chas. W. Shonk Co., minor inpainting **50.00**
National Brewery Co. White Seal Beer, factory scene, horse drawn wagon, early blob top bottle, Griesedieck Bros, proprietors, chipping and scratching **185.00**
Pacific Brewing & Malting Co., Mt. Tacoma illus, orig 1912 work order from Chas. W. Shonk Co. on back.........**50.00**

Tray, Dick's Beer, 12" dia, $65.

Park Brewing Co., factory scene, early railroad, horse drawn carts, and automobilia, Chas. W. Shonk Co. litho, some inpainting, 12" d.................**60.00**
Stahley's Flour, horse and girl, 1905 ....**50.00**
Stegmaier Brewing Co. factory scene, early railroad and automobilia, minor scratching and rubbing.................**70.00**
Terre Haute Brewing Co., room full of colonials raise their empty glasses to flying cherubs who are bringing "that Ever-Welcome Beer" **125.00**

❖ Trivets

Trivets are handy for holding hot irons and pots. Over the years, some have become quite decorative.

Note: All trivets are cast iron, unless otherwise noted.

Iron rest
   Double Point, IWANTU, Comfort Iron, Strause Gas Iron Co., Phila. Pa., embossed image of gas iron **40.00**
   Humphrey Gas Iron & General Specialty Co.............................**42.50**

Fraternal trivet, looped links, heart in hand, painted gold, $15.

Cast iron trivet, George Washington, $125.

Kitchen

Cupids, cast iron, two cupids in center, 4-3/4" w, 8-1/2" l **12.00**

God Bless Our Home, gold, green, red and black paint 4-1/4" dia **14.00**

Good Luck, horseshoe with star in center, mkd 9-35 and VCM, 7" x 4-1/4" **58.00**

Griswold, #7, cast iron, 7-1/4" **45.00**

Peacock, brass **15.00**

Souvenir of San Francisco, hand painted tile in cast iron frame ...**10.00**

Wilton #2, love birds, hearts, brooms and star, painted gold **20.00**

❖ Trolls

Clown troll, purple neck ruffle, pink and yellow satin costume, pink hair, brown eyes, orig Russ label on bottom, one foot imp "© Russ", other imp "China," $12.

These funny looking characters marched onto the scene in the 1960s. With their bright colors and busy hair, they have been bringing collectors good luck.

Periodicals: *Troll Monthly,* 216 Washington St., Canton, MA 02021; *Trollin,* PO Box 601292, Sacramento, CA 95860.

Caveman, Mop-Pets by Sarco, 1960s, 5" h **25.00**

Cinderella, 12" h **15.00**

Marx, talking troll, 18" h.................**45.00**

Wooden, hand-carved, Henning, Norway, 5" h **32.00**

Russ Berrie Troll, baby in pajamas, 7-1/2" h..**6.00**

Treasure Troll, Ace Novelty Co., baby, 11" h **15.00**

❖ Trophies

How many of us have received a trophy for some event and it now resides in the back of a closet. Some trophies find their way to flea markets and then attract new buyers. Look for interesting names or dates on a trophy.

Bowling, Bakelite, 1960s **108.00**

Boy Scouts, figural metal boy on plastic base, 8-1/2" h..............................**35.00**

Dog, Best Hound 1962, cup style, silver-plated **220.00**

Garfield, on his knee, Arlens holding needle, "Get the point," Enesco Corp., 4-1/2" h.......................................**25.00**

Golf

Crystal Lake Country Club, 1931, silver-plated, runner-up, 5" h **5.00**

Figural golfer on marble base, 1973 ....**68.00**

High school

Mercury figure on black base, District Champ, SDHS Exclamatory League, 1933....................................**110.00**

Triumph figure on black base, District High School Exclamatory, 1930 ....**125.00**

Trap shooting, Pennsylvania Trap Shoting, 1930, 6-1/2" h **185.00**

Trophy, plastic, gold tone, small, $.25.

❖ Turtle Collectibles

Turtle collectors will not find a flea market slow-going. There will probably be several interesting examples to add to their growing collections.

Reference: Alan J. Brainard, *Turtle Collectibles,* Schiffer Publishing, 2000.

Bolo tie, figural turtle, crushed turquoise inlay, marked ".925" (sterling silver) and "Taxco," 3" dia **55.00**

Earrings, pr, sterling silver, 1" l **8.50**

Hat, child's, green **5.00**

Pin, Ciner, yellow enameled shell, green rhinestones, red rhinestone eye, 1-1/2" x 1-1/4" **50.00**

Pincushion, green and brown velvet, worn **5.00**

Paperweight, cast iron....................**35.00**

Pill box, sterling silver, 1-1/2" l, 1-1/8" w **35.00**

Planter, McCoy **40.00**

Tape measure, brushed gold metal, red rhinestone eyes, 3" x 2-1/2" **130.00**

Toy, Uncle Timmy Turtle, Fisher-Price #437, 1942 ....**100.00**

❖ TV Guides

These little television-oriented magazines have been steadily growing in value. There is usually an article about the star featured on the cover, plus other interesting tidbits for television memorabilia collectors.

1953, Queen Elizabeth **12.00**

1961, Lawrence Welk **15.00**

1964, America's Long Vigil, Kennedy assassination **4.00**

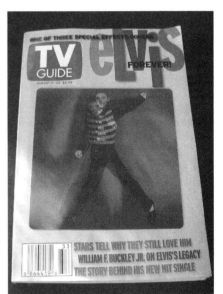

Elvis Forever!, special effects cover, Aug 17-23, 2002, $.50.

1967, Ed Sullivan..............................**7.50**

1973, Bill Cosby.............................**10.00**

1975, Tony Orlando and Dawn **6.00**

1976, George Kennedy.....................**5.00**

1976, Sonny and Cher.....................**18.00**

1977, Frank Sinatra **5.00**

1981, Archie Bunker **6.50**

1982, Michael Landon **7.50**

1984, Pierce Bronsan **12.50**

1985, Cheryl Ladd **4.00**

1986, Farrah Fawcett.........................**5.00**

1986, Nicollette Sheridan **5.00**

1986, Lucille Ball **15.00**

1998, Winter Olympics, set of four ..**30.00**

1999, Star Wars, set of four.............**30.00**

❖ Tupperware

Tupperware was one of the first household products introduced to modern housewives at parties. By gathering with friends, housewives could see the latest in plastic wares and have a good time too. Today, Tupperware is especially sought in Japan and many European countries. Related booklets and other paper ephemera are destined to become collectibles of tomorrow, just as Tupperware is beginning to show up at flea markets.

Advertisement, full color, 1970s, 8" x 10" **17.00**
Bowl, cov, bright green, 8" dia, 3-1/2" h **6.00**
Cake carrier, cov, 9-1/2" x 13".........**24.00**
Coasters, pastel, set of six in orig holder, few scratches, 2-7/8" dia **15.00**
Condiment caddy set, 8 pcs..........**20.00**
Child's cup, solid and sippy lid, name in Spanish on back, 6-1/2" h
  Cinderella **6.00**
  Jasmine, Princess Collection **6.00**
Child's playset
  Mini-mix set, 1979, complete, MIB
  ....**20.00**
  Mini-party set, 1980, complete, MIB
  ....**20.00**
Collector plate, Chrissy's Favorite Toy, little girl with bowl on head, orig certificate, 1993, 7-1/4" dia **8.00**
Cookbook, *Stacked Cooked Meals*, Meredith, 1990, microwave system
  ....**10.00**
Cup, Super Bowl XXIX, January 2, 1995, Joe Robbie Stadium, orig top, 7-1/4" h
  ....**5.00**
Figure, Tupperware lady, 7-3/4" h ...**65.00**
Jello mold, green, 3 pcs.................**16.00**
Microwave set, 3 qt, unused **18.00**
Mustard container, mkd, 7-1/2" h **5.00**
Pastry sheet, 18" w, 21-1/2" l **5.00**
Pepper shaker, light blue, 2-3/4" h ...**4.00**
Salad tongs, blue-green hard plastic, mkd "Tupperware" on handle, 1958, orig box **15.00**

These new Tupperware pieces may someday return to this Pennsylvania flea market since they are durable and now collectible.

Sandwich set, carrier, four 6-1/4" sq containers, one each pink, blue, yellow, and green, 9" h carrier **25.00**
Stacking set, 13 pcs......................**16.00**

❖ Twin Winton

Twin Winton had production facilities in both Pasedena and San Juan Capistrano, Calif., in the early 1950s. Their wares are well known to cookie jar collectors, but don't overlook some of their other table wares and accessories.

Bank, Hillbilly, barrel mkd "Mountain Dew 100 Proof" **85.00**
Candy jar, elephant, 9" h **45.00**
Cookie jar
  Cat..**60.00**
  Dutch girl, 12-3/8" h **45.00**
  Poodle at Cookie Counter, 13-1/2" h
  ....**250.00**
  Pot O' Cookies...........................**115.00**
  Sailor Elephant, 11-1/2" h, small chip on hat....................................**45.00**
Dealers sign **300.00**
Figure, black football player, 6" h, 1972
  ....**75.00**
Mug, Hillbilly, 4" h **35.00**
Napkin holder
  Dutch Girl **20.00**
  Mother Goose **55.00**
Pitcher, Hillbilly, glaze flake on spout
  ....**33.00**
Salt and pepper shakers, pr
  Kittens **46.00**
  Lions...**40.00**
  Racoons **65.00**
  Squirrels **20.00**
Stein, Hillybilly **55.00**

❖ Typewriters & Accessories

Tap, tap, ding. Remember the bell that used to ring as you pecked away on a typewriter? Some collectors still hearing that sound. You can find them searching flea markets for vintage typewriters, accessories, and related ephemera. Vintage typewriters are another collectible where you should thoroughly inspect the keys, motor, and wiring, before trying to use it.

Reference: Michael Adler, *Antique Typewriters*, Schiffer Publishing, 1997.

Periodicals: *Ribbon Tin News,* 28 The Green, Watertown, CT 06795-2118; *The Typewriter Exchange*, 2125 Mount Vernon Street, Philadelphia, PA 19130.

Collectors' Club: Early Typewriter Collectors Association, 2591 Military Ave., Los Angeles, CA 90064.

Advertisement

  Royal, 1962 ....**13.00**
  Royal Portable, 1970s **3.00**
Oil can, Smith Premier Typewriter Oiler, 3-1/2" h..**22.00**
Postcard, Remington Plant.............**15.00**
Ribbon tin
  Columbia Twins **15.00**
  Eberhard **10.00**
  Panama **20.00**
  Remington.....................................**7.50**
  Seagull **23.00**
  Vogue Royale **5.00**
  Webster Star Brand.....................**18.00**
Typewriter
  Adler 7, oak case **335.00**
  Bing #2, German, with case.......**150.00**
  L.C. Smith #8, 12" carriage **20.00**
  L.C. Smith & Corona, Comet........**65.00**
  Remington, portable, #5..............**40.00**
  Simplex...**50.00**
  Tom Thumb, orig case.................**15.00**
  Underwood #5............................**155.00**

Corona typewriter, black metal case, orig label from "Corona Shop, A.L. Johnson" on front, as is, $15.

❖ Umbrellas

While you might not want to open one in your house, it's great fun to find vintage umbrellas and parasols at flea markets. Look for examples in working order with interesting handles and fabrics in good condition.

Blue nylon umbrella, white Quakertown Hospital Flight Festival logo, $5.

Beach, beige cloth, long wooden spiked pole, c1940, some wear and fading **40.00**

Black, large size, "J" shaped Bakelite handle **45.00**

Brown, light beige stripes, clear lucite handle, some wear.......................**10.00**

Golf, bright red and white, wood handle **35.00**

Holly Hobbie, child size, plastic........**7.50**

Newscaster, Comcast, black, white and red **10.00**

Parasol, beige, boa trim, shepherd's crook handle, c1900...................**100.00**

Parasol, white linen, crochet work trim, c1890 ....**120.00**

Penny toy, tin litho, Chinaman seated on cart, holding parasol which spins as toy is pushed, 3-1/4" h **150.00**

Water lilies, adapted from famous painting of the same name, greens, blues, white flowers......................**15.00**

❖ Unicorns

This mystical beast has charmed many hearts. Today collectors search them out and enjoy finding the various ways they are

interpreted in glass, ceramic, and even on paper.

Collectors' Club: Unicorns Unanimous, 248 N. Larchmont Blvd, Los Angeles, CA 90004.

Beanie Baby, Mystic the Unicorn, protector on orig tag.....................**18.00**

Bell, bronzed pot metal, figural unicorn handle, 6-1/2" h............................**20.00**

Candleholder, Vandor, MIB **12.00**

Clipboard, brass **24.00**

Doorknocker, brass........................**30.00**

Figure, ceramic

Hamilton/Enesco, Starlight Starbright Series, Believe in Miracles **60.00**

Hamilton/Enesco, Starlight Starbright Series, Hang on to Your Dreams **60.00**

Lefton, gold horns and hooves, pastel pink ribbons, floral accents, #10912, retired, pair **30.00**

White, ivory, blue, and black, fired-on gold horn, applied silk flowers ..**75.00**

Garden ornament, Unicorn Gargoyle, gypsum, Windstone, 13-3/4" h, orig box **85.00**

Mirror, hand, Vandor, MIB..............**10.00**

Pin, vermeil, black enameled horn, red, green, blue, and pink cabochons, rhinestone accents, mkd "Reinad," 3-1/2" x 3"....................................**450.00**

Print, black and white, sgd "Lisa Johnson, 1979," matted and framed, 11" x 14"......................................**25.00**

Sculpture, glass, hand blown, Scott Hartshorn, 4" h............................**30.00**

Stuffed toy

White plush, satin ribbons, shimmering gold horn, iridescent mane.......**22.00**

White plush, silver horn and hooves, Gund, 10" h **10.00**

Vase, galloping unicorn, light green, mkd "Hull USA," 11-1/2" h **80.00**

❖ Universal Pottery

Organized in 1934 by the Oxford Pottery Company, in Cambridge, Ohio, firm merged and bought several other small potteries over the years. Universal Pottery made dinnerware and kitchenware until 1960, when the company closed. Because of the mergers, several different brand names were used, including Oxford Ware and Harmony House.

References: Timothy J. Smith, *Universal Dinnerware and Its Predecessors*, Schiffer Publishing, 2000.

For additional listings, see *Warman's Americana & Collectibles* and *Warman's American Pottery & Porcelain*.

Batter bowl set, Circus pattern, 4-1/2" d, 5-1/2" d, 6-1/2" d, 3 matching lids, one with nick **25.00**

Bread box, Cattails **40.00**

Casserole, cov, Cattails **20.00**

Cup and saucer, Woodvine............**12.00**

Custard cup, Calico Fruit.................**6.50**

Dessert bowl, Iris **3.00**

Dinner plate

Ballerina **10.00**

Rambler Rose **10.00**

Drip jar, Bittersweet **25.00**

Unicorn hook rack, brass, rearing unicorn, bar with 4 hooks, $5.

Gravy boat
    Highland **35.00**
    Rambler Rose **12.00**
Milk jug, Calico Fruit **30.00**
Mixing bowl, Woodvine, 1 qt **22.50**
Pie server, Cattails **24.00**
Platter
    Bittersweet....................................**35.00**
    Cattails **35.00**
Reamer pitcher, Roses, 8-1/2" h..**330.00**
Refrigerator pitcher, Cattails **40.00**
Salad bowl, Bittersweet **24.00**
Salt and pepper shakers, Calico Fruit,
    pr **20.00**
Saucer, Iris **1.50**
Soup bowl, Rambler Rose...............**6.50**
Sugar bowl, cov
    Baby's Breath **30.00**
    Ballerina **35.00**
    Cattails **30.00**
Utility jar, Windmill.........................**35.00**
Vegetable bowl, cov, Iris, 9-3/4" d..**25.00**
Vegetable bowl, open
    Ballerina **30.00**
    Bittersweet....................................**45.00**
Water jug, orig stopper **35.00**

❖ U.S. Glass

Known to collectors and dealers as U.S. Glass, the United States Glass Company started as a conglomerate of several glass houses in 1891. The first wares under this new company were pressed pattern glass. One innovation was the company's States series, made up of pre-existing patterns that were renamed, while others were new designs. As the years went on, U.S. Glass developed some of the newer, sleeker, more elegant Depression-era patterns. The last of U.S. Glass factories to close was Tiffin Glass.

Prices listed below are for clear pieces, unless otherwise indicated.

Banana stand, Colorado, blue........**65.00**
Bowl, Bull's Eye and Daisy, ruby stained
    ....**30.00**
Bread plate, Daisy and Button with
    Crossbars....................................**30.00**
Bride's basket, Delaware, silver plated
    frame **75.00**
Butter dish, cov
    Almond Thumbprint, non-flint.......**40.00**
    Daisy and Button with Thumbprint
       Panel.......................................**42.00**

Butter pat, Leaf and Dart...............**24.00**
Cake stand
    Connecticut **40.00**
    Louisiana......................................**55.00**
Celery tray
    Daisy and Button with Crossbars
    ....**36.00**
    Vermont, gold trim **30.00**
Compote, cov, New Hampshire, high
    standard, 5" dia **5.00**
Compote, open, Louisiana, high
    standard, 8" dia **30.00**
Cordial, Daisy and Button with
    Crossbars....................................**30.00**
Creamer
    California, emerald green.............**50.00**
    Daisy and Button with Crossbars.**42.00**
    Leaf and Dart **48.00**
    Texas, gold trim **45.00**
    Vermont, gold trim **32.00**
Finger bowl, Nevada **25.00**
Goblet
    California, emerald green.............**55.00**
    Galloway, non-flint **75.00**
    Manhattan **25.00**
Juice tumbler, Pennsylvania **10.00**
Mug, Daisy and Button with Crossbars
    ....**15.00**
Olive, Maryland, gold trim **18.00**
Pickle castor, Galloway, silver plated
    holder and lid **85.00**
Plate, Maryland, 7" dia **30.00**
Punch bowl, Almond Thumbprint, non-
    flint...**75.00**
Punch cup, Iowa.............................**15.00**
Relish, Maryland **15.00**
Rose bowl, Galloway **25.00**
Salt and pepper shakers, pr
    California **45.00**
    Kentucky......................................**24.00**
Sauce dish, Nevada **10.00**
Spooner, Bull's Eye and Daisy **25.00**
Sugar, cov
    Colorado......................................**75.00**
    Vermont, gold trim **35.00**
Syrup, Loop with Dewdrop..............**60.00**
Toothpick, Delaware, rose, gold trim
    ....**45.00**
Tumble, Maryland, gold trim **30.00**
Waste bowl, Lens and Star, frosted
    ....**24.00**
Whiskey, Pennsylvania, gold trim ...**24.00**
    Wine, Connecticut, non-flint **35.00**

❖ Valentines

Collecting Valentine's Day sentiments is a pleasure for many folks. The earliest cards were hand made. After the greeting card business became more fully developed, valentines were included. Many collectors prefer die-cut cards, which are sometimes found with layers or pull-down decorations. Others like mechanical or animated cards, which have a moving part.

Collectors' Club: National Valentine Collectors Association, P.O. Box 1404, Santa Ana, CA 92702.

For additional listings, see *Warman's Antiques and Collectibles Price Guide* and *Warman's Americana & Collectibles.*

Charm string, four hearts, ribbon...**45.00**
Honeycomb tissue
    Children playing house, 1920s, 8" x 5"
    ....**25.00**
    Cupid and flower basket, 1926 ....**32.00**
Mechanical Boxer, "You sure are a Knockout Valentine," 8-3/4" h, 8" w
    ....**24.00**

To My Valentine, teddy bear holding string of heart cutouts spelling I love u, Gibson, Cincinnati, Ohio, USA, on back, mid 1950s, $.50.

Baseball player swinging bat, "I'd sure go to bat for a Valentine Like You," 6-1/4" h...**22.00**
    Girl doing dishes, 8" h, 6" w.........**25.00**
    Saxaphone player, "My dear Sweetheart I'm making a big noise about you," 5" h.........................**10.00**
Novelty, American Fancy, c1900, rect, panel with silk, celluloid, orig box, 7-1/2" x 10".....................................**45.00**
Pull-down, German
    Car and kids, 1920s **35.00**
    Dollhouse, large, 1935 ....**45.00**
Stand-up, easel-back
    Automobile, windows open **12.00**
    Cat with parachute, 4-1/2" x 3-1/2"
    ....**29.00**
    Flower basket, pasteboard, 1918...**9.00**

❖ Van Briggle Pottery

The Van Briggle Pottery was founded in 1869 by an Ohio artist, Artus Van Briggle. For health reasons, he moved his pottery to Colorado Springs in 1901. After his death in 1904, his wife, Anna, continued the pottery for a few years. Reading the marks can give valuable clues as to the date and maker. The really pricey pieces of Van Briggle are early works; prime examples can command hundreds of dollars. However, there are plenty of more ordinary pieces that are great for a beginning collector. Keep in mind, the company is still in business and many current-production pieces turn up at flea markets.

Candlestick, double-socket, mulberry glaze, floral design, 4-1/2" h, pr .**140.00**
Ewer, black glaze, 7-1/4" h..............**60.00**
Lamp base, emb stylized florals under maroon glaze with blue over-spray, orig factory fittings, incised varnished bottom with logo, name, and Colo. Sprgs, c1920, 9" h.....................**115.00**
Low bowl, circular, rolled rim, maroon glaze with blue over-spray, incised marks, logo, and date 1916, 7" dia
    ....**150.00**

Van Briggle Pottery, three turquoise and blue matte glazed pieces: fan vase (repaired); floriform bowl with flower frog; embossed vase, all incised "AA Van Briggle/Colo. Sprgs," 1920s, $195.

Paperweight
    Donkey, mulberry glaze, 3-3/4" h**135.00**
    Owl, black glaze, 1960s, 9-1/2" h
    ....**125.00**
    Shell, mulberry glaze, 9" l **95.00**
Planter, donkey, brown glaze, Anna Van Briggle **70.00**
Plaque, Indian head, ming turquoise, 4-1/2" h..**80.00**
Vase
    4" h, emb stylized florals, maroon glaze with blue over-spray, dirty bottom with incised "VB" logo and Colo Sprgs **225.00**
    5-1/2" h, shape no. 833, molded stylized flowers, under brown glaze with green over-spray, dirty bottom with incised logo, name and Colo Sprgs, c1920 ....**230.00**
    6" h, incised and molded stylized flowers, under blue/gray glaze with turquoise over-spray, dirty bottom with incised logo, name, and date "20", c1920 ....**375.00**
    10-1/4" h, 4-1/4" d, tapering, emb tobacco leaves, covered in matte ochre and umber glaze, incised AA, die-stamped 1915 and 45....**1,380.00**
Wall pocket, daisy design, Mountain Craig Brown glaze, 7-5/8" h **302.50**

❖ Vandor

Vandor is a relatively newcomer to the flea market scene. Their specialized wares bring vintage characters back to life and are well received. Because the wares are mainly from the 1990s, the original box and packaging should be readily available.

Au Gratin dish, Country, farm scene, 12-3/4" l..**26.00**
Bank, Howdy Doody.......................**25.00**
Cookie jar
    Betty Boop, holiday **35.00**
    Greatful Dead, 1998, MIB **125.00**
    Honeymooners, Preston Willingham sculptor, 1998 ....**175.00**
    Mona Lisa...................................**85.00**
Creamer, Country **15.00**
Egg cup, Sweet Pea **45.00**
Mug, Country.................................**15.00**
Music box, Popeye and Olive Oyl...**75.00**
Picture frame, Betty Boop, copyright K.F.S., 1985, orig paper label.......**65.00**
Salad plate, Country, chicken, pig, sheet, and hens **17.00**
Salt and pepper shakers, pr
    Betty Boop and Pup, on motorcycle, 4-1/2" h **24.00**
    Bewitched, stove salt shaker, Samatha pepper shaker, 2-7/8" h, MIB....**20.00**
    Cat Pais, nodders, 1996..............**25.00**
    Country.......................................**10.00**

Greatful Dead, yellow bear salt shaker, train pepper shaker, 2-1/4" h, MIB **22.00**
Man in top hat **15.00**
Poodles, NRFB...........................**20.00**
Popeye **95.00**
Teapot, cov
Betty Boop, car...........................**12.50**
Cherry Woods **5.00**

❖ Van Telligen

Designer Ruth Van Telligen created some fun characters for the Royal China and Novelty Company of Chicago. Produced by Regal China, the items were limited to a few cookie jar designs and salt and pepper shakers. The cookie jars were made in limited numbers and tend to be hard to find.

Salt and pepper shakers, pr
Bears, yellow, 3-1/2" h.................**45.00**
Black boy and dog......................**185.00**
Bunnies, hugging **25.00**
Ducks **75.00**
Dutch boy and girl, 3-3/4" h **70.00**
Mary and lamb **85.00**
Peek-A-Boos, red and white **120.00**
Snuggle Hug Love Bugs **125.00**

❖ Vaseline Glass

Threaded vaseline glass lidded jar with applied amethyst prunts, 7-1/2" h, $75.

Vaseline glass is named for its unusual yellow-green color, which is created by adding uranium salts to the glassware batch. Collectors test their vaseline glass with a black light or even a Geiger counter, as it is somewhat radioactive. Production was restricted in later years because of the lack of uranium. This type of glass was made by early American glassblowers up through the early Depression years. The white swirls of the opalescent highlights create a pleasing contrast to the unusual base color.

References: Sue C. Davis, *Pictorial Guide to Vaseline Glass,* Schiffer Publishing, 2002;

Barrie Skelcher, *The Big Book of Vaseline Glass,* Schiffer Publishing, 2002.

Reproduction Alert

Bread plate, Daisy and Button with Crossbars, pattern glass **35.00**
Celery vase, Daisy and Button with Crossbars, pattern glass **50.00**
Cologne bottle, 5-1/2" h, 2" sq.....**250.00**
Compote, low, Three Panel, pointed rim **70.00**
Console set, 10" d compote, matching 9" h candlesticks............................**500.00**
Creamer, Wreath and Shell, opalescent, dec **135.00**
Cruet, Everglades, opalescent **275.00**
Ice cream set, Daisy and Button, large bowl, serving bowls, some chips, 7 pc set **475.00**
Jelly compote, Iris with Meander, opalescent...................................**95.00**
Knife rest, barbell shape, faceted ends, 4-7/8" l...................................**95.00**
Perfume bottle, Waterfall Nude, Czechoslovakian, 7-1/2" h..........**225.00**
Spooner, Palm Beach, opalescent .**95.00**
Sugar, cov, Diamond Spearhead, opalescent...............................**235.00**
Toothpick holder, Daisy and Button **55.00**
Tumbler, Fluted Scrolls **50.00**
Vase, free blown, 8" h....................**60.00**
Water set, Basketweave, pitcher and 6 goblets.....................................**650.00**

❖ Vending Machines

Got a penny for a gumball? Vending machines with gumballs, peanuts, and other goodies captured many pennies and loose change. These simple vending machines date to about 1910.

References: Several good older reference books exist on this topic and are recommended to those who want to learn more about vending machines.

Periodicals: *Antique Amusements Slot Machines & Jukebox Gazette*, 909 26th St NW, Washington, DC 20037; *Around the Vending Wheel*, 54217 Costana Ave, Lakewood, CA 90712; *Coin Drop International*, 5815 W 52nd Ave, Denver, CO 80212; *Coin Machine Trader*, 569 Kansas SE, P.O. Box 602, Huron, SD 57350; *Coin-Op Classics*, 17844 Toiyabe St, Fountain Valley, CA 9270; *Coin-Op Newsletter*, 909 26th St, NW, Washington, DC, 20037; *Coin Slot*, 4401 Zephyr St, Wheat Ridge, Co 80033; *Gameroom*, 1014 Mt Tabor Rd, New Albany, IN 47150; *Loose Change*, 1515 S Commerce St, Las Vegas, NV 89102; *Pin Game Journal*, 31937 Olde Franklin Dr, Farmington, MI, 48334; *Scopitone Newsletter*, 810 Courtland Dr, Ballwin, MO 63021.

Aspirin, Winthrop Metal Products, 10¢, 1940s **45.00**

Cigar, Malkin Phillies, steel meal, 10¢, 1930s **95.00**
Combs, Advance machine, Model #4, 10¢, 1950s **45.00**
Confection, Master, c1923, 1 cent, 16" h **200.00**
Gum
Adams, c1934, four column, tab gum vendor, chrome, decal, 22" h..**100.00**
Ford, round globe with Ford decal, chrome finish **150.00**
Jumbo, depicts circus elephant, 15" h **295.00**
Mills Automatic Tab, 5-column tab gum vendor, aluminum front, colorful paper sign, green case...........**295.00**
Victor, 1940s, aluminum front, cylindrical glass, 17" h restored **245.00**
Victor, 1950s, red andblack metal case, glass globe, 11" h **195.00**
Matches, Edwards Mfg Co, c1930, Diamond, one to four books, 13-1/2" h **225.00**
Nut
Atlas Bantam tray vendor, 1940s, restored, 11" h **395.00**
Eldridge, aluminum, 1936, 8-1/2" h, 4-1/2" w, 4" d **195.00**
Northwest, 1930s, porcelain base and top, frosted globe, embossed name, 15" h **395.00**
Silver King Hot Nut, c. 1947, red hobnail glass light on top, 15" h **495.00**
Postcard, Exhibit Supply, 1¢, 1930s **125.00**
Stamps, Postage and Stamp Machine Co., metal, 5¢ and 10¢, 1948.......**45.00**

❖ Ventriloquist Dummies

Charlie McCarthy and Jerry Mahoney easily come to mind when thinking about vintage ventriloquist dummies. How fascinated we used to be with this form of entertainment. Becase there were many amateur ventriloquists, their dummies occasionally find their way to flea markets. Look for well-constructed handmade examples or those produced by well-known doll companies.

Bart Simpson, custom made........**200.00**
Boy, hand made, wearing child's blue suit, white shirt **90.00**
Bozo **42.00**
Jerry Mahoney **60.00**
Lester, Paul Winchell, 1973 25" h **142.00**
Groucho Marx, made by Juro, 1977, 30" h **95.00**

Ventriloquist dummy, boy, velvet coat, lined with fabric that matched pants, green shirt, striped socks, lower jaw missing, $95.

Three Stooges.............................**100.00**
Willie Talk, Horsman **42.00**

❖ Vernon Kilns

Founded in Vernon, Calif., the firm was formerly called Poxon China. After it sold to Faye Bennison in 1931, it was renamed Vernon Kilns. The company then flourished and made high-quality dinnerware and other items. Souvenir plates were among their more successful products. The company folded in 1958, when it sold its trade name, molds, and remaining stock.

Periodical: *Vernon Views*, P.O. Box 945, Scottsdale, AZ 85252.

Ashtray, Frontier Days, 5-3/4" w **80.00**
Cake plate, Organdie, 12" d **20.00**
Chop plate, Hawaiian Flowers, blue, 14" d **42.00**
Coffeepot, Style **165.00**
Creamer and sugar, Brown-Eyed Susan **12.00**
Cup and saucer
    Chatelaine, topaz **40.00**
    Moby Dick, brown.........................**22.00**
Dinner plate
    Dolores, 10-1/2" d **18.00**
    Hawaiian Flowers, blue, 9" d........**32.00**
Egg cup, Organdie..........................**27.50**
Flower pot, matching saucer, Tam O'Shanter **80.00**
Mug, Brown-Eyed Susan.................**25.00**
Pitcher
    Raffia, 2 qt...................................**40.00**
    Tweed, half pint, streamline, 5" h....**80.00**

Platter, Painted Rose, oval, 16" l ..**105.00**
Salad plate, Chatelaine, topaz........**25.00**
Salt and pepper shakers, pr, Gingham **15.00**
Souvenir plate
    Georgia, 10" d **15.00**
    Lookout Mountain, made for Livelys Lookout Museum, deep red, 10-1/4" dia...**20.00**
    Nebraska University **30.00**
    Oklahoma State Agricultural and Mechanical College, backstamp "Vernon Kilns, designed especially for Creech's, Stillwater, Oklahoma" **30.00**
    Texas Southwest Methodist University, Dallas, backstamp "Made exclusively for Titche-Goettinger Co." **35.00**
Teapot, Linda **125.00**
Tid-Bit tray, Tam O'Shanter, 3 tiers, wood handle..............................**45.00**

Vernon Kilns, creamer, Plaid pattern, green, brown, and rust, white ground, mkd "Authentic Vernonware, Made in USA," $35.

❖ Victorian

This is one of those topics clearly open to individual interpretation. It takes it name from the reign of Queen Victoria, but clearly lasted for years after her reign ceased. Decorators and dealers use "Victorian" to describe things from that era, especially objects that are ornate, richly colored and often richly textured.

Boudoir chair, lady's, wicker, ornate curliques, bead garlands............**335.00**
Bud vase, sterling silver, unidentified hallmarks, 8" h **90.00**
Dresser set, brush, comb, mirror, silver, monogrammed **125.00**
Fan, ostrich feathers, ribbon, white, some losses **120.00**
Frame, double heart shape openings, wood, brass corners, 12" x 13" **60.00**
Honey dish, cov, beehive shape, opaque green glass, attributed to Vallerystahl **195.00**
Mirror, beveled, ornate, 12" sq **155.00**
Rose bowl, glass, rich cranberry color **65.00**
Sheet, matching pillow case, cutwork and

embroidered cherubs, bows, and flowers, 90" sq...........................**110.00**
Vase, slightly frosted glass shading from clear to deep rose, hand shape holding cornucopia, hand painted gold ring on one finger and dot trim on ruffled top **65.00**
Watch pin, scrolled motif on center raised oval, scalloped body, black enamel trim, hook for watch, tiny C-scroll pin clasp **25.00**

❖ Vienna Art

The Vienna Art Company was responsible for many interesting lithographed-tin items, including numerous advertising pieces. Look for intricate scenes with rich colors. Because this tinware was designed to be used, expect to find scratches or wear.

Calendar, adv Harvard Brewing Co. Pure Malt Beverages, Lowell, Mass USA, lady with large pink ribbons in her hair, white gown, ornamental gilt border **150.00**
Plate, adv, 10" dia
    Anheuser-Busch Malt-Nurtine on back, front with lady in low cut diaphanous top...**95.00**
    Compliments of the American Sheet and Tinplate Co., Pittsburgh, maid with flowing brunette brown hair, plunging neckline, gilt border....**90.00**
    Dr. Pepper, beautiful lady holding stem of lilies, silhouetted against floral background, some rim chips, overall soiling and staining................**650.00**
    Jamestown Exposition, 1907, Pocahontas and John Smith, copyrighted W.H. Owens & Co., Manchester, VA......................**125.00**
    Joslin Dry Goods Co. adv on back, Gypsy lady...............................**90.00**
Tray
    9-1/2" dia, adv Stegmaier Brewing Co. Wilkes Barre, PA, lady with flowing hair dec with flowers, cobalt blue border, sapphire blue and gilt dec **80.00**
    10" dia, adv Anheuser-Busch Malt Nutrine, St. Louis, lady with flowing brown hair, low gown, green, gold, white, and pink on mantel border, dated 1905.............................**200.00**
    10" d, adv Heim Breweries Select, East St. Louis, Ills, art plate #104, Poesie, lady with flowering brown hair, springs of leaves in her hair, pink low-cut gown, gold, cream, brown, and green border.....................**75.00**
    10" d, adv Hotel Majestic, color litho of maiden in rose colored gown, holding vase of flowers, Mucha-tyupe

gilt border.................................**150.00**
10" d, beautiful maid with white gown,
long brown flowing hair, red hat, Art
Nouveau green, gilt, and brown
border, back mkd "Royal Saxony Art
Plate #105, Irene, Chs. W. Shonk
Co.," **60.00**
10" d, bust of beautiful maiden, pink
gown, springs of leaves, multicolored
border, reverse mkd "Royal Saxony
Art Plate #104, Poesie, Chs. W.
Shonk Co"................................**90.00**

❖ Vietnam War

With the passing of time since the Vietnam
War, there is growing interest in military and
civilian items related to the conflict. Items
from "The Name" and those from back in
"The World" are seen with increasing
frequency at flea markets, where good
pieces an still be found at reasonable
prices.

Flight jacket, G-1, US Navy, leather, size
40 ....**260.00**
Magazine, Life, Oct. 20, 1967, "U.S.
Prisoners in North Viet Nam" **5.00**
MIA bracelet, red aluminum, "Maj
Horace H. Fleming III, FL. USMC 10
May 68 SVN" **25.00**
Lighter, Zippo
Vietnam 67-68 Long Binh **300.00**
Vietnam 68-69 Qui Nhon, enamel
decor......................................**300.00**
Pinback button, "Out Now Nov. 6th,
Demonstrate Against the War NPAC,"
1-3/4" dia **17.00**
Poster, cardboard, "Vietnam Moratorium
Oct. 15 No Business As Usual Until
The Troops Are Home," 13" x 10".**15.00**
Shoulder tab, RV Ranger, white silk,
light-red border, "23 Vietnamese
Ranger Bn"..................................**75.00**
Uniform patch.................................**5.00**

❖ View-Master

Gimme, gimme, I want to see too! Since
View-Masters and their reels were first
created in 1939, they have been educating
and entertaining us. During World War II,
shortages caused a cutback in production,
until the Army and Navy recognized that
this would be a good way to train troops.
After the war, demand soared and was met
by several different companies.

Collectors' Club: National Stereoscopic
Association, P.O. Box 14801, Columbus, OH
43214.

Reels

Annie Oakley................................**15.00**
Archie..**8.00**
Brussels World Fair, 1958, four reel set
....**48.00**
Cinderella, GAF, 3 reels **28.00**
Daniel Boone...............................**15.00**
Eight Is Enough, GAF, 1980, MIP ..**15.00**
Fat Albert & Cosby Kids...............**10.00**
Ghostbusters..................................**5.00**
Huckleberry Hound & Yogi Bear.....**5.00**
Inspector Gadget...........................**6.00**
King Kong.......................................**9.00**
Lassie and Timmy, 1958, GAF.....**20.00**
Mickey Mouse Club......................**25.00**
New Zoo Revue **12.00**
Pete's Dragon................................**8.00**
Sleeping Beauty, Swayers FT-10,
©1953...**8.00**
Time Tunnel.................................**75.00**
Tom Sawyer...................................**9.00**
Waltons **10.00**
Zorro, View-Master B 469, 3 reels,
small tear **45.00**

Stereoscope

Sawyer View-Master Model C, 1946-
55, with 2 reels **27.00**
View-Master Model E I.O.B..........**75.00**

❖ Viking Glass

Located in New Martinsville, W.Va., this
glass company has recently ceased
production under the last of the original
family owners, Dalzell-Viking. Viking
produced various brightly colored glassware
items through the years and also made
some crackle glass. Look for a silver and
pink foil label on some items.

Ashtray
Amber, crackle glass, 7" l.............**15.00**
Tea blue, triangular, orig foil label, 3-
3/4" w...................................**17.50**
Bookends, pr, owls, dark green, 7" h
....**65.00**
Bowl, amethyst, 1950s...................**25.00**
Bust, Madonna.............................**30.00**
Candy dish, olive green, Teardrop
pattern, 8" h................................**15.00**
Compote
Amber, part of orig sticker, 8-1/2" dia,
7" h **35.00**
Amberina, 4-3/4" h, 8-3/4" dia......**35.00**
Cruet, applied handle, orig stopper, 6-
1/2" h, Amber or green................**30.00**
Fairy lamp, red satin.......................**55.00**
Figure
Duck, dark blue **40.00**
Elephant, frosted **20.00**
Penguin, dark blue **65.00**
Goblet, orange and gold, 4-5/8" h..**12.00**
Juice set, cobalt blue, 5 pcs **30.00**
Pitcher, orange, applied clear handle
....**30.00**

*Viking Glass Fairy lamp, orange, sawtooth type
pattern, orig foil label, $18.*

❖ Wade Ceramics

The British firm known as The Wade Group originally made industrial ceramics. By the late 1920s, the company started making figurines, which were well received, and then dinnerware and accessories. Many dealers know the name Wade from the Red Rose Tea premiums.

References: Donna Baker, *Wade Miniatures*, Schiffer Publishing, 2000; Pat Murray, *The Charlton Standard Catalogue of Wade, Vol. Three,* 1998; *The Charlton Standard Catalogue of Wade Whimsical Collectibles,* 4th ed., 1998, Charlton Press.

Collectors' Clubs: The Official International Wade Collectors Club, Royal works, Westport, Road, Burslem, Stoke-On-Trent, ST6 4AP England; Wade Watch, 8199 Pierson Court, Arvada, CO 80005.

Baby dish, Quack Quacks, Robert Barlow design, 1930s, 7" dia **85.00**
Circus figures, set of 15 entertainers and animals....................................**35.00**
Decanter, dark blue neck, base with white ground, multicolored coat of arms dec, British rum, orig contents ...**125.00**
Dish, ballerina **12.00**
Figure
   Kissing bunnies **135.00**
   Lucky Leprechaun, cobbler, 1950s **32.00**
   Mary Had A Little Lamb **7.50**
   Storybook Chimp, wearing skirt **5.00**
Ginger jar, red and black flowers, white ground **32.50**
Pitcher, Heath bird, 9" h **175.00**
Red Rose Tea figure
   Buffalo **3.50**
   Camel **3.00**
   Cat...**3.75**
   Cockatoo **8.00**
   Elephant **3.50**
   Hippo **3.00**
   Kangaroo.......................................**2.50**
   Rabbit...**2.25**
   Raccoon..**2.50**
   Tiger...**2.50**
Stein, beer barrel shape, sgd "T. J.," 7-1/2" h...**35.00**
Teapot, Scottie, 8" l **300.00**
Tea set, Golden Turquoise, teapot, creamer, and sugar **125.00**
Turtle, with lid.................................**35.00**

Wall plaque, yacht, green, blue, and beige **45.00**

❖ Waffle Irons

An array of interesting waffle irons can be found at most flea markets. Early cast-iron examples were placed over an open fire. Later versions were electrified. Collectors are especially interested in waffle irons with unusual patterns. Watch out damage irons and those with missing parts.

Birmingham Stove & Range Co., No. 8, cast iron.......................................**65.00**
Coleman Waffle Iron, early 1930s, high Art Deco style, chrome, low profile, small black and white porcelain top impala insert, black Bakelite handles **85.00**
Crescent, No. 8, Fanner Mfg. Co., Cleveland, Ohio, wire handles....**110.00**
Electrahot, 1940s, two 6" sets of plates mounted on oval base..................**30.00**
Rainbow, No. 80W, Precision Mfg., Dover, N.J., chrome, wooden handles, temperature gauge window in top**35.00**
Stover, No. 28, cast iron, wooden handles, Stover Mfg. Co., Freeport, Ill **110.00**
Toastmaster, Model 2D2, electric, McGraw Electric Co., Elgin, Ill......**45.00**
Universal China, electric, replaced cord **65.00**
Wear-Ever Aluminum, No. 340-1, wire handle **25.00**
Wright & Bridgeford, Louisville, cast iron **120.00**

❖ Wagner Ware

Wagner Manufacturing made cast-iron hollow ware, brass castings, and aluminum cookware among other household items. The company prospered from 1891 to the late 1950s under the care of the Wagner family. The firm was bought in 1959 by Textron, which held it until 1969.

Periodical: *Kettles n' Cookware*, Drawer B, Perrysville, NY 14129.

Ashtray, skillet shape, 3" dia **48.00**
Child's teakettle, 6" h...................**290.00**
Corn stick, 13" l............................**68.00**
Muffin pan, 11-hole, 7-1/4" x 10-1/2" **55.00**
Scoop, #912, 9-1/4" l **24.00**
Skillet
   No. 8 ....**30.00**
   No. 12 ....**59.00**
   No. 1101A, sq................................**45.00**
Teakettle, wire handle, 6" h **150.00**
Waffle iron, wooden handles **30.00**

❖ Walgreen's Collectibles

Walgreens is an American institution. Being one of the oldest drug stores in the country contributes to collectors searching for early tins and products with the Walgreen's name. Others concentrate on things relating to other aspects of the store.

Bank, 1913 Ford Model t, Ertl, #9531, 1991, mint **18.50**
Bottle, vitamins, orig box, 3-1/2" h....**5.00**
Box, prescription, 1952 label, Cincinnati **6.50**
Restaurant ware, Syracuse China
   Bowl, dessert 4-1/2" dia **18.00**
   Cup and saucer.............................**8.50**
   Grill plate, 9-1/2" dia....................**26.00**
   Plate, 7-1/4" dia...........................**35.00**
Match cover, 1930s **11.00**
Tin, Epsom salt, 1 lb **9.00**

❖ Wallace China

Wallace China was founded in 1931 in Vernon, Calif., making commercial and residential dinnerware until 1959. The company's western designs are favorites with collectors. The Westward Ho pattern is a good example of the firm's hotel chinaware, while Willow is also popular with Blue Willow collectors. Wallace China is well marked.

Bowl, Chuckwagon, 4" dia **55.00**
Cereal bowl, Magnolia **20.00**
Chili bowl
   Western brands motif **70.00**
   Westward Ho...............................**55.00**
Cup and saucer
   Newport..**8.00**
   Yorkshire......................................**8.00**
Dinner plate
   Bonanza logo, 9-1/2" d...............**20.00**
   Daphne..**16.00**
   Master Pizza, 7" dia **10.00**
   Newport.......................................**15.00**
   Rodeo...**115.00**
   Yorkshire......................................**8.00**
Fruit bowl, Yorkshire **4.00**
Grill plate, Magnolia **20.00**
Mug, California, green border **8.00**
Pitcher, Hibiscus **200.00**
Salad plate, Rodeo **70.00**
Salt and pepper shakers, pr, Rodeo, 5" h **124.00**
Saucer, El Rancho **12.00**
Serving plate
   Old Hawaii, oval **30.00**
   Shadow Leaf **20.00**
Teapot, individual size, Restaurant Ware **12.50**

❖ Wall Pockets

Wall Pocket, bonnet, turquoise, gold trim, English, $43.

Wall pockets are clever pottery holders designed to be hung on walls. Potteries such as Roseville and Weller made wall pockets in the same lines as their vases, bowls, etc. Collectors search for these potteries plus interesting examples from lesser-known makers. Wall pockets were very collectible a few years ago, driven by the decorator market. Today they are becoming easier to find at flea markets, but the prices haven't declined.

Reference: Betty and Bill Newbound, *Collector's Encyclopedia of Wall Pockets, Identification and Values,* Collector Books, 1996, 1998 value update.

Collectors' Club: Wall Pocket Collectors Club, 1356 Tahiti, St. Louis, MO 63128.

Frankoma Acorn, light brown, mkd "Frankoma 190"...........................**25.00**
Cowboy Boot, blue and white, speckled, mkd "Frankoma 133"....................**30.00**
Japan, Harlequin heads, boy and girl **65.00**
McCoy
    Apple on leaf **50.00**
    Fan, white, pink floral **60.00**
    Figure of woman in bonnet and bow, white, red trim..........................**40.00**
    Leaf, blue and pink......................**40.00**
    Morning Glory **50.00**
    Post Box, green...........................**50.00**
    Sunflower, yellow, with bird **45.00**
    Tulip, white...................................**40.00**
    Yellow, pink floral dec **40.00**
Roseville
    Foxglove, brown, #1296-8".........**190.00**
    Gardenia, brown, #666-8"..........**150.00**
    Green, matte, 8" l......................**120.00**
    Maple Leaf, 8-1/2".......................**75.00**
    Three sided, green, 11" l............**110.00**
    Tulips, emb flowers, white **60.00**
Shawnee, teapot, pink apple dec....**32.00**

Wall Pocket, green luster top band, multicolored dec of branch with bird, price for pr, $35.

Unmarked
    Cornucopia shape, cattail and duck dec, blue, 6" h...........................**40.00**
    Plaster, yellow iris dec, homemade, 8" l **20.00**
Weller
    Blue, emb leaf, 7" l **60.00**
    Iris, blue, 8-1/2" l **50.00**
    Klyro, 8" h.................................**110.00**
    Roma, 7" l **130.00**

❖ Watch Fobs

A watch fob is a useful and/or decorative item that is attached to a man's pocket watch by a strap. Its main function is to assist the user in removing the watch from a pocket. The heyday of watch fobs was late in the 19th century, when many manufacturers created them to advertise products, commemorate special events, or serve as decorative and useful objects. Most watch fobs are made of metal and struck from a steel die. Some are trimmed with enamel or may have a celluloid plaque. When found with their original watch strap or original packaging, the value is enhanced.

Collectors' Clubs: Canadian Association of Watch Fob Collectors, PO Box 787, Caledonia, Ontario, NDA IAO Canada; International Watch Fob Association, Inc., RR5, PO Box 210, Burlington, IA 52601; Midwest Watch Fob Collectors, Inc.,6401 W. Girard Ave., Milwaukee, WI 53210.

Reproduction Alert

For additional listings, see *Warman's Americana & Collectibles.*

Advertising
    Anheuser-Busch, diecut silvered brass, enameled red, white, and blue trademark, 1-1/2" dia **60.00**
    Evening Gazette, baseball shape, scorecard back, 1912 ....**95.00**

Bronze watch fobs, leather strap, left: Mack bulldog, $25; center: Caterpillar, heavy equipment, $20; right: Oshkosh, dump truck, $25.

    Foundry & Machine Exhibition Co., 1-3/4" x 1-1/2" **48.00**
    Gardner-Denver Co, jackhammer, silvered brass, tool replica, symbol and name on back, c1950........**25.00**
    Huntingdon Pianos, dark white metal, 7/8" black, white, blue, and gold celluloid with Paderewski, inscription "Paderewski Bought One," early 1900s.......................................**65.00**
    Joliet Corn Shellers....................**150.00**
    Kelly Springfield Tires, white metal, raised illus of female motorist, "Kelly Springfield Hand Made Tires" on back, 2" d.................................**80.00**
    Lima Construction Equipment, copper luster, large excavation tractor, world continents background, inscribed "Lima/Move The Earth With a Lima," back text for shovels, draglines, clamshells, and cranes............**25.00**
    Pontiac, with key chain, 3/4" d **45.00**
    Red Goose Shoes, enameled red goose......................................**100.00**
Commemorative
    American Legion, Cleveland State Convention, 1946, diecut brass **35.00**
    Princeton University, brass, 1908.**48.00**
    World Championship Rodeo Contest, Chicago **45.00**
Political
    Democratic National Convention, Baltimore, 1912, silvered brass, center shield with eagle............**20.00**
    Republican National Convention, brass, 1920, bust of Lincoln **40.00**

❖ Waterford Crystal

Waterford is easily identified with high-quality crystal. The firm was started in 1729 in Waterford, Ireland. Look for a finely etched mark or a foil type label. Waterford continues to make exquisite glassware today.

For additional listings, see *Warman's Antiques and Collectibles* and *Warman's Glass.*

Christmas ornament, c1995..........**17.50**
Claret, Colleen, set of six in orig box, some orig labels.........................**480.00**
Clock, ABC block **60.00**
Figure
    Dolphin **110.00**
    Eagle **140.00**
    Lion **150.00**
    Rocking horse **80.00**
    Shark..**125.00**
Frame, ABC block, 4" x 6"..............**55.00**
Goblet, Colleen **65.00**
Paperweight, Capital **90.00**
Vase, bulbous, top to bottom vertical cuts separated by horizontal slash cuts, sgd, 7" h....................................**140.00**

Waterford Crystal Champagne flutes, orig green and gold foil labels, orig price tags on base, orig box, set of four, $48.

Waterford Crystal pendant, heart shaped crystal, orig box, $18.

❖ Watering Cans

Here's a topic that was really hot at last summer's flea markets. It seemed like everywhere you looked there was a watering can. Again, it's the decorator influence encouraged those with a country-style interior to add a few watering cans. And, while all this flower watering has been going on, more children's vintage lithographed-tin watering cans also appeared on the scene. They too have become an eagerly sought item.

Brass, small dings, 4-3/8" h, 9-3/8" l.**8.00**
Ceramic, Czechoslovakian, white ground, blue-green shading and trim, 2 swans swimming, 5-1/4" h............**60.00**
Child's, litho on tin
    Ohio Art, turquoise and orange flowers, pink hearts, yellow ground, 8-1/4" h
    ....**35.00**
    Pretty garden, bright colors, c1920, very slight use, 6-1/4" h..........**150.00**
    Super Smurf in Shower................**10.00**
    Victorian children in garden, handle loose, scratches, wear, 8" h......**60.00**
Copper, round, long narrow spout, round closed sprinkler head...................**66.00**
Miniature, doll house size, metal, painted red, flower dec, 1" h **5.00**
Sterling silver, narrow spout, small size
    ....**45.00**
Tin
    Brass head **35.00**
    Dover, orig label, no sprinkler **25.00**
    Painted green, wear, orig round sprinkler, long loop handle........**40.00**
    Unmarked, some age darkening..**30.00**
Toleware, some rust and surface abrasion, 16" h, 9-3/4" dia base.**115.00**

Pick your favorite from this great selection of watering cans.

❖ Watt Pottery

Although the name Watt Pottery wasn't used until about 1920, founder W.J. Watt was involved in the pottery business as early as 1886. He worked at several pottery companies before purchasing the Crooksville, Ohio, Globe Stoneware Company. With the help of his sons Harry and Thomas, son-in-law C.L. Dawson, daughter Marion Watt, and numerous other relatives, he began production of this uniquely American pottery. Most Watt dinnerware features underglazed decorations on a sturdy off-white or tan body. Much of Watt dinnerware was sold by Safeway, Woolworth, and grocery chains. A fire destroyed the factory in October 1965, and it was never rebuilt.

Collectors' Club: Watt Pottery Collectors USA, Box 26067, Fairview Park, OH 44126.

> **Reproduction Alert**

For additional listings, see *Warman's Americana & Collectibles.*

Baker, Starflower, #67..................**165.00**
Berry Bowl, Cherry, #4 ....**25.00**
Bowl
    Apple, #04 ....**95.00**
    Raised Pansy, #9 ....**135.00**
    Rooster, #6...............................**105.00**
    Tulip, #64 ....**175.00**
Casserole, individual, Raised Pansy
    ....**145.00**
Cereal bowl, Apple **24.00**
Cookie jar, Autumn Foliage, #76 ....**95.00**
Creamer
    Apple, #62 ....**175.00**
    Tulip, #62 ....**225.00**
Mug, Starflower, #61 ....**285.00**
Pepper shaker, Autumn Foliage, hour-glass shape **90.00**
Pie Plate, Pansy, #33, adv **60.00**

Watts Pottery, creamer, Apple pattern, chip, hairline, $10.

Watts Pottery, two bowls and creamer, Rooster pattern, sold as set, $35.

Pitcher

Apple, #15 ....**165.00**
Bleeding Heart, #15 ....**55.00**
Cherries, #15, with advertising...**180.00**
Rooster, #15.............................**145.00**
Tear Drop, #15 ....**65.00**
Spaghetti bowl, Cherry, #39......**50.00**

❖ Weather Vanes

Weather vanes were originally designed to indicate the direction of the wind, showing farmers which way a potential weather system was coming. Look for large weather vanes made of copper, sheet metal, cast or wrought iron, wood, or zinc. Expect to find some signs of weathered wear on vintage weather vanes.

References: Robert Bishop and Patricia Coblentz, *Gallery of American Weathervanes and Whirligigs*, E.P. Dutton, 1981.

Reproduction Alert: Reproductions of early weathervanes are being expertly aged and then sold as originals.

Collecting Hint: Because they were popular targets for hunters and gun-toting boys, many old weathervanes are riddled with bullet holes. Filled holes generally can be detected with a blacklight.

For additional listings, see *Warman's Country Price Guide* and *Warman's Antiques and Collectibles Price Guide.*

Arrow, copper, ball finial, dents, 13" h, 25" l..**345.00**
Banner, zinc and wrought iron, banner/arrow finial, 54-1/2" h.....**690.00**
Eagle, copper, full bodied, cast zinc feet, wooden base, 21" wing span, 18-1/2" h, one foot loose, arrow bent **250.00**
Fish, flat sheet metal, applied fins, green glass eyes cracked, gilt loss, 13-3/4" h, 16" l..**1,035.00**
Horse
Prancing, cast aluminum, over arrow, bullet holes, small size.............**49.50**
Running, sheet metal, holes, wear, 16" h, 28" l **220.00**
Running, tin, full-bodied, on arrow, 24" l..**825.00**

Standing, sheet metal, large tail to vane, 26" l..............................**110.00**
Rooster, sheet iron, reinforced with riveted iron straps, 36-1/2" h, 27-1/2" l...**977.50**
Schooner, 39" l, 23-3/8" h, wooden, hull painted red and black, cream colored sail, wire rigging, America, 20th C, wooden stand, wear..................**275.00**

❖ Wedgwood

Wedgwood is another name that usually denotes quality. Josiah Wedgwood built a factory at Etruria, England, between 1766 and 1769, after having been in the ceramics business for a few years. Wedgwood's early products included caneware, unglazed earthenware, black basalt, creamware, and jasperware. Bone china was introduced between 1812 and 1822. Over the years these and other wares have been made, marked, and well used. Today, Wedgwood still continues its tradition of fine quality.

Periodical: *ARS Ceramics,* 5 Dogwood Court, Glen Head, NY 11545.

Collectors' Clubs: Wedgwood International Seminar, 22 DeSavry Crescent, Toronto, Ontario M4S 212 Canada; The Wedgwood Society, The Roman Villa, Rockbourne, Fordingbridge, Hants, SP6 3PG, England; The Wedgwood Society of Boston, 28 Birchwood Drive, Hampstead, NH 03841; The Wedgwood Society of New York, 5 Dogwood Court, Glen Head, NY 11545; Wedgwood Society of Southern California, Inc., PO Box 4385, North Hollywood, CA 91617.

For additional listings, see *Warman's Antiques and Collectibles Price Guide* and *Warman's English & Continental Pottery & Porcelain.*

Basket, Queen's Ware, oval, undertray, basketweave molded bodies, pierced galleries, green and black enamel oak leaves and trim, imp mark, early 19th C, 9" l..**290.00**
Biscuit jar, cov Basalt, black, engine-turned body below band of children playing in relief, silver plated rim, handle, and cov, imp mark, late 19th C...**520.00**
Jasper, three color dip, central dark blue band bordered in light blue, applied white classical figures, silver plated rims, cov, and handle, imp mark, handle damaged **250.00**
Bowl, black jasper dip, applied white classical Dancing Hours figures, foliate banding, imp mark, c1962, 10-1/8"...**460.00**
Celery dish, bone china, gilt diamond border, printed mark, foot rim, light gilt wear, c1820..............................**175.00**

Wedgwood Jasperware plate, white portrait of Benjamin Franklin, white stars on rim, gold signature, $25.

Cheese dish, cov, jasper, dark blue dip, applied white classical and foliate relief, imp mark, mid 19th C.................**350.00**
Creamer, jasper, blue, relief of Classical figures making offerings to gods..**60.00**
Dinner plate, lavender on cream, shell edge **35.00**
Egg-shaped box, cov, 1978, incised "Wedgwood, England, V," 2" h, 3" l...**65.00**
Fruit plate, majolica, turquoise basketweave, 6-1/2" d...............**250.00**
Game pie, caneware, oval, molded, rabbit finial, imp mark, 1865, 7" l, orig liner cracked..............................**445.00**
Match box, jasper, dark blue..........**90.00**
Medallion, jasper, light green dip, oval, portrait of Admiral Richard Howe, imp title and mark, 3-1/2" x 4-1/4" **260.00**
Pitcher, black basalt, club, enameled floral dec, imp mark, c1860, 6-1/2" h...**345.00**
Plaque, jasper, solid black, applied white classical relief of muses, imp mark, 19th C, wood frame, rect............**490.00**
Urn, jasper, blue, scene of Classical figures in relief, two handles, acanthus borders, 11" h............................**275.00**
Vase
Creamware, molded grape vines and foliage, painted band of strawberries, mid 19th C, minor damage, 6" h...**90.00**
Diceware, tricolor, pale blue dip, yellow quatrefoils, white ground, pierced flower frog cover with white applied quatrefoils, #82 of limited edition of 200, mkd "Wedgwood, Made in England, H82HB, 74," c1974, 5-1/4" h, 4-5/8" d **1,275.00**
Jasper, black jasper dip, applied white classical relief, Portland, imp "Marshall Field & Co. Wedgwood Exhibition 1918," price for pr, 4" h...**690.00**

Weller Pottery water pitcher, stylized flower, 10-1/2" dia, 8" h, $100.

Wedgwood Pitcher, silver luster band, foot, and handle, pink scene, mkd "Ferrera Wedgwood & Barlaston, Made in England," $48.

Wine cooler, redware, fruiting vines on molded body, raised mask handles, imp mark, early 19th C, 10" h **550.00**

❖ Weller Pottery

Samuel Weller opened a small pottery factory near Zanesville, Ohio, in 1872, originally producing utilitarian stoneware. By 1882, he moved to larger quarters and expanded his lines. As the years continued, more designers arrived and the lines were expanded to include commercial wares. As art pottery became popular, Weller developed lines to answer that need. Today, some of the art pottery lines are highly sought. The company stayed in business during World War II, but by 1948 it had ceased operations.

For additional listings, see *Warman's Antiques and Collectibles Price Guide, Warman's Americana & Collectibles,* and *Warman's American Pottery & Porcelain.*

Weller Pottery Vase, La Sa, tropical landscape, nacreous gold and blue glazes, marked, cracked, 6-1/2" h, $175.

Basket, Florenzo, 5-1/2"..................**75.00**
Console bowl, Sydonia, 17" x 6"....**90.00**
Ewer, Louwelsa, peaches on a vine, decor by Lillie Mitchell, crazed, 12-1/2" h..**595.00**
Flower Frog, Marvo, blue................**55.00**
Mug
   Dickensware II, stag head decor, 5-3/4" h..**375.00**
   Aurelian, grapes and leaves decor, glaze imperfections, 4-1/2" h ..**375.00**
Pitcher, Louwelsa, 14" h, artist sgd, #750 ....**600.00**
Planter, Forest Tub, 4"...................**135.00**
Vase
   Art Nouveau, 5" h.......................**160.00**
   Atlas, 6-1/2" h............................**165.00**
   Dogwood, 9-1/2" h **125.00**
   Forest, fan-shape, blue, tan, and green matte glaze, imp mark, c1920 **200.00**
Wall pocket, Pearl, 8-1/2" l **160.00**

❖ Western Collectibles

The American West has always held a fascination. Whether you're a collector interested in history or a decorator striving to achieve a western motif using authentic items, flea markets yield many items rustling up.

Barbed wire in orig wooden box, state of Texas motif on sides, $50.

Cookbook, Western Cookbook, wooden cover with emb copper panel of cowboy, rawhide lashes, blue pages with recipes, $12.

Periodicals: *American Cowboy,* PO Box 6630, Sheridan, WY 82801; *Boots,* Lone Pine Road, PO Box 766, Challis, ID 83226; *Cowboy Collector Newsletter,* PO Box 7486, Long Beach, CA 90807; *Cowboy Guide,* PO Box 6459, Sante Fe, NM 87502; *Rope Burns,* PO Box 35, Gene Autry, OK 73436; *The Westerner,* PO Box 5253, Vienna, WV 26105.

Collectors' Clubs: American Cowboy Culture Association, 4124 62nd Drive, Lubbock, TX 79413; National Bit, Spur & Saddle Collectors Association, PO Box 3098, Colorado Springs, CO 80934; Western Americana Collectors Society, PO Box 620417, Woodside, CA 94062.

Belt Buckle, bucking bronc, MIB **40.00**
Book
   Famous Sheriffs and Western Outlaws, William MacLeod Raine, Doubleday, 1929, 1st ed., 294 pgs..............**12.00**
   Old Frontiers: The Story of the Cherokee Indians, John P. Brown, 1938..**70.00**
   Two on the Trail, A Story of the Far Northwest, Hubert Footner, Gross & Dunlap, 1912 ....**6.00**
Bookends, pr, "End of the Trail," tired Indian on pony, cast metal **75.00**
Coasters, cowboy, set of four in holder **15.00**
Compact, wooden with boots, hat and cactus..**36.00**
Cowboy hat, Stetson, orig box **150.00**
Figure, cowboy, Stetson..................**35.00**
Glass, frosted, painted cowboy on bucking bronco, 1950s **25.00**
Holster, leather, double, studs, jewels, 1950s **65.00**
Mug, steer head, Western Enamel, 4-3/4" h **22.50**
Pennant, Grand National Livestock Show and Rodeo, San Francisco, 1960s **35.00**
Pinback Button, "Let 'er buck," celluloid, cowboy on bucking horse, 1" d **25.00**
Plate, steer head, Western Enamel, 10" dia **20.00**

Toothpick holder, opaque blue milk glass, cowboy hat shape, $20.

Saddle, western style, tooled decor, 1970s **225.00**

Saddle stand, wood.....................**100.00**

Scarf, horses motif, rayon, 28" sq **24.00**

Spurs, N&J, brass, horse head, pr, ...**225.00**

Vase, wagon wheel shape, stamped "Frankoma" **35.00**

Wall lamp, cast iron silhouette of bronco buster **30.00**

❖ Westmoreland Glass

Founded in 1899 in Grapeville, Pa., the Westmoreland Company originally made handcrafted high-quality glassware. During the 1920s, the company started to make reproductions and decorated wares. Production continued until 1982. Pieces were made in crystal, black, and colored milk glass, among other colors. Milk glass pieces bring the most interest from collectors today.

Collectors' Clubs: National Westmoreland Glass Collectors Club, PO Box 625, Irwin, PA 15692; Westmoreland Glass Collectors Club, 2712 Glenwood, Independence, MO 64052; Westmoreland Glass Society, PO Box 2883, Iowa City, IA 52244.

Animal dish, cov
    Swan on nest, milk glass **185.00**
    Turkey, goofus coloring, chip on lid, some loss to paint **125.00**
Basket
    Princess Feather, 7-1/4" dia.......**125.00**
    Thousand Eye, clear, 8-3/4" h....**300.00**
Bowl
    Dolphin, milk glass, 12" dia........**145.00**
    Hobnail, blue, ftd, two handles, 8" dia **160.00**
    Paneled Grape, milk glass, 10" dia **50.00**
Bud vase, Roses & Bows, milk glass, 10" h, paneled grape dec...........**45.00**
Cake stand, Paneled Grape, milk glass **95.00**

Westmoreland Glass Co., child's creamer and sugar, diamond quilt pattern, white milk glass, orig label, $35.

Candelabra, 3 light, Paneled Grape, milk glass..**285.00**
Candlesticks, pr
    Old Quilt, milk glass, 3" h............**20.00**
    Paneled Grape, milk glass, 2-lite ...**37.50**
Candy dish, cov
    Della Robbia, 7" h **100.00**
    Old Quilt, milk glass, sq, high foot **30.00**
Cheese dish, cov, Old Quilt, milk glass **45.00**
Cologne bottle, Paneled Grape, milk glass..**45.00**
Compote, vaseline, 7" h...............**145.00**
Console set, Crystal Wedding, milk glass, cov compot, pr 4-1/2" h candlesticks, orig label **150.00**
Creamer and sugar, Della Robia, milk glass..**18.00**
Cruet, Old Quilt, milk glass **25.00**
Cup, Della Robia **45.00**
Cup and saucer
    Paneled Grape, milk glass **22.50**
    Plain, beaded edge, milk glass **12.00**
Dresser set, Paneled Grape, milk glass, 4 pcs **250.00**
Dresser tray
    Daisy, milk glass.........................**20.00**
    Paneled Grape, milk glass, decorated **125.00**
    Sunflower, milk glass...................**30.00**
Epergne, Paneled Grape, milk glass, 14" h **235.00**
Goblet
    Della Robia, milk glass.................**18.00**
    Paneled Grape, milk glass **18.00**
    Thousand Eye, crystal..................**12.00**
Honey dish, cov, Beaded Grape, milk glass, sq **20.00**
Iced tea tumbler
    Old Quilt, milk glass, 5-1/4" h, ftd **18.00**
    Paneled Grape, milk glass, 12 oz **22.00**
Pickle jar, frosted flower pattern, 12" h, 4-1/4" dia **95.00**
Pin dish, square, milk glass.............**7.00**
Pitcher, pint, Paneled Grape, milk glass **47.50**
Planter, Paneled Grape, milk glass, 5" x 9"...**40.00**

Plate
    Milk Glass, beaded edge, apple dec **12.00**
    Old Quilt, milk glass, 8" d............**32.00**
Punch set, Della Robia, crystal bell shaped punch bowl, 6 cups **45.00**
Salad plate, Della Robia, crystal, dark stained fruit................................**24.00**
Relish, 3 part, Paneled Grape, milk glass **40.00**
Tidbit, Beaded Grape, milk glass, 2 tiers **45.00**
Tray
    Grape, milk glass **25.00**
    Heavy Scroll, allover gold dec......**25.00**
    Maple Leaf, 9" d **12.00**
Tumbler, milk glass, ftd
    Apple **20.00**
    Old Quilt, 4-1/4" h......................**10.00**
    Peach **20.00**
Vase, Grape and Lattice, milk glass, 10" h **115.00**
Wedding bowl, Roses & Bows, milk glass, 10" h **65.00**

❖ Wheaton Glass

Wheaton Glass is located in central New Jersey and operates a museum and working glass site in Millville. Flea markets are seeing few of their limited-edition bottles and objects. Perhaps this will change as collectors begin to search for Wheaton objects again.

Ashtray, ruby **3.00**
Bottle
    George Washington **5.00**
    Great American Series, Mark Twain, W72, blue carnival **30.00**
    Jenny Lind, set of three, red, green, and cobalt blue **12.00**
    Mother and Daughter, set of two, green **20.00**
    President Series, 12 bottles **50.00**
Bud vase, ruby..............................**10.00**
Decanter, Robert F. Kennedy, green.**5.00**
Paperweight, figural green pepper .**20.00**

❖ Whirligigs

A variation of the weathervane, whirligigs indicate wind direction and velocity. Often constructed by the unskilled, they were generally made of wood and metal and exhibited a rather primitive appearance. Flat, paddle-like arms are characteristic of single-figure whirligigs, but multi-figure examples are usually driven by a propeller that moves a series of gears or rods. Three-dimensional figures are commonly found on 19th-century whirligigs, but silhouette figures are generally indicative of 20th-century construction.

Reference: Robert Bishop and Patricia Coblentz, *Gallery of American*

Weathervanes and Whirligigs, E.P. Dutton, 1981.

Indian in canoe, carved and painted wood, paddle arms, 14" h, 18" l..**440.00**

Man, light-blue outfit, blue hat, rubber arms, composition, looks like weathered wood, contemporary, 24-1/2" h...**605.00**

Man sawing logs, cut tin, wooden base, old worn gold, red, green and black paint, directional in green and black, propeller in green and orange, 32-3/4" l **137.50**

Patriotic motif, black man with hat pumping water for woman in polka-dot bandana and with washboard, wooden, propellers in red, white and blue with stars on the ends, white stars along the base, compass stars on the directional, repairs, weathering, 26-1/2" l ..**1,072.50**

Roosters, 2 facing each other, on tower made resembling an oil derrick, wooden, painted wood, 62" h.....**110.00**

Soldier, painted wood, black, gray, and white, wooden stand, wear, 9-5/8" w, 13" h **355.00**

Woman washing clothes, painted wood, 1930s, 12" h, 15" l......................**185.00**

❖ Whistles

Think referees and police officers are the only ones to use whistles? Think again. During the early 20th century, lithographed-tin whistles made a perfect advertising medium. Fifty years later, plastic examples were advertising pop-culture icons.

Acme Thunderer, mkd "Acme Thunderer, Tryon Trade Mark, Made in England"....................................**40.00**

Benzo-Gas, Blow Out The Carbon, cylindrical, 1-3/8" h......................**58.00**

Chicken Dinner Delicious Candy, litho tin, 2" l **80.00**

Cracker Jack, litho tin, shows trademark boy, 2-5/8" l **110.00**

Dragnet, Official Jack Webb Whistle, plastic **12.00**

Foremost Dairy, plastic, horn shape, 1950s, 5" l **32.00**

Guitar, litho tin, 2" l **12.00**

Pepsi-Cola, 2 miniature bottles.....**150.00**

Robin Hood Shoes, litho tin, flat style, 2-5/8" l **95.00**

Twinkie Shoes For Girls And Boys, litho tin, balloon shape, 1-1/4" l..**125.00**

Uncle Sam riding early bicycle, plastic, chips, 3-1/2" h, 4-1/4" l.....**45.00**

Weatherbird Shoes, cylindrical **60.00**

❖ White Knob Windups

White Knob Wind-Ups Dinosaur, yellow body, red spots, blue eyes, $5.

Just give a twist or two to the little white knob, and these plastic playthings teeter across any hard, flat surface. Because of their small size they are most commonly found in showcases. Only recently have they received much attention, which has tarted to send prices scurrying. Of course, ask permission to test any white knob windup before buying it. Few nonfunctioning examples are worth owning.

Baby Bert and Earnie, crawling, pr..**8.00**

Cat in the Hat, riding scooter pulling carousel, Universal Theme Park exclusive.......................................**10.00**

Cheeseburger wearing sunglasses, exclusive to Restaurant Margaretiville **7.00**

Creature from the Black Lagoon....**3.00**

Donald Duck, Disney Theme Parks**13.00**

Dumbo, Disney's Magic Kingdom ...**11.50**

Ghost, white, black witch's hat, 2-1/4" h **10.00**

Godzilla..**3.00**

Jets football helmet......................**12.00**

King Kong...**3.00**

Mickey Mouse, Tomy, 3-1/2" h........**10.00**

Pluto **20.00**

Pumpkin, orange, black witch's hat, 2-1/4" h **10.00**

Strolling Bowling, Tomy **8.50**

Skull, 3-1/4" h..................................**10.00**

Wind-Up Bunny, Easter theme, MOC **2.50**

❖ Wicker

Wicker furniture evokes a summertime feeling, even in the cold of winter. Wicker can be found in natural rattan or painted. The Victorians loved it. Today the look is still popular. Look for pieces with original upholstery in good condition and without too many layers of paint. Many pieces of wicker cannot be stripped without damaging the materials.

Wicker Miniatures, 2 chairs, table, natural, pale green trim, $95.

Baby basket, painted white, wooden stand with wheels........................**150.00**

Chair

Arm, wide flat arm rests continue to back, broad seat, repainted....**200.00**

Corner, elaborate scrolling, bird cage arms and supports, natural finish **650.00**

Photographer's, elaborate scrolled back and arms, painted white.**450.00**

Ferner, white, metal liner, rectangular, repainted several times **185.00**

Footstool, upholstered seat, painted **195.00**

Music stand, Wakefield Rattan Co., three shelves, orig paper label, c1883 ....**285.00**

Rocking chair, Wakefield Rattan Co., serpentine edges, braided trim, wooden rockers, painted white...**265.00**

Suite, sofa, two matching arm chairs, ottoman, some damage to wicker, worn old upholstery, as found condition ..**300.00**

Table, round wooden top, re-painted ..**120.00**

Wicker Chaise lounge and matching round table, painted black, $450.

Wicker Wicker loveseat, orig white paint, $195, repainted white wicker ferner, $95; reproduction decorative bicycle in front.

✶ Williamsburg

Today Colonial Williamsburg is well known as a living history museum. The plans to reconstruct this colonial capitol started to evolve in 1926. Part of the experience visitors have during their visit to this Virginia re-created area is to watch craftsmen create articles of all kinds, from pewter to silver to hats. The work of the Colonial Williamsburg Foundation is supported by the sale of other items. Many of these items eventually make their way to flea markets.

Plate, blue and white, "Historic Wiliamsburg Virginia," Wren Building, William and Mary College in center, vignettes around rim include Powder Horn, Governor's Palace, Capital, and Bruton Parish Church, mkd "Old English Staffordshire Ware, Jonroth England, imported for Gifts, Duke of Gloucester Street, Williamsburg, Virginia," 10-1/4" dia, $40.

Afghan, woven, children spelling out ABC's **10.00**
Book, *Official Guidebook & Map to Colonial Williamsburg*, 1953, 104 pgs **4.50**
Box, cov, brass, oval, monogrammed **20.00**
Bread and butter plate, Potpourri pattern, Wedgwood, 6-1/2" d **20.00**
Candlestick, brass, Raleigh pattern, mkd "CW" on base, 3-3/4" dia, 5-1/2" h **125.00**
Creamer and sugar, crock shape, salt glazed stoneware, cobalt blue accent, 2-1/2" h..**18.00**
Dinner plate, Potpourri pattern, Wedgwood, 10-1/4" dia **28.00**
Inkwell, pewter, Steiff, mkd "CW," 5" dia, 2-1/2" h......................................**110.00**
Needlework
Capitol, cross-stitched sampler, framed **40.00**
Raleigh Tavern, needlepoint, framed, 13-1/2" x 16-1/2"......................**75.00**
Pitcher, hand blown aqua glass, rolled rim, applied handle, Blenko, 6" h .**55.00**
Print, Governor's Palace, black frame **30.00**
Sebastian figure, colonial couple, mkd "Williamsburg Couple, copyright 1956

P. W. Baston," orig box, 3" h **35.00**
Tankard, pewter, Steiff, 4-3/4" h......**50.00**

❖ Winchester

This favorite American firearms manufacturer has a quite a following with collectors. Those with sharp vision can find all kinds of epherma and advertising.

Collectors' Club: Winchester Club of America, 3070 S. Wyandot, Englewood, Co 80110.

Ammunition, 50-110-300 for Model 1886 rifles, orig box in good condition, orig labels, 20 cartridges..................**200.00**
Banner, Headquarters for Winchester Rifles & Shotguns, fringed hem, wood rod, 19-1/2" x 29" **150.00**
Book, *The Book of Winchester Engraving*, first edition, dust jacket **500.00**
Brochure, Western-Winchester, full color printing, illus and describes western Super-X and Xpert shotgun shells and cartridges, 1957 ....**15.00**
Catalog
Winchester Rifles, John Wayne cover, 1982..**10.00**
Winchester-Western, New Haven, CT, 1976, 5-3/4" x 7-1/2"..................**40.00**
Counter felt, Shoot Where You aim **175.00**
Flashlight, dents, 1923 patent date, 9-1/4" l...**60.00**
Pocket knife, 2-blade, cracked bone-handle, 3-3/4" l closed..................**65.00**
Stickpin, Ask for Winchester Nublack, brass, shotgun shell shape, green enamel shell casing with inscription, early 1900s.............................**125.00**
Tin, J. Goldmark's Percussion Caps, made Winchester, some loss to paper labels, 1-1/2" dia **30.00**

❖ Winnie The Pooh

A. A. Milne's "tubby little cubby all stuffed with fluff" has become a best friend to countless children. It's no wonder Pooh, Piglet, Eeyore, and the rest of the gang are eagerly sought by collectors. Mass marketing of Pooh in recent years has brought a flood of newer collectibles into the market. However, buyers can still find a fair share of vintage Pooh items at flea markets.

Big Golden Book, *Winnie-The-Pooh and Eeyore's Birthday*, E. Dutton, copyright 1964, 1965 by Walt Disney Productions **35.00**
Book
Winnie The Pooh, Fat Bee, puppet included, produced for Buena Vista home video, 1994, mint **12.00**

Winnie the Pooh, cereal bowl, plastic, Tigger the hunter, $2.

Winnie the Pooh and Tigger Too, Disney's Wonderful World of Reading, Grolier, hardcover, 1975, orig cardboard mailer **20.00**
Figure, Eeyore, stamped "Walt Disney Productions Japan," 4" l **45.00**
Little Golden Book, Walt Disney Presents Winne-The-Pooh, The Honey Tree, 1977, 19th printing **1.00**
Pinback button, Winnie, Disneyland souvenir, c1960 ....**12.00**
Plush toy, Winnie, tags removed, 12" h **15.00**
Puzzle blocks, Disney, sold by Sears, bottom missing from orig box.......**10.00**
Record, Winnie the Pooh and Christopher Robin Songs, Disney, 78 rpm, Decca Records **40.00**
Sand pail, tin litho **7.50**
Toy, white knob wind-up, Winnie the Pooh in safari clothing, exclusive to Disney Animal Kingdom................**6.50**
Wall decoration
Train, Disney, particleboard, 35" l.**12.00**
Winnie, Tiger, Eeyore, heavy cardboard, c1960.....................**40.00**

❖ Wizard of Oz

MGM gave birth to an institution when it released *The Wizard of Oz* in 1939, although L. Frank Baum's stories of Oz date to the early part of the 20th century. While vintage Oz items are competitively sought and can be pricey, a variety of contemporary collectibles fit into any person's budget. Among the newer items are numerous pieces commemorating the film's 50th anniversary in 1989.

Periodical: Beyond the Rainbow Collector's Exchange, Elaine Willingham, P.O. Box 31672, St. Louis, MO 63131-0672.

Wizard of Oz action figures, Dorothy, Wicked Witch, and Tin Man, Mego, incomplete, each $5.

Collectors' Clubs: Emerald City Club, 153 E. Main St., New Albany IN 47150; The International Wizard of Oz Club, P.O. Box 10117, Berkeley, CA 94709-5117.

Book

The Road to Oz, Junior Edition, Rand/McNally & Co., 1939 copyright, 5-1/2" x 6-3/4"..........................**24.00**

The Road to Oz, L. Frank Baum, Reilly & Lee, 1909 ....**90.00**

Collector's plate, If I Only Had a Brain, Scarecrow, 1977, orig box, 8-1/2" dia **38.00**

Cookbook, The Wonderful Wizard of Oz Cookbook, Monica Bayley, hardcover, 1st ed, 1981 ....**52.00**

Cookie jar, Dorothy & Toto, Star Jars, limited production of 1,939, 1994 ....**350.00**

Doll, Barbie as Dorothy, Hollywood Legend Series, 1994, MIB **227.50**

Drinking glass, Scarecrow, Coca-Cola, 50th anniversary commemorative, 1989, 6" h..**10.00**

Game, Wizard of Oz Collector's Edition Monopoly Game, Parker Brothers, MIB **85.00**

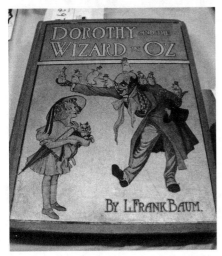

Wizard of Oz book, Dorothy and the Wizard of Oz, L. Frank Baum, $40.

Lunch box and thermos, Aladdin, 50th anniversary...................................**65.00**

Play set, Wizard of Oz, Mego, complete **250.00**

Photograph, Judy Garland, black and white, checkered Wizard of Oz dress, 1940s, 8" x 10" **8.00**

Sheet music, *Over the Rainbow*, 1939 ....**40.00**

Ticket stub, Karlton Theater.............**4.00**

❖ Wolverine Toys

The Wolverine Supply & Manufacturing Company was founded in 1903. The first type of toys produced were lithographed sand toys, followed by girls' housekeeping toys, and then action games, and cars and trucks.

Automatic Coal Loader, litho tin....**80.00**

Canister set, 2-1/2" h flour, 2-1/4" h sugar, 2-3/8" coffee, 2" h tea, white background with white polka dot on red band at bottom, row of green scallops, strawberries, flowers, and leaves, each marked **100.00**

Cap't Sandy Andy sand toy, orig box **200.00**

Corner grocer, 14 orig cardboard adv boxes, metal telephone, working weight scale, and paper roller, 11-1/2" x 30" open **550.00**

Do The Twist, dancer on pedestal, MIB **75.00**

Dollhouse with furniture, litho tin, 2-story house with bay window, 5 rooms, 10 pcs plastic furniture, 15" h, 22" w, 12" d.. **45.00**

Drum Major, #27, round base, c1930, 13-1/4" h..................................**225.00**

Gee Whiz Racehorse Game, 1930s, 15" l **145.00**

Horse-drawn farm wagon, plastic wind-up, orig box **150.00**

Icebox, tin....................................**55.00**

Jet Roller Coaster, 12" l.............**225.00**

Kitchen cabinet, #280, 1949, complete with toy groceries, orig box **195.00**

Le Mans Pinball, orig box, 50.00

Railway car, #129, streamlined, red, beige, and black, orig pull string, orig box, 18" l **495.00**

See and Spell **50.00**

Shooting Gallery, orig box **175.00**

Streamline Railway pull toy, 1930s, 17-3/4" l **220.00**

Sunny Suzy, electric iron, orig box.**25.00**

Washing machine, blue and white Delft design, slight rust, 1940, 9" h **130.00**

❖ Wood Collectibles

Wooden objects of all types are found at flea markets. Look for objects that are interesting, well made, and fit into your decorating scheme. Today's decorators often prefer a weathered look, while others prefer natural finished wood or an aged patina.

Collectors' Club: International Wood Collectors Society, 5900 Chestnut Ridge Road, Riner, VA 24149.

Apple box, pine, old red paint, conical feet, 10" l **310.00**

Bible rack, from old church pew, refinished, affixed to board for hanging, 28" l **45.00**

Bookrack, cherry, refinished, 24" l ..**15.00**

Bowl, treen, old worn brown finish, tight are cracks, 6" d **175.00**

Checkerboard, inlaid, mahogany and maple, 20th C, minor veneer damage, 14-3/4" sq..................................**110.00**

Churn, stave construction, metal bands, turned lid, dasher, old refinishing, 21-1/2" h..**150.00**

Cutting board, round top, shaped base, metal blade, 18" l **35.00**

Drying rack, mortised construction, chamfered, shoe feet, old blue repaint over yellow, 24-1/2" w **220.00**

Easel, folding.................................**200.00**

Egg timer, candlestick telephone shape, wood, stamped "Cornwall Wood Products, So. Paris, Maine," 5" h..**45.00**

Niddy noddy, hardwood, old yellow paint, one end with age crack **110.00**

Picture frame, barn boards, 24" x 32" **15.00**

Plate, some knife marks, 10" dia.....**15.00**

Press, orig hardware, patina, dovetailed construction, carved spout, 17" .**150.00**

Salad bowl, varnished int., bright hand painted flowers, matching serving fork and spoon **25.00**

Towel bar, walnut, three horizontal bars on tapering squared posts, scrolled trestle feet, New England, early 19th C, 37-1/2" w **175.00**

Wall pocket, painted, 8" h..............**20.00**

❖ World's Fairs & Expositions

The first really great world's exposition was the Great Exhibition of 1851 in London. Since that time, there have been many world's fairs, expositions, and celebrations. Today collectors tend to specialize in a particular fair or type of memorabilia.

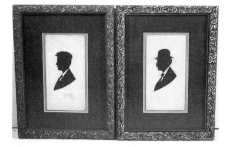

Two framed portraits, silhouettes from St. Louis World's Fair by E.J. Perry 1904, 12"x 9", $175.

World's Fairs & Expos, 1932, bronze token, George Washington on reverse, $20.

World War I drill master's hat, $30.

Periodical: *World's Fair*, PO Box 339, Corte Madera, CA 94976.

Collectors' Club: World's Fair Collectors' Society, PO Box 20806, Sarasota, FL 34276.

Ashtray

1933, brass and emb chrome over copper.....................................**100.00**
1961, Unisphere, "Presented by United States Steel, Made in Japan," 5-3/4" dia...**48.00**
1962, Seattle, Space Needle, mkd "Made in Japan," 4" dia...............**8.00**
1982, Knoxville, clear glass, red decal, 3-1/2" dia **2.50**

Drinking glass, 1982, Knoxville **10.00**

Foil stickers, 1939-40, New York, 4-3/4" x 5-1/2" clear cellophane pack, double-sided sheet with gold, blue, and orange foil stickers on one side, silver, blue, and orange on other side, 12 images on both sides...............................**25.00**

Guide book

1934, "World's Fair 1934 Official Guide Book," 5-1/2" x 8-1/2", full color Art Deco cover, 192 pages.............**25.00**
1939, "Second Edition Official Guide Book," 1939, New York, 5" x 8", soft cover, Art Deco style cover of Trylon/Perisphere at night, 256 black and white pgs **25.00**

Handkerchief, 1939 NY, different world costumes ....:....**20.00**

Key chain, 1962, Seattle, engraved design on front, mkd "Made in Germany" **15.00**

Pennant, 1939 Golden Gate International Exposition, San Francisco Bay, pastel Portals of the Pacific Building, red ground, 14-3/4" l..........................**45.00**

Plate

1904, St. Louis, clear glass, center heavy gold scene of Cascade Gardens, 7" dia.........................**55.00**
1982, Knoxville, TN, 4" dia..........**20.00**

Salt and pepper shakers, pr, 1939, Eneloid plastic, blue Trylon and Perisphere, orange base, inscribed "New York World's Fair" **35.00**

Souvenir Spoon

1892, Administration Building, sterling silver, 4-14" l **50.00**
1939 NY, Theme Building on front, mkd "Pat. Pend., Wm. Rogers Mfg Co." **25.00**

Tapestry, 1939 NY, 16" x 17".........**45.00**

Token, 1974, Expo '74, Spokane, silvered metal, 1-1/2" dia.............**15.00**

Toy, 1933 Century of Progress Greyhound bus, Chicago, Arcade **45.00**

Tray, 1967 Montreal, Expo '67, metal, 7" l **15.00**

Viewmaster reel

1964, New York, International area **28.00**
1967, Expo '67 Montreal, general tour **22.00**

❖ World War I

Fueled by the assassination of Austrian Archduke Franz Ferdinand by a Serbian national in June of 1914, World War I was set off with Germany invading Belgium and France. Shortly after that, Russia, England, and Turkey joined the war. By 1917 the United States and Italy had become involved. When peace was reached in 1919, millions had died damage was wide spread. Memorabilia relating to World War I was carefully laid aside, hoping it would be the last war. Alas, it was not.

Periodicals: *Men at Arms*, 222 W Exchange St, Providence, RI 02903; *Military Collector Magazine*, PO Box 245, Lyon Station, PA, 19536; *Military Collectors' News*, PO Box 702073, Tulsa, OK 74170; *Military Trader*, PO Box 1050, Dubuque, IA 52004; *Wildcat Collectors Journal*, 15158 NE 6 Ave, Miami FL 33162.

Collectors' Clubs: American Society of Military Insignia Collectors, 526 Lafayette Ave, Palmerton, PA 18701; Association of American Military Uniform Collectors, PO Box 1876, Elyria, OH 44036; Company of Military Historians, North Main St, Westbrook, CT 06498; Orders and Medals Society of America, PO Box 484, Glassboro, NJ 08028.

Badge, American Red Cross-Military Welfare, cap, enamel **24.00**

Bayonet, orig case **24.00**

Belt, some emblems........................**35.00**

Gas mask, carrying can, shoulder strap, canister attached to bottom, German **50.00**

Grave marker, unused, bronze, Hampden Bros Aluminum Co.......**45.00**

Handkerchief, Remember Me, soldier and girl in center, red, white, and blue edge **24.00**

Helmet, U.S., 3rd Army insignia......**72.00**

Leather flight cap..........................**60.00**

Magazine, *Red Cross Magazine*, October 1918, battle-scene cover **15.00**

Medal, British, King George V.........**65.00**

Photograph, Officer Training Camp, Chickamuga Park, GA, 1917, 7" x 31" **85.00**

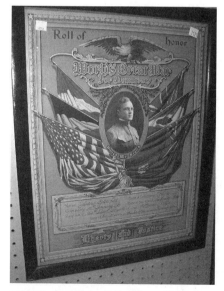

World War I certificate, Roll of Honor, World's Great War for Democracy, Charles P. Ley, 1912, black and white portrait in center, green background, multicolored flags, block with biographical info over "Liberty and Justice", orig frame, $95.

Postcard, real-photo, soldier in uniform
....**5.00**

Poster, *They Gave Their Lives - Do You Lend Your Savings?*, image of battlefield hilltop cemetery, 30" x 20"
....**75.00**

Scarf, silk, sweetheart, white, eagle, flag, sweethearts, etc. **40.00**

Sheet Music
American Patrol March, 1914 ......**15.00**
What Kind of an American Are You?, Uncle Sam design **20.00**

Songbook, *U.S. Army Song Book*, 1918
....**40.00**

Trench art, pencil holder, shell affixed to base of 3 crossed bullets, 4-3/8" h
....**95.00**

Watch fob, flag on pole, USA, beaded, blue...**48.00**

❖ World War II

Several world events came together in 1939, leading to World War II. The German Third Reich was engaged in an arms race; the Depression compounded the situation. After Germany invaded Poland, Allied and Axis alliances were formed. From 1942 to 1945, the whole world was involved, almost all industry was war-related. Peace was not achieved until August 1945. Today collectors are discovering artifacts, equipment, and remembrances of this war.

Reference: Martin Jacobs, *World War II Homefront Collectibles,* Krause Publications, 2000.

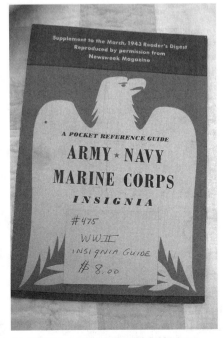

World War II, A Pocket Reference Guide, Army, Navy, Marine Corps Insignia Guide, *Reader's Digest Supplement, March, 1943, red, white, and blue cover, $8.*

Two World War II advertising posters, soldier in water holding rifle over head, "He's up to his neck too but he's giving–Do Your Part Peoria Community and War Fund, October 17 – 25", 22" x 13", $60.

Periodicals: *Men at Arms*, 222 W Exchange St, Providence, RI 02903; *Military Collector Magazine*, PO Box 245, Lyon Station, PA, 19536; *Military Collectors' News*, PO Box 702073, Tulsa, OK 74170; *Military Trader*, PO Box 1050, Dubuque, IA 52062; *Wildcat Collectors Journal*, 15158 NE 6 Ave, Miami FL 33162; *World War II*, 7741 Miller Drive, SE, Suite D2, Harrisburg, PA 20175; *WWII Military Journal,* PO Box 28906, San Diego, CA 92198.

Collectors' Clubs: American Society of Military Insignia Collectors, 526 Lafayette Ave, Palmerton, PA 18701; Assoc of American Military Uniform Collectors, PO Box 1876, Elyria, OH 44036; Company of Military Historians, North Main St, Westbrook, CT 06498; Imperial German Military Collectors Association, 82 Atlantic St., Keyport, NJ 07735; Orders and Medals Society of America, PO Box 484, Glassboro, NJ 08028.

Belt, German, black leather **80.00**

Belt buckle, Navy, Okinawa, 1945, mkd "Solid Brass, Made in USA" **24.00**

Book
Army Songs, 1941, 64 pgs **35.00**
Pilot Rating Book, CAA, U.S. Dept of Commerce **20.00**

Dexterity puzzle, Atom Bomb, silhouette of Japan, A.C. Gilbert Co., 1946...**150.00**

Dogtag, scarce early version with next of kin name/address, ...**10.00**

Drinking glass, Remember Pearl Harbor, artwork of Pearl Harbor and Hawaiian Islands, warships, and aircraft, 4-3/4" h...........................**65.00**

Envelope, shows pilot delivering letter to solider parachuting to ground, caption reads "High-Ho, A Letter for…," unused, 8-7/8" x 3-7/8" **8.00**

Helmet, painted, U.S. Navy Seabees, M1, mint **450.00**

Medal, campaign and service medal, orig box..**25.00**

Poster, Under the Shadow of Their Wings Our Land Shall Dwell Secure, 2 naval aviators in life vests with air battle scene in background, 37" x 27"
....**180.00**

Postcard, Three Dirty Dogs Remember Pearl Harbor, Axis leaders portraits, unused..**30.00**

Punch-out kit, Model Battleship, 7" x 10", full color envelope with scene of battleship on open sea, colorful thin cardboard sheet, Reed & Associates, early 1940s, unused.....................**45.00**

Salt and pepper shakers, pr, figural, Gen MacArthur, glazed ceramic, 2" x 2-1/2", tan hat, long yellow pipe **85.00**

Sheet Music, *What Do You Do In The Infrantry*.......................................**15.00**

Songbook, Army Song Book, 1941, 64 pgs **30.00**

View-Master reel, Naval Aviation Military Training Division, hand-lettered, #51,Fiat G-50 Italian fighter **29.00**

❖ Wrestling Memorabilia

The last sport of this edition is one that involves fewer players than team sports, but is physically demanding. It has also created a unique kind of memorabilia for its collectors and devotees.

Reference: Kristian Pope and Ray Whebbe Jr., *Professional Wrestling Collectibles*, Krause Publications, 2000.

Periodicals: *Sports Cards Magazine & Price Guide,* 700 E State St, Iola, WI 54990; *Sports Collectors Digest*, 700 E State St, Iola, WI 54990.

Autographed photo, 8" x 10"
Bill Goldberg.................................**22.00**
Hulk Hogan **28.00**
Kevin Nash **20.00**
Lex Lugar **18.00**
The Warlord..................................**18.00**

Beanbag toy, Diamond Dallas Page, World Championship Wrestling......**7.00**

Buckle, enameled pewter, wrestling figures, eagle, "Championship," 5-1/2" x 4-1/4"...**70.00**

Flyer, Wrestling Foto Review of Your Wrestling Stars, Carnera, Tarzan Kowalski, Ski Hi Lee photos, 1955, 4 pgs **15.00**

Game, WWF Wrestling Stars, Milton Bradley, 1985 ....**20.00**

Medal, "4th 120 lb 1948," 1" h **5.00**

Pin, 1984 Olympics, Coca-Cola **2.25**

Plaque, autographed
Goldberg **45.00**
Hollywood Hogan **45.00**
Sting..**45.00**

Poster, Dual Anisette Liqueur adv
....**530.00**

Program
Montevideo, Uruguay, Sept, 1913, 11-1/2" x 8-7/8" **20.00**

Sumo, Japanese, photos, diagrams of arena, woodblock prints, 1981, 24 pgs...........**20.00**
Sports Card, WMF Superstars, foil.**30.00**

❖ Wright, L.G.

L.G. Wright was a curious company. It started manufacturing glass using old molds of other companies. Some of the wares were done in colors or textures not originally manufactured in a particular pattern. Some pattern glass collectors embraced this as a way to add color or another form to their collections. However, L.G. Wright also made reproductions in original colors, causing great confusion for unsuspecting collectors. Today, as the factory has closed and production ceased, some folks are collecting L.G. Wright wares as examples of that glass company and are not encumbered by the reproduction aspect. Some of the original glass molds were sold to companies who have plans to use them in the future, creating reproductions of reproductions.

Cocktail, Paneled Grape, #55, blue opalescent...................................**25.00**
Creamer and sugar, Beaded Curtain, cranberry......................................**160.00**
Cruet, Moss Rose, white satin, hp **135.00**
Goblet
  Paneled Grape, #55, blue opalescent
  ....**30.00**
  Wildflower, amber........................**18.50**
Pump and trough, carnival glass reproduction, cobalt blue..............**20.00**
Sherbet
  Bull's Eye, amber **19.00**
  Wedding Ring, amber **17.50**
Toothpick holder, Moon and Star, amber **25.00**
Vase, Cherries, milk glass, cranberry int., hp, 6-1/2" h...............................**195.00**
Wine, Paneled Grape, #55, blue opalescent...................................**30.00**

❖ Wright, Russel

Russel Wright was an American industrial designer who took the streamlined look to new heights. He influenced several companies and their designs, such as Chase Brass and Chrome, and General Electric.

One area where his influence was greatly felt was in dinnerware design. The Steubenville Pottery responded with a pattern called American Modern, made from 1939 to 1959. The original issue colors were Bean Brown, Chartreuse Curry, Coral, Granite Grey, Seafoam Blue, and White. Later color additions included Black Chutney, Cedar Green, Cantalope, Glacier Blue, and Steubenville Blue. Wright also created other dinnerware patterns, but American Modern remains one that is most sought after by collectors.

Russel Wright Iroquois white dinner service: 12 dinner plates, 12 salad plates, 12 soup bowls, 12 cups, 12 saucers, creamer, lidded sugar, salt shakers, 2 oval platters and gravy boat, 67 pcs, $250.

Reference: Ann Kerr, *Collector's Encyclopedia of Russel Wright,* 3rd ed., Collector Books, 2002.

American Modern pattern
Bread and butter plate, 6" d
  Bean Brown.................................**10.00**
  Granite Grey...............................**5.00**
Butter, cov, Coral **285.00**
Carafe, Granite Grey **175.00**
Casserole, cov ....
  Granite Grey................................**65.00**
  Seafoam Blue..............................**45.00**
Celery dish
  Bean Brown.................................**28.00**
  Granite Grey **25.00**
Chop plate
  Chartreuse Curry **35.00**
  Granite Grey................................**30.00**
Cup and saucer
  Coral..**12.00**
  Granite Grey................................**14.00**
Dinner plate
  Cedar Green **10.00**
  Granite Grey................................**13.00**
Fruit bowl, lug
  Coral..**17.50**
  Granite Grey................................**15.00**
Hostess Plate, Granite Grey **85.00**
Iced Tea Tumbler, Coral, glass, slight use **24.00**
Pickle, Chartreuse Curry.................**15.00**
Platter
  Coral..**35.00**
  Granite Grey................................**28.00**
Salad bowl
  Granite Grey................................**85.00**
  Seafoam Blue..............................**90.00**
Salad plate
  Coral..**17.50**
  Granite Grey................................**15.00**
Salt shaker
  Chartreuse Curry **14.00**
  Granite Grey................................**10.00**
Sauceboat, Coral **45.00**
Soup, lug
  Bean Brown.................................**27.50**
  Granite Grey................................**15.00**

Teapot, Coral.................................**95.00**
Tumbler, Granite Grey **85.00**
Vegetable bowl, open
  Coral..**35.00**
  Granite Grey...............................**25.00**
Water pitcher
  Granite Grey...............................**100.00**
  Seafoam Blue..............................**185.00**

❖ Wristwatches

Got the time? The first real wristwatch dates back to about 1850, but it wasn't until around 1880 that wristwatches were the stylish element we consider them to be. By the 1930s, the idea caught on well enough that sales of wrist watches finally surpassed sales of pocket watches. All kinds of watches can be found at flea markets. Don't forget to calculate the price of any required repairs before purchasing a watch.

References: Kahlert Muhe Brunner, *Wristwatches*, 4th ed, Schiffer Publishing, 1999; Cooksey Shugart, Tom Engle and Richard E. Gilbert, *Complete Price Guide to Watches*, 21st ed, Collector Books, 2001.

Periodical: *International Wrist Watch*, 242 West Ave, Darien, CT 06820.

Collectors' Clubs: International Wrist Watch Collectors Chapter 146, 5901C Westheimer, Houston, TX 77057; National Assoc of Watch & Clock Collectors, 514 Poplar Street, Columbia, PA 17512; The Swatch Collectors Club, PO Box 7400, Melville, NY 11747.

Art Deco, lady's, Art Deco, platinum, octagonal case, ivorytone with Roman numerals, platinum and 14kt yellow gold engraved bezel set with nine diamonds, cabochon blue stone winder, monogrammed, 6-3/4" l round woven gold band **300.00**
Bucherer, lady's, 18k yg, Swiss movement, 17 jewel, designed as double-hinged engraved bangle, center covered watch, cream dial, applied goldtone Arabic and abstract indicators, Swiss hallmarks........**165.00**
Garsons, man's, 14kt gold, sq goldtone dial with simulated jewel indicators, 17 jewel nickel movement, subsidiary seconds dial, 8-1/4" l integrated mesh band **345.00**
Gruen
  Man's, 10k wg, precision autowind, Tonneau case, black lizard band
  ....**65.00**
  Man's, 14k yg, orig strap............**300.00**
Hamilton, lady's, Art Deco, bezel and shoulders set with round baguette diamonds, platinum mount, black cord strap, white gold filled clasp, minor discoloration to dial **460.00**

Lorus, Mickey Mouse, c1980, band
simulates animation film of Mickey
walking, MIB...............................**25.00**
Movado, man's, 14K yg, tank, stepped
lugs, slightly bowed sides, gold-tone
dial, Roman numerals and abstract
indicators, subsidiary seconds dial,
worn leather strap, crystal loose **230.00**
Omega, man's, 18k yg, round cream dial,
goldtone Arabic numeral and abstract
indicators.....................................**225.00**
Rolex, man's, perpetual, stainless steel,
Air King, silver-tone dial, applied
abstract indicators, sweep second
hand, oyster bracelet with clasp,
discoloration to dial, scratches to
crystal..**575.00**
Uti, Paris, lady's, 18k yg, silver-tone dial,
applied gold-tone indicators, leather
strap with keyhole form closure,
hallmarks, wear to strap.............**575.00**

❖ Wyandotte

Playthings a kid could be rough with,
Wyandotte's heavy-gauge steel toys were a
favorite with children. The company began
in 1921, taking its name from the town of
Wyandotte, Mich., where it was located. At
first the firm just made toy pistols and rifles,
but soon moved to a line of cars and trucks
with wooden wheels. Wyandotte went out of
business in 1956.

Airliner, 4-engine, 12-3/4" wingspan
....**110.00**
Army truck, 22" l............................**115.00**
Circus truck, No. 503, 11" l..........**650.00**
Coupe, 1930s, 7-1/2" l **160.00**
Ice truck, #348 ....**375.00**
Railway Express Agency Delivery
Truck, green, yellow details, silver roof,
cream, red, and blue logos, operating
tailgate, orig tires and accessories
including dolly and miniature packages,
1950s, 20" l, few scratches and scuffs
....**375.00**
Rocket Racer, #319......................**100.00**
Ship, *U.S.S. Enterprise* **120.00**
Station wagon, Cadillac, #1007, 21" l
....**275.00**
Submarine **165.00**
Toytown Delivery, 21" l **300.00**
Wrecker, 10" l **110.00**

❖ Yard Long Photos and Prints

To most collectors, a long narrow print is considered a "yard long" print. The format can be horizontal or vertical. Yard long prints first appeared about 1900, and some were used as premiums as well as advertising. Many calendars were created in this format.

Many photographs were also made in this format too. These were especially popular with school groups, so that the entire student body could be included in a photo. Military units also favored this size.

Calendar
1911, Pabst Extra, American Girl, C.W. Henning, full length, cardboard roll at bottom..**350.00**
1924 John Clay & Company Live Stock Commission by Frank H. Desch, lady sitting on porch railing **550.00**
1927, Pompeian, The Bride, sgd "Rolf Armstrong".............................**350.00**

Photograph
1919, U.S.S. *Siboney* Arriving at U.S. Naval Base, Aug. 8, 1919 ....**175.00**
1938, Egg Harbor High School, Class of '38, in front of Capital, names identified on back, framed **75.00**

Print
Battle of the Chicks, Ben Austrian, © 1920 by The Art Interchange Co. of New York................................**250.00**
Carnations by Grace Barton Allen, basket of red carnations (BK 2-30) **250.00**
Easter Greetings, Paul DeLongpre, © 1894 by Knapp Co. Litho **400.00**
Hula Girl, sgd "Gene Pressler"...**350.00**

Liberty Girl, Pompeian Beauty, by Forbes, verse by Daniel M. Henderson, date 1919 and information on back (BK 1-28) **400.00**
Yard of Puppies by Guy Bedford, Chicago (BK 2-26) **375.00**

❖ Yellow Ware

This type of utilitarian pottery has been produced in the United States and England since the early 19th century. Because yellowware was quite durable, it became the kitchen pottery of choice, replacing the more fragile redware. Color may range from pumpkin orange to deep yellow to pale cream, and most of the pieces are unmarked. Horizontal bands in white, brown, blue, or a combination thereof were the most common type of decoration.

References: William C. Ketchum Jr., *American Country Pottery: Yellowware and Spongeware*, Alfred A. Knopf, 1987; Joan Leibowitz, *Yellow Ware*, Schiffer Publishing, 1985 (1993 value update); Lisa S. McAllister, *Collector's Guide to Yellow Ware*, Collector Books, 1997; Lisa S. McAllister and John L. Michael, *Collecting Yellow Ware*, Collector Books, 1993.

Museums: Bennington Museum, VT; Henry Ford Museum, Dearborn, MI; Museum of Ceramics, East Liverpool, OH.

For additional listings, see *Warman's Country Price Guide*.

Beater jar, 3 white stripes, base chip, 5-3/4" h..**170.00**
Bowl, mixing
  4 bands of brown slip, 2-3/8" h, 4-1/4" dia..**110.00**
  Nesting set of 5, thick white stripe between thin white stripes **275.00**
Canning jar, barrel shape, 6-3/4" h **110.00**
Creamer, black stripes, white band, green seaweed dec, 3-7/8" h, hairline at base of handle **165.00**
Dish, rectangular, canted sides, 2-1/4" h, 11" l, 8" w..................................**270.00**
Match holder, lion motif, 2 chips to the holder, 5-7/8" h, oval base 7-7/8" x 4-7/8" **280.00**
Miniature, chamber pot, white band, 2-1/4" h..**100.00**

Pie funnel, 2-1/2" h.......................**125.00**
Pie plate, 10" dia............................**90.00**
Pudding mold
  Ear of corn, scalloped designs on interior sides, simple gallery-like foot, oval, 4-3/8" h, 7-3/8" x 9-1/4"....**170.00**
  Sheath of wheat, minor rim chips, 3-1/4" h, 7-5/8" l **110.00**
Rolling pin, wood handles, adv **125.00**
Turk's head, 7-1/2" dia, 2-3/4" h...**185.00**

❖ Yo-Yos

Q: What keeps coming back when you toss it away? A: A yo-yo. Few people can truly throw away a yo-yo, which means there are many examples available on today's market. In addition to vintage items, look for contemporary yo-yos featuring popular cultural figures, advertising yo-yos and commemorative examples. Yo-yo collections can be seen free of charge at The Yozeum in Tucson, Ariz., and the National Yo-Yo Museum in Chico, Cal.

Collectors' Clubs: American Yo-Yo Association, 627 163rd St., South Spanaway, WA98387.

Baseball, white, red stitching dec **4.00**
Big Con, plastic................................**4.00**
Bowling ball, Duncan Sports Line Model, #1070, MOC **55.00**
Butterfly, Duncan, green plastic **5.00**
Campbell's Kids, Duncan **26.00**
Coca-Cola, 1992 Summer Olympics **25.00**
Dr. Pepper, 10-2-4 logo, wooden, red and blue.................................**35.00**
Eleyo, red, MIB................................**5.00**
Glow Imperial, Duncan.....................**6.00**
Grand Prix, wheel............................**5.00**
Hot Wheels, Mattel, tire motif, red chrome hubcaps, 1990, MOC **13.00**
The Iron Giant, Warner Bros., 1990 ....**12.00**
Jurassic Park, 1992, MIP **21.50**
Oreo Cookie **10.00**
Planter's Mr. Peanut......................**20.00**
Pro Flash Boy, pink plastic..............**8.00**
Spider-Man, Duncan, 1978.............**25.00**
Steam Genie, metal **10.00**

❖ Zanesville Pottery

The area around Zanesville, Ohio, was home to several potteries. The Zanesville Art Pottery started production about 1900. Their first wares were utilitarian and they soon ventured into art pottery production. The firm was bought by S.A. Weller in 1920 and became part of Weller Pottery at that time. Another popular company was Peters and Reed.

Bowl, fluted edge, mottled blue glaze, 6-1/2" d **45.00**

Bowl, and figural turtle flower frog, Landsun, blue tones, Peter and Reed, bowl 8" dia.................................**154.00**

Figurine, frog, marbleized, Peters and Reed, 4-7/8" h **220.00**

Jar, cov, marbleized green, Peters and Reed, 4" h **330.00**

Jardiniere, ruffed rim, cream to light amber peony blossoms, shaded brown ground **75.00**

Vase

Arts & Crafts design, teal glaze, shallow base chip, 12" h.........**225.00**

Chromal, dark blue, brown and tan, Peters and Reed, 7-3/4" h **220.00**

Moss Aztec, embossed blackberries, Peters and Reed, 2 glaze nicks, 7-7/8" h **88.00**

❖ Zeppelins

Oh, those fanciful flying machines. Some folks call them dirigibles, while others refer to them as blimps. To collectors they are something to float about, especially when finding that rare piece to add to their coveted possessions.

Book

Aircraft Carrier: Graf Zeppelin, Breyer, 48 pgs.......................................**10.00**

The Zeppelin in Combat, A History of the German Naval Airship Division, Douglas H. Robinson, 400 pgs, black and white photos, charges, drawings **50.00**

Christmas light bulb, milk glass, painted green, red, white, blue, and gold, 1950s, 2-1/2" l, non-working **20.00**

First-day cover, "San Francisco Greets *U.S.A.S. Macon* Upon Arrival at Home Base," 8 cent airmail stamp, postmarked "Moffett Field, Oct 15, 1933"..**30.00**

Flight Schedule, from Germany to America, c1936 ....**60.00**

Magazine print, German *Graf Zeppelin* flying over NY skyscrapers, from New Yorker Magazine, Haupt, 1930, 8" x 11" image, acid-free mat **125.00**

Postcard, Zeppelin flying over Montevideo, Uruguay, black and white **28.00**

Stereoview, Zeppelin flying over German town during World War I, description on back..**60.00**

Toy, plastic, hanging gondola, orig box with narrative printed in German, English, and French, 13" l..........**125.00**

Index

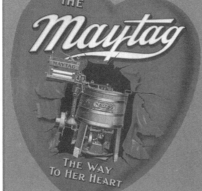

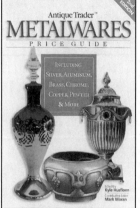

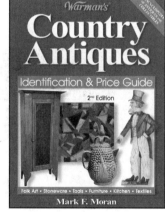